DIGITAL MARKETING

PEARSON

At Pearson, we have a simple mission: to help people make more of their lives through learning.

We combine innovative learning technology with trusted content and educational expertise to provide engaging and effective learning experiences that serve people wherever and whenever they are learning.

From classroom to boardroom, our curriculum materials, digital learning tools and testing programmes help to educate millions of people worldwide - more than any other private enterprise.

Every day our work helps learning flourish, and wherever learning flourishes, so do people.

To learn more please visit us at
www.pearson.com/uk

SIXTH EDITION

DIGITAL MARKETING

DAVE CHAFFEY

FIONA ELLIS-CHADWICK

PEARSON

Harlow, England • London • New York • Boston • San Francisco • Toronto • Sydney • Auckland • Singapore • Hong Kong
Tokyo • Seoul • Taipei • New Delhi • Cape Town • São Paulo • Mexico City • Madrid • Amsterdam • Munich • Paris • Milan

Pearson Education Limited
Edinburgh Gate
Harlow CM20 2JE
United Kingdom
Tel: +44 (0)1279 623623

Web: **www.pearson.com/uk**

First published 2000 (print)
Second edition published 2003 (print)
Third edition published 2006 (print)
Fourth edition published 2009 (print)
Fifth edition published 2012 (print and electronic)
Sixth edition published 2016 (print and electronic)

© Pearson Education Limited 2000, 2003, 2006, 2009 (print)
© Pearson Education Limited 2012, 2016 (print and electronic)

Pearson Education is not responsible for the content of third-party internet sites.

ISBN: 978-1-292-07761-1 (print)
　　　978-1-292-07764-2 (PDF)
　　　978-1-292-07762-8 (eText)
　　　978-1-292-12564-0 (ePub)

British Library Cataloguing-in-Publication Data
A catalogue record for the print edition is available from the British Library

Library of Congress Cataloguing-in-Publication Data
A catalog record for the print edition is available from the Library of Congress
10 9 8 7 6 5 4 3 2 1
19 18 17 16 15

Cover image © Getty Images
Print edition typeset in 10/12 pts and Sabon MT Pro by 76
Print edition printed in Slovakia by Neografia
NOTE THAT ANY PAGE CROSS REFERENCES REFER TO THE PRINT EDITION

Brief contents

Preface   xiii
About the authors   xxiv
Acknowledgements   xxv

Part 1   Digital marketing fundamentals   2

1   Introducing digital marketing   4
2   Online marketplace analysis: micro-environment   54
3   The online macro-environment   118

Part 2   Digital marketing strategy development   174

4   Digital marketing strategy   176
5   The impact of digital media and technology on the marketing mix   248
6   Relationship marketing using digital platforms   298

Part 3   Digital marketing: implementation and practice   352

7   Delivering the online customer experience   354
8   Campaign planning for digital media   418
9   Marketing communications using digital media channels   476
10   Evaluation and improvement of digital channel performance   548
11   Business-to-consumer digital marketing practice   592
12   Business-to-business digital marketing practice   622

Glossary   649
Index   679

Contents

Preface   xiii
About the authors   xxiv
Acknowledgements   xxv

Part 1 Digital marketing fundamentals   2

1 Introducing digital marketing   4

Learning objectives / Questions for marketers /
   Links to other chapters   4
Introduction – how have digital technologies
   transformed marketing?   6
Digital marketing in practice
   The Smart Insights interview: Nick Dutch,
   Head of Digital at Domino's Pizza   9
Definitions – what are digital marketing and
   multichannel marketing?   11
Paid, owned and earned media   11
The growing range of digital marketing platforms   12
Introduction to digital marketing strategy   16
Key features of digital marketing strategy   16
Applications of digital marketing   16
Benefits of digital marketing   17
Alternative digital business models   20
What is the difference between e-commerce
   and e-business?   22
Different forms of online presence   24
Challenges in developing and managing digital marketing
   strategy   25
A strategic framework for developing a digital marketing
   strategy   27
Introduction to digital marketing communications   29
The relationship between digital and traditional
   communications   30
Using digital media channels to support
   business objectives   31
The key types of digital media channels   32
Different types of social media marketing tools   34
Benefits of digital media   37
Key challenges of digital communications   43
Key communications concepts for digital marketing   43
   Case study 1
   eBay thrives in the global marketplace   46

Summary   49
Exercises   49
   Self-assessment exercises   49
   Essay and discussion questions   50
   Examination questions   50
References   50
Weblinks   52

2 Online marketplace analysis: micro-environment   54

Learning objectives / Questions for marketers /
   Links to other chapters   54
Introduction   56
Situation analysis for digital marketing   56
Digital marketing in practice
   The Smart Insights interview: Michael Welch of
   Blackcircles.com   57
The digital marketing environment   59
Understanding customer journeys   61
Customer analysis   68
Demand analysis and implications for
   marketing planning   69
Implications for marketing planning:
   conversion models   69
Consumer choice and digital influence   72
Consumer transactions   74
Online consumer behaviour and implications for
   marketing   76
Customer characteristics   76
Consumer personas   79
The buying process   79
Competitors   88
The shape and nature of online competitive markets   88
Competitor analysis and benchmarking   91
Suppliers   93
Online marketing intermediaries   94
Portals   96
New channel structures   96
Business models for e-commerce   99
Revenue models   103
   Case study 2
   Boo hoo – learning from the largest European
     dot-com failure   108

Summary	111
Exercises	112
Self-assessment exercises	112
Essay and discussion questions	112
Examination questions	112
References	113
Weblinks	116

3 The online macro-environment   118

Learning objectives / Questions for marketers /	
Links to other chapters	118
Introduction	120
Digital marketing in practice	
The Smart Insights interview: Fred Bassett of	
Blue Latitude	121
The rate of environment change	123
Technological forces	123
A short introduction to Internet technology	123
URL strategy	125
How does the Internet work?	125
Infrastructure components of the Internet	126
Web page standards	126
Text information – HTML (Hypertext Markup Language)	127
Text information and data – XML (eXtensible Markup	
Language)	127
Graphical images (GIF, JPEG and PNG files)	128
Animated graphical information (Flash and plug-ins)	128
Audio and video standards	128
The difference between the Internet, intranets	
and extranets	129
Web application frameworks and application servers	129
Digital security	130
Approaches to developing secure systems	133
Technology convergence	135
SMS messaging and applications	135
Mobile apps	136
QR codes	137
Wi-Fi	137
Bluetooth wireless applications	138
Emerging technologies	138
Assessing the marketing value of technology innovation	139
Economic forces	142
Market growth and employment	142
International market growth and emerging economies	143
Economic disruption	143
Political forces	144
Political control and democracy	145
Internet governance	145
Taxation	145
Tax jurisdiction	146
Legal forces	147
Legal activities can be considered unethical	147
1 Data protection and privacy law	148
2 Disability and discrimination law	159

3 Brand and trademark protection	159
4 Intellectual property rights	161
5 Contract law	162
6 Online advertising law	163
Social forces	164
Social exclusion	164
Cultural forces	165
Environmental and green issues related to Internet usage	165
Case study 3	
Zopa launches a new lending model	167
Summary	169
Exercises	169
Self-assessment exercises	169
Essay and discussion questions	170
Examination questions	170
References	170
Weblinks	172

Part 2 Digital marketing strategy development   174

4 Digital marketing strategy   176

Learning objectives / Questions for marketers /	
Links to other chapters	176
Introduction	178
Digital marketing strategy as a channel marketing strategy	178
The scope of digital marketing strategy	179
Digital marketing in practice	
The Smart Insights interview: Sajjad Bhojani	
of Dunelm	182
The need for an integrated digital marketing strategy	184
How to structure a digital marketing strategy	186
Situation analysis	190
Internal audit for digital marketing	191
Customer research	192
Resource analysis	192
Stage models of the digital marketing capability	193
Competitor analysis	194
Intermediary analysis	194
Assessing opportunities and threats	195
Setting goals and objectives for digital marketing	196
The online revenue contribution	200
Setting SMART objectives	203
Frameworks for objective setting	205
Strategy formulation for digital marketing	208
Decision 1: Market and product development strategies	210
Decision 2: Business and revenue models strategies	213
Decision 3: Target marketing strategy	215
Decision 4: Positioning and differentiation strategy	
(including the marketing mix)	220
Decision 5: Customer engagement and social	
media strategy	223
Decision 6: Multichannel distribution strategy	225

Decision 7: Multichannel communications strategy 228
Decision 8: Online communications mix and budget 231
Decision 9: Organisational capabilities (7S framework)
    and governance 232
Strategy implementation 236
Assessing different Internet projects 236
The online lifecycle management grid 238
    Case study 4
    Tesco online development strategy supports
    global expansion 239
Summary 242
Exercises 242
    Self-assessment exercises 242
    Essay and discussion questions 243
    Examination questions 243
References 243
Weblinks 246

**5 The impact of digital media and
    technology on the marketing mix** 248
*Learning objectives / Questions for marketers /
    Links to other chapters* 248
Introduction 250
What is the marketing mix? 250
Digital marketing in practice
    The Smart Insights interview: Roberto Hortal 252
Product 255
1 Options for varying the core product 256
2 Options for offering digital products 257
3 Options for changing the extended product 258
4 Conducting research online 259
5 Velocity of new product development 260
6 Velocity of new product diffusion 260
The long tail concept 261
Branding in a digital environment 262
Price 267
1 Increased price transparency 269
2 Downward pressure on price 270
3 New pricing approaches (including auctions) 274
4 Alternative pricing structure or policies 276
Place 277
1 Place of purchase 277
2 New channel structures 280
3 Channel conflicts 281
4 Virtual organisations 282
Promotion 284
People, process and physical evidence 285
People 286
Process 288
Physical evidence 288
    Case study 5
    Spotify streaming develops new revenue models 290
Summary 293
Exercises 293

    Self-assessment exercises 293
    Essay and discussion questions 293
    Examination questions 293
References 294
Weblinks 297

**6 Relationship marketing using
    digital platforms** 298
*Learning objectives / Questions for marketers /
    Links to other chapters* 298
Introduction 300
From e-CRM to social CRM 302
Structure of this chapter 303
Digital marketing in practice
    The Smart Insights interview:
    Guy Stephens of IBM 304
The challenge of customer engagement 308
Benefits of using e-CRM to support
    customer engagement 308
Marketing applications of e-CRM 311
CRM technologies and data 311
Customer lifecycle management 311
Permission marketing 313
'Right touching' through developing online
    contact strategies 319
The 'emotionally unsubscribed' email list members 320
Personalisation and mass customisation 322
Using digital media to increase customer
    loyalty and value 324
Determining what customers value 324
The relationship between satisfaction and loyalty 325
Measuring the voice of the customer in
    digital media 327
Differentiating customers by value and engagement 328
Lifetime value modelling 331
Recency–frequency–monetary value (RFM) analysis 335
The 'Big Data' concept 339
Product recommendations and propensity modelling 340
Applying virtual communities and social
    networks for CRM 340
Marketing to consumers using independent
    social networks 343
Customer experience – the missing element
    required for customer loyalty 343
    Case study 6
    Dell gets closer to its customers through
    its social media strategy 344
Summary 347
Exercises 347
    Self-assessment exercises 347
    Essay and discussion questions 347
    Examination questions 348
References 348
Weblinks 350

Part 3 Digital marketing: implementation and practice 352

7 Delivering the online customer experience 354

Learning objectives / Questions for marketers /
Links to other chapters 354
Introduction 356
Creating effective digital experiences 356
Structure of the chapter 359
Digital marketing in practice
The Smart Insights interview: Ben Jesson and
Karl Blanks of agency Conversion Rate Experts 360
Planning website design and redesign projects 362
Who should be involved in a website project? 364
Prototyping and agile software development 366
Initiation of the website project 370
Domain name selection and registration 370
Uniform resource locators (URLs) 371
Selecting a hosting provider 372
Website performance optimisation 372
The availability of the website 373
Defining site or app requirements 374
Business requirements 374
Usability requirements 375
Web accessibility requirements 378
Localisation 379
Reviewing competitors' websites 380
Designing the information architecture 381
Card sorting 382
Blueprints 383
Wireframes 383
Landing pages 386
Designing the user experience 388
Evaluating designs 389
Elements of site design 389
Mobile design considerations and techniques 391
Site navigation schemes 395
Development and testing of content 400
Criteria for selecting a content management system 400
Testing the experience 401
Online retail merchandising 402
Site promotion or 'traffic building' 404
Service quality 404
Tangibles 407
Reliability 407
Assurance 407
Multichannel communications preferences 407
Empathy 408
The relationship between service quality, customer
satisfaction and loyalty 410
Case study 7
Refining the online customer experience
at i-to-i.com 410

Summary 412
Exercises 413
Self-assessment exercises 413
Essay and discussion questions 413
Examination questions 413
References 414
Weblinks 416

8 Campaign planning for digital media 418

Learning objectives / Questions for marketers /
Links to other chapters 418
Introduction 420
The structure of this chapter 421
Digital marketing in practice
The Smart Insights interview:
Mike O'Brien of the Jam Partnership 422
The characteristics of digital media 424
1 From push to pull 424
2 From monologue to dialogue to trialogue 424
3 From one-to-many to one-to-some and one-to-one 425
4 From one-to-many to many-to-many
communications 426
5 From 'lean-back' to 'lean-forward' 427
6 The medium changes the nature of standard
marketing communications tools such
as advertising 427
7 Increase in communications intermediaries 428
8 Integration 428
9 Timing of campaign communications have
additional 'always-on' and real-time marketing
components 428
**Step 1. Goal setting and tracking for
interactive marketing communications** 432
Terminology for measuring digital campaigns 432
Examples of digital campaign measures 436
Campaign response mechanisms 438
Step 2. Campaign insight 441
Customer insight for digital marketing campaigns 442
Step 3. Segmentation and targeting 443
Step 4. Offer, message development and creative 447
Focus on content marketing 449
**Step 5. Budgeting and selecting the
digital media mix** 451
1 Level of investment in digital media techniques in
comparison to offline promotion 451
2 Selecting the right mix of digital media
communications tools 454
3 Level of investment in digital assets 460
**Step 6. Integration into overall media
schedule or plan** 463
Planning integrated marketing communications 463
Key activities in media selection and planning 464
Case Study 8
A short history of Facebook 468

Summary 472
Exercises 472
   Self-assessment exercises 472
   Essay and discussion questions 472
   Examination questions 473
References 473
Weblinks 475

9 Marketing communications using digital media channels 476

Learning objectives / Questions for marketers /
   Links to other chapters 476
Introduction 478
How is this chapter structured? 478
Digital marketing in practice
   The Smart Insights interview: Kate Webb,
   online marketing manager at Vision Express 480
Search engine marketing 484
What is SEO? 485
Advantages and disadvantages of SEO 488
Best practice in planning and managing SEO 489
Paid search marketing 495
Advantages and disadvantages of paid
   search marketing 498
Best practice in planning and managing paid search
   marketing 499
Online public relations 502
What is online public relations (e-PR)? 502
Advantages and disadvantages of online
   public relations 504
Best practice in planning and managing
   online public relations 506
Online partnerships including affiliate marketing 510
Affiliate marketing 510
Advantages and disadvantages of affiliate marketing 511
Best practice in planning and managing
   affiliate marketing 512
Online sponsorship 513
Interactive display advertising 515
What is display advertising? 515
Advantages and disadvantages of display advertising 516
Best practice in planning and managing
   display ad campaigns 519
**Opt-in email marketing and mobile
   text messaging** 522
What is email marketing? 522
Opt-in email options for customer acquisition 522
Opt-in email options for prospect conversion
   and customer retention (house list) 523
Advantages and disadvantages of email marketing 524
Best practice in planning and managing
   email marketing 525
Mobile text messaging 528
Social media and viral marketing 528
Developing a social media communications strategy 529

Viral marketing 529
Advantages and disadvantages of social media
   and viral marketing 532
Best practice in planning and managing viral marketing 534
Offline promotion techniques 535
Advantages and disadvantages of using offline
   communications to support e-commerce 536
Incidental and specific advertising of the
   online presence 537
Public relations 537
Direct marketing 538
Other physical reminders 538
Word-of-mouth marketing 538
   Case study 9
   Innovation at Google 539
Summary 541
Exercises 543
   Self-assessment exercises 543
   Essay and discussion questions 543
   Examination questions 543
References 544
Weblinks 546

10 Evaluation and improvement of digital channel performance 548

Learning objectives / Questions for marketers /
   Links to other chapters 548
Introduction 550
Digital marketing in practice
   The Smart Insights interview: Avinash Kaushik,
   analytics evangelist at Google 551
Performance management for digital channels 553
Stage 1: Creating a performance management system 553
Stage 2: Defining the performance metrics framework 555
Stage 3: Tools and techniques for collecting metrics
   and summarising results 560
**Customer experience and content
   management process** 573
How often should content be updated? 574
**Responsibilities for customer experience and
   site management** 575
Who owns the process? 576
Who owns the content? 577
Who owns the format? 579
Who owns the technology? 580
Content management systems 581
   Case study 10
   Learning from Amazon's culture of metrics 582
Summary 587
Exercises 588
   Self-assessment exercises 588
   Essay and discussion questions 588
   Examination questions 588
References 589
Weblinks 590

11 Business-to-consumer digital marketing practice 592

Learning objectives / Questions for marketers / Links to other chapters 592
Introduction 594
Key themes and concepts 596
The consumer perspective: online consumer behaviour 596
Who are the online customers? 596
The retail perspective: online retailing 606
Development of online retailing 607
Online retail formats and strategic approaches 609
Implications for e-retail marketing strategy 612
  Case study 11
  ASOS leads the way with social media and reinvents fashion retailing online 614
Summary 617
Exercises 618
  Mapping your path to purchase 618
  Self-assessment exercises 618
  Essay and discussion questions 618
  Examination questions 619
References 619

12 Business-to-business digital-marketing practice 622

Learning objectives / Questions for marketers / Links to other chapters 622
Introduction 624
Key themes and concepts 625

Types of B2B organisational marketing and trading environments 625
Using digital marketing to support customer acquisition in B2B marketing 627
Lead-generation and conversion optimisation for B2B marketing 629
Customer retention in B2B marketing 630
Options for online inter-organisational trading 633
B2B e-marketplaces 635
Drivers of adoption of e-marketplaces 636
  Case study 12.1
  Covisint – a typical history of a B2B marketplace? 637
How digital technologies can support B2B marketing 639
How organisations make efficiency gains 640
Analysing the factors which influence the degree of adoption of Internet technologies 640
Digital marketing strategies 642
  Case study 12.2
  B2B adoption of the Internet: Inspirational Cosmetics 645
Summary 646
Exercises 646
  Self-assessment exercises 646
  Essay and discussion questions 647
  Examination questions 647
References 647

Glossary 649
Index 679

Preface

Digital media and technology, an opportunity and threat

The development of the Internet, World Wide Web and other digital technologies have transformed marketing. For consumers, they give a much wider choice of products, services and prices from different suppliers and a more convenient way to select and purchase items. There is also a choice of technology platforms from desktops and laptops to smartphone and tablet devices for consumers to use. For organisations, digital media and new technology platforms give the opportunity to expand into new markets, offer new services, apply new online communications techniques and compete on a more equal footing with larger businesses. For those working within these organisations it gives the opportunity to develop new skills and to use these new tools to improve the competitiveness of the company.

At the same time, the Internet and related digital technology platforms give rise to many threats to organisations. For example, online companies such as **ASOS.com** (clothing), **Amazon.com** (books and retail), iTunes (music) and Expedia (travel) have captured a significant part of their market and struck fear into the existing players. Many consumers now regularly use social networks like Facebook, Google+, LinkedIn and Twitter as part of their daily lives. Engaging these consumers is an ongoing challenge, but as we will see, companies like ASOS have taken advantage of these opportunities to interact with customers and this has helped them develop as a worldwide brand.

Management of digital marketing

With the success stories of companies capturing market share following the rapidly increasing adoption of the Internet by consumers and business buyers has come a fast-growing realisation that all organisations must have an effective online presence to prosper, or possibly even survive! Michael Porter said in 2001:

> The key question is not whether to deploy Internet technology – companies have no choice if they want to stay competitive – but how to deploy it.

What are the techniques that businesses need to master to make effective use of digital marketing? Figure P.1 gives an indication of the range of marketing activities that now need to be managed effectively and which are covered in this text. RACE describes the range of tactics needed to reach, interact with, convert and engage online audience across the customer lifecycle from generating awareness, conversion to sale (online and offline) and retention and growth of customers.

The figure shows the range of different marketing activities or operating processes needed to support acquiring new customers through communicating with them on third-party websites and social media, attracting them to a company website, converting website visits into sales and then using online media to encourage further sales. You can see that applying social media is a part of RACE and therefore is one of the key management

| REACH | ACT | CONVERT | ENGAGE |

Situation analysis: How well are we using digital media now?

| Audience and customer analysis | Competitor benchmarking | Partner and influencer analysis | SWOT: own digital marketing review |

Objective setting / Control: Which goals and KPIs should we use?

| Vision and mission setting | Business and marketing goals | SMART objectives and KPIs | Digital Analytics and Dashboards |

Strategy: How can we achieve our goals?

| Segmentation and targeting | Brand positioning and value proposition | Engagement and content strategy | Integrated multichannel communications |

Governance: How do we manage digital marketing?

| Digital Transformation | Investment and Prioritisation | Multichannel Resourcing | Digital Agility |

Tactics: Which digital marketing activities do we optimise?

REACH	**ACT & CONVERT**	**ENGAGE**
Acquisition strategy to build awareness off-site and in offline media to drive to web presences	Conversion strategy to achieve marketing goals of leads & sales on web presences and offline	Retention and growth strategy to build customer and fan advocacy, repeat visits & sales
Search Engine Optimisation (SEO)	Customer journeys Desktop & mobile	Customer Experience
Pay Per Click (PPC)	Content marketing	Customer service & support
Affiliate and Co-marketing	Marketing Automation	Customer contact strategy
Online advertising	Merchandising and Personalisation	Customer service & support
Online PR	Conversion rate optimisation	Big Data
Social media marketing	Social commerce	Social CRM

| Figure P.1 | Key activities needing management for integrated digital marketing
Source: Smart Insights (2015) Introducing RACE: a practical framework to improve your digital marketing. Article by Dave Chaffey, 20 January 2015, **www.smartinsights.com/digital-marketing-strategy/race-a-practical-framework-to-improve-your-digital-marketing/** |

challenges in digital marketing, so we consider approaches to managing social media marketing throughout the text. Applying digital platforms as part of multichannel marketing to integrate customer journeys between traditional and 'new' media is also a major challenge and a theme throughout this text. Management processes related to governance of digital marketing include planning how digital marketing can be best resourced to contribute to the organisation and integrating with other marketing activities. The increased adoption of digital marketing also implies a significant programme of change that needs to be managed. New objectives need to be set, new communications strategies developed and staff developed through new responsibilities and skills.

Digital marketing – new skills required?

The aim of this text is to provide you with a comprehensive guide to the concepts, techniques and best practice to support all the digital marketing processes shown in Figure P.1. This text is based on emerging academic models together with best practice from leading adopters of digital media. The practical knowledge developed through reviewing these concepts and best practice is intended to enable graduates entering employment and marketing professionals to exploit the opportunities of digital marketing while minimising the risks.

Specifically, this text addresses the following needs:

- There is a need to know to what extent digital technology and media changes existing marketing models and whether new models and strategies can be applied to exploit the medium effectively.
- Marketing practitioners need practical digital marketing skills to market their products effectively. Knowledge of the new jargon – terms such as 'marketing automation', 'click-through', 'cookie', 'uniques' and 'page impressions' – and of effective methods of site design and promotion such as search engine marketing will be necessary, either for direct 'hands-on' development of a site or to enable communication with other staff or agencies that are implementing and maintaining the site.
- Given the rapidly changing market characteristics and best practices of digital marketing, web-based information sources are needed to update knowledge regularly. This text and the supporting companion website contain extensive links to websites to achieve this.

The text assumes some existing knowledge of marketing in the reader, perhaps developed through experience or by students studying introductory modules in marketing fundamentals, marketing communications or buyer behaviour. However, basic concepts of marketing, communications theory, buyer behaviour and the marketing mix are outlined.

Summary of changes for the sixth edition

The acclaimed structure of previous editions has been retained since this provides a clear sequence to the stages of strategy development and implementation that are required to plan successfully for digital marketing in existing and start-up companies.

The main changes made for the sixth edition, based on feedback from reviews and our close monitoring of the trends and latest developments are:

Chapter 1 – Introducing digital marketing
- Concept of digital transformation in large organisations introduced at end of chapter.

Chapter 2 – Online marketplace analysis: micro-environment

- Chapter introduction updated to describe customer choice, mobile platform use and customer journeys in the context of buying decision models such as Google's ZMOT and the McKinsey Loyalty Loop.
- Mini case study on *Ecomom* added to give a recent example of an e-retail failure with serious consequences.
- Business model canvas introduced. A useful new tool for students to review online business models for case studies and assignments. Section on portal types deleted.

Chapter 3 – The online macro-environment

- Structure of chapter retained with some discussion of updated laws for cookies, native advertising and distance selling.

Chapter 4 – Digital marketing strategy

- The latest approaches to strategy development including implementing digital transformation programmes and content marketing strategy.

Chapter 5 – The impact of digital media and technology on the marketing mix

- New section on co-marketing with the Napster case study replaced by a new case on Spotify.

Chapter 6 – Relationship marketing using digital platforms

- We introduce terms used to describe CRM in modern marketing including Marketing Automation, Big Data and predictive analytics.
- We have extended the section on social CRM and the concept of Loyalty Loop is described.

Chapter 7 – Delivering the online customer experience

- Change in emphasis from online customer experience to managing digital experiences on other platforms including mobile, social media and in-store retail.
- Explanation and example of DevOps and growth hacking added to the agile development section.
- Government Service Design Manual used as a reference to describe the process for developing online services through Discovery, Beta, Alpha and Live stages (also used in many commercial projects).
- Coverage of mobile site design issues has been extended in a section 'Mobile design considerations and techniques'.

Chapter 8 – Campaign planning for digital media

- New coverage of 'Always-on' communications and real-time marketing and PR including campaign examples from Burger King, Evian and Metro.
- New analysis tools, the Content Distribution and Content Marketing matrix added for reviewing and prioritising content marketing and digital media investments.

Chapter 9 – Marketing communications using digital media channels

- An update on the latest changes in search ranking factors including a review of the importance of Google's algorithm updates like Panda, Penguin and Hummingbird.
- A discussion of the marketing effectiveness of social media in the box 'Is social media 'mostly a waste of time' and an 'infantile delusion'?
- New content on co-marketing, programmatic ad buying and emotions that influence a viral campaign.

Chapter 10 – Evaluation and improvement of digital channel performance

- Change in emphasis from measuring and managing websites to managing digital experiences on other platforms including mobile, social media and in-store retail.
- New discussion of the need for digital agility to update different content types illustrated by a retailer.

Chapter 11 – Business-to-consumer digital marketing practice
- New and updated examples.

Chapter 12 – Business-to-business digital marketing practice
- New and updated examples.

A new series of cases 'Digital marketing in practice – Smart Insights interview' is included at the start of each chapter. These are presented in question-and-answer format and focus on the practical challenges and opportunities facing practitioners working in digital media:

- *Chapter 1* Nick Dutch of Domino's Pizza Group
- *Chapter 2* Michael Welch of **Blackcircles.com**
- *Chapter 3* Fred Bassett of Blue Latitude
- *Chapter 4* Sajjad Bhojani of Dunelm
- *Chapter 5* Roberto Hortal of EDF Energy
- *Chapter 6* Guy Stephens of IBM
- *Chapter 7* Ben Jesson and Karl Blands of Conversion Rate Experts
- *Chapter 8* Mike O'Brien of the Jam Partnership
- *Chapter 9* Kate Webb of Vision Express
- *Chapter 10* Avinash Kaushik of Google.

All interviews are available online at: **www.smartinsights.com**.

Table P.1	In-depth case studies in Digital Marketing, 6th edition	
Chapter	**Case study**	**Themes**
1 Introduction	eBay thrives in the global marketplace	Business and revenue model, proposition, competition, objectives and strategies, risk management
2 Micro-environment	Boo Hoo – learning from the largest European dot-com failure	Assessing a consumer market, business models, marketing communications
3 Macro-environment	Zopa launches a new lending model	Companion vision, branding, target market, communicating the proposition, challenges and reasons for failure
4 Digital marketing strategy	Tesco online development strategy supports global expansion	Business models, proposition and online product range, target market strategy
5 Digital marketing mix	Spotify streaming develops new revenue models	Peer-to-peer services, revenue models, proposition design, strategy, competition, risk factors
6 Relationship marketing	Dell gets closer to its customers through its social media strategy	Influence of website design on conversion, retention marketing, personalisation, e-CRM, RFM analysis
7 Online customer experience	Refining the online customer experience at **i-to-i.com**	Strategy, proposition, site design, on-site search capabilities
8 Campaign planning	A short history of Facebook	Ad revenue models, privacy
9 Digital media channels	Innovation at Google	Technology, ad revenue models, innovation
10 Evaluation and improvement of digital channel performance	Learning from Amazon's culture of metrics	Strategy, measurement, online marketing communications, personalisation approach
11 Business-to-consumer marketing	ASOS reinvents fashion retail	Online consumer profiles, purchasing behaviour and expectations and e-retailing
12 Business-to-business marketing	Covisint – typical history of a B2B marketplace? B2B adoption of the Internet: Inspirational Cosmetics	B2B trading environment, business markets, trading partnerships and digital marketing strategies

The structure and content of this text

The text is divided into three parts, each covering a different aspect of how organisations use the Internet for marketing to help them achieve competitive advantage. Table P.2 shows how the text is related to established marketing topics.

Part 1 Digital marketing fundamentals (Chapters 1–3)

Part 1 relates the use of the Internet to traditional marketing theories and concepts, and questions the validity of existing models given the differences between the Internet and other media.

- Chapter 1 *Introducing digital marketing* considers using the Internet as part of customer-centric, multichannel marketing; it also reviews the relationship between Internet marketing, digital marketing, e-commerce and e-business, and the benefits the Internet can bring to adopters, and outlines differences from other media and briefly introduces the technology.

Table P.2 Coverage of marketing topics in different chapters

Topic	1	2	3	4	5	6	7	8	9	10	11	12
Advertising								✓		✓		
Branding				✓	✓	✓				✓	✓	
Consumer behaviour	✓	✓					✓	✓	✓	✓	✓	✓
Channel and market structure	✓	✓		✓						✓	✓	✓
Communications mix				✓				✓	✓			
Communications theory	✓							✓	✓			
Customer service quality						✓	✓	✓			✓	✓
Direct marketing						✓		✓	✓			
International marketing		✓	✓	✓			✓				✓	✓
Marketing mix		✓		✓	✓			✓				
Marketing research	✓	✓	✓							✓		
Evaluation and measurement	✓			✓			✓	✓	✓	✓		
Pricing strategy		✓		✓	✓							
Promotion	✓	✓		✓				✓	✓			
Public relations								✓	✓			
Relationship marketing						✓	✓					
Segmentation		✓		✓	✓	✓		✓		✓		
Services marketing					✓		✓					
Strategy and planning	✓	✓	✓	✓	✓	✓	✓	✓	✓	✓	✓	✓
Technology background	✓		✓					✓	✓			

Note: A blue tick ✓ indicates fairly detailed coverage; a black tick ✓ indicates a brief direct reference or indirect coverage.

- Chapter 2 *Online marketplace analysis: micro-environment* reviews how digital media and technology changes the immediate environment of an organisation, including the marketplace and channel structure. It describes the type of situation analysis needed to support digital strategy by examining how customers, competitors and intermediaries and the interplay between them can be evaluated.
- Chapter 3 *The online macro-environment* reviews the impact of social, technological, economic, political and legal environmental influences on digital strategy and its implementation. The emphasis is on privacy and data protection regulations and managing technology innovation.

Part 2 Digital marketing strategy development (Chapters 4–6)

Part 2 describes the emerging models for developing strategy and provides examples of the approaches companies have used to integrate the Internet into their marketing strategy.

- Chapter 4 *Digital marketing strategy* considers how the digital strategy can be aligned with business and marketing strategies and describes a generic strategic approach with phases of situation review, goal setting, strategy formulation and resource allocation and monitoring.
- Chapter 5 *The impact of digital media and technology on the marketing mix* assesses how the different elements of the marketing mix can be varied in the online environment as part of strategy formulation.
- Chapter 6 *Relationship marketing using digital platforms* details strategies and tactics for using the Internet to build and sustain 'one-to-one' relationships with customers.

Part 3 Digital marketing: implementation and practice (Chapters 7–11)

Part 3 of the text explains practical approaches to implementing a digital marketing strategy. Techniques for communicating with customers, building relationships and facilitating electronic commerce are all reviewed in some detail. Knowledge of these practical techniques is essential for undergraduates on work placements involving a website, and for marketing managers who are dealing with suppliers such as design agencies.

- Chapter 7 *Delivering the online customer experience* explains how an online presence is developed to support branding and customer service quality objectives. The stages, analysis of customer needs, design of the site structure and layout, and creating the site, are covered together with key techniques such as user-centred design, usability and accessibility design. It also covers different service quality models used to assess experience.
- Chapter 8 *Campaign planning for digital media* describes the novel characteristics of digital media, and then considers different aspects of marketing communications which are important for developing a successful online campaign.
- Chapter 9 *Marketing communications using digital media channels.* Among the techniques covered are banner advertising, affiliate networks, promotion in search engines, co-branding and sponsorship, email, online PR, viral and word-of-mouth marketing with particular reference to social networks.
- Chapter 10 *Evaluation and improvement of digital channel performance* reviews methods for assessing and improving the effectiveness of a site and communications in delivering business and marketing benefits. The chapter briefly covers process and tools for updating sites.

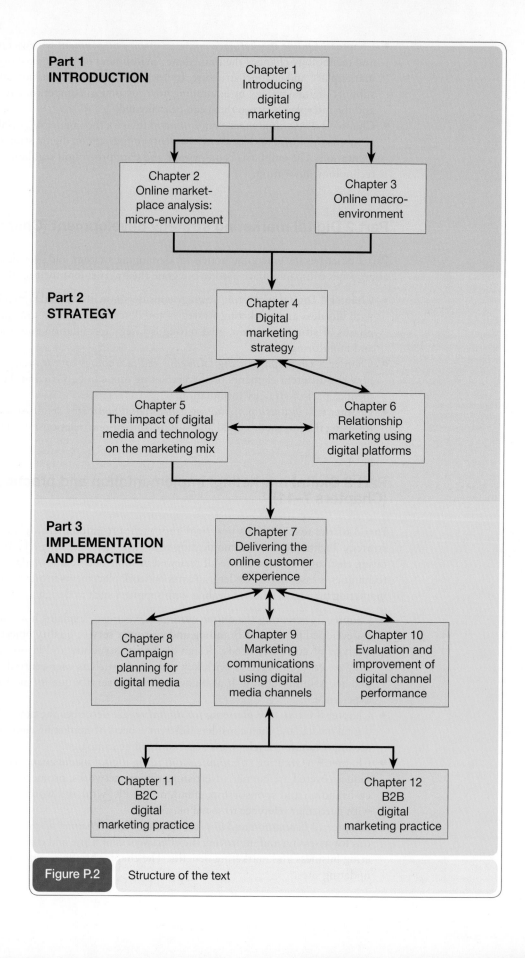

Figure P.2 Structure of the text

- Chapter 11 *Business-to-consumer digital marketing practice* examines models of marketing to consumers and provides case studies of how retail businesses are tackling such marketing.
- Chapter 12 *Business-to-business digital marketing practice* examines the different area of marketing to other businesses and provides many examples of how companies are achieving this to support international marketing.

Who should use this text?

Students

This text has been created primarily as the main student text for undergraduate and postgraduate students taking specialist marketing courses or modules which cover e-marketing, Internet and digital marketing, electronic commerce and e-business. The text is relevant to students who are:

- *undergraduates on business programmes* which include modules on the use of the Internet and e-commerce. This includes specialist degrees such as Internet marketing, electronic commerce, marketing, tourism and accounting or general business degrees such as business studies, business administration and business management;
- *undergraduate project students* who select this topic for final-year projects or dissertations – this text is an excellent supporting text for these students;
- *undergraduates completing a work placement* in a company using the Internet to promote its products;
- *students at college aiming for vocational qualifications* such as the HNC or HND in Business Management or Computer Studies;
- *postgraduate students* taking specialist master's degrees in electronic commerce or Internet marketing, generic MBAs and courses leading to qualifications such as the Certificate in Management or Diploma in Digital Marketing or Management Studies which involve modules on electronic commerce and digital marketing.

Practitioners

Previous editions have been widely used by digital marketing practitioners including:

- *marketing managers or specialists such as e-commerce managers or digital marketing managers* responsible for defining digital marketing strategy and implementing and maintaining the company website;
- *senior managers and directors* wishing to understand the potential of digital marketing for a company and who need practical guidelines on how to exploit this potential;
- *technical project managers or webmasters* who may understand the technical details of building a site, but have a limited knowledge of marketing fundamentals and how to develop an Internet marketing strategy.

What does the text offer to lecturers teaching these courses?

The text is intended to be a comprehensive guide to all aspects of using the Internet and other digital media to support marketing. The text builds on existing marketing theories and concepts, and questions the validity of models in the light of the differences between the Internet and other media. The text references the emerging body of literature specific to Internet marketing. It can therefore be used across several modules. Lecturers will find the text has a good range of case studies, activities and exercises to support their teaching. Website links are given in the text and at the end of each chapter to provide important information sources for particular topics.

Student learning features

A range of features has been incorporated into this text to help the reader get the most out of it. Each feature has been designed to assist understanding, reinforce learning and help readers find information easily, particularly when completing assignments and preparing for exams. The features are described in the order in which you will find them in each chapter.

At the start of each chapter

The 'Chapter at a glance' page provides easy navigation for each chapter. It contains:

- *Main topics:* the main topics and their page numbers.
- *Case studies:* the main cases and their page numbers.
- *Learning objectives:* a list describing what readers can learn through reading the chapter and completing the exercises.
- *Questions for marketers:* explaining the relevance of the chapter for practitioners.
- *Links to other chapters:* a summary of related information in other chapters.

In each chapter

- *Definitions:* when significant terms are first introduced the main text contains succinct definitions in the margin for easy reference.
- *Web references:* where appropriate, web addresses are given to enable readers to obtain further information. They are provided in the main text where they are directly relevant as well as at the end of the chapter.
- *Case studies:* real-world examples of how companies are using the Internet for marketing. Questions at the end of the case study are intended to highlight the main learning points from the example.
- *Mini case studies:* short features which give a more detailed example, or explanation, than is practical in the main text. They do not contain supplementary questions.
- *Activities:* exercises in the main text which give readers the opportunity to practise and apply the techniques described in the text.
- *Chapter summaries:* intended as revision aids to summarise the main learning points from the chapter.

At the end of each chapter

- *Self-assessment exercises:* short questions which will test understanding of terms and concepts described in the chapter.
- *Essay questions:* conventional essay questions.
- *Discussion questions:* these require longer essay-style answers discussing themes from the chapter. They can be used either as topics for individual essays or as the basis for seminar discussion.

- *Examination questions*: typical short-answer questions of the type that are encountered in exams. These can also be used for revision.
- *References*: these are references to books, articles or papers referred to within the chapter.
- *Further reading*: supplementary texts or papers on the main themes of the chapter. Where appropriate, a brief commentary is provided on recommended supplementary reading on the main themes of the chapters.
- *Web links*: these are significant sites that provide further information on the concepts and topics of the chapter. This list does not repeat all the website references given within the chapter, for example company sites. For clarity, the website address prefix '**http://**' is generally omitted.

At the end of the text

- *Glossary*: comprehensive definitions of all key terms and phrases used within the main text, cross-referenced for ease of use.
- *Index*: all key words and abbreviations referred to in the main text.

Support material

Free supplementary materials are available at Dave Chaffey's website at **www.smartinsights .com/book-support** to support all users of the text. This regularly updated website contains advice, comment, support materials and hyperlinks to reference sites relevant to the text. There is a password-protected area for lecturers only to discuss issues arising from using the text; additional examination-type questions and answers; a multiple-choice question bank with answers; additional cases with suggestions for discussion; and a downloadable version of the Lecturer's Guide and OHP Masters.

References

Porter, M. (2001) Strategy and the Internet, *Harvard Business Review* (March), 62–78.

About the authors

Dave Chaffey BSc, PhD, FCIM, MIDM

Dave is CEO of Smart Insights (**www.smartinsights.com**), an online publisher and analytics company providing advice and alerts on best practice and industry developments for digital marketers and e-commerce managers. The advice is also created to help readers of Dave's books. The most relevant information is highlighted at **www.smartinsights.com/book-support**.

Dave also works as an independent digital marketing trainer and consultant for Marketing Insights Limited. He has consulted on digital marketing and e-commerce strategy for companies of a range of sizes from larger organisations like 3M, Barclaycard, HSBC, Mercedes-Benz, Nokia and The North Face to smaller organisations like Arco, **Confused.com**, Euroffice, Hornbill and i-to-i.

Dave's passion is educating students and marketers about latest and best practices in digital marketing, so empowering businesses to improve their online performance through getting the most value from their web analytics and market insight. In other words, making the most of online opportunities and avoiding waste.

He is proud to have been recognised by the Department of Trade and Industry as one of the leading individuals who have provided input and influence on the development and growth of e-commerce and the Internet in the UK over the last ten years. Dave has also been recognised by the Chartered Institute of Marketing as one of 50 marketing 'gurus' worldwide who have helped shape the future of marketing. He is also proud to be an Honorary Fellow of the IDM.

Dave is a visiting lecturer on e-commerce courses at different universities including Birmingham, Cranfield, Derby, Manchester Metropolitan and Warwick Universities. He is also a tutor on the IDM Diploma in Digital Marketing, for which he is senior examiner.

In total, Dave is author of five best-selling business books including *Digital Business and Ecommerce Management*, *Digital Marketing: Strategy, Implementation and Practice*, *eMarketing eXcellence* (with P.R. Smith) and *Total Email Marketing*. Many of these books have been published in new editions since 2000 and translations include Chinese, Dutch, German, Italian and Serbian.

When offline Dave enjoys fell-running, indie guitar music and travelling with his family.

Fiona Ellis-Chadwick PhD, BSc, PGCE

Fiona-Ellis Chadwick (**www.ellis-chadwick.com**) is a Senior Lecturer at Loughborough University School of Business & Economics, where she is the Director of the Institute of Consultancy and Research Application and is an active researcher, lecturer and author. As part of her role Fiona is a leading researcher in the field of online e-commerce in retailing and is an active member of the Town Centre Research Interest Group. She is a leading thinker in the development of innovative blended-learning for undergraduate and postgraduate teaching in the subject areas of retailing and marketing, having built her expertise working with leading international publishers and universities, particularly The Open University over the past 20 years. She had a successful commercial career before becoming an academic and completing her PhD. Having made a significant contribution in the area of online retailing she continues to focus her research and academic publications in the areas of strategic adoption of the Internet. Her work on these topics has been published in *Industrial Marketing Management*, *Journal of Business Research*, *European Journal of Marketing*, *Internet Research*, *International Journal of Retail Distribution and Management*, plus additional textbooks and practitioner journals. She is also a member of the Independent Standards Board for The Retail Ombudsman. Fiona is passionate about how technology and education can help business development in the future.

Acknowledgements

I am fortunate to have shared my journey of understanding how best to use digital marketing with thousands of students and marketing professionals and I thank you for sharing your experiences with me. I'd particularly like to thank all the practitioners who have shared their experiences on applying digital marketing in the opening case study interviews in each chapter and on **SmartInsights.com**.

Likewise, I appreciate the effort made by the digital marketing specialists who have shared their knowledge as expert commentators on Smart Insights including Mike Berry and Richard Sedley (marketing strategy), Dan Barker, Ben Jesson and Pritesh Patel (analytics), Dan Bosomworth, Paul Fennemore, Katy Howell and Marie Page (Social media marketing), Rene Power (B2B marketing), Rob Thurner (mobile marketing), Chris Soames, James Gurd and John Newton (search marketing), Mel Henson (copywriting), Paul Rouke (usability) and Mark Brownlow, Kath Pay and Tim Watson (email marketing). Also to the many occasional contributors who have shared their expertise and experiences.

The authors would like to thank the team at Pearson Education in Harlow for their help in the creation of this text, especially Tom Hill, Eileen Srebernik (our acquisitions editors) and Tim Parker who managed the text through the production process.

As always, special thanks go to my family for supporting me in the ongoing updates.

Dave Chaffey

Publisher's Acknowledgements

The publishers are grateful to the reviewers of this book for their valuable comments.

We are grateful to the following for permission to reproduce copyright material:

Figures

Figure 1.1 from **www.google.com/about/corporate/company/history.html** Google. Google and the Google logo are registered trademarks of Google Inc., used with permission; Figure 1.3 from **chiefmartek.com**, Scott Brinker; Figure 1.4 from **http://www.youtube.com/watch?v=fGaVFRzTTP4**, Tesco Stores Limited; Figure 1.8 from Digital transformation: Why and how companies are investing in the new business models to lead digital customer experiences. Brian Solis., **www.altimetergroupdigitaltransformation.com**, The Altimeter Group. 2014; Figure 1.11 from *Emarketing Excellence, Planning and optimising your digital marketing*, Routledge (Chaffey, D. and Smith P.R. 2008) Taylor and Francis; Figure 1.12 from **http://novaspivack.typepad.com/nova_spivacks_weblog/2007/02/steps_towards_a.html.**, Nova Spivack; Figure 2.4 from **http://www.smartinsights.com/marketplace-analysis/consumer-buying-behaviour/what-influences-purchase/attachment/consumer-decision-journey/**. Published with permission from Digital Marketing advice site **SmartInsights.com** curated by Dave Chaffey; Figure 2.6 from *Googling the Present, Economic and Labour Review*, Office for National Statistics (Chamberlin, G. 2010) ONS, Source: Office for National Statistics licensed under the Open Government Licence v.3.0.; Figure 2.10 from New GfK ROPO study with Vodafone, Published on Google Barometer Blog October 20th 2010, Google. Google and the Google logo are registered trademarks of Google Inc., used with permission; Figure 2.12 from *Googling the Present, Economic and Labour Review* Office for National Statistics (Chamberlin, G. 2010) Office for National Statistics, Source: Office for National Statistics licensed under the

Open Government Licence v.3.0; Figure 2.13 from Online Customer Experience: A Review of the Business-to-Consumer Online Purchase Context *International Journal of Management Reviews*, 13 (1), 24-39 (Rose S., Hair N. and Clark M. 2011), © 2010 Rose S., Hair N. and Clark M. International Journal of Management Reviews © 2010 British Academy of Management and Blackwell Publishing Ltd., Reproduced with permission of Blackwell Publishing; Figures 2.19 and 2.21 from **www.bowencraggs.com**, Bowen Craggs & Co.; Figure 2.26 from **www.SmartInsights.com**, Published with permission from Digital Marketing advice site **SmartInsights.com** curated by Dave Chaffey; Figure 3.3 from Smart Insights (Marketing Intelligence) Limited (2014); Figure 4.3 from *EMarketing Excellence: Planning and optimizing your digital marketing.*, 3 ed., Butterworth Heinemann, Oxford (Chaffey, D. and Smith, P.R. 2008) Copyright © 2008 Elsevier B.V. All Rights Reserved; Figure 4.9 from **www .arenaflowers.com**, Arena Flowers; Figure 6.2 from Social CRM: The New Rules of Relationship Management, Whitepaper published April 2010, Editor Charlene Li; Figure 6.19 from Case Study: Applying RFM Segmentation to the SilverMinds *Journal of Direct Data and Digital Marketing Practice*, 5 (3), 269-275 (Patron M. 2004), Palgrave Macmillan Copyright © 2004, Macmillan Publishers Ltd; Figure 7.2 from Succeeding with brands on the internet, *Journal of Brand Management*, 8 (3), 186-95 (de Chernatony, L. 2001), Palgrave Macmillan; Figure 7.6 from **http://www.webpagetest.org/**, Google, Google and the Google logo are registered trademarks of Google Inc., used with permission; Figure 7.13 from **www.apps.ft.com**, Financial Times, © The Financial Times Limited. All Rights Reserved; Figure 8.6 from Millward Brown Qualitative; Figure 8.13 from **www.centreforintegratedmarketing.com**, CODAR is a registered trademark of Stepping Stones Consultancy Ltd; Figures 1.18, 8.12, 8.14, 9.1, 9.12 published with permission from Digital Marketing advice site **SmartInsights.com** curated by Dave Chaffey; Figure 9.14 from Blog post, **www.amnavigator.com/blog/2011/09/12/back-to-affiliate-cookie-duration-return-days-question/** E Prussakov; Figure 9.18 from *The Hitwise UK Media Impact Report*, Hitwise (2006) Hitwise; Figure 10.5 from *The Multichannel Challenge* Butterworth-Heinemann, Oxford, UK (Wilson, H. 2008) © 2008 Butterworth-Heinemann, Oxford, UK reproduced by permission of Taylor & Francis Books UK; Figure 10.9 from National Express; Figure 10.10 from Test reports courtesy of Maxymiser Content Intelligence, **www.maxymiser.com**, Maxymiser Ltd; Figure 11.1 from Global perspective on retail: online retailing, Euromonitor, **http://www.cushmanwakefield.com**, © Cushman & Wakefield Inc; Figure 11.5 from 20th anniversary of first online sale: how we shop on the web, *The Telegraph*, 11/08/2014 (Spence, P.), The Telegraph, copyright © Telegraph Media Group Limited 2014; Figure 12.8 from Implementing e-value strategies in UK retailing, *International Journal of Retail and Distribution Management*, 33 (6), 426-43 (Nicholls, A. and Watson, A. 2005), International journal of retail & distribution management by EMERALD GROUP PUBLISHING LIMITED. Reproduced with permission of EMERALD GROUP PUBLISHING LIMITED in the format Republish in a book via Copyright Clearance Center.

Screenshots

Screenshot 1.5 from **http://www.tatucouture.com/**, Tatu Couture; Screenshot 1.8 from **https://www.travelrepublic.co.uk/apps/**, Travel Republic; Screenshot 1.17 from **www.travelrepublic .co.uk**, Travel Republic; Screenshot 2.15 from Google (2015), Google and the Google logo are registered trademarks of Google Inc., used with permission; Screenshot 2.20 from **www.taobao.com**, AllThingsGreen; Screenshot 4.14 from **www.ideastorm.com**, © 2015 Dell Inc. All Rights Reserved.; Screenshot 4.16 from **http://www.ap.dell.com/content/default .aspx?c=sg&1=en&s=gen**. © 2015 Dell Inc. All Rights Reserved; Screenshot 5.8 from **www .google.co.uk**, Google and the Google logo are registered trademarks of Google Inc., used with permission; Screenshot 5.11 from **www.spotify.com**, Spotify AB, Spotify does not control the rights to the photograph of the women in the screenshot; Screenshot 6.1 from **http:// about.zappos.com/our-unique-culture/zappos-core-values**, © 2013 **Zappos.com**, Inc. or its affiliates; Screenshot 6.6 from Smart Insights (Marketing Intelligence) Ltd; Screenshot 6.13 from **www.ctshirts.co.uk**, Charles Tyrwhitt LLP; Screenshot 7.11 from **www.csszengarden .com**, CSS Zengarden; Screenshot 7.17 from **www.i-to-i.com**, itoi; Screenshot 8.2 from **www .threadless.com**, Threadless; Screenshot 8.5 from **twitter.com**, Twitter, Tweet and Twitter Bird Logo are trademarks of Twitter, Inc. or its affiliates; Screenshot 8.18 from **www.oktopost.com**,

Oktopost.com; Screenshot 8.22 from **www.lynxeffect.com**, reproduced with kind permission of Unilever PLC and group companies; Screenshot 8.24 from **http:developers.facebook.com/docs/plugins**, Facebook; Screenshot 9.3 from **www.Google.com**, Google, Google and the Google logo are registered trademarks of Google Inc., used with permission; Screenshot 9.4 from Google, Google and the Google logo are registered trademarks of Google Inc., used with permission; Screenshot 9.8 from **https://majestic.com/**, majestic.com; Screenshot 9.10 from You tube Video, Gatorade Co; Screenshot 9.11 from **http://www.smartinsights.com/**, published with permission from Digital Marketing advice site **SmartInsights.com** curated by Dave Chaffey; Screenshot 10.8 from Hootsuite social and media management dashboard Custom Analytics, Hootsuite Media Inc; Screenshot 11.6 from **https://www.shopdirect.com/**, Shop Direct; Screenshot 12.4 from **http://socialmedia.cisco.com**, Courtesy of Cisco Systems, Inc. Unauthorised use not permitted; Screenshot 12.5 from **www.leadforensics.com**, Lead Forensics

Tables

Table 1.2 from *E marketing Excellence, Planning and Optimising Your Digital Marketing* 3ed., Elsevier (Smith P.R. and Chaffey D. 2008) © Elsevier (2008); Table 2.1 from *Googling the Present, Economic and Labour Review* Office for National Statistics (Chamberlin, G. 2010) Office for National Statistics, Source: Office for National Statistics licensed under the Open Government Licence v.3.0.; Table 2.4 from Multi-channel experience consistency: Evidence from Lexus, *Journal of Direct Data and Digital Marketing Practice*, 6 (4), 317-25 (Stuart-Menteth H., Arbuthnot S. and Wilson H. 2005), Copyright © 2005, Macmillan Publishers Ltd; Table 2.5 from *Understanding Influence, and Making It Work For You: A CNET Networks Study*, The Associated Press/YGS Group (2007) The Associated Press/YGS Group; Table 5.1 from A comparison of time-varying online price and price dispersion between multichannel and dot-com DVD retailers, *Journal of Interactive Marketing* 20 (2), 3-20 (Xing, X., Yang, S. and Tang, F., A 2006), Copyright © 2006 Direct Marketing Educational Foundation, Inc. Originally published in [2006] by Wiley Periodicals, Inc. Published by Elsevier Inc. All rights reserved; Table 8.4 from School of Computer Science web research summary, University of Manchester, **www.cs.manchester.ac.uk/research/vicram/studies/eyetracking.php**, Harper, S. (2006); Table 8.7 from **www.iab.net/xmos**, Interactive Advertising Bureau; Table 10.1 from ABCE (**www.abce.org.uk**); Table 11.3 from Allegra Strategies (2005); Table 12.2 from An empirical study of the uptake of performance measurement by internet retailers, *Internet Research*, 18 (4), 361-81 (Gunawan, G., Ellis-Chadwick, F. and King, M. 2008), Emerald Publishing

Text

Interview on pages 9-10 from Nick Dutch Head of Digital at Domino's Pizza Group Limited in the UK& ROI. Published with permission from Digital Marketing advice site **SmartInsights.com** curated by Dave Chaffey; Case Study 1.2 published with permission from Digital Marketing advice site **SmartInsights.com** curated by Dave Chaffey; Case Study 1.3 from **http://www.travelrepublic.co.uk/help/pressReplace_003.aspx**, Travel Republic; Interview on pages 57-59 from Michael Welch, published with permission from Digital Marketing advice site **SmartInsights.com** curated by Dave Chaffey; Interview on pages 121-2 from Fred Bassett of Blue Latitude, published with permission from Digital Marketing advice site **SmartInsights.com** curated by Dave Chaffey; Interview on pages 182-4 from Sajjad Bhojani, Head of Dunelm Direct Trading at Dunelm, published with permission from Digital Marketing advice site **SmartInsights.com** curated by Dave Chaffey; Interviews on pages 252-5, pages 360-1, pages 422-4, 9 and pages 551-3 published with permission from Digital Marketing advice site **SmartInsights.com** curated by Dave Chaffey; Interview on pages 304-7 from Guy Stephens Social Customer Care consultant at IBM, published with permission from Digital Marketing advice site **SmartInsights.com** curated by Dave Chaffey; Interviews pages 252-5, pages 360-1, pages 422-4, 9 and pages 551-3 published with permission from Digital Marketing advice site **SmartInsights.com** curated by Dave Chaffey; Case Study 9.1 from **www.buzzparadise.com/case-studies/pr-2-0-event-for-renault-le-web-2010/**, Buzz Paradise; Case Study 12.3 adapted from Excerpt from Transforming Strategy One Customer at a Time, *Harvard Business Review* (R. Harrington and A. Tjan 2008), Copyright © 2008 by The Harvard Business School Publishing Corporation; all rights reserved.

Part 1
Digital marketing fundamentals

Chapter 1 introduces the opportunities and challenges of digital marketing and explains the different types of digital marketing platforms and media channels available to engage audiences online. It also introduces a planning framework that can be used to structure digital marketing strategies and case studies. Chapters 2 and 3 provide a foundation for developing an integrated digital marketing strategy by reviewing how the online marketplace of an organisation can be assessed as part of situation analysis.

1 Introducing digital marketing 4

- Introduction – how have digital technologies transformed marketing?
- Definitions – what are digital marketing and multichannel marketing?
- Introduction to digital marketing strategy
- Introduction to digital marketing communications

2 Online marketplace analysis: micro-environment 54

- Situation analysis for digital marketing
- The digital marketing environment
- Understanding customer journeys
- Consumer choice and digital influence
- Online consumer behaviour and implications for marketing
- Competitors
- Suppliers
- New channel structures
- Business models for e-commerce

3 The online macro-environment 118

- The rate of environment change
- Technological forces
- Economic forces
- Political forces
- Legal forces
- Social forces
- Cultural forces

Chapter 1
Introducing digital marketing

Chapter at a glance

Main topics

- Introduction – how have digital technologies transformed marketing? 6
- Definitions – what are digital marketing and multichannel marketing? 11
- Introduction to digital marketing strategy 16
- Introduction to digital marketing communications 29

Case studies

Digital marketing in practice

The Smart Insights interview: Nick Dutch, Head of Digital at Domino's Pizza Group Limited shares the approach used to help plan digital strategy development 9

Case study 1: eBay thrives in the global marketplace 46

Learning objectives

After reading this chapter, you should be able to:

- Explain the relevance of different types of digital platforms and digital media to marketing
- Evaluate the advantages and challenges of digital media
- Identify the key differences between customer communications digital marketing and traditional marketing.

Questions for marketers

Key questions for marketing managers related to this chapter are:

- What are the options for digital marketing to grow our business?
- What are the key benefits of digital marketing?
- What differences do digital media introduce compared to existing marketing communications models?

Scan code to find the latest updates for topics in this chapter

Links to other chapters

This chapter provides an introduction to digital marketing, and the concepts introduced are covered in more detail later in the book, as follows:

- Chapters 2 and 3 explain marketplace analysis for digital marketing planning
- Chapters 4, 5 and 6 in Part 2 describe how digital marketing strategy can be developed
- Chapters 7, 8, 10 and 11 in Part 3 describe strategy implementation
- Chapters 11 and 12 in Part 3 describe B2C and B2B applications.

Introduction – how have digital technologies transformed marketing?

The Internet, the web and digital media have transformed marketing and business since the first website (**http://info.cern.ch**) went live in 1991. With over 3 billion people around the world regularly using the web to find products, entertainment and friends, consumer behaviour and the way companies market to both consumers and businesses have changed dramatically.

To succeed in the future, organisations will need marketers, strategists and agencies with up-to-date knowledge of how to apply digital media such as the web, email, mobile and interactive TV. The aim of *Digital Marketing: Strategy, Implementation and Practice* is to support students and professionals in gaining and developing this knowledge. In the text, we will show how traditional marketing models and concepts can be applied to help develop digital marketing strategies and plans and where new models are appropriate. We will also give many practical examples and best practices for applying online communications tools to effectively market an organisation's products and services using the Internet and other digital media.

For the authors of this book, digital marketing is an exciting area to be involved with, since it poses many new opportunities and challenges yearly, monthly and even daily. Innovation is a given, with the continuous introduction of new technologies, new business models and new communications approaches. For example, Google innovates relentlessly. Its service has developed a long way since 1998 (Figure 1.1) with billions of pages now indexed and other services such as web mail, pay-per-click (PPC) adverts, analytics and social networking all part of its offering. Complete Activity 1.1 or view Table 1.1 to see other examples of online startups showing the rate at which new innovations occur.

Figure 1.1	Google timeline
	Source: Google Corporate Timeline: www.google.com/about/company/timeline/

Activity 1.1 | Innovation in digital marketing platforms

Purpose

To introduce some of the most important platforms used for digital marketing today and to illustrate innovation in online business models and communications approaches.

Questions

1 Think about the innovation you have witnessed during the time you have used the Internet, World Wide Web and mobile platforms. What would you say are the main sites used in your country which have changed the way you spend your time online? Table 1.1 shows the sites that we believe have had the biggest influence on online business models in the US and Europe, with more emphasis on the most recent ones.

2 What do these sites have in common with the ones that you have selected and what do you think has made them successful?

Table 1.1 | Timeline of online services indicating innovation in business model or marketing communications approach

Year founded	Company/service	Category of innovation
1994	Amazon	Retailer
1995 (March)	Yahoo!	Directory and portal
1995 (September)	eBay	Online auction
1995 (December)	Altavista	Search engine
1996	Hotmail	Web-based email Viral marketing (using email signatures to promote service) Purchased by Microsoft in 1997
1998	GoTo.com Overture	First pay-per-click search marketing Purchased by Yahoo! in 2003
1998	Google	Search engine
1999	Blogger	Blog publishing platform Purchased by Google in 2003
1999	Alibaba	B2B marketplace with $1.7 billion IPO on Hong Kong stock exchange in 2007 (see case in Chapter 2, p. 94)
1999	MySpace Formerly eUniverse	Social network Purchased by News Corp in 2005
2001	Wikipedia	Open encyclopedia
2002	Last.fm	A UK-based Internet radio and music community website, founded in 2002. On 30 May 2007, CBS Interactive acquired Last.fm for £140m (US$280m)
2003	Skype	Peer-to-peer Internet telephony VOIP – Voice Over Internet Protocol Purchased by eBay in 2005
2003	Second Life	Immersive virtual world

Year founded	Company/service	Category of innovation
2004	Facebook	Social network applications and groups
2005	YouTube	Video sharing and rating
2006	Paypal	Paypal offers first mobile payment service
2007	iPhone	Apple launches the iPhone
2008	Groupon	A group-buying service based on use of discounted gift certificates
2009	Foursquare and Kickstarter	Foursquare was a location-based social media website designed for mobile access through 'check-ins' Kickstarter launches to give momentum crowdsourcing
2011	Snapchat	A mobile photo messaging service where images are deleted after a set number of seconds
2012	SmartThings	Internet of Things service, connects everyday objects — from ovens to thermostats to the Internet
2013	Apple iBeacon and CloudTags	iBeacon uses low-energy Bluetooth to notify shoppers of items of interest. Cloudtags gives shoppers in-depth information about products via tablets
The Future	Digital innovations and business propositions	Innovation drives the digital economy and is set to continue into the future. Digital has become mainstream and although there are opportunities, displacing existing global incumbent platforms will be rare. For the latest developments see: **www.thenextweb.com**

The challenge for marketers is to assess which innovations are most relevant to their organisation and to seek to gain advantage through introducing them to a company such that the digital marketing techniques integrate effectively with traditional marketing communications.

This text will take you through the questions to ask and potential solutions step by step to enable you to develop appropriate strategies. In this introductory chapter, after an initial scoping of digital marketing, we review two main aspects of managing digital marketing. In the first part of this chapter, we review the main strategic challenges and opportunities of digital marketing that must be managed by organisations. We then go on to introduce the communications techniques for promoting companies online through digital technology platforms such as desktop, tablet and smartphone devices (for example, search engine marketing (SEM), and social media and display advertising) using the unique characteristics of digital media. The following practitioner interview with Nick Dutch, Head of Digital at Domino's Pizza Group, highlights some of the challenges and opportunities of marketing an online business.

Nick Dutch is Head of Digital at Domino's Pizza Group Limited in the UK and Republic of Ireland. In this interview he shares the approach used to help plan digital strategy development.

Digital strategy development at Domino's Pizza

Q. Please outline your role and how your team is structured

My role combines all aspects of the online customer experience from media to conversion, both on the desktop site and in mobile. So, I'm responsible for all online marketing activity that drives people to the site and interactions on the customer journey whether on our desktop site, mobile sites and apps and our communities on social media sites which are also part of how the Domino's brand is presented in the digital space. From a strategic point of view, I'm responsible for developing the long-term strategic roadmap for digital and ensuring it contributes to and complements the overall business strategy.

We have six in our digital team in total, with three other manager roles for the three key activities: an e-Commerce Marketing Manager, Digital Campaigns Manager and CRM Manager. The e-Commerce Marketing Manager's remit is performance-based with a focus on generating value through search, affiliate and display marketing and also maximising conversion on-site. They work closely with the Digital Campaigns Manager – imagine the intersecting Yin and Yang of Digital Marketing. The Digital Campaigns Manager ensures integration with broader brand marketing initiatives and is tasked with bringing the brand to life online, so they're responsible for branded digital content on- and off-site. The CRM Manager works with an E-CRM exec and they manage automated triggered email predominantly and in future increased SMS and personalisation anywhere 1:1 communications, including Push notifications on mobile, digital display and of course the website itself. They're also supported by a database marketing analyst.

Our team is relatively small since we're supported on the technical side by the commercial systems team responsible for the development and maintenance of all our e-commerce platforms (in IT services), we're their client. We work with them closely on new features and applications, conversion rate optimisation and they manage on-site product content updates. There are also business analysts in this team who provide reports and insights to support CRO.

Q. How do you set the vision for the long-term contribution of desktop+mobile channels for Dominos?

Our vision for digital is centred on how we can provide convenience to the customer across different channels – convenience has to be platform agnostic.

The rate of consumer adoption of digital technologies informs this vision, so we went into mobile first, because we were already seeing that mobile platforms were popular for customers. We will be tracking take-up of newer technologies like NFC payment options and will add them to a longer-term three-year roadmap based on when we see them entering the mainstream. Then there is a hard roadmap for the next 12 months. What we identify two years out may fall by the wayside if there isn't a clear customer imperative.

We prioritise new developments based on a combination of how it will impact customer convenience and commercial returns through increased conversion rate or average order value. It doesn't have to always be a scientific prioritisation; decisions can be more brand-related: for example, connected TV – opportunity to partner with

TV manufacturer – may be more brand related – innovation is a key element of our brand DNA so we'll always consider those things that may not be 100 per cent commercially viable also.

Q. What is your process for making investment decisions in media?

The starting point is based on integrating with business priorities, which are based on a classic campaign marketing planning process – based on new product introductions for example – so online campaign activities are aligned with these.

At a top level, we make an investment-split decision for search marketing, affiliates and display based on previous performance trends comparing the previous year to different quarters and of course our current business targets and forecasts. We need to use the best mix of media to attract customers who are exhibiting different behaviours in their buying decision. So some customers will be in the process of getting pizza in tonight and are looking for the best deals right now. Affiliates are significant in driving that decision. But others may be considering eating in a few days; display can be important here and we do see a halo-effect of display ads prompting searches for Domino's, so it's important to balance performance and brand investments.

At a practical level, like all e-commerce sites, we look at our year-on-year performance carefully – all decisions are based on beating year-on-year performance mentality. Detailed decisions are involved here – for example around search, we may have a search budget where we have to balance investment in paid and natural search to get the best efficiency. Likewise, depending on the market factors, we will change the balance of targeting different terms in Adwords; some terms are demand creation such as generics, whereas others mop up demand such as brand or local search terms.

Adjusting the media mix month by month is always an ongoing activity because of four factors. First, competitor action such as a promotion or competing on a brand term or other media activity. Second, new marketing options we may want to test to gain advantages – for example, the current targeting options in Gmail or custom audiences in Facebook. Then there are changes to business needs such as weather affecting demand – we have to generate more demand which can be mean upweighting generic or local search targeting for new customers.

Finally, our analysis techniques or tools of which media are effective will improve – for example, we have been looking more recently at purchase attribution and this has given emphasis on display budget against more 'mopping up channels'.

I haven't mentioned social media yet since it's not so important from a direct-sales point of view. That said, we do use content marketing where bespoke content is developed around our audience's passion, for example to associate us with football. But it's critical for other aspects such as community management on the social networks where we create and share content continuously around this. We do offer social sign-in through Facebook Connect, for example, but that isn't used to a significant degree. Of course, social media is also important for customer service where we have to manage this proactively. We use some outsourced services for different social media activities.

Q. How do you manage conversion rate improvements and the implementation of new features on your sites?

We now continually optimise, there has been a change in mindset as sales from the online channels have increased. It was more of a static site originally, but we are now able to review more regularly, for example on a fortnightly or monthly review process. We use Google Analytics as a performance tool for reviewing customer journeys and we use multi-device attribution, but can use journey analysis, e.g. through ad serving to give us something similar.

Definitions – what are digital marketing and multichannel marketing?

Digital media
Communications are facilitated through content and interactive services delivered by different digital technology platforms including the Internet, web, mobile phone, interactive TV, IPTV and digital signage.

Digital marketing
The application of the Internet and related digital technologies in conjunction with traditional communications to achieve marketing objectives.

Online company presence
Different forms of online media controlled by a company including their website, blogs, email list and social media presences. Also known as 'owned media'.

Electronic customer relationship management (E-CRM)
Using digital communications technologies to maximise sales to existing customers and encourage continued usage of online services through techniques including database, personalised web messages, customer services, email and social media marketing.

Multichannel marketing
Customer communications and product distribution are supported by a combination of digital and traditional channels at different points in the buying cycle.

Customer journeys
The sequence of online and offline touchpoints a customer takes during a buying process or broader customer experience. Online this may include a range of digital platforms, communications media, websites, pages and engagement devices.

The use of the Internet and other **digital media** and technology to support 'modern marketing' has given rise to a bewildering range of labels and jargon created by both academics and professionals. It has been called digital marketing, Internet marketing, e-marketing and web marketing. For the fifth edition we changed the title of this text from *Internet Marketing* to *Digital Marketing* since it shows the use of a range of digital platforms to interact with audiences and for other reasons explained in the preface. Of course, what is important within a company is not the term, but the activities that comprise digital marketing, which must be prioritised according to their relevance. So in this chapter we focus on introducing these different digital marketing activities.

Digital marketing can be simply defined as:

Achieving marketing objectives through applying digital technologies and media.

This succinct definition helps remind us that it is the results delivered by technology that should determine investment in Internet marketing, not the adoption of the technology! These digital technologies include the desktop, mobile, tablet and other digital platforms introduced later in the chapter.

In practice, digital marketing includes managing different forms of **online company presence**, such as company websites and social media company pages in conjunction with online communications techniques introduced later in this chapter, including search engine marketing, social media marketing, online advertising, email marketing and partnership arrangements with other websites. These techniques are used to support the objectives of acquiring new customers and providing services to existing customers that help develop the customer relationship through **E-CRM**. However, for digital marketing to be successful there is still a necessity for integration of these techniques with traditional media such as print, TV and direct mail as part of multichannel marketing communications.

The role of digital platforms in supporting integrated **multichannel marketing** is another recurring theme in this text and in Chapter 2 we explore its role in supporting different **customer journeys** through alternative communications and distribution channels. Online channels can also be managed to support the whole buying process from pre-sale to sale to post-sale and further development of customer relationships.

Paid, owned and earned media

To develop a sound digital strategy today involves understanding a more complex, more competitive buying environment than ever before, with customer journeys involving many different forms of online presence. To help develop a strategy to reach and influence potential customers online, it's commonplace to refer to three main types of media channels marketers need to consider today (Figure 1.2):

1 **Paid media.** These are bought media where there is investment to pay for visitors, reach or conversions through search, display ad networks or affiliate marketing. Offline, traditional media like print and TV advertising and direct mail remain important, accounting for the majority of paid media spend.
2 **Owned media.** This is media owned by the brand. Online this includes a company's own websites, blogs, email list, mobile apps or their social presence on Facebook, LinkedIn or Twitter. Offline owned media may include brochures or retail stores. It's useful to think of a company's own presence as media in the sense that they are an alternative investment to other media and they offer opportunities to promote products using similar ad or editorial formats to other media. It emphasises the need for all organisations to become multichannel publishers.

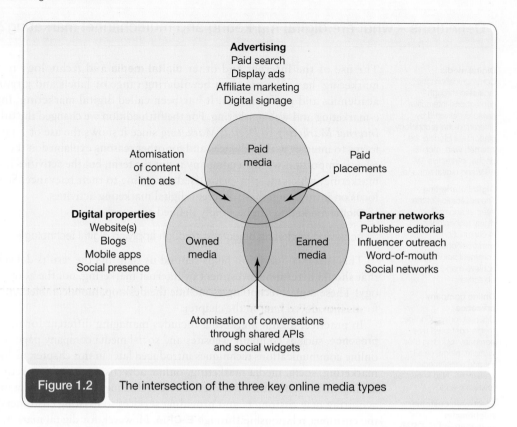

Figure 1.2   The intersection of the three key online media types

Paid media
Also known as bought media, a direct payment occurs to a site owner or an ad network when they serve an ad, a sponsorship or pay for a click, lead or sale generated.

Owned media
Different forms of online media controlled by a company including their website, blogs, email list and social media presence.

Earned media
The audience is reached through editorial, comments and sharing online.

Application Programming Interfaces
Method of exchanging data between systems such as website services.

3 **Earned media**. Traditionally, earned media has been the name given to publicity generated through PR invested in targeting influencers to increase awareness about a brand. Now earned media also includes word-of-mouth that can be stimulated through viral and social media marketing, and conversations in social networks, blogs and other communities. It's useful to think of earned media as the sharing of engaging content developed through different types of partners such as publishers, bloggers and other influencers including customer advocates. Another way of thinking about earned media is as different forms of conversations between consumers and businesses occurring both online and offline.

We will see at the end of this chapter that content marketing has become a core integrated modern marketing approach which involves communications across paid, owned and earned media.

You can see in Figure 1.2 that there is overlap between the three different types of media. It is important to note this since achieving this overlap requires integration of campaigns, resources and infrastructure. Content on a content hub or site can be broken down (sometimes described as microcontent) and shared between other media types through widgets powered by program and data exchange APIs (**Application Programming Interfaces**) such as the Facebook API.

The growing range of digital marketing platforms

If you think of the options to reach and interact with audiences when they are online, we have traditionally used digital media channels like search, social media or display ads on media sites accessed via desktop or laptop-based hardware platforms. The desktop access platform has been dominant for years and remains so for now, but the number of mobile smartphone and tablet visitor sessions now exceed desktop Internet sessions for many consumer businesses. Combining with these hardware platforms, there are also different software platforms which marketers can use to reach and interact with their audience through content marketing or advertising, so let's look at the range of options that are available:

Desktop, laptop and notebook platforms

1 **Desktop browser-based platform.** This is traditional web access through the consumer's browser of choice, whether Internet Explorer, Google Chrome or Safari.

2 **Desktop apps.** We don't hear this platform talked about much; increasingly users are accessing paid and free apps from their desktop via the Apple App Store or the Microsoft equivalent, like Gadgets. This gives opportunities for brands to engage via these platforms.

3 **Email platforms.** While email isn't traditionally considered a platform, it does offer an opportunity separate from browser and app-based options to communicate with prospects or clients, whether through editorial or advertising, and email is still widely used for marketing.

4 **Feed-based and API data exchange platforms.** Many users still consume data through RSS feeds, and Twitter and Facebook status updates can be considered a form of feed or stream where ads can be inserted.

5 **Video-marketing platforms.** Streamed video is often delivered through the other platforms mentioned above, particularly through browsers and plug-ins, but it represents a separate platform. Television channels delivered through streaming over the Internet (known as IPTV) are related to this platform.

It could be argued that the major social networks Facebook, LinkedIn and Twitter also provide a form of platform, but these really exist across all of these technology platforms so they haven't been identified separately.

Mobile phone and tablet platforms

The options on mobile hardware platforms are similar in many ways to the desktop. Since they can be used in different locations there are many new opportunities to engage consumers through **mobile marketing** and **location-based marketing**. The main platforms are:

1 **Mobile operating system and browser.** There are mobile browsers which are closely integrated with the operating system.

2 **Mobile-based apps.** Apps are proprietary to the mobile operating system, whether Apple iOS, Google Android, RIM or Windows. A big decision is whether to deliver content and experience through a browser and/or a specific app which provides an improved experience. If you check the latest research you will see that the majority of mobile media time is app-based.

Other hardware platforms

Apart from desktop and mobile access, there are a host of other and growing platforms through which to communicate with customers. For example:

1 *Gaming platforms.* Whether it's a PlayStation, Nintendo or Xbox, there are increasing options to reach gamers through ads or placements within games, for example in-game ads.

2 *Indoor and outdoor kiosk-type apps.* For example, interactive kiosks and augmented reality options to communicate with consumers.

3 *Interactive signage.* The modern version of signage is closely related to kiosk apps and may incorporate different methods such as touchscreen, Bluetooth or QR codes to encourage interactive. Mini Case Study 1.1 gives a futuristic example.

4 *Wearables.* Smart watches such as the Apple Watch and smart glasses such as Google Glass.

Software platforms for managing modern marketing

There is a bewildering range of software, services and systems available today for managing marketing. Many are now available as **SaaS** platforms which have made services to manage marketing more affordable for smaller businesses and easier to manage for all since no installation is required.

Mobile marketing
Marketing to encourage consumer engagement when using mobile phones (particularly smartphones) or tablet devices.

Location-based marketing
Location or proximity-based marketing is mobile marketing based on the GPS built into phones or based on interaction with other local digital devices.

Mobile-based apps
Designed to run on smartphones and tablet computers, apps provide users with rich mobile content by deploying the handset's multiple native capabilities. Apps are available for download from app stores hosted by the mobile operating systems (e.g. iTunes for iOS, Google Play for Android, Microsoft App Store, BlackBerry App World).

Software as a Service (SaaS)
Business applications and software services are provided through Internet and web protocols with the application managed on a separate server from where it is accessed through a web browser on an end user's computer with data stored within 'The Cloud'.

The range of options have been ably summarised by Scott Brinker, who publishes a summary of the marketing technology landscape each year. The six main categories of system he recommends marketers review for the range of technologies available are:

1 **Marketing experiences.** More specialised technologies that directly affect prospects and customers across their lifecycle, such as advertising, email, social media, search engine optimisation, content marketing, A/B testing, marketing apps – the 'front-office' of modern marketing.
2 **Marketing operations.** The tools and data for managing the 'back-office' of marketing, such as analytics, Marketing Resource Management (MRM), Digital Asset Management (DAM) and agile marketing management.

Activity 1.2	The latest marketing technology landscape

Purpose

To illustrate the range of systems available to support marketers and to explain the main categories of service available.

Activity

1 Search for Scott Brinker's latest technology roadmap for the current year on his **ChiefMartec.com** site. For each of the six categories of service summarised in Figure 1.3, write a layman's description of how they can support digital marketing activities by reviewing the proposition as described on the websites of the most popular services in the category (the most popular are listed first).
2 Make a note to understand the different types of service defined in each category.
3 Choose one or two vendor systems and visit their website to see how they explain the proposition and explain it to others in your group(s). Alternatively identify the most popular service(s) in each category.

Marketing experiences
(Customer experience, digital media channel, voice of customer, personalisation, chat, sales enable, testing and optimisation)

Marketing operations
(Digital analytics, attribution and dashboards asset management, audience and market data)

Marketing middleware
(APIs, data management, tag management, identity)

Marketing backbone platforms
(CRM, marketing automation, content management, Ecommerce)

Infrastructure
(Databases, big data, cloud, mobile and web development)

Internet
(Digital platforms)

Figure 1.3	Scott Brinker's categorisation of modern marketing technology options. Digital Platforms include Facebook, Google, LinkedIn and Twitter

Source: With permission – Chiefmartec.com

3 **Marketing middleware** such as Data Management Platforms (DMPs), tag management, cloud connectors, user management and API services.

4 **Marketing backbone platforms** such as customer relationship management, marketing automation, content management and e-commerce engines. (These are quite different in their application, so need to be reviewed separately.)

5 **Infrastructure services** such as databases, big data management, cloud computing and software development tools.

6 **Internet services** such as Facebook, Google and Twitter that underlie today's marketing environment. (How you integrate with these key platforms.) Complete Activity 1.2 to review the latest technologies.

Mini case study 1.1	Tesco Homeplus opens subway virtual store in South Korea

In South Korea, Tesco Homeplus operates around 600 stores (including franchise store operations) but has significantly fewer stores than the market leader E-mart. Based on research which showed that many Koreans tend to shop in stores near their homes for convenience, Tesco trialled a virtual store to reach these shoppers.

And Tesco now operates 22 virtual stores, where virtual displays were implemented in a similar way to actual stores, from the display to merchandise but with smartphone QR code readers used to shop and the goods delivered home after checkout (Figure 1.4). This approach enables South Koreans to shop – on-the-go.

Source: Homeplus (2014), www.tescoplc.com/index.asp?pageid=314

Figure 1.4	YouTube video explaining the Tesco Homeplus Virtual Subway Store presence in South Korea *Source*: www.youtube.com/watch?v=fGaVFRzTTP4

Introduction to digital marketing strategy

The key strategic decisions for digital marketing are in common with traditional business and marketing strategy decisions. As we will see in Chapter 4, which defines a process for developing a digital marketing strategy, customer segmentation, targeting and **positioning** are all key to effective digital marketing. These familiar **target marketing strategy** approaches involve selecting target customer groups and specifying how to deliver value to these groups as a proposition of services and products. As well as positioning of the core product or brand proposition, online development of a compelling *extended product* or **online value proposition (OVP)** is also important (see Chapter 7). This defines how the online experience of a brand is delivered through content, visual design, interactivity, sharing, rich media and how the online presence integrates with the offline presence. All of the companies referenced in Table 1.1 have a clear, compelling OVP. Strategic decisions about the future OVP a company offers is a key part of Internet marketing strategy.

Positioning
Customers' perception of the product and brand offering relative to those of competitors.

Target marketing strategy
Evaluation and selection of appropriate customer segments and the development of appropriate offers.

Online value proposition (OVP)
A statement of the benefits of online services that reinforces the core proposition and differentiates from an organisation's offline offering and those of competitors.

Key features of digital marketing strategy

The interaction and integration between Internet channels and traditional channels is a key part of digital marketing strategy development. Digital marketing strategy is essentially a channel marketing strategy and it needs to be integrated with other channels as part of multi-channel marketing. It follows that an effective digital marketing strategy should:

- Be aligned with business and marketing strategy (for example, many companies use a rolling three-year plan and vision), with more specific annual business priorities and initiatives.
- Use clear objectives for business and brand development and the online contribution of leads and sales for the Internet or other digital channels. These should be based on models of the number using the channels.
- Be consistent with the types of customers who use and can be effectively reached through the channel.
- Define a compelling, differential **value proposition** for the channel which must be effectively communicated to customers.
- Specify the mix of online and offline communication tools used to attract visitors to the company website or interact with the brand through other digital media such as email or mobile.
- Support the customer journey through the buying process as they select and purchase products using the digital channel in combination with other channels.
- Manage the online customer lifecycle through the stages of attracting visitors to the website, converting them into customers and retention and growth.

Value proposition
The benefits or value a brand offers to customers in its products and services.

Applications of digital marketing

For established multichannel organisations, digital media offer a range of opportunities for marketing products and services across the purchase cycle that companies need to review as part of their digital strategy. Consider the example of a low-cost airline. Digital media and technologies can be used as follows:

- **Advertising medium.** Display ads on publisher sites or social networks can be used to create awareness of brands and demands for products or services.
- **Direct-response medium.** Targeted search advertising enables companies to drive visits to a site when consumers shows intent to purchase, such as searching for a flight to a destination.

- **Platform for sales transactions.** Online flight booking is now the most common method for booking flights both for consumers and business travellers.
- **Lead-generation method.** For booking business flights, tools can be provided which help identify and follow up corporate flight purchases.
- **Distribution channel**, such as for distributing digital products. Today, airlines sell more insurance services than previously, for example.
- **Customer service mechanism.** For example, customers may 'self-serve' more cost-effectively by reviewing frequently asked questions.
- **Relationship-building medium.** Here a company can interact with its customers to better understand their needs and publicise relevant products and offers. For example, easyJet uses its email newsletter and tailored alerts about special deals to encourage repeat flight bookings.

Benefits of digital marketing

The benefits of digital marketing in supporting marketing is suggested by applying the definition of marketing by the Chartered Institute of Marketing (**www.cim.co.uk**):

> Marketing is the management process responsible for identifying, anticipating and satisfying customer requirements profitably.

This definition emphasises the focus of marketing on the customer, while at the same time implying a need to link to other business operations to achieve this profitability. Chaffey and Smith (2012) note that digital marketing can be used to support these aims as follows:

- *Identifying* – the Internet can be used for marketing research to find out customers' needs and wants (Chapters 7 and 10).
- *Anticipating* – the Internet provides an additional channel by which customers can access information and make purchases – evaluating this demand is key to governing resource allocation to e-marketing (as explained in Chapters 2, 3 and 4).
- *Satisfying* – a key success factor in e-marketing is achieving customer satisfaction through the electronic channel, which raises issues such as: is the site easy to use, does it perform adequately, what is the standard of associated customer service and how are physical products dispatched? (These issues of customer relationship management are discussed further in Chapters 6 and 7.)

In Chapter 4, we show how to quantify different goals as part of developing digital marketing strategy. To introduce the typical types of goals for digital marketing, see Table 1.2 which gives a basic framework for setting and reviewing different types of goals for digital strategy development based on the 5Ss of Chaffey and Smith (2012).

A powerful method of evaluating the strategic marketing opportunities of using the Internet is to apply the strategic marketing grid of Ansoff (1957), as discussed in the strategy formulation section of Chapter 4. This shows how the Internet can potentially be used to achieve four strategic directions:

1 *Market penetration.* The Internet can be used to sell more existing products into existing markets.
2 *Market development.* Here the Internet is used to sell into new geographical markets, taking advantage of the low cost of advertising internationally without the necessity for a supporting sales infrastructure in the customers' countries.
3 *Product development.* New products or services are developed which can be delivered by the Internet. These are typically digital products.
4 *Diversification.* In this sector, the Internet supports selling new products which are developed and sold into new markets.

Table 1.2	The 5Ss of Internet marketing

Benefit of e-marketing	How benefit is delivered	Examples of typical objectives
Sell – Grow sales	Includes direct online sales and sales from offline channels influenced online. Achieved through wider distribution to customers you cannot readily service offline or perhaps through a wider product range than in-store, or lower prices compared to other channels	• Achieve 10 per cent of sales online in market • Increase online sales for product by 20 per cent in year
Serve – Add value	Achieved through giving customers extra benefits online or inform product development through online dialogue and feedback	• Increase interaction with different content on site • Increase dwell-time duration on site by 10 per cent (sometimes known as 'stickiness') • Increasing number of customers actively using online services (at least once per month) to 30 per cent
Speak – Get closer to customers	Creating a two-way dialogue through web interactions like forums and surveys and conducting online market research through formal surveys and informally monitoring conversations to learn about them	• Grow email coverage to 50 per cent of current customer database • Survey 1000 customers online each month • Increase visitors to community site section by 5 per cent
Save – Save costs	Achieved through online email communications, sales and service transactions to reduce staff, print and postage costs. Savings also accrue through 'web self-service' where customers answer queries through online content	• Generate 10 per cent more sales for same communications budget • Reduce cost of direct marketing by 15 per cent through email • Increase web self-service to 40 per cent of all service enquiries and reduce overall cost-to-serve by 10 per cent
Sizzle – Extend the brand online	Achieved through providing new propositions, new offers and new experiences online including building communities	• Improve branding metrics such as brand awareness, reach, brand favourability and purchase intent

Source: Chaffey and Smith (2012)

Geyskens *et al.* (2002) suggested an alternative perspective, that there are three main forms of demand expansion for an existing company when they adopt direct Internet channels. These are:

1 *Market expansion*, which occurs when new segments of customers are reached who did not previously buy in a category – they give the example of Estée Lauder, which hopes that the Clinique.com site will attract customers who avoid buying at a cosmetics counter because they find the experience intimidating.

2 *Brand switching*, which is by winning customers from competitors.

3 *Relationship deepening*, which is selling more to existing customers.

For well-established brands with a loyal customer base, price reduction relative to other channels is not necessarily essential or some web-channel price reductions can be used, but they note that often competitive pressures may require lower online prices. These authors also note the potential benefits of reduction in transactional and distribution costs through introducing a direct Internet channel once initial startup costs are incurred. However, for manufacturer brands it important that consideration is given to the advertising expenditure required to move goods through the supply chain once a brand is established online (Pei *et al.*, 2014). It is essential for brands to plan how they will manage potential channel conflict when establishing their brands online.

As well as assisting large corporate organisations develop their markets, perhaps the most exciting potential of the Internet is to help existing small and medium enterprises (SMEs) expand. Read Mini Case Study 1.2, which illustrates how one manufacturer has used digital media and technology to build its brand. There is further discussion of the opportunities of digital communication at the end of the chapter.

Mini case study 1.2	Tatu Couture expands the reach of its brand online

Tatu Couture designs and manufactures luxury British lingerie which is sold through stockists in the UK, Paris and New York. Tatu Couture has a unique vision to push the boundaries of design and innovation with its trend-setting luxury lingerie and designer body wear. All the goods are manufactured and hand finished in the UK.

Overview and digital strategy

Agency Tonica supported Tatu Couture by creating a four-stage strategy to increase digital presence (Figure 1.5). In addition to the stockist route, Tatu Couture was keen to increase its own direct sales, so we

Figure 1.5	Tatu Couture (www.tatucouture.com)

had two simple objectives for the work – to increase visits to **tatucouture.com** and increase sales from the site. The steps to develop the reach of the company are explained by the agency as:

Step 1 – Take control

Like many small to medium sized enterprises (SMEs), Tatu Couture had employed a Web Designer to create their site, but were unfamiliar with some of the standard tools that could help them track success. In this phase of work, we focussed on empowering Tatu Couture to take control so that they could cost-effectively develop their site without spending budget on external resource:

- Suggesting Tatu Couture gain full account control of their Shopify website
- Assisting Tatu Couture in having Google Webmaster Tools access in order to access information about the health of their site
- Setting up Google Analytics in order to track website performance.

Step 2 – Make the most of your contacts

In this phase, we were keen to ensure that Tatu Couture could conduct their own email campaigns using free provider, Mailchimp. During this process we also consolidated their contact data into a new Tatu Couture Mailchimp account, and set up a website 'sign up' so that new prospects could be captured.

Step 3 – Promote (for free when possible!)

In addition to the email campaigns, we identified several low-cost or no-cost promotion options:

- Google Merchant (aka Google Shopping/Google Product Search). In order to increase online presence, we were keen to feed Tatu Couture products into Google Shopping, particularly as this was still a free service in the UK (prior to March 2013). Luckily Shopify had a fairly easy integration option for this, so we were able to activate the integration and add a few settings (such as shipping) for products to be regularly submitted.
- Google Places – a free local service which helps Tatu Couture stand out regionally.
- Google Adwords (pay-per-click advertising). Since the launch campaign, low-cost Google Adwords campaigns have been used at key events in the calendar, continuing to lower the cost per click, increase click-through rates and utilise the best performing keywords.
- We have also used micro-geographic targeting in Google Adword campaigns as a proxy for income – for example, targeting South Kensington and Chelsea postcodes.
- Facebook. Tatu Couture is using this investment to reach the most likely recipients to purchase. The challenge in promoting a luxury product online is reaching an audience likely to purchase and this is where the beauty of Facebook could help.

By targeting Facebook profiles who already liked other luxury or designer products, our Facebook campaign could reach a more tailored market than using Google alone. During the campaign we were able to double Facebook likes for Tatu Couture. In the last three months, Facebook has driven 16 per cent of the traffic to the site.

Step 4 – Search engine optimisation

As well as suggesting search engine optimisation changes along the way, we suggested a more formal search engine optimisation (SEO) review as Step 4. Tatu Couture have begun to implement these SEO changes in an effort to drive more organic traffic to the site. The changes included incorporating more keywords into the product descriptions in addition to the unique Tatu Couture copy.

Source: Smart Insights (2013)

Alternative digital business models

As part of strategy development, organisations require clarity on the type of business model they will develop.

Business and consumer business models

A basic aspect of the types of online business model explored in Chapter 2 is whether the proposition offered appeals to consumers or business. So digital marketing opportunities are often described in terms of the extent to which an organisation is transacting with consumers (**business-to-consumer – B2C**) or other businesses (**business-to-business – B2B**).

Reference to the well-known online companies in Table 1.1 initially suggests these companies are mainly focussed on B2C markets. However, B2B communications are still important for many of these companies since business transactions may occur, as for example with eBay Business (**http://business.ebay.com/**), or the B2C service may need to be sustained through advertising provided through B2B transactions, for example Google's revenue is largely based on its B2B AdWords (**http://adwords.google.com/**). Advertising service and advertising-based revenue is also vital to social network sites such as YouTube, Facebook and Twitter.

Digital media and technologies offer new opportunities for direct-to-customer strategies where brands can communicate directly to their consumers. For example, a publisher and authors can interact with their readers, or food brands can interact directly with their purchasers via their websites or social media.

Figure 1.6 gives examples of different companies operating in the business-to-consumer (B2C) and business-to-business (B2B) spheres. Often companies such as easyJet and BP will have products that appeal to both consumers and businesses, so will have different parts of their site to appeal to these audiences. Figure 1.6 also presents two additional types of

Business-to-consumer (B2C)
Commercial transactions between an organisation and consumers.

Business-to-business (B2B)
Commercial transactions between an organisation and other organisations (inter-organisational marketing).

| | **From: Supplier of content/service** | |
Consumer or citizen	*Business (organisation)*	*Government*
Consumer-to-consumer (C2C) • eBay • Peer-to-peer (Skype) • Blogs and communities • Product recommendations • Social network (Bebo, Facebook Google+)	**Business-to-consumer (B2C)** • Transactional: Amazon • Relationship-building: BP • Brand-building: Unilever • Media owner – News Corp • Comparison intermediary: Kelkoo, Pricerunner	**Government-to-consumer (G2C)** • National government transactional: Tax – HM Revenue & Customs • National government information • Local government information • Local government services
Consumer-to-business (C2B) • Priceline • Consumer-feedback, communities or campaigns	**Business-to-business (B2B)** • Transactional: Euroffice • Relationship-building: BP • Media owned: Emap business productions • B2B marketplaces: EC21 • Social network (Linked-In, Plaxo)	**Government-to-business (B2B)** • Government services and transactions: tax • Legal regulations
Consumer-to-government (C2G) • Feedback to government through pressure group or individual sites	**Business-to-government (B2G)** • Feedback to government businesses and non-governmental organisations	**Government-to-government (G2G)** • Inter-government services • Exchange of information

To: Consumer of content/service — *Consumer or citizen* / *Business (organisation)* / *Government*

| **Figure 1.6** | Summary and examples of transaction alternatives between businesses, consumers and governmental organisations |

craigslist

Consumer-to-consumer (C2C)
Informational or financial transactions between consumers, but usually mediated through a business site.

Consumer-to-business (C2B)
Consumers approach the business with an offer.

E-government
The use of Internet technologies to provide government services to citizens.

transaction – those where consumers transact directly with other consumers (**consumer-to-consumer – C2C**) and where they initiate trading with companies (**consumer-to-business – C2B**). Common C2C interactions include transactional exchange (e.g. eBay, www.ebay.com), financial services (e.g. Zopa, www.zopa.com) and betting (e.g. Betfair, www.betfair.com). In the early stages of the evolution of the web, Hoffman and Novak (1996) highlighted the potential importance of C2C interactions; the significance of their findings have been supported by growth of social networks. More recently, Adjei *et al*. (2010) found how brand communities can be effective tools for influencing sales and retaining customers and building confidence in new customers.

The significance of C2C interactions is shown by Activity 1.3.

Figure 1.6 also includes government and public services organisations which deliver online or **e-government** services. As well as the models shown in the figure, it has also been suggested that employees should be considered as a separate type of consumer through the use of intranets, which is referred to as employee-to-employee or E2E.

Activity 1.3	Why are C2C interactions important?

Purpose

To highlight the relevance of C2C transactions to B2C companies.

Activity

Consult with fellow students and share experience of C2C interactions online. Think of C2C on both independent sites and organisational sites. How can C2C communications assist these organisations?

Direct-to-customer model
A brand which has previously communicated to its customers via intermediaries such as media sites or wholesalers communicates directly via digital media such as social networks, email and websites.

Electronic commerce
All financial and informational electronically mediated exchanges between an organisation and its external stakeholders.

Sell-side e-commerce
E-commerce transactions between a supplier organisation and its customers.

Buy-side e-commerce
E-commerce transactions between a purchasing organisation and its suppliers.

Social commerce
Social commerce is a subset of e-commerce which encourages participation and interaction of customers in rating, selecting and buying products through group buying. This participation can occur on an e-commerce site or on third-party sites.

What is the difference between e-commerce and e-business?

Electronic commerce (e-commerce) refers to *both financial and informational* electronically mediated transactions between an organisation and any third party it deals with (Chaffey, 2014). So e-commerce involves management not only of online sales transactions, but also of non-financial transactions such as inbound customer service enquiries and outbound email broadcasts, so you can argue that e-commerce is open to all online organisations.

E-commerce is often further subdivided into a **sell-side e-commerce** perspective, which refers to transactions involved with selling products to an organisation's customers, and a **buy-side e-commerce** perspective, which refers to business-to-business transactions to procure resources needed by an organisation from its suppliers. This is shown in Figure 1.7.

Social commerce is an increasingly important part of e-commerce for site owners, since incorporating reviews and ratings into a site and linking to social networking sites can help understand customers' needs and increase conversion to sale. It can also involve group buying using a coupon service like Groupon. There is much discussion on the extent to which social media interactions between consumers directly influence sales. Digital marketing insight 1.1 outlines research hinting at the complexity of understanding this relationship. We introduce social media marketing later in this chapter.

E-business or digital business is similar to e-commerce but broader in scope and refers to using digital technology to manage a range of business processes incorporating the sell-side and buy-side e-commerce shown in Figure 1.7, and also other key supporting business processes including research and development, marketing, manufacturing and inbound and outbound logistics.

Digital marketing insight 1.1 Social commerce – how much do social networks influence purchase?

Research published by the Harvard Business School, quoting Iyengar *et al.* (2009), found that in Korea, where social networking and commerce is more established, social networks do influence purchase, but the degree of influence depends on the usage level and connectedness of a user. In summary, the research shows:

- For light users of social networks with few connections (48% of users), purchases are unaffected by social network activity.
- For moderate users of social networks with average connections (40%), purchases are influenced by social network interaction, boosting vendor sales for this group by 5%.
- For heavy users of social networks with a high number of connections (12%), purchases are also influenced by social network interaction, but *negatively*; these users avoid buying what their friends have bought and are talking about, leading to a 14 per cent drop in sales from this group for vendors.

We return to this question in Chapter 9, where we explore the effectiveness of different types of digital media in the Smart Insights (2015b) article 'Is this the social media backlash?'

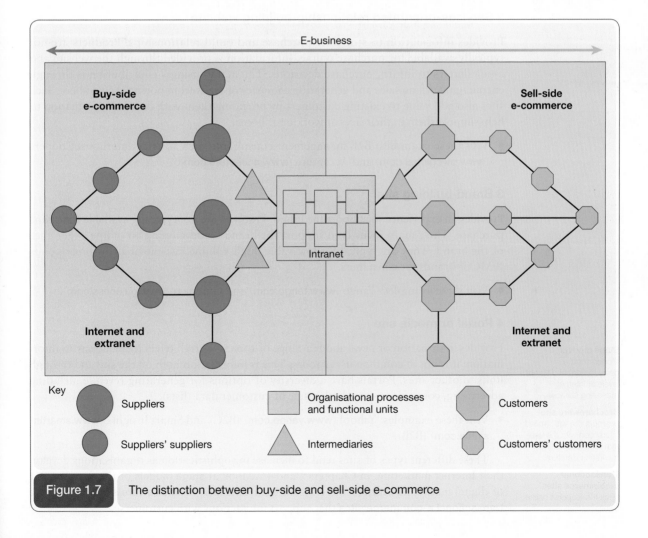

Figure 1.7 The distinction between buy-side and sell-side e-commerce

Electronic business (e-business) or digital business
Electronically mediated information exchanges, both within an organisation and with external stakeholders supporting the range of business processes.

Different forms of online presence

The form of digital strategy developed by a company will depend on the nature of a business. Chaffey (2014) identifies different types of online presence which each have different objectives and are appropriate for different markets. Note that these are not clear-cut categories of websites since any company may combine these types as part of their business model, but with a change in emphasis according to the market they serve. Increasingly companies are using their company pages on social networks such as Facebook, Google+ and LinkedIn to similar purposes. As you review websites and company social presences, note how organisations have different parts of the site focussing on these functions of sales transactions, services, relationship-building, brand-building and providing news and entertainment. The five main types of site or site or mobile app functions are as follows.

1 Transactional e-commerce site

Enables purchase of products online. The main business contribution of the site is through sale of these products. The sites also support the business by providing information for consumers who prefer to purchase products offline.

- Visit these examples: an end-product manufacturer such as Vauxhall (**www.vauxhall .co.uk**) or an online retailer such as Amazon (**www.amazon.com**).

2 Services-orientated relationship-building website

Provides information to stimulate purchase and build relationships. Products are not typically available for purchase online. Information is provided through the website and e-newsletters to inform purchase decisions. The main business contribution is through encouraging offline sales and generating enquiries or leads from potential customers. Such sites also add value to existing customers by providing them with detailed information to help support them in their lives at work or at home.

- Visit these examples: B2B management consultants such as PricewaterhouseCoopers (**www.pwcglobal.com**) and Accenture (**www.accenture.com**).

3 Brand-building site

Provides an experience to support the brand. Products are not typically available for online purchase. Their main focus is to support the brand by developing an online experience of the brand. They are typical for low-value, high-volume fast-moving consumer goods (FMCG) brands for consumers.

- Visit these examples: Tango (**www.tango.com**) and Guinness (**www.guinness.com**).

4 Portal or media site

Stage models
Models for the development of different levels of Internet marketing services.

Brochureware site
A simple site with limited interaction with the user that replicates offline marketing literature.

Transactional e-commerce sites
Sites that support online sales.

Provides information or news about a range of topics. 'Portal' refers to a gateway to information; it is not in common usage today. This is information both on the site and through links to other sites. Portals have a diversity of options for generating revenue including advertising, commission-based sales, sale of customer data (lists).

- Visit these examples: Yahoo! (**www.yahoo.com**) (B2C) and Smart Insights (**www.smartinsights.com**) (B2B).

These different types of sites tend to increase in sophistication as organisations develop their Internet marketing. In Chapters 2 and 4 we look at **stage models** of the development of digital marketing services and capabilities, from static **brochureware sites** to dynamic **transactional e-commerce sites** that support interactions with customers.

5 Social network or community site

These sites or parts of sites focus on enabling community interactions between different consumers (C2C model). Typical interactions include posting comments and replies to comments, sending messages, rating content and tagging content in particular categories.

Well-known examples include Facebook, LinkedIn and Twitter. In addition to distinct social network sites such as these, social networks can also be integrated into other site types.

Challenges in developing and managing digital marketing strategy

Some of the challenges in managing Internet marketing strategy which are commonly seen in many organisations (and should be managed) include:

- Unclear responsibilities for the many different Internet marketing activities (shown in Figure P.1 in the Preface).
- No specific objectives are set for Internet marketing.
- Insufficient budget is allocated for Internet marketing because customer demand for online services is underestimated and competitors potentially gain market share through superior online activities.
- Budget is wasted as different parts of an organisation experiment with using different tools or suppliers without achieving economies of scale.
- New online value propositions for customers are not developed since the Internet is treated as 'just another channel to market' without review of opportunities to offer improved, differentiated online services.
- Results from digital marketing are not measured or reviewed adequately, so actions cannot be taken to improve effectiveness.
- An experimental rather than planned approach is taken to using e-communications with poor integration between online and offline marketing communications.

Research by Smart Insights (2014) investigated the challenges of managing digital marketing. It was found that many businesses do face challenges in these areas:

- **Planning.** Half (50 per cent) of businesses surveyed do not have a defined digital plan or strategy although they are active in digital marketing, while nearly half (44 per cent) also don't have a defined marketing plan in the business against which to align strategy.
- **Organisational capabilities.** Nearly half (43 per cent) of businesses have a well-defined performance improvement process, with 46 per cent having adapted their structure. Many businesses either already have or are planning to introduce a digital transformation programme, although a substantial number (37 per cent) of businesses don't think it's relevant for them.
- **Integration of digital channels into marketing.** Only a quarter of companies (26 per cent) were happy with their level of integration of digital marketing and traditional communications. The main barriers to integration are: 1. Lack of integrated strategy and plans (28 per cent); 2. Teams structured in silos (21 per cent); 3. Lack of skills in integrated communications (17 per cent).
- **ROI evaluation.** A significant proportion (39 per cent) see opportunities from digital marketing, but find ROI measurement challenging – a key area for managers to address.

Digital transformation
A staged programme of business improvements to People, Process and Tools tools used for integrated digital marketing to maximise the potential contribution of digital technology and media to business growth.

Given the future importance of digital marketing, larger organisations have introduced **Digital transformation** programmes to help manage these challenges. The approach has been discussed by many management consulting groups, for example MIT Center for Digital Business and Capgemini Consulting (2011) and Altimeter (2014).

Altimeter produced a visual proposing enablers and barriers to digital transformation (Figure 1.8). It shows how disruptive digital technologies such as social media, mobile platforms and real-time marketing should be harnessed to create an effective digital customer experience.

Applying the 7Ss

The 7Ss are a useful framework for reviewing an organisation's existing and future capabilities to meet the challenges posed by the new digital channels, and some of the aspects of this are shown in Table 1.3.

You may have encountered the 7S framework, summarised by Waterman *et al.* (1980) and developed by McKinsey consultants in the 1980s. It is often referenced when referring to the management of a business. EConsultancy (2005) has summarised some of the strategic resource management issues that require consideration, as shown in Table 1.3.

Table 1.3	Summary of some of the organisational challenges of digital marketing that need to be managed in the context of the 7S framework

Element of 7S model	Application to digital marketing strategy	Key issues from practice and literature
Strategy	The significance of digital marketing in influencing and supporting the organisation's strategy	Gaining appropriate budgets and demonstrating/delivering value and ROI from budgets. Annual planning approach Techniques for using digital marketing to impact organisation strategy Techniques for aligning digital strategy with organisational and marketing strategy

Element of 7S model	Application to digital marketing strategy	Key issues from practice and literature
Structure	The modification of organisational structure to support digital marketing	Integration of digital marketing and e-commerce teams with other management, marketing (corporate communications, brand marketing, direct marketing) and IT staff Use of cross-functional teams and steering groups Insourcing vs outsourcing
Systems	The development of specific processes, procedures or information systems to support digital marketing	Campaign planning approach–integration Managing/sharing customer information Managing content quality Unified reporting of digital marketing effectiveness In-house vs external best-of-breed vs external integrated technology solutions
Staff	The breakdown of staff in terms of their background and characteristics such as IT vs marketing, use of contractors/consultants, age and sex	Insourcing vs outsourcing Achieving senior management buy-in/involvement with digital marketing Staff recruitment and retention. Virtual working Staff development and training
Style	Includes both the way in which key managers behave in achieving the organisation's goals and the cultural style of the organisation as a whole	Relates to role of digital marketing team in influencing strategy – is it dynamic and influential or conservative and looking for a voice
Skills	Distinctive capabilities of key staff, but can be interpreted as specific skill sets of team members	Staff skills in specific areas: supplier selection, project management, content management, specific e-marketing approaches (SEO, PPC, affiliate marketing, email marketing, online advertising)
Superordinate goals	The guiding concepts of the digital marketing organisation which are also part of shared values and culture. The internal and external perception of these goals may vary	Improving the perception of the importance and effectiveness of the digital marketing team among senior managers and staff it works with (marketing generalists and IT)

Source: EConsultancy (2005)

A strategic framework for developing a digital marketing strategy

To realise the benefits of digital marketing and avoid the pitfalls that we have described, an organisation needs to develop a planned, structured approach. Consequently, this text defines a strategic approach to Internet marketing which is intended to manage these risks and deliver the opportunities available from online channels. In Figure 1.9 we suggest a process for developing and implementing a digital marketing plan which is based on our

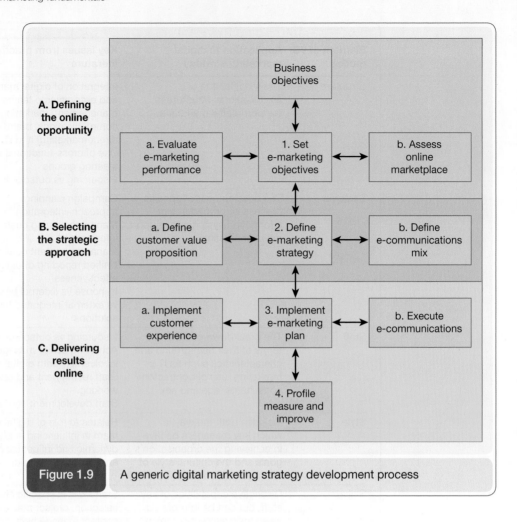

A. Defining the online opportunity

B. Selecting the strategic approach

C. Delivering results online

Business objectives

a. Evaluate e-marketing performance ⟷ 1. Set e-marketing objectives ⟷ b. Assess online marketplace

a. Define customer value proposition ⟷ 2. Define e-marketing strategy ⟷ b. Define e-communications mix

a. Implement customer experience ⟷ 3. Implement e-marketing plan ⟷ b. Execute e-communications

4. Profile measure and improve

Figure 1.9   A generic digital marketing strategy development process

experience of strategy definition in a wide range of companies. This diagram highlights the key activities and their dependencies which are involved for the creation of a typical digital marketing strategy and relates them to coverage in different chapters in this text:

A: Defining the online opportunity

Setting objectives to define the potential is the core of this phase of strategy development. Key activities are:

- *1 Set Digital marketing objectives* (Chapters 4 and 8). Companies need to set specific numerical objectives for their online channels and then resource to deliver these objectives. These objectives should be informed by and influence the business objectives and also the following two activities.
- *1a Evaluate digital marketing performance* (Chapters 4 and 10). Apply web analytics tools to measure the contribution of leads, sales and brand involvement currently delivered by online communications such as search engine marketing, online advertising and email marketing in conjunction with the website.
- *1b Assess online marketplace* (Chapters 2, 3 and 4). Situation analysis review of the micro-environment (customers, competitors, intermediaries, suppliers and internal capabilities and resources) and the broader macro-environment which influences strategy, such as legal requirements and technology innovation.

B: Selecting the strategic approach

- *2 Define digital marketing strategy* (Chapter 4). Select appropriate strategies to achieve the objectives set at stage A1.
- *2a Define customer value proposition* (Chapters 4 to 7). Define the value proposition available through the online channel and how it relates to the core proposition delivered by the company. Review segmentation and targeting options. Review the marketing mix and brand values to evaluate how they can be improved online.
- *2b Define digital communications mix* (Chapters 4, 8 and 9). Select the offline and online communications tools to encourage usage of an organisation's online services and to generate leads and sales. Develop new outbound communications and event-triggered touch strategies to support customers through their relationship with the company.

C: Delivering results online

- *3 Implement digital marketing plan* (Part 3). This details the implementation of the strategy.
- *3a Implement customer experience* (Chapter 7). Build the website and create the email marketing communications which form the online interactions customers make with a company. Create online customer relationship management capabilities to understand customers' characteristics, needs and behaviours and to deliver targeted, personalised value (Chapter 6).
- *3b Execute digital communications* (Chapter 8). Manage the continuous online marketing communications such as search engine marketing, partnership social media marketing, sponsorships and affiliate arrangements, and campaign-based e-marketing communications such as online advertising, email marketing and microsites to encourage usage of the online service and to support customer acquisition and retention campaigns. Integrate the digital media channels with traditional marketing.
- *4 Customer profiling* (Chapter 6), *monitoring and improving online activities and maintaining the online activities* (Chapter 9). Capture profile and behavioural data on customer interactions with the company and summarise and disseminate reports and alerts about performance compared with objectives in order to drive performance improvement.

You will see that in the process diagram, Figure 1.9, many double-headed arrows are used, since the activities are often not sequential, but rather inform each other, so activity 1, set digital marketing objectives, is informed by the activities around it but may also influence them. Similarly, activity 4, profile, measure and improve, is informed by the execution of online activities but there should be a feedback loop to update the tactics and strategies used.

Introduction to digital marketing communications

Digital media channels
Online communications techniques used to achieve goals of brand awareness, familiarity, favourability and to influence purchase intent by encouraging users of digital media to visit a website to engage with the brand or product, and

For many years, marketing campaigns were based on traditional media including TV, print and radio ads, and direct mail supported by public relations. But, in a few short years, since the web concept was first proposed in the late 1980s by Sir Tim Berners-Lee, there have been huge changes in marketing communications. The digital equivalents of these traditional media, which are known as **digital media channels**, are vital components of most marketing campaigns today. For example, in an online campaign, marketers can use ads and content on social media to engage audiences; **display ads**, the familiar banner and skyscraper ads seen on many online publisher sites; **pay-per-click (PPC)** ads such as the ultimately to purchase online or offline through traditional media channels such as by phone or in-store.

Display ads
Use of graphical or *rich media ad units* within a web page to achieve goals of delivering brand awareness, familiarity, favourability and purchase intent. Many ads encourage interaction through prompting the viewer to *rollover* to play videos, complete an online form or to view more details before clicking through to a site.

Pay-per-click
PPC refers to when a company pays for text ads to be displayed on the search engine results pages as a sponsored link (typically above, to the right of or below the natural listings) when a specific keyphrase is entered by the search users. It is so-called because the marketer pays each time the hypertext link in the ad is clicked on. If a link is clicked repeatedly, then this will be detected by the search engine as click fraud and the marketer will not be charged.

Search engine optimisation
A structured approach used to increase the position of a company or its products in search engine natural or organic results listings (the main body of the search results page) for selected keywords or phrases.

Affiliate marketing
A commission-based arrangement where referring sites (publishers) receive a commission on sales or leads by merchants (retailers). Commission is usually based on a percentage of product sale price or a fixed amount for each sale, but may also be on a per-click basis, for example when an aggregator refers visits to merchants.

Email marketing
Typically applied to outbound communications from a company to prospects or customers to encourage

Sponsored Links in Google; **search engine optimisation (SEO)** to gain higher positions in the natural listings of Google; **affiliate marketing** where sites which generate a sale for a merchant gain commission; and **email marketing**, which is most effective when messages are sent to an existing customer base – i.e. customers who have given their permission to receive them. Many of these digital communications techniques are analogous to their traditional equivalents – for example, display ads are broadly equivalent to print or display ads and email marketing is equivalent to direct mail.

But the approaches used to target the online audience are potentially very different, with personalisation based on the customer profile and previous interactions with communications giving many options to deliver more timely, relevant messages. (Personalised communications are also effective on the website, where **landing pages** are commonly used to make the page more relevant to what the customer is seeking.) Leading websites also provide great opportunities to engage the visitor through in-depth text content, **rich media** such as video and audio and participation in customer communities.

The relationship between digital and traditional communications

It is helpful to understand the relationship between the new digital communications techniques and traditional communications, in order that new opportunities are not missed and campaigns can be planned in an integrated fashion. According to Jenkinson (2007), there are important learning opportunities to be derived from understanding the scope of personalisation both on- and offline. To illustrate the relationship between different levels of marketing communications consider Table 1.4, which is based on terminology introduced by Jenkinson and Sain (2001) and increasingly adopted by practitioners and academics.

Table 1.4	Key marketing communications concepts	
Marketing communications term	**Definition**	**Examples from traditional and digital media**
Medium (media)	'Anything that conveys a message' The carrier of the message or method of transmission. Can be conceived as the touchpoint with the customer	Broadcast (television, radio), press, direct mail, cinema, poster, digital (web, email, mobile)
Discipline	'A body of craft technique biased towards a facet of marketing communication' These are traditionally known as 'promotion tools' or the different elements of the communications mix	Advertising, direct marketing, public relations, market research, personal selling, sales promotion, sponsorship, packaging, exhibitions and trade shows. All are also used online
Channel (tools)	The combination of a discipline with a medium	Direct mail, direct response TV, television brand advertising. Digital channels: different forms of search marketing, affiliate marketing, display advertising, email marketing, social media, blogs and feeds

purchase or branding goals. Email marketing is most commonly used for mailing to existing customers on a houselist, but can also be used for mailing prospects on a rented or co-branded list. Emails may be sent as part of a one-off campaign or can be automated event-based, triggered emails such as a welcome strategy which can be broadcast based on rules about intervals and customer characteristics.

Marketing communications term	Definition	Examples from traditional and digital media
Vehicle	A specific channel used to reach a target audience	TV (ITV, Channel 4), newspaper (*The Sun, Metro, The Times*), magazine (*The Economist, Radio Times*), radio (Virgin Radio, BBC Radio 5) and their website equivalents. Different search engines such as Google fit, or aggregators of product from other suppliers such as Money supermarket, also fit here

---

Activity 1.4   Digital media differences?

Purpose

To illustrate similarities and differences between digital and traditional media.

Activity

Make two columns. On the left, write down different digital media channels and on the right, the corresponding communications disciplines such as advertising, direct marketing or PR which are most appropriate.

Landing page
A destination page when a user clicks on an ad or other form of link from a *referring site*. It can be a home page but more typically and desirably, a landing page is a page with the messaging focussed on the offer in the ad. This will maximise conversion rates and brand favourability.

Rich media
Advertisements or site content that are not static, but provide animation, sound or interactivity. An example of this would be a display advertisement for a loan in which a customer can type in the amount of loan required, and the cost of the loan is calculated immediately.

Web or digital analytics
Techniques used to assess and improve the contribution of digital marketing to a business, including reviewing traffic volume, referrals, clickstreams, online reach data, customer satisfaction surveys, leads and sales.

Using digital media channels to support business objectives

Before we explain the different digital media channels, it is important to consider how they can support business goals. RACE (Figure 1.10 and Preface Figure P.1) is a practical framework developed by Smart Insights (2010) to help marketers manage and improve the commercial value that their organisations gain from digital marketing. RACE is an evolution of the REAN (Reach–Engage–Activate–Nurture) framework originally developed by Xavier Blanc and popularised by Steve Jackson in his book *Cult of Analytics* (Jackson, 2009). It is intended to help create a simplified approach to reviewing the performance of online marketing and taking actions to improve its effectiveness. The measures introduced in Figure 1.10 are covered in more depth in Chapters 4 and 10, where we explore the power of using **web analytics** for improving marketing performance.

RACE consists of four steps designed to help engage prospects, customers and fans with brands throughout the customer lifecycle.

- Step 1: Reach – Build awareness of a brand, its products and services on other sites and in offline media and build traffic by driving visits to web and social media presences.
- Step 2: Interact – Engage audience with brand on its website or other online presence to encourage them to act or interact with a company or other customers.
- Step 3: Convert – Achieve conversion to generate leads or sales on web presences and offline.
- Step 4: Engage – Build customer relationships through time to achieve retention goals.

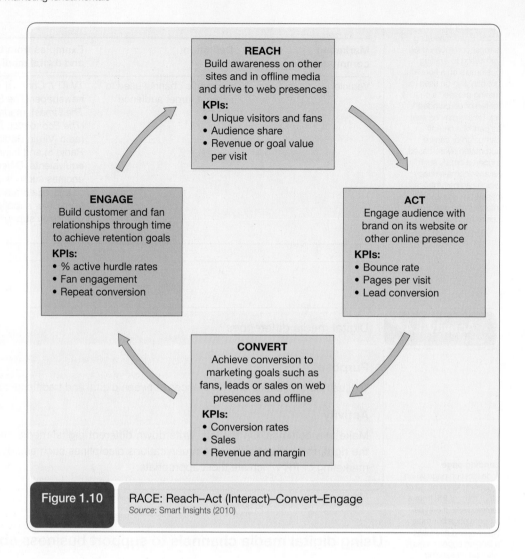

| Figure 1.10 | RACE: Reach–Act (Interact)–Convert–Engage
Source: Smart Insights (2010) |

Digital channels always work best when they are integrated with other channels, so where appropriate digital channels should be combined with the traditional offline media and channels. The most important aspects of integration are, first, using traditional media to raise awareness of the value of the online presences at the Reach and Interact stages and, second, at the 'Convert' and 'Engage' steps where customers may prefer to interact with customer representatives.

The key types of digital media channels

There are many online communications tools which marketers must review as part of their communications strategy or as part of planning an online marketing campaign. To assist with planning, Chaffey and Smith (2012) recommend that these online marketing tools are divided into the six main groups, shown in Figure 1.11.

In Chapters 8 and 9, we review these tools in detail, but this is the essence of each digital media channel:

1 *Search engine marketing*. Placing messages on a search engine to encourage click-through to a website when the user types a specific keyword phrase. Two key search marketing techniques are paid placements or sponsored links using pay-per-click, and

Social network
A site that facilitates peer-to-peer communication within a group or between individuals through providing facilities to develop user-generated content (UGC) and to exchange messages and comments between different users.

Blog
Personal online diary, journal or news source compiled by one person, an internal team or external guest authors. Postings are usually in different categories. Typically comments can be added to each blog posting to help create interactivity and feedback.

Podcast
Individuals and organisations post online media (audio and video) which can be viewed in the appropriate players (including the iPod which first sparked the growth in this technique). The latest podcast updates can be automatically delivered by RSS.

Feed (or RSS feed)
Blog, news or other content is published by an XML standard and syndicated for other sites or read by users in RSS reader services such as Google Reader, personalised home pages or email systems. RSS stands for Really Simple Syndication.

Viral marketing
A marketing message is communicated from one person to another, facilitated by different media, such as word-of-mouth, email or websites, in particular social network or blogsites. Viral marketing implies rapid transmission of messages is intended.

Social media marketing
Monitoring and facilitating customer-to-customer interaction and participation throughout the web to encourage positive engagement with a company and its brands. Interactions may occur on a company site, social networks and other third-party sites.

placements in the natural or organic listings using search engine optimisation where no charge is made for clicks from the search engine.

2 *Online PR*. Maximising favourable mentions of your company, brands, products or websites on third-party websites such as **social networks, blogs, podcasts** or **feeds** that are likely to be visited by your target audience. Also includes responding to negative mentions and conducting public relations via a site through a social media news centre or blog, for example.

3 *Online partnerships*. Creating and managing long-term arrangements to promote your online services on third-party websites or through email communications. Different forms of partnership include link building, affiliate marketing, aggregators such as price comparison sites like Moneysupermarket (**www.moneysupermarket.com**), online sponsorship and co-branding.

4 *Display advertising*. Use of online ads such as banners and rich media ads to achieve brand awareness and encourage click-through to a target site.

5 *Opt-in email marketing*. Renting email lists or placing ads in third-party e-newsletters or the use of an in-house list for customer activation and retention.

6 *Social media marketing*. Companies participate and advertise within social networks and communities to reach and engage their audience. **Viral marketing** or online word-of-mouth messages are closely related to this. Here content is shared or messages are forwarded to help achieve awareness and, in some cases, drive response.

Social media marketing is an important category of digital marketing which involves encouraging customer communications on a company's own site, or social presences such as Facebook or Twitter or in specialist publisher sites, blogs and forums. It can be applied

| Figure 1.11 | Six categories of e-communications tools or media channels |

Source: Chaffey and Smith (2012)

as a traditional broadcast medium – for example companies can use Facebook or Twitter to send messages to customers or partners who have opted in. However, to take advantage of the benefits of social media it is important to start and participate in customer conversations. These can be related to products, promotions or customer service and are aimed at learning more about customers and providing support, thus improving the way a company is perceived.

The growth of social networks has been documented by Boyd and Ellison (2007), who describe social networking sites (SNS) as:

> Web-based services that allow individuals to (1) construct a public or semi-public profile within a bounded system, (2) articulate a list of other users with whom they share a connection, and (3) view and traverse their list of connections and those made by others within the system.

The interactive capabilities to post comments or other content and rate content are surprisingly missing from this definition.

Different types of social media marketing tools

There are many, many sites and tools which comprise what we call 'social media'. To gain an idea of just how many, complete Activity 1.5, which lists many tools in 25 categories.

A social media site is much more than simply a website. From a technology viewpoint, most of these sites can be considered as software applications or web services which give access to users at different levels of permission and then enable management and storage of different forms of user-generated content. Messaging is also an important feature of

---

Digital marketing insight 1.2	Social media matters – the Cluetrain Manifesto sparks the social media marketing revolution

When Levine *et al.* (2000) coined the phrase 'markets are conversations', they perhaps did not realise how fundamental this idea would be to the success of marketing in the digital age. Creating a social media or customer engagement strategy is challenging because it requires a change in mindset for the company wishing to exploit it. The challenge is that the company may have to give up some control of their messaging to enable them to communicate with customers effectively. The change in approach required is clear from a movement that originated in the USA in 1999, known as the Cluetrain manifesto (**www.cluetrain.com**). The authors, Levine *et al.* (2000), say:

> *The cluetrain used email, newsgroups, mailing lists, chat and web pages to facilitate internet based conversations and human interaction in a digital space. Conversations among human beings sound human. They are conducted in a human voice. Most corporations, on the other hand, only know how to talk in the soothing, humorless monotone of the mission statement, marketing brochure, and your-call-is-important-to-us busy signal. Same old tone, same old lies. No wonder networked markets have no respect for companies unable or unwilling to speak as they do. Corporate firewalls have kept smart employees in and smart markets out. It's going to cause real pain to tear those walls down. But the result will be a new kind of conversation, which gives everyone permission to take part in the discussion. And if this is the case it will be the most exciting conversation business has ever engaged in.*

many of these sites, particularly the main social networks which will alert users when new content related to their content or connections is published. APIs for exchanging data with other web services interfaces are also a key feature of social networks which enable them to be more useful and allow them and their members to extend their reach and influence by incorporating social comments into other sites.

Activity 1.5	Assessing social media marketing platforms

Purpose

To explore the range of social media sites and tools, to categorise them and assess their business applications.

Activity

Visit the Conversation Prism (**www.conversationprism.com**), which is a visual map of the social media landscape. Identify the types of social media sites you and your colleagues use. How do you think the popularity of tools would differ for different types of B2B and B2C sites? Discuss how businesses should decide on the most important to invest in to achieve their goals.

According to Weinberg and Ekin (2011), social media is neither a perfect substitute for traditional marketing, nor is it a one-size-fits-all. Marketers can effectively use social media by taking their message directly to consumers and focussing on traditional objectives. Since there are so many types of social presence, it's helpful to simplify the options to manage. You can see there's more to social media than social network...

1 *Social networks.* The core social platforms in most countries where people interact through social networks are Facebook for consumer audiences, LinkedIn for business audiences, Google+ and Twitter for both.
2 *Social publishing and news.* Nearly all newspapers and magazines, whether broad or niche, now have an online presence with the option to participate through comments on articles, blogs or communities.
3 *Social commenting in blogs.* A company blog can form the hub of your social media strategy and you can look at tapping into others' blogs, whether company or personal or through blog outreach.
4 *Social niche communities.* These are communities and forums independent of the main networks, although these do support sub-groups. You can create your own community this way.
5 *Social customer service.* Sites like GetSatisfaction, as well as companies' own customer support forums, are increasingly important for responding to customer complaints.
6 *Social knowledge.* These are reference social networks like Yahoo! Answers, Quora and similar, plus Wikipedia. They show how any businesses can engage their audiences by solving their problems and subtly showing how their products have helped others.
7 *Social bookmarking.* The bookmarking sites like Delicious (**www.delicious.com**), which are relatively unimportant in the UK except if you are engaging technical audiences.
8 *Social streaming.* Rich and streaming media social sites – photos, video and podcasting.
9 *Social search.* Search engines are becoming more social with the ability to tag, comment on results and, most recently, vote for them through Google+1.
10 *Social commerce.* We've left this one until last, because it's mainly relevant for the retail sector. It involves reviews and ratings on products and sharing of coupons about details.

Web 2.0 concept
A collection of web services involving data exchange between sites that facilitate participation and interaction of web users with sites to create user-generated content and encourage behaviours such as community or social network participation, mashups, content rating, use of widgets and tagging.

Video marketing
The use of video to gain visibility in search marketing, video hosting sites and to engage site visitors.

Web 3.0 concept
Next-generation web incorporating high-speed connectivity, complex cross-community interactions and an intelligent or semantic web where automated applications can access data from different online services to assist searchers perform complex tasks of supplier selection.

Web 2.0

The **Web 2.0 concept** emerged in 2004. was summarised in an influential article by Tim O'Reilly (2005). A brief reference to the concept has been retained in this edition, although the term is not used in practice today. The main types of services that developed as part of Web 2.0 which still underpin website–social media interaction are: free to use, ad-support web-hosted services or interactive applications for different media formats such as Flickr for images; YouTube for video; Bing or Google Maps; blogging services such as Wordpress. com; and rating of content and services through rating systems. Data exchange between sites through XML-based data standards, for example RSS, is still used for direct sharing of content from business blogs to social network updates. The 'Ajax' (Asynchronous JavaScript and XML) implementation is still used for developing many interactive features. **Video marketing** was also part of 'Web 2.0' and has grown in importance since.

Since the Web 2.0 concept has been widely applied, it is natural that commentators would try to develop it to the **Web 3.0 concept**, although the term has not been widely used to date. Figure 1.12 summarises the evolution of digital and web-related technologies.

- *Web applications*. Usage of web-based applications and services (like Google word processor and spreadsheets). Using the web in this way is sometimes termed cloud computing where all that is really needed for many activities is a computer with a web browser with local software applications used less widely.
- *Syndication*. Increased incorporation of syndicated content and services from other sites or a network into a site (using tools such as Yahoo! Pipes and XML exchange between widgets). We refer to this concept as 'atomisation' in Chapter 9.
- *Streamed video or IPTV*. Increased use of streamed video from existing TV providers and user-generated content (as suggested by use of YouTube and IPTV services such as Joost).

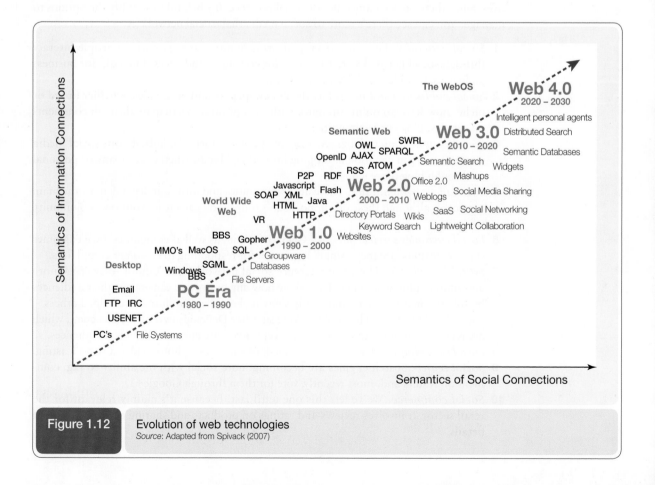

Figure 1.12	Evolution of web technologies

Source: Adapted from Spivack (2007)

- *Virtual worlds*. Increased use of immersive virtual environments such as Second Life.
- *Personal data integration*. Increased exchange of data between social networks fulfilling different needs
- *The semantic web*. Increased use of semantic mark-up leading to the semantic web envisioned by Tim Berners-Lee over ten years ago. It seems semantic mark-up will be needed to develop artificial intelligence applications which recommend content and services to web users without them actively having to seek them and apply their own judgement as to the best products and brands (i.e. an automated shopping comparison service) (as suggested by the use of standardised data feeds between shopping comparison sites and Google Base).

Benefits of digital media

In the section on digital marketing strategy, we described some of the applications of Internet marketing to support communications with customers across the purchase cycle from generating awareness, achieving direct response for lead generation or sale and supporting customer service and relationship marketing. In this section we explore key differences between digital media and traditional media which savvy marketers exploit.

Digital marketing communications differ significantly from conventional marketing communications because digital media enabled new forms of interaction and new models for information exchange. A useful summary of the differences between new media and traditional media originally developed by McDonald and Wilson (1999) and still valid – they describe the '6 Is of the e-marketing mix' which are practical benefits of digital marketing that the marketer should exploit.

1 Interactivity

John Deighton was one of the first authors to identify these characteristics of a digital medium (Deighton, 1996):

- the customer initiates contact
- the customer is seeking information or an experience (pull)
- it is a high-intensity medium – the marketer will have 100% of the individual's attention when he or she is viewing a website
- a company can gather and store the response of the individual
- individual needs of the customer can be addressed and taken into account in future dialogues.

Figure 1.13(a) shows how traditional media are predominantly *push media* where the marketing message is broadcast from company *to* customer, although interaction can be encouraged through direct response to phone, website or social media page. Online it is often the customer who initiates contact and is *seeking* information through researching information on a website. In other words, it is a '*pull*' mechanism where it is particularly important to have good visibility in search engines when customers are entering search terms relevant to a company's products or services. Amongst marketing professionals this powerful new approach to marketing is now commonly known as inbound marketing (Shah and Halligan, 2009). **Inbound marketing** is powerful since advertising wastage is reduced. Content and search marketing can be used to target prospects with a defined need – they are proactive and self-selecting. But this is a weakness since marketers may have less control than in traditional communications where the message is pushed out to a defined audience and can help generate awareness and demand.

Inbound marketing
The consumer is proactive in seeking out information for their needs, and interactions with brands are attracted through content, search and social media marketing.

Figure 1.13(b) shows how digital media should be used to encourage two-way communications, which may be extensions of the direct-response approach. For example, FMCG suppliers use their website or Facebook presence as a method of generating interaction by providing incentives such as competitions and sales promotions to encourage the customer to respond with their names, addresses and profile information such as age and sex.

| Figure 1.13 | Summary of communication models for (a) traditional media, (b) new media |

2 Intelligence

Digital media and technology can be used as a relatively low-cost method of collecting marketing research, particularly about customer perceptions of products and services, as described in Chapter 10 which reviews digital analytics and market research.

3 Individualisation

Personalisation
Delivering individualised content through web pages or email.

Sense and respond communications
Customer behaviour is monitored at an individual level and the marketer responds with communications tailored to the individual's need.

Outbound Internet-based communications
The website and email marketing are used to send personalised communications to customers.

Another important feature of interactive marketing communications is that they can be tailored to the individual (Figure 1.14(b)) at relatively low costs, unlike in traditional media where the same message tends to be broadcast to everyone (Figure 1.14(a)). This individualisation is based on the intelligence collected about site visitors and then stored in a database and subsequently used to target and personalise communications to customers to achieve *relevance* in all media. The process of tailoring is also referred to as **personalisation** – Amazon is the most widely known example where the customer is greeted by name on the website and receives recommendations on site and in their emails based on previous purchases. This ability to deliver 'sense and respond communications' is another key feature of digital marketing and is explored further in Chapter 6.

4 Integration

The Internet provides further scope for integrated marketing communications. Figure 1.15 shows the role of the Internet in multichannel marketing. When assessing the marketing effectiveness of a website, the role of the Internet in communicating with customers and other partners can best be considered from two perspectives. First, there is **outbound Internet-based communications** from *organisation to customer*. We need to ask how does the Internet complement other channels in communicating the proposition for the company's products and services to new and existing customers with a view to generating new leads

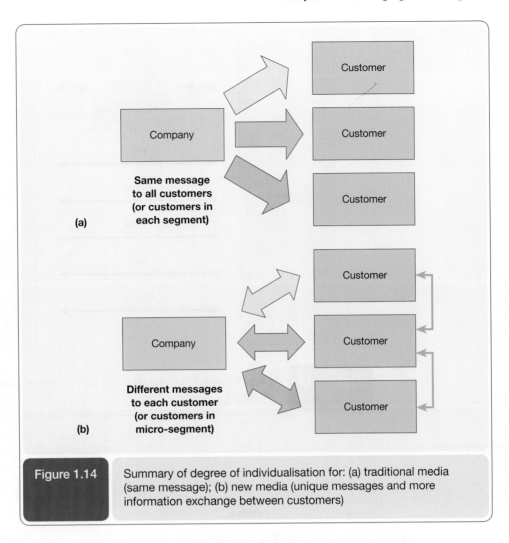

| Figure 1.14 | Summary of degree of individualisation for: (a) traditional media (same message); (b) new media (unique messages and more information exchange between customers) |

Inbound Internet-based communications
Customers enquire through web-based forms and email.

and retaining existing customers? Second, **inbound Internet-based communications** from *customer to organisation*: how can the Internet complement other channels to deliver customer service to these customers? Many companies have now integrated email response and website callback into their existing call centre or customer service operation.

Some practical examples of how the Internet can be used as an integrated communications tool as part of supporting a multichannel customer journey (Figure 1.16) are the following:

- The Internet can be used as a direct-response tool, enabling customers to respond to offers and promotions publicised in other media.
- The website can have a direct response or callback facility built into it. The Automobile Association has a feature where a customer service representative will contact a customer by phone when the customer fills in their name, phone number and a suitable time to ring.
- The Internet can be used to support the buying decision even if the purchase does not occur via the website through assisted selling via live chat or phone. For example, Dell has a prominent web-specific phone number on its website that encourages customers to ring a representative in the call centre for support.

Figure 1.15 Channels requiring integration as part of integrated e-marketing strategy

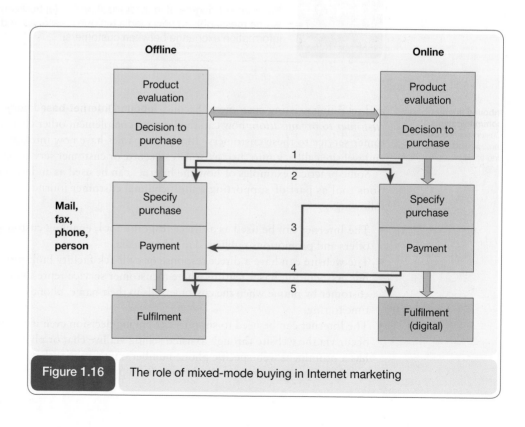

Figure 1.16 The role of mixed-mode buying in Internet marketing

Activity 1.6	Integrating online and offline communications

Purpose

To highlight differences in marketing communications introduced through the use of the Internet as a channel and the need to integrate these communications with existing channels.

Activity

List communications between a PC vendor and a home customer over the lifetime of a product such as a PC. Include communications using both the Internet and traditional media. Refer to channel-swapping alternatives in the buying decision in Figure 1.16 to develop your answer.

5 Industry restructuring

Disintermediation
The removal of intermediaries such as distributors or brokers that formerly linked a company to its customers.

Reintermediation
The creation of new intermediaries between customers and suppliers providing services such as supplier search and product evaluation.

Disintermediation and **reintermediation** are key concepts of industry restructuring that should be considered by any company developing an e-marketing strategy and are explored in more detail in Chapters 2, 4 and 5.

For marketers defining their company's communications strategy it becomes very important to consider the company's representation on these intermediary sites by answering questions such as 'Which intermediaries should we be represented on?' and 'How do our offerings compare to those of competitors in terms of features, benefits and price?'

6 Independence of location

Electronic media also introduce the possibility of increasing the reach of company communications to the global market. This gives opportunities to sell into international markets which may not previously have been possible. The Internet makes it possible to sell to a country without a local sales or customer service force (although this may still be necessary for some products).

Mini case study 1.3	Online pureplay startup Travel Republic achieves growth through taking advantage of benefits of digital marketing

Travel Republic is the highest ranking independent online travel agent in the UK, with over 1 million travellers booking every year. It's an example of a pureplay that has deployed digital marketing techniques like search, social media and email marketing to grow both in the UK and internationally.

Online travel agent Travel Republic topped *The Sunday Times* Virgin Fast Track 100 list four years after the company was launched. The Kingston-upon-Thames based business was set up in 2003 and is the brainchild of three university friends – Paul Furner, managing director, Chris Waite, IT director, and Kane Pirie, finance and operations director.

Today the company can no longer be termed a startup, with revenues increasing 14.5 per cent in 2014 to £67.5 million, giving it an operating profit margin of 20 per cent and with separate sites for local audiences in Spain, Italy and Ireland.

The company employs more than 150 staff. TravelRepublic.co.uk appears in the IMRG-Hitwise Hot Shops List, which ranks the UK's top 50 most popular Internet retailers, across all sectors (ranked by number of web visitors). In the online travel agency sector TravelRepublic.co.uk is more popular than Opodo and ebookers.com, although Expedia.co.uk and lastminute.com rank higher.

A major reason for the growth of Travel Republic is that it has taken advantage of the 'pull' effect of web communications. Through using sponsored links in search networks such as Google AdWords, it has been able to target its offering precisely to an online audience looking for a competitive price on a holiday or a flight to a particular destination. Of course, this has to be backed up by a strong proposition, an easy to use, high-performance website and trust in the brand indicated by user reviews and holiday guarantees (Figure 1.17). TravelRepublic.co.uk caters for a broad range of customers including families, couples and groups. The web-site offers charter, low-cost and scheduled airlines, powerful rate shopping technology for hotel rooms and apartments, plus hotel reviews and resort guides written by its customers.

Customers can save up to 50 per cent on the price of a comparable package holiday purchased online or on the high street. TravelRepublic.co.uk works with over 100 different flight operators and offers flights to more than 200 destinations. The website also offers over 30,000 discounted hotels, apartments and villas plus a wide range of other services such as taxi transfers, airport parking and car hire. The website gives cus-tomers complete flexibility with flights, hotels and durations.

Paul Furner, managing director of TravelRepublic.co.uk explained how the company developed:

Chris, Kane and I met at university but then followed very different careers – Chris in software development, Kane in corporate finance/private equity and me in software quality assurance. These differing back-grounds, all outside of the travel industry, have allowed us to take a fresh new look at the sector and become one of its leading innovators.

However, equally important has been our commitment, from the outset, to deliver gold standard cus-tomer service to our customers. At a time when it is often said that there is no loyalty on the web we would beg to differ. Our levels of repeat and recommended business suggest that we have a real affinity with our customers which we plan to build upon in the coming months.

Source: Travel Republic press release, 2 December 2007, Travel Republic is the UK's Fastest Growing Private Company, **www.travelrepublic. co.uk/help/pressReplace_003.aspx**

| Figure 1.17 | Travel Republic (www.travelrepublic.co.uk) |

In terms of deploying campaigns, these are further benefits of digital communications:

- *Accountability*. Digital media are potentially more accountable through the use of measurement systems known collectively as web analytics. Google provides a free tool known as Google Analytics (**www.google.com/analytics**) to enable its advertisers to test the value generated from its ads.
- *Testing*. Potentially, testing becomes more straightforward at a lower cost with the option to trial alternative creative executions, messaging or offers. Google offers another free tool – the Website Optimiser – to test alternative landing pages.
- *Flexibility*. Campaigns can be more flexible, with the capability to change copy or offers during a campaign. Alternative ads can be served within Google to evaluate which works best. Google AdWords also offers dayparting, where ads can be displayed at different times of the day.
- *Micro-targeting*. Alternative messages can be delivered for different audiences according to what they are searching for. Potentially a company can show a different advert in Google AdWords for each term searched on.
- *Cost-control*. Costs can be controlled for each group of search terms entered by customers through the search engine, managed collectively, and bids made can be increased or decreased with the aid of software.

Key challenges of digital communications

It is sometimes suggested by some suppliers of digital media that they are 'quick, cheap and easy' to deploy. This is a great misconception since there are many challenges which need to be overcome when managing digital campaigns. Again referring to a Google AdWords campaign as an example, these include:

- *Complexity*. To enable the benefits we have mentioned above – such as personalisation, testing and dynamic variation in ads through time – time has to go into configuring the campaign although the search engines provide defaults to enable easy setup. This requires specialist expertise either in-house or at an agency to manage the campaign.
- *Responding to competitors*. Since competitors can also change their approach readily, more resource has to be used to monitor competitor activity. Automated tools known as bid management tools can assist with this – they will automatically check amounts competitors are paying and then adjust them according to pre-defined rules.
- *Responding to changes in technology and marketing platforms*. Google and the other ad-serving companies innovate to offer better capabilities for their customers. This means that staff managing campaigns need training to keep up-to-date. Google offers 'Adwords Qualified Professionals' so that companies can be certain of a minimum skills level.
- *Cost*. Although costs can be readily controlled, in competitive categories the costs can be high, exceeding €10 per click.
- *Attention*. While online paid search ads are highly targeted and there is arguably little wastage, not everyone will view paid adverts, indeed there is a phenomenon known as 'banner blindness' where web users ignore online ads (see Chapter 9 for more details). Engaging with the audience with advertising is also a problem in social networks and other publisher sites, which can lead to a very low rate of people clicking on ads.

Key communications concepts for digital marketing

In this section, we introduce three key concepts which underpin digital communications across the digital media we have introduced in this chapter.

1 Customer engagement.
2 Permission marketing.
3 Content marketing.

1 Customer engagement

This difficulty in gaining attention online on all types of sites has led to the emergence of the concept of **customer engagement** as a key challenge with which digital marketers are increasingly concerned. cScape (2008) describe customer engagement as:

> repeated interactions that strengthen the emotional, psychological or physical investment a customer has in a brand.

While for Haven (2007), customer engagement is:

> the level of involvement, interaction, intimacy, and influence an individual has with a brand over time.

Arguably, the biggest difference in communications introduced by the growth of digital media and the web is the capability, or many would say necessity, to include customer's' conversations as an integral part of communications. Today, proactively managing consumer participation which occurs through social networks such as Facebook, Google+ and LinkedIn, video postings and comments on YouTube and myriad blogs and forums is essential since, when a positive sentiment is expressed by a real person independent from a company this confers credibility on the company.

Equally, there are negative sentiments or comments made by consumers on the web that need to be managed. For example, on one site (**www.haveyoursay.com**) a purchaser of a car was highly critical about a make of car and the comments appeared near the top of the Google search results page when someone searched for the brand, yet for several years the manufacturer did nothing to manage this.

2 Permission marketing

Permission marketing is an established approach to online marketing which is still highly relevant today as a practical foundation for CRM and online customer engagement. "Permission marketing' was a term coined by Seth Godin. Godin (1999) noted that while research used to show we were bombarded by 500 marketing messages a day, with the advent of the web and digital TV this has now increased to over 3000 a day! From an organisation's viewpoint, this leads to a dilution in the effectiveness of the messages – how can the communications of any one company stand out? From the customer's viewpoint, time is seemingly in ever shorter supply; customers are losing patience and expect reward for their attention, time and information. Godin refers to the traditional approach as **interruption marketing**. Permission marketing is about seeking the customer's permission before engaging them in a relationship and providing something in exchange. The classic exchange is based on information or entertainment – a B2B site can offer a free report in exchange for a customer sharing their email address or 'Liking' a brand, while a B2C site can offer a newsletter or access to their wall with valuable content and offers. We cover the principles of permission marketing in more detail and with examples related to CRM in Chapter 6.

3 Content marketing

Success in permission marketing requires exceptional, compelling content. To emphasise the importance of content marketing to gaining permission, encouraging sharing and ongoing engagement through websites and social media, the concepts of **content marketing** and content strategy have developed to describe best practice approaches. Today, by content we refer to the combination of static content forming web pages, but also dynamic rich media content which encourages interaction. Videos, podcasts, user-generated content and interactive product selectors should also be considered as content which should be refined to engage issues.

You can see the challenge content strategy presents since today there are so many different types of content delivered in different forms to different places on different access platforms, yet it is increasingly important to engage customers in social media.

The definition suggests these elements of content management that need to be planned and managed:

1 *Content engagement value*. Which types of content will engage the audience – is it simple product or services information, a guide to buying product, or a game to engage your audience?
2 *Content media*. Plain text, rich media such as Flash or Rich Internet applications or mobile apps (see Chapter 3), audio (podcasts) and hosted and streamed video. Even plain text offers different format options from HTML text to ebook formats and PDFs.
3 *Content syndication*. Content can be syndicated to different types of sites through feeds, APIs, microformats or direct submission by email. Content can be embedded in sites through widgets displaying information delivered by a feed.
4 *Content participation*. Effective content today is not simply delivered for static consumption, it should enable commenting, ratings and reviews. These also need to be monitored and managed both in the original location and where they are discussed elsewhere.
5 *Content access platform*. The different digital access platforms such as desktops and laptops of different screen resolution and mobile devices. Paper is also a content access platform for print media.

Smart Insights (2015a) explain the key elements of a content hub using the diagram shown in Figure 1.18, or, as they put it, a 'content marketing machine' as:

1 Create the right types of sharable content formats to meet customer interests and company commercial goals. The quality and range of content must be sufficient and sustained to compete. (In Chapter 9, the Smart Insights Content Marketing Matrix is presented as a method of reviewing the most appropriate content formats to use.)

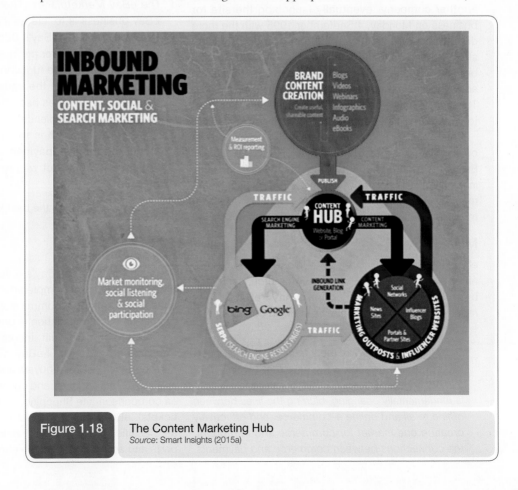

Figure 1.18	The Content Marketing Hub
	Source: Smart Insights (2015a)

Content marketing hub
A central branded location where your audience can access and interact with all your key content marketing assets. In a practical sense, the content hub can be a blog or new section, an online customer magazine or a resource centre.

2 A defined branded **content marketing hub** or repository for accessing all relevant content marketing assets.
3 Invest in seeding content and working with partner sites and influencers to increase awareness and sharing of content.
4 Content marketing should be linked into search marketing and particular search marketing, since if there is a regular stream of quality content Google will favour the site when searchers are looking for information or products.
5 The right people, process and tools need to be in place to monitor content and sharing effectiveness in social media. This should include following up on any comments from social media.

To conclude this chapter, read Case Study 1 for the background on the success factors which have helped build one of the biggest online brands.

Case Study 1   eBay thrives in the global marketplace

Context

It's hard to believe that one of the most well-known dot-coms has now been established 15 years. Pierre Omidyar, a 28-year-old French-born software engineer living in California, coded the site while working for another company, eventually launching the site for business on Monday, 4 September 1995 with the more direct name 'Auction Web'. Legend reports that the site attracted no visitors in its first 24 hours. The site became eBay in 1997. In 2014 eBay had 155 million active buyers, an increase from 90 million active in 2009. This shows how established pureplays have continued to grow with global adoption of the web.

This summary and many others in the text are based on the SEC filing of the business. The Security and Exchange Commission (SEC) required by company law in the US gives deep, relatively hype-free insights on the main online platforms based in the US and is recommended for students studying these types of business.

Mission

eBay describes its purpose as to 'pioneer new communities around the world built on commerce, sustained by trust, and inspired by opportunity'. eBay's 2014 report describes the company's view on current use of e-commerce:

Driven by the ubiquity of the Internet and the proliferation of mobile devices, we believe that the way consumers engage with each other, brands and services is fundamentally changing, blurring the lines between offline retail and online e-commerce, and effectively creating one market for commerce and reinforcing the connections between commerce and payments.

We believe that this trend has expanded our addressable market.

At the time of writing eBay comprises two major businesses:

1 *The eBay Marketplaces*. The mission for the core eBay business is to 'create the world's online marketplace'. In 2008, eBay's SEC filing notes some of the success factors for this business, for which eBay seeks to manage the functionality, safety, ease-of-use and reliability of the trading platform. By 2011 the strategic priorities had changed to trust, value, selection and convenience.
2 *PayPal*. The mission is to 'create the new global standard for online payments'. This company was acquired in 2003 but was repurchased at a later date.

This case focuses on the best known eBay business, the eBay Marketplace.

Revenue model

The vast majority of eBay's revenue is for the listing and commission on completed sales. For PayPal purchases an additional commission fee is charged. The margin on each transaction is phenomenal since once the infrastructure is built, incremental costs on each transaction are tiny – all eBay is doing is transmitting bits and bytes between buyers and sellers. To grow revenue eBay has acquired and developed other sites such as comparison site **Shopping.com** and StubHub (event tickets). eBay has also created vertical formats (such as Classifieds, Daily Deals, Fashion, Motors (vehicles, parts and accessories) and Electronics.

eBay also expanded into providing infrastructure for other retailers in 2011 with its purchase of GSI, a provider of e-commerce and interactive marketing services encompassing websites and fulfilment centres to enterprise clients that include some of the world's leading brands and retailers covering merchandise categories, including apparel, sporting goods, toys and baby, health and beauty and home.

Advertising and other non-transaction net revenues represent a relatively small proportion of total net revenues and the strategy is that this should remain the case.

Proposition

The eBay Marketplace is well known for its core service, which enables sellers to list items for sale on an auction or fixed-price basis giving buyers the opportunity to bid for and purchase items of interest.

Software tools are provided, particularly for frequent traders, including Turbo Lister, Seller's Assistant, Selling Manager and Selling Manager Pro, which help automate the selling process, the Shipping Calculator, Reporting tools, etc. Today over 60 per cent of listings are facilitated by software, showing the value of automating posting for frequent trading.

Fraud is a significant risk factor for eBay. BBC (2005) reported that around 1 in 10,000 transactions within the UK were fraudulent; 0.0001 per cent is a small proportion, but scaling this up across the number of transactions makes a significant volume.

eBay has developed 'Trust and Safety Programs' which are particularly important to reassure customers since online services are prone to fraud. For example, the eBay feedback forum can help establish credentials of sellers and buyers. Every registered user has a feedback profile that may contain compliments, criticisms and/or other comments by users who have conducted business with that user. The Feedback Forum requires feedback to be related to specific transactions and Top Seller status was introduced in 2010 to increase trust in the service. There is also a Safe Harbour data protection method and a standard purchase protection system.

eBay has increased use of mobile commerce since 2009, yet it still only accounts for 20 per cent of purchases in 2014, including sales from 240 million app downloads since inception.

According to the SEC filing, eBay summarises the core messages to define its proposition as follows:

For buyers:

- trust
- value
- selection
- convenience.

For sellers:

- access to broad markets
- cost effective marketing and distribution
- access to large buyer base
- good conversion rates.

In 2007, eBay introduced Neighbourhoods (**http://neighbourhoods.ebay.com**) where groups can discuss brands and products they have high involvement with. This social commerce experiment has now ended.

In January 2008, eBay announced significant changes to its Marketplaces business in three major areas: fee structure, seller incentives and standards, and feedback. These changes have been controversial with some sellers, but are aimed at improving the quality of experience. Detailed Seller Ratings (DSRs) enable sellers to be reviewed in four areas: (1) item as described; (2) communication; (3) delivery time; and (4) postage and packaging charges. This is part of a move to help increase conversion rate by increasing positive shopping experiences, for example by including more accurate descriptions with better pictures and avoiding excessive shipping charges. Powersellers with positive DSRs will be featured more favourably in the search results pages and will gain additional discounts.

Competition

Although there are now few direct competitors of online auction services in many countries, there are many indirect competitors. The SEC filings describe competing channels as including online and offline retailers, distributors, liquidators, import and export companies, auctioneers, catalogue and mail-order companies, classifieds, directories, search engines, products of search engines, virtually all online and offline commerce participants and online and offline shopping channels and networks.

Objectives and strategy

The overall eBay aims are to increase the gross merchandise volume and net revenues from the eBay Marketplace. More detailed objectives are defined to achieve these aims, with strategies focussing on:

1 *Acquisition* – increasing the number of newly registered users on the eBay Marketplace.
2 *Activation* – increasing the number of registered users that become active bidders, buyers or sellers on the eBay Marketplace.
3 *Activity* – increasing the volume and value of transactions that are conducted by each active user on the eBay Marketplace.

The focus on each of these three areas will vary according to strategic priorities in particular local markets.

eBay Marketplace growth is also driven by defining approaches to improve performance in these areas. First, category growth is achieved by increasing the number and size of categories within the marketplace, for example: Antiques, Art, Books and Business & Industrial. Second, formats for interaction: the traditional format is auction listings, but it has been refined now to include the 'Buy-It-Now' fixed-price format. This fixed-price listing now accounts for well over half of all transactions.

eBay's growth strategy

In its SEC filings, success factors eBay believes are important to enable it to compete in its market include:

- ability to attract buyers and sellers;
- volume of transactions and price and selection of goods;
- customer service;
- brand recognition.

According to its 2010 SEC filing:

Our growth strategy is focussed on reinvesting in our customers by improving the buyer experience and seller economics by enhancing our products and services, improving trust and safety and customer support, extending our product offerings into new formats, categories and geographies, and implementing innovative pricing and buyer retention strategies.

It also notes that in the context of its competitors, other factors it believes are important are:

- community cohesion, interaction and size;
- system reliability;
- reliability of delivery and payment;
- website convenience and accessibility;
- level of service fees;
- quality of search tools.

This implies that eBay believes it has optimised these factors, but its competitors still have opportunities for improving performance in these areas which will make the market more competitive.

Risk management

The SEC filing lists the risks and challenges of conducting business internationally as follows:

- regulatory requirements, including regulation of auctioneering, professional selling, distance selling, banking and money transmitting;

- legal uncertainty regarding liability for the listings and other content provided by users, including uncertainty as a result of less Internet-friendly legal systems, unique local laws and lack of clear precedent or applicable law;
- difficulties in integrating with local payment providers, including banks, credit and debit card associations, and electronic fund transfer systems;
- differing levels of retail distribution, shipping and communications infrastructures;
- different employee/employer relationships and the existence of workers' councils and labour unions;
- difficulties in staffing and managing foreign operations;
- longer payment cycles, different accounting practices and greater problems in collecting accounts receivable;
- potentially adverse tax consequences, including local taxation of fees or of transactions on websites;
- higher telecommunications and Internet service provider costs;
- strong local competitors;
- different and more stringent consumer protection, data protection and other laws;
- cultural ambivalence towards, or non-acceptance of, online trading;
- seasonal reductions in business activity;
- expenses associated with localising products, including offering customers the ability to transact business in the local currency;
- laws and business practices that favour local competitors or prohibit foreign ownership of certain businesses;
- profit repatriation restrictions, foreign currency exchange restrictions and exchange rate fluctuations;
- volatility in a specific country's or region's political or economic conditions;
- differing intellectual property laws and taxation laws.

Question

Discuss how eBay uses different parts of their site to focus on certain activities and how this has contributed to continued growth.

Summary

1 Digital marketing refers to the use of digital technology platforms, combined with traditional media, to achieve marketing objectives. Digital marketing involves using paid, owned and earned digital media channels and using other technologies, such as databases for customer relationship management (e-CRM). We reviewed ten key digital hardware platforms including desktop, mobile and tablet.

2 A customer-centric approach to digital marketing considers the needs of a range of customers using techniques such as persona and customer scenarios (**Chapter 2**) to understand customer needs in a multichannel buying process. Tailoring to individual customers may be practical using personalisation techniques.

3 Electronic commerce refers to both electronically mediated financial and informational transactions.

4 Electronic business is a broader term referring to how technology can benefit all internal business processes and interactions with third parties. This includes buy-side and sell-side e-commerce and the internal value chain.

5 E-commerce transactions include business-to-business (B2B), business-to-consumer (B2C), consumer-to-consumer (C2C) and consumer-to-business (C2B) transactions.

6 There are six key digital media channels: search marketing; online PR; partnership (affiliate) marketing; display advertising; email; and social media marketing. These communications techniques are best used in an integrated form by applying the concepts of content, inbound and permission marketing.

7 The Internet is used to develop existing markets through enabling an additional communications and/or sales channel with potential customers. It can be used to develop new international markets with a reduced need for new sales offices and agents. Companies can provide new services and possibly products using the Internet.

8 Digital marketing can support the full range of marketing functions and in doing so can help reduce costs, facilitate communication within and between organisations and improve customer service.

9 Interaction with customers, suppliers and distributors occurs across the Internet. The web and email are particularly powerful if they can be used to create *relevant, personalised communications*.

10 The marketing benefits the Internet confers are advantageous both to the large corporation and to the small or medium-sized enterprise. These include:

- a new medium for advertising and PR;
- a new channel for distributing products;
- opportunities for expansion into new markets;
- new ways of enhancing customer service;
- new ways of reducing costs by reducing the number of staff in order fulfilment.

Exercises

Self-assessment exercises

1 Explain the main types of digital marketing platform.
2 Identify different ways in which a website or social media presence is used for marketing in different markets.
3 Outline different applications of digital marketing which can help meet business goals.
4 Explain what is meant by electronic commerce, social commerce and digital business. How do they relate to the marketing function?

5 Six digital media channels are introduced in this chapter. What are they and how do they work to reach, engage and convert an audience?

6 Summarise the main communications difference between digital and traditional media.

7 Distinguish between social media marketing, inbound and content marketing.

8 How can the Internet and digital media be used to develop new markets and penetrate existing markets? What types of new products can be delivered by the Internet?

Essay and discussion questions

1 Some would see digital media primarily as a means of advertising and selling products. What are the opportunities for other uses of the Internet and digital media for marketing?

2 'The World Wide Web represents a *pull* medium for marketing rather than a *push* medium.' Discuss.

3 You are a newly installed marketing manager in a company selling products in the business-to-business sector. Currently, the company has only a limited website containing electronic versions of its brochures. You want to convince the directors of the benefits of investing in the website to provide more benefits to the company. How would you present your case?

4 Explain the main benefits that a company selling fast-moving consumer goods should derive from its website.

Examination questions

1 Explain electronic commerce and social commerce and how they relate.

2 Which techniques can be used to increase awareness of a brand and encourage interaction with the brand?

3 A digital marketing manager must seek to control and accommodate all the main methods by which consumers may visit a company website. Describe these methods.

4 Imagine you are explaining the difference between the digital marketing and e-commerce to a marketing manager. How would you explain these two terms?

5 What is the relevance of 'conversion marketing' for digital marketing?

6 Explain how digital platforms can be used to increase market penetration in existing markets and develop new markets.

References

Adjei, M.T., Noble, S.M. and Noble, C.H. (2010) The influence of C2C communications in online brand communities on customer purchase behaviour, *Journal of the Academy of Marketing Science*, 38(5), 634–53.

Altimeter (2014) Digital transformation: why and how companies are investing in the new business models to lead digital customer experiences. Author: Brian Solis, www.altimetergroupdigitaltransformation.com.

Ansoff, H. (1957) Strategies for diversification, *Harvard Business Review* (September–October), 113–24.

BBC (2005) eBay's 10-year rise to world fame. Robert Plummer story from BBC News, 2 September, http://news.bbc.co.uk/go/pr/fr/-/1/hi/business/4207510.stm.

Boyd, D. and Ellison, N. (2007) Social network sites: definition, history and scholarship, *Journal of Computer-Mediated Communication*, 13(1), 210–30.

Chaffey, D. (2014) *E-business and E-commerce Management*, 6th edn, Financial Times/ Prentice Hall, Harlow.

Chaffey, D. and Smith, P.R. (2012) *Emarketing Excellence, Planning and optimising your digital marketing*, 4th edn, Taylor & Francis.

cScape (2008) *Second Annual Online Customer Engagement Report 2008*. Produced by EConsultancy in association with cScape, **www.econsultancy.com**.

Deighton, J. (1996) The future of interactive marketing, *Harvard Business Review* (November–December), 151–62.

EConsultancy (2005) Managing an e-commerce team: integrating digital marketing into your organisation. Author: Dave Chaffey, **www.econsultancy.com**.

Geyskens, I., Gielens, K. and Dekimpe, M. (2002) The market valuation of internet channel additions, *Journal of Marketing*, 66 (April), 102–19.

Godin, S. (1999) *Permission Marketing*, Simon and Schuster, New York.

Haven, B. (2007) Marketing's new key metric: engagement, 8 August, Forrester.

Hoffman, D.L. and Novak, T.P. (1996) Marketing in hypermedia computer-mediated environments: conceptual foundations, *Journal of Marketing*, 60 (July), 50–68.

Iyengar, R., Han, S. and Gupta, S. (2009) Do friends influence purchases in a social network? Harvard Business School working paper 09–123.

Jackson, S. (2009) *Cult of Analytics, Driving Online Marketing Strategies using Web Analytics*, Elsevier, Oxford.

Jenkinson, A. (2007) Evolutionary implications for touchpoint planning as a result of neuroscience: a practical fusion of database marketing and advertising, *Journal of Database Marketingand Customer Strategy Management*, 14(3), 164–85.

Jenkinson, A. and Sain, B. (2001) *Getting Words Clear – Marketing Needs a Clear and Consistent Terminology*. White paper available from Centre for Integrated Marketing, **www.integratedmarketing.org.uk**.

Levine, R., Locke, C., Searls, D. and Weinberger, D. (2000) *The Cluetrain Manifesto*, Perseus Books, Cambridge, MA.

McDonald, M. and Wilson, H. (1999) *E-Marketing: Improving Marketing Effectiveness in a Digital World*, Financial Times/Prentice Hall, Harlow.

MIT Center for Digital Business and Capgemini Consulting (2011) *Digital Transformation: A Roadmap for Billion-Dollar Organisations*. White paper, **www.uk.capgemini-consulting.com/digital-transformation**.

O'Reilly, T. (2005) What is Web 2? Design patterns and business models for the next generation of software. Web article, 30 September, O'Reilly Publishing, Sebastopol, CA.

Pei, Z., Toombs, L. and Yan, R. (2014) How does the added new online channel impact the supporting advertising expenditure?, *Journal of Retailing and Consumer Services*, 21(3), 229–38.

SEC (2008) United States Securities and Exchange Commission submission Form 10-K. eBay submission for the fiscal year ended December 31, 2007.

Shah, D. and Halligan, B. (2009) *Inbound Marketing: Get Found Using Google, Social Media, and Blogs*, Wiley, NJ.

Smart Insights (2010) Introducing RACE: a practical framework to improve your digital marketing. Blog post by Dave Chaffey, 15 July 2010, **www.smartinsights.com/ digital-marketing-strategy**.

Smart Insights (2013) A digital campaign example of a startup fashion brand. Blog post, 25 April.

Smart Insights (2014) *Managing Digital Marketing 2014*. Best practices in integrating digital technology and marketing to fuel business growth. Free research report published at SmartInsights.com, January 2014. Author: Dave Chaffey.

Smart Insights (2015a) *Content Marketing Strategy 7 Steps Guide*, **www.smartinsights.com/**.

Smart Insights (2015b) Is this the social media backlash? Blog post by Dave Chaffey, 21 January 2015, **www.smartinsights.com/social-media-marketing/social-media-strategy/social-media-backlash/**.

Spivack (2007) How the WebOS Evolves? Nova Spivack blog posting, 9 February 2007, **http://novaspivack.typepad.com/nova_spivacks_weblog/2007/02/steps_towards_a.html**.

Waterman, R.H., Peters, T.J. and Phillips, J.R. (1980) Structure is not organisation, *McKinsey Quarterly In-house Journal*, McKinsey & Co., New York.

Weinberg, B.and Ekin, P. (2011) Social spending: managing the social media mix, *Business Horizons*, 54(3), 275–82.

Weblinks

Leading portals and blogs covering digital marketing developments

- Altimeter (**http://altimetergroupdigitaltransformation.com**). US analyst with free reports on Digital Transformation and Social Business.
- ClickZ Experts (**www.clickz.com/experts**). An excellent collection of articles on online marketing communications. US-focussed.
- Direct Marketing Association UK (**www.dma.org.uk**). Source of up-to-date data protection advice and how-to guides about online direct marketing.
- Econsultancy.com (**www.econsultancy.com**). UK-focussed portal with extensive supplier directory, best-practice white papers and forum.
- eMarketer (**www.emarketer.com**). Includes reports on media spend based on compilations of other analysts. Fee-based service.
- iMediaConnection (**www.imediaconnection.com**). Articles covering best practice in digital media channels.
- Interactive Advertising Bureau (**www.iab.net**). Best practice on interactive advertising. See also **www.iabuk.net** in the UK.
- The Interactive Media in Retail (**www.imrg.org**). Trade body for e-retailers reporting on growth and practice within UK and European e-commerce.
- Mary Meeker (**www.kpcb.com/insights**). An analyst at Kleiner Perkins Caufield Byers who presents trends and forecasts on digital technology yearly with a focus on mobile channels.
- Marketing Sherpa (**www.marketingsherpa.com**). Case studies and news about online marketing.
- Ofcom (**http://stakeholders.ofcom.org.uk/**). The Office of Communication has an annual Communications Market report on the adoption of digital media including telecommunications and the Internet (including broadband adoption), digital television and wireless services.
- Mashable (**www.mashable.com**). The largest site covering developments in digital media and technology.
- Smart Insights (**www.smartinsights.com**). Covers all developments in digital marketing to support this book. Edited by Dave Chaffey. Digital Transformation is covered on this hub page: **www.smartinsights.com/manage-digital-transformation**.

Chapter 2
Online marketplace analysis: micro-environment

Chapter at a glance

Main topics

- Situation analysis for digital marketing 56
- The digital marketing environment 59
- Understanding customer journeys 61
- Consumer choice and digital influence 72
- Online consumer behaviour and implications for marketing 76
- Competitors 88
- Suppliers 93
- New channel structures 96
- Business models for e-commerce 99

Case studies

Digital marketing in practice

The Smart Insights interview with Michael Welch of Blackcircles.com on creating a new online business 57

Case Study 2: Boo hoo – learning from the largest European dot-com failure 108

Learning objectives

After reading this chapter, you should be able to:

- Identify the elements of an organisation's online marketplace that have implications for developing a digital marketing strategy
- Evaluate techniques for reviewing the importance of different actors in the microenvironment: customers, intermediaries, suppliers and competitors as part of the development of digital marketing strategy
- Review changes to business and revenue models enabled by digital markets.

Questions for marketers

Key questions for marketing managers related to this chapter are:

- What are our capabilities for understanding our online marketplace?
- How relevant is the behaviour of the actors in the micro-environment to the future of our business?
- How do I complete a marketplace analysis and how does this inform our digital marketing planning?
- How are customers' needs changing as digital platforms develop and what are the implications of such changes?
- How do I compare our online marketing with that of our competitors?
- How do we find suitable intermediaries at the planning stage of a digital marketing strategy?

**Scan code
to find the
latest updates
for topics in
this chapter**

Links to other chapters

- Chapters 2 and 3 provide a foundation for later chapters on Internet marketing strategy and implementation
- Chapter 3 builds on the concepts, frameworks and ideas introduced in this chapter
- Chapter 4 explains how environment analysis is used as part of strategy development
- Chapter 5 considers the principal functions of the mix in digital strategy development.

Introduction

Path to purchase
The different sites, channels and devices and information sources that consumers use to inform their purchase decision for a product or service. Also known as conversion pathways on a site.

Online marketplace
Exchanges of information and commercial transactions between consumers, businesses and governments completed through different forms of online presence such as search engines, social networks, comparison sites and destination sites.

Multiscreening
A term used to describe simultaneous use of devices such as digital TV and tablet.

The demands on marketers who are responsible for planning digital marketing strategies are growing significantly as they work out how to manage commercial contributions, the complexities of the competitive marketplace, social communities and innovations in technology. The growth in use of digital media and technology has led to a customer **path to purchase** that is now much more complex since purchase decisions are influenced by many more online touchpoints, which we introduced in Chapter 1. In the **online marketplace**, consumer purchase decisions are influenced by many sources of information, such as search results, customer reviews, social media conversations, and company websites. Additionally, potential customers are using multiple devices (sometimes simultaneously) to garner information that will inform their purchase decisions. For example, using smartphones or tablets while watching TV. This process is known as **multiscreening**. The digital influences are also supplemented by exposure to traditional communications such as TV, print or radio advertising.

In the next two chapters we look at how organisations might assess the digital environment and in doing so identify implications for digital marketing strategy. We begin by looking at online consumer behaviour, focussing on the main forces that influence purchasing and the competitive environment. Then we consider how existing companies and startups can create business and revenue models which take advantage of online marketplace opportunities.

Situation analysis for digital marketing

Situation analysis
Collection and review of information about an organisation's external environment and internal resources and processes in order to refine its strategy.

The online marketplace is complex and dynamic; organisations should carefully analyse the market context in which they operate, identify opportunities and then plan how they can compete effectively. Understanding an organisation's environment is a key part of **situation analysis**, and forms a solid foundation for all types of marketing planning but especially when devising a digital marketing strategy as shown in Figure 1.9.

What should be reviewed in situation analysis? From the perspective of a business creating a digital marketing plan, situation analysis should review these factors which we cover in this chapter:

A **Customers**. Digital proposition and communications should be based around the customer: their characteristics, behaviours, needs and wants. So our view is that marketers should start with the customer when analysing the situation.

B **Marketplace analysis including intermediaries, influencers and potential partners**. This is a summary of the main online influences on purchase during the customer journey or path to purchase. We will see that there is a wide range of influences including search engines, publisher media sites, blogs, review sites and social networks which should all be considered. Marketplace analysis also involves reviewing opportunities and threats from digital media and technology including new business and revenue models.

C **Competitors**. Benchmarking customer propositions and communications activities against competitors can identify opportunities for new approaches and digital marketing activities that need to be improved.

D **Wider macro-environment**. These are the broader strategic influences we cover in Chapter 3, including social, legal, environment, political and technology influences.

Another major part of situation analysis involves an inward-looking, internal review of the effectiveness of existing digital marketing approaches. This will include reviewing current results from digital marketing by review of key performance indicators (KPIs) and dashboards and the organisational capabilities and processes used to manage digital marketing summarised as strengths and weaknesses. We explain how to review performance by selecting relevant goals and key performance indicators in Chapter 4, covering digital strategy, and Chapter 10, covering digital analytics.

To be successful in online trading environments it is important to respond effectively to changes in the marketplace, as the interview with Michael Welch of online startup **Black circles.com** shows.

Digital marketing in practice	The Smart Insights interview

Michael Welch of Blackcircles.com on creating a new online business

Overview and concepts covered

Michael Welch created Blackcircles.com (Figure 2.1) as a new way for consumers to buy tyres at competitive prices either over the Internet or on the telephone. From the site, consumers can find the best deal from a network of over 1000 local dealerships.

Blackcircles.com now has a turnover of £18 million and is growing rapidly, so we thought it would be interesting to learn the approaches its founder, Michael Welch has used to grow and sustain the business.

The interview

Q. Which factors were important to the initial success of Blackcircles.com**?**

Michael Welch: At the very beginning it was mainly about hard work, determination and not 'taking no for an answer'. If I'm honest, there was no real difference between me and the next guy walking down the street – I just wanted it more.

A key factor in the company getting to where it is today though was also having a strong USP (unique selling point). There were a couple of other companies around at the same time with a similar USP and there are now countless smaller operations that seem to have modelled their USP on ours.

Providing a culture of excellent customer service is an obvious way to go, back when you are a new company – at times – it is all you have. When brand awareness is zero to slim, you have to work as hard as possible to show the customers that first use you – and in reality are taking a gamble – that you give a damn and that their gamble has paid off. I worked hard to make sure customers came first.

Q. Which marketing activities are important to your continued growth?

Michael Welch: The base of our continued growth actually hasn't altered much from those early days. Customer satisfaction is still very much key, the desire to make the company a success is there and our USP is just as strong as it was back at the start of the last decade.

I suppose there has been a shift in that we were once the underdogs and now we are leading the pack. Implementing new ideas and technologies has played a major part in helping us to stay on top, i.e. making sure we are up to date with the best SEO techniques, embracing the world of social media and continually trying to offer more attractive services to our customers – the launch of car servicing being one such evolution on the original 'tyre retailer' tag that **Blackcircles.com** started with.

Underneath all that, though, the company is supported by a foundation of 'getting the basics right'.

Figure 2.1   Blackcircles.com

Q. How do you manage and improve service quality?

Michael Welch: It's a vital ongoing process. The most obvious way in which we check on the site's service quality is through customer feedback. This has been the backbone of many changes we've made over the years. Our customers are a great resource and I'm often surprised at the number of people I meet who don't listen to what their customers are saying to them – it's free advice, why wouldn't you take it?

We recently placed Trustpilot on our website, which is the online retail industry's equivalent of Trip Advisor. This shows independent customer reviews and an overall rating. This is a further commitment from us and a great message to customers that we will be doing everything possible to give them a great service. We are passionate about great service.

On top of listening to what our customers are saying we also actively take part in user testing. We've been working with a company recently which records anonymous users (which you can define as a British person in their mid-30s who doesn't often use the Internet to shop) on our site.

Not only are we able to see what they are doing, but they are also giving a narration of their thoughts. It's early days but we've already discovered areas of the site that can be improved due to this.

The newest form of testing we're just beginning to get involved with is a heat map style technology. Seeing where users are clicking and where they are not is great. It makes you ask why certain areas of a page are receiving attention while the rest is being ignored.

Q. How do you review the success of your site? Which approaches do you use?

Michael Welch: As far as I'm concerned, if you don't include web analytics in your marketing plan, then quite simply, you don't have a marketing plan. Gone are the days when all website owners ever worried about was visitor numbers – good riddance too as it means we don't have to put up with those horrible 'visitor counters' that you used to see bandied about everywhere.

Understanding not just how many visitors you have, but also how they are using your site is invaluable. We actively check out this information on a regular basis. A quick example would be: what percentage of our visitors search for tyres? From this, what percentage then adds a set of tyres to their basket and then how many actually end up on the payment confirmation page?

Looking at these stats we can see at what point in an order process people exit our site. Then we ask ourselves what content is on each page, are there enough calls to action? Is there enough information? Is it easy to navigate? Could we add in new content to encourage people to buy? If we come up with a potential change that we believe will help a page perform better, we then track to see the difference. If conversions go up, great – but how can we improve it further? If they drop – back to the drawing board.

Not only do we see the importance on an 'order process' based analysis, but also using it for certain technical aspects. For instance, customers with one browser end up buying in greater percentages than those with a different browser. OK, so is there a piece of code on a page that is affecting the customers' experience? Or is it even a demographic thing?

All this is just scratching the surface. Web analytics can answer so many questions you didn't even know you needed to ask. The trick is not getting overawed – it is too easy to get lost in an ocean of statistics.

Q. Which new approaches in the marketplace are you reviewing currently?

Michael Welch: The use of video is an interesting avenue that we are keenly pursuing at the moment. Audio and visual are right up there in terms of brand development; and with the sheer number of opportunities available on the web, online videos have never been more exciting. We're still testing the water at the moment with a new 'Blackcircles.com TV' channel on YouTube, but I'm pleased with the results so far.

In a bit of a more traditions sense we are also enhancing our email campaigns. However, I'm very wary of over-saturating our customers with information that they will just mark as spam. The key goal for us at the moment is engaging our customers with the brand. Social media is playing a large role in this as well, as you would expect.

The digital marketing environment

Micro-environment
The *players* (stakeholders) and their interactions which influence how an organisation responds in its marketplace.

Macro-environment
Broad forces affecting all organisations in the marketplace, including social, technological, economic, political, legal and ecological influences.

The digital marketing environment refers to the contexts in which firms operate, including how they relate to customers and other businesses participating in their markets. Each firm has its own unique space within the marketing environment, which is shaped by how they interact with internal aspects of their own business, competing businesses and the wider marketing environment.

The digital marketing environment involves two major elements: (1) **micro-environment** and (2) **macro-environment** (Figure 2.2). The micro-environment is known as '*the operating environment*', and focuses on the players which shape the immediate trading environment. These players include the customers whose needs and wants are to be satisfied, along with the competitors, intermediaries and suppliers. These groups of actors shape the online

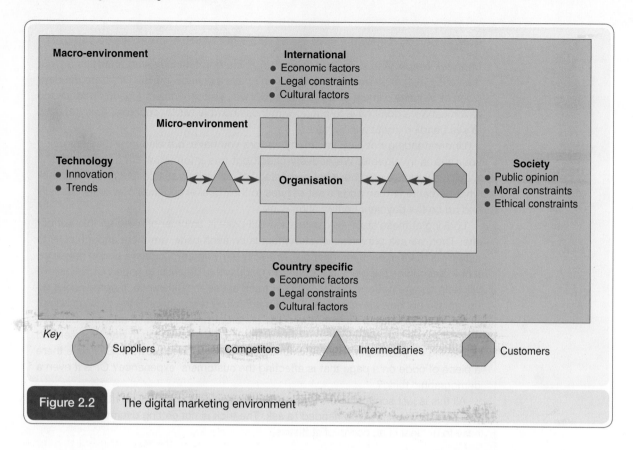

Macro-environment

International
- Economic factors
- Legal constraints
- Cultural factors

Micro-environment

Technology
- Innovation
- Trends

Organisation

Society
- Public opinion
- Moral constraints
- Ethical constraints

Country specific
- Economic factors
- Legal constraints
- Cultural factors

Key

Suppliers | Competitors | Intermediaries | Customers

| Figure 2.2 | The digital marketing environment |

marketplace and a digital marketer needs to understand their behaviour and the implication of changes if an organisation is to develop an effective digital marketing strategy.

The macro-environment is sometimes known as 'the remote environment' and consists of external forces which can significantly affect organisational success. These forces originate from the marketplace, which is largely beyond the immediate control of an organisation – e.g. economic conditions, changes to international trade legislation, technological developments and innovations, social change and political interventions. We study the parts of the macro-environment at are significant to developing digital strategy in Chapter 3.

The trading environment can have a profound impact on performance; consequently an organisation should continually monitor the environment (micro and macro). This process is often referred to as **environmental scanning**. Online marketplace analysis helps to define the nature of the competitive market or **click ecosystem**. In Chapter 1 we saw that there are a range of digital technology platforms within the mobile and desktop hardware platforms. Major online players such as Facebook, Google and Salesforce have developed their own infrastructure or **online market ecosystem** which connects websites through data exchange, giving opportunities to enhance the customer experience and extend their reach and influence. For example, Facebook has developed an API system known as the Facebook platform to enable exchange of data between websites and applications including mobile apps. This enables other site owners to incorporate information about consumer Facebook interactions into their own websites and apps and share social objects across the Facebook ecosystem to extend their reach. Google has developed its own ecosystem related to search marketing and mobile – the Android ecosystem. As part of marketplace analysis, companies have to evaluate the relative importance of these ecosystems and the resources they need to put into integrating their online services with them, to create a plan.

Environmental scanning
The process of continuously monitoring and analysing events in an organisation's environment(s) which have implications for planning.

Click ecosystem
Describes the customer behaviour or flow of online visitors between search engines, media sites, other intermediaries to an organisation and its competitors.

Online market ecosystem
Interactions between different online systems related to a specific hardware or software technology which may be independent or developed by a particular brand.

Purpose

To explore the increasing importance of facilitating communications through online platforms and service providers.

Activity

Discuss in a group, or make notes to identify the main companies (e.g. Facebook) and platforms (e.g. tablet devices) used by consumers that are important for companies to review their presence on. Once you have identified the main company or service types, group them together so that their overall importance can be reviewed.

Understanding customer journeys

Customer journeys is a term commonly used by digital marketers to describe 'touchpoints' or different types of paid, owned and earned media which influence consumers as they access different types of website and content when selecting products and services. It is the modern marketers' job to make the best investments to feature their brands and provide relevant content to support this decision making. To help understand different customer journeys to purchase, customer journey maps are a technique used to model behaviour of different audience personas (see the consumer behaviour section in this chapter for an explanation). A generic example is shown in Figure 2.3.

Google has developed a retail-specific model for understanding customer journeys, widely discussed in marketing of this consumer decision making known as the **Zero Moment**

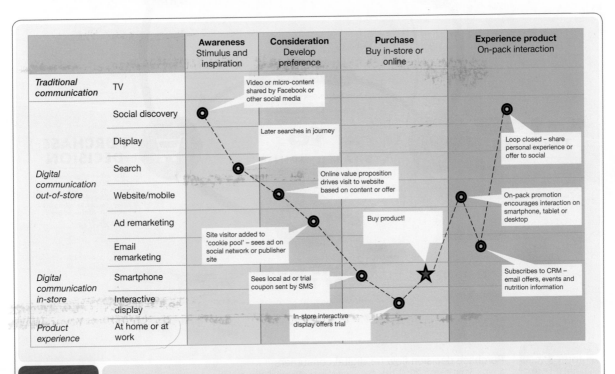

| Figure 2.3 | An example of a customer journey map |

Zero Moment of Truth (ZMOT)

A summary of today's multichannel consumer decision making for product purchase where they search, review ratings, styles, prices comments on social media before visiting a retailer.

of Truth (ZMOT) (Lecinski, 2012). ZMOT describes the combination of online and offline influences on purchase, shown visually in Figure 2.4. The use of search engines and social media means that there is more choice, so consumers will expand their consideration of products. Court *et al.* (2009) showed in the classic *McKinsey Quarterly* paper 'The Consumer Decision Journey' how the number of brands added to the consideration list differs by industry. Their research showed that people actively evaluating personal computers added an average of one brand to their initial-consideration set of 1.7, while automobile shoppers added 2.2 to their initial set of 3.8. The paper also discusses the 'Loyalty loop', which shows opportunities for brands to reinforce the loyalty for their own products or encourage switching from others, as discussed further at the start of Chapter 6.

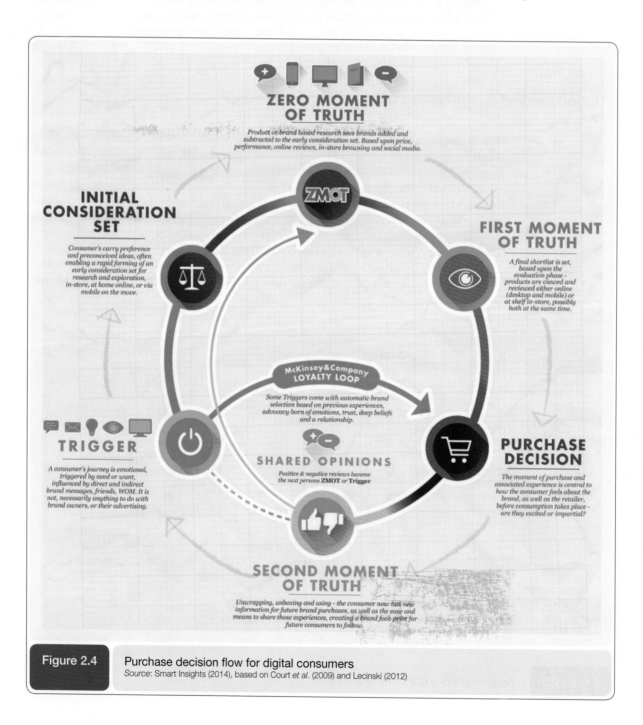

Figure 2.4	Purchase decision flow for digital consumers
	Source: Smart Insights (2014), based on Court *et al.* (2009) and Lecinski (2012)

To help understand the influences on online customer journeys in more detail it is useful to produce an online marketplace map, as shown in Figure 2.5. This summarises different customer groups and how they seek new products and services and the different types of search results that may influence them.

The main elements of the online marketplace map presented in Figure 2.5 are:

1 *Customer segments.* The marketplace analysis helps identify and summarise different target segments for an online business in order to understand their online media consumption, behaviour and the type of content and experiences they want online. In a digital campaign or website design project, personas are used to understand the preferences, characteristics and online behaviours of different groups (as described in the section on online buyer behaviour later in this chapter).

2 *Search intermediaries.* These are the main search engines in each country. Typically Google, Yahoo!, Bing and Ask, but others are important in some markets such as China (Baidu), Russia (Yandex) and South Korea (Naver). There are companies which provide specialist audience data to enable a digital marketer to discover the relative importance of particular search engines (and other types of site) in different countries, e.g. ComScore, Experian Hitwise and Nielsen online. Indeed, search engines have become so significant that search trends are used to predict future sales volumes. Choi and Varian

Figure 2.5 An online marketplace map

(2009) note that Google Trends data on search volumes through time is very useful for predicting levels of spending. They argue that:

> because Google Trends data are practically available in real time, any statistical relationship between actual sales and Google Trends can be exploited to produce more timely estimates of data. For example, official retail sales data are only available with a lag of several weeks, whereas a model based on Google Trends data could produce estimates much faster. This approach to producing more rapid estimates of present data is commonly referred to as nowcasting, as the idea is to predict the present rather than the future (forecasting).

Figure 2.6 shows Office for National Statistics sales data for textile clothing and footware mapped against historic clothing-related searches, e.g. top searches for dress, clothes, shoes and boots.

Companies need to know which sites are effective in harnessing search traffic and either partner with them or try to obtain a share of the search traffic using the search engine marketing and affiliate marketing techniques explained in Chapter 9. Well-known, trusted brands which have developed customer loyalty are in a good position to succeed online since a common consumer behaviour is to go straight to the site through entering a URL or from a bookmark or email. Alternatively they may search for the brand or URL. By evaluating the type and volume of phrases used to search for products in a given market, it is possible to calculate the total potential opportunity and the current share of search terms for a company. **Share of search** can be determined from Google Search Console reports from the company site which indicate the precise key phrases used by visitors to actually reach a site from different search engines.

3 *Intermediaries, influencers and media or publisher sites.* Media sites and other intermediaries such as individual influencers, social networks, **aggregators** and **affiliates** are often successful in attracting visitors via customer search or direct to their websites

Share of search
The audience share of Internet searchers achieved by a particular audience in a particular market.

Aggregators
An alternative term to price comparison sites. Aggregators include product, price and service information comparing competitors within a sector such as financial services, retail or travel. Their revenue models commonly include affiliate revenues (CPA), pay-per-click advertising (CPC) and display advertising (CPM).

Affiliates
Companies promoting a merchant typically through a commission-based arrangement either direct or through an affiliate network.

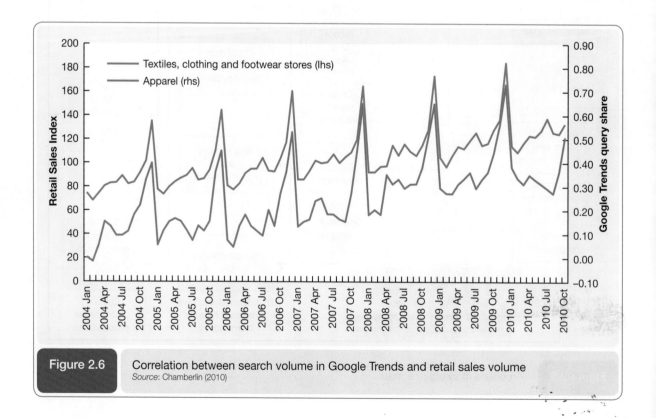

Figure 2.6   Correlation between search volume in Google Trends and retail sales volume
Source: Chamberlin (2010)

Table 2.1	Top ten search terms for all retailing and for apparel			
Search term	Food retailers	Volume of search relative to the top term	Textiles, clothing and footware	Volume of search relative to the top term
1 top term	Tesco	100	Shoes	100
2	Asda	50	Boots	75
3	Tesco Direct	15	Dress	55
4	Morrison's	10	Clothes	45
5	Sainsbury's	10	Next	40
6	Aldi	5	Dresses	35
7	Clubcard	5	Nike	35
8	George Asda	5	River Island	35
9	Ocado	5	Watches	35
10	Sainsbury	5	New Look	30

Source: Chamberlin (2010)

if they are mainstream brands. Companies need to assess potential online media and distribution partners in the categories shown in Figure 2.2, such as:

- *Mainstream news media sites or portals*. These include traditional (for example, **FT. com**, *The Times*, *Guardian*) or pureplay (like Google News).
- *Niche/vertical media sites*. For example Econsultancy, **ClickZ.com** Marketing Land are in a business-to-business niche in marketing.
- *Social networks*. For example, Facebook, Google+, Twitter and LinkedIn. We saw through Digital marketing insight 1.1 that there is discussion on how influential interactions between consumers in social networks are in driving sales.
- *Price comparison sites (also known as aggregators)*. For example, Moneysupermarket, Kelkoo, gocompare, **Shopping.com**, **confused.com**, **mysupermarket.com**.
- *Super-affiliates*. Affiliates gain revenue from a merchant they refer traffic to by being paid commission based on a proportion of the sale or a fixed amount. They are important in e-retail markets, accounting for double digit percentages of sales.
- *Niche affiliates or bloggers*. These are often individuals but they may be very influential – for example, in the UK Martin Lewis of **Moneysavingexpert.com** receives millions of visits every month. Smaller affiliates and bloggers can be important collectively. With the growth in readership and social interactions on blogs, identifying **key online influencers** within a market is important to help reach and engage target audiences.

Key online influencers
Celebrities, individuals well known in their niche, or publishers that an online target audience listens to and interacts with. Online influencer outreach or 'blogger outreach' can help companies reach and engage a wider audience. Recently, video bloggers ('vloggers' or 'YouTubers') have become popular amongst teenage audiences.

Can also boost credibility

4   *Destination sites and platforms*. These are the sites that the marketer is trying to attract visitors to, including transactional sites by retail, financial service, travel, manufacturers and other companies or non-transactional sites, such as brand or relationship-building sites as introduced in Chapter 1. Destination sites also include presence on other social sites like Facebook and Twitter or mobile apps. Figure 2.5 refers to OVP or 'online value proposition', which is a summary of the unique features offered by brands in their online services and presences which are described in more detail in Chapter 4. The OVP is a key aspect to consider within planning – marketers should evaluate their OVPs against competitors and think about how they can refine them to develop a unique online experience.

Digital marketing insight 2.1   Resources for analysing the online marketplace

How to make sense of the volume of available data can be a big challenge for any online marketer. However, it makes sense when planning digital marketing campaigns to take up the opportunity to plan based on the actual marketplace characteristics rather than intuition. Nevertheless, in order to do this a digital marketer needs to know how and where they can tap into the wealth of research about current Internet use and future trends. Typically, businesses use different tools for analysis of the online marketplace and customer behaviour as they access different websites as part of their customer journey. There are both free and paid-for analytical services available to help. Table 2.2 shows a selection of free and paid-for services available for online marketplace analysis, and these resources can be used to assess the number of people searching for information and the popularity of different types of sites measured by the number of **unique visitors**.

By scanning the detailed results from searching information providers, a digital marketing planner can build an informed picture of what is happening at any given time and also make forecasts for strategic planning.

Unique visitors
Individual visitors to a site measured through cookies or IP addresses on an individual computer.

Table 2.2   Research tools for assessing digital markets

Search tool provider and sources of information	Focus and services
1 Google tools	Google is one of the best sources of accurate tools for marketplace analysis including: • *Campaign Planner* (this Adwords tool shows relative size and audience of publishers in the Google programme) • *Google Trends* – trends in search volume by country – no sign-in required • *Keyword Planner* – this tool available within AdWords gives additional detail.
2 SimilarWeb (www.similarweb.com)	Freemium tool providing traffic ranking of individual sites and their sources of traffic. Works best for larger sites. Alternatives are Alexa and Compete.
3 Experian Hitwise (www.hitwise.com)	Paid-for tool available in many countries to compare audience size and search/site use. Works through monitoring IP traffic to different sites through ISPs.
4 Nielsen (www.nielsen.com)	Paid-for tool but free data on search engines and intermediaries available from press release section focus in on what consumers buy. Panel service based on at-home and at-work users who have agreed to have their web use tracked by software. Top rankings on site gives examples of most popular sites in several countries.
5 Comscore (www.comscore.com)	Paid-for tool but free data on search engines and intermediaries available from press release section. Source of global digital marketing intelligence. Services provide insight into behaviour and lifestyle of consumers, e.g. demographics, attitudes, offline behaviour.

6	**Google Analytics**	Free and paid-for service, which provide insights into website traffic.
7	**Internet or Interactive Advertising Bureau (IAB)** US: **www.iab.net** UK: **www.iabuk.net** Europe: **www.europe.uk.net**	Research focussing on investment in different digital media channels, in particular display ads and search marketing. Paid-for services.
8	**Internet Media in Retail Group (IMRG) (www.imrg.org)**	The IMRG provides statistics on UK e-retail sales, mostly limited to members.
9	**Government sources**	Useful government sources include Eurostat (EU, **http:// epp.eurostat.ec.europa.eu**), Ofcom (UK, **www.ofcom .org.uk** and **Statistics.gov.uk**) and **Data.gov** for the US.
10	**Non-government organisations**	Include Pew Internet Surveys (US, **www.pewinternet .org**) and International Telecoms Union (**www.itu.int**)

In the remainder of this chapter we examine the players who shape the micro-environment. We also consider ideas and methods of analysis and highlight implications for digital marketing planning. Table 2.3 provides an overview of the issues.

Table 2.3	The micro-environment: issues for digital marketers

Micro-environment	Issues
Customers	• Access to digital platforms • Level of use of digital platforms and services • Behaviour as they seek and buy products and services (intent), influences they respond to, and their characteristics • Service expectations, satisfaction ratings and advocacy
Suppliers and intermediaries	• Level of technology adoption • Integration and connectedness • Service provision • Trading relationships
Competitors	• Strategic intentions and planning • Communications and promotional techniques used • Resources and capabilities • Levels of service provision • Supplier and intermediary relationships • Performance

Customer analysis

We have explained that situation analysis should start with and centre on the customer. In marketing, understanding the trading situation is very important for setting realistic business and marketing objectives. Customers' attitudes towards the Internet have changed significantly during the last two decades. In consumer markets, shoppers are becoming more attuned to buying online and digital technologies enable them to be well-informed when making purchasing decisions. Research suggests that 'there will be a significant struggle for power between the retailer and the consumer' (Doherty and Ellis-Chadwick, 2011) in the future as the consumer becomes more informed and demanding. In business markets, some of the same principles apply but the balance of power is less likely to be determined by the Internet per se, as the technology plays a more facilitative role in purchasing and communication; this is because personal relationships currently tend to be of greater importance when negotiating sales than remotely transacted arrangements. However, social networks play an increasingly important role in linking together both consumers and potential business partners. Complete Activity 2.2 to get a feel for how business networks are changing the way we make connections.

Activity 2.2	LinkedIn: making professional connections

Purpose

To consider the business potential of online networks.

Activity

Businesses rely on their connections to other businesses and key individuals to develop their business. In 2002, Reid Hoffman had an idea which he turned into the largest professional network in the world: LinkedIn. In March 2015, there were over 332 million professional individuals signed up to the network, in 200 countries worldwide.

Visit **http://press.linkedin.com/success-stories** and read 'Success stories of LinkedIn members' who have used this network to grow their business.

Now answer these questions:

1 How have the successful LinkedIn members used the network to their advantage?
2 Suggest how being a member of the LinkedIn network might help a company to develop better customer knowledge.

Consumer behaviour analysis
In digital markets, this type of analysis involves research into the motivations, media consumption preferences and selection processes used by consumers as they use digital channels together with traditional channels to purchase online products and use other online services.

Customer insight
Knowledge about customers' needs, profile, preferences and digital experiences from analysis of qualitative and quantitative data. Specific insights can be used to inform marketing tactics directed at groups of customers with shared characteristics.

Customer segments
Groups of customers sharing similar characteristics, preferences and behaviours that are meaningful in terms of various market propositions, and which are defined as part of *target marketing strategy and planning*.

From the micro-environment perspective, customers are important actors in a company's immediate trading environment, and analysis of their behaviour is central to understanding of the trading situation and ultimately digital planning. **Consumer behaviour analysis** can be considered from two perspectives:

1 *Demand analysis*. This involves understanding the potential and actual volume of visitors to an online presence and the extent to which prospects convert to tactical and strategic outcomes, e.g. lead generation and sales.
2 *Digital consumer behaviour*. Here a marketer wants to understand the needs, characteristics and digital experiences or behaviours of target consumers. These variables are often collectively referred to as **customer insight**. Based on this analysis, **customer segments** can be created which will be used to develop targeting approaches as part of strategy and planning (described in Chapter 4 onwards).

We summarised the tools for finding customer insight in Digital marketing insight 2.1.

Demand analysis and implications for marketing planning

Digital marketing managers should understand current trends and levels of use of the Internet and different online services and how they relate to services and products the organisation wishes to deliver online. Additionally, marketers need to be aware of factors that affect how customers actively use the digital services on offer. This evaluation process is called **demand analysis**. The benefits of this form of analysis are that companies can identify opportunities for influencing and delivering sales online based on actual use of digital media by individuals in the company's target market. Demand analysis can reduce guesswork and improve the effectiveness of digital marketing communications campaigns.

Demand analysis
Quantitative determination of the potential use and business value from online customers of an organisation. Qualitative analysis of perceptions of online channels is also assessed.

Assessing demand for digital services by looking at these generic factors can enable marketers to set more realistic strategic objectives for each target segment, but in order to do this the digital marketer also needs to assess the volume and share of customers who:

- have access to the digital channel;
- use specific online services which may affect the purchase decision, like price comparison sites, social networks and specialist blogs;
- are influenced by using the digital channel but purchase using another channel as part of the multichannel buyer behaviour;
- purchase or use other services using the digital channel.

Using information sources and tools like those suggested in Table 2.2, plus any primary research a company decides to carry out, a digital marketer should be able to develop a sound understanding of the characteristics, needs and wants of the individuals (and/or companies) in the target market and their propensity to engage with digital channels. Once this foundation level of understanding is developed it is possible to consider how to achieve marketing goals and objectives through the use of digital communications.

Implications for marketing planning: conversion models

As part of situation analysis and objective setting, experienced digital marketers build conversion or waterfall models of the efficiency of their web marketing. Using this approach, the total potential online demand for a service in a particular market can be estimated and then the success of the company in achieving a share of this market can be determined. **Conversion marketing** tactics can be used to convert as many *potential* site visitors into *actual* visitors and then into leads, customers and repeat customers.

Conversion marketing
Using marketing communications to maximise conversion of potential customers to actual customers.

Berthon *et al.* (1998) suggested the online purchasing decision process could be looked at using the hierarchy of effects model (originally developed for assessing the efficiency of offline marketing communications). The model assumes that different types of communications can be used based on where the customer is in the purchasing decision process e.g. at the beginning of the purchasing process advertising can be used to raise awareness; further through the process, sales promotion techniques can be used to elicit action.

Figure 2.7 shows an adapted version of the Berthon *et al.* (1998) model from Chaffey (2001) and it highlights the conversion metrics, which act as drivers of performance. The key ratios to consider are:

- *awareness efficiency*: target web users/all web users;
- *attractability efficiency*: number of individual visits/number of seekers;
- *engagement efficiency*: number of active visitors/number of visits;
- *conversion efficiency*: number of purchases/number of active visits.

This model is instructive for improving digital marketing within an organisation since these different types of conversion efficiencies are key to understanding how effective online and offline marketing communications are in achieving marketing outcomes.

Figure 2.7	A model of the Internet marketing conversion process. It shows key traffic or audience measures (Q_0 to Q_4), first-time visitors (Q_2) and repeat visitors (Q_{2R}) and key conversion efficiency ratios

An additional and important ratio is *retention efficiency*, which involves calculating the relationship between the *number of repurchases/number of purchases*.

The model is useful to the digital marketer as it highlights the significance of how conversion effectiveness differs between first-time users and repeat users. It also shows the stages a customer may take in a virtual purchasing journey. An additional important aspect of online buyer behaviour not shown in the figure is the site path or **clickstream** for different audience types or segments. Analysing the clickstream reveals which pages a website visitor looks at before leaving the site.

Figure 2.8 shows an example of how measuring conversion rates can be used to improve web marketing. Numbers are across a fixed time period of one month. If for a particular market there is a potential audience (market) of 200,000 (Q_1), then if online and offline promotion techniques achieve 100,000 visitors to the site (Q_2), marketers have achieved an impressive conversion rate of 50 per cent. The online marketers are then looking to convert these visitors to action. Before this is achieved, the visitors must be engaged. Data from log files show that many visitors leave when they first visit the home page of a site if they do not find the site acceptable or they are not happy with the experience. The number of visitors engaged (Q_3) is 50,000, which is half of all visitors. For the visitors that are engaged, the next step is to convert them to action. This is achieved for 500 visitors (Q_4), giving a conversion rate (Q_4/Q_3) of 1 per cent. If what is calculated (as is most common) is (Q_4/Q_2), this gives a conversion rate of 0.5 per cent.

An organisation in the position depicted in Figure 2.8 is attracting visitors to the site, but not converting them into active customers. Many companies fall into the trap of building websites which are aesthetically pleasing but fail to deliver the marketing objectives of leads and sales. By looking more closely at the conversion ratios of an organisation and running conversion rate optimisation programmes (**as described in Chapter 7**), businesses can considerably improve the returns on their media investments that drive visitors to a site.

| Figure 2.8 | An example of a conversion model |

Multichannel conversion models

In reality, conversion modelling is complex because it needs to take into account both online and offline behaviour. Figure 2.9 is simplified as it does not take account of offline influences. For example, an advertiser may use Google AdWords to promote their product but some shoppers will buy online while others will prefer to use other channels to make their purchases, e.g. use the phone or buy in-store.

In the busy third quarter trading period of 2014, John Lewis saw online sales rise by 19 per cent while store sales showed no growth. However, 'click and collect' accounted for over 50 per cent of deliveries, showing the complexity of the online shopping journey and the increased opportunities to connect with the shopper (Bold, 2015).

Therefore, it is useful to put in place the means of monitoring cross-channel conversions at different stages in the buying process as it can help a business to understand how

example
showrooming

| Figure 2.9 | Model showing conversion between the digital channel and traditional channels during the buying process |

ROPO models highlight consumer behaviour in the consumer phone market

ROPO ('Research Online Purchase Offline') is a term coined to describe research published by Google (2010). This study reviewed the role of the Internet in the decision process for mobile and broadband contracts involving the Vodafone website and stores in Germany based on a panel of 16,000 web users and questionnaires about their intent and purchase. For both of these services, the contract was signed online by around a third of the audience. However, a significant proportion signed the contract offline. The matrix presented in Figure 2.10 is a good framework for evaluating and summarising multichannel behaviour since it also shows the situation where research is offline and purchase occurs online. This behaviour is particularly common where products such as in this case, handsets, where consumers want to evaluate their purchase online.

Figure 2.10 Research Online Purchase Online example
Source: Google (2010)

it might improve performance in both online and offline channels by making the marketing spend more effective.

Figure 2.9 shows a model of how this might work. For example, phone numbers which are unique to the website can be used as an indication of the volume of callers to a contact centre influenced by the website. This insight can then be built into budget models of sales levels such as that shown in Figure 2.9. This shows that of the 100,000 unique visitors in a period we can determine that 5000 (5 per cent) may actually become offline leads.

In this section we have been discussing complex models for analysing customer conversion strategies. There are however three core dimensions at the heart of such models which it is important to be aware of: 'Access: Choose: Transact' (ACT). We will now review each dimension, first from the perspective of B2C marketplace and then B2B.

Consumer choice and digital influence

Consumer choice is a crucial step in the purchasing process and digital media now play an increasingly important role in buying decisions. For many consumers the Internet is the first place to look for information that will inform what they buy, so the Internet:

- is a vital part of the research process, as Internet users now spend longer researching products online;
- is used at every stage of the research process from the initial scan to the more detailed comparison and final checking of specifications before purchase.

The result of this change in behaviour means that consumers are more knowledgeable and they are referring to a multiplicity of sources to find information which will inform their final purchasing decision – e.g. brand websites, social media, review sites, traditional print media, personal recommendations which are part of a customer journey such as that shown in Figure 2.3. Digital sources of information now play a more important role in shaping purchase decisions. So companies have to think carefully how they can maximise the value of positive comments and reviews and reinforce customer perceptions through product quality, and service experiences both on- and offline.

The implications of the growth in the use of digital media in the selection process means that digital markets need to aim to ensure that the products and services they wish to market through digital channels are well-represented. Furthermore, the demand for information is likely to continue to intensify with the use of smartphones and other mobile devices.

Understanding the potential reach of a website and its role in influencing purchasing is clearly important in setting digital marketing budgets. Moreover, as consumers become more familiar with using the Internet, especially while on the move through mobile devices, the more likely they are to turn to the Internet to inform their decision making. See Digital marketing insight 2.3.

Digital marketing insight 2.3   **M-shoppers can be thoughtful, motivated and reluctant**

Mobile shopping (M-shopping) has grown rapidly as the penetration of mobile phones, smart phones and tablets has increased dramatically. Smartphone penetration – at 1.75 billion in 2014 – will increase to two-fifths of the world's population by 2017. Indeed, mobile phone adoption has outstripped landline ownership and in some nations mobile phone penetration is over 90 per cent. While lower income countries such as in Latin America, the Middle East and Africa have lower penetration rates, mobile technology is liberating these markets as mobile technology provides wireless Internet access. Despite this rapid expansion in uptake of mobile phones, marketers need to understand consumers' barriers and motivators to using a phone as a means of shopping if they are to effectively access their target markets. San-Martine *et al.* (2013) found that there are three distinct groups of M-shoppers:

1 *Thoughtful m-shoppers* – this group are reflective about the value of m-shopping and are not entirely sure about the value of this form of buying. They are concerned about the lack of interpersonal interactions but they are motivated by value. So to engage this type of shopper, marketers need to develop additional motivating offers through the mobile channel.

2 *Motivated m-shoppers* – this group do not envisage any barriers to shopping in this way, they are frequent users of technology and confident with remote shopping. This group can also be motivated by special offers but to a much lesser extent than the Thoughtful group as they do not need to be incentivised in the same way.

3 *Reluctant m-shoppers* – this group sees no advantage to m-shopping. They are concerned about lack of interpersonal interaction, and find it difficult to shop via a mobile phone. Marketers will find this group difficult to access via m-shopping.

Source: oneMarketer (2014); San-Martine *et al.* (2013)

Figure 2.11 shows that when consumers first use the web they tend to limit it to searching for product information, but as they become more confident they are not only likely to involve the Internet at a greater number of points in the purchasing process but also to increase the value of the products they buy and the frequency with which they make purchases.

Developing an understanding of the processes involved in customer choice should enable marketers to identify how to tailor services to meet the needs of the customers so that they move to the transaction dimension.

Consumer transactions

The proportion of Internet users who will purchase different types of products online varies considerably based on the characteristics and demographic profile of the consumers, the product category and the past experiences of the shopper. There have also been many predictions about the development of online retailing and how it might fuel demand for online transactions. Convenience remains the biggest driver for online shoppers, whilst preferring to shop in-store and not seeing the need to shop online are the largest barriers to adoption. Figure 2.12 shows influences on consumer purchasing made in the UK.

By understanding the dimensions which affect how consumers interact with online trading environments, digital markets can identify key points where they can seek to manage conversion. By studying online consumers, marketers can garner a great deal of insight into online behaviour. But for marketers working in business-to-business environments there are further considerations. See Digital marketing insight 2.4.

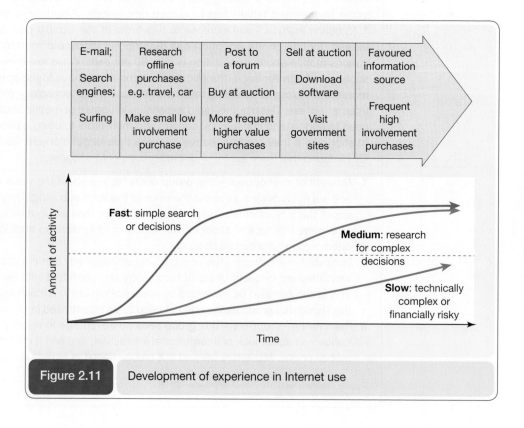

E-mail; Search engines; Surfing	Research offline purchases e.g. travel, car Make small low involvement purchase	Post to a forum Buy at auction More frequent higher value purchases	Sell at auction Download software Visit government sites	Favoured information source Frequent high involvement purchases

Fast: simple search or decisions

Medium: research for complex decisions

Slow: technically complex or financially risky

Amount of activity

Time

| Figure 2.11 | Development of experience in Internet use |

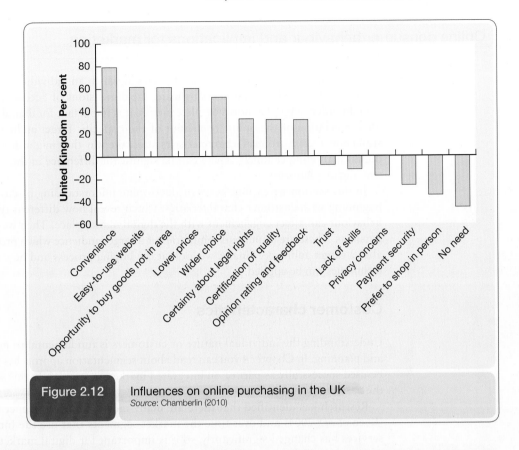

Figure 2.12	Influences on online purchasing in the UK

Source: Chamberlin (2010)

Digital marketing insight 2.4	Business access and digital influence

Assessing online customer demand and characteristics for business services requires additional considerations. The B2B market is more complex than B2C markets insofar as variation in online demand or research in the buying process will occur according to different types of organisation and people within the buying unit in the organisation. We need to profile business demand according to:

Variation in organisation characteristics:

- size of company – employees or turnover;
- industry sector and products;
- organisation type – private, public, government, not-for-profit;
- application of service – which business activities do purchased products and services support?;
- country and region.

Individual role:

- role and responsibility – job title, function or number of staff managed;
- role in buying decision – purchasing influence;
- department;
- product interest;
- demographics – age, sex and possibly social group.

Online consumer behaviour and implications for marketing

So far we have considered the different stages at which an individual or a business might engage with digital environments by using the dimensions of access choice and transaction. In order to build a more complete picture it is important for digital marketers to gain an appreciation of the online behaviour of their specific target audiences and to understand how their customers' characteristics affect the way they might interact with different digital marketing channels. There can be significant difference in the ways an individual uses digital platforms.

In this section we explore ways of developing understanding of customer behaviour, beginning with customer characteristics, which reveal how different types of individual behaviour can affect engagement with the digital marketplace. Then we explore customer personas. These are thumbnail summaries of a target audience which provide ways to visualise a target audience. Finally, we look at the buying process and how digital marketing techniques can be applied.

Customer characteristics

Understanding the individual nature of customers is fundamental to marketing practice and planning. In Chapter 4 you can read about segmentation approaches and how they can be used successfully as part of an integrated marketing strategy. In this section we explore the actual consumer behaviour variables which help build segmentation profiles.

Research has identified that there are many factors which influence online behaviour (Keen *et al.*, 2004) and over time the market segments that use the Internet and digital services has changed significantly, so it is important for digital markets (a) to be aware of important behaviour variables, and (b) to understand how to model online consumer behaviour.

According to Doherty and Ellis-Chadwick (2010), it is possible to look back and see that the types of individuals using the web have changed significantly since 1995. In those early days, online shoppers tended to be young males, who were generally better educated and wealthier than their contemporaries. They also had both the confidence and desire to experiment with the Internet, which at the time was an exciting new channel (Donthu and Garcia, 1999; Korgaonkar and Wolin, 1999). Some companies specifically targeted these types of customers and developed services to suit their needs. Research suggests there are two key areas which can prove very fruitful when aiming to identify consumer variables:

1 *Demographic variables*. Doherty and Ellis-Chadwick (2010) suggest that any personal attributes that tend to remain static throughout an individual's lifetime, or evolve slowly over time – such as age, gender, race etc. – can be defined as *demographic variables*. Key elements of a consumer's demographic profile that have been found to influence online behaviour include variables such as income, education, race, age (Hoffman *et al.*, 2000); gender (Slyke, 2002); and life-style (Brengman *et al.*, 2005), cultural and social make-up that influences online behaviour (e.g. Shiu and Dawson, 2004).

2 *Psychographic and behavioural variables*. Any aspect of a consumer's perceptions, beliefs and attitudes that might influence online behaviour, and in particular a consumer's intention to shop, can be defined as a *psychographic/behavioural variable*. Indeed, there has now been a significant amount of research exploring how the consumer's character or personality might influence their online behaviour (George, 2004). Cheung *et al.* (2005) suggest that the impact of a wide range of behavioural characteristics, such as knowledge, attitude, innovativeness and risk aversion, can have a significant effect on a consumer's intention to shop. For example, it has been found that consumers who are primarily motivated by convenience were more likely to make purchases online, while those who value social interactions were found to be less interested (Swaminathan *et al.*, 1999).

By studying the variables which influence the consumer's experiences in the online environment 'it becomes possible to analyse their future intentions to continue to use digital services and to shop online' (Wolfinbarger and Gilly, 2003). For example, the impact of consumers' personal experiences of, say, convenience, site design and security might affect their overall satisfaction with a particular website. Another important point is that by studying variables associated with a consumer's experiences, digital marketers begin to understand how to increase loyalty and trust through websites and online services. As use of the digital environment has grown, further research has been carried out which gives us an even greater understanding of the online customer experience.

According to Rose and Hair (2011) 'customer interactions with an organisation's website creates opportunities for positive experiences that can lead to long-term relationship building'.

The concept of online customer experience has been widely studied in contexts ranging from service delivery to retailing and tourism (e.g., Arnold *et al.*, 2005; Tsai, 2005). Figure 2.13 shows a framework for understanding the concepts which motivate and influence the online consumer. An important point to consider is that past experiences will provide the basis for future evaluations. According to Arnold *et al.* (2005), the antecedents or background to the online experience consist of an important list of concepts which can positively or negatively influence or motivate the consumer to engage with a digital offer:

1 **Information processing** (IP) is very important as it shapes how a consumer deals with available data and information that will influence their future behaviour. IP involves the mental processes and senses an individual uses to interpret the world they inhabit.

2 **Perceived ease of use** also needs consideration by digital marketers, as the easier a website or mobile site is to use the more likely a customer will have a positive online experience (Cheung *et al.*, 2005).

3 **Perceived usefulness** refers to the extent to which the digital offer fits with the customer's daily life, for instance, shopping, booking train tickets, banking (Arnold *et al.*, 2005). It is here that digital marketers can really start to develop a path to consumer benefits.

4 **Perceived benefits**: if a customer feels they will be rewarded in some positive way by engaging with a digital offer this is likely to generate support for an online brand (Arnold *et al.*, 2005).

5 **Perceived control**: if a customer is a skilled user of the digital technology in question then they will feel they are able to function successfully in this environment. Earlier in

Figure 2.13	Framework for understanding online customer experiences

Source: Rose and Hair (2011)

the chapter we discussed how some mobile shoppers are confident whereas others are not (see Digital marketing insight 2.3).

6 **Skill** refers to the customer's ability to use the technology to achieve their desired goals (Klein and Ford, 2002). It has been found that individuals learn by doing in the Internet environment and so build their skill set over time – e.g. the more frequent the visitor to a website the higher their exposure and the greater their ability to engage with this digital content.

7 **Trust and risk** play an important role in how a customer behaves online. Inexperienced Internet users can feel vulnerable and fear the unknown (Tan and Sutherland, 2004). Customers should be able to achieve their buying goals without feeling they are exposed to undue risk – e.g. financial risk, social risk, personal risk. Marketers should seek to find ways to limit the risk of engaging with their online offer and seek to build trust through developing online relationships.

8 **Enjoyment** is an outcome of a positive online experience.

A digital marketer should consider how each of these antecedents can influence a customer's motivations to engage with the digital offer and also look for opportunities to create competitive advantage by overcoming potential barriers. These eight antecedents can influence how the customer thinks (cognitive state) and feels (affective state) about their online experience and affect the outcomes of any subsequent behaviour. If the customer has a positive experience this will increase the likelihood of the customer being satisfied and having positive repurchase intentions. Arnold *et al.* (2005) propose that digital marketers need to be aware that it is important not only to develop the functional aspects of an online offer (e.g. website) but also to consider how the emotional state and past experiences of the customer can affect customers' levels of engagement.

Digital marketing insight 2.5	Online segments

Consumers on and offline are largely similar (Jaywardhena *et al.*, 2007) and therefore it is important for digital marketers to consider the Internet as an extension of an existing business. In the case of new pureplay businesses it is also important to understand the offline as well as the online world because the physical world will inform behaviour in the digital world regardless of where a business operates. There are many ways to define customers in the digital marketplace: for example, Green (2013) identified the avid shopper, early adopters of the Internet and savvy online buyers, who know where to shop for the best deals (friends often refer to them as shopaholics); the emotional shopper, who buys when emotional triggers – stress, boredom, upset – prompt them to seek gratification, which they do by going to buy online. The impulse buyer sees a deal and buys it. Retailers across the Internet have picked up on this type of buyer and often list 'other items you might be interested in'.

Business buyers are also individuals, who work within a corporate framework, so many of the functional and emotional triggers which influence online consumer behaviour apply. But just as with consumers, B2B buyers are influenced by the physical circumstances they work in. Business buying tends to be done by a decision-making unit (DMU), which means the purchase decision is likely to be more complex than a consumer purchase (Hague, 2014). Business buyers are knowledgeable and focus their attention on price and value, so selling organisations not only need to consider the B2B buyers as individuals but also to focus on their buying objects and touch the '*hot butting* of all decision makers' (Hague, 2014).

Looking at the characteristics of buyers and target segments is part of well-established traditional marketing practices. Online marketers use these techniques but have also taken them to a new level and in doing so have developed a way to better understand a target audience by building consumer personas.

[handwritten margin note: similar to profiling criminals]

Consumer personas

A persona is a fictional profile typically informed by research that represents a particular target audience. **Personas** are a tool which can help in understanding online customer characteristics and behaviour. Creating personas is a powerful technique for developing customer-centred online strategies, company presences and campaigns and forms part of marketplace analysis.

They have been used for a long time in research for segmentation and advertising, but in recent years have also proved effective for improving website design by companies that have applied the technique.

For an example of the application of personas, see Mini case study 2.1.

Marketers can also develop secondary personas and complementary personas to provide a fuller range of options.

The buying process

According to Kotler *et al.* (2001), there are different stages in the buying process. At each stage the purpose (from both the buyer's and supplier's perspective) is a particular outcome:

- awareness;
- interest;

Personas
A fictional profile that represents a particular target audience. A thumbnail summary of the characteristics, needs, motivations and environment of typical website users.

Customer scenarios (online customer journeys)
Alternative tasks or outcomes required by a customer. Typically accomplished in a series of stages or different tasks involving different information needs across different sites and platforms.

Mini case study 2.1	Personas 'with wings'

AMP is a marketing agency which offers a full suite of services from brands wishing to communicate in the digital marketplace. They use customer personas as a way of developing understanding of their clients target audiences. They use the persona to create a visual and contextual representation of the target audience, using demographics and psychographics. In building this representation AMP also look at the use of social media and technology, which gives an understanding of the likely touchpoints the target audience will encounter.

According to Stokes (2015), the Red Bull Student persona is:

- *'The thrill seeker'*
- *He's 24 years old*
- *Graduated from college, 2 years ago with an English degree*
- *He is currently the assistant manager at a ski & board shop*
- *He makes £$30,000 a year.*
- *Whether it's jumping over cliffs into powder snow on a snowboard, racing down treacherous trails on a mountain bike or hitting the half-pike skateboard, he's there because he's a daredevil. He welcomes the new experiences and loves taking risks with adventurous activities like skydiving and windsurfing. He likes to live a fast-paced life existence and he's always on the go. No matter how daring the challenge, he will always be there with a Red Bull in hand, on high energy and ready to jump.*

By developing a persona using data from a number of different variables it should become possible for marketers who are developing digital campaigns to begin to empathise with a particular target audience and develop digital campaigns which not only attract but also meet the needs of the audience as well as delivering benefits for engaging with the campaign, thereby creating a win–win outcome for the company and its customers.

Additionally customer scenarios (online customer journeys) can be developed for different personas which describe their overall online customer journeys. Seybold and Marshak (2001) originally described such journeys as:

A customer scenario is a set of tasks that a particular customer wants or needs to do in order to accomplish his or her desired outcome.

Customer scenarios can be developed for each persona. For an online bank, scenarios might include:

- new customer opening an online account;
- existing customer transferring an account online;
- existing customer finding an additional product.

The customer persona/scenario approach has the following benefits:

- fosters customer-centricity;
- identifies detailed information needs and steps required by customers;
- can be used to test existing website designs or prototypes and to devise new designs;
- can be used to compare and test the strength and clarity of communication of proposition on different websites;
- can be linked to specific marketing outcomes required by site owners.

Here are some guidelines and ideas on what can be included when developing a persona. The start or end point is to give each persona a name.

1 Build personal attributes into personas:
   - demographic – age, sex, education, occupation and, for B2B, company size, position in buying unit;
   - psychographic – goals, tasks, motivation;
   - webographics – web experience (months), usage location (home or work), usage platform (dial-up, broadband), usage frequency, favourite sites.
2 Remember that personas are only models of characteristics and environment:
   - design targets;
   - stereotypes;
   - three or four usually suffice to improve general usability, but more may be needed for specific behaviours;
   - choose one *primary persona* whom, if satisfied, means others are likely to be satisfied.
3 Different scenarios can be developed for each persona, as explained further below. Write three or four, for example:
   - information-seeking scenario (leads to site registration);
   - purchase scenario – new customer (leads to sale);
   - purchase scenario – existing customer (leads to sale).

Once different personas have been developed that are representative of key site-visitor types or customer types, a primary persona is sometimes identified. Wodtke (2002) says:

Your primary persona needs to be a common user type who is both important to the business success of the product and needy from a design point of view – in other words, a beginner user or a technologically challenged one.

- evaluation;
- trial;
- adoption.

This set of outcomes, sometimes known as the hierarchy of response model, have been considered in the digital market. Chaffey and Smith (2012) describe them as:

1 problem recognition;
2 information search;
3 evaluation;
4 decision;
5 action (sale or use of online service);
6 post-purchase.

Figure 2.14 gives a summary of how digital media can be used to support the different stages in the buying process. The boxes on the left show the typical stages that a new prospect passes through, according to, for example, Robinson *et al.* (1967). A similar analysis was performed by Berthon *et al.* (1998), who speculated that the relative communications effectiveness of using a website in this process gradually increased from 1 to 6.

It is worthwhile reviewing each of the stages in the buying process referred to in Figure 2.14 in order to highlight how effective the Internet can be when used at different stages to support the marketing communications objectives. Of course, the exact stage of the buying decision varies for different products and different types of customers, so an alternative approach is to develop channel chains (Figure 2.23 below), which reflect these differences. In general, digital media support the consumer buying process as follows.

1 Consumer: unaware. Company: generates awareness (of need, product or service)

Generating awareness of need is conventionally achieved principally through the mass media used in offline advertising. The Internet is relatively ineffective at this since it tends to have a more limited impact and reach than television, radio or print media. However, display advertising or paid search marketing can be used to supplement offline awareness-building, as explained in Chapter 8. Online equivalents of word-of-mouth or

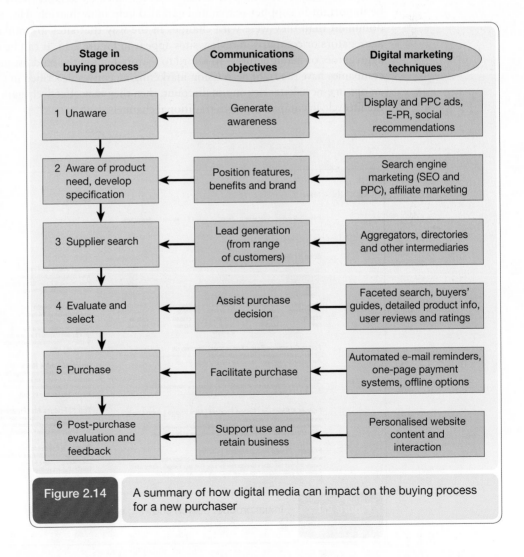

| Figure 2.14 | A summary of how digital media can impact on the buying process for a new purchaser |

recommendations from friends or colleagues, perhaps influenced by a viral marketing campaign, can also create awareness of need. Some companies have effectively developed brand awareness by means of PR and media mentions concerning their success on the Internet, with the result that even if a customer does not have a current need for a product, that customer may be aware of the source when the need develops.

2 Consumer: aware of need, develops specification. Company: position features, benefits and brand

Once a consumer is aware of a need and is considering what features and benefits are required from a product or online service, then they may turn straight to the web to start identifying the range of features available from a particular type of product through using a generic search using search engines such as Google or Yahoo! So influencing consumers through search engine marketing and affiliate marketing is important at this stage. Specification development effectively happens at the same time as supplier search and more suppliers can be evaluated in greater depth than traditionally. For example, Figure 2.15 shows the e-retailers available in an initial product search on fridges. Retailers such as John Lewis and Currys are displayed in the natural listings (see Chapter 8), while others such as **AO. com** and Euronics are displayed in Google AdWords. The image-based ads are known as Product Listing Ads (PLAs).

Intermediaries well known within a sector, such as Kelkoo (**www.kelkoo.com**), can be important in supplier search and can also help in evaluation. However, they are less dominant than they were with changes in the way that sites are ranked. For example, aggregators or comparison review sites appear in Figure 2.15. It can be difficult for these aggregators or manufacturers to afford to feature high in the paid listings. On the web, if companies have the right permission marketing incentives described in Chapter 6, such as an opt-in e-newsletter or coupon discount, then they may effectively gain interest earlier in the lifecycle in comparison with traditional channels.

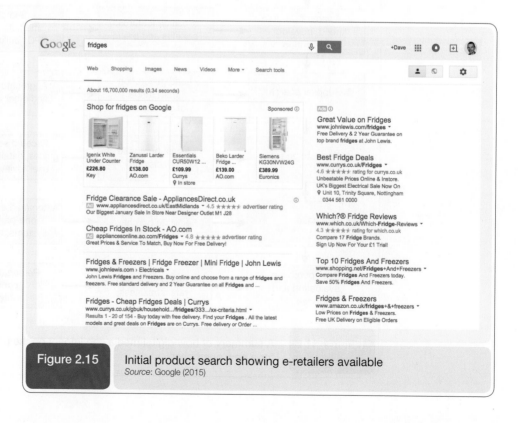

Figure 2.15	Initial product search showing e-retailers available

Source: Google (2015)

3 Consumer: supplier search. Company: generate leads (engage and capture interest)

Once customers are actively searching for products, the web provides an excellent medium to help them do this. It also provides a good opportunity for companies to describe the benefits of their websites and obtain qualified leads. The digital marketer must consider the methods that a customer will choose for searching and then ensure that the company or its product is featured prominently on these sites whether they are search engines, aggregators or affiliate intermediaries.

4 Consumer: evaluate and select. Supplier: assist purchase decision

One of the most powerful features of websites is their facility to carry a large amount of content at relatively low cost. This can be turned to advantage when customers are looking to identify the best product. By providing relevant information in a form that is easy to find and digest, a company can use its website to help in persuading the customer. For example, the Currys site (Figure 2.16) enables customers to readily compare product features side-by-side, so they can decide on the best products for them. Thanks to the web, this stage can now overlap with earlier stages. Brand issues are important here, as proved by research in the branding section of Chapter 5, since a new buyer naturally prefers to buy from a familiar supplier with a good reputation – it will be difficult for a company to portray itself in this way if it is unknown and has a slow, poorly designed or shoddy website.

5 Consumer: purchase. Company: facilitate purchase

Once a customer has decided to purchase, then the company will not want to lose the custom at this stage! The website should enable standard credit-card payment mechanisms with the option to place the order by phone or mail. Online retailers pay great attention to identifying factors that encourage customers to convert once they have added a product to their 'shopping basket'. Security guarantees, delivery choices and free delivery offers, for example, can help increase conversion rates.

| Figure 2.16 | Currys' product category page (**www.currys.co.uk**) |

6 Consumer: post-purchase evaluation and feedback.
Company: support product use and retain business

The Internet also provides great potential for retaining customers, as explained in Chapter 6, since:

- value-added services such as free customer support can be provided by the website and these encourage repeat visits;
- feedback on products can be provided to customers – the provision of such information will indicate to customers that the company is looking to improve its service;
- email can be used to give regular updates on products and promotions and encourage customers to revisit the site;
- repeat visits to sites provide opportunities for cross-selling and repeat selling through personalised sales promotions messages based on previous purchase behaviour.

Activity 2.3	Changes in consumer buyer behaviour caused by digital channels

Although the model shown in Figure 2.14 provides a useful starting point for assessing buyer behaviour, it should be remembered that the Internet has changed behaviour and in some ways the model is not an accurate reflection of reality. What do you think are its main weaknesses? We would suggest:

- The process is not necessarily sequential.
- The process is compressed – for low-involvement products, the decision can be made straight away. The process will often start with a search and is mediated through search engines throughout, with the searches refined iteratively from generic to specific plus brand, for example 'fridge', 'upright fridge', 'comets fridge', 'whirlpool fridge', 'whirlpool 20TB L4'.
- The participation on the web and the creation of user-generated content (UGC), such as reviews and ratings on the retail site and comparison intermediaries such as Revoo (www.revoo.com), are important in the decision process.
- Viral marketing and online PR can be important for generating awareness. In a virtual environment, trust becomes important, as we will see below, so the strength and familiarity of brands will be important.

In this section we have reviewed simple models of the online buying process that can help Internet marketers convert more site visitors to lead and sale; however, in many cases the situation is not as simple as the models.

Multichannel buying models

It's important to recognise that a user journey through a website is only part of a wider customer experience which involves multiple channels (Brashear *et al.*, 2009). The importance of multichannel strategies should also be built into assessing customer behaviour and their perception of the online customer experience. The importance of digital channels in influencing the overall customer experience is indicated in Digital marketing insight 2.6.

Since online interactions on a website often happen with limited consumer experience of a site, site owners and designers need to understand how they can develop trusting relationships with target audiences through the use of multiple channel strategies.

Trust-based models focus on trust and commitment

Online, purchasers lack the physical reassurance they have when purchasing from a store or talking to someone over a phone. This is compounded by stories of fraud and security problems. It follows that consumers are looking for cues of trust when they are on a site and

Digital marketing insight 2.6   Lexus assesses multichannel experience consistency

The luxury car brand Lexus has worked with the Multichannel Marketing Best Practice Club at the Cranfield School of Management, UK to assess the relative importance of consistency between channels. The pertinent results of this study are presented in Table 2.4. It can be seen that, as might be expected, the showroom experience is very important to the overall attitude towards the brand and purchase intent. The importance of the website experience quality is also notable and especially its role in the propensity to recommend – the Lexus customer can readily recommend the website to a friend or a colleague. So it is the interactive channels that deliver the best experience, as would be expected.

Table 2.4   The impact of channel experience on customer relationship

Lexus communication channel	Attitude towards the brand	Future purchase intention	Propensity to recommend
TV experience quality	0.362**	0.360**	0.185
Print experience quality	0.203	0.133	0.023
Direct mail experience quality	0.343*	0.204	0.072
Showroom experience quality	0.447**	0.292*	0.217
Contact centre experience quality	0.431*	0.566	0.147
Website experience quality	0.452**	0.315*	0.309*

*Correlation is significant at the 0.05 level
**Correlation is significant at the 0.01 level
Source: Menteth et al., 2005. Reprinted by permission of Macmillan Publishers Ltd: *Interactive Marketing*, 6(4) 317–25, copyright 2005, published by Palgrave Macmillan. (The new name of this journal is *Journal of Direct Data and Digital Marketing Practice*)

[handwritten note: Social listening can identify some of the same info]

Digital marketing insight 2.7   Using real-time experience tracking (RET) to assess the influence of different omnichannel communications on customer touchpoints

Real-time experience tracking (RET) involves asking a consumer panel to send text messages on their mobile phones every time they see a message or reference to a given brand or one of its competitors over a period of a week to a month, depending on the length of the purchase process. The structured four-character message captures the brand, the touchpoint type (Saw a tweet about it? Saw it in a shop window?), how positive the customer felt about the encounter, and how persuasive it was. Respondents add further detail online, and fill in surveys at the start and end of the study to record brand attitude changes.

Examples of RET in action

RET can be used to assess how consumers perceive brands in different markets – for example, Unilever could not understand why a campaign for Axe body spray wasn't working in Italy when it was performing well in Poland. In both countries, TV advertising was positively received. But whereas in Poland the ads were followed by high street touchpoints such as the 'Axe Police' – attractive women who would 'arrest' young men and spray them with Axe – such reminders close to potential purchase moments were missing in Italy. RET can also diagnose how attitudes lead to the next step in the chain, as one major international charity discovered. The charity, which relies on a large network of stores selling second-hand and new goods to raise both revenue and awareness, recently applied RET in an effort to understand why direct donations (as opposed to store profits) to the charity were falling. The RET project revealed that the in-store experience of customers was rather mixed; quite a few people felt that the stores were poorly organised and deduced from this that the charity probably wasn't very good at helping its beneficiaries either.

RET can also help highlight the relative influence of channels, including those that are less easy to track than online channels. In another example, PepsiCo used RET to fine-tune its re-launch of Gatorade in Mexico, repositioning the brand around sports nutrition. It soon found that experiences in gyms and parks (seeing posters or seeing other people drinking Gatorade, for instance) were twice as effective in shifting brand attitudes as similar encounters elsewhere. The company was able to quickly shift more ad and distribution resources into these touchpoints and pass on what it had learnt as Gatorade was re-launched in other Latin American countries.

Source: MacDonald *et al*. (2012)

marketers need to understand the nature of these. These cues can include brand familiarity, site design, type of content, accreditation and recommendations by other customers. Bart *et al*. (2005) developed a conceptual model that links website and consumer characteristics, online trust and behaviour and found that external sources indicated are very important in building trust – e.g. search engines listing, personal recommendations, brand identity. Figure 2.17 summarises the key drivers of trust identified by Bart *et al*. (2005) and the model has been adapted to show how elements of trust can be substantiated online.

When reviewing products on a destination site, web users will differ in their decision-making style, which will vary according to their knowledge of the web and their attitude to risk and trust. To evaluate these issues, a useful framework has been developed by Forrester for the financial services market to segment customers. This is summarised in Figure 2.18. It shows how customers will generally fall into four groups, first based on those who gather detailed information and those who rely on less information and then based on those who value advice from advisers.

Social interaction communication models update

Throughout this section we have seen evidence of the increased role of digital media in our daily lives (both socially and in the workplace). The use of social media, such as Facebook and Twitter, has risen substantially in the last four years. Social media have become important as means of communicating and interacting online and also as a source of peer recommendations. Generally, as humans we are keen to join together and participate in sharing information. This human wish to socialise and share experiences is an important underlying driver of the growing popularity of social networks. In 2007, Microsoft conducted a study looking at motivations and found that individuals use social networks:

- 59 per cent – to keep in touch with friends and family;
- 57 per cent – I like looking at other people's spaces;

Key Elements of trust & how to Substantiate

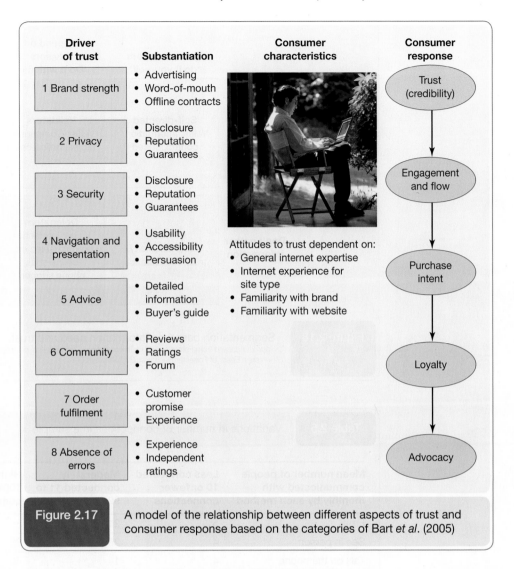

Driver of trust	Substantiation	Consumer characteristics	Consumer response

1 Brand strength
- Advertising
- Word-of-mouth
- Offline contracts

2 Privacy
- Disclosure
- Reputation
- Guarantees

3 Security
- Disclosure
- Reputation
- Guarantees

4 Navigation and presentation
- Usability
- Accessibility
- Persuasion

5 Advice
- Detailed information
- Buyer's guide

6 Community
- Reviews
- Ratings
- Forum

7 Order fulfilment
- Customer promise
- Experience

8 Absence of errors
- Experience
- Independent ratings

Attitudes to trust dependent on:
- General internet expertise
- Internet experience for site type
- Familiarity with brand
- Familiarity with website

Consumer response:
- Trust (credibility)
- Engagement and flow
- Purchase intent
- Loyalty
- Advocacy

Figure 2.17	A model of the relationship between different aspects of trust and consumer response based on the categories of Bart *et al.* (2005)

- 47 per cent – I want to meet people with similar interests;
- 46 per cent – to express my opinions and views on topics;
- 20 per cent – it is a good way to date;
- 17 per cent – using it for a specific reason, e.g. wedding, job networking.

Members of a community or social network will differ in the extent to which they are connected with others. The most influential network members will be highly connected and will discuss issues of interest with a wider range of contacts than those who are less connected (Table 2.5).

It is generally believed by PR professionals seeking to influence marketplace perceptions that it is important to target the highly connected individuals since they are typically trusted individuals that other members of the community may turn to for advice. However, Watts and Dodds (2007) suggest that consideration should also be given to the *herding* instinct, as 'most social change is driven not by influentials, but by easily influenced individuals influencing other easily influenced individuals'.

Although there is a clear wish to socialise online, site owners need to remember that it is not straightforward to engage an online audience as they move between different sites.

This section has considered customers and their behaviour, as well as how to analyse demand for digital services and the models a digital market might apply to gain better understanding of customers in the micro-environment. The next section explores another set of actors, who shape the micro-environment: competitors.

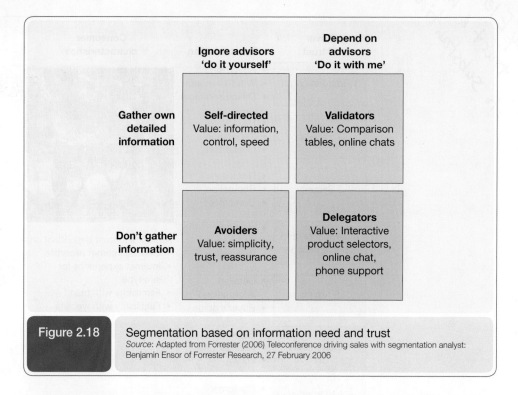

Figure 2.18	Segmentation based on information need and trust

Source: Adapted from Forrester (2006) Teleconference driving sales with segmentation analyst: Benjamin Ensor of Forrester Research, 27 February 2006

Table 2.5	Variations in number of connections in a sample

Mean number of people communicated with monthly by each method	Less connected 10 or fewer connections	Moderately connected 11 to 99 connections	Highly connected 100+ or fewer connections
Email	5	21	84
See in person	4	20	88
Talk on the phone	4	14	46
Instant message	1	5	16
Text message	1	4	15

Source: Understanding Influence, and Making It Work For You: A CNET Networks Study, 2007

Competitors

For any marketer, a key consideration is developing an understanding of how to satisfy customers better than the competition. In Chapter 4 we explore developing competitive advantage and the value chain in some detail. In this chapter, the focus is on the structure of competitive markets and way the competitors behave.

The shape and nature of online competitive markets

According to Jobber and Ellis-Chadwick (2013), 'an industry is a group of firms that market products that are close substitutes for each other'. However, some industries are more profitable than others, some are reasonably stable, while others are highly volatile. The variance between industrial sectors and specific markets is not all down to the abilities of the companies within the market to produce customer satisfaction. There are various forces that *shape the rules of competition*. Porter's five forces model has been widely used to help analyse the shape and competition and it is the nature of the forces and how they combine, he suggests, that ultimately determine how companies compete. In 2001, Porter updated his model to encompass the influence of the Internet. The rest of this sub-section explores his ideas following the five forces which make up the model. Table 2.6 summarises the impact of the Internet on the five forces.

Bargaining power of buyers

The increase in customer power and knowledge is perhaps the single biggest threat posed by electronic trading. This force is important in both B2C and B2B trading situations. From a B2C perspective, the bargaining power of retail shopper is greatly increased when they are using the Internet as they are able to evaluate products and compare prices. This is particularly true for standardised products where offers from different suppliers can be readily compared through online intermediaries such as search engines and price comparison sites, e.g. Kelkoo or Pricerunner, Compare the market and Confused.com. From a B2B

Table 2.6	Impact of the Internet on the five competitive forces

Bargaining power of buyers	Bargaining power of suppliers	Threat of substitute products and services	Barriers to entry	Rivalry between existing competitors
• The power of online buyers is increased since they have a wider choice and prices are likely to be forced down through increased customer knowledge and price transparency (see Chapter 5)	• When an organisation purchases, the bargaining power of its suppliers is reduced since there is a wider choice and increased commoditisation due to e-procurement and e-marketplaces	• Substitution is a significant threat since new digital products or extended products can be readily introduced	• Barriers to entry are reduced, enabling new competitors, particularly for retailers or service organisations that have traditionally required a high-street presence or a mobile sales force	• The Internet encourages commoditisation, which makes it less easy to differentiate products
• For a B2B organisation, forming electronic links with customers may deepen a relationship and it may increase switching costs, leading to 'soft lock-in'	• The reverse arguments regarding bargaining power of buyers	• The introduction of new substitute products and services should be carefully monitored to avoid erosion of market share • Internet technology enables faster introduction of products and services • This threat is related to new business models which are covered in a later section in this chapter	• New entrants must be carefully monitored to avoid erosion of market share • Internet services are easier to imitate than traditional services, making it easy for 'fast followers'	• Rivalry becomes more intense as product lifecycles decrease and lead times for new product development decrease • The Internet facilitates the move to the global market, increasing the number of competitors

perspective, online auctions and business-to-business exchanges can also have a similar effect of driving down price of commodities. The Internet has not only opened up opportunities for more customers (in both sectors B2C and B2B) to take advantage of comparing prices but has also extended the scope to commodities products. Purchase of some products that have not traditionally been thought of as commodities, may become more price-sensitive. This process is known as **commoditisation**. Examples of goods that are becoming commoditised include electrical goods and cars.

In the business-to-business arena, a further issue is that the ease of use of the Internet channel makes it potentially easier for customers to swap between suppliers – switching costs are lower. With the Internet, which offers a more standard method for purchase through web browsers, the barriers to swapping to another supplier will be lower. With a specific EDI (electronic data interchange) link that has to be set up between one company and another, there may be reluctance to change this arrangement (**soft lock-in** due to switching costs). Commentators often glibly say 'online, your competitor is only a mouse click away', but it should be remembered that soft lock-in still exists on the web – there are still barriers and costs to switching between suppliers since, once a customer has invested time in understanding how to use a website to select and purchase a particular type of products, they may not want to learn another service.

A significant downstream channel threat is the potential loss of partners or distributors if there is a channel conflict resulting from disintermediation (see the sections on new channel structures, pages 97 and 98). For example, a car distributor could switch to an alternative manufacturer if its profitability were threatened by direct sales from the manufacturer.

Bargaining power of suppliers

This can be considered as an opportunity rather than a threat. Companies can insist, for reasons of reducing cost and increasing supply chain efficiency, that their suppliers use certain technologies and software solutions to process orders Additionally, the Internet tends to reduce the power of suppliers since barriers to migrating to a different supplier are reduced, particularly with the advent of **business-to-business exchanges**. However, if suppliers insist on proprietary technology to link companies, then this creates soft lock-in due to the cost or complexity of changing suppliers.

Threat of substitute products and services

This threat can occur from established or new companies. The Internet is particularly good as a means of providing information-based services at a lower cost. The greatest threats are likely to occur where digital product and/or service fulfilment can occur over the Internet. These substitutes can involve a new online channel essentially replicating an existing service, as is the case with online banking or e-books. But, often, online can involve adding to the proposition. For example, compared to traditional music retailers, online legal subscription music services such as iTunes (**www.iTunes.com**) offer a much wider choice of products with different delivery modes (real-time streaming to a PC or the capability to burn onto a CD or download to a portable music device such as an MP3 player). In banking, new facilities have been developed to help customers manage their finances online by aggregating services from different providers into one central account. Such added-value digital services can help lock customers into a particular supplier.

Barriers to entry

For traditional companies, new online entrants have been a significant threat for retailers selling products such as books and financial services. For example, for the banking sector in Europe, traditional banks were threatened by the entry of completely new startup competitors, such as First-e (**www.first-e.com**) which later became financially unviable, or

Commoditisation
The process whereby product selection becomes more dependent on price than on differentiating features, benefits and value-added services.

Soft lock-in
Electronic linkages between supplier and customer that increase switching costs.

Business-to-business exchanges or marketplaces
Virtual intermediaries with facilities to enable trading between buyers and sellers.

of traditional companies from one country that use the Internet to facilitate their entry into another country. US company Citibank (**www.citibank.com**) and ING Direct (**www.ingdirect.co.uk**) from the Netherlands used the latter approach. New companies were also created by traditional competitors – for example, Prudential created Egg (**www.egg.com**), Abbey National created Cahoot (**www.cahoot.com**), and the Co-operative bank created Smile (**www.smile.co.uk**). ING Direct acquired millions of customers in new markets such as Canada, Australia and the UK through a combination of offline advertising, online advertising and an online or phone application process and account servicing.

In the past it has been argued that it is particularly easy and low cost for new entrants to challenge the market. The logic behind the argument is that these new entrants have been able to enter the market rapidly since they do not have the cost of developing and maintaining a distribution network to sell their products and these products do not require a manufacturing base.

However, to succeed, new entrants need to be market leaders in executing marketing and customer service. These are sometimes described as *barriers to success* or *hygiene factors* rather than *barriers to entry*. The costs of achieving these will be high. For example, First-e has not survived as an independent business. This competitive threat is less common in vertical business-to-business markets involving manufacture and process industries such as the chemical or oil industries since the investment barriers to entry are much higher.

Intensity of rivalry

The Internet has encouraged the commoditisation of more products, making it harder to differentiate between product offers. However, as digital markets have evolved so has the number of companies providing services via the Internet. As a result, in some market sectors there is an increasing number of companies (existing and new entrants) competing for their share of the available business. The nature of the rivalry between the companies trading online is largely determined by the number of players in a market and their relative sizes, the structure of costs and pricing, the switching costs customers will encounter if they change, strategic objectives and exit barriers. For example, in the online book market, Amazon is a major player accounting for a large proportion of the spend on books. Many book retailers find it hard to compete as their operating costs are higher than Amazon's, which restricts the opportunity to cut costs and sell at lower prices for sustained periods, Amazon has also differentiated from its competitors as it is able to offer the largest selection of books on the planet and speedy delivery services. Shoppers are also encouraged to stay with Amazon as the online interface makes it very easy for the shopper to buy and pay for books. Moreover, Amazon has developed the Kindle, an electronic book reader, which is now accounting for more sales of e-books than paper printed ones. In the UK, where Amazon launched its Kindle Store only in 2010, the company has sold 242 e-books for every 100 hardbacks since 1 April 2011, even though there has been a growth in hardback sales (Edgecliffe-Johnson, 2011). The Internet has also increased the opportunity for global players to expand into new local markets.

By using the five forces model for analysing the structure and nature of the competition, digital marketers can gain an understanding of the marketplace. However, it is important to be aware that actions have consequences. For example, a price reduction may stimulate a response from a competitor (the same applies to promotional activities and advertising) – and *wars* can be very costly. Therefore, the next step for the digital marketer is to develop understanding of their competitors and how they might respond. The next sub-section explores how to analyse competitors and assess their potential.

Competitor analysis
Involves identifying the companies which are competing for our business and then reviewing what they are good at, what are their strengths, where are their weaknesses; what are they planning, where do they want to take the company and how do they behave when other companies try to take their market share.

Competitor analysis and benchmarking

Competitor analysis and benchmarking of competitor use of digital marketing for acquisition and retention of customers is especially important because of the dynamic nature of the Internet medium. As Porter (2001) has pointed out, this dynamism enables new services to be launched and elements of the marketing mix, such as price and promotion, to be changed much more frequently than was traditionally the case. Copying of concepts and approaches within sectors is rife, but can sometimes be controlled through patenting. For example, **Amazon.com** has patented the 'One Click' approach to purchase, so this term and approach is not seen on other sites. The implications of this dynamism are that competitor benchmarking is not a one-off activity while developing a strategy, but needs to be continuous.

Competitor benchmarking is the term used for structured comparison of digital marketing approaches of an organisation's services within a market. Its purpose is to identify threats posed by changes to competitor offerings, but also to identify opportunities for enhancing a company's own web services through looking at innovative approaches in non-competing companies. Competitor benchmarking is closely related to developing the customer proposition and brand experience and is informed by understanding the requirements of different customer personas, as introduced earlier in this chapter.

Benchmarking of services has different perspectives which serve different purposes:

Competitor benchmarking
A structured analysis of the online services, capabilities and performance of an organisation within the areas of customer acquisition, conversion, retention and growth.

1 *Internal capabilities* such as resourcing, structure and processes vs *external customer facing* features of the sites.
2 *Different aspects of the customer lifecycle*: customer acquisition, conversion to retention. Capabilities are benchmarked in all the activities of each aspect (shown in Figure P.1 in the Preface). For example, what are the capabilities of a competitor within search marketing through reviewing their presence in the paid and natural listings of the search engines.
3 *Qualitative to quantitative*: from qualitative assessments by customers through surveys and focus groups through to quantitative analysis by independent auditors of data across customer acquisition (e.g. number of site visitors or reach within market, cost of acquisition, number of customers, sales volumes and revenues and market share); conversion (average conversion rates) and retention such as repeat conversion and number of active customers.
4 *In-sector and out-of-sector*: benchmarking against similar sites within sector and reviewing out-of-sector to sectors which tend to be more advanced, such as online publishers, social networks and brand sites. Benchmarking services are available for this type of comparison from analysts such as Bowen Craggs Index (**www.bowencraggs .com**) that specialise in the review of corporate communications websites. An example of one of their benchmark reports is shown in Figure 2.19. You can see that this is based on the expert evaluation of the suitability of the site for different audiences as well as measures under the overall construction (which includes usability and accessibility), message (which covers key brand messages and suitability for international audiences)

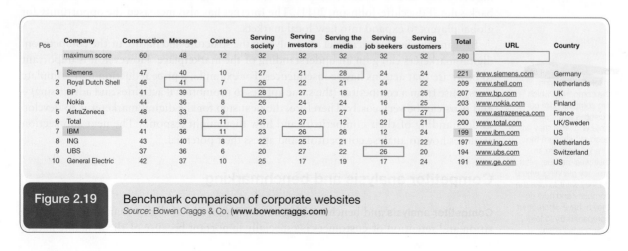

Pos	Company	Construction	Message	Contact	Serving society	Serving investors	Serving the media	Serving job seekers	Serving customers	Total	URL	Country
	maximum score	60	48	12	32	32	32	32	32	280		
1	Siemens	47	40	10	27	21	28	24	24	221	www.siemens.com	Germany
2	Royal Dutch Shell	46	41	7	26	22	21	24	22	209	www.shell.com	Netherlands
3	BP	41	39	10	28	27	18	19	25	207	www.bp.com	UK
4	Nokia	44	36	8	26	24	24	16	25	203	www.nokia.com	Finland
5	AstraZeneca	48	33	9	20	20	27	16	27	200	www.astrazeneca.com	France
6	Total	44	39	11	25	27	12	22	21	200	www.total.com	UK/Sweden
7	IBM	41	36	11	23	26	26	12	24	199	www.ibm.com	US
8	ING	43	40	8	22	25	21	16	22	197	www.ing.com	Netherlands
9	UBS	37	36	6	20	27	22	26	20	194	www.ubs.com	Switzerland
10	General Electric	42	37	10	25	17	19	17	24	191	www.ge.com	US

Figure 2.19 Benchmark comparison of corporate websites
Source: Bowen Craggs & Co. (**www.bowencraggs.com**)

and contact (which shows integration between different audiences). Although some research into site types is based on the presence or absence of a feature, Figure 2.19 is based on an expert review taking ten hours. The methodology states: 'it is not "tick box": every metric is judged by its existence, its quality and its utility to the client, rather than "Is it there or is it not?"'

5 *Financial to non-financial measures.* Through reviewing competitive intelligence sources such as company reports or tax submissions, additional information may be available on turnover and profit generated by digital channels. But other forward-looking aspects of the company's capability which are incorporated on the balanced score measurement framework (see Chapter 4) should also be considered, including resourcing, innovation and learning.

6 *From user experience to expert evaluation.* Benchmarking research should take two alternative perspectives, from actual customer reviews of content and usability to expert evaluations.

In the physical world, a company's competitors tend to be visibly active in any given market and therefore are well known. However, in digital environments there may be new entrants that have the potential to achieve significant market share, which are less visible until they grow to a significant size. This is particularly the case with retail sales. For example, successful new companies have developed on the Internet that sell books, music, CDs and electronic components. As a consequence, companies need to review the Internet-based performance of both existing and new players. Companies should review:

- well-known local competitors (for example, UK or European competitors for British companies);
- well-known international competitors;
- new Internet companies – local and worldwide (within sector and out of sector).

As well as assessing competitors on performance criteria, it is also worthwhile categorising them in terms of their capability to respond. Deise *et al.* (2000) suggest an equation that can be used in combination to assess the capability of competitors to respond:

'Agility' refers to the speed at which a company is able to change strategic direction and respond to new customer demands. 'Reach' is the ability to connect to or to promote products and generate new business in new markets. 'Time-to-market' is the product lifecycle from concept through to revenue generation or, more generally, it can be considered how long it takes to implement new digital marketing services – e.g. social network integration. Companies with a high competitive capability within their market and competitive markets are arguably the most important ones to watch.

In summary, it is important for digital markets to be able to identify and understand their competitors and in doing so be able to infer what their strategies and future activities might be. (We revisit competitor benchmarking in more detail in Chapters 4, 7 and 10.)

Suppliers

Suppliers deliver the goods and services a business needs to carry out its activities further down the supply chain. In the digital marketplace, the supply chain can take many different forms depending on whether physical or digital products are involved. The most significant aspect of monitoring suppliers in the context of digital marketing is with respect to the effect suppliers have on the value of the quality of the product or service delivered to the end customer. Key issues include the effect of suppliers on product price, availability and features. This topic is not discussed further since it is less significant than other factors in an Internet marketing context. However, the Internet has had a significant impact in some business activity sectors insofar as it has resulted in new channel structures for supply chains and new types of suppliers, which offer specialist services to the digital industry as a whole. The new suppliers act as intermediaries and offer a wide range of specialist services: website development, technology management and integration.

Online marketing intermediaries

Marketing intermediaries
Firms that can help a company to promote, sell and distribute its products or services, for example media sites, comparison sites, search engines, social networks and blogs.

Destination sites
Sites typically owned by merchants, product manufacturers or retailers providing product information.

Online intermediary sites
Websites that facilitate exchanges between consumer and business suppliers.

Online social network
A service facilitating the connection, collaboration and exchange of information between individuals.

Marketing intermediaries are firms that can help a company to promote, sell and distribute its products or services. They should not be confused with Internet service providers, which develop websites and provide hosting services. In the Internet context, online marketing intermediaries can be contrasted with destination sites, which are typically merchant sites owned by manufacturers or retailers that offer information and products (in reality any type of site can be a **destination site**, but the term is generally used to refer to merchant and brand sites).

Online intermediary sites provide information about destination sites and are a means of connecting Internet users with product information. The best known online intermediaries are the most popular sites such as Google, MSN and Yahoo! These are known as 'portals' and are described further below. Other consumer intermediaries such as Kelkoo (**www.kelkoo.com**) and Bizrate (**www.bizrate.com**) provide price comparison for products, as described earlier in this chapter. Most newspapers – e.g., *The Times*, *Guardian*, *The Telegraph* – and magazine publishers, and Emap (**www.greatmagazines.co.uk**), now provide online versions of their publications. These are as important in the online world in promoting products as newspapers and magazines are in the offline world.

Online intermediaries are businesses which support business and consumer audiences, so they can serve both B2B and B2C information exchanges. Auction sites are another type of online intermediary that support the B2B and the C2C exchanges introduced in Chapter 1. Online intermediaries sometimes support **online social networks,** which are a form of online community described in more detail in the section on virtual communities at the end of Chapter 6. The Google Orkut service (**www.orkut.com**) is an example of a personal social network, while LinkedIn (**www.linkedin.com**) and Ecademy (**www.ecademy .com**) are examples of business networks.

Mini case study 2.2	Alibaba provides a global market for all

Alibaba.com is one of the leaders of e-commerce transactions in China. It provides a marketplace connecting small and medium-sized buyers and suppliers from China and around the world. Its web presence includes an international marketplace (www.alibaba.com) which focuses on global importers and exporters and a China marketplace (www.alibaba.com.cn) which focuses on suppliers and buyers trading domestically in China.

From a launch in 1999 the marketplaces have grown such that Alibaba's consumer-to-consumer portal Taobao, similar to **eBay.com**, features nearly a billion products and is one of the 20 most visited websites globally.

In November 2007, Alibaba launched on the Hong Kong stock exchange and raised HK$13.1 billion (US$1.7 billion) in gross proceeds before offering expenses, making it the largest Internet IPO in Asia and the second largest globally. In September 2014, Alibaba's market value was measured as US$231 billion at a US IP.

Jack Ma, the founder of Alibaba, first saw the Internet in 1995 when he went to Seattle as an interpreter for a trade delegation and a friend showed him the Internet. They searched for the word 'beer' on Yahoo! and discovered that there was no data about China. He decided to launch a website and registered the name China Pages.

He borrowed $2000 to set up his first company. At the time he knew nothing about personal computers or emails and had never touched a keyboard before. He described the experience as a 'blind man riding on the back of a blind tiger'.

Initially the business did not fare well, since it was a part of China Telecom, and Jack Ma reflects that 'everything we suggested, they turned us down; it was like an elephant and an ant'.

He resigned, but in 1999 he gathered 18 people in his apartment and spoke to them for two hours about his vision. Everyone put their money on the table, and he got $60,000 to start Alibaba. He chose Alibaba as the name since it was easy to spell and associated with 'Open Sesame', the command that Ali Baba used to open doors to hidden treasures in *One Thousand and One Nights*.

During the dot-com bubble there were layoffs, such that by 2002 there was only enough cash to survive for 18 months. But they then developed a product for China exporters to meet US buyers online, which Ma said saved the company. By the end of 2002, Alibaba made $1 in profits! Each year since it has improved in profitability to the position where it was launched on the stock market.

Jack Ma's driving vision was to build an e-commerce ecosystem that allows consumers and businesses to do all aspects of business online. By 2006 he had done so well it caused one of Alibaba's major competitors eBay to close its operation in China. The Alibaba Group's flagship company is a world-leading B2B e-commerce company and Taobao (part of the group – see Figure 2.20) is China's largest online retail website, which provides a portal for shopping, socialising and sharing information. Alibaba also now provides cloud computing, and a range of other computing services and has become one of China's leading Internet portals.

Figure 2.20   Taobao (www.taobao.com)

Sarkar *et al.* (1996) identified many different types of potential online intermediaries (mainly from a B2C perspective) which used to be referred to as 'cybermediaries'. While this term is no longer widely used the types of intermediaries remain relevant and include:

Directories
Structured listings of registered sites in different categories.

- **directories** (such as Yahoo! directory, Open Directory, **Business.com**);
- search engines (Google, Yahoo! Search, Bing);
- virtual resellers (own inventory and sells direct, e.g. Amazon, CDWOW);
- financial intermediaries (offering digital cash and payment services such as PayPal);
- forums, fan clubs and user groups (referred to collectively as 'virtual communities') or social networks such as HabboHotel for youth audiences (**www.habbo.com**);
- evaluators (sites which act as reviewers or comparison of services) such as **www.trip advisor.com**.

Since Sarkar *et al.* (1996) identified the different types of intermediaries there has been much diversification and new intermediaries provide services to other intermediaries.

Activity 2.4	Tripadvisor.com

VisitBritain, the UK's national tourist board, is promoting travel review site TripAdvisor. The idea is that travellers who use the VisitBritain website can now click on a link to a 'dedicated UK tourism destination page in TripAdvisor (**www.tripadvisor.co.uk/ Tourism-g186216-United_Kingdom-Vacations.html**). Each attraction, hotel and tourist destination is given a rating based on customers' reviews. A great idea or an own goal? Some hoteliers are very dissatisfied. Traditionally, in Britain, hotels are rated from one star to five stars, and these stars are given out by tourist board hotel inspectors who (unannounced) stay overnight to do an assessment of a hotel and then award (if applicable) the appropriate star rating. Hotels pay to be included in the scheme and generally feel that there is a guarantee of standards across the industry. Hoteliers feel the TripAdvisor system is open to corruption, does not offer consistent standards, and they have no form of recourse if a customer gives a bad review.

Purpose

To examine the marketing opportunities provided by an Evaluator intermediary site.

Activity

1 Visit the TripAdvisor for your country and search for a hotel in your home town. See how TripAdvisor reviews rate the hotel.
2 Now imagine you are responsible for the online communications for the hotel. Make a list of the positive and negative points raised in the reviews
3 Suggest how you might use these comments positively to generate visitor traffic to the hotel website.

Portals

Portal
An online publisher that acts as a gateway to information and services available on the Internet by providing search engines, directories and other services such as personalised news or free email.

An Internet **portal** is a type of publisher that acts as a gateway to information and services available on the Internet. However, the term is no longer in common usage since directories are no longer favoured by users or Google as they were in the first ten years of the web.

For marketers to extend the visibility or reach of their company online, they need to be well represented on a range of publishers through using sponsorships, online adverts and search marketing, as explained in Chapter 8.

New channel structures

Channel structure
The configuration of partners in a distribution channel.

Channel structures describe the way a manufacturer or selling organisation delivers products and services to its customers. The distribution channel will consist of one or more intermediaries, such as wholesalers and retailers. For example, a music company is unlikely to distribute its CDs directly to retailers, but will use wholesalers that have a large warehouse of titles that are then distributed to individual branches according to demand. A company selling business products may have a longer distribution channel involving more intermediaries.

The relationship between a company and its channel partners can be dramatically altered by the opportunities afforded by the Internet. This occurs because the Internet offers a means of bypassing some of the channel partners. This process is known as **disintermediation** or, in plainer language, 'cutting out the middleman'.

Disintermediation
The removal of intermediaries such as distributors or brokers that formerly linked a company to its customers.

Figure 2.21 illustrates disintermediation in a graphical form for a simplified retail channel. Further intermediaries, such as additional distributors, may occur in a business-to-business market. Figure 2.21 shows the former position where a company marketed and sold its products by 'pushing' them through a sales channel. Figure 2.21 shows two different types of disintermediation in which the wholesaler (b) or the wholesaler and retailer (c) are bypassed, allowing the producer to sell and promote direct to the consumer. The benefits of disintermediation to the producer are clear – it is able to remove the sales and infrastructure cost of selling through the channel, and some of these cost savings can be passed on to the customer in the form of cost reductions.

The Internet's potential to change channel structures has been debated and, in disintermediation, the rise of a new breed of virtual merchants and the cannibalising of customers were all quoted as potential threats to the high street. More specifically, according to Doherty and Ellis-Chadwick (2010):

> 'Disintermediation' was the word on many commentators' lips, in the early days of Internet retailing, when it was envisaged that manufacturers could simply target their consumers directly, and in so doing, cut the retailer, as 'middle man', out of the equation [Malone *et al.*, 1997].

By interacting directly with customers, via the Internet, manufacturers would have the opportunity to dramatically change the structure and dynamic of retail channels (Ettorre, 1996), and in so doing, allow both producers and customers to benefit from a more direct form of contact (Benjamin and Wigand, 1995). It was envisaged that this form of 'pirating the value chain' (Ghosh, 1998) could ultimately change the balance of power within electronic retail channels. Indeed, Alba *et al.* (1997) suggested that 'disintermediation' might be the 'the most important structural change brought about by interactive home selling'.

Moreover, since purchasers of products still require assistance in the selection of products, this led to the creation of new intermediaries, a process referred to as **reintermediation**.

Reintermediation
The creation of new intermediaries between customers and suppliers providing services such as supplier search and product evaluation.

Figure 2.22 shows the operation of reintermediation in a graphical form. Following disintermediation, where the customer goes direct to different suppliers to select a product, this becomes inefficient for the consumer. Take the example of someone buying insurance – to decide on the best price and offer, they would have to visit, say, five different insurers

Figure 2.21 Disintermediation of a consumer distribution channel showing: (a) the original situation, (b) disintermediation omitting the wholesaler, and (c) disintermediation omitting both wholesaler and retailer

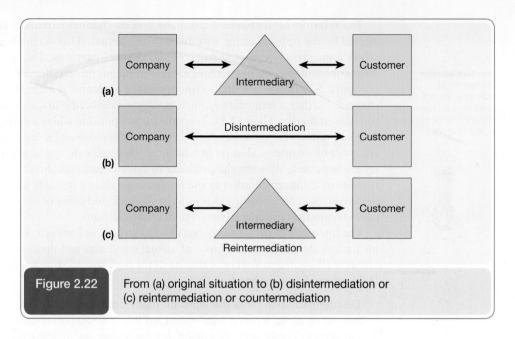

Figure 2.22 From (a) original situation to (b) disintermediation or (c) reintermediation or countermediation

and then return to the one they decide to purchase from. Reintermediation removes this inefficiency by placing an intermediary between the purchaser and seller. This intermediary performs the price evaluation stage of fulfilment since its database has links updated from prices contained within the databases of different suppliers.

What are the implications of reintermediation for the Internet marketer? First, it is necessary to make sure that a company, as a supplier, is represented with the new intermediaries operating within your chosen market sector. This implies the need to integrate, using the Internet, databases containing price information with that of different intermediaries. Secondly, it is important to monitor the prices of other suppliers within this sector (possibly by using the intermediary website for this purpose). Thirdly, long-term partnering arrangements such as sponsorships need to be considered. Finally, it may be appropriate for businesses to create their own intermediary to compete with existing intermediaries or to pre-empt similar intermediaries. For example, the Thomson Travel Group set up **Latedeals.com** (**www.thomson.co.uk/late-deals/late-deals.html**) in direct competition with **Lastminute.com** (**www.lastminute.com**). A further example is that, in the UK, Boots the Chemist set up its own intermediaries, Handbag (**www.handbag.com**) and Wellbeing (**www.wellbeing.com**). This effectively created barriers to entry for other new intermediaries wishing to operate in this space. Such tactics to counter or take advantage of reintermediation are sometimes known as **countermediation**.

Countermediation
Creation of a new intermediary by an established company.

Market mapping and developing channel chains is a powerful technique recommended by McDonald and Wilson (2002) for analysing the changes in a marketplace introduced by the Internet. A market map can be used to show the flow of revenue between a manufacturer or service provider and its customers through traditional intermediaries and new types of intermediaries. For example, Thomas and Sullivan (2005) give the example of a US multichannel retailer that used cross-channel tracking of purchases through assigning each customer a unique identifier to calculate channel preferences as follows: 63 per cent bricks-and-mortar store only, 12.4 per cent Internet-only customers, 11.9 per cent catalogue-only customers, 11.9 per cent dual-channel customers and 1 per cent three-channel customers.

A channel chain is similar – it shows different customer journeys for customers with different channel preferences. It can be used to assess the current and future importance of these different customer journeys. An example of a channel chain is shown in Figure 2.23.

	Offline journey	Mixed-mode journey		Online journey
Awareness of agent	Local property paper	Word-of-mouth	Search engine	Search engine
Search and select agents	Go to agents	Estate agents site		Portal: Rightmove
Negotiation	At home	At home		Book online
Viewings feedback	Monthly letter	Phone/e-mail		E-mail/text

Figure 2.23 Example of a channel chain map for consumers selecting an estate agent to sell their property

Business models for e-commerce

Defining a clear **online business model** is essential for a new startup online business to be successful. But it's also important for existing businesses thinking about options to refine their business model or add new services to their offerings in the light of new opportunities made possible by the Internet. The Business Model Canvas developed by Osterwald and Pigneur (2010) is a valuable framework for summarising strategy for online businesses. It was published as part of a co-creation project involving 470 practitioners from 45 countries. It's also available as an app and downloadable templates on the Business Model Generation site (**www.businessmodelgeneration.com**).

The main sections of the canvas, in a logical order to consider them, are:

1 **Value proposition.** This is at the heart of what the business offers to its audiences and is arguably most to important success. More details are provided in a follow-up book by Osterwalder *et al.* (2014).
2 **Customer segments.** Different target audiences the value propositions will appeal to. In the business model canvas, the alternatives recommended are mass market, niche market, segmented (broken down further) or a range of diverse segments.
3 **Customer relationships.** The types of relationships that will be formed, for example self-service, automated services, communities or more personal assistance. Co-creation of content may be part of this.
4 **Channels.** The methods by which the organisation's services will be delivered and the audiences reached.
5 **Key partners.** To exploit online and offline value networks, forming partnerships gives an opportunity of expanding reach and taking advantage of existing organisations and online influencers that have built an audience.
6 **Activities.** Which are the main activities that need to be performed to deliver the value proposition to develop revenue.
7 **Resources.** Different types of process and people to complete the activities to create and deliver the value proposition.
8 **Cost structure.** Different cost elements, these should be checked against activities and resources. Costs are classically broken down into fixed and variable costs and economies of scale.

9   **Revenue stream**. This is the method by which a business derives income. Common online options are: ad revenue, subscription fees, sales of physical or virtual goods or affiliate-based commission arrangements. Licensing and leasing are other alternatives.

An example of how these nine different elements of a business model can be applied is shown in Figure 2.24.

It's a great framework, but it's always worth considering what the missing elements of frameworks are. It's arguably missing a method of specifying key performance indicators for evaluating performance of the business model. I recommend adding these to the relevant sections, in particular for revenue stream, cost structure and key activities. It also doesn't directly consider the impact of different forms of competitors. To help here, it's useful to think through how the canvas would look for successful companies already active in this market.

We will look further at how to define elements of the business model such as value proposition and targeting in Chapters 5 and 8.

Online business model
A summary of how a company will generate a profit identifying its core product or service value proposition, target customers in different markets, position in the competitive online marketplace or value chain and its projections for revenue and costs.

A review of the different **online business models** made available through e-commerce is of relevance to existing companies, but in particular, startup companies and online intermediaries. Venkatram (2000) pointed out that existing businesses needed to use the Internet to build on current business models, while at the same time experimenting with new business models. New business models may be important to gain a competitive advantage over existing competitors, while at the same time heading off similar business models created by new entrants. More commonly, they may simply offer a different revenue stream through advertising or charging for services in a new way. For Internet startups the viability of a business model and in particular their sources of revenue will be crucial to funding from venture capitalists. But what is a business model? Timmers (1999) defines a 'business model' as:

> An architecture for product, service and information flows, including a description of the various business actors and their roles; and a description of the potential benefits for the various business actors; and a description of the sources of revenue.

| **Figure 2.24** | Different types of online trading location |

Investors will require eight key elements of the business model to be defined which will summarise the organisation's e-business strategy:

1 *Value proposition.* Which products and or services will the company offer? This is supplemented by the added value defined using the online value proposition described in Chapter 5.

2 *Market or audience.* Which audience will the company serve and target with its communications? For example, business-to-business, business-to-consumer or not-for-profit? Within these categories are there particular audience segments that will be targeted. The scope of geographical markets such as countries, regions or towns needs to be defined. A communications plan as described in Chapters 8 and 9 will detail how the audience will be reached and influenced using online communications and offline communications such as advertising and public relations.

3 *Revenue models and cost base.* What are the specific revenue models that will generate different income streams? What are the main costs of the business forming its budget? How are these forecast to change through time?

4 *Competitive environment.* Who are the direct and indirect competitors for the service and which range of business models do they possess?

5 *Value chain and marketplace positioning.* How is the company and its services positioned in the value chain between customers and suppliers and in comparison with direct and indirect competitors?

6 *Representation in the physical and virtual world.* What is its relative representation in the physical and virtual world, e.g. high-street presence, online only, intermediary, mixture? How will the company influence its audience through a multichannel buying process?

7 *Organisational structure.* How will the organisation be internally structured to create, deliver and promote its service (see Chapter 10)? How will it partner with other companies to provide services, for example through outsourcing?

8 *Management.* What experience in similar markets and companies do the managers have? Will they attract publicity?

Timmers (1999) identified no fewer than 11 different types of business model that can be facilitated by the web and generally remain relevant. You will notice that many of these are in common with the intermediary types identified by Sarkar which we reviewed earlier in the chapter:

1 *e-shop* – marketing of a company or shop via the web;

2 *e-procurement* – electronic tendering and procurement of goods and services;

3 *e-malls* – a collection of online retailers (the virtual mall model didn't prove effective online, but comparison sites could be considered their equivalent);

4 *e-auctions* – eBay (**www.ebay.com**) is the best-known example and offers both B2B and B2C offerings;

5 *virtual communities* – these can be B2C communities such as the major social networks or B2B communities such as those built around trade publishers (these are important for their potential in e-marketing and are described in the section on virtual communities in Chapter 9;

6 *collaboration platforms* – these enable collaboration between businesses or individuals, e.g. e-groups, now part of Yahoo! (**www.yahoo.com**) services;

7 *third-party marketplaces* – marketplaces are described in Chapter 7;

8 *value-chain integrators* – offer a range of services across the value chain;

9 *value-chain service providers* – specialise in providing functions for a specific part of the value chain, such as the logistics company UPS (**www.ups.com**);

10 *information brokerage* – provide information for consumers and businesses, often to assist in making the buying decision or for business operations or leisure;

11 *trust and other services* – examples of trust services include Internet Shopping is Safe (ISIS) (**www.imrg.org/isis**) or TRUSTe (**www.truste.org**) which authenticate the quality of service provided by companies trading on the web.

Publishers are a major type of business model that is not clearly represented in the Timmers categories. We examine the revenue models for these below. Regardless of the descriptors used, the important point is that as part of strategy development, organisations should identify relevant partners and develop tactics for working with them appropriately.

Figure 2.25 suggests a different perspective for reviewing alternative business models. There are three different perspectives from which a business model can be viewed. Any individual organisation can operate in different categories, as the examples below show, but most will focus on a single category for each perspective. Such a categorisation of business models can be used as a tool for formulating e-business strategy. The three perspectives, with examples, are:

1 *Marketplace position perspective*. The book publisher here is the manufacturer, Amazon is a retailer and Yahoo! is both a retailer and a marketplace intermediary.
2 *Revenue model perspective*. The book publisher can use the web to sell direct while Yahoo! and Amazon can take commission-based sales. Yahoo! also has advertising as a revenue model.
3 *Commercial arrangement perspective*. All three companies offer fixed-price sales, but, in its place as a marketplace intermediary, Yahoo! also offers alternatives.

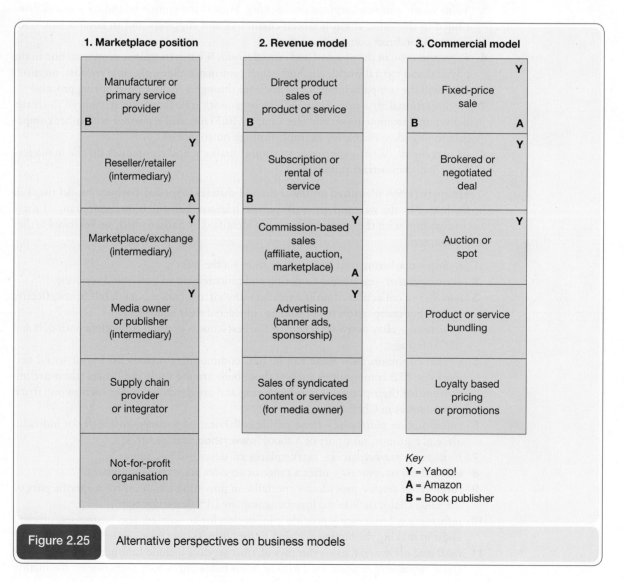

| Figure 2.25 | Alternative perspectives on business models |

Revenue models

Revenue models
Describe methods of generating income for an organisation.

Revenue models specifically describe different techniques for generation of income. For existing companies, revenue models have mainly been based upon the income from sales of products or services. This may be either for selling direct from the manufacturer or supplier of the service or through an intermediary that will take a cut of the selling price. Both of these revenue models are, of course, still crucial in online trading. There may, however, be options for other methods of generating revenue; a manufacturer may be able to sell advertising space or sell digital services that were not previously possible.

Online publisher and intermediary revenue models

For a publisher, there are many options for generating revenue online based around advertising and fees for usage of the online service. These options, particularly the first four in the list below, can also be reviewed by other types of business such as price comparison sites, aggregators, social networks and destination sites which can also carry advertising to supplement revenue. The main types of online revenue model are:

CPM (cost per thousand)
The cost to the advertiser (or the revenue received by the publisher) when an ad is served 1000 times.

1   *CPM display advertising on site.* **CPM** stands for 'cost per thousand', where M denotes 'mille'. This is the traditional method by which site owners charge a fee for advertising. The site owner charges advertisers a rate card price (for example £50 CPM) according to the number of times ads are served to site visitors. Ads may be served by the site owner's own ad server or more commonly through a third-party ad network service such as DoubleClick (which is owned by Google).

CPC (cost per click)
The cost to the advertiser (or the revenue received by the publisher) of each click of a link to a third-party site.

2   CPC advertising on site (pay-per-click text ads). **CPC** stands for 'cost per click'. Advertisers are charged not simply for the number of times their ads are displayed, but according to the number of times they are clicked upon. These are typically text ads served by a search engine such as Google (**www.google.com**) on what is known as its content network. Google has its AdSense (**http://adsense.google.com**) program for publishers, which enables them to offer text- or image-based ads typically on a CPC basis, but optionally on a CPM basis. Typical costs per click can be surprisingly high – i.e they are in the range £0.10 to £4, but sometimes up to £20 for some categories such as 'life insurance'. The revenue for search engines and publishers from these sources can also be significant: Google's annual reports (**http://investor.google.com**) show that this is between a quarter and a third of Google's revenue.

3   *Sponsorship of site sections or content types (typically fixed fee for a period).* A company can pay to advertise a site channel or section. For example, the bank HSBC sponsors the Money section on the Orange broadband provider portal (**www.orange.co.uk**). This type of deal is often struck for a fixed amount per year. It may also be part of a reciprocal arrangement, sometimes known as a 'contra-deal' where neither party pays.

Cost per acquisition (CPA)
The cost to the advertiser (or the revenue received by the publisher) for each outcome such as a lead or sale generated after a click to a third-party site.

4   *Affiliate revenue (CPA, but could be CPC).* Affiliate revenue is commission-based – for example, I display Amazon books on my site **DaveChaffey.com** and receive around 5 per cent of the cover price as a fee from Amazon. Such an arrangement is sometimes known as **cost per acquisition (CPA)**. Increasingly, this approach is replacing CPM or CPC approaches where the advertiser has more negotiating power. For example, manufacturing company Unilever negotiates CPA deals with online publishers where it paid for every email address captured by a campaign rather than a traditional CPM deal. However, it depends on the power of the publisher, which will often receive more revenue overall for CPM deals. After all, the publisher cannot influence the quality of the ad creative or the incentivisation to click which will affect the click-through rate and so earnings from the ad.

5   *Transaction fee revenue.* A company receives a fee for facilitating a transaction. Examples include eBay and PayPal, which charge a percentage of the transaction cost between buyer and seller.

6 *Subscription access to content or services.* A range of documents can be accessed from a publisher for a fixed period. These are often referred to as premium services on websites.

7 *Pay-per-view access to documents.* Here payment occurs for single access to a document, video or music clip which can be downloaded. It may or may not be protected with a password or **digital rights management (DRM)**. I pay to access detailed best-practice guides on Internet marketing from Marketing Sherpa (**www.marketingsherpa.com**).

8 *Subscriber data access for email marketing.* The data a site owner has about its customers are also potentially valuable since it can send different forms of email to its customers if they have given their permission to receive email from either the publisher or third parties. The site owner can charge for adverts placed in its newsletter or can deliver a separate message on behalf of the advertiser (sometimes known as 'list rental'). A related approach is to conduct market research with the site customers.

Digital rights management (DRM)
The use of different technologies to protect the distribution of digital services or content such as software, music, movies or other digital data.

Calculating revenue for an online business

Site owners can develop models of potential revenue depending on the mix of revenue-generating techniques from the four main revenue options they use on the site given in the options above.

Consider the capacity of a site owner to maximise revenue or 'monetise' their site – which factors will be important? The model will be based on assumptions about the level of traffic and number of pages viewed plus the interaction with different types of ad unit. Their ability to maximise revenue will be based on these factors which can be modelled in the spreadsheet shown in Figure 2.26:

- *Number and size of ad units.* This is a delicate balance between the number of ad units in each site section or page – too many obtrusive ad units may present a bad experience for site users; too few will reduce revenue. Figure 2.26 has a parameter for the number of ad units or containers in each ad revenue category. There is a tension with advertisers who know that the awareness and response they generate from their ads is maximised when they are as large as practical and in prominent placements. A more accurate revenue model would develop revenue for different page types such as the home page and different page categories, e.g. the money or travel sections.
- *Capacity to sell advertising.* Figure 2.26 also has a parameter for the percentage of ad inventory sold in each category – for example, for the CPM ad display revenue only 40 per cent of inventory may be sold. This is why you may see publisher sites with their own 'house ads' – it is a sign they have been unable to sell all their ad space. A benefit of using the Google AdSense publisher program is that inventory is commonly all used.
- *Fee levels negotiated for different advertising models.* These will depend on the market competition or demand for advertising space. For 'pay-per-performance' advertising options such as the CPC and CPA models, it also depends on the response. In the first case, the site owner only receives revenue when the ad is clicked upon and in the second case, the site owner only receives revenue when the ad is clicked upon and a product is purchased on the destination merchant site.
- *Traffic volumes.* More visitors equate to more opportunities to generate revenue through serving more pages (which helps with CPM-based advertising) or more clicks to third-party sites (which helps generate revenue from CPC and CPA deals).
- *Visitor engagement.* The longer visitors stay on a site (its 'stickiness'), the more page views that will accumulate, which again gives more opportunities for ad revenue. For a destination site a typical number of page views per visit would be in the range 5–10, but for a social network, media site or community the figure could be greater than 30.

Considering all of these approaches to revenue generation together, the site owner will seek to use the best combination of these techniques to maximise the revenue. An illustration of this approach is shown in Figure 2.26.

Ad revenue option	Measure	Site
	Pages served	**100,000**
Display advertising (CPM)	CPM (Cost Per Thousand)	£2
	% Inventory served	40%
	Avg. Clickthrough (CTR %)	0.10%
	Ad units served per page	2
	Clicks – CPM ads	80
	Revenue – display ads	**£160**
	Earnings per 100 clicks (EPC)	**£200.0**
	eCPM – display ads	**£1.60**
Fixed run-of-site sponsorship	% Inventory served	100%
	Avg. Clickthrough (CTR %)	0.30%
	Ad units served 1	1
	Clicks – fixed	300
	Revenue – fixed sponsorship	**£3,000**
	Earnings per 100 clicks (EPC)	**£1,000.0**
	eCPM – fixed	**£30.00**
Text ad advertising (CPC)	% Inventory served	100%
	Avg. Clickthrough (CTR %)	1.00%
	Avg. Cost Per Click	£0.30
	Ad units served per page	1
	Clicks – CPC ads	1,000
	Revenue – CPC ads	**£300**
	Earnings per 100 clicks (EPC)	**£30.0**
	eCPM – CPC ads	**£3**
Affiliate commission	% Inventory served	100%
	Avg. Clickthrough (CTR %)	0.50%
	Ad units served per page	1
	Clicks – Affiliates	500
	Destination conversion rate (%)	3%
	Average order value	£100
	Commission %	10%
	Revenue – affiliates	**£150**
	Earnings per 100 clicks (EPC)	**£30.0**
	eCPM – affiliates	**£1.50**
Overall metrics for site	**Clicks – total**	**1,880**
	Revenue – total	**£3,610**
	Earnings per 100 clicks (EPC) – total	**£192.02**
	eCPM – total	**£36.10**

Blue cells = input variables – vary these for 'what-if' analysis

Orange cells = Output variables (calculated – **do not overtype**)

Figure 2.26	Revenue model spreadsheet
	Source: SmartInsights.com

To assess how effective different pages or sites in their portfolio are at generating revenue using these techniques, site owners will use two approaches. The first is eCPM, or effective cost per thousand. This looks at the total the advertiser can charge (or cost to advertisers) for each page or site. Through increasing the number of ad units on each page this value will increase. The other alternative to assess page or site revenue-generating effectiveness is revenue per click (RPC), also known as 'earnings per click' (EPC). Alternatively, revenue can be calculated as ad revenue per 1000 site visitors. This is particularly important for affiliate marketers who make money through commission when their visitors click through to third-party retail sites, and then purchase there.

Activity 2.5 explores some of the revenue models that are possible.

Activity 2.5	Revenue models at marketing membership sites

Purpose

To illustrate the range of revenue-generating opportunities for an online publisher. This site looks at three alternative approaches for publishing, referencing three different types of portal.

Visit **Econsultancy.com**, **SmartInsights.com** and **MarketingProfs.com** and

1 Summarise the revenue models which are used for each site by looking at the information for advertisers and affiliates.
2 Give the advantages and disadvantages of the different revenue models for the site audience and the site owner.

Examples of e-commerce failures

We can learn from examples of failure. They're not written up that commonly since naturally those involved don't want to share their failures.

Boo.com is an interesting case of the potential and pitfalls of an e-commerce startup and criteria for success, or one could say of 'how not to do it'. The **boo.com** site was launched in November 1999 following two significant delays in launching and in January 2000 it was reported that 100 of its 400 employees had been made redundant due to disappointing initial revenues of about £60,000 in the Christmas period. Boo faced a high '**burn rate**' because of the imbalance between promotion and site development costs and revenues. As a consequence, it appeared to change its strategy by offering discounts of up to 40 per cent on fashions from the previous season. Closure followed in mid-2000 and the **boo.com** brand was purchased by an American entrepreneur who still continues to use it, as you can see on **www.boo.com**. Boo.com features as Case study 2. Investors provided a reported £74 million in capital. This enthusiasm is partly based on the experience of two of the founders in creating **bokus.com**, a relatively successful online bookseller.

Mini case study 2.3 gives a more recent example of an e-retail failure with serious consequences.

To conclude this chapter, read the following Case study 2 about dot-com failure **Boo. com**. We can learn from studying the mistakes of others, and have chosen this example since it shows what can happen when a company does not understand the marketplace and does not have clear goals.

Mini case study 2.3	Ecomom fails to control its revenue model

Ecomom was a small startup Internet retail company selling earth-friendly mum and maternity products including food, toys, apparel and other baby-related items. With headquarters in Las Vegas and San Francisco and a third-party fulfilment in Los Angeles, any volume could be shipped within 24 hours. Founded in 2007, by 2011 it had turnover of just over $1 million. A further round of investment of $12 million required further growth, but at what cost?

Business Insider (2013) describes the story of the eventual failure of the company in 2013. With hindsight it's difficult to understand investment in the company, but perhaps this was buoyed by the success story of Tony Hsieh building Las Vegas-based Zappos into an online shoe and retail business that Amazon acquired for $1.2 billion. Of course, investors require growth and Ecomom did achieve revenues of nearly $4 million in 2013. But investors also require a return on their investment and, as you'll see, the way growth was achieved was far from profitable.

Philip Prentiss, who joined the company in 2011 as financial controller, was the first dedicated finance person. As with many startups, payroll, tax and accounts are outsourced to third-party bookkeepers. Many company failures are not written up because employees don't want to share the story of failure. But in a candid summary of his time at the failed company, Prentiss (2013) describes the reasons, starting with the lack of financial prudence. Describing Ecomom, CEO Jody Sherman says:

> He was not a numbers guy. I would bring the financial statements to Jody who would glance at them so cursorily and wave me away with 'no one can understand this without extensive analysis'. Critically, he did not understand margin. At the end of December when things were getting truly desperate, he said to me 'Phil, just bring me a forecast that shows how much we need to sell to break even.' He did not understand, after three years of negative margin, that increased sales resulted in increased losses.

In this open letter describing the failure of the company, Prentiss shows how the financial presentation format hid a contribution margin of −48 per cent which he identified when he joined the company. In other words, for every additional $60 average order shipped, the variable cost was $89 and the company lost $29. This situation was caused by heavy discounting, with common use of 50 per cent discounts on daily deal sites like Groupon. To make matters worse, although discounts were meant to be one time only, the company couldn't limit them by customer, so every discounted order had a 50 per cent reduction regardless whether they were from a new company or an existing company. The company sales manager was paid based on sales achieved *before* discounting. As the same time, there were no premium lines or own-label items where margin could have been better. Add to this that this is a fiercely competitive growing sector with established retail brands such as Whole Foods or general retailers such as Amazon selling similar goods.

By mid-Autumn 2012 a $860K loss for the previous quarter was the result of the discounting strategy. Prentiss notes that no substantive changes were made to the business strategy and, starting from $4.8 million capital raised in August, for the five months to 31 December the company lost $1.1 million after variable cost, spent $1.7 million more on overhead, and locked up another $1.2 million in inventory, leaving less than $1 million in the bank.

Sadly, the company closed early in 2013 and shortly afterwards the CEO, Jody Sherman, took his own life.

But the legacy of the company and its founder may be how it has highlighted the pressure of running a startup. *Business Insider* quotes Dave McClure, an investor in Ecomom and the entrepreneur behind investment firm 500Startups, who says:

> Oh Jesus, [founding a company] can suck. I can remember facing extremely 'dark days' as an entrepreneur. I went through layoffs, co-founder battles, and wife battles, and not for much gain. It was a hell of a lot of work for not a hell of a lot of return. Then there are days when you sit in a corner and cry. You can't really do anything else. You don't have a social life. You don't really want to interact with family and friends because there's just not much context for them. Your world revolves around your startup and it's all about trying to survive and not look like an idiot in front of employees.

Context

'Unless we raise $20 million by midnight, boo.com is dead.' So said boo.com CEO Ernst Malmsten on 18 May 2000. Half the investment was raised, but this was too little, too late, and at midnight, less than a year after its launch, Boo.com closed. The headlines in the *Financial Times* the next day read: 'Boo.com collapses as investors refuse funds. Online sports retailer becomes Europe's first big Internet casualty.'

Boo.com remains a valuable case study for all types of businesses, since it doesn't only illustrate the challenges of managing e-commerce for a clothes retailer, but rather highlights failings in e-commerce strategy and management that can be made in any type of organisation.

Company background

Boo.com was founded in 1998 by three Swedish entrepreneurs, Ernst Malmsten, Kajsa Leander and Patrik Hedelin. Malmsten and Leander had previous business experience in publishing, where they created a specialist publisher and had also created an online bookstore, bokus.com, which in 1997 became the world's third largest book e-retailer behind Amazon and Barnes& Noble. They became millionaires when they sold the company in 1998. At Boo.com, they were joined by Patrik Hedelin, who was also the financial director at bokus, and at the time they were perceived as experienced European Internet entrepreneurs by the investors who backed them in their new venture.

Company vision

The vision for Boo.com was for it to become the world's first online global sports retail site. It would be a European brand, but with a global appeal. Think of it as a sports and fashion retail version of Amazon. At launch it would open its virtual doors in both Europe and America with a view to 'amazoning the sector'. Note, though, that Amazon did not launch simultaneously in all markets. Rather it became established in the US before providing local European distribution.

The Boo.com brand name

According to Malmsten *et al.* (2001), the boo brand name originated from film star Bo Derek, best known for her role in the movie *10*. The domain name 'bo.com' was unavailable, but adding an 'o', they managed to procure the domain 'boo.com' for $2500 from a domain name dealer. According to Rob Talbot, director of marketing for Boo.com, Boo was 'looking for a name that was easy to spell across all the different countries and easy to remember . . . something that didn't have a particular meaning'.

Target market

The audience targeted by Boo.com can be characterised as 'young, well-off and fashion-conscious' 18-to-24-year-olds. The concept was that globally the target market would be interested in sports and fashion brands stocked by Boo.com.

The market for clothing in this area was viewed as very large, so the thought was that capture of only a small part of this market was required for Boo.com to be successful. The view at this time on the scale of this market and the basis for success is indicated by *New Media Age* (1999):

> The $60b USD industry is dominated by Gen Xers who are online and according to market research in need of knowing what is in, what is not and a way to receive such goods quickly. If boo.com becomes known as the place to keep up with fashion and can supply the latest trends then there is no doubt that there is a market, a highly profitable one at that, for profits to grow from.

The growth in market was also supported by retail analysts, with *Verdict* predicting online shopping in the United Kingdom to grow from £600 million in 1999 to £12.5 billion in 2005.

However, *New Media Age* (2005) does note some reservations about this market, saying:

> Clothes and trainers have a high rate of return in the mail order/home shopping world. Twenty-year-olds may be online and may have disposable income but they are not the main market associated with mail order. To date there is no one else doing anything similar to boo.com.

The Boo.com proposition

In its proposal to investors, the company stated that its 'business idea is to become the world-leading Internet-based retailer of prestigious brand leisure and sportswear names'. It listed brands such as Polo, Ralph Lauren, Tommy Hilfiger, Nike, Fila, Lacoste and Adidas. The proposition involved sports and fashion goods alongside each other. The thinking was that sports clothing has more standardised sizes with less need for a precise fit than designer clothing.

The owners of **Boo.com** wanted to develop an easy-to-use experience which re-created the offline shopping experience as far as possible. As part of the branding strategy, an idea was developed of a virtual salesperson, initially named Jenny and later Miss Boo. She would guide users through the site and give helpful tips. When selecting products, users could drag them onto models, zoom in and rotate them in 3D to visualise them from different angles. The technology to achieve this was built from scratch along with the stock control and distribution software. A large investment was required in technology, with several suppliers being replaced before launch – which was six months later than promised to investors, largely due to problems with implementing the technology.

Clothing the mannequin and populating the catalogue was also an expensive challenge. For 2000, about $6 million was spent on content about spring/summer fashion wear. It cost $200 to photograph each product, representing a monthly cost of more than $500,000.

Although the user experience of **Boo.com** is often criticised for its speed, it does seem to have had that wow factor that influenced investors. Analyst Nik Margolis, writing in *New Media Age* (1999), illustrates this by saying:

> What I saw at *Boo.com* is simply the most clever web experience I have seen in quite a while. The presentation of products and content are both imaginative and offer an experience. Sure everything loads up fast in an office but I was assured by those at *Boo. com* that they will keep to a limit of eight seconds for a page to download. Eight seconds is not great but the question is will it be worth waiting for?

Of course, today, the majority of European users have broadband, but in the late 1990s the majority were on dial-up and had to download the software to view products.

Communicating the Boo.com proposition

Early plans referred to extensive 'high-impact' marketing campaigns on TV and newspapers. Public relations were important in leveraging the novelty of the concept and human side of the business – Leander was previously a professional model and had formerly been Malmsten's partner. This PR was initially focussed within the fashion and sportswear trade and then rolled out to publications likely to be read by the target audience. The success of this PR initiative can be judged by the 350,000 email pre-registrations who wanted to be notified of launch. For the launch Malmsten *et al*. (2001) explains that 'with a marketing and PR spend of only $22.4 million we had managed to create a worldwide brand'.

To help create the values of the **Boo.com** brand, Boom, a lavish online fashion magazine, was created, which required substantial staff for different language versions. The magazine wasn't a catalogue which directly supported sales; rather it was a publishing venture competing with established fashion titles. For existing customers the *Look Book*, a 44-page print catalogue, was produced which showcased different products each month.

The challenges of building a global brand in months

The challenges of creating a global brand in months are illustrated well by Malmsten *et al*. (2001). After an initial round of funding, including investment from JP Morgan, LMVH Investment and the Benetton family, which generated around $9 million, the founders planned towards launch by identifying thousands of individual tasks, many of which needed to be completed by staff yet to be recruited. These tasks were divided into 27 areas of responsibility familiar to many organisations including office infrastructure, logistics, product information, pricing, front-end applications, call centres, packaging, suppliers, designing logos, advertising/PR, legal issues and recruitment. At its zenith, **Boo.com** had 350 staff, with over 100 in London and new offices in Munich, New York, Paris and Stockholm. Initially boo.com was available in UK English, US English, German, Swedish, Danish and Finnish with localised versions for France, Spain and Italy added after launch. The website was tailored for individual countries using the local language and currency and also local prices. Orders were fulfilled and shipped out of one of two warehouses: one in Louisville, Kentucky and the other in Cologne, Germany. This side of the business was relatively successful, with on-time delivery rates approaching 100 per cent achieved.

Boo possessed classic channel conflicts. Initially, it was difficult getting fashion and sports brands to offer their products through **Boo.com**. Manufacturers already had a well-established distribution network through large high-street sports and fashion retailers and many smaller retailers. If clothing brands permitted **Boo.com** to sell their clothes online at discounted prices, then this would conflict with retailers' interests and would also portray the brands in a negative light if their goods were in an online 'bargain bucket'. A further pricing issue is where local or *zone pricing* in different markets exists – for example, lower prices often exist in the US than Europe and there are variations in different European countries.

Making the business case to investors

Today it seems incredible that investors were confident enough to invest $130 million in the company and, at the high point, the company was valued at $390 million. Yet much of this investment was based on the vision of the founders to be a global brand and achieve 'first-mover advantage'. Although there were naturally revenue projections, these were not always based on an accurate, detailed analysis of market potential. Immediately before launch, Malmsten *et al.* (2001) describe a meeting with would-be investor Pequot Capital, represented by Larry Lenihan, who had made successful investments in AOL and Yahoo! The **Boo.com** management team were able to provide revenue forecasts, but unable to answer fundamental questions for modelling the potential of the business, such as 'How many visitors are you aiming for? What kind of conversion rate are you aiming for? How much does each customer have to spend? What's your customer acquisition cost? And what's your payback time on customer acquisition cost?' When these figures were obtained, the analyst found them to be 'far-fetched' and reputedly ended the meeting with the words: 'I'm not interested. Sorry for my bluntness, but I think you're going to be out of business by Christmas.'

When the site launched on 3 November 1999, around 50,000 unique visitors were achieved on the first day, but only four in 1000 placed orders (a 0.25 per cent conversion rate). This shows the importance of modelling conversion rates accurately. This low conversion rate was also symptomatic of problems with technology, which gave rise to negative PR. One reviewer explained how he waited: 'Eighty-one minutes to pay too much money for a pair of shoes that I still have to wait a week to get?' These rates did improve as problems were ironed out – by the end of the week 228,848 visits had resulted in 609 orders with a value of $64,000. In the six weeks from launch, sales of $353,000 were made and conversion rates had more than doubled to 0.98 per cent before Christmas. However, a relaunch was required within six months to cut download times and to introduce a 'low-bandwidth version' for those using dial-up connections. This led to conversion rates of nearly 3 per cent on sales promotion. Sales results were disappointing in some regions, with US sales accounting for 20 per cent compared to the planned 40 per cent.

The management team felt that further substantial investment was required to grow the business from a presence in 18 countries and 22 brands in November to 31 countries and 40 brands the following spring. Turnover was forecast to rise from $100 million in 2000/01 to $1350 million by 2003/04, which would be driven by $102.3 million in marketing in 2003/04. Profit was forecast to be $51.9 million by 2003/04.

The end of Boo.com

The end of **Boo.com** came on 18 May 2000, when investor funds could not be raised to meet the spiralling marketing, technology and wage bills.

Source: Prepared by Dave Chaffey from original sources including Malmsten *et al.* (2001) and *New Media Age* (1999).

Questions

1 Which strategic marketing assumptions and decisions arguably made **Boo.com**'s failure inevitable? Contrast these with other dot-com-era survivors that are still in business, for example **lastminute.com**, **Egg.com** and Fire **box.com**.

2 Use the framework of the marketing mix to appraise the marketing tactics of **Boo.com** in the areas of product, pricing, place, promotion, process, people and physical evidence.

3 In many ways, the vision of Boo's founders were 'ideas before their time'. Give examples of e-retail techniques used to create an engaging online customer experience which Boo adopted that are now becoming commonplace.

Summary

1 The constantly changing online environment should be monitored by all organisations in order to be able to respond to changes in the micro-environment or the immediate marketplace. The micro-environment is largely within the reach of an organisation and therefore digital marketers should be aware of the management implications that arise from this arena. To be successful it is important to understand consumer and competitor behaviour and which suppliers and intermediaries offer services that will enable a company to achieve its digital marketing goals.

2 In this chapter, we have explored each of the groups of players in the micro-environment. From a consumer perspective we have identified variables that are likely to be the most effective foundation for developing targeting strategies. We have also considered how to analyse consumer demand and the importance of developing conversion strategies.

3 Competitors are an importance group of actors in the micro-environment and the Internet has created major changes to the competitive environment. This chapter has considered how organisations should deploy tools such as Porter's five forces to assess the nature and structure of competition in online markets.

4 We have examined techniques for competitive benchmarking and how to analyse competitor behaviour, which has highlighted how important it is to understand the potential strengths and weaknesses of the companies a business might compete with online.

5 Suppliers and intermediaries also have an important role to play in digital marketing. We have explored the services provided by these actors and considered the opportunities provided.

6 Finally, we considered the impact of the Internet on marketing channels. The Internet can encourage the formation of new channel structures. These include *disintermediation* within the marketplace as organisations' channel partners such as wholesalers or retailers are bypassed. Alternatively, the Internet can cause *reintermediation* as new intermediaries with a different purpose are formed to help bring buyers and sellers together in a *virtual marketplace* or *marketspace*.

7 This chapter has provided a foundation for analysing the immediate trading environment and provides a foundation for Chapter 3, which focuses on the macro-environment.

8 A business model is a summary of how a company will generate revenue, identifying its product offering, value-added services, revenue sources and target customers. Exploiting the range of business models made available through the Internet is important to both existing companies and startups.

9 The Internet may also offer opportunities for new revenue models such as commission on affiliate referrals to other sites or banner advertising.

10 The opportunity for new commercial arrangements for transactions includes negotiated deals, brokered deals, auctions, fixed-price sale, and pure spot markets; barters should also be considered.

11 Customer analysis is an important part of situation analysis. It involves assessing demand for online services, characteristics of existing online customers and the multichannel behaviour of customers as they select and purchase products.

12 Regular competitive benchmarking should be conducted to compare services.

13 The role of intermediaries like publishers, media sites, comparison sites and bloggers should also be carefully reviewed as part of strategic analysis.

Exercises

Self-assessment exercises

1 Explain the components of the digital market environment.
2 Why is environmental scanning necessary?
3 Summarise how each of the micro-environment factors may directly drive the content and services provided by a website.
4 How would you analyse demand for digital marketing services?
5 Why is it important to understand conversion marketing models?
6 What is the difference between demographic variables and behavioural variables?
7 What are the main aspects of customer adoption of the Internet that managers should be aware of?
8 What are the main changes to channel structures that are facilitated through the Internet?
9 How should a marketing manager benchmark the online performance of competitors?
10 How can the Internet be used to support the different stages of the buying process?

Essay and discussion questions

1 Competition is intensified when trading online. Discuss the extent to which you feel this assertion is true.
2 Internet access varies from country to country; explain the key factors which might influence different levels of access.
3 Discuss how an Internet entrepreneur might identify market opportunities online.
4 Perform a demand analysis for e-commerce services for a product sector and geographical market of your choice.
5 Perform competitor benchmarking for online services for an organisation of your choice.

Examination questions

1 The relationship between intermediaries, suppliers and resellers are crucial to every business. Discuss how the Internet potentially changes supply-chain relationships?
2 Trading online increasingly involves developing multichannel strategies. Give three examples of potential channel conflicts that might arise from using the Internet. Illustrate your answer with examples.
3 Discuss the extent to which it is possible to operate as a *virtual* organisation.
4 Using examples, suggest different ways that a company might use the Internet to build market share.
5 There are numerous variables which can be used to identify potential target segments that can be used for marketing strategy and planning. Suggest which variables have the most potential for identifying online consumers and justify your answer with examples.
6 Discuss the extent to which Porter's five forces model is applicable for analysing competition in digital markets.
7 Compare the physical and digital trading environments by identifying the similarities and differences.
8 Imagine you are about to set up a business online. Explain how you would go about investigating the micro-environment as part of your situation analysis.
9 Suggest how you would advise a business that has a website which is not delivering a benefit to the company.

References

Alba, J., Lynch, J., Weitz, B., Janiszewski, C., Lutz, R., Sawyer, A. and Wood, S. (1997) Interactive home shopping: consumer, retailer and manufacturer incentives to participate in electronic market places, *Journal of Marketing*, 61, 38–53.

Arnold, M., Reynolds, K., Ponder, N. and Lueg, J. (2005) Customer delight in a retail context: investigating delightful and terrible shopping experiences, *Journal of Business Research*, 58, 1132–45.

Bart, Y., Shankar, V., Sultan, F. and Urban, G. (2005) Are the drivers and the role of online trust the same for all websites and consumers? A large-scale exploratory empirical study, *Journal of Marketing* (October), 133–52.

Benjamin, R. and Wigand, R. (1995) Electronic markets and virtual value-chains on the information superhighway, *Sloan Management Review* (Winter), 62–72.

Berthon, P., Lane, N., Pitt, L. and Watson, R. (1998) The World Wide Web as an industrial marketing communications tool: models for the identification and assessment of opportunities, *Journal of Marketing Management*, 14, 691–704.

Bold, B. (2015) Black Friday bolsters Christmas online sales at John Lewis, *Marketing*, 5 January, www.marketingmagazine.co.uk/article/1327802/black-friday-bolsters-christmas-online-sales-john-lewis.

Brashear, T.G., Kashyap, V., Musante, M.D. and Donthu, N. (2009) A profile of the internet shopper: evidence from six countries, *Journal of Marketing Theory and Practice*, 17(3), 267–81.

Brengman, M., Geuensb, M., Weijtersc, C., Smith, S. and Swinyardd, W. (2005) Segmenting Internet shoppers based on their web-usage-related lifestyle: a cross-cultural validation, *Journal of Business Research*, 58(1), 79–88.

Business Insider (2013) The story of a failed startup and a founder driven to suicide, by Alyson Shontell, 4 April 2013, 8:43 PM, www.businessinsider.com/jody-sherman-ecomom-2013-4.

Chaffey, D. (2001) Optimising e-marketing performance – a review of approaches and tools, in *Proceedings of IBM Workshop on Business Intelligence and E-marketing*, Warwick, 6 December.

Chaffey, D. and Smith, P.R. (2008) *Emarketing Excellence. Planning and Optimising your Digital Marketing*, 3rd edn, Butterworth-Heinemann, Oxford.

Chamberlin, G. (2010) Googling the present, *Economic and Labour Review*, December 2010, Office for National Statistics.

Cheung, C.M.K., Chan, G.W.W. and Limayem, M. (2005) A critical review of online consumer behaviour: empirical research, *Journal of Electronic Commerce in Organisations*, 3(4), 1–19.

Choi, H. and Varian, H. (2009) Predicting the present with Google Trends, Google Inc., http://static.googleusercontent.com/external_content/untrusted_dlcp/www.google.com/en//googleblogs/pdfs/google_predicting_the_present.pdf.

Court, D., Elzinga, D., Mulder, S. and Jørgen Vetvik, O. (2009) The consumer decision journey, *McKinsey Quarterly*, June, www.mckinsey.com/insights/marketing_sales/the_consumer_decision_journey.

Deise, M., Nowikow, C., King, P. and Wright, A. (2000) *Executive's guide to e-business. From tactics to strategy*, John Wiley and Sons, New York.

Doherty, N.F and Ellis-Chadwick, F.E (2010) Internet retailing: the past the present and the future, *International Journal of Retail and Distribution Management*, 38(11–12), 943–65.

Donthu, N. and Garcioa, A. (1999) The Internet shopper, *Journal of Advertising Research*, 39(3), 316–33.

Edgecliffe-Johnson, A. (2011) Kindle e-book sales soar for Amazon, 19 May, **www.ft.com/cms/s/0/efb8670a-8240–11e0–961e-00144feabdc0.html**.

eMarketer (2014) Smartphone users worldwide will total 1.75 billion in 2014, *eMarketer* (**www.emarketer.com/Article/Smartphone-Users-Worldwide-Will-Total-175-Billion-2014/1010536**).

Ettorre, B. (1996) 2002: what's the world coming to (how technological developments affect industries)?, *Management Review*, 85(9), 33.

George, J. (2004) The theory of planned behaviour and Internet purchasing, *Internet Research*, 14(3), 198–211.

Ghosh, S. (1998) Making business sense of the Internet, *Harvard Business Review* (March–April), 126–35.

Google (2010) New GfK ROPO study with Vodafone. Published on Google Barometer Blog, 20 October, **http://googlebarometer.blogspot.com/2010/10/new-gfk-ropo-study-with-vodafone.html**.

Green, D. (2013). The five types of online shopper, *Huffington Post*, 24 February, **www.huffingtonpost.ca/drew-green/online-shopping-canada_b_2742950.html**.

Hague, N. (2014) Why adding value should not be confined to the margins, *Marketing*, **www.marketingmagazine.co.uk/article/1322497/greater-insight-why-adding-value-not-confined-margins**.

Hoffman, D., Novak, T. and Schlosser, A. (2000) 'The evolution of the digital divide: how gaps in Internet access may impact electronic commerce, *Journal of Computer-Mediated Communications* 5(3).

Jaywardhena, C., Wright, L. and Dennis, C. (2007) Consumers online: intentions, orientations and segmentation, *International Journal of Retail and Distribution Management*, 35(6), 515–26.

Jobber, D. and Ellis-Chadwick, F. (2013) *Principles and Practice of Marketing*, 7th edn, McGraw-Hill, Maidenhead.

Keen, C., Wetzels, M., de Ruyter, K. and Feinberg, R. (2004) E-tailers versus retailers: which factors determine consumer preferences?, *Journal of Business Research*, 57(7), 635–95.

Klein, L. and Ford, G. (2002) Consumer research for information in the digital age: an empirical study of pre-purchase search for automobiles, *Advances in Consumer Research*, 29, 100–101.

Korgaonkar, P.K. and Wolin, L.D. (1999) A multivariate analysis of web usage, *Journal of Advertising Research*, 39(2), 53–68.

Kotler, P., Armstrong, G., Saunders, J. and Wong, V. (2001) *Principles of Marketing*, 3rd European edn, Financial Times/Prentice Hall, Harlow.

Lecinksi, J. (2012) Winning the zero moment of truth. Published by Google, **www.zeromomentoftruth.com**.

Macdonald, E., Wilson, H. and Konus, U. (2012) Tracking the customer's journey to purchase, *Harvard Business Review*. Blog by Emma Macdonald, Hugh Wilson, and Umut Konus, 11:12 am, 17 August.

Malmsten, E., Portanger, E. and Drazin, C. (2001) *Boo Hoo. A* **Dot.com** *Story from Concept to Catastrophe*, Random House, London.

Malone, T.W., Yates, J. and Benjamin, R.I. (1997) Electronic markets and electronic hierarchies, *Communications of the ACM*, 30(6), 484–97.

McDonald, M. and Wilson, H. (2002) *New Marketing: Transforming the Corporate Future*, Butterworth-Heinemann, Oxford.

Menteth, H., Arbuthnot, S. and Wilson, H. (2005) Multi-channel experience consistency: evidence from Lexus, *Interactive Marketing*, 6(4), 317–25.

New Media Age (1999) Will **boo.com** scare off the competition? by Budd Margolis, 22 July.

New Media Age (2005) Personal lender, by Dominic Dudley, 18 August.

Osterwald, A. and Pigneur, Y. (2010) Business model generation site: A handbook for visionaries, game changers and challengers(**www.businessmodelgeneration.com**), Wiley, London.

Osterwalder, A., Pigneur, Y., Bernarda, G., Smith, A. and Papadakos, T. (2014) Value proposition design: how to create products and services customers want (Strategyzer), **https://strategyzer.com/value-proposition-design**.

Porter, M. (2001) Strategy and the Internet, *Harvard Business Review*, March, 62–78.

Prentiss, P. (2013). Implosion at Ecomom. An unedited letter by Phillip Prentiss, Scribd, **www.scribd.com/doc/137629166/Ecomom-Post-Mortem,** and later published on Business Insider (2013).

Robinson, P., Faris, C. and Wind, Y. (1967) *Industrial Buying and Creative Marketing*, Allyn and Bacon, Boston.

Rose, S. and Hair, N.C. (2011) Online customer experience: a reveiw of the busienss-to-consumer online purchase context, *International Journal of Management Reviews*, 13(1), 24–39. doi:**10.1111/j.1468–2370.2010.00280.x.**

San-Martine, S., Lopez-Catalan, B. and Ramon-Jeronimo, M. (2013) Mobile shoppers: types, drivers and impediments, *Journal of Organisational Computing and Electronic Commerce*, 23(4), 350–371. doi:**10.1080/10919392.2013.837793.**

Sarkar, M., Butler, B. and Steinfield, C. (1996) Intermediaries and cybermediaries. A continuing role for mediating players in the electronic marketplace, *Journal of Computer Mediated Communication*, 1(3).

Seybold, P. and Marshak, R. (2001) *The Customer Revolution*, Crown Business, New York.

Shui, E. and Dawson, J. (2004) Comparing the impacts of technology and national culture on online usage and purchase from a four country perspective, *Journal of Retailing and Consumer Services*, 11(6), 385–94.

Slyke, C.V. (2002) Gender differences in perceptions of web-based shopping, *Communications of the ACM*, 47, 82–6.

Stokes, K. (2015) What's a brand's consumer persona? *AMP Blog* (**www.ampagency.com/blog/insights-lab-incubator-consumer-persona**).

Smart Insights (2014) What influences purchase of your product or service? [Infographic]. Blog post by Dan Bosomworth, 12 August, **www.smartinsights.com/marketplace-analysis/consumer-buying-behaviour/what-influences-purchase/**.

Swaminathan, V., Lepkowska-White, E. and Rao, B.P. (1999) Browsers or buyers in cyberspace? An investigation of factors influencing electronic exchange, *Journal of Computer-Mediated Communication*, 5(2), 1–19.

Tan, F. and Sutherland, P. (2004). Online consumer trust: a multi-dimensional model, *Journal of Electronic Commerce in Organisations*, 2, 41–59.

Thomas, J. and Sullivan, U. (2005) Managing marketing communications with multichannel customers, *Journal of Marketing*, 69(October), 239–51.

Timmers, P. (1999) *Electronic Commerce Strategies and Models for Business-to-Business Trading*, Wiley, Chichester.

Tsai, S.-P. (2005) Integrated marketing as management if holistic customer experience, *Business Horizons*, 8, 431–41.

Venkatraman, N. (2000) Five steps to a dot-com strategy: how to find your footing on the web, *Sloan Management Review*, Spring, 15–28.

Watts, D. and Dodds, S. (2007) Influentials, networks, and public opinion formation, *Journal of Consumer Research*, 34(4), 441–58.

Wodtke, C. (2002) *Information Architecture: Blueprints of the Web*, New Riders, Indianapolis.

Wolfinbarger, M. and Gilly, M (2003) etailQ: dimensionalizing, measuring and predicting etail Quality, *Journal of Retailing*, 79(3), 183–98.

Weblinks

A directory of Internet marketing links, including sources for statistics from the Internet environment, is maintained by Dave Chaffey at **www.smartinsights.com**. Latest updates are available at **http://bit.ly/smartstatistics**.

Sources for Internet adoption statistics

Online research aggregators and publishers

* ClickZ Internet research (**www.clickz.com/stats**).
* eMarketer (**www.emarketer.com**). Includes reports on media spend based on compilations of other analysts. Fee-based service with some free data available.
* Internet World Stats (**www.internetworldstats.com**). Compiles global statistics by region country from other sources on this list.
* Marketing Charts (**www.marketingcharts.com**). Has an online media section with visual summaries of reports mainly from the audience media panels.

Government sources on Internet use and adoption

* European government (**http://europa.eu.int/comm/eurostat**).
* OECD (**www.oecd.org**). OECD broadband research (**www.oecd.org/sti/ict/broadband**).
* UK government (**wwww.statistics.gov.uk**).
* Ofcom (**www.ofcom.org.uk**). Ofcom is the independent regulator and competition authority for the UK communications industries, with responsibilities across television, radio, telecommunications and wireless communications services and has in-depth reports on communications markets.
* US government (**www.usa.gov**) government business and general national statistics.

Online audience panel media consumption and use data

These are fee-based data, but contain useful free data within press release sections.
* Comscore (**www.comscore.com**).
* ExperianHitwise (**www.hitwise.com**). Hitwise blog (**http://weblogs.hitwise.com**). Sample reports from Hitwise on consumer search behaviour and importance of different online intermediaries. Netratings (**www.netratings.com**).

Other major online research providers

* The European Interactive Advertising Association (**www.eiaa.net**). The EIAA and IAB have merged to form a powerful pan-European trade organisation with surveys of media consumption.
* The Pew Internet & American Life Project (**www.pewinternet.org**), produces reports that explore the impact of the Internet on families, communities, work and home, daily life, education, healthcare, and civic and political life.

Chapter 3
The online macro-environment

Chapter at a glance

Main topics

- The rate of environment change 123
- Technological forces 123
- Economic forces 142
- Political forces 144
- Legal forces 147
- Social forces 164
- Cultural forces 165

Case studies

Digital marketing in practice
The Smart Insights interview with Fred Bassett of Blue Latitude on online marketplace analysis 121
Case study 3: Zopa launches a new lending model 167

Learning objectives

After reading this chapter, you should be able to:

- Identify how the macro-environment affects an organisation's digital marketing strategy, planning, implementation and performance
- Consider legal, moral and ethical constraints of digital marketing
- Identify aspects of each of the macro-environmental forces that are particularly relevant to digital marketing.

Questions for marketers

Key questions for marketing managers related to this chapter are:

- How important are macro-environmental changes to my digital marketing strategy?
- How can I ensure my online marketing activities are consistent with evolving culture and ethical standards of online communities?
- How important is it for me to understand technological innovations?
- Which laws am I subject to when marketing online?
- How is social media marketing likely to impact on my business and what changes do I need to make in order to react to social changes in the online marketplace?
- What are the political influences which could influence my digital marketing planning?
- How do I keep up in a constantly changing marketing environment?

**Scan code
to find the
latest updates
for topics in
this chapter**

Links to other chapters

This chapter provides a foundation for later chapters on digital marketing strategy and implementation:

- Chapter 4 looks at the development of a digital marketing strategy
- Chapter 5 considers the Internet and the marketing mix
- Chapter 6 explores relationship marketing using the Internet
- Chapter 7 looks at how to deliver the online customer experience
- Chapter 8 describes campaign planning for digital media.

Introduction

In Chapter 2, we reviewed the influences on customers which shape the online marketplace or trading environment. In this chapter, we review how broader, macro-economic forces can influence digital marketing. These are forces which affect the trading environment but companies operating have limited direct influence over.

An indication of the challenge of assessing the macro-environment factors is presented in Figure 3.1. This figure of the 'waves of change' shows how fluctuations in the characteristics of different aspects of the environment vary at different rates through time. The manager has to constantly scan the environment and assess which changes are relevant to their sphere of influence. Changes in social culture, and particularly pop culture (what's hot and what's not), tend to be very rapid. Introduction of new technologies and changes in their popularity tend to be frequent too and need to be assessed. Governmental and legal changes tend to happen over longer timescales, although, since this is only a generalisation, new laws can be introduced relatively fast. The trick for managers is to identify those factors which are important in the context of e-commerce which are critical to competitiveness and service delivery and monitor these. We believe it is the technological and legal factors which are most important to managing e-commerce, so we focus on these.

In the marketing literature, there are widely used mnemonics, which aim to act as an *aide-memoire* for the macro-environmental forces, e.g. PEST, SLEPT and PESTLE, where each letter represents a slightly different arrangement of the following macro forces:

- Political forces
- Economic forces
- Social forces
- Technological forces
- Legal forces
- Environmental forces

For the digital marketer, the most important to task is to carry out a thorough assessment of the forces that are shaping the online marketing environment and identify which forces

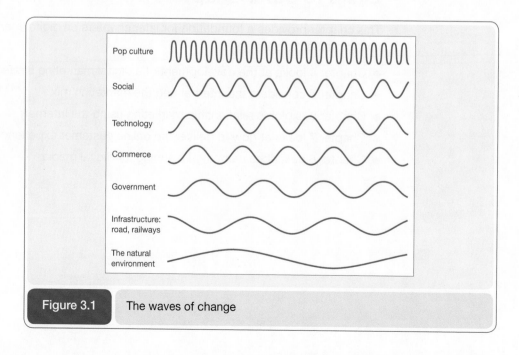

| Figure 3.1 | The waves of change |

have implications for their own marketing planning and strategic initiatives. The chapter proceeds by exploring each of the macro-environmental forces in the following order:

- *Technological forces:* changes in technology which influence marketing opportunities; create new product development opportunities; introduce new ways to access target markets through channel integration; create new forms of access platforms and applications.
- *Economic forces:* cause variation in economic conditions; affect trading opportunities; influence consumer spending and business performance; have significant implications for digital marketing planning.
- *Political forces:* national governments and transnational organisations have an important role in determining the future adoption and control of the Internet and the rules by which it is governed.
- *Legal forces:* determine the methods by which products can be promoted and sold online. Laws and ethical guidelines that seek to safeguard individuals' rights to privacy and businesses' to free trade.
- *Social forces:* cultural diversity among digital communities, which influences use of the Internet and the services businesses provide online.

The main reason for keeping track of changes in the macro-environment is to be aware of how changes in social behaviour, new laws and technological innovation can create opportunities or threats. Organisations that monitor and respond effectively to their macro-environment can create differentiation and competitive advantages which enable the business to survive and prosper. Given the significance of technology, we begin with this force as it is arguably a top priority for digital marketing planning.

Digital marketing in practice   The Smart Insights interview

Fred Bassett of Blue Latitude on online marketplace analysis

Overview and main concepts

This interview with Fred Bassett of digital strategy consulting strategy firm Blue Latitude outlines a structured approach to online marketplace analysis in order to inform digital marketing strategy.

The interview

Q. Fred, you say there is an increasing demand for online marketplace analysis today. Why do you think this is? Surely most companies already understand their marketplace

Fred Bassett: The main driver is simply competitive pressure. Many companies have now optimised essential processes such as search marketing, email marketing and site conversion. This has led to many online markets becoming highly competitive environments in which improving performance is increasingly challenging.

Marketplace analysis helps identify opportunities for growth from discovering gaps in the market that competitors aren't exploiting. In strategic terms, situation analysis helps identify gaps where customer segments aren't well served by existing propositions.

At a more tactical level, we also identify quick wins in terms of online media allocation, PR and partnership opportunities – where media investments such as paid search or display ads could be better spent.

Q. What process do you follow in your environment analysis and mapping?

Fred Bassett: We have developed a five-stage situation analysis process. This starts with Business Insight Analysis which aims to identify the current goals and the challenges of the business as highlighted by an online-specific SWOT analysis. Next is User Insight; since our approach is centred on the customer, we spend a lot of time understanding different customer clusters. We use existing research and data, or perform new qualitative and quantitative research to define segments and personas for different customer groups.

Then we turn to Competitive Insight, where we analyse purchase behaviour in the context of the journeys web users take as they select products or seek information online and offline. For example, what sequence of search terms do they use as they visit different sites, which types of sites do they visit and how does the whole customer journey map out? The competitive insight analysis also involves benchmarking of the propositions of different competitors and sites.

We use a proprietary predictive modelling tool to assess which are the most influential types of site that make an impact on purchase. This could involve analysis of tens of thousands of user journeys.

For each persona, we then create a probability model which indicates the influencing effect of each type of site. This is validated against data available from web analytics.

The final output is an environment mapping for each persona which summarises the influence of different sites such as portals, blogs, social media sites, search engines, etc. against their current and future potential value for the business in terms of opportunities for partnering, PR or media spend.

Q. Wow that must require integration of many data sources. Which data sources typically inform the predictive model?

Fred Bassett: Well, it will vary a fair bit between sectors, but there are certainly many sources we leverage – over 20 in some cases.

Typical external data includes audience data from the likes of Hitwise and comScore and keyword usage tools. This is blended with internal data such as historical search data, web analytics and purchase data. For customer insights within a sector we will also use analyst sources such as Forrester or Gartner.

One of the benefits of using data in this way is that we can work in and compare a brand's online activities in different territories. We have performed situation analyses in over 22 territories across Europe, Asia, North and South America.

Q. How is the output from the model used by businesses?

Fred Bassett: We find the environment map [similar to those recommended at the start of Chapter 2] gives marketing directors the confidence to present a clear digital strategy based on evidence-based insights. We use the environment map to help formulate a strategy with the client and then we map this strategy against different business objectives in areas of customer acquisition, conversion and retention.

Within each of these areas, tactics are developed which may cover a number of areas from targeting new audiences, refining customer propositions and content or developing long-term partnership arrangements.

The visual mapping we use makes it easier for others in the business to understand and buy into the approaches used.

Q. Which types of sectors have you applied this model to?

Fred Bassett: The model scales well across different markets. We have used this approach on markets as varied as retail, pharmaceutical, not-for-profit and financial services.

The rate of environment change

In the 'digital world', changes in social culture and particularly pop culture (what's 'hot' and what's not) tend to be very rapid. Introduction of new technologies and changes in their popularity tend to occur frequently. Government and legal changes tend to happen over longer time scales. Therefore, digital marketers need to be alert to the forces that are important in the context of their own trading environment so they can aim to ensure the competitiveness of the business. They should also develop the capacity to respond to environmental changes and the emerging opportunities and threats by developing **strategic agility**, a concept strongly associated with knowledge management theory and based on developing a sound process for reviewing marketplace opportunities and threats and then selecting the appropriate strategy options.

Strategic agility is important for digital marketers to understand and they should consider how to ensure:

Strategic agility
The capability to innovate and so gain competitive advantage within a marketplace by monitoring changes within an organisation's marketplace, and then efficiently evaluating alternative strategies, selecting, reviewing and implementing appropriate candidate strategies.

1 collection, dissemination and evaluation of different information sources from the micro- and macro-environment;
2 processes for generating and reviewing the relevance of new strategies based on creating new value for customers;
3 research into potential customer value against the business value generated;
4 implementation of prototypes of new functionality to deliver customer value;
5 measurement and review of results from prototypes to revise further to improve proposition or to end a trial.

Technological forces

Marketers need to understand digital and Internet technology and terminology, as making mistakes can have significant consequences. In this section, we explore digital technology, the Internet and web technology; we will also consider digital security, technology convergence and emerging technology. These are key factors, which currently have significant implications for digital marketing planning. As an example of the impact of the opportunities afforded by technology, Activity 3.1 explores the options for delivering mobile services to customers, which is a current concern for marketers.

Internet
The physical network that links computers across the globe. It consists of the infrastructure of network servers and communication links between them that are used to hold and transport the vast amount of information.

World Wide Web
The World Wide Web is a medium for publishing information and providing services on the Internet. It is accessed through *web browsers*, which display site *content* on different *web pages*. The content making up *websites* is stored on web servers.

Web server
Used to store the web pages accessed by web browsers. They may also contain databases of customer or product information, which can be queried and retrieved using a browser.

A short introduction to Internet technology

The **Internet** has existed since the late 1960s, when a limited number of computers were connected for military and research purposes in the United States to form the ARPAnet. The recent dramatic growth in the use of the Internet occurred because of the development of the **World Wide Web**. This became a commercial proposition in 1993 after development of the original concept by Tim Berners-Lee, a British scientist working at CERN in Switzerland in 1989. Today, the main principles of web technology hold true. Web content is stored on **web server** computers and then accessed by users who run **web browser** software such as Google Chrome, Microsoft Internet Explorer, Apple Safari or Mozilla Firefox which display the information and allow users to interact and select links to access other websites. Rich media, such as Flash applications, audio or video content, can also be stored on a web server, or a specialist **streaming media server**.

Promoting website addresses is important to marketing communications. The technical name for web addresses is **uniform (universal) resource locator (URL)**.

Activity 3.1	Environmental forces: the importance of the mobile web

Context

Many years have been heralded as 'The year of mobile', where adoption of mobile web access and mobile commerce would grow rapidly. As long ago as 1999/2000 this was the case, yet if companies had invested in mobile facilities then, it's unlikely they would have seen a return from their investment. Today, use of mobile devices and smartphones is more commonplace, so it's important for companies to consider how they can use these technologies within their marketing. This activity reviews the demand for popularity of mobile experiences in your country.

Activity

Use publicly available data to assess the importance of consumer access to mobile devices for different types of business. Determine for your country:

- The percentage of consumers accessing websites through mobile (divided into table and smartphone users and for different demographics).
- The percentage of visits buying online via smartphones and tablets (ideally broken down into different product categories).
- The proportion of readers who access their email and social media via a smartphone.
- The relative popularity of mobile sites compared with mobile apps for different purposes.

Web browser
Browsers such as Google Chrome, Mozilla Firefox, Apple Safari and Microsoft Internet Explorer provide an easy method of accessing and viewing information stored as HTML web documents on different web servers.

Streaming media server
A specialist server used to broadcast audio (e.g. podcasts) or video (e.g. IPTV or webcast presentations). Served streams can be unicast (a separate copy of stream is served for each recipient), multicast (recipients share streams) or peer-to-peer.

Uniform (universal) resource locator (URL)
A web address used to locate a web page on a web server.

Web addresses are structured in a standard way as follows: **www.domain-name.extension/filename.html**

The 'domain-name' refers to the name of the web server and is usually selected to be the same as the name of the company, and the extension will indicate its type. The 'extension' is also commonly known as the generic top-level domain (gTLD).

Common gTLDs are:

- **.com** represents an international or American company (e.g. **www.travelocity.com**);
- **.org** are not-for-profit organisations (e.g. **www.greenpeace.org**);
- **.mobi** was introduced in 2006 for sites configured for mobile phones;
- **.net** is a network provider (e.g. **www.amakai.net**).

There are also country code top-level domains (ccTLDs) maintained by the Internet Corporation for Assigned Names and Numbers (ICANN), e.g.:

- **.co.uk** represents a company based in the UK (e.g. **www.thomascook.co.uk**);
- **.au, .ca, .de, .es, .fi, .fr, .it, .nl**, etc. represent other countries (the **co.uk** syntax is an anomaly!);
- **.ac.uk** is a UK-based university or other higher education institution (e.g. **www.cranfield.ac.uk**);
- **.org.uk** is for an organisation focussing on a single country (e.g. **www.mencap.org.uk**).

In 2011, the Internet Corporation for Assigned Names and Numbers, the not-for-profit organisation dedicated to registering, maintaining and coordinating the Internet addressing system, began a programme of expansion for gTLD names. According to Beckstrom (2011), their aim is to give Internet users more choice and create business opportunities. Between 1998 and 2010, 22 gTLDs came into general use but ICANN's expansion programme for new gTLDs will allow the introduction of many more domains. However, the use of gTLDs, country-level domain names (ccTLDs) such as .au, .ca, .cn, co.uk, co.nz,

.de, .fr and the universal **.com** for US and pureplay companies is likely to remain dominant since marketers perceive that consumers like the familiarity and trust of companies using these domains. By 2015 ICANN had released more than 1000 new gTLDs, This created an opportunity for brands to take more control over their corporate image online but also increases the potential risk for fraud and counterfeiting. ICANN has set up the Trademark Clearing House to help brands set up their own gTLD and also to help protect brands' identities. The new gTLDs to give some flexibility for startups to create brand names consistent with a web address. The lack of names had given rise to many creative brand names since web addresses for gTLDs were typically not available for dictionary-related words.

Domain names are part of a company's brand property and digital brand managers should protect brand abuse of domains by other companies that might register variants of competitors' brand domain names.

URL strategy
A defined approach to forming URLs including the use of capitalisation, hyphenation and sub-domains for different brands and different locations. This has implications for promoting a website offline through promotional or vanity URLs, search engine optimisation and findability.

A clean URL which fits many of these aims is **www.domain.com/folder-name/document-name**. Care must be taken with capitalisation since Linux servers parse capitals differently from lower-case letters.

URL strategy

Today marketers often need to discuss different options for describing addresses for their content for campaigns. For example, is a country or blog referenced on a sub-domain or a sub-folder? How are different types of content or products structured within a folder hierarchy? The defined methods used are known for businesses as **URL strategy**. Digital marketing insight 3.1 describes some of the terminology you may encounter, as explained by Google.

How does the Internet work?

In this section, we briefly examine some of the fundamental aspects of Internet technology. It's important that marketers understand the technological underpinning of digital

---

Digital marketing insight 3.1   **What's in a URL?**

A great example of different URL components is provided by Google engineer Matt Cutts (2007). He gives this example: **http://video.google.co.uk:80/videoplay?docid=-7246927612831078230&hl=en#00h02m30s**

Here are some of the components of the url:

- The *protocol* is http. Other protocols include https, ftp, etc.
- The *host* or *hostname* is **video.google.co.uk**.
- The *sub-domain* is **video**.
- The *domain name* is **google.co.uk**.
- The *top-level domain or TLD* is uk (also known as gTLD). The uk domain is also referred to as a country-code top-level domain or ccTLD. For **google.com**, the TLD would be com.
- The *second-level domain* (SLD) is **co.uk**.
- The *port* is 80, which is the default port for web servers (not usually used in URLs, when it is the default although all web servers broadcast on ports).
- The *path* is **/videoplay**. Path typically refers to a file or location on the web server, e.g. **/directory/file.html**.
- The URL parameter is docid and the value of that parameter is – 724692761 2831078230. These are often called the name, value pair. URLs often have lots of parameters. Parameters start with a question mark (?) and are separated with an ampersand (&).
- The *anchor* or fragment is '**#00h02m30s**'.

Client–server
The client–server architecture consists of client computers such as PCs sharing resources such as a database stored on a more powerful server computer.

Internet service provider
A provider enabling home or business users a connection to access the Internet. They can also host web-based applications.

Backbones
High-speed communications links used to enable Internet communications across a country and internationally.

Static (fixed) web page
A page on the web server that is invariant.

Dynamic web page
A page that is created in real time, often with reference to a database query, in response to a user request.

Transaction log file
A web server file that records all page requests.

Web analytics
Techniques used to assess and improve the contribution of e-marketing to a business, including reviewing traffic volume, referrals, clickstreams, online reach data customer satisfaction surveys, leads and sales.

Content
Content is the design, text and graphical information that forms a web page. Good content is the key to attracting customers to a website and retaining their interest or achieving repeat visits

marketing. This enables them to discuss technology options with systems vendors and technical staff and take the right decisions about which technologies to adopt. Many digital marketers are active bloggers or engaged in social networks since this enables them to experience, first-hand, the latest developments and use tools to analyse what works and what doesn't.

The Internet is a large-scale **client–server** system where content is transmitted from client PCs whose users request services from server computers that hold content, rich media and host business applications that deliver the services in response to requests. Client PCs within homes and businesses are connected to the Internet via local **Internet service providers (ISPs)** which, in turn, are linked to larger ISPs with connection to the major national and international infrastructure or **backbones**.

Infrastructure components of the Internet

Figure 3.2 shows the basic process by which web browsers communicate with web servers. A request from the client PC is executed when the user types in a web address, clicks on a hyperlink or fills in an online form such as a search. This request is then sent to the ISP and routed across the Internet to the destination server. The server then returns the requested web page if it is a **static (fixed) web page**. If it requires reference to a database, such as a request for product information, it will pass the query on to a database server and will then return this to the customer as a **dynamic web page**. Information on all file requests such as images, rich media and pages is stored in a **transaction log file** or via a **web analytics** system such as Google Analytics (**www.google.com/analytics**), which records the page requested, the time it was made and the source of the enquiry, as explained in Chapter 9.

Web page standards

The information, graphics and interactive elements that make up the web pages of a site are collectively referred to as **content**. Different standards exist for text, graphics and multimedia, many coordinated by the W3C (Digital marketing insight 3.2).

http 'send' communication

Server returns page requested

User requests page

http 'get' communication

ISP   'The Internet'   ISP

Server running web server software

Client PC running web browser

Transaction log file

HTML and graphics files

Database and applications servers

| Figure 3.2 | Information exchange between a web browser and a web server |

Digital marketing insight 3.2	W3C

The World Wide Web Consortium (W3C, www.w3.org) community enables the web to expand and develop by building an Open Web Platform to support and foster innovations and future sustainability for the web. Founded by Tim Berners-Lee, the inventor of HTTP protocol, which underpins web technology, W3C is an organisation which works to maintain international standards for the web. W3C provides a forum for discussion on the development and growth of the web, facilitates software development and acts as an educational platform. W3C aims to ensure that protocols and standards are maintained between its members and organisations across the globe. It is important for managers of company websites to be familiar with the latest standards which are being proposed, so they can assess and plan compliance with standards in the future.

Source: www.w3.org/2011/01/w3c2011.html; and http://en.wikipedia.org/wiki/World_Wide_Web_Consortium

Text information – HTML (Hypertext Markup Language)

HTML (Hypertext Markup Language)
A standard format used to define the text and layout of web pages. HTML files usually have the extension.HTML or .HTM.

Web page content is formatted and rendered by the browser software using **HTML** (or XHTML) **Hypertext Markup Language.** HTML is an international standard established by the W3C and is intended to ensure that any web page written according to the definitions in the standard will appear the same in any web browser.

A description of HTML markup is outside the scope of this text (see **www.w3schools. com** for tutorials). In brief, HTML code is used to construct pages using codes or instruction tags, such as <title>, to indicate to the web browser what is displayed. The <title> tag indicates what appears at the top of the web browser window. Each starting tag has a corresponding end tag, usually marked by a '/', for example bold text is used to embolden 'bold text'.

Cascading style sheets (CSS)
Enable web designers to define standard styles (e.g. fonts, spacing and colours) to hypertext mark-up language documents. By separating the presentation style of documents from the content of documents, CSS simplifies web authoring and site maintenance since style can be defined across a whole site (or sections of sites).

Cascading Style Sheets (CSS) are now used by most websites to enable standard styling and interaction features across a site. Visit CSS Zen Garden (**www.csszengarden.com**) or view Figure 7.11 to see examples of how CSS effectively decouples style from content.

Text information and data – XML (eXtensible Markup Language)

Metadata
Literally, data about data – a format describing the structure and content of data.

XML or eXtensible Markup Language
A standard for transferring structured data, unlike HTML which is purely presentational.

When the early version of HTML was designed by Tim Berners-Lee at CERN, he based it on the existing standard for representation of documents. This standard was SGML, the Standard Generalised Markup Language, which was ratified by the ISO in 1986. SGML uses tags to identify the different elements of a document such as title and chapters. While HTML proved powerful in providing a standard method of displaying information that was easy to learn, it was purely presentational. It lacked the ability to describe the data on web pages. A **metadata** language providing information about data contained within pages is much more powerful and is provided by **XML** or **eXtensible Markup Language**, produced in February 1998. This is also based on SGML. The key word describing XML is 'extensible'. This means that new markup tags can be created that facilitate the searching and exchange of information. For example, product information on a web page could use the XML tags <NAME>, <DESCRIPTION>, <COLOUR> and <PRICE>. The tags can effectively act as a standard set of database field descriptions so that data can be exchanged through price comparison sites.

The importance of XML for data integration is indicated by its incorporation by Microsoft into its BizTalk server for B2B integration and the creation of the ebXML (electronic business XML) standard by Microsoft's rival, Sun Microsystems. We will see in Chapter 9 that the basic metadata that each page of a website can use is important for search engine optimisation (SEO). SEO is increasingly used by digital markets to ensure their websites get noticed by target audiences.

Graphical images (GIF, JPEG and PNG files)

GIF (Graphics Interchange Format)
A graphics format and compression algorithm best used for simple graphics.

JPEG (Joint Photographic Experts Group)
A graphics format and compression algorithm best used for photographs.

Graphics produced by graphic designers or captured using digital cameras can be readily incorporated into web pages as images. **GIF (Graphics Interchange Format)** and **JPEG (Joint Photographic Experts Group)** refer to two standard file formats most commonly used to present images on web pages. GIF files are limited to 256 colours and are best used for small, simple graphics, such as banner adverts, while JPEG is best used for larger images where image quality is important, such as photographs. Both formats use image compression technology to minimise the size of downloaded files. Portable Network Graphics (**.PNG**) is growing in popularity since it is a patent- and licence-free standard file format approved by the World Wide Web Consortium to replace the GIF file format.

Animated graphical information (Flash and plug-ins)

Plug-in
An add-on program to a web browser providing extra functionality such as animation.

Plug-ins are additional programs, sometimes referred to as 'helper applications', and work in association with the web browser to provide features not present in the basic web browser. The best-known plug-in is probably that for Adobe Acrobat which is used to display documents in **.pdf** format (**www.adobe.com**) and the Macromedia Flash and Shockwave products for producing interactive graphics (**www.macromedia.com**).

Audio and video standards

Traditionally, sound and video or 'rich media' have been stored as the Microsoft standards .WMA and .AVI. Alternative standards are RM3, MP3 or MP4 MPEG. Film is now widely used for both personal and corporate communications.

Activity 3.2	Using video for digital marketing

Purpose

To consider the scope for using video for digital marketing communications.

Activity

1 Identify all the different types of site that incorporate video. You should include broad video hosting sites like YouTube or Vimeo, but also specialist sites.
2 Identify different ways in which businesses can use video to engage audiences to support awareness-building and conversion and plot them on Figure 3.3. This is a blank version of the Content Marketing Matrix which is described in Chapter 8 as a method of reviewing different types of content.

Identify applications for the different focus of sites defined in Chapter 1, i.e. Transactional e-commerce site (e.g. retail, travel, financial services), relationship building site, brand site and publisher.

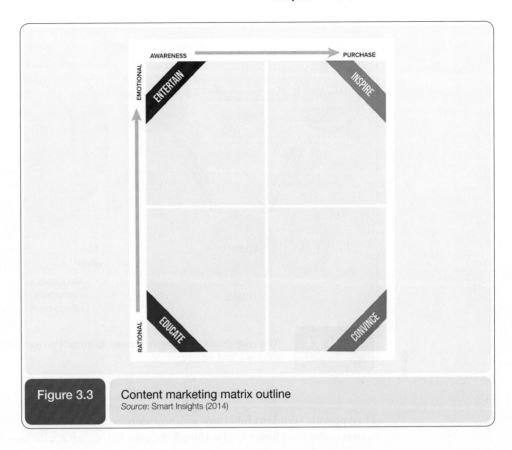

Figure 3.3	Content marketing matrix outline
	Source: Smart Insights (2014)

The difference between the Internet, intranets and extranets

Intranet
A network within a single company that enables access to company information using the familiar tools of the Internet such as email and web browsers. Only staff within the company can access the intranet, which will be password-protected.

Intranet and **extranet** are two terms that arose in the 1990s to describe applications of Internet technology with specific audiences, rather than anyone with access to the Internet. They are still used within marketing for describing access to content. Access to an intranet is limited by username and password to company staff, while an extranet can only be accessed by authorised third parties such as registered customers, suppliers and distributors. This relationship between the Internet, intranets and extranets is shown in Figure 3.4. You can see that an intranet is effectively a private company internet with access available to staff only. An extranet permits access to trusted third parties, and the Internet provides global access.

Extranet
Formed by extending the intranet beyond a company to customers, suppliers, collaborators or even competitors. This is again password-protected to prevent access by general Internet users.

Extranets such as Dell's Premier Pages provide exciting opportunities to communicate with major customers since tailored information such as special promotions, electronic catalogues and order histories can be provided on a web page personalised for each customer.

Web application frameworks and application servers

Web application frameworks
A standard programming framework based on reusable library functions for creating dynamic websites through a programming language.

Web application frameworks provide a foundation for building dynamic interactive websites and web services. They use standard programming conventions or Application Programming Interface (APIs) in combination with data storage to achieve different tasks such as simply adding a user to a system or rendering the different page elements of a site.

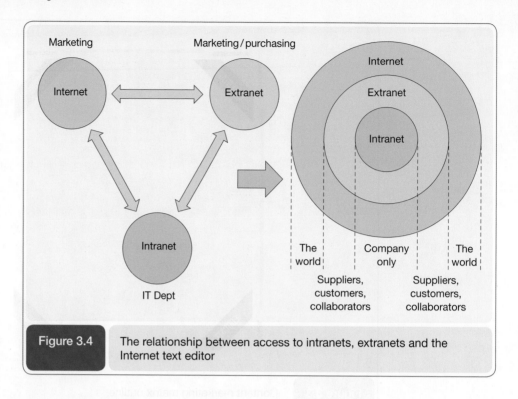

| Figure 3.4 | The relationship between access to intranets, extranets and the Internet text editor |

They provide standard functions in libraries to make it quicker to develop functionality than starting from lower-level coding. Functions in the web application framework are executed by **web application servers** which are software processes running on the server that accept and action requests via the principal web server software (e.g. Apache or Microsoft Information Server). The Common Gateway Interface (CGI) was a forerunner of this concept since it enabled standard functions to be accessed on a server, for example to perform form validation.

Web application server
Software processes which is accessed by a standard programming interface (API) of a web application framework to serve dynamic website functionality in response to requests received from browsers.

Digital security

Security is a key technology factor for marketers consider as it is a major concern for Internet users everywhere. Digital marketers need to understand security issues and the risks they might encounter in order to manage their online operations effectively. This is part of the reason why we are discussing security in this chapter. From a consumer or merchant point of view, these are the main security risks involved in an e-commerce transaction:

- confidential details or passwords accessed on user's computer, for example through keylogging software or malware;
- transaction or credit card details stolen in transit, for example through 'packet sniffing' software;
- customer's credit card details stolen from merchant's server, for example through hacking;
- customer's details accessed by company staff (or through a hacker who is in the building and has used 'social engineering' techniques to find information);
- merchants or customers are not who they claim to be and the innocent party can be drawn into a fraudulent trading situation.

As Internet-derived commerce and communications play an increasingly important role in economic growth, the burden of ensuring secure and safe passage through the Internet is increasing. According to Rueda-Sabater and Derosby (2011) there are five features of the Internet's evolution to consider which add to risks of what they call the *Axes of uncertainty*:

1 Growth in the global economy and in the markets around the Internet will occur primarily in countries that we now categorise as 'emerging'.
2 Governance of the Internet with its loose structure will be open to occasional Internet disruptions, including malicious ones.
3 Digital natives – people who have been raised on the Internet since late 1990 – will relate to the Internet in markedly different ways than do most of today's adults. Members of these web-savvy 'Net generations' will tend to view the Internet as an extender of their own cognitive capabilities and as a portal to a virtual experience.
4 Today's QWERTY keyboard and the language and interface hurdles it represents will no longer be the primary means of relating to the Internet. A combination of voice recognition, bio-sensing, gestural interfaces, touch-screen versatility and other technologies will allow us to input data and commands without keys. One major consequence of this change will be an explosion in the number of people who can use the Internet, as well as in the types of things they can do.
5 Consumers will pay for Internet connectivity in a much wider range of ways, both direct and indirect, compared to today's predominantly flat-price subscriptions. As high bandwidth applications explode, the need to allocate available network capacity efficiently across time and users will be a major issue. The spread of wireless connectivity will also open up many new pricing models for network access, such as easily bundling connectivity and services.

The potential increase in security risks reinforces the need for everyone, not just digital marketers, to understand and be able to assess security risks. In this sub-section we assess the measures that can be taken to reduce the risk of these breaches of e-commerce security. We start by reviewing some of the theory of online security and then review the techniques used.

For a summary of the main security risks for a website owner that must be managed within the design, see the summary in Digital marketing insight 3.3.

Digital marketing insight 3.3   The main website security risks

This summary is provided by specialist website security consultants Watson Hall (www.watsonhall.com). They consider the top ten Internet security risks to be:

1 Validation of input and output data

All data used by the website (from users, other servers, other websites and internal systems) must be validated for type (e.g. numeric, date, string), length (e.g. 200 characters maximum, or a positive integer), syntax (e.g. product codes begin with two letters and are followed by five digits) and business rules (e.g. televisions can only cost between £100 and £2000, an order can contain at most 20 items, daily credit limit must not be exceeded). All data written as output (displayed) needs to be safe to view in a browser, email client or other software and the integrity of any data that is returned must be checked. Utilising Asynchronous JavaScript and XML (AJAX) or Adobe Flex increases complexity and the possible attack vectors.

2 Direct data access (and theft)

If data exists, it can potentially be viewed or extracted. Avoid storing data that you do not need on the website and its database(s), for example some data relating to payment cards should never be stored. Poorly developed systems may allow access to data through SQL injection compromises, insufficient input and output data validation (see point 1 above) or poor system security.

3 Data poisoning

If users can amend or delete data inappropriately and this is then used to update your internal systems, business information is being lost. This can be hard to detect and it is important that the business rules are examined and enforced to validate data changes to ensure that poisoning is not occurring. If poisoning is not detected until well after it has occurred, it may be impossible to recover the original data.

4 Malicious file execution

Uploaded files or other data feeds may not be what they seem. Never allow user-supplied input to be used in any file name or path (e.g. URLs or file system references). Uploaded files may also contain a malicious payload so should not be stored in web accessible locations.

5 Authentication and session management

Websites rely on identifying users to provide access permissions to data and functions. If authentication (verification of identity, registration and logging in), authorisation (granting access rights) and session management (keeping track of the identity of a logged in user while browsing a website) can be circumvented or altered, then a user could access resources that are prohibited. Beware especially of how password reminders, remember-me, change password, log out and updating account details are handled, how session tokens are used and always have login forms on dedicated and encrypted (SSL) pages.

6 System architecture and configuration

The information system architecture model should address the sensitivity of data identified during the requirements and specification phase of a website project. This may entail having separate web, application and database servers or involve clustering, load balancing or virtualisation. Additional security issues can be created through the way the live environment is configured. Sufficient and safe logging, monitoring and alerting facilities need to be built in to allow audit.

7 Phishing

Phishing, where users are misled into believing some other entity is or belongs to an own organisation (email messages and websites are the most common combination), is best tackled through user education, but the way the website is designed, its architecture and how it communicates with users can reduce the risk.

8 Denial of service

While malicious users might try to swamp the web server with a vast number of requests or actions that degrade its performance (filling up logs, uploading large files, repeatedly undertaking tasks that require a lot of memory), **denial of service attacks** include locking out valid user accounts or those caused by coding problems (e.g. memory leaks, resources not being released).

9 System information leakage

Web servers, errors, staff, partner organisations and search engines can all be the source of important information about your website – its technologies, business logic and security methods. An attacker can use such information to their advantage so it is important to avoid system information leakage as far as possible.

Phishing
(Pronounced 'fishing') is a specialised form of online identity theft. The most common form of 'phishing' is where a spam email is sent out purporting to be from an organisation such as a bank or payment service.

Denial of service attack
Also known as a distributed denial of service (DDOS) attack, these involve a hacker group taking control of many 'zombie' computers attached to the Internet whose security has been compromised. This 'botnet' is then used to make many requests to a target server, so overloading it and preventing access to other visitors.

10 Error handling

Exceptions such as user data validation messages, missing pages and server errors should be handled by the code so that a custom page is displayed that does not provide any system information to the user (see item 9 above). Logging and alerting of unusual conditions should be enabled and these should allow subsequent audit.

Activity 3.3	Security breaches

Purpose

To reflect on the significance of security risks to the digital trading environment.

Activity

Choose two of the top ten security risks listed above and find an example reported in the news, e.g. leading high street banks have been exposed to phishing attacks when spoof emails are sent inviting recipients to provide the banking details and security passwords, which will then allow the cyber-criminals to gain access to bank accounts.

An alternative resource is to access the annual Information Security Breaches survey from PwC by searching at **www.pwc.co.uk**.

Make a list of the threats the security risk posed to the business in your examples, e.g. loss of trade, disruption to services, business closure.

Finally, assess the severity and long-term impact of these incidents.

Approaches to developing secure systems

Faced with the growing likelihood of security risks there are various actions which might help reduce the risks.

Digital certificates

Digital certificates (keys)
Consist of keys made up of large numbers that are used to uniquely identify individuals.

Symmetric encryption
Both parties to a transaction use the same key to encode and decode messages.

Asymmetric encryption
Both parties use a related but different key to encode and decode messages

There are two main methods of encryption using **digital certificates** or 'keys':

1 Secret-key or **symmetric encryption** involves both parties having an identical (shared) key known only to them. Only this key can be used to encrypt and decrypt messages. The secret key has to be passed from one party to the other before use. This method is not practical for general e-commerce since it would not be safe for a purchaser to give a secret key to a merchant because control of it would be lost and it could not then be used for other purposes. A merchant would also have to manage many customer keys.

2 Public-key or **asymmetric encryption**. Asymmetric encryption is so called since the keys used by the sender and receiver of information are different. The two keys are related by a numerical code, so only the *pair* of keys can be used in combination to encrypt and decrypt information. Figure 3.5 shows how public-key encryption works in an e-commerce context. A customer can place an order with a merchant by automatically looking up the public key of the merchant and then using this key to encrypt the message containing their order. The scrambled message is then sent across the Internet and on receipt is read using the merchant's private key. In this way only the merchant who has the only copy of the private key can read the order. In the reverse case the merchant could confirm the customer's identity by reading identity information such as a digital signature encrypted with the private key of the customer using their public key.

Digital signatures

Digital signatures can be used to create commercial systems by using public-key encryption to achieve authentication: the merchant and purchaser can prove they are genuine. The purchaser's digital signature is encrypted before sending a message using their private key, and on receipt the public key of the purchaser is used to decrypt the digital signature. This proves the customer is genuine. Digital signatures are not widely used currently due to the difficulty of setting up transactions, but will become more widespread as the public-key infrastructure (PKI) stabilises and the use of certificate authorities increases.

The public-key infrastructure (PKI) and certificate authorities

For digital signatures and public-key encryption to be effective it is necessary to ensure the public key intended for decryption of a document actually belongs to the genuine person who you believe is sending you the document. A system of Trusted Third Party (TTP) certificates are used as a means of containing owner identification information and a copy of the public key used to unlock the information. The TTPs are usually referred to as **certificate authorities (CAs)** – an example is VeriSign (**www.verisign.com**). The message is called a **certificate** and typically includes user and issuing authority identification data, user, public key, date and class of certificate.

In addition to validating identification technology software solutions are also available to ensure the security of e-commerce transactions.

Secure Sockets Layer protocol (SSL)

SSL is the most common security mechanism used on transactional websites in association with CAs like VeriSign that issue an SSL certificate verifying the identity of the certificate owner. The SSL approach enables encryption of sensitive information during online transactions using PKI and digital certificates to ensure privacy and authentication. SSL is more widely used than the rival S-HTTP method. Here, when encryption is occurring they will see that the web address prefix in the browser changes from '**http://**' to '**https://**' and a padlock appears at the bottom of the browser window.

Secure Electronic Transaction (SET)

Secure Electronic Transaction (SET) is a security protocol based on digital certificates, originally developed by a consortium led by Mastercard and Visa, which allows parties to a transaction to confirm each other's identity. Due to complexity of implementation, SET is not widely used and SSL has become the de facto standard.

Ultimately, digital marketers should ensure safe passage for its users. Once the security measures are in place, content on the merchant's site can be used to reassure the

| Figure 3.5 | Public-key or asymmetric encryption |

customer. Some of the approaches used indicate good practice in allaying customers' fears. These include:

- use of customer guarantee to safeguard purchase;
- clear explanation of SSL security measures used including badges of known security verification groups;
- highlighting the rarity of fraud ('ten million customers have shopped safely without credit card fraud');
- the use of alternative ordering mechanisms such as phone or fax;
- the prominence of information to allay fears – the guarantee is one of the main menu options.

Companies can also use independent third parties that set guidelines for online privacy and security. The best-known international bodies for privacy are TRUSTe (**www.truste .org**) and VeriSign for payment authentication (**www.verisign.com**). McAfee (**www.mcafee .com**) and Avast (**www.avast.com**) are examples of commercial organisations which provide encryption, antivirus software, **firewalls** and a range of protection services. Avast provides maps showing infected domains around the globe at **www.avast.com/en-gb/maps**.

Technology convergence

Technology convergence is an important consideration for the digital marketer as consumers are increasingly using multiple platforms to access digital services. Mobile phone and tablet computer technology is rapidly developing and facilitating access to millions of different apps and online services, which go far beyond texting and making phone calls.

SMS messaging and applications

The **Short Message Service (SMS)**, commonly known as 'texting', is, of course, a simple form of person-to-person communication that enables messages to be transferred between mobile phones. Its use grew for many years, but it is now on the decline as consumers turn to messaging via social networks and new mobile messaging applications such as What's App and Viber, which are billed as SMS replacement.

Texting became increasingly popular as a means for brands to communicate with customers. High street banks notify customers of current account balances when they approach an overdraft limit, retailers send delivery notifications and airlines send boarding and flight details using SMS. Text is also used by consumer brands to market their products and texting can be used in supply chain management applications for notifying managers of problems or deliveries.

SMS applications

For the creative marketer who respects opt-in and privacy legislation, SMS has proved a great way to get closer to customers, particularly those in the youth market who are difficult to reach with other media. These are some of the applications:

1 *Database building/direct response to ads/direct mail or on-pack.* This is one of the most significant applications.
2 *Location-based services.* Text for the nearest pub, club, shop or taxi. In London you can now text for the nearest available taxi, and pay the congestion charge through texting, once accounts are set up via the web!
3 *Sampling/trial.* Use for encouraging consumers to trial new products through promotions.
4 *Sales promotions.* Timed e-coupons can be sent out to encourage footfall in real and virtual stores.

Firewall
A specialised software application mounted on a server at the point where the company is connected to the Internet. Its purpose is to prevent unauthorised access into the company from outsiders.

Technology convergence
A trend in which different hardware devices such as TVs, computers and phones merge and have similar functions.

Short Message Service (SMS)
The formal name for text messaging.

Short code

Five-digit number combined with text that can be used by advertisers or broadcasters to encourage consumers to register their interest. They are typically followed up by an automated text message from the advertiser with the option to opt in to further information by email or to link through to a WAP site.

Mobile apps

A software application that is designed for use on a mobile phone, typically downloaded from an App store. iPhone apps are best known, but all smartphones support the use of apps which can provide users with information, entertainment or location-based services such as mapping.

5 *Rewarding with offers for brand engagement.* Valuable content on mobiles can be offered via SMS, for example free ringtones, wallpaper, Java games or credits can be offered to consumers via text.

6 *Short codes.* **Short codes** are easy-to-remember five-digit numbers combined with text that can be used by advertisers or broadcasters to encourage consumers to register their interest.

7 *Offering paid-for WAP services and content.* Any service such as a ringtone delivered by WAP can be invoked from a text message.

Mobile apps

Mobile apps are a highly significant development in mobile communications, indeed all digital communications, since they highlight a change in the method of delivering interactive services and content via mobile phones. Until the advent of apps, popularised by the Apple iPhone App Store and then on Android phones via the Google Play Store, the web browser had been seen as the main model by most for delivering content via mobile phones.

Through reviewing the types of apps which have proved popular, businesses can assess the potential for them to develop applications for their audiences.

The key questions to ask are:

1 *Are apps a strategic priority for us?* The goal of apps for most organisations will be to increase awareness and sales, or for publishers' revenue from advertising or subscriptions. For many companies, this won't be a priority because they will have to put budget into higher priority areas such as improving the experience on their desktop or mobile site, or in their social network presence. Owing to the volume of users reached through these other platforms, incremental improvements here are likely to give better returns. But the figures presented above show the potential benefits of apps to marketers in reaching audiences and potentially in selling apps, although the latter will be generally limited to publishers or specialist software developers. For these types of organisations, apps are likely to be a priority.

2 *Do we build our own app and/or leverage existing apps?* Creating an app is only one of the marketing options – advertising and sponsorship options may be a more cost-effective method to build reach and awareness of a brand. A good example of sponsorship fit is the Canon Sponsorship of the excellent Guardian Eyewitness photography app. There are also options of new iAds from Apple and Google AdSense mobile display networks.

3 *Free or paid apps?* Retailers will generally offer free apps providing choice and convenience in return for loyalty. Brands offering entertainment will most likely also go the free route to increase customer engagement. But for publishers or software houses, a freemium approach of free app showcasing the service and paid app for improved features or content is the standard approach.

4 *Which category of application to target?* As you would expect, accessing social networks and music via apps is popular, but for most organisations games and entertainment are the main options.

5 *How to best promote mobile apps?* The options for marketing apps were also research by Nielsen (2010), who found that the most popular methods of app discovery are:

- searching the app store;
- recommendations from friends and family;
- mention on device or network carrier page;
- email promotion;
- offline mention in TV and print.

6 *How to refine apps in line with feedback.* The success of apps is very dependent on feedback in the App stores and the need to fix bugs and add enhancements to compete shows the need for an ongoing development cycle with frequent updates. A whole new area of app analytics and new solutions will no doubt develop, but a challenge with apps similar to that of Flash apps before them is that measurement functionality needs to be specified in advance. Careful review of hurdle rates for the percentage of user base who are using the app or its different functions is going to be a KPI here.

Social location-based marketing through mobile

In **social location-based marketing** there is a fusion of social and mobile marketing. Foursquare, Facebook Places, Google+ Local, TripAdvisor and Yelp are all options available to consumers. If businesses can encourage consumers to leave favourable reviews and recommendations, then this may encourage new customers through 'social proof' and can increase visibility in local listings such as search engine results.

QR codes

Quick Response (QR) codes are barcodes published in newspapers or billboards which can be scanned by a mobile phone camera and then linked directly through to a website. Figure 3.6 shows an example. They give exciting opportunities for integrating customer journeys. QR codes can be used in promotional initiatives to allow target consumers to have quick access to a variety of information – for example, instant access to email addresses, phone number or business card.

Wi-Fi

Wi-Fi (wireless fidelity) is the shorthand often used to describe a high-speed wireless local area network. Wi-Fi can be deployed in an office or home environment, where it removes the need for cabling and adds flexibility. However, it has attracted most attention for

---

Mini case study 3.1	Location-based marketing

If you're thinking that location-based marketing is just for corporates with large budgets, the likes of Starbucks and McDonalds, then think again. ClickZ (2010) has reported how AJ Bombers, a speciality burger bar in Milwaukee, attributed a sale increase of 110 per cent to Foursquare. It has 1400 people on its Foursquare page who have checked in 6000 times. The mayor gets a free burger, and currently that's 'Amy' – who has had to check in 40 times in the last 60 days at the one-location establishment in order to achieve the distinction.

Engagement is also increased through people who add a tip to the restaurant's Foursquare page getting rewarded with a free cookie when they show it to a waiter or cashier.

The sales increase figure is based on a single campaign which saw 161 check-ins on 28 February – a 110 per cent sales increase when compared to a normal Sunday. Joe Sorge, owner of the restaurant, promoted an AJ Bombers-branded 'Swarm Badge' event to his Foursquare-using regulars. Such a custom badge is awarded to users who check in at a location where at least 50 other users are simultaneously checked in.

The restaurant owner advised that success involves implementing Foursquare as a regular part of operations:

Our staff encourages the use and engagement of Foursquare by virtue of our Foursquare specials being very prominent throughout our business. It encourages our customers to ask questions of our staff. Education of that staff is the key.

| Figure 3.6 | QR codes |

its potential for offering wireless access in airports, shopping centres, cities and towns without the need for a fixed connection.

Bluetooth wireless applications

Bluetooth technology
A wireless standard for transmission of data between devices over short ranges (less than 10m).

Bluetooth technology has potential for different forms of local marketing campaigns known as **proximity marketing**: (1) viral communication; (2) community activities (dating or gaming events); (3) location-based services – electronic coupons as you pass a store.

Emerging technologies

Proximity marketing
Marketing messages are delivered in real time according to customers' presence based on the technology they are carrying, wearing or have embedded. Bluecasting is the best-known example.

In addition to mobile and Wi-Fi access, Internet access technologies to television and radio is available digitally. Internet TV, or IPTV, is increasingly popular and as bandwidth, download speeds and access devices improve, the number and range of users is increasing. This technology creates challenges for the digital marketer as they need to access which technology their target audience is using to access which type of content, information and or digital services.

Activity 3.4   Assessing new technology options

Purpose

To illustrate the process for reviewing the relevance of new technology options.

Activity

You work for a FMCG (fast-moving consumer goods) brand and are attending an industry trade show where you see a presentation about the next-generation (4G) mobile phones which are due to launch in your country in one year's time. You need to decide whether your organisation adopts the new phone and if so when. Complete the following:

1 How would you assess the significance of this new technology?
2 Summarise the proposition of the new access devices for both consumers and your organisation.
3 What recommendations would you make about when to adopt and which services to offer?

Assessing the marketing value of technology innovation

One of the challenges for digital marketers is how to successfully assess which new technological innovations can be applied to give competitive advantage. For example, personalisation technology (Chapter 6) is intended to enhance the customer's online experience and increase their loyalty. However, personalisation may require a large investment in proprietary software and hardware technology for effective implementation. How does the manager decide whether to proceed and which technological solutions to adopt? There is more to digital marketing than establishing and managing a website, and in Chapter 4 strategy decisions are examined while in Chapter 8 how to make decisions to achieve the best media mix is considered.

A manager may have read articles in the trade and general press or spoken to colleagues that have highlighted the potential of a new technology-enabled marketing technique. They then face a difficult decision as to whether to:

- ignore the use of the technique completely, perhaps because it is felt to be too expensive or untried, or because they simply don't believe the benefits will outweigh the costs;
- ignore the technique for now, but keep an eye on the results of other companies that are starting to use it;
- evaluate the technique in a structured manner and then make a decision whether to adopt it according to the evaluation;
- enthusiastically adopt the technique without a detailed evaluation since the hype alone convinces the manager that the technique should be adopted.

Depending on the attitude of the manager, this behaviour can be summarised as:

1 Cautious, a 'wait and see' approach.
2 Intermediate, sometimes referred to as 'fast-follower' approach. Let others take the majority of the risk, but if they are proving successful then rapidly adopt the technique, i.e. copy them.
3 Risk-taking, an early-adopter approach.

Early adopters
Companies or departments that invest in new technologies and techniques.

Different behaviours by different adopters will result in different numbers of adopters through time. This diffusion–adoption process (represented by the bell curve in Figure 3.7) was identified by Rogers (1983), who classified those trialling new products as being innovators, **early adopters**, early majority, late majority, through to the laggards.

1. Innovators (2.5%)
2. Opinion leaders (13.5%)
3. Early majority (34%)
4. Late majority (34%)
5. Laggards (16%)

Conservative adopters

Leading edge

Number of new adopters

Time

| Figure 3.7 | Diffusion–adoption curve |

The diffusion–adoption curve can be used in two main ways as an analytical tool to help managers:

1 to understand the stage at which customers are in adoption of a technology, or any product. For example, the Internet is now a well-established tool and in many developed countries we are into the late majority phase of adoption, with large numbers of users of services. This suggests it is essential to use this medium for marketing purposes. But if we look at WAP technology (see below) it can be seen that we are in the innovator phase, so investment now may be wasted since it is not clear how many will adopt the product.

2 to look at adoption of a new technique by other businesses – from an organisational perspective. For example, an online supermarket could look at how many other e-tailers have adopted personalisation to evaluate whether it is worthwhile adopting the technique.

A commercial application of the diffusion of innovation curve was developed by technology analyst Gartner (2011) and has been applied to different technologies since 1995. They describe a **hype cycle** as a graphic representation of the maturity, adoption and business application of specific technologies.

Hype cycle
A graphic representation of the maturity, adoption and business application of specific technologies.

Gartner (2011) recognises the following stages within the hype cycle (Figure 3.8):

1 *Technology trigger.* The first phase of a hype cycle is the 'technology trigger' or breakthrough, product launch or other event that generates significant press and interest.

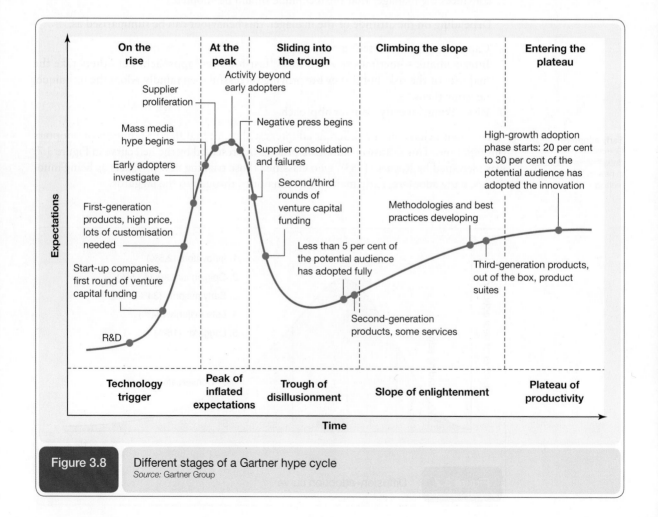

Figure 3.8	Different stages of a Gartner hype cycle
	Source: Gartner Group

2 *Peak of inflated expectations*. In the next phase, a frenzy of publicity typically generates over-enthusiasm and unrealistic expectations. There may be some successful applications of a technology, but there are typically more failures.

3 *Trough of disillusionment*. Technologies enter the 'trough of disillusionment' because they fail to meet expectations and quickly become unfashionable. Consequently, the press usually abandons the topic and the technology.

4 *Slope of enlightenment*. Although the press may have stopped covering the technology, some businesses continue through the 'slope of enlightenment' and experiment to understand the benefits and practical application of the technology.

5 *Plateau of productivity*. A technology reaches the 'plateau of productivity' as the benefits of it become widely demonstrated and accepted. The technology becomes increasingly stable and evolves in second and third generations. The final height of the plateau varies according to whether the technology is broadly applicable or benefits only a niche market.

The problem with being an early adopter (as an organisation) is that being at the leading edge of using new technologies is often also referred to as the 'bleeding edge' due to the risk of failure. New technologies will have bugs or may integrate poorly with the existing systems or the marketing benefits may simply not live up to their promise. Of course, the reason for risk taking is that the rewards are high – if you are using a technique that your competitors are not, then you will gain an edge on your rivals. For example, RS Components (**www.rswww.com**) was one of the first UK suppliers of industrial components to adopt personalisation as part of their e-commerce system. The company has learnt the strengths and weaknesses of the product and now knows how to position it to appeal to customers. It offers facilities such as customised pages, access to previous order history and the facility to place repeat orders or modified re-buys. This has enabled it to build up a base of customers who are familiar with using the RS Components online services and are then less likely to swap to rival services in the future.

It may also be useful to identify how rapidly a new concept is being adopted. When a product or service is adopted rapidly this is known as *rapid diffusion*. Access to the Internet is an example of this. In developed countries the use of the Internet has become widespread more rapidly than the use of TV, for example. It seems that interactive digital TV and Internet-enabled mobile phones are relatively slow-diffusion products! Activity 3.1 (**page** 124) considers this issue further.

So, what action should marketing and e-commerce managers take when confronted by new techniques and technologies? There is no straightforward rule of thumb, other than that a balanced approach must be taken. It would be easy to dismiss many new techniques as fads, or classify them as 'not relevant to my market'. However, competitors are likely to be reviewing new techniques and incorporating some, so a careful review of new techniques is required. This indicates that benchmarking of 'best of breed' sites within a sector and in different sectors is essential as part of environmental scanning. However, by waiting for others to innovate and review the results on their website, a company has probably already lost 6–12 months. Figure 3.9 summarises the choices. The stepped curve I shows the variations in technology through time. Some changes may be small incremental ones such as a new operating system; others, such as the introduction of personalisation technology, are more significant in delivering value to customers and so improving business performance. Line A is a company that is using innovative business techniques, adopts technology early, or is even in advance of what the technology can currently deliver. Line C shows the conservative adopter whose use of technology lags behind the available potential. Line B, the middle ground, is probably the ideal situation where a company monitors new ideas as an early adopter, trials them and then adopts those that will positively impact the business.

Technological forces are significant and can influence digital marketing success significantly. In this section we have considered major factors which make up the forces likely to affect the digital marketer. In the next section, we examine economic forces.

Figure 3.9 Alternative responses to changes in technology

Economic forces

Globally economic influences affect the level of success of business. Economic forces affect supply and demand and consequently it is important for digital markets to identify which economic influences they need to monitor. Classic economic factors such as growth and unemployment, interest and exchange rates can affect every aspect of business activity and are equally pertinent to offline and online businesses. International market growth and emerging economies – for example central and eastern European markets and the BRIC economies – also have the potential to influence digital marketing activities. In this section we explore the implications of the classic economic factors, market growth and emerging markets for digital marketers.

Market growth and employment

According to Varley (2001), 'Modern societies are organised around consumption and so the trends in patterns of consumption that emerge over time are very important for marketers to observe and understand.' The impact of changes in demand can have far-reaching implications for digital marketing initiatives as this will affect the strength of market growth, so it is important to anticipate demand. Sophisticated technology enables companies to analyse purchasing patterns and forecast future demand. But this is only part of the picture of consumption that drives modern global economies. It is also important to monitor changes to trends (which affect market growth) in order to be able to make realistic predictions about how consumers and companies are going to behave in the future.

The changing nature of a population's age profile, changes to working life and changing lifestyles are beyond the control of the digital marketer but such changes are relatively slow-moving so as long as these trends are identified they can be accommodated in long-term strategic plans.

Demographics is the study of populations, which uses measurable variables to monitor and analyse population trends. Demographic variables include:

- age profiles;
- birth rates;
- education levels;

- gender;
- household structures;
- lifestage (e.g. single, married, divorced);
- total income and expenditure;
- working patterns and occupations.

In developed economies, populations are living longer and the age profile of a consumer market can be very important for the digital marketer's business.

Nevertheless, Tim Berners-Lee (inventor of the web) had a vision that everyone everywhere should be able to access the web; the reality is that there is significant variation in the ability of the users based on their age profile. W3C (2008) suggests that web developers and marketers should not stereotype older adults as technophobes. In fact Fox (2004) goes as far as stating: 'Wired seniors are often as enthusiastic as younger users in the major activities which define online life such as email and the use of search engines to answer specific questions.' However, while enthusiasm for using the web may be similar across age groups, what the users are doing online and how they do it varies. Baby boomers, born between 1946 and 1964, regularly use the Internet and mobile phones (although smart phone uptake has been slow) for product research, and to make travel reservations. They are also avid users of digital video and nearly six out of ten *boomers* regularly downloaded or streamed video but are less inclined to engage with social media than younger web users (E-Marketer, 2013). Furthermore, there are age-related functional limitations – e.g. visual decline, hearing loss, motor skills diminishment and cognitive effects – which have implications for web design (W3C, 2008). This means developers and marketers should pay careful attention to the level of interaction, the information architecture and organisation and visual design (Chapter 7).

International market growth and emerging economies

Globalisation
The increase of international trading and shared social and cultural values.

Globalisation refers to the move towards international trading in a single global marketplace and the blurring of social and cultural differences between countries. In Chapter 2 we saw that there is wide variation in the level of use of the Internet in different continents and countries, particularly from the consumer perspective. Furthermore, according to Doherty *et al.* (2003), a major driver of Internet adoption by commercial organisations is the opportunity for market expansion in domestic and international markets. However, digital marketers need to be aware of the implications of trading in global markets and consider whether to develop bespoke branding and marketing campaigns or whether to apply a standardised approach. These issues are considered in more detail in Chapter 5.

Economic disruption

Throughout history there have been periods of strong economic growth followed by economic downturn and recession. The dot-com period of boom and bust at the beginning of the twenty-first century highlighted the fragility of high-tech markets and many of the emerging Internet companies, which had high stock market valuations, crashed and no longer exist. However, from such disruption has emerged an online economy which is fuelling growth. According to Gorell (2011) there are lessons leading innovators can learn, which can help them to steer their businesses through economic turbulence and take advantage of emerging markets. Gorell's observations are that in order to be able to manage in periods of economic change business leaders should focus on developing the ability to:

1 anticipate and act on market uncertainty and unmet customer needs by applying a focussed business model;
2 focus on innovations and how they can deliver value to the company's business model.
3 expect opportunities to emerge from uncertainty and develop strategies which can maximise any emerging market advantage (Gorell, 2011).

The world's best-performing companies are adept at spotting opportunities in times of economic disruption but, according to Gorell (2011): 'By adoption of their best practices, almost any company can learn to out-compete their rivals by creating new products, finding white-space markets and imagining new business models even in the toughest of times.' However, in order to achieve success companies should:

- focus on improving opportunities and innovations which already exist within the business;
- be selective about which innovations are likely to bring early gains and carefully manage company resources – innovations which require limited resources can be very useful in challenging economic times;
- involve everyone in the company in working towards a common goal.

These ideas pose challenges for digital marketers; on the one hand, the advice suggests economic restraint and engaging in low-cost initiatives but, on the other hand, it suggests developing high-growth innovations. According to Inder Sidh (vice president of worldwide strategy and planning, Cisco Systems Inc.), it is possible to do both, and this approach is followed throughout the organisation by looking at 'every opportunity not as a choice between apparent conflicting goals but rather a way of obtaining a multiplier effect by seeking and meeting two apparently conflicting goals' (Davidson, 2011).

In Chapter 4 strategic implications and planning issues are explored further.

This section has identified key economic factors and considered their potential impact for digital marketers and the online trading environment. There are close links between economic factors such as interest rates and inflation on political influences. Some of the issues raised will be returned to later in this chapter. In the next section we explore social forces and how online communities are changing.

Political forces

The political environment is shaped by the interplay of government agencies, public opinion and consumer pressure groups and industry-backed organisations such as TRUSTe (**www.truste.org**). Interaction between these organisations helps to create a trading environment with established regulations. The political environment has many factors which influence the trading environment, such as taxation, investment and management of business and public affairs. Political forces are closely intertwined with economic forces – for example, the government sets financial goals for the Bank of England, which in turn sets interest rates to control inflation. The government's influence over the economy has an impact on overall economic performance and also business investment.

It is important for digital marketers to be aware that political action enacted through government agencies to control the adoption of the Internet includes:

- promoting the benefits of adopting the Internet for consumers and business to improve a country's economic prosperity;
- sponsoring research leading to dissemination of best practice among companies, for example the DTI international benchmarking survey;
- enacting legislation to regulate the environment, for example to protect privacy or control taxation;
- involvement in setting up international bodies to coordinate the Internet, such as ICANN (the Internet Corporation for Assigned Names and Numbers, **www.icann.com**), which has introduced new domains such as **.biz** and **.info**.

The type of initiative launched by government is highlighted by the launch in the UK in September 1999 of a new 'UK online' campaign, a raft of initiatives and investment aimed

E-government
The use of Internet technologies to provide government services to citizens.

at moving people, business and government itself online (**e-government**). E-envoy posts and an e-minister have also been appointed. The prime minister said in 1999:

> There is a revolution going on in our economy. A fundamental change, not a dot.com fad, but a real transformation towards a knowledge economy. So, today, I am announcing a new campaign. Its goal is to get the UK online. To meet the three stretching targets we have set, for Britain to be the best place in the world for e-commerce, with universal access to the Internet and all government services on the net. In short, the UK online campaign aims to get business, people and government online.

The government continued to invest in developing their online proposition and by 2005 billions of pounds had been invested in getting public services online. The 2000 strategy was designed to build a smarter and more efficient public service infrastructure. However, the government faces challenging issues: how to identify citizens online; sharing of information between departments; how to establish 'online' as the main channel of communication for all UK citizens.

A central plank of the e-government regulatory strategy is the Digital Economy Act. However, the Act has been at the centre of a controversy, led by telecoms companies BT and Talk Talk, which were appealing to the High Court that the Act contravened European law on commerce and privacy (BBC, 2011). The heart of the problem is illegal downloading of copyrighted material such as music and film and, prior to the introduction of the Act, content producers argued for legislation to control this type of Internet piracy. The Act requires Internet service providers to make provision for policing this type of action. However, opponents of the Act are unhappy that it can sanction individual computer users and favour the demands of large corporations. One group that is very happy that the Act is in line with European law is the British Phonographic Institute, and Geoff Taylor, Chief Executive, feels this is a positive move that 'gives the green light for action to tackle illegal downloading in the UK' (BBC, 2011).

Political control and democracy

Government action that can have a significant impact on the online marketplace is control of intermediaries. This depends on the amount of regulation in a given country and in individual markets. Taking the UK as example, regulation of different marketplaces occurs through these groups:

- *Financial Services Authority* – controls providers of banking products such as current accounts, savings and loans.
- *Ofcom* – controls providers of mobile phone and broadband services.

In the financial services market, it is not necessary for a price comparison intermediary to show all providers, so, for example, one major insurance provider, Direct Line, has decided not to be included. However, in the energy industry it is required that all providers be included due to the industry regulators, although links between the intermediary and the suppliers do not.

Internet governance

Internet governance
Control of the operation and use of the Internet.

Internet governance describes the control put in place to manage the growth of the Internet and its usage. Governance is traditionally undertaken by government, but the global nature of the Internet makes it less practical for a government to control online.

Taxation

How to change tax laws to reflect globalisation through the Internet is a problem that many governments are grappling with. The fear is that the Internet may cause significant reductions in tax revenues to national or local governments if existing laws do not cover changes in purchasing patterns. In Europe, the use of online betting in lower-tax areas such as Gibraltar has resulted in lower revenues to governments in the countries where consumers would have formerly paid gaming tax to the government via a betting shop. Large UK bookmakers such as William Hill and Victor Chandler are offering Internet-based betting from 'offshore' locations such as Gibraltar. The lower duties in these countries offer the companies the opportunity to make betting significantly cheaper than if they were operating under a higher-tax regime. This trend was dubbed LOCI or Location Optimised Commerce on the Internet by Mougayer (1998). Meanwhile, the government of the country from which a person places the bet will face a drop in its tax revenues. In the UK the government has sought to reduce the revenue shortfall by reducing the differential between UK and overseas costs.

According to Omar *et al.* (2009):

> The tax-free status of most items purchased online has resulted in significant loss of tax revenues to state and local government. Our research indicated that the loss of taxes amounting to $13.3 billion in 2001 will rise to $62.1 billion by 2011, unless taxation policies are changed. Changing the tax laws governing online trading is problematic. One significant aspect concerns the one who collects the revenues: should the taxes on items purchased online be collected by the state and local government, as is now done in traditional brick-and-mortar trades, or should this be done by a concerted, standardised federal effort?

Since the Internet supports the global marketplace, it could be argued that it makes little sense to introduce tariffs on goods and services delivered over the Internet. Such instruments would, in any case, be impossible to apply to products delivered electronically. This position is currently that of the USA. In the document 'A Framework for Global Electronic Commerce', former President Clinton stated that:

> The United States will advocate in the World Trade Organization (WTO) and other appropriate international fora that the Internet be declared a tariff-free zone.

Tax jurisdiction

Tax jurisdiction determines which country gets the tax income from a transaction. Under the current system of international tax treaties, the right to tax is divided between the country where the enterprise that receives the income is resident ('residence' country) and that from which the enterprise derives that income ('source' country). Laws on taxation are rapidly evolving and vary dramatically between countries. A proposed EU directive intends to deal with these issues by defining the place of establishment of a merchant as where they pursue an economic activity from a fixed physical location. At the time of writing, the general principle that is being applied is that tax rules are similar to those for a conventional mail-order sale; for the UK, the tax principles are as follows:

a if the supplier (residence) and the customer (source) are both in the UK, VAT will be chargeable;
b exports to private customers in the EU will attract either UK VAT or local VAT;
c exports outside the EU will be zero-rated (but tax may be levied on import);
d imports into the UK from the EU or beyond will attract local VAT, or UK import tax when received through customs;
e services attract VAT according to where the supplier is located. This is different from products and causes anomalies if online services are created. For example, a betting service located in Gibraltar enables UK customers to gamble at a lower tax rate than with the same company in the UK.

This section has explored some factors that contribute to the economic forces which can affect digital marketing initiatives. The next section considers legal forces.

Legal forces

Laws develop in order to provide a framework of control and regulations that aim to enable individuals and businesses to go about their business in a legal and ethical manner. However, laws are open to interpretation and there are many legal and ethical considerations in the online trading environments. Many laws aim to prevent unethical marketing practices, so marketers have to understand and work within this regulatory framework. This section considers six of the most important legal issues for digital marketers (see Table 3.1).

Legal activities can be considered unethical

Ethical standards
Practices and behaviours which are morally acceptable to society.

Digital marketers should be compliant with the law and adhere to **ethical standards** but the rate of technological innovation is rapid and consequently the law is often unclear.

Table 3.1	Significant laws which control digital marketing

Legal issue	Digital marketing activities affected
1 Data protection and privacy law	• Collection, storage, usage and deletion of personal information directly through data capture on forms and indirectly through tracking behaviour through web analytics • Email marketing and SMS mobile marketing • Use of viral marketing to encourage transmission of marketing messages between consumers • Use of cookies and other techniques for personalising content and tracking on site • Use of cookies for tracking between sites, for example for advertising networks • Use of digital assets installed on a user's PC for marketing purposes, e.g. toolbars or other downloadable utilities sometimes referred to as 'malware'

2 Disability and discrimination law	• Accessibility of content such as images for the visually impaired within Different digital environments:
	  – website
	  – email marketing
	  – mobile marketing
	  – IPTV
	• Accessibility affecting other forms of disability including hearing difficulties and motor impairment

3 Brand and trademark protection	• Use of trademarks and brand names within:
	  – domain names
	  – content on site (for search engine optimisation)
	  – natural search results
	  – paid search advertising campaigns (e.g. Google AdWords)
	• representation of a brand on third-party sites including partners, publishers and social networks
	• defamation of employees

4 Intellectual property rights	• Protection of digital assets such as text content, images, audio and sounds through digital rights management (DRM)

5 Contract law	• Validity of electronic contracts relevant to:
	  – cancellations
	  – returns
	  – errors in pricing
	• distance-selling law
	• international taxation issues where the e-commerce service provider is under a different tax regime to the purchaser

6 Online advertising law	• similar issues to traditional media:
	  – representation of offer
	  – causing offence (e.g. viral marketing)

In this case, marketers need to tread carefully since unethical action can result in serious damage to the reputation of a company and negative sentiment can result in a reduction in online audience or sales.

1 Data protection and privacy law

Privacy
A moral right of individuals to avoid intrusion into their personal affairs.

Identity theft
The misappropriation of the identity of another person, without their knowledge or consent.

Privacy refers to a moral right of individuals to avoid intrusion into their personal affairs by third parties. Privacy of personal data, such as our identities, likes and dislikes, is a major concern to consumers, particularly with the dramatic increase in **identity theft**.

Digital marketers can better understand their customers' needs by using this type of very valuable information. Through collecting personal information it becomes possible to develop highly targeted communications and develop products that are more consistent with users' needs. Therefore, how should marketers respond to this dilemma? An obvious step is to ensure that marketing activities are consistent with the latest data protection and privacy laws. Although compliance with the laws may sound straightforward, in practice different interpretations of the law are possible and since these are new laws they have not been tested in court. As a result, companies have to make their own business decisions based on the business benefits of applying particular marketing practices against the financial and reputational risks of less strict compliance. There is also the challenge of compliance with different laws prevalent in different countries.

Activity 3.5	Security, censorship on the web and the Electronic Frontier Foundation

Purpose

To consider the right to privacy and freedom of information argument.

Activity

Visit: The Virtual Revolution and hear what John Perry Barlow, former member of the rock band The Grateful Dead and founding member of the Electronic Frontier Foundation, has to say about the freedom of information: **www.bbc.co.uk/blogs/legacy/digitalrevolution/2009/10/rushes-sequences-john-perry-ba.shtml**

Now reflect on whether you agree with John's views on the freedom of information and then suggest what implications his views have for digital marketing.

Effective e-commerce requires establishing a balance between the benefits the individual customer will add to their online experience through providing personal information and the amount and type of information that they are prepared for companies to hold about them.

The main information types used by the digital marketer which are governed by ethics and legislation, are:

1 *Contact information.* This is the name, postal address, email address and, for B2B companies, website address.
2 *Profile information.* This is information about a customer's characteristics that can be used for segmentation. They include age, sex and social group for consumers, and company characteristics and individual role for business customers (see Chapter 6).
3 *Platform usage information.* Through web analytics systems it is possible to collect information on type of computer, browser and screen resolution used by site users (see Chapter 7).
4 *Behavioural information (on a single site).* This is purchase history and the whole of the buying process. Web analytics (Chapter 10) can be used to assess the web and email content accessed by individuals.

5 *Behavioural information (across multiple sites)*. This can potentially show how a user accesses multiple sites and responds to adverts across sites. Typically this data is collected and used through an anonymous profile based on cookie or IP addresses which is not related to an individual.

Table 3.2 summarises how these different types of customer information are collected and used through technology. The main issue to be considered by the marketer is disclosure of the types of information collection and tracking data used. The first two types of information in the table are usually readily explained through a privacy statement at the point of data collection and, as we will see, this is usually a legal requirement. However, with the other types of information, users would only know they were being tracked if they have cookie monitoring software installed or if they seek out the privacy statement of a publisher which offers advertising.

All of these issues arise in the next section, which reviews actions that marketers should take to achieve privacy and trust.

Data protection law

Data protection legislation is enacted to protect the individual, to protect their privacy and to prevent misuse of their personal data. Indeed, the first article of the European Union Directive 95/46/EC (see **http://ec.europa.eu/justice_home/fsi/privacy/**), on which legislation in individual European countries is based, specifically refers to **personal data**. It says:

> Member states shall protect the fundamental rights and freedoms of natural persons [i.e. a named individual at home or at work], and in particular their right to privacy with respect to the processing of personal data.

Personal data
Any information about an individual stored by companies concerning their customers or employees.

Table 3.2	Types of information collected online and the related technologies

Type of information	Approach and technology used to capture and use information
1 Contact information	• Online forms – online forms linked to a customer database • Cookies – are used to remember a specific person on subsequent visits
2 Profile information including personal information	• Online registration forms collect data on social networks and company sites • Cookies can be used to assign a person to a particular segment by linking the cookie to a customer database record and then offering content consistent with their segment
3 Access platform usage	• Web analytics system – identification of computer type, operating system and screen characteristics based on http attributes of visitors
4 Behavioural information on a single site	• Purchase histories are stored in the sales order database • Web analytics store details of IP addresses against clickstreams of the sequence of web pages visited • Web beacons in email marketing – a single-pixel GIF is used to assess whether a reader opened an email • First-party cookies are also used for monitoring visitor behaviour during a site visit and on subsequent visits • **Malware** can collect additional information such as passwords
5 Behavioural information across multiple sites	• Third-party cookies used for assessing visits from different sources such as online advertising networks or affiliate networks (Chapter 9) • Search engines such as Google use cookies to track advertising through its AdWords pay-per-click programme • Services such as Hitwise (**www.hitwise.com**) monitor IP traffic to assess site usage of customer groups within a product category

Malware
Malicious software or toolbars, typically downloaded via the Internet, which act as a 'Trojan horse' by executing unwanted activities such as keylogging of user passwords or viruses which may collect email addresses.

In the UK, the enactment of the European legislation is the Data Protection Acts 1984 and 1998 (DPA), which is managed by the legal requirements of the 1998 UK Data Protection Act and the Information Commissioner's office is the UK's independent authority which 'upholds information rights in the public interest, promoting openness by public bodies and data privacy for individuals' (ICO, 2011). The ICO provides detailed information at **www.ico.gov.uk**. This law is typical of laws that have evolved in many countries to help protect personal information. Any company that holds personal data on computers or on file about customers or employees must be registered with a data protection registrar (although there are some exceptions which may exclude small businesses). This process is known as **notification**.

Notification
The process whereby companies register with the data protection registrar to inform about their data holdings

The guidelines on the eight data protection principles which marketers need to consider are produced by Information Commissioner (1998), on which this overview is based. These principles state that personal data should be:

1 Fairly and lawfully processed
In full:

> Personal data shall be processed fairly and lawfully and, in particular, shall not be processed unless at least one of the conditions in Schedule 2 is met; and in the case of sensitive personal data, at least one of the conditions in Schedule 3 is also met.

The Information Commissioner has produced a 'fair processing code' which suggests how an organisation needs to achieve 'fair and lawful processing' under the details of Schedules 2 and 3 of the Act. This requires:

Data controller
Each company must have a defined person responsible for data protection.

Data subject
The legal term to refer to the individual whose data are held.

- appointment of a **data controller** who is the person with defined responsibility for data protection within a company;
- clear details in communications such as on a website or direct mail of how a **data subject** can contact the data controller or a representative;
- before data processing, 'the data subject has given his consent' or the processing must be *necessary* either for a 'contract to which the data subject is a party' (for example, as part of a sale of a product) or because it is required by other laws. Consent is defined in the published guidelines as 'any freely given specific and informed indication of his wishes by which the data subject signifies his agreement to personal data relating to him being processed';
- sensitive personal data requires particular care, this includes:
  - the racial or ethnic origin of the data subject
  - political opinions
  - religious beliefs or other beliefs of a similar nature
  - membership of a trade union
  - physical or mental health or condition
  - sexual life
  - the commission or alleged commission or proceedings of any offence;
- no other laws must be broken in processing the data.

2 Processed for limited purposes
In full:

> Personal data shall be obtained only for one or more specified and lawful purposes, and shall not be further processed in any manner incompatible with that purpose or those purposes.

This implies that the organisation must make it clear why and how the data will be processed at the point of collection. For example, an organisation has to explain how your data will be used if you provide your details on a website when entering a prize draw. You would also have to agree (give consent) for further communications from the company.

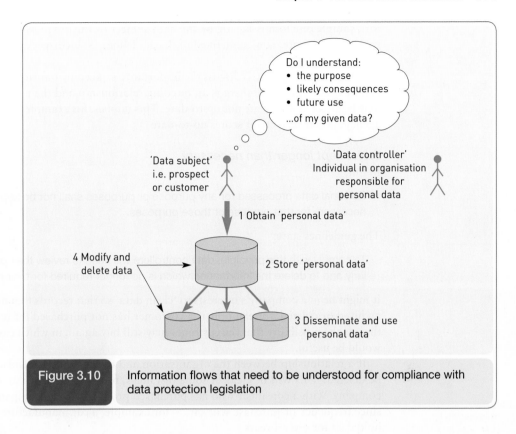

| Figure 3.10 | Information flows that need to be understood for compliance with data protection legislation |

Figure 3.10 suggests some of the issues that should be considered when a data subject is informed of how the data will be used. Important issues are:

- whether future communications will be sent to the individual (explicit consent is required for this in online channels; this is clarified by the related Privacy and Electronic Communications Regulation Act which is referred to below);
- whether the data will be passed on to third parties (again explicit consent is required);
- how long the data will be kept.

3 Adequate, relevant and not excessive
In full:

> Personal data shall be adequate, relevant and not excessive in relation to the purpose or purposes for which they are processed.

This specifies that the minimum necessary amount of data is requested for processing. There is difficulty in reconciling this provision between the needs of the individual and the needs of the company. The more details that an organisation has about a customer, then the better they can understand that customer and so develop products and marketing communications specific to that customer which they are more likely to respond to.

4 Accurate
In full:

> Personal data shall be accurate and, where necessary, kept up to date.

It is clearly also in the interest of an organisation in an ongoing relationship with a partner that the data be kept accurate and up-to-date. The guidelines on the Act suggest that additional steps should be taken to check that data are accurate, in case they are in error, for example due to mis-keying by the data subject or the organisation or for some other reason. Inaccurate data are defined in the guidelines as 'incorrect or misleading as to any matter of fact'.

The guidelines go on to discuss the importance of keeping information up-to-date. This is only necessary where there is an ongoing relationship and the rights of the individual may be affected if they are not up-to-date. This implies, for example, that a credit-checking agency should keep credit scores up-to-date.

5 Not kept longer than necessary

In full:

> Personal data processed for any purpose or purposes shall not be kept for longer than is necessary for that purpose or those purposes.

The guidelines state:

> To comply with this principle, data controllers will need to review their personal data regularly and to delete the information which is no longer required for their purposes.

It might be in a company's interests to 'clean data' so that records that are not relevant are archived or deleted, for example if a customer has not purchased for ten years. However, there is the possibility that the customer may still buy again, in which case the information would be useful.

If a relationship between the organisation and the data subject ends, then data should be deleted. This will be clear in some instances, for example when an employee leaves a company. With a consumer who has purchased products from a company this is less clear since frequency of purchase will vary – for example, a car manufacturer could justifiably hold data for several years.

6 Processed in accordance with the data subject's rights

In full:

> Personal data shall be processed in accordance with the rights of data subjects under this Act.

Subject access request
A request by a data subject to view personal data from an organisation.

One aspect of the data subject's rights is the option to request a copy of their personal data from an organisation; this is known as a **subject access request**. For payment of a small fee, such as £10 or £30, an individual can request information which must be supplied by the organisation within 40 days. This includes all information on paper files and on computer. If you requested this information from your bank there might be several boxes of transactions!

Other aspects of a data subject's rights which the law upholds are designed to prevent or control processing which:

- causes damage or distress (for example, repeatedly sending mailshots to someone who has died);
- is used for direct marketing (for example, in the UK consumers can subscribe to the mail, email or telephone preference services to avoid unsolicited mailings, emails or phone calls); this invaluable service is provided by the Direct Marketing Association (**www.dmaconsumers.org**) – if you subscribe to these services, organisations must check against these 'exclusion lists' before contacting you; if they don't, and some don't, they are breaking the law;
- is used for automatic decision making – automated credit checks, for example, may result in unjust decisions on taking a loan. These can be investigated if you feel the decision is unfair.

7 Secure

In full:

> Appropriate technical and organisational measures shall be taken against unauthorised or unlawful processing of personal data and against accidental loss or destruction of, or damage to, personal data.

The Data Protection Law guidelines place a legal imperative on organisations to prevent unauthorised internal or external access to information and also its modification or destruction. Of course, most organisations would want to do this anyway since the information has value to the organisation and the reputational damage of losing customer information or being subject to a hack attack can be severe. For example in late 2006, online clothing retail group TJX Inc. (owner of TK Maxx) was hacked resulting in loss of credit card details of over 45 million customers in the US and Europe. TJX later said in its security filing that its potential liability (loss) from the computer intrusion(s) was $118 million.

8 Not transferred to countries without adequate protection

In full:

> Personal data shall not be transferred to a country or territory outside the European Economic Area, unless that country or territory ensures an adequate level of protection of the rights and freedoms of data subjects in relation to the processing of personal data.

Transfer of data beyond Europe is likely for multinational companies. This principle prevents export of data to countries that do not have sound data processing laws. If the transfer is required in concluding a sale or contract, or if the data subject agrees to it, then transfer is legal. Data transfer with the US is possible through companies registered through the Safe Harbor Scheme (**http://export.gov/safeharbor/index.asp**).

Anti-spam legislation

Laws have been enacted in different countries to protect individual privacy and with the intention of reducing **spam** or unsolicited commercial email (UCE). For example, see Digital marketing insight 3.4. Originally, the best-known spam was tinned meat (a contraction of 'spiced ham'), but a modern version of this acronym is 'sending persistent annoying email'. Spammers rely on sending out millions of emails in the hope that even if there is only a 0.01 per cent response they may make some money, if not get rich.

Anti-spam laws do not mean that email cannot be used as a marketing tool, but the recipient has to agree to receive the mailing. This approach is called Permissive Marketing. Permissive email marketing is based on consent or **opt-in** by customers, and the option to unsubscribe or **opt-out** is the key to successful email marketing. Email lists can also be rented where customers have opted in to receive email. This is known as a **cold list**, so called because the company that purchases the data from a third party does not know you. Your name will also potentially be stored on an opt-in **house list** within companies you have purchased from where you have given your consent to be contacted by the company or given additional consent to be contacted by its partners.

European regulations on privacy and electronic communications

While the Data Protection Directive 95/46 and Data Protection Act afford a reasonable level of protection for consumers, they were quickly superseded by advances in technology and the rapid growth in spam. As a result, in 2002 the European Union passed the '2002/58/EC Directive on Privacy and Electronic Communications' to complement previous data

Spam
Unsolicited email (usually bulk-mailed and untargeted).

Opt-in
A customer proactively agrees to receive further information.

Opt-out
A customer declines the offer to receive further information.

Cold list
Data about individuals that are rented or sold by a third party.

House list
Data about existing customers used to market products to encourage future purchase.

protection law. This Act is significant for marketers since it applies specifically to electronic communications such as email and the monitoring of websites.

Clauses 22 to 24 are the main clauses relevant to email communications.

| Activity 3.6 | Privacy and social media |

Purpose

To consider the implications of government intervention in privacy online.

Activity

Visit the RUSI website and read about how a new electronic listening station has triggered controversy as government authorities demand more cooperation from Internet companies.

Question

After reading the article at www.rusi.org/analysis/commentary/ref:C545CB576F0A7D/#.VLu5n0esV8E discuss the extent to which you agree with the statement 'privacy is not an absolute right' (Pritchard, 2014).

| Digital marketing insight 3.4 | UK and European email marketing law |

As an example of European privacy law which covers use of email, SMS and cookies for marketing, we review the implications for managers of the UK enactment of 2002/58/EC Directive on Privacy and Electronic Communications. We will contrast this with the law in other European countries. This came into force in the UK on 11 December 2003 as the Privacy and Electronic Communications Regulations (PECR) Act. The law is published at: www.legislation.gov.uk/uksi/2003/2426/contents/made. Consumer marketers in the UK also need to heed the Code of Advertising Practice from the Advertising Standards Agency (www.asa.org.uk/advertising-codes.aspx). This has broadly similar aims and places similar restrictions on marketers to the PECR law. We will summarise the main implications of the law by picking out key phrases. The new PECR law:

1 Applies to consumer marketing using email or SMS text messages

22(1) applies to *individual subscribers*. 'Individual subscribers' means consumers, although the Information Commissioner has stated that this may be reviewed in future to include business subscribers, as is the case in some other countries such as Italy and Germany.

Although this sounds like great news for business-to-business (B2B) marketers – and some take the view 'great, the new law doesn't apply to us' – this could be dangerous. There has been adjudication by the Advertising Standards Agency which found against a B2B organisation that had unwittingly emailed consumers from what they believed was an in-house list of B2B customers.

2 Is an 'opt-in' regime

The law applies to 'unsolicited communications' (22(1)). It was introduced with a view to reducing spam, although we all know its impact will be limited on spammers beyond

Europe. The relevant phrase is part of 22(2) where the recipient must have 'previously notified the sender that he consents' or has proactively agreed to receive commercial email. This is opt-in. Opt-in can be achieved online or offline through asking people whether they want to receive email. Online this is often done through a tick-box.

The approach required by the law has, in common with many aspects of data protection and privacy law, been used by many organisations for some time. In other words, sending unsolicited emails was thought to be unethical and also not in the best interests of the company because of the risk of annoying customers. In fact, the law conforms to an established approach known as **permission marketing**, a term coined by US commentator Seth Godin (1999, Chapter 6 – first four chapters available free from **www.permission.com**).

Viral marketing

One widespread business practice that is not covered explicitly in the PECR law is **viral marketing** (Chapter 9). In the guidelines for marketers for the law, the commissioner states that it 'takes a dim view' of viral marketing, especially when it is incentivised, and the marketer needs to be careful that consent of the friend is agreed.

3 Requires an opt-out option in all communications

An opt-out or method of 'unsubscribing' is required so that the recipient does not receive future communications. In a database this means that a 'do not email' field must be created to avoid emailing these customers. The law states that a 'simple means of refusing' future communications is required both when the details were first collected and in each subsequent communication.

4 Does not apply to existing customers when marketing similar products

This common-sense clause (22(3)(a)) states that previous opt-in is not required if the contact details were obtained during the course of the sale or negotiations for the sale of a product or service. This is sometimes known as the 'soft or implied opt-in exception'. This key soft opt-in caveat is interpreted differently in different European countries, with seven countries – Italy, Denmark, Germany, Austria, Greece, Finland and Spain – not including it. The differences mean that marketers managing campaigns across Europe need to take the differences in different countries into account.

Clause 22(3)(b) adds that when marketing to existing customers, the marketer may market 'similar products and services only'. Case law will help in clarifying this. For example, for a bank, it is not clear whether a customer with an insurance policy could be targeted for a loan.

5 Requires contact details must be provided

It is not sufficient to send an email with a simple sign-off from 'the marketing team' or 'the web team' with no further contact details. The law requires a name, address or phone number where recipients can direct complaints.

6 Requires the 'from' identification of the sender to be clear

Spammers aim to disguise the email originator. The law says that the identity of the person who sends the communication must not be 'disguised or concealed' and that a valid address to 'send a request that such communications cease' should be provided.

7 Applies to direct marketing communications

The communications that the legislation refers to are for 'direct marketing'. This suggests that other communications involved with customer service, such as an email

---

Permission marketing
Customers agree (opt in) to be involved in an organisation's marketing activities, usually as a result of an incentive

Viral marketing
A marketing message is communicated from one person to another, facilitated by different media, such as word-of-mouth, email or websites. It implies rapid transmission of messages is intended.

Cookies
Cookies are small text files stored on an end user's computer to enable websites to identify the user.

about a monthly phone statement, are not covered, so the opt-out choice may not be required here.

8 Restricts the use of cookies

Some privacy campaigners consider that the user's privacy is invaded by planting **cookies** or electronic tags on the end user's computer. The concept of the cookie and its associated law is not straightforward, so it warrants separate discussion.

Digital marketing insight 3.5 | Understanding cookies

A cookie is a data file placed on your computer which identifies that individual computer. 'Cookie' derives from the Unix operating system term 'magic cookie', which meant something passed between routines or programs that enables the receiver to perform some operation.

Types of cookies

The main cookie types are:

Persistent cookies
Cookies that remain on the computer after a visitor session has ended. Used to recognise returning visitors.

Session cookies
A cookie used to manage a single visitor session.

First-party cookies
Served by the site currently in use – typically for e-commerce sites.

Third-party cookies
Served by another site to the one being viewed – typically for portals where an ad network will track remotely or where the web analytics software places a cookie.

- **Persistent cookies** – these stay on a user's computer between multiple sessions and are most valuable for marketers to identify repeat visits to sites.
- Temporary or **session cookies** (single session) – useful for tracking within pages of a session such as on an e-commerce site.
- **First-party cookies** – served by the site visitors are accessing. These can be persistent or session cookies.
- **Third-party cookies** – served by another site to the one being viewed, typically for publishers where an ad network will track remotely or where the web analytics software places a cookie. These are typically persistent cookies.

Cookies are stored as individual text files in a directory on a personal computer. There is usually one file per website. For example: dave_chaffey@british-airways.txt. This file contains encoded information as follows:

FLT_VIS|K:bapzRnGdxBYUU|D:Jul-25–1999| british-airways.com/0425259904 29357426 1170747936 29284034*

Although many web users may think personally identifiable information is stored. The information in the cookie file is essentially just an identification code which may link to a customer database and the date of the last visit, although other information could be stored.

Cookies are specific to a particular browser and computer, so if a user connects from a different computer, such as at work, or starts using a different browser, the website will not identify him or her as a similar user.

What are cookies used for?

Common marketing applications of cookies include:

- *Personalising a site for an individual*. Cookies are used to identify individual users and retrieve their preferences from a database according to an identifier stored in the cookie. For example, I subscribe to the Econsultancy service (www.econsultancy.com);

each time I return I do not have the annoyance of having to log in because it remembers my previous visit. Many sites feature a 'Remember Me' option which implies using a cookie to recognise a returning visitor. Retailers such as Amazon can use cookies to recognise returning visitors and can recommend related books purchased by other readers.

- *Online ordering systems*. This enables a site such as **Tesco.com** to track what is in your basket as you order different products.
- *Tracking within a site*. Web analytics software such as Google Analytics, Adobe Analytics or Webtrends analyses statistics on visitors to websites and relies on persistent cookies to find the proportion of repeat visitors to a website. Webtrends and other tools increasingly use first-party cookies since they are more accurate and less likely to be blocked. Marketers should check whether use of first-party cookies is possible on their site.
- *Tracking across sites*. Advertising networks use cookies to track the number of times a particular computer user has been shown a particular banner advertisement; they can also track adverts served on sites across an ad network. There was an individual rights outcry in the late 1990s since Doubleclick was using this to profile customers. Doubleclick no longer operates an ad network, partly due to this.

Affiliate networks and pay-per-click ad networks such as Google AdWords and Yahoo! Search services may also use cookies to track through from a click on a third-party site to a sale or lead being generated on a destination or merchant site. These approaches tend to use third-party cookies. For example, if conversion tracking is enabled in Google Adwords, Google sets a cookie when a user clicks through on an ad. If this user buys the product, then the purchase confirmation page will include script code supplied by Google to make a check for a cookie placed by Google. If there is a match, the sale is attributed to AdWords. An alternative approach using third-party tracking is that different online campaigns have different tracking parameters or codes within the links through to the destination site, and when the user arrives on a site from a particular source (such as Google AdWords) this is identified and a cookie set. When purchase confirmation occurs, this can then be attributed back to the original source (e.g. Google AdWords) and the particular referrer.

Owing to the large investments made now in pay-per-click marketing and affiliate marketing by many companies, cookie privacy laws and deletion are an area of concern for marketers since the tracking can become inaccurate. However, a sale should still occur even if the cookies are blocked or deleted, so the main consequence is that the ROI (return on investment) of online advertising or pay-per-click marketing may look lower than expected. In affiliate marketing, this phenomenon may benefit the marketer in that payment may not need to be made to the third party if a cookie has been deleted (or blocked) between the time of original click-through and sale.

Privacy issues with cookie use

The problem for digital marketers is that, despite these important applications, blocking by browsers or security software and deletion by users has increased dramatically. Research by Global Web Index (2014) suggests that almost half of online shoppers are now deleting cookies while one in five say they are using tools such as DoNotTrackMe to prevent companies from monitoring their Internet activities.

It seems that many distrust cookies since they indicate that a 'big brother' is monitoring their actions. Others fear that their personal details or credit card details may be accessed by other websites.

Legal constraints on cookies

The PECR law, particularly its update in May 2012, gives companies guidance on their use of cookies. The original 2003 law states:

a person shall not use an electronic communications network to store information, or to gain access to information stored, in the terminal equipment of a subscriber or user unless the following requirements are met.

The requirements are: (a) the user is provided with clear and comprehensive information about the purposes of the storage of, or access to, that information; and (b) is given the opportunity to refuse the storage of or access to that information; (a) suggests that it is important that there is a clear **privacy statement** and (b) suggests that explicit opt-in to cookies is required – this is what we now see on many sites following the implementation of the law in 2013. This was thought by many commentators to be a curious provision since this facility to delete cookies is available in the web browser. A further provision clarifies this. The law states: 'where such storage or access is strictly necessary for the provision of an information society service requested by the subscriber or user'. This indicates that for an e-commerce service session cookies are legitimate without the need for opt-in. It is arguable whether the identification of return visitors is 'strictly necessary' and this is why some sites have a 'remember me' tick box next to the log-in. Through doing this they are compliant with the law. Using cookies for tracking return visits alone would seem to be outlawed, but we will have to see how case law develops over the coming years before this is resolved.

With continuing use of cookies with limited information about their usage, another attempt was made in 2011 by European legislators to control their usage for marketing. Smart Insights (2011a) describes the guidance on this law to be enforced from 25 May 2012. This new law could have significant implications for marketers who currently make use of display advertising, behavioural targeting and web analytics. The new law followed press articles about cookie-based targeting and the 'Do Not Track Us' (http://donottrack.us/) campaign in the US supported by the Electronic Frontier Federation which aims to introduce a universal web tracking opt-out.

Privacy statement
Information on a website explaining how and why individuals' data are collected, processed and stored.

Worldwide regulations on privacy and electronic communications

In the US in January 2004, a new federal law known as the CAN-SPAM Act was introduced to assist in the control of unsolicited email. CAN-SPAM stands for 'Controlling the Assault of Non-Solicited Pornography and Marketing' (an ironic juxtaposition between pornography and marketing). This harmonised separate laws in different US states, but was less strict than in some states such as California. The Act requires unsolicited commercial email messages to be labelled (though not by a standard method) and to include opt-out instructions and the sender's physical address. It prohibits the use of deceptive subject lines and false headers in such messages. Current details of CAN-SPAM act compliance guidelines can be found at: **http://business.ftc.gov/documents/bus61-can-spam-act-compliance-guide-business**. Anti-spam legislation in other countries can be accessed at:

- **www.privacy.gov.au** (Australia enacted a SPAM act in 2003);
- **www.privcom.gc.ca** (Canada has a privacy act);
- **www.privacy.org.nz** (New Zealand Privacy Commissioner);
- **www.spamlaws.com** (summary for all countries).

We conclude this section on privacy legislation with a checklist summary of the practical steps that are required to audit a company's compliance with data protection and privacy legislation. Companies should:

1 Follow privacy and consumer protection guidelines and laws in all local markets. Use local privacy and security certification where available.

2 Notify or inform the site visitor before asking for information on:

- who the company is;
- what personal data are collected, processed and stored;
- the purpose of collection;
- how the site visitor can opt out (be unsubscribed from email lists or cookies);
- how the site visitor can obtain information held about them.

3 Ask for consent for collecting sensitive personal data, and it is good practice to ask before collecting any type of data.

4 Reassure customers by providing clear and effective privacy statements and explaining the purpose of data collection.

5 Let individuals know when 'cookies' or other covert software are used to collect information about them.

6 Never collect or retain personal data unless it is strictly necessary for the organisation's purposes. For example, a person's name and full address should not be required to provide an online quotation. If extra information is required for marketing purposes this should be made clear and the provision of such information should be optional.

7 Amend incorrect data when informed and tell others. Enable correction on site.

8 Only use data for marketing (by the company or third parties) when a user has been informed this is the case and has agreed to this. (This is opt-in.)

9 Provide the option for customers to stop receiving information. (This is opt-out.)

10 Use appropriate security technology to protect the customer information on your site.

2 Disability and discrimination law

Accessibility legislation
Legislation intended to protect users of websites with disabilities including visual disability.

Laws relating to discriminating against disabled users who may find it more difficult to use websites because of audio, visual or motor impairment are known as **accessibility legislation**. This is often contained within disability and discrimination acts. In the UK, the relevant act is the Disability Discrimination Act 2010.

Web accessibility refers to enabling all users of a website to interact with it regardless of disabilities they may have or the web browser or platform they are using to access the site. The visually impaired or blind are the main audience that designing an accessible website can help. Coverage of the requirements that accessibility places on web design are covered in Chapter 7.

3 Brand and trademark protection

Online brand and trademark protection covers several areas, including use of a brand name within domain names and use of trademarks within other websites and in online adverts.

Domain name registration

Domain name registration
The process of reserving a unique web address that can be used to refer to the company website

Most companies are likely to own several domains, perhaps for different product lines or countries or for specific marketing campaigns. Domain name disputes can arise when an individual or company has registered a domain name which another company claims they have the right to. This is sometimes referred to as 'cybersquatting'.

One of the best-known cases was brought in 1998 by Marks and Spencer and other high street retailers, since another company, 'One In a Million Limited', had registered names such as **marks&spencer.com, britishtelecom.net** and **sainsbury.com**. It then tried to sell these names for a profit. The companies already had sites with more familiar addresses, such as **marksandspencers.co.uk**, but had not taken the precaution of registering all related domains with different forms of spelling and different top-level domains, such as **.net**. Unsurprisingly, an injunction was issued against One in a Million, which was no longer able to use these names.

The problem of companies' names being misappropriated was common during the 1990s, but companies still need to be sure to register all related domain names for each brand since new top-level domain names are created through time, such as .biz and .eu.

If you are responsible for websites, you need to check that domain names are automatically renewed by your hosting company (as most are today). For example, the .co.uk domain must be renewed every two years. Companies that don't manage this process potentially risk losing their domain name since another company could register it if the domain name has lapsed. A further option with domain registration is to purchase generic domain names of established sites which historically have performed well in the search engines. Digital marketing insight 3.6 shows the potential value of different generic domains.

Using competitor names and trademarks in meta-tags (for search engine optimisation)

Meta-tags, which are part of the HTML code of a site, are used to market websites by enabling them to appear more prominently in search engines as part of search engine optimisation (SEO) (see Chapter 8). Some companies have tried putting the name of a competitor company within the meta-tags. This is not legal since case law has found against companies that have used this approach. A further issue of marketing-related law is privacy law for email marketing, which was considered in the previous section.

Digital marketing insight 3.6   How much is a domain worth?

One of the highest values attached to a domain in Europe was paid in 2008 when the website **cruise.co.uk** paid the German travel company Nees Reisen £560,000 for the rival name **cruises.co.uk**. *Guardian* (2008) reported the new owner of **cruises.co.uk** as saying that he hopes to use the new domain differently – by turning the site into an online intermediary or community for cruising enthusiasts while its existing **cruise.co.uk** will concentrate on offering the best deals for voyages. Explaining the valuation, **cruise.co.uk**'s managing director, Seamus Conlon stated:

> *'Cruises' is consistently ranked first on Google, with 'cruise' just behind. We wanted the top positions so that when Internet users are searching for cruise deals, reviews or news we are the first port of call. The cruise market is one of the fastest and most consistently growing sectors in the travel industry.*

Since the commercialisation of the web, domain names have changed hands for high prices, for example:

- **business.com** for $7.5 million, December 1999;
- **AsSeenOnTv.com** for $5.1 million, January 2000;
- **Credcards.com** for $2.7 million, July 2004;
- **Insure.com** for $16 million in 2009;
- **sex.com** for $14 million, October 2010;
- **casino.tt** for $2.0 million, May 2011.

However, the release of many new gTLDs by ICANN means the relative value of domains has been drifting downwards. Recently, **DVDs.com**, which was registered in 1996 and sold publicly for $300,000, was listed in the auction at a starting bid of $50,000. Even at this dramatically reduced price the domain did not sell (Jacobs, 2013).

Using competitor names and trademarks in pay-per-click advertising

Pay-per-click search marketing
Refers to when a company pays for text ads to be displayed on the search engine results pages when a specific keyphrase is entered by the search users. It is so called since the marketer pays for each time the hypertext link in the ad is clicked on.

A similar approach can potentially be used in **pay-per-click marketing** (explained in Chapter 9) to advertise on competitors' names and trademarks. For example, if a search user types 'Dell laptop', can an advertiser bid to place an ad offering an 'HP laptop'? There is less case law in this area and differing findings have occurred in the US and France (such advertising is not permitted in France).

Reputational damage in advertising

Companies fear reputational damage through advertising on sites with which they wouldn't want their brand associated because of ad buys on social networks or ad networks (Chapter 9) where it was not clear what content their ads would be associated with. For example, Vodafone removed all its advertising from the social network Facebook after its ads appeared on the group profile for the British National Party. Many other advertisers withdrew their advertising as a result.

Monitoring brand conversations in social networks and blogs

Online brand reputation management and alerting software tools offer real-time alerts when comments or mentions about a brand are posted online in different locations, including blogs and social networks. Some basic tools are available including:

- Googlealert (**www.googlealert.com**) and Google Alerts (**www.google.com/alerts**) which will alert companies when any new pages appear that contain a search phrase such as your company or brand names.
- Nielsen BuzzMetrics' BlogPulse (**www.blogpulse.com**) gives trends and listings of any phrase and individual postings can be viewed.

There are also more sophisticated online reputation-management services which offer more in-depth analysis on whether the sentiment is positive or negative and cover other issues such as unauthorised use of logos and use of trademarks. Examples include Mark Monitor, Reputation Intelligence, Brand Intelligence, Big Mouth Media and Market Sentinel.

Policing online trademark infringement, given the range of opportunities for this and the lag between what the law stipulates and what is possible through the technology, is challenging.

4 Intellectual property rights

Intellectual property rights
Protect the intangible property created by corporations or individuals that is protected under copyright, trade secret and patent laws.

Intellectual property rights (IPRs) protect designs, ideas and inventions and include content and services developed for e-commerce sites. Closely related is copyright law which is designed to protect authors, producers, broadcasters and performers by ensuring they see some returns from their works every time they are experienced. The European Directive of Copyright (2001/29/EC) came into force in many countries in 2003. This is a significant update to the law which covers new technologies and approaches such as streaming a broadcast via the Internet.

IP can be misappropriated in two senses online. First, an organisation's IP may be misappropriated and you need to protect against this. For example, it is relatively easy to copy web content and re-publish on another site, and this practice is not unknown among smaller businesses. Reputation management services can be used to assess how an organisation's content, logos and **trademarks** are being used on other websites.

Trademark
A trademark is a unique word or phrase that distinguishes your company. The mark can be registered as plain or designed text, artwork or a combination. In theory, colours, smells and sounds can also be trademarks.

Secondly, an organisation may misappropriate content inadvertently. Some employees may infringe copyright if they are not aware of the law. Additionally, some methods of designing transactional websites have been patented. For example, Amazon has patented its 'One-click' purchasing option, which is why you do not see this labelling and process on other sites.

5 Contract law

We will look at two aspects of forming an electronic contract – the country of origin principle and distance selling laws.

Country of origin principle

The contract formed between a buyer and a seller on a website will be subject to the laws of a particular country. In Europe, many such laws are specified at the regional (European Union) level, but are interpreted differently in different countries. This raises the issue of the jurisdiction in which law applies – is it that for the buyer, for example located in Germany, or the seller (merchant), whose site is based in France? Although this has been unclear, in 2002 attempts were made by the EU to adopt the 'country of origin principle'. This means that the law for the contract will be that where the merchant is located. The Out-Law site produced by lawyers Pinsent Mason gives more information on jurisdiction (**www.out-law.com/page-479**).

Distance-selling law

Sparrow (2000) advises different forms of disclaimers to protect the retailer. For example, if a retailer made an error with the price or the product details, then the retailer is not bound to honour a contract, since it was only displaying the products as 'an invitation to treat', not a fixed offer.

A well-known case was when an e-retailer offered televisions for £2.99 due to an error in pricing a £299 product. Numerous purchases were made, but the e-retailer claimed that a contract had not been established simply by accepting the online order, although the customers did not see it that way! Unfortunately, no legal precedent was established since the case did not come to trial.

Disclaimers can also be used to limit liability if the website service causes a problem for the user, such as a financial loss resulting from an action based on erroneous content. Furthermore, Sparrow suggests that terms and conditions should be developed to refer to issues such as timing of delivery and damage or loss of goods.

The distance-selling directive also has a bearing on e-commerce contracts in the European Union. It was originally developed to protect people using mail order (by post or phone). The main requirements, which are consistent with what most reputable e-retailers would do anyway, are that e-commerce sites must contain easily accessible content which clearly states:

- the company's identity including address;
- the main features of the goods or services;
- price information, including tax and, if appropriate, delivery costs;
- the period for which the offer or price remains valid;
- payment, delivery and fulfilment performance arrangements;
- right of the consumer to withdraw, i.e. cancellation terms;
- the minimum duration of the contract and whether the contract for the supply of products or services is to be permanent or recurrent, if appropriate;
- whether an equivalent product or service might be substituted, and confirmation as to whether the seller pays the return costs in this event.

After the contract has been entered into, the supplier is required to provide written confirmation of the information provided. An email confirmation is now legally binding provided both parties have agreed that email is an acceptable form for the contract. It is always advisable to obtain an electronic signature to confirm that both parties have agreed the contract, and this is especially valuable in the event of a dispute. The default position for services is that there is no cancellation right once services begin.

Distance selling laws have taken some time to be updated to reflect online trading, particularly of digital products. For example, new EU rules on consumer rights initially proposed in 2008, then detailed in 2011, only came into force in some countries such as the UK in 2014. These changes to protect consumers were intended to:

Eliminate hidden charges and costs on the Internet

This is protection against online 'cost traps' on the Internet. This happens when fraudsters try to trick people into paying for 'free' services, such as horoscopes or recipes. Consumers must explicitly confirm that they understand that they have to pay a price.

Increased price transparency

Traders have to disclose the total cost of the product or service, as well as any extra fees. Online shoppers will not have to pay charges or other costs if they were not properly informed before they place an order.

Banning pre-ticked boxes on websites

When shopping online – for instance buying a plane or content ticket – it's common to be offered additional options during the purchase process, such as travel insurance or car rental. These additional services may be offered through 'pre-ticked' boxes. With the new Directive, pre-ticked boxes will be banned across the European Union.

Better consumer protection in relation to digital products

Information on digital content including the application of any technical protection measures, for example limiting the right for the consumers to make copies of the content. Consumers will have a right to withdraw from purchases of digital content, such as music or video downloads, but only up until the moment the actual downloading process begins.

6 Online advertising law

Advertising standards that are enforced by independent agencies such as the UK's Advertising Standards Authority Code also apply in the Internet environment (although they are traditionally less strongly policed, leading to more 'edgy' creative executions online which are intended to have a viral effect). In the UK, the ASA maintains a list of 'noncompliant advertisers' until the offending sites have been updated **www.asa.org.uk/Rulings/Non-compliant-online-advertisers.aspx**. At the time of writing, non-compliant advertisers were diverse, including: traditional Chinese medicine, car accessories, ticket agencies, clothing retail, online prize promotions and spas.

One particular challenge of online advertising for consumers is that marketing communications must be obviously identifiable. Guidance covers these cases:

- Unsolicited email marketing communications must be obviously identifiable as marketing communications without the need to open them.
- Marketing communications must not falsely claim or imply that the marketer is acting as a consumer (i.e. marketers should not leave reviews about their companies or competitors on behalf of their business).
- Marketers and publishers must make clear that advertorials are marketing communications – for example, by heading them 'advertisement feature'. This guidance is necessary since the increase in **native advertising** has meant that many pieces of content masquerading as ads haven't been disclosed.

Native advertising
Online content that it is created to promote or enhance a brand such as a publisher article or social media update. Such content should be disclosed as advertising by law in many countries, but often it isn't.

In the US, the Federal Trade Commission (FTC) has defined 'native advertising' as 'blending advertisements with news, entertainment, and other editorial content in digital media'– that is, it is synonymous with 'sponsored content'.

Examples of native advertising that have broken advertising guidelines

- In 2012 England footballer Wayne Rooney used his Twitter feed to mention his sponsor Nike, passing off a promotional message as a personal comment without clearly showing it was an advertisement.
- In 2013, *The Atlantic*, the 157-year-old magazine, carried a story about the Church of Scientology on its website celebrating the church's past year of worldwide expansion.
- In 2014, Buzz feed featured an infographic '10 Quotes Every Grad Needs to Read' sponsored by HarperCollins.
- In 2014 British 'vloggers' or 'YouTubers', including Phil Lester and Dan Howell, were censured after featuring an Oreo promotion 'Oreo Lick Race'.

Social forces

Social forces are closely linked with culture and have significant implications for digital marketing. Broadly speaking, the key factors which make up these forces are: social communities based on demographic profile, social exclusion, and cultural factors.

In the previous chapter, we looked at demographics and consumer adoption of the web and found great variation in terms of levels of Internet access, amount of usage and engagement in online purchases. In this chapter, our interest is in the wider impact of demographic influences: changes in populations. Why this is important is that the size and growth rates of populations have implications for digital marketing strategy and planning. One highly important shift in demographic trends is that for the first time in the history of the world over 50 per cent of the population lives in an urban setting.

The world population is estimated at just under 7 billion, with 26.3 per cent being 14 and under, 65.9 per cent between the ages of 15 and 64 and 7.9 per cent over the age of 65. Population growth is estimated to be 1.09 per cent. The expanding population means there is increasing demand on finite resources. Changes in population are important to marketers as they create new market opportunities. Currently, emerging markets in Russia, India, Brazil and China represent market growth but there are other demographic factors before making a major investment in developing and accessing emerging markets – for example, two-thirds of the world's illiterate adults live in just eight countries: Bangladesh, China, Egypt, Ethiopia, India, Indonesia, Nigeria and Pakistan (CIA, 2011).

Analysis of demographic trends can reveal important issues, such as that there is a significant group in each national population of at least a quarter of the adult population that does not envisage ever using the Internet. Clearly, the lack of demand for Internet services from this group needs to be taken into account when forecasting future demand. Furthermore, this raises the questions of social isolation, or what the Oxford Internet Institute called in its research into Internet usage: 'Internet disengagement'. Others consider this to be an aspect of 'social exclusion'.

Social exclusion

Social exclusion
Part of society is excluded from the facilities available to the remainder.

The social impact of the Internet has also concerned many commentators because the Internet has the potential effect of accentuating differences in quality of life, both within a society in a single country and between different nations, essentially creating 'information haves' and 'information have-nots'. This may accentuate **social exclusion** where one part of society is excluded from the facilities available to the remainder and so becomes isolated. The United Nations noted, as early in the growth of the Internet as 1999, that parallel worlds are developing where:

those with income, education and – literally – connections have cheap and instantaneous access to information. The rest are left with uncertain, slow and costly access . . . the advantage of being connected will overpower the marginal and impoverished, cutting off their voices and concerns from the global conversation.

Developed countries with the economies to support it are promoting the use of IT and the Internet through social programmes, such as the UK government's UK Online initiative, which operated between 2000 and 2004 to promote the use of the Internet by business and consumers. The European Commission (2007) believes that 'e-Inclusion policies and actions have made significant progress in implementing the goal of an inclusive knowledge-based society'. The Commission recommends that governments should focus on three aspects of e-inclusion:

1 The access divide (or 'early digital divide'), which considers the gap between those with and those without access. Governments will encourage competition to reduce costs and give a wider choice of access through different platforms (e.g. mobile phone or interactive TV access in addition to fixed PC access).
2 The usage divide ('primary digital divide'), concentrating on those who have access but are non-users. Governments promote learning of basic Internet skills through ICT courses to those with the highest risks of disengagement.
3 The divide stemming from quality of use ('secondary digital divide'), focussing on differentials in participation rates of those people who have access and are users. Training can also be used to reduce this divide.

Cultural forces

The local language and culture of a country or region can dramatically affect the requirements of users of a web service. We discuss this issue further in Chapter 7 on website design. The types of sites used (media consumption) and search engines used can also vary dramatically by country, as discussed in Chapter 9. So it is important for situation analysis to review country differences.

Environmental and green issues related to Internet usage

The future state of our planet is a widely held social concern that is closely related to economic issues. Although technology is generally seen as detrimental to the environment – think long- and short-haul flights, TVs and electronic gadgets burning fuel when left on standby – there are some arguments that e-commerce and digital communications can have environmental benefits. These benefits are also often beneficial to companies in that they can make cost savings while positioning themselves as environmentally concerned – see Digital marketing insight 3.7. If companies trading online can explain these benefits to their customers effectively, as HSBC has done, then this can benefit these online channels.

But what does the research show about how much e-shopping reduces greenhouse gas emissions? A study by Finnish researchers Siikavirta *et al.* (2003), limited to e-grocery shopping, has suggested that, depending on the home delivery model used, it is theoretically possible to reduce the greenhouse gas emissions generated by grocery shopping between 18 per cent to 87 per cent compared with the situation in which household members go to the store. Some of the constraints that were used in the simulation model include: maximum of 60 orders per route, maximum of 3000 litres per route, working time maximum 11 hours per van, working time maximum 5 hours per route, loading time 20 minutes per route, drop-off time 2 minutes per customer.

Digital marketing insight 3.7   HSBC customers plant virtual forest

HSBC has committed to improving the environment since it became a climate-neutral company globally. Through the use of green technologies and emission-offset trading, HSBC counteracts all CO2 emissions generated by its building operations and corporate travel. In 2006, 35 per cent of operations in North America were offset by investments in Renewable Energy Certificates from wind power alone.

Another aspect of its green policy is its online banking service, where it encourages paperless billing. For example, in the UK in 2007 over 400,000 customers switched from paper statements to online delivery, creating a virtual tree each time, and for every 20 virtual trees HSBC promised to plant a real one.

Potentially, online shopping through transactional e-commerce can also have environmental benefits. Imagine a situation where we no longer travelled to the shops, and 100 per cent of items were efficiently delivered to us at home or at work. This would reduce traffic considerably! Although this situation is inconceivable since most of us enjoy shopping in the real world too much, online shopping is growing and it may be having an impact. Research by the Internet Media in Retail Group (**www.imrg.org**) shows the increasing importance of e-commerce in the UK, where over 10 per cent of retail sales are now online. In 2007 it launched a Go Green, Go Online campaign where it identified six reasons why it believes e-commerce is green. These are:

1   *Fewer vehicle miles*. Shopping is the most frequent reason for car travel in Great Britain, accounting for 20 per cent of all trips, and for 12 per cent of mileage. A study by the Swiss Online Grocer LeShop.ch calculated that each time a customer decides to buy online rather than go shopping by car, 3.5 kg of CO2 emissions are saved.
2   *Lower inventory requirements*. The trend towards pre-selling online – i.e. taking orders for products before they are built, as implemented by Dell – avoids the production of obsolete goods that have to be disposed of if they don't sell, with associated wastage in energy and natural resources.
3   *Fewer printed materials*. Online e-newsletters and brochures replace their physical equivalent, so saving paper and distribution costs. Data from the Direct Mail Information Service shows that direct mail volumes have fallen in recent years. This must be partly due to marketing emails, which the DMA email benchmarks (**www .dma.org.uk**) show to number in their billions in the UK alone.
4   *Less packaging*. Although theoretically there is less need for fancy packaging if an item is sold online, this argument is less convincing, since most items like software or electronic items still come in packaging to help convince us we have bought the right thing – to reduce post-purchase dissonance. At least those billions of music tracks downloaded from iTunes and Napster don't require any packaging or plastic.
5   *Less waste*. Across the whole supply chain of procurement, manufacturing and distribution, the Internet can help reduce product and distribution cycles. Some even claim that auction services like eBay and Amazon Marketplace, which enable redistribution of second-hand items, can promote recycling.
6   *Dematerialisation*. Better known as digitisation, this is the availability of products like software, music and video in digital form.

The researchers estimated that this would lead to a reduction of all Finland's greenhouse gas emissions by as much as 1 per cent, but in reality the figure is much lower since only 10 per cent of grocery shopping trips are online. Cairns (2005) completed a study for the UK which shows the importance of grocery shopping – she estimates that car travel for food and other household items represents about 40 per cent of all UK shopping trips by car, and about 5 per cent of all car use. She considers that a direct substitution of car trips by van trips could reduce vehicle-km by 70 per cent or more. A broader study by Ahmed and Sharma (2006) has used value-chain analysis to assess the role of the Internet in changing the amount of energy and materials consumed by businesses for each part of the supply chain. However, no estimates of savings are made.

As a conclusion to this chapter, consider Case study 3, which highlights the marketplace issues faced by a new e-business launched in 2005.

Case Study 3	Zopa launches a new lending model

This case shows how it is still possible to develop radical new online business models. It shows how an online business can be launched without large-scale expenditure on advertising and how it needs to be well targeted at its intended audience.

Context

It might be thought that innovation in business models was left behind in the dot-com era, but still fledgling businesses are launching new online services. Zopa is an interesting example of a pureplay social or peer-to-peer lending service launched in March 2005 with US and Italian sites launching in 2007 and a Japanese site launched in 2008.

Zopa is an online service which enables borrowers and lenders to bypass high street banks. There are over 150,000 UK members and 200,000 worldwide. Zopa is an example of a consumer-to-consumer (peer-to-peer) exchange intermediary.

Zopa stands for 'zone of possible agreement', which is a term from business theory. It refers to the overlap between one person's bottom line (the lowest they're prepared to receive for something they are offering) and another person's top line (the most they're prepared to pay for something). This approach underpins negotiations about the majority of types of products and services.

The business model

The exchange provides a matching facility between people who want to borrow with people who want to lend. Each lender's money is parcelled out between at least 50 borrowers. Zopa revenue is based on charging borrowers 1 per cent of their loan as a fee, and from commission on any repayment protection insurance that the borrower selects. At the time of launch, Zopa estimated it needed to gain just a 0.2 per cent share of the UK loan market to break even, which it could achieve within 18 months of launch.

In 2007, listings were launched (**www.zopa.com/ loans**) where loans can be requested by individuals in a similar way to eBay listings.

Borrowers can borrow relatively cheaply over shorter periods for small amounts. This is the reverse of banks, where if you borrow more and for longer it gets cheaper. The service will also appeal to borrowers who have difficulty gaining credit ratings from traditional financial services providers.

For lenders, returns are in the range of 20 to 30 per cent higher than putting money in a deposit account, but there is the risk of bad debt. Lenders choose the minimum interest rate that they are prepared to accept after bad debt has been taken into account for different markets within Zopa. Borrowers are placed in different risk categories with different interest rates according to their credit histories (using the same Equifax-based credit ratings as used by the banks) and lenders can decide which balance of risk against return they require.

Borrowers who fail to pay are pursued through the same mechanism as banks use and also get a black mark against their credit histories. But, for the lender, their investment is not protected by any compensation scheme, unless they have been defrauded.

The *Financial Times* reported that banks don't currently see Zopa as a threat to their high-street business. One financial analyst said Zopa was 'one of these things that could catch on but probably won't'.

Zopa does not have a contact centre. According to its website, enquiries are restricted to email in order to keep its costs down. However, there is a service promise of answering emails within three hours during working hours.

Although the service was launched initially in the UK in 2005, *Financial Times* (2005) reported that people in 20 countries want to set up franchises, including China, New Zealand, India and some South American countries.

The peer-to-peer lending marketplace now has several providers. The social lending site Kiva allows lenders to give to a specific entrepreneur in a poor or developing world country. In the US, Prosper (www.prosper.com) has over 600,000 members and uses a loan listing model.

About the founders

The three founders of Zopa were chief executive Richard Duvall, chief financial officer James Alexander and David Nicholson, inventor of the concept and business architect. All were involved with Egg, with Richard Duvall creating the online bank for Prudential in 1998. Mr Alexander had been strategy director at Egg after joining in 2000, and previously had written the business plan for Smile, another online bank owned by the Co-operative Bank. The founders were also joined by Sarah Matthews, who was Egg's brand development director.

Target market

The idea for the business was developed from market research that showed there was a potential market of 'freeformers' to be tapped.

Freeformers are typically not in standard employment; rather they are self-employed or complete project-based or freelance work. Examples include consultants and entrepreneurs. Consequently, their incomes and lifestyles may be irregular, although they may still be assessed as creditworthy. According to James Alexander, 'they're people who are not understood by banks, which value stability in people's lives and income over everything else'. Institute of Directors (IOD) (2005) reported that the research showed that freeformers had 'much less of a spending model of money and much more of an asset model'.

Surprisingly, the research indicated a large number of freeformers. *New Media Age* (2005) reported Duvall as estimating that in the UK there may be around 6 million freeformers (of a population of around 60 million). Duvall is quoted as saying: 'It's a group that's growing really quickly. I think in 10 or 15 years' time most people will work this way. It's happening right across the developed world. We've been doing some research in the US and we think there are some 30 or 40 million people there with these attitudes and behaviours.'

Some of the directors see themselves as freeformers: they have multiple interests and do not only work for Zopa; James Alexander works for one day a week in a charity and Sarah Matthews works just three days a week for Zopa. You can see example personas of typical borrowers and lenders on the website: www.zopa.com/ZopaWeb/public/how/zopamembers.shtml.

From reviewing the customer base, lenders and borrowers are often united by a desire to distance themselves from conventional institutions. James Alexander says: 'I spend a lot of time talking to members and have found enormous goodwill towards the idea, which is really like lending to family members or within a community.' But he also says that some of the lenders are simply entrepreneurs who have the funds, understand portfolio diversification and risk and are lending on Zopa alongside other investments.

Business status

The *Financial Times* (2005) reported that Zopa had just 300 members at launch, but within four months it had 26,000 members. This grew to 50,000 lenders in 2015 and since launch it had made loans to over 80,000 people. Although Zopa says it is the UK's biggest peer-to-peer lender, revenues are modest. With the scale of the US market, the leading player, America's Lending Club, is larger. The company floated at a value of $5.4bn (£3.6bn); it has revenues 12 times that of Zopa.

In 2015 Zopa was ten. The most recently reported revenues at the company rose from £2.97m in 2012 to £5.38m in 2013, although the group made its first loss in three years in 2013 after an expansion drive that saw it hire staff and move to new London offices.

Marketing communications

The launch of Zopa was quite different from Egg and other dot-coms at the turn of the millennium. Many companies at that time invested large amounts in offline media such as TV and print to rapidly increase awareness and to explain their proposition to customers.

Instead, Zopa relied on word of mouth and PR, with some online marketing activities where the cost of customer acquisition can be controlled. The launch of such a model and the history of its founders made it relatively easy to have major pieces about the item in relevant newspapers and magazines such as the *Guardian*, *Financial Times*, *The Economist* and the Institute of Directors house magazine, which its target audience may read. Around launch, IOD (2005) reported that Duvall's PR agency, Sputnik, achieved 200 million opportunities for the new company to be read about. Of course, not all coverage is favourable: many of the articles explored the risk of lending and the viability of the startup. However, others pointed out that the rates for the best-rated 'A category' borrowers are better than any commercial loan offered by a bank and, for lenders, rates are better than any savings account. The main online marketing activities that Zopa uses are search engine marketing and affiliate marketing. In 2007 Zopa created its own Facebook application 'People Like You', which lets

Facebookers compare their personality with other people's. Zopa communicates with its audience in an informal way through its blogs (http://blog.zopa.com).

Funding

Zopa initially received funding from two private equity groups, Munich-based Wellington Partners and Benchmark Capital of the US. Although the model was unique within financial services, its appeal was increased by the well-publicised success of other peer-to-peer Internet services such as Betfair, the gambling website, and eBay, the auction site.

Sources: *Financial Times* (2005), *New Media Age* (2005), Institute of Directors (2005), Zopa website (**www.zopa.com**) and blog (**http://blog.zopa.com**).

Question

Imagine you are a member of the team at the investors reviewing the future viability of the Zopa business. On which criteria would you assess the future potential of the business and the returns in your investment based on Zopa's position in the marketplace and its internal capabilities?

Summary

1 Environmental scanning and analysis of the macro-environment are necessary in order that a company can respond to environmental changes and act on the forces which shape the trading environment.

2 Technological forces are arguably the most likely and most important for digital marketers to watch and assess. Rapid variation in technology requires constant monitoring of adoption of the technology by customers and competitors and appropriate responses.

3 Economic forces considered in this chapter include classic economic factors, i.e. employment, interest rates and market growth and emerging markets for digital marketers. Different economic conditions in different markets are considered in developing e-commerce budgets.

4 Political forces involve the role of governments in promoting e-commerce, but also in trying to restrict it, which raises the question of democracy and the Internet.

5 Legal forces to be considered by e-commerce managers include privacy and data protection, distance-selling rules, taxation, brand reputation protection including domain name registration and copyright.

6 Social forces include variation in usage of the Internet while ethical issues include the need to safeguard consumer privacy and security of details. Privacy issues include collection and dissemination of customer information, cookies and the use of direct email. Marketers must act within current law, reassure customers about their privacy and explain the benefits of collection of personal information.

Exercises

Self-assessment exercises

1 Summarise the key elements of the macro-environment that should be scanned by an e-commerce manager.

2 Give an example of how each of the macro-environment forces may directly drive the content and services provided by a website.

3 What actions should e-commerce managers take to safeguard consumer privacy and security?

4 Give three examples of techniques websites can use to protect users' privacy.

5 How do governments attempt to control the adoption of the Internet and to what extent does this impact on the democracy of information?

6 Suggest approaches to managing the rapid change of technological innovation.

Essay and discussion questions

1 You recently started a job as e-commerce manager for a bank. Produce a checklist of all the different legal issues that you need to check for compliance on the existing website of the bank.

2 How should the e-commerce manager monitor and respond to technological innovation?

3 Benchmark different approaches to achieving and reassuring customers about their privacy and security using three or four examples for a retail sector such as travel, books, toys or clothing.

4 Select a new Internet-access technology (such as phone, kiosks or TV) that has been introduced in the last two years and assess whether it will become a significant method of access.

Examination questions

1 Summarise the macro-environment variables a company needs to monitor when operating an e-commerce site.

2 Discuss the potential significance of economic influences on the development of digital marketing initiatives.

3 Explain the purpose of environmental scanning in an e-commerce context.

4 Give three examples of how websites can use techniques to protect the user's privacy.

5 Explain the significance of the diffusion–adoption concept to the adoption of new technologies to:

a consumers purchasing using technological innovations;

b businesses deploying technological innovations.

6 What action should an e-commerce manager take to ensure compliance of their site with ethical and legal standards?

References

Ahmed, N.U. and Sharma, S.K. (2006) Porter's value chain model for assessing the impact of the internet for environmental gains, *International Journal of Management and Enterprise Development*, 3(3), 278–95.

BBC (2011) Digital Economy Act court challenge fails, 20 April, **www.bbc.co.uk/news/technology-13141986**.

Beckstrom (2011) gTLD applicant guide book, **www.icann.org/en/topics/new-gtlds/rfp-new-gtld-global-awareness-campaign-05jul11-en.pdf**.

Cairns, S. (2005) Delivering supermarket shopping: more or less traffic?, *Transport Reviews*, 25(1), 51–84.

CIA (2011) *The World Factbook*, September 2011, **www.cia.gov/library/publications/the-world-factbook/geos/xx.html**.

ClickZ (2010) Foursquare marketing hits and misses: 5 case studies, Christopher Heine, 28 September (**www.clickz.com/clickz/news/1735591/foursquare-marketing-hits-misses-case-studies**).

Cutts, M. (2007) Talk like a Googler: parts of a url, Blog posting, 14 August, www
.mattcutts.com/blog/seo-glossary-url-definitions/.

Davidson, A. (2011) Interviewing innovation by 'doing both': Cisco manages contra-
diction that drive growth and profit, www.emeraldinsight.com.libezproxy.open.ac.uk/
journals.htm?issn=1087–8572&volume=39&issue=1&articleid=1896872&show=html.

Doherty, N.F., Ellis-Chadwick, F. and Hart, C.A. (2003) An analysis of the factors affecting the adoption of the Internet in the UK retail sector, *Journal of Business Research*,
56(11), 887–97.

E-Marketer (2013) How digital behaviour differs among Millennials, Gen Xers and
Boomers. *E-Marketer*, 21 March, www.emarketer.com/Article/How-Digital-
Behavior-Differs-Among-Millennials-Gen-Xers-Boomers/1009748.

European Commission (2007) i2010 Annual Information Society Report 2007, http://
ec.europa.eu/information_society/eeurope/i2010/index_en.htm.

Fox, S. (2004) Older Americans and the Internet, Pew Internet Project, 24 March 2004, presented at 'Older Adults and the Web' event for usability.gov, 19–20 July 2004.

Financial Times (2005) Lending exchange bypasses high street banks, Paul J. Davies,
22 August.

Gartner (2011) Hype cycle special report for 2011, 2 August, www.gartner.com/Display
Document?id=1758314&ref=g_noreg.

Global Web Index (2014) Almost half of online shoppers are deleting cookies, Blog
article posted by Jason Mander, 11 November, http://blog.globalwebindex.net/
online-shoppers-privacy-measures.

Godin, S. (1999) *Permission Marketing*, Simon and Schuster, New York.

Gorell, C. (2011) Quick takes, *Strategy and Leadership*, 39(1).

Guardian (2008) Porn? Sex? Britons value cruises much more, *Guardian*, Richard Wray,
6 February.

ICO (2011) Promoting openness by public bodies and data privacy for individuals: An
information rights strategy for the Information Commissioner's Office, May 2011 v1.0.

Information Commissioner (1998) *Legal Guidelines on the 1998 UK Data Protection Act*,
www.informationcommissioner.gov.uk.

Institute of Directors (IOD) (2005) Profile – Richard Duvall, IOD house magazine,
Director, 51–5.

Jacobs, D. (2013) After the gold rush: domain names have lost their glitter, *Forbes*,
www.forbes.com/sites/deborahljacobs/2013/11/22/after-the-gold-rush-domain-
names-have-lost-their-glitter/.

Mougayer, W. (1998) *Opening Digital Markets – Battle Plans and Strategies for Internet
Commerce*, 2nd edn, CommerceNet Press, McGraw-Hill, New York.

New Media Age (2005) Personal lender, Dominic Dudley, 18 August.

Nielsen (2010) Homes add even more TV sets in 2010, blog post, 28 April, http://
blog-nielsen/nom/nielsenwire.

Omar, A., Khurrum, M., Bhutta, S. and Sanchez, T. (2009) The impact of e-taxation
policy on state and local government revenue, *Electronic Government, an International
Journal*, 6(4), 378–90.

Pritchard, R. (2014) Are security authorities justified in demanding more cooperation
from Internet companies? *RUSI Corporate Pages*, 7 November, www.rusi.org/analysis/
commentary/ref:C545CB576F0A7D/#.VLu5n0esV8E.

Rogers, E. (1983) *Diffusion of Innovations*, 3rd edn, Free Press, New York.

Rueda-Sabater, E. and Derosby, D. (2011) The evolving Internet in 2025: four scenarios,
Strategy and Leadership, 39(1), 32–8.

Siikavirta, H., Punakivi, M., Karkkainen, M. and Linnanen, L. (2003) Effects of
e-commerce on greenhouse gas emissions: a case study of grocery home delivery in
Finland, *Journal of Industrial Ecology*, 6(2), 83–97.

Smart Insights (2011) New privacy law on cookies – do we need to take action? Blog post by Dave Chaffey, 1 March 2011, **www.smartinsights.com/marketplace-analysis/digital-marketing-laws/cookie-privacy-law**.

Smart Insights (2014) The content marketing matrix. Blog post by Dan Bosomworth, 12 January 2014, **www.smartinsights.com/content-management/content-marketing-strategy/the-content-marketing-matrix-new-infographic/**.

Sparrow, A. (2000) E-commerce and the law. The legal implications of doing business online, *Financial Times* Executive Briefings.

Varley, R. (2001) *Retail Product Management*, Routledge, London.

W3C (2008) Web accessibility for older users: a literature review, **www.w3.org/TR/wai-age-literature/#arfl**.

Weblinks

- **Oxford Internet Survey (OxIS)** (**www.oii.ox.ac.uk/microsites/oxis**). Research and statistics from the Oxford Internet Institute is designed to offer detailed insights into the influence of the Internet on society in Britain, including 'Internet disengagement'.
- **Pew Internet and American Life Project** (**www.pewinternet.org**). Funds and publishes original, academic-quality research that explores the impact of the Internet on society. Also highlights adoption trends such as social networks, online video and chat.
- **Brand Republic** (**www.brandrepublic.com/**). A weekly magazine available for the UK, covering a range of new media platforms.
- **Smart Insights Digital Marketing Statistics sources** (**www.smartinsights.com/digital-marketing-statistics**) A compilation of the top ten statistics sources and a custom search engine to search them.
- **Dark Patterns** (**http://darkpatterns.org/journey_map**) Dark Patterns are digital marketing approaches which are questionable ethically. This journey map summarises some of the tactics used.

New digital law developments

- **Marketing Law** (**www.marketinglaw.co.uk**). Up-to-date source on all forms of law related to marketing activities.
- **Privacy International** (**www.privacyinternational.org**). Group campaigning for privacy which contains information on legal developments in different countries.

Country-specific privacy laws

- Australia also enacted a SPAM act in 2003 (**www.privacy.gov.au**).
- Canada also has a privacy act (**www.privcom.gc.ca**).
- European Commission Data Protection and privacy legal resources (**http://ec.europa.eu/justice_home/fsj/privacy**).
- New Zealand Privacy Commissioner (**www.privacy.org.nz**).
- United States (CAN-SPAM Act, **www.ftc.gov/spam**).
- United Kingdom (Information Commissioner, **www.ico.gov.uk**).
- Summary of all countries (**www.spamlaws.com**).

Part 2
Digital marketing strategy development

In Part 2, approaches for developing a digital marketing strategy are explored. These combine traditional approaches to strategic marketing planning with specific Internet-related issues that need to be considered by digital marketers. Chapter 4 presents a framework for developing digital marketing strategies, Chapter 5 discusses the opportunities for varying the marketing mix online and Chapter 6 reviews strategies for online customer relationship management.

4 Digital marketing strategy 176

- The need for an integrated digital marketing strategy
- How to structure a digital marketing strategy
- Situation analysis
- Setting goals and objectives for digital marketing
- Strategy formulation for digital marketing
- Strategy implementation

5 The impact of digital media and technology on the marketing mix 248

- Product
- Price
- Place
- Promotion
- People, process and physical evidence

6 Relationship marketing using digital platforms 298

- The challenge of customer engagement
- Customer lifecycle management

Chapter 4
Digital marketing strategy

Chapter at a glance

Main topics

- The need for an integrated digital marketing strategy 184
- How to structure a digital marketing strategy 186
- Situation analysis 190
- Setting goals and objectives for digital marketing 196
- Strategy formulation for digital marketing 208
- Strategy implementation 236

Case studies

Digital marketing in practice

The Smart Insights interview with Sajjad Bhojani, Head of Dunelm Direct Trading at Dunelm, on their approach to digital marketing 182

Case study 4: Tesco online development strategy supports global expansion 239

Learning objectives

After reading this chapter, you should be able to:

- Relate digital marketing strategy to marketing and business strategy
- Identify opportunities and threats arising from digital media and technology platforms
- Evaluate alternative strategic approaches for using digital platforms.

Questions for marketers

Key questions for marketing managers related to this chapter are:

- What approaches can be used to create digital marketing strategies?
- How does digital marketing strategy relate to other strategy development?
- What are the key strategic options for digital marketing?

Scan code
to find the
latest updates
for topics in
this chapter

Links to other chapters

This chapter is related to other chapters as follows:

- It builds on the evaluation of the Internet environment from Chapters 2 and 3
- Chapter 5 describes the potential for varying different elements of the marketing mix as part of digital marketing strategy
- Chapter 6 describes customer relationship management strategies
- Options for segmenting online customers by activity levels are covered in Chapter 6. Options for segmenting site visitors through web analytics systems are covered in Chapter 10
- Chapter 8 gives examples of goal setting for digital campaigns and strategies for developing the right communications mix.

Introduction

The importance of the Internet to modern business strategy was underlined by Michael Porter (2001), who famously said:

> The key question is not whether to deploy Internet technology – companies have no choice if they want to stay competitive – but how to deploy it.

Digital marketing strategy
Definition of the approach by which applying digital technology platforms will support marketing and business objectives.

A **digital marketing strategy** is needed to provide consistent direction for an organisation's online marketing activities so that they integrate with its other marketing activities and support its overall business objectives. The digital marketing strategy has many similarities to the typical aims of traditional marketing strategies, in that it will:

- provide a future direction to digital marketing activities;
- involve analysis of the organisation's external environment, internal resources and capabilities to inform strategy;
- define digital marketing objectives that support marketing objectives;
- involve selection of strategic options to achieve digital marketing objectives and create sustainable differential competitive advantage;
- include strategy formulation to address typical marketing strategy options such as target markets, positioning and specification of the marketing mix;
- help identify which strategies NOT to pursue and which marketing tactics are not suitable to implement;
- specify how resources will be deployed and how the organisation will be structured to achieve the strategy.

This chapter examines each of these elements of strategy and begins by considering an appropriate process for developing a digital marketing strategy, and then looks at the following aspects of strategy development:

1 situation review (drawing on our coverage in Chapters 2 and 3);
2 goal and objective setting;
3 strategy formulation.

Figure 4.1 indicates the context for digital marketing strategy development. The internal influences include business objectives and strategy and these in turn influence marketing strategy that should directly influence the digital marketing strategy. Key external influences include the market structure and demand, competitor strategies and the current and evolving opportunities and threats, in particular those enabled by new digital technologies (e.g. mobile marketing and social TV) and marketing approaches (e.g. search engine marketing and use of social media). Methods for monitoring the external environment to anticipate external opportunities and threats and competitors' actions have been introduced in Chapters 2 and 3, as were methods of assessing the demand of the market for Internet-delivered services.

Channel marketing strategy
Defines how a company should set specific objectives for digital channels, including web, mobile and social media, and vary its proposition and communications for this channel.

Digital marketing strategy as a channel marketing strategy

Digital marketing strategy is primarily a **channel marketing strategy** which defines how a company should set *channel-specific objectives* and develop a *differential channel proposition* and *channel-specific communications* consistent with the characteristics of the channel and end user requirements. Note that digital channel strategy has two components – many may see it simply as a digital communications strategy (reviewed in

| | **Figure 4.1** | Internal and external influences on digital marketing strategy |

Chapters 6 to 9), but it should also define changes to the proposition enabled by digital channel (reviewed in Chapter 5 on the marketing mix) including Product, Pricing, Place, Promotion and changes to customer service.

The digital strategy determines the strategic significance of the digital channels relative to other communications channels that are used to communicate directly with customers at different **customer touchpoints**. Some organisations, such as low-cost airlines, use virtual channels, such as websites and email marketing, for delivering services and communicating with customers, whereas others may follow a strategy which uses a mix of digital and offline channels – for example, retailers which use face-to-face, telephone, mobile, direct mail communications and the web. We saw in Chapter 2 that the ROPO (research online–purchase offline) behaviours and 'Click-and-Collect' services remain important.

So the focus of digital marketing strategy is decisions about how to use the channel to support existing marketing strategies, how to exploit its strengths and manage its weaknesses, and to use it in conjunction with other channels as part of a **multichannel marketing strategy**. This multichannel marketing strategy defines how different marketing channels should integrate and support each other in terms of their proposition development and communications based on their relative merits for the customer and the company. Indeed, Keith Weed, Head of communications at Unilever, predicts that omni-connectivity is a major technology trend and suggests that in the future connections will not only be between computers, phones and tablets but also home appliances, heating controls, smart watches and health monitors (Weed, 2015).

The scope of digital marketing strategy

When reviewing options for online strategy, it is useful to consider that this now involves more than the narrow focus of a strategy to develop website functionality and attract

Customer touchpoints
Communications channels with which companies interact directly with prospects and customers. Traditional touchpoints include face-to-face (in-store or with sales representatives), phone and mail. Digital touchpoints include web services, email and, potentially, mobile phone.

Multichannel marketing strategy
Defines how different marketing channels should integrate and support each other in terms of their proposition development and communications based on their relative merits for the customer and the company.

visits to it. Although enhancing a desktop and mobile-responsive website and mobile site will be a central part of the strategy, digital marketers should also examine broader issues of how to:

- Use marketing automation tools for customer relationship development (as described in Chapter 6). These may include email, mobile and web-based personalisation based on CRM databases.
- Develop the overall customer experience across multiple channels (as described in Chapter 7 in the section on customer experience management (CXM)).
- Maximise the results from partnering with online intermediaries such as publishers and influencers such as bloggers (as described in Chapters 8 and 9).
- Harness social media marketing both through use on its own site through user-generated content and within the main social networks like Facebook, Google+, LinkedIn and Twitter.

Developing a digital marketing strategy may also involve redesigning business processes to integrate with partners such as suppliers and distributors. Sultan and Rohm (2004) suggested that digital technology created opportunities for new business processes, which could also deliver business benefits. Their study looked at three major organisations representing printing, sportswear and automotive industries, and identified different forms of aligning online strategies with business goals. Their framework identified these strategic objectives:

- *Cost reduction and value chain efficiencies*. In printing industry technology was used to improve customer service processes and the efficiency of traditionally labour intensive processes.
- *Revenue generation*. Sportswear industry through introduction of direct licensed sales of products.
- *Channel partnership*. Partnering with distributors using extranets (all three industries).
- *Communications and branding*. All three industry examples were using technology to foster close relationships with customers.

As the Internet and digitally enhanced trading environments are more widely adopted, the scope for redesigning business processes extends even further. Marketers not only need to look for opportunities to use technology to enhance their offer but must also ensure they protect their competitive positioning.

Figure P.1 in the Preface suggests the range of digital marketing activities that must be managed as part of a digital marketing strategy structured around the customer lifecycle defined as the four steps in RACE Planning (Smart Insights, 2015). The figure shows that the operational activities which need to be implemented and managed as part of strategy can be usefully divided into those focussing on (1) customer acquisition, (2) customer conversion, proposition and experience development, and (3) customer retention and growth. Improving the capability to execute many of these activities will be decided upon through the review process of creating a digital marketing strategy. An output from the digital strategy will be a series of strategic digital marketing initiatives in the areas of customer acquisition, conversion or retention such as those shown in Table 4.1. These initiatives will typically be prioritised and placed as part of a long-term e-commerce 'roadmap' defining required developments over a longer period, say one to three years.

Table 4.1	Summary of typical focus for main types of strategic digital marketing initiatives

Type of digital marketing strategy initiative	Commentary	Examples
New customer proposition (product and pricing)	New site features or other online communications which are directly related to offering new products or services that will generate revenue	• Bank – introducing new product requiring different quotations • Publisher – introducing a price comparison service
Customer acquisition or inbound marketing strategic initiatives	Strategic projects designed to enhance a site's capability and deliver different online marketing techniques aimed to attract new customers	• Content marketing • search engine optimisation (SEO) • pay-per-click (PPC) • Affiliate marketing • Aggregators
Customer conversion and customer experience strategic initiatives	Investments in new customer features designed to engage the audience and increase conversion rates and average order values New functionality, e.g. new online store components; special functionality, e.g. real-time stock checking Strategic initiatives aimed at improving the customers' brand experience	• Implement online shop/secure payment • Introduce customer reviews and ratings • Merchandising capability for offer tailored promotions • Interactive tools to help product selection • Buyers' guides
Customer development and growth strategic initiatives	Investments to improve the experience and delivery of offers to existing customers	• Personalised recommendations and services for existing customers • Email contact strategy focussed on the customer journey and level of brand awareness • Communities, social media, blogs or to encourage advocacy and repeat purchase
Social media, content marketing or social business initiatives	A narrow social media initiative will look at how social media can support acquisition, conversion and retention. A broader social business strategy also includes improving product and service	• Social media listening • Developing content hub • Encouraging review • Influencer outreach • Communities
Enhance marketing capabilities through site infrastructure improvements	These typically involve 'back-end or back-office features' which won't be evident to users of the site, but will help in the management or administration of the site	• CRM or personalisation • Content management system • Performance improvement – improve management information, web analytics systems including systems for multivariate and AB testing • Improve customer feedback facilities
Resourcing and governance strategies	Changes need to marketing management given the increased importance of digital media and technology	• Process change • Skills development • Team structure

| Digital marketing in practice | The Smart Insights interview |

Sajjad Bhojani, Head of Dunelm Direct Trading at Dunelm, explains their approach to digital marketing

Digital strategy development at Dunelm

Dunelm Mill is the UK's largest homewares retailer with a portfolio of established out-of-town superstores with the 'Simply Value for Money' proposition. Its online store features over 17,500 products under the brand name Dunelm Mill.

Q. What is your process for creating a digital marketing strategy?

The business has an ongoing three-year plan, which is revised every 18 months or so. It has the standard Profit and Loss projections for the online sales part of the business. Project P and L is based on estimates of growth in traffic and sales based on conversion models. These targets stay fairly fixed within that period, but are re-reviewed as part of the annual planning process.

For introducing new features to the site and improving our digital marketing we have a 12-month cycle for development of new features.

Q. How do you define your e-commerce strategy?

I see the 4Ps of the Marketing Mix as still vital to take strategic decisions for multi-channel retailers. Product relates to the range of products we offer on our site compared to the stores and how we prioritise them through merchandising such as featured offers on the home page or different categories.

With Price, multichannel retailers need to consider whether they have consistent pricing with stores; this is the approach we have. The right approach will vary by market. For example, I don't believe that in our sector, channel-specific pricing such as online discounts is right. But it may be in other sectors such as electrical, where price checking can be important. That's less relevant for us since we offer own-branded products.

We aim to have competitive pricing, but don't tend to offer web exclusives – these were more relevant earlier on in the development of e-commerce to encourage use of web, but we don't want to erode margin now. There's also the risk that differential channel pricing can be confusing. Customers are multichannel – they don't see Dunelm as two different companies. We offer free delivery for consistency too, although this is currently for orders over £50 or £150 for furniture.

For me, Place online is about offering the right experience, but also offering the right product for each search visitor. Merchandising as people search ('searchandising') the first listings page is really important. You have to decide the combination of featuring offers or best-sellers which will vary as our brand runs different promotions. With our Websphere platform we also have the flexibility for offers such as BOGOF – buy one, get one free.

Place, today, also involves mobile access to our site. This has grown significantly so that it is now 20 per cent of our traffic. But it is a browsing channel, so conversion rates will be lower. It's used for different applications depending where the consumer is. If you look at our target audience of busy females, they are always on the go and are increasingly using their smartphones and tablets for research and store location while shopping. We try to encourage use of mobile through in-store features like point-of-sale posters and shelf-ticket labels explaining the benefits of mobile.

We use different forms of qualitative and quantitative research both online and in-store about usage of website. However, it is difficult to have a complete 'single view of channel', since it's not possible to collect email address consistently across channels, for example.

Place also relates to how you combine online and in-store experiences. We want to provide a service that fits around the varied needs of our customers, that's why we've expanded our delivery options to include Reserve and Collect, where customers can reserve products online for free and then collect in-store at a convenient time.

Promotion is about driving visitors using the channels available to all, such as search, affiliate and display. There is also promotion to existing customer using email marketing, where we look to encourage increases in average order frequency and breadth of categories purchased in; those are our KPIs here. Many customers will have bought in single category, so the CRM programme will encourage that, for example by offering free delivery in a category. This is another area we're looking to refine and we have a specific role for this.

Q. How do you manage conversion rate improvements and the implementation of new features on the site?

We're not that advanced at this stage in our use of conversion rate optimisation since we're currently updating our e-commerce platform to IBM Websphere. For example, we're not yet using AB or multivariate testing. We see it as more of a priority to introduce better personalisation features onto the site. We do have basic product recommendations based on wisdom of crowd but human intervention is required to implement the rules.

We're around 12 months from an active customer experience improvement programme, but the intention is to implement a tool to help use these approaches. It's not simply a case of choosing the right tool – resource is a big challenge too; we need a specific analytics resource and content/copy creation resource to make the updates.

Instead, what we currently do when we introduce new features is we involve users to check that the experience is effective. This is typically a two-phase process where we review the experience with customers based on an initial working version of the page. For example, we may be improving our product page template, so we will create working wireframes for review before building the full template. We will then test again to make minor changes when in User Acceptance Testing (UAT).

Q. What is your process for getting the right investment in marketing channels?

How we assign our online marketing budget overall is simple overall – it's based on return on investment (ROI): for every £1 of investment we have to return £X either through the site or in-store, although we need to understand contribution to in-store better. Within this you have to think about different types of investment, for example brand investments such as display advertising and direct response elements such as paid search (Google AdWords). Direct response is directed at hitting the sales target with investment re-reviewed each month. What's important is how you test and learn. It's an evolving strategy with separate budgets identified for each and different KPIs for search and display since the intent is different.

Search is hugely important; it's core to most retailers including us, but you have to separate investments and analysis for brand and non-search behaviour. Brand searches are where people know about us already and they search for Dunelm on its own or with a product name or category. It's important to connect these searchers with the right product, but even more important to attract visitors searching more generally. To help here we have invested in a non-brand SEO strategy, which has involved improve to site content and architecture, on-site optimisation and off-site optimisation looking at linking patterns. This is a fixed-line investment, which has seen significant improvements year-on-year.

> We have a 12 months sales and profit target, then have flexibility of how that is changed within – separated into brand and direct response.
>
> We can vary between test and responsibility – and have a display retargeting budget where we conduct different trials each month. We are reviewing budget for prospecting – attracting new customers via Ad networks too.
>
> We also have an affiliate programme within the last 12 months. At the same time we need to review investment.
>
> As we review the effectiveness of our media spend we review relative return on investment from different categories, for example focussing on higher average order items. With the breadth of our product range we need to! For each category we review brand, non-brand, direct response and email sales for the previous year and then compare to the current year to evaluate the year-on-year changes.
>
> With the importance of branded search, non-branded search visits are separated out in our analysis. The team has a weekly visit and sales target to hit. Year-on-year performance weekly review is a key part of setting performance targets and spend analysis. We also have separate targets for Reserve and Collect against home delivery, linking through to the profitability of these channels.

The need for an integrated digital marketing strategy

The scope of digital marketing is widening and becoming increasingly pervasive, yet the integration of a digital marketing strategy into business and marketing strategies often represents a significant challenge for many organisations. A possible explanation for this is that typically organisations have considered digital media and technology in isolation and sometimes try to bolt on digital marketing initiatives, often creating separate teams to manage digital marketing. Econsultancy (2008) research highlighted the challenges of digital marketing strategy. The research involved interviewing e-commerce and digital marketing directors at retail, travel, media and telecoms businesses. Aspects of managing digital media and technology which are still a challenge for many larger organisations included:

- *gaining buy-in and budget* consistent with audience media consumption and value generated;
- *conflicts of ownership and tensions* between a digital marketing team and other teams such as traditional marketing, IT, finance and senior management;
- *coordination with different channels* in conjunction with teams managing marketing programmes elsewhere in the business;
- *managing and integrating customer information* about characteristics and behaviours collected online;
- *achieving consistent reporting*, review, analysis and follow-up actions of digital marketing results throughout the business;
- *structuring the specialist digital team* and integrating into the organisation by changing responsibilities elsewhere in the organisation;
- '*time to market*' for implementing new functionality on a site;
- insourcing vs outsourcing online marketing tactics, i.e. search, affiliate, email marketing, PR;
- staff recruitment and retention.

Ultimately, it is important for organisations to integrate all of their strategic plans and it is important to understand clearly how and where the digital marketing strategy fits into the organisation's overall business plan. Figure 4.2 shows a planning hierarchy for an

| Figure 4.2 | Hierarchy of organisation plans including e-marketing plans |

organisation, from a corporate or business plan which informs a marketing plan which in turn informs a communications plan and campaign briefs for different markets or brands. The figure suggests that a digital marketing plan may be useful to improve the planning and execution of 'e-campaign components', which refers to online communications tools such as online advertising or email marketing and continuous or 'always-on' digital marketing activities which may be conducted throughout the year to achieve awareness or engagement on a website or social media presence – e.g. affiliate, search engine or social media marketing. (See Chapter 8 for further discussion of these techniques.) We see a specific digital marketing plan as a temporary, interim tool to support digital transformation by defining the major changes needed for processes, resourcing, structure, media investment and proposition development. Once these issues have been addressed then digital channel activities can and should be integrated within the broader marketing and communications plans. A digital marketing specialist or consultant can create a digital marketing plan to help inform and influence not only senior managers or directors and other non-marketing functions, but also to achieve buy-in from fellow marketers. Failure to plan how to manage digital channels can lead to a number of problems:

1 Customer demand for online services will be underestimated if this has not been researched and it is under-resourced, and no or unrealistic objectives are set to achieve online marketing share.
2 Existing and startup competitors will gain market share if insufficient resources are devoted to digital marketing and no clear strategies are defined.
3 Duplication of resources can occur, e.g. different parts of the marketing organisation purchasing different tools or different agencies for performing similar online marketing tasks.
4 Insufficient resources will be devoted to planning and executing e-marketing and there is likely to be a lack of specific specialist e-marketing skills, making it difficult to respond to competitive threats effectively.
5 Insufficient customer data are collected online as part of relationship building and these data are not integrated well with existing systems.

6 Efficiencies available through online marketing will be missed, e.g. lower communications costs and enhanced conversion rates in customer acquisition and retention campaigns.

7 Opportunities for applying online marketing tools, such as search marketing or email marketing, will be missed or the execution may be inefficient if the wrong resources are used or marketers don't have the right tools.

8 Changes required to internal IT systems by different groups will not be prioritised accordingly.

9 The results of online marketing are not tracked adequately on a detailed or high-level basis.

10 Senior management support of e-marketing is inadequate to drive what often needs to be a major strategic initiative.

Activity 4.1	Benefits of digital-marketing planning

Business commentators suggest that to survive it is vital to have a 'strong digital footprint' (Forbes, 2014). Furthermore, without a digital marketing strategy new business, brand exposure and revenues can all be significantly affected.

Purpose

To consider the barriers and benefits to the adoption of digital marketing planning.

Task

Imagine you are a marketing manager responsible for the development of your organisation's digital marketing strategy. Using an organisation you are familiar with, outline the barriers and potential benefits of digital marketing planning.

How to structure a digital marketing strategy

Michael Porter (2001) thought that the Internet and the digital era have heightened the importance of strategy, but he encouraged business to be cautious and suggested where businesses should focus when developing their strategy. He believed that the growth in the use of digital media and technology would make it harder to create and sustain competitive advantage and suggested six principles which could help to sustain a distinctive strategic position:

1 Start with the *right goal* which is grounded in real economic value.
2 Define a *value proposition*, which is unique but, importantly, deliverable.
3 Do things differently; create *a distinctive value chain*.
4 Be prepared to make *trade-offs*, tailoring a firm's activities to outperform rivals.
5 Create a *fit* between what the company does, where it wants to be and the resources available.
6 Establish *continuity*. Planning decisions follow the distinctive position set out by the original goals.

These all remain fundamental to a digital marketing strategy. More recently, he has recommended that innovative technologies are forcing companies to ask the question 'what business am I in?' (Porter and Heppelmann, 2014) as competition intensifies due to increased data processing power and almost universal connectivity.

In addition to these functional elements of a digital marketing strategy, brand development is also important, including developing the online value proposition explained in this chapter and Chapter 5. Rohit Bhargava, a VP at Ogilvy New York and author of *Personality Not Included* (**www.personalitynotincluded.com**), stresses the importance of developing a brand that is sufficiently distinctive and energetic to encourage interaction and discussion that will amplify brand messages through social media and word-of-mouth. Bhargava describes personality as: 'the unique, authentic, and talkable soul of your brand that people can get passionate about'. He goes on to say:

> Personality is not just about what you stand for, but how you choose to communicate it. It is also the way to reconnect your customers, partners, employees, and influencers to the soul of your brand in the new social media era.

Strategy process model
A framework for approaching strategy development.

Marketing planning
A logical sequence and a series of activities leading to the setting of marketing objectives and the formulation of plans for achieving them.

A **strategy process model** provides a framework that gives a logical sequence to follow to ensure inclusion of all key activities of strategy development and implementation. In a marketing context, these strategy development and implementation activities are coordinated through a marketing plan, and the process of creating this is known as **marketing planning**. McDonald (2003) defined marketing planning simply as:

> the planned application of marketing resources to achieve marketing objectives . . . Marketing planning is simply a logical sequence and a series of activities leading to the setting of marketing objectives and the formulation of plans for achieving them.

McDonald (2003) distinguished between strategic marketing plans which cover a period beyond the next financial year (typically three to five years) and tactical marketing plans which cover detailed actions over a shorter time period of one year or less, and this is equally applicable to digital marketing planning. In a similar way, we suggest that a strategic digital marketing plan, often known in large companies as a digital transformation plan, should place emphasis on four areas:

1 Identification of changes to competitive forces in the micro-environment and macro-environment which will influence customer demand for online experiences and products.
2 Developing value propositions for customers using online services as part of their buying process.
3 Definition of the technology infrastructure and information architecture to deliver these value propositions as a customer experience.
4 Changes to governance of marketing activities affecting the 7Ss summarised in Table 1.3, including structure, skills and systems or processes.

Such an approach requires a long-term plan that can provide a *roadmap* to guide digital marketing activities for 18 months to three years. While many organisations produce longer-term plans of say three to five years, it is important to consider that digital environments are highly dynamic and operational plans should aim to promote strategic agility (see Chapter 3), so a strategy development approach such as that described in Digital marketing insight 4.1 can help.

Digital marketing insight 4.1   Using a cluster-based approach for developing strategy

A generic strategic approach can aid a business in putting together the basic elements of a strategy, but new thinking on strategy development suggests that the interplay between industry structure and a firm's resources can vary significantly depending on the location of a business – e.g. in emerging economies industry structure is more influential than in established economies (Karabag and Berggren, 2014). Moreover, the trading environment has become highly complex and increasingly competitive and as a result firms will have multiple departments which can act independently in response to corporate goals rather than using a more prescriptive 'top-down' approach. Hadighi *et al*. (2013) suggest that the three main elements of strategy formulation are goals, factors and strategies. And how the interconnections between these three elements are dealt with is fundamental to success. These authors argue that a SWOT analysis is more likely to consider the generic strategic views of the firm rather than the specific strategic view of the departments which make up the firm. Consequently, Hadighi *et al*. (2013) suggest there is a more accurate and objective way of looking at all of the strategic elements of a firm and in doing so produce a cluster-based approach towards strategy development.

In order to implement the clustering approach towards strategy development there are a number of steps to follow:

Step 1 Collect factors and goals from individual departments.
Step 2 Form factor–goals matrices for individual departments (by determining interaction among departmental factors and goals).
Step 3 Apply the proposed clustering approach to create integrated organisational clusters.
Step 4 Find the position of the clusters by identifying the most important factors.
Step 5 Generate strategies according to each cluster.
Step 6 Assign strategies to departments for making action plans (tactics) (Hadighi et al., 2013).

Figure 4.3 shows an overall strategy process model for developing a digital marketing strategy recommended by Chaffey and Smith (2012). PR Smith's SOSTAC® Planning framework (explained at **www.prsmith.org**) stands for Situation, Objectives and Strategy, Tactics, Action and Control. Chaffey and Smith (2012) note that each stage is not discrete; rather there is some overlap during each stage of planning – previous stages may be revisited and refined, as indicated by the reverse arrows in Figure 4.3. The elements of SOSTAC® planning in the context of how they are described in this text with respect to digital marketing strategy are:

1 *Situation analysis means 'where are we now?'* Planning activities involved at this stage include performing an Internet-specific SWOT analysis, and reviewing the different aspects of the micro-environment (Chapter 2) including customers, competitors and intermediaries. Situation analysis also involves review of the macro-environment (Chapter 3).

2 *Objectives means 'where do we want to be?'* This can include a vision for digital channels, and also specific numerical objectives for the digital channels such as projections of sales volumes and cost savings (see Chapter 9).

3 *Strategy means 'how do we get there?'* Strategy summarises how to achieve the objectives for the different decision points explained in this chapter, including segmentation, targeting, proposition development (including the elements of the marketing mix described in more detail in Chapter 5 and CRM described in Chapter 6).

4 *Tactics defines the usage of tactical digital communications tools.* This includes specific details of the marketing mix (Chapter 5), CRM (Chapter 6), experience (Chapter 7) and digital communications (Chapters 8 and 9).

5 *Actions refers to action plans, change management and project management skills.* We refer to some of the issues of modifications to organisational roles and structures later in this chapter.

6 *Control looks at the use of management information including web analytics to assess whether strategic and tactical objectives are achieved and how improvements can be made to enhance results further.* This is closely related to goal setting as described in this chapter and in Chapter 8, and also the coverage of web analytics and tracking in Chapter 9.

Where are we now?
- Goal performance (5 Ss)
- Customer insight
- E marketplace SWOT
- Brand perception
- Internal capabilities and resources

Where do we want to be?
5 Ss objectives:
- Sell – customer acquisition and retention targets
- Serve – customer satisfaction targets
- Sizzle – site stickiness, visit duration
- Speak – trialogue; number of engaged customers
- Save – quantified efficiency gains

How do we monitor performance?
- 5 Ss + web analytics – KPIs
- Usability testing/mystery shopper
- Customer satisfaction surveys
- Site visitor profiling
- Frequency of reporting
- Process of reporting and actions

The details of tactics, who does what and when
- Responsibilities and structures
- Internal resources and skills
- External agencies

How do we get there?
- Segmentation, targeting and positioning
- OVP (online value proposition)
- Sequence (credibility before visibility)
- Integration (consistent OVP) and database
- Tools (web functionality, e-mail, IPTV etc.)

How exactly do we get there?
(the details of strategy)
- E-marketing mix, including: the communications mix, social networking, what happens when?
- Details of contact strategy
- E-campaign initiative schedule

Situation analysis → Objectives → Strategy → Tactics → Actions → Control

| Figure 4.3 | The SOSTAC® planning framework applied to digital marketing strategy development
Source: Chaffey and Smith (2012) |

Prescriptive strategy
The three core areas of strategic analysis, strategic development and strategy implementation are linked together sequentially.

Emergent strategy
Strategic analysis, strategic development and strategy implementation are interrelated and are developed together in a more agile fashion.

Strategic windows
Opportunities arising through a significant change in environment.

We will now look at each of the steps involved in strategy development.

Arguably, due to the speed of development of digital technologies, there is a need for a more responsive, more agile approach to strategy planning (as discussed at the start of Chapter 3). Rather than a top-down, **prescriptive strategy** development approach, similar to Figures 4.1, 4.2 and 4.3, a more agile, **emergent strategy** approach is required, where strategic analysis, strategic development and strategy implementation are interrelated. In reality, most organisational strategy development and planning processes have elements of prescriptive and emergent strategy reflecting different planning and strategic review timescales. The prescriptive elements are the structured annual or six-monthly budgeting process or a longer-term three-year rolling marketing planning process. But on a shorter timescale, organisations naturally also need an emergent process to enable strategic agility and the ability to rapidly respond to marketplace dynamics.

An emergent strategy approach is essential in a highly dynamic technology environment as this should enable organisations to respond to sudden environmental changes which can open **strategic windows**. Strategic windows may occur through changes such as introduction of new technology – e.g. mobile and wireless technology or cloud computing – changes in regulation of an industry, changes to distribution channels in the industry (again the Internet has had this impact), emerging target groups of customers who have a new set of needs and demands.

Digital Capacity	ONE. Initial	TWO. Managed	THREE. Defined	FOUR. Quantified	FIVE. Optimized
A. Strategic Approach	No strategy	Prioritised marketing activities	Defined vision and strategy	Business-aligned strategy and roadmap	Agile strategic approach
B. Performance Improvement Process	No KPIs	Volume-based KPIs No dashboards	Quality-based KPIs 'Last click' attribution Business dashboards	Value-based KPIs Weighted attribution Ad hoc CRO	Lifetime-value KPIs Continuous CRO
C. Management Buy-in	Limited	Verbal support, but inadequate resourcing	Sponsorship and increased investment	Active championing and appropriate investment	Integral part of strategy development
D. Resourcing and Structure	No specific skills	Core skills centralised or agencies	Centralised hub and spoke Dedicated resources	Decentralisation and reskilling	Balanced blend of marketing skills
E. Data and Infrastructure	Limited / no customer database	Separate data, tools and IT services	Partially integrated systems and data	Integrated CRM systems and 360° data sources	Flexible approach to optimise resources
F. Integrated Customer Communications	Not integrated	Core push activities synchronised	Integrated inbound approach	Integrated, personalised, Paid-Owned-Earned media	Media optimised for ROI and to maximize CLV
G. Integrated Customer Experience	Website not integrated	Desktop and mobile support, not personalised	Partially personalised desktop and mobile experience	Integrated, personalised, web, mobile, email and social media	Full contextual personalised experiences and recommendations
	'Laggard'	'Developing capability'	'Competent average capability'	'Above-sector average capability'	'Market leading capability'

Figure 4.4 A digital marketing capability model
Source: Smart Insights (http://bit.ly/smartbenchmarking)

Competitive intelligence (CI)
A process that transforms disaggregated information into relevant, accurate and usable strategic knowledge about competitors, position, performance, capabilities and intentions.

One example of an approach to collecting this market event data is **competitive intelligence** or **CI**. We look at some examples of the wealth of competitive intelligence available to digital marketers in Figure 4.4.

Situation analysis

Situation analysis
Collection and review of information about an organisation's internal processes and resources and external marketplace factors in order to inform strategy definition.

The **situation analysis** in classic marketing planning is an audit of current effectiveness of a firm's activities but also for individual departments such as marketing. The analysis involves a review of internal and external factors (for example, the marketing environment) that have implications for strategy development. More specifically, situation analysis involves:

- Assessment of internal capabilities, resources and processes of the company and a review of its activity in the marketplace. The 7S framework introduced in Chapter 1 (Table 1.3) is a useful way of considering these internal capabilities to deliver strategy.
- Consideration of the immediate competitive environment (micro-environment) including customer demand and behaviour, competitor activity, marketplace structure and relationships with suppliers and partners. (These micro-environment factors were reviewed in Chapter 2.)
- Investigation of the wider environment in which a company operates, including economic development, government regulations, legal issues and taxation, social and ethical issues, e.g. data protection and consumer privacy. (These macro-environment factors were reviewed in detail in Chapter 3.)

Now complete Activity 4.2, which illustrates the type of analysis that needs to be performed for a digital marketing situation analysis.

Activity 4.2	Situation analysis for an e-commerce operation

Purpose

To introduce the different types of Internet marketing analysis required as part of the situation review.

Activity

You are a new e-commerce manager in an organisation that has operated a B2B e-commerce presence for two years in all the major European countries. The organisation sells office equipment and has had an established mail-order catalogue operation for 25 years. The UK, Germany, France and Italy each have their own localised content. List the e-commerce-related questions you would ask of your new colleagues and the research you would commission under these headings:

- internal analysis;
- external analysis (micro-economic factors);
- external analysis (macro-economic factors).

Internal audit for digital marketing

The internal audit involves reviewing the existing contribution that the digital channels are currently delivering.

Assessing the current contribution of the digital marketing to the organisation

To assess the contribution and effectiveness of digital marketing involves the organisation in reviewing how well its online presence is meeting its goals. So this activity overlaps with that on strategic goal setting discussed in the next section. Assessing effectiveness also requires a performance measurement or web analytics system to collect and report on marketing effectiveness. These different levels of measures can be useful to assess effectiveness.

1 Business effectiveness
This will include the financial or commercial contribution from digital channels, including online leads, sales and profit and offline-influenced leads and sales and how well it is supporting business objectives. The relative costs of developing and maintaining digital experiences and communications will also be reviewed as part of a cost–benefit analysis.

2 Marketing effectiveness
These measures may include:

- leads (qualified enquiries);
- sales;
- customer retention, satisfaction and loyalty, including lifetime value;
- online market (or audience share);
- brand enhancement;
- customer service.

For large organisations, these measures can be assessed for each of the different markets a company operates in or for product lines produced on the website.

3 Digital marketing effectiveness

These are specific measures that are used to assess the way in which the website is used, and the characteristics of the audience. They are described in more detail in Chapter 9. According to Chaffey and Smith (2012), key performance indicators (KPIs) for an online presence include:

- *unique visitors* – the number of separate, individual visitors to the site;
- total numbers of *sessions* or *visits* to the website;
- *repeat visits* – average number of visits per individual;
- *duration* – average length of time visitors spend on the site;
- *conversion rates* – the percentage of visitors converting to subscribers (or becoming customers);
- *attrition rates* through the online buying process;
- *churn rates* – percentage of subscribers lapsing or unsubscribing.

According to Marketing Magazine.co.uk (2014), leading brands such as Lego, IBM, Lebrara and E.ON are seeking ways to enhance customer experiences as the key to future success. Conny Kalcher, Vice President for Marketing and Consumer Experiences at Lego says:

> 'More and more companies are moving away from measuring consumer satisfaction to measuring consumer engagement and loyalty as the understanding spreads, that consumer satisfaction in itself does not give the answers to what you, as a brand, can do better to improve your service delivery or consumer experience. The implications are that brands must "aim to get under the skin" of their customers if they wish to become great brands in the future'.

Customer research

Persona
A thumbnail summary of the characteristics, needs, motivations and environment of a typical website user.

Customer scenarios
Alternative tasks or outcomes required by a visitor to a website. Typically accomplished in a series of stages of different tasks involving different information needs or experiences.

Research into customers should not be restricted to quantitative demand analysis. Varianini and Vaturi (2000) point out that qualitative research about existing customers provides insights that can be used to inform strategy. Research suggests using user profiling to capture the core characteristics of target customers involves more than using demographics. It also includes customer needs, attitudes experiences and abilities of using digital technologies and the Internet (Doherty and Ellis-Chadwick, 2010). In Chapter 2 we reviewed how customer **personas** and **customer scenarios** are developed to help inform understanding of online buyer behaviour.

Resource analysis

Resource analysis
Review of the technological, financial and human resources of an organisation and how they are utilised in business processes.

Resource analysis involves assessing the capabilities of the organisation to deliver its digital services. The 7S framework introduced in Chapter 1 (Table 1.3) is a useful way of considering the suitability of internal capabilities to achieve strategic aims. Other aspects of resource analysis that can be reviewed include:

- *Financial resources* – the cost components of running an online presence, including site development, promotion and maintenance. Mismatch between current spend and required spend to achieve visibility within the online marketplace should be reviewed using tools such as Hitwise and Netratings which can be used to assess online market share.
- *Technology infrastructure resources* – availability and performance (speed) of website and service-level agreements with the ISP. The need for different applications to enhance the customer experience or increase conversion rates can be assessed (e.g. on-site search, customer review or customisation facilities). The infrastructure to manage sites such

as content management, customer relationship management and web analytics should also be considered.

- *Human resources* – availability for an e-retailer includes service and fulfilment resources for answering customer queries and dispatching goods. For all companies there is a challenge of possibly recruiting new staff or re-skilling marketing staff to manage online marketing activities such as merchandising, search engine marketing, affiliate marketing and email marketing. We return to this topic later in this chapter.
- *Structure* – what are the responsibilities and control mechanisms used to coordinate Internet marketing across different departments and business units? We again return to this topic later in the chapter.
- *Strengths and weaknesses* – SWOT analysis is referred to in the next section where generic strengths and weaknesses are summarised in Figure 4.6 and an example is given in Figure 4.7. Companies will also assess their distinctive competencies.

Stage models of the digital marketing capability

Stage models of capability delivered through the online presence can help assess digital marketing capabilities. Companies tend to follow a natural progression in developing their digital media and experiences to support their marketing activities. Most larger businesses now have an interactive, content-managed corporate site with a range of customer-facing sites for different brands. However, for smaller businesses the following levels of digital marketing can be identified:

- **Level 0.** No website or social presence. Some small businesses may still not have any online presence, although the numbers in this category are decreasing.
- **Level 1.** Company places an entry in a directory website that lists company names and has reviews and photos such as Yellow Pages (**www.yell.com**), Yelp (**www.yelp.com**) or Google My Business (**www.google.com/business**, previously known as Google+ Local and Google Places) to make people searching the web aware of the existence of the company or its products.
- **Level 2.** Simple static website created containing basic company contact and product information (sometimes referred to as **brochureware**). Alternatively they may just have a Facebook page or both.

Brochureware
A website in which a company has simply transferred ('migrated') its existing paper-based promotional literature on to the Internet without recognising the differences required by this medium.

- **Level 3.** Simple interactive site where users are able to search the site and make queries to retrieve information such as product availability and pricing. Enquiries submitted by a form and transmitted by email will also be supported. Today all sites should be designed to be mobile-responsive (as described in Chapter 7).
- **Level 4.** Interactive site supporting transactions with users. The functions offered will vary according to the company. If products can be sold direct then an electronic commerce or online store option for online sales will be available. Other functions might include user-generated content, social sharing of blog or product pages or an interactive customer-service helpdesk or Livechat.
- **Level 5.** Fully interactive site and marketing automation providing relationship marketing with individual customers and facilitating the full range of marketing functions relevant for the sector.

A variety of online stage models have been produced since the classic stage model created by Quelch and Klein (1996) with stages of:

1 image/product information;
2 information collection;
3 customer support/service;
4 internal support and service;
5 transactions.

They noted the sequence in which websites develop for existing and pureplay companies.

Dave Chaffey writing for Smart Insights has developed a modern stage-model framework for assessing internal digital marketing capabilities in larger organisations (Figure 4.4). This was inspired by the capability maturity models devised by the Carnegie Mellon Software Engineering Institute (**www.sei.cmu.edu/cmm/cmm.html**) to help organisations improve their software development practices.

Competitor analysis

In Chapter 2 we showed that competitor analysis or the monitoring of competitor use of e-commerce to acquire and retain customers is especially important in the online marketplace due to the dynamic nature of the Internet medium. This enables new services to be launched and prices and promotions changed much more rapidly than through print communications. Benchmarking is intended to:

1 Review current approaches to digital marketing to identify areas for improvement.
2 Benchmark with competitors who are in the same market sector or industry and in different sectors.
3 Identify best practice from more advanced adopters.
4 Set targets and develop strategies for improving capabilities.

Intermediary analysis

Chapter 2 highlighted the importance of web-based intermediaries such as publisher sites and blogs in increasing awareness and driving traffic to an organisation's website. Situation analysis will also involve identifying relevant intermediaries for a particular marketplace and look at how the organisation and its competitors are using the intermediaries to build traffic and provide services. For example, an e-tailer needs to assess where its target customers might encounter their competitors or know whether competitors have any special sponsorship arrangements or microsites created with intermediaries. The other aspect of situation analysis for intermediaries is to consider the way in which the marketplace is operating. To what extent are competitors using disintermediation or reintermediation? How are existing channel arrangements being changed?

There are now many freemium online services available to companies to understand their effectiveness in attracting and retaining new customers and competitors and intermediaries. We explored some of these tools in Chapter 2. Complete Activity 4.3 to discuss how they can be applied from a strategic perspective to support digital agility.

Activity 4.3	Strategic insight or analysis paralysis?

Purpose

Figure 4.5 shows the range of tools available to review and improve audience engagement compared to competitors and intermediaries. The tools are structured around how they relate to the Smart Insights RACE Planning framework. This activity reviews how these tools can be deployed effectively for a more agile, emergent approach to digital marketing.

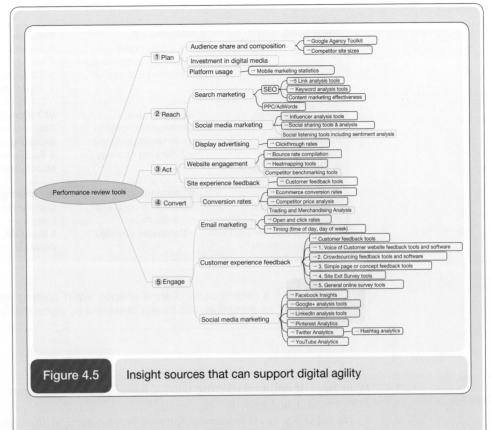

| Figure 4.5 | Insight sources that can support digital agility |

Questions

1 To understand the range of tools available, identify one or two tools in each category that you believe are most important to inform action.
2 How important do you think these tools are to informing strategic decisions?
3 Given your answer to 2, what are the implications for the timing of reviewing digital strategy?

Assessing opportunities and threats

Performing a structured SWOT analysis to summarise the external opportunities and threats that are presented by digital platforms is a core activity for situation analysis. Companies should also consider their own strengths and weaknesses in the Internet marketing environment. Summarising the results through digital channel-specific SWOT analysis (internal Strengths and Weaknesses and external Opportunities and Threats) will clearly highlight the opportunities and threats. Appropriate planning to counter the threats and take advantage of the opportunities can then be built into the Internet marketing plan. An example of a typical SWOT analysis of digital marketing-related strengths and weaknesses is shown in Figure 4.6. As is often the case with SWOT analysis, the opportunities available to a company are the opposites of the threats presented by other companies. The strengths and weaknesses will vary according to the company involved, but many of the strengths and weaknesses are dependent on the capacity of senior management to acknowledge and act on change. The SWOT can be reviewed in the

The organisation	Stengths – S 1. Existing brand 2. Existing customer base 3. Existing distribution	Weaknesses – W 1. Brand perception 2. Intermediary use 3. Technology/skills 4. Cross-channel support
Opportunities – O 1. Cross-selling 2. New markets 3. New services 4. Alliances/co-branding	SO strategies Leverage strengths to maximise opportunities **= Attacking strategy**	WO strategies Counter weaknesses through exploiting opportunities **= Build strengths for attacking strategy**
Threats – T 1. Customer choice 2. New entrants 3. New competitive products 4. Channel conflicts	ST strategies Leverage strengths to minimise threats **= Defensive strategy**	WT strategies Counter weaknesses and threats **= Build strengths for defensive strategy**

Figure 4.6 A generic digital channel-specific SWOT analysis showing typical opportunities and threats presented by digital media

main areas of online marketing activity, namely areas of customer acquisition, conversion, retention and growth.

This 'TOWS' (as it is known) form of presentation of the digital channel-specific SWOT shown in Figure 4.6 is a powerful technique since it not only indicates the SWOT, but can be used to generate appropriate strategies. Often, the most rewarding strategies combine Strengths and Opportunities or counter Threats through Strengths. Figure 4.7 gives an example of typical digital SWOT analytics for an established multichannel brand.

Setting goals and objectives for digital marketing

Any marketing strategy should be based on clearly defined corporate objectives, but there has been a tendency for digital marketing to be conducted separately from other business and marketing objectives. Porter (2001) has criticised the lack of goal setting when many organisations have developed Internet-related strategies. He notes that many companies, responding to distorted market signals, have used 'rampant experimentation' that is not economically sustainable. This resulted in the failure of many 'dot-com' companies and also poor investments by many established companies. He suggests that economic value or sustained profitability for a company is the final arbiter of business success. We have found that goals and objectives are often defined and used differently within different companies or parts of a business and this can lead to confusion when creating processes to track and improve marketing performance. Typically in businesses you see that objectives are specific, they cover the SMART criteria which ensure specific targets for a time period and measure against these using sales or analytics systems. Goals are broader aims which are informed by a vision. In Figure 4.8 the typical relationship between goals, objectives and KPIs is defined.

The organisation	Strengths – S 1 Existing brand 2 Existing customer base 3 Existing distribution	Weaknesses – W 1 Brand perception 2 Intermediary use 3 Technology/skills (poor web experience) 4 Cross-channel support 5 Churn rate
Opportunities – O 1 Cross-selling 2 New markets 3 New services 4 Alliances/co-branding	SO strategies Leverage strengths to maximise opportunities = attacking strategy **Examples:** 1 Migrate customers to web strategy 2 Refine customer contact strategy across customer lifecycle or commitment segmentation (e-mail, web) 3 Partnership strategy (co-branding, linking) 4 Launch new web-based products or value-adding experiences, e.g. video streaming	WO strategies Counter weaknesses through exploiting opportunities = build strengths for attacking strategy **Examples:** 1 Countermediation strategy (create or acquire) 2 Search marketing acquisition strategy 3 Affiliate-based acquisition strategy 4 Refine customer contact strategy (e-mail, web)
Threats – T 1 Customer choice (price) 2 New entrants 3 New competitive products 4 Channel conflicts 5 Social network	ST strategies Leverage strengths to minimise threat = defensive strategy **Examples:** 1 Introduce new Internet-only products 2 Add value to web services – refine OVP 3 Partner with complementary brand 4 Create own social network/customer reviews	WT strategies Counter weaknesses and threats: = build strengths for defensive strategy **Examples:** 1 Differential online pricing strategy 2 Acquire/create pure-play company with lower cost-base 3 Customer engagement strategy to increase conversion, average order value and lifetime value 4 Online reputation management strategy/E-PR

Figure 4.7   An example of a digital channel specific SWOT for an established multichannel brand showing how the elements of SWOT can be related to strategy formulation

So, if you are going to define objectives and goals closely, how should you do this? Use clear definitions that show the relationship between these terms and use examples. For digital marketing you can define different types of performance targets and measures as follows:

1 **Vision.** A high-level statement of how digital marketing will contribute to the organisation.
2 **Goals** are broad aims to show how the business can benefit from digital channels. They describe how your digital marketing will contribute to the business in key areas of growing sales, communicating with your audience and saving money.

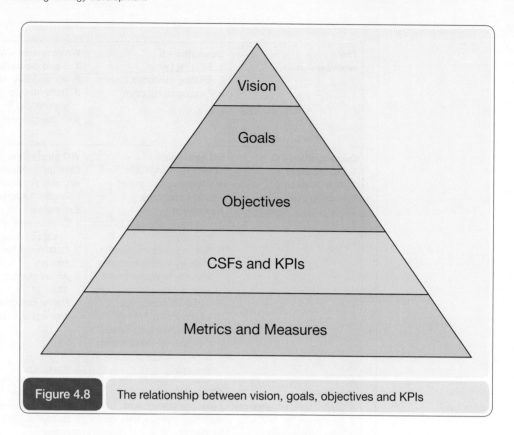

| Figure 4.8 | The relationship between vision, goals, objectives and KPIs |

3　**Objectives.** Specific SMART objectives to give clear direction and commercial targets. Objectives are the SMART targets for digital marketing which can be used to track performance against target.

4　**KPIs.** Key performance indicators (KPIs) are used to check you are on track. KPIs are specific metrics which are used to track performance to make sure you are on track to meet specific objectives. They are sometimes known as performance drivers or critical success factors for this reason.

As a starting point for setting specific objectives, it is useful to think through the benefits of the Internet channel so that these benefits can be converted into objectives. It is useful to identify both *tangible benefits*, for which monetary savings or revenues can be identified, and *intangible benefits*, for which it is more difficult to calculate financial benefits and costs, but they are still important, e.g. customer service quality. Table 4.2 presents a summary of typical benefits of digital marketing.

An alternative way of thinking through the broad goals of digital marketing is to review the 5Ss of Chaffey and Smith (2012), who suggest there are five broad benefits of e-marketing:

● *Sell* – grow sales through wider distribution to customers you can't service offline, or perhaps through a wider product range than in-store, or better prices.
● *Serve* – add value by giving customers extra benefits online, deliver customer service by 'web self-service' or social media and inform them of product development through online dialogue and feedback, for example in blogs or customer communities.
● *Speak* – get closer to customers, learn about their interests by monitoring them through web analytics and social media monitoring, asking them questions in surveys and, creating a dialogue in online customer communities or panels.
● *Save* – save costs of customer service, sales transactions and administration, print and post. Can you reduce transaction costs and therefore either make online sales more

Table 4.2	Tangible and intangible benefits from Internet marketing

Tangible benefits	Intangible benefits
Increased sales from new sales leads giving: • New customers, new markets • Existing customers (repeat-selling) • Existing customers (cross-selling) Cost reductions from: • reduced time in customer service • (customer self-service online) • online sales • reduced printing and distribution costs of marketing communications	Corporate image communication rise due to increased revenue from: • Enhanced brand • More rapid, more responsive marketing communications including PR • Improved customer service • Learning for the future • Meeting customer expectations to have a website • Identifying new partners, supporting existing partners better • Better management of marketing information and customer information • Feedback from customers on products

profitable or use cost savings to enable you to cut prices, which in turn could allow you to generate greater market share?

● *Sizzle* – extend the brand online. Reinforce brand values using interactive digital media and content. Develop an online value proposition which can help inform or entertain customers in ways which aren't possible in traditional media.

Mini case study 4.1	Arena Flowers expands overseas

Arena Flowers (Figure 4.9) is an online florist based in London. The business was incorporated in July 2006 and went live with a transactional website in September 2006. In 2008, the company began moving into European markets, e.g. the Netherlands, Germany, Belgium, France. Overseas sales now represent about a fifth of the company's annual sales (Graham, 2011). The essence of the Arena Flowers' business proposition is to cut out all middlemen and buy direct from growers, so they can get great prices and because the flowers are exceedingly fresh.

There are no 'relay' fees with us and, because of our high stock turnover, we get fresh flowers in daily and they go straight to the customer, rather than sitting in a hot shop window. Arena Flowers offer free delivery on all of our products and we were the first online florist in the UK to offer FFP-accredited, ethically sourced flowers.

That has been a good 'unique selling point' and enables Arena to offer something different from other suppliers such as supermarkets.

Strategic development

The company delivered £2 million net sales in its first year and broke even within the first 12 months of trading. Arena forecast sales of £4 million in year 2, which would bring a healthy profit. The head of design and development, Sam Barton, explained how he sees opportunities to keep growing both sales and profitability at a similar rate in the future through various initiatives. The company developed a Facebook application that provided 15 per cent of the site traffic – an opportunity that has been missed by many of its more established rivals.

| Figure 4.9 | Will Wynne, Arena Flowers (www.arenaflowers.com) |

A can-do approach to developing its business online has enabled Arena Flowers to enter European and other international markets even though the competition is very tough. Will Wynne, Arena's co-founder and current managing director, feels strongly about the importance of getting the language right in order to be successful online in European markets:

I think the language is a no-brainer. You're not going to have any success if you don't adapt to the local language.

It's almost a matter of respect. If you think there's 60 million people in France and 80 million in Germany, and the idea that they would use our website if we didn't translate is probably a bit ambitious.

See more about the team at Arena Flowers at by watching Nick discussing the development of the business and what it stands for at: www.youtube.com/watch?v=4SsnC5dRklg&NR=1.

Sources: Econsultancy (2008); Graham (2011)

The online revenue contribution

Online revenue contribution
An assessment of the direct contribution of the Internet or other digital media to sales, usually expressed as a percentage of overall sales revenue.

A key objective for digital marketing is the **online revenue contribution** since this gives a simple measure of the proportion of online sales achieved in different product categories. This is a measure of the extent to which a company's online presence directly impacts on the sales revenue (or better profit) of the organisation. By understanding the contribution of online revenue, business planners should be able to determine future resource needs to online channels. Online revenue contribution objectives can be specified for different types of products, customer segments and geographic markets. For example, in 1997, low-cost airline easyJet set an online contribution objective of 50 per cent by the year 2000. This established a clear vision and resources could be put in place to achieve this. EasyJet now has an online revenue contribution of 95 per cent.

Allowable cost per acquisition
A target maximum cost for generating leads or new customers profitably.

It is important that companies set sales and revenue goals for online channels for which costs are controlled through an **allowable cost per acquisition**. This takes into account the cost of attracting visitors through techniques such as affiliate marketing, paid search advertising or display advertising, as explained in budget models presented in Chapter 8.

For some companies, such as a FMCG manufacturer, a beverage company or a B2B manufacturer, it is unrealistic to expect a direct online revenue contribution. In this case, an indirect online contribution can be stated. This considers the Internet as part of the promotional mix and its role in reaching and influencing a proportion of customers to purchase the product, generating trials or, in the case of a B2B company, leads. In this case a company could set an **online promotion contribution** or indirect online revenue contribution of 5 per cent of its target market visiting the website or social media presence and interacting with the brand (see Digital marketing insight 4.2)

Online promotion contribution
This is an assessment of the proportion of customers (new or retained) who are influenced and reached by online communications.

Digital marketing insight 4.2 | **Black Friday, boost sales**

The moniker 'Black Friday' is attributed to the Philadelphia Police Department in the 1950s, which gave this name to the day after Thanksgiving due to the mayhem that happened as shoppers flocked to the high street sales. Hearsay evidence suggests the name Black Friday was used as increased sales enabled retailers to go into the 'black' with their accounts for the first time in the year and to generate profits. It wasn't until 2010 that Amazon brought Black Friday to the attention of online shoppers in the UK. Since then this promotional discount day has gathered momentum and led to frenzied scenes in stores across the UK as shoppers fight one another to get at the best bargains. Awareness of this promotional event has been online but it has quickly spread to the physical high street and many retailers have relied on this event to kick-start the third quarter sales. Dixons Carphone reported a positive impact of the Black Friday promotional event.

Source: Based on Butler (2015)

Complete Activity 4.4 to explore the factors that impact online revenue contribution in different markets.

Activity 4.4 | **Assessing the significance of digital channels**

Purpose
To illustrate the issues involved with assessing the suitability of the Internet for e-commerce.

Activity
For each of the products and services in Table 4.3, assess the suitability of the Internet for delivery of the product or service and position it on the grid in Figure 4.10 with justification. Make estimates in Table 4.3 for the direct and indirect online revenue contribution in five and ten years' time for different products in your country. Choose specific products within each category shown.

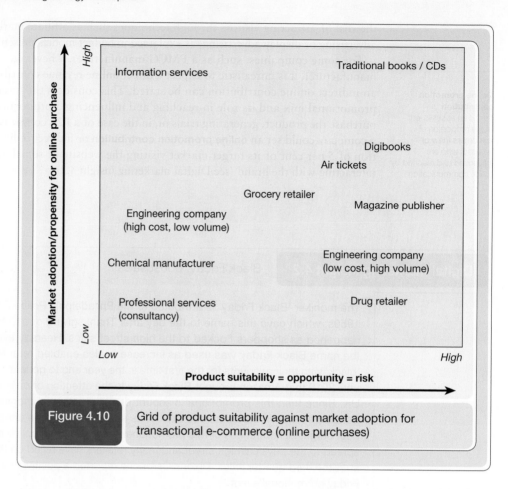

| **Figure 4.10** | Grid of product suitability against market adoption for transactional e-commerce (online purchases) |

| **Table 4.3** | Vision of online revenue contribution for different types of company |

Products/services	Now	2 years' time	5 years' time	10 years' time
Example: Cars, US				
Direct online sales	5%	10%	25%	50%
Indirect online sales	50%	70%	90%	95%
Financial services				
Direct online sales				
Indirect online sales				
Clothing				
Direct online sales				
Indirect online sales				
Business office supplies				
Direct online sales				
Indirect online sales				

Setting SMART objectives

You have probably heard before that effective objectives and measures to set objectives and assess performance against these goals are SMART. SMART is used to assess the suitability of objectives set to drive different strategies or the improvement of the full range of business processes.

- *Specific*. Is the objective sufficiently detailed to measure real-world problems and opportunities?
- *Measurable*. Can a quantitative or qualitative attribute be applied to create a metric?
- *Actionable*. Can the information be used to improve performance? If the objective doesn't change behaviour in staff to help them improve performance, there is little point in it!
- *Relevant*. Can the information be applied to the specific problem faced by the manager?
- *Time-related*. Can the information be constrained through time?

With SMART objectives, everyone is clearer what the target is and progresses towards it and, if necessary, action can be taken to put the company back on target. For SMART digital marketing objectives for an online presence such as a website, mobile app or marketing, consider the VQVC mnemonic as a test or check that you have the right type of measures.

Digital marketing insight 4.3   Check objectives and KPIs using the VQVC mnemonic

VQVC relates to the conversion funnel we introduced in Chapter 2. It stands for:

1 Traffic volume measures

Digital Analytics systems like Google Analytics have specific measures for volume for which objectives which can be set using monthly planning models to sum across to give an annual total.

- *Unique visits* – the number of individuals who visit the site in the specified period.
- *Visits* – the total number of times the site was accessed by different individuals.
- *Page views* – the total number of pages viewed by individuals.

2 Quality measures

To understand the effectiveness of the online experience, conversion measures are essential which combine to assess the quality of the visitors and the quality of the experience. These measures give an indication of how a visitor has engaged with a site. These examples of site engagement benchmarks show the typical range for these metrics.

- *Bounce rate* – The percentage of visitors who leave immediately after viewing only one page. Generally, unless they're on the site for specific information such as a support question, a high bounce rate is a sign of poor quality traffic and/or experience.
- *Duration* – The dwell time – measured as average time on page or average time on site.
- *Pages per visit* – I find this more useful than dwell time since it gives you an idea of how many pages your visitor views on average. It's an opportunity for a marketer to communicate their message.
- *Conversion rates to lead and sale*. These are the most important of the quality measures since they show what proportion of visits convert to commercial outcomes.

3 Value measures

Value shows the communications effectiveness and commercial contribution of digital marketing to a business. Here we're looking for outcomes which show intent to purchase or purchase itself. For an e-commerce site this is straightforward, we can look at measures like sales transactions and average order value. However, it's less obvious for the many non-transactional sites, like B2B sites. Here it's necessary to set up goals customised for the business in Google Analytics for when user actions are completed for qualified leads. Taking the example of a brochure or white paper download, you specify the thank you page address, give the goal a name and specify your goal.

- *Goal value per visit*. If you assign a value to a goal such as a download, you can then compare how different visitor sources contribute value to the site. For example, how does social media marketing compare to email, is LinkedIn more or less valuable than Twitter – this is very powerful for checking your marketing investments.
- *Revenue per visit*. For sites with e-commerce tracking, Google will report revenue per visit, which enables you perform similar analysis to that for goal value.
- *Page value*. If marketers review this measure for pages they can determine which pages are prompting the creation of value, enabling you to improve customer journeys and messaging.

4 Cost measures

Cost includes the cost of content and experience creation and promotion – i.e. paid, owned and earned media costs. Cost per acquisition is typically used to assess media effectiveness.

Here are some typical examples of SMART objectives across VQVC, including those to support goal setting in customer acquisition, conversion and retention categories for digital marketing strategy:

- *Digital channel contribution objective*. Achieve 10 per cent online revenue (or profit) contribution within two years.
- *Acquisition objective*. Acquire 50,000 new online customers this financial year at an average cost per acquisition (CPA) of £30 with an average profitability of £5.
- *Acquisition or conversion objective*. Migrate 40 per cent of existing customers to using online 'paperless' bill payment services within three years (e.g. for a bank or utilities company).
- *Acquisition objective*. Increase by 20 per cent within one year the number of sales arising from a certain target market, e.g. 18–25-year-olds.
- *Conversion objective*. Increase the average order value of online sales to £42 per customer.
- Conversion objective. Increase site conversion rate to 3.2 per cent (would be based on model of new and existing customers in different categories).
- *Conversion objective*. Increase percentage of online service enquiries fulfilled online by 'web self-service' from 85 to 90 per cent.
- *Retention objective*. Increase annual repeat new customer conversion rate by 20 per cent.
- *Retention objective* (existing customers). Increase percentage of active users of the service (purchasing or using of other electronic services) within a 180-day period from 20 to 25 per cent.

- *Retention objective*. Increase customer satisfaction rating for channel from 70 to 80 per cent.
- *Growth objective*. Increase new prospects recommended by friends (viral marketing or 'member get member') by 10,000 per annum.
- *Growth objective*. Increase propensity to recommend online service from 60 to 70 per cent.
- *Penetration objective*. Achieve first or second position in category penetration in the countries within which the company operates (this is effectively online audience or market share and can be measured through visitor rankings such as Hitwise or Netratings (Chapter 2) or, better, by online revenue share).
- *Cost objective*. Achieve a cost reduction of 10 per cent in marketing communications within two years.
- Improve customer service by providing a response to a query within two hours, 24 hours per day, seven days a week.

Specific digital communications objectives are also described in Chapter 8.

Frameworks for objective setting

A significant challenge of objective setting for digital marketing is that there will potentially be many different measures, such as those listed above, and these will have be to grouped to be meaningful and presented on performance dashboards. In this chapter, we have already seen two methods of categorising objectives. First, objectives can be set at the level of business effectiveness, marketing effectiveness and Internet marketing effectiveness, as explained in the section on internal auditing as part of the situation analysis. Second, the 5S framework of Sell, Speak, Serve, Save and Sizzle provides a simple framework for objective setting. A further five-part framework for goal setting and analysis is presented in Chapter 10.

Balanced scorecard
A framework for setting and monitoring business performance. Metrics are structured according to customer issues, internal efficiency measures, financial measures and innovation.

Some larger companies will identify objectives for digital marketing initiatives which are consistent with existing business measurement frameworks, e.g. the **balanced scorecard**, but research has identified widespread variation in the use and level of uptake of performance measures (Gunawan *et al.*, 2008). Nevertheless, the balanced business scorecard is a well-known and widely used framework and it can be helpful as a guide.

Efficiency
Minimising resources or time needed to complete a process. 'Doing the thing right.'

The balanced scorecard was popularised in a *Harvard Business Review* article by Kaplan and Norton (1993). It can be used to translate vision and strategy into objectives and then, through measurement, to assess whether the strategy and its implementation are successful. In addition to financial data, the balanced scorecard uses operational measures such as customer satisfaction, efficiency of internal processes and also the organisation's innovation and improvement activities including staff development. This framework has since been applied to IT (Der Zee and De Jong, 1999), e-commerce (Hasan and Tibbits, 2000) and multichannel marketing (Bazett *et al.*, 2005).

Effectiveness
Meeting process objectives, delivering the required outputs and outcomes. 'Doing the right thing.'

Table 4.4 illustrates specific Internet marketing measures within the four main areas of organisational performance managed through the balanced scorecard. In our presentation we have placed objectives within the areas of **efficiency** ('doing the thing right') and **effectiveness** ('doing the right thing'), e.g. efficiency involves increasing conversion rates and reducing costs of acquisition. Effectiveness involves supporting broader marketing objectives and often indicates the contribution of the online channel.

Performance metrics
Measures that are used to evaluate and improve the efficiency and effectiveness of business processes.

Performance drivers

Key performance indicators (KPIs)
Metrics used to assess the performance of a process and/or whether set goals are achieved.

Specific **performance metrics** are used to evaluate and improve the efficiency and effectiveness of a process. **Key performance indicators (KPIs)** are a special type of performance metric which indicate the overall performance of a process or its sub-processes. An example of KPIs for an online electrical goods retailer is shown in Figure 4.11. Improving the results from the e-commerce site involves using the techniques on the left of the diagram to improve

Table 4.4	Example allocation of Internet marketing objectives within the balanced scorecard framework for a transactional e-commerce site

Balanced scorecard sector	Efficiency	Effectiveness
Financial results (Business value)	• Channel costs Channel profitability	• Online contribution (direct) • Online contribution (indirect) • Profit contributed
Customer value	• Online reach (unique visitors as% of potential visitors) • Cost of acquisition or cost per sale (CPA/CPS) • Customer propensity	• Sales and sales per customer • New customers • Online market share • Customer satisfaction ratings • Customer loyalty index
Operational processes	• Conversion rates • Average order value • List size and quality • Email active (%)	• Fulfilment times • Support response times
Operational processes	• Conversion rates • Average order value • List size and quality • Email active (%)	• Fulfilment times • Support response times

the performance drivers, and so the KPI. The KPI is the total online sales figure. For a traditional retailer, this could be compared as a percentage to other retail channels such as mail order or retail stores. It can be seen that this KPI is dependent on performance drivers such as number of site visits or average order value which combine to govern this KPI.

Leading and lagging performance indicators

When developing goals and measurement systems used to review and improve performance of digital channels, it is also helpful to consider which are leading and lagging indicators of performance. Trends should be identified within these – e.g. are they increasing or decreasing year-on-year (often used as a good like-for-like comparison) – or compared to the previous week, month or average for a recent period.

A **leading performance indicator** is a metric that is suggestive of future performance – think of the amber preceding the green light on traffic lights on a short timescale. The benefit of leading indicators is that they enable managers to be proactive in shaping future performance. There tend to be fewer leading performance indicators, but these can be applied to e-commerce:

● *Repeat sales metrics.* If repeat conversion rates are falling or the average time between sales (sales latency) is falling, then these are warning signs of future declining sales volume for which proactive action can be taken, e.g. through a customer email marketing programme.

● *Customer satisfaction or advocacy ratings such as the Net Promoter Score.* If these are trending downwards or return rates are increasing, this may be a sign of a future decline in repeat sales since more customers are dissatisfied.

● *Sales trends compared to market audience trends.* If, for example, online sales are increasing at a lower rate than overall online audiences for a product category are indicated, e.g. through panel data, Hitwise or searches in particular categories, then this is a warning sign that needs to be acted upon.

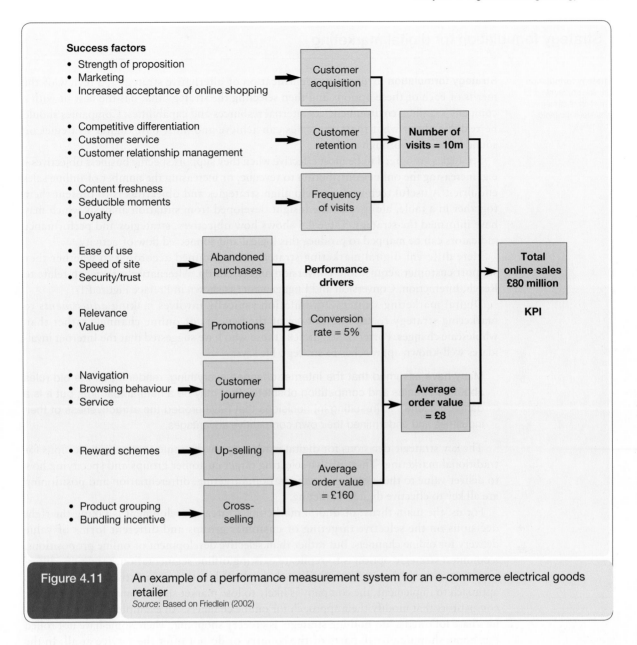

An example of a performance measurement system for an e-commerce electrical goods retailer
Source: Based on Friedlein (2002)

Lagging performance indicator
A measure which indicates past performance. Corrective action can then be applied to improve performance.

A **lagging performance indicator** is one where the measure indicates past performance. Lagging indicators enable corrective action to be taken. Some also identify a coincident performance indicator which is more suggestive of current performance. Lagging performance indicators for a transactional retail site include:

- *Sales volume, revenue and profitability*. These are typically compared against target or previous periods.
- *Cost per acquisition (CPA)*. The cost of gaining each new customer will also be compared against target. Variations in trends in CPA for different referrers (traffic sources) and between different product categories can potentially be used as leading indicators.
- *Conversion efficiency metrics*. For an e-commerce site these include process efficiency metrics such as conversion rate, average order and landing page bounce rates.

These lagging indicators are used operationally on a daily or weekly basis so that performance can be diagnosed and reviewed.

Strategy formulation for digital marketing

Strategy formulation
Generation, review and selection of strategies to achieve strategic objectives.

Strategy formulation involves the identification of alternative strategies, a review of the merits of each of these options and then selecting the strategy that has the best fit with a company's trading environment, its internal resources and capabilities. Companies should be realistic about what their strategies can achieve and must base digital strategies on sound logic and thorough analysis.

Strategies are agreed to be most effective when they support specific business objectives – e.g. increasing the online contribution to revenue, or increasing the number of online sales enquiries. A useful technique to help align strategies and objectives is to present them together in a table, along with the insight developed from situation analysis which may have informed the strategy. Table 4.5 shows how objectives, strategies and performance indicators can be mapped to produce this logical and connected flow of activity.

Here different digital marketing strategies are grouped according to whether they support customer acquisition, conversion and retention. Alternatively, they can relate to Reach, Interaction, Conversion and Engagement (as shown in Preface Figure P1).

Digital marketing strategy formulation typically involves making *adjustments* to marketing strategy to take advantage of the benefits of online channels rather than wholescale changes. Porter (2001) attacks those who have suggested that the Internet invalidates well-known approaches to strategy. He says:

> Many have assumed that the Internet changes everything, rendering all the old rules about companies and competition obsolete. That may be a natural reaction, but it is a dangerous one . . . [resulting in] decisions that have eroded the attractiveness of their industries and undermined their own competitive advantages.

The key strategic decisions for digital marketing are the same as strategic decisions for traditional marketing. They involve selecting target customer groups and specifying how to deliver value to these groups. Segmentation, targeting, differentiation and positioning are all key to effective digital marketing.

For us, the main thrust of digital marketing strategy development is taking the right decisions on the selective targeting of customer groups and different forms of value delivery for online channels. But rather than selective development of online propositions, a common strategic option is to replicate existing offline segmentation, targeting, differentiation and positioning in the online channels. While this is a relatively easy strategic approach to implement, the company is likely to lose market share relative to more nimble competitors that modify their approach for online channels. An example of where companies have followed a 'do-nothing strategy' is grocery shopping, where some have not rolled out home shopping to all parts of the country or do not offer the service at all. In the United Kingdom, Morrisons is a latecomer to the online market and has struggled to make an impact as the most enthusiastic adopters of online channels have already formed relationships with more proactive online grocery brands, such as **Tesco.com** and Sainsbury. Morrisons will face a tough time trying to win back market share online in the future.

As mentioned at the start of the chapter, we should remember that digital marketing strategy is a channel marketing strategy and it needs to operate in the context of multichannel marketing. It follows that it is important that the digital marketing strategy should:

- be based on objectives for online contribution of leads and sales for this channel;
- be consistent with the types of customers that use and can be effectively reached through the channel;
- support the customer journey as they select and purchase products using this channel in combination with other channels;
- define a unique, differential proposition for the channel;

Table 4.5	An example of the relationship between objectives, strategies and performance indicators

Objectives	Substantiation (informed by situation analysis or insight, example)	Strategies to achieve goals	Key performance indicators (critical success factors)
1 *Acquisition objective.* Acquire 50,000 new online (based on current sales) customers this financial year at an average cost per acquisition (CPA) of £30 with an average profitability of 5%	Based on growth forecast 40,000 sales per year, but with incremental sales arising from new affiliate programme and SEO development	Start affiliate marketing programme and improve SEO. Existing media mix based on pay-per-click and display advertising supported by offline media. Use social media engagement to generate leads	Overall CPA for online sales Incremental number and % of sales from affiliate marketing programme
			Number of strategic keywords ranked in top positions in natural search results page
2 *Acquisition (or conversion) objective.* Migrate 40% of existing customers to using online 'paperless' bill payment services and email communications within three years	Extrapolation of current natural migration coupled with increased adoption from offline direct marketing campaign	Direct marketing campaign using direct mail, phone prompts and online persuasion to encourage adoption. Use of incentive to encourage change	Number and percentage of existing customers registering to use online service Number and percentage of customers actively using online services at different points after initially registering
3 *Conversion objective.* Increase the average order value of online sales to £42 per customer	Growth estimate based on current AOV of £35 plus model suggesting 20% increase in AOV	Use of new merchandising system to show users related 'next best product' for different product categories	% of site visitors responding to merchandising/cross-selling messages
4 *Conversion objective.* Increase site conversion rate to 3.2%	Model showing separate increase in conversion for new and existing customers based on strategies shown right	Combination of strategies: • Incentivised email follow-up on checkout abandonments for new customers • Introduction of more competitive pricing strategy on best-sellers • AB and multivariate messaging improvement of landing pages • Refinement to quality of traffic purchased through pay-per-click programme	Variations in conversion rates for new and existing customers in different product categories
5 *Retention objective.* Increase annual repeat new customer conversion rate by 20%	Business case based on limited personalisation of offers to encourage repeat purchases via email	• Delivery of personalised product offers by email • 5% second purchase discount voucher	• Increased conversion rate of retention email contact programme • Conversion to sale for second purchase discount campaigns
6 *Growth objective.* Increase new prospects recommended by friends (viral marketing or 'member get member') by 10,000 per annum	Model based on encouraging 2% of customers to recommend friends annually (based on trial scheme)	Supported by direct mail and email recommendation programme	Response rate to direct mail campaign

- specify how we communicate this proposition to persuade customers to use online services in conjunction with other channels;
- manage the online customer lifecycle through the stages of attracting visitors to the website, converting them to customers and retention and growth.
- be consistent with the types of customers that use and can be effectively reached through the digital communications channels and targeted using **online tactical marketing segmentation**.

Online tactical marketing segmentation
Tactical segmentation enables targeting based on customer journey behaviour such as search behaviour, content accessed and contribution to social media.

Furthermore, digital marketing strategy development involves reappraising a company's approach to strategy based on familiar elements of marketing strategy. We believe there are nine important decisions to consider:

- *Decision 1*: Market and product development strategies.
- *Decision 2*: Business and revenue models strategies.
- *Decision 3*: Target marketing strategy.
- *Decision 4*: Positioning and differentiation strategy (including the marketing mix).
- *Decision 5*: Customer engagement and social media strategy.
- *Decision 6*: Multichannel distribution strategy.
- *Decision 7*: Multichannel communications strategy.
- *Decision 8*: Online communications mix and budget.
- *Decision 9*: Organisational capabilities and governance (7S framework).

The first four decisions are concerned with fundamental questions of how an organisation delivers value to customers online and which products are offered to which markets online. The next four decisions are more concerned with the mix of marketing communications used to communicate with customers across multiple channels.

Decision 1: Market and product development strategies

In Chapter 1, we introduced the Ansoff matrix as a useful analytical tool for assessing online strategies for manufacturers and retailers. This tool is also fundamental to marketing planning and it should be the first decision point because it can help companies think about how online channels can support their marketing objectives, and also suggest innovative use of these channels to deliver new products and more markets (the boxes help stimulate 'out-of-box' thinking which is often missing with digital marketing strategy). Fundamentally, the market and product development matrix (Figure 4.12) can help identify strategies to increase sales volume through varying what is sold (the product dimension on the horizontal axis of Figure 4.12) and who it is sold to (the market dimension on the vertical axis). Specific objectives need to be set for sales generated via these strategies, so this decision relates closely to that of objective setting. Let us now review these strategies in more detail.

1 Market penetration

This strategy involves using digital channels to sell more existing products into existing markets. The Internet has great potential for achieving sales growth or maintaining sales by the market penetration strategy. As a starting point, many companies will use the Internet to help sell existing products into existing markets, although they may miss opportunities indicated by the strategies in other parts of the matrix. Figure 4.12 indicates some of the main ways in which the Internet can be used for market penetration:

- *Market share growth* – companies can compete more effectively online if they have websites that are efficient at converting visitors to sale, as explained in Chapter 7, and mastery of the online marketing communications techniques reviewed in Chapter 8, such as search engine marketing, affiliate marketing and online advertising.

Market development strategies	**Diversification strategies**
Use the Internet for targeting:	Using the Internet to support:
• New geographic markets	• Diversification into related businesses
• New customer segments	• Diversification into unrelated businesses
	• Upstream integration (with suppliers)
	• Downstream integration (with intermediaries)
Market penetration strategies	**Product development strategies**
Use the Internet for:	Use the Internet for:
• Market share growth – compete more effectively online	• Adding value to existing products
• Customer loyalty improvement – migrate existing customers online and add value to existing products, services and brand	• Developing digital products (new delivery/usage models)
• Customer value improvement – increase customer profitability by decreasing cost to serve and increase purchase or usage frequency and quantity	• Changing payment models (subscription, per use, bundling)
	• Increasing product range (especially e-retailers)

Market growth (New markets / Existing markets)

Existing products — *New products*

Product growth

Figure 4.12	Using the Internet to support different organisational growth strategies

- *Customer loyalty improvement* – companies can increase their value to customers and so increase loyalty by migrating existing customers online by adding value to existing products, services and brand by developing their online value proposition (see Decision 4).
- *Customer value improvement* – the value delivered by customers to the company can be increased by increasing customer profitability through decreasing cost to serve (and so price to customers) and at the same time increasing purchase or usage frequency and quantity. These combined effects should drive up sales. Many companies will offer competitive online prices or discounts to help increase their market share. Approaches to specifying online pricing are covered in Chapter 5.

2 Market development

Online channels are used to sell into new markets, taking advantage of the low cost of advertising internationally without the necessity for a supporting sales infrastructure in the customer's country. The Internet has helped low-cost airlines such as easyJet and Ryanair to cost-effectively enter new markets served by their routes. This is a relatively conservative use of the Internet but is a great opportunity for SMEs to increase exports at a low cost, though it does require overcoming the barriers to exporting.

Existing products can also be sold to new market segments or different types of customers. Virtual inventory enables new offerings to be made available to smaller segment sizes, an approach known as micro-targeting. This may happen simply as a by-product of having a website – e.g. RS Components (**www.rswww.com**), a supplier of a range of MRO (maintenance, repair and operations) items, found that 10 per cent of the web-based sales were to individual consumers rather than traditional business customers. It also uses the website to offer additional facilities for customers placing large orders online. The UK retailer Argos found the opposite was true, with 10 per cent of website sales being from businesses when their traditional market was consumer-based. EasyJet also has a section of its website to serve business customers. The Internet may offer further opportunities for selling to market sub-segments that have not been previously targeted. For example, a product sold to large businesses may also appeal to SMEs that they have previously been unable to serve because of the cost of sales via a specialist sales force. Alternatively, a product targeted at young people could also appeal to some members of an older audience and vice versa. Many companies have found that the audience and customers of their website are quite different from their traditional audience.

3 Product development

The web can be used to add value to or extend existing products for many companies. For example, a car manufacturer can potentially provide car performance and service information via a website. Facilities can be provided to download tailored brochures, book a test drive or tailor features required from a car model. But truly new products or services that can be delivered only by the Internet are typically digital media or information products – e.g. online trade magazine *Construction Weekly* diversified to a B2B portal Construction Plus (**www.constructionplus.com**) which had new revenue streams. Similarly, music and book publishing companies have found new ways to deliver products through a new development and usage model such as subscription and pay-per-use, as explained in Chapter 5 in the section on the product element of the marketing mix. Retailers can extend their product range and provide new bundling options online also.

4 Diversification

In this sector, new products are developed which are sold into new markets. The Internet alone cannot facilitate these high-risk business strategies, but it can facilitate them at lower costs than have previously been possible. The options include:

- *Diversification into related businesses*. A low-cost airline can use the website and customer emails to promote travel-related services such as hotel booking, car rental or travel insurance at relatively low costs either through its own brand or through partner companies – e.g. Ryanair offers its customers discounts if they book car hire with Hertz car rentals.
- *Diversification into unrelated businesses*. Again the website can be used to promote less-related products to customers, which is the approach used by the Virgin brand, although it is relatively rare.
- *Upstream integration with suppliers*. This is achieved through data exchange between a manufacturer or retailer and its suppliers to enable a company to take more control of the supply chain.
- *Downstream integration with intermediaries*. Again, this is achieved through data exchange with distributors such as online intermediaries.

The benefits and risks of market and product development are highlighted by the creation of Smile (Figure 4.13), an Internet-specific bank set up by the Co-operative Bank in the UK. It opened for business in October 1999 and in its first year added 200,000 customers at a rate of 20,000 per month. Significantly, 80 per cent of these customers were market development in the context of the parent, since they were not existing Co-operative Bank customers and typically belonged to a higher-income segment.

The risks of the new approach to banking were highlighted by the cost of innovation, with it being estimated that in its first year, the creation and promotion of Smile increased overall costs at the Co-operative Bank by 5 per cent. However, within five years Smile was on target, profitable and growing strongly.

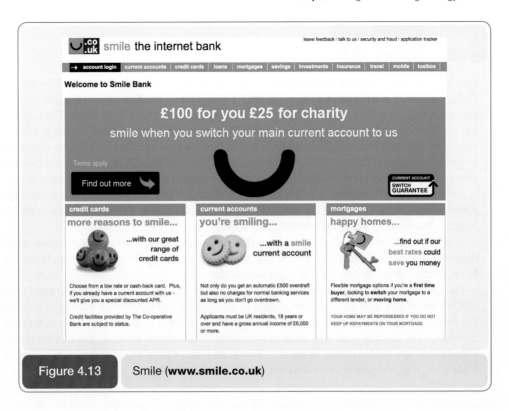

| Figure 4.13 | Smile (**www.smile.co.uk**) |

Decision 2: Business and revenue models strategies

Strategy formulation often requires companies to evaluate new models since to survive in the digital age means companies need to constantly innovate in order to defend market share for competitors and new entrants. Andy Grove of Intel famously said: 'Only the paranoid will survive', alluding to the need to review new revenue opportunities and competitor innovations. A willingness to test and experiment with new **business models** using calculations like those covered in Chapter 2 is also required. Dell is another example of a technology company that regularly reviews and modifies its business model as shown in Mini case study 4.2. Companies at the leading edge of technology such as Facebook and Google constantly innovate through acquiring other companies and internal research and development. Case study 4 on **Tesco.com** at the end of this chapter also highlights innovation in the Tesco business model facilitated through online channels.

This approach to supporting strategic agility through ongoing research and development is sometimes known as a **Skunkworks**, Digital Labs or Digital Innovation centres also in larger businesses.

Surprisingly, the term is not new. It originated from a Second World War R&D project known as the Lockheed Martin Skunk Works, over 70 years ago. Since then, its Skunkworks has helped enhance its global reputation as a pioneer in creating breakthrough technologies and continually to redefine flight.

Ideally, a Skunkworks has sufficient autonomy that it does not get sidetracked by current business needs. So it can operate as an off-shoot of the main organisation, protected from cultures and processes that inhibit progress and has a remit to create, develop and concept test new opportunities, products and services.

Another approach to developing new approaches is to encourage other companies in your sector, this is the approach taken by John Lewis with the JLabs (**www.jlabs.co.uk**).

Business model
A summary of how a company will generate revenue, identifying its product offering, value-added services, revenue sources and target customers.

Skunkworks
A loosely structured group of people who research and develop innovative opportunities and business benefits.

'Early- (first-) mover advantage
An early entrant into the marketplace.

Mini case study 4.2	Innovation in the Dell business model

One example of how companies can review and revise their business model is provided by Dell Computers. Dell gained **early-mover advantage** in the mid-1990s when it became one of the first companies to offer PCs for sale online. Its sales of PCs and peripherals rapidly grew from the mid-1990s with online sales of $1 million per day to sales of $50 million per day in 2000. Based on this success it has looked at new business models it can use in combination with its powerful brand to provide new services to its existing customer base and also to generate revenue through new customers. In September 2000, Dell announced plans to become a supplier of IT consulting services through linking with enterprise resource planning specialists such as software suppliers, systems integrators and business consulting firms. This venture will enable the facility of Dell's PremierPages to be integrated into the procurement component of ERP systems such as SAP and Baan, thus avoiding the need for rekeying and reducing costs.

In a separate initiative, Dell launched a B2B marketplace (formerly **www.dellmarketplace.com**) aimed at discounted office goods and services procurements including PCs, peripherals, software, stationery and travel. This strategic option did not prove sustainable.

Dell launched Ideastorm (**www.ideastorm.com**, see Figure 4.14), as a site encouraging user participation where anyone can suggest new products and features which can be voted on. Importantly, Dell 'closes the loop' through a separate *Ideas in Action* section where it updates consumers on actions taken by the company. For example, as well as improvements to customer service, the company explains how it has introduced new systems such as a non-Windows Linux operating system in response to suggestions on Ideastorm. It also explains ideas it hasn't implemented and why.

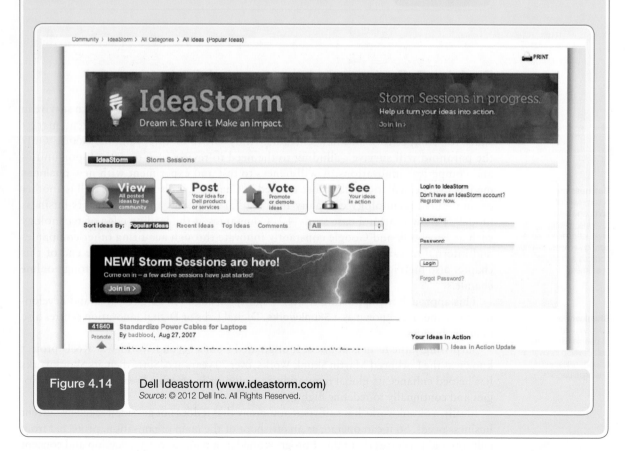

Figure 4.14	Dell Ideastorm (www.ideastorm.com)

Source: © 2012 Dell Inc. All Rights Reserved.

Furthermore, where companies, including transactional sites such as **Amazon.com** or **Lastminute.com**, have introduced advertising as part of their revenue model, the amount of revenue generated tends to be low compared to overall revenue (although it may be used as leverage for other co-branding work) or insight generated about customer response.

So with all strategy options managers should also consider the 'do-nothing option'. Here, a company will not risk a new business model, but adopt a 'wait-and-see' or 'fast-follower' approach to see how competitors perform, and then respond rapidly if the new business model proves sustainable.

Revenue model
Describes methods generating income organisation.

Finally, we can note that companies can make less radical changes to their **revenue models** through the Internet which are less far-reaching, but may nevertheless be worthwhile. For example:

- Transactional e-commerce sites (e.g. **Tesco.com** and **Lastminute.com**) can sell advertising space or run co-branded promotions on site or through their email newsletters or lists to sell access to their audience to third parties.
- Retailers or media owners can sell-on white-labelled services through their online presence such as ISP, email services or photo-sharing services.
- Companies can gain commission through selling products which are complementary (but not competitive to their own); e.g. a publisher can sell its books through an affiliate arrangement through an e-retailer.

Decision 3: Target marketing strategy

Deciding on which markets to target is a key strategic consideration when planning a digital marketing strategy in the same way it is key to marketing strategy. We will see that a company's web presence and email marketing enables it to target more focussed audiences than may be possible with other channels. **Target marketing strategy** involves the four stages shown in Figure 4.15, but the most important decisions are:

Target marketing strategy
Evaluation and selection of appropriate segments and the development of appropriate offers.

- *Segmentation/targeting strategy* – a company's online customers will often have different demographic characteristics, needs and behaviours from its offline customers. It follows

Informed by	Stage of target marketing	Informs
Market research and analysis of customer data	**Segmentation** Identify customer needs and segment market	• Market segment definition • Persona development • Customer experience requirements
Demand analysis	**Target marketing** Evaluate and select target segments	• Select online targeting • Target segments • Online revenue contribution for each segment • Customer lifecycle targeting
Competitor analysis Internal analysis	**Positioning** Identify proposition for each segment	• Core brand proposition • Online value proposition • Online marketing mix • Lifecycle brand development and proposition messaging
Evaluation of resources	**Planning** Deploy resources to achieve plan	• Online marketing mix • Restructuring • Automated online customer contact strategy

Figure 4.15   Stages in target marketing strategy development

that online different approaches to **strategic market segmentation** may be an opportunity and specific segments may need to be selectively targeted through online media channels, the company website or email communications. As we will see, personal development and lifecycle targeting are common approaches for online targeting.

- *Positioning/differentiation strategy* – competitors' product and service offerings will often differ in the online environment. Developing an appropriate online value proposition as described below is an important aspect of this strategy. However, there should also be clarity on the core brand proposition.

The first stage in Figure 4.15 is *segmentation*. Segmentation is a management technique which allows businesses to focus their efforts on the customers they can serve best. When creating digital marketing plans it is useful to distinguish between strategic market segmentation and online tactical segmentation which is used for online targeting.

Strategic market segmentation can be defined as (Jobber and Ellis-Chadwick, 2013):

the identification of individuals or organisations with similar characteristics that have significant implications for determining marketing strategy.

In an Internet marketing planning context, market segments should be reviewed to assess:

- the current market size or value, future projections of size;
- the organisation's current and future market share within the segment;
- needs of each segment, in particular unmet needs;
- competitor market shares within the segment;
- organisation and competitor offers and propositions;
- likelihood of a segment engaging with the organisation's offer across all aspects of the buying process;
- usage of the site and conversion to action through web analytics.

Options for segmenting online customers by activity levels, which is an online tactical marketing segmentation approach, are covered in more detail in Chapter 6 and segmenting site visitors through web analytics systems are covered in Chapter 10.

Stage 2 in Figure 4.15 is target marketing. Here we can select segments for targeting online that are most attractive in terms of growth and profitability. These may be similar or different compared with groups targeted offline. Some examples of customer segments that are targeted online include:

- *The most profitable customers* – using the Internet to provide tailored offers to the top 20 per cent of customers by profit may result in more repeat business and cross-sales.
- *Larger companies (B2B)* – an extranet could be produced to service these customers and increase their loyalty.
- *Smaller companies (B2B)* – large companies are traditionally serviced through sales representatives and account managers, but smaller companies may not warrant the expense of account managers. However, the Internet can be used to reach smaller companies more cost-effectively. The number of smaller companies that can be reached in this way may be significant, so although the individual revenue of each one is relatively small, the collective revenue achieved through Internet servicing can be large.
- *Particular members of the buying unit (B2B)* – the site should provide detailed information for different interests which supports the buying decision, e.g. technical documentation for users of products, information on savings from e-procurement for IS or purchasing managers, and information to establish the credibility of the company for decision makers.
- *Customers that are difficult to reach using other media* – an insurance company looking to target younger drivers could use the web as a vehicle for this.

- *Customers that are brand-loyal* – services to appeal to brand loyalists can be provided to support them in their role as advocates of a brand.
- *Customers that are not brand-loyal* – conversely, incentives, promotion and a good level of service quality could be provided by the website to try and retain such customers.

Some segments can be targeted online by using navigation options to different content groupings such that visitors *self-identify*. This is the approach used as the main basis for navigation on the Dell site (Figure 4.16) and has potential for subsidiary navigation on other sites. Dell targets by geography and then tailors the types of consumers or businesses according to country, the US Dell site having the most options. Other alternatives are to set up separate sites for different audiences – e.g. Dell Premier is targeted at purchasing and IT staff in larger organisations. Once customers are registered on a site, profiling information in a database can be used to send tailored email messages to different segments, as we explain in the Euroffice example in Mini case Study 4.3.

The most sophisticated online tactical segmentation and targeting schemes are often used by e-retailers, which have detailed customer profiling information and purchase history data and seek to increase customer lifetime value through encouraging increased use of online services through time. However, the general principles of this approach can also be used by other types of companies online. The segmentation and targeting approach used by e-retailers is based on five main elements which in effect are layered on top of each other. The number of options used or segment layers, and so the sophistication of the

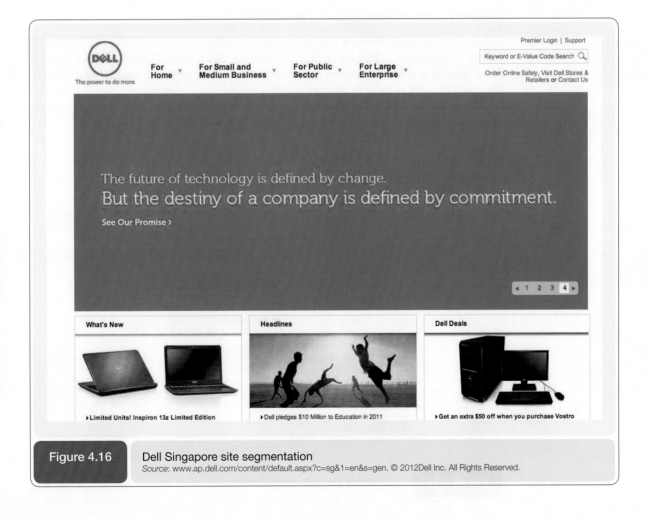

| Figure 4.16 | Dell Singapore site segmentation |

Source: www.ap.dell.com/content/default.aspx?c=sg&1=en&s=gen. © 2012 Dell Inc. All Rights Reserved.

approach, will depend on resources available, technological capabilities and opportunities afforded by the following.

1 Identify customer profile-based demographic characteristics

This is a traditional segmentation based on the type of customer. For B2C companies this will include age, sex and geography. For B2B companies, it will include size of company and the industry sector or application they operate in.

2 Identify customer lifecycle groups

Figure 4.17 illustrates this approach. As visitors use online services they can potentially pass through seven or more stages. Once companies have defined these groups and set up the customer relationship management infrastructure to categorise customers in this way, they can then deliver targeted messages, either by personalised on-site messaging or through emails that are triggered automatically by different rules. First-time visitors can be identified by whether they have a cookie placed on their PC. Once visitors have registered, they can be tracked through the remaining stages. Two particularly important groups are customers that have purchased one or more times. For many e-retailers, encouraging customers to move from the first purchase to the second purchase and then on to the third purchase is a key challenge. Specific promotions can be used to encourage further purchases. Similarly, once customers become inactive (i.e. they have not purchased for a defined period such as three months) further follow-ups are required.

3 Identify behaviour in response and purchase value

As customers progress through the lifecycle shown in Figure 4.17, database analysis can be used by the marketer to build up a detailed response and purchase history which considers the details of recency, frequency, monetary value and category of products purchased. Grouping customers by their current and future value and techniques such as FRAC and RFM analysis can be used to develop strategies to retain valuable customers and migrate lower value customers to higher value in future (see Chapter 6).

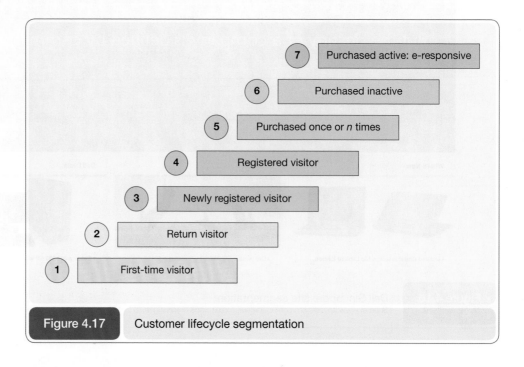

Figure 4.17   Customer lifecycle segmentation

Figure 4.18	Euroffice email (www.euroffice.co.uk)
	Source: Adapted from the company website press releases and Revolution (2005a)

4 Identify multichannel behaviour (channel preference)

Regardless of the enthusiasm of the company for online channels, some customers will prefer using online channels and others will prefer traditional channels. Drawing a channel chain (**Figure 2.24**) for different customers is useful to help understand this. It is also useful to have a flag within the database which indicates the customer's channel preference and, by implication, the best channel to target them through. Customers who prefer online channels can be targeted mainly by online communications such as email, while those who prefer traditional channels can be targeted by traditional communications such as direct mail or phone.

5 Tone and style preference

In a similar manner to channel preference, customers will respond differently to different types of message. Some may like a more rational appeal, in which case a detailed email explaining the benefits of the offer may work best. Others will prefer an emotional appeal based on images and with warmer, less formal copy. Sophisticated companies will test for this in customers or infer it using profile characteristics and response behaviour and then develop different creative treatments accordingly. Companies that use polls can potentially use this to infer style preferences. To summarise this section, read Mini case study 4.3, which illustrates the combination of these different forms of communication.

Euroffice (www.euroffice.co.uk) targets small and medium-sized companies. According to George Karibian, CEO, 'getting the message across effectively required segmentation' to engage different people in different ways. The office sector is fiercely competitive with relatively little loyalty since company purchasers will often simply buy on price. However, targeted incentives can be used to reward or encourage buyers' loyalty. Rather than manually developing campaigns for each segment, which is time-consuming, Euroffice mainly uses an automated event-based targeting approach, with the system identifying the stage at which a consumer is in the lifecycle – i.e. how many products they have purchased and the types of product within their purchase history. Karibian calls this a 'touch marketing funnel' approach – i.e. the touch strategy is determined by customer segmentation and response. Three main groups of customers are identified in the lifecycle and these are broken down further according to purchase category. Also layered on this segmentation is breakdown into buyer type – are they a small home-user, an operations manager at a mid-size company or a purchasing manager at a large company? Each will respond to different promotions.

   The first group, at the top of the funnel and the largest, is 'Group 1: Trial customers', who have made one or two purchases. For the first group, Euroffice believes that creating impulse buying through price promotions is most important. These will be based on categories purchased in the past. The second group, 'Group 2: The nursery', have made three to eight purchases. A particular issue, as with many e-retailers, is encouraging customers from the third to fourth purchase – there is a more significant drop-out at this point which the company uses marketing to control. Karibian says: 'When they get to Group 2: it's about creating frequency of purchase to ensure they don't forget you'. Euroffice sends a printed catalogue to Group 2 separately from their merchandise as a reminder about the company. The final group, 'Group 3: Key accounts', have made nine or more orders. They also tend to have a higher basket value. These people are 'the Crown Jewels' and will spend an average of £135 per order compared to an average of £55 for trial customers. They have a 90 per cent probability of reordering within a six-month period. For this group, tools have been developed on the site to make it easier for them to shop. The intention is that these customers find these tools help them in making their orders and they become reliant on them, so achieving 'soft lock-in'. However, targeted incentives can be used to reward or encourage buyers' loyalty (Figure 4.18).

Decision 4: Positioning and differentiation strategy (including the marketing mix)

Positioning
Customers' perception of the product offer relative to those of competitors.

Stage 3 in Figure 4.15 is **positioning**. Deise *et al*. (2000) suggest that in an online context, companies can position their products relative to competitor offerings according to four main variables: product quality, service quality, price and fulfilment time. They suggest it is useful to review these through an equation of how they combine to influence customer perceptions of value or brand:

$$\text{customer value (brand perception)} = \frac{\text{product quality} \times \text{service quality}}{\text{price} \times \text{fulfilment time}}$$

Strategies should review the extent to which increases in product and service quality can be balanced against variations in price and fulfilment time. Chaston (2000) argues that there are four options for strategic focus to position a company in the online marketplace. It is evident that these are related to the different elements of Deise *et al*. (2000) findings. He says that online these should build on existing strengths, and can use the online facilities to enhance the positioning as follows:

- *Product performance excellence*. Enhance by providing online product customisation.
- *Price performance excellence*. Use the facilities of the Internet to offer favourable pricing to loyal customers or to reduce prices where demand is low (e.g. British Midland Airlines uses auctions to sell under-used capacity on flights).

- *Transactional excellence*. A site such as that of software and hardware e-tailer **dabs.com** offers transactional excellence through combining pricing information with dynamic availability information on products, listing number in stock, number on order and when they are expected.
- *Relationship excellence*. Personalisation features to enable customers to review sales order history and place repeat orders. An example is RS Components (**www.rswww.com**).

These positioning options have much in common with Porter's generic competitive strategies of cost leadership or differentiation in a broad market and a market segmentation approach focussing on a more limited target market (Porter, 1980). Porter has been criticised because many commentators believe that to remain competitive it is necessary to combine excellence in all of these areas. It can be suggested that the same is true for sell-side e-commerce. These are not mutually exclusive strategic options; rather they are prerequisites for success. Customers will be unlikely to judge on a single criterion, but on the balance of multiple criteria. This is the view of Kim *et al.* (2004), who concluded that for online businesses, 'integrated strategies that combine elements of cost leadership and differentiation will outperform cost leadership or differentiation strategies'. It can be seen that Porter's original criteria are similar to the strategic positioning options of Chaston (2000) and Deise *et al.* (2000). Figure 4.19 summarises the positioning options described in this section, showing the emphasis on the three main variables for online differentiation – price, product and relationship-building services. The diagram can be used to show the mix of the three elements of positionings. EasyJet has an emphasis on price performance, but with a component of product innovation. Amazon is not positioned on price performance, but rather on relationship building and product innovation. We will see in Chapter 5, in the section on price, that although it would be expected that pricing is a key aspect determining online retail sales, there are other factors about a retail brand, such as familiarity, trust and service, which are also important.

Differential advantage

Differential advantage
A desirable attribute of a product offering that is not currently matched by competitor offerings.

The aim of positioning is to develop a **differential advantage** over competitors. Jobber and Ellis-Chadwick (2013) suggest that market segmentation is at the heart of developing a differential marketing strategy. Marketing strategists use elements from the marketing mix

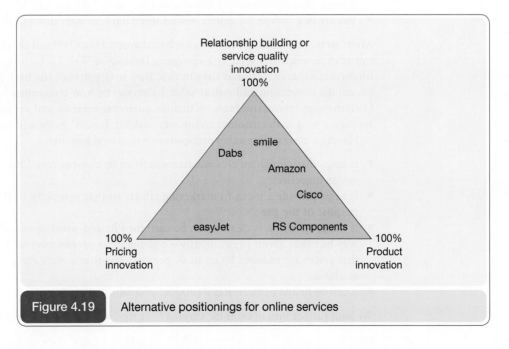

| Figure 4.19 | Alternative positionings for online services |

to establish the difference between their company and their rivals. Many businesses' have differentiated their own line offer by using price, for example:

- *Retailers* offering lower prices online. Examples: **Tesco.com** (price promotions on selected products), Comet (discounts relative to instore pricing on some products).
- *Airlines* offering lower-cost flights for online bookings. Examples: easyJet, Ryanair, BA.
- *Financial services companies* offering higher interest rates on savings products and lower interest rates on credit products such as credit cards and loans. Examples: Nationwide, Alliance and Leicester.
- *Mobile phone network* providers or utilities offering lower-cost tariffs or discounts for customer accounts that are managed online without paper billing. Examples: O_2, British Gas.

It is important to note that price is not the only way to stand out online, quality of brand experience and quality of service is equally important for creating differential advantage.

In a digital marketing context, differential advantage and positioning can be clarified and communicated by developing an **online value proposition (OVP)**. Developing an OVP, involves:

Online value proposition (OVP)
A statement of the benefits of online services reinforces the core proposition and differentiates from an organisation's offline offering and those of competitors.

- developing online content and service and explaining them through messages which:
  - reinforce core brand proposition and credibility;
  - communicate what a visitor can get from an online brand that they can't get from the brand offline and they can't get from competitors or intermediaries.
- communicating these messages to all appropriate online and offline customers with touch points in different levels of detail from straplines to more detailed content on the website or in print.

Communicating the OVP on the site can help create a customer-centric website. Look at how **Webuyanycar.com** does this for different types of visitors and services in Figure 4.20. Virgin Wines used an OVP to communicate its service promise as follows:

- And what if... *You are out during the day*? We promise that our drivers will find a safe place to leave your wine; but if it does get stolen, we just replace it.
- *You find it cheaper elsewhere*? We will refund the difference if you are lucky enough to find a wine cheaper elsewhere.
- *You live somewhere obscure*? We deliver anywhere in the UK, including Northern Ireland, the Highlands and Islands, and the Scilly Isles for £5.99.
- *You are in a hurry*? We deliver within seven days, or your delivery is free.

Many strategic planning decisions are based around the OVP and the quality of online customer experience delivered by a company. Interactive Web 2.0 features can be particularly important for transactional sites in that they may enhance the user's experience and so encourage conversion and repeat sales. Examples of how companies have developed their OVP through interactive features include customer reviews and ratings; podcast product reviews; a blog with customer comments enabled; buyers' guide and video reviews.

Having a clear online value proposition has several benefits:

- It helps distinguish an e-commerce site from its competitors (this should be a website design objective).
- It helps provide a focus to marketing efforts so that company staff are clear about the purpose of the site.
- If the proposition is clear, it can be used for PR, and word-of-mouth recommendations may be made about the company – e.g. the clear proposition of Amazon on its site is that prices are reduced by up to 40 per cent and that a wide range of 3 million titles Is available.
- It can be linked to the normal product propositions of a company or its product.

We look further into options for varying the proposition and marketing mix in Chapter 5.

Figure 4.20 WeBuyAnyCar (www.webuyanycar.co.uk) clearly communicates its proposition

---

Activity 4.5   Online value proposition

Visit the websites of the following companies and, in one or two sentences each, summarise their Internet value proposition. You should also explain how they use the content of the website to indicate their value proposition to customers.

- Tektronix (www.tek.com)
- AO.com (www.ao.com)
- Drowned In Sound (www.drownedinsound.com)
- Harrods (www.harrods.com)
- Guinness (www.guinness.com)

Multichannel prioritisation
Assesses the strategic significance of the Internet relative to other communications channels and then deploys resources to integrate with marketing channels.

Customer communications channels
The range of media used to communicate directly with a customer.

Decisions 5 and 6 relate to **multichannel prioritisation** which assesses the strategic significance of the Internet relative to other communications channels. In making this prioritisation it is helpful to distinguish between **customer communications channels** and distribution channels.

Decision 5: Customer engagement and social media strategy

Each day there are millions of social network status updates, new blog posts, videos and news articles published. As consumers spend more time online reading and interacting with this content, the challenge of engaging them increases. Given this, we believe that

Customer engagement strategy
A strategy to encourage interaction and participation of consumers with a brand through developing content and experiences with the aim of meeting commercial objectives. It is closely related to the development of content marketing and social media strategy.

Social media strategy
A definition of the marketing communications used to achieve interaction with social network users to meet business goals. The scope of social media optimisation also includes incorporation of social features such as status updates and sharing widgets into company websites.

every company must develop a **customer engagement strategy** as a key part of their digital marketing strategy. This customer engagement strategy reviews approaches to create compelling content and experiences that form the online value proposition.

Increasingly, it's most straightforward to achieve online engagement not on a company website, but a social presence in one of the main social networks like Facebook, Google+, LinkedIn, Twitter or specialist networks. Given the popularity of these social networks, many companies will seek to develop an overall **social media strategy**.

When developing an approach for using each social network to build engagement and community, there are some common decisions across the networks that focus on the types of content and how it is published. The answers for each social network will vary, but there are some common themes that should be part of an overall engagement and content marketing strategy. We recommend that companies review these 12 questions to help define their social media marketing strategy.

- *Question 1. Who are our target audience?* For a single company, the typical audience of each social network will differ in terms of demographics. If you review a sample of profiles for your own followers or competitors, you will get a feel for the typical audience and can develop typical customer personas you are targeting.
- *Question 2. What are the content preferences of our audiences?* The type of content that audiences like to see on each network is shown by the content they share or rate highly. For example, on Facebook it may be that videos work well, on Twitter infographics and on LinkedIn posting a provocative statement. Benchmarking to establish the popularity of different types of messages is worthwhile.
- *Question 3. Strategic business goals for social network presences?* Ask which of the 5Ss is the emphasis on: Sell, Speak, Serve, Save or Sizzle. On some platforms such as Twitter, a separate presence can be created for sales and service. But the majority of communications are to engage through speaking, so it's important to establish which types of content will help create sharing and dialogue.
- *Question 4. Which content types should have priority?* Based on your analysis of customer needs and competitor benchmarking, you can set out the topics that will work best when covered in your content stream. For example, for the American Express Open Forum (**www.openforum.com**, a community that is independent of social networks) their content focuses on innovation, marketing and finance, though it can cover health and lifestyle too.
- *Question 5. How to differentiate the social channel from other communications channels?* We have seen that the audience for each network will differ and will have different preferences for types of content that fit the channel. If you can define a powerful offer for the social channel, it will encourage people to subscribe to that channel even if they are already using other channels. It's important to communicate clearly what the channel offers to encourage sign-up. For example, retailer Asda (**www.facebook.com/GeorgeatAsdaOfficial**) offers 'Previews, competitions and exclusive offers' if someone 'Likes' its page. It also has more tactical campaigns to encourage sign-up; this requires email addresses to be collected, which can be assigned to a Facebook user. Communicating the value offered can happen both on the page and in other channels such as email, direct mail or print advertising.
- *Question 6. How to integrate social channels?* This is a complex question since customers use social media sites in combination with other channels like the website, email, apps and traditional communications like advertising. Since the user-generated content of social media is engaging, companies will often want to incorporate social content within their website or emails. This is facilitated by APIs created by the social networks to enable sharing such as the Facebook platform. Incorporating social sign-on (Chapter 6) is increasingly important to enable integration.
- *Question 7. Content frequency and editorial calendar?* To engage an audience requires regular content, but what does regular mean? Will there be several status updates a day

or only several updates a week? How do these link to other content like that on a blog? There will be many different types of content, some will be quick to create, others will take much longer and need planning or resourcing; this is where an editorial calendar is essential.

- *Question 8. Sourcing content?* Creating content takes time, even if it is only a 140-character tweet or status update. Often the content will need to link to more in-depth content on the company website or blog. This will take yet more time to create and will have to be of sufficient quality to engage the audience to encourage sharing and will reflect well on the brand. Some of this can be originated in-house, but it may need an agency to create it.
- *Question 9. How to manage publication and interaction?* Each social platform needs someone to update the content, but also to respond and interact on other social networks. A decision has to be taken as to whether this happens in-house or whether some of it can be outsourced to a third party.
- *Question 10. Software for managing the publishing process?* Software can't create content for you, but it can streamline the process. Tools like Hootsuite or Tweetburner enable status updates to be shared across different networks. For example, status updates can be shared across Facebook, LinkedIn or Twitter. However, a personalised approach is recommended also.
- *Question 11. Tracking the business impact of social network activity?* Tools are available from each of the platforms to help marketers review their effectiveness. For example, Facebook Insights is a service available to page owners on Facebook. There are also analytics features within tools like Hootsuite showing which messages were popular based on sharing and click-through rate. To review how these translate to business value, tagging of messages to show the source of visitors in analytics systems are also needed.
- *Question 12. How to optimise the social presence?* Tracking isn't worthwhile unless it is reviewed and acted upon. The insights available will enable you to test, learn and refine marketing activities. This is known as **social media optimisation (SMO)**. To get the most from social media marketing requires time to be ring-fenced to make changes and then review them.

Social media optimisation (SMO)
A process to review and improve the effectiveness of social media marketing through reviewing approaches to enhance content and communications quality to generate more business value.

Decision 6: Multichannel distribution strategy

Distribution channels
The mechanism by which products are directed to customers either through intermediaries or directly.

Distribution channels refer to flow of products from a manufacturer or service provider to the end customer. At the centre of any distribution channel are the movement of goods and the flow of information between different organisations involved in moving goods from the point of manufacture and the point of consumption. Depending on the *players* that make up the supply chain its structure can vary and this structure will determine whether goods get to the right place at the right time. Players in a supply chain can include: retailers, suppliers, intermediaries, third-party logistic solution providers and transportation companies that provide transportation, warehousing and distribution management facilities for their retailer clients. In retailing, the principal function of a distribution channel is the *breaking of bulk*. Fernie *et al.* (2010) tell us that:

> the aim for retailers (and their supply partners) is to manage this chain to create value for the customer at an acceptable cost. The managing of this so-called 'pipeline' has been a key challenge for logistics professionals, especially with the realisation that the reduction of time not only reduces costs, but also gives competitive advantage.

Mini case study 4.4 discusses how Tesco plc leveraged competitive advantages from making effective decisions for their multichannel strategy.

Mini case study 4.4	Distribution and the online grocery retailer

Fernie *et al*. (2010) identified many challenges which grocery retailers face when setting up and managing online sales operations. Grocery retailers wanting to sell online must typically decide how to select goods that will fulfil customer orders. On average, a typical customer order will be about 60–80 items. But the complexity of managing the products is more than just selecting items: selling groceries means selling products which are from three different temperature zones (ambient, chilled and frozen) from a total range of 10–25,000 products within 12–24 hours for delivery to customers within one- to two-hour time-slots. For example, Tesco is currently picking and delivering an average of 250,000 such orders every week. New logistical techniques have had to be devised to support e-grocery retailing on this scale. Tesco has a logistical network, which links into satellite technology and enables the organisation to know precisely where all of its goods are all of the time in order to ensure availability of goods to fulfil individual orders, which are selected in-store. Adopting this strategy has enabled Tesco to rapidly expand its online operation in the UK and Europe.

According to Ellis-Chadwick *et al*. (2007), Tesco's channel strategy decisions were critical to its future success. The company maximised the benefits of having a national network of retail stores and trained its staff well to establish store-based product selection for all its online shopping orders. This strategy facilitated rapid expansion of its online shopping operation across Britain. Other retailers, such as Sainsbury's, initially adopted a centralised distribution network to support its online shopping operation and this strategy decision limited growth and expansion. Tesco has been able to leverage advantage from being a first-mover and by establishing highly efficient systems to support its online operations. This strategic approach to distribution channels has enabled Tesco to become the No. 1 grocery retailer in the world.

The general options for the mix of 'bricks and clicks' are shown in Figure 4.21. The online revenue contribution estimate is informed by the customer demand analysis of propensity to purchase a particular type of product. If the objective is to achieve a high

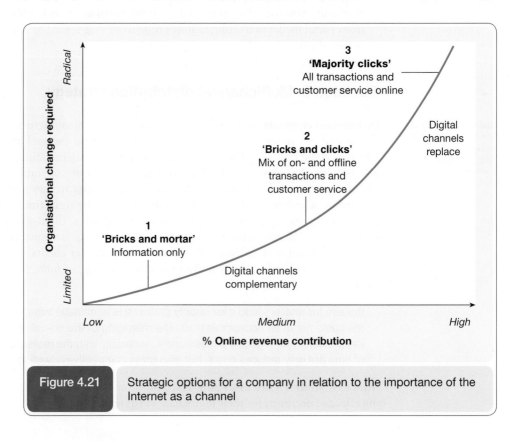

Figure 4.21	Strategic options for a company in relation to the importance of the Internet as a channel

Clicks and mortar
A business combining an online and offline presence.

Clicks-only (Internet pureplay)
An organisation with principally an online presence. It does not operate a mail-order operation or promote inbound phone orders.

online revenue contribution of greater than 70 per cent then this will require fundamental change for the company to transform to a **clicks and mortar** or **clicks-only (Internet pure-play)** company.

Kumar (1999) suggested that a company should decide whether the Internet will primarily *complement* the company's other channels or primarily *replace* other channels. Clearly, if it is believed that the Internet will primarily replace other channels, then it is important to invest in the promotion and infrastructure to achieve this. This is a key decision as the company is essentially deciding whether the Internet is 'just another communications and/or sales channel' or whether it will fundamentally change the way it communicates and sells to its customers.

Figure 4.22 summarises the main decisions on which a company should base its commitment to the Internet. Kumar (1999) suggests that replacement is most likely to happen when:

- customer access to the Internet is high;
- the Internet can offer a better value proposition than other media;
- the product can be delivered over the Internet (it can be argued that this condition is not essential for replacement, so it is not shown in the figure);
- the product can be standardised (the user does not usually need to view to purchase).

Only if all four conditions are met will there primarily be a replacement effect. The fewer conditions met, the more likely it is that there will be a complementary effect.

From an analysis such as that in Figure 4.22 it should be possible to state whether the company strategy should be directed as a complementary or as a replacement scenario. As mentioned in relation to the question of the contribution of the Internet to its business, the company should repeat the analysis for different product segments and different markets. It will then be possible to state the company's overall commitment to the Internet. If the future strategic importance of the Internet is high, with replacement likely, then a significant investment needs to be made in the Internet, and a company's mission needs to be directed towards replacement. If the future strategic importance of the Internet is low then this still needs to be recognised and appropriate investment made.

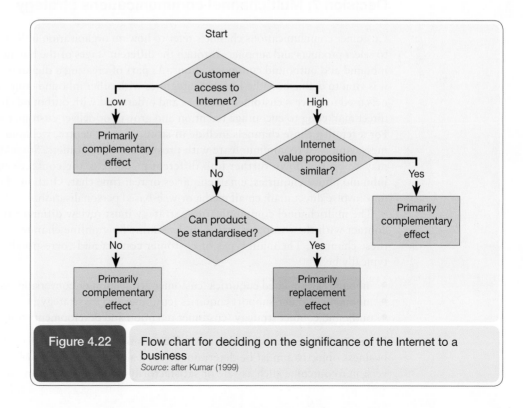

Figure 4.22	Flow chart for deciding on the significance of the Internet to a business

Source: after Kumar (1999)

Changes to marketplace structure

Strategies to take advantage of changes in marketplace structure should also be developed. These options are created through disintermediation and reintermediation (Chapter 2) within a marketplace. The strategic options have already been discussed in Chapter 2, e.g.:

- disintermediation (sell direct);
- create new online intermediary (countermediation);
- partner with new online or existing intermediaries;
- do nothing!

Prioritising strategic partnerships as part of the move from a value chain to a value network should also occur as part of this decision. For all options, tactics will be needed to manage the channel conflicts that may occur as a result of restructuring.

Technological integration

To achieve strategic Internet marketing goals, organisations will have to plan for integration with customers' and suppliers' systems. Chaffey (2014) describes how a supplier (in a B2B market) may have to support technical integration with a range of customer e-procurement needs, e.g.:

- *Links with single customers.* Organisations will decide whether a single customer is large enough to enforce such linkage – e.g. supermarkets often insist that their suppliers trade with them electronically. However, the supplier may be faced with the cost of setting up different types of links with different supermarket customers.
- *Links with intermediaries.* Organisations have to assess which are the dominant intermediaries, such as B2B marketplaces or exchanges, and then evaluate whether the trade resulting from the intermediary is sufficient to set up links with this intermediary.

Decision 7: Multichannel communications strategy

Customer communications channels refer to how an organisation influences its customers to select products and suppliers through the different stages of the buying process through inbound and outbound communications. As part of creating a digital marketing strategy, it is vital to define how the Internet integrates with other inbound communications channels used to process customer enquiries and orders and with outbound channels which use direct marketing to encourage retention and growth or deliver customer service messages. For a retailer, these channels include in-store, contact-centre, web and outbound direct messaging used to communicate with prospects and customers. Some of these channels may be broken down further into different media, e.g. the contact-centre may involve inbound phone enquiries, email enquiries or real-time chat. Outbound direct messaging may involve direct mail, email media or web-based personalisation.

The multichannel communications strategy must review different types of customer contact with the company and then determine how online channels will best support these channels. The main types of customer contact and corresponding strategies will typically be:

- inbound sales-related enquiries (customer acquisition or conversion strategy);
- inbound customer-support enquiries (customer service strategy);
- outbound contact strategy (customer retention and development strategy).

For each of these strategies, the most efficient mix and sequence of media to support the business objectives must be determined. Typically the short-term objective will be conversion to outcome such as sale or satisfactorily resolved service enquiry in the shortest possible time with the minimum cost. However, longer-term objectives of customer loyalty and growth also need to be considered. If the initial experience is efficient, but unsatisfactory to the customer, then they may not remain a customer!

The multichannel communications strategy must assess the balance between:

- *Customer channel preferences* – some customers will prefer online channels for product selection or making enquiries while others will prefer traditional channels.
- *Organisation channel preferences* – traditional channels tend to be more expensive to service than digital channels for the company; however, it is important to assess effectiveness and the ability of channels to convert the customer to sale (e.g. a customer who responds to a TV ad to buy car insurance may be more likely to purchase if they enquire by phone in comparison to web enquiry) or in developing customer loyalty (the personal touch available through face-to-face or phone contact may result in a better experience for some customers which engenders loyalty).

Channels and media have become increasing sophisticated and diverse in recent years and these developments have led to increasingly complex patterns of consumer behaviour. For an organisation to begin to understand customer behaviour online they need to identify target market segments, develop customer profiles, and select channels and media which might be suitable for communicating with the chosen segment. As 'consumer segmentation is a critical aspect of effective multichannel strategy design' (Neslin *et al.*, 2006), organisations are faced with making difficult and challenging decisions.

Figure 4.23 is based on the work of Dholakia *et al.* (2010), who suggest that there are eight dimensions to consider when making channel choice. This figure shows these dimensions and suggests the factors that affect consumer decision making. The channel dimensions have implications for planning and point to key decision areas for an organisation that is developing its channel and communication strategies. For example, dimension 3 – accessibility – is becoming increasingly important with the

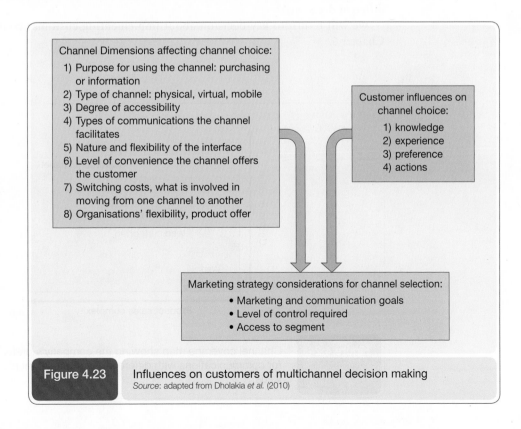

Figure 4.23	Influences on customers of multichannel decision making

Source: adapted from Dholakia *et al.* (2010)

widespread adoption of wireless technology and mobile phones; dimension 5 – flexibility of the interface – some channels offer limited flexibility whereas others can be instantaneously tailored (e.g. advertising which through emotional recognition software can potentially provide a personal message as a customer passes by an outdoor billboard). Customer influences affect their channel choice based on their personal characteristics which affect how they interact with technology. Both the channel dimensions and customers will shape the strategy decisions a marketer makes but there are also marketing strategy considerations which will influence final channels selection, e.g. goals and objectives.

Multichannel communications strategy needs to specify the extent of communications choices made available to customers and the degree to which a company uses different channels to communicate with particular customer segments. Deciding on the best combination of channels is a complex challenge for organisations. Consider your mobile phone company – when purchasing you may make your decision about handset and network supplier in-store, on the web or through phoning the contact centre. Any of these contact points may either be direct with the network provider or through a retail intermediary. After purchase, if you have support questions about billing, handset upgrades or new tariffs you may again use any of these touchpoints to resolve your questions. Managing this multichannel challenge is vital for the phone company for two reasons, both concerned with customer retention. First, the experience delivered through these channels is vital to the decision whether to remain with the network supplier when their contract expires – price is not the only consideration. Second, outbound communications delivered via website, email, direct mail and phone are critical to getting the customer to stay with the company by recommending the most appropriate tariff and handset with appropriate promotions, but which is the most appropriate mix of channels for the company (each channel has a different level of cost-effectiveness for customers which contributes different levels of value to the customer) and the customer (each customer will have a preference for the combinations of channels they will use for different decisions)?

We will return to key decision about implementing customer contact strategies in Chapter 6.

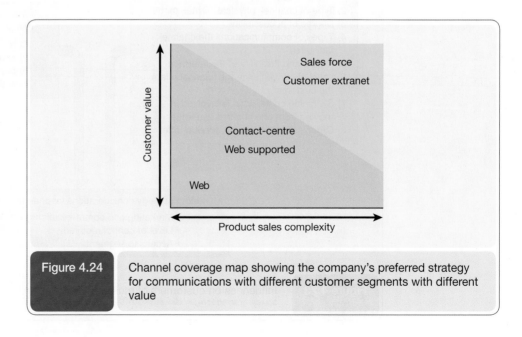

| Figure 4.24 | Channel coverage map showing the company's preferred strategy for communications with different customer segments with different value |

Decision 8: Online communications mix and budget

The decision on the amount of spending on online communications and the mix between the different communications techniques such as search engine marketing, affiliate marketing, email marketing and online advertising closely relates to Decision 6. In Chapter 2 we discussed the changes in levels of adoption of different channels and media and these changes have a cascade effect in terms of implications for planning the communication mix.

Making these decisions requires digital marketers to decide the focus of their communications and whether the primary purpose is customer acquisition, retention or relationship building.

In the case of e-commerce operations Agrawal *et al.* (2001) suggest that success can be modelled and controlled based on the customer lifecycle of customer relationship management. They suggest using a scorecard, which is based on **performance drivers** or critical success factors, e.g. costs for acquisition and retention, conversion rates of visitors to buyers to repeat buyers, together with churn rates. There are three main parts to their scorecard:

1 *Attraction.* Size of visitor base, visitor acquisition cost and visitor advertising revenue (e.g. media sites).
2 *Conversion.* Customer base, customer acquisition costs, customer conversion rate, number of transactions per customer, revenue per transaction, revenue per customer, customer gross income, customer maintenance cost, customer operating income, customer churn rate, customer operating income before marketing spending.
3 *Retention.* This uses similar measures to those for conversion customers.

Agrawal *et al.* (2001) also used a net present value model to show the relative importance of these drivers:

1 Attraction
 • Visitor acquisition cost: 0.74 per cent change in NPV.
 • Visitor growth: 3.09 per cent change in NPV.
2 Conversion
 • Customer conversion rate: 0.84 per cent change in NPV.
 • Revenue per customer: 2.32 per cent change in NPV.
3 Retention
 • Cost of repeat customer: 0.69 per cent change in NPV.
 • Revenue per repeat customer: 5.78 per cent change in NPV.
 • Repeat customer churn rate: 6.65 per cent change in NPV.
 • Repeat customer conversion rate: 9.49 per cent change in NPV.

This research remains important as it highlights on-site marketing communications and the quality of service delivery in converting browsers to buyers and buyers into repeat buyers. It is apparent that marketing spend is large relative to turnover initially, to achieve customer growth, but is then carefully controlled to achieve profitability.

We will return to this topic in Chapter 8, where we will review the balance between **campaign-based e-communications** which are often tied into a particular event such as the launch or re-launch of a website or a product – e.g. an interactive (banner) advert campaign may last for a period of two months following a site re-launch or for a five-month period around a new product launch.

In addition to campaign-based e-communications, we also need **continuous e-communications**. Organisations need to ensure that there is sufficient investment in continuous online marketing activities such as search marketing, affiliate marketing and sponsorship.

Performance drivers
Critical success factors that determine whether business and marketing objectives are met.

Campaign-based e-communications
Digital communications that are executed to support a specific marketing campaign such as a product launch, price promotion or a website launch.

Continuous e-communications
Long-term use of e-marketing communications for customer acquisition (such as search engine and affiliate marketing) and retention (e.g. e-newsletter marketing).

Companies wishing to advertise using digital channels are also making changes; they are having to invest in new staff with the required skills to understand the new media and many established brand images need to be changed to be succeed online.

Decision 9: Organisational capabilities (7S framework) and governance

A useful framework for reviewing an organisation's capabilities to implement digital marketing strategy is shown in Table 1.3 (page 26) applied to digital marketing. Which are the main challenges in implementing strategy? Econsultancy (2008) surveyed UK e-commerce managers to assess their views on the main challenges of managing e-commerce within an organisation. In the context of the 7Ss, we can summarise the main challenges as follows:

- *Strategy* – limited capabilities to integrate into Internet strategy within core marketing and business strategy as discussed earlier in this chapter is indicated by frustration on gaining appropriate budgets.
- *Structure* – structural and process issues are indicated by the challenges of gaining resource and buy-in from traditional marketing and IT functions.
- *Skills and staff* – these issues were indicated by difficulties in finding specialist staff or agencies.

To help manage the internal capabilities for improving the results from digital channels, Econsultancy (2008) has developed a useful checklist for auditing current internal capabilities, resources and processes and then putting in place a programme to improve results. Econsultancy (2008) recommends these steps in a digital channel performance audit and improvement plan:

- *Step 1 – Senior management commitment*. Assess and encourage senior management commitment. What is the level of understanding of digital channels and physical commitment and sponsorship among the senior management team? Develop a plan to educate and influence the senior management team.
- *Step 2 – Digital channel contribution*. What are the digital channels delivering across different markets and product categories now to support business goals in terms of sales, cost of acquisition, profitability and customer loyalty?
- *Step 3 – Brand alignment*. Reviewing how digital channels and website functionality can support traditional brand values but also enhance the brand through development of online value propositions (OVP).
- *Step 4 – Marketplace analysis*. Customer insight is key, i.e. qualitative and quantitative research of customer characteristics, behaviours and opinions. Also includes benchmarking of competitors' proposition, marketing communications and capabilities. Develop detailed understanding of online intermediaries, e.g. key portals, search engines and social networks which influence audience.
- *Step 5 – Technology infrastructure*. Review capability of technology infrastructure to support online marketing innovation. Is an acceptable 'time to market' for new functionality available dependent on legacy system integration, business case authorisation and prioritisation, dedicated development resource and agile technical development processes?
- *Step 6 – Vision and goals*. Develop a long-term vision for how digital channels will contribute to the development business. Set short-term goals for digital channels in areas of customer acquisition, conversion and customer experience, retention and growth.
- *Step 7 – Strategy and planning*. Ensure digital marketing is integrated into different planning cycles (i.e. long-term three- to five-year plans, annual plans and quarterly/monthly operational planning reviews). Establish method and budget sources for identifying, reviewing business case and prioritisation for new site and campaign functionality.

- *Step 8 – Review capability of marketing resources to deliver efficient, integrated cross-channel communications*. Include organisation structure, staff roles and responsibilities, skills levels of staff, agency capability, marketing campaign management and review process.
- *Step 9 – Refine management information and reporting*. Ensure that web analytics and other business reporting tools maximise understanding of the influence of different digital media channels on delivering leads or sales. Implement a culture and process for integrating review and action based on defined key performance indicators and structured tests.
- *Step 10 – Identify and implement 'quick wins'*. Based on strategic analysis performed, identify short-term projects to deliver business results across areas of customer acquisition (e.g. improvements to digital media channels such as search engine marketing, aggregators or affiliate marketing); conversion (improvements to landing page messaging and usability through small findability improvements to navigation or search labelling possibly based on AB or multivariate testing or customer journey improvements on home page, category, product or other landing pages and basket, registration or checkout process) or retention and growth (encouraging repeat site visits or purchases through email marketing or on-site merchandising).

Organisational structure decisions form two main questions. The first is 'How should internal structures be changed to deliver e-marketing?'; and the second is 'How should the structure of links with partner organisations be changed to achieve e-marketing objectives?' Once structural decisions have been made, attention should be focussed on effective **change management**. Many e-commerce initiatives fail not in their conceptualisation, but in their implementation. Chaffey (2012) describes approaches to change management and risk management in Chapter 10.

Change management
Controls to minimise the
risks of project-based and
organisational change.

Internal structures

There are several alternative options for restructuring within a business, such as the creation of an in-house digital marketing or e-commerce group. This issue has been considered by Parsons *et al.* (1996) from a sell-side e-commerce perspective. They recognise four stages in the growth of what they refer to as 'the digital marketing organisation' which are still useful for benchmarking digital marketing capabilities. A more sophisticated e-commerce capability assessment was presented earlier in this chapter on situation review (Figure 4.4). The stages are:

1 *Ad hoc activity*. At this stage there is no formal organisation related to e-commerce and the skills are dispersed around the organisation. It is likely that there is poor integration between online and offline marketing communications. The website may not reflect the offline brand, and the website services may not be featured in the offline marketing communications. A further problem with ad hoc activity is that the maintenance of the website will be informal and errors may occur as information becomes out of date.
2 *Focussing the effort*. At this stage, efforts are made to introduce a controlling mechanism for Internet marketing. Parsons *et al.* (1996) suggest that this is often achieved through a senior executive setting up a steering group which may include interested parties from marketing and IT and legal experts. At this stage the efforts to control the site will be experimental, with different approaches being tried to build, promote and manage the site.
3 *Formalisation*. At this stage the authors suggest that Internet marketing will have reached a critical mass and there will be a defined group or separate business unit within the company that will manage all digital marketing.
4 *Institutionalising capability*. This stage also involves a formal grouping within the organisation, but is distinguished from the previous stage in that there are formal links created between digital marketing and the company's core activities.

Although this is presented as a stage model with evolution implying that all companies will move from one stage to the next, many companies will find that true formalisation with the creation of a separate e-commerce or e-business department is unnecessary. For small and medium companies with a marketing department numbering a few people and an IT department perhaps consisting of two people, it will not be practical to have a separate group. Even large companies may find it is sufficient to have a single person or small team responsible for e-commerce with their role being to coordinate the different activities within the company using a matrix management approach.

Table 4.6 reviews some of the advantages and disadvantages of each type of organisational structures for e-commerce.

Where the main e-commerce function is internal, the Econsultancy (2008) research suggested that it was typically located in one of four areas (see Figure 4.25) in approximate decreasing order of frequency:

a Main e-commerce function in separate team.
b Main e-commerce function part of operations or direct channel.
c Main e-commerce function part of marketing, corporate communications or other central marketing function.
d Main e-commerce function part of information technology.

There is also often one or several secondary areas of e-commerce competence and resource – e.g. IT may have a role in applications development and site build and each business, brand or country may have one or more e-commerce specialists responsible for managing e-commerce in

Table 4.6	Advantages and disadvantages of the organisational structures shown in Figure 4.25		
Organisational structure	**Circumstances**	**Advantages**	**Disadvantages**
(a) No formal structure for e-commerce	Initial response to e-commerce or poor leadership with no identification of need for change	Can achieve rapid response to e-commerce	Poor-quality site in terms of content quality and customer service responses (email, phone). Priorities not decided logically. Insufficient resources
(b) A separate committee or department manages and coordinates e-commerce	Identification of problem and response in (a)	Coordination and budgeting and resource allocation possible	May be difficult to get different departments to deliver their input because of other commitments
(c) A separate business unit with independent budgets	Internet contribution (Chapter 6) is sizeable (>20%)	As for (b), but can set own targets and not be constrained by resources. Lower-risk option than (d)	Has to respond to corporate strategy. Conflict of interests between department and traditional business
(d) A separate operating company	Major revenue potential or flotation. Need to differentiate from parent	As for (c), but can set strategy independently. Can maximise market potential	High risk if market potential is overestimated due to startup costs

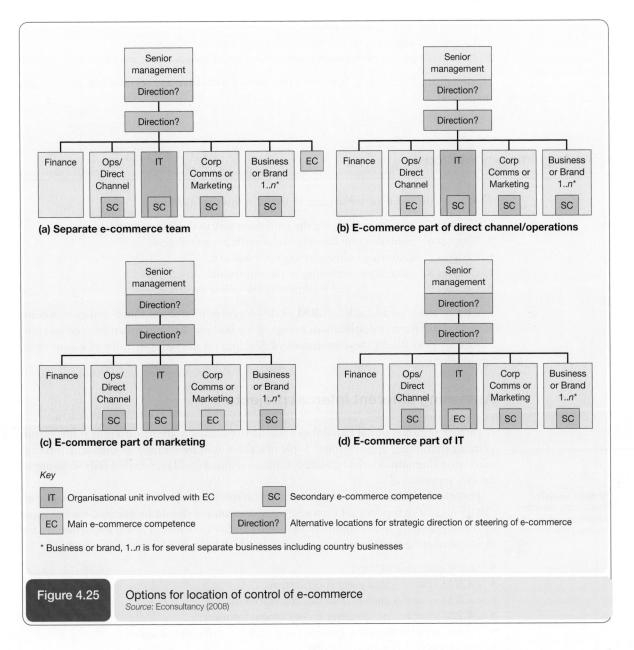

Key

| IT | Organisational unit involved with EC | | SC | Secondary e-commerce competence |

IT Organisational unit involved with EC   **SC** Secondary e-commerce competence

EC Main e-commerce competence   **Direction?** Alternative locations for strategic direction or steering of e-commerce

* Business or brand, 1..*n* is for several separate businesses including country businesses

Figure 4.25 Options for location of control of e-commerce
Source: Econsultancy (2008)

their unit. Which was appropriate depended strongly on the market(s) the company operated in and their existing channel structures.

For the specialist skills needed to plan and manage digital marketing, it may be more efficient to outsource some skills. These are some of the main options for external suppliers for these Internet marketing skills:

1 Full-service digital agency.
2 Specialist digital agency.
3 Traditional agency.
4 In-house resource.

When deciding on supplier or resource, the company needs to consider the level and type of marketing activities it will be covering. The level typically ranges through:

1 Strategy.
2 Analysis and creative concepts.

3 Creative or content development.

4 Executing campaign, including reporting analysis and adjustment.

5 Infrastructure (e.g. web hosting, ad-serving, email broadcasting, evaluation).

Options for outsourcing different e-marketing activities are reviewed in Activity 7.1 (page 364).

Strategy implementation

This forms the topic for subsequent chapters in this text as follows:

- Chapter 5 – options for varying the marketing mix in the Internet environment.
- Chapter 6 – implementing customer relationship management.
- Chapter 7 – delivering online services via a website.
- Chapter 8 – interactive marketing communications.
- Chapter 9 – monitoring and maintaining the online presence.

In each of these areas, such as CRM or development of website functionality, it is common that different initiatives will compete for budget. The next section reviews techniques for prioritising these projects and deciding on the best portfolio of e-commerce applications.

Assessing different Internet projects

A further organisational capability issue is the decision about different information systems marketing applications. Typically, there will be a range of different Internet marketing alternatives to be evaluated. Limited resources will dictate that only some applications are practical.

Portfolio analysis
Identification, evaluation and selection of desirable marketing applications.

Portfolio analysis can be used to select the most suitable projects. For example, Daniel *et al*. (2001) suggest that potential e-commerce opportunities should be assessed for the value of the opportunity to the company against its ability to deliver. Typical opportunities for digital marketing strategy for an organisation which has a brochureware site might be:

- online catalogue facility;
- e-CRM system – lead generation system;
- e-CRM system – customer service management;
- e-CRM system – personalisation of content for users;
- partner relationship management extranet for distributors or agents;
- transactional e-commerce facility.

Such alternatives can then be evaluated in terms of their risk against reward. Figure 4.26 shows a possible evaluation of strategic options. It is apparent that, with limited resources, the e-CRM lead generation, partner extranet and customer services options offer the best mix of risk and reward.

For information systems investments, the model of McFarlan (1984) has been used extensively to assess the future strategic importance applications in a portfolio. This model has been applied to the e-commerce applications by Daniel *et al*. (2008) and Chaffey (2011). Potential e-commerce applications can be assessed as:

- *Key operational* – essential to remain competitive. Example: partner relationship management extranet for distributors or agents.
- *Support* – deliver improved performance, but not critical to strategy. Example: e-CRM system – personalisation of content for users.

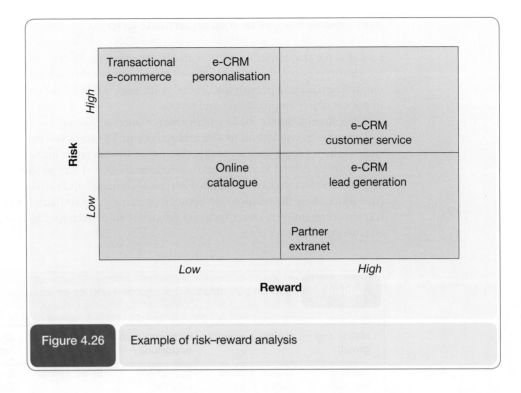

	Transactional e-commerce	e-CRM personalisation

Figure 4.26   Example of risk–reward analysis

- *High-potential* – may be important for achieving future success. Example: e-CRM system – customer service management.
- *Strategic* – critical to future business strategy. Example: e-CRM system – lead generation system is vital to developing new business.

A further portfolio analysis suggested by McDonald and Wilson (2002) is a matrix of attractiveness to customer against attractiveness to company, which will give a similar result to the risk–reward matrix. Finally, Tjan (2001) has suggested a matrix approach of viability (return on investment) against fit (with the organisation's capabilities) for Internet applications. He presents five metrics for assessing viability and fit. Viability is ideally based on a quantitative business case assessment of the value of a new application that will be generated through increasing conversion and retention rates. Fit is a more subjective measure based on the ease of implementation given the fit of an application with an organisation's existing processes, capabilities and culture. Additional criteria are developed for viability and fit. For 'viability', the criteria used to assess the potential value of an investment are rated between 100 (positive) and 0 (unfavourable) in each of these areas:

- market value potential;
- time to positive cash flow;
- personnel requirement;
- funding requirement.

For 'fit', the criteria are rated as low to medium to high to assess the value of a potential investment:

- alignment with core capabilities;
- alignment with other company initiatives;
- fit with organisational structure;
- fit with company's culture and value;
- ease of technical implementation.

The online lifecycle management grid

Earlier in the chapter, in the section on objective setting, we reviewed different frameworks for identifying objectives and metrics to assess whether they are achieved. We consider the online lifecycle management grid at this point since Table 4.7 acts as a good summary that integrates objectives, strategies and tactics.

The columns isolate the key performance areas of site visitor acquisition, conversion to opportunity, conversion to sale and retention. The rows isolate more detailed metrics such as the tracking metrics and performance drivers from higher-level metrics such as the customer-centric key performance indicators (KPIs) and business-value KPIs. In the bottom two rows we have also added in typical strategies and tactics used to achieve objectives which show the relationship between objectives and strategy. Note, though, that this framework mainly creates a focus on efficiency of conversion, although there are some effectiveness measures also.

Table 4.7	Online performance management grid for an e-retailer			
Metric and growth	**Visitor acquisition**	**Conversion to opportunity**	**Conversion to sale**	**Customer retention**
Tracking metrics	Unique visitors New visitors Conversation volume	Opportunity volume	Sales volume	Email list quality Email response quality transactions
Performance drivers (diagnostics)	Bounce rate Conversion rate: new visit to start quote Brand/direct visits	Macro-conversion rate to opportunity and micro-conversion efficiency	Conversion rate to sale Email conversion rate	Active customers (%) (site and email active) Repeat conversion rate for different purchases
Customer-centric KPIs	Cost per click and per sale Brand awareness Conversion polarity	Cost per opportunity Customer satisfaction	Cost per sale Customer satisfaction Average order value (AOV)	Lifetime value Customer loyalty index and advocacy Products per customer
Business value KPIs	Audience share Share of voice	Online product requests (n, £,% of total)	Online originated sales (n, £,% of total)	Retained sales growth and volume
Strategy	Online targeted reach strategy Offline targeted reach strategy	Lead generation strategy	Online sales generation Offline sales impact strategy	Retention and customer growth strategy
Tactics	Continuous communications mix Campaign communications mix Online value Proposition	Usability Personalisation Inbound contact strategy (customer service)	Usability Personalisation Inbound contact strategy (customer service) Merchandising Triggered emails	Database/list quality Targeting Outbound contact strategy (email) Personalisation

Source: Adapted from Neil Mason's Applied Insights (**www.applied-insights.co.uk**) Acquisition, Conversion, Retention approach

These are some of the generic Internet marketing main strategies to achieve the objectives in the grid which apply to a range of organisations:

- *Online value proposition strategy* – defining the value proposition for acquisition and retention to engage with customers online. Includes informational and promotional incentives used to encourage trial. Also defines programme of value creation through time, e.g. business white papers published on partner sites.
- *Online targeted reach strategy* – the aim is to communicate with relevant audiences online to achieve communications objectives. The communications commonly include campaign communications such as online advertising, PR, email, viral campaigns and continuous communications such as search engine marketing or sponsorship or partnership arrangements. The strategy may involve (1) driving new, potential customers to the company site, (2) migrating existing customers to online channels or (3) achieving reach to enhance brand awareness, favourability and purchase intent through ads and sponsorships on third-party sites. Building brand awareness, favourability and purchase intent on third-party sites may be a more effective strategy for low-involvement FMCG brands where it will be difficult to encourage visitors to the site.
- *Offline targeted reach strategy* – the objective is to encourage potential customers to use online channels, i.e. visit website and transact where relevant. The strategy is to communicate with selected customer segments offline through direct mail, media buys, PR and sponsorship.
- *Online sales efficiency strategy* – the objective is to convert site visitors to engage and become leads (e.g. through registering for an e-newsletter or placing the first item in the shopping basket) to convert them to buy products and maximise the purchase transaction value.
- *Offline sales impact strategy* – the aim is to achieve sales offline from new or existing customers. Strategy defines how online communications through the website and email can influence sales offline, i.e. by phone, mail-order or in-store.

| Case Study 4 | Tesco online development strategy supports global expansion |

Context

Tesco is a leading global retail operation and is Britain's leading food retail group. Tesco has a substantial European and international network of retailer operations and has recently begun selling non-food goods – e.g. clothing – in over 20 countries. In recent years Tesco's online operation has enjoyed significant growth in online sales; its non-food operation, Tesco Direct, saw sales rise by 30 per cent. International sales are a fundamental part of Tesco's growth strategy and in Korea, for example, sales grew by 15 per cent. Tesco states that its vision for online retailing takes account of customer needs (Tesco 2014 annual report):

Well, our multichannel approach is already helping customers shop wherever, however and whenever they need to. In the future, the shopping experience will become even more seamless, convenient and effortless. Tesco Labs are already working on turning that vision into a reality for millions of our customers. (McNamara, 2014)

Currently, Tesco Plc is one of the world's top three retailers, competing with WalMart and Carrefour for the leading position. Tesco's 2014 report described how international markets beyond the UK were grouped into three 'cohorts' depending on their current performance and potential:

- *South Korea, Malaysia and Thailand* – markets with significant future potential;
- *Ireland, Czech Republic, Hungary, Poland and Slovakia* – markets where we are focussed on holding our position and improving returns;
- *China, India and Turkey* – markets where we know we must refocus on a more profitable approach to growth.

Founded in 1919 by Jack Cohen, the company grew rapidly and has a history of delivering innovations to the UK retail sector, so it is no surprise that once it became feasible to offer online shopping Tesco was quick to determine how it might trade online. By the early 1990s, Tesco was one of the few UK retailers that had invested in a specialist e-commerce department to spearhead its online developments. In 1994 Tesco started offering online shopping to its customers but strategically the organisation had big plans for online shopping.

Tesco's former chief executive, Terry Leahy, was quoted in the *Sunday Times* as saying: 'We will be the world's biggest online grocery retailer and we intend to become the UK's No. 1 e-commerce business'. This goal was quickly achieved; by December 2000, Tesco offered a wide range of products to 90 per cent of the UK population. The online shopping service, **Tesco.com**, was established soon afterwards and operated as an independent subsidiary to Tesco. Tesco then started to diversify its online product range, offering many non-food products ranges, and the result was a significant increase in sales. To support logistical operations, Tesco developed a sophisticated semi-automated in-store picking service, supported by local refrigerated delivery vans using existing facilities rather than building high-tech dedicated warehouses and, according to Ellis-Chadwick *et al*. (2007), this created a strategic advantage that enabled faster geographical expansion of the online shopping services and a distinct advantage of extended national coverage of Tesco's online shopping service provision. By 2003, 96 per cent of the UK population could shop online with **Tesco.com**, giving the company 65 per cent of the UK online grocery shopping market and further diversification of product ranges, e.g. financial services and telecoms. It started to expand and offered its online services internationally, for example, in South Korea through **Homeplus.co.kr**.

Previously, Tesco has constantly focused on technology innovation in order to streamline services, provide new features and extend the range of points at which customers can access (Ellis-Chadwick *et al*., 2007). Diversification and expansion of the online product portfolio and customer services continues with the addition of a series of innovations such as: DVDs to your door (a rental service), energy utilities (thousands of customers save money on their gas and electricity bills), getting healthy online by using the e-diets service (which helps customers tailor their eating plans to what's right for them, taking into account lifestyles, food preferences and health recommendations) and Internet telephony. However, in 2015 Tesco's new chief executive, Dave Lewis, has begun to restructure Tesco' in response to poor performance, previous diversification (e.g. broadband services, Blinkbox) and aggressive market entrants (e.g. discounters Aldi and Lidl).' (Wood 2015).

The online grocery market and competitors

While Tesco remains the second largest online retailer after Amazon in Europe, there are legacy issues, which Dave Lewis has to deal with if the company is to continue to hold its own online (Warner, 2014)(Warner, 2014). Tesco currently leads the UK's other top grocery retailers in terms of offline and online market share but, according to Wood (2011), Clarke (former CEO of Tesco):

has promised to nurture its domestic business, which despite ringing up almost one pound in every seven spent on the UK high street has lagged behind rivals such as Sainsbury's and Morrisons in sales growth. Despite its recent underperformance, Tesco remains the dominant force in UK retail, with a market share of more than 30 per cent. It is estimated that 13 per cent of all the MasterCard and Visa credit card transactions in the UK are made on a Tesco credit card.

Tesco has been at the forefront of the development of online shopping and while it has been making a significant contribution to the growth in online retail, it has also enabled more retailers and consumers to feel that they can shop and trade online. Tesco is likely to face challenges from different sources of competition as the online shopping market grows and matures.

Staying ahead: how does Tesco promote its online offer?

As with other online retailers, Tesco.online operations rely to a certain extent on instore advertising and marketing to the supermarket's Clubcard loyalty scheme's customer base. The linkages between Clubcard mailings (off- and online) act as a trigger for shoppers to engage with both channels. Email marketing is an important part of Tesco's promotions and, according to Doherty and Ellis-Chadwick (2010), using email marketing is a complex activity, which is largely focussed on 'grabbing customer attention' but it can be used to achieve a number of communication and sales objectives. Humby and Hunt (2003) describe how **Tesco.com** uses 'commitment-based segmentation' or 'loyalty ladder' based on recency of purchase, frequency of purchase and value to drive Tesco's communication campaigns. They identified six lifecycle categories which are then further divided to target communications:

- 'Logged-on'
- 'Cautionary'
- 'Developing'
- 'Established'
- 'Dedicated'
- 'Logged-off' (the aim here is to win back).

Tesco then uses automated event-triggered messaging which can be created to encourage continued purchase – e.g. **Tesco.com** has a touch strategy which includes a sequence of follow-up communications triggered after different events in the customer lifecycle.

In the example given below, communications after event 1 are intended to achieve the objective of converting a website visitor to action; communications after event 2 are intended to move the customer from a first-time purchaser to a regular purchaser, and for event 3 to reactivate lapsed purchasers.

Trigger event 1: Customer first registers on site (but does not buy)

Auto-response (AR) 1: Two days after registration email sent offering assistance and discounts to encourage the first purchase.

Trigger event 2: Customer first purchases online

AR1: Immediate order confirmation.

AR2: Five days after purchase email sent with link to online customer satisfaction survey asking about quality of service from driver and picker (e.g. item quality and substitutions).

AR3: Two weeks after first purchase – direct mail offering tips on how to use service and £5 discount on next purchases, intended to encourage re-use of online services.

AR4: Generic monthly e-newsletter with online exclusive offers encouraging cross-selling.

AR5: Bi-weekly alert with personalised offers for customer.

AR6: After two months – financial discount to encourage the next shop.

AR7: Quarterly mailing of coupons encouraging repeat sales and cross-sales.

Trigger event 3: Customer does not purchase for an extended period

AR1: Dormancy detected – reactivation email with survey of how the customer is finding the service (to identify any problems) and a £5 incentive.

AR2: A further discount incentive is used in order to encourage continued usage to shop after the first shop after a break.

By using this stages approach to keeping track of its customers online Tesco has established a robust strategy for attracting attention and retaining customers using email marketing. According to Doherty and Ellis-Chadwick (2010), this form of digital communication is increasingly important as a mechanism for developing and maintaining mutually beneficial relationships with customers. Furthermore, advertising research discovered a large proportion of the message recipient's attention is determined by the structural, executional elements of a message rather than its content – e.g. length, size, layout (Rossiter and Bellman, 2005) – which has implications for developing effective email marketing messages.

One of the marketing challenges for international campaigns is that Tesco, although a household name in the UK, is entering new markets with its online grocery delivery service without a good level of awareness. It is looking to raise awareness among a younger generation who are using TV less than traditionally. Part of the solution is to use the 'viral marketing' available through social media to share humorous videos. This example (**www.youtube.com/watch?v=BX5EXJwlSpQ**) shows how these videos 'went viral' in Poland. It's a great example of a campaign to show how entertaining and tongue-in-cheek content can appeal to different cultures. It started off as a low-budget trial in Poland, and the videos reached over 740,000 views in a couple of months, peaking to 1.5 million views, at a cost of a few thousand euros for each video. Speaking at the 2014 Smart Insights Digital Impact conference, Niall Walsh, Head of Group Digital and Ecommerce, admitted that it 'exceeded even their own expectations, and have replicated this across other markets. We needed to wean our market away from price and promotion driven videos, and certainly achieved this through more entertaining videos'.

Question

Based on the case study and your own research, discuss where you think Tesco should focus to ensure it can continue to achieve success online and protect market share.

Summary

1 The development of the online presence follows stage models from basic static 'brochureware' sites through simple interactive sites with query facilities to dynamic sites offering personalisation of services for customers.

2 The digital marketing strategy should follow a similar form to a traditional strategic marketing planning process and should include:

- goal setting;
- situation review;
- strategy formulation;
- resource allocation and monitoring.

A feedback loop should be established to ensure the site is monitored and modifications are fed back into the strategy development.

3 Strategic goal setting should involve:

- setting business objectives that the Internet can help achieve;
- assessing and stating the contribution that the Internet will make to the business in the future, both as a proportion of revenue and in terms of whether the Internet will complement or replace other media;
- stating the full range of business benefits that are sought, such as improved corporate image, cost reduction, more leads and sales, and improved customer service.

4 The situation review will include assessing internal resources and assets, including the services available through the existing website.

5 Strategy formulation involves defining a company's commitment to the Internet, setting an appropriate value proposition for customers of the website and identifying the role of the Internet in exploiting new markets, marketplaces and distribution channels and in delivering new products and services. In summary:

- Decision 1: Market and product development strategies.
- Decision 2: Business and revenue models strategies.
- Decision 3: Target market strategy.
- Decision 4: Positioning and differentiation strategy (including the marketing mix).
- Decision 5: Customer engagement and social media strategy.
- Decision 6: Multichannel distribution strategy.
- Decision 7: Multichannel communications strategy.
- Decision 8: Online communications mix and budget.
- Decision 9: Organisational capabilities (7S framework).

Exercises

Self-assessment exercises

1 What is meant by the 'Internet contribution', and what is its relevance to strategy?
2 What is the role of monitoring in the strategic planning process?
3 Summarise the main tangible and intangible business benefits of the Internet to a company.
4 What is the purpose of a digital marketing audit? What should it involve?
5 What does a company need in order to be able to state clearly in the mission statement its strategic position relative to the Internet?
6 What are the market and product positioning opportunities offered by the Internet?
7 What are the distribution channel options for a manufacturing company?

Essay and discussion questions

1 Discuss the frequency with which a digital marketing strategy should be updated for a company to remain competitive.
2 'Setting long-term strategic objectives for a website is unrealistic since the rate of change in the marketplace is so rapid.' Discuss.
3 Explain the essential elements of a digital marketing strategy.
4 Summarise the role of strategy tools and models in formulating a company's strategic approach to the Internet.

Examination questions

1 How might a retail business use the Internet to develop an effective digital marketing strategy?
2 Discuss the extent to which Porter's five forces model can help to identify sources of competition online.
3 Which factors will affect whether the Internet has primarily a complementary effect or a replacement effect on a company?
4 Describe different stages in the sophistication of development of a website, giving examples of the services provided at each stage.
5 Briefly explain the purpose and activities involved in an external audit conducted as part of the development of a digital marketing strategy.
6 Which factors would a financial services sector company consider when assessing the suitability of its product for Internet sales?
7 Explain what is meant by the online value proposition, and give two examples of the value proposition for websites with which you are familiar.

References

Agrawal, V., Arjona, V. and Lemmens, R. (2001) E-performance: the path to rational exuberance, *McKinsey Quarterly*, 1, 31–43.

Bazett, M., Bowden, I., Love, J., Street, R. and Wilson, H. (2005) Measuring multichannel effectiveness using the balanced scorecard. *Interactive Marketing*, 6(3), 224–31.

Butler, S. (2015). Dixons Carphone positive over Black Friday performance, *The Guardian*, 18 January, www.theguardian.com/business/2015/jan/18/dixons-carphone-black-friday-retailer-shares-argos-john-lewis-electrical-goods.

Chaffey, D. (2014) *Digital Business and E-Commerce Management*, 6th edn, Financial Times/Prentice Hall, Harlow.

Chaffey, D. and Smith, P.R. (2012) *EMarketing Excellence: Planning and Optimising Your Digital Marketing*, 4th edn, Butterworth-Heinemann, Oxford.

Chaston, I. (2000) *E-Marketing Strategy*, McGraw-Hill, Maidenhead.

Daniel, E., Wilson, H., McDonald, M. and Ward, J. (2001) *Marketing Strategy in the Digital Age*, Financial Times/Prentice Hall, Harlow.

Daniel, E., Wilson, H., Ward, J. and McDonald, M. (2008) Innovation and integration: developing an integrated e-enabled business strategy. Preliminary findings from an industry-sponsored research project for the Information Systems Research Centre and the Centre for E-marketing. Cranfield University School of Management, January.

Deise, M., Nowikow, C., King, P. and Wright, A. (2000) *Executive's Guide to E-Business. From Tactics to Strategy*, Wiley, New York.

Der Zee, J. and De Jong, B. (1999) Alignment is not enough: integrating business and information technology management with the balanced business scorecard, *Journal of Management Information Systems*, 16(2), 137–57.

Dholakia, U., Kahn, B., Reeves, R., Rindfleisch, A., Stewart, D. and Taylor, E. (2010) Consumer behaviour in a multichannel, multimedia retailing environment, *Journal of Interactive Marketing*, 24, 86–95.

Doherty, N.F. and Ellis-Chadwick, F. (2010) Internet retailing: the past, the present and the future, *International Journal of Retail and Distribution Management*, 38(11–12), 943–65.

Econsultancy (2008) Managing Digital Channels Research Report. Author: Dave Chaffey, **www.e-consultancy.com**.

Ellis-Chadwick, F., Doherty, N.F. and Anastasakis, L. (2007) E-strategy in the UK retail grocery sector: a resource-based analysis, *Managing Service Quality*, 17(6), 702–27.

Fernie, J., Sparks, L. and Mckinnon, A.C. (2010) Retail logistics in the UK: past, present and future, *International Journal of Retail and Distribution Management*, 38(11–12), 894–914.

Forbes (2014) Five important digital marketing elements to consider, *Forbes*, 13 October, **www.forbes.com/sites/thesba/2014/10/13/five-important-digital-marketing-elements-to-consider/**.

Friedlein, A. (2002) *Maintaining and Evolving Successful Commercial Websites: Managing Change, Content, Customer Relationships, and Site Measurement*, Morgan Kaufmann, London.

Graham, F. (2011) Firms ignore the foreign language Internet at their peril, BBC News, **www.bbc.co.uk/news/business-13878064**.

Gunawan, G., Ellis-Chadwick, F. and King, M. (2008) An empirical study of the uptake of performance measurement by Internet retailers, *Internet Research*, 18(4), 361–81.

Hadighi, S., Sahebjamnia, N., Mahdavi, I. and Shirazi, M. (2013). A framework for strategy formulation based on clustering approach: a case study in a corporate organization, *Knowledge-Based Systems*, 49 (September), 37–49. **doi:http://dx.doi.org/10.1016/j.knosys.2013.04.008**.

Hasan, H. and Tibbits, H. (2000) Strategic management of electronic commerce: an adaptation of the balanced scorecard, *Internet Research*, 10(5), 439–50.

Humby, C. and Hunt, T. (2003) *Scoring Points. How Tesco Is Winning Customer Loyalty*, Kogan Page, London.

Jobber, D. and Ellis-Chadwick (2013) *Principles and Practice of Marketing*, 7th edn, McGraw-Hill.

Kaplan, R.S. and Norton, D.P. (1993) Putting the balanced scorecard to work, *Harvard Business Review* (September–October), 134–42.

Karabag, S. and Berggren, C. (2014) Antecedents of firm performance in emerging economies: Business groups, strategy, industry structure, and state support, *Journal of Business Research*, 67(10), 2212–33. doi:**http://dx.doi.org/10.1016/j.jbusres.2014.01.004**.

Kim, E., Nam, D. and Stimpert, D. (2004) The applicability of Porter's generic strategies in the digital age: assumptions, conjectures and suggestions, *Journal of Management*, 30(5).

Kumar, N. (1999) Internet distribution strategies: dilemmas for the incumbent, *Financial Times*, Special Issue on mastering information management, no. 7. Electronic Commerce, **www.ftmastering.com**.

Marketingmagazine.co.uk (2014). Digital transformations: moving beyond customer centric – watch the full debate, *Marketing Magazine*, 3 March, **www.brandrepublic.com/news/1282895/Digital-transformations-Moving-beyond-customer-centric-watch-full-debate/?DCMP=ILC-SEARCH**.

Marketingweek.co.uk (2014) Great brands go beyond 'satisfaction', says Lego marketer Conny Kalcher, *MarketingWeek*, 26 February, **www.brandrepublic.com/news/1282579/Great-brands-go-beyond-satisfaction-says-Lego-marketer-Conny-Kalcher/?HAYILC=RELATED**.

McDonald, M. (2003) *Marketing Plans: How To Prepare Them, How To Use Them*, 5th edn, Butterworth-Heinemann, Oxford.

McDonald, M. and Wilson, H. (2002) *New Marketing: Transforming the Corporate Future*. Butterworth-Heinemann, Oxford.

McFarlan, F.W. (1984) Information technology changes the way you compete, *Harvard Business Review* (May–June), 54–61.

McNamara, M. (2014) Innovation labs and the future of retail, *Tesco: Talking Shop*, **www.tescoplc.com/talkingshop/index.asp?blogid=211**.

Mintzberg, H. and Quinn, J.B. (1991) *The Strategy Process*, 2nd edn, Prentice Hall, Upper Saddle River, NJ.

Neslin, S., Grewal, D., Leghorn, R., Venkatesh, S., Teerling, L. and Thomas, J. (2006) Challenges and opportunities in multichannel customer management, *Journal of Science Research*, 9(2), 95–112.

Parsons, A., Zeisser, M. and Waitman, R. (1996) Organising for digital marketing, *McKinsey Quarterly*, 4, 183–92.

Porter, M. (1980) *Competitive Strategy*, Free Press, New York.

Porter, M. (2001) Strategy and the Internet, *Harvard Business Review* (March), 62–78.

Porter, M.E. and Heppelmann, J.E. (2014) How smart, connected products are transforming competition, *Harvard Business Review*, 92(11), 64–88.

Quelch, J. and Klein, L. (1996) The Internet and international marketing, *Sloan Management Review* (Spring), 61–75.

Revolution (2005a) Email marketing report, by Justin Pugsley, *Revolution* (September), 58–60.

Rossiter, J.R. and Bellman, S. (2005) *Marketing Communications: Theory and Practice*, Pearson Prentice-Hall, Sydney.

Ruddick, G. (2014) Black Friday 2014 explained – retailers gearing up for day of deals, *The Telegraph*, 19 November, **www.telegraph.co.uk/finance/newsbysector/retailandconsumer/11217839/Black-Friday-2014-Get-ready-for-the-biggest-online-shopping-day-in-history.html**.

Smart Insights (2015) Introducing RACE: a practical framework to improve your digital marketing. By Dave Chaffey, originally in July 2010, updated 20 January 2015, **www.smartinsights.com/digital-marketing-strategy/race-a-practical-framework-to-improve-your-digital-marketing/**.

Sultan, F. and Rohm, A. (2004) The evolving role of the Internet in marketing strategy, *Journal of Interactive Marketing*, 19(2).

Tesco (2011) **www.tescoplc.com/media/417/tesco_annual_report_2011_final.pdf**.

Tjan, A. (2001) Finally, a way to put your Internet portfolio in order, *Harvard Business Review* (February), 78–85.

Varianini, V. and Vaturi, D. (2000) Marketing lessons from e-failures, *McKinsey Quarterly*, 4, 86–97.

Warner, J. (2014) Tesco's Dave Lewis has a monumental mountain to climb, *The Telegraph*, 13 December, **www.telegraph.co.uk/finance/comment/jeremy-warner/11292449/Tescos-Dave-Lewis-has-a-monumental-mountain-to-climb.html**.

Weed, K. (2015) Unilever CMO Keith Weed's five tech trends for 2015, *Campaign*, 20 January, **www.campaignlive.co.uk/news/1330056/unilever-cmo-keith-weeds-five-tech-trends-2015/?DCMP=ILC-SEARCH**.

Wood, Z. (2011) Tesco Boss: Internet sales and stores can work together, *The Guardian*, 8 June, **www.guardian.co.uk/business/2011/jun/08/new-tesco-boss-says-internet-sales-and-stores-must-support-each-other**.

Wood, Z. (2015) Tesco chief unveils dramatic shakeup at troubled supermarket, *The Guardian*, 8 January, **www.theguardian.com/business/2015/jan/08/tesco-chief-unveils-dramatic-shake-up-troubled-supermarket**.

Weblinks

- **SmartInsights.com** (**www.smartinsights.com**). Updates about all aspects of digital marketing including strategy edited by Dave Chaffey.
- **PR Smith's SOSTAC** (**www.prsmith.org**)
- **Altimeter** (**www.altimeter.com**). Analysis and recommendations covering Digital Transformation and Social Business.
- **Econsultancy.com** (**www.Econsultancy.com**). A good compilation of reports and white papers many of which are Digital Transformation-related.
- **Forrester Marketing Blog** (**http://blogs.forrester.com/marketing**). Forrester analysts write about developments in technology.
- **Gartner** (**www.gartner.com/marketing/digital/research/commerce/**) Research and recommendations about Digital Business initiatives.
- **McKinsey Quarterly** (**www.mckinseyquarter.com**). Articles regularly cover digital marketing strategy.
- **PwC Digital IQ** (**www.pwc.com/us/en/advisory/digital-iq-survey**) An annual survey on digital transformation by larger businesses.

Chapter 5
The impact of digital media and technology on the marketing mix

Chapter at a glance

Main topics

- Product 255
- Price 267
- Place 277
- Promotion 284
- People, process and physical evidence 285

Case studies

Digital marketing in practice
The Smart Insights interview with Roberto Hortal, EDF Energy, who explains why the marketing mix remains relevant today 252

Case study 5: Spotify streaming develops new revenue models 290

Learning objectives

After reading this chapter, the reader should be able to:

- Apply the elements of the marketing mix in an online context
- Evaluate the opportunities that the Internet makes available for varying the marketing mix
- Assess the opportunities for online brand-building.

Questions for marketers

Key questions for marketing managers related to this chapter are:

- How are the elements of the marketing mix varied online?
- What are the implications of the Internet for brand development?
- Can the product component of the mix be varied online?
- How are companies developing online pricing strategies?
- Does 'place' have relevance online?

Scan code
to find the
latest updates
for topics in
this chapter

Links to other chapters

This chapter is related to other chapters as follows:

- Chapter 2 introduces the impact of the Internet on market structure and distribution channels
- Chapter 4 describes how digital marketing strategies can be developed
- Chapters 6 and 7 explain the service elements of the mix in more detail
- Chapter 7 explains site design can be used to support and enhance brand values
- Chapters 8 and 9 explain the promotion elements of the mix in more detail.

Introduction

Marketing mix
The series of seven key variables – Product, Price, Place, Promotion, People, Process and Physical evidence – that are varied by marketers as part of the customer offering.

Online branding
How online channels are used to support brands that, in essence, are the sum of the characteristics of a product or service as perceived by a user.

This chapter shows how the well-established strategic framework of the **marketing mix** can be applied by marketers to inform their digital marketing strategy. It explores this key issue of digital marketing strategy in more detail than was possible in Chapter 4. As part of our discussion of product we will review how the Internet can be used to support and impact on the way brands are developed. The chapter is structured by taking a look at each element of the marketing mix in turn, reviewing the implications of digital technology, with **online branding** covered under Product.

What is the marketing mix?

Marketers will be familiar with the marketing mix, but this introduction is included for context for digital marketers who are unfamiliar with it. The marketing mix – widely referred to as the 4Ps of Product, Price, Place and Promotion – was originally proposed by Jerome McCarthy (1960) and is still used as an essential part of formulating and implementing marketing strategy by many practitioners. The popularity of the mix as a guide for the application of marketing techniques is driven by the apparent simplicity of the framework. However, in the 1980s the 4Ps was challenged for not referencing the importance of customer service. The result was that the mix was extended to 7Ps, which include three further elements (the service mix) that better reflect service delivery: People, Process and Physical evidence (Booms and Bitner, 1981). Some writers argue that the service mix should be subsumed within the 4Ps. Figure 5.1 summarises the different sub-elements of the 7Ps. Since the 1990s there have been more changes in marketing thinking and research and the outcome has been a shift in emphasis in the application of the marketing mix towards the development of relationship building. Some writers even argue that this is a paradigm shift altering the underlying marketing philosophy guiding the application of marketing tools and concepts (Berry, 2008). Whereas others suggest the move to more relationship-orientated marketing is in response to growing customer demands and increasingly complex technology-driven trading environments (Singh et al., 2011)(Singh, Agrariya and Deepali, 2011).

Using the Internet to vary the marketing mix						
Product	**Promotion**	**Price**	**Place**	**People**	**Process**	**Physical evidence**
• Quality	• Marketing	• Positioning	• Trade	• Individuals	• Customer	• Sales/staff
• Image	communications	• List	channels	on marketing	focus	contact
• Branding	• Personal	• Discounts	• Sales	activities	• Business-led	experience
• Features	promotion	• Credit	support	• Individuals	• IT-supported	of brand
• Variants	• Sales	• Payment	• Channel	on customer	• Design	• Product
• Mix	promotion	methods	number	contact	features	packaging
• Support	• PR	• Free or	• Segmented	• Recruitment	• Research	• Online
• Customer	• Branding	value-	channels	• Culture/	and	experience
service	• Direct	added		image	development	
• Use	marketing	elements		• Training		
occasion				and skills		
• Availability				• Remuneration		
• Warranties						

Figure 5.1	The elements of the marketing mix

Note that the marketing mix concept has been criticised for not being customer-centric. Lautenborn (1990) suggested the 4Cs framework, which considers the 4Ps from a customer perspective. In brief, the 4Cs are:

- customer needs and wants (from the product);
- cost to the customer (price);
- convenience (relative to place);
- communication (promotion).

It is not the aim of this text to debate current thinking on marketing philosophy but it is important to acknowledge the rise in importance of relationship building as this is key to the application of digital marketing strategies and the application of the marketing mix shown in Activity 5.1.

Digital media and technology provides many new opportunities for the marketer:

- to vary the application of marketing mix;
- to develop new routes to delivering competitive advantage;
- to create new market positions;
- to build and service relationships in increasing innovative ways;
- to cut through the barriers of time and space and offer continuous and instantaneous access to products and services.

Think about these opportunities while tackling Activity 5.1.

Activity 5.1 **How can digital media and technology be used to vary the marketing mix?**

Purpose

An activity which highlights the scope for applying digital technology as a strategic marketing tool.

Activity

Review Figure 5.1 and select two opportunities that give potential for varying the marketing mix. For each opportunity suggest how each of the elements of the mix (Figure 5.1):

- provide new opportunities for varying the mix;
- give rise to possible negative implications (threats) for each opportunity;
- create opportunities to use the mix to develop relationships.

Digital marketing also has far-reaching implications for the relative importance of different elements of the mix for many markets, regardless of whether an organisation is involved directly in transactional e-commerce. Consequently, the marketing mix is a useful framework to inform strategy development. First, it gives a framework for comparing an organisation's existing services with competitors' and can also be used as a mechanism for generating alternative strategic approaches. Digital marketing affects all aspects of the traditional and service marketing mix and in this chapter we explore:

- *Product* – looking at opportunities for modifying the core or extended product for digital environments.
- *Price* – focussing on the implications for setting prices in digital markets; new pricing models and strategies.
- *Place* – considering the implications for distribution for digital marketing.
- *Promotion* – exploring promotional techniques in advance of more detailed coverage of new techniques in Chapters 8 and 9.

- *People, process and physical evidence* – reviewing the principal ideas in advance of more detailed discussion in Chapters 6, 7 and 10, where the focus is on how these elements of the mix relate to customer relationship management and managing an organisation's digital presence.

In 2001, Chaffey and Smith recognised the growing importance of relationships, especially within the digital marketing arena and proposed that an eighth element should be added to the digital marketing mix: partnerships. They suggested that their eighth P was very important as it enabled digital marketers to extend reach, and build affiliations (Chaffey and Smith, 2012). This approach is today often known as **co-marketing**, where a strategic or informal agreement is reached for two brands to work together to increase awareness of their partner. Co-marketing, also known as 'contra-deals', has the advantage that it is low-cost since the main cost is staff time to develop joint campaigns and share content. For example, publisher Smart Insights has formed strategic partnerships with vendors such as Hubspot, publishers such as **MyCustomer.com**, services such as Eventbrite, events companies such as UBM and marketing membership bodies such as The IDM to help generate awareness from the audience of the partner. Co-marketing can also involve working with individual bloggers as part of influencer outreach (see Chapter 8).

As you read this chapter, you should consider which are the key elements of the mix that vary online for the different types of online presence introduced in Chapter 1 – i.e. transactional e-commerce, relationship-building, brand-building, media owner portals and social networks. Allen and Fjermestad (2001) and Harridge-March (2004) have reviewed how digital media and technology has impacted on the main elements of the marketing mix, particularly for digital products. The opportunities they describe remain relevant.

Co-marketing
A partnership agreement reached between different businesses to promote each other, typically based on sharing content (and potentially promotions) principally to the audience of owned media channels such as social media, blog and email marketing.

| Digital marketing in practice | The Smart Insights interview |

Roberto Hortal explains why the marketing mix remains relevant today

Overview and main concepts

Roberto Hortal has worked as an e-business director with many years of experience in different types of businesses operating in different countries. Examples of the UK and global enterprises he has worked for include EDF Energy, RSA insurance group, MORE THAN, easyJet and Nokia. He shares his experience of how the marketing mix concept is applied when taking real-world decisions, when companies seek to shape their online value proposition and performance in the digital marketplace.

The interview

Q. We often hear that the concept of the marketing mix isn't that useful any longer in this era of customer-first. What's your view on its relevance today? Are there any particular aspects of the mix which lend themselves to refining online?

Roberto Hortal: The marketing mix is a conceptual framework, and as such it is useful since it enables a common language to be used in the planning, execution and measurement of a number of coordinated activities that deliver the desired marketing outcomes. Customer-centricity demands that organisations becomes a lot better at collecting and reacting to customer insight and adapt their offering to best suit an ever growing number of narrowing customer segments – ever approaching the ideal of the completely personalised product. As complexity increases exponentially, it is crucial to be able to rely on tried and tested concepts like the marketing mix.

I use the basic components of the marketing mix (such as the 4Ps) at work daily, and as such, for me, the marketing mix remains a practical tool. In a digital environment routinely identifying and profiling individual consumers over time and adapting to their needs and wants, the 4Ps become elastic. Is my website a Place, or is it an integral part of the Product? When more efficient digital channels directly influence my ability to Price, do Place and Price become synonymous? This elasticity needs to be managed effectively to avoid the pitfalls of too rigidly applying the model. One must always challenge the validity of every tool in the Digital Marketing armoury; adding, changing and discarding as business and customers evolve. Proposed evolutions of the marketing mix concept (such as the 4Cs) may ensure it remains relevant today. My personal view is we're still some distance from seeing the end of its useful life.

Q. Could you give some examples of where you introduced new ways of applying the mix online.

Roberto Hortal: In my view, the key insight is that digital media can contribute to every element of the mix. Therefore, we must avoid a narrow categorisation of digital as contributing solely (or even primarily) to a single component of the mix.

While I haven't come across an organisation that fundamentally disagrees with that view, some organisations find it easier than others to put it into practice. I have worked in organisations where the mix is embedded in the corporate structure with separate Pricing, Product, Distribution (Place) and Marketing (Promotion) departments. Embedding a digital mindset across those silos can be a daunting task.

I've experimented with channel pricing, as pricing is a critical driver of conversion and business value in a services organisation. Straight online discounts have proven difficult to justify. Online discounts aren't valued by customers (in the age of price comparison, they focus on the total price, rather than its components) and often do not reflect a real lower cost to the business (lower costs to sell and serve are offset by lower transaction value and lower retention rates). Using channel data as a pricing factor has proven a lot more successful: as historical data is accumulated, it is possible to really offer competitive prices to those customers identified as high value at the point of application. An accurate value/propensity model can use the wealth of information available from digital visitors (geography, visit trigger/campaign, past visits, customer history, etc.) to drive truly personalised pricing. In this example, price follows place and both price and promotion reflect the individual customer.

I've successfully extended the data-driven approach to other elements of the mix: dynamic packaging (the creation of a personalised offering from the basis of a modular product) has proven successful many times: at easyJet we built a product that included car hire recommendations based on a predictive model that took destination, seasonality and party size as inputs – increasing car hire uptake very significantly. More recently I've applied the same insight-driven dynamic packaging approach to RSA's Central and Eastern European businesses, increasing sales of optional covers and add-ons very significantly.

Further opportunities exist around selecting which default base products to present: are you more likely to want a cheap energy tariff that tracks price rises or a fixed price deal that ensures protection against future rises? What we know about you from your digital 'shadow' may provide the clues we need.

Q. Online channels bring great opportunities to test propositions online. Can you advise on approaches to testing propositions?

Roberto Hortal: I have used online channels to test propositions in a couple of ways. I assign propositions randomly to visitors on first arrival to test interest/sales. I would typically run this against a large control group (being offered the current main proposition) to both protect commercial results and detect the effect of any external influences that maybe otherwise wrongly influence the experiment. This approach can be extended beyond the site, via randomised allocation of marketing messages on Display, Search etc. to measure a proposition's attractiveness. It's important to test all aspects of the proposition: a proposition successful at attracting interest may convert badly if it can't be priced at a level that matches customer expectations. I also provide a modular proposition platform and allow customers to combine proposition elements. We can easily analyse popular combinations as well as secondary correlations such as the propensity to add a certain ancillary product to a particular proposition configuration, and understand the compound impact on profitability, retention and advocacy from what we know about each of the modular components in isolation.

I've found that proposition testing rarely fits neatly an A/B scenario, with tests quickly developing into complex multivariate experiments with a significant number of variables. It is important to ensure the tests are solidly planned, rigorously executed and statistically significant. Free tools like Google Website Optimiser provide information to test and get the best out of website contact. However, such tools will not prevent badly designed experiments from yielding wrong data. In my experience, the only way to ensure valid tests and improved business results is to bring in the best analytical brain you can find. Analytics is the first role I fill when I build a digital team from scratch, it's that important.

Q. Many organisations are now developing social media strategies. How do you see the intersection between social media and the marketing mix since it clearly impacts on product decision making and service?

Roberto Hortal: If I only had the answer … I take a radically different view of social media than many of my peers. While most people see social media as a branding and customer service channel, I see social media's largest potential in the areas of awareness, consideration and acquisition. This is not to say the best way to use social media sites is to advertise in them. Far from it. The social nature of the Internet demands that brands engage in conversation, and identify and incentivise brand ambassadors to help amplify our messages. There is general acceptance of this, but also a general shyness about steering conversations and seeking to extract immediate commercial value in the form of direct sales. Risk-aversion takes over and anecdotes used to prove the point that there is a risk that poor execution may lead to a social backlash.

The risk is clearly real but there is also an opportunity to execute well and generate significant amounts of business and positive buzz. I recently ran a campaign with Poland's largest social network (Nasza Klassa). A fairly simple personality quiz mechanism was executed beautifully by my Polish team, resulting in what our partners characterised as the country's most successful campaign in terms of reach and engagement, one that generated levels of sales comparable to those contributed by mainstream e-marketing channels.

Social media spaces require nurture and respect, but we must not forget that so do physical locations. In the same way that people like to go to the village Post Office for a chat but also to do their banking, branded social media environments have the potential to merge conversation and commerce in a seamless, altogether better proposition for both consumers and brands.

Q. Many organisations now are looking at providing new mobile propositions. A key decision is whether to implement them as mobile app or mobile site. How do you approach this platform decision?

Roberto Hortal: I start from the point of view of the user: Why would they use this proposition? Where would they use the proposition? How would they find it first time, and subsequently? Would they accept/appreciate the added engagement possibilities of an app (alerts, updates, a permanent place on the home screen)?

Some scenarios where I have used this approach in the past include:

- **Insurance/energy sales**. Website – neither mobile app nor mobile site. In this particular case I think the best option is to provide a solidly usable, accessible web sales capability that works well across devices. Rather than building separate sites/capabilities for separate devices I prefer to ensure the basis of the experience is optimised – this principle ensures that device-specificity doesn't catch me off-guard: sales websites I have managed worked well on iPhone the day it came out as they were built of solid principles and standards that apply across devices. I do use extensively the principles of progressive enhancement to provide a great experience to segments of people on particular channels/devices such as modern PC browsers and mobile browsers. However, the underlying principle of a solid, accessible, easy-to-use site has never let me down.

- **Regular/emergency transaction**. Apps – I look at regular events such as submitting an electricity meter reading or unpredictable ones such as registering a motor insurance claim as ideal candidates for a mobile app. Regularity breeds familiarity, and regular events can benefit from app characteristics such as local storage, transparent login, notifications and a permanent place on the user's screen. These same characteristics, together with the reassurance of being completely contained on the device and not requiring uninterrupted Internet access, support the use of apps for functionality perceived as critical. HTML5 may make these distinctions technically irrelevant, but I expect customer behaviour will lag significantly so they will effectively apply for a long while yet.

- **Seamless access vs perceived value**. An app's installation is quite a disruptive process: you need to open the shop interface, confirm credentials, find the app, start a possibly long download (which may impact on your monthly limits), find the app on the phone screens, start it, watch it initialise (including possibly entering username and password for initial configuration) and finally access it – and from now on it will take space permanently on your device, competing with your music and movies. Quite an expensive process, from a usability point of view. Therefore an app must have quite a high perceived value in order to get installed. On the other hand, if casual use (particularly in conjunction with web searching/browsing) is what is sought, then a mobile site is the best solution.

- **Fragmentation is finally the last of my current worries**. We used to have to contend with the iPhone and the iPad – two screen sizes in a universal app is manageable. Suddenly we have myriad versions of iOS, Android, Windows Phone on a continuum of screen sizes and very variable device capabilities (processor speed, camera/s, GPS, NFC, etc.). This is turning into a big argument for HTML5 and mobile sites. Major platform/device combos will continue to be relevant for apps, but I also expect the relative size of this group of devices to shrink in relation to the universe of mobile devices – serving most of which will only be practical through mobile web.

Product

Product variable
The element of the marketing mix that involves researching customers' needs and developing appropriate products. (*See* **Core product** and **Extended product**.)

The **product variable** of the marketing mix refers to characteristics of a product, service or brand. Product decisions should be informed by market research where customers' needs are assessed and the feedback is used to modify existing products or develop new products. There are many alternatives for varying the product in the online context when a company is developing its online strategy. Internet-related product decisions can be usefully divided into decisions affecting the **core product** and the **extended product**. The core product refers to the main product purchased by the consumer to fulfil their needs, while the extended or augmented product refers to additional services and benefits that are built around the core of the product.

The main implications of the Internet for the product element of the mix are:

1 options for varying the core product;
2 options for offering digital products;
3 options for changing the extended product;
4 conducting research online;
5 speed of new product development;
6 speed of new product diffusion.

1 Options for varying the core product

For some companies, there may be options for new digital products which will typically be information products that can be delivered over the web. Ghosh (1998) talked about developing new products or adding 'digital value' to customers. The questions he posed still prove useful today:

- *Can I offer additional information or transaction services to my existing customer base*? For example, a bookseller can provide customer book reviews, new title previews or sell books online. A travel company can provide video tours of resorts and accommodation.
- Can I address the needs of new customer segments by repackaging my current information assets or by creating new business propositions using the Internet? For an online bookseller, creating an electronic book service, or a DVD rental service.
- Can I use my ability to attract customers to generate new sources of revenue such as advertising or sales of complementary products? **Lastminute.com**, which sells travel-related services, has a significant advertising revenue; it can also sell non-travel services.
- Will my current business be significantly harmed by other companies providing some of the value I currently offer? Consider the consequences if other companies use some of the product strategies described above.

Of course, the markets transformed most by the Internet are those where products themselves can be transformed into digital services. Such products include music (download or streaming of digital tracks – see the iTunes case study at the end of the chapter), books (electronic books), newspaper and magazine publishing (online access to articles) and software (digital downloads and online subscription services).

The Internet also introduces options for **mass customisation** of products, particularly digital products or products that can be specified online. The Internet has provided a channel through which manufacturers can not only sell the personalised products but also use the Internet as a source of information for developing the latest catwalk designs. ASOS has revolutionised the way *fashionistas* shop in the UK (and around the globe). This online brand, launched in 2002 and now a leading online fashion retailer in the UK, introduced the 'catwalk view', where fashion-hungry online shoppers can watch products being walked down the runway before they buy. ASOS sells fashionable clothing from a range of designers and its own in-house team. Their business model relies on quick turnover of 'on trend' fashion items to the mid and lower ends of the clothing market (Swash, 2014).

Mass customisation (Davis, 1997; Pine, 1993)has been heralded as a business strategy which derives benefits from the personalisation of products in which a customer takes a more active role in product design (Kamail and Loker, 2002).

Digital marketing insight 5.1 discusses Alvin Toffler's futuristic predictions about the rise of the prosumer in 1980.

Companies can also consider how the Internet can be used to change the range or combination of products offered. Some companies, such as online fashion retailers, may only offer a subset of products online. Alternatively, a company may have a fuller catalogue available online than is available through offline brochures. **Bundling** is a further

Digital marketing insight 5.1	The prosumer

The prosumer concept was introduced in 1980 by futurist Alvin Toffler in his book *The Third Wave*. According to Toffler, the future would once again combine production with consumption. In *The Third Wave*, Toffler saw a world where interconnected users would collaboratively 'create' products. Note that he foresaw this over ten years before the web was invented!

Alternative notions of the prosumer, all of which are applicable to e-marketing, are catalogued at Logophilia WordSpy (**www.wordspy.com**):

1　A consumer who is an amateur in a particular field, but who is knowledgeable enough to require equipment that has some professional features: ('professional' + 'consumer').

2　A person who helps to design or customise the products they purchase: ('producer' + 'consumer').

3　A person who creates goods for their own use and also possibly to sell: ('producing' + 'consumer').

4　A person who takes steps to correct difficulties with consumer companies or markets and to anticipate future problems: ('proactive' + 'consumer').

An example of the application of the prosumer is provided by BMW, which used an interactive website prior to launch of its Z3 roadster where users could design their own preferred features. The information collected was linked to a database and as BMW had previously collected data on its most loyal customers, the database could give a very accurate indication of which combinations of features were the most sought after and should therefore be put into production.

alternative. Koukova *et al.* (2008) found that the Internet has encouraged the bundling of information-based products, such as newspapers, books, music videos, in physical and digital formats. Amazon offered buyers of physical books the opportunity to buy the digital version at a minimal price (Koukova *et al.*, 2008). At the time of writing, Sky Box Office, TalkTalk Box Office and Blinkbox offer various bundles of film, from downloads, buy, rent and or keep (Recombu, 2015). The benefits for the sellers are that digital products provide opportunities to leverage advantage as there are marginal costs involved with supplying digital versions and considerable cost savings if customers switch to the digital offer. Therefore, the introduction of physical and digital product bundles offers much scope for new approaches to product delivery and pricing strategies (Koukova *et al.*, 2008) (Koukova, Kannan & Ratchford, 2008).

Finally, the Internet is a platform for providing information about the core features of the product. However, the availability of information can impact on price as the price has become more transparent. Comparison sites like **Comparethemarket.com** enable online shoppers to assess the price of car insurance from many suppliers in one location.

2 Options for offering digital products

Companies such as publishers, TV companies and other media owners who can offer digital products such as published content, music or videos now have great flexibility to offer a range of product purchase options at different price points, including:

- *Subscription*. This is a traditional publisher revenue model, but subscription can potentially be offered for different periods at different price points, e.g. three months, twelve months or two years.

- *Pay-per-view.* A fee for a single download or viewing session at a higher relative price than the subscription service – e.g. music products from iTunes. Customers can enjoy instant download in a similar way to a mobile company 'pay-as-you-go' model. Travel publisher Lonely Planet enables visitors to a destination to download an introduction for a fraction of the price of a full printed guide.
- *Bundling.* Different channels or content can be offered as individual products or grouped at a reduced price compared to pay-per-view.
- *Ad-supported content.* There is no direct price set here. Instead, the publisher's main revenue source is through adverts on the site (CPM display advertising on-site using banner ads and skyscrapers) a fixed sponsorship arrangement or CPC, which stands for 'cost-per-click' – more typical when using search ad network publishing such as Google Adsense (**www.google.com/adsense.com**), which accounts for around a third of Google's revenue. Other options include affiliate revenue from sales on third-party sites or offering access to subscriber lists.

The digitisation of products presents opportunities to some industries and threats to others. Newspapers is an example of an industry where the Internet has had a far-reaching impact. Most popular quality newspapers are now successfully using subscription-based business models to maintain their readership. Indeed, the *Guardian*, the *Daily Telegraph* and the *Independent* (popular UK newspapers) have a larger online readership than the equivalent print versions (Reid, 2014).

3 Options for changing the extended product

When a customer buys a new computer, it consists not only of the tangible computer, monitor and cables, but also the information provided by the computer salesperson, the instruction manual, the packaging, the warranty and the follow-up technical service. These are elements of the extended product. Chaffey and Smith (2012) suggest these examples of how the Internet can be used to vary the extended product:

| Digital marketing insight 5.2 | Digital players enter Hollywood? |

The Internet has begun to change the way we watch movies. For years the film industry has not been significantly affected by the shift towards digital in the same way that the music and newspaper industries have, but that is all about to change. While the Internet has all but eliminated the distribution costs for film makers, the industry has been protected due to the high costs of film production (Levine, 2014). At Amazon studios, you are invited to submit a script a video or an idea for a comedy series (Amazonstudios, 2015). And you can also become a reviewer of existing productions. It appears that Amazon is aggressively expanding its offer in the world of film production as it is currently developing over 14 movies. Arguably, the underlying business idea is that Amazon will become recognised as a content producer and then be able to charge subscription fees for its services (Jarvey and McClintock, 2015). In doing so, Amazon probably hopes to compete with the large media corporations. Traditionally, the movie industry had relatively high entry barriers, due to distribution and production costs, and other contractual barriers. Amazon appears to be a new entrant which is seeking to change the rules and others are set to follow. Vessel is a startup business which also has ambitions to shake up the world of online videos through online subscriptions. Vessel has launched a service whereby viewers can sign up for early access to top 'YouTubers, musicians and production companies' (Dredge, 2015).

- endorsements;
- awards;
- testimonies;
- customer lists;
- customer comments;
- warranties;
- guarantees;
- money-back offers;
- customer service (see people, process and physical evidence);
- incorporating tools to help users during their selection and use of the product.

Peppard and Rylander (2005) have researched how people assimilate information online when selecting products and point out that it is important that the site replicates information about product selection that would normally be provided by interaction in other channels by a member of sales staff by phone or face-to-face. These facilities can be replicated online. For example, the bank First Direct uses an interactive dialogue to recommend the best options on their portfolio of financial products, e.g. savings, investments, mortgage insurance.

Organisations should aim to identify sources of value to engage customers before they have to pay for the products and services on offer. Ghosh (1998) suggested this was an important trigger to encourage site visitors to engage with a brand on a first visit to a site and/or to encourage return visits. He refers to this process as 'building a customer *magnet*' and the concepts he identified remain central to 'portal' or 'community' websites. Once customers are attracted to a site and have begun to learn about the brand offer, the next step is to provide extensions to the freely available offer. Ideally, customers will be encouraged to enter into a paid-for relationship with the organisation. In other cases a premium may be charged for new services – e.g. at Amazon Web Services there are limited offers for new (qualifying) customers who are looking for unlimited capacity for support of software, data migration and cloud services (AmazonWebServices, 2015).

4 Conducting research online

The Internet provides many options for learning about product preferences and it can be used as a relatively low-cost method of collecting marketing research, particularly when trying to discover customer perceptions of products and services. Sawhney *et al.* (2005) have reviewed the options for using digital media for new product innovation where they contrast the traditional new product research process with a digitally augmented co-creation process. They suggest that online research tools should be evaluated according to how they can be used: (1) front-end developments of ideation and concept against back-end developments involving product design and testing, and (2) the nature of collaboration – broad/high reach against deep/high richness.

Options for performing new product development research online include:

- *Online focus group*. A moderated focus group can be conducted to compare customers' experience of product use. Many companies now have permanent customer panels they can use to ask about new ideas.
- *Online questionnaire survey*. These typically focus on the site visitors' experience, but can also include questions relating to products.
- *Customer feedback or support forums*. Comments posted to the site or independent sites such as social networks may give suggestions about future product innovation. Freshdesk (**freshdesk.com**) has developed a platform to enable a company to communicate and collaborate inside and outside the company. The platform also has the capacity to integrate with CRM, e-commerce and analytics systems. Companies using freshdesk include Honda, 3M, Hugo Boss, Kuoni and Unicef.

- *Web analytics*. A wealth of marketing research information is also available from response data from email and search campaigns and the website itself, since every time a user clicks on a link offering a particular product, this indicates a preference for products and related offers. Such information can be used indirectly to assess customers' product preferences.

Approaches for undertaking these types of research are briefly reviewed in Chapter 10.

5 Velocity of new product development

The Internet provides a platform which enables new products to be developed more rapidly as it is possible to test new ideas and concepts and explore different product options through online market research. Companies can use their own panels of consumers to test opinion more rapidly and often at lower costs than for traditional market research. Google is a highly innovative company and it has had many successes and failures, e.g. GoogleAdwords (success) and Google Buzz and Wave (failure), Google Glass (enhanced wearable technology and augmented reality glasses – shelved (Gibbs, 2015)). Another aspect of the velocity of new product development is that the network effect of the Internet enables companies to form partnerships more readily in order to launch new products.

6 Velocity of new product diffusion

In the early days of the Internet, Quelch and Klein (1996) noted that to remain competitive, organisations will have to roll out new products more rapidly to international markets. Additionally, Malcolm Gladwell, in his book *The Tipping Point* (2000), emphasised the importance of word-of-mouth communication on the impact of the rate of adoption of new products, especially through the Internet. In Chapter 9, we will see how marketers seek to influence this effect through what is known as 'viral marketing'.

Tipping point
Using the science of social epidemics explains principles that underpin the rapid spread of ideas, products and behaviours through a population.

Marsden (2004) provides a good summary of the implications of the **tipping point** for marketers. He says that 'using the science of social epidemics, *The Tipping Point* explains the three simple principles that underpin the rapid spread of ideas, products and behaviours through a population'. He advises how marketers should help create a 'tipping point' for a new product or service, the moment when a domino effect is triggered and an epidemic of demand sweeps through a population like a highly contagious virus.

There are three main laws that are relevant from *The Tipping Point*:

1 The law of the few

This suggests that the spread of any new product or service is dependent on the initial adoption by 'connectors' who are socially connected and who encourage adoption through word-of-mouth and copycat behaviour. In an online context, these connectors may use personal blogs, email newsletters and podcasts to propagate their opinions.

2 The stickiness factor

Typically, this refers to how 'glued' we are to a medium such as a TV channel or a website, but in this context it refers to attachment to the characteristics and attributes of a product or a brand. Gladwell stresses the importance of testing and market research to make the product effective. Marsden suggests that there are certain cross-category attributes which are key drivers for product success – e.g.,

- *Excellence*: being perceived as best of breed;
- *Uniqueness*: clear one-of-a-kind differentiation;
- *Engagement*: fosters emotional involvement;
- *Cost*: perceived value for money.

3 The power of context

Gladwell (2000) suggests that like infectious diseases, products and behaviours spread far and wide only when they fit the physical, social and mental context into which they are launched. He gives the example of a wave of crime in the New York subway that came to an abrupt halt by simply removing the graffiti from trains and clamping down on fare-dodging. It can be suggested that products should be devised and tested to fit their context, situation or occasion of use.

The long tail concept

Long tail concept
A frequency distribution suggesting the relative variation in popularity of items selected by consumers.

The **long tail concept** is useful for considering the role of Product, Place, Price and Promotion online. The phenomenon, now referred to as the 'long tail', following an article by Anderson (2004), was arguably first applied to human behaviour by George Kingsley Zipf, professor of linguistics at Harvard, who observed the phenomenon in word usage. He found that if the variation in popularity of different words in a language is considered, there is a systematic pattern in the frequency of usage or popularity. Zipf's 'law' suggests that if a collection of items is ordered or ranked by popularity, the second item will have around half the popularity of the first one and the third item will have about a third of the popularity of the first one and so on (Newitz, 2013). In general:

The kth item is 1/k the popularity of the first.

Look at Figure 5.2, which shows how the 'relative popularity' of items is predicted to decline according to Zipf's law from a maximum count of 1000 for the most popular item to 20 for the 50th item.

In an online context, application of this 'law' is now known as 'the long tail' thanks to Anderson (2004). It can be applied to the relative popularity of a group of websites or web pages or products on an individual site, since they tend to show a similar pattern of popularity. There are a small number of sites (or pages within sites) which are very popular (the head which may account for 80 per cent of the volume) and a much larger number of sites or pages that are less popular individually, but still collectively important. Returning to the

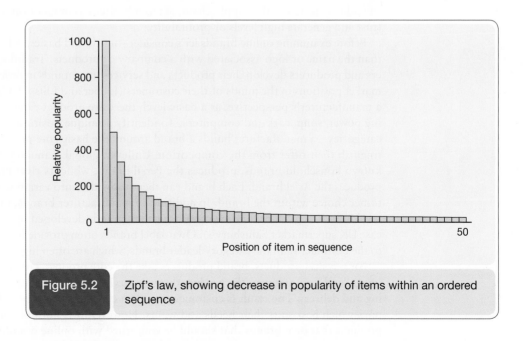

Figure 5.2 Zipf's law, showing decrease in popularity of items within an ordered sequence

product context, Anderson (2004) argued that for a company such as Amazon, the long tail or Zipf's law can be applied to describe the variation in preferences for selecting or purchasing from a choice of products as varied as books, CDs, electronic items, travel or financial services. This pattern has also been identified by Brynjolfsson *et al*. (2003), who presented a framework that quantifies the economic impact of increased product variety made available through electronic markets. They say:

> One reason for increased product variety on the Internet is the ability of online retailers to catalogue, recommend, and provide a large number of products for sale. For example, the number of book titles available at **Amazon.com** is more than 23 times larger than the number of books on the shelves of a typical Barnes & Noble superstore, and 57 times greater than the number of books stocked in a typical large independent bookstore.

Looking at the issue from another perspective, they estimate that 40 per cent of sales are from relatively obscure books with a sales rank of more than 100,000 (if you visit Amazon, you will see that every book has a sales rank from 1 for the most popular to over 1 million for the least popular). This indicates the importance of the long tail for online retailers like Amazon, since 40 per cent of sales are from these less popular books which cannot be stocked in a conventional bookstore (a large real-world book store would typically hold about 100,000 books). In a Pricing context, another benefit for online retailers is that less popular products cannot be readily obtained in the real world, so Amazon can justify higher prices for these books. Brynjolfsson *et al*. (2003) estimated that average Amazon prices for an item in the top 100,000 is $29.26 and in less popular titles $41.60.

Branding in a digital environment

Branding
The process by which companies distinguish their product offerings from the competition by the sum of the characteristics of product or service as perceived by the customer.

Branding is important online and offline as it helps customers differentiate between products and services from different manufacturers and producers. Furthermore, branding is how companies set themselves apart from their competitors. Perhaps most importantly, 'branding affects perceptions since it is well-known that in blind product testing consumers fail to distinguish between brands' (Jobber and Ellis-Chadwick, 2013). Consequently, how a brand is developed and presented online is particularly important because a website visitor has limited physical cues to help form an opinion about a company and its services, such as talking to a sales representative or the ambiance of the physical store. Branding can add value across the supply chain, act as a barrier to competition, increase consumer trust and generate high levels of profitability.

Before examining online brands let's consider some brand basics. A brand is much more than the name or logo associated with a company or products. Traditionally, manufacturers and producers develop their products and services into brands in order to create unique market positions in the minds of their customers (Jobber and Ellis-Chadwick, 2013). From a manufacturer's perspective, at a basic level, there are product categories such as washing power, soup, cars and computers. To identify a unique position – within such basic categories – a manufacturer builds a brand around the basic core product in order to distinguish their offer from the competition. Unilever, global manufacturer of many well-known household brands, produces the Persil brand, while its rival Procter & Gamble, produces the Ariel brand. Each brand can then be divided into variants, which extend customer choice within the brand. In addition to manufacturer brands, there are also own-label brands (e.g. Sainsbury's *basics*), which are brands developed by distributors (in this case UK supermarket Sainsbury's). Own-label brands often provide lower-cost alternatives to the customer than the category leader brands, which are often highly priced.

For physical products, brand producers take the core product, create a brand name and image, and then augment the product through service, guarantees, design quality, packaging and delivery. The result is customers can then choose between brands by selecting the ones which best suits their needs and wants. However, it is not only manufacturers and products that own brands that should be concerned with online branding. All businesses are perceived as brands and the online presence is increasingly important in governing brand perception. The company's website, mobile apps and social media presence all affect the perception of the brand and are part of the experience of a brand (see Chapter 7). Social media provide a new platform to interact with brands.

A key concept at the heart of creating a brand is positioning and, according to Jobber and Ellis-Chadwick (2013) 'creating a unique position in the marketplace involves a careful choice of target market and establishing a clear differential in the minds of the people'. Offline brands are able to get into the minds of the customers, to position their brands using a range of brand elements contributing to **brand equity**:

Brand equity
The assets (or liabilities) linked to a brand's name and symbol that add to (or subtract from) a service.

- Brand domain – key target markets, where the brand competes;
- Brand heritage – the background and culture of the brand;
- Brand values – the core characteristics, e.g., price, quality, performance;
- Brand assets –distinctive names, symbols, images;
- Brand personality – the character of the brand;
- Brand reflection – how the customer perceives themselves as a result of buying the brand.

Online brands face a different set of challenges. However, it is important to differentiate between physical brands that are migrating online and virtual brands. For established physical brands, the online environment is often an extension of a well-established offline business. Since the early days, the online environment has developed and markets have become more stable, many brands have developed online. For example, the supermarket brand Tesco has developed **Tesco.com**. In this instance, Tesco has been able to leverage some advantage from its long-established offline brand to build credibility online. Since 1995, Tesco has grown its online offer into the world's largest online grocery retailer (Ellis-Chadwick, 2013). The brand has focussed on maintaining the quality of the offline service online using all the traditional elements of brand building to position **Tesco.com**. Migrating a brand in the other direction from online to offline is not as straightforward. Now read Mini case study 5.1 to find out more.

| Mini case study 5.1 | Expansion of an online brand offline |

According to Bravo *et al.* (2011), 'in recent years the offline and online spheres of strategic brand management are becoming more and more interconnected'. Part of the reason for this is that when offline companies decide to sell their product online they also need to establish the logistical and technical networks to support the operation. However, as companies seek to commercialise their products by using digital channels, the crossover from offline to online can lead to the creation of new online products and extend a brand's reach to a wider target audience. By operating offline, brands can build value in both environments, by extending their existing brand. For an offline brand a core reason for expanding online is accessing new markets, adding customer value and increasing flexibility through the use of multichannels. According to Burt (2010), established brands are 'getting more, rather than less important'. However, for a brand moving from online to offline the focus and opportunities are slightly different. Online brands can create awareness for their product and service offers and it may be possible to enhance consumer trust in the online brand (Delgado and Hernandez, 2008). But online brands must *get it right* if they are to enhance their brand positioning by going offline. Ebay, Amazon and Google have all experimented with physical stores. Ebay and Google set up shop in London, Amazon in New York. The Google store sold Chromebook laptops and accessories from a 'zone' within the Curry's PC World shop. Head of consumer marketing at Google UK said they have 'found anecdotally that when people tried the Chromebook and played with it, that it made a huge difference to their understanding of what the Chromebook is all about' (Meyer, 2011).

Online brands have yet to match up with their competitors in the physical high street. Even among the less well-established newer technology brands, for example, Apple has over 400 stores, Microsoft has stores in 63 locations and Samsung has plans for over 60 stores in Europe (Kelly, 2014).

For startup and established online brands, the issue of branding is more complex. The Internet and digital technologies have changed the global brand landscape. Since 1998, online brands have emerged and become household names in less than 15 years – e.g. Google, Amazon, eBay, Facebook (Interbrand, 2014). Digital technology has also brought distinctive features to the online **brand experience** (Morgan-Thomas and Veloutsou, 2013). An online brand is very similar to its offline counterparts insofar as it incorporates a name, set of symbols and product/service components. But according to Morgan-Thomas and Veloutsou (2013), the major difference is the context in which the customer experiences the brand. Online context tends to be:

Brand experience
The frequency and depth of interactions with a brand can be enhanced through the Internet.

- information rich;
- dynamic;
- characterised by excessive information flows;
- technologically innovative.

These authors (Morgan-Thomas and Veloutsou, 2013) expand further on the implications for online brand experiences. On the negative side, the virtual nature of the digital marketplace means there is a lack of physical cues and heightened challenges due to the intangibility of the environment and increased uncertainty of what engaging in an online experience will deliver. However, on the positive side, digital environments create opportunities for increased interactivity and real-time brand experiences, which can be empowering for the customer. Therefore, an online brand should seek to build links with customers by delivering positive online experiences, which then lead to satisfaction and positive intentions to interact with the brand in the future.

Consequently, positioning online brands requires marketers to think creatively about the traditional elements of a brand and also consider new elements.

- *Online brand domain* – where the brand competes. Google has established and maintained its market-leading position in the search engine marketplace by following the company's mission to 'organise the world's information and make it universally accessible'.
- *Online brand heritage* – Guinness is a brand with heritage going back over 200 years; use of the Internet has only been possible on a commercial scale since 1989, so online brands must look for other ways to develop their heritage. One way to do this is by offering genuine value. Online brands can get very close to their customers through use of digital technology and should seek to develop genuinely valuable relationships.
- *Online brand values* – the core characteristics, that the users of the brand value. AltaVista (launched 1995) was an early free search engine, which originally provided a clean user interface, similar to Google. But AltaVista soon lost market share when its search experience was rated lower than that of its new rival Google and it added other new services rather than focussing on the core deliverables the brand had to offer. It is important for online brands to emphasise the benefits of engaging with the brand and also to develop a unique personality that is engaging and shareable (Brown, 2014).
- *Online brand assets* – distinctive names, symbols, images. Twitter is an example of an online brand name which is distinctive, and with the bird symbol the brand assets help its users quickly assimilate with the brand. It is important to ensure that a company presents a standardised message at whatever touchpoint they interact with the online brand (Brown, 2014).
- *Online brand personality* – the character of the brand, which its customers use to determine the added value offered by the brand and also to express their own individual personalities through association with the brand (Valette-Florence *et al.*, 2011). Online brands need to understand their brands from the customer's perspective.
- *Online brand reflection* – how the customer perceives themselves as a result of buying the brand. Being authentic and transparent about what the brand stands for is important if an online brand is to create positive brand associations.

We return to the concept of brand promise at the start of Chapter 7 since this is closely related to delivering customer experience.

Success factors for brand sites

In Chapter 1, we identified a 'brand website' as one of five classes of website or parts of sites which support different organisational goals. Although other types of sites were mentioned, including transactional sites, relationship-building sites, portals and social networks all seek to provide a favourable brand experience. In the case of manufacturer 'brand sites', the manager of the site needs to carefully think of the best way the brand can engage with consumers given lack of content naturally associated with low-involvement products.

For the site itself, it is not the quantity of visitors that is important; rather it is about the quality of visitors, since brand sites are most likely to attract **brand advocates,** who can be important in influencing others to make them aware of the brand or trial the brand. Ries and Ries (2000) suggested that it is important that brand sites provide a home for the brand loyalists and advocates. It follows that brand owners should determine the type of content on a brand site which will encourage brand loyalists (and also the brand-neutral consumer) to visit and then return to the brand site. Flores (2004) has said that encouraging visitors to return is key and he suggests different aspects of a quality site experience to achieve this. Some of the methods he suggests to encourage visitors to return include:

> **Brand advocate**
> A customer who has favourable perceptions of a brand who will talk favourably about a brand to their acquaintances to help generate awareness of the brand or influence purchase intent.

- *creating a compelling, interactive experience including rich media which reflects the brand*. The research by Flores (2004) showed that a site which delivers an unsatisfactory experience will negatively affect brand perception. He notes that some brand sites which often contain rich media or video, although visually engaging, may have poor usability or download speeds.
- *considering how the site will influence the sales cycle by encouraging trial*. Trial will often be fulfilled offline so approaches such as samples, coupons or prize draws can be used. These response activators should be integrated throughout the site. For example, car brands will all have prominent options for taking a test drive, receiving a brochure or the option to win a car or a visit to a race circuit.
- developing an exchange (permission marketing) programme on your website to begin a 'conversation' with the most valuable customer segments. Permission-based email or text messages can be used to update consumers about new products or promotions.

Additionally we would stress the importance of achieving customer engagement with brand sites to encourage participation or co-creation of content. For example, brands can encourage users to share and submit their comments, stories, photos or videos. Once engaged in this way, visitors are more likely to return to a site to see others' comments.

Dorset Cereals (Figure 5.3, **www.dorsetcereals.co.uk**) gives a good example of how the opportunities for a consumer brand to engage its audiences have been well thought through. Some of the approaches they used are indicated by titles on the menu bar and the associated goals can be inferred. For example:

- *Buy things*. Goals – increase product usage. Provide content for brand advocates.
- *We make*. Goals – increase sales for new adoptions since product distribution is not as widespread as some brands.
- *Win stuff*. Goals: encourage trial and reward loyalists. The company has not used sampling to date, but instead has run prize draws related to the rural nature of its brand, e.g. win a Land Rover, win trips to flower shows, photo competitions. The current featured promotion is the 'naturally light-hearted challenge' which is a seven-day permission email supported programme to eat more healthily.
- *Blog (the notice board)*. Goal: engage site visitors and encourage involved customers to keep brand 'front-of-mind' through comments and posts.
- *Get in touch*. Goals: encourage feedback and dialogue.

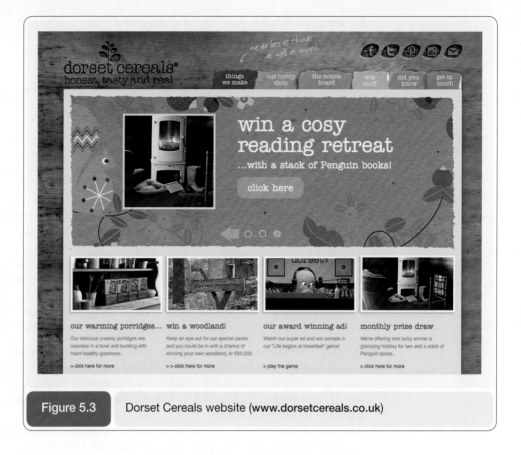

Figure 5.3 Dorset Cereals website (www.dorsetcereals.co.uk)

- *Online shop*. Goals: Direct sales of cereal and branded merchandise such as cereal bowls.
- *Social media* Goals: interact with target audiences and extend reach and customer understanding.
- *Sell our cereals*. Goal: Find additional distributors.

The success factors a brand uses should closely interlink with the brand's identity.

Brand identity

Brand identity
The totality of brand associations including name and symbols that must be communicated

Aaker and Joachimsthaler (2000) also emphasise the importance of developing a plan to communicate the key features of the **brand identity** and increase brand awareness. Brand identity is again more than the name. These authors refer to it as a set of brand associations that imply a promise to customers from an organisation.

Brand names for online brands

Ries and Ries (2000) suggest two rules for naming online brands.

1 The Law of the Common Name – they say 'the kiss of death for an Internet brand is a common name'. The idea is that common names such as **Art.com** or **Advertising.com** are poor since they are not sufficiently distinctive.
2 The Law of the Proper Name – they say 'your name stands alone on the Internet, so you'd better have a good one'. This suggests that proper names are to be preferred to generic names, e.g. **PinkMoods.com** against **Woman.com**.

More recent research has found that the characteristics of the word chosen to represent a brand can influence consumer behaviour (Vitevitch and Donoso, 2011) and be linked to the propensity with which a buyer will engage with a brand. This study suggests that in order to increase the likelihood that a consumer will engage with a new brand, it should be easy to pronounce, have interesting arrangements of syllables and consonants so as to make the name easy to recall but should not be too similar to other words (thereby causing confusion with other brand names).

In essence good brand names are those which are easy to remember and pronounce but also have potential to catch the attention of customers (Brand Name Generator, 2015).

Activity 5.2	How to develop a new brand name

Purpose

To illustrate how non-words (those not recognised in everyday language) can be used as brand names.

Activity

Visit the Brand name generator at **http://business-name-generators.com/generator. php?gen=brand-name-generator**; and then generate new brand names which you feel have potential as online brands. Evaluate your choice using the following criteria:

1 Easy to pronounce Y/N
2 Easy to remember Y/N
3 Intriguing word pattern (syllables and consonants) Y/N
4 Has the potential to attract attention Y/N
5 Not close to existing known word(s) Y/N
6 Creates a feeling of trust Y/N
7 Has an 'air' of professionalism Y/N

Once you have a name which you feel has potential to be successful (more than five Ys) suggests some products which could fit with the name.

From a practical perspective, if you are registering a domain for a new company it is also worth remembering that search engines tend to favour sites in their listings which include the name of the service which is searched for within the domain name. For example, a domain name such as MyVoucherCodes (**www.myvouchercodes.com**) will tend to rank well for 'voucher codes' since the search engine will see sites linking to it which contains the words 'voucher codes' (note that due to changes in Google's algorithm this is true to a lesser extent than previously).

Price

Price variable
The element of the marketing mix that involves defining product prices and pricing models.

Pricing models
Describe the form of payment such as outright purchase, auction, rental, volume purchases and credit terms.

The **Price variable** of the marketing mix refers to an organisation's pricing policies which are used to define **pricing models** and, of course, to set prices for products and services. The Internet has dramatic implications for pricing in many sectors. Initially, research suggested that two approaches have been commonly adopted for pricing on the Internet: startup companies have tended to use low prices to gain a customer base, while many existing companies have transferred their existing prices to the web (Baker *et al.*, 2000; Xing *et al.*, 2006). However, as organisations are increasingly developing multichannel strategies in order to give their customers more opportunities to interact with brands, it becomes more difficult to justify online and offline pricing policies, especially in consumer markets. Dixons Carphone Warehouse, for example, not only offers uniform pricing across its brands but also has a Price Comparison App which allows its users to search for products by key word or bar codes and then get instant price comparisons for other retailers selling identical products (PC World, 2015). Low-cost airlines sell the majority of their products online and penalise consumers with higher prices if they do not buy online. However, for companies selling tangible goods, it is becoming harder to legitimise differential online pricing.

The Pricing element mix invariably relates to the Product element (even when the offer is a service), since online pricing depends on the range of products offered and the point at which a product is in its lifecycle. Extending the product range may allow these products to be discounted online. Some organisations have launched new products online which have a lower Price element; for example, banks have launched 'eSavings' products where higher interest rates are offered to online customers in order to attract new customers. Alternatively, they may offer insurance products with a 10 per cent online discount in order to encourage customers to switch to the digital channel. Often these agreements are dependent on the customer servicing their account online, which helps reduce the cost-base of the bank. This then relates to the service elements of the mix since service has to be delivered online. See Digital marketing insight 5.3.

The main implications of the Internet for the price aspect of the mix, which we will review in this section, are:

1 increased price transparency and its implications on differential pricing;
2 downward pressure on price (including commoditisation);
3 new pricing approaches (including dynamic pricing, price testing and auctions);
4 alternative pricing structure or policies.

Digital marketing insight 5.3   **Discounting options for online services**

Some service industry providers face a challenge with regard to pricing due to the nature of their products: their inventory – e.g. theatre, airline and event tickets – cannot be stored for future use in the same way that products can. So the service provider faces the constant dilemma of how much and when to discount prices to maximise the sales of *perishable* services. In the hotel industry, in the low season there are many un-booked rooms due to low demand but these cannot be stored for the high season. However, the profit margins of hotel rooms are relatively high for each let room. So the challenge is how to increase use of the *perishable* rooms (Guo *et al.*, 2013). The authors suggest that profits in the hotel industry can be increased significantly 'with a proper pricing strategy provided by market segmentation'. The Internet and online reservation systems (ORS) have enabled this approach and are now widely used around the globe. ORS have become increasingly sophisticated and offer dynamic pricing based on target segments and lead times. This has enabled hoteliers to engage in sophisticated pricing strategies in an attempt to maximise sales. Some offer variable discounts for booking in advance (e.g. Marriott International, Hilton), while others offer fixed discounts. The pricing approaches can vary depending on the target segments, frequency of use, loyalty and many other related variables. Dynamic pricing strategies used in conjunction with ORS have benefited the hotel industry and where applied effectively increased profitability. However, the book anytime, any place, anywhere model which underpins this new way of booking rooms also has its limitations. The hotel industry has to deal with 'cancellations and no-shows', so sometimes hotels add into their ORS the capacity to overbook (Ling *et al.*, 2014). Or a more innovative approach of 'Name Your Own Price'.

1 Increased price transparency

Quelch and Klein (1996) described two contradictory effects of the Internet on price that are related to **price transparency**. First, a supplier can use the technology for **differential pricing** – for example, for customers in different countries (or as discussed in Digital marketing insight 5.3). However, if precautions are not taken about price, the customers may be able to quickly find out about the price discrimination through price comparison and they will object to it.

Pricing online has to take into account the concept of **price elasticity of demand**. This is a measure of consumer behaviour based on economic theory that indicates the change in demand for a product or service in response to changes in price. Price elasticity of demand is determined by the price of the product, availability of alternative goods from alternative suppliers (which tends to increase online) and consumer income. A product is said to be 'elastic' (or responsive to price changes) if a small change in price increases or reduces the demand substantially. A product is 'inelastic' if a large change in price is accompanied by a small amount of change in demand.

Although, intuitively, we would think that price transparency enabled through the Internet price comparison services such as **Shopping.com** (owned by eBay), which leads to searching by product rather than by store level, would lead to common comparisons of price and the selection of the cheapest product – but the reality seems different. Pricing online is relatively inelastic. There are two main reasons for this. First, pricing is only one variable – consumers also decide on suppliers according to other aspects about the brand such as familiarity, trust and perceived service levels. Second, consumers often display **satisficing behaviour**. The term 'satisfice' was coined by Herbert Simon in 1957 when he said that people are only 'rational enough' and that they suspend or relax their rationality if they feel it is no longer required. This is called 'bounded rationality' by cognitive psychologists. In other words, although consumers may seek to minimise some variable (such as price) when making a product or supplier selection, most may not try too hard. Online, this is supported by research (Johnson *et al.*, 2004; Allan, 2012) which has shown that shoppers visit a number of web stores before making their purchase decisions. In the early days of online shopping, choices were limited and consumer confidence in the digital marketplace was relatively low. Currently, consumers – on average – visit at least three websites prior to making their purchase decisions and there is an indication that the more sites they visit the more likely they are to make a purchase.

Retailers or other transactional e-commerce companies operating in markets where their products are readily reviewed online need to review their strategy towards the impact of **aggregators** which facilitate price comparison. One strategy for companies in the face of increased price transparency is to highlight the other features of the brand – such as the quality of the retail experience, fulfilment choice or customer service – to reduce the emphasis on cost as a differentiator. Another strategy is to educate the market about the limitations in aggregators such as incomplete coverage or limited information about delivery or service levels.

Arguably, this conflict shows the importance of companies that are featured within aggregators possessing a strong brand which can offer additional value in terms of customer service or trust. It also shows the continuing importance of offline advertising in shaping consumer perceptions of brands and to drive visitors directly to a destination site.

For business commodities, auctions on business-to-business exchanges can also have a similar effect of driving down price. Purchase of some products that have not traditionally been thought of as commodities may become more price sensitive. This process is known as **commoditisation**. Examples of goods that are becoming commoditised include electrical goods and cars.

Activity 5.3	Assessing price ranges on the Internet

Purpose

To illustrate the concept of price transparency.

Activity

Visit a price comparison site, e.g. **www.pricerunner.com**; **www.confused.com**; **money-supermarket.com** (Figure 5.4); **www.gocompare.com** and then find the products below and examples of the best and worst offers:

- insurance
- a personal loan
- a savings product

Figure 5.4	My Supermarket aggregator (www.mysupermarket.co.uk)

2 Downward pressure on price

The competition caused by price transparency and increased number of competitors is the main reason for downward pressure on price. Many aggregators or comparison sites have benefited from this approach (e.g. **mysupermarket.com**). For example, Figure 5.4 shows an example of this website comparing four different supermarkets showing the variation in prices between Tesco, ASDA, Sainsbury's and Ocado. However, you should be aware when looking at price comparisons that you are not always seeing a like-for-like comparison; products can vary, especially when supermarket own-brands are in the shopping basket.

The Internet also tends to drive down prices since Internet-only retailers that do not have a physical presence do not have the overheads of operating stores and a retailer distribution network. This means that, in theory, online companies can operate at lower

Pricing level
The price set for a specific product or range of products.

pricing levels than offline rivals. This phenomenon is prevalent in the banking sector where many banks have set up online companies or online-only accounts offering better rates of interest on savings products. Online purchase discounts are a common approach in many markets.

Price elasticity of demand (see Digital marketing insight 5.4) assesses the extent to which a change in price will influence the demand for a product. It is calculated as the change in quantity demanded (expressed as a percentage) divided by the change in price as a percentage. Different products will naturally have different coefficients of price elasticity of demand depending on where they lie on the continuum of consumer tastes from relatively undifferentiated commodities to luxury, highly differentiated products where the brand perception is important.

Digital marketing insight 5.4   **Price elasticity of demand**

The formula for the price elasticity of demand is:

$$\text{Price elasticity of demand coefficient} = \frac{(\% \text{ change in quantity demanded})}{(\% \text{ change in price})}$$

Price elasticity for products is generally described as:

- *Elastic (coefficient of price elasticity > 1).* Here, the percentage change in quantity demanded is greater than the percentage change in price. In elastic demand, the demand curve is relatively shallow and a small percentage increase in price leads to a reduction in revenue. On balance overall, when the price is raised, the total revenue of producers or retailers falls since the rise in revenue does not compensate for the fall in demand; and when the price is decreased, total revenue rises because the income from additional customers compensates in the decrease in revenue from reduced prices. Figure 5.5 shows the demand curve for a relatively elastic product (price elasticity = 1.67).

Price reduced from £50 to £250
% change in price = 60%
% change in demand = 100%
Price elasticity = 1.67
i.e. demand is price elastic

Figure 5.5   Price elasticity of demand for a relatively elastic product

- *Inelastic demand (coefficient of price elasticity < 1).* Here, the percentage change in quantity demanded is smaller than the percentage change in price. In inelastic demand, the demand curve is relatively steep and a small percentage increase in price causes a small decrease in demand. On balance overall revenue increases as the price increases and falls as the price falls. Figure 5.6 shows the demand curve for a relatively inelastic product (price elasticity = 0.3125).

When the price elasticity coefficient is close to 1, this is described as unit elastic or unitary elastic. At the limits of elasticity, products will vary from:

- *perfectly elastic (coefficient is not infinite),* effectively shown as a horizontal line on demand curve graphs such as Figure 5.5 where any increase in the price will cause demand (and revenue for the goods) to drop to zero.
- *perfectly inelastic (coefficient of price elasticity is zero),* effectively shown as a vertical line on demand curve graphs such as Figure 5.6 where changes in the price do not affect the quantity demanded for the good.

When the price elasticity value is 1 of the demand for a good it is known as *unit elastic (or unitary elastic).*

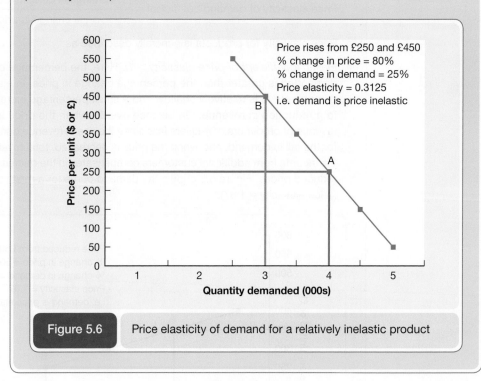

| Figure 5.6 | Price elasticity of demand for a relatively inelastic product |

Discounting of the most popular products is another pricing approach used by both online and traditional retailers to acquire customers or drive sales. For example, online booksellers may decide to offer a discount of 50 per cent on the top 25 best-selling books in each category, for which no profit is made, but offer a smaller discount on less popular books to give a profit margin.

Xing *et al.* (2006) reported in their study of pricing levels for DVD merchants, summarised in Table 5.1, that traditional multichannel marketing companies tend to charge higher prices than pureplays or dot-com only companies, although pureplays will adjust their prices upwards more rapidly. However, they noted that this is market-specific and

Table 5.1	A summary of the differences in pricing among DVD retailers from the research of Xing *et al.* (2006)					
All titles			**Popular titles**		**Random titles**	
Retailer type	**Average**	**Standard deviation**	**Average**	**Standard deviation**	**Average**	**Standard deviation**
Pureplay example – Amazon	21.51Q	3.90	21.05	3.72	21.99	4.02
Multichannel example – Borders	22.95	4.44	22.57	4.01	23.34	4.81
Pureplay average	20.54	3.75	20.42	3.60	20.6	63.90
Multichannel retailer average	22.28	4.27	22.02	4.19	22.55	4.33

Price dispersion
The distribution or range of prices charged for an item across different retailers.

when sales tax and shipping are taken into account, pureplays often charge more than multichannel merchants, as they found in a previous study of the consumer electronic market. They also found that **price dispersion** tended to be less for pureplays.

Baker *et al.* (2000) suggest that companies should use the following three factors to assist in pricing.

1 *Precision*. Each product has a price-indifference band, where varying price has little or no impact on sales. The authors report that these bands can be as wide as 17 per cent for branded consumer beauty products, 10 per cent for engineered industrial components, but less than 10 per cent for some financial products. The authors suggest that while the cost of undertaking a survey to calculate price indifference is very expensive in the real world, it is more effective online.

2 *Adaptability*. This refers simply to the fact that it is possible to respond more quickly to the demands of the marketplace with online pricing. For some product areas, such as ticketing, it may be possible to dynamically alter prices in line with demand. **Tickets .com** adjusts concert ticket prices according to demand and has been able to achieve 45 per cent more revenue per event as a result. Arguably, in this case, and for other sought-after items such as computer games or luxury cars, the Internet can actually increase the price since there it is possible to reach more people.

3 *Segmentation*. This refers to pricing differently for different groups of customers. This has not traditionally been practical for B2C markets since at the point of sale, information is not known about the customer, although it is widely practised for B2B markets. One example of pricing by segments would be for a car manufacturer to vary promotional pricing, so that rather than offering every purchaser discount purchasing or cash-back, it is only offered to those for whom it is thought necessary to make the sale. A further example is where a company can identify regular customers and fill in customers who only buy from the supplier when their needs can't be met elsewhere. In the latter case, up to 20 per cent higher prices are levied.

What then are the options available to marketers given this downward pressure on pricing? We will start by looking at traditional methods for pricing and how they are affected by the Internet. Bickerton *et al.* (2000) identify a range of options that are available for setting pricing.

1 *Cost-plus pricing*. This involves adding on a profit margin based on production costs. As we have seen above, a reduction in this margin may be required in the Internet era.

2 *Target-profit pricing*. This is a more sophisticated pricing method that involves looking at the fixed and variable costs in relation to income for different sales volumes and unit prices. Using this method, the breakeven amount for different combinations can be calculated. For e-commerce sales the variable selling cost (i.e. the cost for each transaction) is small. This means that once breakeven is achieved each sale has a large margin. With this model differential pricing is often used in a B2B context according to the volume of goods sold. Care needs to be taken that differential prices are not evident to different customers. One company, through an error on its website, made prices for different customers available for all to see, with disastrous results.

3 *Competition-based pricing*. This approach is common online. The advent of price comparison engines such as Kelkoo (**www.kelkoo.com**) for B2C consumables has increased price competition and companies need to develop online pricing strategies that are flexible enough to compete in the marketplace, but are still sufficient to achieve profitability in the channel. This approach may be used for the most popular products, such as the top 25 CDs, but other methods, such as target-profit pricing, will be used for other products.

4 *Market-orientated pricing*. Here the response to price changes by customers making up the market are considered. This is known as 'the elasticity of demand'. There are two approaches. *Premium pricing* (or *skimming the market*) involves setting a higher price than the competition to reflect the positioning of the product as a high-quality item. Penetration pricing is when a price is set below the competitors' prices to either stimulate demand or increase penetration. This approach was commonly used by dot-com companies to acquire customers. The difficulty with this approach is that if customers are price-sensitive then the low price has to be sustained – otherwise customers may change to a rival supplier. This has happened with online banks – some customers regularly move to reduce costs of overdrafts, for example. Alternatively, if a customer is concerned by other aspects such as service quality, it may be necessary to create a large price differential in order to encourage the customer to change supplier.

While there is much research evidence that suggests the Internet has had a downwards impact on pricing, this may not be so prevalent in the future. As the Internet has become a more mainstream shopping channel, consumers are tending to focus more on the quality of the services provided rather than the price.

3 New pricing approaches (including auctions)

The Internet has proved to have the technological capacity to create new pricing options. Figure 5.7 summarises different pricing mechanisms, which have been used effectively online. While many of these were available before the advent of the Internet and are not new, the Internet has made some models easier to apply. In particular, the volume of users makes traditional or **forward auctions** (B2C) and **reverse auctions** (B2B) more tenable – these have become more widely used than previously.

An **offer** is a commitment for a trader to sell under certain conditions, such as a minimum price. A **bid** is made by a trader to buy under the conditions of the bid, such as a commitment to purchase at a particular price. In a sealed-bid arrangement, suppliers submit their bids in response to an RFP posted to a website at a set time. In an open-bid arrangement, suppliers bid sequentially through a series of product lots or subgroups and can view their competitors' bids and respond in real time. A moving end-time (a 'soft close') is used for each lot, which means that any bid within the last minute of the closing time automatically extends the end time for a few minutes to allow other bidders to respond.

Forward auctions
Item purchased by highest bid made in bidding period.

Reverse auctions
Item purchased from lowest-bidding supplier in bidding period.

Offer
A commitment by a trader to sell under certain conditions.

Bid
A commitment by a trader to purchase under certain conditions.

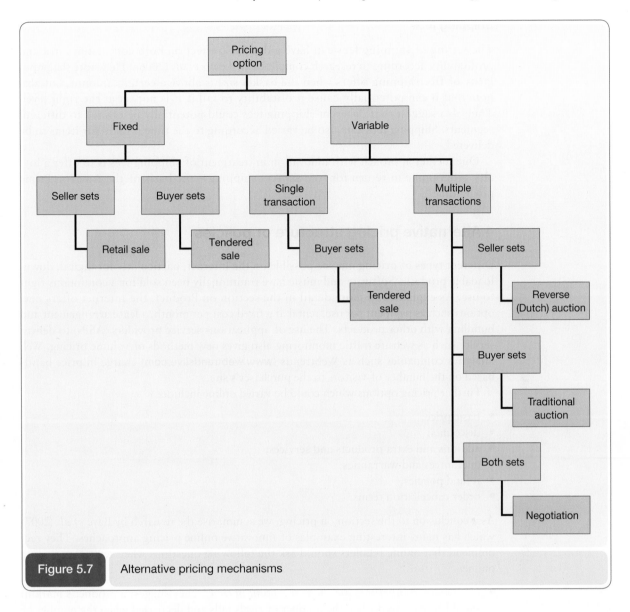

| Figure 5.7 | Alternative pricing mechanisms |

Price testing and dynamic pricing

Dynamic pricing
Prices can be updated in real time according to the type of customer or current market conditions

The Internet introduces new opportunities for **dynamic pricing** – for example, new customers could automatically be given discounted purchases for the first three items. Care has to be taken with differential pricing since established customers will be unhappy if significant discounts are given to new customers. Amazon trialled such a discounting scheme and it received negative press and had to be withdrawn when people found out that their friends or colleagues had paid less. If the scheme had been a clear introductory promotion this problem may not have arisen.

Baye *et al.* (2007) reported that European electronics online retailer Pixmania (**www .pixmania.com**) used price experimentation to learn about its customers' price sensitivity. They noted that for a PDA, Pixmania adjusted its product price 11 times in a 14-week period, from a low of £268 to a high of £283, as part of a series of small experiments that enabled it to learn about the price sensitivities of its customers. This pricing strategy also provides an additional strategic benefit – unpredictability.

Shipping fees

The setting of shipping fees can have a dramatic effect on both conversion rates and profitability according to research completed by Lewis *et al.* (2006). They note the popularity of free shipping offers when the basket size is above a certain amount, but also note that it can potentially cause profitability to fall if it is not set at the right level. They also suggest that different shipping fees could potentially be offered to different segments. Shipping fees can also be varied according to the time it takes for items to be delivered.

One further approach with innovation in treatment of shipping fees is to offer a loyalty programme in return for free express shipping – the basis of the Amazon Prime programme.

4 Alternative pricing structure or policies

Different types of pricing may be possible on the Internet, particularly for digital, downloadable products. Software and music have traditionally been sold for a continuous right to use. As explained in more detail in the section on Product, the Internet offers new options such as payment per use, rental at a fixed cost per month, a lease arrangement and bundling with other products. The use of applications service providers (ASPs) to deliver service such as website traffic monitoring also gives new methods of volume pricing. Web analytics companies such as Webtrends (**www.webtrendslive.com**) charge in price bands based on the number of visitors to the purchaser's site.

Further pricing options which could be varied online include:

- basic price;
- discounts;
- add-ons and extra products and services;
- guarantees and warranties;
- refund policies;
- order cancellation terms.

As a conclusion to the section on pricing, we summarise the research by Baye *et al.* (2007) which has many interesting examples of innovative online pricing approaches. They recommend that online retailers should ask the following questions when reviewing pricing online:

- *How many competitors are there at a point in time?* They suggest a product's markup should be increased when the number of rivals falls and decreased when the number of rivals increases. They also recommend that since the identity of competitors online will differ from traditional offline rivals it is important to include key online competitors.
- *What is the position in the product lifecycle?* A product's markup should be decreased over its lifecycle or when new versions are introduced.
- *What is the price sensitivity or elasticity of a product?* They suggest continuously experimenting to learn from changes in the price sensitivity of a product.
- *What level is pricing set?* The optimal markup factor should be applied at the product rather than category or firm level based on price testing at the product level. They also note the variation of conversion rates and click-through fees from paid search engines and aggregators at the category or product level which makes it important to have micro-management of pricing.
- *Are rivals monitoring my price?* Be unpredictable if rivals are watching; exploit 'blind spots' if rivals are not watching.
- *Are we stuck in the middle?* A middle pricing point is suboptimal, particularly if prices can be set to target the lowest point in the market.

Place

Place variable
The element of the marketing mix that involves distributing products to customers in line with demand and minimising cost of inventory, transport and storage.

The **Place variable** of the marketing mix refers to how the product is distributed to customers. Typically, for offline channels, the aim of Place is to maximise the reach of distribution to achieve widespread availability of products while minimising the costs of inventory, transport and storage. In an online context, thanks to ease of navigating from one site to another, the scope of Place is less clear since Place also relates to Promotion and Partnerships. Take the example of a retailer of mobile phones. For this retailer to reach its potential audience to sell and distribute its product, it has to think beyond its own website to third-party websites where it can promote its services. Successful retailers are those that maximise their representation or visibility on third-party sites which are used by their target audiences. These third-party sites will include search engines, online portals reviewing mobile phones and product comparison sites. When thinking about representation on third-party sites, it is useful to think of the long-tail concept (Anderson, 2004) referenced in Figure 5.2. Across all Internet sites, there are a small number of sites including portals such as Google, MSN and Yahoo! which are very popular (the head, which may theoretically account for 80 per cent of the volume of visitors) and a much larger number of sites that are less popular individually, but still collectively important. Similarly within a category of sites, such as automotive, there will be a few very popular sites, and then many niche sites which are collectively important in volume and may be more effective at reaching a niche target audience. When considering Place and Promotion, it is important to target both the head and the tail to maximise reach and to attract quality visitors to the destination site.

The main implications of the Internet for the Place aspect of the mix, which we will review in this section, are:

1 place of purchase;
2 new channel structures;
3 channel conflicts;
4 virtual organisations.

1 Place of purchase

Suggesting the concept of place in relation to the Internet may seem peculiar; as it is a global virtual environment that crosses geographical boundaries, the issues associated with distribution, logistics and the point at which sales and other transactions take place are important for digital marketers. For example, when selling physical goods there are cost and time issues associated with fulfilment (local, regional and international) together with issues of trust, culture and local support networks. However, in the case of sellers of digital products there is no physical limitation on fulfilment. For example, Apple iTunes has proved successful in offering this service worldwide. Read Mini case study 5.2.

Evans and Wurster (1999) argued there are three aspects of 'navigational advantage' that are key to achieving competitive advantage online. These three, which all relate to the Place elements of the mix, are:

- *Reach*. Evans and Wurster say: 'It [reach] means, simply, how many customers a business can connect with and how many products it can offer to those customers'. Reach can be increased by moving from a single site to representation with a large number of different intermediaries. Allen and Fjermestad (2001) suggest that niche suppliers can readily reach a much wider market due to search-engine marketing (Chapter 8). Evans and Wurster also suggest that reach refers to the range of products and services that can be offered since this will increase the number of people the company can appeal to.

Mini case study 5.2	Internet retailing: the past, present and future

Retailers make a good case for exploring the impact of the Internet on the place element of the marketing. Since the beginning of the online shopping era there have been many predictions made about the likely impact of the Internet. However, according to Doherty and Ellis-Chadwick (2010), not all of these have come to fruition. They state, 'Retailers are not cannibalising their own custom, virtual merchants do not dominate the market place and the high street has not been put out of business', but they are seeing a rise in the role of one to one marketing, increasing competition and a shift in power from the retailer to the consumer (Doherty and Ellis-Chadwick, 2010).

Currently, many academic studies are 'beginning to play down the chances of the Internet having a significant destabilising effect on the viability of the high street' (Doherty and Ellis-Chadwick, 2010). However, certain product activity sectors such as music, entertainment, print publishing and travel agents have significantly reduced their high street presence due to the impact of the Internet. Furthermore, although in the majority of retail sectors the Internet is having less impact on the physicality of retailing, it is widely agreed that consumer behaviour is changing in so far as shoppers are going online to find information about the products and services they wish to buy.

Whilst it may not be possible to determine the degree to which the Internet is going to impact on the physical high street it is clear that the influence of online shopping is set to rise.

Now listen to where UK retailers think they are going to be in the next five years: www.open.edu/openlearn/money-management/management/retail-management-and-marketing?track=13.

Source: Based on Doherty and Ellis-Chadwick (2010)

- *Richness*. This is the depth or detail of information which is both collected about the customer and provided to the customer. The latter is related to the richness of product information and how well it can be personalised to be relevant to the individual needs.
- *Affiliation*. This refers to whose interest the selling organisation represents – consumers' or suppliers' – and stresses the importance of forming the right partnerships. This particularly applies to retailers. The authors suggest that successful online retailers will reward customers who provide them with the richest information on comparing competitive products. They suggest this tilts the balance in favour of the customer.

Table 5.2	Different places for virtual marketplace representation

Place of purchase	Examples of sites
A Seller-controlled	• Vendor sites, i.e. home site of organisation selling products – e.g. **www.dell.com**
B Seller-orientated	• Intermediaries controlled by third parties to the seller such as distributors and agents – e.g. Opodo (**www.opodo.com**) represents the main air carriers. Amazon marketplace where third-parties can sell products
C Neutral	• Intermediaries not controlled by buyer's industry • Product-specific search engines – e.g. CNET (**www.cnet.com**) • Comparison sites – e.g. uSwitch (**www.uswitch.com**) energy industry
D Buyer-orientated	• My Supermarket (**www.mysupermarket.com**) • Intermediaries controlled by buyers – e.g. the remaining parts of the Covisint network of motor manufacturers • Discount sites for consumers such as voucher code sites – e.g. **www.myvouchercodes.com** – and Cashback sites – e.g. GreasyPalm (**www.greasypalm.com**)
E Buyer-controlled	• Website procurement posting or reverse auctions on company's own site

Syndication

Traditionally, **syndication** referred to articles or extracts from books being included in other publications such as newspapers and magazines. In an online context, this practice related to Place and partnerships needs to be reviewed for online content owners since there may be opportunities to generate additional revenue by re-publishing content on third-party sites through feeds, widgets or data exchange, or it may be possible to increase exposure on partner sites and so generate awareness or visits to the company site. For example, through its Connect service, **Amazon.com** enables authors to publish a blog on their site based on an RSS feed (see Chapter 1) from their own blog, so increasing awareness of the blog.

But syndication also has implications for other companies, and in particular retailers, since syndication of information from their product catalogues to third-party aggregators is important to extend their reach. Retailers need to consider participating in Google Shopping so that Product Listing Ads (PLAs, Figure 5.8) are displayed to increase awareness (see Chapter 9, the section on search marketing).

Since integrating product data with a range of aggregators that will require formats can be time-consuming, some companies such as Channel Advisor (**www.channeladvisor.com**) now offer a service to upload data and track results across a range of aggregators.

Payment mechanisms – purchase place

Traditionally, online purchase will occur at the retailer through a partnership with an online secure payment provider such as Worldpay (**www.worldpay.com**). Effectively, the purchase transaction occurs on a different domain, but it is important that customers are reassured that the payment process is secure and to make it seamless. Retailers often offer payment mechanisms where the purchaser has already set up payment with another payment provider, such as PayPal (**www.paypal.com**). This approach can assist with reassurance about

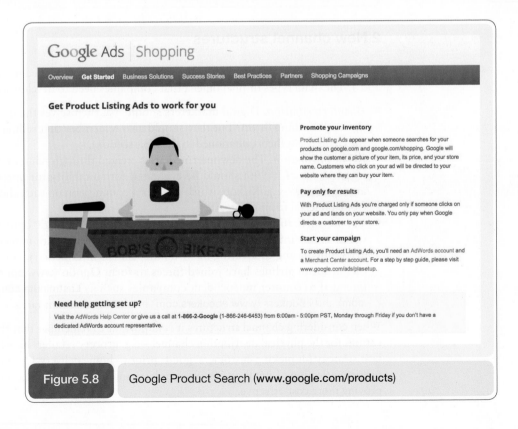

| Figure 5.8 | Google Product Search (www.google.com/products) |

privacy and security and increase purchase convenience and choice for the user, so these options also have to be reviewed.

Localisation

Localisation
Tailoring of website information for individual countries or regions. Localisation can include simple translation, but also cultural adaptation.

Providing a local site, with or without a language-specific version and additional cultural adaptations, is referred to as **localisation**. A site may need to support customers from a range of countries with:

* different product needs;
* language differences;
* cultural adaptation.

Some approaches used for cultural adaptation and localisation are described further in Chapter 7 in the section on localisation.

Activity 5.4	Place of purchase on the Internet

Purpose

To explore connections between physical and virtual locations.

Activity

Imagine you are going to purchase a second-hand car. Set out the stages in the process you might go through from thinking about the car you might buy to finding a place to purchase your car and then identifying the final car you might buy.

While you are going through this process try to identify when you will be using the Internet (virtual environment) and when you will be in the physical environment (e.g. visiting car dealers).

---

2 New channel structures

New channel structures enabled by the Internet have been described in detail in Chapters 2 and 4. The main types of phenomena that companies need to develop strategies for are:

* *Disintermediation.* Digital marketers should ask themselves the question: is there an option for selling direct? But they should also remember that selling direct can lead to the channel conflicts (mentioned in the next section).
* *Reintermediation.* The new intermediaries created through reintermediation described by Sarkar *et al.* (1996) should be evaluated for suitability for partnering in affiliate arrangements – e.g. Kelkoo, which receives a commission on each click or sale resulting from a referral from its site.
* *Countermediation.* Countermediation refers to the strategic options to make better use of online intermediaries, such as through partnering with independent intermediaries, purchasing or creating its own independent intermediary. For example, a group of European airlines have joined forces to form Opodo (**www.opodo.com**), which is intended to counter independent companies such as **Lastminute.com** (**www.lastminute .com**) and eBookers (**www.ebookers.com**) in offering discount fares.

When considering channel structures it is important to remember that there may be implications for the physical distribution channel – e.g. grocery retailers have had to identify the best strategy for picking customers' goods prior to home delivery. Options include in-store picking (selection of items on customer orders) and regional picking centres. The former is proving more cost-effective.

3 Channel conflicts

A significant threat arising from the introduction of an Internet channel is that while disintermediation gives a company the opportunity to sell direct and increase profitability on products, it can also threaten distribution arrangements with existing partners. Such channel conflicts are described by Frazier (1999), and need to be carefully managed. Frazier identifies some situations when the Internet should only be used as a communications channel. This is particularly the case where manufacturers offer an exclusive, or highly selective, distribution approach. To take an example, a company manufacturing expensive watches costing thousands of pounds will not in the past have sold direct, but will have used a wholesaler to distribute watches via retailers. If this wholesaler is a powerful player in the watch distribution supply chain, they will react against the watch manufacturer selling directly to the consumer. The wholesaler may even refuse to act as distributor and may threaten to distribute only a competitor's watches, which are not available over the Internet. Furthermore, direct sales may damage the product's brand or change its price positioning.

Further channel conflicts involve other stakeholders including sales representatives and customers. Sales representatives may see the Internet as a direct threat to their livelihood. In some cases, such as Avon cosmetics and Encyclopaedia Britannica, this has proved to be the case, with this sales model being partly or completely replaced by the Internet. For many B2B purchases, sales representatives remain an essential method of reaching the customer to support them in the purchase decision. Here, following training of sales staff, the Internet can be used as a sales support and customer education tool. Customers who do not use the online channels may also respond negatively if lower prices are available to their online counterparts. This is less serious than other types of channel conflict.

To assess channel conflicts it is necessary to consider the different forms of channel the Internet can take. These are:

- a communication channel only;
- a distribution channel to intermediaries;
- a direct sales channel to customers;
- any combination of the above.

To avoid channel conflicts, the appropriate combination of channels must be arrived at. For example, Frazier (1999) notes that using the Internet as a direct sales channel may not be wise when a product's price varies considerably across global markets. In the watch manufacturer example, it may be best to use the Internet as a communication channel only.

Digital channel strategy will, of course, depend on the existing arrangements for the market. If a geographical market is new and there are no existing agents or distributors, there is unlikely to be channel conflict in that there is a choice of distribution through the Internet only or appointments of new agents to support Internet sales, or a combination of the two. Often SMEs will attempt to use the Internet to sell products without appointing agents, but this strategy will only be possible for retail products that need limited pre-sales and after-sales support. For higher-value products such as engineering equipment, which will require skilled sales staff to support the sale and after-sales servicing, agents will have to be appointed.

For existing geographical markets in which a company already has a mechanism for distribution in the form of agents and distributors, the situation is more complex, and there is the threat of channel conflict. The strategic options available when an existing reseller arrangement is in place have been described by Kumar (1999):

- *No Internet sales.* Neither the company nor any of its resellers makes sales over the Internet. This will be the option to follow when a company, or its resellers, feel that the number of buyers has not reached the critical mass thought to warrant the investment in an online sales capability.

- *Internet sales by reseller only*. A reseller who is selling products from many companies may have sufficient aggregated demand (through selling products for other companies) to justify the expense of setting up online sales. The manufacturer may also not have the infrastructure to fulfil orders direct to customers without further investment, whereas the reseller will be set up for this already. In this case it is unlikely that a manufacturer would want to block sales via the Internet channel.
- *Internet sales by manufacturer only*. It would be unusual if a manufacturer chose this option if it already had existing resellers in place. Were the manufacturer to do so, it would probably lead to lost sales as the reseller would perhaps stop selling through traditional channels.
- *Internet sales by all*. This option is arguably the logical future for Internet sales. It is also likely to be the result if the manufacturer does not take a proactive approach to controlling Internet sales.

Strategy will need to be reviewed annually and the sales channels changed as thought appropriate. Given the fast rate of change of e-commerce, it will probably not be possible to create a five-year plan! Kumar (1999) notes that history suggests that most companies have a tendency to use existing distribution networks for too long. The reason for this is that resellers may be powerful within a channel and the company does not want to alienate them, for fear of losing sales.

4 Virtual organisations

Benjamin and Wigand (1995) state that 'it is becoming increasingly difficult to delineate accurately the borders of today's organisations' and a further implication of the introduction of electronic networks such as the Internet is that it becomes easier to outsource aspects of the production and distribution of goods to third parties. This can lead to the boundaries within an organisation becoming blurred. Employees may work in any time zone, and customers are able to purchase tailored products from any location. The absence of any rigid boundary or hierarchy within the organisation should lead to a company becoming more responsive and flexible, and having a greater market orientation. Davidow and Malone (1992) describe the virtual corporation as follows:

> To the outside observer, it will appear almost edgeless, with permeable and continuously changing interfaces between company, supplier and customer. From inside the firm, the view will be no less amorphous, with traditional offices, departments, and operating divisions constantly reforming according to need. Job responsibilities will regularly shift.

Kraut *et al.* (1998) suggest the following features of a **virtual organisation**:

Virtual organisation
A virtual organisation uses information and communications technology to allow it to operate without clearly defined physical boundaries between different functions. It provides customised services by outsourcing production and other functions to third parties.

- Processes transcend the boundaries of a single form and are not controlled by a single organisational hierarchy.
- Production processes are flexible, with different parties involved at different times.
- Parties involved in the production of a single product are often geographically dispersed.
- Given this dispersion, coordination is heavily dependent on telecommunications and data networks.

Introna (2001) notes that a key aspect of the virtual organisation is strategic alliances or partnering. The ease of forming such alliances in the value network (as described in Chapter 2) is one of the factors that has given rise to the virtual organisation.

All companies tend to have some elements of the virtual organisation. The process whereby these characteristics increase is known as **virtualisation**. Malone *et al.* (1987) argued that the presence of electronic networks tends to lead to virtualisation since they enable the governance and coordination of business transactions to be conducted effectively at lower cost.

Virtualisation
The process whereby a company develops more of the characteristics of a virtual organisation.

What are the implications for a marketing strategist of this trend towards virtualisation? Initially it may appear that outsourcing does not have direct relevance to market orientation.

However, an example shows the relevance. Michael Dell relates (in Magretta, 1998) that Dell does not see outsourcing as getting rid of a process that does not add value; rather it sees it as a way of 'coordinating their activity to create the most value for customers'. Dell has improved customer service by changing the way it works with both its suppliers and its distributors to build a computer to the customer's specific order within just six days. This *vertical integration* has been achieved by creating a contractual vertical marketing system in which members of a channel retain their independence, but work together by sharing contracts.

So, one aspect of virtualisation is that companies should identify opportunities for providing new services and products to customers looking to outsource their external processes. The corollary of this is that it may offer companies opportunities to outsource some marketing activities that were previously conducted in-house. For example, marketing research to assess the impact of a website can now be conducted in a virtual environment by an outside company rather than by having employees conduct a focus group.

Referring to small and medium businesses, Azumah *et al.* (2005) indicate three levels of development towards what they term an e-organisation:

- 1/2-fusion organisations – minimum use of the Internet and network technologies.
- Fusion organisation – committed and intensive use of the Internet and network technologies.
- E-organisation – uses technologies as the core of the business for managing the entire business processes, from the point of receiving a customer order to processing the order and parts, and supplying and delivery.

Marshall *et al.* (2001) provide useful examples of different structures for the virtual organisation. These are:

- *Co-alliance model* – effort and risk are shared equally by partners.
- *Star alliance model* – here the effort and risk are centred on one organisation that subcontracts other virtual partners as required.
- *Value alliance model* – this is a partnership where elements are contributed across a supply chain for a particular industry. This is effectively the value network of Chapter 2.
- *Market alliance model* – this is similar to the value alliance, but is more likely to serve several different marketplaces.

Using the Internet to facilitate such alliances can provide competitive advantage to organisations operating in business-to-business markets since their core competences can be complemented by partnerships with third parties. This can potentially help organisations broaden their range of services or compete for work that on their own they may be unable to deliver. Such approaches can also be used to support business-to-consumer markets. For example, Dell can compete on price and quality in its consumer markets through its use of a star alliance model where other organisations are responsible for peripherals such as monitors or printers or distribution.

At a more practical level, electronic partnerships can be used to deliver the entire marketing mix referenced in this chapter through standardised data exchange interfaces, which include:

- advertising through Paid Search networks (e.g. Google AdWords);
- promoting services through feeds on price comparison search engines (e.g. Kelkoo or Google Product Search);
- promoting services through affiliate networks (e.g. Commission Junction) or advertising networks (e.g. Google AdSense publishers programme);
- procuring expertise for short-term digital marketing work through an online web skills marketplace such as Elance (**www.elance.com**), **Guru.com** (**www.guru.com**), Scriptlance (**www.scriptlance.com**) or oDesk (**www.oDesk.com**);
- use of secure payment system services such as Paypal or Google Checkout;
- analysis of web performance through online web analytics services (e.g. Google analytics).

Promotion

Promotion variable
The element of the marketing mix that involve communication with customers and other stakeholders to inform them about the product and the organisation.

The **Promotion variable** of the marketing mix refers to how marketing communications are used to inform customers and other stakeholders about an organisation and its products. The Internet and digital marketing techniques are highly important and have significant implications for marketing communication planning and for this reason digital promotions are covered in depth in Chapters 8 and 9. In this chapter the aim is to briefly outline the core components of Promotions.

According to Jobber and Ellis-Chadwick (2013), 'Good communications are the life-blood of successful market-orientated companies and their brands. But creating good communications presents many challenges'. Digital technology is changing the way individuals and business communicate, the channels through which they communicate and the number of touchpoints encountered. Modern businesses are developing more integrated approaches towards the use of communications tools in order to maximise the opportunities to deliver messages to their target audiences. The main elements of the promotional mix a business might use to communicate and their online equivalents summarised by Chaffey and Smith (2012) are shown in Table 5.3.

Specification of the Promotion element of the mix is usually part of a communications strategy. This will include selection of target markets, positioning and integration of different communications tools. The Internet offers a new, additional marketing communications channel to inform customers of the benefits of a product and assist in the buying decision. These are different approaches for looking at how the Internet can be used to vary the Promotion element of the mix:

1 reviewing new ways of applying each of the elements of the communications mix – such as advertising, sales promotions, PR and direct marketing;
2 assessing how the Internet can be used at different stages of the buying process;
3 using promotional tools to assist in different stages of customer relationship management from customer acquisition to retention. In a web context this includes gaining initial visitors to the site and gaining repeat visits through these types of communications techniques:

Table 5.3	The main elements of the promotional mix

Communications tool	Online implementation
Advertising	Interactive display ads, pay-per-click search advertising
Selling	Virtual sales staff, site merchandising, chat and affiliate marketing
Sales promotion	Incentives such as coupons, rewards, online loyalty schemes
Public relations	Online editorial, blogs, feeds, e-newsletters, newsletters, social networks, links and viral campaigns
Sponsorship	Sponsoring an online event, site or service
Direct mail	Opt-in email using e-newsletters and e-blasts (solus emails)
Exhibitions	Virtual exhibitions and white-paper distribution
Merchandising	Promotional ad-serving on retail sites, personalised recommendations and e-alerts
Packaging	Virtual tours, real packaging is displayed online
Word-of-mouth	Social, viral, affiliate marketing, email a friend, links

Digital marketing insight 5.5   Using data to shape advertising

Arguably, the promotional element of the mix has been affected significantly by the advent of the Internet. Marketing communications in digital environments are a dialogue rather than a monologue and there can also be a high level of interaction. The implications of these changes are that marketers can create more focussed, targeted and individual communication messages and campaigns. A key driver of such communications is data and the information it can reveal.

Listen to what Matt Brittin, head of Google operations has to say about the importance of data and how it can be used to shape advertising at: www.open.edu/openlearn/body-mind/matt-brittin-on-the-value-data.

- reminders in traditional media campaigns why a site is worth visiting – such as online services and unique online offers and competitions;
- direct email reminders of site proposition – new offers;
- frequently updated content – including promotional offers or information that helps your customer do their job or reminds them to visit.

The Promotion element of a marketing plan also requires three important decisions about investment for the online promotion or the online communications mix:

- *Investment in site promotion compared to site creation and maintenance.* Since there is often a fixed budget for site creation, maintenance and promotion, the e-marketing plan should specify the budget for each to ensure there is a sensible balance and the promotion of the site is not underfunded.
- *Investment in online promotion techniques in comparison to offline promotion.* A balance must be struck between these techniques. Typically, offline promotion investment often exceeds that for online promotion investment. For existing companies, traditional media such as print are used to advertise the sites, while print and TV will also be widely used by dot-com companies to drive traffic to their sites.
- *Investment in different online promotion techniques.* For example, how much should be paid for banner advertising as against online PR about online presence, and how much for search engine registration?

People, process and physical evidence

The people, process and physical evidence elements of the mix are closely related and often grouped as 'the service elements'. They are significant since the level of perceived service will impact on a customer's loyalty and the probability of their recommending the service. Since this issue is closely related to the online customer experience, we also look at issues of website performance and response to customer emails in Chapter 7, including review of frameworks such as WEBQUAL and E-SERVQUAL for assessing service effectiveness.

Some of the key issues in improving the delivery of service online have been summarised by Rayport *et al.* (2005). They identify these questions that senior executives and managers should ask to assess the combination of technology and human assistance that is used to deliver service. We have added some typical examples of applications for each type:

1 *Substitution.* Deploying technology instead of people (or the opposite situation), for example:
   - frequently asked questions section on a website;
   - in-site search engine;

- interactive sales dialogue recommending relevant products (Figure 5.3) based on human response;
- avatar offering answers to questions, as in the Ikea Ask Anna feature;
- automated email response or a series of 'Welcome' emails educating customers about how to use a service;
- using video to demonstrate products online.

2   *Complementarity*. Deploying technology in combination with people, for example:
   - call-back facility where the website is used to set up a subsequent call from contact centre;
   - online chat facility – the user chats through text on the website;
   - an employee using a WiFi-enabled hand-held device to facilitate easy rental car returns.

3   *Displacement*. Outsourcing or 'off-shoring' technology or labour, for example:
   - a fast-food chain centralising drive-through order taking in a remote call centre;
   - the online chat or call-back systems referred to above can be deployed at a lower cost through outsourcing.

Note that this perspective doesn't stress another important aspect of the service elements of the online marketing mix, namely the participation by other customers in shaping a service through their feedback and the collaboration that occurs as customers will answer other customers' questions in a forum.

We will now review the different elements of the service elements of the mix in more detail.

People

People variable
The element of the marketing mix that involves the delivery of service to customers during interactions with customers

The **People variable** of the marketing mix relates to how an organisation's staff interact with customers and other stakeholders during sales and pre- and post-sales communications with them.

Chaffey and Smith (2012) make a similar point to Rayport *et al.* (2005) when they suggest that, online, the main consideration for the People element of the mix is the review of how staff involvement in the buying is changed, either through new roles such as replying to emails or online chat enquiries or through their being replaced through automated online services.

While the options for this form of customer service outlined above are straightforward, what is challenging is to implement the applications effectively. For example, if an FAQ doesn't have sufficient relevant answers or a call-back does not occur at the right time, then the result will be a dissatisfied customer who is unlikely to use a service again or will tell others about their experience either through ratings in shopping comparison engines (e.g. Figure 5.4) or sites created for this purpose such as Blagger (**www.blagger.com**).

To manage service and quality, organisations must devise plans to accommodate the five stages shown in Figure 5.9.

Stage 1: Customer defines support query

Companies should consider how easily the customer can find contact points and compose a support request on site. Best practice is clearly to find email support options. Often, finding contact and support information on a website is surprisingly difficult. Standardised terminology on site is 'Contact Us', 'Support' or 'Ask a Question'. Options should be available for the customer to specify the type of query on a web form or provide alternative email addresses such as **products@company.com** or **returns@company.com** on site, or in offline communications such as a catalogue. Providing FAQs or automated diagnostic tools should be considered at this stage to reduce the number of inbound enquiries.

| Figure 5.9 | Stages in managing inbound email |

Epson (**www.epson.co.uk**) provides an online tool to diagnose problems with printers and to suggest solutions.

Finally, the website should determine expectations about the level of service quality. For example, inform the customer that 'your enquiry will be responded to within 24 hours'.

Avatars are increasingly being used to reduce the need for enquiries such as 'Ask Anna' on the Ikea site. Research by Holzwarth *et al.* (2006) found that use of an avatar-based sales agent can lead to more satisfaction with the retailer, a more positive attitude towards the product and a greater purchase intent. They investigated the usage of 'attractive' versus 'expert' advisers dependent on the complexity of the purchase decision.

Stage 2: Receipt of email and acknowledgement

Best practice is that automatic message acknowledgement occurs. This is usually provided by **autoresponder** software. While many autoresponders only provide a simple acknowledgement, more sophisticated responses can reassure the customer about when the response will occur and highlight other sources of information.

Stage 3: Routeing of email

Best practice involves automated routeing or workflow. Routeing the email to the right person is made easier if the type of query has been identified through the techniques described for Stage 1. It is also possible to use pattern recognition to identify the type of enquiry.

Stage 4: Compose response

Best practice is to use a library of pre-prepared templates for different types of query. These can then be tailored and personalised by the contact centre employee as appropriate.

Avatar
A term used in computer-mediated environments to mean a 'virtual person'. Derived from the word's original meaning: '*n*. the descendant of a Hindu deity in a visible form; incarnation; supreme glorification of any principle'.

Autoresponder or 'mailbots'
Software tool or 'agent' running on web servers that automatically sends a standard reply to the sender of an email message

The right type of template can again be selected automatically using the software referred to in Stage 2.

Stage 5: Follow-up

Best practice is that if the employee does not successfully answer the first response, then the email should suggest callback from an employee or a live chat. Indeed, to avoid the problem of 'email ping-pong' where several emails may be exchanged, the company may want to proactively ring the customer to increase the speed of problem resolution, and so solve the problem. Finally, the email follow-up may provide the opportunity for outbound contact and marketing, perhaps advising about complementary products or offers.

Process

Process variable
The element of the marketing mix that involves the methods and procedures companies use to achieve all marketing functions.

The **Process variable** of the marketing mix refers to the methods and procedures companies use to achieve all marketing functions – such as new product development, promotion, sales and customer service (as described in the previous section). The restructuring of the organisation and channel structures to accommodate online marketing which were described in the previous chapter are part of Process.

Customer contact strategies are a compromise between delivering quality customer service with the emphasis on customer choice and minimising the cost of customer contacts. Typical operational objectives that should drive the strategies and measure effectiveness are:

- to minimise average response time per email and the range of response time from slowest to fastest. This should form the basis of an advertised service quality level;
- to minimise clear-up (resolution) time, for example, number of contacts and elapsed time to resolution;
- to maximise customer satisfaction ratings with response;
- to minimise average staff time and cost per email response.

Customer contact strategies for integrating web and email support into existing contact centre operations usually incorporate elements of both of the following options:

- *Customer-preferred channel.* Here the company uses a customer-led approach where customers use their preferred channel for enquiry, whether it be phone call-back, email or live chat. There is little attempt made to influence the customer as to which is the preferable channel. Note that while this approach may give good customer satisfaction ratings, it is not usually the most cost-effective approach, since the cost of phone support will be higher than customer self-service on the web, or an email enquiry.
- *Company-preferred channel.* Here the company will seek to influence the customer on the medium used for contact. For example, easyJet encourages customers to use online channels rather than voice contact to the call centre for both ordering and customer service. Customer choice is still available, but the company uses the website to influence the choice of channel.
- *Delivering customer services and assisted sales through Livechat is increasingly popular.* For example, mobile phone company EE uses Liveperson for customer service and assisted sales as explained in Mini case study 5.3.

Physical evidence

Physical evidence variable
The element of the marketing mix that involves the tangible expression of a product and how it is purchased and used.

The **Physical evidence variable** of the marketing mix refers to the tangible expression of a product and how it is purchased and used. In an online context, 'physical evidence' refers to the customer's experience of the company through the website. It includes issues such as site ease of use or navigation, availability and performance, which are discussed further in Chapter 7.

Mini case study 5.3	Online customer service at EE

Established as a joint venture, bringing together the UK businesses of Orange and T-Mobile, EE (formerly Everything Everywhere) is now the UK's largest mobile phone company.

EE employs more than 11,000 customer-facing employees, covering both service and sales, and all are experts in mobile devices and operating systems. In the course of a year, the company registers around 86 million customer conversations via online and offline channels.

EE wants to be considered best in service across all channels and saw Live Chat as an important new way to establish high levels of customer satisfaction in relation to transactional queries and general enquiries on the site.

Digital engagement solutions provided by LivePerson (Figure 5.10) support the online sales operation and customer upgrades operations by enabling meaningful, real-time connections with website visitors. Using Live Chat to engage directly with customers, EE is driving conversions, increasing incremental sales and improving the online experience. LivePerson also provides predictive modelling and analytics, enabling EE to identify customers whose behaviours indicate they may require help with the purchase decision. This is achieved by tracking the activity of individuals as they move through the site. Behaviours such as lingering on a page for a longer than average time or the triggering of multiple error messages can be a strong indicator that assistance is needed. At these points, invitations to chat are served proactively. By offering help when it is most needed, EE has succeeded in raising sales, while also improving customer satisfaction rates and enhancing perception of the EE brand. Equally important, each engagement is unique to the individual, ensuring a personalised and therefore relevant experience.

In 2013, when the service was introduced, real-time engagement via chat resulted in 30,000 contract sales, running at a rate of 0.5 sales per agent per hour. This rate is roughly twice as productive as the average for telephone sales agents and ten times more effective than the rates achieved by agents in bricks-and-mortar stores. Customers who generally self-serve convert at around 1 per cent, whereas with real-time sales

Figure 5.10	Liveperson Chat (www.liveperson.com)

engagement the conversion rate is five times higher. The upgrade team consistently converts at over 40 per cent, with CSAT measured at above 80 per cent. The all-important customer satisfaction (CSAT) score for the chat channel currently stands at 83 per cent. At the same time, by deflecting direct contact from call centres onto an online channel with support from chat agents, EE is reinforcing its status as a service-focussed digital brand. The success of real-time engagement in the sales channel has also prompted innovation. Customers searching for EE via Google now have the option of clicking through to a chat agent from the search engine itself, and similar direct links are to be established with selected affiliate and price comparison sites.

Source: LivePerson customer success story. Available online at **www.liveperson.com/resources/customer-success-story**

Case Study 5 | Spotify streaming develops new revenue models

Spotify is a streaming music service originally developed in 2006 in Sweden and launching in 2008. Spotify Ltd now operates as the parent company in London while Spotify AB manages research and development in Stockholm.

This case study about the online music subscription service illustrates how different elements of the mix can be varied online. It also highlights success factors for developing an online marketing strategy.

In early 2015, Spotify was valued at more than $5 billion. Investments in the growth of the company have been $1–2 billion in seven rounds of funding from 17 investors.

Context

Spotify was not the first online entrant to online music services, but it was an innovator in marketing approaches, technology and subscription options that have enabled it to become a market leader in music subscription. The first major entrant was in 1999 through Napster which we have featured in previous editions of this text in this chapter. Its initial incarnation was as the first widely used service for 'free' peer-to-peer (P2P) music sharing. The record companies mounted a legal challenge to Napster due to lost revenues on music sales which eventually forced it to close. But the Napster brand was purchased and its second incarnation still offers a legal music service, although following bankruptcy in 2008 it has had several owners such as Roxio and Best Buy. Napster now focus on the music subscription service as part of the Rhapsody music services in direct competition to Spotify.

Revenue model and value proposition

Spotify operates a freemium model, with the majority of its users streaming music to their mobiles or desktop via apps or web browsers. Users who subscribe for free get ads between tracks, which are part of the Spotify revenue model. Users of the free service encounter audio ads every five or six songs, or approximately three minutes of advertising for every hour of listening.

Since many users enjoyed the unlimited free music option, Spotify moved to limit this in April 2011, when it announced that audio streaming would be limited to ten hours per month after an initial unlimited listening period of six months. This restriction was removed in 2014.

Spotify Premium users who pay a fixed monthly fee get additional features (Figure 5.11) including offline listening and no ads.

The Wikipedia entry for Spotify has charted the growth of Spotify:

In November 2011 more than 2.5 million paying subscribers signed up to its service. This followed 500,000 premium users signing up since its partnership with Facebook's 'Open Graph', which allows people to share the tracks they were listening to with friends. It also launched in the United States in 2011.

In August 2012 there were four million paying Spotify subscribers responsible for at least €20 million per month in revenue.

By March 2013, Spotify had grown to six million paying customers globally (a figure that remained in December 2013) and 24 million total active users.

By May 2014, Spotify had grown to ten million paying customers and 30 million free users.

By January 2015, Spotify had grown to 15 million paying customers and 45 million free users.

Through licensing the service to other businesses there are further opportunities for revenue. For example, in January 2015, PlayStation announced that Spotify would power its new music service called PlayStation Music.

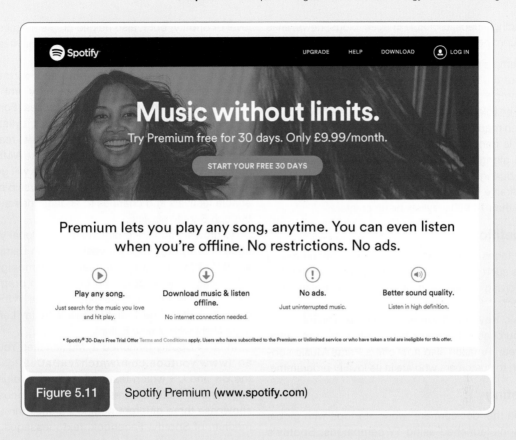

| Figure 5.11 | Spotify Premium (www.spotify.com) |

The company pays roughly 70 per cent of its revenue for royalties to artists and companies that hold the rights to the music. Spotify pays artists and labels per streamed track, with the Spotify artists' page (**www.spotifyartists.com/spotify-explained/**) explaining that there is an average 'per stream' payout to rights holders of between $0.006 and $0.0084. Artists have questioned the value that Spotify returns, with some major global artists such as Taylor Swift and AC/DC withdrawing some or all of their music from the platform. However, for many others it provides a way to reach new audiences through recommendations and playlists and gain royalties from listeners they would previously not have received any revenue from. Spotify makes the case that it aims to regenerate lost value by converting music fans from these poorly monetised formats (e.g. illegal download services) to the paid streaming format, which produces far more value per listener.

Value proposition

In addition to the core music listening service Spotify has developed other features to add to the value of the service which have also given opportunities to spread awareness of the site through co-marketing.

Spotify claims that its users are highly engaged, with the average multiplatform user spending 146 minutes a day using the service. Between 2013 and 2014 the share of users listening on mobile tripled, although more than 50 per cent of sessions are still on desktop.

Advertising

Spotify has developed a range of innovative advertising formats to build its revenue, mainly from its free subscribers. These formats are described as:

● Audio Ad – A cross-platform, unavoidable format comprised of an audio spot, cover art and clickable campaign name.
● Display – Leaderboard ads in the Spotify player are served when the user is interacting with Spotify.
● Homepage Takeover – Block out a full day for your brand on our Homepage.
● Branded Playlist – Custom user-generated playlists with brand logo, custom text and optional link to your campaign.
● Sponsored Session – Users choose to watch a video to receive a 30-minute, ad-free session.
● Video Takeover – Sponsor the ad break experience with video and display.
● Advertiser Page – A microsite seamlessly integrated into the Spotify player. The Advertiser Page can contain practically any content you'd find on a webpage,

including videos, clickable images, blogs, news, links and comments.

One example of a campaign run on Spotify was for the launch of the BMW 320i for which an 'American Road Trip' campaign was developed. A branded app on Spotify enabled users to select from one of five iconic American road trips. Based on their selection, a custom playlist is generated featuring songs and artists from regions along the selected route. A BMW video was served during playlist generation and the final playlist was sharable via social media. The campaign resulted in more than 14,000 playlists being created.

Competition

Spotify faces competition from existing online music services such as iTunes and Napster, but given that this is an evolving marketplace, other major competitors can be expected. For example, in late 2014 Google launched its Music Key subscription service via YouTube and Apple purchased the Beats subscription service earlier in the year. Amazon also now offers Prime Music subscription to customers who are in its loyalty programme.

Marketing

Unlike in the 'dot-com era' when startups with global aspirations launched using TV campaigns, Spotify's growth has been a more modest approach relying on word-of-mouth, PR and co-marketing rather than big ad budgets.

The launch of Spotify in the US used private 'Beta' invites to create a buzz, as those with access shared their use of it in social media (and through word-of-mouth)

The music streaming service went live in October 2008, and it kept its free service invitation only, something that had been in place while it was in the final stages of development prior to public launch.

The invitation-only element was a vital part of the platform's rise. Not only did it help manage the growth

level of Spotify, but it also helped create a viral element to the service, with users each having five invites at first to share with their friends.

Spotify has used co-marketing and partnerships with publishers to increase its reach by embedding different formats of widgets on other sites. For example, Drowned In Sound has a monthly playlist that it embeds within its blog which encourages its readers to engage with Spotify. A music magazine like *NME* offers apps with a range of playlists which again will generate awareness and engagement. Other partnership services enable festivals and charities to engage their audience through Spotify playlists.

To grow its audience beyond its traditional younger audience, Spotify today invests more in campaigns. In 2013 it launched a multiplatform campaign, with a 30-second ad spot during the season premiere of NBC's 'The Voice'. Sixty-second versions of the commercial aired in 'The Tonight Show with Jay Leno' and 'Late Night with Jimmy Fallon'.

In 2014 Spotify launched a 'Music takes You Back' ad (www.youtube.com/watch?v=BaDe9PgkpI4) in the UK and US which featured in cinema, digital signage and online. It centres around three videos which showcase three different people's stories through the medium of Spotify, Facebook, text messages, Skype and Instagram. Its aim is to show how Spotify can bring people together through its integration with social media. Spotify decided not to use TV, creating 75- to 90-second videos rather than the typical 30-second TV ad break slots.

Question

Assess how Spotify competes with traditional and online music providers by reviewing the approaches it uses for different elements of the marketing mix.

Summary

1 Evaluating the opportunities provided by the Internet for varying the marketing mix is a useful framework for assessing current and future digital marketing strategy.

2 *Product*. Opportunities for varying the core product through new information-based services and also the extended product should be reviewed.

3 *Branding*. Is an important concept in the digital marketplace but in addition, each of the established elements of a brand offline (e.g. domain, value, assets, heritage) need careful consideration as to how they relate to the online world. Additionally the context in which we encounter online brands is an important consideration.

4 *Price*. The Internet leads to price transparency and commoditisation and hence lower prices. Dynamic pricing gives the ability to test prices or to offer differential pricing for different segments or in response to variations in demand. New pricing models such as auctions are available.

5 *Place*. This refers to place of purchase and channel structure on the Internet. There are three main locations for e-commerce transactions: seller site, buyer site and intermediary. New channel structures are available through direct sales and linking to new intermediaries. Steps must be taken to minimise channel conflict.

6 *Promotion*. This aspect of the mix is discussed in more detail in Chapter 8.

7 *People, process and physical evidence*. These aspects of the mix are discussed in more detail in Chapters 6 and 7 where customer relationship management and service delivery are discussed.

Exercises

Self-assessment exercises

1 Select the two most important changes introduced by the Internet for each of the 7Ps.

2 What types of product are most amenable to changes to the core and extended product?

3 Explain the implications of the Internet for Price.

4 What are the implications of the Internet for Place?

Essay and discussion questions

1 'The marketing mix developed as part of annual planning is no longer a valid concept in the Internet era.' Discuss.

2 Critically evaluate the impact of the Internet on the marketing mix for an industry sector of your choice.

3 Explain how the Internet has affected pricing policies.

4 Does 'Place' have any meaning for marketers in the global marketplace enabled by the Internet?

Examination questions

1 Describe three alternative locations for transactions for a B2B company on the Internet.

2 Explain two applications of dynamic pricing on the Internet.

3 How does the Internet impact an organisation's options for core and extended (augmented) product?

4 Briefly summarise the implications of the Internet on each of these elements of the marketing mix:
   a Product
   b Price
   c Place
   d Promotion.
5 Explain the reasons why the Internet could be expected to decrease prices online.
6 How can an organisation vary its promotional mix using the Internet?

References

Aaker, D. and Joachimsthaler, E. (2000) *Brand Leadership*, Free Press, New York.

Allan, S. (2012) Consumer behaviour and today's publishers: why advertisers love the Affiliate Channel, *Content Marketing*, 10 August, **http://marketingland.com/consumer-behaviour-and-todays-publishers-why-advertisers-love-the-affiliate-channel-18048**.

Allen, E. and Fjermestad, J. (2001) E-commerce marketing strategies: a framework and case analysis, *Logistics Information Management*, 14(1–2), 14–23.

Amazonstudios (2015) Amazon pilot season, **http://studios.amazon.com/**.

AmazonWebServices (2015) Deploy a hybrid storage solution using Avere's Edge Filer and Amazon S3, *AWS Official Blog*, **https://aws.amazon.com/blogs/aws/?nc1=f_so_bl&tag=viglink121320–20**.

Anderson, C. (2004) The long tail, *Wired*, 12 October, **www.wired.com/wired/archive/12.10/tail.html**.

Azumah, G., Loh, S. and McGuire, S. (2005) E-organisation and its future implication for SMEs, *Production Planning and Control*, 6(6), 555–62.

Baker, W., Marn, M. and Zawada, C. (2000) Price smarter on the Net, *Harvard Business Review* (February), 2–7.

Baye, M., Gatti, J., Kattuman, P. and Morgan, J. (2007) Dashboard for online pricing, *The California Management Review*, 50(1), 202–16.

Benjamin, R. and Wigand, R. (1995) Electronic markets and virtual value-chains on the information superhighway, *Sloan Management Review* (Winter), 62–72.

Berry, L. (2008) Relationship marketing perspectives 1983 and 2000, *Journal of Relationship marketing*, 1(1), 59–77.

Bickerton, P., Bickerton, M. and Pardesi, U. (2000) *CyberMarketing*, 2nd edn, Butterworth-Heinemann, Oxford.

Booms, B. and Bitner, M. (1981) Marketing strategies and organisation structures for service firms, in J. Donnelly and W. George (eds), *Marketing of Services*, American Marketing Association, New York.

Brand Name Generator (2015) **http://business-name-generators.com/generator.php?gen=brand-name-generator**.

Bravo, R., Iversen, N. and Pina, J. (2011) Expansion strategies for online brands going offline, *Marketing Intelligence and Planning*, 29(2), 195–213.

Brown, D. (2014) 8 ways to develop a successful online brand for your small business, *Huffington Post*, 17 September, **www.huffingtonpost.com/david-brown/8-ways-to-develop-a-succe_b_5832280.html**.

Brynjolfsson, E., Smith, D. and Hu, Y. (2003) Consumer surplus in the digital economy: estimating the value of increased product variety at online booksellers, *Management Science*, 49(11), 1580–96, **http://ebusiness.mit.edu/research/papers/176_ErikB_OnlineBooksellers2.pdf**.

Burt, S. (2010) Retailing in Europe: 20 years on, *International Review of Retail, Distribution and Consumer Research*, 20(1), 9–27.

Chaffey, D. and Smith, P.R. (2012) *E-marketing Excellence: Planning and Optimising Your Digital Marketing*, 4th edn, Butterworth-Heinemann, Oxford.

Davidow, W.H. and Malone, M.S.C. (1992) *The Virtual Corporation. Structuring and Revitalising the Corporation for the 21st Century*, HarperCollins, New York.

Davis, S. M. (1997) *Future Perfect*. doi: **http://onlinelibrary.wiley.com/doi/10.1111/j.1083–6101.2002.tb00155.x/full#b5**.

Delgado, E. and Hernandez, M. (2008) Building online brands through brand alliances in Internet, *European Journal of Marketing*, 42(9–10), 954–76.

Doherty, N.F. and Ellis-Chadwick, F. (2010) Internet retailing: the past, the present and the future, *International Journal of Retail and Distribution Management*, 38(11–12), 943–65.

Dredge, S. (2015) Vessel sets sail with ambitions to shake up the online video market, *The Guardian*, 22 January, **www.theguardian.com/technology/2015/jan/21/vessel-video-service-youtube-app**.

Ellis-Chadwick, F. (2013) History of online retail, **www.open.edu/openlearn/money-management/management/business-studies/history-online-retail**.

Evans, P. and Wurster, T.S. (1999) Getting real about virtual commerce, *Harvard Business Review* (November), 84–94.

Flores, L. (2004) 10 facts about the value of brand websites, *AdMap* (February), 26–8, **www.imediaconnection.com/content/wp/admap.pdf**.

Frazier, G. (1999) Organising and managing channels of distribution, *Journal of the Academy of Marketing Science*, 27(2), 222–40.

Ghosh, S. (1998) Making business sense of the Internet, *Harvard Business Review* (March–April), 127–35.

Gibbs, S. (2015) I enjoyed my week in Google Glass, but those around me weren't so keen, *The Guardian*, 16 January, **www.theguardian.com/technology/2015/jan/16/my-week-in-google-glass**.

Gladwell, M. (2000) *The Tipping Point: How Little Things can Make a Big Difference*, Little, Brown, New York.

Guo, X., Ling, L., Yang, C., Li, Z. and Liang, L. (2013) Optimal pricing strategy based on market segmentation for service, *International Journal of Hospitality Management*, 35, 274–81. doi: **http://dx.doi.org/10.1016/j.ijhm.2013.07.001**.

Harridge-March, S. (2004) Electronic marketing, the new kid on the block, *Marketing Intelligence and Planning*, 22(3), 297–309.

Holzwarth, M., Janiszewski, C. and Neumann, M. (2006) The influence of avatars on online consumer shopping behaviour, *Journal of Marketing*, 70(October), 19–36.

Interbrand (2014) 2014 – Best global brands, **www.bestglobalbrands.com/2014/ranking/**.

Introna, L. (2001) Defining the virtual organisation, in S. Barnes and B. Hunt (eds), *E-Commerce and V-Business: Business Models for Global Success*, Butterworth-Heinemann, Oxford.

Jarvey, N. and McClintock, P. (2015). Amazon Studios' Movie Push: Another Blow to Theatre Owners, *The Hollywood Reporter*, 30 January, **www.hollywoodreporter.com/news/amazon-studios-movie-push-blow-765066**.

Jobber, D. and Ellis-Chadwick, F. (2013) *Principles and Practices of Marketing*, 7th edn, McGraw-Hill, Maidenhead.

Johnson, E., Moe, W., Fader, P., Bellman, S. and Lohse, G. (2004) On the depth and dynamics of online search behaviour, *Management Science*, 50(3), 299–308.

Kamail, N. and Loker, S. (2002) Mass customisation: on-line consumer involvement in product design, *Journals of Computer-Mediated Communication*, 7(4). doi: **10.1111/j.1083–6101.2002.tb00155.x**.

Kelly, S. (2014) Google eyes first U.S. retail location near NYC Apple store, *Mashable.com*, 12 March, **http://mashable.com/2014/03/12/google-retail-store-new-york/**.

Koukova, N., Kannan, P. and Ratchford, B. (2008) Product form bundling: implications for marketing digital products, *Journal of Retailing*, 84(2), 181–94. doi: http://dx.doi.org/10.1016/j.jretai.2008.04.001.

Kraut, R., Chan, A., Butler, B. and Hong, A. (1998) Coordination and virtualisation: the role of electronic networks and personal relationships, *Journal of Computer Mediated Communications*, 3(4).

Kumar, N. (1999) Internet distribution strategies: dilemmas for the incumbent, *Financial Times*, Special issue on mastering information management, no. 7. Electronic Commerce (www.ftmastering.com).

Lautenborn, R. (1990) New marketing litany: 4Ps passes; C-words take over, *Advertising Age*, 1 October, 26.

Levine, R. (2014) How the internet has all but destroyed the market for films, music and newspapers, *The Guardian*, 14 August, www.theguardian.com/media/2011/aug/14/robert-levine-digital-free-ride.

Lewis, M., Singh, V. and Fay, S. (2006) An empirical study of the impact of nonlinear shipping and handling fees on purchase incidence and expenditure decisions, *Marketing Science*, 25(1), 51–64.

Ling, L., Guo, X. and Yang, C. (2014) Opening the online marketplace: an examination of hotel pricing and travel agency on-line distribution of rooms, *Tourism Management*, 45, 234–43. doi: http://dx.doi.org/10.1016/j.tourman.2014.05.003.

Magretta, J. (1998) The power of virtual integration. An interview with Michael Dell, *Harvard Business Review* (March–April), 72–84.

Malone, T., Yates, J. and Benjamin, R. (1987) Electronic markets and electronic hierarchies: effects of information technology on market structure and corporate strategies, *Communications of the ACM*, 30(6), 484–97.

Marsden, P. (2004) Tipping point marketing: a primer, *Brand Strategy* (April), www.viralculture.com/pubs/tippingpoint2.htm.

Marshall, P., McKay, J. and Burn J. (2001) Structure, strategy and success factors in the virtual organisation, in S. Barnes and B. Hunt (eds), *E-Commerce and V-Business. Business Models for Global Success*, Butterworth-Heinemann, Oxford.

McCarthy, J. (1960) *Basic Marketing: A Managerial Approach*, Richard D. Irwin, Homewood, IL.

Meyer, D. (2011) Google opens a 'Chrome Zone' shop in London, www.zdnet.co.uk/blogs/communication-breakdown-10000030/google-opens-a-chrome-zone-shop-in-london-10024474/.

Morgan-Thomas, A. and Veloutsou, C. (2013) Beyond technology acceptance: brand relationships and online brand experience, *Journal of Business Research*, 66(1), 21–7. doi: http://dx.doi.org/10.1016/j.jbusres.2011.07.019.

Newitz, A. (2013) A mysterious law that predicts the size of the world's biggest cities, 9 December, http://io9.com/the-mysterious-law-that-governs-the-size-of-your-city-1479244159.

PC World (2015) www.pcworld.co.uk/gbuk/price-promise-875-theme.html?intcmp=nav~price-promise~service.

Peppard, J. and Rylander, A. (2005) Products and services in cyberspace, *International Journal of Information Management*, 25(4).

Pine, B.J. (1993) *Mass Customisation: The New Frontier in Business Competition*, Harvard Business School Press, Boston, MA.

Quelch, J. and Klein, L. (1996) The Internet and international marketing, *Sloan Management Review* (Spring), 61–75.

Rayport, J., Jaworski, B. and Kyung, E. (2005) Best face forward: improving companies' service interfaces with customers, *Journal of Interactive Marketing*, 19(4), 67–80.

Recombu (2015) TalkTalk Box Office vs Sky Box Office vs Blinkbox, http://recombu.com/digital/article/talktalk-box-office-vs-sky-box-office-vs-blinkbox.

Reid, A. (2014) Guardian sees most monthly web-only UK readers, *The Guardian*, 28 August, **www.journalism.co.uk/news/report-guardian-maintains-lead-with-most-monthly-web-only-uk-readers/s2/a562273/**.

Ries, A. and Ries, L. (2000) *The 11 Immutable Laws of Internet Branding*, HarperCollins Business, London.

Sarkar, M., Butler, B. and Steinfield, C. (1996) Intermediaries and cybermediaries: a continuing role for mediating players in the electronic marketplace, *Journal of Computer Mediated Communication*, 1(3).

Sawhney, M., Verona, G. and Prandelli, E. (2005) Collaborating to create: the Internet as a platform for customer engagement in product innovation, *Journal of Interactive Marketing*, 19(4), 4–17.

Singh, A., Agrariya, K. and Deepali, I. (2011) What really defines relationship marketing? A review of definitions and general and sector specific defining constructs, *Journal of Relationship Marketing*, 10(4), 203–37.

Swash, R. (2014) Asos share slump not sign of public turning its back on fashion retailer, *The Guardian*, 5 June, **www.theguardian.com/business/2014/jun/05/asos-share-slump-public-fashion-retailer-trends**.

Valette-Florence, P., Guizana, H. and Merunka, D. (2011) The impact of brand personality and sales promotions on brand equity, *Journal of Business Research*, 64(1), 24–8.

Vitevitch, M., & Donoso, A. (2011) Phonotactic probability of brand names: I'd buy that! *Psychological Research*, 76 (1 November), 693–8. doi: **10.1007/s00426–011–0374-z**.

Xing, X., Yang, S. and Tang, F. (2006) A comparison of time-varying online price and price dispersion between multichannel and dotcom DVD retailers, *Journal of Interactive Marketing*, 20(2), 3–20.

Weblinks

- **Chris Anderson** has a blog site (**www.thelongtail.com**), the Long Tail, to support his book on the topic published in 2006 by Hyperion, New York.
- **CIM 10-minute guide to achieving an effective marketing mix.** (**www.cim.co.uk/filestore/resources/10minguides/marketingmix.pdf**). A fairly detailed introduction to the marketing mix with further links.
- **ClickZ** (**www.clickz.com**). An excellent collection of articles on online marketing communications, US-focussed. Relevant section for this chapter: brand marketing.
- **The culturally customised website** (**www.theculturallycustomizedwebsite.com**). Resources supporting the authors' book of this title.
- **Gladwell.com** (**www.gladwell.com**). Author's site with extracts from *The Tipping Point* and other books.
- **Paul Marsden's** Viral Culture site (**www.viralculture.com**). Articles related to *The Tipping Point* and connected marketing.

Chapter 6
Relationship marketing using digital platforms

Chapter at a glance

Main topics

- The challenge of customer engagement 308
- Customer lifecycle management 311

Case studies

Digital marketing in practice

The Smart Insights interview: Guy Stephens, Social Customer Care consultant at IBM on using social media platforms to enhance customer service   304

Case Study 6: Dell gets closer to its customers through its social media strategy   344

Learning objectives

After reading this chapter, the reader should be able to:

- Assess the relevance and alternative approaches for using digital platforms for customer relationship management and Marketing Automation
- Evaluate the potential of the digital technology and applying the concept of 'Big Data' to support one-to-one marketing
- Assess how to integrate social and mobile interactions to develop social CRM capabilities.

Questions for marketers

Key questions for marketing managers related to this chapter are:

- How can Marketing Automation be used to increase the value of customers through the customer lifecycle?
- How do I implement permission marketing with mobile, social and messaging applications?
- How can I apply personalisation and mass customisation cost-effectively in my marketing?

Scan code
to find the
latest updates
for topics in
this chapter

Links to other chapters

This chapter is related to other chapters as follows:

- Chapter 4 introduces customer lifecycle-based segmentation models
- Chapter 7 has guidelines on how to develop the right customer experience to assist in forming and maintaining relationships
- Chapter 8 describes methods of acquiring customers for one-to-one marketing
- Chapters 10 and 11 give examples of relationship marketing in the business-to-consumer and business-to-business markets.

Introduction

Customer relationship management (CRM)
A marketing-led approach to building and sustaining long-term business with customers.

Marketing automation
Enables businesses to automate tasks in the marketing and sales process to make the process to deliver more relevant communications typically delivered as personalised emails and website messages.

One-to-one marketing
A unique dialogue occurs between a company and individual customers (or groups of customers with similar needs).

Building long-term relationships with customers is essential for any sustainable business, and this applies equally to online elements of a business. Failure to build relationships to gain repeat visitors and sales largely caused the failure of many dot-coms following huge expenditure on customer acquisition. Research summarised by Reichheld and Schefter (2000) showed that acquiring online customers is so expensive (he suggested 20–30 per cent higher than for traditional businesses) that startup companies may remain unprofitable for at least two to three years. The research also shows that by retaining just 5 per cent more customers, online companies can boost their profits by 25 per cent to 95 per cent.

Over the last three decades or more, relationship marketing, direct marketing and database marketing have combined to enable **customer relationship management (CRM)**. In recent years, **marketing automation** technology has been used to create rules that schedule more relevant emails and personalised communications on company websites. Marketing automation is the term currently used to describe a closely related approach known as **one-to-one marketing**. However, owing to the costs of managing relationships on an individual level, many companies will apply marketing automation to tailor communications and offers to customer segments or groups, rather than individuals.

Marketing automation techniques can also be used to deliver customer service online, although personal interactions to give a tailored response are often used. How to achieve the levels of customer satisfaction necessary to encourage customer loyalty is a major focus within this chapter. Mini case study 6.1 shows an inspiring example of how relentless focus on the customer has helped build a company.

Mini case study 6.1	Zappos delivers customer happiness

Zappos is a US online clothing retailer often referred to as a pioneer in online marketing. Zappos' primary product category is shoes, which accounts for about 80 per cent of its business. There are currently more than 50,000 varieties of shoes sold in the Zappos store, from brands like Nike, Ugg boots, ALDO Shoes, and Steve Madden. They also serve the niche shoe markets, including narrow and wide widths, hard-to-find sizes, American-made shoes, and vegan shoes.

Tony Hsieh, CEO of Zappos, puts the company's success down to a customer-centric approach. He says simply 'We pay more attention to our customers'. He explains: 'People may not remember exactly what you did or what you said, but they will always remember how you made them feel'. Tony's summary of the evolution of the Zappos brand has seen it go from simply having a strong customer focus to being really passionate about how they make their customers feel (Figure 6.1).

The customer focus is encapsulated in ten core values (**http://about.zappos.com/our-unique-culture/ zappos-core-values**, Figure 6.1). In 2007, Zappos expanded its inventory to include clothing, handbags, eyewear, watches and kids' merchandise, which currently account for 20 per cent of annual revenues. Zappos expects that clothing and accessories will bring in an additional $1 billion worth of revenue from 2015, as the clothing market is four times the size of the footwear market.

Overall, the approach seems to be successful. In 2009, Amazon purchased Zappos for $1.2 billion. Here is our summary of the five success factors based around the core values of Zappos that can be applied to other businesses:

1 **Customers come back, order more and more often**
   - On any given day, about 75 per cent of purchases from Zappos are from returning customers.
   - Repeat customers order over 2.5 times more in the following 12 months.
   - Repeat customers spend more.

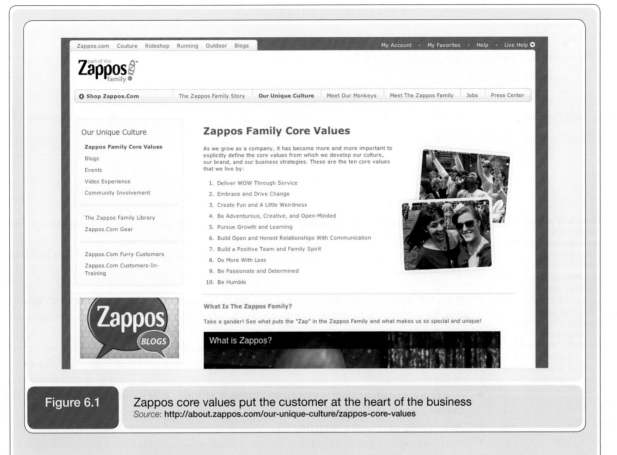

2 Make it easy for customers to build your brand
- Superior experience drives word-of-mouth, so do the unexpected.
- Remove the risk of purchase and make it easy to return products for free.
- Fast, accurate fulfilment is worth talking about.
- Deliver an 'above and beyond' customer service.
- Drive people to the phone; be contactable and be open.

3 Talk to people!
- 'The telephone is one of the best branding devices available.'
- Take time to talk to people properly.
- At Zappos there are no call times and no sales-based performance goals for sales reps.
- Zappos will also pay you $2000 to quit, so only the best people who enjoy the job stay.
- The Culture Book makes it clear how Zappos do business and even underpins performance management.
- According to the company's Wikipedia entry, to support the 6th core value, on average, Zappos employees answer 5000 calls a month, and 1200 emails a week (except in the holiday season, when call frequency increases significantly). Call centre employees don't have scripts, and there are no limits on call times. The longest call reported is 10 hours 29 minutes.

4 Build a culture that envelops customers and internal staff
- Zappos has 'committable core values' that are clear, exciting and simple.
- It doesn't matter what your core values are as long as you commit to them and get internal alignment.
- Commit to a culture of transparency: 'An Ask Anything Culture'.
- Zappos' insights.com focuses on lifting the lid for customers and future employees.

---

5 Have a vision ...

- 'Whatever you're thinking, think bigger', comments Tony.
- Does your company vision have real meaning? Without it there is little chance of achieving any of the above.
- 'What would you be passionate about doing for ten years even if you never made a dime?'

In 2014 Zappos was reported to have introduced a 'holacracy' with 'no job titles, no managers, no hierarchy'.

Sources: Hsieh (2010); Wikipedia entry for company (**http://en.wikipedia.org/wiki/Zappos**)

Electronic customer relationship management (E-CRM)
Using digital communications technologies to maximise sales to existing customers and encourage continued usage of online services through techniques including database, personalised web messages, customer services, email and social media marketing.

Electronic customer relationship management (E-CRM) involves creating strategies and plans for how digital technology and digital data can support CRM.

Digital marketing activities that are within the scope of E-CRM which we will cover in this chapter include:

- Using the *website and online social presences for customer development* from generating leads through to conversion to an online or offline sale using email and web-based content to encourage purchase.
- *Managing customer profile information and email list quality* (coverage of email addresses and integration of customer profile information from other databases to enable targeting).
- Managing customer contact options through mobile, *email and social networks* to support up-sell and cross-sell.
- *Data mining* to improve targeting.
- Providing online personalisation or *mass customisation* facilities to automatically recommend the 'next-best product'.
- Providing *online customer service facilities* (such as frequently asked questions, callback and chat support).
- Managing *online service quality* to ensure that first-time buyers have a great customer experience that encourages them to buy again.
- Managing the *multichannel customer experience* as they use different media as part of the buying process and customer lifecycle.

From e-CRM to social CRM

The interactive nature of the web combined with email and mobile communications provides an ideal environment in which to develop customer relationships, and databases provide a foundation for storing information about the relationship and providing information to strengthen it by improved, personalised services. This online approach to CRM is often known as electronic customer relationship management (e-CRM). E-CRM, can be characterised as sense and respond communications. The classic example of this is the personalisation facilities provided by Amazon where personal recommendations are provided through email marketing and personalised messages to site visitors.

Social CRM
The process of managing customer-to-customer conversations to engage existing customers, prospects and other stakeholders with a brand and so enhance customer-relationship management.

In previous chapters, we have seen the growing popularity of social media with consumers and as a marketing technique. It's natural that a new marketing approach, **social CRM** has developed to determine how social media can be applied to develop customer relationships and customer value. The scope of e-CRM and social CRM crosses many business processes, as suggested by Figure 6.2.

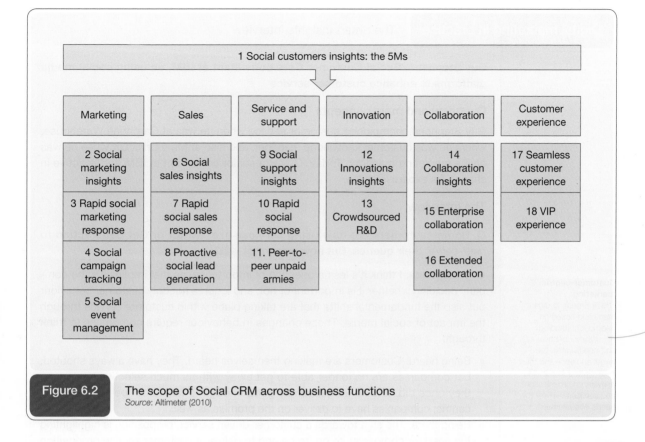

Figure 6.2	The scope of Social CRM across business functions
	Source: Altimeter (2010)

The scope of each area shown in Figure 6.2 is:

1 *Marketing*. Monitoring, analysis and response of customer conversations through social listening tools.
2 *Sales*. Understanding where prospects are discussing selection of products and services offered by you and competitors and determining the best way to get involved in the conversation to influence sales and generate leads. Within B2B, LinkedIn is an obvious location that should be monitored.
3 *Service and support*. Customer self-help through forums provided by you and neutral sites.
4 *Innovation*. Using conversations to foster new product development or enhance online offerings is one of the most exciting forms of social CRM.
5 *Collaboration*. This is e-business collaboration within an organisation through an intranet and other software tools to encourage all forms of collaboration which support business process.
6 *Customer experience*. This references the use of social CRM to enhance the customer experience and add value to a brand which is implied by many of the other aspects above. It gives the examples of using VIP programmes offering collaboration between customers with shared characteristics to add value and create advocacy.

Structure of this chapter

We started the chapter by reviewing the challenges of customer engagement and introducing how e-CRM can be used to help encourage engagement. We then considered how e-CRM, permission marketing and social CRM can support customer marketing activities through the customer lifecycle. In the final part of the chapter, we show how advanced techniques are used to assess and increase customer value.

| Digital marketing in practice | The Smart Insights interview |

Guy Stephens, Social Customer Care consultant at IBM, on using social media platforms to enhance customer service

Overview and main concepts

Guy Stephens championed customer service when he was at Carphone Warehouse, where he was customer knowledge manager, and also at Mars Drink UK when he was online marketing manager. Today, Guy is a senior consultant at IBM and is active in sharing his expertise online.

The interview

Q. Some customers are now using services like Twitter or Get Satisfaction to 'self-serve' their queries. But how important is it?

Guy Stephens: I think it's less a question of importance, as that implies it's the company deciding whether it is important or not, and ignores not only customer behaviour but also the fundamental shifts that are taking place within customer service through the impact of social media. These changes in behaviour require companies to think through:

- Being heard: Customers are making themselves heard. They have always shouted, but companies are no longer able to get away with as much selective hearing as they once did. It is no longer simply good enough to talk about being customer-centric; companies have to deliver on the promise as well.
- Being there: The shift towards a customer-driven service proposition is highlighting the need for companies to go, to be and to deliver a customer service proposition that can feasibly take place wherever a customer is, whenever a customer wants it and however a customer so chooses.
- Being now: The increasing ubiquity of smartphones and apps is condensing the customer service experience to the point at which it takes place. This brings with it implications on resourcing, agent skill levels, collaborative working amongst others.
- Being seen: Customer service has always had a PR capability, but this has traditionally been overlooked. Social media forces the customer service interaction into a public arena where a fine line between opportunity and risk is an inherent part of operating in this space. The real-time characteristic of this adds a further layer of complexity that needs to be understood.

Social media is changing the way not only customer service is being provided, but how business is conducted between companies and customers. My view is that we will continue to see the mainstreaming of social media, and, with it, the gradual questioning and subsequent erosion of the lines between customer service, sales, marketing, compliance, business operations.

Q. Which are the most common online service options companies should consider?

Guy Stephens: From what I have seen over the last two years, if a company is looking to deliver customer service through the use of social media, then the platforms they have got to include are: Twitter, blogs, YouTube and now Facebook.

For some reason, Facebook has come back into the frame and companies are interestingly treating it as a help destination point in its own right. In the UK, Thomas Cook has a help and support page within its Facebook offering. We are seeing a shift in thinking towards a deeper understanding and appreciation of the need to provide 'service at source' for customers. Traditionally, companies would have looked to

Customer-centric marketing
The approach to digital marketing based on deep understanding of customer behaviour and needs within the target audience and then seeking to deliver more relevant communications and services to meet the needs of customers.

bring the interaction back to their website or into the contact centre as soon as possible.

Take the case of BestBuy's Twelpforce. The next iteration of Twelpforce, according to John Bernier of Best Buy, is: 'for us to enable customers to answer questions that come from anywhere so that the customer doesn't have to find us, we find them. We don't want someone to have to leave Facebook to ask a question, we want them to ask it there.'

What I would say to companies looking to move into this space, is that while there exist what could loosely be termed a core set of tools, you've got to see what your customers are doing and where they are doing it. You set up a Twitter account or offer help and support on Facebook because your customers are there and in doing so you are meeting their needs, not yours.

Q. Many examples of customer service provided through social channels often involve retail. How important is customer service in other sectors?

Guy Stephens: There are some sectors which have a natural affinity with it because of the nature of their product or service. But in my mind it is simply understanding what you want to achieve, observing how your customers behave and then matching that to the available toolset.

Furthermore, I think there needs to be less thinking about sector and more about what it is that you are trying to do. Every sector requires the passing of information at some point between customer and company. Whether that is keeping people updated if their train is delayed, through to informing customers about changes to a returns policy, through to apologising for poor service.

On this point, and as a quick aside, I think companies also shouldn't overlook or underestimate the power of being 'signposts to the mundane' in a sense. What I mean by this is that many of the calls or emails that come into the contact centre every day are simple requests for information about delivery times, new products, product specifications etc. – information that can be responded to easily and quickly, without the need to really come into the call centre. Social channels like Twitter, Facebook and YouTube are fantastic assets for this and the upside in terms of immediate PR value often outweighs the actual issue itself.

Take the financial services or legal sectors. Traditionally we would have looked at these sectors and concluded that social media wouldn't work. We have a very open system in social media on the one hand, and come up against two heavily regulated sectors on the other. And yet, think about when you want to get a mortgage, renew your car insurance or understand some legal requirement relating to your work. Up until the point at which you actually have to pass sensitive data through to someone, I would have thought there's probably quite a lot of space in which social media could have a role to play in simply explaining a process or pointing someone in the right direction.

Think about someone buying a mortgage for the first time or a student opening up their first bank account. A lot of research is undertaken, particularly in the case of choosing a mortgage. A lot of hand-holding and explaining of terminology is needed. A lot of this hand-holding could be handled on the platforms that these potential customers use. So for a student opening their first bank account are they more likely to go to your website or Facebook?

Q. What about the smaller to mid-size business? Can social CRM help here?

Guy Stephens: Absolutely, social media isn't an exclusive 'one size fits all' solution. There are many different platforms to choose from, and they can all be used individually or in combination in any number of different ways.

What's key is that in taking part you are offering something relevant and meaningful to your customers, whether that's a Wiggly Wrigglers recording a podcast,@ OverheardAtMoo responding to customers' queries, or the Carphone Warehouse employees publishing helpful tips and hints about mobile phones via their Eyeopeners channel on YouTube.

I think these types of adopters share an openness to explore, an awareness of what their customers want, backed up by a willingness to actually respond. From a customer service point of view, there are obvious benefits in handling queries' and complaints via social channels. Not only are you handling and often resolving the issues or complaints at source, but you are also wrapping into the way you engage with your customers an automatic PR layer. For a small- to medium-sized company, this type of automatic PR, almost like a continual reputation feed, brings with it clear cost-saving implications as well.

At this point, many companies may well raise the spectre of negative comments as a reason for either not going down this route or at the very least being cautious of it. My response to them is this. People, your customers will complain – that is their right, and that is what we all do. But the reason we complain is that a company has got it wrong somewhere along the way. Customers are simply letting you know where. This gives all companies the opportunity not only to respond in a positive and empathetic way, but also to actually rectify the problem as well. I think we need to re-evaluate not only the way we look at complaints, but also how we define them as well, regardless of the size of your company.

Q. How should companies develop strategies to change the way they deliver customer service enquiries?

Guy Stephens: Fundamentally, for me, this is all about a change in mindset. Companies have long talked about being **customer-centric**, without having to really prove that they are or deliver on it. Customers are now holding mirrors up and exposing all parts of a company to scrutiny.

For me, once again it's about creating an open, enquiring and responsive environment to your customers' needs. This doesn't equate to chaos, or not being in control of what you are doing, or not understanding what success looks like. I like to think of this approach as 'freedom within a framework'.

It's not about looking at it in terms of what the company wants to achieve, but approaching it from the perspective of what your customers are trying to achieve, and then working that backwards. Once again, how well do you understand your customers? Do you understand what social platforms they are using? Do you understand what they are using them for? Do you understand what traditional platforms they are using and what they are using those for? Are they achieving what they set out to achieve? If not, why not? What are the barriers? Then flip it round and ask yourself: what are we trying to achieve?

Only then can you start to understand the gaps and begin to make changes. It's important that you understand what your baseline is before trying to plug in a new channel and avoid unintentionally creating subsequent issues around channel or process integration. If I think back to my time at the Carphone Warehouse, the reason we could try things out was simply because of our approach. Part of this is having people who 'get social'. And this touches on an important issue. From a resourcing perspective, it's apparent from talking to those who are going down this route that their approach is very much around hiring people who understand social media, and then training them in terms of the customer service skills they will need.

If we move onto the practical issues surrounding the use of social media for customer service, the key issues for me are communication and integration.

- *Communicating expectations*: keeping customers informed so that you can manage their expectations. This is where empathy comes into the picture as well. We are certainly seeing customers expecting companies to imbue a greater sense of empathy into customer service interactions than ever before. For a company, how do you 'productise' empathy in a way?
- *Integration*: ensuring the holistic customer experience helps them achieve what they set out to achieve without, bluntly, 'pissing them off' along the way. How do all the different channels – Twitter, phone, store visit, web, chat – that a customer might use in any one interaction work together? What takes precedence over another channel? How do you, or even do you, build a response mechanism to Stephen Fry tweeting about your products, against any other customer tweeting in about the same product? What channels will you offer? What are your opening hours?

For me, it comes back to looking to, working with and trusting your customers to help you find the answers to these questions. Companies no longer hold the dominant position they once did, and we are in a period where companies are being forced to re-evaluate, and in some instances re-engineer, the way in which they engage with their customers.

Q. What is the future potential of web self-service?

Guy Stephens: Companies must try to understand how people seek help. Traditionally, if something went wrong we would go into a store, call or email that company about it, or else ask our friends. Now, if something goes wrong we often turn to Google as our first port of call. From there we go to Twitter, forums, YouTube, blogs etc. Calling a company isn't necessarily your first step any more. The idea of self-sufficiency is a very real threat and in some instances the role of the company is being marginalised; customer service in a sense is decentralising. But this decentralisation also brings with it opportunities.

I think what we will see are a few trends emerge which will require us to recognise and define new ways of working, and which will influence how support is provided both by customers to each other and by companies to customers, and even to wider networks at large:

- Customer service will continue its move into the frontline, becoming a truly strategic part of the business. This is likely to be characterised by an element of friction at the point at which the customers' call for a greater degree of 'socialised' engagement rubs against the traditional drive for cost savings and lean efficiencies.
- There will be a continued move towards collaborative 'help/support' spaces built around the exchange of information and knowledge between people. This will continue the gradual erosion of the way we currently work. A by-product of this will be a blurring between the traditional divisions that separate not only a company from its customers, but also in the actual provision of the services themselves.
- The rise of 'ubiquitous connectivity' not to only one's own network, but to networks in general will continue. The idea that I can literally plug in anytime anywhere. With this comes the idea of 'empowered me' – I am my own work force. Not only am I self-sufficient, but I am also able to offer help as and when the inclination takes me.
- Social media will become increasingly embedded in the processes that underpin the products and services 'companies provide. The current novelty and associated awkwardness in the way we talk about and define customer service as being made up of traditional and social channels will gradually ebb as we simply see the customer service proposition as a natural combining of the two.

Read the full interview with Guy Stephens at: http://goo.gl/WS2W2.

The challenge of customer engagement

Customer engagement
Repeated interactions that strengthen the emotional, psychological or physical investment a customer has in a brand.

Media fragmentation
Describes a trend towards increasing choice and consumption of a range of media in terms of different channels such as web and mobile and also within channels, for example more TV channels, radio stations, magazines, more websites. Media fragmentation implies increased difficulty in reaching target audiences.

Forrester (2007) heralded **customer engagement** as 'marketing's new key metric', given the rapidly increasing online **media fragmentation** and the challenges of keeping customers engaged with brands given the proliferation of choice. Customer engagement is sometimes used to refer to engaging customers on a single touchpoint, such as whether someone dwells on the site for a significant time or whether they convert to sale or other outcome. Instead engagement really refers to the long-term ability of a brand to gain a customer's attention on an ongoing basis whether the engagement could occur on-site, in third-party social networks or in email or traditional direct communications. Richard Sedley, commercial director of customer experience consultancy Foviance (**www.foviance.com**), an international design consultancy, has developed the definition of customer engagement as: 'Repeated interactions that strengthen the emotional, psychological or physical investment a customer has in a brand.'

The commercial aim of engagement is to maximise customer value through using customer interactions to lead to more profitable relationships.

Forrester (2007) developed a framework to measure online engagement through the customer lifecycle and also away from a brand's own site, such as on publisher sites or social networks.

According to Forrester, engagement has four parts which can be measured both online and offline:

- *Involvement*. Forrester says that online this includes website visits, time spent, pages viewed.
- *Interaction*. This is contributed comments to blogs, quantity/frequency of written reviews, and online comments as well as comments expressed in customer service. (We could add the recency, frequency and category of product purchases, and also ongoing engagement in email marketing programmes, as discussed later in this chapter; all are important here.)
- *Intimacy*. This is sentiment tracking on third-party sites including blogs and reviews, as well as opinions expressed in customer service calls.
- *Influence*. This is advocacy indicated by measures such as likelihood to recommend, brand affinity, content forwarded to friends, etc.

It should be measured by data collected both online and offline. Forrester analyst Brian Haven says (Forrester, 2007):

> Using engagement, you get a more holistic appreciation of your customers' actions, recognising that value comes not just from transactions but also from actions people take to influence others. Once engagement takes hold of marketing, marketing messages will become conversations, and dollars will shift from media buying to customer understanding.

Benefits of using e-CRM to support customer engagement

Using digital platforms for relationship marketing involves integrating the customer database with websites and messaging to make the relationship targeted and personalised. Through doing this, marketing can be improved through:

- *Targeting more cost-effectively*. Traditional targeting, for direct mail for instance, is often based on mailing lists compiled according to criteria that mean that not everyone contacted is in the target market. For example, a company wishing to acquire new affluent consumers may use postcodes to target areas with appropriate demographics, but within the postal district the population may be heterogeneous. The result of poor targeting will be low response rates, perhaps less than 1 per cent. *Permission marketing* or **inbound marketing** has the benefit that the list of contacts is *self-selecting* or pre-qualified. A company will only aim to build relationships with those who have visited a website and expressed an interest in its products by registering their name and address.

Inbound marketing
The customer is proactive in actively seeking out a solution and interactions with brands are attracted through content, search and social media marketing.

- *Mass customisation of the marketing messages* (and possibly the product). This tailoring process is described in a subsequent section. Technology makes it possible to send tailored emails at much lower cost than is possible with direct mail and also to provide tailored web pages to smaller groups of customers (microsegments).

- *Increased depth and breadth of information and improve the nature of relationship.* Digital media enables more information to be supplied to customers as required through content marketing. For example, special pages such as Dell's Premier can be set up to provide customer groups with specific information. The nature of the relationship can be changed in that contact with a customer can be made more frequently. The frequency of contact with the customer can be determined by customers – whenever they have the need to visit their personalised pages – or they can be contacted by email by the company.

Sense and respond communications
Delivering timely, relevant communications to customers as part of a contact strategy based on assessment of their position in the customer lifecycle and monitoring specific interactions with a company's website, emails and staff.

- *Deeper customer understanding and more relevant communications can be delivered through a sense and respond approach.* Examples of **sense and respond communications** include tools that summarise products purchased on-site and the searching behaviour that occurred before these products were bought; online feedback forms about the site or products are completed when a customer requests free information; questions asked through forms or emails to the online customer service facilities; online questionnaires asking about product category interests and opinions on competitors; new product development evaluation – commenting on prototypes of new products.

- *Lower cost.* Contacting customers by email or through their viewing web pages costs less than using physical mail, but, perhaps more importantly, information needs to be sent only to those customers who have expressed a preference for it, resulting in fewer mail-outs. Once personalisation technology has been purchased, much of the targeting and communications can be implemented automatically.

- *Delivering loyalty programmes.* Loyalty schemes are often used to encourage customer extension and retention. You will be familiar with schemes run by retailers such as the Tesco Clubcard or Nectar schemes or those of airlines and hotel chains. Such schemes are often used for e-CRM purposes, as follows:

  a initial bonus points for sign-up to online services or initial registration;

  b points for customer development or extension – more points awarded to encourage second or third online purchase;

  c additional points to encourage reactivation of online services.

- Popular products are offered for a relatively low number of points to encourage repeat purchases.

Gamification
The process of applying game thinking and mechanics to engage an audience by rewarding them for achievements and sharing.

- *Opportunities for gamification.* **Gamification** involves applying game-based thinking to a brand, business or organisation to engage and develop loyalty. Research shows that game play itself stimulates the human brain (releasing dopamine) and the now proven mechanics from gaming can be brought into marketing, and especially mobile marketing. Some key features of gamification applied to digital marketing are:

  - creative and concept to engage;

  - game mechanics to encourage play (badges, points, leader-boards, levels, interactions);

  - game dynamics can be altered to reward and even penalise;

  - game currencies to provide the motivation – this can be financial, status, need for doing good, pleasure and influence.

Mini case study 6.2	Chiquita uses gamification with film tie-in

The aim of this campaign, according to Scott Faucheux, North America consumer marketing manager at Chiquita Brands, was to 'create an engaging online playground for our Chiquita Banana consumer where the whole family could share in the fun of Chiquita-branded products, the film Rio, and win great prizes including tasty Chiquita Bananas and other nutritious products. The movie's colourful and exciting story continues online for Chiquita Banana consumers'.

Consumers that signed into the site received a virtual passport and earned virtual badges for exploring pages including video clips from the movie, recipes, colouring pages, product information, games and a sweepstake. The game mechanics includes five concepts from game designers to motivate player behaviour:

1 *Badges* are used as a way to reward players for accomplishing missions. They use the badges to fill their passports and complete levels of game play.
2 Players *work as a team*, collaborating to complete missions. Each time one player earns a badge, the total number of earned badges increases. As that total number of badges goes up, more prizes are unlocked with the prize packages becoming progressively better.
3 The *news feed* shows all player activity, a way of surfacing and cross-promoting all of the content being consumed. It shows life and activity in the game and that there are other people playing. Players can see what others are doing and get clues to what they should do next.
4 *The leader board* shows the high scorers to help ramp up competition among players and sustain interest.
5 *Notification* – players get real-time feedback via an icon that pops up in the bottom of the window. This is an immediate reinforcement of the behaviour and the reward with a recommendation for the next action.

Figure 6.3	Chiquita Rio film campaign applies gamification *Source*: www.bunchball.com/chiquita

Source: www.empowermm.com/blog/2011/05/18/chiquita-rio-empower-gamification/

Marketing applications of e-CRM

E-CRM systems support the following marketing applications:

1 *Sales force automation (SFA).* Sales representatives are supported in their account management through tools to arrange and record customer visits.
2 *Customer service management.* Representatives in contact centres respond to customer requests for information by using an intranet to access databases containing information on the customer, products and previous queries. It is more efficient and may increase customer convenience if customers are given the option of **web self-service**, i.e. accessing support data through a web interface.
3 *Managing the sales process.* This can be achieved through e-commerce sites, or in a B2B context by supporting sales representatives by recording the sales process (SFA).
4 *Customer communications management.* Managing communications integrated across different channels like direct mail, email, mobile messaging, personalised web messages and social networks.
5 *Analysis.* Through technologies such as data warehouses and approaches such as data mining, which are explained further later in the chapter, customers' characteristics, their purchase behaviour and campaigns can be analysed in order to optimise the marketing mix.

Web self-service
Customers perform information requests and transactions through a web interface rather than by contact with customer support staff.

CRM technologies and data

Database technology is at the heart of delivering these CRM applications. Often the database is accessible through an intranet website by employees or an extranet by customers or partners providing an interface onto the entire customer relationship management system. Email is used to manage many of the inbound, outbound and internal communications managed by the CRM system. A workflow system is often used for automating CRM processes. For example, a workflow system can remind sales representatives about customer contacts or can be used to manage service delivery, such as the many stages of arranging a mortgage. The three main types of customer data held as tables in customer databases for CRM are typically:

1 *Personal and profile data.* These include contact details and characteristics for profiling customers, such as age and sex (B2C), and business size, industry sector and the individual's role in the buying decision (B2B).
2 *Transaction data.* A record of each purchase transaction including specific product purchased, quantities, category, location, date and time and channel where purchased.
3 *Communications data.* A record of which customers have been targeted by campaigns and their response to them (outbound communications). Also includes a record of inbound enquiries and sales representative visits and reports (B2B).

The behavioural data available through 2 and 3 are very important for targeting customers to more closely meet their needs.

Customer lifecycle management

Customer lifecycle
The stages each customer will pass through in a long-term relationship through acquisition, retention and extension.

In this section we will review methods of assessing the position of customers in the lifecycle and the use of 'sense and respond' communications to build customer loyalty at each stage of the customer lifecycle.

A high-level view of the classic **customer lifecycle** of select, acquire, retain, extend is shown in Figure 6.4.

Customer extension
- 'Sense and respond'
- Cross-selling and up-selling
- Optimise service quality
- Use the right channels

Customer selection
- Who do we target?
- What is their value?
- What is their lifecycle?
- Where do we reach them?

Customer retention
- Understand individual needs
- Relevant offers for continued usage of online services
- Maximise service quality
- Use the right channels

Customer acquisition
- Target the right segments
- Minimise acquisition cost
- Optimise service quality
- Use the right channels

| Figure 6.4 | The four classic marketing activities of customer relationship management |

Customer selection
Identifying key customer segments and targeting them for relationship building.

Customer acquisition
Strategies and techniques used to gain new customers.

1 **Customer selection** means defining the types of customers that a company will market to. It means identifying different groups of customers for which to develop offerings and to target during acquisition, retention and extension. Different ways of segmenting customers by value and by their detailed lifecycle with the company are reviewed.

2 **Customer acquisition** refers to marketing activities to form relationships with new customers while minimising acquisition costs and targeting high-value customers. Service quality and selecting the right channels for different customers are important at this stage and throughout the lifecycle. For an online business, acquisition may involve a single-step conversion, for example, if a new visitor arrives on a site and purchases on the first visit. Typically, a longer, multi-step process is needed for conversion to sale where a visitor returns to the site. To facilitate conversion, customer lifecycle marketing should seek to form an initial relationship through asking for contact details for communication such as email address, mobile number or a social media contact. This is the permission marketing approach which we explain in the next section. For online SaaS startups, there is an additional step of **activation**, which means that a person registered with an online brand takes further action(s), such as trying the service.

Activation
A prospect or customer takes the first step in actively using an online service after initial registration or purchase.

Customer retention
Techniques to maintain relationships with existing customers.

3 **Customer retention** refers to the marketing activities taken by an organisation to keep its existing customers, i.e. to encourage them to buy again or continue a contract which renews for a service. Identifying relevant offerings based on their individual needs and detailed position in the customer lifecycle (e.g. number and value of purchases) is key.

4 **Customer extension** refers to increasing the depth or range of products that a customer purchases from a company. This is often referred to as 'customer development'.

Customer extension
Techniques to encourage customers to increase their involvement with an organisation.

There is a range of customer extension techniques that are particularly important to online retailers:

- *Re-sell*. Selling similar products to existing customers – particularly important in some B2B contexts as rebuys or modified rebuys.
- *Cross-sell*. Selling additional products which may be closely related to the original purchase, but not necessarily so.
- *Up-sell*. A subset of cross-selling, but in this case selling more expensive products.
- *Reactivation*. Customers who have not purchased for some time, or have lapsed, can be encouraged to purchase again.
- *Referrals*. Generating sales from recommendations from existing customers – for example, member-get-member deals.

You can see that this framework distinguishes between customer retention and customer extension. Retention involves keeping the most valuable customers by selecting relevant customers for retention, understanding their loyalty factors that keep them buying and then developing strategies that encourage loyalty and cement the relationship. Customer extension is about developing customers to try a broader range of products to convert the most growable customers into the most valuable customers. You will also see that there are common features to each area – balancing cost and quality of service through the channels used according to the anticipated value of customers. Peppers and Rogers (1993) brought to our attention the notion of one-to-one marketing and discussed how it could be facilitated through the use of digital technologies. This was a new model of consumer marketing in the early 1990's but remains pertinent.

Peppers and Rogers (1997) recommend the following stages to achieve these goals, which they popularised as the 5Is:

- *Identification.* Learn the characteristics of customers in as much detail as possible to be able to conduct the dialogue.
- *Individualisation.* Individualising is using mass customisation and personalisation to define the company's approach to each customer, offering a benefit to the customer based on the identification of customer needs. The effort expended on each customer should be consistent with the value of that customer to the organisation.
- *Interaction.* Continued dialogue to understand both the customer's needs and the customer's strategic value.
- *Integration.* Integration of the relationship and knowledge of the customer must extend throughout all parts of the company, harnessing data integrated from different systems.
- *Integrity.* Since all relationships are built on trust, it is essential not to lose the trust of the customer. Efforts to learn from the customer should not be seen as intrusive, and privacy should be maintained. (See Chapter 3 for coverage of privacy issues related to e-CRM.)

Marketers still recognise the importance of Peppers and Rogers' (1993)(Peppers & Rogers, 1993) model and say that it is a critical component when interacting with consumers on their shopping journeys (Tomei, 2010). Tomei (2010) suggests there are three stages where understanding how to interact on a 1:1 basis is important. The stages are:

1 *Prior to the store visit* – shoppers are researching and looking for purchase options, often looking at reviews through social media. Marketers need to integrate all available data to provide better insight for the shopper.
2 *On the road* – marketers need to stay in touch with the prospective customer throughout their journey to purchase. GPS technology enables on-the-move communications, which can be highly targeted.
3 *In the store* – marketers are able to stay in touch and in doing so customise individual shoppers' experiences. Apple has developed iBeacons, which through mobile phones enables retailers to alert shoppers to products, discounts and rewards within their stores (Shellaker, 2014).

Permission marketing

Permission marketing
Customers agree (opt-in) to be involved in an organisation's marketing activities, usually as a result of an incentive.

Permission marketing is a significant concept that underpins online CRM in management of the customer lifecycle. 'Permission marketing' is a term coined by Seth Godin (1999). It is best characterised with just three (or four) words:

> Permission marketing is …
>   anticipated, relevant and personal [and timely].

Interruption marketing
Marketing communications that disrupt customers' activities.

Godin (1999) noted that while research used to show we were bombarded by 500 marketing messages a day, with the advent of the web and digital TV this has now increased to over 3000 a day! From the marketing organisation's viewpoint, this leads to a dilution in the effectiveness of the messages – how can the communications of any one company stand out? Godin refers to the traditional approach as **interruption marketing**. Permission marketing is about seeking the customer's permission before engaging them in a relationship and providing something in exchange. The classic exchange is based on information or entertainment – a B2B site can offer a free report in exchange for a prospect sharing their email address which will be used to maintain a dialogue; a B2C site can offer a screensaver in exchange.

From a practical e-commerce perspective, we can think of a customer agreeing to engage in a relationship when they check a box on a web form to indicate that they agree to receive further communications from a company. This approach is widely known as **opt-in**. This is preferable to **opt-out**, the situation where a customer has to consciously request not to receive further information.

The importance of incentivisation in permission marketing has also been emphasised by Seth Godin, who likens the process of acquisition and retention to dating someone. Likening customer relationship building to social behaviour is not new, as O'Malley and Tynan (2001) note; the analogy of marriage has been used since the 1980s at least. They also report on consumer research which indicates that while marriage may be analogous to business relationships, it is less appropriate for B2C relationships.

Godin (1999) suggests that dating the customer involves:

1 offering the prospect an *incentive* to volunteer;
2 using the attention offered by the prospect, offering a curriculum over time, teaching the consumer about your product or service;
3 reinforcing the *incentive* to guarantee that the prospect maintains the permission;
4 offering additional *incentives* to get even more permission from the consumer;
5 over time, using the permission to change consumer behaviour towards profits.

In practice, new forms of 'interruption' are required. To attract prospects to a website or social media presence, the inbound marketing techniques described in Chapter 9, such as search marketing, social media and remarketing using display ads, are still needed to gain attention.

Figure 6.5 gives a summary of a common, effective process for permission-based online relationship building to support engagement through the different stages of the customer lifecycle.

The stages are:

- *Stage 1. Attract new and existing customers to online presence.* The online and offline communications channels described in Chapter 9, such as search, social media marketing and direct mail, are used to drive visitors to a website, Facebook or other form of presence such as an app that enables opt-in.
- *Stage 2a. Prompt and incentivise visitors to action.* Two key types of incentives to consider are: **lead generation offers** and **sales generation offers**. On Facebook, companies used gated pages where the visitor must 'Like' the brand before they can gain the incentive.

Types of offers marketers can devise include information value, entertainment value, monetary value and privileged access to information (such as that only available on an extranet). The beauty of digital marketing is that different offers can be tested for different audiences using AB or multivariate testing (Chapter 10) and the offers refined to increase response.

To get visitors to take notice, prominent calls-to-action or pop-ups can boost conversion rates. For example, the pop-up shown in Figure 6.6, which was resisted by Dave Chaffey for several years, increased lead conversion by 40 per cent when deployed on Smart Insights. Many web users will be annoyed by pop-ups, yet for site owners they do increase the number of leads, so the number of pop-ups is now increasing and is likely to do so further.

- *Stage 2b: Capture customer information to maintain relationship.* Capturing profile information is commonly achieved through an online form such as shown in Figure 6.6,

---

Opt-in
A customer proactively agrees to receive further information.

Opt-out
A customer declines the offer to receive further information.

Lead generation offer
Offered in return for customers providing their contact details and characteristics. Commonly used in B2B marketing where free information such as a report or a seminar will be offered.

Sales generation offer
Encourage product trial. A coupon redeemed against a purchase is a classic example.

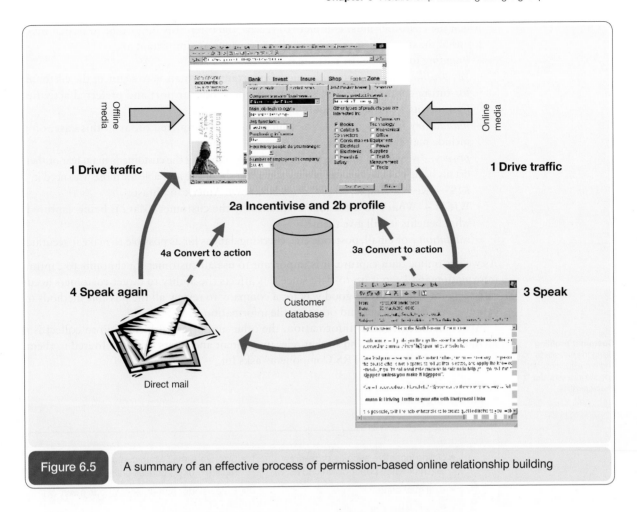

| Figure 6.5 | A summary of an effective process of permission-based online relationship building |

| Figure 6.6 | Example of a pop-up on SmartInsights.com |

which the customer must complete to receive the offer. It is important to design these forms to maximise their completion. Factors which are important are:

- *branding* to reassure the customer;
- *key profile fields* to capture the most important information to segment the customer for future communications – in this case postcode, airport and preferred activities (not too many questions should be asked);
- *mandatory fields* – mark fields which must be completed or, as in this case, only include mandatory figures;
- *privacy* – 'we will not share' is the magic phrase to counter the customer's main fear of their details being passed on; a full privacy statement should be available for those who need it;
- *KISS* – 'Keep it simple, stupid' is a well-known American phrase;
- *WIFM* – 'What's in it for me?' Explain why the customer's data is being captured; what benefits it will give them?
- *validation* – of email, postcode etc., checking data as far as possible to make it accurate.

As well as online data capture, it is important to use all customer touchpoints to capture information and keep it up-to-date since this affects the ability to target customers accurately. Figure 6.7 provides a good way for a company to review all the possible methods of capturing email addresses and other profile information.

Apart from the contact information, the other important information to collect is a method of **customer profiling** so that relevant content and offers can be delivered to them. For example, B2B company RS Components asks for:

- industry sector;
- purchasing influence;

Customer profiling
Using the website to find out a customer's specific interests and characteristics.

	New customers	**Existing customers**
Online touch points	• Online incentive such as prize-draw (B2C) or white paper download (B2B) • Viral marketing • E-newsletter opt-in on site • Registration to view content or submit content to a community forum • Renting list, co-branded e-mail or advertising in third-party e-newsletter to encourage opt-in • Co-registration with third party sites	• Capture e-mail when customer first registers or purchases online • E-newsletter and other methods given on left
Offline touch points	• Direct mail offer perhaps driving visitors to web • Trade shows or conference • Paper response to traditional direct mail communication • Phone response to direct mail or ad	• Paper order form, customer registration/product warranty form • Sales reps – face-to-face • Contact centre – by phone • Point of sale for retailers

Figure 6.7 Matrix of customer touch points for collecting and updating customer email contact and other profile information

- specific areas of product interest;
- how many people you manage;
- total number of employees in company.

Once data has been initially collected, it should be added to gain a better understanding of customer needs and behaviours. The risk here is that if data is entered into different systems, data quality issues may arise with inaccurate data. Management measures should be put in place to create an accurate **single customer view**. This is a significant risk with e-CRM systems since data can be collected offline and in different online systems such as on the website, transactional e-commerce or within social media and a separate email system.

Single customer view
Customer profile information is kept consistent across systems to maintain customer data quality.

- *Stage 3: Maintain dialogue using online communication.* To build the relationship between company and customer there are many digital methods of communication. These are:
  1 Send an email to the customer which can be tailored based on the customer's' disclosed profile information or information inferred from the type of content they have accessed on the site.
  2 Display specific information on the website when the customer logs in. This is referred to as 'personalisation'.
  3 Use syndication technology such as RSS feeds or sharing via social networks to deliver content to the customer. Social networks have the limitation currently of not having a level of permission where profile information can be accessed, and messages can't be personalised. Integration of email and social network profiles is possible using a technique known as **social sign on** (Smart Insights, 2011) where a user logs in to a site using their social network profile and this can be linked with profile information captured through traditional web forms. Smart Insights (2011) give the example of Sears Social (**http://social.sears.com**), where users' reviews and ratings about products are included as part of their profile. This is an example of social commerce.

Social sign-on
A user logs in to a site using a social network service user name and password. This can enable connection between social memberships and company profile information.

- *Stage 4. Maintain dialogue using offline communication.* Direct mail or phone contact may still be cost-effective forms of communication since these can also be tailored and may have more 'cut-through' compared to an email. With direct mail campaigns the aim may be to drive traffic to the website in a web response campaign using techniques such as:
  - online competition;
  - online web seminar (webinar);
  - sales promotion.

A further objective in stage 3 and stage 4 is to improve customer information quality. In particular, emails may bounce – in which case offline touchpoints, as indicated in Figure 6.7, need to be planned to determine the latest addresses.

With the advent of social media marketing, the permission marketing concept has been applied to social networks where opt-in involves 'liking' a brand on Facebook or following a company on Twitter, LinkedIn or Google+. Within Facebook, 'Liking' or exchange of email address can be encouraged through company pages as in Mini case study 6.3 about Princess Cruises. Of course, email offers a key benefit over social media channels since it can be tailored to the individual.

Writing for *What's New in Marketing*, Chaffey (2004) extended Godin's principles to e-CRM with his 'e-permission marketing principles', which remain relevant for reviewing use of email marketing and social CRM communications strategy:

- **Principle 1** – *Consider selective opt-in to communications.* In other words, offer choice in *communications preferences* to the customer to ensure more relevant communications. Some customers may not want a weekly e-newsletter; rather, they may only want to hear about new product releases. Remember opt-in is a legal requirement in many countries. Four key communications preferences options, selected by tick box are:
  - *Content* – news, products, offers, events.
  - *Frequency* – weekly, monthly, quarterly, or alerts.

| Mini case study 6.3 | Princess Cruises integrate Facebook and email marketing activities |

In this campaign, Princess Cruises used a classic 'blog to win' or 'share to win' campaign asking readers about their favourite travel destination and based around the hub of the company Facebook page (Figure 6.8).

The different waves of this integrated campaign were:

Step 1 Promote to existing customers through email

Subject line: *Just one week left to enter to win a dream holiday!*

The aim is to encourage subscribers to like the company on Facebook and then encourage entries – both which will have a viral effect.

Step 2 Facebook contest tab encourages like

The campaign is based around a 'Travel Bucket' wish list in which customers are encouraged to share through videos and write-ups.

Step 3 Engage through contest tabs to create, share and win

Company Facebook pages have different tabs like a company microsite within Facebook which encourage customers to interact and return to the site.

Step 4 Inspire through blog

Within the company site, the blog also generates ongoing interest through articles written about cruise destination positioned as written by staff rather than journalists to add a personal touch.

| Figure 6.8 | Princess Cruises campaign Facebook Page |

- *Channel* – email, social network, direct mail, phone or SMS.
- *Format* – text vs HTML.
- **Principle 2** – *Create a 'common customer profile'*. A structured approach to customer data capture is needed, otherwise some data will be missed – as is the case with the utility company that collected 80,000 email addresses, but forgot to ask for the post-code for geo-targeting! This can be achieved through a common customer profile – a definition of all the database fields that are relevant to the marketer in order to understand and target the customer with a relevant offering. The customer profile can have different levels to set targets for data quality (Level 1 is contact details and key profile fields only, Level 2 includes preferences and Level 3 includes full purchase and response behaviour).
- **Principle 3** – *Offer a range of opt-in incentives*. Many websites now have 'free–win–save' incentives to encourage opt-in, but often it is one incentive fits all visitors. Different incentives for different audiences will generate a higher volume of permission, particularly for business-to-business websites. We can also gauge the characteristics of the respondent by the type of incentives or communications they have requested, without the need to ask them.
- **Principle 4** – *Don't make opt-out too easy*. Often marketers make it too easy to unsubscribe. Although offering some form of opt-out is now a legal requirement in many countries due to privacy laws, a single click to unsubscribe is making it too easy. Instead, wise e-permission marketers such as Amazon use the concept of 'My Profile' or a 'selective opt-out'. Instead of unsubscribe, they offer a link to a 'communications preferences' or 'customer centre' web form to update a profile that includes the options to reduce communications, which may be the option taken rather than unsubscribing completely.
- **Principle 5** – *Watch, don't ask (or 'Sense and Respond')*. The need to ask interruptive questions can be reduced through the use of monitoring clicks to better understand customer needs and to trigger follow-up communications. Some examples:
  - monitoring click-through to different types of content or offer;
  - monitoring the engagement of individual customers with email communications;
  - follow-up reminder to those who don't open the email first time.
- **Principle 6** – *Create an outbound contact strategy*. Online permission marketers need a plan for the number, frequency and type of online and offline communications and offers. This is a **contact** or **touch strategy** which is particularly important for large organisations with several marketers responsible for email communications. We describe contact strategies in more depth in the next section.

Contact strategy
Definition of the sequence and type of outbound communications required at different points in the customer lifecycle.

An example of permission marketing in practice, and how to set goals for permission". 'Say and Southwell (2006) give an example of a permission-based campaign to promote a new interactive banking service, the campaign objectives and results (in brackets) were to:

- capture 5000 mobile phone numbers from customers (200 per cent of plan);
- acquire 3000 email addresses (176 per cent of plan);
- raise awareness about the new service (31,000 customers view demonstration);
- create 1000 new registrations (576 per cent of plan).

'Right touching' through developing online contact strategies

Given the difficulty in achieving customer engagement, with the increase in media fragmentation and the development of high attention media such as social networks, the need for developing a structured approach to communicating with customers across the lifecycle has become more urgent. Dave Chaffey has emphasised the importance for companies to build and refine an integrated multichannel touch or contact strategy which delivers customised communications to consumers using different media including display ads, social media, email and web recommendations and promotions. (Digital marketing insight 6.1)

Contextual marketing
Relevant communications
are delivered consistent
with the context of the
recipient which can
depend on their location,
time or place.

Every customer interaction or response to a communication should be followed up by a series of relevant communications delivered by the right combinations of channel (web, email, phone, direct mail) to elicit a response or further dialogue. This is **contextual marketing**, where the aim is to deliver relevant messages which fit the current context of what the customer is interested in according to the searches they have performed, the type of content they have viewed or the products they have recently purchased.

A contact policy should be developed to manage and control communications so that they are at an acceptable level. The contact strategy should indicate the following:

- *Frequency* – e.g. minimum once per quarter and maximum once per month.
- *Interval* – e.g. there must be a gap of at least one week or one month between communications.
- *Content and offers* – we may want to limit or achieve a certain number of prize draws or information-led offers.
- *Links* – between online communications and offline communications.
- *A control strategy* – a mechanism to make sure these guidelines are adhered to, for example using a single 'focal point' for checking all communications before creation dispatch.

Examples of contact strategies for Euroffice and **Tesco.com** were discussed in Chapter 4. A simpler example of a contact strategy is shown in the following Mini case study 6.4.

Table 6.1 shows a recommended approach for developing a contact strategy or email communications sequence involving different behavioural trigger events which prompt broadcast of a personalised email.

The 'emotionally unsubscribed' email list members

The inactive members of an email list are sometimes called the 'emotionally unsubscribed'. They represent a significant issue in the management of customer email marketing programmes. Although unsubscribe rates are usually low (for example, less than 0.1 per cent per campaign) there can be upwards of 50 per cent of a list who are 'emotionally unsubscribed' – i.e. they are not actually unsubscribed but rarely open or click, suggesting that email is not an effective communications channel. To avoid this and to maintain the dialogue, it is important to ensure that the contact strategy has been planned and

---

| Digital marketing insight 6.1 | Right touching can be summarised as: |

A **Multichannel Communications Strategy**

Customised for Individual Prospects and Customers forming segments

Across a **defined customer lifecycle**

Which ...

Delivers the **Right Message**

Featuring the **Right Value Proposition** (product, service or experience)

With the **Right Tone**

At the **Right Time** or context

With the Right **Frequency and Interval**

Using the Right **Media/Communications channels**

To achieve ...

Right **balance of value between both parties**

Mini case study 6.4	WHSmith use behavioural email to encourage engagement

Behavioural email marketing or remarketing is a classic 'sense and respond' e-CRM approach. In this case, a classic abandoned shopping cart follow-up email, but with three alternative communications which were tested with these results:

1 *Generic branded follow-up email*: + 10 per cent conversion rate.
2 *Personalised remarketing email with a promotional code for a 5 per cent discount time-limited to 72 hours*: + 100 per cent conversion rate.
3 *Personalised remarketing email with a promotional code for a 5 per cent discount time-limited to 48 hours*: + 200 per cent conversion rate.

A survey was conducted (VE interactive) of those customers who had clicked through from the remarketing emails and had made a purchase, but who hadn't actually used the promotional codes! Interestingly, it was found:

● These customers had still reacted to the remarketing email as a prompt to return to the WHSmith website.
● It was the expiry date of the call to action that had prompted them to return, even though they then did not take advantage of the 5 per cent discount promo code.

Source: VE Interactive Case Study published on SmartInsights: www.smartinsights.com/email-marketing-ecrm-alerts/email-remarketing-an-example-of-how-to-test/, accessed January 2015.

Table 6.1	Example welcome contact strategy

	Message type	Interval/trigger condition	Outcomes required	Medium for message/sequence
1	Welcome message	Guest site membership signup Immediate	● Encourage trial of site services ● Increase awareness of range of commercial and informational offerings	Email, post transaction pa
2	Engagement message	1 month inactive (i.e. <3 visits)	● Encourage use of forum (good enabler of membership) ● Highlight top content	Email, home page, side panels deep in site
3	Initial cross-sell message	1 month active	● Encourage membership ● Ask for feedback	Email
4	Conversion	2 days after browsing content	● Use for range of services for guest members or full	Phone or email

implemented to deliver relevant messages. Some other steps that can be taken to manage this issue include:

● Measure the level of activity in email response at a more granular level, e.g. review open, click, purchase rates or other actions at different points in time compared to when the subscribers first signed up. Response rates from different segment types who have taken different actions can also be reviewed to see how engaging they find the e-newsletter.
● Test different frequencies. It may be appropriate to reduce frequency if customers become 'emotionally unsubscribed' and then emails received will have a large impact. List members can also be surveyed for their preferences, possibly as part of a reactivation campaign.

- Develop automated customer lifecycle emails as part of the contact strategy which are relevant and tailored according to the interests of the subscriber. Lifecycle emails will include welcome email contact strategies, reactivation email strategies and other service messages such as customer feedback surveys.
- Ensure the fields that are used to customise messages are those that are most likely to be relevant. Often these won't be the obvious fields such as gender, but contextual information related to content or products which have been recently consumed, as shown by Figure 6.9.
- Use offline communications such as direct mail and phone where list members express a preference for these (and see Stage 4 below).

Personalisation and mass customisation

Personalisation
Web-based personalisation involves delivering customised content for the individual, through web pages, email or push technology.

Mass customisation
The creation of tailored marketing messages or products for individual customers or groups of customers typically using technology to retain the economies of scale and the capacity of mass marketing or production.

Customer preference centre
Profile page(s) which enables customers to tailor the type and frequency of communications they receive.

Increasingly companies gather much personal data through the application of digital technology and then use it to develop personalised communication messages, with the aim of making the content appear more aligned to an individual's interests. However, not all individuals respond favourably; indeed some react negatively towards advertisers that adopt this approach due to fears over security of personal data and the feeling they are being manipulated (Tucker, 2014). This leaves online marketers with a dilemma: should they strengthen privacy controls but in doing so reduce the opportunity to personalise their advertising messages and thereby reduce the potency of personalised communications? Tucker (2014) investigates the question of 'How strengthening privacy controls affects advertising performance' using Facebook advertising campaigns. The findings support earlier research by Fournier and Avery (2011), who suggested that 'to succeed in the new world of social media, brands must relinquish control'. Tucker (2014) found that when individuals were given more control over privacy settings they were more likely to respond positively to personalised communications. So to derive maximum benefits from the use of personal information advertisers should consider giving individuals more control over how their information is used.

A way to manage **personalisation** and **mass customisation** on a website is to tailor information content email through a **customer preferences centre**. 'Personalisation' and 'mass customisation' are terms that are often used interchangeably. In the strict sense, personalisation refers to customisation of information requested by a site customer at an *individual* level. Mass customisation involves providing tailored content to a *group* or *individuals*

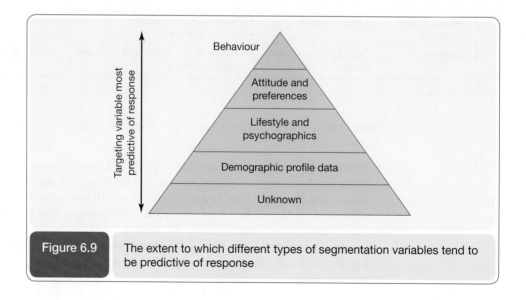

Figure 6.9 The extent to which different types of segmentation variables tend to be predictive of response

with similar interests. It uses technology to achieve this on an economical basis. An example of mass customisation is when Amazon recommends similar products according to what others in a segment have offered, or if it sent a similar email to customers who had an interest in a particular topic such as e-commerce.

Other methods of profiling customers include collaborative filtering and monitoring the content they view. With **collaborative filtering**, customers are openly asked to indicate what their interests are by checking boxes. A database then compares the customer's preferences with those of other customers in its database, and makes recommendations or delivers information accordingly. The more information a database contains about an individual customer, the more useful its recommendations can be. The best-known example of this technology in action can be found on the Amazon website (**www.amazon.com**), where the database reveals that customers who bought book X also bought books Y and Z.

Figure 6.10 summarises the options available to organisations wishing to use the Internet for mass customisation or personalisation. If there is little information available about the customer and it is not integrated with the website then no mass customisation is possible (A). To achieve mass customisation or personalisation, the organisation must have sufficient information about the customer. For limited tailoring to groups of customers (B), it is necessary to have basic profiling information such as age, sex, social group, product category interest or, for B2B, role in the buying unit. This information must be contained in a database system that is directly linked to the system used to display website content. For personalisation on a one-to-one level (C) more detailed information about specific interests, perhaps available from a purchase history, should be available.

An organisation can use Figure 6.10 to plan their relationship marketing strategy. The symbols X_1 to X_3 show a typical path for an organisation. At X_1 information collected about customers is limited. At X_2 detailed information is available about customers, but it is in discrete databases that are not integrated with the website. At X_3 the strategy is to provide mass customisation of information and offers to major segments, since it is felt that the expense of full personalisation is not warranted.

Collaborative filtering
Profiling of customer interests coupled with delivery of specific information and offers, often based on the interests of similar customers.

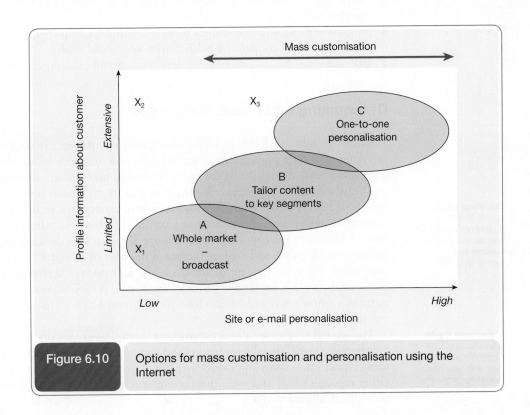

Figure 6.10 Options for mass customisation and personalisation using the Internet

Using digital media to increase customer loyalty and value

Customer loyalty
The desire on the part of the customer to continue to do business with a given supplier over time.

The ultimate commercial aim of relationship marketing approaches such as e-CRM and social CRM is to increase engagement with customers leading to increased **customer loyalty** and so direct sales from these customers and indirect sales through advocacy. Understanding the different levers that contribute to increased engagement and loyalty amongst different customer groups should be the starting point in developing a customer retention and growth strategy.

In Chapter 2 we introduced the Loyalty Loop described by Court *et al.* (2009) in the classic McKinsey Quarterly white paper *The Consumer Decision Journey*. The paper discusses 'Loyalty loop', which shows opportunities for brands to reinforce the loyalty of their own customers or encourage switching after purchase during what it calls the 'Enjoy, Advocate, Bond' stage. They found that more than 60 per cent of consumers of facial skin care products conduct online research about the products *after* purchase – a touchpoint not normally considered in the classic marketing funnel. When consumers are pleased with a purchase, they'll advocate for it by word-of-mouth including social media, but if a consumer is disappointed by the brand, they may criticise it through social media. Part of social CRM activities are to encourage online advocacy and limited negative word-of-mouth. Presi *et al.* (2014) explored how customers who share their negative service experience by creating UGC in social media can be segmented according to their motivation. They found that altruistic, vengeance and economic motivations are strong drivers for user-generated content (UGC) creation after a negative service experience.

In their book, *Groundswell* (Li and Bernoff, 2011), advising on social CRM, Forrester analysts Charlene Li and Josh Bernoff advise using these five activities to manage CRM:

1 **Listening** – developing an analytics capability enabling you to monitor social conversations.
2 **Talking** – improving customer engagement capabilities (in both social and other channels) that enable you to respond to what you've heard.
3 **Energising** – harnessing the power of your 'best' customer to be active advocates for your brand.
4 **Support** – using social channels to help customers help themselves and others via collaborative and cooperative behaviours across social media.
5 **Embrace** – involve customers in the development and tailoring of your products.

Determining what customers value

Emotional loyalty
Loyalty to a brand is demonstrated by favourable perceptions, opinions and recommendations.

Consider the different forms of online interaction a consumer can have with a brand that can determine their perceptions of satisfaction and influence loyalty. Figure 6.11 shows how, when using digital media for online retention marketing, our ultimate goal on the right of the diagram is customer loyalty. The factors on the left help to deliver two main drivers of loyalty. First, **emotional loyalty,** where loyalty to a brand is demonstrated by favourable perceptions, opinions and recommendations including social sharing. The success factors at the top of the diagram are all related to the customer experience of online services (as we will explore further at the start of Chapter 7). These tend to influence emotional loyalty the most, and these are important in determining customer satisfaction. Of course, a favourable customer experience is very important to achieving repeat purchases – how many online sites have you continued to use after a poor level of service was delivered?

Behavioural loyalty
Loyalty to a brand is demonstrated by repeat sales and response to marketing campaigns.

The second type of loyalty is **behavioural loyalty**, where loyalty relates to repeat sales, repeated site visits, social interactions and response to marketing campaigns. To achieve these repeat sales, companies work hard to deliver relevant marketing communications either through email and social media communications, web-based personalisation or through traditional media.

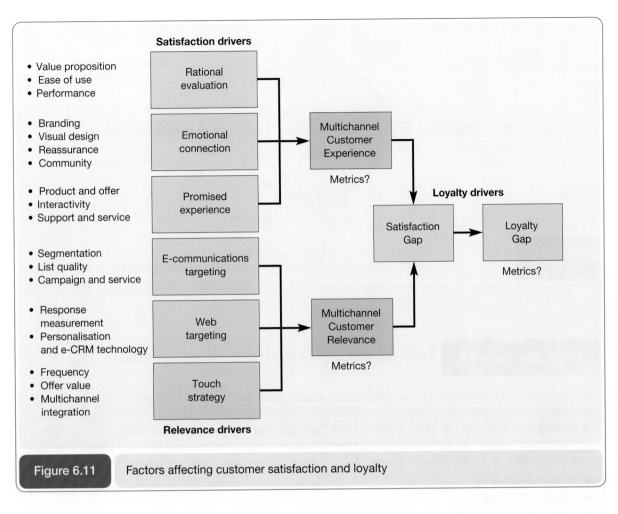

Satisfaction drivers

- Value proposition
- Ease of use
- Performance

- Branding
- Visual design
- Reassurance
- Community

- Product and offer
- Interactivity
- Support and service

- Segmentation
- List quality
- Campaign and service

- Response measurement
- Personalisation and e-CRM technology

- Frequency
- Offer value
- Multichannel integration

Relevance drivers

| Figure 6.11 | Factors affecting customer satisfaction and loyalty |

Figure 6.11 shows typical loyalty drivers to review, but customer research is essential to understand how specific factors affect loyalty and how satisfaction influences loyalty.

The relationship between satisfaction and loyalty

Customer satisfaction
The extent to which a customer's expectations of product quality, service quality and price are met.

Although the terms 'satisfaction' and 'loyalty' are sometimes used interchangeably, we have seen that they do not necessarily correspond. **Customer satisfaction** refers to how happy a customer is about the quality of products and services. As a customer's satisfaction with products and/or services increases, so should their behavioural and emotional loyalty, together with advocacy (Table 6.2 and Mini case study 6.5).

As we have seen, though, there may be customers with a high degree of satisfaction who don't exhibit behavioural loyalty and, conversely, customers who are loyal according to their behaviour that may be at risk of defection since they are not satisfied. The implications are that it is important not only to measure satisfaction with online services, but loyalty also. In this way we are able to identify customers at risk of defection who are likely to choose an alternative and those in the zone of indifference. This is an important category of customer who, although they may have a high degree of satisfaction, is not necessarily loyal.

To measure satisfaction ratings meaningfully, satisfaction must be benchmarked against other companies in and out of sector using standard questions. In the US, the American Satisfaction Index uses a standard methodology for different types of e-businesses, as shown in Figure 6.12. This diagram illustrates how behavioural measures which reveal how customers interact with brands online are often recorded through web analytics systems as

Figure 6.12 Alternative methods for reviewing customer feedback
Source: Foresee Results (2011), Annual Ebusiness Report, published 19 July 2011, edited by Larry Freed

Mini case study 6.5   How car manufacturers use loyalty-based segmentation

An approach to reconciling customer satisfaction, loyalty, value and potential is to use a value-based segmentation. This modelling approach is often used by car manufacturers and other companies that are assessing strategies to enhance the future value of their customer segments. This approach involves creating a segmentation model combining real data for each customer about their current value and satisfaction, and modelled values for future loyalty and value. Each customer is scored according to these four variables:

- current satisfaction;
- repurchase loyalty;
- current value;
- future potential.

Table 6.2   Loyalty-based segmentation for car manufacturer

SLVP score	Nature of customer	Segment strategy
Moderate satisfaction and loyalty. Moderate current and future potential value	An owner of average loyalty who replaces their car every three to four years and has a tendency to repurchase from brand	Not a key segment to influence. But should encourage to subscribe to e-newsletter club and deliver targeted messages around time of renewal
High satisfaction, moderate loyalty. Low future and potential value	A satisfied owner but tends to buy second-hand and keeps cars until they have a high mileage	Engage in dialogue via email newsletter and use this to encourage advocacy and make aware of benefits of buying new
Low satisfaction and loyalty. High current and future potential value	A dissatisfied owner of luxury cars who is at risk of switching	A key target segment who needs to be contacted to understand issues and reassure about quality and performance

described in Chapter 10, but they are lagging indicators that don't predict future success. Satisfaction measures tend to be more predictive of future success and purchase intent.

Measuring the voice of the customer in digital media

Online voice of customer (VoC)
Qualitative assessments of the effectiveness of digital presence based on direct customer feedback. They answer 'who and why' questions about how customers interact with brands online.

Net Promoter Score (NPS)
A measure of the number of advocates a company (or website) has who would recommend it compared to the number of detractors.

Online voice of customer (VoC) measures are useful for reviewing customer sentiment online. The satisfaction ratings we have reviewed are one example of VoC measures. Another approach, which we will explore in Chapters 7 and 10, is intent-satisfaction surveys where the reasons for why a customer is visiting a site are compared against their success in completing tasks and their satisfaction ratings. This is a key technique for improving online customer journeys.

Net Promoter Score (NPS) is a key VoC measure of advocacy originally popularised by Reichheld (2006) in his book: 'the Ultimate Question' is essentially 'would you recommend us?' The aim is to work out techniques to maximise this NPS. Reichheld explains the main process for NPS as follows:

1 Systematically categorise customers into promoters, passives or detractors. If you prefer, you can call them loyal advocates, fair-weather friends and adversaries.
2 Creating closed-loop processes so that the right employees will directly investigate the root causes that drive customers into these categories.
3 Making the creation of more promoters and fewer detractors a top priority so employees up and down the organisation take actions based on their findings from these root-cause investigations.

In practice, consumers are asked 'Would you recommend [Brand/Company X] to a friend or colleague?', answered on a scale between 0 (not at all likely) and 10 (extremely likely). The actual score is calculated by subtracting the percentage of detractors (those giving 0–6 answers) from promoters (9–10s). The middle section, between 7 and 8, are the so-called passives.

The concept of NPS is based on economic analysis of the customer base of a company. For Dell, Reichheld estimates that the average consumer is worth $210 (five-year, Net Present Value), whereas a detractor costs the company $57 and a promoter generates $328. Online, Dell uses software from Opinion Labs (**www.opinionlabs.com**) to both gather feedback and follow up on negative experiences and so reduce the number of detractors with major negative sentiment.

So, the idea is that after surveying as many customers as possible (to make it representative) and show you are listening, you then work backwards to determine which aspects of the experience of interacting with a brand creates 'promoters' or 'detractors'. Some specific approaches that can be used to help manage NPS in the online environment are:

1 Facilitating online advocacy:
   - Page template contains 'Forward/recommend to a friend' options.
   - Email templates contain 'Forward to a friend option'.
   - Facilitate customer feedback through a structured programme of emailing customers for their opinions and NPS evaluations and by making it easy for site owners to comment.
   - Showcase positive experiences – for example, e-retail sites often contain options for rating and commenting on products.
   - Involve customers more in shaping your web services and core product offerings, such as the approach used by Dell in their IdeaStorm site (**www.ideastorm.com**).
2 Managing online detractors:
   - Use online reputation management tools for notification of negative (and positive) comments.
   - Develop a process and identify resources for rapidly responding to negative comments using a natural and open approach.

- Assess and manage the influence of negative comments within the natural listings of search engines.
- Practise fundamental marketing principles of listening to customer comments about products and services and aim to rectify them to win back the situation!

An example of a company that seeks feedback from customers and then makes this feedback available to all customers is shirt retailer Charles Tyrwhitt (Figure 6.13).

Kirby and Samson (2007) have critiqued the use of the NPS in practice. For example, they ask:

> is an NPS of 40, consisting of 70% promoters and 30% detractors, the same as the same NPS consisting of 40% promoters and 0% detractors?

They also quote research by Kumar *et al.* (2007) which shows that while about three-quarters of US telecoms and financial service customers may intend to recommend when asked, only about one-third actually follow through and only about 13 per cent of those referrals actually generate new customers. Keiningham *et al.* (2007) have assessed the value of recommendation metrics as determinants of customer lifetime value and also believe that the use of NPS could be misleading. They say the consequences of a simple focus on NPS are:

> the potential misallocation of customer satisfaction and loyalty resources due to flawed strategies that are guided by a myopic focus on customers' recommend intentions.

Differentiating customers by value and engagement

A core approach to relationship marketing is to focus our limited resources and marketing activities on the most valuable customers. Within the online customer base of an

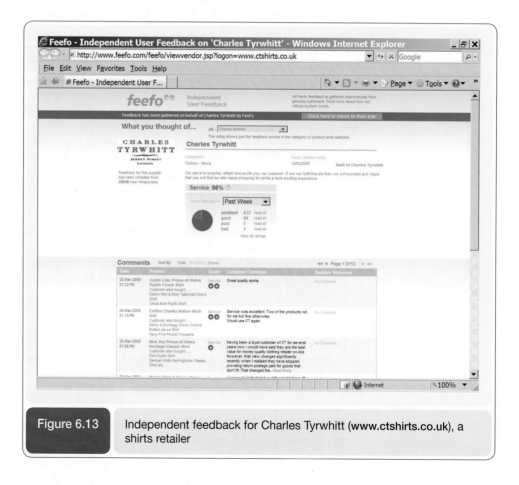

| Figure 6.13 | Independent feedback for Charles Tyrwhitt (**www.ctshirts.co.uk**), a shirts retailer |

organisation, there will be customers who have different levels of activity or engagement with online services and purchasing. A good example is a bank – some customers may use the online account once a week, others much less frequently and some not at all. Figure 6.14 illustrates the different levels of activity in this case.

A key part of e-CRM strategy is to define measures that indicate activity levels and then develop tactics to increase activity levels through more frequent use. An online magazine could segment its customers in this way, also based on returning visitors. Even for companies without transactional service a similar concept can apply if they use email marketing – some customers will regularly read and interact with the email and others will not.

Objectives and corresponding tactics can be set for:

- Increasing the number of new users per month and annually (separate objectives will be set for existing bank customers and new bank customers) through promoting online services to drive visitors to the website.
- Increasing the percentage of active users (an appropriate threshold can be used – for different organisations it could be set at 7, 30 or 90 days). Using direct communications, such as email, personalised website messages, direct mail and phone communications to new, dormant and inactive users increases the percentage of active users.
- Decreasing the percentage of dormant users (once new or active – could be sub-categories) who have not used the service or responded to communications within a defined time period, such as three months.
- Decreasing the percentage of inactive users (or non-activated) users. These are those who signed up for a service such as online banking and had a username issued, but have not used the service.

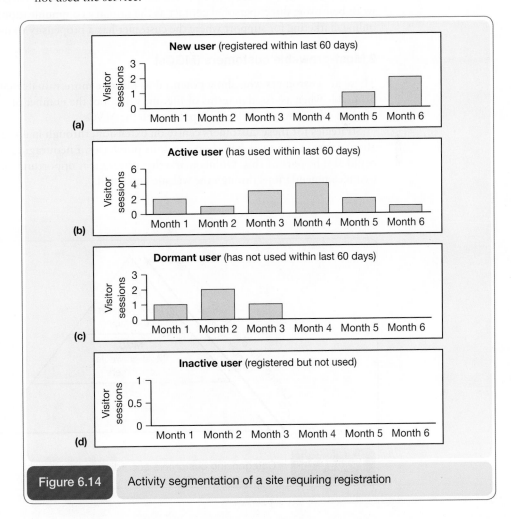

| Figure 6.14 | Activity segmentation of a site requiring registration |

You can see that corresponding strategies can be developed for each of these objectives.

Another key metric, in fact the *key* retention metric for e-commerce sites, refers to repeat business. The importance of retention rate metrics was highlighted by Agrawal *et al.* (2001). The main retention metrics they mention which influence profitability are:

- *repeat-customer base* – the proportion of the customer base that has made repeat purchases;
- *number of transactions per repeat customer* – this indicates the stage of development of the customer in the relationship (another similar measure is number of product categories purchased);
- *revenue per transaction of repeat customer* – this is a proxy for lifetime value since it gives average order value.

Figure 6.15 gives a visual indication of this approach using the terminology suggested by Peppers and Rogers (2002). They identify three groups of customers with corresponding communications strategies:

1 Most-valuable customers (MVCs)

These are the customers who contribute the most profit and are typically a small proportion of the total customer base as suggested by their position in the pyramid. These customers will most likely have purchased more or higher-value products. The strategy for these customers focuses on retention rather than extension. In the case of a bank, personal relationship managers would be appointed for customers in this category to provide them with guidance and advice and to make sure they remain loyal. Often this strategy will work best using direct personal contact as the primary communication channel, but using online marketing for support where the customer has a propensity to use online channels.

2 Most-growable customers (MGCs)

These are customers who show potential to become more valuable customers. They are profitable when assessed in terms of lifetime value, but the number of product holdings or lifetime value is relatively low compared with the MVCs.

Strategies for these customers centre on extension, through making recommendations about relevant products based on previous purchases. Encouraging similar repurchases could also be part of this. Online marketing offers great opportunities to make personalised recommendations through the website and email.

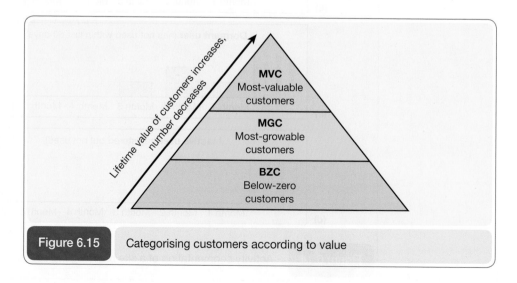

Figure 6.15   Categorising customers according to value

Below-zero customers (BZCs)

BZCs are simply unprofitable customers. The strategy for these customers may vary – they can be encouraged to develop towards MGCs, but more typically expenditure will be minimised if it is felt that it will be difficult to change their loyalty behaviour or the source of their being unprofitable. Again, digital media can be used as a lower-cost form of marketing expenditure to encourage these customers to make repeat purchases or to allow them to self-serve online.

Lifetime value modelling

Lifetime value (LTV)
Lifetime value is the total net benefit that a customer or group of customers will provide a company over their total relationship with a company

An appreciation of **lifetime value (LTV)** is key to the theory and practice of customer relationship management.

Digital technology has enabled marketers to become more sophisticated in how they can identify and target valuable customers. Kumar *et al.* (2007) explain it this way:

> By applying statistical models, they can predict not only when each customer is likely to make a future purchase but also what he or she will buy and through which channel. Managers can use these data to estimate a potential lifetime value for every customer and to determine whether, when and how to contact each one to maximise the chances of realising (and even increasing) his or her value.

However, while the term is often used, calculation of LTV is not straightforward, so many organisations do not calculate it. You are referred to Kumar *et al.* (2007) for an explanation of LTV calculations. Lifetime value is defined as the total net benefit that a customer, or group of customers, will provide a company over their total relationship with the company. Modelling is based on estimating the income and costs associated with each customer over a period of time, and then calculating the net present value in current monetary terms using a discount rate value applied over the period.

There are different degrees of sophistication in calculating LTV. These are indicated in Figure 6.16. Option 1 is a practical way or approximate proxy for future LTV, but the true LTV is the future value of the customer at an individual level.

Lifetime value modelling at segment level (4) is vital within marketing since it answers the question:

> How much can I afford to invest in acquiring a new customer?

| Figure 6.16 | Different representations of lifetime value calculation |

If online marketers try to answer this from a short-term perspective, as is often the case – i.e. by judging it based on the profit from a single sale on an e-commerce site – there are two problems:

- They become very focussed on short-term return on investment (ROI) and so may not invest sufficiently to grow the business.
- They assume that each new customer is worth precisely the same and ignore differentials in loyalty and profitability between differing types of customer.

Lifetime value analysis enables marketers to:

- plan and measure investment in customer acquisition programmes;
- identify and compare critical target segments;
- measure the effectiveness of alternative customer retention strategies;
- establish the true value of a company's customer base;
- make decisions about products and offers;
- make decisions about the value of introducing new e-CRM technologies.

Figure 6.17 gives an example of how LTV can be used to develop a CRM strategy for different customer groups. Four main types of customers are indicated by their current and future value as bronze, silver, gold and platinum. Distinct customer groupings (circles) are identified according to their current value (as indicated by current value) and future value (as indicated by lifetime value calculations). Each of these groups will have a customer profile signature based on their demographics, so this can be used for customer selection. Different strategies are developed for different customer groups within the four main value groupings. Some bronze customers, such as groups A and B, realistically do not have development potential and are typically unprofitable, so the aim is to reduce costs in communications and if they do not remain as customers this is acceptable. Some bronze customers, such as group C, may have potential for growth so for these the strategy is to extend their purchases. Silver customers are targeted with customer extension offers and gold customers are extended where possible, although they have relatively little growth

| Figure 6.17 | An example of an LTV-based segmentation plan |

potential. Platinum customers are the best customers, so it is important to understand the communication preferences of these customers and not to over-communicate unless there is evidence that they may defect.

To illustrate another application of LTV and how it is calculated, take a look at the last example in Activity 6.1.

Activity 6.1 | **Charity uses lifetime value modelling to assess returns from new e-CRM system**

A charity is considering implementing a new email marketing system to increase donations from its donors. The charity's main role is as a relief agency which aims to reduce poverty through providing aid, particularly to the regions that need it most. Currently, its only email activity is a monthly e-newsletter received by its 200,000 subscribers which features its current campaigns and appeals. It hopes to increase donations by using a more targeted approach based on previous customer behaviour. The email system will integrate with the donor database which contains information on customer profiles and previous donations.

The company is considering three solutions which will cost between £50,000 and £100,000 in the first year. In the charity, all such investments are assessed using lifetime value modelling.

Table 6.3 is a lifetime value model showing customer value derived from using the current system and marketing activities.

A *Donors* – this is the number of initial donors. It declines each year dependent on the retention rate (row B).

Table 6.3 | Lifetime value model for customer base for current system

		Year 1	Year 2	Year 3	Year 4	Year 5
A	Donors	100,000	50,000	27,500	16,500	10,725
B	Retention	50%	55%	60%	65%	70%
C	Donations per annum	£100	£120	£140	£160	£180
D	Total donations	£10,000,000	£6,000,000	£3,850,000	£2,640,000	£1,930,500
E	Net profit (at 20% margin)	£2,000,000	£1,200,000	£770,000	£528,000	£386,100
F	Discount rate	1	0.86	0.7396	0.636	0.547
G	NPV contribution	£2,000,000.0	£1,032,000.0	£569,492.0	£335,808.0	£211,196.7
H	Cumulative NPV contribution	£2,000,000.0	£3,032,000.0	£3,601,492.0	£3,937,300.0	£4,148,496.7
I	Lifetime value at net present value	£20.0	£30.3	£36.0	£39.4	£41.5

→

B   *Retention rate* – in lifetime value modelling this is usually found to increase year-on-year, since customers who stay loyal are more likely to remain loyal.

C   *Donations per annum* – likewise, the charity finds that the average contributions per year increase through time within this group of customers.

D   *Total donations* – calculated through multiplying rows A and C.

E   *Net profit (at 20 per cent margin)* – LTV modelling is based on profit contributed by this group of customers, row D is multiplied by 0.2.

F   *Discount rate* – since the value of money held at a point in time will decrease due to inflation, a discount rate factor is applied to calculate the value of future returns in terms of current-day value.

G   *NPV contribution* – this is the profitability after taking the discount factor into account to give the net present value in future years. This is calculated by multiplying row E by row F.

H   *Cumulative NPV contribution* – this adds the previous year's NPV for each year.

I   *Lifetime value at net present value* – this is a value per customer calculated by dividing row H by the initial number of donors in Year 1.

Based on preliminary tests with improved targeting, it is estimated that with the new system, retention rates will increase from 50 to 51 per cent in the first year, increasing by 5 per cent per year as currently. It is estimated that in year 1 donations per annum will increase from £100 per annum to £120 per annum, increasing by £20 per year as currently.

Question

Using the example of the lifetime value for the current donor base with the current system, calculate the LTV with the new system.

Kumar *et al.* (2007) note that the capability of a customer to generate value is divided into lifetime value of purchases (CLV) and what they term CRV, customer referral value. This concept is closely related to that of the 'net promoter score' identified earlier in the chapter. These authors stress that there is not a clear correlation between CLV and CRV. For example, in their study they found that customers with the highest CLV did not have the highest CRV. So they suggest that customers should be segmented according to both attributes and then tactics developed. For one company they studied, they identified four groupings of customers presented in a customer value matrix plotting average CRV at one year on the *x*-axis and average CLV after one year on the *y*-axis to give these segments:

- *Champions (top-right) – 21% of customers*, CLV = $370, CRV = $590
- *Misers (bottom-left) – 21% of customers*, CLV = $130, CRV = $64
- *Affluents (top-left) – 29% of customers*, CLV = $1219, CRV = $49
- *Advocates (bottom-right) – 29% of customers*, CLV = $180, CRV = $670

You can see that it would be worthwhile using different tactics for each segment to encourage recommendation or purchase – for example to migrate misers to affluents or advocates, and advocates and affluents to champions.

In-depth analysis of customer data has traditionally been completed by catalogue retailers such as Argos, Littlewoods Index or retailers such as Boots using a technique known as 'RFM analysis'. This technique tends to be little known outside retail circles, but e-CRM gives great potential to apply it in a range of techniques since we can use it not only to analyse purchase history, but also visit or log-in frequency to a site or online service and response rates to email communications.

Recency–frequency–monetary value (RFM) analysis

RFM is sometimes known as FRAC, which stands for: Frequency, Recency, Amount (obviously equivalent to monetary value), Category (types of product purchased – not included within RFM). We will now give an overview of how RFM approaches can be applied, with special reference to online marketing. We will also look at the related concepts of latency and hurdle rates.

Recency

This is the recency of customer action, e.g. purchase, site visit, account access, email response. Novo (2003) stresses the importance of recency when he says:

> Recency, or the number of days that have gone by since a customer completed an action (purchase, log-in, download, etc.), is the most powerful predictor of the customer repeating an action ... Recency is why you receive another catalogue from the company shortly after you make your first purchase from them.

Online applications of analysis of recency include monitoring through time to identify vulnerable customers, and scoring customers to preferentially target more responsive customers for cost savings.

Frequency

Frequency is the number of times an action is completed in a period of a customer action – e.g. purchase, visit, email response(for example, five purchases per year, five visits per month, five log-ins per week, five email opens per month, five email clicks per year). Online applications of this analysis include combining with recency for 'RF targeting'.

Monetary value

The monetary value of purchase(s) can be measured in different ways – for example, average order value of £50, total annual purchase value of £5000. Generally, customers with higher monetary values tend to have a higher loyalty and potential future value since they have purchased more items historically. One example application would be to exclude these customers from special promotions if their RF scores suggested they were actively purchasing. Frequency is often a proxy for monetary value per year since the more products purchased, the higher the overall monetary value. Ultimately it is possible to simplify analysis by just using recency and frequency. Monetary value can also skew the analysis with high-value initial purchases.

Mini case study 6.6 explains how pet charity PDSA is applying RFM analysis to better understand donation patterns.

Latency

Latency
The average length of time that different customer types take between different activities, e.g. log-ins, paying bills, first and second purchase.

Latency is a powerful concept, closely related to frequency – it is the average time between customer events in the customer lifecycle. Examples include the average time between website visits, second and third purchase and email click-throughs. Online applications of latency include putting in place triggers that alert companies to customer behaviour outside the norm, such as increased interest or disinterest, and then to manage this behaviour using e-communications or traditional communications. For example, if a B2B or B2C organisation with a long interval between purchases found that latency decreased for a particular customer, then they may be investigating an additional purchase via email or website (their recency and frequency would probably increase also). Emails, phone calls or direct mail could then be used to target this person with relevant offers according to what they were searching for.

Mini case study 6.6	Charity PDSA refines its understanding of its members using RFM analysis

The context for this case is provided by Robin Prouse, who is the training manager of Apteco Ltd (www.apteco.com), a company that specialises in analytical marketing software. He is in a unique position to understand the difficulties and challenges facing many organisations in making sense of their customer data and has worked with PDSA.

Robin says:

The starting place for most organisations is to gather and organise their data in one place. Once the data is available and in a suitable software tool such as FastStats Discoverer, the question then arises, what do you do with it? Understanding and being able to visualise who your current customers are is the springboard to effective marketing.

Software functionality allows for RFM information to be found and in turn calculate valuable knowledge, such as lifetime value, and identify segments at risk of attrition or churn. When you know your customers, the opportunities for cross-sell or up-sell become more apparent. Once these important customer segments have been identified, profiling tools give you the ability to find the key characteristics of their members, which can then be applied to other existing customers or prospects.

Integrated software now makes it easier for the marketer to take their segmented data and present their message through a number of different channels. Email broadcasting is becoming increasingly popular and being able to upload your contact list and content directly from your marketing software adds another link to the marketing cycle. By capturing and adding responses to your data, the marketing cycle is made complete.

PDSA (www.pdsa.org) is the UK's leading veterinary charity providing free veterinary care for the sick and injured pets of those unable to afford veterinary fees. The charity, which is entirely funded by public support, operates a UK-wide network of 47 PetAid hospitals and branches and also works through some 348 contracted private veterinary practices. PDSA also operates 180 charity shops UK-wide, but its main income is derived from direct marketing and relationship-building programmes that result in gifts in wills, voluntary donations and trading activities.

The charity uses Discoverer for detailed marketing analytics, supporter profiling, database segmentation and predictive modelling. The direct marketing and legacy teams also make extensive use of Discoverer's Cascade module for campaign planning and management.

PDSA holds a huge database of past transactional and promotional histories on nearly 6 million supporters. This dataset is used to report lifetime value, patterns and trends in support, and for the identification of cross-sell and up-sell opportunities. In conjunction with third-party geo-demographic data, Discoverer has been used to build sophisticated legacy propensity models, donor profiles and channel attrition analysis.

As PDSA improves its online presence via its website (www.pdsa.org.uk) and dedicated email marketing campaigns, Discoverer has increasingly been used to monitor and classify donor email addresses. This allows marketers to combine online knowledge with that contained in transactional and operational systems – linking offline lifetime value, demographics and product propensity models with online marketing permissions and click-through analysis.

Hurdle rate

Hurdle rate
The proportion of customers that fall within a particular level of activity. For example, the percentage of members of an email list that click on the email within a 90-day period, or the number of customers that have made a second purchase.

According to Novo (2003), **hurdle rate** refers to the percentage of customers in a group (such as in a segment or on a list) who have completed an action. It is a useful concept since it can be used to compare the engagement of different groups or to set targets to increase engagement with online channels, as the examples below show:

- 20 per cent of customers have visited in the past six months;
- 5 per cent of customers have made three or more purchases this year;
- 60 per cent of registrants have logged onto system this year;
- 30 per cent have clicked through on email this year.

Grouping customers into different RFM categories

In the examples above, each division for recency, frequency and monetary value is placed in an arbitrary position to place a roughly equal number of customers in each group. This approach is also useful since the marketer can set thresholds of value relevant to their understanding of their customers.

RFM analysis involves two techniques for grouping customers:

1 *Statistical RFM analysis*

This involves placing an equal number of customers in each RFM category using quintiles of 20 per cent (10 deciles can also be used for larger databases), as shown in Figure 6.18. The figure also shows one application of RFM with a view to using communications channels more effectively. Lower-cost e-communications can be used to correspond with customers who use only services more frequently since they prefer these channels, while more expensive offline communications can be used for customers who seem to prefer traditional channels.

2 *Arbitrary divisions of customer database*

This approach is also useful since the marketer can set thresholds of value relevant to their understanding of their customers.

For example, RFM analysis can be applied for targeting using email according to how a customer interacts with an e-commerce site. Values could be assigned to each customer as follows:

Recency:
1 – Over 12 months
2 – Within last 12 months
3 – Within last 6 months
4 – Within last 3 months
5 – Within last 1 month

Frequency:
1 – More than once every 6 months
2 – Every 6 months
3 – Every 3 months
4 – Every 2 months
5 – Monthly

Figure 6.18 RFM analysis

Monetary value:
1 – Less than £10
2 – £10–£50
3 – £50–£100
4 – £100–£200
5 – More than £200

Simplified versions of this analysis can be created to make it more manageable – for example, a theatre group uses these nine categories for its direct marketing:

Oncers (attended theatre once):
- Recent oncer   attended <12 months
- Rusty oncer   attended >12 but <36 months
- Very rusty oncer   attended in 36+ months

Twicers:
- Recent twicer   attended <12 months
- Rusty twicer   attended >12 but <36 months
- Very rusty twicer   attended in 36+ months

2+ subscribers:
- Current subscribers   booked 2+ events in current season
- Recent   booked 2+ last season
- Very rusty   booked 2+ more than a season ago

Another example, with real-world data, is shown in Figure 6.19. You can see that plotting customer numbers against recency and frequency in this way for an online company gives a great visual indication of the health of the business and groups that can be targeted to encourage more repeat purchases.

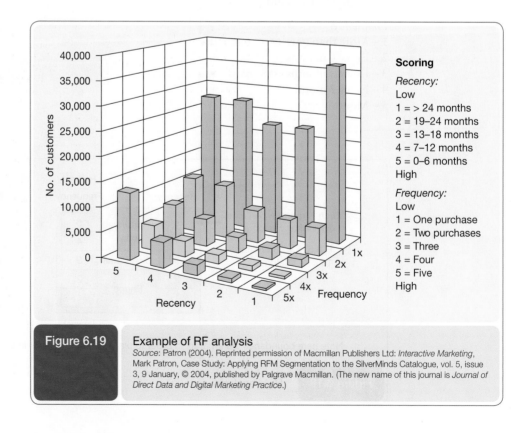

Figure 6.19	Example of RF analysis

Source: Patron (2004). Reprinted permission of Macmillan Publishers Ltd: *Interactive Marketing*, Mark Patron, Case Study: Applying RFM Segmentation to the SilverMinds Catalogue, vol. 5, issue 3, 9 January, © 2004, published by Palgrave Macmillan. (The new name of this journal is *Journal of Direct Data and Digital Marketing Practice*.)

The 'Big Data' concept

'Big Data' is a term used to describe analysis techniques and systems which exploit the larger volumes of data that are now available for marketers.

The opportunity and challenge of **Big Data for marketing** is often described using the three dimensions or vectors shown in Figure 6.20:

'Big Data' applications in marketing
'Big Data' refers to applications to gain value from the increasing Volume, Velocity and Variety of data integrated from different sources. These enhance insight to deliver more relevant communications through techniques such as marketing automation and social CRM.

- *Data Volume* refers to the increase in data which is now available for online interactions with websites and social media.
- *Data Velocity* shows how marketers now have access to real-time data, such as real-time analytics of interactions on web and mobile sites and also social media interactions.
- *Data Variety* shows how new types of unstructured data, including, again, social media interactions, offer potential too. This also suggests the potential of integrating different sources of data to gain more customer insight.

The key question for marketers given access to the potential new types of data is: how do we harness it? Through integrating new types of data from different systems and sources there is clearly the option to mine new data about how businesses interact with customers to encourage purchase. Ultimately, the main application of Big Data in marketing is used to increase the relevance of communications using the marketing automation techniques discussed earlier in the chapter. Techniques such as predictive modelling are used to send more relevant, contextual emails or web personalised banners to customers in order to generate response.

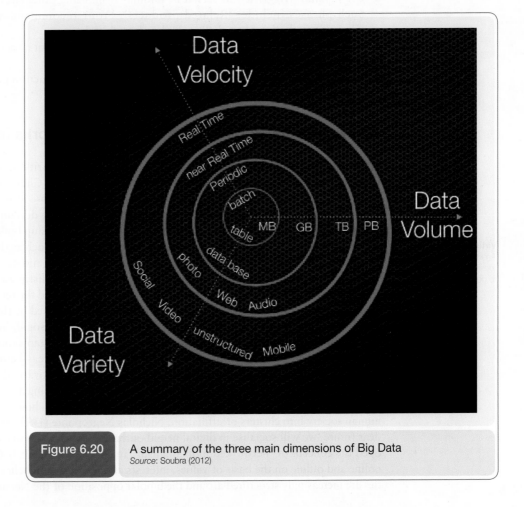

Figure 6.20	A summary of the three main dimensions of Big Data
	Source: Soubra (2012)

Some have argued that 'Big Data' is a classic example of 'The Emperor's New Clothes' fable – i.e. it is a term created by systems vendors and consultants to generate demand for services which have been previously available under another label. Others note that many marketers are not exploiting the 'Small Data' available through campaign reporting and digital analytics discussed in Chapters 8 and 10.

Product recommendations and propensity modelling

Propensity modelling
The approach of evaluating customer characteristics and behaviour and then making recommendations for future products.

Propensity modelling is one name given to the approach of evaluating customer characteristics and behaviour, in particular previous products or services purchased, and then making recommendations for the next suitable product. However, it is best known as recommending the 'Next best product' to existing customers.

A related acquisition approach is to target potential customers with similar characteristics through renting direct mail or email lists or advertising online in similar locations.

The following recommendations are based on those in van Duyne *et al.* (2003):

1 *Create automatic product relationships* (i.e. next best product). A low-tech approach to this is, for each product, to group together products previously purchased together. Then for each product, rank product by number of times purchased together to find relationships.
2 *Cordon off and minimise the 'real estate' devoted to related products*. An area of screen should be reserved for 'Next best product prompts' for up-selling and cross-selling. However, if these can be made part of the current product they may be more effective.
3 *Use familiar 'trigger words'*. That is, familiar from using other sites such as Amazon. Such phrases include: 'Related products', 'Your recommendations', 'Similar', 'Customers who bought ...', 'Top 3 related products'.
4 *Editorialise about related products*. That is, within copy about a product.
5 *Allow quick purchase of related products*.
6 *Sell related product during checkout*. And also on post-transaction pages, i.e. after one item has been added to the basket or purchased.

Applying virtual communities and social networks for CRM

We discussed some of the psychological reasons for the popularity of social networks in Chapter 2 in the section on consumer buyer behaviour and in Chapter 9 we will review some of the related Web 2.0 marketing techniques that can be used for customer acquisition. But in this section, we consider why social networks have developed and how they can be used to develop customer understanding and for relationship building.

Virtual community
An Internet-based forum for special-interest groups to communicate.

The reasons for the popularity of **virtual communities** today such as the social networks Facebook, Google+ and LinkedIn can be traced back to the nineteenth century. The German sociologist Ferdinand Tonnies (1855–1936) made the distinction between public society and private community (Loomis, 1957). Tonnies employed the terms *Gemeinschaft*, meaning 'community' (informal, organic or instinctive ties typified by the family or neighbourhood), and *Gesellschaft*, meaning 'society' (formal, impersonal, instrumental, goal-orientated relations typified by big cities, the state and large organisations). Membership of *Gemeinschaft* is self-fulfilling (intrinsic motivation), whereas being a member of a *Gesellschaft* is a means to further individual goals (extrinsic motivation).

Marshall McLuhan (1964) posited that 'cool' (meaning on-going and shared) and inclusive 'electric media' (meaning telephone and television, rather than books) would 'retribalise' human society into clusters of affiliation. Nicholas Negroponte (1995) predicted that in the near future 'we will socialise in digital neighbourhoods'. Manuel Castells (1996) has developed the concept of 'networked individualism', in which individuals build their networks online and offline on the basis of values, interests and projects, and believes that 'our societies are increasingly structured around the bipolar opposition of the Net and the Self'.

Mini case study 6.7	Taking the guesswork out of CRM – how Guess uses predictive analytics

In an interview with Guess Director of Marketing – CRM, Victoria Graham, Custora (2014) describes different opportunities for the brand in the way the company uses **predictive analytics**. The first opportunity is combining multiple customer and transaction data sources. Graham explains:

> *All of our analysis was based on past purchases behaviour. We're not data scientists, we don't have PhDs in our office, so any predictive analysis – like who might buy in the future, and what a customer might buy in the future – was not something that we were able to capture.*

Guess applied predictive analytics by first identifying and understanding its customers across two dimensions: purchase-based customer personas, and high-value customers. These insights were then applied to predict future purchase response to acquisition and retention campaigns. This has prompted a change in the Guess email strategy. Three years ago we were emailing customers three, possibly four times a week. Graham says:

> *We were very much 'batch and blast', and our email calendar was driven by our merchant team: If there's a product launch, or a big promotion, like 40% off all sweaters, that was driving the email calendar. We're now in the process of changing that.*
>
> *We've been cognizant of the fact that it is quite likely that we were irritating our customers with constantly talking to them. We had two options when we talked about getting personalised with our emails: One option was to cut back on emails. If today's email is about denim, and you like accessories, you just don't get today's email. But the thought of cutting down the number of emails we send out was scary. The other option was, if we're going to email everyone every day, let's talk to them in a way that's meaningful and relevant to them.*

In a test, they isolated the accessories persona and the non-accessories persona. They compared the accessories customers who received the accessories-focussed email (group A) to accessories customers who received the regular email (group B). The CTR and conversion rate of group A far exceeded those of group B.

Another analytical approach was identifying high-value customers to optimise acquisition. This dispelled a lot of assumptions according to Graham, such as assuming that top customers were metropolitan customers, who liked core products like denim, but also loved accessories. But this wasn't necessarily the case, Graham explains:

> *when we looked at where our customers really over-index and differentiate themselves from the rest of our customer database, they found that they were more likely to live in suburban areas. Arizona popped as a big state for high lifetime value customers. Their first purchase tended to be a knit or a sweater or denim.*

Note that techniques do not necessarily require an expensive recommendations engine except for very large sites.

Predictive analytics
Using data mining and statistical modelling to predict future outcomes, for example by scoring customer propensity to respond to a specific offer.

Virtual communities are the emerging construct of the traditional social marketplaces where groups of people who share common interests and needs come together online. Most are drawn together by the opportunity to share a sense of community with like-minded individuals, regardless of where they live.

Virtual communities also provide opportunities for some companies to develop relationships with their customers. Since the publication of the article by Armstrong and Hagel in 1996 entitled 'The real value of online communities' and John Hagel's subsequent book (Hagel, 1997), there has been much discussion about using digital media to create virtual communities.

The power of the virtual communities, according to Hagel (1997), is that they exhibit a number of positive feedback loops (or 'virtuous circles'). Focussed content attracts new members, who in turn contribute to the quantity and quality of the community's pooled knowledge. Member loyalty grows as the community grows and evolves. The purchasing power of the community grows and thus the community attracts more advertisers to fund it. The growing revenue potential attracts yet more vendors, providing more choice and attracting more members. As the size and sophistication of the community grow (while it still remains tightly focussed) its data-gathering and profiling capabilities increase – thus enabling better-targeted marketing and attracting more vendors,… and so on. In such positive feedback loops there is an initial startup period of slow and uneven growth until critical mass in members, content, vendors and transactions is reached. The potential for growth is then exponential – until the limits of the focus of the community as it defines itself are reached.

All of these predictions are now a reality, particularly within the social networks which support rich interactions. When deciding on a strategic approach to online communities, companies essentially have two main options if they decide to use them as part of their efforts in relationship building. They can either create community through other sites (earned media, Chapter 1) or provide community facilities on their own site (owned media). We will look at the options for each separately, but it's worth noting that the overlap between the two is increasing due to capability for social sign-on that we introduced earlier in the chapter with the Sears Social example (SmartInsights, 2011).

1 Creating community through social networks

The main social media platforms which can offer a presence for companies are Facebook, Twitter, LinkedIn, Google+ and YouTube. Other social media platforms do exist, but they tend to have a smaller audience reach as they have a niche focus. The most commonly used options are:

1 *Facebook company page.* These are popular with customers for many types of companies as catalogued by Social Bakers (**www.socialbakers.com/statistics/facebook**). Facebook pages are designed to help businesses engage an audience and so promote their products and services. The members of the page are referred to as 'fans' who 'Like' the page. These fans can then receive status update information from the business page within their news feeds. Paid Facebook ads can be used to recruit new fans, but fans will also be attracted as other fans like the page or share information.

2 *Twitter page.* Twitter enables companies to set up their own page with communication made through messages that can contain up to 140 characters. Currently the pages for companies are the same as those for individuals with a short bio featuring the company. Crucially for communication, as with Facebook status updates, these messages can contain links through to the company website which contain relevant content or offers to engage the audience. Twitter is also commonly used for customer service. Some companies such as retailers Dell and ASOS have separate channels for customer offers and support.

3 *LinkedIn Company pages and groups.* LinkedIn is the most popular network to track and maintain professional contacts within the business world. Therefore, it is often utilised by academics, corporate executives and professionals. It allows users to promote their experience and expertise through resumes and professional recommendations. Companies can set up a company page which. similar to other networks, has status updates to communicate new products and services and users can comment on these. Many companies also set up their own group on LinkedIn which can cover a topic but is branded by the company. For example, jobs company **OnlyMarketingJobs.com** set up a group called Digital/Online Marketing Professionals (DOMP) which raises awareness of the brand although discussions are about digital marketing practice more widely.

4 *Google+.* Google+ is more recently established and also has company pages from companies like H&M and Cadbury. While these 'flagship' company pages are popular, others are less so and in 2014 Google declared that it wasn't seeking to rival Facebook with Google+.

5 *YouTube channels.* These enable companies to post and host videos which users can comment on. The level of usage of these channels tends to be lower than that for other social networks so consequently they are not so widely used.

Before investing a lot of time in trying to build a community within a social network, it's important for business to establish strategic priorities and processes that will give the best results. (We covered some of these decisions in Chapter 4.)

2 Creating your own presence

If a company sets up a community facility on its own site or sets up a separately branded community like the American Express Open Forum (**www.openforum.com**), which is targeted towards small and medium-sized businesses, it is more closely aligned to the goals and brand values of the website. Since registered members of the community will be on the company database, the community will provide opportunities for email marketing and research about the company and its products as part of the learning relationship. However, the brand may be damaged if customers criticise products, so some moderation is required. Honda UK (**www.honda.co.uk/cars**) gave a good example of a community created by their brand on their site. Rather than having a separate community section, the community is integrated within the context of each car as a 'second opinions' review menu option in the context of each car. Interestingly, some negative comments are permitted to make the discussion more meaningful. However, they have not continued this approach at the time of writing this edition. Another approach used by Kia (**www.kia.co.uk**) is to feature selected reviews from an independent review service (**www.revoo.com**).

A potential problem with a company-hosted forum is that it may be unable to get sufficient people to contribute to give the community 'critical mass'. Communities are best suited to high-involvement brands, such as a professional body like CIPD, or those related to sports and hobbies and business-to-business.

Marketing to consumers using independent social networks

One potential benefit of marketing to virtual communities is that they are naturally formed around problems shared, benefits sought, interests etc. and so are naturally self-segmented. Segmentation develops organically around particular topics and interests – e.g. aficionados of quality coffee might debate the merits of various strains of coffee beans, of methods of preparation, of coffee machines and of service quality at coffee shop brands such as Starbucks. The owners of many specialist communities could be seeking advertising revenue (see Case Study 8 on Facebook), so they may accept links to merchants and display advertising if the match of product/service and community interests is close enough and the advertising doesn't divert from the community. Although social networks such as Facebook and Google+ use advertising as a revenue source, for the advertisers responses tend to be low because the focus of users is on interacting, not on the ads.

Customer experience – the missing element required for customer loyalty

We have in this chapter shown how delivering relevant timely communications as part of permission marketing is important to developing loyalty. However, even the most relevant communications will fail if another key factor is not taken into account – this is the *customer experience*. If a first-time or repeat customer experience is poor due to a slow-to-download difficult-to-use site, then it is unlikely that loyalty from the online customer will develop. In the next chapter we review techniques used to help develop this experience.

Case Study 6 — Dell gets closer to its customers through its social media strategy

Dell is well known as a technology company, offering a broad range of product categories, including desktop computer systems, storage, servers and networking products, mobility products, software and peripherals, and services to manage IT infrastructure for large organisations.

Dell business strategy

Dell's vision is to 'strive to provide the best possible customer experience by offering: superior value; high-quality, relevant technology; customised systems; superior service and support; and differentiated products and services that are easy to buy and use'.

The core elements of the strategy which are evident in Dell's marketing communications are:

- *We simplify information technology for customers.* Making quality personal computers, servers, storage and services affordable is Dell's legacy. We are focussed on making information technology affordable for millions of customers around the world. As a result of our direct relationships with customers, or 'customer intimacy', we are best positioned to simplify how customers implement and maintain information technology and deliver hardware, services and software solutions tailored for their businesses and homes.
- *We offer customers choice.* Customers can purchase systems and services from Dell via telephone, kiosks and our website, **www.dell.com**, where they may review, configure and price systems within our entire product line; order systems online, and track orders from manufacturing through shipping. We have recently launched a retail initiative and plan to expand that initiative by adding new distribution channels to reach additional consumers and small businesses through retail partners and value-added resellers globally.
- *Customers can purchase custom-built products and custom-tailored services*. Historically our flexible, build-to-order manufacturing process enabled us to turn over inventory every five days on average, thereby reducing inventory levels and rapidly bring the latest technology to our customers. The market and our competition has evolved and we are now exploring the utilisation of original design manufacturers and new distribution strategies to better meet customer needs and reduce product cycle times. Our goal is to introduce the latest relevant technology more quickly and to rapidly pass on component cost savings to a broader set of our customers worldwide.

- *We are committed to being environmentally responsible in all areas of our business.* We have built environmental consideration into every stage of the Dell product lifecycle – from developing and designing energy-efficient products, to reducing the footprint of our manufacturing and operations, to customer use and product recovery.

Dell's sales and marketing

Dell sells products and services directly to customers through dedicated sales representatives, telephone-based sales and online at **www.dell.com**. Customer segments include large corporate, government, healthcare and education accounts, as well as small-to-medium businesses and individual consumers.

Dell stresses the importance of its direct business model in providing direct and continuous feedback from customers, thereby allowing products and marketing programmes to be developed and refined for specific customer groups.

In its SEC filing, Dell emphasises how it listens to customers to develop relevant innovative technology and services they trust and value. Evidence for using the participative nature of Web 2.0 is that customers can offer suggestions for current and future Dell products, services and operations on an interactive portion of the Dell website called Dell IdeaStorm. It says: 'This constant flow of communication, which is unique to our direct business model, also allows us to rapidly gauge customer satisfaction and target new or existing products.'

For large business and institutional customers, Dell maintains a field sales force throughout the world. Dedicated account teams, which include field-based system engineers and consultants, form long-term relationships to provide our largest customers with a single source of assistance and develop specific tailored solutions for these customers. Dell also maintains specific sales and marketing programmes targeted at federal, state and local governmental agencies as well as specific healthcare and educational markets.

Dell Premier

For its large organisational customers, Dell offers Premier (**http://premier.dell.com**), which is a secure, customisable procurement and support site or extranet designed to save organisations time and money through all phases of I/T product ownership. The main benefits of Dell Premier are described as:

- *Easy ordering* – a custom online store ensures access to your products at your price.
- *Easy tracking* – view real-time order status, online invoices and purchase history details.
- *Easy control* – custom access groups define what users can see and do within Premier.

Marketing communications

Dell markets its products and services to small-to-medium businesses and consumers primarily by advertising on television and the Internet, advertising in a variety of print media and by mailing a broad range of direct marketing publications, such as promotional pieces, catalogues and customer newsletters. In certain locations Dell also operate stores or kiosks, typically located within shopping centres, that allow customers to view its products in person and purchase online with the assistance of a Dell expert.

Dell online communications

The management of the consumer site was presented to EConsultancy (2008). Dell has a three-stage order funnel:

- marketing communications execution measured by site visits;
- site merchandising measured by consideration% (site visits to e-store visits);
- store merchandising measured by conversion% (e-store visits to e-receipts).

The presenter explained how Dell aims to understand and act on customer behaviour based on identification of a series of consideration drivers – for example, the quality of online advertising; path quality through site; merchandising/offers – and conversion drivers – for example, configurator 'ease of use'; accessibility of decision support tools and consistency of message through the entire path.

Dell will invest in strategic improvements to the site to improve these levers – examples mentioned included new merchandising approaches such as customer ratings and reviews, videos, major 'path' or customer journey changes created through decision support tools to 'Help me choose'. There are also more tactical initiatives to help deliver the right message to each customer including customisation/personalisation, real estate optimisation and message balancing.

More tactical persuasion of site visitors is based on price moves/optimised price position to market and the mix of product features. A wide range of different offers need to be managed. Tactical promotions which are driven by promotional 'end dates' which are weekly or bi-weekly include varying:

- free shipping;
- money-off discounts;

- free upgrades (e.g. memory);
- free accessories;
- finance offers;
- service upgrades.

The presenter also noted how, across Europe, the promotional mix has to vary to reflect the differences in buying psychology. He summarised the main differences between customers as follows:

- UK – all about price;
- CH – add value over price;
- DE – all about high-end products in mix;
- IT – design is important (!);
- DK – cheap is good;
- NO – added value is key;
- FR – tailored for France.

Dell's use of digital media channels

The main digital media channels used by **Dell.com** in Europe are:

- Paid search through programmes such as Google AdWords, which are used to promote value through time-limited offers related to the phrase searched upon. For example, a Google search for 'cheapest Dell' displays an ad: 'Discount Dell Laptops **www. dell.co.uk/laptop** – Save up to £300 on selected Dell Laptops from £329. Buy online now!'
- Display advertising – for example, advertising on technology websites – is particularly important for the corporate market.
- Affiliate marketing – used to protect the Dell brand by enabling affiliates to bid on terms such as 'Dell laptops' and to target niche audiences such as owners of gaming machines.
- Email marketing – an e-newsletter is used to keep in touch with existing customers and deliver targeted offers when their hardware may be renewed.

How Dell use social media marketing

Cory Edwards, director of social media and reputation team (SMART) at Dell has explained Dell's approach to social media marketing. He stresses the importance of commitment from senior managers which is exemplified for Dell by CEO Michael Dell, who frequently emphasises the importance of social media marketing to Dell. Edwards (2011) contains this quote from Michael Dell:

Engaging in honest, direct conversations with customers and stakeholders is a part of who we are, who we've always been. The social web amplifies our opportunity to listen and learn and invest ourselves in a two-way dialogue, enabling us to become a better company with more to offer the people who depend on us.

Edwards simply says, 'If content is king, then listening is queen'.

As an indication of the importance of social media listening to Dell, Dell has created a Social Media Listening Command Centre which has six wall monitors tracking what Dell's most influential customers are saying, trending topics relating to Dell, market performance including share of voice and ratings of sentiment expressed about Dell. Around 25,000 posts in 11 languages are monitored daily by Dell's 'Ground Control Team'.

Dell has a social media governance workflow which reviews the potential importance of these customer comments and identifies those it is worth following up with. The Ground Control Team is tightly integrated with the@DellCares Twitter team who engage around 1000 customers per week. Their role is to reach out to people complaining about Dell on Twitter. Edwards notes that the team has a 30 per cent rate of converting ranters to ravers.

As well as responding to negative mentions as part of customer service, Dell has created an Online Influencer Relations Program. This is managed by identifying influencers across business unit, region or topic area. Key influencers are identified using a Conversation tracker, which is part of Dell's social media listening tool Radian 6. Influencers are provided with content and products which they may review or share. Dell has gone beyond virtual relationships introducing Dell Customer Advisory Panel (CAP) which Edwards describes as 'a ranters and ravers event'. Invitees are prioritised based on size of social media reach and their affinity with Dell.

Relationship owners are designated and involved with ongoing efforts to build advocates. Within CAP days, Dell not only listens, but gives feedback on how problems are addressed. For example, Dell heard that there were too many dropped calls and unnecessary transfers, so it explained how ePhone CRM software is being launched across sites, which will improve reporting capability to track telecom issues and queue mergers to eliminate certain types of transfer.

The reputation management we have described is only part of the social media marketing activities. If we review these activities according to the RACE framework (Chapter 1), we can see that Dell is involved in social media marketing activities across the customer lifecycle:

- *Reach*: Research, network and advertise to reach and interact with customers and prospects on the social outposts, communities and blogs relevant to your audience.
- *(Inter) Act*: This involves determining your goals and then working out the engagement tools that

will encourage your customers to interact and will inspire them. Dell has clear goals around a number of financial and non-financial measures. They look at measures including operational savings through paid search and support savings and boosting customer loyalty measured through the Net Promoter Score.

When customers interact with Dell, their experiences are shared via their social graph of followers or fans, so there is this viral effect which helps customer acquisition.

- *Convert*: Here Dell is trying to leverage initial interaction to go through into real value of leads or sales. At a practical level, Dell has a clearance channel, Dell Outlet, that it uses to sell through Twitter. It may also offer promotional coupons through social media like Groupon or deals sites to encourage sales.
- *Engage*: This is the big challenge with social media: how to keep customers engaged. For Dell, engagement occurs on several platforms, but in particular within community forums, which are user-to-user support postings where topics range from support to pre-purchase or enthusiast discussions. There are millions of members with tens of thousands of discussions and accepted solutions each week. The Direct2Dell Network is also used for B2B customers with separate blogs for Enterprise IT, Small Business, Education, Investors, etc. They encourage guest influencers to join the discussion. Finally, another big part of engagement for Dell is IdeaStorm – one of the best examples of crowdsourcing through social media, which encourages ideas, feedback, innovation and dialogue. Over tens of thousands of ideas have been generated, with around 100,000 comments added, and a viral effect occurring through a Facebook app. Only several hundred ideas have been implemented, but the secret is that Dell closes the loop by feeding back to customers what has worked and what hasn't.

Source: 2011 SEC Filing Econsultancy (2008); Dell case study; Online Marketing Masterclass, presented at the Royal Institute of British Architects, November 2008. Edwards (2011); Tackling corporate reputation with social media, presentation by Cory Edwards, director of social media and reputation team (SMART) February 2011, available to view online at **www.slideshare.net/KerryatDell/dell-social-media-nma-event-london-v2-feb-2011** See also: **www.slideshare.net /KerryatDell/dells-social-media-journey-econsultancy-master-classes-november-2009 http://content.dell.com/us/en/corp /our-story-company-timeline.aspx**

Question

Describe approaches used by Dell within its site design and promotion to deliver relevant offers for different types of online customers.

Summary

1 E-CRM enables 'sense and respond' communications where personalised emails or web-based messages can be delivered based on disclosed or inferred customers preferences stored as customer profiles.
2 E-CRM also involves management of online services to deliver customer service which is aimed at improving brand loyalty.
3 The classic model for permission marketing to support e-CRM is:
   - Step 1 – Attract customers to website, partner microsite or social presence such as Facebook.
   - Step 2a – Incentivise in order to gain contact and profile information.
   - Step 2b – Capture customer information to maintain the relationship and profile the customer.
   - Step 3 – Maintain dialogue through using online communications to achieve repeat site visits.
   - Step 4 – Maintain dialogue consistent with customer's profile using email, social media messaging or where cost-effective, direct mail or outbound phone contact.
4 Personalisation technologies enable customised emails (or direct mails) to be sent to each individual (or related groups) and customised web content to be displayed or distributed using push technology.
5 E-CRM also involves review of customer advocacy through techniques such as Net Promoter Score (NPS) and development of programmes to encourage customer advocacy.
6 The development of online communities through social networks, particularly Facebook company pages and LinkedIn groups or independent communities linked to the company site, is a key part of social CRM.
7 Development of an independent customer community may give additional benefits since the community will be more aligned with company goals and customer brand experience.
8 Management of customer value through customer lifetime value and Recency–Frequency–Monetary (RFM value analysis) is a core technique for targeting marketing programmes at customers who will generate the most future value for an organisation.

Exercises

Self-assessment exercises

1 Why are digital platforms so suitable for relationship marketing?
2 Explain 'personalisation' in a digital marketing context.
3 What is meant by 'customer profiling'?
4 Explain the concept and benefits of the 'sense and respond' approach to customer communications.
5 How can customer concerns about privacy be responded to when conducting one-to-one marketing using the Internet?
6 What are the key decisions when creating or improving an online community?
7 Explain the concept and applications of RFM analysis to different types of web presence.
8 Explain the concept and applications of lifetime analysis.

Essay and discussion questions

1 Explain the factors that influence the development of multichannel customer contact strategies.

2 Explain how customer lifetime value analysis can be applied to improve all aspects of the customer lifecycle.

3 Write a report summarising for a manager the necessary stages for transforming a static brochureware site to e-CRM and the benefits that can be expected.

4 Explore the legal and ethical constraints on implementing relationship marketing using the digital media.

Examination questions

1 Define and explain the scope and applications of e-CRM.

2 What characteristics of the Internet make it so conducive to the direct marketing approach?

3 Suggest how an organisation could review its e-CRM capabilities.

4 Explain the benefits to businesses of creating virtual communities and how such communities can be used as part of relationship marketing.

5 Suggest three measures a company can take to ensure that a customer's privacy is not infringed when conducting one-to-one marketing.

6 Explain how digital media can support customer advocacy. Suggest how advocacy can be proactively managed.

7 What is 'web self-service'? What are typical challenges in managing this?

8 Explore opportunities and methods for personalising the interactive web session and adding value for that individual customer.

References

Agrawal, V., Arjona, V. and Lemmens, R. (2001) E-performance: the path to rational exuberance, *McKinsey Quarterly*, 1, 31–43.

Altimeter (2010) Social CRM: the new rules of relationship management. White paper published April 2010, Editor Charlene Li.

Armstrong, A. and Hagel, J. (1996) The real value of online communities, *Harvard Business Review* (May–June), 134–41.

Castells, M. (1996) *The Rise of the Network Society*, Blackwell, Oxford.

Chaffey, D. (2004) E-permission marketing, Chartered Institute of Marketing, *What's New in Marketing*, e-newsletter, Issue 25, **www.wnim.com**.

Court, D., Elzinga, D., Mulder, S. and Vetvik, O.J. (2009) The consumer decision journey, *McKinsey Quarterly* (June).

Custora (2014) *Taking the guesswork out of marketing – how Guess uses predictive analytics*. Blog post by Netta Kivilis on the Custora blog, 10 December 2014, **http://blog .custora.com/2014/12/taking-the-guesswork-out-of-marketing-how-guess-uses-predictive-analytics/**.

EConsultancy (2008) Managing digital channels. Integrating digital marketing into your organisation (190-page report). Author: Dave Chaffey.

Edwards, C. (2011) Tackling corporate reputation with social media, presentation by Cory Edwards, director of social media and reputation team (SMART) February 2011, **www. slideshare.net/KerryatDell/dell-social-media-nma-event-london-v2-feb-2011**. See also: **www.slideshare.net/KerryatDell/dells-social-media-journey-econsultancy-masterclasses-november-2009; http://content.dell.com/us/en/corp/our-story-company-timeline.aspx**.

Forrester (2007) Marketing's new key metric: engagement, marketers must measure involvement, interaction, intimacy, and influence, *Forrester Analyst report*, Brian Haven, 8 August.

Fournier, S. and Avery, J. (2011) The uninvited brand, *Business Horizons*, 54, 197–207.

Godin, S. (1999) *Permission Marketing*, Simon and Schuster, New York.

Hagel, J. (1997) *Net Gain: Expanding Markets through Virtual Communities*, Harvard Business School Press, Boston.

Hsieh, T. (2010) Delivering customer happiness: a presentation by Zappos CEO Tony Hsieh with Tony Robbins, **www.slideshare.net/zappos/ zappos-tony-robbins-business-mastery-011610**.

Keiningham, T., Cooil, B., Aksoy, L., Andreassen, T. and Weiner, J. (2007) The value of different customer satisfaction and loyalty metrics in predicting customer retention, recommendation and share-of-wallet, *Managing Service Quality*, 17(4).

Kirby, K. and Samson, A. (2007) Customer advocacy metrics: the NPS theory in practice, *AdMap*, February 2007, 17–19.

Kumar, V., Petersen, J. and Leone, R. (2007) How valuable is word of mouth?, *Harvard Business Review*, 85(10), 139–46.

Li, C. and Bernoff, J. (2011) *Groundswell: Winning in a world Transformed by Social Technologies*, Harvard Business Press, Boston.

Loomis, C.P. (1957) *Community and Society: Gemeinschaft und Gesellschaft*, Michigan State University Press.

McLuhan, M. (1964) *Understanding Media*, Routledge, London.

Negroponte, N. (1995) *Being Digital*, Hodder and Stoughton, London.

Novo, J. (2003) Drilling down: turning customer data into profits with a spreadsheet, **www.jimnovo.com**.

O'Malley, L. and Tynan, C. (2001) Reframing relationship marketing for consumer markets, *Interactive Marketing*, 2(3), 240–46.

Peppers, D. and Rogers, M. (1993) *The One to One Future: Building Relationships One Customer at a Time*, Currency/Doubleday, New York.

Peppers, D. and Rogers, M. (1997) *Enterprise One-to-One: Tools for Building Unbreakable Customer Relationships in the Interactive Age*, Piatkus, London.

Peppers, D. and Rogers, M. (2002) *One to One B2B: Customer Relationship Management Strategies for the Real Economy*, Capstone, Oxford.

Presi, C., Saridakis, C. and Hartmans, S. (2014) User-generated content behaviour of the dissatisfied service customer, *European Journal of Marketing*, 48(9–10).

Reichheld, F. (2006) *The Ultimate Question: Driving Good Profits and True Growth*, Harvard Business School Publishing, Boston.

Reichheld, F. and Schefter, P. (2000) E-loyalty, your secret weapon, *Harvard Business Review* (July–August), 105–13.

Say, P. and Southwell, J. (2006) Case study: Beep-beep-beep-beep, that'll be the bank then – Driving sales through mobile marketing, *Journal of Direct, Data and Digital Marketing Practice*, 7(3), 262–5.

Shellaker, M. (2014) Is 2014 the year of iBeacons?, *The Guardian*, **www.theguardian.com/ media-network/marketing-agencies-association-partner-zone/ibeacons-shopping-2014**.

Smart Insights (2011) Why social sign-on matters. Blog post by Dave Chaffey, 26 September, **www.smartinsights.com/social-media-marketing-alerts/why-social-sign-on-matters**.

Soubra, D. (2012) *The 3Vs that define Big Data*. Blog post published 5 July 2012, **www .datasciencecentral.com/forum/topics/the-3vs-that-define-big-data**.

Tomei, R. (2010) Doing one-to-one marketing one better, *Brandweek*, 51(44). doi:**10644318, 12/13/2010**.

Tucker, C. (2014). Social networks, personalised advertising and privacy controls, *Journal of Marketing Research*, 51(5), 546–62. doi:**10.1509/jmr.10.0355**.

Van Duyne, D., Landay, J. and Hong, J. (2003) *The Design of Sites. Patterns, Principles, and Processes for Crafting a Customer-centred Web Experience*, Addison-Wesley, Reading, MA.

Weblinks

- **ClickZ** (**www.clickz.com**). An excellent collection of articles on online marketing communications. US-focussed. Relevant section for this chapter: CRM strategies.
- **CRM Today** (**www.crm2day.com**). A portal with articles about the practical aspects of deploying CRM technology.
- **Database Marketing Institute** (**www.dbmarketing.com**). Useful collection of articles on best practice.
- **Dataversity** (**www.dataversity.net**). An aggregator site for articles discussing Big Data.
- **Infoworld** (**www.infoworld.com/category/big-data/**). Resources on the latest developments in Big Data.
- **Jim Novo** (**www.jimnovo.com**). A site by a US consultant that has a lot of detail on techniques to profile and target customers online.
- **MyCustomer** (**www.mycustomer.com**). Articles about the principles and technology of customer relationship management.
- **Net Promoter Score blog** (**http://netpromoter.typepad.com/fred_reichheld**). Multi-author blog and forum discussing the practicalities of implementing NPS.
- **Peppers and Rogers One-to-One marketing website** (**www.1to1.com**). A site containing a lot of information on the techniques and tools of relationship marketing.

Part 3
Digital marketing: implementation and practice

In Part 3, particular issues regarding the execution of digital marketing strategy are described, including development of a website and ensuring a quality customer experience (Chapter 7), marketing communications to promote a site (Chapters 8 and 9) and the maintenance and evaluation as online presence (Chapter 10). In Chapters 11 and 12, specific examples are given of how business-to-consumer and business-to-business companies are using the Internet.

7 Delivering the online customer experience 354

- Planning website design and redesign projects
- Initiation of a website project
- Defining site or app requirements
- Designing the user experience
- Development and testing of content
- Online retail merchandising
- Site promotion or 'traffic building'
- Service quality

8 Campaign planning for digital media 418

- The characteristics of digital media
- Step 1. Goal setting and tracking for interactive marketing communications
- Step 2. Campaign insight
- Step 3. Segmentation and targeting
- Step 4. Offer, message development and creative
- Step 5. Budgeting and selecting the digital media mix
- Step 6. Integration into overall media schedule or plan

9 Marketing communications using digital media channels 476

- Search engine marketing
- Online public relations
- Online partnerships including affiliate marketing
- Interactive display advertising
- Opt-in email marketing and mobile text messaging
- Social media and viral marketing
- Offline promotion techniques

10 Evaluation and improvement of digital channel performance 548

- Performance management for digital channels
- Customer experience and content management process
- Responsibilities for customer experience and site management

11 Business-to-consumer digital marketing practice 592

- The consumer perspective: online consumer behaviour
- The retail perspective: online retailing
- Implications for e-retail marketing strategy

12 Business-to-business digital marketing practice 622

- Types of B2B organisational marketing and trading environments
- Using digital marketing to support customer acquisition in B2B marketing
- Options for online inter-organisational trading
- How digital technologies can support B2B marketing
- Digital marketing strategies

Chapter 7
Delivering the online customer experience

Chapter at a glance

Main topics

- Planning website design and redesign projects 362
- Initiation of the website project 370
- Defining site or app requirements 374
- Designing the user experience 388
- Development and testing of content 400
- Online retail merchandising 402
- Site promotion or 'traffic building' 404
- Service quality 404

Case studies

Digital marketing in practice

The Smart Insights interview with Ben Jesson and Karl Blanks of agency Conversion Rate Experts on conversion rate optimisation 360

Case study 7: Refining the online customer experience at i-to-i.com 410

Learning objectives

After reading this chapter, the reader should be able to:

- Describe the different stages needed to create an effective website, mobile app or social media presence
- Define the requirements that contribute to an effective digital experience delivered as a website, mobile app or online presence
- Identify the similarities and differences in creating a website and other forms of online presence.

Questions for marketers

Key questions for marketing managers related to this chapter are:

- Which activities are involved in creating or redeveloping a new desktop or mobile site?
- What are the key factors of online service quality and site design that will help our goals of customer acquisition and retention?
- Which techniques can I use to determine visitors' requirements and whether they are met?
- How should I integrate the different forms of online presence?

Scan code
to find the
latest updates
for topics in
this chapter

Links to other chapters

Related chapters are:

- Chapters 4 and 5, which describe the development of the strategy and tactics that inform online experiences
- Chapters 8 and 9, which describe approaches to promoting websites
- Chapter 10, which describes the analysis of digital customer experience and their maintenance.

Introduction

Managing the **digital customer experience** for a brand used to be relatively straightforward; businesses simply had a website and an email newsletter alongside offline channels to sale. Today, the picture is far more complex, with the combination of touchpoints where marketers seek to influence consumers stretching across paid, earned and owned media on different devices. Consider the customer-facing touchpoints of a brand's online experience. These can include a desktop or mobile optimised site, mobile apps and company pages on social media. Company pages on social media today have a strong visual, interactive emphasis including Facebook or Google+ (text updates, video and image posts plus apps), Twitter (text updates can include images; video and Twitter cards enable interaction), LinkedIn (company pages and groups), YouTube (branded video channels), Instagram and Pinterest (image emphasis). Most companies seek to maintain a presence across all seven of these networks, although LinkedIn may be limited to careers. Even within offline channels, digital devices are being used to supplement the digital experience, as shown in Mini case study 7.1 on NFC in-store integration. For example, Debenhams, a leading UK retail adopter of mobile, shared this retrospective of their mobile development over the last two years or so. Speaking at the 2014 Mobile Marketing conference, Debenhams' mobile marketing manager, Sarah Bailie, explained:

> Integrating online in store should be top priority for all multichannel retailers looking to create an experiential and destination shopping experience. Debenhams' most valuable customers engage with the brand via multiple channels.

Creating effective digital experiences

Given the popularity of digital devices for finding out about brands and services, improving the capability to create and maintain these effective online brand presences is a key part of digital marketing. In the introduction we have described the range of different types of digital devices that offer digital interactions between a brand and its audience. For most businesses, the majority of interactions still occur on desktop and mobile websites, so this is where we focus in this chapter. Although social media have grown in importance, they are relatively unimportant in prompting website visits. 'Effective' means that the presence must deliver relevance and a satisfactory digital customer experience for its audience. At the same time, 'effective' means the presence must support and add value to the brand to deliver results for the company. **Conversion rate optimisation (CRO)** is increasingly being used by companies to improve the commercial contribution of online presence to a business, as the Smart Insights interview introducing this chapter shows.

In this chapter, we will explore different practical actions that companies can take to create and maintain satisfactory online experiences. An indication of the need to produce a customer-centric online presence is given by Alison Lancaster, at the time the head of marketing and catalogues at John Lewis Direct and then marketing director at Charles Tyrwhitt (**www.ctshirts.co.uk**), who said:

> A good site should always begin with the user. Understand who the customer is, how they use the channel to shop, and understand how the marketplace works in that category. This includes understanding who your competitors are and how they operate online. You need continuous research, feedback and usability testing to continue to monitor and evolve the customer experience online. Customers want convenience and ease of ordering. They want a site that is quick to download, well-structured and easy to navigate.

You can see that creating effective online experiences is a challenge since there are many practical issues to consider, which we present in Figure 7.2. This is based on a diagram

Mini case study 7.1	CloudTags integrates in-store digital experiences

CloudTags is working with a number of retailers to create an innovative, omni-channel experience using mobile devices and NFC technology. The retailers, among them Harvey Nichols and MADE (an online furniture retailer), have been putting tablet computers in stores for consumers to pick up and use. The customer simply enters their email address, which creates a customer profile, and by interacting with physical products via tapping on NFC icons in store they get rich, in-depth product content such as images, videos and recommendations. There is also a separate tool that allows users to send details of the products to the inbox.

If assisted by staff, the store is able to track and attribute activity online (should the user go home and purchase) so the original salesperson is included in the credit for the sale.

Results

Harvey Nichols found that 90 per cent of shoppers engaged in-store were not previously known to them; 16 per cent of all shoppers engaged with the experience and 18 per cent took further action after receiving an email.

MADE also used the technology at its Notting Hill showroom (Figure 7.1): 21 per cent of consumers opted to have their in-store collections sent to their inbox; 41 per cent went on to browse products online; and over the course of the trial the average order value increased 15 per cent.

This example shows how, today, consumers are happy to interact with a company using technology. Ease of purchase, good customer experience and strong engagement are moving beyond attractive extras and are becoming standard expectations.

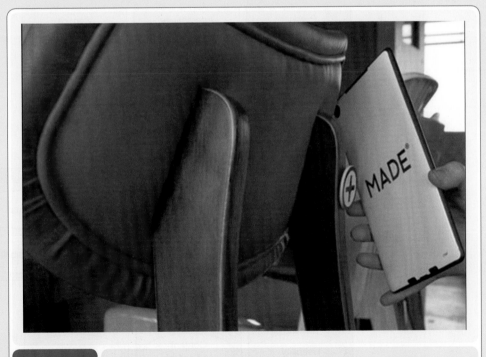

Figure 7.1	Cloudtags tablets used to assist in-store digital experience

by de Chernatony (2001), who suggested that delivering the online experience promised by a brand requires delivering rational values, emotional values and promised experience (based on rational and emotional values). The factors that influence the online customer experience can be presented in a pyramid form of success factors, as is shown in Figure 7.2 (the different success factors reflect current best practice and differ from those of de

Chernatony). The diagram also highlights the importance of delivering service quality on-line, as has been indicated by Trocchia and Janda (2003). More recently, Christodoulides *et al.* (2006) have tested the importance of a range of indicators of online brand equity for online retail and service companies. This analysis was performed across these five dimensions of brand equity, assessed by asking the questions below – they provide an excellent framework which can be applied to assess and benchmark the quality of brand experience for different types of website:

1 **Emotional connection**
   Q1: I feel related to the type of people who are [X]'s customers.
   Q2: I feel as though [X] actually cares about me.
   Q3: I feel as though [X] really understands me.
2 **Online experience**
   Q4: [X]'s website provides easy-to-follow search paths.
   Q5: I never feel lost when navigating through [X]'s website.
   Q6: I was able to obtain the information I wanted without any delay.
3 **Responsive service nature**
   Q7: [X] is willing and ready to respond to customer needs.
   Q8: [X]'s website gives visitors the opportunity to 'talk back' to [X].

Figure 7.2 The online customer experience pyramid – success factors

Source: Reprinted by permission of Macmillan Publishers Ltd.: *Journal of Brand Management*, based on a diagram in de Chernatony, L. (2001) 'Succeeding with brands on the internet', 8(3), pp.186–95, © 2001, published by Palgrave Macmillan

4 Trust

Q9: I trust [X] to keep my personal information safe.

Q10: I feel safe in my transactions with [X].

5 Fulfilment

Q11: I got what I ordered from [X]'s website.

Q12: The product was delivered in the time promised by [X].

WEBQUAL is a similar framework for e-commerce sites covering 14 dimensions across four broad areas of ease of use, ease of information gathering, ease of transactions and entertainment value (Loiacono *et al.*, 2000, 2007). We detail these and cite alternative frameworks such as SITEQUAL at the end of the chapter.

Consider how these elements of effective online brand experience might differ today? Differences could include support for interactions with other customers including rating of content or products, support for different digital devices and integration with other online and offline channels. More recent research into assessing company digital capabilities in the context of **Customer Experience Management (CXM)** is limited. Klaus (2014) notes that 'there remains a need for both theoretical and conceptual development, and empirical research to determine which digital CX strategies and practices have the most positive influence on organisational performance'. He identifies three levels of company approach to CXM, Preservers, Transformers and Vanguards. He categorises Vanguards as having a 'clear strategic model of CX management impacting all areas of the organisation, and developing commensurate business processes and practices to ensure its effective implementation. While Transformers merely acknowledge the broad-based challenges of CX management, Vanguards integrate functions and customer touchpoints to ensure consistency of the desired customer experiences across their own business'.

Figure 7.2 incorporates many of the factors that are relevant for a transactional e-retail site such as price and promotions which together form **web merchandising** (see the end of the chapter), but you can see that many of the rational and emotional values are important to any website. You may not be familiar with some of the terms, such as 'usability' and 'accessibility' (which are delivered through an effective website design), but these will all be explained later in this chapter.

In Figure 7.2 these factors are all associated with using the website, but the online customer experience extends beyond this, so effective designs are based on integrating with the entire **customer journey** for different audiences and different scenarios to achieve the best result. So design of online presence also needs to look at the bigger picture:

- ease of locating the site through search engines (Chapter 8);
- services provided by partners online on other websites;
- quality of outbound communications such as e-newsletters;
- quality of processing inbound email communications from customers;
- integration with offline communications and touchpoints like store and phone as part of multichannel marketing.

Alternative frameworks, such as WEBQUAL and E-SERVQUAL, for assessing website effectiveness are covered in the section on service quality.

Customer Experience Management (CXM)
A holistic approach to managing customer experience and customer engagement across digital and non-digital touchpoints including web, mobile and social digital platforms, in-store and by call-centres.

Web merchandising
The aims of web merchandising are to maximise the sales potential of an online store for each visitor. This means connecting the right products with the right offer to the right visitor, and remembering that the online store is part of a broader experience including online and offline advertising, in-store visits, customer service and delivery.

Customer journey
A description of modern multichannel buyer behaviour as consumers use different media to select suppliers, make purchases and gain customer support.

Structure of the chapter

We start the chapter by considering the requirements for a presence that delivers appropriate rational and emotional values. We then look at the processes and stages involved in managing a project to improve the customer experience. Our coverage on website design is integrated with consideration of researching online buyer behaviour since an appropriate experience can only be delivered if it is consistent with customer behaviour, needs and wants. We then go on to review delivery of service quality online. This includes aspects such as speed and availability of the site itself which support the rational values, and also fulfilment and support which are a core part of the promised experience.

Digital marketing in practice   The Smart Insights interview

Ben Jesson and Karl Blanks of agency Conversion Rate Experts on conversion rate optimisation

Overview and main concepts covered

Ben Jesson and Karl Blanks of agency Conversion Rate Experts discuss how to optimise business and generate revenue with their ideas on Conversion Rate Optimisation.

The interview

Q. We're seeing a lot more companies working now on CRO. What is it and why is its use increasing?

Ben Jesson: Yes, it should be. Landing page optimisation focuses on one page. We coined the term Conversion Rate Optimisation (CRO) in 2007 to describe the process of optimising the business itself. It's really commercial optimisation. A proper job of CRO includes the review of the entire process from the initial lead-generation ad, all the way through to the post-sale follow-up. The real goal is to identify which parts of the sales funnel will yield the greatest wins with the least work.

That means it's necessary to bring a lot of disciplines to the party, including understanding traffic sources, visitor psychology and the company's position in the marketplace, including its core strengths and weaknesses. On top of that there's usability testing, copywriting and web design factors to look at.

All these elements go into creating hypotheses for testing. We're maniacal about testing, because we've seen too many businesses merely throw a series of 'best practices' against the wall to see if anything sticks. Best practices should not be the answer to optimising a website, but merely one starting point for formulating a test strategy.

Once we determine what truly works for a particular website, then we examine how our findings might be used in other media channels. For instance, a better series of benefit statements might be transferable to direct mail or email autoresponder campaigns – subject to testing in those media, of course.

Q. How do you help companies build a business case for returns from CRO?

Karl Blanks: It's easy. We explain that CRO allows companies to generate more revenue without spending more on advertising. It's about getting a higher return from the existing ad spend. Unlike certain industries like public relations, the entire foundation of CRO is based on data, measurement and testing. You don't need to present arguments when the data can do the talking for you. Once you measure the value of visitors, conversions and sales, then it's simple arithmetic to show how, say, a 10 per cent boost in conversions would help the bottom line.

Here's another powerful side-benefit: when you optimise your funnel and bring in more revenues, you then have earned a luxury. You get to decide whether to pocket those profits or plough them back into even more advertising, thus distancing yourself even further from your competitors. It's a nice problem to have.

Q. Which approaches do you use to decide which part of a site needs most urgent attention?

Ben Jesson: *FORTUNE* magazine called what we do 'a combination of multi-variate statistical analysis and good old-fashioned detective work' and that pretty well describes our approach.

It's often very useful to map out your entire sales/conversion funnel and make sure it's being comprehensively measured in whatever web analytics package you prefer.

Then you should look for the biggest drop-offs from one step to the next. We like to say that we look for the 'blocked arteries' (that is, pages – or page elements – that get loads of visitors but are underperforming). How do you know if something is underperforming? Clues come from a range of feedback mechanisms: the analytics data, usability tests, surveys, customer support feedback … and, of course, gut feel. Of course, we have the advantage of having been engaged by companies on several continents and in many industries, so we have a good knowledgebase of what's good and what's bad.

Q. What can limit conversion? Give some examples of the most common 'conversion rate killers' you see.

Karl Blanks: These are some of the most common mistakes we see:

- Killer #1: not split testing. Many people think they're done if they take action to make changes to their site. In reality they're only 'done' when tests show that the changes in fact improved conversions. Installing a 'best practice' magic button that another site swears by might actually lower conversions. Despite the popularity of video, Google once discovered through tests that video reduced conversions on one of its pages. You simply must test to find out.

  Not long ago, multivariate testing software cost more than £5000 per month. Now you can use Google Website Optimiser and other software packages for free, so there's really no excuse. We created a tool, called Which Multivariate, which helps you to select the best software for multivariate testing.
- Killer #2 is 'meek tweaking' – in other words, making changes that are never likely to have a significant effect.
- Killer #3 is asking for the sale on the first visit. It's often a good idea to test the creation of a multi-step conversion funnel, in which you provide great value before you ask for the order. Comparison charts, forums, special reports, and email marketing are examples of elements that allow you to provide good information, ask for names, cultivate a relationship and thereby improve the chances of a sale.

Q. Could you share some tools that readers could use on their sites?

Karl Blanks: Excellent design is a prerequisite for conversion, but the biggest breakthroughs tend to be the new tools and techniques for gathering insights into the visitor's mindset. For determining how visitors interact with a site we often use both Clicktale and CrazyEgg.

KISSInsights and Ethnio are both good for asking your visitors to give you immediate feedback on your site. GazeHawk enables you to conduct an eye-tracking study on your site for a tiny fraction of the traditional cost.

Many of your readers will already know about how wireframing is important in order to get agreement on functional aspects before you take the time to make a site look good. We like Balsamiq for that purpose.

Planning website design and redesign projects

Despite the growth in social media, the company website, which today must be effective for users accessing via desktop, smartphone and tablet devices, is still at the heart of online communications. For the experience to be effective, a sound process is needed to design, build and refresh the online experience. In the past, it has been a common mistake among those creating a new website for the first time to 'dive in' and start creative design and content creation without sufficient forward planning. This is still a risk today, but new website design and build projects for existing businesses are less common, although still needed for new startups, new brands or new campaigns. Instead, what has become more common are website redesigns and relaunches and the continuous approach of Conversion Rate Optimisation referenced in the Digital Marketing in Practice interview at the start of this chapter. This change in emphasis is illustrated by many larger businesses in the retail sector which now have teams to continuously boost conversion rates. For example, speaking at Ecommerce Expo in 2014, Gareth Jones, Deputy CEO of Shop Direct, explained how, as part of a programme of digital transformation, they had increased the number of experiments to test improvements to conversion to over 50 per month with the aspiration to more than double them. He says:

By July 2016, we'll have more challengers live in a visit than competitors launch in a year.

He also reported that you need to invest in a range of tests since naturally not all will be successful, with around one-third giving a significant improvement in revenue, one-third failing and one-third neutral.

Regardless of timescale, the design and optimisation process (Figure 7.2) involves analysing the needs of owners and users of a site and then deciding on the best way to build the site to fulfil these needs. Without a structured plan and careful design, costly reworking is inevitable, as the first version of a site will not achieve the needs of the end users or the business. Follow Activity 7.1 to think through the problems you have experienced when using a site that does not meet your needs.

The process of website development summarised in Figure 7.3 is idealised because, for efficiency, many of these activities have to occur in parallel. Figure 7.4 gives an indication of the relationship between these tasks, and how long they may take, for a typical website project. We will explain some of the specialist design terminology later in this chapter. The main development tasks which need to be scheduled as part of the planning process are as follows:

1 *Pre-development tasks*. For a new site, these include domain name registration and deciding on the company to host the website. They also include preparing a brief setting out the aims and objectives of the site, and then – if it is intended to outsource the site – presenting the brief to rival agencies to bid for and pitch their offering.

2 *Discovery, analysis and design*. This is a research phase involving detailed analysis and design of the site, and includes clarification of business objectives, market research to identify the audience and typical customer personas and user journeys and their needs, defining the information architecture of different content types and prototyping different functional and visual designs to support the brand.

3 *Content development and testing*. Developing the site to create prototypes including integration of content management systems, database integration, usability and performance testing.

4 *Publishing or launching the site or improvement*. This is a relatively short stage. Often a **soft launch** is used where the site is updated, but the version is not widely communicated until the owners are sure the site is stable. Some site owners such as Google test features with a limited number of users to assess their impact before the features are rolled out more widely.

Soft launch
A trial version of a site launched with limited publicity.

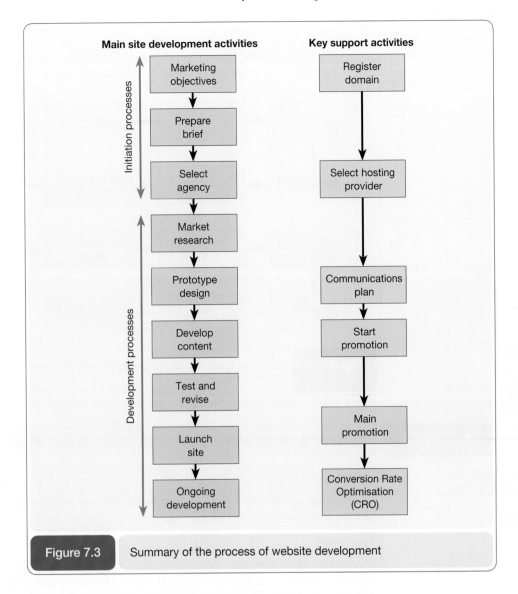

| **Figure 7.3** | Summary of the process of website development |

5 *Pre-launch promotion or communications.* Search engine registration and optimisation is most important for new sites. Although search engines can readily index a new site, they don't give the same level of visibility to new sites (sometimes known as 'the Google sandbox effect'), where the site is effectively on trial until it is established with links from other sites indicating its credibility. Briefing the PR company to publicise the launch is another example of pre-launch promotion.

6 *Ongoing promotion.* The schedule should also allow for promotion after site launch. This might involve structured discount promotions on the site, or competitions which are planned in advance. Many now consider search engine optimisation, content marketing and pay-per-click marketing (Chapter 9) as a continuous, 'always-on', process, and will often employ a third party to help achieve this.

7 *Ongoing development.* It used to be commonplace for there to be a time gap of several years between major website redesigns involving new layout and typography. Although content relating to products, services and promotions would be updated, the layout of page templates remained static. Increased adoption of CRO, which we described at the start of the chapter, means that the process of 1 to 5 is repeated between major updates using an agile development process, as explored further in the next section.

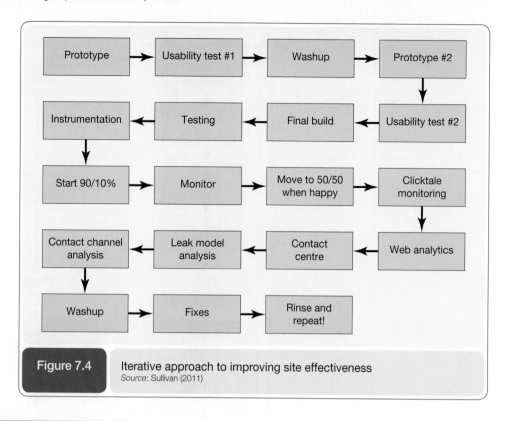

Figure 7.4 Iterative approach to improving site effectiveness
Source: Sullivan (2011)

Activity 7.1 What can go wrong without a planned approach to website design?

Purpose

To indicate potential problems to customers, partners and staff if the design of an online presence is not carefully planned.

Activity

Make a list of the potential problems related to a poorly planned design which may be faced by customers of an online retailer. Base your answer on problems you have experienced on a website that can be related to planning and implementation of site design.

The answers you identify all define the requirements for a new website design including: relevant content, acceptable performance, renders correctly in browser, findable within search engines (search engine optimisation (SEO)).

It's important to realise that Figure 7.3 is a simplification of real-world optimisation approaches. In reality, iteration of designs in a prototyping phase is required. Then once a working version is finalised it should be tested through user testing and then live testing using the AB/multivariate testing approach (as described in Chapter 10).

Who should be involved in a website project?

The success of a website is dependent on the range of people involved in its development, and how well they work as a team. Typical profiles of team members follow:

- *Site sponsors*. These will be senior managers who will effectively be paying for the system from their budgets. They will understand the strategic benefits of the system and

Digital marketing insight 7.1

Figure 7.4 defines an iterative approach to improving site effectiveness recommended by Sullivan (2011). At that point Craig Sullivan was e-business manager at Belron, an international windscreen repair service with local country brands such as Autoglass. He is now an independent consultant. You can hear him explain the increasing importance of user experience and the challenges marketers face when trying to optimise customer experiences, both on- and offline.

Hear Craig speak at: www.youtube.com/watch?v=VRYbpfrrxbg

will be keen that the site is implemented successfully to achieve the business objectives they have set.

- *Site owner.* 'Ownership' will typically be the responsibility of a marketing manager or e-commerce manager, who may be devoted full-time to overseeing the site in a large company; it may be part of a marketing manager's remit in a smaller company. In larger companies – for example, UK retail appliances brand **AO.com** – there is a separate team for desktop, mobile and tablet platforms with separate team members covering all these skills.
- *Project manager.* This person is responsible for the planning and coordination of the website project. They will aim to ensure that the site is developed within the budget and time constraints that have been agreed at the start of the project, and that the site delivers the planned-for benefits for the company and its customers.
- *Site designer.* The site designer will define the 'look and feel' of the site, including its styling through Cascading Style Sheets (CSS), layout and how company brand values are transferred to the web.
- *Content developer.* The content developer will write the copy for the website and convert it to a form suitable for the site. In medium or large companies this role may be split between marketing staff or staff from elsewhere in the organisation who write the copy and a technical member of staff who converts it to the graphics and HTML documents forming the web page and does the programming for interactive content.
- *Webmaster.* This is a technical role. The webmaster is responsible for ensuring the quality of the site. This means achieving suitable availability, speed, working links between pages and connections to company databases. In small companies the webmaster may also take on graphic design and content developer roles.
- *Digital experience analyst or CRO expert.* Familiar with how to analyse digital analytics to identify site effectiveness and how to run conversion rate optimisation experiments (as explained further in Chapter 10).
- *Stakeholders.* The impact of the website on other members of the organisation should not be underestimated. Internal staff may need to refer to some of the information on the website or use its services.

While the site sponsor and site owner will work within the company, many organisations outsource the other resources since full-time staff cannot be justified in these roles. There are a range of different choices for outsourcing which are summarised in Activity 7.2.

We are seeing a gradual blurring between these different types of supplier as they recruit expertise so as to deliver a 'one-stop shop' or 'full-service agency', but they still tend to be strongest in particular areas. Companies need to decide whether to partner with the 'best of breed' in each, or to perhaps compromise and choose the one-stop shop that gives the best balance and is most likely to achieve integration across different marketing activities – this would arguably be the new media agency, or perhaps a traditional marketing agency that has an established new media division. Which approach do you think is best?

Observation of the practice of outsourcing suggests that two conflicting patterns are evident:

- *Outside-in*. A company often starts using new digital marketing technologies by outsourcing some activities where there is insufficient in-house expertise. The company then builds up skills internally to manage these areas as digital marketing becomes an important contributor to the business. An outside-in approach will probably be driven by the need to reduce the costs of outsourcing, poor delivery of services by the supplier or simply a need to concentrate resources for a strategic core competence in-house.
- *Inside-out*. A company starts to implement digital marketing using existing resources within the IT department and marketing department in conjunction with recruitment of digital media specialists. They may then find that there are problems in developing a site that meets customers' needs or in building traffic to the site. At this point they may turn to outsourcing to solve the problems.

These approaches are not mutually exclusive and an outside-in approach may be used for some activities, such as SEO or content development, while an inside-out approach is used for other functions such as site promotion.

Activity 7.2	Options for outsourcing different digital marketing activities

Purpose

To highlight the outsourcing available for digital marketing and to gain an appreciation of how to choose suppliers.

Activity

A B2C company is trying to decide which of its e-business activities it should outsource. Select a single supplier that you think can best deliver each of these services indicated in Table 7.1. Justify your decision.

Table 7.1	Options for outsourcing different digital marketing activities

E-marketing function	Traditional marketing agency	Digital marketing agency	Traditional IT supplier	Management consultants
1 Strategy				
2 Design				
3 Content and service development				
4 Online promotion				
5 Offline promotion				
6 Infrastructure				

Prototyping and agile software development

Prototypes are trial versions of an entire website or a part of the site being refined that are gradually refined through an iterative process to become closer to the final version. Initial prototypes or 'mockups' may simply be paper prototypes or storyboards, perhaps of a 'wireframe' or screen layout. These may then be extended to include visuals of key static pages. Finally, working prototypes will be produced as HTML code is developed. The idea is that the design agency or development team and the marketing staff who commissioned the work can review and comment on prototypes, and changes can then be made to the site to incorporate these comments. Prototyping should result in a more effective final site which can be developed more rapidly than a more traditional approach with a long period of requirements determination.

Each iteration of the prototype typically passes through the stages shown in Figure 7.5, which are:

1 *Discovery or analysis*. Understanding the requirements of the audience of the site and the requirements of the business, defined by business and marketing strategy (and comments input from previous prototypes).

2 *Design*. Specifying different features of the site that will fulfil the requirements of the users and the business as identified during analysis.

3 *Develop*. The creation of the web pages and the dynamic content of the website.

4 *Test and review*. Structured checks are conducted to ensure that different aspects of the site meet the original requirements and work correctly.

Agile software development

Today, the concept of prototyping has been extended across the whole lifecycle for developing website functionality or software applications, where it is known as **agile software development**. The goal of agile development is to be able to create stable releases more frequently than traditional development methodologies, i.e. new functionality will be introduced through several releases each month rather than a more significant release every few weeks, months or even years. The approach is sometimes known as 'permanent beta'. Another difference with agile development is the emphasis on face-to-face communication to define requirements rather than detailed requirements specifications.

Scrum is a methodology that supports agile software development. Scrum involves stakeholders including the *scrum master* who is effectively a project manager, the *product owner* who represents the stakeholders such as the business owners and customers and the *scrum team* which includes the developers.

Scrum is based on focussed sprints of a 15–30-day period where the team creates an increment of potentially releasable software. Potential functionality for each sprint is agreed at a *sprint planning meeting* from the *product backlog*, a prioritised set of high-level requirements. The sprint planning meeting is itself iterative, with the product owner stating their requirements from the product backlog and the technical team then determining how much of this they can commit to complete during the forthcoming sprint. The term 'scrum' refers to a daily project status meeting during the sprint. (See **www.softhouse .se/hploads/scrum_eng_webb.pdf** for an overview of the process.)

The principles of agile development are encapsulated in the *Agile Manifesto* (**http:// agilemanifesto.org/**), which was agreed in 2001 by proponents of previous rapid development methodologies including the Dynamic Systems Development Methodology and Extreme Programming. The Agile Manifesto is useful in illustrating the principles of agile programming it contrasts with traditional approaches. The text of the manifesto is:

We are uncovering better ways of developing software by doing it and helping others do it. Through this work we have come to value:

- individuals and interactions over processes and tools
- working software over comprehensive documentation
- customer collaboration over contract negotiation
- responding to change over following a plan.

That is, while there is value in the items on the right, we value the items on the left more.

Prototype
A preliminary version of part, or a framework of all, of a website, which can be reviewed by its target audience or the marketing team. Prototyping is an iterative process in which website users suggest modifications before further prototypes and the final version of the site are developed.

Wireframe
A simplified outline of a single-page template used to define new layout or functionality for part of a website for discussion, iteration and then a brief for implementation.

Agile software development
An iterative approach to developing software and website functionality with the emphasis on face-to-face communications to elicit, define and test requirements. Each iteration is effectively a mini-software project including stages of planning, requirements analysis, design, coding, testing and documentation.

Scrum
Scrum is a methodology that supports agile software development based on 15–30-day sprints to implement features from a product backlog. 'Scrum' refers to a daily project status meeting during the sprint.

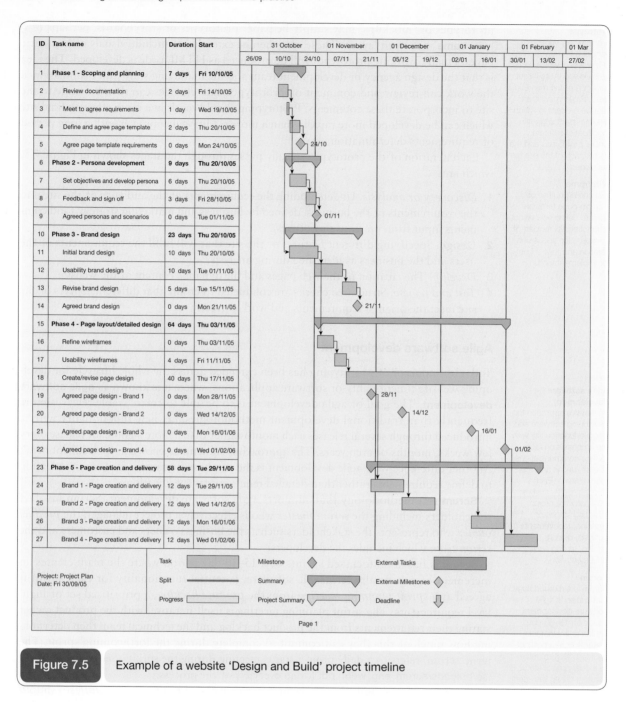

ID	Task name	Duration	Start			31 October		01 November		01 December		01 January		01 February		01 Mar
				26/09	10/10	24/10	07/11	21/11	05/12	19/12	02/01	16/01	30/01	13/02	27/02
1	**Phase 1 - Scoping and planning**	**7 days**	**Fri 10/10/05**												
2	Review documentation	2 days	Fri 14/10/05												
3	Meet to agree requirements	1 day	Wed 19/10/05												
4	Define and agree page template	2 days	Thu 20/10/05												
5	Agree page template requirements	0 days	Mon 24/10/05			24/10									
6	**Phase 2 - Persona development**	**9 days**	**Thu 20/10/05**												
7	Set objectives and develop persona	6 days	Thu 20/10/05												
8	Feedback and sign off	3 days	Fri 28/10/05												
9	Agreed personas and scenarios	0 days	Tue 01/11/05				01/11								
10	**Phase 3 - Brand design**	**23 days**	**Thu 20/10/05**												
11	Initial brand design	10 days	Thu 20/10/05												
12	Usability brand design	10 days	Tue 01/11/05												
13	Revise brand design	5 days	Tue 15/11/05												
14	Agreed brand design	0 days	Mon 21/11/05					21/11							
15	**Phase 4 - Page layout/detailed design**	**64 days**	**Thu 03/11/05**												
16	Refine wireframes	0 days	Thu 03/11/05												
17	Usability wireframes	4 days	Fri 11/11/05												
18	Create/revise page design	40 days	Thu 17/11/05												
19	Agreed page design - Brand 1	0 days	Mon 28/11/05						28/11						
20	Agreed page design - Brand 2	0 days	Wed 14/12/05							14/12					
21	Agreed page design - Brand 3	0 days	Mon 16/01/06									16/01			
22	Agreed page design - Brand 4	0 days	Wed 01/02/06										01/02		
23	**Phase 5 - Page creation and delivery**	**58 days**	**Tue 29/11/05**												
24	Brand 1 - Page creation and delivery	12 days	Tue 29/11/05												
25	Brand 2 - Page creation and delivery	12 days	Wed 14/12/05												
26	Brand 3 - Page creation and delivery	12 days	Mon 16/01/06												
27	Brand 4 - Page creation and delivery	12 days	Wed 01/02/06												

Project: Project Plan
Date: Fri 30/09/05

Task		Milestone	External Tasks
Split		Summary	External Milestones
Progress		Project Summary	Deadline

Page 1

Figure 7.5   Example of a website 'Design and Build' project timeline

DevOps
An approach to development of systems which involves a more collaborative and closer relationship between development and operations teams with the aim of reducing deployment times and frequency of system updates and improving their stability.

Closely related to the agile approach is restructuring using the **DevOps** approach. Wikipedia (2015) explains the reasons behind this:

The specific goals of a DevOps approach span the entire delivery pipeline, they include improved deployment frequency, which can lead to faster time to market, lower failure rate of new releases, shortened lead time between fixes, and faster mean time to recovery in the event of a new release crashing or otherwise disabling the current system. Simple processes become increasingly programmable and dynamic, using a DevOps approach, which aims to maximise the predictability, efficiency, security, and maintainability of operational processes.

Digital marketing insight 7.2

The Government Service Design Manual (www.gov.uk/service-manual) describes the process for developing online services using an agile approach covering Discovery, Beta, Alpha and Live stages. The UK Government Digital Service takes each new service they want to bring online or relaunch through four main phases and a retirement phase. These mirror those used in commercial projects who use similar terminology in agile. These are:

- *Discovery* (4–8 weeks) – The discovery phase gives a high-level understanding of user needs, defines KPIs and scopes initial prototypes which may be needed.
- *Alpha* (6–8 weeks) – The alpha involves exploring solutions for user challenges. More developers and designers will be brought into the team, and will help you to build and test prototypes and possible solutions for your users' needs.
- *Beta* – The objective of the beta phase is to build a fully working prototype which is tested with users and may involve private and public betas.
- *Live* – The government service manual explains: 'The work doesn't stop once your service is live. You'll be iteratively improving your service, reacting to new needs and demands, and meeting targets set during its development.'

In an article (O'Neill, 2014), one of the project managers explains the success factors for delivery, he picks out the 26 criteria (www.gov.uk/service-manual/digital-by-default) for an effective project, the majority of which also apply to commercial projects.

Growth hacking

Growth hacking
A mindset which focuses marketing activities on increasing the scale and profitability of a business through testing and improving techniques for improving the value of audience touchpoints across the customer lifecycle of Reach, Interactions, Conversion and Engagement.

Recently, the concept of **growth hacking** has developed as a way of supporting the profitable growth of businesses through using an agile approach. Andrew Chen (2012), an entrepreneur who is an advisor and investor to many startups, describes a growth hacker as follows in his post *Is the Growth Hacker the New VP Marketing?*

> *Growth hackers are a hybrid of marketer and coder, one who looks at the traditional question of 'How do I get customers for my product?' and answers with A/B tests, landing pages, viral factor, email deliverability, and Open Graph. On top of this, they layer the discipline of direct marketing, with its emphasis on quantitative measurement, scenario modelling via spreadsheets, and a lot of database queries.*

This quote shows that many of the features such as a focus on testing and learning through conversion rate optimisation (CRO) are not new, indeed they have been featured in this book for several editions; it shows a change in mindset in how business transformation can be achieved. Another key feature of growth hacking is applying techniques for how to achieve viral growth through encouraging users to share their experience. The growth of Hotmail from 0 to 12 million users before it was bought by Microsoft is a favourite anecdote of growth hackers. For Hotmail the sharing was rapid due to the email signature: 'PS I love you. Get your free email at Hotmail. Signature.' Today encouraging sharing through social sign-on and social sharing is more an approach sought by growth hackers. These techniques have helped companies like LinkedIn grow from 13 million to 175 million users according to Schranz (2012), who explained that Facebook's growth team started by establishing a simple framework of things to measure and improve to make it easier for everyone to understand what to focus on and why it matters:

- *Acquisition* – Get people in front of your product.
- *Activation* – Provide a great initial experience.

- *Engagement* – Keep people engaged, deliver value.
- *Virality* – Get people to recommend your product.

Some of the principles of growth hacking are being adopted by existing businesses, looking to enhance the sales from their digital channels. For example, *The Guardian*'s advertising for a Head of Growth Hacking described the growth in the role as:

> The Guardian is committed to a 'digital-first' strategy and in order to support this, we are seeking a Head of Growth Hacking to manage a virtual, cross functional team focussed on GNM's growth hacking plan. This role is responsible for finding innovative ways to accelerate adoption, use, and retention to drive up audiences to the Guardian's digital product portfolio.

Initiation of a website project

Initiation of the website project
This phase of the project should involve a structured review of the costs and benefits of developing a website (or making a major revision to an existing website). A successful outcome to initiation will be a decision to proceed with the site development phase, with an agreed budget and target completion date.

Before the analysis, design and creation of the website, all major projects will have an initial phase in which the aims and objectives of the website are reviewed, to assess whether it is worthwhile investing in the website and to decide on the amount to invest. The **initiation of the website project** provides a framework for the project that ensures:

- there is management and staff commitment to the project;
- objectives are clearly defined;
- the costs and benefits are reviewed in order that the appropriate amount of investment in the site occurs;
- the project will follow a structured path, with clearly identified responsibilities for different aspects such as project management, analysis, promotion and maintenance;
- the implementation phase will ensure that important aspects of the project, such as testing and promotion, are not skimped.

Domain name selection and registration

Domain name registration
The process of reserving a unique web address that can be used to refer to the company website, in the form of **www.<company name>. com** or **www.<company name>.co.uk**.

If a project or campaign involves a new site rather than an upgrade, it will be necessary to **register a new domain name**, more usually referred to as a 'web address' or 'uniform (or universal) resource locator' (URL).

Choosing a domain name is a relatively simple decision, since there is some basic terminology that marketers need to be aware of. Companies typically have many digital services located on different address domains, particularly for companies with different domains for different countries. The domain name refers to the address of the web server and is usually selected to be the same as the name of the company, and the extension will indicate its type.

The extension is commonly known as the generic top-level domain (gTLD). Common gTLDs are:

i .**com** represents an international or American company, such as **www.travelocity.com**.
ii .**org** are not-for-profit organisations (e.g. **www.greenpeace.org**).
iii .**mobi** – introduced in 2006 for sites configured for mobile phones.
iv .**net** is a network provider such as **www.demon.net**.

There are also specific country-code top-level domains (ccTLDs):

v .**co.uk** represents a company based in the UK, such as **www.thomascook.co.uk**.
vi .**au, .ca, .de, .es, .fi, .fr, .it, .nl**, etc. represent other countries (the co.uk syntax is an anomaly!).

vii .ac.uk is a UK-based university or other higher education institution (e.g. **www.cran field.ac.uk**).

viii .org.uk is for an organisation focussing on a single country (e.g. **www.mencap.org.uk**).

The 'filename.html' part of the web address refers to an individual web page – for example 'products.html' for a web page summarising a company's products.

It is important that companies define a URL strategy which will help customers or partners find relevant parts of the site containing references to specific products or campaigns when printed in offline communications such as adverts or brochures.

Uniform resource locators (URLs)

The technical name for web address is **uniform (or universal) resource locator (URL)**. URLs can be thought of as a standard method of addressing, similar to postcodes, that make it straightforward to find the name of a domain or a document on the domain.

In larger businesses, particularly those with many sites, it's important to develop a **URL strategy** so that there is a consistent way of labelling online services and resources.

There is further terminology associated with a URL which will often be required when discussing site implementation or digital marketing campaigns, as shown in Digital marketing insight 7.3.

Domain names are registered using a hosting company or domain broker using a domain name service, such as:

- *InterNIC* (**www.internic.net**). Registration for the .com, .org and .net domains.
- Nominet (**www.nominet.org.uk**). Registration for the .co.uk domain. All country-specific domains, such as .fr (France) or .de (Germany), have their own domain registration authority.

Uniform (universal) resource locator (URL)
A web address used to locate a web page on a web server.

URL strategy
A defined approach to forming URLs including the use of capitalisation, hyphenation and subdomains for different brands and different locations. This has implications for promoting a website offline through promotional or vanity URLs, search engine optimisation and findability.
A clean URL which fits many of these aims is **www.domain.com/ folder-name/document-name**. Care must be taken with capitalisation since Linux servers parse capitals differently from lower-case letters.

| **Digital marketing insight 7.3** | What's in a URL? |

A great example of different URL components is provided by Google engineer Matt Cutts (2007). He gives this example:

http://video.google.co.uk:80/videoplay?docid=-7246927612831078230&hl=en#00h02m30s

Here are some of the components of the url:

- The *protocol* is http. Other protocols include https, ftp, etc.
- The *host* or *hostname* is **video.google.co.uk**.
- The *subdomain* is **video**.
- The *domain name* is **google.co.uk**.
- The *top-level domain* or *TLD* is uk (also known as gTLD). The uk domain is also referred to as a country-code top-level domain or ccTLD. For **google.com**, the TLD would be com.
- The *second-level domain* (SLD) is co.uk.
- The *port* is 80, which is the default port for web servers (not usually used in URLs when it is the default, although all web servers broadcast on ports).
- The *path* is /videoplay. Path typically refers to a file or location on the web server, e.g. /directory/file.html.
- The URL parameter is docid and the value of that parameter is -7246927612831078230. These are often called the 'name, value' pair. URLs often have lots of parameters. Parameters start with a question mark (?) and are separated with an ampersand (&).
- The *anchor* or *fragment* is '#00h02m30s'.

The following guidelines should be borne in mind when registering domain names:

1 *Campaign microsites may hinder findability and give maintenance problems.* If a new site is created specifically for a campaign this can cause problems since although Google's robots will crawl it rapidly, it will probably not rank highly without backlinks from other sites, so it will have poor visibility (as described in Chapter 8 in the section on SEO). For this reason it is often better to redirect visitors typing in the domain name to a campaign subfolder on an existing site.

2 *Organisations should register multiple ccTLDs to protect their reputation.* As described in Chapter 3, 'domaineers' may seek to purchase domain extensions or ccTLDs which would rightly belong to the brand such as **.org.uk** or their equivalents in other countries.

3 *New startup companies should consider whether the company and domain name can assist in SEO.* While existing brands will use their main company or brand name for a site, new companies may benefit if the domain name contains a key phrase that searchers will seek. As we saw in Chapter 3, about the legal constraints on domain purchase, companies may pay a lot to register a domain such as **cruises.com** for this reason.

Managers or agencies responsible for websites need to check that domain names are automatically renewed by the hosting company (as most are today). For example, the **.co.uk** domain must be renewed every two years. Companies that don't manage this process potentially risk losing their domain name since another company could potentially register it if the domain name lapsed.

Selecting a hosting provider

Selecting the right partner to host a website is an important decision since the quality of service provided will directly impact on the quality of service delivered to a company's customers. The partner that hosts the content will usually be a specialist hosting provider such as Rackspace (**www.rackspace.com**) for the majority of small and medium-sized companies, but for larger companies the web server used to host the content may be inside the company and managed by the company's IT department.

The quality of service of hosted content is essentially dependent on two factors: the performance of the website and its availability.

Website performance optimisation

Bandwidth
Indicates the speed at which data are transferred using a particular network medium. It is measured in bits per second (bps).

Content distribution (or delivery) networks (CDNs)
A system of servers distributed globally with copies of data stored locally to enable more rapid download of content. Their use has increased with increased use of streaming video and more complex web applications.

It's important for site owners to recognise that page download performance is essential to the success of a site even when many users have broadband connections and sites are hosted to Internet with high **bandwidth**. Research by Strangeloop (2011) showed that the average user perception of acceptable download time is three seconds, while for the average Fortune 500 site it is seven seconds.

Research by Trilibis (2014) of over 150 prominent mobile responsive sites showed that only 21 per cent of these modern websites were loading in less than four seconds on a smartphone, and that 32 per cent of the sites required between 8 and 48 seconds to load.

Trilibis investigated the reason for this sluggish page-load time of responsive sites and found that image size was the primary cause. By analysing page composition, they determined that the mean home page weight of the sites in the sample was 1.7MB, with a median weight of 1.2MB.

The Strangeloop (2011) research also reveals that these larger sites often have poor performance despite use of **content distribution networks (CDNs)** like Akamai and Cloudflare, indicating underlying technical issues in delivering content from the server.

Google clearly takes this area of website management seriously; it wants users to access relevant content quickly as part of the service and has stated that if a site is particularly slow its ranking will be affected. To help site owners, Google has made available tools such as that illustrated in Figure 7.6 to show the relevant performance, so marketers should ask their agency to assess their performance.

The length of time is dependent on a number of factors, some of which cannot be controlled, but primarily depends on the bandwidth of the hosting company's connection to the Internet and the performance of the web server hardware and content management platform. It also depends on the 'page weight' of the site's pages measured in kilobytes (which is dependent on the number and complexity of images and animations).

Another factor for a company to consider when choosing a hosting provider is whether the server is *dedicated* to one company or whether content from several companies is located on the same server. A dedicated server is best, but it will attract a premium price.

The availability of the website

The availability of a website is an indication of how easy it is for a user to connect to it. In theory this figure should be 100 per cent but sometimes, for technical reasons such as failures in the server hardware or upgrades to software, the figure can drop substantially below this.

SciVisum, a web-testing specialist, found that three-quarters of Internet marketing campaigns are impacted by website failures, with 14 per cent of failures so severe that they prevented the campaign meeting its objectives. The company surveyed marketing professionals from 100 UK-based organisations across the retail, financial, travel and online gaming sectors. More than a third of failures were rated as 'serious to severe', with many customers complaining or being unable to complete web transactions. These are often seen by marketers as technology issues which are owned by others in the business, but marketers need to ask the right questions. The SciVisum (2005) research showed that nearly two-thirds of marketing professionals did not know how many users making transactions

| Figure 7.6 | WebPage Test service results (www.webpagetest.org) |

their websites could support, despite an average transaction value of £50 to £100, so they were not able to factor this into campaign plans. Thirty-seven per cent could not put a monetary value on losses caused by customers abandoning web transactions. A quarter of organisations experienced website overloads and crashes as a direct result of a lack of communication between the two departments.

SciVisum recommends that companies do the following:

- Define the peak visitor throughput requirements for each customer journey on the site. For example, the site should be able to support at the same time: approximately ten checkout journeys per second, 30 add-to-basket journeys per second, five registration journeys per second, two check-my-order-status journeys per second.
- Service-level agreement – more detailed technical requirements need to be agreed for each of the transaction stages. Home-page delivery time and server uptime are insufficiently detailed.
- Set up a monitoring programme that measures and reports on the agreed journeys 24/7.

Defining site or app requirements

Discovery or analysis phase
The identification of the requirements of an online service. Techniques to achieve this may include quantitative analysis of digital analytics data and qualitative analysis involving focus groups, questionnaires sent to existing customers or interviews with key accounts.

The **discovery or analysis phase** involves using different marketing research techniques to find out the needs of the business and audience, whether it's a website, mobile site, app or company social page. These needs can then be used to drive the design and content of the website.

Analysis is not a 'one-off' exercise, but is likely to be repeated for each iteration of the prototype. Although analysis and design are separate activities, there tends to be considerable overlap between the two phases. In analysis we are seeking to answer the following types of 'who, what, why, how, when, where' questions, each of which has an associated analysis technique:

- Who are the key audiences for the site (personas)?
- Why should they use the site (what will appeal to them)?
- What should the content of site be? Which services will be provided (value proposition)?
- How will the content of the site be structured (information architecture)?
- How will navigation around the site occur (findability)?
- What are the main marketing outcomes we want the site to deliver, such as registration, leads and sales, and how will we increase them (persuasion and CRO)?
- When, where and on which device is the online presence accessed: at home, at work or while mobile?

User-centred design
A design approach which is based on research of user characteristics and needs.

To help answer these questions, web designers commonly use a research-based approach known as **user-centred design**, which uses a range of techniques to ensure the site meets user needs. This often involves ethnographic research used to build the website design or customer personas (as described in Chapter 2). (See Chapter 2 for more details on creating personas which summarise different customer journeys.)

A structured approach to user-centred design is defined in the standard *ISO 13407: Human-centred design processes for interactive systems*. This was published in 1999 and also covers software and hardware systems.

We will now explore the key requirements for an online presence: business requirements and user requirements which comprise usability, accessibility and information needs.

Marketing-led site design
Site design elements are developed to achieve customer acquisition, retention and communication of marketing messages.

Business requirements

With a focus on user-centred design, there is a risk that business requirements to achieve marketing outcomes may be marginalised. A **marketing-led site design** is informed by marketing objectives and tactics. A common approach is to base the design on achieving the performance drivers of successful digital marketing (**referred to in Chapter 4**) and the loyalty drivers referred to at the start of this chapter. Design will be led by these performance drivers as follows:

- *Customer acquisition* – the online value proposition must be clear. Appropriate incentives for customer acquisition and permission marketing such as those described in Chapter 6 must be devised.
- *Customer conversion* – the site must engage first-time visitors. Call to action for customer acquisition and retention offers must be prominent with benefits clearly explained. The fulfilment of the offer or purchase must be as simple as possible to avoid attrition during this process.
- *Customer retention* – appropriate incentives, content and customer service information to encourage repeat visits and business must be available (see Chapter 6).
- *Service quality* – this has been covered in this chapter. Service quality is affected by site navigation, performance, availability and responsiveness to enquiries.
- *Branding* – the brand offer must be clearly explained and interaction with the brand must be possible.

Persuasion marketing
Using design elements such as layout, copy and typography together with promotional messages to encourage site users to follow particular paths and specific actions rather than giving them complete choice in their navigation.

Marketing-led site design is also known as **persuasion marketing**. Consultant Bryan Eisenberg (**www.bryaneisenberg.com**) was an early advocate of persuasion marketing alongside other design principles such as usability and accessibility. He says this type of focus on marketing outcome is required:

> during the wireframe and storyboard phase we ask three critical questions of every page a visitor will see:
>
> 1 What action needs to be taken?
> 2 Who needs to take that action?
> 3 How do we persuade that person to take the action we desire?

Fogg (2009) has developed a model to inform persuasive design. The Fogg Behaviour Model (**www.behaviormodel.org**) asserts that for a person to perform a target behaviour, they must (1) be sufficiently motivated, (2) have the ability to perform the behaviour and (3) be triggered to perform the behaviour. These three factors must occur at the same moment, otherwise the behaviour will not happen.

Before we review user-centred design processes, consider Mini case study 7.2, which shows how one company has developed a site that blends marketing-led and user-centric design.

Usability requirements

Usability
An approach to website design intended to enable the completion of user tasks.

Usability is a concept that can be applied to the analysis and design of a range of products which defines how easy they are to use. The British Standard/ISO Standard (1999) *Human-centred design processes for interactive systems* defines usability as:

> the extent to which a product can be used by specified users to achieve specified goals with effectiveness, efficiency and satisfaction in a specified context of use.

You can see how the concept can be readily applied to website design – web visitors often have defined *goals* such as finding particular information or completing an action such as booking a flight or viewing an account balance.

In Jakob Nielsen's classic book *Designing Web Usability* (2000), he describes usability as follows:

> An engineering approach to website design to ensure the user interface of the site is learnable, memorable, error free, efficient and gives user satisfaction. It incorporates testing

Mini case study 7.2	Ultralase

Ultralase is one of the UK's largest laser eye treatments companies. The first Ultralase clinic was opened in January 1991 and there are now 31 locations in the UK. Its growth has been supported through its website and digital media since the content available online is a key part of the consumer decision-making process and for the company lead generation.

Figure 7.7 shows how Ultralase combines persuasion, usability and accessibility within its home page to help meet business needs.

These are some of the design elements used by Ultralase to help it achieve its goals:

1 *Carousel area (centre top of page)*. Use to deliver key brand messages and position the brand through imagery.
2 *Customer journey highlighted (buttons below carousel)*. The 'call-to-action' buttons for 'book a consultation', 'request a brochure' and 'find your local clinic' help highlight what the customer can do on the site and its goals.

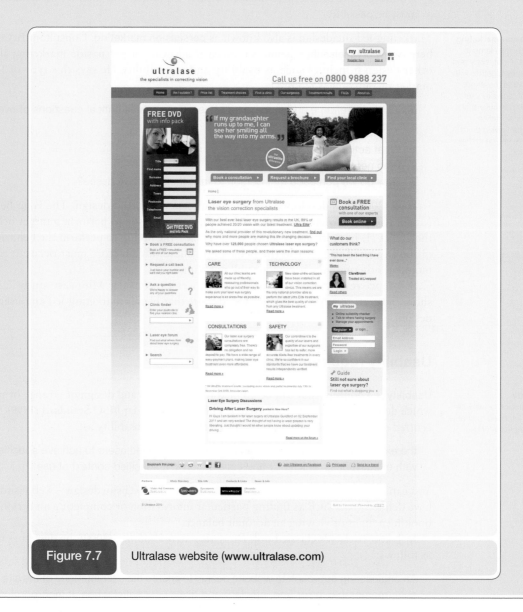

Figure 7.7	Ultralase website (www.ultralase.com)

3 *Intro text*. This helps show relevance for users, communicates key brand messages and is used for search engine optimisation to target the key phrases laser eye surgery and treatment.

4 *Incentivised response-form (left sidebar)*. Multiple incentives and prominent position consistent with eye-tracking studies.

5 *Clear calls-to-action*. Again, prominent on the left-hand side, these are likely to be set up as conversion goals in Google Analytics. Containers blend image and text to avoid banner blindness. These containers all highlight the site's online value proposition.

6 *Common questions answered (centre panel)*. These 'points of resolution' are often hidden in a FAQ, but it is interesting that Ultralase highlights them on the home page. Key concerns are also highlighted in the main navigation.

7 *Prominent phone response (top right)*. Vital for high-value, complex products since conversion tends to be higher via the phone channel. A unique web number can be used for tracking online influence.

8 *Social proof (right sidebar)*. The right sidebar is used for the map to show the scale of the company through number of clinics and engaging containers for customer testimonials.

9 *MyUltralase (top right and right sidebar)*. This site registration facility again shows the online value proposition. This is intended to encourage a deeper relationship and return visits.

and evaluation to ensure the best use of navigation and links to access information in the shortest possible time. A companion process to information architecture.

In practice, usability involves two key project activities. **Expert reviews** are often performed at the beginning of a redesign project as a way of identifying problems with a previous design. **Usability testing** involves:

1 identifying representative users of the site (see, for example, Table 7.2) and identifying typical tasks;

2 asking them to perform specific tasks such as finding a product or completing an order;

3 observing what they do and how they succeed.

For a site to be successful, the user tasks or actions need to be completed:

- *Effectively* – web usability specialists measure task completion; for example, only three out of ten visitors to a website may be able to find a telephone number or other piece of information.
- *Efficiently* – web usability specialists also measure how long it takes to complete a task on-site, or the number of clicks it takes.

Jakob Nielsen explains the imperative for usability well in his 'Usability 101' (**www.useit.com/alertbox/20030825.html**). He said:

> On the web, usability is a necessary condition for survival. If a website is difficult to use, people leave. If the homepage fails to clearly state what a company offers and what users can do on the site, people leave. If users get lost on a website, they leave. If a website's information is hard to read or doesn't answer users' key questions, they leave. Note a pattern here?

For these reasons, Nielsen suggests that around 10 per cent of a design project budget should be spent on usability, but often actual spend is significantly less.

Some would also extend usability to including testing of the visual or brand design of a site in focus groups, to assess how well consumers perceive it reflects the brand. Often, alternative visual designs are developed to identify those which are most appropriate.

Additional website design research activities include the use of *personas* and *scenario-based design* (as introduced in Chapter 2).

Expert review
An analysis of an existing site or prototype by an experienced usability expert who will identify deficiencies and improvements to a site based on their knowledge of web design principles and best practice.

Usability/user testing
Representative users are observed performing representative tasks using a system.

Mini case study 7.3	Thomas Cook Netherlands use 4Q to review and improve its customers' experience

To find out the customer satisfaction ratings for visitors to its site compared to their intent, Thomas Cook Netherlands used Voice of Customer Tool 4Q (Figure 7.8).

A sample of visitors were asked four questions after they had used the site to determine the gap between what they were looking for and whether they were successful. Thomas Cook noticed that website visitors were not able to find certain seasonal travel content such as destinations and specific accommodations from the homepage. Visitors also validated other research into web performance by suggesting that page load times could be improved. Using not only their own research, but also the voice of their customers, they were able to build a much stronger case to focus optimisation improvements in these areas.

'Because our work is very seasonal, we are constantly monitoring feedback in order to meet our visitors' content expectations', said Matthew Niederberger, conversion specialist at Thomas Cook Netherlands. 'Thanks to our visitors' insights, we have been able to improve much of the content on the homepage to better meet their needs. We have also increased priority to several web performance improvement projects as we could clearly see that this was a major concern among our visitor base.'

Source: iPerceptions (2011)

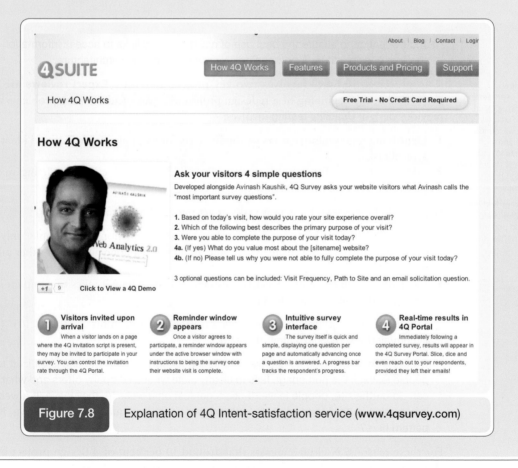

Figure 7.8	Explanation of 4Q Intent-satisfaction service (www.4qsurvey.com)

Web accessibility requirements

Web accessibility is another core requirement for websites. It is about allowing all users of a website to interact with it regardless of disabilities they may have, or the web browser or platform they are using to access the site. The visually impaired are the main audience that

Web accessibility
An approach to site design intended to accommodate site usage using different browsers and settings – particularly required by the visually impaired and visitors with other disabilities including motor control, learning difficulties and deaf users. Users whose first language is not English can also be assisted.

Accessibility legislation
Legislation intended to protect users of websites with disabilities including visual disability.

designing an accessible website can help. However, increased usage of mobile devices also makes consideration of accessibility important.

The following quote shows the importance of accessibility to a visually impaired user who uses a screen-reader which reads out the navigation options and content on a website.

> For me being online is everything. It's my hi-fi, it's my source of income, it's my supermarket, it's my telephone. It's my way in.
>
> (Lynn Holdsworth, screen-reader user, web developer and programmer)
> Source: RNIB

Remember, as we explained in Chapter 3, that many countries now have specific **accessibility legislation** to which website owners are subject. This is often contained within disability and discrimination acts. In the UK, the relevant act is the Disability and Discrimination Act (DDA) 1995. Recent amendments to the DDA make it unlawful to discriminate against disabled people in the way in which a company recruits and employs people, provides services or provides education. Providing services is the part of the law that applies to website design. Providing accessible websites is a requirement of Part II of the Disability and Discrimination Act published in 1999 and required by law from 2002.

Guidelines for creating accessible websites are produced by the governments of different countries and non-government organisations such as charities. Internet standards organisations, such as the World Wide Web Consortium, have been active in promoting guidelines for web accessibility through the Website Accessibility Initiative (see **www.w3.org/WAI**). This describes common accessibility problems such as:

> Images without alternative text; lack of alternative text for imagemap hot-spots; misleading use of structural elements on pages; uncaptioned audio or undescribed video; lack of alternative information for users who cannot access frames or scripts; tables that are difficult to decypher when linearised; or sites with poor colour contrast.

A fuller checklist for accessibility compliance for website design and coding using HTML is available from the World Wide Web Consortium (**http://www.w3.org/WAI/**).

Localisation

Localisation
Tailoring of website information for individual countries.

A further aspect of customer-centricity for website design is the decision whether to include specific content for particular countries. This is referred to as **localisation**. A site may need to support customers from a range of countries with:

- different product needs;
- language differences;
- cultural differences – this approach is also referred to as 'cultural adaptation'.

Localisation will address all these issues. It may be that products will be similar in different countries and localisation will simply involve converting the website to suit another country. However, in order to be effective this often needs more than translation, since different promotion concepts may be needed for different countries. Note that each company prioritises different countries according to the size of the market, and this priority then governs the amount of work it puts into localisation.

Singh and Pereira (2005) provide an evaluation framework for the level of localisation:

- *Standardised websites (not localised).* A single site serves all customer segments (domestic and international).
- *Semi-localised websites.* A single site serves all customers; however, contact information about foreign subsidiaries is available for international customers. Many sites fall into this category.
- *Localised websites.* Country-specific websites with language translation for international customers, wherever relevant. 3M (**www.3m.com**) has adapted the websites for many countries to local language versions. It initially focussed on the major websites.

- *Highly localised websites*. Country-specific websites with language translation; they also include other localisation efforts in terms of time, date, postcode, currency formats, etc. Dell (**www.dell.com**) provides highly localised websites.
- *Culturally customised websites*. Websites reflecting complete 'immersion' in the culture of target customer segments; as such, targeting a particular country may mean providing multiple websites for that country depending on the dominant cultures present. Durex (**www.durex.com**) is a good example of a culturally customised website.

Deciding on the degree of localisation is a difficult challenge for managers since while it has been established that local preferences are significant, it is often difficult to balance localisation costs against the likely increase or conversion rate through localisation. In a survey published in *Multilingual* (2008), localisation was seen as important with 88 per cent of managers at multinational companies stating that localisation is a key issue and 76 per cent of them saying that it is important specifically for international customer satisfaction. Yet over half of these respondents also admitted that they allocate only between 1 per cent and 5 per cent of their overall budget for localisation.

An indication of the importance of localisation in different cultures has been completed by Nitish *et al*. (2006) for the German, Indian and Chinese cultures, assessing localised websites in terms not only of content, but cultural values such as collectivism, individualism, uncertainty avoidance and masculinity. The survey suggests that without cultural adaptation, confidence or flow decreased so resulting in lower purchase intent.

A further aspect of localisation to be considered is search engine optimisation (see Chapter 9), since sites which have local language versions will be listed more prominently within the search engine results pages for local versions of the search engines. Many specialist companies have been created to help manage these content localisation issues for companies – for example, agency Web Certain maintains a forum advising on localisation (**www.multilingual-seo.com**).

Reviewing competitors' websites

Benchmarking of competitors' websites is vital in positioning a website to compete effectively with competitors that already have websites. Given the importance of this activity, criteria for performing benchmarking have been described in Chapters 2 and 4.

Benchmarking should not only be based on the obvious tangible features of a website such as its ease of use and the impact of its design. Benchmarking criteria should include those that define the companies' marketing performance in the industry and those that are specific to web marketing, as follows:

- *Financial performance* (available from About Us, investor relations and electronic copies of company reports) – this information is also available from intermediary sites such as finance information or share dealing sites such as Bloomberg (**www.bloomberg.com**) for major quoted companies.
- *Conversion efficiency* – sites can be compared to published results of average conversion rates (see, for example, **SmartInsights.com**).
- *Marketplace performance* – market share and sales trends and, significantly, the proportion of sales achieved through the Internet. This may not be available directly on the website, but may need the use of other online sources. For example, new entrant to European aviation easyJet (**www.easyjet.com**) achieved over two-thirds of its sales via the website and competitors needed to respond to this.
- *Business and revenue mo*dels (see Chapter 5) – do these differ from other marketplace players?
- *Marketplace positioning* – the elements of the marketing mix covered in Chapter 5, including Product, Pricing and Place.

- *Marketing communications techniques* – is the customer value proposition of the site clear? Does the site support all stages of the buying decision from customers who are unfamiliar with the company through to existing customers? Are special promotions used on a monthly or periodic basis? Beyond the competitor's site, how do they promote their site? How do they make thorough use of intermediary sites to promote and deliver their services?
- *Services offered* – what is offered beyond brochureware? Is online purchase possible? What is the level of online customer support and how much technical information is available?
- *Implementation of services* – these are the practical features of site design that are described in this chapter, such as aesthetics, ease of use, personalisation, navigation, availability and speed.

A review of corporate websites suggests that, for most companies, the type of information that can be included on a website will be fairly similar. Many commentators make the point that some sites miss out the basic information that someone who is unfamiliar with a company may want to know, such as:

- *Who are you?* 'About Us' is now a standard menu option.
- *What do you do?* What products or services are available?
- *Where do you do it?* Are the products and services available internationally?
- *What makes you different?* Why should I use your site/services compared to your competitors'? This includes communicating the online value proposition (OVP) (see Chapter 4).

Designing the information architecture

Information architecture
The combination of organisation, labelling and navigation schemes constituting an information system.

Rosenfeld and Morville (2002) emphasised the importance of **information architecture** to an effective website design. They said:

> It is important to recognise that every information system, be it a book or an intranet, has an information architecture. 'Well developed' is the key here, as most sites don't have a planned information architecture at all. They are analogous to buildings that weren't architected in advance. Design decisions reflect the personal biases of designers, the space doesn't scale over time, technologies drive the design and not the other way around.

In their book, which is still the basis for good practice in web design, Rosenfeld and Morville (2002) give these alternative definitions of an information architecture:

1 The combination of organisation, labelling and navigation schemes within an information system.
2 The structural design of an information space to facilitate task completion and intuitive access to content.
3 The art and science of structuring and classifying websites and intranets to help people find and manage information.
4 An emerging discipline and community of practice focussed on bringing principles of design and architecture to the digital landscape.

Site map
A graphical or text depiction of the relationship between different groups of content on a website.

Findability
Supporting users to locate the content or offers they are looking for through search engines or when browsing or searching on a site.

In practice, information architecture involves creating a plan to group information logically – it involves creating a site structure which is often represented as a **site map**. A well-developed information architecture is very important to usability since it determines navigation options and **findability** (Morville, 2005). Mini case study 7.4 shows how research to improve findability and in particular through optimising on-site search engines can yield major benefits to site owners.

A planned information architecture is essential to large-scale websites such as transactional e-commerce sites, media owner sites and relationship-building sites that include a large volume of product or support documentation. Information architectures are less

Mini case study 7.4	Travel company Thomson improves findability through analytics and user feedback

This case study of TUI travel company Thomson highlights the importance of site search. It is based on a presentation by Sandra Leonhard, Head of Ecommerce.

When Thomson calculates improvements derived from usability, two of the main measures used are:

'Look to Book%' = Number of bookings/Unique users

'Search to Book%' = Number of bookings/Number of unique searches

Below is usability testing and customer feedback obtained as part of the project to optimise search. Customers tend to be frank – these are some examples of the direct feedback you can get from tests like these which can be used to refine messaging and usability on a site to improve results:

● 'Your search and book could allow a range of dates and selection of details from all brochures. A dropdown for regional airports would help.'
● 'Search would be better if you could input destinations relevant to your departure airport.'
● 'It won't let me select any destination in search.'
● 'This is my third try. It will not show me anything!!! Useless site.'
● 'Search facility restricted to brochure. I wanted to search for any holidays within a date period but I had to state a destination – why when I wanted a good deal to any destination.'
● 'I find the website appalling to search for a holiday due to the fact that it appears to search in a very specific manner. I always get the message "sorry we aren't able…" I booked through <a competitor> instead.'

Basic analytics showed the scope for improvement and the optimisation project delivered this. Although these problems have now been resolved we have included this example since many sites have not been optimised in this way.

important to small-scale websites and brand sites, but even here the principles can be readily applied and can help make the site more visible to search engines and more usable. It is also important for search engine optimisation (Chapter 8), since it determines how different types of content that users may search for are labelled and grouped.

The benefits of creating an information architecture include:

● A defined structure and categorisation of information will support user and organisation goals, i.e. it is a vital aspect of usability.
● It helps increase 'flow' on the site – a user's mental model of where to find content should mirror that of the content on the website.
● Search engine optimisation – a higher listing in the search rankings can often be used through structuring and labelling information in a structured way.
● Applicable for integrating offline communications – offline communications such as ads or direct mail can link to a product or campaign landing page to help achieve direct response, sometimes known as 'web response'. A sound URL strategy (as explained in Chapter 8) can help this.
● Related content can be grouped to measure the effectiveness of a website as part of design for analysis, which is also explained below.

Card sorting

Card sorting or web classification
The process of arranging a way of organising objects on the website in a consistent manner.

Using card sorting is a way in which users can become actively involved in the development process of information architecture.

Card sorting is a useful approach since websites are frequently designed from the perspective of the designer rather than the information user, leading to labels, subject grouping and categories that are not intuitive to the user. **Card sorting or web classification** should categorise web objects (e.g. documents) in order to facilitate information task completion or information goals the user has set.

Robertson (2003) explains an approach to card sorting which identifies the following questions when using the technique to aid the process of modelling web classification systems:

- Do the users want to see the information grouped by subject, task, business or customer groupings, or type of information?
- What are the most important items to put on the main menu?
- How many menu items should there be, and how deep should it go?
- How similar or different are the needs of the users throughout the organisation?

Selected groups of users or representatives will be given index cards with the following written on them, depending on the aim of the card sorting process:

- types of documents;
- organisational key words and concepts;
- document titles;
- descriptions of documents;
- navigation labels.

The user groups may then be asked to:

- Group together cards that they feel relate to each other.
- Select cards that accurately reflect a given topic or area.
- Organise cards in terms of hierarchy – high-level terms (broad) to low-level terms.

At the end of the session the analyst must take the cards away and map the results into a spreadsheet to find out the most popular terms, descriptions and relationships. If two or more different groups are used, the results should be compared and reasons for differences should be analysed.

Blueprints

Blueprint
Shows the relationships between pages and other content components, and can be used to portray organisation, navigation and labelling systems.

According to Rosenfeld and Morville (2002), **blueprints**:

> show the relationships between pages and other content components, and can be used to portray organisation, navigation and labelling systems.

They are often thought of, and referred to, as 'site maps' or 'site structure diagrams' and have much in common with these, except that they are used as a design device clearly showing grouping of information and linkages between pages, rather than a page on the website to assist navigation.

Refer to Figure 7.9 for an example of a site structure diagram for a toy manufacturer website which shows the groupings of content and also an indication of the process of task completion.

Wireframes

Wireframe
Also known as 'schematics', a way of illustrating the layout of an individual web page.

A related technique to blueprints is the **wireframes** which are used by web designers to indicate the eventual layout of a web page. Figure 7.10 shows that the wireframe is so called because it just consists of an outline of the page with the 'wires' of content separating different areas of content or navigation shown by white space.

Wodtke (2002) describes a wireframe (sometimes known as a 'schematic') as:

> a basic outline of an individual page, drawn to indicate the elements of a page, their relationships and their relative importance.

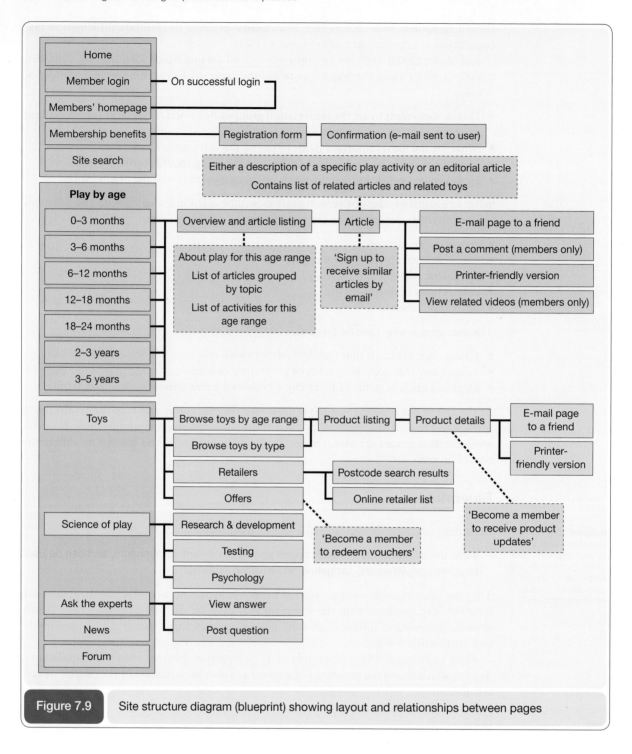

Figure 7.9 Site structure diagram (blueprint) showing layout and relationships between pages

A wireframe will be created for all types of similar page groups, identified at the blueprint (site map) stage of creating the information architecture.

Wireframes are then transformed into physical **site design page templates**, which are now traditionally created using standardised **cascading style sheets (CSS)** that enable a standard look and feel to be enforced across different sections of the site. Complete Activity 7.3 to see the power of using CSS.

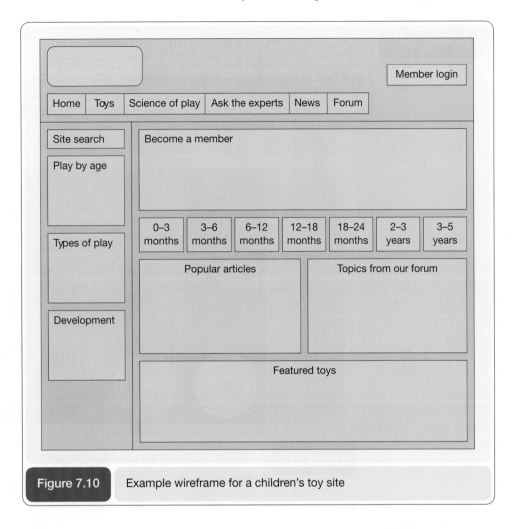

| Figure 7.10 | Example wireframe for a children's toy site |

Site design page template

A standard page layout format which is applied to each page of a website. Typically defined for different page categories (e.g. category page, product page, search page).

Cascading style sheets (CSS)

A simple mechanism for adding style (e.g. fonts, colours, spacing) to web documents. CSS enables different style elements to be controlled across an entire site or section of site. Style elements that are commonly controlled include typography, background colour and images, and borders and margins.

The standards body W3C (**www.w3.org**) defines cascading style sheets as:

a simple mechanism for adding style (e.g. fonts, colours, spacing) to Web documents.

CSS enable different style elements to be controlled across an entire site or section of site. Style elements that are commonly controlled include:

- typography;
- background colour and images;
- borders and margins.

For example, CSS will use this syntax to enforce the standard appearance of body copy on a site:

```
body {
    margin:0;
    padding:0;
    colour:#666666;
    background-colour:#f3f3f3;
    font-family: Arial, 'Trebuchet MS', Verdana;
    font-size: 70%;
    background-repeat:repeat-x;
    background-position:top;
    }
```

Visit CSS ZenGarden (**www.csszengarden.com**), which shows how CSS can be used to separate content from how it is presented. You can select different designs to see how the new design changes radically as different styles are applied. The example shown is a current 'flat' or 'metro' design (Figure 7.11).

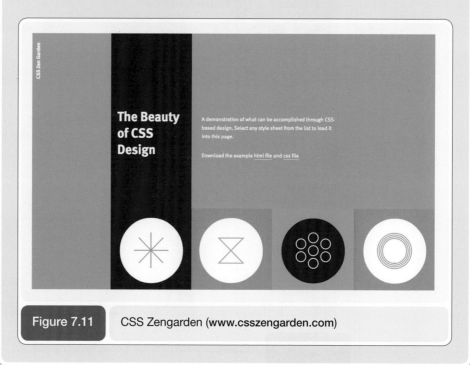

| Figure 7.11 | CSS Zengarden (www.csszengarden.com) |

The benefits of CSS are:

- *Bandwidth* – pages download faster after initial page load since style definitions only need to be downloaded once as a separate file, not for each page.
- *More efficient development* – through agreeing site style and implementing in CSS as part of page templates, it is more efficient to design a site.
- *Reduces updating and maintenance time* – presentational markup is stored in one place separate from the content, making it quicker to update the site globally with less scope for errors.
- *Increased interoperability* – by adhering to W3C recommendations; helps with support of multiple browsers.
- *Increases accessibility* – users can more readily configure the way a site looks or sounds using browsers and other accessibility support tools. The site is more likely to render on a range of access platforms like PDAs and smartphones.

Landing page
An entrance page to the site when a user clicks on an ad or other form of link from a referring site. It can be a home page but more typically, and desirably, a landing page is a page with the messaging focussed on the offer in the ad. This will maximise conversion rates and brand favourability.

Landing pages

Deciding on the page template design for different forms of **landing pages** is particularly important for site owners seeking to maximise conversion rate since many first-time visitors don't arrive on the home page, they arrive deeper in the site from search engines or links from other sites. Chaffey and Smith (2012) suggest these are typical aims and corresponding questions to consider for increasing landing page conversion rate:

- *Aim 1 – Generate response (online lead or sale and offline callback).* Does the page have a prominent call-to-action, such as a prominent button above the fold; and repeated in text and image form?
- *Aim 2 – Engage different audience types (reduce bounce rate, increase value events, increase return rate).* Does the page have a prominent headline and subheads showing the visitor is in the right place? Does the page have scent-trail trigger messages, offers or images to appeal to different audiences? For example, Dell has links on its site to appeal to consumers and different types of businesses. A landing page containing form fields to fill in is often more effective than an additional click since it starts committed visitors on their journey.
- *Aim 3 – Communicate key brand messages (increase brand familiarity and favourability).* Does the page clearly explain who you are, what you do, where you operate and what makes you different? Is your online value proposition compelling? Do you use customer testimonials or ratings to show independent credibility? To help with this, use run-of-site messages (on all pages) across the top of the screen or in the left or right sidebars.
- *Aim 4 – Answer the visitor's questions (reduce bounce rates, increase conversion rates).* Different audiences will want to know different things. Have you identified personas (Chapter 4) and do you seek to answer their questions? Do you use FAQ or messages which say 'New to company'?
- *Aim 5 – Showcase range of offers (cross-sell).* Do you have recommendations on related or best-selling products and do you show the full range of your offering through navigation?
- *Aim 6 – Attract visitors through search engine optimisation (SEO).* How well do you rank for relevant search terms compared to competitors? Do your navigation, copy and page templates indicate relevance to search engines through on-page optimisation?

Blueprints illustrate how the content of a website is related and navigated while a wireframe focuses on individual pages; with a wireframe the navigation focus becomes where it will be placed on the page. Wireframes are useful for agencies and clients to discuss the way a website will be laid out without getting distracted by colour, style or messaging issues which should be covered separately as a creative planning activity.

Storyboarding
The use of static drawings or screenshots of the different parts of a website to review the design concept with user groups. It can be used to develop the structure – an overall 'map' with individual pages shown separately.

The process of reviewing wireframes is sometimes referred to as **storyboarding**, although the term is often applied to reviewing creative ideas rather than formal design alternatives. Early designs are drawn on large pieces of paper, or mock-ups are produced using a drawing or paint program.

At the wireframe stage, emphasis is not placed on use of colour or graphics, which will be developed in conjunction with branding or marketing teams and graphic designers and integrated into the site after the wireframe process.

According to Chaffey and Wood (2010), the aim of a wireframe will be to:

- integrate consistently available components on the web page (e.g. navigation, search boxes);
- order and group key types of components together;
- develop a design that will focus the user onto core messages and content;
- make correct use of white space to structure the page;
- develop a page structure that can be easily reused by other web designers.

Common wireframe or template features you may come across are:

- navigation in columns on left or right and at top or bottom;
- header areas and footer areas;
- containers, 'slots' or 'portlets' – these are areas of content such as an article or list of articles placed in boxes on the screen. Often slots will be dynamically populated from a content management system;

- containers on the homepage may be used to:
  - summarise the online value proposition;
  - show promotions;
  - recommend related products;
  - feature news, etc.;
  - contain ads.

Designing the user experience

Design phase
The design phase defines how the site will work in the key areas of website structure, navigation and security.

Once analysis has determined the business and user needs for a site, the site can be designed. The **design phase** is critical to a successful website since it will determine the quality of experience users of a site have; if they have a good experience they will return, if not they will not! A 'good experience' is determined by a number of factors such as those that affect how easy it is to find information: for example, the structure of the site, menu choices and searching facilities. It is also affected by less tangible factors such as the graphical design and layout of the site.

As mentioned at the start of the chapter, design is not solely a paper-based exercise, but needs to be integrated into the prototyping process. The design should be tested by review with the client and customer to ensure it is appropriate. Since the main reason given for returning to a website is high-quality content, and content effects conversion too, it is important to determine, through analysis, that the content is correct. However, the quality of content is determined by more than the text copy. It is important to achieve high-quality content through design. Nigel Bevan (1999a) says:

> Unless a website meets the needs of the intended users it will not meet the needs of the organisation providing the website. Website development should be user-centred, evaluating the evolving design against user requirements.

User-centred design
Design based on optimising the user experience according to all factors, including the user interface, which affect this.

How can this customer-orientated or user-centred content be achieved? **User-centred design** starts with understanding the nature and variation within the user groups. According to Bevan (1999a), key issues to consider which are still fundamental for digital experiences, whether desktop or mobile site, app or social network company page, include:

- Who are the important users?
- What is their purpose for accessing the site?
- How frequently will they visit the site?
- What experience and expertise do they have?
- What nationality are they? Can they read your language?
- What type of information are they looking for?
- How will they want to use the information: read it on the screen, print it or download it?
- What type of browsers will they use? How fast will their communication links be?
- How large a screen or window will they use, with how many colours?

Rosenfeld and Morville (2002) suggest four stages of site design that also have a user-centred basis:

1 Identify different audiences.
2 Rank importance of each to business.
3 List the three most important information needs of audience.
4 Ask representatives of each audience type to develop their own wish lists.

We noted in Chapter 2 that customer persona and scenario analysis is a powerful technique of understanding different audiences which can be used to inform and test website design which looks at additional factors from those in the lists above such as device usage, location and context of usage and integration with other online services including social media.

Evaluating designs

A test of effective design for usability is dependent on three areas according to Bevan (1999b):

- *Effectiveness* – can users complete their tasks correctly and completely?
- *Productivity (efficiency)* – are tasks completed in an acceptable length of time?
- *Satisfaction* – are users satisfied with the interaction?

Elements of site design

Once the requirements of the user and marketer are established we turn our attention to the design of the human–computer interface. Nielsen (2000) structures his book on web usability according to three main areas, which can be interpreted as follows:

1 *site design and structure* – the overall structure of the site;
2 *page design* – the layout of individual pages;
3 *content design* – how the text and graphic content on each page is designed.

There is also the additional area of branding and messaging which is a key part of persuasion, as explained earlier in this chapter.

Site design and structure

The structures created by designers for websites will vary greatly according to their audience and the site's purpose, but we can make some general observations about common approaches to site design and structure and their influence on consumers. These are often known as best practice principles of website design and in this section we will summarise some of the main factors. Of course, there are exceptions to such rules of thumb or 'heuristics', but often a design approach that works on one type of site will work on another, particularly if it is a common feature across the majority of sites.

Rosen and Purinton (2004) assessed the design factors which influence a consumer (based on questionnaires of a group of students). They believe there are some basic factors that determine the effectiveness of an e-commerce site. They group these factors as follows:

- *Coherence* – simplicity of design, easy to read, use of categories (for browsing products or topics), absence of information overload, adequate font size, uncrowded presentation.
- *Complexity* – different categories of text.
- *Legibility* – use of 'mini home page' on every subsequent page, same menu on every page, site map.

You can see that these authors suggest that simplicity in design is important. Another example of research into website design factors supports the importance of design. Fogg *et al.* (2003) asked students to review sites to assess the credibility of different suppliers based on the website design. They considered these factors most important:

Design look	46.1%
Information design/structure	28.5%
Information focus	25.1%
Company motive	15.5%
Usefulness of information	14.8%
Accuracy of information	14.3%
Name recognition and reputation	14.1%

Advertising	*13.8%*
Bias of information	*11.6%*
Tone of the writing	*9.0%*
Identity of site sponsor	*8.8%*
Functionality of site	*8.6%*
Customer service	*6.4%*
Past experience with site	*4.6%*
Information clarity	*3.7%*
Performance on a test	*3.6%*
Readability	*3.6%*
Affiliations	*3.4%*

However, it should be borne in mind that such generalisations can be misleading based on the methodology used. Reported behaviour (e.g. through questionnaires or focus groups) may be quite different from actual observed behaviour. Leading e-retail sites (for example **Amazon.com** and **eBay.com**) and many media sites typically have a large amount of information and navigation choices available on-screen since the site designers know from testing alternative designs that consumers are quite capable of finding content relevant to them, and that a wider choice of links means that the user can find the information they need without clicking through a hierarchy. When performing a real-life product search, in-depth information on the products and reviews of the product are important in making the product decision and are one of the benefits that online channels can give. Although design look is top of the list of factors presented by Fogg *et al.* (2003), you can see that many of the other factors are based on the quality of information.

In the following coverage, we will review the general factors which designers consider in designing the style, organisation and navigation schemes for the site.

Site style

An effective website design will have a style that is communicated through use of colour, images, typography and layout. This should support the way a product is positioned or its brand.

Site personality

The style elements can be combined to develop a personality for a site. We could describe a site's personality in the same way we can describe people, such as 'formal' or 'fun'. This personality has to be consistent with the needs of the target audience. A business audience often requires detailed information and prefers an information-intensive style such as that of the Cisco site (Example: **www.cisco.com**). A consumer site is usually more graphically intensive. Before the designers pass on their creative designs to developers, they also need to consider the constraints on the user experience, such as screen resolution and colour depth, browser used and download speed.

Visual design

Despite modern browsers and broadband access, graphic design of websites still represents a challenge since designers of websites are severely constrained by a number of factors:

- *The speed of downloading graphics* – designers still need to allow for page download speed, as we explained earlier in the chapter.
- *The screen resolutions of the computer* – designing for different screen resolutions is particularly important today with the range of resolutions from smartphone to tablet to desktop.

- *The number of colours on screen* – the colour palettes available on web browsers.
- *The type of web browser used* – different browsers, such as Google Chrome, Microsoft Internet Explorer IE and Apple Safari, and different versions of browsers, such as IE8.0 or 9.0, may display graphics or text slightly differently or may support different plug-ins.
- *Different access devices* – with the increase in popularity of mobile and tablet browsers it has become very important to support users of these sites using techniques such as **adaptive web design**.

Adaptive web design
Also known as progressive enhancement, this design technique delivers different layouts and features according to what is supported by browser and screen resolution of the device.

As a result of these constraints, the design of websites is a constant compromise between what looks visually appealing and modern on the most advanced hardware platforms and highest speed network connections and what works for other systems. This is referred to as the 'lowest common denominator problem' since this is what the designer has traditionally had to do – design for the old browsers, using slow links and low screen resolutions.

Mobile design considerations and techniques

In Chapter 2 we explained that it's important to research the level of adoption of mobile devices such as smartphones and tablets. For many site types such as social networks and news sites, the proportion of mobile users has been well above 50 per cent for several years. At the time of writing this edition, many retail sites now see more than half of their traffic from mobile and this will naturally increase. So designing websites such that they are effective across desktop and mobile devices is now a key consideration for all businesses. The challenge of the many options for mobile site design has been nicely summarised by ex-eBay designer Luke Wroblewski, as shown in Digital marketing insight 7.4.

We will now review five common options for mobile site development identified by Thurner and Chaffey (2013):

A Simple mobile site (different content).
B Screen-scrape (same content).
C Responsive Design (same content, different mobile styling).
D HTML5 site (same content, different mobile styling).
E Adaptive design (potentially different content, different styling on different mobile devices)

These are not mutually exclusive, so an HTML5 site can typically offer adaptive and responsive design too.

Mobile site design option A. Simple mobile site
The quickest method of creating a mobile site is to create a completely separate mobile site on a domain **http://m.company.com** which has a different design, build, hosting and content. This option may be appropriate for very small businesses looking for a simple mobile site which they don't update frequently, but we would advise this not a viable long-term option for most companies for these reasons:

- Updates to content have to be duplicated across each site.
- Different tools and resources often needed to manage each site.
- Future updates to styling have to be duplicated too.
- May not give a consistent brand experience for users.

Mobile site design option B. Screen-scrape
Although it's not an option we can recommend as best practice, it's worth noting that a number of high-profile retail brands like ASOS and John Lewis opted for a temporary 'screen-scrape' approach, which involves dropping existing web content into a basic mobile

site template without opting for back-end integration. The advantage of the screen-scrape approach is that it presents a quick route to market, and avoids potential conflict between PC web and mobile web developers.

Think through the widespread disadvantages of screen-scraping when compared with the fully integrated approach, which provides the better long-term solution.

- The screen-scrape option incurs additional time and cost to manage the site, as changes to the back-end CMS will need to be updated manually on the mobile site, rather than benefiting from automatic updates.
- A review of 'screen-scrape' sites reveals an alarming degree of standardisation across the sites, which lack the differentiation brands demand across their PC websites.

Mobile site design option C. Responsive design

Responsive Web Design (RWD)
Layout and formatting of website content is modified at the point of rendering to suit different screen resolutions and capabilities to produce a better experience to users of a range of desktop, tablet and smartphone devices using web development methods like CSS and image scaling.

Today's multiple-device-using consumers need content in the right format in real time, which presents challenges as the form factor and operating system varies across most of their devices. Enter **Responsive Design**, which automates the overlay of contextually relevant content matching the profiles of mobile users – allowing you to access social media feeds, loyalty offers and other data feeds triggered by your preferences to maximise engagement and to optimise sales conversion.

First introduced as a concept in 2010, Responsive Design is the principle web developers deploy to design website styling that changes the display layout to suit users of a range of mobile devices using modern web development methods like CSS3 and image scaling. Blocks of content are moved and rescaled based on screen resolution, as shown in Figure 7.12.

Responsive Design is an increasingly popular approach to building mobile sites since it enables a single version of the site and content to be maintained which adapts for different resolutions. It was formerly called a 'fluid design' since the layout 'flows' as resolution is

| Figure 7.12 | Responsive design showing updated layout for different content blocks |

changed (as you change the size of a browser for instance). Contrast this to what we often see when browsing using a smartphone on a non-responsive site: tiny text and difficult to select buttons and navigation which require us to zoom in to select the next page.

Technically speaking, Responsive Design uses cascading stylesheets, in particular an approach called **media queries** to specify how the page is laid out based on device type and resolution. (See for example, Knight (2011) for an introduction to the technical approaches.) This will produce an improved experience for users across a range of devices, but there are limitations such as break points where less common devices may not be supported or sites which aren't 'upwardly responsive' – i.e. high resolution displays may be less well supported than lower resolution. Responsive design disadvantages include its being more technically complex to implement and test which leads to higher costs and a larger codebase (particularly of stylesheets) to load which can harm page load times. Despite this, it is now implemented for many new sites and site redesigns. The disadvantages of responsive design can be overcome at cost through adaptive design.

Mobile site design option D. HTML5

HTML5 blurs the line between sites and apps, and challenges the prominence and cash-flow of the appstore hosts. Companies operating in the main sectors who were enthusiastic adopters of mobile, such as retail, packaged goods, travel, financial services, publishing, are turning to HTML5 'web apps' in order to build once and target all mobile platforms at once. This is more cost-effective and less labour-intensive than building different native apps for iOS, Android, Windows Phone and BlackBerry.

As Mini case study 7.5 shows, HTML5 web apps allow developers and publishers to circumnavigate the 30 per cent commission charged by Apple and Google on app download costs and a further 30 per cent on products and subscriptions sold 'in-app'. Both costs can be eliminated with HTML5-based sites.

From the technical perspective, HTML5 apps have some problems that native apps do not. HTML5 apps are typically slower than native apps and it is more costly to support a range of apps. **FT.com** still uses native apps for Android and Windows platforms.

Of course, the other big benefit for publishers, not mentioned here, is that they can take a bigger share of subscription revenues. The app was launched in June 2011 in response to Apple's introduction of new rules governing subscription-based iOS apps – Apple is looking for a 30 per cent cut of subscription revenues for people signing up from its native app and keeping access to those subscribers.

Rob Grimshaw of **FT.com** told *The Guardian* (2013) that switching to HTML5 wasn't just about a spat with Apple, but was an attempt to ensure the FT could scale quickly across different devices and platforms:

> The origins of the web app come from thinking more broadly about our mobile strategy, and particularly how we are going to cope with developing for numerous different platforms. There are at least five [native mobile platforms] out there that you reasonably have to cover, and a web app is the obvious solution. We just accelerated it because of some of the things Apple did with their subscriptions.

Mobile site design option E. Adaptive design

The **adaptive mobile web design** is a hybrid approach combining different client- and server-based logic to give the best performance with the best experience on priority devices without the speed limitations of the responsive approach. The approach is contrasted with responsive web design in Table 7.2. You can see that by only serving code and styling need for a specific mobile device the approach can result in a faster experience, although development times and costs can be higher, so it is an approach best suited to the largest businesses.

Media queries
A styling approach within Cascading Style Sheets (CSS3) enabling the layout to change based on type of device at its scale.

Adaptive mobile web design
Generally a more sophisticated approach than Responsive web design that involves delivering an experience optimised for handsets targeted and splits the code and processing to render on different devices between the client and the server.

Mini case study 7.5	FT.com adopts HTML5 for its iOS Web App

FT.com proves that HTML5 web apps are now providing clear benefits over OS-specific apps.

The success of the **FT.com** web app for iOS shows that developing mobile platform-specific apps isn't the only option; in future, the dependence on app stores for each mobile native OS may seem quaint. The figures on digital publishing by **FT.com** a year after the app was launched certainly show the importance of mobile platforms for publishers:

- Digital subscriptions to the title, which operate behind a metered paywall increased 31 per cent year-on-year to more than 300,000.
- The number of registered users climbed 29 per cent to 4.8 million.
- Mobile devices account for 25 per cent of traffic to **FT.com**, while there are 2.7 million FT web app users.

FT.com HTML5 mobile site, it's not a native mobile app

The FT does a great job in explaining the benefits of non-OS apps (Figure 7.13). When launched, as 'a better, faster app', the FT explained these benefits:

- *Web browser access* – No app store download needed.
- *Automatic enhancements* – No need to visit an app store for the latest version.
- *Reading offline* – The latest edition is automatically stored for offline access (this is possible with native OS apps).
- *Speed* – Improved performance on most connections.
- *Greater range of content* – Including video on iPhone – this gets around the problem of Flash players.
- *Use your existing account* – no additional registration required.

Figure 7.13	FT.com app proposition

Table 7.2	A summary of the advantages and disadvantages of different options for mobile-optimised websites

	Approach	Advantages	Disadvantages
Responsive Web Design (RWD)	CSS Media Queries modify presentation for device resolution	Single template for all devices gives speed and cost benefits	Bigger page weight Compromises experience for higher resolutions?
Client-side Adaptive	Javascript on the user's device loads different templates based on device resolution	• Complete rebuild of CSS not needed • Only resources needed loaded onto client • Experience customised for devices	Maintenance of additional code
Server-side Adaptive	Dynamic serving of styles based on device detection	Smaller mobile pages than other approaches	Multiple templates must be maintained

Personalisation

Mobile sites featuring personalisation are still relatively unusual. This is surprising if you consider that one phone has one user. Ask a group of strangers to pass their phones round the room and you'll detect a potent sense of anxiety. We don't share our phones, with anyone. We don't want others seeing the texts we send and receive, the photos we've taken, our social media pages, the sites we've browsed or the apps we've downloaded.

This means that we can develop highly personalised and customised sites. Back-end integration, with application programming interfaces (APIs) exposing individual customer records, can be used to build bespoke sites which match the profile of each user. Look no further than Amazon to see how brands can use purchase history data and apply intelligence to develop sites with highly targeted product offers. To make your sites highly relevant to users, you can apply behavioural targeting, with time- and location-sensitive messaging.

A personalised mobile-optimised site has the benefit that specific features can be developed for mobile users. This is not the case with a basic Responsive Design approach. Back-end integration enabling linkage to individual customer records can be used to build bespoke sites which match the profile of each user. Amazon is well known for integrating purchase history data and applying intelligence to its desktop site with highly targeted product offers. Of course, it now also does this for its mobile site.

Separate from these mobile website approaches, mobile apps are a further option which must be considered separately. While most would agree that a website accessible on mobile is essential it's not clear whether a **mobile app** is essential for all but the larger organisations, particularly with the development of responsive and adaptive website design.

Site navigation schemes

Devising a site that is easy to use is critically dependent on the design of the **site navigation scheme**. Hoffman and Novak (1997) and many subsequent studies (e.g. Rettie, 2001; Smith and Sivakumar, 2004) have stressed the importance of the concept of **flow** in governing site usability. The concept of 'flow' was first brought to prominence by Mihaly Csikszentmihalyi, a psychology professor at the University of Chicago. In his book, *Flow: The Psychology of Optimal Experience*, he explains his theory that people

Mobile app
Designed to run on smartphones and tablet computers, apps provide users with rich mobile content by deploying the handset's multiple native capabilities. Apps are available for download from app stores hosted by the mobile operating systems (e.g. iTunes for iOS, Google Play for Android, Microsoft App Store, BlackBerry App World).

Site navigation scheme
Tools provided to the user to move between different information on a website.

Flow
Describes how easy it is for users of a site to move between the different pages of content of the site.

Digital marketing insight 7.4 — Taking the mobile site vs app decision

Despite advances in web development, frameworks such as CSS, the challenge of developing for different platforms has increased with the advent of new platforms such as smartphones and tablets. Consequently, key technology options include:

- mobile version of website (full site);
- mobile version of site (most popular pages linking through to traditional pages);
- separate mobile app;
- which device formats and so screen sizes to support;
- which mobile operating systems and mobile browser versions to support (for example, Android, iOS, Symbian, etc.).

It will only be cost-effective for the very largest organisations to design for all of these target platforms and devices, so companies need to balance the costs against the benefits and select carefully. The decision is complicated by the improving quality of screen resolution through smartphones and tablets. Many of these now have a size that enables viewing of sites designed for desktops, although zooming and panning can be frustrating.

The challenge has been nicely summarised by former eBay designer Luke Wroblewski (2011), now lead designer at startup BagCheck, who says:

As use of mobile devices continues to skyrocket across the globe, we're seeing more ways to tackle the challenge of creating great web experiences across multiple devices. But which approach is right for any given project?

For us site performance and speed of development were crucial. So many of the decisions we made were designed to make both of these as fast as possible. As part of our focus on performance, we also had a philosophy of 'just what's necessary'. This meant sending things to devices (and people) that didn't actually need them made us squeamish. We liked to optimise. With a dual template system we felt we had more optimisation of: source order, media, URL structure, and application design.

are most happy when they are in a state of flow – a Zen-like state of total oneness with the activity at hand. In an online marketing context, 'flow' essentially describes how easy it is for users to find the information or experiences they need as they move from one page of the site to the next, but it also includes other interactions such as filling in on-screen forms. Rettie (2001) has suggested that the quality of navigation is one of the prerequisites for flow, although other factors are also important. They include quick download time, alternative versions, auto-completion of forms, opportunities for interaction, navigation that creates choices, predictable navigation for control and segmenting content by Internet experience.

It can be suggested that there are three important aspects to a site that is easy to navigate. These are:

- *Consistency*. A site will be easier to navigate if the user is presented with a consistent user interface when viewing the different parts of the site. For example, if the menu options in the support section of the site are on the left side of the screen, then they should also be on the left when the user moves to the 'news section' of the site.
- *Simplicity*. Sites are easier to navigate if there are limited numbers of options. It is usually suggested that two or possibly three levels of menu are the most that are desirable. For example, there may be main menu options at the left of the screen that take the user

to the different parts of the site, and at the bottom of the screen there will be specific menu options that refer to that part of the site. (Menus in this form are often referred to as 'nested'.)

- *Context.* Context is the use of 'signposts' to indicate to users where they are located within the site – in other words, to reassure users that they are not 'lost'. To help with this, the website designer should use particular text or colour to indicate to users which part of the site they are currently using. Context can be provided by the use of JavaScript 'rollovers', where the colour of the menu option changes when the user positions the mouse over the menu option and then changes again when the menu option is selected. Many sites also have a site-map option that shows the layout and content of the whole site so the user can understand its structure. When using a well-designed site it should not be necessary to refer to such a map regularly.

Deep linking
Jakob Nielsen's term for a user arriving at a site deep within its structure.

Nielsen (2000) pointed out what many people reviewing sites still forget – that many users will not arrive on the home page, but may be referred from another site or according to a print or TV advert to a particular page. He calls this process **deep linking** and site designers should ensure that navigation and context are appropriate for users arriving on these pages.

As well as compromises on depth of links within a site, it is also necessary to compromise on the amount of space devoted to menus. Nielsen (1999) points out that some sites devote so much space to navigation bars that the space available for content is limited. Nielsen suggests that the designer of navigation systems should consider the following information that a site user wants to know:

- *Where am I?* The user needs to know where they are on the site and this can be indicated by highlighting the current location and clear titling of pages. This can be considered as *context. Consistency* of menu locations on different pages is also required to aid cognition. Users also need to know where they are on the web. This can be indicated by a logo, which by convention is at the top or top-left of a site.
- *Where have I been?* This is difficult to indicate on a site, but for task-orientated activities such as purchasing a product it can show the user that they are at the *n*th stage of an operation, such as making a purchase.
- *Where do I want to go?* This is the main navigation system which gives options for future operations.

To answer these questions, clear succinct labelling is required. Widely used standards such as Home, Main page, Search, Find, Browse, FAQ, Help and About Us are preferable.

Since using the navigation system may not enable the user to find the information they want rapidly, alternatives have to be provided by the site designers. These alternatives include search, advanced search, browse and site map (a simplified site map in the footer is common today). **Whatis.com** (**www.whatis.com**) illustrates these features well.

Menu options

Designing and creating the menus to support navigation present several options. A combination of text-based menus, graphical buttons or images is usually preferred in modern sites to meet the requirements of accessibility, persuasion, SEO and usability. Yet some sites are still based solely on Flash or image-based menus, which will reduce the business effectiveness of the site. Most large retail sites now use 'mega-menus' where there are a wide range of products and promotions to communicate.

Page design

The page design involves creating an appropriate layout of page elements to meet the goals of findability and usability, as illustrated in the example in Activity 7.3. The main elements of a particular page layout are the title, navigation and content. Standard content, such as copyright information, may be added to every page as a footer. Common page templates will be created for pages which share similar characteristics, such as home page, category/sub-category page, product page, search results page and checkout pages for a retail site. Through use of common templates improvements can be implemented more efficiently.

Issues in page design include:

- *Page elements.* We have to consider the proportion of a page devoted to content compared to all other material such as headers, footers and navigation elements. The location of these elements also needs to be considered. It is conventional for the main menu to be at the top or on the left. The use of a menu system at the top of the browser window allows more space for content below.
- *Resizing.* A good page layout design should allow for the user to change the size of text or work with different monitor resolutions.
- *Consistency.* Page layout should be similar for all areas of the site unless more space is required – for example for a discussion forum or product demonstration. Standards of colour and typography can be enforced through cascading style sheets.
- *Printing.* Layout should allow for printing or provide an alternative printing format.

Content design

It's evident that a compelling customer experience demands exceptional, compelling content and a well-planned **content strategy**. Today, by content we refer to the combination of static content forming web pages, but also dynamic rich media content which encourages interaction. Videos, podcasts, user-generated content and interactive product selectors should also be considered as content which should be refined to engage issues.

To create such resources requires a content strategy since there is a challenge of delivering so many different types of content in different forms to different places on different access platforms.

The definition suggests these elements of content management that need to be planned and managed:

1 *Content engagement value.* Which types of content will engage the audience – is it simple product or services information, a guide to buying product or a game to engage your audience.
2 *Content media.* Plain text, rich media such as Flash or Rich Internet applications or mobile apps, audio (podcasts) and hosted and streamed video. Even plain text offers different format options from HTML text to ebook formats and PDFs.
3 *Content syndication.* Content can be syndicated to different type of sites through feeds, APIs, microformats or direct submission by email. Content can be embedded in sites through widgets displaying information delivered by a feed.
4 *Content participation.* Effective content today is not simply delivered for static consumption, it should enable commenting, ratings and reviews. These also need to be monitored and managed both in the original location and where they are discussed elsewhere.
5 *Content access platform.* The different digital access platforms such as desktops and laptops of different screen resolution and mobile devices. Paper is also a content access platform for print media.

Halvorson (2010) describes the importance of these activities. It can be seen that managing the creation of quality content is part of a broader customer engagement strategy which

Content strategy
The management of text, rich media, audio and video content aimed at engaging customers and prospects to meet business goals published through print and digital media including web and mobile platforms which is repurposed and syndicated to different forms of web presence such as publisher sites, blogs, social media and comparison sites.

looks at delivering effective content across the whole customer lifecycle. As such it is an integral part of the CRM strategy development which we covered in Chapter 6. It is also an important marketing activity affecting conversion optimisation, social media engagement and SEO, so increasing attention is directed at content strategy today.

To help implement a content strategy requires a change of mindset for many companies (Pulizzi and Barrett, 2010). They need to think more like a publisher and so invest in quality content that's superior to that of their competitors. This requires:

- Quality, compelling content – content is still king!
- Quality writers to create quality content who may be internal staff or external freelance writers.
- An editorial calendar and appropriate process to schedule and deliver the content.
- Investment in software tools to facilitate the process.
- Investment in customer research to determine the content their different audiences will engage with.
- Careful tracking of which content engages and is effective for SEO and which doesn't.

Pulizzi and Barrett (2010) recommend creating a content marketing roadmap which is underpinned by the BEST principles. BEST stands for:

- *Behavioural*. Does everything you communicate with customers have a purpose? What do you want them to do as a result of interacting with content?
- *Essential*. Deliver information that your best prospects need if they are to succeed at work or in life.
- *Strategic*. Your content marketing efforts must be an integral part of your overall business strategy.
- *Targeted*. You must target your content precisely so that it's truly relevant to your buyers. Different forms of content will need to be delivered through different social platforms.

Copywriting for the web is an evolving art form, but many of the rules for good copywriting are as for any media. Common errors we see on websites are:

- too much knowledge assumed of the visitor about the company, its products and services;
- using internal jargon about products, services or departments – using undecipherable acronyms.

Web copywriters also need to take account of the user reading the content on-screen. Approaches to dealing with the limitations imposed by the customer using a monitor include:

- writing more concisely than in brochures;
- chunking, or breaking text into units of five to six lines at most, which allows users to scan rather than read information on web pages;
- use of lists with headline text in larger font;
- never including too much on a single page, except when presenting lengthy information such as a report which may be easier to read on a single page;
- using hyperlinks to decrease page sizes or help achieve flow within copy, either by linking to sections further down a page or linking to another page.

Hofacker (2000) described five stages of human information processing when a website is being used. These can be applied to both page design and content design to improve usability and help companies get their message across to consumers. Each of the five stages summarised in Table 7.3 acts as a hurdle, since if the site design or content is too difficult to process then the customer cannot progress to the next stage. It is useful to consider the stages in order to minimise these difficulties.

Table 7.3	A summary of the characteristics of the five stages of information processing described by Hofacker (2000)	
Stage	**Description**	**Applications**
1 Exposure	Content must be present for long enough to be processed	Content on banner ads may not be on-screen long enough for processing and cognition
2 Attention	User's eyes will be drawn towards headings and content, not graphics and moving items on a web page (Nielsen, 2000)	Emphasis and accurate labelling of headings is vital to gain a user's attention. Evidence suggests that users do not notice banner adverts, suffering from 'banner blindness'
3 Comprehension and perception	The user's interpretation of content	Designs that use common standards and metaphors and are kept simple will be more readily comprehended
4 Yielding and acceptance	Is information (copy) presented accepted by customers?	Copy should refer to credible sources and present counter arguments as necessary
5 Retention	As for traditional advertising, this describes the extent to which the information is remembered	An unusual style or high degree of interaction leading to flow and user satisfaction is more likely to be recalled

Development and testing of content

It is not practical to provide details of the methods of developing content since marketers do not need an in-depth understanding of development technologies as they will use specialists for this. What marketers do have to know is the aspects of customer experience that can be affected by the tools and development methodologies used. Then, when selecting suppliers, they can ask questions so that the type of constraints on the customer experience described in Activity 7.1 are accounted for. They can also test to make sure the systems have been built successfully. Selecting the right **content management system (CMS)** is important to provide a good user experience and is also important for an efficient method of publishing content since the facility can be made available to people throughout the company. Today there are two main forms of CMS, both of which are delivered as web services which can be accessed through a web browser. Enterprise CMSs can be used for large, complex sites (and other corporate documents); as well as the standard page creation and editing facilities these offer version control and review of documents through workflow systems which notify reviewers when new documents are ready for editing. CMS for smaller companies traditionally lack workflow or multi-author facilities, but offer many of the other features to create content. However blogging platforms such as WordPress and Moveable Type are increasingly used by smaller businesses for managing their entire site since they have enterprise features.

Content management system (CMS)
A software tool for creating, editing and updating documents accessed by intranet, extranet or Internet.

Criteria for selecting a content management system

A professional content management system should provide these facilities:

* *Easy authoring system.* Editing of new and existing documents should be possible through a WYSIWYG (what you see is what you get) facility similar to a word processor which makes it easy to embed images and supports a range of markups necessary for SEO.
* *Search engine robot crawling.* The content must be stored and linked such that it can be indexed by search engine crawlers to add it to their index. Sometimes URL rewriting

to a search-engine-friendly format without many parameters is required. The Google Webmaster pages describe the requirements: **www.google.com/webmasters**.

- *Search-engine-optimisation-friendly markup.* Some bespoke content management systems created by design agencies do not enable easy editing of the key fields, such as <title>, <h1> and <meta name = 'description' content = 'page description'>.
- *Different page templates.* The design and maintenance of content structure (subcomponents, templates, etc.), web page structure and website structure. It should be possible to create different layouts and designs for different site sections or categories of pages.
- *Link management.* The maintenance of internal and external links through content change and the elimination of dead links.
- *Input and syndication.* The loading (spidering) of externally originating content and the aggregation and dissemination of content from a variety of sources.
- *Versioning.* The crucial task of controlling which edition of a page, page element or the whole site is published. Typically this will be the most recent, but previous editions should be archived and it should be possible to roll back to a previous version.
- *Security and access control.* Different permissions can be assigned to different roles of users and some content may only be available through log-in details. In these cases, the CMS maintains a list of users.
- *Use of plug-ins and widgets.* Mashups are possible through embedding widgets such as links to social networks or third-party applications. But a content management system may not readily support embedding within the main content or sidebars.
- *Publication workflow.* Content destined for a website needs to pass through a publication process to move it from the management environment to the live delivery environment. The process may involve tasks such as editorial authorisation and the construction of composite documents in real time (personalisation and selective dissemination).
- *Tracking and monitoring.* Providing logs and statistical analysis of use to provide performance measures, tune the content according to demand and protect against misuse. It should also be possible to rapidly add tags to the page templates for web analytics tools such as Google Analytics.
- *Navigation and visualisation.* Providing an intuitive, clear and attractive representation of the nature and location of content using colour, texture, 3D rendering or even virtual reality. It should be possible to make changes to the navigation and containers holding content within the page template.
- *Flexibility to test new approaches.* It should be possible to test alternative designs and messaging using techniques such as AB and multivariate testing (as described in Chapter 11).

Testing the experience

Development
The creation of a website by programmers. It involves writing the HTML content, creating graphics and writing any necessary software code such as JavaScript or ActiveX (programming).

Testing
Involves different aspects of the content such as spelling, validity of links, formatting on different web browsers and dynamic features such as form filling or database queries.

Marketing managers responsible for websites need to have a basic awareness of website **development** and **testing**. We have already discussed the importance of usability testing with typical users of the system. In brief, other necessary testing steps include:

- test that the content displays correctly on different types and versions of web browsers;
- test plug-ins;
- test all interactive facilities and integration with company databases;
- test spelling and grammar;
- test adherence to corporate image standards;
- test to ensure all internal and links to external sites are valid.

Testing often occurs on a separate test web server (or directory) or *test environment*, with access to the test or prototype version being restricted to the development team. When complete, the website is released or published to the main web server or *live environment*.

Post-launch, ongoing improvements to site effectiveness can be made through review of the web analytics and testing of different page layouts, messaging and offers using the AB and multivariate testing tools (as described in Chapter 10).

Online retail merchandising

Findability
An assessment of how easy it is for a web user to locate a single content object or to use browse navigation and search system to find content. Like usability it is assessed through efficiency – how long it takes to find the content and effectiveness – how satisfied the user is with the experience and relevance of the content they find.

Faceted navigation
Enables users to rapidly filter results from a product search based on different ways of classifying the product by their attributes or features. For example by brand, by sub-product category, by price bands.

For online retail site owners, merchandising is a crucial activity, in the same way it is for physical retail store owners. In both cases, the aims are similar – to maximise sales potential for each store visitor. Online, this means presenting relevant products and promotions to site visitors which should help boost key measures of site performance such as conversion rate and average order value. You will see that many of these approaches are related to the concept of **findability**. Some of the most common approaches used are:

- *Expanding navigation through synonyms*. Through using a range of terms which may apply to the same product, the product may become easier to find if a site visitor is searching using a particular expression.
- *Applying faceted navigation or search approaches*. Search results pages are important in online merchandising since conversion rates will be higher if relevant products and offers are at the top of the list. **Faceted navigation** enables website users to 'drill-down' to easily select a relevant product by selecting different product attributes (Figure 7.14).
- *Featuring the bestselling products prominently*. Featuring strongest product lines prominently is a common approach, with retailers showing 'Top 10' or 'Top 20' products.
- *Use of bundling*. The classic retail approach of buy-one-get-one-free (BOGOF) is commonly applied online through showcasing complementary products. For example, Amazon discounts two related books it offers. Related products are also shown on the product page or in checkout, although care has to be taken here since this can reduce conversion rates.

| Figure 7.14 | Faceted navigation at **Euroffice.com** |

- *Use of customer ratings and reviews.* Reviews can be important in influencing sales. Research from online ratings service Bazaar Voice showed that for one of its clients, CompUSA, the use of reviews achieved:
  - 60 per cent higher conversion;
  - 50 per cent higher order value;
  - 82 per cent more page views per visitor.
- Mini case study 7.6, 'Figleaves.com uncovers customer feedback to increase conversion', shows another example.
- *Use of product visualisation systems.* These systems enable web users to zoom in and rotate on products.

Weathers and Makienko (2006) have also investigated the effect of merchandising on online store success rate based on a study of users of review site **Bizrate.com**. They found that features to enable searching for products were particularly important, as was a choice of ordering options.

Mini case study 7.6	**figleaves.com** uncovers customer feedback to increase conversion

figleaves.com (Figure 7.15) explains its online value proposition as follows:

- *figleaves.com is the world's largest online seller of branded intimate apparel. The retailer offers branded underwear, swimwear, exercisewear, nightwear and hosiery for men and women. [Core proposition and audience]*
- *While the choice is huge, it couldn't be easier to find what you are looking for. You can shop by brand, size, price, colour, style or occasion; or, if you know exactly what you are looking for, we will take you directly to it in one click. [Ease of use/findability]*

Figure 7.15	Example of customer ratings at figleaves.com

- *You can easily return goods if they don't fit or if they don't meet your expectation. It's our famous 'no hassle' returns policy. If you're in the UK we even pay the returns postage. [Returns policy]*
- *What's more, you can check out your purchases at home – no queuing for or embarrassing moments in luridly lit changing rooms. [Unique channel-specific advantage of online service]*
- *Underwear makes a great gift for both men and women. If you are buying for a loved one then we can send your present in a beautiful gift box along with a personalised message. Alternatively, you can send a gift certificate so that the recipient can choose exactly what they want themselves. [Gifting]*
- *We know how much you appreciate speedy delivery – in-stock items are usually dispatched within 24 hours. [Delivery]*

This research by Bazaarvoice shows the value of using customer reviews:

- Overall, products with reviews have a 12.5 per cent higher conversion rate than those without.
- Products with 20+ reviews have an 83.85 per cent higher conversion than those products without reviews. Note that products prompting the most reviews tend to be the best sellers and thus are generally higher converting.
- Analysing the session conversion for the same products before and after going live, the same products with reviews have a 35.27 per cent higher overall session conversion rate.
- Conversion was not negatively affected for products without reviews.
- The look-to-book ratio is four times lower (better) for products with reviews compared to those without.
- Overall look-to-book is 32.6 per cent higher (worse) for products without reviews.
- Since going live, products with reviews have seen a significant decrease (better) in the look-to-book ratio.
- Products without reviews saw no significant decrease.

Source: Bazaar Voice case study: http://bazaarvoice.com/cs_rr_conversion_figleaves.html

Site promotion or 'traffic building'

Promotion of a site in order to boost visitors is a significant topic that is part of the strategy of developing a website. It will follow the initial development of a site and is described in detail in Chapters 8 and 9. Particularly important issues that must be considered during the course of site design are search engine optimisation and the experience delivered on landing pages where the visitor arrives not on the home page, but deeper within the site.

Service quality

Delivering service quality in e-commerce can be assessed through reviewing existing marketing frameworks for determining levels of service quality. Those most frequently used are based on the concept of a 'service–quality gap' that exists between the customer's expected level of service (from previous experience and word-of-mouth communication) and their perception of the actual level of service delivery. We can apply the elements of service quality on which Parasuraman *et al.* (1985) suggest that consumers judge companies. Note that there has been heated dispute about the validity of this SERVQUAL instrument framework in determining service quality – see, for example, Cronin and Taylor (1992). Despite this it is still instructive to apply these dimensions of service quality to customer service on the web (see, for example, Chaffey and Edgar, 2000; Kolesar and Galbraith, 2000; Zeithaml *et al.*, 2002; and Trocchia and Janda, 2003):

- *tangibles* – the physical appearance of facilities and communications;
- *reliability* – the ability to perform the service dependably and accurately;
- *responsiveness* – a willingness to help customers and provide prompt service;
- *assurance* – the knowledge and courtesy of employees and their ability to convey trust and confidence;
- *empathy* – providing caring, individualised attention.

As well as applying these academic frameworks, organisations can use benchmarking services such as Foresee (**www.foreseeresults.com**) based on the American Customer Satisfaction Index methodology which assess satisfaction scores based on the gap between expectations and actual service (see Chapter 6, Figure 6.12).

It should also be remembered that the level of service selected by an online transactional service is based on the relationship between the costs to serve, the value of the product and the likelihood of the channel to increase conversion. Figure 7.16 shows the typical situation for a bank. Typically costs to serve increase to the top-right of the diagram, as does the capability to convert through a more extended dialogue and the value generated from sale. The figure shows a general pattern, but the options are often not mutually exclusive – for example, phone contact may be available for all levels, but emphasised for the most complex products. We introduced some of these methods of delivering service in Chapter 5:

1 *Straight-through processing.* Transaction typically occurs without intervention from staff for a relatively simple product such as a savings account.
2 *Call-backs.* The customer has the option to specify the bank call if there is anything they are unclear on.
3 *Live chat.* Online discussion between service representative and the client. This may be invoked proactively if analysis suggests the customer is having difficulty in deciding.
4 *Co-browsing.* Sharing of screen to walk through application process.
5 *Phone.* Typically this has the highest cost, but often the highest conversion rate.

Two of the most significant frameworks for assessing online service quality are:

- WEBQUAL (Loiacono *et al.*, 2000, 2007) which considers 14 dimensions. It has been criticised for relating too much to functional design issues rather than service issues. Consider other limitations which could include rating of content or products, trust

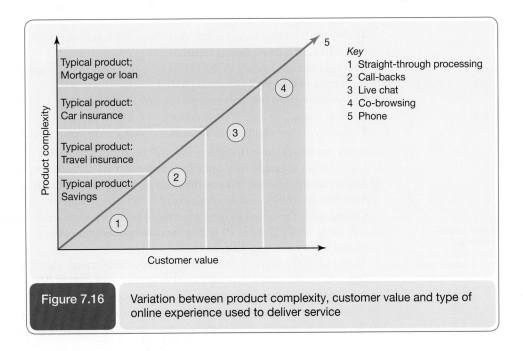

| Figure 7.16 | Variation between product complexity, customer value and type of online experience used to deliver service |

factors, support for different digital devices or integration with other online and offline channels. Green and Pearson (2011), for example, cover the trust factors and perceived risk. The dimensions of WEBQUAL are:

1 *Information quality* – the concern that information provided is accurate, updated and appropriate.
2 *Functional fit to task* – the extent to which users believe that the website meets their needs.
3 *Tailored communications* – communications can be tailored to meet the user's needs.
4 *Trust* – secure communication and observance of information privacy.
5 *Response time* – time to get a response after a request or an interaction with a website.
6 *Ease of understanding* – easy to read and understand.
7 *Intuitive operations* – easy to operate and navigate.
8 *Visual appeal* – the aesthetics of the site.
9 *Innovativeness* – the creativity and uniqueness of the website.
10 *Emotional appeal* – the emotional affect of using the website and intensity of involvement.
11 *Consistent image* – the website does not create dissonance for the user by an image incompatible with that projected by the firm through other media.
12 *Online completeness* – allowing all or most necessary transactions to be completed online (for example, purchasing over the website).
13 *Relative advantage* – equivalent to or better than other means of interacting with the company.
14 *Customer service* – the response to customer inquiries, comments and feedback when such response requires more than one interaction.

- E-SERVQUAL (Zeithaml *et al*., 2002) which contains seven dimensions. The first four are classified as the core service scale, and the latter three dimensions are regarded as a recovery scale, since they are only relevant when online customers have questions or problems:

1 *Efficiency* refers to the ability of the customers to get to the website, search for information or transact as required.
2 *Fulfilment* involves the accuracy of service promises, including products' in-stock availability and delivering the products in the promised time.
3 *Reliability* is associated with the technical functioning of the site, including availability and performance.
4 *Privacy* is related to assurance that shopping behaviour data are not shared and that credit card information is secure.
5 *Responsiveness* refers to the ability of e-tailers to provide appropriate support information to customers when requested.
6 *Compensation* involves returns facilities for refunds and return shipping and handling costs.
7 *Contact* is the ability of customers to talk to a live service agent online.

Both are useful frameworks which can still be applied to evaluate online service quality today, although arguably they omit the importance of accessibility, findability techniques, multichannel integration and customer reviews and ratings (as discussed in the later section on merchandising as a determinant of satisfactory experience).

Online marketers should assess what customers' expectations are in each of these areas, and identify where there is an **online service–quality gap** between the customer expectations and what is currently delivered.

Online service–quality gap
The mismatch between what is expected and delivered by an online presence.

As noted at the start of the chapter, Klaus (2014) notes that there have been limited attempts to review more holistic digital customer experiences despite the development of broader customer experience management assessment such as EXQ: a multiple-item scale for assessing service experience developed by Klaus and Maklan (2012).

We will now examine how the five determinants of online service quality apply online.

Tangibles

It can be suggested that the tangibles dimension is influenced by ease of use and visual appeal based on the structural and graphic design of the site. Design factors that influence this variable are described later in this chapter.

Reliability

The reliability dimension is dependent on the availability of a website – in other words, how easy it is to connect to the website as a user. Many companies fail to achieve 100 per cent availability and potential customers may be lost for ever if they attempt to use the site when it is unavailable.

Reliability of email response is also a key issue. Transversal (2008), found the following reliability of response in a survey of UK businesses:

- Websites could only provide answers to 50 per cent of questions asked (when testing against FAQ and service content).
- The average response to an email was 46 hours.
- Meanwhile 60 per cent of calls to contact centres were answered within three minutes.

Among business-to-business communications, InsideSales (2011) reviewed response and found a similarly poor picture of response. Of the US companies surveyed, 55.3 per cent of the 159 companies never responded, but 40.1 per cent responded within 24 hours, suggesting that these companies do have an acceptable response policy in place.

Responsiveness is closely related to the reliability of response to email as described above. Responsiveness is also indicated by the performance of the website – the time it takes for a page request to be delivered to the user's browser as a page impression. Data from monitoring services such as Keynote (**www.keynote.com**) indicate that there is a wide variability in the delivery of information and hence service quality from web servers hosted at ISPs, and companies should be careful to monitor this and specify levels of quality with suppliers in service-level agreements (SLAs).

Assurance

In an email context, assurance can best be considered as the quality of response. In a survey reported by Chaffey and Edgar (2000), of 180 responses received, 91 per cent delivered a personalised human response, with 9 per cent delivering an automated response which did not address the individual enquiry; 40 per cent of responses answered or referred to all three questions, with 10 per cent answering two questions and 22 per cent one. Overall, 38 per cent did not answer any of the specific questions posed!

Multichannel communications preferences

Upton (2008) reports on research where 1000 UK consumers aged 18+ were surveyed to identify the role and importance of customer services and communications for online businesses. Despite the growing popularity of email as a communication tool, 53 per cent of those interviewed still prefer to communicate with businesses over the telephone, particularly for service enquiries, compared with 48 per cent for email and 16 per cent for traditional mail. However, when asked about their experiences, three out of ten UK consumers stated they found it difficult to locate contact details on websites.

Surprisingly, 53 per cent of consumers consider three minutes waiting time a satisfactory period to speak with an agent over the telephone. Consumers particularly disliked ringing a contact centre only to be met with a computerised answering service. As Upton notes, replacing a skilled operator with an automated service might save money in the short term – however, in the long term companies risk losing brand advocacy and sales. Additionally, customers believe 24 hours is a respectable amount of time to wait for a response when contacting a business via email.

He concludes:

> Overall the research shows that in this era of multi-communication, consumers are no longer allied to any particular mode of communication. They will select the most convenient or appropriate channel even if the retailer trades solely online.
>
> As a result, brands need to provide their contact centre agents with the tools to seamlessly combine different communication channels such as telephone, email, v-mail, web chat and SMS to communicate with the consumer and meet their expectations of service.
>
> Agents also need to have real-time access to all past interactions with a customer. This should include text transcriptions of conversations and emails, scanned copies of letters received and despatched, as well as call recordings, comments and outcomes ensuring that the agent is fully briefed on the existing relationship that the customer has with the brand. Importantly, this information can be further used to tailor all future contact with the customer, delivering greater levels of customer satisfaction. By employing the customer's preferred channel of communication, which has been identified using the data from real conversations with individuals, it is possible to meet customer expectations, and as a result maximise retention and brand advocacy.

A further assurance concern of e-commerce websites is the privacy and security of customer information (see Chapter 3). A company that adheres to the UK Internet Shopping Is Safe (ISIS) (**www.imrg.org/isis**) or TRUSTe principles (**www.truste.org**) will provide better assurance than one that does not. For security, 'hacker safe' accreditation is available from Scan Alert (**www.scanalert.com**) which is owned by McAfee security products. This involves automated daily scans to test site security.

Chaffey and Smith (2012) suggest that the following actions can be used to achieve assurance in an e-commerce site:

- provide clear and effective privacy statements;
- follow privacy and consumer protection guidelines in all local markets;
- make security of customer data a priority;
- use independent certification bodies;
- emphasise the excellence of service quality in all communications.

Empathy

Although it might be considered that empathy requires personal human contact, it can still be achieved, to an extent, through email and web communications.

Provision of personalisation facilities is also an indication of the empathy provided by the website, but more research is needed as to customers' perception of the value of web pages that are dynamically created to meet a customer's information needs.

It can be suggested that for managers wishing to apply a framework such as SERVQUAL in an e-commerce context there are three stages appropriate to managing the process:

1 *Understanding expectations*. Customer expectations for the e-commerce environment in a particular market sector must be understood. The SERVQUAL framework can be used with market research and benchmarking of other sites to understand requirements such as responsiveness and empathy. Scenarios can also be used to identify customer expectations of using services on a site.

2 *Setting and communicating the service promise*. Once expectations are understood, marketing communications can be used to inform the customers of the level of service. This can be achieved through customer service guarantees or promises. It is better

to under-promise than over-promise. A book retailer who delivers a book in two days when three days were promised will earn the customer's loyalty better than the retailer who promises one day but delivers in two! The enlightened company may also explain what it will do if it doesn't meet its promises – will the customer be recompensed? The service promise must also be communicated internally and combined with training to ensure that the service is delivered.

3 *Delivering the service promise*. Finally, commitments must be delivered through on-site service, support from employees and physical fulfilment. Otherwise, online credibility is destroyed and a customer may never return.

Tables 7.4 and 7.5 summarise the main concerns of online consumers for each of the elements of service quality. Table 7.4 gives the main factors in the context of SERVQUAL and Table 7.5 presents the requirements from an e-commerce site that must be met for excellent customer service.

Table 7.4	Online elements of service quality		
Tangibles	**Reliability**	**Responsiveness**	**Assurance and empathy**
Ease of use	Availability	Download speed	Contacts with call centre
Content quality	Reliability	Email response	Personalisation
Price	Email replies	Call-back	Privacy
		Fulfilment	Security

Table 7.5	Summary of requirements for online service quality
Email response requirements	**Website requirements**
Defined response times and named individual responsible for replies	Support for customer-preferred channel of communication in response to enquiries (email, phone, postal mail or in person)
Use of autoresponders to confirm query is being processed	Clearly indicated contact points for enquiries via email mailto: and forms
Personalised email where appropriate	Company internal targets for site availability and performance
Accurate response to inbound email by customer-preferred channel: outbound email or phone call-back	Testing of site usability and efficiency of links, HTML, plug-ins and browsers to maximise availability
Opt-in and opt-out options must be provided for promotional email with a suitable offer in exchange for a customer's provision of information	Appropriate graphic and structural site design to achieve ease of use and relevant content with visual appeal
Clear layout, named individual and privacy statements in email	Personalisation option for customers
	Specific tools to help a user to answer specific queries such as interactive support databases and frequently asked questions (FAQ)

Source: Chaffey and Edgar (2000)

The relationship between service quality, customer satisfaction and loyalty

As we discussed in Chapter 6 (see Figure 6.11), it is key for organisations to understand not only the levers that determines service quality and customer satisfaction, but also loyalty or repeat purchases.

Rigby *et al.* (2000) assessed repeat-purchase drivers in grocery, clothing and consumer electronics e-tail. It was found that the key loyalty drivers were similar to those of Dell, including correct delivery of order, but other factors such as price, ease of use and customer support were more important.

Case Study 7 | **Refining the online customer experience at i-to-i.com**

This case is about a specialist travel and education company, focussing on its online TEFL (Teaching English as a Foreign Language) courses. The company's site (Figure 7.17) combines many of the features we have described in this chapter blending accessibility, usability and persuasion. This case considers the challenges of delivering an effective design across different markets for different audiences.

i-to-i background

i-to-i (www.i-to-i.com) is an international organisation with offices in the UK, USA, Ireland and Australia. Around 20,000 people have selected i-to-i as they travel on ventures to support 500 worthwhile projects in five continents and it has also trained a further 80,000 people as TEFL (Teaching English as a Foreign Language)

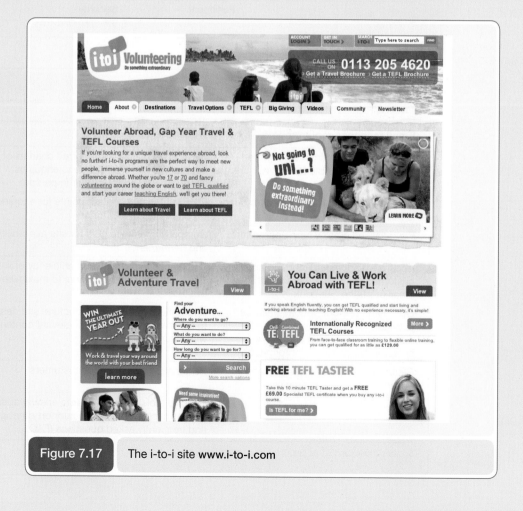

Figure 7.17 | The i-to-i site **www.i-to-i.com**

teachers. This service is offered through the main site and also through a specialist online TEFL site (www. onlinetefl.com), on which this case focuses.

The history of i-to-i

The founder of i-to-i, Deirdre Bounds, was inspired to create the company following a career break which took her to teach English in Japan, China and Greece and drive a backpackers' bus in Sydney. The company initially started through creating TEFL courses eventually leading to organising volunteer projects. Since 2003, the company has supported the i-to-i Foundation, a registered charity committed to providing funds to the most needy community and ecological projects in the i-to-i family. In 2007, i-to-i became part of the TUI travel group.

Proposition

The main features of the i-to-i TEFL proposition communicated through its site are:

- *International accreditation*: i-to-i is externally accredited by the ODLQC in order to ensure that its courses are rigorously monitored and always meet the highest industry standards.
- *World-class reputation*: i-to-i has four offices worldwide and it has over 12 years' experience teaching TEFL.
- *Partnership*: i-to-i is preferred TEFL course provider for STA Travel, Opodo and Lonely Planet.
- *Complete student support*: students receive advice on how to get work abroad, how best to prepare for their time away and up-to-the-minute advice on current job opportunities.
- *Highly experienced tutors*: all i-to-i tutors have at least three years' overseas teaching experience.

This proposition is backed up by 'the i-to-i TEFL Promise' which is communicated on the site.

- We will beat any equivalent and cheaper course by 150%.
- If you're not entirely satisfied after the first seven days, we'll give you a full refund.
- Our experience, our high academic standards and the quality of our courses means that i-to-i TEFL certificates are recognised by thousands of language schools worldwide.
- Additionally i-to-i can offer to help students find TEFL jobs abroad.

Audience segmentation

The main segmentation used by i-to-i is geographic:

- UK;
- North America;
- Europe;
- Australia and New Zealand;
- Rest-of-world (same as UK).

Different brochures are available for each geographical area. Information is also collected on an optional basis about prospects' age and status, although these are not used for targeting emails. Status categories are:

- Student;
- employed;
- self-employed;
- career break;
- unemployed;
- retired.

Since optional information is restricted to certain lead tools it is not used to target emails. For weekend TEFL – postcode/city is used to target courses to the nearest location of prospects.

Competitors

Some of the main competitors for online TEFL courses based in the UK and Australia include:

- www.cactustefl.com
- www.teflonline.com
- www.eslbase.com

In the US, competitors who also operate in the UK and other countries include:

- www.teflcorp.com/
- ITTP (International Tefl-Tesol-Online): www.tefl-tesol-online.com

Media mix

i-to-i uses a combination of these digital media channels to drive visits, leads and sales:

- pay per click (PPC) (mainly Google AdWords);
- social media marketing using Facebook, Twitter and i-to-i's own traveller community;
- natural search;
- affiliate marketing;
- display advertising;
- email marketing.

Customer experience and conversion process

Detailed content to help visitors decide on purchasing a course is available on the site. This includes module outlines and videos. Specific landing pages are used to convert visitors from paid search or affiliates for example.

A number of engagement devices are blended into the design used to generate leads, including brochures, 'TEFL tasters', an email guide and campaign promotions such as winning a course. Customers have the choice of requesting a brochure (post or download), requesting a callback or a live chat.

Such leads are followed up through a series of welcome emails. Results are monitored, but emails are not proactively followed up on. There is no phone follow-up of leads due to the relative low value of the products, but site visitors are encouraged to ring or setup a callback which often leads to higher conversion rates.

Marketplace challenges

The main marketplace challenges faced by i-to-i are:

- Increasing its presence and conversion effectiveness in a competitive market in different geographies.
- i-to-i has good exposure in the UK, its primary market, but operates in a cluttered marketplace with price being the main differentiator (products are similar and some competitors are just as established etc.).
- Research suggests that there is good opportunity within the US, but exposure is more limited because of the cost of pay-per-click advertising and because presence in natural search favours the US.
- Rest-of-world sales (outside of the UK, USA, Canada, Ireland/Europe, Australia, New Zealand) are increasing and is believed to be a growing market. i-to-i seeks to penetrate these markets, but in a cost-effective way that will not distract attention from the main markets.
- Increasing demand through reaching and educating those considering travel, who are not aware of TEFL courses and the opportunities they unlock. For example, many will look for casual work in other countries, e.g. in bars or in agriculture, but will be unaware of TEFL.

Questions

1 Select one country that i-to-i operates in closest to the area where you live. Define a persona based on their age and product needs and then identify the main customer journeys that form the customer for this persona. Which routes through the site would this user follow?

2 Review the range of engagement devices on the i-to-i website to engage the audience to generate leads.

3 Identify key areas for improvement for i-to-i based on your use of the site.

Summary

1 An effective online customer experience is dependent on many factors, including the visual elements of the site design and how it has been designed for persuasion, usability, accessibility and performance.

2 Careful planning and execution of website implementation is important, in order to avoid the need for extensive reworking at a later stage if the design proves to be ineffective.

3 Analysis, design and implementation should form an iterative, prototyping approach based on usability testing that meets business and user requirements.

4 A feasibility study should take place before the initiation of a major website project. A feasibility study will assess:

- the costs and benefits of the project;
- the difficulty of achieving management and staff commitment to the project;
- the availability of domain names to support the project;
- the responsibilities and stages necessary for a successful project.

5 The choice of host for a website should be considered carefully since this will govern the quality of service of the website.

6 Options for analysis of users' requirements for a website include:

- interviews with marketing staff;
- questionnaire sent to companies;
- usability and accessibility testing;
- informal interviews with key accounts;
- focus groups;
- reviewing competitors' websites.

7 The design phase of developing a website includes specification of:

- the information architecture, or structure, of the website using techniques such as site maps, blueprints and wireframes;
- the flow, controlled by the navigation and menu options;
- the graphic design and brand identity;
- content strategy;
- country-specific localisation;
- the service quality of online forms and email messages.

Exercises

Self-assessment exercises

1 Explain the term 'prototyping' in relation to website creation.
2 What tasks should managers undertake during initiation of a web page?
3 What factors should be considered for domain name registration?
4 List the factors that determine website 'flow'.
5 Which requirements are important to an effective website?
6 List the options for assessing online service quality.
7 Which issues should be considered when developing a content strategy?
8 What are the factors that control the performance of a website?

Essay and discussion questions

1 Discuss the relative effectiveness of the different methods of assessing the customer's needs from a website.
2 Select three websites of your choice and compare their design effectiveness. You should describe design features such as navigation, structure and graphics.
3 Explain how strategy, analysis, design and implementation of a website should be integrated through a prototyping approach. Describe the merits and problems of the prototyping approach.
4 When designing the interactive services of a website what steps should the designer take to provide a quality service to customers?

Examination questions

1 What is website prototyping? Give three benefits of this approach.
2 What requirements should be defined at the initiation phase of an online project?
3 Which factors are important in selecting a web design agency?
4 How can customer analysis be used to develop a more effective online service?
5 Name, and briefly explain, four characteristics of an online service that will govern whether a user recommends it.
6 What are the constraints on web service design depending on the technology platform the service is accessed on?

References

Bevan, N. (1999a) Usability issues in website design, *Proceedings of the 6th Interactive Publishing Conference*, November, **www.usability.serco.com**.

Bevan, N. (1999b) Common industry format usability tests, *Proceedings of UPA'98*, Usability Professionals Association, Scottsdale, Arizona, 29 June–2 July 1999, **www.usability.serco.com**.

BSI (1999) BSc 13407 Human-centred design processes for interactive systems, British Standards Institute.

Chaffey, D. and Edgar, M. (2000) Measuring online service quality, *Journal of Targeting, Analysis and Measurement for Marketing*, 8(4), 363–78.

Chaffey, D. and Smith, P.R. (2012) *E-marketing Excellence. Planning and Optimising your Digital Marketing – at the Heart of E-Business*, 4th edn, Butterworth-Heinemann, Oxford.

Chaffey, D. and Wood, S. (2010) *Business Information Management*, 2nd edn, Financial Times/Prentice Hall, Harlow.

Christodoulides, G., de Chernatony, L., Furrer, O., Shiu, E. and Temi, A. (2006) Conceptualising and measuring the equity of online brands, *Journal of Marketing Management*, 22(7–8), 799–825.

Chen, A. (2012) Is the growth hacker the new VP marketing? Blog post by Andrew Chen, 27 April 2012.

Cronin, J. and Taylor, S. (1992) Measuring service quality: a re-examination and extension, *Journal of Marketing*, 56, 55–63.

Csikszentmihalyi, M. (1990) *Flow: The Psychology of Optimal Experience*, Harper and Row, New York.

Cutts, M. (2007) Talk like a Googler: parts of a url, Blog posting, 14 August 2007, **www.mattcutts.com/blog/seo-glossary-url-definitions/**.

de Chernatony, L. (2001) Succeeding with brands on the Internet, *Journal of Brand Management*, 8(3), 186–95.

Fogg, B. (2009) In Proceedings of the 4th International Conference on Persuasive Technology, pp. 1–7, **www.behaviormodel.org**.

Fogg, B., Soohoo, C., Danielson, D., Marable, L., Stanford, J. and Tauber, E. (2003) How do people evaluate a website's credibility? A Consumer WebWatch research report, prepared by Stanford Persuasive Technology Lab.

Green, D.T. and Pearson, M.J. (2011) Integrating website usability with the electronic commerce acceptance model, *Behaviour and Information Technology*, 30(2), 181–99.

Guardian (2013) *Financial Times*: there is no drawback to working in HTML5, Interview with Stuart Dredge, *Guardian*, 29 April.

Halvorson, K. (2010) *Content Strategy for the Web*, New Riders, Berkeley, CA.

Hofacker, C. (2000) *Internet Marketing*, Wiley, New York.

Hoffman, D.L. and Novak, T.P. (1997) A new marketing paradigm for electronic commerce, *The Information Society*, Special issue on electronic commerce, 13, 43–54.

InsideSales (2011) Audit of response to sales leads, **www.insidesales.com/resources**.

iPerceptions (2011) iPerceptions' 4Q Suite helps improve Thomas Cook Netherlands website performance and content, **www.iperceptions.com/news/iperceptions%E2%80%99-4q-suite-helps-improves-thomas-cook-netherlands-website-performance-and-content/**.

Kolesar, M. and Galbraith, R. (2000) A services-marketing perspective on e-retailing, *Internet Research: Electronic Networking Applications and Policy*, 10(5), 424–38.

Klaus, P. (2014) Towards practical relevance – Delivering superior firm performance through digital customer experience strategies, *Journal of Direct, Data and Digital Marketing Practice*, 15(4), 306–316.

Klaus, P. and Maklan, S. (2012) EXQ: a multiple-item scale for assessing service experience, *Journal of Service Management*, 23(1), 5–33.

Knight, K. (2011). Responsive web design: what it is and how to use it, Smashing Magazine blog post, 12 January 2011, **http://coding.smashingmagazine.com/2011/01/12/guidelines-for-responsive-web-design/**.

Loiacono, E., Watson, R. and Goodhue, D. (2000) WEBQUAL: a measure of website quality, in K. Evans and L. Scheer (eds), *Marketing Theory and Applications*, American Marketing Association, Chicago, Vol. 13, 432–9.

Loiacono, E.T., R.T. Watson and D.L. Goodhue (2007) WebQual: an instrument for consumer evaluation of web sites, *International Journal of Electronic Commerce*, 11(3), 51–87.

Morville, P. (2005) *Ambient Findability, What We Find Changes Who We Become*, O'Reilly Media, Sebastopol, CA.

Multilingual (2008) Localising a localizer's website: the challenge, *Multilingual* (January/February), 30–33.

Nielsen, J. (1999) Details in study methodology can give misleading results, Jakob Nielsen's Alertbox, 21 February, **www.useit.com/alertbox/990221.html**.

Nielsen, J. (2000) *Designing Web Usability*, New Riders Publishing, Berkeley, CA.

Nitish, S., Fassott, G., Zhao, H. and Boughton, P. (2006) A cross-cultural analysis of _ German, Chinese and Indian consumers' perception of website adaptation, *Journal of Consumer Behaviour*, 5, 56–68.

O'Neill, M. (2014) 5 lessons learnt: getting services live. Blog post, 24 November 2014, **https://digitaltransformation.blog.gov.uk/2014/11/24/5-lessons-learnt-getting-services-live/**.

Parasuraman, A., Zeithaml, V. and Berry, L. (1985) A conceptual model of service quality and its implications for future research, *Journal of Marketing*, 49(Fall), 48.

Pulizzi, J. and Barrett, T. (2010) *Get Content. Get Customers*, McGraw-Hill, Columbus, OH.

Rettie, R. (2001) An exploration of flow during Internet use, *Internet Research*, 11(2), 103–13.

Rigby, D., Bavega, S., Rastoi, S., Zook, C. and Hancock, S. (2000) The value of customer loyalty and how you can capture it, Bain and Company/Mainspring white paper, 17 March, **www.mainspring.com**.

Robertson, J. (2003) Information design using card sorting, Step Two, **www.steptwo.com.au/papers/cardsorting/index.html**.

Rosen, D. and Purinton, E. (2004) Website design: viewing the Web as a cognitive landscape, *Journal of Business Research*, 57(7), 787–94.

Rosenfeld, L. and Morville, P. (2002) *Information Architecture for the World Wide Web*, 2nd edn, O'Reilly, Sebastopol, CA.

Schranz, T. (2013) Growth Hackers Conference: lessons learnt. Blog post, 1 November 2012 by Thomas Schranz published at **www.blossom.io/blog/2012/11/01/growth-hackers-conference-lessons-learnt.html**.

SciVisum (2005) Internet campaign effectiveness study, press release, July, **www.scivisum.co.uk**.

Singh, N. and Pereira, A. (2005) *The Culturally Customised Website, Customising Websites for the Global Marketplace*, Butterworth-Heinemann, Oxford.

Smith, D. and Sivakumar, K. (2004) Flow and Internet shopping behaviour: a conceptual model and research propositions, *Journal of Business Research*, 57(10), 1199–208.

Strangeloop (2011) Report State of the Union: study of the top 2000 retail websites reveals that the top sites are getting slower not faster, **www.strangeloopnetworks.com/resources/research/report-state-of-the-union-for-page-speed-and-website-performance/key-findings/**.

Sullivan (2011) Web design process infographic. SmartInsights blog post, 6 September, **www.smartinsights.com**.

Thurner, R. and Chaffey, D. (2013) *Winning with Mobile: Creating a Strategy for Mobile Marketing, Mobile Commerce and Mobile CRM*, Smart Insights.

Transversal (2008) Email black hole causing customer service crisis, **www.transversal.com/html/news/viewpress.php?article=81**.

Trilibis (2014) Trilibis web performance survey finds 69 per cent of responsive design websites fail to deliver acceptable load times on mobile devices. Press release, 21 April 2014.

Trocchia, P. and Janda, S. (2003) How do consumers evaluate Internet retail service quality?, *Journal of Services Marketing*, 17(3).

Upton, N. (2008) Online customer service, What's new in marketing, e-newsletter, 66, February 2008, **www.wnim.com**.

Weathers, D. and Makienko, I. (2006) Assessing the relationships between e-tail success and product and website factors, *Journal of Interactive Marketing*, 2, 41–54.

Wikipedia (2015) DevOps, **http://en.wikipedia.org/wiki/DevOps**.

Wodtke, C. (2002) *Information Architecture: Blueprints for the Web*, New Riders, Indianapolis.

Wroblewski, L. (2011) Why separate mobile and desktop web design, blog post, 1 September, **www.lukew.com/ff/entry.asp?1390**.

Zeithaml, V., Parasuraman, A. and Malhotra, A. (2002) Service quality delivery through websites: a critical review of extant knowledge, *Academy of Marketing Science*, 30(4), 368.

Weblinks

Accessibility

- **Royal National Institute for the Blind** (**www.rnib/org.uk/accessibility**) Web accessibility guidelines.
- **W3C** (**www.w3.org/WAI**) Guidelines and resources from the World Wide Web Consortium (W3C).

Retail e-commerce effectiveness compilations

- Custora Pulse (**www.custora.com/pulse**)
- Monetate Ecommerce Quarterly (**www.monetate.com/research/**)
- IMRG (**http://imrg.org**)

Information architecture

- **Boxes and Arrows** (**www.boxesandarrows.com**). A great collection of best practice articles and discussions about IA topics such as controlled vocabularies.
- **Peter Morville** (**www.semanticstudios.com/publications**). Blog of the author of the classic information architecture book. In-depth best practice articles.
- **Louis Rosenfeld site** (**www.louisrosenfeld.com**). Rosenfeld is also author of the classic Information Architecture book.
- **Jesse James Garrett** (**http://jjg.net/ia**). Design expert JJG's Articles on IA.
- **Step Two** (**www.steptwo.com.au**). This design company has introductory outlines and more detailed articles on information architecture and other aspects of usability.

Usability

- **UsabilityNet** (**www.usabilitynet.org**) A portal about usability with good links to other sites and an introduction to usability terms and concepts.

- **Usability.Gov** (**www.usability.gov**) A comprehensive US portal site covering every aspect of usability, from planning and analysing to designing, followed by testing and refining.
- **UseIt** (**www.useit.com/alertbox**) Ten years on, it is still worth subscribing for Jakob Nielsen's often trenchant views on web design, which are typically based on his user research.
- **UIE** (**www.uie.com/articles**) Jared Spool's user interface engineering articles provide good best practice summary articles.

Web development

- **Web Developers Handbook** (**www.alvit.de/handbook**) A simple, comprehensive directory of the web development, how-to resources and blogs.
- **Government Service Design Manual** (**www.gov.uk/service-manual**) Describes the process for developing online services through Discovery, Beta, Alpha and Live stages.
- **Webby Awards** (**www.webbyawards.com**) Best practice. The Oscars for the web – international.

Web standards

- **A List Apart** (**www.alistapart.com**) Explores the design, development and meaning of web content, with a special focus on web standards and best practices.
- **Web Standards Project (WASP)** (**www.webstandards.org**) A consortium that promotes web standards.
- **The World Wide Web Consortium** (**www.w3.org**) The global standards body prominent in defining web standards.
- **Zeldman.com** (**www.zeldman.com**) The blog of web standards advocate, Jeffrey Zeldman.

Chapter 8
Campaign planning for digital media

Chapter at a glance

Main topics

- The characteristics of digital media 424
- Step 1. Goal setting and tracking for interactive marketing communications 432
- Step 2. Campaign insight 441
- Step 3. Segmentation and targeting 443
- Step 4. Offer, message development and creative 447
- Step 5. Budgeting and selecting the digital media mix 451
- Step 6. Integration into overall media schedule or plan 463

Case studies

Digital marketing in practice

The Smart Insights interview with Mike O'Brien of the Jam Partnership on the ingredients for creating engaging digital campaigns 422

Case study 8: A short history of Facebook 468

Learning objectives

After reading this chapter, the reader should be able to:

- Assess the difference in communications characteristics between digital and traditional media
- Identify the main success factors in managing a digital campaign
- Understand the importance of integrating online and offline communications
- Relate promotion techniques to methods of measuring site effectiveness.

Questions for marketers

Key questions for marketing managers related to this chapter are:

- How do the characteristics of digital media differ from those of traditional media?
- How should I plan an online marketing campaign?
- How do I choose the best mix of online and offline communications techniques?

Scan code
to find the
latest updates
for topics in
this chapter

Links to other chapters

Related chapters are:

- Chapter 1 describes the 6Is, a framework that introduces the characteristics of Internet marketing communications
- Chapter 2 introduces portals and search engines – one of the methods of online traffic building discussed in this chapter
- Chapter 3 introduces some of the legal and ethical constraints on online marketing communications
- Chapter 4 provides the strategic basis for Internet marketing communications.
- Chapter 7 describes on-site communications
- Chapter 9 reviews the different digital media channels in detail
- Chapter 10 considers the measurement of communications effectiveness.

Introduction

A company that has developed an effective online customer experience as discussed in Chapter 7 is only part-way to success in digital marketing. In the days of the dot-com boom a common expression was: 'If you build it, they will come.' This famous line proved true of a baseball stadium built in the film *Field of Dreams*, but unfortunately it doesn't apply to websites or other forms of online presence like mobile apps or social media sites. Berthon *et al.* (1998) make the analogy between online communications and a trade fair. Effective promotion and achieving visibility of the stand is necessary to attract some of the many show visitors to that stand and encourage them to interact. Similarly, if you want to maximise quality visitors within a target audience to your online presences to acquire new customers online, Internet marketers have to select the appropriate online and offline marketing communications.

Planning for how digital media are used includes both short-term campaigns to support a particular goal such as launching a new product, promoting a sale or encouraging prospects to attend an event, and longer-term 'always-on' or **continuous e-communications activities** which review the best mix of communications to use to drive visitors to a site and achieve the main outcomes for the site such as product sales (for a retailer), lead generation (for a business-to-business company), engagement with a brand or subscriptions or ad revenue (for an online publisher or consumer brand).

Chaffey and Smith (2012) refer to the relevance of timing for traffic building. They say:

> Some e-marketers may consider traffic building to be a continuous process, but others may view it as a specific campaign, perhaps to launch a site or a major enhancement. Some methods tend to work best continuously; others are short term. Short-term campaigns will be for a site launch or an event such as an online trade show.

A similar sentiment is expressed on the Alliance & Leicester, which refers to use of 'drip' as against 'burst' communications. Speaking to *New Media Age* (2006), Graham Findlay, Customer Acquisition Manager at bank Alliance & Leicester (now part of Santander), highlighted the importance of continuous e-communications when he said:

> A big part of my team's job is to continually monitor traffic to and from our sites. We work to maintain the bank's profile. Some of our competitors don't always have a full online presence, settling instead for bursts of activity. That's certainly not our strategy.

The article reported that Alliance & Leicester have increased their search engine marketing budget from £10,000 in 2001 to £3 million in 2006 as part of a £13 million budget. Explaining the importance of visibility in search he says:

> I believe there's volume to be made from search and it's only right that a direct bank like us features in the top listings through search.

Planning for digital media includes both short-term campaigns to support a particular goal such as launching a new product, promoting a sale or encouraging prospects to attend an event, and longer-term 'always-on' or continuous e-communications activities which seek to tap into consumer intent for products and services as they search for information about brands, suppliers and reviews to inform their decision. Always-on communications review the best mix of communications investment to use to drive visitors to a site and achieve the main outcomes for the site such as product sales (for a retailer), lead generation (for a business-to-business company), engagement with a brand or subscriptions or ad revenue (for an online publisher or consumer brand).

An example of the benefits that can accrue through a continuous focus on improving results is explored in Mini case study 8.1. This is an example of the approach of growth

Continuous e-communications activities
Long-term use of e-marketing communications intended to generate site visitors for customer acquisition (such as search engine, affiliate marketing and online sponsorship) and retention (for example, e-newsletter marketing).

Mini case study 8.1   A focus on 'always-on' marketing and growth hacking increases Metro audience by 16 million monthly unique visitors in one year

This mini case study shows how businesses can tap into the continuous demand for content via search engines and social media to grow their audience. In this case, the business is a news publisher which many other types of online brands must compete with for a share of audience. In VIP Wordpress (2014), **Metro. co.uk**'s Head of Development Dave Jensen shares some insights into how the company increased unique visitors from 9 million to 25 million uniques in a single year. He explains what the article describes as '10 Growth Hacks' that helped support the increase in visitors. Some of these 'hacks' are technology and hosting related, such as adopting a responsive design, improving site performance and improving indexing of the site by Google to increase search referral from 2 million to 10 million visits a month. Other changes involve opening the platform up to offer more 'user generated content' such as contributed blog articles. Social media optimisation was also a contributor of growth. Methods to encourage sharing via Facebook saw Facebook Page likes increase from 173,000 in February 2013 to 562,000 Facebook Page Likes in February 2014 with this social amplification also contributing to traffic.

Summarising the process behind the increase in visits, Dave Jensen says:

None of the above would have been possible without the adoption of a lean mindset and the approach of build, measure, learn, iterate. It has been an amazing 12 months of growth at Metro and a great feeling to be part of a team that came up with and then executed a plan which delivered these results.

---

hacking introduced in the previous chapter which blends improvements to communications and experience.

The structure of this chapter

We begin Chapter 8 by reviewing the unique characteristics of digital media which must be applied for success in online campaigns. We then look at the different practical aspects of communications which must be reviewed as part of planning always-on communications or managing a campaign and integrating it with traditional media. These are the sections of this chapter and the main questions we will be answering.

Digital media channel
Online communications technique used to achieve goals of brand awareness, familiarity, favourability, and to influence purchase intent by encouraging users of digital media to visit a website, where they will engage with the brand or product and ultimately purchase online or offline through traditional media channels such as by phone or instore.

1 *Goal setting and tracking* – which specific goals should be set for online campaigns and how do we measure success? What response mechanisms will be most effective?
2 *Campaign insight* – which data about customer and competitor behaviour is available to inform our decision?
3 *Segmentation and targeting* – how can we target and reach our different audiences?
4 *Offer and message development* – how do we specify our offer and key messages?
5 *Budgeting and selecting the digital media mix* – how should we set the budget and invest in different forms of digital media?
6 *Integration into overall media schedule or plan* – how should we plan the media schedule which incorporates different waves of online and offline communications?

Referrer or referring site
The source of a visitor to a site delivered via a digital media channel. Typically a specific site, e.g. Google AdWords, or a media site or an individual ad placement on the site.

In Chapter 9, we will review the success factors for the main **digital media channels** such as affiliate, search and social media marketing (shown in Figure 1.9) which make up the tactics of digital marketing campaigns. When a visitor is directed to a site from another third-party site via a digital media channel, the origin is known as a **referrer or referring site**.

Digital marketing in practice | The Smart Insights interview

Mike O'Brien of the Jam Partnership on the ingredients for creating engaging digital campaigns

Overview and main concepts covered

Quality campaign creative engages. But creating quality creative is far from simple. Mike O'Brien has been involved in creating many campaigns and this interview shows the power of digital media in creating engaging campaigns. As Mike says:

> I think we have reached the point where creative platforms are no longer hindering the free-flow of ideas. They are opening up to the point where even the most obscure brand, regardless of budget can create, execute and evaluate the most incredible interpersonal ideas and campaigns and create real time engagements with customers.

The interview

Q. What are the ingredients for successful digital creative of a campaign?

Mike O'Brien: We should be on the lookout for campaigns that put the customer, not the brand, product or service, at the heart of everything. The future belongs to campaigns that transcend one-sided linear communication and push the boundaries of client/customer relationships into the realm of interpersonal communication. In linear communication, brands put themselves in a superior position to customers. They believe their job is to anticipate and satisfy customer needs, wants and desires, while the customer's subordinate role is simply to learn, spend and be grateful. Interpersonal communication, on the other hand, is a two-way process in which the brand and the customer learn to anticipate and satisfy each other's needs, wants and desires together in a process that rewards both parties for facilitation and engagement.

Q. Which campaign creative mistakes do you see most often?

Mike O'Brien: The total lack of relevance to the customer is all too apparent in most campaigns, especially in online display which seems, despite the billions being poured into it at the moment, to have virtually no demonstrable impact on the clients' business. I am also convinced that we tend to have too much interest in the platform and technology and not enough in the customer's journey. Whole page takeovers and interstitials that add nothing to the customer's context of engagement really make me blow a fuse. Our job is not to interrupt the customer but to work with them to achieve their key tasks. A great example of this supporting role is the Mini Banner campaign that drops a Cherished Mini search tab into the site's (Autotrader, MSN etc.) search tab structure. For the same reason, I like simple but effective dynamic, data feed and capture, contextual and RSS feed ads that augment and give direction to the customer's on-screen experience in the way that the Domino's app does on my iPhone when I am hungry. Don't expect me to look at car ads when my stomach is grumbling.

I suppose the other gripe I have is creative that shows little or no understanding of state of play between the brand and the customer. Are we in the awareness, conversion or engaged phase? How do I change my mode of engagement accordingly? Am I in a position to make the communication more relevant and individuated as the engagement deepens?

Q. What process do you recommend for getting the right creative for your audience?

Mike O'Brien: We need to help everyone involved in creating campaigns to see the world from the customer's perspective. We have a tribe of young digital creative specialists trying to communicate with an increasingly ageing population and the apparent disconnect is as misguided as Saga sending me a 'Welcome to the Club' mailing on my 50th birthday that all but suggested the onset of incontinence pants was imminent.

The root of this kind of creative incongruence is a lack of empathy and life experience and, to make matters worse, an industry-wide inability to bridge the gap through informative and inspirational briefing. I see far too many briefs written with little or no enthusiasm for the task, an optimistically heroic focus on the brand, product or service, a patronising and meagre view of the customer and an abundance of cut and paste edits from earlier scribbles and brain dumps.

So, let's look for briefs that are 80 per cent customer and 20 per cent us. Let's make sure that campaigns can be segmented into groups that allow us to create very specific responses to very specific audiences. Out there in the world of the customer are rich sources of unique campaign ideas that are relevant, original and impactful waiting to be discovered.

Q. With the walled garden of Facebook a component of many campaigns do you think this hinders campaign creative?

Mike O'Brien: No. Facebook can be a great source of inspiration to the creative thinker. What better chance to engage with the language, visual culture and interests of the customer? As a young creative 30 years ago, I would have needed to virtually invent the world of the customer or, frankly, be indifferent to any reality that existed

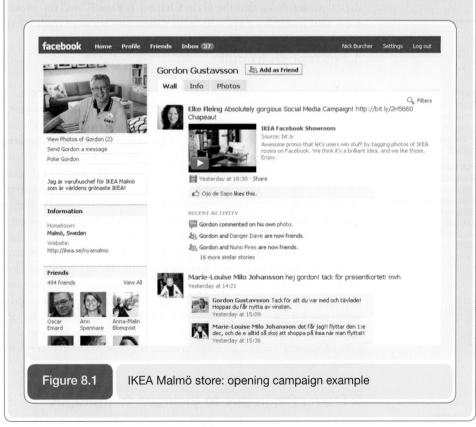

| Figure 8.1 | IKEA Malmö store: opening campaign example |

outside of my elitist agency experience. I'm not sure a lot has changed. Perhaps social marketing will help to bridge the gap. One campaign that works the social channel brilliantly is the IKEA Malmö store campaign (Figure 8.1).

When IKEA launched a brand new store in Malmö, Sweden, their agency chose to use an existing and very popular platform (Facebook) and technology (photo tagging) in an innovative way. They created a Facebook account for Gordon Gustavsson, the General Manager of the new store. Over the course of two weeks, they added a dozen photos of in-store showrooms filled with IKEA products. Once the first photo was posted, they announced that people were free to tag the items in the photos, and the first person to tag an item would win said item. By tagging the photos, they would appear on the taggers' profile pages, links and news feeds, therefore exposing the 'campaign' to all of their Facebook friends. Soon everybody was anticipating the next photo in the series, spreading the word about the IKEA promotion. This is a stunning example of facilitated leverage campaigns built around ideas that see customers as an integral part of the creative process. If you make an idea sufficiently engaging the customers will do the heavy lifting for you.

The characteristics of digital media

By understanding the key interactive communications characteristics enabled through digital media we can exploit these media while guarding against their weaknesses. In this section, we will describe eight key changes in the media characteristics between traditional and digital media. Note that the 6Is in Chapter 1 (page 37 and on) provide an alternative framework that is useful for evaluating the differences between traditional media and new media.

1 From push to pull

Push media
Communications are broadcast from an advertiser to consumers of the message, who are passive recipients.

Pull media and inbound marketing
The consumer is proactive in actively seeking out a solution and interactions with brands and are attracted through content, search and social media marketing.

Traditional media such as print, TV and radio are **push media** – one-way streets where information is mainly unidirectional, from company to customer, unless direct response elements are built in. In contrast, many digital marketing activities like content, search and social media marketing involve **pull media and inbound marketing**. Among marketing professionals this powerful new approach to marketing is now commonly known as inbound marketing (introduced in Chapter 1) (Shah and Halligan, 2009). Inbound marketing is powerful since advertising wastage is reduced. It involves applying content and search marketing to target prospects with a defined need – they are proactive and self-selecting. But this is a weakness since marketers may have less control than in traditional communications where the message is pushed out to a defined audience and can help generate awareness and demand. Advocates of inbound marketing argue that content, social media and search marketing do have a role to play in generating demand. The implications are that stimuli to encourage online interactions are still important through online or traditional ads, direct mail, physical reminders or encouraging word-of-mouth. 'Push' from email marketing remains important and is part of the inbound or permission marketing approach (Chapter 6): it should be an aim of websites and social media presences to capture customers' email addresses in order that opt-in email can be used to push relevant and timely messages to customers.

2 From monologue to dialogue to trialogue

Interactivity
The medium enables a dialogue between company and customer.

Creating a dialogue through **interactivity** is the next important feature of the web and digital media which provide the opportunity for two-way interaction with the customer.

This is a key distinguishing feature of the medium according to Peters (1998), and Deighton (1996) proclaimed the interactive benefits of the Internet as a means of developing long-term relationships with customers through what would later be defined as permission marketing by Godin (1999).

Walmsley (2007) believes that the main impact of digital media has not been to find new ways to connect brands to consumers as originally anticipated, but in connecting those consumers to each other. In the age of **trialogue**; brands need to reinterpret themselves as facilitators. Walmsley believes this trialogue will influence every aspect of marketing, from product design through to product recommendation. An example where product design is influenced is **Threadless.com**, the online T-shirt store, which only carries designs its users have uploaded, and manufactures only those that get a critical mass of votes (see Figure 8.2).

3 From one-to-many to one-to-some and one-to-one

Traditional push communications are one-to-many, from one company to many customers, often the same message to different segments and often poorly targeted. With digital media 'one-to-some' – reaching a niche or micro-segment becomes more practical – e-marketers can afford to tailor and target their message to different segments through providing different site content or email for different audiences through **mass customisation** and **personalisation** (Chapter 6).

Figure 8.3 illustrates the opportunities for mass customisation as interaction occurs between an organisation (O) communicating a message (M) to customers (C) for a single-step flow of communication. It is apparent that for traditional mass marketing in (a) a single message (M_1) is communicated to all customers (C_1 to C_5).

Trialogue
The interaction between company, customer and other customers facilitated through online community, social networks, reviews and comments.

Mass customisation
The creation of tailored marketing messages or products for individual customers or groups of customers typically using technology to retain the economies of scale and the capacity of mass marketing or production.

Personalisation
Web-based personalisation involves delivering customised content for the individual through web pages, email or push technology.

| Figure 8.2 | Threadless (www.threadless.com) |

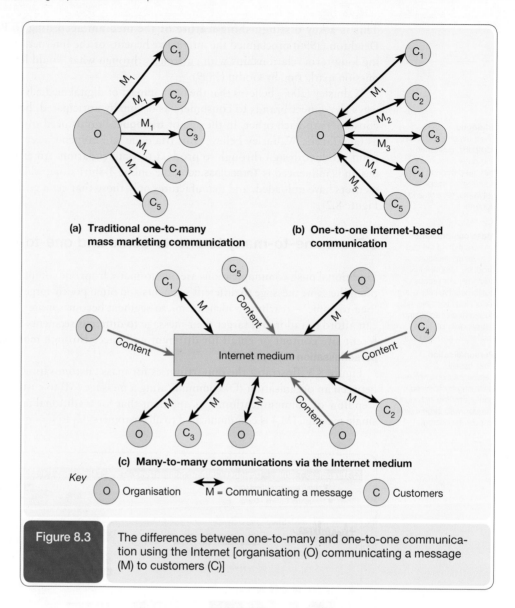

(a) **Traditional one-to-many mass marketing communication**

(b) **One-to-one Internet-based communication**

(c) **Many-to-many communications via the Internet medium**

Key

O Organisation   M = Communicating a message   C Customers

Figure 8.3	The differences between one-to-many and one-to-one communication using the Internet [organisation (O) communicating a message (M) to customers (C)]

Hoffman and Novak (1997) believed that this change was significant enough to represent a new model for marketing, or a new 'marketing paradigm' (Figure 8.3 (c)). They suggest that the facilities of the Internet, including the web, represent a computer-mediated environment in which the interactions are not between the sender and receiver of information, but with the medium itself. Their vision of the future is now apparent in the popularity of social networks, blogs and specialist communities.

> consumers can interact with the medium, firms can provide content to the medium, and in the most radical departure from traditional marketing environments, consumers can provide commercially-orientated content to the media.

4 From one-to-many to many-to-many communications

Digital media also enable many-to-many communications. Hoffman and Novak (1996) noted that new media are many-to-many media. Here customers can interact with other customers via a website, in independent communities or on their personal websites and blogs. We will see in the section on online PR that the implications of many-to-many communications are a loss of control of communications requiring monitoring of information sources, but it opens more opportunities to reach out to influencers to expand reach.

5 From 'lean-back' to 'lean-forward'

Digital media are also intense media – they are interactive, lean-forward media where the customer wants to be in control and wants to experience flow and responsiveness to their needs. First impressions and devices to encourage the visitor to interact are important. If the visitor to your site does not find what they are looking for immediately, whether through poor design or slow speed, they will move on, probably never to return.

6 The medium changes the nature of standard marketing communications tools such as advertising

Pay-for-performance communications
The wastage from traditional media buys can be reduced online through advertising models where the advertisers only pay for a response (cost-per-click) as in pay-per-click search marketing or for a lead or sale as in affiliate marketing.

In addition to offering the opportunity for one-to-one marketing, the Internet can be, and widely still is, used for one-to-many advertising. The website or social media site can be considered as similar in function to an advertisement (since it can inform, persuade and remind customers about the offering, although it is not paid for in the same way as a traditional advertisement). Berthon *et al.* (1996) consider a website as a mix between advertising and direct selling since it can also be used to engage the visitor in a dialogue. Constraints on advertising in traditional mass media, such as paying for time or space, become less important. The wastage in traditional advertising where ads are either ignored or are not relevant for an audience is reduced in online marketing and search marketing in particular. In pay-per-click (PPC) advertising, display of ads can be controlled according to user need based on what searchers are looking for and cost is only incurred where interest is indicated by a click. Affiliate marketing is also a **pay-for-performance communications** technique where cost is only incurred where there is a response.

Peters (1998) suggested that communication via the new medium is differentiated from communication using traditional media in four ways. First, *communication style* is changed with *immediate*, or synchronous, transfer of information through online customer service. Asynchronous communication, where there is a time delay between sending and receiving information as through email, also occurs. Second, *social presence* or the feeling that a communications exchange is sociable, warm, personal and active may be lower if a standard web page is delivered, but can be enhanced, perhaps by personalisation. Third, the consumer has more *control of contact*; and fourth the user has control of *content*, for example through personalisation facilities or posting their own user-generated content.

Although Hoffman and Novak (1996) pointed out that with the Internet the main relationships are not *directly* between sender and receiver of information, but with the web-based environment, the classic communications model of Schramm (1955) can still be used to help understand the effectiveness of marketing communication using the Internet. Figure 8.4 shows the model applied to the Internet. Four of the elements of the model that can constrain the effectiveness of Internet marketing are:

- *Encoding* – this is the design and development of the site content or email that aims to convey the message of the company, and is dependent on understanding of the target audience.
- *Noise* – this is the external influence that affects the quality of the message; in an Internet context this can be slow download times, the use of plug-ins that the user cannot use or confusion caused by too much information on-screen.
- *Decoding* – this is the process of interpreting the message, and is dependent on the cognitive ability of the receiver, which is partly influenced by the length of time they have used the Internet.
- *Feedback* – this occurs through online forms and through monitoring of on-site behaviour through web analytics (Chapter 10).

| Figure 8.4 | The communications model of Schramm (1955) applied to the Internet |

7 Increase in communications intermediaries

If we contrast traditional advertising and PR with the options available in paid, owned and earned digital media, there is an increase in options to reach audiences online through a large number of options for media and influencers. Traditional radio channels, newspapers and print titles have migrated online, but in addition there are a vast number of online-only publishers, bloggers and individual sharing through social networks. The concept of the long tail (Chapter 5) also applies to websites in any sector. There are a handful of key sites, but many others can also be used to reach customers. The online marketer needs to select the most appropriate of this plethora of sites which customers visit to drive traffic to their website.

8 Integration

Although digital media have distinct characteristics compared to traditional media, it does not follow that we should concentrate our communications solely on digital media. Rather we should combine and integrate traditional and digital media according to their strengths as explained in Step 6 in this chapter.

9 Timing of campaign communications have additional 'always-on' and real-time marketing components

Always-on communications
Continuous investment in paid, owned and earned digital media to engage prospects and customers and meet purchase intent as they research products through search, social media and publisher sites.

Real-time marketing (and PR)
Brands develop an agile, proactive approach to PR, content marketing and advertising to participate in current news and trends to help increase their visibility and influence through positive brand mentions. They also develop a reactive approach to respond to negative brand mentions through social media reputation management.

Earlier in this chapter and in previous chapters we have described the need for '**always-on**' or continuous communications activity across paid, owned and earned media to tap into consumer intent to research new products through search engines, publisher sites and social media. Alongside this, investment in traditional 'burst' marketing campaigns is, of course, still needed to promote new products, seasonal promotions, brand engagement and demand (lead) generation. See Mini case study 8.2, which shows how a modern marketing campaign can blend offline experiential marketing with digital activation.

Another change in the timing of marketing campaigns and communications is from forward planning of campaigns to a more agile, dynamic approach now known as **real-time marketing (and PR)**. Online PR specialist David Meerman-Scott (2010) describes Real-time marketing this way.

Real-time means news breaks over minutes, not days. It means ideas percolate, then suddenly and unpredictably go viral to a global audience. It's when companies develop

Memes
An idea, theme or trend that engages an audience and spreads through viral communications.

Newsjacking
A publisher or other brand seeks to take advantage of current topical interest in a story and then add to or subvert it to increase their own publicity.

(or refine) products or services instantly, based on feedback from customers or events in the marketplace. And it's when businesses see an opportunity and are the first to act on it.

Although not mentioned in the Meerman-Scott definition, social media and word-of-mouth are typically the means by which news and ideas spread virally. Brands can be proactive in creating their own viral news, **memes** or storytelling through campaigns to make proactive use of real-time marketing such as through **newsjacking**, but also need to be reactive when their brand is presented negatively. This is part of reputation management and crisis communications which are described in the next chapter in the sections on online PR and social media.

Mini case study 8.2	Evian uses uses real-time social media to create an impact in New York, London and Paris

Evian began this real-time, local marketing campaign over three days in August 2014 under the hashtag #Evianbottleservice. In New York it targeted consumers in city parks like Bryant Park and Madison Square Park at hot times of day (http://youtu.be/4EscVUOoFTw). AdWeek (2014) explained how to participate in the programme: consumers had to use the hashtag to tweet a message to Evian describing their current location. Evian's community managers, social media agency Team Epiphany, and staffers from PR company Edelman then responded to the tweets, triggering a team of brand ambassadors on the streets to deliver a bottle of water within five to seven minutes to each participant. Evian also bought Promoted Tweets to target postcodes around the neighbourhoods to amplify the real-time efforts (Figure 8.5).

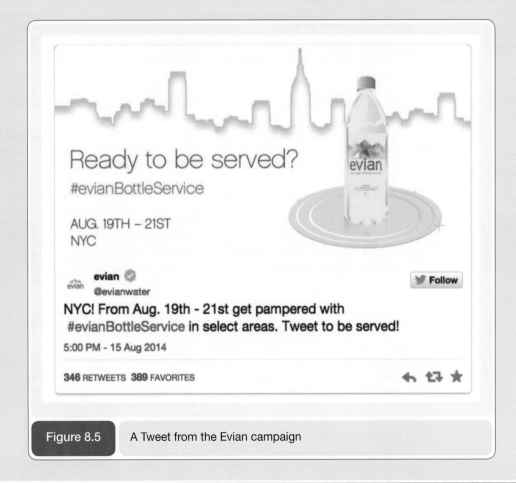

Figure 8.5	A Tweet from the Evian campaign

A week after the Manhattan campaign ended, the initiative spread to the Billie Jean King National Tennis Centre in Queens, NY as part of Evian's sponsorship of the US Open.

Before the campaign launched, Evian teased it via social media on 15 August, earning 147 followers per day to 21 August. The number of new followers represents an 11-fold increase from the same time period in July. Evian has roughly 19,200 followers on Twitter.

The water company also claims that there were 3.5 times more daily mentions of the brand between 15 and 21 August compared to competitors. And, the engagement on tweets passed the benchmark for CPG brands by 80 per cent. Overall, 2.8 million impressions and 75,000 engagements were generated on Twitter.

We conclude this section with our summary of some of the main differences between traditional and digital media (Table 8.1) and a review of how consumers perceive the Internet in comparison to traditional media (Digital marketing insight 8.1).

Table 8.1	Summary of differences in characteristics of traditional media and digital media (note that rows 10–12 are similarities between the two media types

Traditional media	Digital media
1 Push emphasis (e.g. TV and print ads and direct mail)	Pull emphasis. Relevance to context (search engine marketing (SEM))
2 One-way communications	Dialogue and interactivity and trialogue through user-generated content (UGC)
3 Targeting cost constrained by media placements	Micro-targeting and personalisation through SEM and media placements on niche sites
4 Limited customer-to-customer interactions	Participation: through communities and social networks
5 Static campaigns – once campaigns have been booked with a media agency it is difficult to adjust them	Dynamic campaigns where it is possible to test alternative creative and targeting and then revise during campaign according to performance
6 Burst campaigns maximise ad impact over a short period	Continuous, 'always-on' media where a permanent 'real-time' presence is required in online media (e.g. in search, social media and on publishers sites)
7 Limited media-buying opportunities with high degree of wastage	Limitless paid media-buying opportunities with pay-per-performance options plus owned and earned media (see Chapter 1 for definitions)
8 Detailed response measurement often limited to qualitative research	Potentially measurable at micro-level through web analytics and ad tracking systems
9 Pre-testing	Can also test and refine during campaign
10 Most communications to reach audience via media owners	Media owners are still important but communications also possible via website and non-media-owned blogs and social networks
11 Integrated communications vital	Integrated communications vital
12 Not cheap, quick or easy	Not cheap, quick or easy

| Digital marketing insight 8.1 | Consumer perceptions of the Internet and different media |

This study was completed when the web was a relatively new medium, but it's still worth referencing since it contrasts the differences between different media channels well. Review whether you think these differences remain valid in this era when social media marketing is dominant. Branthwaite *et al.* (2000) conducted a global qualitative project covering a sample of 18–35 year olds in 14 countries across North and South America, East and West Europe, Asia and Australia to investigate consumer perceptions of the Internet and other media. Consumers' perceptions of the Internet, when asked to explain how they felt about it in relation to different animals, were as follows:

The dominant sense here was of something exciting, but also inherently malevolent, dangerous and frightening in the Internet.

The positive aspect was expressed mainly through images of a bird but also a cheetah or dolphin. These captured the spirit of freedom, opening horizons, versatility, agility, effortlessness and efficiency.

In comparison with other media, the Internet was described as follows:

The Internet seemed less like a medium of communication than the others, and more like a reservoir of information.

This distinction was based on differences in the mode of operating: other media communicated to you whereas with the Internet the user had to actively seek and extract information for themselves. In this sense, the Internet is a recessive medium that sits waiting to be interrogated, whereas other media are actively trying to target their communications to the consumer.

Table 8.2 and Figure 8.6 present the final evaluation of the Internet against other media.

| Table 8.2 | Comparison of the properties of different media |

	TV	Outdoor	Print	Internet
Intrusiveness	High	High	Low	Low
Control/ selectivity	Passive	Passive	Active, selective	Active, selective of consumption
Episode attention	Long	Short	Long	Restless, fragmented span
Active processing	Low	Low	High	High
Mood	Relaxed, seeking exceptional gratification	Bored, under-stimulated	Relaxed, seeking interest, stimulation	Goal-orientated, needs-related
Modality	Audio/visual	Visual	Visual	Visual (auditory increasing)
Processing	Episodic, superficial	Episodic/ semantic	Semantic, deep	Semantic, deep
Context	As individual in interpersonal setting	Solitary (in public space)	Individual, personal	Alone, private

Source: Branthwaite et al. (2000)

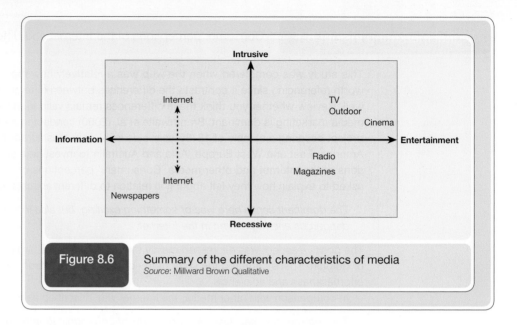

Figure 8.6	Summary of the different characteristics of media
	Source: Millward Brown Qualitative

We will now recommend a series of steps that can be used when taking a structured approach to planning an integrated campaign or an online customer acquisition plan. Our emphasis is to focus on how digital media will be managed when integrated with other media.

Step 1. Goal setting and tracking for interactive marketing communications

Digital marketers develop communications objectives for different timescales:

- *Annual marketing communications objectives*. For example, achieving new site visitors or gaining qualified leads could be measured across an entire year since this will be a continuous activity based on visitor building through search engines and other campaigns. Annual budgets are set to help achieve these objectives.
- *Campaign-specific communications objectives*. Digital marketing campaigns such as to support a product launch through online advertising and viral marketing. Specific objectives can be stated for each in terms of gaining new visitors, converting visitors to customers and encouraging repeat purchases. Campaign objectives should build on traditional marketing objectives, have a specific target audience and have measurable outcomes which can be attributed to the specific campaign.

The measures we cover in this section can be applied to both short and long term. More depth on tracking through analytics and the specific measures used for measuring social media ROI is available in Chapter 10.

Terminology for measuring digital campaigns

There are a bewildering series of terms used to set goals and track the effectiveness of digital campaigns, so we start this section by explaining the main measures you will encounter in models for campaign planning and reports from online campaigns. Remember that as we explained in the goal-setting section with regard to strategy in Chapter 4, it's important that when setting goals and tracking we go beyond the volume measures of visitors attracted to a site and use the full range of VQVC measures, that's Volume, Quality, Value and Cost of visitors.

Figure 8.7 shows different measures for goal setting and tracking digital media campaigns from least sophisticated to more sophisticated, as shown under the following headings.

0 Volume measures including clicks, visitor session and unique visitors

Visitor session (visit)
A series of one or more page impressions, served to one user, which ends when there is a gap of 30 minutes or more between successive page impressions for that user.

Traffic volume is usually measured as the number of click-throughs or visits to a site (**visitor sessions**) to a site or better **unique visitors**. Unique visitors is preferable to using page views or hits as a measure of effectiveness, since it represents opportunities to communicate with individuals but, as we will explain in Chapter 10, it may be technically difficult to calculate 'uniques' accurately as measurement is based on cookies. A more sophisticated measure is reach (%) or online audience share. This is only possible using panel data/audience data tools such as **www.netratings.com**, **www.comscore.com** or **www.hitwise.com**.

Unique visitor
Individual visitor to a site measured through cookies or the IP address on an individual computer.

Example: An online bank has 1 million unique visitors per month.

1 Quality measures including conversion rates to action and bounce rate

Visit or session conversion rate
An indication of the capability of a site in converting visitors to defined outcomes such as registration. Calculated by dividing the number of conversion events by the number of visitor sessions within a time period.

Traffic volume measures give no indication of whether the audience referred to the site engages with it or leaves straight away, so we need quality measures to show us this. Conversion rate is the best known quality measure which shows what proportion of visitors from different sources within a defined time period convert to specific marketing outcomes on the web, such as lead, sale or subscription.

Example: 10 per cent of visitors convert to an outcome such as logging in to their account, or asking for a quote for a product.

Conversion rates can be expressed in two different ways – at the visit level (**visit or session conversion rate**) or the unique visitor level (**visitor conversion rate**).

Eric Petersen (2004) explains it this way:

Visitor conversion rate
An indication of the capability of a site in converting visitors to defined outcomes such as registration. Calculated by dividing the number of conversion events by the number of unique visitors within a defined time period.

the denominator you use [to calculate conversion rate] will depend on whether you're trying to understand how people behave during visits or the people themselves. If you're

Step 6	Lifetime value
Step 5	Branding metrics
Step 4	Campaign ROI (%)
Step 3	Cost-per-acquisition (CPA)
Step 2	Cost = cost-per-click (CPC)
Step 1	Quality = conversion rate
Step 0.	Volume = unique visitors / Reach (%)

Figure 8.7   Measures used for setting campaign objectives or assessing campaign success increasing in sophistication from bottom to top

interested in people [and the overall buying process] use unique visitors, if you're interested in behaviour [on a single visit] use visits.

Examples:

$$\text{Visit conversion rate} = \frac{10 \text{ conversion events}}{1000 \text{ visits}} = 1\%$$

For an e-retailer this is the order conversion rate:

$$\text{Order conversion rate} = \frac{10 \text{ sales}}{1000 \text{ visits}} = 1\%$$

$$\text{Visitor conversion rate} = \frac{10 \text{ conversion events}}{800 \text{ visits}} = 1.25\%$$

For an e-retailer, this can be called the buyer conversion rate, also known as the browse-to-buy ratio or for a travel company 'look to book':

$$\text{buyer conversion rate} = \frac{10 \text{ sales}}{800 \text{ unique visitors}} = 1.25\%$$

Bounce rate
Proportion of visitors to a page or site who exit after visiting a single page only, usually expressed as a percentage.

A related measure that is useful to monitor during campaigns is the **bounce rate** which indicates the proportion of referred visitors to a page or site who exit after visiting a single page only, usually expressed as a percentage (i.e. that arrive at the site and bounce off it since they don't discover relevance!).

Reviewing bounce or engagement rates can improve the effectiveness of landing pages and the quality of referrers to a page. The benefit of using bounce rates rather than conversion rates is that there is a much wider variation in bounce rates for a page (i.e. typically 20 to 80 per cent, compared to under 10 per cent), which enables problems with individual referrers, keywords or landing page conversions to be more readily identified. Bounce rates are calculated as follows:

$$\text{Bounce rate \%} = \frac{100 \times \text{single page visits to a page (or site)}}{\text{all visits starting on page (or site)}}$$

$$\text{Engagement rate \%} = (100 - \text{bounce rate \%})$$

2 Media cost measures including cost-per-click and cost-per-thousand

Cost-per-click (CPC)
The cost of each click from a referring site to a destination site, typically from a search engine in pay-per-click search marketing.

The cost of visitor acquisition is usually measured as the **cost-per-click (CPC)** specific to a particular digital media channel, such as pay-per-click search engine marketing, since it is difficult to estimate for an entire site with many visitors referred from offline advertising.

Example: £2 CPC (500 clicks delivered from Google Adwords costing £1000).

Cost-per-thousand (CPM)
The cost of placing an ad viewed by 1000 people.

Cost-per-thousand (CPM) ($M = mille$) is usually used as the currency when buying display ad space, for example, £10 CPM will mean that the ad will be served to 1000 visitors (technically visitor sessions). An effective CPM can also be calculated for other media channels, such as pay-per-click advertising, for comparison.

3 Acquisition cost measures including cost-per-action or acquisition

Cost-per-acquisition (CPA)
The cost of acquiring a new customer or achieving a sale. Typically limited to the communications cost and refers to cost per sale for new customers. May also refer to other outcomes such as cost per quote or enquiry.

A digital campaign will not be successful if it meets its objectives of acquiring site visitors and customers but the cost of achieving this is too high. So it is essential to have specific objectives and measures for the cost of using different digital media channels to drive visitors to the site and convert to transaction. This is stated as the **cost-per-acquisition (CPA)** (sometimes cost-per-action). Depending on context and market, CPA may refer to different outcomes. Typical cost targets include:

- cost-per-acquisition – of a visitor;
- cost-per-acquisition – of a lead;
- cost-per-acquisition – of a sale (most typical form of CPA, also known as CPS).

Allowable cost-per-acquisition
A target maximum cost for generating leads or new customer's profitably.

To control costs, it is important for managers to define a target **allowable cost-per-acquisition** such as £30 for generating a business lead or £50 for achieving sign-up to a credit card. When the cost of visitor acquisition is combined with conversion to outcomes this is the cost of (customer) acquisition.

Example: £20 CPA (for £2 CPC, 10% conversion with one-in-ten visits resulting in sale).

4 Return on investment (ROI) *or value* measures

Return on investment is used to assess the profitability of any marketing activity, or indeed any investment. You will also know that there are different forms of ROI, depending on how profitability is calculated. Here we will assume it is just based on sales value or profitability based on the cost per click and conversion rate.

$$ROI = \frac{profit\ generated\ from\ referrer}{amount\ spent\ on\ advertising\ with\ referrer}$$

A related measure, which does not take profitability into account is return on advertising spend (ROAS), which is calculated as follows:

$$ROAS = \frac{total\ revenue\ generated\ from\ referrer}{amount\ spent\ of\ advertising\ with\ referrer}$$

5 Branding measures

These tend to be most relevant to interactive advertising or sponsorship. They are the equivalent of offline advertising metrics, i.e. brand awareness (aided and unaided), ad recall, brand familiarity, brand favourability and purchase intent.

6 Lifetime value-based ROI measures

Here the value of gaining the customer is not just based on the initial purchase, but the lifetime value (and costs) associated with the customer. This requires more sophisticated models which can be most readily developed for online retailers and online financial services providers. The technique for the calculation of LTV was outlined in Chapter 6.

Example: A bank uses a net present value model for insurance products which looks at the value over ten years but whose main focus is on a five-year result and takes into account:

- acquisition cost;
- retention rates;
- claims;
- expenses.

This is valuable since it helps give them a realistic 'allowable cost per sale' which is needed to get a return over five years. They track this in great detail – for example, they will know the ROI of different Google Adwords keywords and will then select keyphrases and bid strategies accordingly.

Figure 8.8 shows an example of an online ad campaign for an insurance product placing many of the core volume, quality and cost measures covered in this section in context. Here an opportunity or lead is when a quote is requested. Note that the cost of acquisition is high but this does not take into account the synergies of online advertising with offline campaigns, i.e. those who are influenced by the ad, but do not click through immediately.

	Results	
REACH of e-communications	21,700,000	Ad impressions
	£700,000	Media cost
Attraction efficiency	0.23%	Click-through rate
	£32.26	Cost-per-mille/thousand (CPM/CPT)
Website VISITS	50,000	Clicks (approximately equivalent to visitors)
	£14.00	Cost-per-click (CPC)
Site conversion efficiency	33.40%	Conversion rate (Click to quote)
LEADS or opportunities generated	16,700	Opportunity response
	£41.92	Cost-per-opportunity (CPO)
Lead conversion efficiency	10.60%	Conversion rate (opportunity to sale)
Number of OUTCOMES delivered	1,770	Sales
	£395.58	Cost-per-sale (CPS)

Figure 8.8 An example of effectiveness measures for an online ad campaign

Examples of digital campaign measures

An interactive marketing communications plan should have five main types of goals included.

1 *Audience or traffic building goals.* These define targets for using **online site promotion** and **offline site promotion** to drive quality visitors or traffic to a website or other social presence which convert to the outcomes required (sales, lead, newsletter sign-up, social interaction) at an acceptable cost.

   Examples of **SMART traffic building** objectives which can be expressed as visitors, visits or sales:

   * Achieve 100,000 unique visitors or 200,000 visitor sessions within one year.
   * Deliver 20,000 online sales at an average order value of £50 and a cost-per-acquisition of £10.
   * Convert 30 per cent of existing customer base to active use (at least once every 90 days) of online service.
   * Achieve 10 per cent 'share of searches' within a market.

2 *Conversion or interaction goals.* Use onsite communications to deliver an effective message to the visitor which helps influence perceptions or achieves a required marketing outcome. The message delivered on-site will be based on traditional marketing communications objectives for a company's products or services. For example:

   * encourage trial (for example, achieve 10 per cent conversion of new unique visitors to registration or downloads of a music service such as iTunes or Spotify);

- build in-house permission-based list (increase email database by 10,000 during year through data capture activities);
- encourage engagement with content (conversion of 20 per cent of new unique visitors to product information area);
- persuade customer to purchase (conversion of 5 per cent of unique new visitors);
- encourage further purchases (conversion of 30 per cent of first-time buyers to repeat purchasers within a six-month period).

To estimate a realistic number of conversions, we recommend creating conversion-based models like that shown in Figure 8.9. Take, for example, the objectives of a campaign for a B2B services company such as a consultancy company, where the ultimate objective is to achieve 1000 new clients using the website in combination with traditional media to convert leads to action. To achieve this level of new business, the marketer will need to make assumptions about the level of conversion that is needed at each stage of converting prospects to customers. This gives a core objective of 1000 new clients and different critical success factors based on the different conversion rates.

If there are no products available for sale online, such as a luxury car manufacturer or a high-value B2B service offering white paper downloads, then it is less clear how to calculate ROI.

To get the most from campaigns which don't result in sales online and optimise their effectiveness, it is useful to put a value or points score on different outcomes – for example in the case of the car manufacturer, values could be assigned to brochure requests (5 points or £20), demonstration drive requests (20 points or £100) or simply visits to the site involving reviewing product features information (1 point or £1). This approach is known as value event scoring.

Through knowing the average percentage of online brochure requests or demo drive requests that convert to sales, and the average order value for customers referred from the website, then the value of these on-site outcomes can be estimated. This is only an estimate, but it can help inform campaign optimisation, by showing which referring sites, creative or PPC keywords and pages visited on the site are most likely to generate desirable outcomes. Mini case study 8.3 gives an example of different types of events for a photo-sharing site.

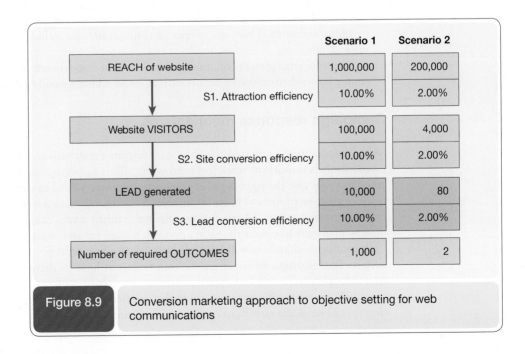

	Scenario 1	Scenario 2
REACH of website	1,000,000	200,000
S1. Attraction efficiency	10.00%	2.00%
Website VISITORS	100,000	4,000
S2. Site conversion efficiency	10.00%	2.00%
LEAD generated	10,000	80
S3. Lead conversion efficiency	10.00%	2.00%
Number of required OUTCOMES	1,000	2

Figure 8.9 Conversion marketing approach to objective setting for web communications

---

Mini case study 8.3	Spanish photo-sharing website measures value events

Fotonatura (**www.fotonatura.org**), a Spanish photo-sharing website, uses these micro-conversion goals in Google Analytics which give an overall conversion rate of 1.72 per cent:

- Goal 1 – Registration (503 conversions)
- Goal 2 – Photo publication (3788 conversions)
- Goal 3 – Premium service registration (9 conversions)
- Goal 4 – Camera sales page (1049 conversions)

Source: Kaushik (2008)

---

3 *Third-party site reach and branding goals.* Reach, influence and engage with prospective customers on third-party sites such as online news and magazines sites, portals and social networks.

- Reach a targeted audience of 500,000 during the campaign.
- Create awareness of a product or favourability towards a brand (measured through brand research of brand awareness, brand favourability or purchase intent through using an online brand-tracking service such as Dynamic Logic, **www.dynamic logic.com**).

4 *Multichannel marketing goals.* Integrate all communications methods to help achieve marketing objectives by supporting mixed-mode buying.

> Examples of **mixed-mode buying** objectives:

Mixed-mode buying
The customer's purchase decision is influenced by a range of media such as print, TV and Internet.

- Achieve 20 per cent of sales achieved in the call centre as a result of website visits.
- Achieve 20 per cent of online sales in response to offline adverts.
- Increase average amount spent in store for every active site visitor from £3 to £4.
- Reduce contact-centre phone enquiries by 15 per cent by providing online customer services.

5 *Longer-term brand engagement goals.* One of the biggest challenges of online marketing, indeed marketing through any channel, is to sustain long-term interactions leading to additional sales. These are measured through lifetime value, loyalty and customer interactions.

> Customer engagement communication shows the importance of capturing and maintaining up-to-date customer details such as email addresses and mobile phone numbers.

Campaign response mechanisms

Digital media have increased the choice of response mechanisms. Reviewing response mechanisms is important since too narrow may limit response, but too broad and unfocused may not give the right types of response – marketers need to emphasise the response types or customer journeys most favourable to the overall success of the campaign in their creative and messaging. Policies for response mechanism across campaigns should be specified by managers to ensure the right approach is used for all campaigns.

Response mechanisms will naturally vary depending on type of product. So, brands such as fast-moving consumer goods brands do not have to drive visitors to their own site; through advertising and creating interactive microsites on third-party sites, they can potentially be more effective in reaching their audience who are more likely to spend their time on online media sites than on destination brand sites.

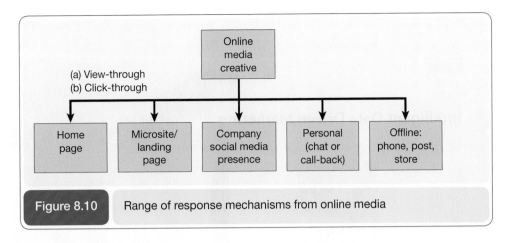

| Figure 8.10 | Range of response mechanisms from online media |

Online response mechanism

The required response mechanisms should be specified in the digital campaign plan and the number of responses from each model. Figure 8.10 suggests the typical options of outcomes to online campaign media. From the creative shown using media such as a display ad, pay-per-click ad or rented email newsletter, there are five main options.

1 Home page

In the majority of cases, investment in online media will be wasted if visitors are driven from the **media site** to the home page of the **destination website**. Typically it is appealing to many audiences and offering too much choice – it won't effectively reinforce the message of the online creative or convert to further action.

2 Microsite/landing page

A focussed **landing page** or specially created microsite can more effectively convert visitors to the action to help gain a return on the online campaign investment. Figure 8.11 shows an example of a landing page giving a range of response mechanisms, although offline is omitted. A **URL strategy** is used to make the page easy to label in offline creative. This specifies how different types of content on a site will be placed in different folders or directories of a website (this can also help with search engine optimisation). For example, if you visit the BBC site (**www.bbc.co.uk**), look at how the web address details vary as you move from one section to another such as News or Sport. An individual destination page on a website may be labelled, for example, **www.company.com/products/insurance/car-insurance**. A further example is where site owners have to make a decision how to refer to content in different countries, either in the form:

    http://<country-name>.<company-name>.com

or the more common

    http://www.<companyname.com>.com/<country-name>

Campaign URLs or CURLs are less widely used today, the idea being that they will be more memorable than the standard company address and blend in with the campaign concept. For example, an insurer used the CURL **www.quotemehappy.com**, which represents memorable elements of the campaign. Also memorable is **www.subservientchicken.com** – a viral hit from ten years ago for Burger King and reinvigorated for 2015 under the hashtag #ChickenRedemption.

Media site
Typical location where paid-for ads are placed.

Destination website
Site typically owned by a retailer or manufacturer brand which users are encouraged to click through to.

Landing page
A destination page when a user clicks on an ad or other form of link from a referring site. It can be a home page but more typically and desirably, it is a page with the messaging focussed on the offer in the ad. This will maximise conversion rates and brand favourability.

URL strategy
A defined approach to how content is labelled through placing it in different directories or folders with distinct web addresses.

Campaign URL or CURL
A web address specific to a particular campaign.

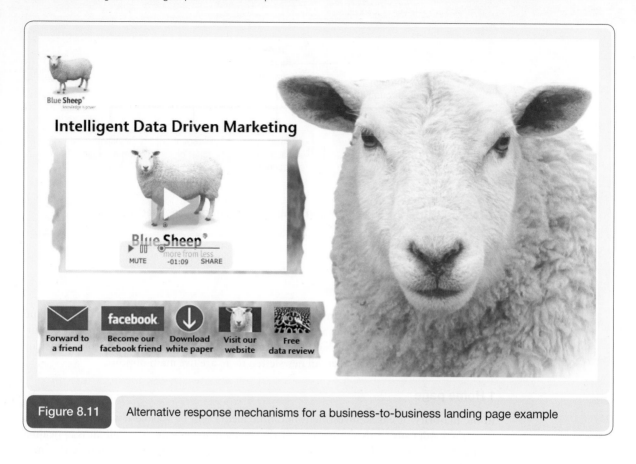

| **Figure 8.11** | Alternative response mechanisms for a business-to-business landing page example |

3 Personal (chat or call-back)

Call-back service
A facility available on the website for a company to contact a customer at a later time as specified by the customer.

In this case the creative or landing page encourages campaign respondents to 'talk' directly with a human operator. It is usually referred to as a **call-back service** and integrates web and phone. Buttons or hyperlinks encourage a call-back from a telephone operator or an online chat. The advantage of this approach is that it engages the customer more and will typically lead to a higher conversion-to-sale rate since the customer's questions and objections are more likely to be answered and the personal engagement is more likely to encourage a favourable impression.

4 Offline: phone, post or store

Because part of a campaign is run online does not mean that offline responses should be excluded. Offline response mechanisms should not be discarded unless the cost of managing them cannot be justified, which is rarely the case.

Offline response goals for multichannel integration

Web response model
The website is used as a response mechanism for offline campaign elements such as direct mail or advertising.

We also need to include the right response mechanism for the offline media element of the campaigns such as TV ads, print ads or direct-mail pieces. The permission-based **web response model** is one that is frequently used today in direct marketing (Chapter 6). For example, this process could start with a direct mail drop or offline advert. The website is used as the direct response mechanism, hence 'web response'. Ideally, this approach will use targeting of different segments. For example, a Netherlands bank devised a campaign targeting six different segments based on age and income. The initial letter was delivered by post and contained a PIN (personal identification number) which had to be typed in

| Digital marketing insight 8.2 | What's in a hashtag – #! |

No major campaign today is complete without a hashtag, but where did the trend start? Here's the timeline:

- August 2007 – Hashtags first proposed for use on Twitter
- July 2009 – Twitter officially embraces the hashtag linking to a list of all tweets for anything proceeded by #
- January 2011 – Instagram adds hashtag support
- Spring 2011 – Twitter plays a role in the civil unrest of the Arab Spring. #Bahrain becomes one of the most used hashtags of all time
- October 2011 – Google+ begins automatically linking all hashtags in posts
- January 2013 – Half of Superbowl ads include a hashtag
- June 2013 – Facebook begins supporting hashtags
- October 2013 – celebrity use of Twitter for ads (discussed in Chapter 3). The Advertising Standards Authority (UK) and the Federal Trade Commission (USA) state that adverts made via a celebrities Twitter page should incorporate the hashtag '#ad'.

Hashtags can help make the connection between a social media concept and a campaign such as an offer or regular content. Some social media users follow specialist hashtags so they can help a little in increasing visibility.

Which are your favourite or memorable hashtags? A good way to investigate them is through searching on a brand in Twitter. We think @ASOS makes good use of them to feature regular offers and events. For example #OOTD and #UNiDAYSXASOS. Here are some examples of how they work them into their copy:

- There's £500 up for grabs, whoop! RT& follow for your chance to win #ASOSMidseasonsale. http://asos.to/SVWvYq
- Countdown for #ASOSonXfactor. Free garms, just for seeing us on your fave TV show – sweet
- HURRY, the #ASOSDailyEdit competition finishes real soon.
- Fun#LookOfTheDay (and Halloween outfit inspiration): http://goo.gl/xKqKm@DelevingnePoppy
- Who wants to see a private screening of #DarkShadowsDVD? Tweet a pic of how you style the gothic trend using #ASOSLoves to win tickets.

when the customer visited the site. The PIN had the dual benefit that it could be used to track responses to the campaign, while at the same time personalising the message to the consumer. When the PIN was typed in, a 'personal page' was delivered for the customer with an offer that was appropriate to their particular circumstances.

Step 2. Campaign insight

Client discovery process
An initiative to learn what a client or brands needs from a campaign, their strategic initiatives which it must align with, their goals and their marketing outcomes.

Research into the target audience and how they select products and services within the marketplace is core to a campaign planning approach. When a company is working with an agency, the marketer at the client company will incorporate initial customer insight into a brief as part of the agency completing a **client discovery process**. This will give agency staff valuable information about the audience and marketplace.

Fill (2007) describes this stage of communications planning as context analysis. He identifies these aspects of context which should be researched:

- *Customer context* including dimensions of segment characteristics; levels of awareness, perception and attitudes towards the brand or organisation; level of involvement; types of perceived risk and influence of different members of the decision-making unit.
- *Business context* including corporate and marketing strategy and plans; brand/organisation analysis and competitor analysis.
- *Internal context* including financial constraints; organisation identity; culture, value and beliefs; marketing expertise; agency availability and suitability.
- *External context* including key stakeholders; communications and needs; social, political, economic, legal and technological restraints and opportunities.

So, the context analysis references all existing plans such as business and marketing plans, internal and external information sources. Information from these will be collated and put into a campaign brief.

More detailed campaign insight will be accessed and analysed once the agency or internal team are working on the campaign. Large agencies use 'data planners' or 'customer communications planners' to review all available external data sources such as market, audience and internal data on customer profiles, past campaign results on the most effective channels in generating product sales to assist clients in strategic development and execution of campaigns. This data is then used to inform campaign targeting and media selection.

For example, a brief might specify that a FMCG client wants to run an online promotional campaign, with the goal of stimulating trial of products and adding to a prospect database through encouraging online registration. The campaign strategy or offer is based around offering daily prizes. The data planner involved uses all transactional data collected from previous similar campaigns campaign to be linked to socio-demographic data which is coupled with transactional information.

Customer insight for digital marketing campaigns

There is a wealth of customer insight information available for digital marketing campaigns, but it varies by sector. So it is important during the briefing or pre-planning stage to list all the possible information sources and then evaluate which are worthwhile, since some are free and some are paid syndicated research. We have introduced many of the techniques in Chapter 2, such as persona and customer scenario analysis, and also some of the information sources (see Table 2.2, Research tools for assessing digital markets).

Examples of the types of customer insight related to online competitor and audience behaviour that might be accessed at this stage in the campaign from third-party syndicated research sources include:

- *Site audience reach and composition.* What is the breakdown of audiences by age, gender or socio-economic group on different sites? This data is available from online audience panel providers such as Nielsen Netrating, Comscore and Hitwise.
- *Online buying behaviour and preferences.* For example, from the Forrester Internet User Monitor or **TGI.net**. In the UK, **TGI.net** gives information on typical product preferences for a particular site – for example, the percentage of the audience whose last holiday was a city break. Additional surveys can be conducted via publisher sites.
- *Customer media consumption.* The usage of different offline and online media for different target demographics can be accessed from sources such as Hitwise.
- *Customer search behaviour.* The proportion of different phrases and their importance can be used to inform messaging.
- *Competitor campaign activity.* The activity of current advertising campaigns and previous seasonal campaigns. For example, in the UK, this is available from Thomson Intermedia.

- *Competitor performance.* This will give information on the audience size (reach) and composition of competitor sites and services like Hitwise can show which marketing techniques such as search engine marketing or affiliate marketing are successful in driving visitors to a competitor since referring sites and search terms can be accessed.

Wertime and Fenwick (2008) suggest a similar technique to persona development (see Chapter 7) for campaigns which they describe as a 'participant print'. The main elements of the participant print are:

- *General profile.* This is basic demographic and psychographic information about customers. It may also include insight from previous online campaigns and activities such as search keywords and propensity to respond for different demographic groups (response rates).
- *Digital profile.*
  - *Digital usage habits.* The authors say this includes the usage of different digital media channels, types of sites used and digital platforms they use.
  - *Content consumption preferences.* This includes favoured sources of information related to the product category from portals specific to the product, comparison sites and specialist blogs.
  - *Content creation profile.* This reviews the propensity of the group to participate online. For example, in contests where they upload photos or ringtones, blogs or forums they comment on including neutral sites and competitor sites.
- *Individual profiles.* This is information about existing prospects and customers including profile information from customer databases, content preferences from web analytics and qualitative research with customers about their needs, wants and how they prefer to use digital channels.

An example of the type of in-depth research available is the IPA Touchpoints survey which covers both surveyed usage of websites and other media, and opinions including why they use particular media. Hussein (2006) describes the purpose of this – he says the aim is to enable campaign planners to identify relevant target markets (demographic groups, attitudinal groups, activity groups, and so on) and fully understand them in terms of:

- how they spend their day (shopping, work, travelling);
- who they spend it with (friends, family, work colleagues);
- what they believe in (views and opinions on life, brands, media, advertising);
- what is important to them (time spent on activities, family values);
- how, when, where and why they consume particular media.

Further information on marketplace analysis, including links to the main data sources for digital campaign insights, is provided in Table 2.3.

Step 3. Segmentation and targeting

Campaign targeting strategy defines the target audience or type of people that you need to reach with your campaign communications. It's about defining, selecting and reaching specific audiences online. Targeting methods vary according to the market, campaign and e-communications tools involved. The key targeting issues to define for the online elements of a campaign are:

- quality of insight about customer or prospect available to assist with targeting;
- range of variables or parameters used to target – e.g. audience characteristics, value, needs and behaviours;
- identifying the targeting attributes or variables which will influence response;

- specific targeting approaches available for the key e-communications tools – e.g. online advertising, search engine marketing and email marketing.

The targeting approaches used for acquisition and retention campaigns will naturally depend on established segmentations and knowledge about customers. (We have also discussed targeting approaches from a strategic basis in Chapters 4 and 6.) From a campaign point of view, Table 8.3 shows some of the main targeting variables which can be reviewed in digital campaign planning.

Let's look at each targeting variable in a little more depth.

1 *Relationship with company*. Campaigns will often be intended to target new contacts *or* existing contacts. But remember, some communications – such as e-newsletters and email campaigns – will reach both. Marketers have to consider whether it will be cost-effective to have separate communications for new, existing and lapsed contacts – or to target each of these groups in the same communications but using different content aimed at each.

    When visitors click through to your website from online and offline campaigns, copy should be presented that recognises the relationship or, again, provides a range of content to recognise each different relationship. Visit Microstrategy (**www.microstrategy. com**) to see how its registration page establishes the relationship.

2 *Demographic segmentation*. This is typically based on age, gender or social group. Online demographics are often used as the basis for which sites to purchase display advertising or for renting email lists. Demographics can also be used to limit or focus who pay-per-click search ads are displayed to.

3 *Psychographic or attitudinal segmentation*. This includes attitudes to risk and value when buying – e.g. early adopter, brand loyal or price conscious. It is less straightforward to target on these attributes of a consumer since it is easier to buy media based on demographic breakdown. However, certain sites may be more suitable for reaching a particular psychographic audience. The psychographic characteristics of the audience

Table 8.3	A range of targeting and segmentation approaches for a digital campaign
Targeting variable	**Examples of online targeting attributes**
1 Relationship with company	New contacts (prospects), existing customers, lapsed customers
2 Demographic segmentation	B2C: Age, gender, social group, geographic location B2B: Company size, industry served, individual members of decision-making unit
3 Psychographic or attitudinal segmentation	Attitudes to risk and value when buying, e.g. early adopter, brand loyal or price conscious
4 Value	Assessment of current or historical value and future value
5 Lifecycle stage	Position in lifecycle, related to value and behaviour, i.e. time since initial registration, number of products purchased, categories purchased in
6 Behaviour	Search term entered into search engine Responsiveness to different types of offers (promotion or product type). Responsiveness to campaigns in different channels (channel preference). Purchase history in product categories including recency, frequency and monetary value (Chapter 6)

are still an important part of the brief, to help develop particular messages. It is possible to collect attitudinal information on a site and add it to the customer profile. For example, Wells Fargo asks investors to select:

- the type of investment preferred (individual stocks or mutual funds); and
- what type of investor best describes you? (aggressive growth to more cautious).

4 *Value*. The higher-value customers (indicated by higher average order value and higher modelled customer lifetime values) will often warrant separate communications with different offers. Sometimes digital channels are not the best approach for these customers – relationship managers will want direct contact with their most valuable customers; while digital channels are used to communicate more cost-effectively with lower value customers. It is also worth considering reducing the frequency of emails to this audience.

5 *Lifecycle stage*. This is very useful where customers follow a particular sequence in buying or using a service, such as online grocery shopping or online banking. As explained in Chapter 6, automated, event-triggered email marketing can be developed for this audience. For example, bank First Direct uses a six-month welcome strategy based on email and direct mail communications. For other campaigns, the status of a customer can be used for targeting – for example not purchased or used service, purchased once, purchased more than five times and active, purchased more than five times and inactive, etc.

6 *Behavioural*. Behavioural targeting is one of the big opportunities provided by digital marketing. It involves assessing customers' past actions in following links, reading content, using online services or buying products, and then follows up on these with a more relevant message based on the propensity to act estimated on the previous action.

Online options for behavioural targeting can be illustrated by a travel company such as **lastminute.com**:

- *Pay-per-click search engine marketing* makes targeting possible according to the type of keyphrase typed when a potential customer searches for information. A relevant ad specific to a holiday destination the prospect is looking for –e.g. 'Hotel New York' – can then be shown.
- *Display advertising* makes behavioural targeting possible since cookies can be used to track visitors across a site or between sites and display relevant ads. If a site user visits the travel section of a newspaper site, then the ad about 'lastminute' can be served as they visit other content on this site, or potentially on other sites.
- *Email marketing* can be targeted based on customer preferences indicated by links they have clicked on. For example, if a user has clicked a link on a holiday in North America, then a targeted email can be delivered relevant to this product or promotion. More sophisticated analysis based on RFM (Recency, Frequency and Monetary value) analysis (Chapter 6) can also be used.

When reviewing the options for which variables to use, the campaign planner must keep in mind that those selected for targeting should be those that are most likely to influence the level of response for the campaign. It is possible to target on many variables, but the incremental benefit of targeting on additional variables may not be worth the cost and effort. Figure 6.9 (page 322) indicates the general improvement in campaign response dependent on the type of targeting variables used.

Within digital media campaigns there are many options for targeting which we will explore in more detail in the next chapter, for example:

1 *Targeting using search marketing*. Targeting via intent or the types of keywords people search on as they look for products, information or experiences.
2 *Targeting using display advertising*. As with targeting using traditional publications, targeting is possible using audience composition of different websites.

3 *Targeting using social media.* Each main social media platform offers opportunities for granular targeting as shown in Figure 8.12 for Facebook. Similarly, LinkedIn enables targeting of LinkedIn members by location, company type and size, role, seniority and group membership.

4 *Targeting using affiliate marketing.* This will use a combination of search, display and social media techniques.

Figure 8.12 shows a tool related to content marketing aimed at helping marketers to review the effectiveness of different types of paid, owned and earned media to promote or distribute their content. Its aim is to review existing and potential use of different digital media in generating site visits, leads or sales compared to the level of investment in applying the media measured as paid media costs and the costs of marketing team members.

It uses a similar 'gap analysis' approach to the content marketing matrix (Figure 8.14) to compare current use of media to promote content against existing investment in content.

Step 1. Current use of media for content distribution.
Step 2. Review promotion gap against competitor or sector use of content distribution techniques.
Step 3. Select and prioritise new methods of content promotion.

The four types of media shown on the matrix are:

- *Wasteful media (lowest volume, highest cost).* Your aim here should be to reduce costs through budget reallocation and/or efficiency improvements.
- *Slow and steady media (lowest volume, lowest cost).* The least important to act on, but you need to make sure you are not distracted by these. Here, the aim is to minimise costs and review potential of techniques for improvement.

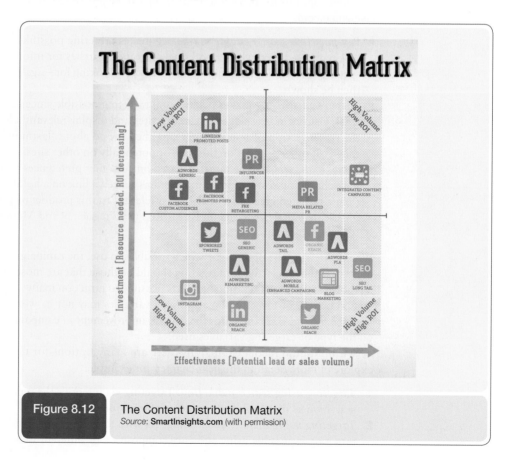

Figure 8.12	The Content Distribution Matrix
	Source: **SmartInsights.com** (with permission)

- *High-cost volume driver media (highest volume, highest cost).* You should aim to reduce costs and make efficiency improvements.
- *Star performers (highest volume, lowest cost).* The aim here is to add more focus to scale volume further.

Companies use this template in combination with analytics or lead reporting systems to identify which media are driving volume and how cost-effective they are.

Step 4. Offer, message development and creative

Many digital campaigns have direct response as the primary objective. Defining the right offer is vital to achieving these response objectives. But there are also likely to be brand objectives, to communicate the 'big idea' or concept behind the campaign or to position the brand.

In an online environment, there is very little time for the message to be delivered. Eye-tracking studies suggest average gaze or dwell times for a whole page may be around ten seconds, as suggested by Table 8.4, but individual fixation times on page elements such as page headlines or ads are much lower, so it is important the message is succinct and powerful.

So given the limited page dwell times and fixations, a clear primary message is needed in the different forms of digital media where it is delivered:

- *Paid search* – within the headline of the ad.
- *Natural search* – within the <title> tag and meta description tag (see Chapter 9).
- *Email marketing* – within the subject line and the headline or title of the email supported by images.
- *Display ads* – within the opening frame and possibly repeated in all frames.

The primary message should deliver relevance according to the context, so within paid search the primary message should be consistent with the search term entered by the

Table 8.4	Variation in fixation time for different websites				
Web page name	**Visual complexity level**	**Average gaze time (seconds)**	**First fixation**	**Longest fixation**	**Scanpath shape**
BBC UK	Complex	10.3	Forthcoming show picture	Forthcoming show picture	U, Z
Computer Science Manchester	Complex	10.1	Wide graphic/ picture	Wide graphic/picture	Z
Gene Ontology	Complex	12.5	Title	Title	C, I
IMG Group	Complex	11.4	Horizontal menu	Right menu	Z, U
Vodafone UK	Complex	11.3	Flashing image	Flashing image	*
Google Results	Simple	9.3	Results	Logo, search keyword	Z, U
John Rylands Library Catalogue	Simple	6.0	Horizontal menu	Search source	Z
MINT Group	Simple	9.1	Logo	Logo	U
Peve Group	Simple	8.9	Centre graphic	Centre graphic	Z, I

Source: Harper (2006)

user and should highlight the value proposition clearly. To successfully communicate our offer and message, we also need to ensure that the creative and copy helps achieve the five stages of information processing shown in Table 7.3 – i.e. Exposure, Attention, Comprehension and Perception, Yielding and Acceptance, and Retention (page 400). Similarly, we also need to deliver a response as shown by well-known AIDA mnemonic, which stands for:

A wareness/Attention
I nterest
D esire
A ction.

Having captured attention and developed interest with a primary offer and message, the creative needs to stimulate desire and action with the secondary offer and message, which:

- reassures prospects by giving a little more evidence of the offer or product benefits;
- convinces the sceptic and encourages them to click;
- can appeal to different types of person to the primary offer;
- again, should have a clear call-to-action.

Jenkinson (2003) proposes that every marketing communication should contain a blend of five elements related to customer experience, with the significance or intensity of each element varying. He believes that this is useful for briefing the communication requirements from different communications media. The elements of this 'CODAR' framework are illustrated by the example in Figure 8.13.

- *Idea forming*. Generating ideas in the consumer's or client's mind, such as the brand promise, a value proposition or brand values.
- *Relationship building*. Building a relationship including affinity, emotional bonding, brand know-how or expertise, and database and/or personal knowledge about the customer.
- *Sales activation*. Stimulating the customer towards further investigation, trial or purchase.

Figure 8.13	Example of CODAR framework for integrated communications
	Source: www.centreforintegratedmarketing.com

- *Help*. Providing service and assistance to the customer relevant to their needs and wants – from informing the customer about availability of new technology/product to consultancy in the purchase process, in use status reporting or resolution of a post-purchase problem.
- *Product experience*. Using and interacting with the brand's deliverables, including store and website design, product availability, information such as a bank statement, value or pleasure in use.

Many lessons from direct marketing can be applied to digital communications. In his book, *Commonsense Direct Marketing*, Drayton Bird (2000) identified 'twenty-five pointers before you write a word or sketch a layout'. Here are the most relevant ones to be considered when developing online creative work:

- *What is the objective?* Gather names? Produce qualified leads? Make firm sales? Get free trials?
- *Are you clear on the positioning?* What will your message tell the prospect about your product or service? Does it fit in with the positioning?
- *Who are you selling to?* What are their hopes, fears, likes, dislikes, needs? Are they male or female? Young or old, rich or poor? Until you know these facts, you will not know what tone to adopt, let alone what to say.
- *What is it? And what does it do?* Obvious, but…
- *What need in your prospect does your product or service fulfil?* How many of the nine basic human motivations are relevant to potential customers of your product or service: make money, save money, save time and effort, help their families, feel secure, impress others, gain pleasure, improve themselves and belong to a group?
- *What makes it so special?* Interrogate your product or service. How does it differ from the alternatives? These are its features.
- *What benefits are you offering?* What it does rather than what it is.
- *What do you consider the most important benefit to be?* Ideally a unique benefit, but certainly the most appealing combination of benefits.

Perceptual mapping is a useful tool to review positioning and differentiation within the marketplace. It summarises how customers see a company's brand in relation to others in the marketplace. In perceptual mapping, two axes define fundamental characteristics of how people see products, services or brands. A classic method is to include a more rational dimension like price against a more emotional dimension such as making you feel safe.

Focus on content marketing

We introduced the growing role of content marketing within digital marketing communications in Chapter 1. We believe that content marketing should be at the heart of digital marketing for all types of brands, because content fuels all the main digital marketing channels we use to communicate with our audiences. Search, social media, conversion rate optimisation and email marketing all require content which helps a brand increase its visibility, engage its audience and drives leads and sales. Within a campaign, content is vital as the method of engaging the audience and generating demand, whether this is educational content as part of a business-to-business campaign or video content as part of a consumer campaign. The only case where the role of content is diminished is where the main campaign offer is a price cut, discount or sale.

Given the importance of content marketing, many businesses now look to develop a content marketing strategy as part of their digital marketing tactics. As with all strategies, this will involve review of the current approach, setting specific objectives and developing strategies to create and share content. To review how content can best support digital marketing, Dave Chaffey developed the Content Marketing Matrix with Dan Bosomworth of Smart Insights. The activity explains how this can be used to identify the right content types.

Activity 8.1	Using the Content Marketing Matrix to audit and improve content effectiveness

We recommend the *Content Marketing Matrix* (Figure 8.14) as a key technique to review current use of different content formats and to identify new types of content that could be useful for a business.

The matrix is structured to help you think through the dimensions of different content based on how an audience could find content valuable and what you're trying to achieve as a business.

Activity

Complete this process to review a company's use of different types of content to support marketing:

1 Review current use of content within company through plotting different content types on the grid.
2 Repeat this review for two to three competitors (direct or indirect), again plotting on the grid.
3 Brainstorm future content types possible.
4 Define criteria for investing in content (e.g. generating reach, helping conversion, existing customers).
5 Use your criteria from Step 4 to prioritise the two or three types of content needed to trial in content campaigns.

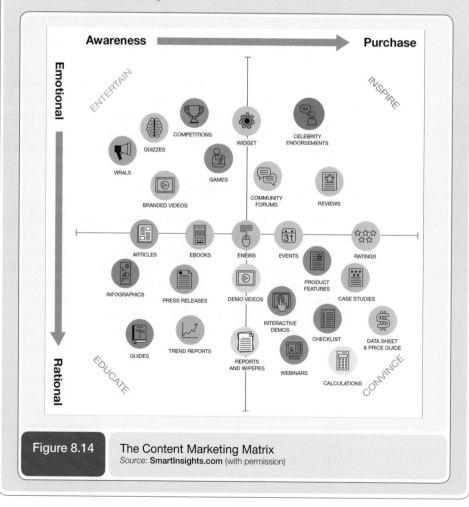

Figure 8.14	The Content Marketing Matrix
	Source: **SmartInsights.com** (with permission)

Step 5. Budgeting and selecting the digital media mix

Traditional approaches such as those suggested by Kotler *et al.* (2001) can be used to set overall communications budgets. For example:

- *Affordable method* – the communications budget is set after subtracting fixed and variable costs from anticipated revenues.
- *Percentage-of-sales methods* – the communications budget is set as a percentage of forecast sales revenues.
- *Competitive parity methods* – expenditure is based on estimates of competitor expenditure. For example, e-marketing spend is typically 10–15 per cent of the marketing budget.
- *Objective and task method* – this is a logical approach where budget is built up from all the tasks required to achieve the objectives in the communications plan. This is a bottom-up approach that is often based on a model of the effectiveness of different digital media channels based on the measures of campaign effectiveness described in the objective setting section at the start of this chapter. Complete Activity 8.2 to understand how these models are created.

Digital marketing campaign plans require three important decisions to be made about investment for the online promotion or the online communications mix. These are:

1 Level of investment in digital media as opposed to traditional media.
2 Mix of investment in digital media channels or e-communications tools.
3 Level of investment in digital assets.

1 Level of investment in digital media techniques in comparison to offline promotion

A balance must be struck between online and offline communications techniques based on the strengths and weaknesses of the different media options. A useful framework for considering the media characteristics which influence decisions on which to invest in has been developed by Coulter and Starkis (2005). Offline media are often superior in generating attention, stimulating attention and gaining credibility. Online media tend to be better at engagement due to personalisation, interaction and support of word-of-mouth. The offer can also often be fulfilled online for products that can be bought online. However, there are limits to the number of people that can be reached through online media (a limit to number searching on particular terms) and the cost is not necessarily always lower in competitive markets.

Activity 8.2	A framework for selecting media

Coulter and Starkis (2005) identify these factors for media selection. We have added comments.

Quality

1 *Attention-getting capability (Attention)* – ability of an ad placed in this specific media to 'grab the customer's attention' due to the nature of that media.
2 *Stimulating emotions (Stimulation)* – ability of an ad placed in this specific media to convey emotional content and/or elicit emotional responses.
3 *Information content and detail (Content)* – ability of an ad placed in this specific media to convey a large amount of information and/or product description.
4 *Credibility/prestige/image (Credibility)* – ability of a specific media to lend prestige to a product through association (i.e. because that product is advertised within the media).

5 *Clutter* – degree to which it is difficult for a product advertised within a specific media to 'stand out' due to the large number of competitive offerings/messages.

[*Comment*: We would stress the capability of the media to generate a response, which is dependent on the combination of factors mentioned here that relate to brand awareness and influence. For online media, certain media such as pay-per-click search marketing tends to be more responsive than media buys of ads on portals since there is less clutter and the relevance is higher since the web user is searching.]

Time

1 *Short lead time* – degree to which an ad can be created and/or placed within a specific media in a relatively short period of time.
2 *Long exposure time* – degree to which the communication recipient is able to examine the advertising message within a specific media for an extended period of time.

[*Comment*: The ability to dynamically alter an ad during a campaign to select the best performing creative for each placement is particularly important online – for example optimising different creative executions of a display ad or a Google AdWords ad.]

Flexibility

1 *Appeal to multiple senses (Appeal)* – degree to which an ad placed within this specific media can communicate via sight, sound, taste, touch and/or smell concurrently.
2 *Personalisation* – degree to which an advertising message placed within this specific media can be customised in order to target a specific individual or group of individuals.
3 *Interactivity* – degree to which the customer can respond to information conveyed in an advertisement placed within this specific media.

Coverage

1 *Selectivity* – degree to which an ad placed within this specific media is able to target a specific group of people.
2 *Pass-along audience (Pass-along)* – degree to which an ad placed within this specific media is seen by those other than the original message recipient.

[*Comment*: This is the viral marketing effect.]

3 *Frequency/repeat exposure (Frequency)* – degree to which any single ad placed within this specific media may be seen by any one particular individual on more than one occasion.

[*Comment*: Online this capability is available through behavioural targeting of display ads where cookies can be used to serve ads to the same person and develop the message with each new exposure if appropriate.]

4 *Average media reach (Reach)* – degree to which an ad placed within this specific media reaches a relatively wide audience.

Cost

1 *Development/production cost (Development cost)* – relative cost of developing or producing an ad for this specific media.
2 *Average media delivery cost (Delivery cost)* – average cost-per-thousand associated with this specific media.

[*Comment*: We should also add cost-per-response which is dependent on the click-through rate for each media and placement.]

The relative importance of these characteristics and the investment in different digital media will be dependent on the product and the type of campaign – whether it is direct-response-orientated or brand-orientated – and the scale of budget.

Figure 8.15 outlines typical options that companies have during a campaign, quarterly or annually. Which do you think would be the best option for an established company as compared to a dot-com 'pureplay' company? It seems that in both cases, offline promotion investment often exceeds that for online promotion investment. However, some pureplays do invest the majority of their budget in paid search and affiliate marketing, although they are likely to find there are limits to growth that this will impose. There are also increases to buying digital media, as suggested by Mini case study 8.3, which need to be considered. For existing companies, traditional media such as print are used to advertise the sites, while print and TV will also be widely used by dot-com companies to drive traffic to their sites.

Econometric modelling

Econometric modelling
A quantitative technique to evaluate the past influence or predict the future influence on a dependent variable (typically sales in a marketing context) of independent variables which may include product price, promotions and the level and mix of media investments.

Econometrics or **econometric modelling** is an established approach to understanding the contribution of different media in influencing consumers and ultimately generating sales and profit. It can also be used in a predictive way to plan for future campaigns. It is increasingly used in integrated campaigns to assess the appropriate media mix (see Cook, 2004, for further explanation).

One of its main benefits is its ability to separate the effects of a range of influences such as offline or online media usage or other variables such as price or promotions used and to quantify these individual effects. A simple example might be for the sales of a drinks brand:

$$
\begin{aligned}
\text{Sales} = 100\ & + \\
& + 2.5 \times \text{own TVRs (television ratings)} \\
& - 1.4 \times \text{own price} \\
& + 1.6 \times \text{competitor price} \\
& + 1.0 \times \text{distribution} \\
& - 0.8 \times \text{temperature} \\
& - 1.2 \times \text{competitor TVRs}
\end{aligned}
$$

These relationships are typically identified using multiple linear regression models where a single dependent variable (typically sales) is a function of one or more explanatory or independent variables such as price, temperature, level of promotion.

Econometric models are developed from historic time-series data which record fluctuations dependent on different variables including seasonal variables, but most importantly, variations in media spend levels and the mix of media. In econometrics, sales fluctuations are expressed in terms of the factors causing them.

| Figure 8.15 | Options for the online vs offline communications mix: (a) online> offline, (b) similar online and offline, (c) offline> online |

Digital marketing insight 8.3 | Econometrics applications according to the Institute of Practitioners in Advertising

1 *Overall communication effectiveness (payback)*. This is the aggregate response of consumers to an advertising campaign over the entire period of its influence. Effects can often be reported by individual media. Sometimes it is also possible to quantify secondary effects where advertising increases (say) distribution, that in turn generates additional sales.

2 *Comparative campaign effects*. Econometric modelling can help to determine which campaign is the most potent influence on sales or other key measures.

3 *Efficiency*. Efficiency covers a diversity of issues:
- How big a budget is needed to:
  - reach sales targets;
  - maintain adstock levels.
- How advertising should be flighted or scheduled:
  - press vs television vs other media;
  - burst vs drip;
  - by time of year (media cost and relative effectiveness may be issues);
  - relative to previous activity (recency).
- What are the most effective coverage or frequency levels?
- Are particular weights of advertising more effective per unit of advertising – i.e. at what point do diminishing returns set in? The issue of diminishing marginal returns to scale with respect to advertising weight is one of the aspects of efficiency most often raised. It can imply ratings becoming less effective per additional rating point. It could refer to costs or responses that differ by region or time of year. All imply a resource allocation issue where econometrics can be helpful.

4 *Cross-brand effects: portfolio, umbrella and halo*. In some markets operators have a portfolio of products that may even be direct competitors – for example brewing or financial products. Advertising one of these could positively or adversely affect others. Thorough evaluation of advertising should investigate both the effects on the advertised brand and its stablemates.

5 *Competitive effects*. Competitive effects can be measured:
- on your own brand;
- on the competitor by modelling their sales (also showing your brand's effects on them).

Once the relative effects of own and competitive media activity are understood it becomes possible to calculate the budget levels required to offset competitive actions.

Source: Summarised from IPA (2004)

2 Selecting the right mix of digital media communications tools

When selecting the mix of digital media for a campaign or longer-term investments, marketers will determine the most appropriate mix based on their knowledge built up through experience of previous campaigns and taking input from their advisers such as experienced colleagues or agency partners.

Varianini and Vaturi (2000) have suggested that many online marketing failures have resulted from poor control of media spending. The communications mix should be optimised to minimise the cost of acquisition. If an online intermediary has a cost acquisition of £100 per customer while it is gaining an average commission on each sale of £5 then, clearly, the company will not be profitable unless it can achieve a large number of repeat orders from the customer.

Agrawal *et al.* (2001) suggested that e-commerce sites should focus on narrow segments that have demonstrated their attraction to a business model. They believe that promotion techniques such as affiliate deals with narrowly targeted sites and email campaigns targeted at segments grouped by purchase histories and demographic traits are 10–15 times more likely than banner ads on generic portals to attract prospects who click through to purchase. Alternatively, pay-per-click ads on Google may have a higher success rate.

When this experience isn't there, which is often the case with new digital media opportunities, it is important to do a more structured evaluation including factors such as the ability of each medium to influence perceptions, drive a response, the cost of response and the quality of response – are respondents more likely to convert to the ultimate action such as sale? What is their likely lifetime value? For example, some digital media channels such as affiliates are more likely to attract customers with a lower lifetime value who are more likely to switch suppliers.

Media planning and buying agency Zed Media has produced a useful summary of how a media mix might typically vary according to budget (see Figure 8.16).

The figure shows that for a direct response campaign with limited budget, investment in controllable, targeted media which typically have a lower cost-per-acquisition such as affiliates and paid search should be the main focus. If more budget is available, it may not be possible to buy further keywords or there may be benefits from generating awareness of the offering through more display advertising.

| Figure 8.16 | Recommendations of the mix of investment in digital media for direct and brand response campaigns
Source: Zed Media (**www.zedmedia.com**) |

With a brand campaign where the focus is on generating awareness, the recommendations of Zed Media are reversed where they recommend that, even at lower budgets, more investment should be made in display advertising.

Deciding on the optimal expenditure on different communication techniques will be an iterative approach since past results should be analysed and adjusted accordingly. Marketers can analyse the proportion of the promotional budget that is spent on different channels and then compare this with the contribution from purchasing customers who originated using the original channel. This type of analysis, reported by Hoffman and Novak (2000) and shown in Table 8.5, requires two different types of marketing research. First, **tagging** of customers can be used. Here, we monitor, using specifically coded URLs or cookies, the numbers of customers who are referred to a website through different online techniques such as search ads, affiliate or banner ads, and then track the money they spend on purchases. Digital marketing insight 8.4 gives more details of how the Google Analytics system is used.

Tagging
Tracking of origin of customers and their spending patterns.

Attributing influence on sales to digital media channel

It is seldom the case that a customer will go straight to a site and purchase, or that they will perform a single search and then purchase. Instead, they will commonly perform multiple searches and will be referred to the ultimate purchase site by different types of site. This consumer behaviour is indicated by Figure 8.17. This shows that someone looking to purchase a car may be referred to a site several times via different digital communications channels.

A common approach to attributing the influence of different online media a customer consumes before purchase has been the **last-click method of digital media channel attribution** introduced well by Lee (2010). Figure 8.18 gives an example of using a social media marketing tool to assess effectiveness on a last click basis. It shows that when a business shares content across different social networks they can review how many clicks and conversion to leads are generated. In this example, Facebook is most effective by volume.

Last-click method of digital media channel attribution
The site which referred a visitor immediately before purchase is credited with the sale. Previous referrals influenced by other customer touch points on other sites are ignored.

However, Lee explains that this can give a misleading picture of which marketing channels are effective. In an analysis of visitors to an airline site (Figure 8.19), he shows that although the overall patterns of referrers to the site at first appear similar, there are some major differences. If you refer to Figure 8.19 you can see that email marketing, SEO

Table 8.5	Relative effectiveness of different forms of marketing communications for a B2C company

Medium	Budget	Contribution	Effectiveness
Print (off)	20%	10%	0.5
TV (off)	25%	10%	0.25
Radio (off)	10%	5%	0.5
PR (off)	5%	15%	3
Word-of-mouth (off)	0%	25%	Infinite
Banners (on)	20%	20%	1
Affiliate (on)	20%	10%	0.5
Links (on)	0%	3%	Infinite
Search engine registration (on)	0%	2%	Infinite

Digital marketing insight 8.4 Campaign tracking in Google Analytics

Defining a standard set of online marketing source codes is essential to determining the value of different referral sources such as ad campaigns or email campaigns.

Many companies track AdWords because of its automated integration enabled from Google AdWords, but they may not track other codes or have a standard notation which needs to be defined and then added to all links involving media placements.

Google Analytics uses five standard dimensions for a campaign which need to be incorporated into the query string of the URL for each ad placement as this example shows: http://www.domain.com/landing_page.php?utm_campaign=spring-sale&utm_medium=banner&utm_source=<mediasitename>.com

The campaigns report in Google Analytics will then enable you to compare the value generated by differerent campaigns and media within them.

The meaning of each of the five dimensions is:

- *utm_campaign (Required)*. The name of the marketing campaign, e.g. Spring Campaign.
- *utm_medium (Required)*. Media channel (i.e. email, banner, CPC, etc.).
- *utm_source (Required)*. Who are you partnering with to push your message, for example a partner site.
- *utm_content (Optional)*, The version of the ad (used for A/B testing) or in AdWords. You can identify two versions of the same ad using this variable. This is not always used and is NOT included in the above example.
- *utm_term (Optional)* The search term purchased (if the link refers to keywords).This is not always used and is NOT included in the above example.

Many email and social media marketing tools now set these up automatically, but you can set them up manually – search for the 'The Google URL builder' to see how to create these links.

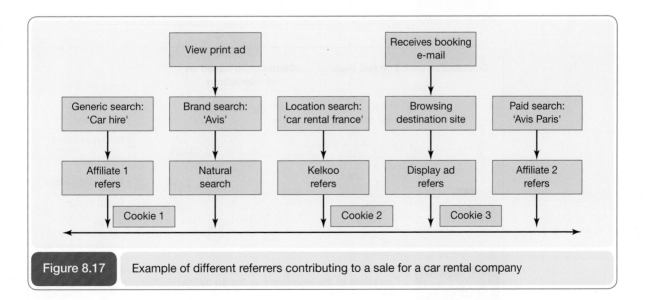

Figure 8.17 Example of different referrers contributing to a sale for a car rental company

for non-brand terms and PPC for brand terms are more significant when looking at the contribution of all sources.

Referring to Figure 8.17, you can see this has the benefit that we don't credit multiple affiliates with sale for affiliate marketing – only Affiliate 2 is credited with the sale, a process known as **digital media de-duplication**. But it has the disadvantage that it simplifies the reality of previous influence or **digital media 'assists'** and previous referrals influenced by other customer touchpoints on other sites are ignored, such as the natural search or display ad.

So, for the most accurate interpretation of the contribution of different media, the online marketer needs to use tagging and analysis tools to try to build the best picture of which channels are influencing sales and then weight the media accordingly. For example, a more sophisticated approach is to weight the responsibility for sale across several different referrers according to a model – so just considering the affiliates, Affiliate 1 might be credited with 30 per cent of the sales value and Affiliate 2 with 70 per cent, for example. This approach is useful since it indicates the value of display advertising – a common phenomenon is the halo effect where display ads indirectly influence sales by creating awareness and stimulating sale at a later point in time. These are sometimes known as 'viewthrough' or post-impression effects.

Digital media de-duplication
A single referrer of a visit leading to sale is credited with the sale based on the last-click method of digital media channel attribution.

Digital media 'assist'
A referrer of a visit to a site before the ultimate sale is credited with the sale, often through a weighting system.

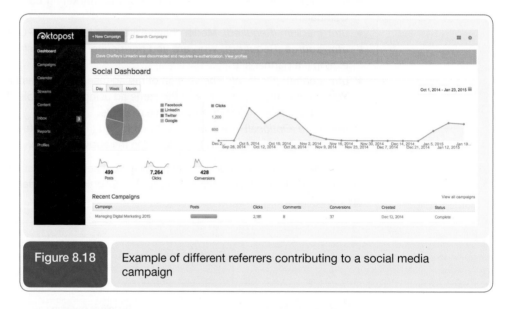

| Figure 8.18 | Example of different referrers contributing to a social media campaign |

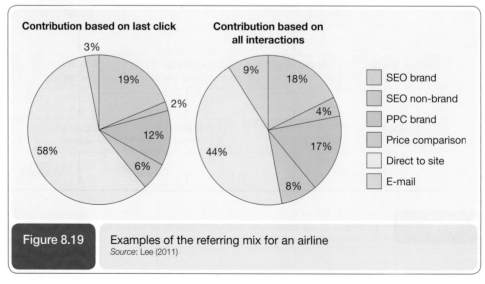

| Figure 8.19 | Examples of the referring mix for an airline |

Source: Lee (2011)

These allocation approaches won't be possible if agencies are using different tracking tools and reporting separately on different media channels – for example, the ad agency reports on display advertising, the search agency on pay-per-click, the affiliate manager on affiliate sales. Instead it is important to use a unified tracking system which typically uses common tags across all media channels. Common unified tracking solutions that consider all media are available from the likes of Atlas, Doubleclick Dart and some of the larger media agencies.

Further sophistication of tracking will be worthwhile for companies investing millions in digital media in order to understand the customer journey and the contribution of media. A useful analysis to perform is in the form shown in Figure 8.20. This anonymised example shows the importance of display ads, for example, and how different channels support each other.

It can then be worthwhile understanding the role of individual channels better, and in particular paid search. Marketers need to understand how consumers use different types of terms. Table 8.6 shows the repeated use of different types of search terms for a single customer (other digital channels such as affiliates are ignored here). The two columns on the right show how it is unrealistic to attribute the sale to the last search since the influence of the assists isn't shown.

Channels	Sequence	% Conversions	Channel allocation
2	DS	34.01%	74.75%
	SD	20.98%	
	XS	8.35%	
	SX	7.33%	
	DX	2.24%	
	XD	1.83%	
3	DDS	7.74%	18.53%
	SDS	5.30%	
	SXS	3.05%	
	DXD	1.02%	
	DXS	0.81%	
	XSX	0.41%	
	SDX	0.20%	
4	SDSD	1.63%	4.48%
	DSDS	1.43%	
	DXDX	0.41%	
	DSDX	0.20%	
	DSXD	0.20%	
	DXDS	0.20%	
	DXSD	0.20%	
	SDSX	0.20%	
5	DSDSD	1.02%	1.43%
	SDSDS	0.41%	
6	DSDSDS	0.20%	0.61%
	SDSDSD	0.20%	
	SDSDXS	0.20%	
7	DSDSDSD	0.20%	0.20%

Figure 8.20   Example of the sequence of visits to a site in generating conversions where two or more digital media channels were involved (Codes for channels: D = Display, S = Search, X = Aggregator)

Table 8.6	Example of weighted allocation of different searches			
User id	**Search query**	**Sale?**	**Value attributed: last click method**	**Value attributed: weighted method**
123	Mobile phone (generic search)	No	£0	£40
123	Best camera phone (category generic search)	No	£0	£40
123	Nokia phone (product search)	No	£0	£40
123	Nokia N91 Orange (product + supplier search)	No	£0	£40
123	E-retailer brand name (branded search)	Yes	£200	£40

Achieving and measuring repeat visits is worthwhile since, according to Flores and Eltvedt (2005), on average, purchase intent sees a double-digit increase after someone has been to a site more than once.

For some promotional techniques, tagging of links on third-party sites will not be practical. These will be grouped together as unattributed referrers. For word-of-mouth referrals, we have to estimate the amount of spend for these customers through traditional market research techniques such as questionnaires or asking at point of sale. The use of tagging enables much better insights on the effectiveness of promotional techniques than is possible in traditional media, but due to its complexity it requires a large investment in staff time and tracking software to achieve it. It is also very dependent on cookie deletion rates.

To see how a budget can be created for a digital campaign, complete Activity 8.3.

Activity 8.3	Creating a digital campaign budget

Purpose

To illustrate the type of budget created internally or by digital marketing agencies. Figure 8.21 shows an extract.

Activity

Download the spreadsheet from **http://blog.davechaffey.com/spreadsheet** to understand how the different calculations relate to each other. Try changing the cost of media (blue cells) and different click-through rates (blue cells) for which typical values are shown for a competitive retail product. View the formulas to see how the calculations are made.

How would you make this model more accurate (i.e. how would you break down each digital media channel further?)

Digital asset
The graphical and interactive material that supports a campaign displayed on third-party sites and on microsites. Includes display ads, email templates, video, audio and other interactive media such as Flash animations.

3 Level of investment in digital assets

The **digital assets** are the creative that support a campaign such as that shown in Mini case study 8.4, they include:

- display ad or affiliate marketing creative such as banners and skyscrapers;
- microsites;

Input parameter table	Overall budget	£10,000	Blue cells = input variables – vary these for 'what-if' analysis
	Average order value	£50	Orange cells = output variables (calculated – do not overtype)
	Gross profit margin	30.0%	

		Advertising		Search		Partners	
		Ad buys (CPM)	Ad network (CPM)	Paid search (CPC)	Natural search	Affiliates (CPA)	Aggregators
Media cost	Setup / creative / Mgt costs	£0	£0	£0	£0	£0	£0
	CPM	£10.0	£10.0	£4.0	£0.4	£10.0	£20.0
	CPC	£5.0	£5.0	£0.20	£0.20	£5.0	£10.0
	Media costs	£10,000	£10,000	£30,000	£10,000	£10,000	£10,000
	Total cost setup and media	£10,000	£10,000	£30,000	£10,000	£10,000	£10,000
	Budget %	10%	10%	30%	10%	10%	10%
Media impressions and response	Impressions or names	1,000,000	1,000,000	7,500,000	25,000,000	1,000,000	500,000
	CTR	0.2%	0.2%	2.0%	0.2%	0.2%	0.2%
	Clicks or site visits	2,000	2,000	150,000	50,000	2,000	1,000
Conversion to opportunity (lead)	Conversion rate to opportunity	100.0%	100.0%	100.0%	100.0%	100.0%	100.0%
	Number of opportunities	2,000	2,000	150,000	50,000	2,000	1,000
	Cost per opportunity	£5.0	£5.0	£0.2	£0.2	£5.0	£10.0
Conversion to sales	Conversion rate to sale	100.0%	100.0%	100.0%	100.0%	50.0%	100.0%
	Number of sales	2,000	2,000	150,000	50,000	1,000	1,000
	% of sales	1.0%	1.0%	72.7%	24.2%	0.5%	0.5%
	Cost per sale (CPA)	£5.0	£5.0	£0.2	£0.2	£10.0	£10.0
Revenue	Total revenue	£100,000	£100,000	£7,500,000	£2,500,000	£50,000	£50,000
Costs	Cost of goods sold	£70,000	£70,000	£5,250,000	£1,750,000	£35,000	£35,000
	Media costs	£10,000	£10,000	£30,000	£10,000	£10,000	£10,000
	Total costs (inc media)	£80,000	£80,000	£5,280,000	£1,760,000	£45,000	£45,000
Profitability	Profit	£20,000	£20,000	£2,220,000	£740,000	£5,000	£5,000
	Return on investment	25.0%	25.0%	42.0%	42.0%	11.1%	11.1%

Figure 8.21 Spreadsheet template for digital campaign budgeting
Source: http://blog.davechaffey.com/spreadsheet

- email templates;
- video, audio and other interactive media such as Flash animations, games or screensavers which form a microsite.

As with traditional media, there is a tension between spend on the advertising creative and the media space purchased to run the executions. There is a danger that if spend on media is too high, then the quality of the execution and the volume of digital assets produced will be too low.

Mini case study 8.4   Lynx uses microsite to promote its 'Get More' campaign

In 2004 a new deodorant brand, Lynx Pulse, used online games, screensavers, viral emails, video clips and soundtracks, to extend the brand experience – from applying deodorant to interacting with the brand – for 1.4 million unique users.

A similar approach was repeated in 2008 using a similar range of digital assets in the 'Get In There' campaign, which was part of a long-term 'Lynx Effect' brand concept supported at a campaign-specific URL (www.lynxeffect.com, Figure 8.22). Rather than a short-term campaign, to maximise the impact the brief was to 'create a consistent long-term presence for the Lynx-Axe brand online'. Another difference from previous campaigns was the greater use of video and user-generated content.

The reason for the campaign was highlighted by Karen Hamilton, regional VP of marketing Lynx-Axe Europe, who explained the thinking behind the campaign to NMA (2008) when she said:

With our new campaign we feel we now have a digital presence that not only continues to give young guys the edge in the mating game but also provides us with an ongoing platform to deliver cutting-edge

Figure 8.22 | Lynx Effect campaign microsite (www.lynxeffect.com)

digital creativity. With Get In There, BBH came to us with a big idea that's rooted in the heart of our brand and understands the role of digital in our target audience's life. We have specifically created a large amount of exciting, diverse and tailored content that works across many different platforms.

For the agency Jonathan Bottomley, planning director BBH, said:

Get In There is a rallying cry from the brand to get guys away from their computers, out of the chat rooms and to start meeting real girls rather than virtual girls.

The idea had to break into the heart of guys' digital lives, so we created an extended network of linked content to sit on partner sites that guys visit all the time: YouTube, FHM, Flickr, Bebo. At the heart of the network is lynxeffect.com, *which provides guys with tips, tools and widgets that they can use to approach girls. The idea is to give them an 'in', something to break the ice so that the fear of wondering what to say is reduced.*

There are killer weapons, such as the Lynx FX soundboard, which you can download to your mobile phone to turn it into a pulling machine. There are downloadable business cards, magic tricks and email tools, all of which are refreshed regularly. For guys in need of inspiration, hidden camera footage showcases the exploits of the Lynx Guys, characters who are getting in there with the ladies, trying to show how it's done.

The Unilever owned brand Lynx continues to stick with the brand and is currently focussing on its 18th birthday with the **LynxEffect.com/Africa18** (Eleftheriou-Smith, 2013). The latest digital campaign celebrates the longevity of the product and has a set up a campaign to get users to engage with the brand online: see **http://lynxafrica18.tumblr.com/the-project**.

Source: Eleftheriou-Smith (2013)

Step 6. Integration into overall media schedule or plan

Integrated marketing communications
The coordination of communications channels to deliver a clear, consistent message to achieve marketing goals.

In common with other communications media, digital media are most effective when they are deployed as part of an **integrated marketing communications** approach. Kotler *et al.* (2001) describe integrated marketing communications as:

> the concept under which a company carefully integrates and coordinates its many communications channels to deliver a clear, consistent message about the organisation and its products.

The characteristics of integrated marketing communications have been summarised by Pickton and Broderick (2001) as the 4Cs of:

Coherence – different communications are logically connected.
Consistency – multiple messages support and reinforce, and are not contradictory.
Continuity – communications are connected and consistent through time.
Complementary – synergistic, or the sum of the parts is greater than the whole!

The 4Cs also act as guidelines for how communications should be integrated.

Further guidelines on integrated marketing communications from Pickton and Broderick (2001) that can be usefully applied to digital marketing are the following.

- Integrated communications planning is based on *clearly identified marketing communications objectives* (see later section).
- Digital marketing should involve *management of all forms of contact*, which includes management of both outbound communications, such as banner advertising or direct email, and inbound communications such as email enquiries.
- Internet marketing should utilise a *range of promotional tools*. These are the digital media channels illustrated in Figure 1.9 (page 28).
- A *range of media* should be used to communicate consistent messages about opportunities for customers to interact with a brand online. Marketing managers need to consider the most effective mix of online and offline media channels shown in Figure 1.9 to encourage interactions and drive traffic to their online presence.
- The communications plan should involve careful selection of the *most effective promotional and media mix*. This is discussed at the end of the chapter.

Additionally, we can say that integrated marketing communications should be used to support customers through the entire buying process, across different media.

Planning integrated marketing communications

The Account Planning Group (**www.apg.org.uk**), in its definition of media planning, highlights the importance of the role of media planning when they say that the planner:

> Needs to understand the customer and the brand to unearth a key ***insight*** for the communication/solution [Relevance].

> As media channels have mushroomed and communication channels have multiplied, it has become increasingly important for communication to cut through the cynicism and ***connect*** with its audience [Distinctiveness].

> …the planner can provide the edge needed to ensure the solution reaches out through the clutter to its ***intended audience*** [Targeted reach].

> …needs to ***demonstrate*** how and why the communication has performed [Effectiveness].

Media-neutral planning (MNP)

Media-neutral planning
An approach to planning ad campaigns to maximise response across different media according to consumer usage of these media.

The concept of **media-neutral planning (MNP)** has been used to describe an approach to planning integrated marketing campaigns including online elements. To read a review of the different interpretations see Tapp (2005), who notes that there are three different aspects of planning often encompassed with media-neutral planning:

- *Channel planning*, i.e. which route to market shall we take: retail, direct, sales partners etc. (we would say this emphasis is rare).
- *Communications-mix planning*, i.e. how do we split our budget between advertising, direct marketing, sales promotions and PR.
- *Media planning*, i.e. spending money on TV, press, direct mail and so on.

In our view, MNP is most usually applied to the second and third elements and the approach is based on reaching consumers across a range of media to maximise response. For example, Crawshaw (2004) says:

> The simple reason we would want media-neutral communications is so that we can connect the right message with our target audience, at the right time and place to persuade them to do what we want. This will lead to powerful, effective, value for money communications that solve clients' business challenges.

A customer-centric media-planning approach is key to this process. Anthony Clifton, Planning Director at WWAV Rapp Collins Media Group, is quoted by the Account Planning Group as saying (quoted in Crawshaw, 2004):

> Real consumer insight has to be positioned at the core of the integrated planning process and the planner must glean a complete understanding of the client's stakeholders, who they are, their mindset, media consumption patterns and relationship with the business – are they 'life-time' consumers or have they purchased once, are they high value or low value customers etc. This requires lifting the bonnet of the database, segmentation and market evaluation.

Key activities in media selection and planning

The starting point for media planning, selection and implementation is to have clearly defined campaign objectives:

- For direct response campaigns, the most important are response volume, quality and cost.
- For campaigns where awareness and branding are the main outcomes, branding metrics become important.

Pickton and Broderick (2001) identify six activities in media implementation: target audience selection, media objectives, media selection, media scheduling, media buying and media evaluation.

A particularly important aspect for online media is that this evaluation and adjustment can – and should – occur during the campaign, in order to identify the best placements and creatives and to refine the ongoing media plan.

Learning from cross-media optimisation studies

Cross-media optimisation studies (XMOS)
Studies to determine the optimum spend across different media to produce the best results.

Many **cross-media optimisation studies (XMOS)** have shown that the optimal online spend for low-involvement products is surprisingly high at 10–15 per cent of total spend. Although this is not a large amount, it compares to previous spend levels below 1 per cent for many organisations.

XMOS research is designed to help marketers and their agencies answer the (rather involved) question: 'What is the optimal mix of advertising vehicles across different media,

---

| Digital marketing insight 8.5 | Different forms of campaign integration |

The IPA (2011) report showed the popularity of alternative options for campaign integration. There was analysis of over 250 IPA Effectiveness Awards case studies, entered over a seven-year period (2004–2010), including examples from Hovis, O_2, Virgin Atlantic, HSBC, E4 Skins, Johnnie Walker and more.

The report defines four options for integration:

1 *No integration* – single channel or campaigns using a number of channels but not integrating consistently across them. Analysis suggests that campaigns with no obvious integration or who use only one channel are good at reducing price sensitivity but have little impact on market share.
2 *Advertising-led integration* – channels unified around a common creative idea/'matching luggage' approach. Traditionally integrated advertising-led campaigns were reported to be more effective at share gain and customer acquisition.
3 *Brand idea-led 'orchestration'* – unified around a shared brand concept or need-state platform, often built around core brand values of the organisation. Analysis of campaigns suggests that brand idea-led campaigns are highly effective in retention, share defence and profit gain.
4 *Participation-led 'orchestration'* – goal is to create a common dialogue or conversation, it has emerged in recent years, partly driven by digital media. The analysis in the report suggests that participation-led campaigns underperform on hard sales measures but excel in rewarding existing users and on brand fame. Since they are relatively new, they are a small proportion of the total.

The research also found that multichannel campaigns are better at driving effectiveness than single-channel activity: 78 per cent of cases with three channels demonstrate hard business effects versus 67 per cent of those with only one channel; there is, however, a point of diminishing returns beyond three channels. It's surprising this difference isn't larger, but multiple channels fare well when considering other measures.

---

in terms of frequency, reach and budget allocation, for a given campaign to achieve its marketing goals?'

The mix between online and offline spend is varied to maximise campaign metrics such as reach, brand awareness and purchase intent. Table 8.7 summarises the optimal mix identified for four famous brands. For example, Dove (IAB, 2004) found that increasing the level of interactive advertising to 15 per cent would have resulted in an increase in overall branding metrics of 8 per cent. The proportion of online is small, but remember that many companies are spending less than 1 per cent of their ad budgets online, meaning that offline frequency is too high and they may not be reaching many consumers.

The reasons for using and increasing the significance of online in the media mix are similar to those for using any media mix as described by Sissors and Baron (2002):

- *Extend reach* – adding prospects not exposed by a single medium/other media.
- *Flatten frequency distribution* – if audiences viewing TV ads are exposed too many times, there is a law of diminishing returns and it might prove better to reallocate that budget to online media.
- *Reach different kinds of audiences.*
- *Provide unique advantages in stressing different benefits* – based on the different characteristics of each medium.
- *Allow different creative executions to be implemented.*
- *Add gross impressions if the other media is cost-efficient.*
- *Reinforce messages by using different creative stimuli.*

Table 8.7	Optimum media mix suggested by XMOS studies		
Brand	**TV**	**Magazine**	**Online**
Colgate	75%	14%	11%
Kleenex	70%	20%	10%
Dove	72%	13%	15%
McDonald's	71%	16% (radio)	13%

Source: Briggs et al. (2005)

Briggs *et al*. (2005) give the example of the launch of a new model of car. Their XMOS study provides these insights:

- Advertising works, but the price of some media has been bid up to make it inefficient compared to alternatives.
- TV generates the greatest level of absolute reach and produces high levels of purchase-consideration impact, but is less cost effective compared to magazine and online.
- Magazines and online category-related sites are similar in their impact, being very selective and efficiently delivering 'in-market' prospects.
- Electronic roadblocks are the most cost-efficient, and can produce significant daily reach (40 per cent or more); however, they are not as scalable as TV.
- While roadblocks delivered 40 per cent reach in a day, TV can deliver nearly twice the level in a single day.
- Due to changing media habits of consumers, Ford's campaign could be fine-tuned to increase sales by 5 per cent without spending a dollar more.

For integrated communications to be successful, the different techniques should be successfully integrated through time as part of a campaign or campaigns.

Figure 8.23 shows how communications can be planned around a particular event. (SE denotes 'search engine'; C1 and C2 are campaigns 1 and 2.) Here we have chosen the launch of a new version of a website, but other alternatives include a new product launch or a key seminar. This planning will help provide a continuous message to customers. It also ensures a maximum number of customers are reached using different media over the period.

In keeping with planning for other media, Pincott (2000) suggests there are two key strategies in planning integrated Internet marketing communications. First, there should be a media strategy which will mainly be determined by how to reach the target audience. This will define the online promotion techniques described in this chapter and where to advertise online. Second, there is the creative strategy. Pincott says that 'the dominant online marketing paradigm is one of direct response'. However, he goes on to suggest that all site promotion will also influence perceptions of the brand.

Finally, here are five questions about integration you must ask when creating a campaign:

1 *Consistent branding and messaging*. Is the branding and messaging sufficiently similar (coherent) throughout the campaign?
2 *Varying the offer, messaging and creative through the campaign*. Is offer and messaging varied sufficiently through the campaign? With each different medium and wave of the campaign, it can improve results to subtly vary the offer, message and creative. This might appear to conflict with the first guideline, but the two can be compatible, since:

- different treatments and offers will appeal to different people and achieve different results;

| Figure 8.23 | Integration of different communications tools through time |

- if each communication in a campaign is identical, then future campaign waves will be ignored;
- escalating or improving offers during a campaign can achieve better response.

3 *Frequency (number) and interval of communications.* Are you exposing the audience sufficiently or too much to your messages? This is a difficult balance to strike. In our view, some marketers often undercommunicate for fear of overcommunicating!

   With online media buys, it's also important to think about frequency as well as reach. Increases in frequency will usually increase awareness as for any medium – though direct response will usually peak quite quickly before ebbing away.

   If you have defined touch strategies that mandate a minimum or maximum number of communications within a period – and the interval between them – you should check that your plans fit in with these or that they do not constrain your campaign.

4 Sequencing of communications. You have the option to:

- launch your campaigns online first;
- launch your campaigns offline first;
- launch your campaigns simultaneously online and offline.

Here are some examples where your online and offline activities might not launch simultaneously:

- a campaign for an event promotion starts with a direct mail or an email;
- e-communications are reserved as contingency – in case offline response volumes are not high enough;
- a promotion is launched online first (notified by email) to appeal to loyal customers;
- an unusual ad execution is launched online first to create a buzz;
- a press release is announced first online so that it can be transmitted by particular advocates;
- a timed or limited offer is launched online, because timing of receipt can be more accurately assured.

5 *Optimising timing.* Do communications get delivered and received at the optimal time? For online display advertising, PPC and email marketing there are specific times of the day, days of the week or times of the month that your message will work best.

Case Study 8 A short history of Facebook

Context

This case is about the social network Facebook, which hardly needs an introduction. However, when we first featured it in an earlier edition of his text, it was a niche service mainly used in colleges and universities. It is still a good case study in that it shows many of the success factors needed for launch of a new digital business, along with the risks of alienating users when their privacy needs are not listened to. It's incredible that it now has more than a billion monthly active users worldwide, yet has fewer than 5000 employees.

Value proposition

In 2015, the Facebook mission as stated on its company page is simply: 'We want to give you the power to share and to make the world more open and connected'. Previously, Facebook described itself in a more functional sense as

> a social utility that helps people communicate more efficiently with their friends, family and coworkers. The company develops technologies that facilitate the sharing of information through the social graph, the digital mapping of people's real-world social connections. Anyone can sign up for Facebook and interact with the people they know in a trusted environment.

Consumer value proposition

You may well have seen the 2010 film *The Social Network*, which describes how Facebook was founded while Mark Zuckerberg was a student at Harvard University. Initially membership was limited to Harvard students. The initial viral effect of the software was indicated since more than half of the undergraduate population at Harvard registered on the service within the first month! Zuckerberg used open-source software PHP and the MySQL database to create the original 'TheFacebook.com' site and these technologies are still in use today. The film also describes the long-running dispute on ownership of Facebook since another Harvard-originated social networking site 'HarvardConnection', which later changed its name to ConnectU, alleged in September 2004 that Zuckerberg had used their source code to develop Facebook when they originally contracted him to help in building their site.

When Facebook first launched in February 2004, there were just three things that users could do on the site which are still core to its functionality. Users could create a profile with their picture and information, view other people's profiles, and add people as friends.

The latest SEC update (2014) explains these core consumer benefits defined by the company:

- *Connect and share with your friends*. Staying connected is the core feature as we would expect, but note the more emotional underpinnings of the other elements of the value proposition.
- *Discover and learn*. Facebook references public figures and organisations that interest them – available through Facebook company pages.
- *Express yourself*. A fundamental need. Facebook does this through its key features which it describes as the Timeline, News Feed, Photos and Videos and messaging through Email, Chat and Text.
- *Stay connected everywhere*. Referencing the importance of mobile use and use on other sites to Facebook's users and business model: *People can access Facebook through the website, mobile sites, smartphone apps, and feature phone products*.

Value proposition for marketers and businesses

Facebook works hard to monetise its audience, particularly since Facebook held its initial public offering (IPO) on 18 May 2012. This was the biggest IPO for an Internet company, with a peak market capitalisation of over $104 billion. Facebook describes its offer to business as follows:

> Marketers can engage with more than one billion monthly active users on Facebook or subsets of our users based on information people have chosen to share with us such as their age, location, gender, or interests. We offer marketers a unique combination of reach, relevance, social context, and engagement to enhance the value of their ads.

Commercial companies or not-for-profit organisations (e.g. www.facebook.com/joinred) can also create their own Facebook pages for their company (currently free). Facebook users can then express their support by adding themselves as a fan, writing on the company Wall, uploading photos, and joining other fans in discussion groups. When users become fans, they can optionally agree to be kept up-to-date about developments which then appear in their news feeds.

To encourage companies to advertise, Facebook uses an algorithm known as EdgeRank, which determines the percentage of company status updates appear in a user's newsfeed.

Revenue model

Facebook has an ad-based revenue model. Some of the features of Facebook Ads (www.facebook.com/ads) include:

- Targeting by age, gender, location, interests and more.
- Alternative payment models: cost per click (CPC) or impression-based (CPM).
- 'Trusted Referrals' or 'Social Ads' – ads can also be shown to users whose friends have recently engaged with a company's Facebook page or engaged with the company website.

At the time of the launch of ads, the Facebook blog made these comments, which indicate the delicate balance between advertising revenue and user experience. They said, first of all, 'what's not changing':

- Facebook will always stay clutter-free and clean.
- Facebook will never sell any of your information.
- You will always have control over your information and your Facebook experience.
- You will not see any more ads than you did before this.

And what is changing:

- You now have a way to connect with products, businesses, bands, celebrities and more on Facebook.
- Ads should be getting more relevant and more meaningful to you.

Facebook's strategy

Facebook describes the key elements of its strategy in its SEC filing as:

1 *Expand global community.* Facebook names specific 'relatively less-penetrated, large markets' such as Brazil, India, Mexico and Japan.
2 *Develop social products to provide the most compelling user experience.* As with many SEC filings of successful Internet businesses, there is a clear commitment to user experience. Facebook's approach is based on Insight:

> *To provide the most compelling user experience, we continue to develop products and technologies focussed on optimising our social distribution channels to deliver the most useful content to each user by analysing and organising vast amounts of information in real time.*

Smart Insights (2012) quotes Andrew (Boz) Bosworth, who is the Director of Engineering at Facebook, as saying

> *Every day, we run hundreds of tests on Facebook, most of which are rolled out to a random sample of people to test their impact. For example, you may have seen a small test for saving news feed stories last week.*

> *Other products might require network effects to be properly tested, so in those cases we launch to everyone in a specific market, like a whole country.*

3 *Mobile products.* Facebook is seeking to make these more engaging and more easily available. In April 2014 Facebook passed 1 billion million average monthly users of mobile services. The acquisition of photo sharing app Instagram in August 2012 was part of this strategy.
4 *Facebook Platform.* Facebook notes the importance of developing an open system through apps and websites built by developers using the Facebook Platform including API (Application Programming Interfaces) and Social Plugins (for example, Like and Share buttons; Figure 8.24) to help integration with other services such as websites. The Facebook Platform was introduced in 2007 and by January 2008 over 18,000 applications had been built on Facebook Platform with 140 new applications added per day. More than 95 per cent of Facebook members have used at least one application built on Facebook Platform.

Facebook Platform for mobile applications was launched in October 2007, although many Facebook users already interacted with their friends through mobile phones

5 *Improve ad products.* With the IPO this is a vital aim for Facebook, but it has to be balanced against the other elements of the strategy, particularly 2. Facebook states: 'Our advertising strategy centres on the belief that ad products that are social, relevant, and well-integrated with other content on Facebook can enhance the user experience while providing an attractive return.'
6 *Build a scalable infrastructure.* Facebook describes its investment in software and hardware infrastructure that enables its aim to provide a 'unique, personalised experience to each of our users around the world'. To do this Facebook explains its technology investments as focussing on analytics and

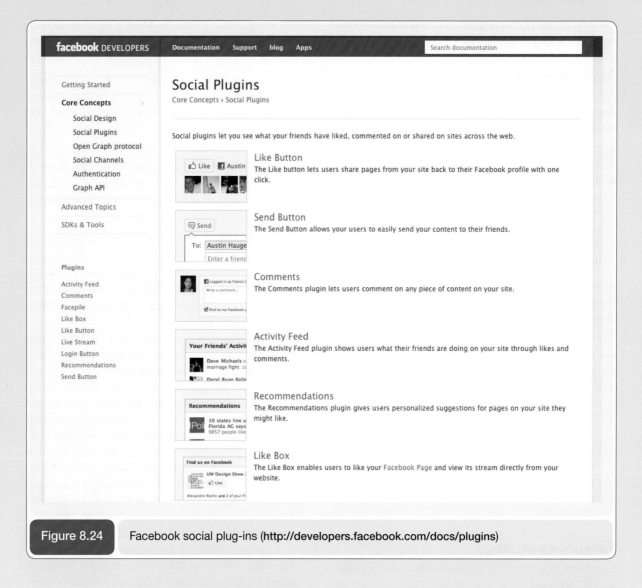

| Figure 8.24 | Facebook social plug-ins (http://developers.facebook.com/docs/plugins) |

development in areas including content optimisation and delivery, graph query, media storage and serving, large-scale data management, and software performance.

Facebook's competitors

Although it seems curious to think of a company as large as Facebook having competitors, it has new global rivals and local rivals. It mentions Google+, which Google has integrated with certain of its products, including search and Android, as well as other, largely regional, social networks that have strong positions in particular countries, such as Mixi in Japan and vKontakte and Odnoklassniki in Russia. It also describes companies that offer microblogging (Twitter), developers of platforms such as Apple iOS and Google Android and games developers as key competitors. It has taken the decision not to create a competing mobile platform, instead in 2013 launching Facebook Home on Android to increase usage of Facebook on these devices.

Risk factors

Today Facebook states that: 'Trust is a cornerstone of our business' and it now dedicates significant resources to the goal of building user trust through developing and implementing programs designed to protect user privacy, promote a safe environment and assure the security of user data. Facebook has to some extent learnt this lesson from early mistakes, with incidents including:

● *New feed functionality launched – September 2006.* New information feeds were launched in mid-2006 which show the challenges of balancing the benefit of new functionality against disrupting existing user habits.

- Writing in the Facebook blog in September 2006 Mark Zuckerberg said:

  We really messed this one up. When we launched News Feed and Mini-Feed we were trying to provide you with a stream of information about your social world. Instead, we did a bad job of explaining what the new features were and an even worse job of giving you control of them. I'd like to try to correct those errors now.

- *Privacy concerns sparked by 'Beacon technology' – November 2007*. Facebook received a lot of negative publicity on its new advertising format related to the 'Beacon' tracking system. Mark Zuckerberg was forced to respond to on the Facebook blog (5 December 2007). He said:

  About a month ago, we released a new feature called Beacon to try to help people share information with their friends about things they do on the web. We've made a lot of mistakes building this feature, but we've made even more with how we've handled them. We simply did a bad job with this release, and I apologise for it. While I am disappointed with our mistakes, we appreciate all the feedback we have received from our users. I'd like to discuss what we have learnt and how we have improved Beacon.

- *Privacy setting concerns – autumn 2009 to spring 2010*. In December 2009, Facebook implemented new privacy settings. This meant some information, including 'lists of friends', was 'publicly available', when it was previously possible to restrict access to this information. Photos and some personal information were also public unless users were sufficiently knowledgeable and active to limit access. Privacy campaigners including the Electronic Frontier Foundation and American Civil Liberties Union criticised the changes. In May 2010 further changes were made to give users greater control and simplify the settings.

Facebook lists some of its other key risk factors as:

- users increasingly engage with other products or activities;
- we fail to introduce new and improved products or if we introduce new products or services that are not favourably received;
- users feel that their Facebook experience is diminished as a result of the decisions we make with respect to the frequency, prominence, and size of ads that we display;
- we are unable to continue to develop products for mobile devices that users find engaging, that work with a variety of mobile operating systems and networks, and that achieve a high level of market acceptance;
- we are unable to manage and prioritise information to ensure users are presented with content that is interesting, useful, and relevant to them;
- users adopt new technologies where Facebook may not be featured or otherwise available.

Key sources for the latest information on Facebook:

- All Facebook (www.allfacebook.com) and Inside Facebook (www.insidefacebook.com) are sites specialising in reporting all developments at Facebook.
- Key Facts – updated quarterly at close of year (http://newsroom.fb.com/Key-Facts)'
- SEC updates – Security and Exchange Commission annual report filings give great insights into how Facebook positions itself and what it sees as its risk factors (http://investor.fb.com/)'
- Smart Insights Facebook updates and advice (http://www.smartinsights.com/social-media-marketing/facebook-marketing/) cover the major developments that marketers need to be aware of'
- Social Bakers (www.socialbakers.com/facebook-statistics/) Facebook statistics by country and brand popularity.
- Wikipedia Pages for Facebook (http://en.wikipedia.org/wiki/Facebook).

Questions

1 As an investor in a social network such as Facebook, which financial and customer-related metrics would you use to assess and benchmark the current business success and future growth potential of the company?

2 Complete a situation analysis for Facebook focussing on an assessment of the main business risks which could damage the future growth potential of the social network.

3 For the main business risks to Facebook identified in Question 2, suggest approaches the company could use to minimise these risks.

Summary

1 Key characteristics of interactive communications are the combination of push and pull media, user-submitted content, personalisation, flexibility and, of course, interactivity to create a dialogue with consumers.

2 We reviewed these elements of a digital marketing communications plan:

- *Step 1. Goal setting and tracking.* These can include goals for campaign volume (unique visitors and visits), quality (conversion to value events), cost (including cost-per-acquisition) and profitability.
- *Step 2. Campaign insight.* Information to feed into the campaign plan includes potential site audience reach and compositions, online buying behaviour and preferences, customer search behaviour and competitor campaign activity.
- *Step 3. Segmentation and targeting.* Key segmentation approaches are relationship with company, demographic segmentation, psychographic or attitudinal segmentation, value, lifecycle stage and behaviour.
- *Step 4. Offer and message development.* Includes identification of primary and secondary offers.
- *Step 5. Budgeting and selecting the digital media mix.* Should be based on conversion models reviewing all the digital media channels.
- *Step 6. Integration into overall media schedule or plan.* The principles of integration include coherence, consistency, continuity and complementarities.

Exercises

Self-assessment exercises

1 Review the reasons why continuous marketing activity involving certain digital media channels is preferable to more traditional burst or campaign-based activity.
2 Describe the unique characteristics of digital media in contrast to traditional media.
3 Give example goals for an online acquisition campaign in terms of response rates or engagement with creative, cost and overall campaign effectiveness.
4 Review the options for targeting particular audience groups online with different digital media.
5 How should a company decide on the relative investment between digital media and traditional media in a marketing campaign?
6 What are the options for integrating different types of digital media channels with traditional media?
7 How can different forms of customer insight be used to inform campaign execution?
8 What are the issues that a marketer should consider when defining their offer and message for an online campaign?

Essay and discussion questions

1 Discuss Berthon *et al.*'s (1998) suggestion that effective Internet promotion is similar to a company exhibiting at an industry trade show attracting visitors to its stand.
2 Select a company of your choice and assess the effectiveness of the integration between their traditional communications, digital media channels and their website.
3 Select a recent campaign from a charity and with reference to their website campaign pages, identify how they should set campaign goals and review effectiveness.

4 How should companies decide on the granularity of targeting in digital media campaigns? Select two digital media channels to illustrate your examples.

Examination questions

1 Outline the range of goals that should be used to define success criteria for an online marketing campaign.
2 Using an example from a business-to-business company, describe the options available for targeting an audience through an email newsletter.
3 Explain why integration between online and traditional media will make a campaign more effective overall.
4 Describe different options for testing the effectiveness of competing offers online.
5 Which do you think are the three most important changes in campaign communications introduced by the emergence of digital media channels?
6 Which considerations would determine the suitability of incorporating a mobile 'text-to-win' promotion into an offline campaign?
7 In which ways is the long tail concept relevant to campaign planning?
8 How should a confectionary brand assess the success of a campaign microsite in uplift of branding metrics?

References

Adweek (2014) Evian's real-time marketing reaps big social stats, targets New Yorkers with Twitter-enabled service, Lauren Johnson, 5 September 2014, www.adweek.com/news/technology/evians-real-time-marketing-reaps-big-social-stats-159898.

Agrawal, V., Arjona, V. and Lemmens, R. (2001) E-performance: the path to rational exuberance, *McKinsey Quarterly*, 1, 31–43.

Berthon, P., Lane, N., Pitt, L. and Watson, R. (1998) The World Wide Web as an industrial marketing communications tool: models for the identification and assessment of opportunities, *Journal of Marketing Management*, 14, 691–704.

Berthon, P., Pitt, L. and Watson, R. (1996) Resurfing W3: research perspectives on marketing communication and buyer behaviour on the World Wide Web, *International Journal of Advertising*, 15, 287–301.

Bird, D. (2000) *Commonsense Direct Marketing*, 4th edn, Kogan Page, London.

Branthwaite, A., Wood, K. and Schilling, M. (2000) The medium is part of the message – the role of media for shaping the image of a brand, *ARF/ESOMAR Conference*, Rio de Janeiro, Brazil, 12–14 November.

Briggs, R., Krishnan, R. and Borin, N. (2005) Integrated multichannel communication strategies: evaluating the return on marketing objectives – the case of the 2004 Ford F-150 launch, *Journal of Interactive Marketing Communications*, 19(3).

Chaffey, D. and Smith, P.R. (2012) *E-marketing Excellence: Planning and Optimising Your Digital Marketing*, 4th edn, Butterworth-Heinemann, Oxford.

Cook, L. (2004) Econometrics and integrated campaigns, *AdMap*, June, 37–40.

Coulter, K. and Starkis, J. (2005) Development of a media selection model using the analytic network process, *International Journal of Advertising*, 24(2), 193–215.

Crawshaw, P. (2004) Media neutral planning – what is it? Online article, Account Planning Group, www.apg.org.uk.

Deighton, J. (1996) The future of interactive marketing, *Harvard Business Review* (November–December), 151–62.

Eleftheriou-Smith, L.-M. (2013) Lynx celebrates 18 years of Africa with 'The can becomes the man' work, *Campaign*, 19 November 2013, **www.campaignlive.co.uk/news/1221418/ Lynx-celebrates-18-years-Africa-The-becomes-man-work/?DCMP=ILC-SEARCH**.

Facebook (2014) SEC updates – Security and Exchange Commission annual report filings give great insights into how Facebook positions itself and what it sees as its risk factors, **http://investor.fb.com/**.

Fill, C. (2007) *Marketing Communications: Engagement, Strategies and Practice*, Financial Times Prentice Hall, Harlow.

Flores, L and Eltvedt H. (2005) Beyond advertising – lesson about the power of brand new websites to build and expand brands, ESOMAR, Montreal. ESOMAR, Online Conference, Montreal, June 2005.

Godin, S. (1999) *Permission Marketing*, Simon and Schuster, New York.

Harper, S. (2006) Pilot Eye Tracking Study, University of Manchester, School of Computer Science web research summary, **http://hcw.cs.manchester.ac.uk/research/vicram/studies/ eyetracking.php**.

Hoffman, D.L. and Novak, T.P. (1996) Marketing in hypermedia computer-mediated environments: conceptual foundations, *Journal of Marketing*, 60 (July), 50–68.

Hoffman, D.L. and Novak, T.P. (1997) A new marketing paradigm for electronic commerce, *The Information Society*, Special issue on electronic commerce, 13 (January–March), 43–54.

Hoffman, D.L. and Novak, T.P. (2000) How to acquire customers on the web, *Harvard Business Review* (May–June), 179–88, **http://ecommerce.vanderbilt.edu/papers.html**.

Hussein, I. (2006) IPA TouchPoints, *AdMap*, July–August, 46–8.

IAB (2004) XMOS research case studies, **www.iab.net/insights_research/1672/1678/1690**.

IPA (2004) Econometrics explained, by Louise Cook and Mike Holmes, edited by Les Binet, a white paper published by the Institute of Practitioners in Advertising, **www.ipa .co.uk**.

IPA (2011) Integration: how to get it right and deliver results, Summary of a Institute of Practitioners in Advertising members report, 21 June 2011.

Jenkinson, A. (2003) Seeboard. A case study from the Centre for Integrated Marketing, **www.centreforintegratedmarketing.com**.

Kaushik (2008) Excellent analytics tip#13: measure macro and micro conversions. Blog post, 26 March 2008, Avinash Kaushik: **www.kaushik.net/avinash/**.

Kotler, P., Armstrong, G., Saunders, J. and Wong, V. (2001) *Principles of Marketing*, 3rd European edn, Financial Times/Prentice Hall, Harlow.

Lee, G. (2010) Death of 'last click wins': media attribution and the expanding use of media data, *Journal of Direct, Data and Digital Marketing Practice*, 12(1), 16–26.

Meerman-Scott, D. (2010) *Real-time Marketing and PR How to Instantly Engage Your Market, Connect with Customers, and Create Products that Grow Your Business*, Wiley, New York.

NMA (2006) Banking on search, *New Media Age*, 16 March 2006.

NMA (2008) Ad Watch – Lynx makes successful pass at digital with Get In There, *New Media Age*, 7 February, 14–15.

Peters, L. (1998) The new interactive media: one-to-one but to whom?, *Marketing Intelligence and Planning*, 16(1), 22–30.

Petersen, E. (2004) *Web Measurement Hacks. Tips and Tools to Help Optimise your Online Business*, O'Reilly, Sebastapol, CA, **www.oreilly.com/catalogue/webmeasurehks/ chapter/index.html**.

Pickton, A. and Broderick, D. (2001) *Integrated Marketing Communications*, Financial Times/Prentice Hall, Harlow.

Pincott, G. (2000) Website promotion strategy, white paper from Millward Brown, **www .intelliquest.com**.

Schramm, W. (1955) How communication works, in W. Schramm (ed.), *The Process and Effects of Mass Communications*, University of Illinois Press, Urbana, IL, 3–26.

Shah, D. and Halligan, B. (2009) *Inbound Marketing: Get Found Using Google, Social Media and Blogs*, John Wiley, Hoboken, NJ.

Sissors, J. and Baron, R. (2002) *Advertising Media Planning*, 6th edn, McGraw-Hill, Chicago.

Smart Insights (2012) Ship early, ship often. Blog post, 4 September 2012 by Dave Chaffey.

Tapp, A. (2005) Clearing up media neutral planning, *Interactive Marketing*, 6(3), 216–21.

Varianini, V. and Vaturi, D. (2000) Marketing lessons from e-failures, *McKinsey Quarterly*, 4, 86–97.

VIP Wordpress (2014) 10 growth hacks that helped **metro.co.uk** achieve 27 million monthly visitors, article by Sara Rosso, posted on 11 March 2014.

Walmsley, A. (2007) New media; the age of the trialogue, *The Marketer* (September), 12.

Wertime, K. and Fenwick, I. (2008) *DigiMarketing – The Essential Guide to New Media and Digital Marketing*, John Wiley and Sons, Singapore.

Weblinks

Links on specific digital media channels such as email marketing and search engine marketing are at the end of Chapter 9.

Sites focussing on approaches to running interactive marketing campaigns

- **ClickZ** (**www.clickz.com/experts/**). Has columns on different aspects of interactive communications including media planning.
- **iMediaConnection** (**www.imediaconnection.com**). Media site reporting on best practice in online advertising.
- **US Internet Advertising Bureau** (**www.iab.net**). The widest range of studies about Internet advertising effectiveness. In UK: **www.iabuk.net**.
- **Journal of Computer Mediated Communications** (**www.blackwell-synergy.com/loi/jcmc**). A free online per-reviewed journal describing developments in interactive communications.
- **Media Buyer Planner** (**www.buyerplanner.com**). Developments in media planning with strong focus on online media.
- **Marketing Sherpa** (**www.marketingsherpa.com**). Articles and links on Internet marketing communications including email and online advertising.
- **SmartInsights.com** (**www.smartinsights.com**). Advice on creating effective marketing campaigns include customer insight and attribution modelling.
- **World Advertising Research Centre** (**www.warc.com**). Covers offline and online media. Mainly subscription service, but with some free resources.

Chapter 9
Marketing communications using digital media channels

Chapter at a glance

Main topics

- Search engine marketing 484
- Online public relations 502
- Online partnerships including affiliate marketing 510
- Interactive display advertising 515
- Opt-in email marketing and mobile text messaging 522
- Social media and viral marketing 528
- Offline promotion techniques 535

Case studies

Digital marketing in practice

The Smart Insights interview with Katie Webb, Online Marketing Manager at Vision Express, who explains how the multichannel retailer prioritises its use of social media to meet its business goals 480

Case study 9: Innovation at Google 539

Learning objectives

After reading this chapter, the reader should be able to:

- Distinguish between the different types of digital media channels
- Evaluate the advantages and disadvantages of each digital media channel for marketing communications
- Assess the suitability of different types of digital media for different purposes.

Questions for marketers

Key questions for marketing managers related to this chapter are:

- Which digital communications media should we select for different types of market?
- What are the success factors for using digital media that will make our campaigns more effective?

Scan code to find the latest updates for topics in this chapter

Links to other chapters

Related chapters are:

- Chapter 1 introduces the main options for communications with across paid, owned and earned digital media types
- Chapter 8 reviews how to plan campaigns which use digital media channels. The section towards the end of the chapter on 'Selecting the right mix of digital media communications tools' in 'Step 5. Budgeting and selecting the digital media mix', is particularly relevant
- Chapter 10 also considers the measurement of communications effectiveness.

Introduction

Digital media channel
Online communications technique such as search engine marketing, affiliate marketing and display advertising used to engage web users on third-party sites; encourage them to visit an organisation's site or purchase through traditional channels such as by phone or in-store.

Digital marketing managers use many different **digital media channels,** such as affiliate, email, social and search engine marketing, to attract visitors to their website. They also have options such as display advertising and widget marketing for communicating brand values to visitors of third-party websites. Traditional communications disciplines such as advertising, direct mail and PR remain important in generating awareness and favourability about brands and in encouraging visits to a business's online presence.

Choosing the most effective digital communications techniques and refining them to attract visitors and new customers at an efficient cost is now a major marketing activity, for both online business and multichannel businesses. In this chapter, we explain the differences between the different digital media options and review the strengths, weaknesses and success factors for using the communications techniques.

How is this chapter structured?

This chapter is structured around the six main digital media channels we have identified in Table 9.1 (Figure 1.9 on page 28 portrays a graphical summary). To enable easy comparison of the different techniques and to assist with assignments and revision, we have structured each section the same way:

- *What is it*? A description of the digital media channel.
- *Advantages and disadvantages*? A structured review of the benefits and drawbacks of each channel.
- *Best practice in planning and management*. A summary of the issues such as targeting, measurement and creative which need to be considered when running a campaign using each digital channel. This expands on the coverage given in the previous chapter on these issues.

As you read each section, you should compare the relative strengths and weaknesses of the different techniques and how consumers perceive different options in terms of trust (Activity 9.1). In the final section, we summarise their strengths and weaknesses for different applications.

Table 9.1	Summary of different digital media channels	
Digital media channel	**Description**	**Different communications techniques**
Search engine marketing (SEM)	Gaining listings in the search engine results pages of the major search engines, Google, Bing, YouTube and popular country-specific engines. Also includes advertising on third-party publisher sites which are part of the search display networks to generate awareness and for remarketing	• Search Engine Optimisation (SEO) listing in the natural listing which does not attract a fee per click. Based on on-page optimisation and link-building • Pay-per-click advertising sponsored listings using Google AdWords, for example
Online public relations (E-PR)	Maximising favourable mentions of your company, brands, products or websites on third-party sites such as media sites, social networks or blogs that are likely to be visited by your target audience. Also includes monitoring and, where necessary, responding to negative mentions and conducting public relations via a site through a press centre or blog, for example	• Syndicating content (e.g. press releases), gaining positive mentions, managing reputation on third-party sites, particularly forums and social networks • Use of owned media – own company feeds, blogs and feeds • Blogger and influencer outreach for earned media

Digital media channel	Description	Different communications techniques
Online partnerships including affiliate marketing and co-marketing	Creating and managing long-term arrangements to promote your online services on third-party websites or through email communications. Different forms of partnership include co-marketing, link building, affiliate marketing, aggregators such as price comparison sites, online sponsorship and co-branding	• Commission-based affiliate marketing for transactional e-commerce sites • Creating long-term partnership relationships such as sponsorship, link-building or editorial
Interactive display advertising	Use of online display ads such as banners and rich media ads to achieve brand awareness and encourage click-through to a target site	• Site-specific media buys • Use of ad networks • Behavioural re-targeting or remarketing based on action
Opt-in email marketing	Using legal, permission-based emailing to prospects or customers who have agreed to receive emails from an organisation. Solus emails can be booked where a publisher sends an email on behalf of a brand or the brand can be featured in an e-newsletter. Companies can build up their own 'house list' containing customer or prospect details and company emails encourage purchase	• Acquisition email activity including list rental (rarely permitted by law today), co-branded publisher campaigns, advertising on e-newsletters • Retention and growth activity, e.g. house list for e-newsletters and customer email campaigns • Automatic or event-triggered email campaign activity
Social media marketing including viral and electronic word-of-mouth marketing	Social media marketing and viral marketing is effectively online word-of-mouth – compelling brand-related content is shared, forwarded or discussed electronically or discussed offline to help achieve awareness and, in some cases, drive response. Strong link with online PR activity	• Branded presence of company page or advertising on social network • Creating 'viral agents' or compelling interactive content • Encouraging amplification of viral messages • Using customer advocacy effect • Widget marketing

The importance of each of these digital media channels in driving visitors will vary from company to company, but to give you an indication of how important they are on average see Digital marketing insight 9.1. You can see why search engine marketing is an important channel and this is why we start our coverage in this chapter with this. You can also see that direct traffic is high, reflecting the importance of visits driven by traditional channels or visits from email or social networks that are not being tracked separately. You can also see that links from other sites are also quite significant.

Digital marketing insight 9.1   How balanced is your referrer mix?

One approach to determining the most appropriate mix of digital media channels is this compilation across all sites that use the web analytics tool Google Analytics to measure site effectiveness (see Chapter 10 for a description of how these tools work). Figure 9.1 shows the average mix of referrers or 'traffic sources' for sites tracked by Google Analytics.

This is a summary of the different terms in the pie chart:

• *Search engine* – this groups both natural and paid search (AdWords).
• *Referral* – this is traffic from other sites which have direct links to a site. This can include social media sites, but Google and other analytics services now separate out 'social traffic'.

Figure 9.1	Average percentage of traffic from different sources referred to a website
	Source: Smart Insights (2011a)

- *Direct* – direct traffic results from URL type-ins, bookmarks or when email marketing isn't tracked by marketers adding specific link tracking to their email so that they show up in analytics. These days direct traffic will also include non-browser traffic from visitors clicking on apps for reading social media updates like Hootsuite or Tweetdeck or other mobile apps linking to a site. This traffic is sometimes called 'Dark Social' since it is difficult to attribute to social media updates.
- *Other* – campaigns include AdWords when linked to the Google Account and any other campaigns like affiliates, display ads and email campaigns when these have had marketing campaign tags attached. In this compilation AdWords is included under search engines.

Note: This industry benchmark data is no longer updated and published by Google. Marketers can use the Benchmarks feature in Google Analytics to compare their mix of referrers to their website or reference the Similar Web compilation (**www.similarweb .com**) which is also useful for students reviewing the traffic sources for case study companies they are reviewing in assignments.

Kate Webb, online marketing manager at Vision Express, explains how the multichannel retailer prioritises its use of social media to meet business goals.

The Interview

Q. How big an impact has the increase in popularity of social media with consumers had on Vision Express?

Kate Webb: It's had quite an impact in terms of time and resource, especially in the early days. As a company we're relatively new to social media; we've only been active for just over a year. We spent a lot of time during the first three to six months listening, watching and learning what consumers were saying about our brand/looking for from our brand, in order to decide on how we should communicate, and where – which platforms.

During this time we have seen our follower/fan numbers grow, but more importantly the engagement with our customers is increasing and we feel that our customers are really starting to converse with us as a brand.

Since being involved in social media we have seen an increase in the number of customers who mention us directly, or seek us out, rather than simply mentioning our brand name in passing conversation. To us this is an important development in building our customer relationship.

At Vision Express our social media activities are based on engaging with our existing customer base; we want to improve on relationships, or continue offline relationships, with our customers, online. In the optical industry we have a long purchase cycle, on average our customers come back to us every two years, so it is a long period during which to maintain our social media relationships.

We have found that for probably about 1–2 per cent of our customer base, social media is their main point of contact with us. The type of communication varies between the different social media platforms, for example we find that Twitter is more of a customer service tool, while Facebook is a fun and engaging platform, suitable for promotional outreach.

There is still progress to be made, especially as social media grows and platforms are developed/changed, but we're confident we're on the right track to providing the same high level of service that our customers get in our stores, online.

Q. What do you see as the key parts of a social media strategy that require management?

Kate Webb: I find that too often businesses think that social media is just about posting messages about the company on Twitter or Facebook, or getting an agency in to handle everything for them. But the key to making social media work, for me, is to have a strong strategy behind it, and to manage that strategy.

For me the key areas of focus in this strategy should be:

- *Brand/business persona*: I feel it's key to define a persona or personality for your business and to identify how you want to position your brand on social media, is the brand/business fun/funky, calm/serious, sensitive/nurturing or brash/loud? You need flexibility to evolve this over time as your relationship with customers grows.
- *Which platforms*: There are hundreds of social media platforms that we could all be involved in, so it's key to identify which platforms support your business objectives, and which ones you are going to get involved with. Otherwise resources and communication will simply be spread too thinly.
- *Goals/objectives*: It is important to ensure that your social media objectives or goals are aligned with that of your organisation. What is it that you want to achieve via social media. For Vision Express, our three critical goals are to:
  - Add value and service to our online customers, via informative dialogue, responsive customer service and feedback. This also works as a two-way path, in that we then pass onto our store network all/any feedback we have received from our online customers.
  - Engage with our online customers, and build relationships with them. In order to do this effectively, we are working towards a one-customer-view database, which will enable us to match social media activity to in-store activity by our customers, thus enabling us to provide a tailored approach in our conversations.
  - Build brand awareness and consumer knowledge about our service offering. We want our customers to understand our company, and to recognise our values, ethics and personality, online and offline.
- *Analytics/results*: Be this sentiment or engagement levels, reporting on results/analytics needs to be regular, managed and analysed in order to adapt future strategy.
- *Technology advancements*: Social media platforms are changing all the time. Because of this it is imperative that we understand and gain knowledge of how these advancements/changes will affect our business's social media presence going forward.

Q. How should a company assess the relevance of different social media opportunities to prioritise their focus?

Kate Webb: Having clear objectives and a clear strategy will help. Enabling you, on a case-by-case basis, to identify what social media opportunities work for which promotion/aspect of the business.

It's important for any business/brand not to spread their actions/activities too thinly, identify where the majority of your customers are and focus on engaging well with your customers on a few platforms.

As well as identifying which platforms to be active on, it's important to also understand to what extent you work with these platforms; does your business need/require interactive apps or games? Or is simple communication the key to your social media engagement?

I feel it is also important to identify where social media fits in with your overall online and offline presence, and ensure that it complements your other activities. Recently I have seen an increase in brands advertising both online and on TV their Facebook and Twitter presences, but not their website? To me, a brands website should take precedence, and social media presences should complement the website messaging and be aimed at engaging customers with the website.

If through doing these engagement activities we acquire customers, then great, but this isn't our primary focus.

Q. What advice would you give to a company starting a social media listening/reputation management initiative?

Kate Webb: Listen, listen and listen some more. Social media isn't about who shouts the loudest, it's about engaging in conversation with your customers/prospective customers and about keeping them informed.

If you are really serious about social media, and I think companies need to be these days, you need to enlist a social media monitoring platform, which will enable you to listen to what consumers are saying about your brand across micromedia (Twitter/Facebook), blogs and forums.

You won't be able to respond to all consumer mentions, due to forum rules, but you can at least listen and feed this back into the business, so you can modify activities, or continue doing popular ones! Start small, don't overstretch your resources, and be realistic about the amount of time/resource and money social media can take up.

A few key things to remember are, once you start talking, you need to continue the commitment to maintain the conversations, and ensure you gain inter-company awareness, there is nothing worse than talking to a customer via Twitter, and then having them go into store to be presented with 'We're on Twitter? I didn't know that'.

You will also need to get to know your customers. The ideal solution here is to integrate social media activities into your core customer database, so you have one customer view, but this can take time, money and resource. In the interim, the better social media monitoring tools these days are offering engagement platforms, which allow you to add notes and assign tasks, so you can build up a reasonable knowledge of your social media customers.

Q. Where do you think the responsibilities for managing social media marketing in a company should lie? How is it managed at Vision Express?

Kate Webb: By spending our first three to six months listening to what our customers were saying about our brand and what they were looking for from our brand, we managed to identify that our social media activities needed to be part of the whole business, not just an 'add-on' to our marketing activities.

It is important that social media activities have management 'buy-in' in any business. It needs to be integrated into core business activities if it is going to work properly.

To integrate these activities into different departments correctly requires management support, the management structure need to understand why/how/who social media impacts on and affects both internally and within our customer base.

As a result, so far, we've integrated social media into a couple of key departments within the business, with the online marketing team as social media 'owners', in that we will identify the next strategic steps, bring in agency support, provide understanding of new developments and report on analytics and progress.

We have involvement from our customer care team, who respond on a day-to-day basis to customer enquiries/queries and feedback. We integrate social media into our marketing planning activities from the outset, identifying whether a promotion is suitable for social media and, if so, which platform it suits best, and we have our product department involved to provide a great level of product information and advice.

To have social media as purely a marketing tool/activity will restrict a business in providing the right level of customer care, and will lead to sporadic/untimely and unfocused outreach.

Activity 9.1   How do consumers rate communications?

Figure 9.2 shows consumer ratings of different forms of advertising. Review the alternatives and then discuss the implications for a marketer of using these communication channels.

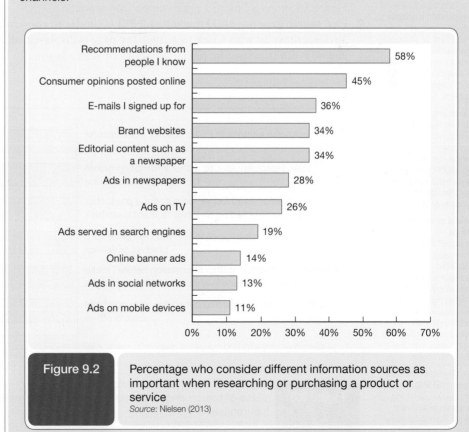

Figure 9.2   Percentage who consider different information sources as important when researching or purchasing a product or service
Source: Nielsen (2013)

Search engine marketing

Search engine marketing (SEM)
Promoting an organisation through search engines to meet its objectives by delivering relevant content in the search listings for searchers and encouraging them to click through to a destination site. The two key techniques of SEM are *search engine optimisation (SEO)* to improve results from the natural listings, and *paid-search marketing* to deliver results from the sponsored listings within the search engines. Note, in the US and some European countries the acronym SEM is sometimes used just to describe paid search advertising. Confusing!

Navigational (or brand) search
Searchers use a search engine such as Google to find information deeper within a company site by appending a qualifier such as a product name to the brand or site name. Organisations need to check that relevant pages are available in the search results pages for these situations.

Search engine optimisation (SEO)
A structured approach used to increase the position of a company or its products in search engine natural or organic results listings for selected keywords or phrases.

Natural or organic listings
The pages listing results from a search engine query which are displayed in a sequence according to relevance of match between the keyword phrase typed into a search engine and a web page according to a ranking algorithm used by the search engine.

Search engine results pages (SERPS)
The page(s) containing the results after a user types a keyphrase into a search engine. SERPS contain both natural or

Search engine marketing (SEM) is a key technique for generating quality visitors to a website, as suggested by Figure 9.1. We all now naturally turn to a search engine when we are seeking a new product, service or entertainment, as shown by the research presented in Figure 9.3. The main options include Google, Bing, the Google-owned YouTube, which is the second largest search engine by volumes of searches in many countries, or other regional search engine. We also turn to search when we are familiar with a brand, short-cutting site navigation by searching for a brand, appending a brand name to a product or typing a URL into Google. This is known as **navigational (or brand) search**. Given the obvious importance of reaching an audience during their consideration process for a product or when they are locating a brand, search engine marketing (SEM) has become a fiercely competitively area of digital marketing.

There are two main types of SEM that are quite distinct in the marketing activities needed to manage them, so we will study them separately, although in practice they should be integrated:

1 **Search engine optimisation (SEO)** involves achieving the highest position or ranking practical in the **natural or organic listings** shown in Figure 9.4 as the main body of the **search engine results pages (SERPS)** across a range of specific combination of keywords (or keyphrases) entered by search engine users.

As well as listing pages which the search engine determines as relevant for the search performed based on the text it contains and other factors, such as links to the page, the SERPs also contain other tools which searchers may find useful. Google terms these tools part of a strategy known as **universal search** or blended search. For example, Figure 9.4 shows a link to a price comparison service.

2 **Paid search (pay-per-click) marketing (PPC)** is similar to conventional advertising; here a relevant text ad with a link to a company page is displayed when the user of a search engine types in a specific phrase. A series of text ads usually labelled as 'sponsored

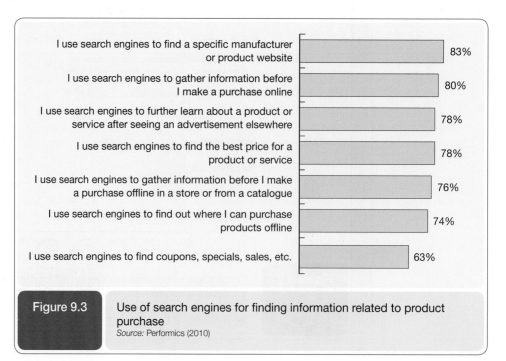

Figure 9.3	Use of search engines for finding information related to product purchase *Source:* Performics (2010)

organic listings and paid
or sponsored listings.

Universal search
The natural listings
incorporate other
relevant results from
vertical searches related
to a query, such as
video, books, news,
real-time social media
recommendations, site
links and images.

**Paid search marketing
(pay-per-click) market-
ing (PPC)**
A relevant text ad with
a link to a company
page is displayed on the
SERPs when the user of
a search engine types
in a specific phrase. A
fee is charged for every
click of each link, with the
amount bid for the click
mainly determining its
position. Additionally, PPC
may involve advertising
through a display network
of third-party sites (which
may be on a CPC, CPM
or CPA basis).

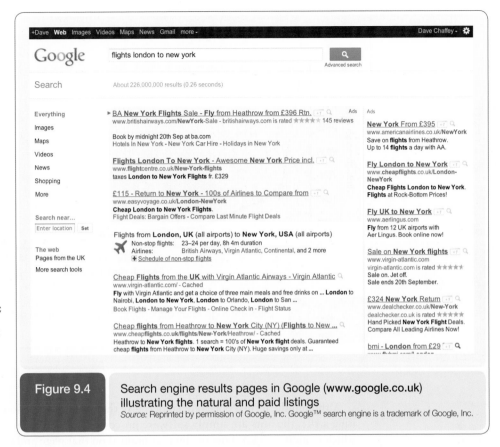

Figure 9.4 Search engine results pages in Google (www.google.co.uk) illustrating the natural and paid listings
Source: Reprinted by permission of Google, Inc. Google™ search engine is a trademark of Google, Inc.

links' are displayed above or to the right of the natural listings, as in Figure 9.4. Although many searchers prefer to click on the natural listings, a sufficient number do click on the paid listings (typically around a quarter or a third of all clicks) such that they are highly profitable for companies such as Google and a well-designed paid search campaign can drive a significant amount of business for companies. There are also opportunities to create awareness and response from pay-per-click ads displayed on third-party sites as we will see in the section on paid search marketing.

The importance of effective search engine marketing is suggested by Figure 9.5, which shows that generating the highest rankings for a company in the search engine results pages (SERPs) can generate many more visits because of a higher click-through rate. Note that click-through rate according to position will vary dramatically by type of keyword such as brand or generic keyword, but this research is based on 10,000 keywords across 250 B2C and B2B companies.

What is SEO?

Robots or spiders
Spiders are software
processes, technically
known as robots,
employed by search
engines to index web
pages of registered sites
on a regular basis. They
follow or crawl links
between pages and
record the reference
URL of a page for future
analysis.

Improving positions in the natural listings is dependent on marketers understanding the process whereby search engines compile an index by sending out spiders or robots to crawl around sites that are registered with that search engine (Figure 9.6). The figure shows that the technology harnessed to create the natural listings involves these main processes:

1 *Crawling.* The purpose of the crawl is to identify relevant pages for indexing and assess whether they have changed. Crawling is performed by **robots** (bots) that are also known as **spiders**. These access web pages and retrieve a reference URL of the page for later analysis and indexing.

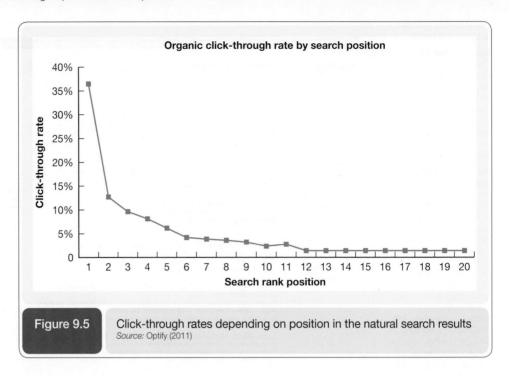

Figure 9.5	Click-through rates depending on position in the natural search results
	Source: Optify (2011)

Although the terms 'bot' and 'spider' give the impression of something physical visiting a site, the bots are simply software processes running on a search engine's server which request pages, follow the links contained on that page and create a series of page references with associated URLs. This is a recursive process, so each link followed will find additional links which then need to be crawled.

2 *Indexing.* An index is created to enable the search engine to rapidly find the most relevant pages containing the query typed by the searcher. Rather than searching each page for a query phrase, a search engine 'inverts' the index to produce a lookup table of documents containing particular words.

The index information consists of phases stored within a document and also other information characterising a page such as the document's title, meta description, PageRank, trust or authority, spam rating, etc. For the keywords in the document, additional attributes will be stored such as semantic markup (<h1>, <h2> headings denoted within HTML), occurrence in **link anchor text**, proximity, frequency or density and position in document, etc. The words contained in link anchor text 'pointing' to a page are particularly important in determining search rankings.

3 *Ranking or scoring.* The indexing process has produced a lookup of all the pages that contain particular words in a query, but they are not sorted in terms of relevance. Ranking of the document to assess the most relevant set of documents to return in the SERPs occurs in real time for the search query entered. First, relevant documents will be retrieved from a runtime version of the index at a particular data centre, then a rank in the SERPs for each document will be computed based on parsing many ranking factors, of which we highlight the main ones in later sections.

4 *Query request and results serving.* The familiar search engine interface accepts the searcher's query. The user's location is assessed through their IP address and the query is then passed to a relevant data centre for processing. Ranking then occurs in real time for a particular query to return a sorted list of relevant documents and these are displayed on the search results page.

Link anchor text
The text used to form the blue underlined hyperlink viewed in a web browser defined in the HTML source. For example, a link: Visit Dave Chaffey's Digital Marketing site is created by the HTML code: <A href="**http://www. smartinsights.com**">Visit Dave Chaffey's Digital Marketing site</A>.

Search engine ranking factors

Google has stated that it uses more than 200 factors or signals within its search ranking algorithms. These include positive ranking factors that help boost position and negative factors or filters which are used to remove search engine spam (also known as webspam) from the index where SEO companies have used unethical approaches such as automatically creating links to mislead the Google algorithms. The importance of ranking factors are much disputed by SEOs since with so many factors it is difficult to isolate their impact to prove a correlation, or more important a causative relationship between. The interested should read the balanced article by Fiorelli (2014) discussing the *The Myth of Google's 200 Ranking Factors*. In this coverage we will summarise the current thinking based on Dave Chaffey's more than 15 years of experience as an SEO consultant and publisher.

At a top level, the two most important factors for good ranking positions in all the main search engines are:

- *Matching between web page copy and the key phrases searched*. The main factors to optimise on are 'keyword density', keyword formatting, keywords in anchor text and the document meta-data including page title tags. The SEO process to improve results in this area is known as **on-page optimisation**. We will cover some of details of best practice for this process in a topic later in this section.
- *Links into the page (inbound or **backlinks**)*. Google counts each link to a page from another page or another site as a vote for this page. So pages and sites with more external links from other sites will be ranked more highly. The quality of the link is also important, so if links are from a site with a good reputation and relevant context

On-page optimisation
Writing copy and applying markup such as the <title> tag and heading tag <h1> to highlight to search engine relevant keyphrases within a document.

Backlink
Hyperlink which links to a particular web page (or website). Also known as an inbound link. Google PageRank and Yahoo! WebRank are methods of enumerating this.

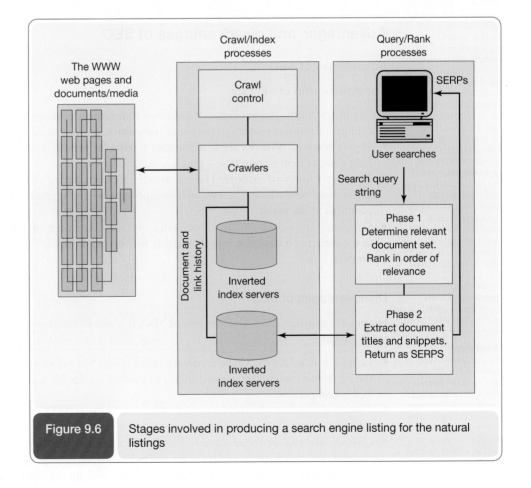

| Figure 9.6 | Stages involved in producing a search engine listing for the natural listings |

for the keyphrase, then this is more valuable. Internal links are also assessed in a similar way. The processes to improve this aspect of SEO are **external link building** and **internal link architecture**. To reduce the impact of webspam, search engines introduced **nofollow tags**, which means that links added to comments in blogs and social media blogs have a limited impact, although it seems that many search spammers aren't aware of this.

When we first wrote about SEO in the first edition of this text, the concept of content marketing didn't exist. Today amongst practising marketers it is now recognised that the best, scalable way to gain quality backlinks is through content marketing described in the 'Focus on Content Marketing' section in Chapter 8. This involves developing quality content and then working with partner sites through a process of 'outreach'. Some have suggested that SEO has become less important, but the reality is that SEO has always involved a combination of technical SEO to ensure pages are indexed, development of content and working with other site owners. This hasn't changed.

With the growing importance of sharing of links through social media the search engines now use the number of social mentions to a page and across a site to determine ranking positions (Smart Insights, 2010). For example, a representative of Bing said of assessment of Twitter:

> We take into consideration how often a link has been tweeted or retweeted, as well as the authority of the Twitter users that shared the link.

The implications of this are that if companies can get influencers with a larger influence to recommend their content or offers through social networks this can have the dual effect of reaching more people through their **social graph** and improving rankings.

Advantages and disadvantages of SEO

Advantages of SEO

The main benefits of SEO are:

- *Significant traffic driver*. Figure 9.1 showed that search marketing can attract a significant proportion of visitors to the site *if* companies are successful in implementing it.
- *Highly targeted*. Visitors are searching for particular products or services so will often have a high intent to purchase – they are qualified visitors.
- *Potentially low-cost visitors*. There are no media costs for ad display or click-through. Costs arise solely from the optimisation process where agencies are paid to improve positions in the search results.
- *Dynamic*. The search engine robots will crawl the home page of popular sites daily, so new content is included relatively quickly for the most popular pages of a site (less so for deep links).

Disadvantages of SEO

Despite the targeted reach and low cost of SEO, it is not straightforward as these disadvantages indicate:

- *Lack of predictability*. Compared with other media SEO is very unreliable in terms of the return on investment – it is difficult to predict results for a given investment and is highly competitive.
- *Time for results to be implemented*. The results from SEO may take months to be achieved, especially for new sites.
- *Complexity and dynamic nature*. The search engines take hundreds of factors into account, yet the relative weightings are not published, so there is not a direct correlation between marketing action and results – 'it is more of an art than a science'. Furthermore, the ranking factors change through time.

- *Ongoing investment.* Investment needed to continue to develop new content and generate new links.
- *Poor for developing awareness in comparison with other media channels.* Searchers already have to be familiar with a brand or service to find it. However, it offers the opportunity for less well-known brands to 'punch above their weight' and to develop awareness following click-through.

For these reasons, investment in paid search may also be worthwhile.

Best practice in planning and managing SEO

In this section we will review six of the main approaches used to improve the results from SEO covering different search engine ranking factors. We describe these in some detail since is one of the most cost-effective digital marketing techniques, so it's important to understand that SEO is a technical discipline and that the techniques used change through time. For this reason SEO is often outsourced to a specialist SEO agency, although some companies believe they can gain an edge through having an internal specialist who understands the company's customers and markets well. You will see that some of the on-page optimisation techniques recommended in this section are relatively straightforward and it is important to control brand and proposition messages. Content editors and reviewers within a company therefore need to be trained to understand these factors and incorporate them into their copywriting.

1 Search engine submission

While some unscrupulous search marketing companies offered to register companies in the 'Top 1000 search engines', in reality registering in the top 5–10 search engines of each country an organisation operates in will probably account for more than 95 per cent of the potential visitors. Most existing companies and even startups will be automatically included in the search index since the search engine robots will follow links from other sites that link to them and do not require submission services. Google allegedly places new sites in a review status sometimes referred to as the *Google sandbox effect*. However, Google search engineers deny the existence of this and explain it is a natural artefact produced by new sites having limited links, history and so reputation. Either way, it is important to remember this constraint when creating startup companies or separate unlined microsites for a campaign since you may have to rely on paid search to gain SERPS visibility.

2 Index inclusion

Index inclusion
Ensuring that as many of the relevant pages from your domain(s) are included within the search engine indexes you are targeting to be listed in.

Duplicate content
Different pages which are evaluated by the search engine to be similar and so don't rank highly, even though they may be for distinct products or services.

Although a search engine robot may visit the home page of a site, it will not necessarily crawl all pages or assign them equal weight in terms of page rank or relevance. So when auditing sites as part of an SEO initiative, SEO agencies will check how many pages are included within the search engine index for different search engines. This is known as **index inclusion**.

Among the potential reasons for not gaining complete index inclusion are:

- Technical reasons why the search robots do not crawl all the pages, such as the use of SEO-unfriendly content management system with complex URLs.
- Pages identified as webspam or of less importance or considered to be **duplicate content** which are then contained in what used to be known as the supplemental index in Google which don't rank so highly. In these cases it is sometimes best to use a specific 'canonical' meta tag which tells the search engine which the primary page is. If you are a multinational company with different content sites for different countries, then it is challenging to deliver the relevant content for local audiences with use of regional domains tending to work best.

Companies can check the index inclusion through:

- Reviewing web analytics data which will show the frequency with which the main search robots crawl a site.
- Using web analytics referrer information to find out which search engines a site's visitors originate from, and the most popular pages.
- Checking the number of pages that have been successfully indexed on a site. For example, in Google the search 'inurl:www.smartinsights.com' or 'site:www.smartinsights.com' lists all the pages of Dave's site indexed by Google and gives the total number in the top-right of the SERPs.
- Using Google Webmaster Tools, a free service that site owners can register with which shows pages indexed and potential webspam problems such as a penalty described in Digital marketing insight 9.2.

Digital marketing insight 9.2 **Is SEO a zoo of Panda and Penguins?**

Since it was launched, Google has named many of the major updates to its algorithm. The best source to review the latest changes is the Moz Algorithm change history (**moz. com/google-algorithm-change**). Some of the earlier updates such as Florida (2003) and Jagger (2005) mark the start of Google proactively combatting webspam. In the entry for Florida, Moz explains:

Figure 9.7	Google Algorithm change history
	Source: Moz (2015)

This was the update that put updates (and probably the SEO industry) on the map. Many sites lost ranking, and business owners were furious. Florida sounded the death knell for low-value late 90s SEO tactics, like keyword stuffing, and made the game a whole lot more interesting.

Each year has seen hundreds of minor changes which SEO specialists have to assess the importance of and review the impact on their sites using analytics. This is one reason that so many people work within SEO.

More recently the **Panda and Penguin algorithm updates** have had a large impact which has reduced the visits to many companies and can potentially destroy the business for an online pureplay or a small business. For an example, see the story of Joe, a plumber, related by Haynes (2012).

Panda involves a series of major algorithm updates by Google dating from 2011 aimed at reducing the visibility of low-quality sites with 'thin' content. It was originally known as Farmer to reduce the visibility of 'article farm' sites where webmasters could submit low quality keyword stuffed articles to sites targeting specific anchor text. Some also said penalised 'scraper' sites where content was copied from other sites, but this was, in fact an existing filter.

Penguin was another series of major algorithm updates by Google dating from April 2012 to Autumn 2014 aimed at reducing the visibility of sites involved in aggressive link building. Google described it as an 'important algorithm change targeted at webspam. The change will decrease rankings for sites that we believe are violating Google's existing quality guidelines'. Specific techniques to avoid which could result in penalties include:

1 A link profile with too many links with similar exact-match anchor text, i.e. the same keyphrases from multiple sites.
2 Keyword stuffing in inbound and outbound links.
3 Use of keywords in 'exact match domains (EMD)' where the domain name targeted a specific phrase.
4 Related on-page factors where Google penalised poor-quality pages violating its guidelines.

Google has also developed many specialist updates such as Pigeon in 2014 which governs Local SEO – search results related to a service in a region – and Pirate in 2014, which targeted sites offering downloads of videos and software. In addition to changes intended to combat spam there are also algorithm updates related to infrastructure such as Caffeine and Hummingbird which developed a concept called the **Knowledge Graph**.

Panda and Penguin algorithm updates
Changes to Google's algorithm aimed at reducing the impact at webspam. They caused the rankings of many sites to fall. Panda targeted low-quality sites with 'thin' content. Penguin targeted sites using aggressive link building.

Knowledge Graph
An infrastructure developed by Google to display related information about people, places and objects.

---

3 Keyphrase analysis

Keyphrase (keyword phrase)
The combination of words users of search engines type into a search box which form a search query.

The key to successful search engine marketing is achieving **keyphrase** relevance since this is what the search engines strive for – to match the combination of keywords typed into the search box to the most relevant destination content page. Notice that we say 'keyphrase' (short for 'keyword phrase') rather than 'keyword' since search engines such as Google attribute more relevance when there is a phrase match between the keywords that the user types and a phrase on a page.

Key sources for identifying the keyphrases your customers are likely to type when searching for your products include your market knowledge, competitors' sites, keyphrases from visitors who arrive at your site (from web analytics), the internal site search tool and the keyphrase analysis tools such as the Google Keyword Planner listed at **www.smartin sights.com/search-engine-optimisation-seo**. When completing keyphrase analysis we need to understand different qualifiers that users type in. Here are examples of common types of qualifiers for 'car insurance':

- *comparison/quality* – compare car insurance;
- *adjective* (price/product qualifiers) – cheap car insurance, woman car insurance;
- *intended use* – high mileage car insurance;
- *product type* – holiday car insurance;
- *vendor* – Churchill car insurance;
- *location* – car insurance UK;
- *action request* – buy car insurance.

According to the Google Keyword tool for a single month in 2015, for searches completed in the UK, the most popular exact phrases related to car insurance were:

- car insurance: 450,000;
- car insurance quotes: 161,000;
- classic car insurance: 151,000;
- cheap car insurance: 145,000;
- compare car insurance: 109,660;
- temporary car insurance: 47,000;
- young drivers car insurance: 9,000.

These data suggest the importance of ranking well for high-volume 'generic' keyphrases such as 'car insurance quotes' and to consider products and services that target a need such as 'temporary' or 'young drivers insurance' and name them accordingly.

4 On-page optimisation

Although each search engine has its own algorithm with many weighting factors that change through time, fortunately there are common factors in the match between search terms entered and the occurrence of the words on the page that influence search engine rankings.

Occurrence of search term in body copy

The number of times the keyphrase is repeated in the text of the web page is a factor in determining the position for a keyphrase, but it is less important than when search engines were first developed as discussed by Fiorelli (2014). Copy can be written to increase the number of times a word or phrase is used (technically, keyword density) and this can have a limited impact to boost position in the search engine. Note though that search engines carry out checks that a phrase is not repeated too many times such as 'cheap flights … cheap flights … cheap flights … cheap flights … cheap flights … cheap flights … cheap flights … cheap flights …' or the keyword is hidden using the same colour text and background and will not list the page if this keyphrase density is too high or it believes 'keyword stuffing' or 'search engine spamming' has occurred. Today, other ranking factors like anchor text of backlinks pointing to the page from other sites and the occurrence of synonyms within the page body copy, headings and title are more important.

In its guidance for Webmasters, Google states:

> Google goes far beyond the number of times a term appears on a page and examines all aspects of the page's content (and the content of the pages linking to it) to determine if it's a good match for your query.

These other factors include:

- frequency (which must be not too excessive, i.e. less than 2–4 per cent);
- occurrence in title and headings: <title>, <h1>, <h2>;
- occurrence in anchor text of hyperlinks;
- markup such as bold;

- density (the number of times);
- proximity of phrase to start of document and the gap between individual keywords;
- links out to other related sites;
- alternative image text (explained below);
- document meta-data (explained below).

Alternative image text

Graphical images can have hidden text associated with them that is not seen by the user (unless graphical images are turned off or the mouse is rolled over the image) but will be seen and indexed by the search engine and is a minor ranking factor, particularly in images linking to other pages. For example, text about a company name and products can be assigned to a company logo using the 'ALT' tag or attribute of the image tag as follows:

```
<img name="Logo" src="logo.gif" alt="Car insurance">
```

Document meta-data

'Meta' refers to information 'about' the page which characterises it. The three most important types of meta-data are the document <title> tag, the document 'descriptions' meta tag and the document 'keywords' meta tag. These need to be unique for each page on a site, otherwise the search engine may assess the content as duplicate and some pages may be down-weighted in importance. Let's look at it in a little more detail:

1 *The document title.* The <title> tag is arguably the most important type of meta-data since each search engine places significant weighting on the key phrases contained within it *and* it is the call-to-action hyperlink on the search engine results page (Figure 9.4). If it contains powerful, relevant copy, you will get more clicks and the search engine will assess relevance relative to other pages which are getting fewer clicks.

2 *The 'description' meta tag.* A meta tag is an attribute of the page within the HTML <head> section which can be set by the content owner. It doesn't directly affect ranking, but shows the information which will typically be displayed in the search engine results page. If it is absent or too short, relevant 'snippets' will be used from within the body copy, but it is best to control messages and this can help identify the page as unique to prevent duplicate content problems. So, the page creator can modify this to make a stronger call-to-action in the search engine listings as in this case:

```
<meta name="description" content="Direct Line offers you great value car insurance
by cutting out the middleman and passing the savings directly on to you. To find out if
you could save, why not get a car insurance quote? Breakdown Cover Insurance also
available.">
```

To see how relevant and unique your <title> and meta descriptions are, use the Google 'site': syntax with a keyphrase – this will return all the pages on your site about a particular topic. For example:

```
<seo site:smartinsights.com>
```

To view meta tags for a site, select View, Source or Page Source in your browser.

3 *The 'keywords' meta tag.* The meta keywords meta tag is used to summarise the content of a document based on keywords. Some unscrupulous SEOs can still be heard to say to potential clients ('we will optimise your meta tags'). But this is not significant today since the keywords meta tag is relatively unimportant as a ranking factor (Google has never used them), although these keywords may be important to internal search engines. For example:

```
<meta name="keywords" content="Car insurance, Home insurance, Travel insurance,
Direct line, Breakdown cover, Mortgages personal loans, Pet insurance, Annual holi-
day insurance, Car loans, uk mortgages, Life insurance, Critical illness cover">
```

4 **Semantic markup**. In order to better manage the interrelationships between different data on the web, the W3C has introduced specific HTML markup in a format defined by **Schema.org** known as **microformats** which can be used to reinforce the semantics, or meaning, of the information on web pages so that it can be better understood and managed by search engines. These are particularly important in some markets since they give more prominence to businesses in the search results, as described by Smart Insights (2014), for example:

- local business information such as names and addresses;
- product details such as pricing, size;
- ratings awarded for articles, products or service quality.

5 External linking

Boosting externals links is vital to SEO in competitive markets – on-page optimisation is insufficient, although it is less easy to control and often neglected. The founders of Google realised that the number of links into a page and their quality was a great way of determining the relevance of a page to searchers, especially when combined with the keyphrases on that page (Brin and Page, 1998). Although the Google algorithm has been upgraded and refined continuously since then, the number and quality of external links is still recognised as the most important ranking factor and this is similar for other search engines. As we mentioned above, links shared through social media are now also used as ranking factors.

Generally, the more links a page has from good-quality sites, the better its ranking will be. **PageRank** is one factor that helps Google deliver relevant results since it counts each link from another site as a vote. However, not all votes are equal – Google gives greater weight to links from pages which themselves have a high PageRank and where the link anchor text or adjacent text contains text relevant to the keyphrase. It has been refined to identify sites that are 'authority sites' or hub sites for a particular type of search. For keyphrases where there is a lot of competition, such as 'car insurance', the quantity and quality of inbound links will be much more important than keyphrase density in determining ranking.

While natural links will be generated if content is useful, a proactive approach to link-building is required in competitive markets. Chaffey and Smith (2012) recommend these steps to help boost your external links.

1 *Identify and create popular content and services.* By creating more valuable content and then showcasing them within your navigation, or grouping it within a few pages such as a 'Useful Resources' or a more extensive 'Resource Centre', you can encourage more people to link to your content naturally, or approach them and suggest they link or bookmark not only to the home page, but directly to the useful tools that have been created. This is part of the Content Marketing approach described in Chapter 8.

2 *Identify potential partner sites.* There are several options to find partner sites. It is helpful to try to identify the types of sites that you may be able to link with, for example:

- directories of links (often less valuable);
- traditional media sites;
- niche online-only media sites;
- trade associations;
- manufacturers, suppliers and other business partners;
- press release distribution sites;
- bloggers including customers and partners;
- social networks.

Note: The section on online PR later in this chapter has more guidance on approaches for link-building and influencer outreach which is the technical term for this activity and is one method of 'Content Distribution' described in the 'Focus on Content Marketing' section in Chapter 8.

Microformats
A semantic definition of a specific information type such as a product, event, recipe or review. **Schema. org** manages some of the most common definitions.

PageRank
A scale between 0 to 10 used by Google named after Google founder Larry Page which is used to assess the importance of web pages according to the number of inbound links or backlinks.

3 *Contact partner sites as part of link-building.* A typical sequence is:
 - Step 0 – Develop relevant content or offer to encourage linking as part of Content Marketing.
 - Step 1 – write email encouraging link (or phone call to discuss from someone inside the company will often work best).
 - Step 2 – follow-up link.
 - Step 3 – set up links

Google suggests that site owners should rely on organic linking to their content because of its value and has criticised many approaches to proactive link-building which marketers have found effective. For example, Google has cautioned that 'guest blogging', where a writer creates an article for another site linking back to their own site, shouldn't be used. Yet it is a common, effective practice and is essentially a form of PR, so it is no surprise that marketers persist with this practice. However, Google has put filters such as the Penguin algorithm in place to reduce the impact of links from other sites which are clearly used to 'game' the system. So if an ignorant link-builder has created many identical links to a site from different sites with the same anchor text, such as 'car insurance quotes' for example, then Google will see this as an unnatural 'backlink profile' for the site. Google has put tools in place to 'undo the damage' created by link-building, such as a Disavow link tool in Google Webmaster Tools.

Given that the quality (and quantity) of inbound or backlinks is one of the main factors that determines SEO success it is important that an in-house or agency specialist uses the types of tools shown in Digital marketing insight 9.3 to review their approach.

Many of the principles of external link-building can also be applied to links within sites. The most important principle is to include keyphrases used by searchers within the anchor text of a hyperlink to point to relevant content. It's also important to consider how to increase the number of internal links to pages which you want to rank well. A meshed structure with lots of interlinks can work better than a simple hierarchy.

To summarise the complexities of SEO, see the compilation of the most important ranking factors based on correlation studies and the viewpoints of a panel of experts in Moz (2013).

Paid search marketing

Although SEO has proved a popular form of digital marketing, paid search marketing is still of great relevance since it gives much more control on the appearance in the listings subject to the amount bid and the relevance of the ad.

Each of the main search engines has its own paid advertising programme:

 - Google Adwords (**www.google.com/adwords**);
 - Microsoft Bing and Yahoo! adCenter (**http://advertise.bingads.microsoft.com**).

Display (or content) network
Sponsored links are displayed by the search engine on third-party sites such as online publishers, aggregators or social networks. Ads can be paid for on a CPC, CPM or a CPA basis. There are also options for graphical or video ads as well as text-based ads

Contextual ad
Ad relevant to page content on third-party sites brokered by search ad networks.

What is paid search marketing?

We explained the principles of paid search marketing or sponsored links in the introduction to the section on search engine marketing. Although we said that the main model for paying for sponsored listings in the search engines is pay-per-click marketing, we have called this section paid search marketing since there are, increasingly, other options for payment on what is known as the content network.

Paid search content network

Paid listings are also available through the **display network** of the search engines such as Google AdSense and Yahoo! Content Match. These **contextual ads** are automatically displayed according to the page content. They can be paid for on a CPC, CPM or CPA

Digital marketing insight 9.3   Reviewing the links into a site

You can use the syntax link:site in Google to see examples of links into a page on a site as judged by Google, e.g. **link:www.smartinsights.com**. But note that this also includes internal links and is not comprehensive. A better option to display links is the Moz Site Open Site Explorer tool (**www.opensiteexplorer.com**) or Majestic (**www.majestic.com**, Figure 9.8), which has a free backlink history tool to show the growth in links. Note that it is the growth in *unique* linking domains which is more important to review for ranking competitiveness. For alerts of new links or new mentions on other sites, Google's own alerts (**www.google.com/alerts**) are useful tools. Other free services such as BuzzSumo (**www.buzzsumo.com**), Social Crawlytics (**www.socialcrawlytics.com**) and Topsy (**www.topsy.com**) are recommended for seeing the popularity of content as it is shared.

Figure 9.8   Backlink analysis
Source: Majestic

(pay-per-action) basis and include not only text ads but also options for graphical display ads or video ads. Google generates around a third of its revenue from the content network, so there is a significant amount of expenditure on the network.

Trusted feeds

Trusted feeds or paid for inclusion is no longer significant to search advertising. However, we include reference to them since a similar approach is used by retailers to include their products in **Google's Product Listing Ads (PLAs)**, where product information such as pricing and images are uploaded to Google's servers for display in Google AdWords and within Google Shopping (see documentation for Google Merchant Blog for the latest techniques).

What controls position in paid search?

In early pay-per-click programs, the relative ranking of sponsored listings was simply based on the highest bidded cost-per-click (CPCs) for each keyword phrase. So it was a pure

---

Trusted feed
An automated method of putting content into a search engine index or an aggregator database.

Google's Product Listing Ads (PLAs)
Product information such as pricing and images are uploaded to Google's servers using a product feed in XML or text formats for display in ads within Google AdWords or Google Shopping

auction arrangement with the cost-per-click dependent on the balance of the extent of competition in the marketplace against the revenue or profit that can be generated dependent on conversion rates to sale and retention. The inflated CPCs (Table 9.2) at the time of writing in different product sectors show how competitive Google AdWords is. Since only a small proportion of visitors to a site clicking from the ad will convert, it is difficult to generate a positive return-on-investment for these generic terms.

Contrary to what many web users may believe, today it is not necessarily the company which is prepared to pay the most per click that will get top spot. The search engines also take the relative click-through rates of the ads dependent on their position (lower positions naturally have lower click-through rates) into account when ranking the sponsored links, so ads which do not appear relevant, because fewer people are clicking on them, will drop down or may even disappear off the listing. The analysis of CTR to determine position is part of the **quality score**, a concept originally developed by Google but now integrated as part of the Microsoft Bing and Yahoo! search networks.

Google quality score

Understanding quality score is the key to successful paid search marketing. You should consider its implications when you structure the account and write copy or review performance with an agency. Google developed the quality score because it understood that delivering *relevance* through the sponsored links was essential to its user's experience, and the company's profits. Google's AdWords help system explains:

> The AdWords system works best for everybody; advertisers, users, publishers and Google too when the ads we display match our users' needs as closely as possible. We call this idea 'relevance'.
>
> We measure relevance in a simple way: Typically, the higher an ad's quality score, the more relevant it is for the keywords to which it is tied. When your ads are highly relevant, they tend to earn more clicks, move higher in Ad Rank and bring you the most success.

A summary formula for the Google quality score is:

> Quality score = (keyword's click-through rate, ad text relevance, keyword relevance, landing page relevance, speed and other methods of assessing relevance)

So, higher click-through rates achieved through better targeted creative copy are rewarded, as is relevance of the landing page (Google now sends out AdBots-Google to check them out). More relevant ads are also rewarded through ad text relevance, which is an assessment of the match of headline and description to the search term. Finally, the keyword relevance is the match of the triggering keyword to the search term entered.

Quality score
An assessment in paid search by Google AdWords (and now other search engines) of an individual ad triggered by a keyword which, in combination with the bid amount, determines the ranking of the ad relative to competitors. The primary factor is the click-through rate for each ad, but quality score also considers the match between the keyword and the occurrence of the keyword in the text, historical click-through rates, the engagement of the searcher when they click through to the site and the speed at which the page loads.

Table 9.2	Example variation in cost-per-click for different keywords in UK campaigns

Category	CPC (£)
Car insurance	£6.93
iPhone	£1.98
Winter coat	£0.63
Holiday barbados	£2.53
Laser eye treatment	£7.20
Digital Marketing Agency	£8.94

Source: Suggested position 1 bids from the Google Keyword Planner in 2015

If you have ever wondered why the number of paid ads above the natural listings varies from none to three, then it's down to the quality score – you can only get the coveted positions for keywords which have a sufficiently high quality score – you can't 'buy your way to the top' as many think.

Advantages and disadvantages of paid search marketing

Paid search listings, or sponsored links, are very important to achieve visibility in search engines when an organisation is in a competitive market, given the competition to appear on the first page of the natural listing for target keyphrases.

As a result, many companies with an established paid search programme may generate more visits from paid search than SEO, although this wouldn't be true for companies that are class leaders in SEO.

Advantages of paid search marketing

The main benefit of paid search marketing are:

Google Display Network (GDN)
Different types of online publishers agree for Google to display contextual ads on their sites for a fee, for example as part of the AdSense programme.

- *The advertiser is not paying for the ad to be displayed*. As we explained at the start of Chapter 8, wastage is much lower with paid search compared to traditional advertising. Cost is only incurred when an ad is clicked on and a visitor is directed to the advertiser's website. Hence it's a cost-per-click (CPC) model! However, there are increasingly options for paid search marketing using other techniques – Google also offers CPM (site targeting) and CPA (pay-per-action) options on the **Google Display Network (GDN)**, where contextual ads are displayed on third-party sites relevant to the content on a page.
- *PPC advertising is highly targeted*. The relevant ad with a link to a destination web page is only displayed when the user of a search engine types in a specific phrase (or the ad appears on the content network, triggered by relevant content on a publisher's page), so there is limited wastage compared to other media. YouTube users can also be targeted through Google's 'promoted video' PPC option. Users responding to a particular keyphrase or reading related content have high intent or interest and so tend to be good-quality leads.
- *Good accountability*. With the right tracking system, the ROI for individual keywords can be calculated.
- *Predictable*. Traffic, rankings and results are generally stable and predictable in comparison with SEO.
- *Technically simpler than SEO*. Position is based on combination of bid amount and quality score. Whereas SEO requires long-term, technically complex work on page optimisation, site re-structuring and link building.
- *Remarketing*. Google offers retargeting through cookies placed on the searchers computer to display ads on the content network after someone has clicked on a paid search ad or visited a specific page on a site as a reminder to act. These can be effective in boosting the conversion rate to lead or sale.
- *Speed*. PPC listings get posted quickly, usually in a few days (following editor review). SEO results can take weeks or months to be achieved. Moreover, when a website is revised for SEO, rankings will initially drop while the site is re-indexed by the search engines.
- *Branding*. Tests have shown that there is a branding effect with PPC, even if users do not click on the ad. This can be useful for the launch of products or major campaigns.

Disadvantages of paid search marketing

However, there disadvantages to be managed:

- *Competitive and expensive*. Since pay-per-click has become popular, some companies may get involved in bidding wars that drive bids up to an unacceptable level. Some phrases such as 'life insurance' can exceed £10 per click.

- *Inappropriate*. For companies with a lower budget or a narrower range of products on which to generate lifetime value, it might not be cost-effective to compete.
- *Requires specialist knowledge*. PPC requires a knowledge of configuration, bidding options and of the reporting facilities of different ad networks. Internal staff can be trained, but they will need to keep up-to-date with changes to the paid search services.
- *Time-consuming*. To manage a PPC account can require daily or even hourly checks on the bidding in order to stay competitive. This can amount to a lot of time. The tools and best practice varies frequently, so keeping up-to-date is difficult.
- *Irrelevant*. Sponsored listings are only part of the search engine marketing mix. Many search users do not click on these because they don't trust advertisers, although these are mainly people involved in marketing!

Best practice in planning and managing paid search marketing

With PPC, as for any other media, media buyers carefully evaluate the advertising costs in relation to the initial purchase value or lifetime value they feel they will achieve from the average customer. As well as considering the cost-per-click (CPC), you need to think about the conversion rate when the visitor arrives at your site. Clearly, an ad could be effective in generating click-throughs or traffic, but not achieve the outcome required on the website such as generating a lead or online sale. This could be because there is a poor-incentive call-to-action or the profile of the visitors is simply wrong. One implication of this is that it will often be more cost-effective if targeted microsites or landing pages are created specifically for certain keyphrases to convert users to making an enquiry or sale. These can be part of the site structure, so clicking on a 'car insurance' ad will take the visitor through to the car insurance page on a site rather than a home page.

Table 9.3 shows how cost-per-click can differ between different generic (e.g. 'car insurance') and specific (e.g. 'women's car insurance') keywords, as well as the impact of different conversion rates on the overall CPA. The table also shows the cost of PPC search in competitive categories and why companies will strive to maximise their quality score to help reduce costs.

The cost per customer acquisition (CPA) can be calculated as follows:

$$\text{Cost per acquisition} = \frac{100}{\text{conversion rate \%}} \times \text{cost-per-click}$$

Given the range in costs, two types of strategy can be pursued in PPC search engine advertising. If budget permits, a premium strategy can be followed to compete with the major competitors who are bidding the highest amounts on popular keywords. Such a strategy is based on being able to achieve an acceptable conversion rate once the customers are driven through to the website. A lower-cost strategy involves bidding on lower-cost, less popular phrases. These will generate less traffic, so it will be necessary to devise a lot of these phrases to match the traffic from premium keywords.

Table 9.3	Examples of cost-per-click and CPA figures				
Keywords	**Clicks/day**	**Avg. CPC**	**Cost/day**	**CPA @ 25% conversion**	**CPA @ 10% conversion**
'car insurance'	1323	€15.6	€20,640	€62	€156
'cheap car insurance'	199	€14.6	€2905	€58	€146
'woman car insurance'	4	€11.6	€46	€46	€116

Optimising pay-per-click

Each PPC keyphrase ideally needs to be managed individually in order to make sure that the bid (amount per click) remains competitive in order to show up in the top of the results. Experienced PPC marketers broaden the range of keyphrases to include lower-volume phrases. Since each advertiser will typically manage thousands of keywords to generate click-throughs, manual bidding soon becomes impractical.

Some search engines include their own bid management tools, but if an organisation is using different pay-per-click schemes, it makes sense to use a single tool to manage them all. It also makes comparison of performance easier too. Bid management software such as Acquisio (**www.acquisio.com**) and WordStream (**www.wordstream.com**) can be used across a range of PPC services to manage keyphrases on multiple PPC ad networks and optimise the costs of search engine advertising. The current CPC is regularly reviewed and your bid is reduced or increased to maintain the position you want according to different strategies and ROI limits, with amounts capped such that advertisers do not pay more than the maximum they have deposited.

Although pay-per-click marketing does not initially appear as complex as search engine optimisation, in reality there are many issues to consider. In the next section we explain some of the main techniques and questions for the digital marketer to ask.

1 Targeting

- *Search ad network strategy.* Which of the search networks mentioned above do you use? Which are used in different countries?
- *Content network strategy.* How do you treat the content network? Do you disable it? Create separate campaigns? Target specific sites using the Placement tool? Develop different creative? Use placement targeting in Google?
- *Campaign structure strategy.* Campaign structure is important to ensure that searches using a specific search term trigger the relevant ad creative. Are AdGroups small enough to deliver a message relevant for the keyphrase entered? To understand the type of targeting that is possible, look at these two examples. First, in Figure 9.9(a) we have a campaign structure for an online clothes retailer. They monitor spend and budget by product type, so structure their campaigns accordingly and target them nationally. Keywords related to each product will trigger ads defined within each AdGroup. In Figure 9.9(b) is an example of a campaign for a restaurant chain. They monitor spend and budget by outlet, so structure their campaigns accordingly and target them to local areas.
- *Keyword matching strategy.* How is creative targeted using the combination of broad match and negative match, phrase match and exact match?
- *Search-term targeting strategy.* What are the strategies for targeting different types of keyphrases such as brand, generic, product-specific and different qualifiers (cheap, compare, etc.)?

2 Budget and bid management

- *Budgeting strategy.* Is budget set as maximum cost-per-click (CPC) at the appropriate level to deliver satisfactory return on investment? Is daily budget sufficient that ads are served at full delivery (always present)?
- *Listing position strategy.* Which positions are targeted for different keywords?
- *Bidding strategies.* What is the appropriate maximum cost per click for different target keywords and campaigns to maximise effectiveness?
- *Dayparting strategy.* Are ads delivered continuously through the day and week or are different certain days and times targeted (e.g. office hours, evening after ad breaks)?

| **Figure 9.9** | AdWords campaign structures (a) Clothing retailer; (b) Restaurant chain |

Google AdWords Enhanced campaigns
An approach introduced by Google in 2013 to simplify the management of ads displayed in different locations, different day parts (times of day) and on different devices

- *Use of enhanced campaigns.* **Google AdWords Enhanced campaigns** is a tool to simplify the complexity of advertising when different types of mobile devices can be targeted in different locations at different times.
- *Bid management tool strategy.* Is a tool used to automate bidding? Which?
- *Importance of fake clicks.* Whenever the principle of PPC marketing is described to marketers, very soon a light bulb switches on and they ask, 'So we can click on competitors and bankrupt them?' Well, actually, no. The PPC ad networks detect multiple clicks from the same computer (IP address) and filters them out.

3 Creative testing and campaign optimisation

- *Ad creative and copy strategy.* How are the 95 characters forming ad headlines, description and creative used to encourage click-through (and reduce click-through from unqualified visitors if necessary)? Is alternative copy tested? How are ads tested?
- *Destination or landing page strategy.* How are landing pages improved?
- *Campaign review and optimisation strategy.* What is the workflow for reviewing and improving success? Which reports are used? How often are they reviewed? By whom? Which tests are used? What are the follow-ups?
- *Specialist and innovative paid search techniques.* These include local, international, pay-per-call, mobile search.

4 Communications integration

- *SEO integration strategy.* How is SEO integrated with paid search to maximise ROI?
- *Affiliate integration strategy.* How is affiliate marketing integrated with paid search to maximise ROI?
- *Marketing campaign integration strategy.* How is budget and creative changed during offline campaigns?

Online public relations

What is online public relations (e-PR)?

Digital media have become a very important element of **public relations (PR)** and the Internet has influenced PR practices (Ye and Ki, 2012). More funds have been allocated to online PR projects especially through corporate and social blogs and its contribution to branding strategies has increased significantly (Bush, 2010). Mike Grehan, a UK search engine marketing specialist, explains (Grehan, 2004):

> Both online and off, the process is much the same when using PR to increase awareness, differentiate yourself from the crowd and improve perception. Many offline PR companies now employ staff with specialist online skills. The web itself offers a plethora of news sites and services. And, of course, there are thousands and thousands of newsletters and zines covering just about every topic under the sun. Never before has there been a better opportunity to get your message to the broadest geographic and multi-demographic audience. But you need to understand the pitfalls on both sides to be able to avoid.

Online PR activity is closely associated with improving results from many of the other communications techniques described in this chapter, in particular SEO (link-building), partnership marketing and social media marketing. It is also closely related to content marketing described in the 'Focus on content marketing' section in Chapter 8 since a core activity in content marketing is 'content distribution' which can involve working with influencers to feature content that has been developed. Furthermore, online PR has witnessed much innovation of Web 2.0-based approaches such as blogs, feeds, social networks and widgets, which we will explore in this section.

But let's start with an understanding of traditional public relations – itself somewhat intangible. As you will know, 'PR' and 'public relations' are often used interchangeably. Unfortunately, PR is also an abbreviation for 'press release' or 'press relations'. Of course, the scope of PR is much wider than press releases. On its website, the UK Institute of PR defines PR as follows:

> Public relations is about reputation – the result of what you do, what you say and what others say about you. Public relations is the discipline which looks after reputation, with the aim of earning understanding and support and influencing opinion and behaviour. It is the planned and sustained effort to establish and maintain goodwill and mutual understanding between an organisation and its publics [its target audience including potential customers and stakeholders].

From a marketing communications and traffic building perspective, the main activities we are interested in are media relations with different types of **online influencers** or **Key Opinion Leaders** (KOLs) which can be used to reach and influence potential customers. While websites are important tools for promoting investor relations and CSR (corporate social responsibility), this is not our main focus here.

Online PR or e-PR leverages the network effect of the Internet. Remember that Internet is a contraction of 'interconnected networks'! Mentions of a brand or site on other sites are powerful in shaping opinions and driving visitors to your site. The main element of online PR is maximising favourable mentions of an organisation, its brands, products or websites on third-party websites which are likely to be visited by its target audience. Furthermore, as we noted in the section on search engine optimisation, the more links there are from other sites to your site, the higher your site will be ranked in the natural or organic listings of the search engines. **Online influencer outreach** is now an important activity to identify companies or individuals with a strong online following and then using

Online reputation management
Controlling the reputation of an organisation through monitoring and controlling messages placed about the organisation.

these contacts to influence their audience. Minimising unfavourable mentions, for example monitoring and influencing conversations in blogs and social networks through **online reputation management**, is also an aspect of online PR.

Differences between online PR and traditional PR

Researchers suggest that digital media tends to bolster stakeholders' strength and increase organisations' ability to collect information, monitor public opinion and engage in direct dialogue with their publics regarding key issues (McAllister and Taylor, 2007). Ranchhod *et al.* (2002) identify four key differences between online PR and traditional PR which are fundamentals of online PR that remain true today.

1 *The audience is connected to organisations.* Previously, there was detachment – PR people issued press releases which were distributed over the newswires, picked up by the media, and then published in their outlets. These authors say:

> The communication channel was unidirectional. The institutions communicated and the audiences consumed the information. Even when the communication was considered a two-way process, the institutions had the resources to send information to audiences through a very wide pipeline, while the audiences had only a minuscule pipeline for communicating back to the institutions.

2 *The members of the audience are connected to each other.* Through publishing their own blogs, social profiles or e-newsletters or contributing to reviews or discussions on others, information can be rapidly distributed from person to person and group to group. Consumers will also have their own conversations about their needs and brands which will shape brand perception and purchase intent. The authors say:

> Today, a company's activity can be discussed and debated over the Internet, with or without the knowledge of that organisation. In the new environment everybody is a communicator, and the institution is just part of the network.

Mini case study 9.1	Renault uses influencer outreach to support growth

In 2010, Renault launched a new range of zero emission vehicles. Renault's objective was to get people talking about the range, and especially the star model, the TWIZY. Renault wanted to create links with opinion leaders sensitive to the automotive sector but also to ecology and new technologies.

To reach influencers and help spread the word about the new model, agency BuzzParadise organised a special meeting at an international event, LeWeb. The idea was for Renault to use this platform to set up viral advertising aimed at a target sensitive to technological advances. Invitations were sent to 13 bloggers from France, Germany, Great Britain, Italy and Spain writing about High-Tech, Trends, Innovation and Scientific themes. These partners met for a conference session and tests of vehicles in the ZE range.

As a result, 22 articles were created across the blogs and, through these, 900,000 exposures to the message were generated. This increased visibility for Renault and its TWIZY in the European blogosphere, social networks (Facebook, Twitter) and SEO (Google). The amplification effect of a relatively small number of bloggers is illustrated well by this reach figure. But it's worth remembering that visibility on blogs and social networks like this is usually ephemeral, meaning that the message is only visible for a short time within the blogosphere. So other techniques are also needed to give a more sustained delivery of messages and reminders to the audience. This is where traditional advertising and remarketing through displaying advertising to those who have already visited a company microsite play an important role.

Source: Buzz Paradise (2010)

3 *The audience has access to other information.* Often in the past, the communicator was able to make a statement that it would be difficult for the average audience member to challenge – the Internet facilitates rapid comparison of statements. The authors say:

> It takes a matter of minutes to access multiple sources of information over the Internet. Any statement made can be dissected, analysed, discussed and challenged within hours by interested individuals. In the connected world, information does not exist in a vacuum.

4 *Audiences pull information.* Today this is often known as inbound marketing. Previously there were limited channels in terms of television and press. Today there are many sources and channels of information – this makes it more difficult for the message to be seen. The authors say:

> Until recently, television offered only a few channels. People communicated with one another by post and by phone. In these conditions, it was easy for a public relations practitioner to make a message stand out.

For the marketer or PR professional, managing PR, the main differences are:

- *Less easy to control.* There are many more places a brand can be discussed online, such as in blogs and forums, compared to traditional media where there are a smaller number of media outlets with news filtered through journalists and other editorial staff.
- *More options to create their own stories.* Since a company will have its own site, press centre, feeds and blogs, it is possible to bypass other media owners to some extent. Many companies have now created a 'social media newsroom'.
- *Need for faster response.* It is often said that 'bad news travels fast'. This has been facilitated online and a 'blogstorm' can soon arise where many bloggers are critical of a brand's action. Rapid response teams are needed. Some brands have created a social media command centre as part of a **social media governance** process based on **social media listening**. For examples of social media governance policies in a range of sectors, see **www.socialmediagovernance.com**.
- *Easier to monitor.* Since Google and online reputation management tools index many pages, it is arguably easier to identify when a brand is discussed online.

Social media governance
A definition of how companies should respond to social mentions that may give rise to leads or reputational damage.

Social media listening
The process of using monitoring tools to review mentions of a brand and related keywords within social networks and other online sites.

Advantages and disadvantages of online public relations

Advantages of online public relations

The advantages of the proactive online public relations techniques which seek to build a buzz around a campaign or to gain favourable mentions and links on third-party sites are:

- *Reach.* E-PR can be a relatively low-cost method of directly reaching a niche audience or a mass audience if the brand is amenable to stories that are of interest to publishers. This is often the case for new online brands and startups such as Zopa (**www.zopa.com**). If buzz around an online campaign orchestrated through online PR is successful then additional reach and impact may also be generated by traditional media such as TV, print and radio.
- *Cost.* The costs for online PR are the agency or internal staff fees for developing the online PR plan, concepts and content. Since there are no media placement costs, this can be cost-effective.
- *Credibility.* Comments that are made by a person independent from a company are considered more authentic and so can help raise trust about an online provider such as a retailer. You can see that personal recommendations are particularly important and seem to be trusted more than content sites giving reviews and opinions (although these are still given credence by many web users).
- *Search engine optimisation.* E-PR can help generate backlinks to a site which are favourable for SEO, often from large sites such as online newspapers or magazines which have good link equity.

- *Brand-enhancement and protection*. Favourable stories can enhance the reputation of a brand among its target audience and amplification through influencers can help reach a new audience. But since unfavourable media mentions may damage a brand, so monitoring and response to these is a necessity for most brands.

Mini case study 9.2	Dell and Gatorade launch social media command centres

In 2010/2011 Dell and Gatorade (Figure 9.10) independently launched 'social media command centres'. Watch the videos (available from the links for this chapter) to see how they planned to use them for reputation managing and reviewing the impact of social media.

Clearly, these are big brands. What does this mean for smaller organisations? Some have even questioned their relevance for larger companies, calling them white elephants. These are some implications of the need for social media listening highlighted by the approach of these big brands:

1 Put in place free or paid listening tools.
2 Use free tools initially to check the volume of conversation. If it's not significant, you probably don't need a 'mission control centre', but you should use a free tool to monitor your brand and respond appropriately – it's not just about monitoring the negatives as some seem to think, it's about reaching out to potential partners and collaborators too.
3 Set up social governance policies.
4 Find a method such that you can follow up on potential partnership options – remember that Partnerships is the 8th P in the marketing mix.
5 Integrate your social media monitoring and reporting with other business and campaign reporting and web analytics systems.

Source: **SmartInsights.com** (2011b)

| Figure 9.10 | Gatorade social media command centre video |

Disadvantages of online public relations

The main disadvantage of e-PR is that it is not a controlled discipline like online advertising techniques such as pay-per-click marketing or display advertising where the returns generated will be known for a given expenditure. In other words, it could be considered a high-risk investment.

Many marketers are also wary of creating blogs or forums on their sites which may solicit negative comments. However, there are counter-arguments to this, namely that it is best to control and be involved with conversations about a brand on the site rather than when it is less controlled on third-party sites. For example, brands such as Dell (**www.ideastorm.com**) and Honda enable web users to make comments about their brands; this shows they are listening to customer comments and gains valuable sentiment that can feed into new product development ideas.

Best practice in planning and managing online public relations

In this section we will review the different types of online PR activities and techniques to improve results from these activities. The main activities that can be considered to be specifically involved with online PR include:

- collaborating with marketers to define content and stories which will be sharable and help support the brand's objectives;
- communicating with media owners online (influencer outreach to support link-building and SEO);
- managing how your brand is presented on third-party sites;
- creating a buzz – online viral marketing.

Communicating with online media owners (influencer outreach)

Forming relationships with publishers of media online gives a way to expand the reach of a brand. These influencers may include traditional journalists, but also, as we saw in Mini case study 9.1 about Renault, bloggers or celebrities.

Journalists can be influenced online through a press-release area or social media newsroom on the website; creating email alerts about news that journalists and other third parties can sign up to; news stories or releases submitted to online news feeds. Examples of feeds include PR Newswire: (**www.prnewswire.com**), PressBox (**www.pressbox.co.uk**), PRWeb (**www.prweb.com**) and Business Wire (**www.businesswire.com**). Press releases can also be written for search engine optimisation (SEO) since they will link back to the site.

An increasing number of journalists rely on blogs and feeds for finding sources for stories rather than traditional press releases, so engaging influencers through these is also important. Charles Arthur (**www.charlesarthur.com/blog/**), contributor to the *Guardian*, in a posting 'Why I'm not reading PR emails to get news stories any more', says:

> I'm not going to read things that are obviously press releases because the possibility of it just being annoying or irrelevant is too great; I'm going to go to my aggregator instead, because I've chosen every feed there for its potential interest. I pay more attention to my RSS feeds because they're sources I've chosen, rather than the emails I get from PR companies.

Web 2.0 concept
A collection of web services that facilitate interaction of web users with sites to create user generated content and encouraging behaviours such as community or social network participation, mashups, content rating, use of widgets and tagging.

Web 2.0 PR techniques

Many specialist online PR techniques such as blogs, podcasting and RSS feeds are collectively referred to as **Web 2.0**, which we introduced in the first chapter. When it was in vogue around 2004, Web 2.0 represented a revolution in web usage where previously passive consumers of content become active contributors.

In this section we give a brief review of some of the tools and techniques that developed as part of the Web 2.0 revolution which are still relevant.

Blogs and blogging

Blog
An online diary or news source prepared by an individual or a group of people. From 'Web log'. Business blogs are created by an organisation for communication to their audiences.

Blogs give an easy method of regularly publishing web pages as online journals, diaries or news or events listings. Many blogs provide commentary or news on a particular subject; others function as more personal online diaries. A typical blog combines text, images and links to other blogs, web pages and other media related to its topic. The capability for readers to leave comments in an interactive format is an important part of many blogs. Feedback (trackback) comments from other sites are also sometimes incorporated. Frequency can be hourly, daily, weekly or less frequently, but several updates daily is typical.

There are many free services which enable anyone to blog (for example **www.wordpress. com** and **www.blogger.com**. The blogging format enables the content on a website to be delivered in different ways. For example, the Smart Insights blog has a lot of rich content related to Internet marketing which can be delivered in different ways:

- *By topic* (in categories or topics to browse). For example, social media marketing category (Figure 9.11).
- *By tag* (more detailed topics – each article will be tagged with several tags to help them appear in searches). For example, 'B2B' or 'case studies'.
- *By author* (features from different columnists who can be internal or external). Guest posting is an effective method for both guest author and blog to increase reach.
- *By time* (all posts broken down by the different methods above are in reverse date order).

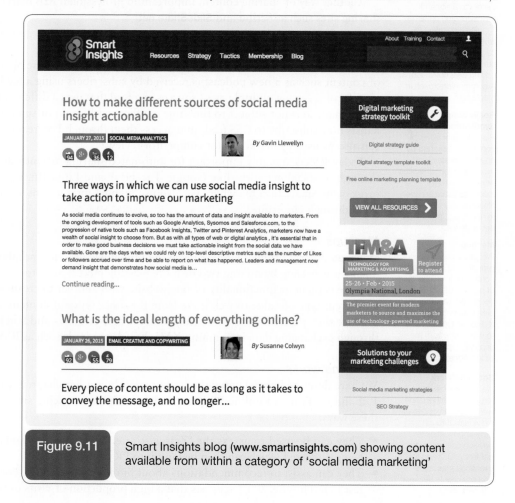

Figure 9.11   Smart Insights blog (**www.smartinsights.com**) showing content available from within a category of 'social media marketing'

Although some forecast that blogs would become less important with the publishing of content on social networks, they remain important in many business and consumer sectors since they enable a more in-depth exploration of interest in topics and many influencers have their own blog.

Social bookmarking

Social bookmarking
Web users keep a shared version of favourite sites ('Favourites') online. This enables the most popular sites in a category to be identified.

Sites like Digg, Google, Reddit, StumbleUpon and Del.icio.us allow users to store, organise, search and manage favourite web pages on the Internet rather than on their PC. With such **social bookmarking** systems, users save links to web pages that they want to remember and/or share on bookmark hosting sites. These bookmarks are usually public but can be saved privately, shared only with specified people or groups, shared only inside certain networks, or some other combination of public and private domains.

Podcasts are related to blogs since they can potentially be generated by individuals or media organisations to voice an opinion either as audio (typically MP3) or less commonly currently as video (video podcasts).

Podcast
Individuals and organisations post online media (audio and video) which can be viewed in the appropriate players including the iPod which first sparked the growth in this technique.

Photo, video and slide sharing sites

Tagging
Tracking of the origin or referring site or of visitors to a site and their spending patterns. Tagging also refers to where users or web page creators categorise content on a site through adding descriptive terms. A common approach in blog posts.

Photo sharing sites which are popular include Flickr (a Yahoo! service), Picasa (a Google service) and SnapFish. These rely on **tagging** to enable users to find related shots they are interested.

Video sharing sites include YouTube, Google Videos, Jumpcut, Grouper, Revver, Blip.tv, VideoEgg and Daily Motion.

Another way of sharing content important in professional B2B markets is through slide sharing sites such as Scribd and **SlideShare.net**.

Really Simple Syndication feeds

Really Simple Syndication feed (RSS)
Blog, news or other content is published by an XML standard and syndicated for other sites or read by users in RSS reader software services. Now typically shortened to 'feed', e.g. news feed or sports feed.

Really Simple Syndication (RSS) is closely related to blogging, where blog, news or any type of content such as a new podcast is received by subscribers using a feed reader. It offers a method of receiving multiple news sources in a feed that uses a different broadcast method from email, so is not subject to the same conflicts with spam or spam filters. Many journalists now subscribe to RSS feeds and access them through Feedreaders like Feedly which can also be used by marketers for competitor review.

Today, RSS is arguably important for automated sharing or syndication or from a blog through to social networks like Google, Facebook and LinkedIn. Figure 9.12 shows the process for Smart Insights where we also use manual interactions such as tailoring messages through Hootsuite.

Mashups

Mashup
Websites, pages or widgets that combine the content or functionality of one website or data source with another to create something offering a different type of value to web users from the separate types of content or functionality.

Mashups (a term originally referring to the pop music practice, notably hip-hop, of producing a new song by mixing two or more existing pieces) are sites or widgets that combine the content or functionality of one website with another to create something offering a different type of value to web users from the other types of content or functionality. In practice they provide a way of sharing content between sites and stitching together sites through exchanging data in common XML-based standards such as RSS.

Social networks

Social network
A site that facilitates peer-to-peer communication within a group or between individuals through providing facilities to develop user-generated content (UGC) and to exchange messages and comments between different users.

We have described **social networks** in more depth in other chapters (including Chapters 1, 2 and 6). From an online PR perspective, social networking sites can be valuable in these ways:

- They can be used to assess the 'Zeitgeist', i.e. what current trends and opinions are being discussed which can then be built into PR campaigns.
- They can assist in recommendations about brands and products. For example, Hitwise research (Hitwise, 2007) suggests that a high proportion of visits to fashion retail stores

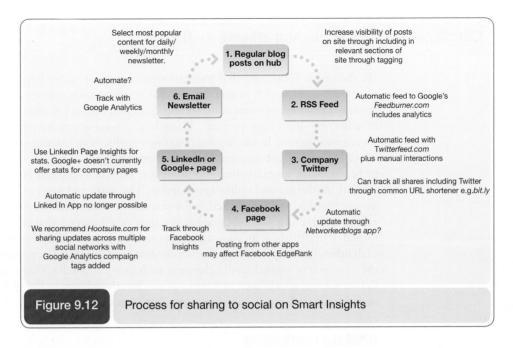

| Figure 9.12 | Process for sharing to social on Smart Insights |

such as Top Shop were preceded by usage of social networks, suggesting that some visits are prompted by discussions.

● They can be used to solicit feedback about product experiences and brand perception, either by explicit requests or observing what is discussed.

Widgets

Widget

A badge or button incorporated into a site or social network space by its owner, with content or services typically served from another site making a widget effectively a mini-software application or web service. Content can be updated in real time since the widget interacts with the server each time it loads.

Widgets are different forms of tools made available on a website or on a user's desktop. They either provide some functionality, like a calculator, or they provide real-time information, for example on news or weather.

Site owners can encourage partners to place them on their sites and this will help educate people about your brand, possibly generating backlinks for SEO purposes and also engaging with a brand when they're not on the brand owner's site. Widgets offer partner sites the opportunity to add value to their visitors through the gadget functionality or content, or to add to their brand through association with you (co-branding).

The main types of widgets are:

● *Web widgets*. Web widgets have been used for a long time as part of affiliate marketing, but they are getting more sophisticated by enabling searches on a site, real-time price updates or even streaming video.

● *Google gadgets*. Different content can be incorporated into a personalised Google 'iGoogle' homepage.

● *Desktop and operating system gadgets*. Microsoft Windows and Apple Operating systems provide dashboard gadgets which make it easier to subscribe to information updates.

● *Social sharing widgets*. These encourage site visitors to share content they like, effectively voting on it. Share buttons provided by the networks or aggregators like **AddThis.com** or **ShareThis.com** are now an essential part of many sites to assist in 'viral amplification'.

● *Facebook applications*. Facebook created an API known as the Facebook platform (application programming interface) to enable developers to create small interactive programs that site owners can add to their sites to personalise them. Charitable site Just Giving has a branded app with several hundred users.

Online partnerships including affiliate marketing

We showed in Chapter 5 that partnerships are an important part of today's marketing mix. We have also seen in this chapter that working with partner sites in influencer outreach is a key part of content marketing, SEO and online PR. Resources must be devoted to managing your online partners. Many large organisations have specific staff to manage these relationships. In smaller organisations partnership management is often neglected, which is a missed opportunity. There are three key types of online partnerships which need to be managed: co-marketing and influencer outreach (covered in the previous section), affiliate marketing and online sponsorship. The main and most important form of partnership marketing for transactional e-commerce sites which we review in this section is affiliate marketing. We explained at the start of Chapter 5 that co-marketing involves a formal or informal partnership agreement reached between different businesses to promote each other, typically based on sharing content (and potentially promotions) principally to the audience of owned media channels such as social media, blog and email marketing. Co-marketing, also known as 'contra-deals', has the advantage that it is low-cost since the main cost is staff time to develop joint campaigns and share content.

Affiliate marketing

Affiliate marketing divides marketers and agencies as to its value. The discussion revolves around the value of affiliate marketing in generating incremental sales. There is no doubt that affiliates can generate more sales at a controlled cost, the question is whether these sales would have occurred anyway if a brand is well known. For example, Amazon has an affiliate programme but it could be argued that its brand is so well known and it has such a large customer base that it would receive many sales anyway. However, Amazon has run its programme for over ten years and although it has reduced commissions, it is still running and is used to promote new product offerings such as music downloads.

What is affiliate marketing?

Affiliate marketing
A commission-based arrangement where referring sites (publishers) receive a commission on sales or leads by merchants (retailers or other transactional sites). Commission is usually based on a percentage of product sale price or a fixed amount for each sale (CPA or cost per acquisition), but may also sometimes be based on a per-click basis, for example when an aggregator refers visits to merchants.

Affiliate marketing is the ultimate form of marketing communications since it is what is known as a 'pay-per-performance marketing' method and it's a commission-based arrangement where the merchant only pays when they make the sale or get a lead. Compare this to the wastage with traditional advertising or direct mail! It can also drive a volume of business in a range of sectors – many banks, travel companies and online retailers get more than 10 per cent of their sales from a well-run affiliate marketing programme. It's not so suitable though for business products or lower-priced consumer products since it will not be sufficiently profitable for the affiliates, and it may be difficult to recruit sufficient affiliates.

Figure 9.13 summarises the affiliate marketing process. You can see that when a visitor to an affiliate site (who may be an online publisher or aggregator) clicks through to a merchant site, this prospect will be tracked through a cookie placed on the visitor's PC. If the prospect later transacts within an agreed period, usually 1, 7, 30, 60 or 90 days, the affiliate will be credited with the sale through an agreed amount (percentage of sale or fixed amount).

Digital marketers need to be selective in choosing the right forms of affiliate marketing and not all may be desirable. These are the options of affiliate marketing models for you to consider.

- *Aggregators*. These are the major comparison sites like Kelkoo, USwitch and Moneysupermarket. These aren't strictly affiliates since some, such as Kelkoo and Shopzilla, charge on a cost-per-click, but USwitch and Moneysupermarket have a CPA model

| Figure 9.13 | The affiliate marketing model (note that the tracking software and fee payment may be managed through an independent affiliate network manager) |

as well. Google Product Search (formerly Froogle) uses a similar model, but is a free option for retailers to submit a feed for which products may then be featured in the top of the Google SERPs.

- *Review sites.* For example CNet software or hardware reviews, or maybe startups like Reevoo or Review Centre. These all link to merchants based on cost-per-click or cost-per-acquisition deals.
- *Rewards sites.* These split the commission between the reward site and its visitors. Examples are GreasyPalm or QuidCo.
- *Voucher code sites.* MyVoucherCodes or Hot UK Deals are typical. If you have some great deals to entice first-time shoppers you should generate business, although many search by well-known brand.
- *Über-bloggers.* Martin Lewis's **MoneySavingExpert.com** is an incredibly popular site due to his PR efforts and great content. Although he has no ads, he is an affiliate for many sites he recommends.
- *Everyone else.* They don't tend to be high-volume super-affiliates like all the above, but they're collectively important and you can work them via affiliate networks like Commission Junction or Tradedoubler. They often specialise in SEO or PPC.

Advantages and disadvantages of affiliate marketing

Advantages of affiliate marketing

Many of the benefits of affiliate marketing are closely related to search engine marketing since affiliates are often expert at deploying SEO or PPC to gain visibility in the search results pages. The main benefits of affiliate marketing are:

- *SERPS visibility.* Gain more visibility in the paid and natural listings of the SERPs (increase 'share of search' page).
- *Reach different audiences.* Can use different affiliates to target different audiences, product categories and related phrases.
- *Responsiveness to marketplace changes.* Affiliates may be more responsive than your in-house or agency teams in terms of algorithm changes for SEO or changes in bidding approaches for PPC. They are also great at identifying gaps in your search strategy. For example, they may be quicker at advertising on new products, or may use keyphrase variants that you haven't considered.
- *Target generic phrases in SERPs.* Enables you to reach customers through generic phrases (e.g. 'clothing') at a relatively low cost if the affiliates secure better positions in natural listings.

- *Increase reach in SERPs*. Increase the reach of your brand or campaign since affiliate ads and links featuring you will be displayed on third-party sites.
- *Generate awareness*. Can be used to generate awareness of brand or new products for which a company is not well known.
- *Diversity risk*. Use of affiliates reduces the risk caused by temporary or more fundamental problems with your SEM management or other digital marketing programmes.
- *Pay-per-performance*. The costs of acquisition can be controlled well.

Disadvantages of affiliate marketing

But there can be substantial drawbacks to an affiliate marketing programme which arise from the fact that your affiliates are mainly motivated by money. It follows that some of them may use unethical techniques to increase their revenue. Potential disadvantages are:

- *Incremental profit or sales may be limited*. You may be cannibalising business you would have achieved anyway.
- *Affiliates may exploit your brand name*. This is particularly the case where affiliates exploit brand names by bidding on variations of it (for example 'Dell', 'Dell Computers' or 'Dell laptop') or by gaining a presence in the natural listings. Here there is already awareness. It is important to prevent this and many affiliate programmes exclude brand bidding, although affiliates can have a role in displacing competitors from the listings for brand terms.
- *May damage brand reputation*. Your ads may be displayed on sites inconsistent with your brand image, such as gambling or pornography sites. Alternatively, creative may be out-of-date, which could be illegal.
- *Programme management fees*. If using an affiliate network to manage your campaigns they may take up to 30 per cent of each agreed affiliate commission as additional 'network override'.
- *Programme management time*. Affiliate marketing is founded on forming and maintaining good relationships. This cannot be done through the agency alone and marketers within a company need to speak to their top affiliates.

Best practice in planning and managing affiliate marketing

In this section we will review how affiliate networks can be used to improve the results from affiliate marketing and the main controls on affiliate marketing, i.e. commission, cookie periods and creative. It is important that these parameters are clearly defined in the affiliate agreement to reduce the likelihood of abuse.

Affiliate networks

Affiliate network
Third-party brokers also known as affiliate managers who manage recruitment of affiliates and infrastructure to manage a merchant's affiliate programme in the form of links, tracking and payment of a range of affiliates.

To manage the process of finding affiliates, updating product information, tracking clicks and making payments many companies use an **affiliate network** or affiliate manager such as the US/European networks Commission Junction (**www.cj.com**), Link Share (**www.link-share.com**) or Trade Doubler (**www.tradedoubler.com**, mainly European). Since the affiliate network takes a cut on each sale, many merchants also try to set up separate relationships with preferred affiliates, often known as 'super-affiliates'.

Since many of the important affiliates are members of more than one affiliate network programme, it is usually found that it is not worthwhile for a merchant to join more than two affiliate networks. They also need to be careful that several affiliates are not credited for multiple sales since this quickly becomes unprofitable for the merchant.

Commission

In affiliate marketing, it is vital that commission is set at such a level that it incentivises affiliates to preferentially promote a merchant's products, while at the same time being profitable.

Earnings per click (EPC)
A relative measure of the effectiveness of a site or section of a site in generating revenue for the site owner through affiliate marketing for every 100 outbound clicks generated.

The affiliates or publishers are naturally obsessive about their **earnings per click (EPC)**. This is average earnings per click and is usually measured across 100 clicks.

EPC is a crucial measure in affiliate marketing since an affiliate will compare merchants on this basis and then usually decide to promote those with the highest EPC, which will be based on the commission levels and the conversion rates to sale for different merchants.

A merchant will set commission levels according to a product's awareness level within a merchant's portfolio of products or how much they feel they need to promote them. It will also be worth increasing commissions when there is a favourable promotion on a product since affiliates will then promote it, knowing that their EPC is more likely to increase. Less well-known products or newly launched products will often have more favourable commissions. For example at the time of writing, **Tesco.com** used affiliates for different products with different commission as follows:

- e-diets commission from £12 on 1–9 sales to £20 on 61+ sales;
- wine at 2 per cent on lowest tier to 3 per cent on the Gold tier of sales of >£2500;
- grocery and utilities – flat fee of £5 for first-time purchase only.

Cookie expiry period

Affiliates' EPC will also depend on the cookie expiry period agreed on the time between a visitor clicking on the affiliate link and the sale being accredited to the affiliate. Common times are 7, 30 or 90 days. A longer cookie period will result in a higher EPC. Prussakov (2011a) recommends that 60 to 90 days is often best to incentivise affiliates in competitive markets with a longer decision-making period. Merchants don't typically want to pay multiple affiliates for a single sale. Instead, it is usually the last referring affiliate that is credited or a mix between the first and last. So a good tracking system is required to resolve this. Prussakov (2011b) uses the data presented in Figure 9.14 to argue that the majority purchase within a shorter period, so a longer period gives a better incentive without adversely affecting profitability.

Creative and links

Managing the creative which affiliates use to promote a merchant is a challenge since creative needs to be up-to-date in line with different promotions or it may be misleading, or even illegal. So this needs to be monitored by the affiliate manager. Many merchants now provide live product feeds to affiliate networks in order to keep their promotions and product pricing up-to-date.

There are risks of brand damage through affiliates displaying creative on content which a merchant might feel was not complementary to their brand (for example, a gambling site). This needs to be specified in the affiliate agreement – sites need to be reviewed carefully before affiliates are permitted to join a specific programme and additional sites used by each affiliate should be monitored.

Another form of brand or trademark abuse is when an affiliate bids on a merchant's brand name such that they may receive credit for a sale when a prospect was already aware of the merchant (as explained in Chapter 3 in the legal section). The limits of this should also be specified within the affiliate agreements and monitored carefully.

Online sponsorship

Online sponsorship is not straightforward. It's not just a case of mirroring existing 'real-world' sponsorship arrangements in the 'virtual world', although this is a valid option. There are many additional opportunities for sponsorship online which can be sought out, even if you don't have a big budget at your disposal.

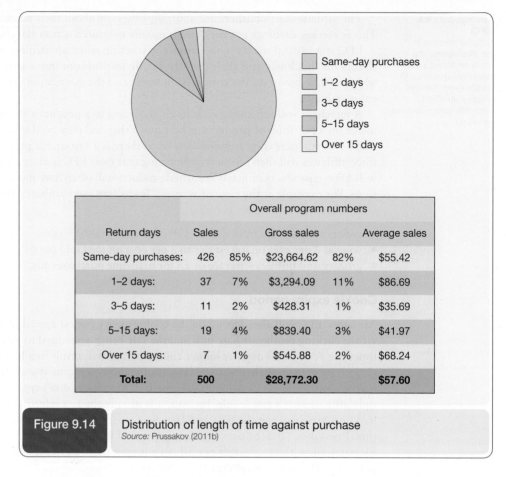

	Overall program numbers					
Return days	Sales		Gross sales		Average sales	
Same-day purchases:	426	85%	$23,664.62	82%	$55.42	
1–2 days:	37	7%	$3,294.09	11%	$86.69	
3–5 days:	11	2%	$428.31	1%	$35.69	
5–15 days:	19	4%	$839.40	3%	$41.97	
Over 15 days:	7	1%	$545.88	2%	$68.24	
Total:	**500**		**$28,772.30**		**$57.60**	

Figure 9.14	Distribution of length of time against purchase
	Source: Prussakov (2011b)

Ryan and Whiteman (2000) define online sponsorship as:

the linking of a brand with related content or context for the purpose of creating brand awareness and strengthening brand appeal in a form that is clearly distinguishable from a banner, button or other standardised ad unit.

For the advertiser, online sponsorship has the benefit that their name is associated with an online brand that the site visitor is already familiar with. So, for users of a publisher's site, with which they are familiar, sponsorship builds on this existing relationship and trust.

Paid-for sponsorship of another site, or part of it, especially a portal, for an extended period is another way to develop permanent links. Co-branding is a lower-cost method of sponsorship and can exploit synergies between different companies. Note that sponsorship does not have to directly drive visitors to a brand site – it may be more effective if interaction occurs on the media owner's microsite.

A great business-to-business example of online sponsorship is offered by WebTrends which sponsors the customer information channel on **ClickZ.com** (**www.clickz.com/experts**). It combined this sponsorship with different ads each month offering e-marketers the chance to learn about different topics such as search marketing, retention and conversion marketing through detailed white papers and a 'Take 10' online video presentation by industry experts which could be downloaded by registered users. The objective of these ads was to encourage prospects to subscribe to the WebTrends WebResults e-newsletter and to assess purchase intent at sign-up enabling follow-up telemarketing by regional distributors. WebTrends reported the following results over a single year of sponsorship:

- list built to 100,000 WebResults total subscribers;
- 18,000 Take 10 presentations;
- 13,500 seminar attendees.

Co-branding
An arrangement between two or more companies which agree to jointly display content and perform joint promotion using brand logos, email marketing or banner advertisements. The aim is that the brands are strengthened if they are seen as complementary. Co-branding is often a reciprocal arrangement which can occur without payment as part of a wider agreement between partners.

Co-branding and contra-deals

Contra-deals
A reciprocal agreement in the form of an exchange where payment doesn't take place. Instead services or ad space to promote another company as part of co-branding occurs.

Co-branding of sites or emails are closely related to online sponsorship. These **contra-deals**, as they are sometimes referred to, typically occur where there is an association between two brands and they are complementary but not competitive.

For example, one online publisher may offer subscribers the chance to sign up with newsletters from another company, a process known as 'co-registration'.

Co-branding can be a cost-effective form of online marketing, but specific resources such as 'online partnership manager' have to be put in place to set up and manage the relationships between partners. This will often be part of an affiliate manager's role.

Interactive display advertising

What is display advertising?

Display advertising
Display ads are paid ad placements using graphical or *rich media ad units* within a web page to achieve goals of delivering brand awareness, familiarity, favourability and purchase intent. Many ads encourage interaction through prompting the viewer to interact or rollover to play videos, complete an online form or to view more details by clicking through to a site.

Ad serving
The term for displaying an advertisement on a website. Often the advertisement will be served from a web server different from the site on which it is placed.

Destination site
The site reached on click-through.

Microsite
A small-scale destination site reached on click-through which is part of the media owner's site.

Run-of-site
Cost per 1000 ad impressions. CPM is usually higher for run-of site advertisements where advertisements occur on all pages of the site.

Results-based payment
Advertisers pay according to the number of times the ad is clicked on.

Display advertising involves an advertiser paying for an advertising placement on third-party sites such as publishers or social networks. The process usually involves **ad serving** from a different server from that on which the page is hosted (ads can be served on destination sites in a similar way). Ad serving uses a specialist piece of software, possibly mounted on an independent server such as Doubleclick (now owned by Google). In 2008, Google launched its free ad manager service (**www.google.com/admanager**) to help site owners sell, schedule, optimise revenue, serve ads and measure directly sold and network-based inventory.

Advertising is used on a range of sites in order to drive traffic to an organisation's **destination site,** or alternatively a **microsite** or nested ad content on the media owner's site or on the destination site. The destination page from a banner ad will usually be designed as a specifically created direct-response page to encourage further action. For example, the nappy supplier Huggies placed an advertisement on a childcare site that led the parents clicking on this link to more detailed information on Huggies contained on the site and encouraging them to opt in to a loyalty programme.

Display advertising is still colloquially known as banner advertising, but practitioners such as the trade body the Internet Advertising Bureau (**www.iab.net** and **www.iabuk.net**), media owners such as publishers, advertisers and their agencies now commonly refer to 'display advertising'. This reflects the increasing range of ad formats we will discuss below.

Purchasing ad placements

When media is purchased, it is either purchased on a specific site such as *The Times* or *New York Times*, or it is purchased across several sites, which are known as an ad network.

Display advertising is purchased for a specific period. It may be purchased for the ad to be served on:

- the **run-of-site** (the entire site);
- a section of site;
- according to keywords entered on a search engine.

Traditionally, the most common payment is according to the number of customers who view the page as a cost-per-thousand (CPM) ad or page impressions. Typical CPM is in the range £10–£30. Other options that benefit the advertiser if they can be agreed are per click-through or per action such as a purchase on the destination site. Although initially media owners were able to control charging rates and largely used a per-exposure model, with the increase in unused ad inventory there has been an increase in **results-based payment** methods particularly within ad networks.

Programmatic ad buying
Describes the purchase online display advertising that is aggregated, booked, flighted, analysed and optimised via demand-side software interfaces and algorithms. It includes RTB and also non-RTB methods and buy types such as Facebook Ads API and the Google Display Network.

Demand Side Platforms (DSPs)
A service that enables ads to be managed across multiple ad networks and ad exchanges through a single interface designed for managing reporting and performance.

Real-time bidding (RTB)
Bids for buying ads against keywords can be managed in real time in conjunction with a DSP.

Programmatic ad buying

The options for purchasing and managing display advertising are now much more complex, as suggested by the summary in Figure 9.15 of the ad buying ecosystem created by the IAB.

A major change in online advertising is through the use of new **programmatic ad buying** techniques, known as **Demand Side Platforms (DSPs)**, which use an approach called **real-time bidding (RTB)**. The purpose of these is to exploit efficiencies through using technology to automatically bid on the most cost-effective ad inventory in an auction. Since individuals are tracked across different sites they can be targeted according to their interests shown by content view using a technique known as behavioural targeting. However, it is unclear whether privacy concerns such as those we covered in Chapter 3 will prevent this in future.

Advantages and disadvantages of display advertising

Robinson *et al.* (2007) have noted that the two primary goals of online display advertising are, first, using display adverts as a form of marketing communication used to raise brand awareness; and, second, as a direct response medium focussed on generating a response. Cartellieri *et al.* (1997) refer to a wider range of goals for online campaigns including:

| Figure 9.15 | Ad buying ecosystem |

- *Delivering content.* This is the typical case where a click-through on a banner advertisement leads to a destination site giving more detailed information on an offer. This is where a direct response is sought. Today ads often embed videos or whitepapers to deliver content directly within the ad.
- *Enabling transaction.* If a click-through leads to a merchant such as a travel site or an online bookstore this may lead directly to a sale. A direct response is also sought here.
- *Shaping attitudes.* An advertisement that is consistent with a company brand can help build brand awareness.
- *Soliciting response.* An advertisement may be intended to identify new leads or as a start for two-way communication. In these cases an interactive advertisement may encourage a user to type in an email address or other information.
- *Encouraging retention.* The advertisement may be placed as a reminder about the company and its service and may link through to on-site sales promotions such as a prize draw.

These objectives are not mutually exclusive, and more than one can be achieved with a well-designed ad campaign.

Advantages of online advertising

- *Direct response.* Display advertising can generate an immediate direct response via click-through to a website enabling transaction for retail products, for example.
- *Advertising now available for smaller advertisers.* Previously, ad buying online was limited to larger advertisers. But now a small business can purchase a small-scale, highly targeted ad campaign for a few dollars using the Google Display Network options in Google AdWords or the advertising programmes available on the social networks such as Facebook, Twitter or LinkedIn. They can now use self-service tools like AdRoll (www.adroll.com) to remarket across all of these to boost conversion.

XMOS (cross-media optimisation studies) Research designed to help marketers and their agencies answer the question 'What is the optimal mix of advertising vehicles across different media, in terms of frequency, reach and budget allocation, for a given campaign to achieve its marketing goals?' The mix between online and offline spend is varied to maximise campaign metrics such as reach, brand awareness and purchase intent.

Media multiplier or halo effect The role of one media channel on influencing sale or uplift in brand metrics. Commonly applied to online display advertising, where exposure to display ads may increase click-through rates when the consumer is later exposed to a brand through other media, for example sponsored links or affiliate ads. It may also improve conversion rates on destination sites through higher confidence in the brand or familiarity with the offer.

- *Indirect response.* We will see in the section on the disadvantages of display advertising that click-throughs are so low that it suggests display advertising is not worthwhile. However, the indirect response should not be underestimated. This is where viewers of an ad later visit a website or search on the brand or category. Research by OPA Europe (2010) showed that for members' sites, one-third exposed to display advertising conducted searches for the advertised brands while 42 per cent visited advertised brand sites. Note that these results are for well-known brands and control figures were not presented to show the uplift compared to those not exposed.
- *Enhancing brand awareness and reach.* The visual imagery of a display ad can generate awareness about a brand, product or need. This is less practical in search engine marketing where searchers are already seeking a specific brand, product or need, although there are opportunities to make searchers aware of other, unknown suppliers. We also saw at the end of Chapter 8 that **XMOS (cross-media optimisation studies)** showed that online was useful for reaching audiences whose consumption of traditional media has decreased.
- *Media-multiplier or halo effect.* Repeated exposure to ads online, particularly in association with other media, can increase brand awareness and ultimately purchase intent. Furthermore, practitioners report a **media multiplier or halo effect** of buying online ads which can help increase the response rates from other online media. For example, if a web user has been exposed to banner ads, this may increase their response to paid search ads and may also increase their likelihood of converting on a site since brand awareness and trust may be higher. Attribution modelling, which we introduced in Chapter 8, can help determine the contribution of display ads, as shown in Digital marketing insight 9.2.
- This is suggested by research reported by MAD (2007) in the travel market which involved asking respondents what their response to an online ad that appealed to them would be. Surely it would be a click? In fact the results broke down as follows:
  - search for a general term relating to the advertisement (31 per cent);
  - go straight to advertiser's site (29 per cent);
  - search for the advertiser's name (26 per cent);

- click on banner to respond (26 per cent);
- visit a retail store (4 per cent).

Of course, this methodology shows us reported behaviour rather than actual behaviour, but it is still significant that more than twice as many people are being driven to a search engine by banner advertising than by clicking directly on the banner! The research concludes that paid search marketing needs to be optimised to work with banner advertising, by anticipating searches that are likely to be prompted by the banner and ensure a higher rank for search results. For example, a brand featuring a Cyprus holiday offer will generate generic search terms like 'package holiday Cyprus' rather than brand searches.

Abraham (2008) has also shown that online ads can stimulate offline sales. For one retailer with a turnover of $15 billion, research showed that over a three-month period, sales increased (compared to a control group) by 40 per cent online and by 50 per cent offline among people exposed to an online search – and display – ad campaign promoting the entire company. Because its baseline sales volumes are greater in physical stores than on the Internet, this retailer derived a great deal more revenue benefit offline than the percentages suggest.

- *Achieving brand interactions.* Many modern display ads comprise two parts – an initial visual encouraging interaction through a rollover and then another visual or application encouraging interaction with a brand. This enables advertisers to calculate an interaction rate (IR) to assess the extent to which viewers interact with a brand ad.
- *Targeting.* Media buyers can select the right site or channel within a site to reach the audience (e.g. a specialist online car magazine or review site or the motoring channel within an online newspaper or TV channel site). Audiences can also be targeted via their profile through serving personalised ads, or ad in email if visitors have registered on a site.

  Behavioural re-targeting options is used in an ad network to preferentially serve an ad to someone who seems to have an interest in a topic from the content they consume. Effectively the ad follows the viewer around the site. For example, if someone visits the car section of a site, then the ad is served to them when they view other sections of the site. Re-targeting can work across an ad network too and can even be sequential, where the messages are varied for an individual the more times they are exposed to the ad. Search re-targeting offers the option to display an ad after a visitor has searched on a particular term such as a car marque. Tracking of individuals is achieved through use of cookies.

- *Cost.* There are opportunities to buy online media at a cheaper rate compared to traditional media, although this is less true in focussed, competitive markets such as financial services where there is limited premium inventory for media buyers to purchase.

  Ad networks from suppliers such as Blue Lithium or 24–7 Media give advertisers the options of advertising across a network of sites to reach a particular demographic, e.g. female 18–25, but at a lower cost than media buys on a specific site since the actual site used for the ad placement isn't known (hence these are sometimes known as '*blind network buys*'). Lower CPMs are achievable and in some cases CPC or CPA payment options are available. Site owners such as publishers use ad networks since it gives them a method of gaining fees from unused ad inventory which has not sold at premium rates.

- *Dynamic updates to ad campaigns.* In comparison with traditional media, where media placements have to be bought weeks or months in advance, online ads are more flexible since it is possible to place an advertisement more rapidly and make changes during the campaign. Experienced online advertisers build in flexibility to change targeting through time. Best practice is to start wide and then narrow to a focus – allow 20 per cent budget for high-performing ad placements (high CTR and conversion).

  In an iMediaConnection (2003) interview with ING direct VP of marketing, Jurie Pieterse, the capability to revise creative is highlighted:

  Another lesson we learnt is the importance of creative. It's critical to invest in developing various creative executions to test them for best performance and constantly introduce new challengers to the top performers. We've also learnt there's no single top creative unit – different creative executions and sizes perform differently from publisher to publisher.

- *Accountability*. As we will discuss later in the section, it is readily possible to measure reach, interaction and response to ads. However, it is more difficult to measure brand impact.

Disadvantages of online advertising

- *Relatively low click-through rates*. When discussing online ads, many web users will state they ignore ads and find them intrusive. Published click-through rates support this, with most compilations showing response rates of around 0.1 to 0.2 per cent, but with rich media formats such as video ads attracting higher click-through rates. This phenomenon is known among practitioners as banner blindness The first 468 × 68 pixel banner ad was placed on Hotwired in 1995 and the call-to-action 'Click here!' generated a click-through of 25 per cent. Since then, the click-through rate (CTR) has fallen dramatically, with many consumers suffering from 'banner blindness' – they ignore anything on a website that looks like an ad. Remember, though, that for reasons such as awareness generation and the media multiplier effect, digital marketers should not dismiss online advertising as ineffectual based on click-through rates alone. It should also be remembered that the use of new ad formats such as **native advertising** (which we introduced in Chapter 3) and widget marketing mean that there are other ways to get cut-through.

- *Relatively high costs or low efficiency*. When the low response rates are combined with relatively high costs of over £10 per thousand, this makes online ads an inefficient medium.

- *Brand reputation*. Brands can potentially be damaged in the consumers' mind if they are associated with some types of content such as gambling, pornography or racism. It is difficult to monitor precisely which content an ad is served next to when millions of impressions are bought across many sites, this is particularly the case when using ad networks.

Native advertising
Online content that it is created to promote or enhance a brand such as a publisher article or social media update. Such content should be disclosed as advertising by law in many countries, but often it isn't.

Best practice in planning and managing display ad campaigns

In this section we will review how measurement, targeting and creative can be used to improve the results from display ad campaigns.

Measurement of display effectiveness

Page and ad impressions
One page impression occurs when a member of the audience views a web page. One ad impression occurs when a person views an advertisement placed on the web page.

Reach
Reach defines the number of unique individuals who view an advertisement.

CPM
The cost of placing an ad viewed by 1000 people.

Interaction rate (IR)
The proportion of ad viewers who interact with an online ad through rolling over it. Some will be involuntary depending on where the ad is placed on the screen, so it is highly dependent on placement.

Different terms are used for measuring banner ad effectiveness. Each time an advertisement is viewed is referred to as an advertisement or **ad impression** – also known as **page impressions** (page views). Since some people may view the advertisement more than once, marketers are also interested in the **reach**, which is the number of unique individuals who view the advertisement. This will naturally be a smaller figure than that for ad impressions. Cost of ads is typically based on **CPM** or cost-per-thousand (*mille*) ad impressions as with other media. However, the popularity of CPC search advertising and CPA affiliate deals mean that these are options too.

As with other digital media, direct response to ads is measured through click-through rate. **Interaction rate (IR)** is a form of measurement that is unique to display ads. It refers to the many ads which encourage the site visitor to interact through a prompt to 'rollover' and another Flash creative will be loaded which may offer a clear brand message rendered in large font, a response form such as an insurance quote or a request to obtain a SIM or a game or poll. The engagement of the ad campaign for different placements can then be assessed through the interaction rate which will typically be ten times higher than the click-through rate if the targeting, offer and creative is right.

When payment is made according to the number of viewers of a site it is important that the number of viewers be measured accurately. To do this independent **website auditors** are required. The main auditing body in the UK is the Audit Bureau of Circulation Electronic, ABCelectronic (**www.abce.org.uk**).

There is much discussion about how many impressions of an advertisement an individual has to see for it to be effective. Novak and Hoffman (1997) note that for traditional media it is thought that fewer than three exposures will not give adequate recall. For new media, because of the greater intensity of viewing a computer screen, recall seems to be better with a smaller number of advertisements compared with old media. The technical term for adequate recall is **effective frequency**.

When a user clicks on the advertisement, he or she will normally be directed to further information, viewing of which will result in a marketing outcome. Usually the user will be directed through to part of the corporate website that will have been set up especially to deal with the response from the advertisement. When a user clicks on an advertisement immediately this is known as a **click-through**, but adserving systems (using cookies) also measure **view-through**, which indicates when a user views an ad and subsequently visits a website within a defined period, such as 30 days. This increases overall response, but it should be borne in mind that users may have visited the site in response to other stimuli.

Interactive ad formats

As well as the classic 468 × 60 rotating GIF banner ad which is decreasing in popularity, media owners now provide a choice of larger, richer formats which web users are more likely to notice. Research has shown that message association and awareness building are much higher for flash-based ads, rich-media ads and larger-format rectangles (multipurpose units, MPUs) and skyscrapers. Other online ad terms you will hear include **interstitials** (intermediate adverts before another page appears) and the more common **overlays** (formerly more often known as *superstitials* or *overts*) that appear above content and, of course, *pop-up windows* that are now less widely used because of their intrusion. Online advertisers face a constant battle with users who deploy pop-up blockers or less commonly ad-blocking software, but they will persist in using rich-media formats where they generate the largest response.

Interactive ad targeting options

Online ads can be targeted through placing ads:

- *On a particular type of site (or part of site)* which has a specific visitor profile or type of content. So a car manufacturer of a car preferred by single female drivers can place ads on a publisher site appealing a young female audience. A financial services provider can advertise in the money section of the site to target those interested in these products. To reach large mass-market audiences, advertisers can place an ad on a large portal home page such as MSN which has millions of visitors each day (sometimes known as a 'road-block' if they take all ad inventory).
- *To target a registered user's profile.* A business software provider could advertise on the FT to target registrants' profiles such as finance directors or IT managers.
- *At a particular time of day or week.*
- *To follow users' behaviour.* **Behavioural ad targeting** is all about relevance – dynamically serving relevant content, messaging or ad which matches the interests of a site visitor according to inferences about their characteristics. These inferences are made by anonymously tracking the different types of pages visited by a site user during a single visit to a site or across multiple sessions. Other aspects of the environment used by the

Glossary (margin definitions)

Website auditors
Auditors accurately measure the usage of different sites in terms of the number of ad impressions and click-through rates.

Effective frequency
The number of exposures or ad impressions (frequency) required for an advertisement to become effective.

Click-through
A click-through (ad click) occurs each time a user clicks on a banner advertisement to direct them to a web page that contains further information. The click-through rate is expressed as a percentage of total ad impressions, and refers to the proportion of users viewing an advertisement who click on it. It is calculated as the number of click-throughs divided by the number of ad impressions.

View-through
Indicates when a user views an ad and subsequently visits a website.

Interstitial ads
Ads that appear between one page and the next.

Overlay
Typically an animated ad that moves around the page and is superimposed on the website content.

Behavioural ad targeting
Enables an advertiser to target ads at a visitor as they move elsewhere on the site, visit other sites on an ad network return to the site, the process of remarketing to increase the frequency or number of impressions served to an individual in the target market.

visitor can also be determined, such as their location, browser and operating system. For example, **FT.com** using software from Revenue Science can identify users in eight segments: Business Education, Institutional Investor, Information Technology, Luxury and Consumer, Management, Personal Finance, Travel and Private Equity. The targeting process is shown in Figure 9.16. First the ad serving system detects whether the visitor is in the target audience (media optimisation), then creative optimisation occurs to serve the best ad for the viewer type.

In 2010 behavioural targeting became available through Google's AdWords platform as Remarketing which made it available to many more advertisers.

Ad creative

As with any form of advertising, certain techniques will result in a more effective advertisement. Robinson *et al.* (2007) conducted research on the factors which increased click-through response to banner ads. The main variables they (and previous studies they reference) include are:

- banner size;
- message length;
- promotional incentive;
- animation;
- action phrase (commonly referred to as a call-to-action);
- company brand/logo.

Their research indicated that the design elements which made the most effective banner ads included a larger size, longer message, absence of promotional incentives and the presence of information about casino games. Surprisingly, the inclusion of brand name was not favourable in increasing click-through, although, as we noted, this may be because the ad generates a subsequent search on the brand. Please note that this study was restricted to online gambling ads.

Figure 9.16   Behavioural ad targeting process

Anecdotal discussions by the authors with marketers who have advertised online indicate the following are also important and worth considering:

- *Appropriate incentives are needed to achieve click-through.* Banner advertisements with offers such as prizes or reductions can achieve higher click-through rates by perhaps as much as 10 per cent.
- *Creative design needs to be tested extensively.* Alternative designs for the advertisement need to be tested on representatives of a target audience. Anecdotal evidence suggests that the click-through rate can vary greatly according to the design of the advertisement, in much the same way that recall of a television advertisement will vary in line with its concept and design.
- *Placement of advertisement and timing need to be considered carefully.* The different types of placement options available have been discussed earlier in the chapter, but it should be remembered that audience volume and composition will vary through the day and the week.

Different styles of ad creative can be viewed by visiting the Ad Gallery of an ad serving company such as DoubleClick (**www.richmediagallery.com/**) or a site that reviews ads such as Digital Buzz Blog (**www.digitalbuzzblog.com**)

Opt-in email marketing and mobile text messaging

We have grouped email marketing with text messaging since these are both 'push media' which share much in terms of their applications for prospect and customer communications. In this coverage we concentrate on email marketing since mobile marketing was covered in Chapter 3.

What is email marketing?

When devising plans for email marketing communications, marketers need to plan for:

Outbound email marketing
Emails are sent to customers and prospects from an organisation.

Inbound email marketing
Management of emails from customers by an organisation.

- **Outbound email marketing**, where email campaigns are used as a form of direct marketing to encourage trial and purchases and as part of a CRM dialogue.
- **Inbound email marketing**, where emails from customers, such as service enquiries, are managed (this was discussed in Chapters 3 and 5 and isn't discussed further in this chapter).

The applications of outbound email marketing communications broadly break down into customer acquisition and retention activities. Email activities within organisations tend to focus on customer acquisition as these ratings (on a five-point scale) on the relative merits of different applications of email by Chittenden and Rettie (2003) suggest:

- customer retention (4.5);
- sales promotion (4.4);
- gathering customer data (3.0);
- lead generation (3.0);
- brand awareness (2.7);
- customer acquisition (2.1).

Opt-in email options for customer acquisition

For acquiring new visitors and customers to a site, there are three main options for email marketing. From the point of view of the recipient, these are:

- *Cold email campaign.* In this case, the recipient receives an opt-in email from an organisation that has rented an email list from a consumer email list or trade publisher and event provider. Although they have agreed to receive offers by email, the email is effectively cold. For example, a credit card provider could send a cold email to a list member who is not currently their member. It is important to use some form of 'statement of origination', otherwise the message may be considered spam.

- *Co-branded email.* Here, the recipient receives an email with an offer from a company they have a reasonably strong affinity with. For example, the same credit card company could partner with a mobile service provider such as Vodafone and send out the offer to their customer (who has opted in to receive emails from third parties). Although this can be considered a form of cold email, it is warmer since there is a stronger relationship with one of the brands and the subject line and creative will refer to both brands. Co-branded emails tend to be more responsive than cold emails to rented lists since the relationship exists and fewer offers tend to be given. Digital marketing insight 9.4 gives an example of where email marketing is used to increase awareness as part of an integrated campaign combined with display advertising.
- *Third-party e-newsletter.* In this visitor acquisition option, a company publicises itself in a third-party e-newsletter. This could be in the form of an ad, sponsorship or PR (editorial) which links through to a destination site. These placements may be set up as part of an interactive advertising ad buy since many e-newsletters also have permanent versions on the website. Since e-newsletter recipients tend to engage with them by scanning the headlines or reading them if they have time, e-newsletter placements can be relatively cost effective. Viral marketing, which is discussed in the next main section, also uses email as the mechanism for transferring messages.

Opt-in
An individual agrees to receive email communications.

House list
A list of prospect and customer names, email addresses and profile information owned by an organisation.

Opt-in email options for prospect conversion and customer retention (house list)

Email is most widely used as a prospect conversion and customer retention tool using an **opt-in house list** of prospects and customers that have given permission to an organisation

---

Digital marketing insight 9.4	SEAT combines email with display advertising to increase awareness

This study analysed the advertising effectiveness of email marketing and display advertising, looked at responses from over 1000 consumers to SEAT Ibiza ST campaigns. It used a classic 'hold out' approach where different respondents were reached through different combinations of media:

- contact through an email campaign;
- contact with display advertising;
- contact with both campaign channels.

The main results from the campaign which showed the integrated benefits of the campaign were:

1 The combination of display and email advertising improves advertising recall by 13 per cent compared with just display advertising (Figure 9.17).
2 Email increases disposition to buy in 47 per cent of cases and is therefore ideal for increasing conversions.
3 Spending power as a target group – by using email you can precisely reach your target group.
4 Email allowed the required reach of advertising to be reached three times more quickly than display advertising.

Source: eCircle (2011)

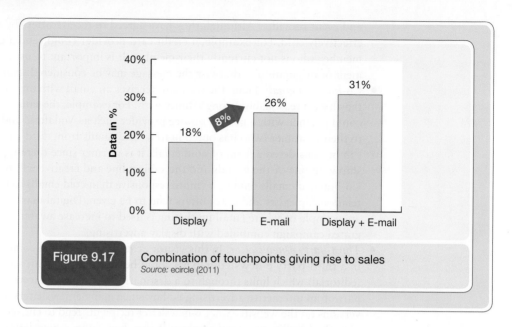

Figure 9.17 Combination of touchpoints giving rise to sales
Source: ecircle (2011)

to contact them. For example, **Lastminute.com** has built a house list of over 10 million prospects and customers across Europe. Successful email marketers adopt a strategic approach to email and develop a contact or touch strategy which plans the frequency and content of email communications (as explained in Chapters 4 and 6). Some options for in-house email marketing include:

- *Conversion email.* Someone visits a website and expresses interest in a product or service by registering and providing their email address, although they do not buy. Automated follow-up emails can be sent out to persuade the recipient to trial the service. For example, betting company William Hill found that automated follow-up emails converted twice as many registrants to place their first bet compared to registrants who did not receive an email.
- *Regular e-newsletter type.* Options are reviewed for different frequencies such as weekly, monthly or quarterly with different content for different audiences and segments. These are commonly used to update consumers on the latest products or promotions or business customers on developments within a market.
- *House-list campaign.* These are periodic emails to support different objectives such as encouraging trial of a service or newly launched product, repeat purchases or reactivation of customers who no longer use a service.
- *Event-triggered or behavioural emails.* These tend to be less regular and are sent out perhaps every three or six months when there is news of a new product launch or an exceptional offer.
- *Email sequence.* Software can send out a series of emails with the interval between emails determined by the marketer.

Advantages and disadvantages of email marketing

Advantages of email marketing

We saw in Chapter 6 that permission-based email is an effective tool for building relationships with customers online. Despite the increase in spam, such that the vast majority of emails are spam or viruses (most estimates exceed 80 per cent), email can still drive good response levels, particularly for house lists (retention email marketing). Opt-in email communications provide a controlled push message which encourages response.

Owing to these advantages, in many countries the volume of email marketing exceeds direct mail volumes. However, no one is suggesting direct mail will disappear immediately since it will typically have a higher impact than email marketing and the two work best when integrated.

The main advantages of email marketing are:

- *Relatively low cost of fulfilment.* The physical costs of email are substantially less than direct mail.
- *Direct response medium encourages immediate action.* Email marketing encourages click-through to a website where the offer can be redeemed immediately – this increases the likelihood of an immediate, impulsive response. For this reason, it is one of the best methods of attracting existing customers to return to a site (it's a push media).
- *Faster campaign deployment.* Lead times for producing creative and the whole campaign lifecycle tends to be shorter than traditional media.
- *Ease of personalisation.* It is easier and cheaper to personalise email than for physical media and also than for a website.
- *Options for testing.* It is relatively easy and cost-effective to test different email creative and messaging.
- *Integration.* Through combining email marketing with other direct media that can be personalised, such as direct mail, mobile messaging or web personalisation, campaign response can be increased as the message is reinforced by different media.

Disadvantages of email marketing

Some of the disadvantages of email marketing which marketers need to manage as they run their campaigns so that they are closely related to best practice are:

- *Deliverability.* Difficulty of getting messages delivered through different Internet service providers (ISPs), corporate firewalls and web mail systems.
- *Renderability.* Difficulty of displaying the creative as intended within the in-box of different email reading systems.
- *Email response decay.* Email recipients are most responsive when they first subscribe to an email. It is difficult to keep them engaged.
- *Communications preferences.* Recipients will have different preferences for email offers, content and frequency which affect engagement and response. These have to be managed through communications preferences.
- *Resource intensive.* Although email offers great opportunities for targeting, personalisation and more frequent communications, additional people and technology resources are required to deliver these.

Best practice in planning and managing email marketing

In this section we will review how measurement, targeting and creative can be used to improve the results from email marketing.

Email service providers

Email service providers (ESPs)
Provide a web-based service used by marketers to manage their email activities including hosting email subscription forms, broadcast and tracking.

Email service providers (ESPs) or marketing automation services are a popular method companies use to manage their email marketing. ESPs provide a web-based service used by marketers to manage their email activities with less recourse to an agency. Rather than buying software that you host and manage on your server, the software is effectively used on a subscription basis, with a cost based on number of emails sent and runs on another company's server. The ESP manages four key capabilities including hosting of forms for managing email subscriptions and landing pages, the broadcast tools for dispatching the emails and a database containing the prospect or customer profiles.

Measuring email marketing

The key measures for email marketing are:

- *Delivery rate* (here indicated by 'non-bounce rate'). Emails will bounce if the email address is no longer valid or a spam filter blocks the email.
- *Open rate.* This is measured for HTML messages through downloaded images. It is an indication of how many customers open an email, but is not accurate since some users have preview panes in their email readers which load the message even if is deleted without reading, and some email readers such as Outlook Express now block images by default (this has resulted in a decline in open rates through time). Open rates for particular types of email address, e.g. **Hotmail.com**, is also an indication of deliverability problems.
- *Click-through or click rate.* This is the number of people who click through on the email of those delivered (strictly unique clicks rather than total clicks). You can see that response rates are quite high at around 10 per cent.

Additionally, and most important, are the marketing outcomes or value events (Chapter 8) such as sales and leads achieved when an email recipient clicks through to the website. Retailers will also have additional methods of comparing email campaigns such as revenue/profit per email or thousand emails and average order value (AOV).

Email marketing success factors

Effective email marketing shares much in common with effective direct email copy. Chaffey (2006) uses the mnemonic CRITICAL for a checklist of questions that can be used to improve the response of email campaigns. It stands for:

- *Creative.* This assesses the design of the email including its layout, use of colour and image and the copy (see below).
- *Relevance.* Does the offer and creative of the email meet the needs of the recipients? This is dependent on the list quality and targeting variables used.
- *Incentive (or offer).* The WIFM factor ('What's in it for me?') for the recipient. What benefit does the recipient gain from clicking on the hyperlink(s) in the email? For example, a prize draw is a common offer for B2C brands.
- *Targeting and timing.* Targeting is related to the relevance. Is a single message sent to all prospects or customers on the list or are emails with tailored creative, incentive and copy sent to the different segments on the list? Timing refers to when the email is received: the time of day, day of the week, point in the month and even the year; does it relate to any particular events? There is also the relative timing – when it is received compared to other marketing communications – this depends on the integration.
- *Integration.* Are the email campaigns part of your integrated marketing communications? Questions to ask include: are the creative and copy consistent with my brand? Does the message reinforce other communications? Does the timing of the email campaign fit with offline communications?
- *Conversation.* This is to remind us that email shouldn't just be considered as a broadcast medium and opportunities should be taken to encourage response, for example through social media.
- *Attributes (of the email).* Assess the message characteristics such as the subject line, from address, to address, date/time of receipt and format (HTML or text). Send out Multipart/MIME messages which can display HTML or text according to the capability of the email reader. Offer choice of HTML or text to match users' preferences.
- *Landing page (or microsite).* These are terms given to the page(s) reached after the recipient clicks on a link in the email. Typically, on click-through the recipient will be presented with an online form to profile or learn more about them. Designing the page so the form is easy to complete can affect the overall success of the campaign.

A relevant incentive, such as free information or a discount, is offered in exchange for a prospect providing their email address by filling in an online form. Careful management of email lists is required since, as the list ages, the addresses of customers and their profiles will change, resulting in many bounced messages and lower response rates. Data protection law also requires the facility for customers to update their details.

Practical issues in managing email marketing

Deliverability
Refers to ensuring email messages are delivered and aren't blocked by spam filters because the email content or structure falsely identifies a permission-based email as a spammer, or because the sender's IP address has a poor reputation for spam.

Renderability
The capability of an email to display correctly formatted in different email readers on desktop and mobile devices.

Two of the main practical challenges for email marketers or their agencies to manage are **deliverability** and **renderability**.

Email marketers have to ensure their emails are delivered given the increase in efforts by ISPs and web-email companies to reduce spam into their end users' in-boxes. Email marketers do not want to be identified as a 'False positive' where permission-based emails may be bounced or placed into junk-mail boxes or simply deleted if the receiving system assesses that they are spam.

Web-based email providers such as Hotmail and Yahoo! Mail have introduced standard authentication techniques known as Sender ID and Domain Keys which email marketers should use to make sure the email broadcaster is who they say they are and doesn't spoof their address as many spammers do. Email providers also assess the reputation of the email broadcasters using services such as SenderScore (**www.senderscore.org**) based on the number of complaints and quality of emails sent.

It is also important that email marketers do not use keywords in their emails which may identify them as spam. For example, email filter such as Spam Assassin (**www.spamassassin.org**) have these types of rules which are used to assess spam:

- SUB_FREE_OFFER
- SUBJECT_DRUG_GAP_VIA
- TO_ADDRESS_EQ_REAL
- HTML_IMAGE_RATIO_04
- HTML_FONT_BIG

- Subject starts with 'Free'
- Subject contains a gappy version of 'viagra'
- To: repeats address as real name
- BODY: HTML has a low ratio of text to image area
- BODY: HTML tag for a big font size

Although the word 'free' in a subject line may cause a problem, this is only one part of the signature of a spam, so it may still be possible to use this word if the reputation of the sender is good.

Renderability refers to how the email appears in different email readers. Often images are blocked by readers in an effort to defeat spammers who use the fact that images are downloaded as the user views the email to detect that the email is a valid address. So emails that are only made up of images with no text are less likely to be effective than hybrid messages combining text and images. Formatting can also differ in different readers, so designers of emails have to test how emails render in common email readers such as Hotmail and Yahoo! Mail.

A further challenge is trying to achieve ongoing engagement with list members. Some approaches that are commonly used include:

- Develop a welcome programme where over the first three to six months targeted, automatically triggered emails educate subscribers about your brand, products and deliver targeted offers.
- Use offers to re-activate list members as they become less responsive.
- Segment list members by activity (responsiveness) and age on list and treat differently, either by reducing frequency or using more offline media.
- Follow-up on bounces using other media to reduce problems of dropping deliverability.
- Best practice when renting lists is to request only emails where the opt-in is within the most recent six to nine months when subscribers are most active.

List management

Email marketers need to work hard to improve the quality of their list (as explained in Chapter 6). DMA (2008) reports that companies often fail to collect the most recent address, with UK companies having email addresses for only 50 per cent of their database.

Respondents believed that the data and its selection accounted for over half of a campaign's success. The creative and offer are still considered significant, while timing is viewed as having the least impact, accounting for just 10 per cent of the success of an email campaign. The report noted that the majority of respondents gather new email addresses through organic website traffic with offline (paper-based) activity accounting for 40 per cent and telemarketing for 31 per cent.

Mobile text messaging

We have concentrated our coverage on email marketing in this section since the amount of marketing investment and levels of activity in email marketing is much higher than mobile text messaging because it seems that receiving permission-based emails is more acceptable than receiving what may be perceived as an intrusive text message on a mobile device. Additionally, it enables more complex, visual messages to be delivered. However, Rettie *et al.* (2005) in an analysis of 26 text marketing campaigns (5401 respondents) demonstrated surprising levels of effectiveness. Her team found that overall acceptability of SMS advertising was 44 per cent, significantly higher than the acceptability of telemarketing, and found relatively high response rates and brand recall compared to direct mail and email marketing.

Social media and viral marketing

Social media marketing
Monitoring and facilitating customer interaction and participation throughout the web to encourage positive engagement with a company and its brands. Interactions may occur on a company site, social networks and other third-party sites.

Social media marketing is an important category of digital marketing which involves encouraging customer communications on a company's own site, or social presences such as Facebook or Twitter or in specialist publisher sites, blogs and forums. It can be applied as a traditional broadcast medium – for example, companies can use Facebook or Twitter to send messages to customers or partners who have followed them. However, to take advantage of the benefits of social media it is important to start to participate in customer conversations. These can be related to products, promotions or customer service and are aimed at learning more about customers and providing support, so improving the way a brand is perceived.

We've seen throughout this text that the opportunities of communicating with customers through social network sites, online communities and interactions on company sites are so great today that a social media strategy has become a core element of digital business strategy. Yet creating a social media or customer engagement strategy is challenging since it requires a change in mindset for the company as they may have to give up some control on their messaging to enable them to communicate with customers effectively. The change in approach required is clear from a movement that originated in the USA in 1999, known as the Cluetrain manifesto (**www.cluetrain.com**). The authors, Levine *et al.* (2000), say:

> Conversations among human beings sound human. They are conducted in a human voice. Most corporations, on the other hand, only know how to talk in the soothing, humourless monotone of the mission statement, marketing brochure, and your-call-is-important-to-us busy signal. Same old tone, same old lies. No wonder networked markets have no respect for companies unable or unwilling to speak as they do. Corporate firewalls have kept smart employees in and smart markets out. It's going to cause real pain to tear those walls down. But the result will be a new kind of conversation. And it will be the most exciting conversation business has ever engaged in.

Of course, more than a change in mindset is required – to achieve change on this scale requires senior management sponsorship, investment and changes to processes and tools as described in the next chapter on change management.

You can see that the Cluetrain manifesto is a call-to-action encouraging managers to change their culture and provide processes and tools to enable employees of an organisation to interact with and listen to customer needs in a responsible way.

Developing a social media communications strategy

When developing a social media strategy there seems to be a tendency for managers to turn straight to the tools they'll be using – should we start with Twitter or Facebook, or should we create a blog? This is the worst possible way to develop strategy; indeed it's not strategy, it's tactics! Strategy development for social media should be informed by demand analysis of customer channel adoption and the commercial potential of the approach.

Customer adoption of social media tools will vary according to customer segments and markets. So it's important to start by completing a marketplace analysis (as described in Chapter 2) to see which social tools and engagement techniques are most effective for the target audience.

Next, the commercial benefits of social media need to be reviewed and goals defined. Some marketers will see social media primarily as a way of gaining new customers through the viral effect of social media as existing customers or contacts discuss or recommend your content or products. For others, the benefits may be centred more around how recommendations, reviews and ratings can increase conversion rate. Public relations specialists will want to listen to the conversations for positive and negative sentiment about brand and then seek to manage this by increasing the positives and managing the negatives. Finally, social media can be viewed as a customer engagement and retention tool. Here social media are used to deliver customer service or are used as alternative channels to email marketing to inform customers about new product launches or promotions.

POST is a useful framework for businesses to apply to help them develop a social media strategy, summarised by Forrester (2007). POST is a simplified version of the SOSTAC framework introduced at the start of this chapter:

- *People*. Understanding the adoption of social media within an audience is an essential starting point. The Forrester social media profiling tool shows how usage varies for different demographic groups: **www.forrester.com/Groundswell/profile_tool.html**.
- *Objectives*. Set different goals for different options to engage customers across different aspects of the customer lifecycle from customer acquisition to conversion to retention. Josh Bernoff of Forrester recommends, 'Decide on your objective before you decide on a technology. Then figure out how you will measure it.'
- *Strategy*. How to achieve your goals. Bernoff suggests that because social media are a disruptive approach you should imagine how social media will support change. He says: 'Imagine you succeed. How will things be different afterwards? 'Imagine the endpoint and you'll know where to begin.'
- *Technology*. Finally, decide on the best social media platforms and tools to achieve your goals (we reviewed the options for building communities and generating awareness through social networks at the end of Chapter 6).

Viral marketing

Viral marketing
Online viral marketing, or buzz marketing, is a form of electronic word-of-mouth marketing. Brands and promotions are discussed and awareness of them transmitted in two main forms, either as pass-along email or discussion in a social network.

Social media marketing is closely related to **viral marketing** since social media naturally involves 'social media amplification' where content is shared. Viral marketing is a specific approach that involves harnessing the network effect of the Internet and can be effective in reaching a large number of people rapidly as a marketing message is quickly transmitted to many people in the same way as a natural virus or a computer virus. It is effectively an online form of word-of-mouth communications which is sometimes also known as 'buzz marketing'. When planning integrated campaigns, it is important to note that the online viral affect can be amplified through offline media mentions or advertising either on TV and radio or in print.

Word-of-mouth (WOM) marketing is an established concept closely related to viral marketing, but broader in context. The Word-of-Mouth Marketing Association (**www.womma.org/wom101**) explain how WOM can be harnessed:

> Word-of-mouth can be encouraged and facilitated. Companies can work hard to make people happier, they can listen to consumers, they can make it easier for them to tell their friends, and they can make certain that influential individuals know about the good qualities of a product or service.

They go on to explain that all word-of-mouth marketing techniques are based on the concepts of customer satisfaction, two-way dialogue and transparent communications. The basic elements are:

- educating people about your products and services;
- identifying people most likely to share their opinions;
- providing tools that make it easier to share information;
- studying how, where and when opinions are being shared;
- listening and responding to supporters, detractors and neutrals.

WOMMA identify different approaches for facilitating WOM. The ones that are most relevant to online marketing are:

- *Buzz marketing.* Using high-profile entertainment or news to get people to talk about your brand.
- *Viral marketing.* Creating entertaining or informative messages that are designed to be passed along in an exponential fashion, often electronically or by email.
- *Community marketing.* Forming or supporting niche communities that are likely to share interests about the brand (such as user groups, fan clubs and discussion forums); providing tools, content and information to support those communities.
- *Influencer marketing.* Identifying key communities and opinion leaders who are likely to talk about products and have the ability to influence the opinions of others.
- *Conversation creation.* Interesting or fun advertising, emails, catchphrases, entertainment or promotions designed to start word-of-mouth activity.
- *Brand blogging.* Creating blogs and participating in the blogosphere, in the spirit of open, transparent communications; sharing information of value that the blog community may talk about.
- *Referral programmes.* Creating tools that enable satisfied customers to refer their friends.

Positive WOM is believed to increase purchase intent. For example, Marsden *et al.* (2005) found that brands such as HSBC, Honda and O₂ with a greater proportion of advocates measured through Net Promoter Score (NPS, Chapter 6) tended to be more successful. They recommend eight ways to encourage word-of-mouth, most of which can be facilitated online:

- *Implement and optimise referral programmes.* Reward customers for referring new customers, and reward the referee as well as the referrer.
- *Set up brand ambassador schemes.* Recruit brand fans as ambassadors who receive exclusive merchandise/offers to share with their contacts.
- *Use tryvertising.* A combination of 'try' or 'trial' and 'advertising', this is a twist on product sampling. The idea is that rather than provide free samples or trials to anyone in a target market, tryvertising involves sampling on a selective and exclusive basis to lead users – ideally with new products or services before they become widely available.
- *Use causal marketing.* Associate your brand with a good cause that builds on brand values (e.g. Nike anti-racism in sport).

Word-of-mouth (WOM) marketing
According to the Word-of-Mouth Marketing Association it is giving people a reason to talk about your products and services, and making it easier for that conversation to take place. It is the art and science of building active, mutually beneficial consumer-to-consumer and consumer-to-marketer communications

- *Measure your Net Promoter Score (NPS).* Track your NPS at all brand touchpoints to find out what you are doing right, and what needs to be improved.
- *Start an influencer outreach programme.* Reach out to the 10 per cent who tell the other 90 per cent what to try and buy with special offers and programmes.
- *Harness the power of empowered involvement.* Create advocacy – let your lead clients, customers or consumers call the shots on your innovation and marketing with VIP votes and polls.
- *Focus innovation on doing something worth talking about.* Do something new that delivers an experience that exceeds expectations.

In an online context, word-of-mouth marketing is important since there is great potential for facilitating electronic word-of-mouth. It is very important for online marketers to understand how WOM can be generated and influenced since research, such as that conducted by Forrester (2007) quoted in the section on online public relations, shows that recommendations from friends, family or even other online consumers are trusted and are a major consideration in product and supplier selection.

Social network-related viral marketing

Dee *et al.* (2007) note the importance of social networks in influencing perceptions about brands, products and suppliers. Their research shows large differences in gender and age

---

| Mini case study 9.3 | Research reveals which emotions make content 'go viral' |

The 'holy grail' for many marketers today is 'viral content'. Marketers talk about wanting a 'goes viral!' Academic research into the types of emotion has yielded evidence into the types of emotions that content must leverage to create a successful viral campaign. For example, two University of Pennsylvania Marketing Professors, Jonah Berger and Katherine L. Milkman, published an article 'What makes content viral?' (2012) describing how they had used a web crawler to analyse three months of articles written on the *New York Times* news website. Examining results from nearly 7000 articles, they found that *Emotional arousal* was the single biggest factor in determining whether a campaign 'went viral'. Articles that inspired, caused anger or awe-inspiring emotions, were all far more likely to end up on the 'most emailed list' on the site. Although negative articles actually evoked slightly more email responses than positive ones did, both emotional groupings were dependent on the intensity of arousal resulting from the expressed emotions. In other words, those articles that were either *really positive* or *really negative* were more likely to evoke email responses than those which were *less* positive or *less* negative – i.e. by extension, less emotive and therefore more aligned to the neutral middle line.

Similar findings resulted from a 2013 study led by Associate Professor of Emerging Media and Communication, Rosanna E. Guadagno (Guadagno *et al.*, 2013), which looked at the factors that caused YouTube videos to go viral. This research team also concluded that a video was much more likely to be shared in cases where it aroused emotions – either positive or negative – in participants. This study also found that videos which resulted in high levels of human emotion had a tendency to be shared. Whether participants viewed them positively or negatively mattered little in this regard; what mattered was that they had an overwhelming emotional attachment to the content, one way or the other.

Writing in the *Harvard Business Review*, Kelsey Libert and Kristin Tynski of Fractl explored the emotions that make marketing campaigns go viral. To understand the best emotional drivers to use in the content, they reviewed 30 of the top 100 images of the year from **imgur.com** as voted on social sharing site **Reddit.com**. They then surveyed 60 viewers to find out which emotions each image activated for them, classified using Robert Plutchik's comprehensive Wheel of Emotion. They found that certain specific emotions were common in highly viral content, while others were less common. Emotions that fit into the surprise and anticipation segments of Plutchik's wheel were overwhelmingly represented.

on the types of products discussed, but recommendations on restaurants, computers, movies and vehicles are popular in all categories.

Microsoft (2007), which part-owns Facebook, has developed these approaches for taking advantage of social networking through buying ad space, creating a brand space or brand channels that enable consumers to interact with or promote a brand:

- *Understand consumers' motivations for using social networks.* Ads will be most effective if they are consistent with the typical lifestage of networkers or the topics that are being discussed.
- *Express yourself as a brand.* Use the web to show the unique essence of your brand, but think about how to express a side of the brand that it is not normally seen.
- *Create and maintain good conversations.* Advertisers that engage in discussions are more likely to resonate with the audience, but once conversations are started they must be followed through.
- *Empower participants.* Social network users use their space and blogs to express themselves. Providing content or widgets to associate themselves with a brand may be appealing. For example, in the first six months of launching charity donation widgets, 20,000 have been used online and they became one of the biggest referrers to the JustGiving website and driving more people to fundraising pages to make donations (JustGiving, 2007).
- *Identify online brand advocates.* Use reputation management tools to identify influential social network members who are already brand advocates. Approach the most significant ones directly. Consider using contextual advertising such as Microsoft content ads or Google AdSense to display brand messages within their spaces when brands are discussed.
- *The golden rule: behave like a social networker.* Microsoft recommends this simple fundamental principle which will help the content created by advertisers to resonate with social networkers: behave like the best social networkers through:
  - being creative;
  - being honest and courteous (ask permission);
  - being individual;
  - being conscious of the audience;
  - updating regularly.

Advantages and disadvantages of social media and viral marketing

The advantages and disadvantages of viral marketing are shared with those with online PR, as covered earlier in the chapter. However, it can be argued that the risk in investment in viral marketing is higher since it is difficult to predict the success of a particular viral agent.

Advantages of social media and viral marketing

The main advantage of social media and viral marketing is that an effective viral agent can reach a large audience in a cost-effective way. We have also seen how consumers rate the opinions of their peers, friends and family highly, so they can be highly influential. Kumar *et al.* (2007) have discussed the potential value that can be generated through customer referrals in several case studies. Within social networks, major influencers can help spread the message more widely.

Disadvantages of social media and viral marketing

The main disadvantage of viral marketing is that this is a high-risk marketing communications technique, since it requires significant initial investment in the viral agent and seeding. However, there is no guarantee that the campaign will 'go viral', in which case the investment will be wasted.

With marketing within social networks it is challenging to engage audiences when they are socialising with their contacts and may not wish to interact with brands. It is also difficult to find the right types of content which will engage audiences and they will share with their contacts. Seeding to key influencers can help with distributing content, but seeding is a time-consuming specialist activity.

Of course, although positive viral marketing can spread rapidly, so can negative sentiments about a company, which we referred to in the section on online reputation management (see page 502).

Now social media is established and we have experienced a lot of 'hype' about its benefits for marketing we would expect to see its impact evaluated and it criticised. This has indeed happened with some strong viewpoints on both sides described in Digital marketing insight 9.5. What do you think?

| Digital marketing insight 9.5 | Is social media 'mostly a waste of time' and an 'infantile delusion'? |

Here are three examples of social media being criticised in what you could say is a 'backlash'.

First, take a look at Mark Ritson, Associate Professor of Marketing and Branding and Columnist on *Marketing Week*, speaking in this video: **www.youtube.com/watch?v=S2NUayn2vP0**. He acknowledges that 'social media is an amazing tool' but states that it is 'mostly a waste of time' and suggests that marketers' focus is wrong, he says:

> Marketers are putting too much emphasis on social media due to the hype in the media, and are forgetting how powerful traditional advertising and marketing can be.

Some marketers and PR professionals like Nicola Swankie (2014) from Society felt the need to respond to his video on behalf of Social Media Practitioners. She responded in a long post reminding him that:

> Social media has given us the new power that people have is vital to consider for any marketer, because it's shifted marketing forever – it's given us the control to personalise and choose the media we see and it's given us a voice.

She says that great marketing should engage, it shouldn't be something people want to ignore:

> Social is the most honest of any media and so it's where lazy, unengaging marketing is most in evidence. That is not a reason to ignore Social, it should be a challenge to us all to think about how to make our marketing more compelling and relevant.

Well said?

Here's another case where a respected marketer criticises social media marketing. Bob Hoffman, described as 'a traditional ad man', is the publisher of the Ad Contrarian blog. He delivered a withering quote at Advertising Week Europe which featured in AdRants (and you can see it in this video: **www.youtube.com/watch?v=EyTn_DgfcFE**):

> The theory that people want to engage with brands online and share their enthusiasm with their friends, and that their friends will share their enthusiasm with other friends through social media channels has turned out to be an infantile fantasy.

Of course, these are only opinions from people who can't be considered active marketing practitioners. The opinion of people who are actively working using digital marketing counts for more you could argue. When we survey Smart Insights readers we find that social media marketing is usually rated positively as cost-effective, although typically behind search and email marketing (Smart Insights, 2015). But for definitive proof in a business or across a sector we have to turn to analytics.

Benchmarking data from SimilarWeb also reported in Smart Insights (2015) presents traffic sources for different sectors and this shows that in the retail sector for the UK and US social is indeed insignificant (less than 5 per cent of site visits) compared with search, direct and referrals from other sites, although some 'dark social' social media traffic may be masked in direct traffic. A last-click approach to reviewing the impact of social media in sales can be misleading since often social media updates may generate initial awareness, but conversion occurs in a subsequent visit following a search or direct visit.

If we review media attribution analytics, there is a similar pattern for retailers with a low impact for social media behind the other main digital marketing channels. This analysis was summarised in a blog post for a report titled 'Facebook and Twitter do almost nothing for Sales?', described in Smart Insights (2014).

Best practice in planning and managing viral marketing

Much discussion of practice in viral and word-of-mouth marketing centres around how and who to reach to achieve influence. Some, such as Malcom Gladwell (2000) and Seth Godin (2001) in their popular books *The Tipping Point and Unleashing the Idea Virus*, have suggested that influentials are important. Godin (2001) writes about the importance of what he terms 'the ideavirus' as a marketing tool. He describes it as 'digitally augmented word-of-mouth'. What differences does the ideavirus have from word-of-mouth? First, transmission is more rapid; second, transmission tends to reach a larger audience; and third, it can be persistent – reference to a product on a service. Godin emphasises the importance of starting small by seeding a niche audience he describes as a 'hive' and then using advocates in spreading the virus – he refers to them as 'sneezers'. Traditionally, marketers would refer to such a grouping as 'customer advocates' or 'brand loyalists'.

Others believe that the role of influencers in achieving word-of-mouth can be overstated. Balter and Butman (2005), in their book *Grapevine*, say:

Everybody talks about products and services, and they talk about them all the time. Word-of-mouth is NOT about identifying a small subgroup of highly influential or well-connected people to talk up a product or service. It's not about mavens or bees or celebrities or people with specialist knowledge. It's about everybody.

While the influencers will have a greater impact, academics Watts and Dodds (2007) argue that the 'influentials hypothesis' is based on untested assumptions and in most cases does not match how diffusion operates in the real world. They comment that 'most social change is driven not by influentials, but by easily influenced individuals influencing other easily influenced individuals'. The role of social media in influencing consumers is discussed further in Chapter 2 in the section on consumer behaviour (see page 72).

To make a viral campaign effective, Justin Kirby of viral marketing specialists DMC (**www.dmc.co.uk**) suggested these three things are needed (Kirby, 2003):

- *Creative material – the 'viral agent'*. This includes the creative message or offer and how it is spread (text, image, video).

- *Seeding*. Identifying websites, blogs or people to send email to start the virus spreading. Seeding can also be completed by email to members of a house list or renting a list with the likely audience.
- *Tracking*. To monitor the effect, to assess the return from the cost of developing the viral agent and seeding.

Today, these factors are still relevant within online PR campaigns although we talk about 'shareable social objects' rather than 'viral agent' and 'influencer outreach' rather than 'seeding'.

Offline promotion techniques

The importance of offline communications in driving visitors to a website is well-known by site owners who find that greater levels of investment in offline advertising using TV, print or radio results in a greater numbers of direct visitors to websites (Figure 9.1). This can be tracked by web analytics which shows an increase in searches containing the brand or campaign name or the web address, or direct visitors who enter the site URL into the address bar.

Research has identified that there is a clear correlation between investment in offline advertising and visits to a website. For example, Hitwise (2006) found in a study of brands including BSkyB, Orange and the AA that searches on brand terms and URLs increased when offline media investment was combined with online. For example, when Sky's media campaign included both online and offline advertising (in September to November of 2005) the strongest result was achieved online with searches for the Sky brand increasing +20 per cent and searches for the Sky URL more than doubling. When offline ran without the integration of online in March 2006, the same lift in searches was not evident. This research also shows the need for significant offline spend, with Sky spending around 20 per cent online, with print, TV and radio still remaining significant (see Figure 9.18).

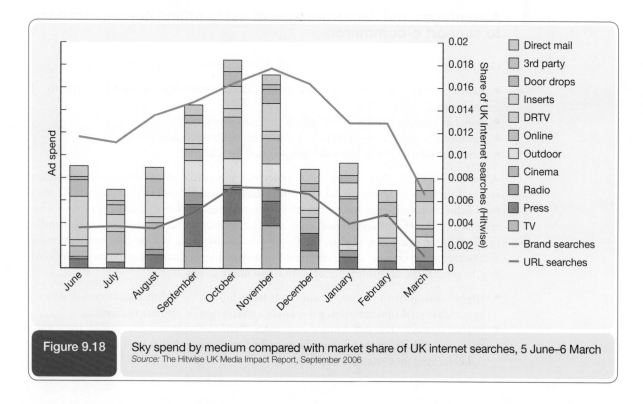

| Figure 9.18 | Sky spend by medium compared with market share of UK internet searches, 5 June–6 March |

Source: The Hitwise UK Media Impact Report, September 2006

The linkage between advertising and search has also been investigated by Graham and Havlena (2007), who additionally studied the role of advertising in generating word-of-mouth discussion online. They found 'strong evidence that advertising does stimulate increased visitation to the websites of advertised brands – an indicator of consumer interest and involvement with a brand'.

Online website promotion techniques such as search engine marketing and banner advertising often take prominence when discussing methods of traffic building. But we start with using offline communications to generate site visitors since it is one of the most effective techniques to generate site traffic and the characteristics of offline media are such (Figure 8.6, page 432) that they often have a higher impact and are more creative, which can help explain the online value proposition. **Offline promotion** refers to using communications tools such as advertising and PR delivered by traditional media such as TV, radio and print in order to direct visitors to an online presence.

Offline promotion
Using traditional media such as TV, radio and print to direct visitors to an online presence.

Despite the range of opportunities for using new online communications tools, traditional communications using offline media such as TV, print and direct mail and others shown in Figure 1.9 (page 28) remain the dominant form of investment in marketing communications for most. Even organisations which transact a large proportion of their business online continue to invest heavily in offline communications. EConsultancy's (2008) research into advanced adopters showed that even here the average expenditure on digital media channels as a proportion of communications budget was only 23 per cent. Consider the travel sector, where both travel suppliers such as BA, Thomson and easyJet and intermediaries such as Expedia and Opodo transact an increasing proportion of their sales online, but are still reliant on offline communications to drive visitors to the web to transact.

When the web analytics data about referring visitors is assessed, for most companies that are not online-only businesses, we find that over half the visitors are typically marked as 'No referrer'. This means that they visited the site direct by typing the web address into the address bar in response to awareness of the brand generated through real-world communications (others may have bookmarked the site or clicked through from a search engine).

Advantages and disadvantages of using offline communications to support e-commerce

Offline communications work; they are effective in achieving four critical things:

- *Reach* – since newspaper, TV and postal communications are used by virtually all consumers.
- *Brand awareness* – through using high-impact visuals.
- *Emotional connection* – with brand again through visuals and sounds.
- *Explanation* – of the online value proposition for a brand.

A further benefit is that for any given objective, integrated marketing communications received through different media are more effective in achieving that objective. We mentioned this cumulative reinforcement effect of integrated marketing communications when referring to the 4Cs of coherence, consistency, continuity and complementarities earlier in the chapter. Having said this, the disadvantages of using offline communications to encourage online channel usage compared to many online communications tools are obvious. In general the disadvantages of offline communications are:

- *Higher cost.* Return on investment tends to be higher for online communications such as search engine optimisation, pay-per-click marketing or affiliate marketing.
- *Higher wastage.* The well-known expression: 'half my advertising is wasted, but I don't know which half', may be true about offline marketing, but it isn't true online if the right tracking processes are in place.

- *Poorer targeting*. Targeting by behaviour, location, time, search keyword, site and site content is readily possible online. This tends to be more targeted compared to most offline media (apart from direct marketing).
- *Poorer accountability*. It is straightforward to track response online – offline it is expensive and error-prone.
- *Less detailed information*. The detailed information to support a decision can only be cost-effectively delivered online.
- *Less personalised*. Although direct mail can be personalised, personalisation is more straightforward online.
- *Less interactive experience*. Most offline communications are one-way – interaction is possible online with the right creative.

Incidental and specific advertising of the online presence

Incidental offline advertising
Driving traffic to the website is not a primary objective of the advert.

Specific offline advertising
Driving traffic to the website or explaining the online proposition is a primary objective of the advert.

Two types of offline advertising can be identified: incidental and specific. Reference to the website is **incidental offline advertising** if the main aim of the advert is to advertise a particular product or promotion and the website is available as an ancillary source of information if required by the viewer. Traditionally, much promotion of the website in the offline media by traditional companies has been incidental – simply consisting of highlighting the existence of the website by including the URL at the bottom of an advertisement. Reference to the website is **specific offline advertising** if it is an objective of the advert to explain the proposition of the website in order to drive traffic to the site to achieve direct response. Here the advert will highlight the offers or services available at the website, such as sales promotions or online customer service. Many state 'Visit our website!!', but clearly a more specific strapline can be developed which describes the overall proposition of the site ('detailed information and product guides to help you select the best product for you') or is specific to the campaign ('we will give you an instant quote online, showing how much you save with us').

Offline response mechanisms

The different response mechanics such as web response and URL strategy which we discussed in Chapter 8 in the section on campaign response mechanisms have to be used to maximise response since this helps to direct potential customers to the most appropriate content on the website. Different URLs are also useful for measuring the response of offline media campaigns since we can measure the number of visitors arriving directly at the URL by entering the domain name.

Public relations

Public relations can be an important tool for driving traffic to the website if changes to online services or online events are significant or if a viral campaign is discussed online. The days of the launch of a website being significant are now gone, but if a site is re-launched with significant changes to its services, this may still be worthy of mention. Many newspapers have regular features listing interesting entertainment or leisure sites or guides to specific topics such as online banking or grocery shopping. Trade magazines may also give information about relevant websites.

Jenkins (1995) argues that one key objective for public relations is its role in transforming a negative situation into a positive achievement. The public relations transfer process, he suggests, is as follows:

- from ignorance to knowledge;
- from apathy to interest;

- from prejudice to acceptance;
- from hostility to sympathy.

These are, of course, goals of online PR, which was discussed in more detail earlier in this chapter.

Direct marketing

Direct marketing can be an effective method of driving traffic to the website. As mentioned earlier, a web response model can be used where the website is the means for fulfilling the response, but a direct mail campaign is used to drive the response. Many catalogue companies will continue to use traditional direct mail to mail out a subset of their offering, with the recipient tempted to visit the site through the fuller offering and incentives such as competitions or web-specific offers.

Other physical reminders

Since we all spend more time in the real rather than the virtual world, physical reminders explaining why customers should visit websites are significant. What is in customers' hands and on their desktop will act as a prompt to visit a site and counter the weakness of the web as a pull medium. This is perhaps most important in the B2B context where a physical reminder in the office can be helpful. Examples, usually delivered through direct marketing, include brochures, catalogues, business cards, point-of-sale material, pens, postcards, inserts in magazines and password reminders for extranets.

Word-of-mouth marketing

It is worth remembering that, as we stated in the section on viral and word-of-mouth marketing, word-of-mouth plays an important role in promoting sites, particularly consumer sites where the Internet is currently a novelty. Opinion Research Corporation International, ORCI (1991), reported on a study among US consumers which showed that the typical Internet consumer tells 12 other people about his or her online shopping experience. This compares with the average US consumer, who tells 8.6 additional people about a favourite film and another 6.1 people about a favourite restaurant! It has been said that if the online experience is favourable then a customer will tell 12 people, but if it is bad they will tell twice as many, so word-of-mouth can be negative also. Parry (1998) reported that for European users, word-of-mouth through friends, relatives and colleagues was the most important method by which users found out about websites, being slightly more important than search engines and directories or links from other sites.

Activity 9.2	Selecting the best digital media channel mix techniques

Suggest the best mix of online (and offline) promotion techniques to build traffic for the following situations:

1 Well-established B2C brand with high brand awareness.
2 Dot-com startup.
3 Small business aiming to export.
4 Common B2C product, e.g. household insurance.
5 Specialist B2B product.

Case Study 9	Innovation at Google

In addition to being the largest search engine on Earth, mediating tens of billions of searches daily, Google is an innovator and has diversified from being an ad-supported search platform with the development of its Android operating system and Chromebook and Nexus. All online marketers should follow Google to see the latest approaches it is trialling.

Google's mission

Google's mission is encapsulated in the statement 'to organise the world's information ... and make it universally accessible and useful'. Google explains that it believes that the most effective, and ultimately the most profitable, way to accomplish its mission is to put the needs of its users first. Offering a high-quality user experience has led to strong word-of-mouth promotion and strong traffic growth. In its most recent SEC filing Google highlighted its commitment to research for new product development to release 'early and often':

> Our product development philosophy is to launch innovative products early and often, and then iterate rapidly to make those products even better. We often post early-stage products at test locations online or directly on **Google.com**. We then use data and user feedback to decide if and how to invest further in those products.
>
> Our research and development expenses were $5.2 billion, $6.8 billion, and $8.0 billion in 2011, 2012, and 2013, respectively.

Culture and ethics

Further details on the culture and ethics of Google is available at **www.google.com/intl/en/corporate/ten-things.html** (may no longer be available, but kept for historic context). Notable tenets of the Google philosophy are:

1 Focus on the user and all else will follow.
2 It's best to do one thing really, really well.
3 You can make money without doing evil.

Putting users first is reflected in three key commitments in the Google SEC filing:

1 *We will do our best to provide the most relevant and useful search results possible, independent of financial incentives. Our search results will be objective*

and we will not accept payment for inclusion or ranking in them.

2 *We will do our best to provide the most relevant and useful advertising. Advertisements should not be an annoying interruption. If any element on a search result page is influenced by payment to us, we will make it clear to our users.*

3 *We will never stop working to improve our user experience, our search technology and other important areas of information organisation.*

In the SEC filing, the company explains 'how we provide value to our users':

> We serve our users by developing products that quickly and easily find, create, organise, and share information. We place a premium on products that matter to many people and have the potential to improve their lives.

Some of the key benefits which are explained are: Comprehensiveness and Relevance; Objectivity; Global Access; Ease of Use; Pertinent, Useful Commercial Information; Multiple Access Platforms and Improving the Web.

The range of established Google services is well known and is listed at **www.google.com/options/**. Google's commitment to innovation is indicated by these more recent additions:

- Google+ announced 2011 – the social network to rival Facebook?
- Google TV (announced 2010) as part of a partnership agreement with Sony.
- Nexus One Phone using the Google Android mobile operating system launched in January 2010 (**www.google.com/phone**).
- Google Mobile advertising (although Google has offered text ads for some time, the 2009 acquisition of AdMob enables improvements in sophistication of this approach).
- Google Chrome OS (a lightweight operating system announced in 2009 and targeted initially at Netbooks).
- Google Chrome (a browser announced as a beta in 2008 and a full product for Windows in 2009).
- In 2014 the number of Android users worldwide passed a billion.

Google revenue models

You will realise that the majority of Google's revenue is from its AdWords program, amounting to over $60 billion in 2014. However, you may not realise that Google has to pay many of its publisher partners for the advertising clicks they drive on its Display network (GDN). In 2014, this partner revenue amounted to nearly one-quarter of all Google ad revenue. In 2014, 69 per cent of Google's revenue came from its own sites with 'network revenue' from publisher partners amounting to 20 per cent (this has been as high as one-third previously). Other revenue from undisclosed sources represented 11 per cent of total revenue.

These include enterprise search products where companies can install search technology through products such as the Google Appliance and Google Mini and paid analytics services such as Google Analytics Premium. Other sources include hardware sales and the Music Key subscription service.

Google AdWords, the auction-based advertising program, is the main source of revenue. Advertisers pay on a 'pay-per-click' cost basis within the search engines and some other services, but with cost-per-thousand payment options available on Google Networks members' websites. Google has experimented with a range of classified style ad programmes for other media, including:

- Google Audio Ads (ads are placed in radio programmes);
- Google Print Ads;
- Google TV Ads;
- Google Promoted Video Ads within YouTube, user-initiated click-to-play video ads.

Of these only YouTube ads have been successful.

Google's revenues are critically dependent on how many searches it achieves in different countries and the proportion of searchers who interact with Google's ads (the click-through rate). The competition for commercial terms affecting the cost-per-click (CPC) in bidding by advertisers is also critical, so Google discloses these in its earnings reports.

International revenues accounted for approximately 56 per cent of total revenues in Q4 2014, 9 per cent of ad revenue was from the UK alone.

31 per cent of Google's revenue is from the Network of content partners subscribing to the Google Adsense programme.

Risk factors

Some of the main risk factors that Google declares include:

1 New technologies could block Google ads. Ad-blocking technology could, in the future, adversely affect Google's results, although there has not been widespread adoption of these approaches.

2 New devices which don't feature Google search. It says:

> More people are using devices other than personal computers to access the internet and accessing new platforms to make search queries. If manufacturers and users do not widely adopt versions of our web search technology, products, or operating systems developed for these devices, our business could be adversely affected.

3 Litigation and loss of confidence through click fraud. Click fraud can be a problem when competitors click on a link, but this is typically small-scale. A larger problem is structured click fraud where site owners on the Google content network seek to make additional advertising feeds.

4 Index spammers could harm the integrity of Google's web search results. This could damage Google's reputation and cause its users to be dissatisfied with products and services.

At 31 December 2013, Google had 47,756 full-time employees, consisting of 18,593 in research and development, 15,348 in sales and marketing, 6563 in general and administrative, and 7252 in operations. All of Google's employees are also equity holders, with significant collective employee ownership. As a result, many employees are highly motivated to make the company more successful. Google's engineers are encouraged to spend up to 10 per cent of their time identifying new approaches.

Question

Explain how Google generates revenue and exploits innovation in digital technology to identify future revenue growth. You should also consider the risk factors for future revenue generation.

Source: SEC (2008)

Summary

1 Online promotion techniques include:

- *Search engine marketing* – search engine optimisation (SEO) and content marketing improves position in the natural listings and pay-per-click marketing features a company in the sponsored listings of a search engine or on the display network.
- *Online PR* – including techniques such as influencer outreach, link building, blogging, and reputation management.
- *Online partnerships* – including affiliate marketing (commission-based referral), co-branding and sponsorship.
- *Online advertising* – using a range of formats including banners, skyscrapers and rich media such as overlays.
- *Email marketing* – including rented lists, co-branded emails, event-triggered emails and ads in third-party e-newsletters for acquisition, and e-newsletters and campaign emails to house lists.
- *Social media marketing* – engaging audiences on different social networks and on a company's own site through sharing content and developing great creative concepts which are transmitted by online word-of-mouth or viral marketing.

2 Offline promotion involves promoting the website address, highlighting the value proposition of the website and achieving web response through traditional media advertisements in print or on television.

3 Interactive marketing communications must be developed as part of integrated marketing communications for maximum cost-effectiveness.

4 Key characteristics of interactive communications are the combination of push and pull media, user-submitted content, personalisation, flexibility and, of course, interactivity to create a dialogue with consumers.

5 Objectives for interactive communications include direct sales for transactional sites, but they also indirectly support brand awareness, favourability and purchase intent.

6 Important decisions in the communications mix introduced by digital media include:

- the balance between spend on media and creative for digital assets and ad executions;
- the balance between spend in traditional and offline communications;
- the balance between investment in continuous and campaign-based digital activity;
- the balance of investment in different interactive communications tools.

Table 9.4 provides a summary of the strengths and weaknesses of the tools discussed in this chapter.

Table 9.4	Summary of the strengths and weaknesses of different communications tools for promoting an online presence	
Promotion technique	**Main strengths**	**Main weaknesses**
Search engine optimisation (SEO)	Highly targeted, relatively low cost compared to PPC. High traffic volumes if high volume of search intent and is SEO effective. Considered credible by searchers	Requires significant ongoing investment in content marketing and due to intense competition, complexity and changes to ranking algorithm. Investment won't necessarily guarantee returns and top three position in results needed for volume

Promotion technique	Main strengths	Main weaknesses
Pay-per-click (PPC) marketing	Highly targeted to reach audience when searching for products or solutions. Controlled cost of acquisition. Can extend reach and remarket using the display network	Relatively costly in competitive sectors, particularly where others are paying 'over the odds' lower volumes compared with organic visits
Online PR	Relatively low cost and good targeting. Can assist with SEO through creation of backlinks	Identifying online influencers and setting up partnerships can be time-consuming. Need to invest in content marketing to encourage sharing
Affiliate marketing	Performance marketing approach of payment is by results (e.g. 5 per cent of sale or leads goes to referring site)	Only relevant for businesses with online sales. Costs of payments to affiliate networks for setup and management fees. Changes to ranking algorithm have reduced volume from affiliates using search.
Online sponsorship	Most effective if low-cost, long-term co-branding arrangement with synergistic site	May increase awareness, but does not necessarily lead directly to sales
Interactive advertising	Main intention to achieve visit, i.e. direct response model. But also role in branding through media multiplier effect. New 'native Advertising' formats based on content can be more effective	Response rates have declined historically because of 'banner blindness'
Email marketing	Push medium – can't be ignored in user's inbox (compared to social updates). Can be used for direct response link to website	Requires opt-in for effectiveness. Better for customer communications than for acquisition Since can't buy prospect lists. Inbox cut-through – message diluted among other emails. Limits on deliverability
Social media marketing, viral and word-of-mouth marketing	With an effective viral agent, possible to reach a large number at relatively low cost. Influencers in social networks can be significant	Difficult to create powerful viral concepts and control targeting. Risks damaging brand since unsolicited messages may be received
Traditional offline advertising (TV, print, etc.)	Larger reach than most online techniques and sometimes more cost-effective. Greater creativity possible, leading to greater impact	Targeting arguably less easy than online. Typical high cost of acquisition, but more cost-effective local options may be available

Exercises

Self-assessment exercises

1 Briefly explain and give examples of online promotion and offline promotion techniques.
2 Explain the different types of payment model for banner advertising.
3 Which factors are important in governing a successful online banner advertising campaign?
4 How can a company promote itself through a search engine?
5 Explain the value of social media marketing.
6 How can online PR help to promote a new product?
7 How should websites be promoted offline?
8 What do you think the relative importance of these Internet-based advertising techniques would be for an international chemical manufacturer?
   a display advertising;
   b paid search marketing;
   c affiliate marketing.

Essay and discussion questions

1 How should companies evaluate the relevance and effectiveness of the digital media channels discussed in this chapter to their organisation?
2 Discuss the merits of the different models of paying for banner advertisements on the Internet for both media owners and companies placing advertisements.
3 Explain the factors that control the position of a company's products and services in the search engine results pages of a search engine such as Google.
4 Compare the effectiveness of different methods of online advertising including display advertisements, paid search marketing and affiliate marketing.

Examination questions

1 Give three examples of digital media channels and briefly explain their communications benefits.
2 Describe four different types of site on which online display advertising for a car manufacturer's site could be placed.
3 Click-through is one measure of the effectiveness of online advertising.
   a What is 'click-through'?
   b Which factors are important in determining the click-through rate of a banner advertisement?
   c Is click-through a good measure of the effectiveness of online advertising?
4 What is meant by co-branding? Explain the significance of co-branding.
5 What are 'meta tags'? How important are they in ensuring a website is listed in a search engine?
6 Name three alternative types of email marketing that can be used for customer acquisition.
7 Briefly evaluate the strengths and weaknesses of affiliate marketing for a well-known retailer.
8 Which techniques can be used to promote a website in offline media?

References

Abraham, M. (2008) The off-line impact of online ads, *Harvard Business Review*, 86(4), 28.

Balter, D. and Butman, J. (2005) *Grapevine: The New Art of Word-of-Mouth Marketing*, Portfolio, New York.

Berger, J. and Milkman, K.L. (2012) What makes online content viral?, *Journal of Marketing Research*, 49(2), 192–205.

Brin, S. and Page, L. (1998) The anatomy of a large-scale hypertextual web search engine, *Computer Networks and ISDN Systems*, 30(1–7), 107–17, **www-db.stanford. edu/~backrub/google.html.**

Bush, M. (2010) How Social media is helping public-relations sector not just survive, but thrive, Advertising Age, 23 August, **http://adage.com/article/news/ social-media-helping-public-relations-sector-thrive/145507/.**

Buzz Paradise (2010) PR 2.0 for Renault, Case study, **www.buzzparadise.com/case-studies/ pr-2-0-event-for-renault-le-web-2010/.**

Cartellieri, C., Parsons, A., Rao, V. and Zeisser, M. (1997) The real impact of Internet advertising, *McKinsey Quarterly*, 3, 44–63.

Chaffey, D. (2006) *Total Email Marketing*, 2nd edn, Butterworth-Heinemann, Elsevier, Oxford.

Chaffey, D. and Smith, P.R. (2012) *E-marketing Excellence*, 4th edn, Butterworth-Heinemann Elsevier, Oxford.

Chittenden, L. and Rettie, R. (2003) An evaluation of email marketing and factors affecting response, *Journal of Targeting, Measurement and Analysis for Marketing*, 11(3), 203–17.

Dee, A., Bassett, B. and Hoskins, J. (2007) Word-of-mouth research: principles and applications, *Journal of Advertising Research*, 47(4), 387–97.

DMA (2008) UK National Client Benchmarking Report, **www.dma.org.uk.**

Ecircle (2011) Display versus email. The SEAT Ibiza campaign illustrating how to effectively allocate your online advertising budgets. Research study published March.

EConsultancy (2008) *Managing Digital Channels Research Report*, Dave Chaffey, **www. e-consultancy.com.**

Fiorelli, G. (2014) The myth of Google's 200 ranking factors, blog post, 30 September 2014, **http://moz.com/blog/the-myth-of-googles-200-ranking-factors.**

Fitzgerald, M. (2006) The name game: tagging tools let users describe the world in their own terms as taxonomies become folksonomies, *CIO Magazine*, 1 April.

Forrester (2007) Consumer trends survey North America – leveraging user-generated content, January, Brian Haven.

Gladwell, M. (2000) *The Tipping Point: How Little Things Can Make a Big Difference*, Little Brown, New York.

Godin, S. (2001) Unleashing the Ideavirus, **www.ideavirus.com.**

Graham, J. and Havlena, W. (2007) Finding the 'missing link': advertising's impact on word of mouth, web searches, and site visits, *Journal of Advertising Research*, 47(4), 427–35.

Grehan, M. (2004) Increase your PR by increasing your PR, *E-marketing News e-newsletter*, November, **www.e-marketing-news.co.uk/november.html#pr.**

Guadagno, R.E., Rempala, D.M., Murphy, S. and Okdie, B.M.(2013) What makes a video go viral? An analysis of emotional contagion and Internet memes, *Computers in Human Behavior*, 29(6), 2312–19.

Haynes, M. (2012) Are SEOs destroying small businesses? A Penguin story, 1 October 2012, posted by Marie Haynesat, **http://moz.com/ugc/ are-seos-destroying-small-businesses-a-penguin-story.**

Hitwise (2006) UK media impact report, Analyst Heather Hopkins, **www.hitwise.com.**

Hitwise (2007) Social networks can drive traffic – case study of ASOS and TopShop, blog posting by analyst Heather Hopkins, 1 March, **http://weblogs.hitwise.com/heather-hopkins/2007/03/social_networks_can_drive_taf.html.**

iMediaConnection (2003) Interview with ING Direct VP of Marketing, Jurie Pietersie, www.mediaconnection.com/content/1333.asp.

Jenkins, F. (1995) *Public Relations Techniques*, 2nd edn, Butterworth-Heinemann, Oxford.

JustGiving (2007) Justgiving Widget version 2.0, blog posting, 24 July, http://justgiving. typepad.com/charities/2007/07/justgiving-widg.html.

Kirby, J. (2003) Online viral marketing: next big thing or yesterday's fling?, *New Media Knowledge*, www.newmediaknowledge.co.uk.

Kumar, V., Petersen, J. and Leone, R. (2007) How valuable is word of mouth?, *Harvard Business Review*, 85(10), 139–46.

Levine, R., Locke, C., Searls, D. and Weinberger, D. (2000) *The Cluetrain Manifesto*, Perseus Books, Cambridge, MA.

Libert, K. and Tynski, K. (2013) Research: the emotions that make marketing campaigns go viral, 24 October 2013, *Harvard Business Review* blog, https://hbr.org/2013/10/ research-the-emotions-that-make-marketing-campaigns-go-viral/

MAD (2007) How online display advertising influences search volumes, 4 June, MAD Network (*Marketing Week*), Centaur Communications, http://technologyweekly.mad.co.uk/ Main/InDepth/SearchEngineMarketing/Articles/f66d813eeab74e93ad8f252ae9c7f02a/How-online-display-advertising-influences-search-volumes.html.

Marsden, P., Samson, A. and Upton, N. (2005) Advocacy drives growth, *Brand Strategy*, 198 (December 2005/January 2006).

Microsoft (2007) Word of the web guidelines for advertisers: understanding trends and monetising social networks. Research report, http://advertising.microsoft.com.

Moz (2013) Google search engine ranking factors, www.seomoz.org/article/ search-ranking-factors.

Moz (2015) Google Algorithm Change History page, http://www.seomoz.org/ google-algorithm-change.

New Media Age (2008) Measuring Buzz. By Sean Hargrave, 17 January.

Nielsen (2013) Under the influence: consumer trust in advertising. Blog post, 19 September 2013, www.nielsen.com/us/en/insights/news/2013/under-the-influence-consumer-trust-in-advertising.html.

Novak, T. and Hoffman, D. (1997) New metrics for new media: towards the development of web measurement standards, *World Wide Web Journal*, 2(1), 213–46.

OPA Europe (2010) The silent click. building brands online in Europe, www.opa-europe. org/news/press-releases/265.

Optify (2011) The changing face of SERPS: organic clickthrough rate, white paper, www. optify.net/wp-content/uploads/2011/04/Changing-Face-of-SERPS-Organic-CTR.pdf.

ORCI (1991) Word-of-mouth drives e-commerce. Survey summary, May, Opinion Research Corporation International, www.opinionresearch.com.

Parry, K. (1998) Europe gets wired. A survey of Internet use in Great Britain, France and Germany, Research Report 1998. KPMG Management Consulting, London.

Performics (2010) Search engine usage study: 92% of searchers click on sponsored results, press release, www.performics.com/news-room/press-releases/ Search-Engine-Usage-Study-92-percent/1422.

Prussakov, E. (2011a) *A Practical Guide to Affiliate Marketing. Quick Reference for Affiliate Managers and Merchants*, Self-published.

Prussakov (2011b) Back to affiliate cookie duration return days question. Blog post by Geno Prussakov, 12 September, www.amnavigator.com/blog/2011 Ö 09 Ö 12/ back-to-affiliate-cookie-duration-return-days-question/.

Ranchhod, A., Gurau, C. and Lace, J. (2002) Online messages: developing an integrated communications model for biotechnology companies, *Qualitative Market Research: An International Journal*, 5(1), 6–18.

Rettie, R., Grandcolas, U. and Deakins, B. (2005) Text message advertising: response rates and branding effects, *Journal of Targeting, Measurement and Analysis for Marketing*, 13(4), 304–12.

Robinson, H., Wysocka, A. and Hand, C. (2007) Internet advertising effectiveness: the effect of design on click-through rates for banner ads, *International Journal of Advertising*, 26(4), 527–41.

Ryan, J. and Whiteman, N. (2000) Online advertising glossary: sponsorships. ClickZ Media Selling channel, 15 May.

SEC (2008) Annual report filing on form 10–K to US Securities and Exchange Commission (SEC) for Google Inc., 15 February.

Smart Insights (2010) 'Official': Facebook and Twitter DO influence natural search rankings, Chris Soames, December 2010.

Smart Insights (2011a) How balanced is your traffic mix? Blog post, Dave Chaffey, 4 July, www.smartinsights.com/digital-marketing-strategy/customer-acquisition-strategy/how-balanced-is-your-traffic-mix/.

Smart Insights (2011b), Social media command centres. Blog post, 13 July, Dave Chaffey, www.smartinsights.com/analytics-conversion-optimisation-alerts/social-media-command-centres/; http://www.smartinsights.com/search-engine-optimisation-seo/seo-strategy/customer-acquisition-strategy/facebook-twitter-influence-natural-search-rankings/.

Smart Insights (2014) 5 options for semantic markup to improve SEO. Blog article by Yusuf Bhana, 27 May 2014, www.smartinsights.com/search-engine-optimisation-seo/blended-or-universal-search/semantics-markup-future-seo/.

Smart Insights (2015) Is this the social media backlash? Blog post by Dave Chaffey, 21 January 2015, www.smartinsights.com/social-media-marketing/social-media-strategy/social-media-backlash/.

Swankie, N. (2014) 'Social media a waste of time'? No chance says Nicola Swankie. Blog post, 10 December 2014, www.pria.com.au/priablog/social-media-a-waste-of-time-no-chance-says-nicola-swankie.

Watts, D. and Dodds, S. (2007) Influentials, networks and public opinion formation, *Journal of Consumer Research*, 34(4), 441–58.

Ye, L. and Ki, E.-J. (2012) The status of online public relations research: an analysis of published articles in 1992–2009, *Journal of Public Relations Research*, 24, 409–34. doi: 10.1080/1062726X.2012.723277.

Weblinks

General digital media channel-related email newsletters and portals

- ClickZ Experts (www.clickz.com/experts). Has columns on email marketing, email marketing optimisation and email marketing case studies.
- Econsultancy.com (www.econsultancy.com). Best practice sections on different e-communications tools.
- Marketing Sherpa (www.marketingsherpa.com). Articles and links on online marketing communications including examples of email and online advertising.
- Smart Insights (www.smartinsights.com) Advice on best practice and the latest updates on all digital marketing channels covered in this chapter edited by Dave Chaffey.

Email-related advice sites

- Direct Marketing Association UK (www.dma.org.uk). Best practice guidelines and benchmarks of response rates.
- Email Experience Council (www.emailexperience.org). A US organisation with compilations of practical tips on email marketing.

Affiliates and aggregator advice sites

- **A4UForum** (www.a4uforum.co.uk). Used by affiliates to discuss approaches and compare programmes.
- **Affiliate marketing blog** (http://blog.affiliatetip.com). Practical tips and the latest developments from affiliate Shawn Collins.
- **AM Navigator** (www.amnavigator.com/blog). Advice on managing affiliate programmes from Geno Prussakov).

Internet advertising research sites

- **AtlasSolutionsInstitute** (www.atlassolutions.com). Microsoft owned ad-serving and tracking provider with research about consumer behaviour and optimising ad effectiveness.
- **Doubleclick** (www.google.com/doubleclick/insights/research.html). Google owned ad-serving and tracking provider with research about consumer behaviour and optimising ad effectiveness.
- **iMediaConnection** (www.imediaconnection.com). Media site reporting on best practice in online advertising.
- **US Internet Advertising Bureau** (www.iab.net). The widest range of studies about Internet advertising effectiveness. In UK: **www.iabuk.net**.
- **Tangozebra** (www.tangozebra.co.uk) is a UK-based provider of ad-serving technology which showcases many of the most recent ad campaigns by industry category.
- **World Advertising Research Centre** (www.warch.com). Mainly subscription service, but some free resources.

Search-engine-related links

- **Google Webmaster tools** (www.google.com/webmasters). Provides a useful set of tools for sites verified by their owners including index inclusion, linking and ranking for different phrases in different locations.
- **Moz** (www.moz.com). Formerly focussing exclusively on SEO, but not broadened to content marketing and other inbound marketing techniques. The most popular site globally with SEO specialists.
- **Search Engine Land** (www.searchengineland.com). A blog resource covering the latest developments in Search marketing. The sister site Marketing Land (www.marketing-land.com) is recommended for a broader audience.
- **Webmasterworld** (www.webmasterworld.com). A forum where search practitioners discuss best practice.

Viral marketing/Word-of-mouth research sites

- **Mashable** (www.mashable.com). Site focussing on developments and statistics related to social networks.
- **Word-of-mouth marketing association** (www.womma.org). A US-orientated community of word-of-mouth marketing specialists.
- **O'Reilly Radar** (http://radar.oreilly.com). Commentary on the development of Web 2.0 approaches technologies from publishers O'Reilly, whose founder Tim O'Reilly coined the term Web 2.0.

Chapter 10
Evaluation and improvement of digital channel performance

Chapter at a glance

Main topics

- Performance management for digital channels 553
- Customer experience and content management process 573
- Responsibilities for customer experience and site management 575

Case studies

Digital marketing in practice
The Smart Insights interview with Avinash Kaushik, analytics evangelist at Google 551

Case study 10: Learning from Amazon's culture of metrics 582

Learning objectives

After reading this chapter, the reader should be able to:

- Understand terms and tools used to measure and improve digital marketing effectiveness
- Develop an appropriate process to collect measures for digital marketing effectiveness
- Identify the activities necessary when managing an online presence.

Questions for marketers

Key questions for marketing managers related to this chapter are:

- How do I measure and improve the effectiveness of digital marketing?
- How much resource do I need to put into managing and improving the site?

Scan code
to find the
latest updates
for topics in
this chapter

Links to other chapters

This chapter should be read in conjunction with these chapters:

- Chapter 4 describes the development of a digital marketing strategy. The aim of measurement is to quantify whether the objectives of this strategy have been achieved

- Chapter 7 describes issues involved in creating an effective digital experience including websites and mobile platform, and should be read before this chapter to introduce the reader to the concepts of website management

- Chapter 8 describes methods of increasing brand awareness online. It should be read before this chapter since one aspect of measuring the effectiveness of digital marketing is aimed at assessing the different online communications methods.

Introduction

Companies that have a successful approach to online marketing often seem to share common characteristics. They attach great importance and devote resources to monitoring the success of their online marketing, putting in place the processes to continuously improve the performance of their digital channels. This approach has been fundamental to the growth of Amazon, as Case study 10 in this chapter explains about their culture of metrics.

The importance of defining an appropriate approach to measurement and improvement is such that the term **web or digital analytics** has developed to describe this key digital marketing activity. A Digital Analytics association (formerly web analytics, **www.digitalanalyt icsassociation.org**) has been developed by vendors, consultants and researchers in this area to manage best practice. Their definition of web analytics is:

> Web analytics is the measurement, collection, analysis and reporting of Internet data for the purposes of understanding and optimising web usage.

You can see this is a 'catch-all' definition. How do you think it could be improved? We think it could reference the commercial aims of optimisation and the measurement of multichannel usage.

To succeed in a measured approach to improving results from Internet marketing we suggest that there are four main organisational prerequisites, which are broken down as shown in Figure 10.1 into the quality of the web analytics processes including defining the right improvement measures and purchasing the right tools and the management processes – such as putting in place a process where staff review results and then modify their marketing activities accordingly.

This chapter is in two parts – the first part is about performance management, where we review the approach to improving performance through assessing appropriate measures, tools and the right process to apply them as suggested by Figure 10.1. In the second part, we review some of the issues involved with maintaining an online presence, looking at the tools and process for improving different company web presences.

Web or digital analytics
Techniques used to assess and improve the contribution of digital marketing to a business, including reviewing traffic volume, referrals, clickstreams, online reach data, customer satisfaction surveys, leads and sales.

Figure 10.1 Key questions in evaluating process, metrics and tools for improving the contribution of digital marketing within an organisation

| Digital marketing in practice | The Smart Insights interview |

Avinash Kaushik, analytics evangelist at Google

Overview and main concepts covered

Avinash Kaushik is Google's analytics evangelist, well-known for his books *Web Analytics An Hour a Day*, *Analytics 2.0* and his *Occam's Razor Blog*.

The interview

Q. Some have criticised online customer engagement as being an abstract concept that can't be readily applied in the real world. Can you give some practical examples of how a site owner can apply the engagement concept to get better results?

Avinash Kaushik: Engagement is a nice goal to have. Create sites that customers will find engaging and they'll stick around or come back again or maybe do business with you.

But that term has been manipulated to a point where it means nothing any more (or everything to everyone) and is often used as an excuse to not do the hard work of figuring out what the real outcomes of the site are for the company and the website visitors.

My encouragement to website owners is to be initially sceptical when someone is trying to pawn off 'engagement' on them and ask the tough question: 'What do you really mean by engagement and how does it specifically apply to my business?'

Secondly, I encourage people to realise that on the most glorious spring day when the birds are chirping the right song, web analytics tools can measure the degree of engagement but they fall quite a bit short of measuring the kind of engagement. So they can report that visitors saw 19 pages on your site (degree) but they can't tell you if that was because the visitors were frustrated with your crappy navigation or thrilled with your content.

People use Google Analytics (or other tools) to measure easily various elements of the degree of engagement. Perhaps the simplest example is using the bounce rate for the core landing pages to identify pages that won't even entice visitors to make one click! In two clicks you can also get loyalty (recency), frequency, length of visit and depth of visit to get a solid feel for if visitors are making repeat visits to the site or if they visit it more frequently and marry that up with content consumption. Doing this by looking at trends over time is a fantastic way to understand if the site is delivering value for your customers.

For many 'social' websites, website owners also measure the number of people who sign up and then contribute by writing reviews or comments etc. These are all really good examples of (1) measuring the degree of engagement and (2) not confusing the real metric being measured by calling it engagement.

Q. Which are the best measures or reports you could point to which help marketers understand how well an e-commerce site is performing for retention?

Avinash Kaushik: I touched on some of the obvious ones above, the loyalty metrics (specifically recency and frequency). They immediately tell you if you are acquiring traffic that comes back again and again, and since GA will tell you recency by going as far back in history as you have data, that is a great way to know when customers come back (and perhaps also understand why). The other obvious thing to do for shorter time periods is to look at the trends for percentage of new visits, especially by the sources of your traffic.

Some retailers want to do retention analysis by looking at repeat purchases. For this, Google Analytics, like pretty much every tool out there, provides a very strong complement of e-commerce reports that allow you to segment the data by the types of purchasers (new or returning) which will help you understand their purchase behaviour and by applying filters to your data you can dig deeper into sources of traffics, trends in number of visits, content consumed etc.

This in conjunction with using even simple on-exit website surveys can give you a great picture of what is happening on your website and where you are missing the boat.

Q. Conversion optimisation. Today there is a lot more talk in large organisations about using techniques like AB or multivariate testing. How would you advise a small business owner to set out on this journey?

Avinash Kaushik: This might surprise you, but I am seeing a lot more traction in using optimisation techniques with smaller companies than with larger companies. There are a couple of interesting reasons:

1 A/B or MVT is now free with tools like Google Website Optimiser, so you can dispense with RFP's and all that 'stuff' and just go try the tool.
2 Smaller companies are much more willing to try new things and have less politics and entrenched opinions (and HiPPO's) that are hard to overcome. This is of course a bit sad because given the traffic and the sheer opportunities it really is a crime for larger companies to leave so much more revenue on the table, or the chance to optimise the customer experience which will improve loyalty and satisfaction.

My recommendations for any company are perhaps similar:

● Start with A/B testing. In my experience starting simple will ensure that you will get out of the gates fast and be able to start the critical process of cultural shift with easily understandable experiments. Then you can move to the 1.8 billion combination page test.
● For the highest impact try dramatic differences in your test versions. Trying shades of blue might sound interesting but the test might take a very, very long time to provide you with statistically significant differences. But trying a page with only text and one with text and images might get you on the path to understanding your customers faster.
● Run a report for your top 25 landing pages (entry pages) on your site, then look at the bounce rates for each of them. Pick three with the highest bounce rates, these are the pages letting you down the most. You'll win big by testing these first.
● Have an active 'customer listening channel'. Remote usability testing, market research, customer call centres or surveys (even a free excellent solution like 4Q, which I helped create with iPerceptions). The best focus points about what is not working on your site come from your customers (sadly not you) and likewise the greatest ideas on how to improve your site (and hence test) also come from your customers. Listen and you will prosper.

Q. What excites you most about potential developments in web analytics in the future?

Avinash Kaushik: The thing that excites me most is that no one has a clue where this is all headed. We have no idea what 'web analytics' will look like in five years. That is exciting because there is a tonne of change and growth to come and being a part of that change is simply fantastic.

There are new data collection methods to come, there are new ways of doing superior analysis of data, there is so much more we could do with Artificial Intelligence in optimising customer experiences, there are opportunities to bridge the various islands of data (on the web or outside) to create something amazing, there are … it goes on and on.

They are going to get a lot better about what you should look at. Visualisation is great and tables are good but what is killing analysts right now is their ability to figure out, from megabytes and megabytes of data, what is actually worth looking at. Most tools still simply spew data out relying on the analyst (or the data consumer) to figure things out. That is a bad strategy, yet most tools follow it.

Visualisation has got a lot better – but I'm not seeing any form of intelligent recommendations. It's very tricky and the web analytics companies are too busy copying other functionality! It's good you mention that ClicksTracks features though. Using ClickTracks as an example, I demonstrated how to look at only the data that has shifted in importance by a statistically significant amount. Your top 20 of anything never changes, but using this type of report, What's Changed, you can look at just the data that really matters. Now it is easier to take action.

I expect all tools to get much, much better at applying advanced mathematics and statistics to help their users identify where to focus their attention. The other thing I would highlight as an evolution for web analytics tools is that they are going to do a lot more than page view reporting on your site. I don't mean doing clever things like event logging to measure Web 2.0 experiences – that is cool of course. I am referring to their ability to measure content no matter how it is distributed (widgets, rss, etc.) and where it is consumed (websites, feed readers, mobile phones, your home refrigerator or washing machine!).

Opportunity is, I suppose, what I find most exciting about the future of web analytics.

Performance management for digital channels

Performance management system
A process used to evaluate and improve the efficiency and effectiveness of an organisation and its processes.

Performance measurement system
The process by which metrics are defined, collected, disseminated and actioned.

Digital marketing metrics
Measures that indicate the effectiveness of digital marketing activities integrated across different channels and platforms in meeting customer, business and marketing objectives.

To improve results for any aspect of any business, performance management is vital. As Bob Napier, Chief Information Office, Hewlett-Packard was reported to have said back in the 1960s, 'You can't manage what you can't measure'. The processes and systems intended to monitor and improve the performance of an organisation are known by business operations researchers as **performance management systems** and are based on the study of **performance measurement systems**.

Today, nearly all organisations have different forms of online presence, but the questions highlighted in Figure 10.1 aren't answered adequately. So, a good starting point is to understand the current improvement process and the organisational barriers which prevent a suitable improvement process.

In this section, we will review approaches to performance management by examining three key elements of an Internet marketing measurement system. These are, first, the *process* for improvement and, secondly, the measurement framework which specifies groups of relevant **digital marketing metrics** and, finally, an assessment of the suitability of tools and techniques for collecting, analysing, disseminating and actioning results. We will review three stages of creating and implementing a performance management system.

Stage 1: Creating a performance management system

The essence of *performance management* is suggested by the definition for performance *measurement* used by Andy Neely and co-workers of Cranfield School of Management's

Centre for Business Performance. They defined performance measurement as (Neely *et al.*, 2002):

> the process of quantifying the efficiency and effectiveness of past actions through acquisition, collation, sorting, analysis, interpretation and dissemination of appropriate data.

Performance management extends this definition to the process of analysis and actioning change in order to drive business performance and returns. Online marketers can apply many of the approaches of business performance management to digital marketing. As you can see from the definition, performance is measured primarily through information on process **effectiveness** and **efficiency**, as introduced in Chapter 4 in the section on objective setting, where we noted that it is important to include both effectiveness and efficiency measures.

Effectiveness
Meeting process objectives, delivering the required outputs and outcomes, 'doing the right thing'.

Efficiency
Minimising resources or time needed to complete a process 'doing the thing right'.

The need for a structured performance management process is clear when we examine the repercussions if an organisation does not have one. These include: poor linkage of measures with strategic objectives or even absence of objectives; key data not collected; data inaccuracies; data not disseminated or analysed; or no corrective action. Many of the barriers to improvement of measurement systems reported by respondents in Adams *et al.* (2000) also indicate the lack of an effective process. The barriers can be grouped as follows:

- *senior management myopia* – performance measurement not seen as a priority, not understood or targeted at the wrong targets – reducing costs rather than improving performance;
- unclear responsibilities for delivering and improving the measurement system;
- *resourcing issues* – lack of time (perhaps suggesting lack of staff motivation), the necessary technology and integrated systems;
- *data problems* – data overload or of poor quality, limited data for benchmarking.

The Web Analytics Association (2011) Outlook survey of companies using web analytics gives insights on the specific challenges of performance management for digital marketing. The top five challenges were:

- actionability of the data (36 per cent);
- business decisions driven by analytics (35.3 per cent);
- social media (34.9 per cent);
- executive management awareness and support for web analytics (34.9 per cent);
- failure to take action on the data (31.0 per cent).

The top two issues reported suggest the problems of performance management, taking action based on the data.

To avoid these pitfalls, a coordinated, structured measurement process such as that shown in Figure 10.2 is required. Figure 10.2 indicates four key stages in a measurement process. These were defined as key aspects of annual marketing plan control by Kotler (1997). Stage 1 is a goal-setting stage where the aims of the measurement system are defined – this will usually take the strategic digital marketing objectives as an input to the measurement system. The aim of the measurement system will be to assess whether these goals are achieved and specify corrective marketing actions to reduce variance between target and actual key performance indicators. Stage 2, performance measurement, involves collecting data to determine the different metrics that are part of a measurement framework, as discussed in the next section. Stage 3, performance diagnosis, is the analysis of results to understand the reasons for variance from objectives and selection of marketing solutions to reduce variance.

In a digital marketing context, corrective action is the implementation of these solutions as updates to content, design, ongoing marketing communications and CRO. At this stage the continuous cycle repeats, possibly with modified goals.

| **Figure 10.2** | A summary of the performance measurement process |

Stage 2: Defining the performance metrics framework

Measurement for assessing the effectiveness of digital marketing should assess the contribution of digital marketing at different levels:

1 Are corporate objectives defined in the digital marketing strategy being met?
2 Are marketing objectives plans achieved?
3 Are marketing communications objectives achieved?

These measures can also be related to the different levels of marketing control specified by Kotler (1997). These include strategic control (question 1), profitability control (question 1), annual-plan control (question 2) and efficiency control (question 3).

Efficiency measures are more concerned with minimising the costs of online marketing while maximising the returns for different areas of focus such as acquiring visitors to a website, converting visitors to outcome or achieving repeat business.

Chaffey (2000) suggested that organisations define a measurement framework or create a management dashboard which defines groupings of specific metrics used to assess digital marketing performance. He suggested that suitable measurement frameworks will fulfil these criteria:

- Include macro-level effectiveness metrics which assess whether strategic goals are achieved and indicate to what extent e-marketing contributes to the business (revenue contribution and return on investment). This criterion covers the different levels of marketing control specified by Kotler (1997), including strategic control, profitability control and annual-plan control.
- Include micro-level metrics which assess the efficiency of digital marketing tactics and implementation. Wisner and Fawcett (1991) note that organisations typically use a hierarchy of measures and they should check that the lower-level measures support the macro-level strategic objectives. Such measures are often referred to as *performance drivers*, since achieving targets for these measures will assist in achieving strategic objectives. Digital marketing performance drivers help optimise online marketing by attracting more site visitors and increasing conversion to desired marketing outcomes. These achieve the marketing efficiency control specified by Kotler (1997). The research by Agrawal *et al.* (2001), who assessed companies on metrics defined in three categories

of attraction, conversion and retention as part of an e-performance scorecard, uses a combination of macro- and micro-level metrics.

- Assess the impact of digital marketing on the satisfaction, loyalty and contribution of key stakeholders (customers, investors, employees and partners) as suggested by Adams *et al.* (2000).
- Enable comparison of performance of different digital channels with other channels as suggested by Friedman and Furey (1999).
- The framework can be used to assess e-marketing performance against competitors' or out-of-sector best practice.

Since 2000, many marketing and digital marketing dashboard services have been introduced, but it is difficult to understand which are the best types of solution and whether they are worthwhile beyond the main dashboard system such as Google Analytics or Adobe Analytics. Complete Activity 10.1 to explore the types of dashboards available and their benefits.

Activity 10.1	Selecting the right type of digital marketing dashboard

Purpose

To assess the benefits and disadvantages of dashboards and review some of the options available.

Activity

1 Review some of the most commonly used dashboards by digital marketers to understand their features and how they differentiate.
   - Google Analytics (which offers standard and customised dashboards)
   - Geckoboard
   - Kissmetrics
   - Klipfolio
   - Sproutsocial
   - Tableau
2 Identify different types of dashboard solutions.
3 List essential requirements of dashboard solutions which differentiate them from tools such as Google Analytics.
4 What are the potential disadvantages of dashboard systems which require management?

When identifying metrics it is common practice to apply the widely used SMART mnemonic and it is also useful to consider three levels – business measures, marketing measures and specific digital marketing measures (see the objective setting section in Chapter 4).

Figure 10.3 shows a framework of measures, which can be applied to a range of different companies. The groupings of measures remain relevant, although they are centred on sites or online presence, measures for engagement with social media should also be considered. In Chapter 4, we also reviewed two alternative frameworks (see Tables 4.6 and 4.9) that can also be used for creating a performance dashboard.

Channel promotion

Channel promotion
Measures that assess why customers visit a site – which adverts they have seen, which sites have they been referred from.

These measures evaluate the volume, quality and value of where the website, social presence or mobile site visitors originate – online or offline – and what are the sites or offline media that prompted their visit. Web analytics can be used to assess which intermediary

The WebInsights™ diagnostics framework includes these key metrics:

1. **Business contribution:**
   Online revenue contribution (direct and indirect), category penetration, costs and profitability.

2. **Marketing outcomes:**
   Leads, sales, service contacts, conversion and retention efficiencies.

3. **Customer satisfaction:**
   Site usability, performance/availability, contact strategies. Opinions, attitudes and brand impact.

4. **Customer behaviour (web analytics):**
   Profiles, customer orientation (segmentation), usability, clickstreams and site actions.

5. **Site promotion:**
   Attraction efficiency. Referrer efficiency, cost of acquisition and reach. Search engine visibility and link building. E-mail marketing. Integration.

| **Figure 10.3** | The five diagnostic categories for digital marketing measurement |

Referrer
The site that a visitor previously visited before following a link.

sites customers are referred from (**the referrer**) and which keywords they typed into search engines when trying to locate product information. Similar information on referrer is not typically available for visits to social media sites. Promotion is successful if traffic meets objectives of volume, quality, value and cost (as explained in Chapter 8). Quality will be determined by whether visitors are in the target market and have a propensity for the service offered (through reviewing conversion (online or offline), bounce rates and cost of acquisition for different referrers).

Key measure

Referral mix. For each referral source such as paid search or display ads it should be possible to calculate:

- percentage of all referrals or sales (and influence in achieving sale last click or assist);
- cost-per-acquisition (CPA) or cost-per-sale (CPS);
- contribution to sales or other outcomes.

Channel buyer behaviour
Describes which content is visited and the time and duration.

Channel buyer behaviour

Once customers have been attracted to the site we can monitor content accessed, when they visit and how long they stay, and whether this interaction with content leads to satisfactory marketing outcomes such as new leads or sales. If visitors are incentivised to register on-site it is possible to build up profiles of behaviour for different segments. Segments can also be created according to visitor source and content accessed. It is also important to recognise return visitors for whom cookies or login are used. In Chapter 6 we saw how hurdle rates can be used to assess activity levels for return visits, e.g. 30 per cent of customers return to use the online service within 90 days.

Key ratios

- Bounce rates for different pages, i.e. proportion of single page visits.
- Home page views/all page views, e.g. 20 per cent = (2000/10,000).

Stickiness
An indication of how long
a visitor stays on-site.

- **Stickiness**: page views/visitor sessions, e.g. 2 = 10,000/5000.
- **Repeats**: visitor sessions/visitors, e.g. 20 per cent = 1000/5000.

Channel satisfaction
Evaluation of the
customer's opinion of the
service quality on the site
and supporting services
such as email.

Channel satisfaction

Customer satisfaction with the online experience is vital in achieving the desired channel outcomes. Online methods such as online questionnaires, focus groups and interviews can be used to assess customers' opinions of the website content and customer service and how it has affected overall perception of brand. Benchmarking services such as Foresee (**www. foreseeresults.com**) based on the American Customer Satisfaction Index methodology are published for some industries. These assess scores based on the gap between expectations and actual service.

Key measure

Customer satisfaction indices. These are discussed in Chapter 7 and include ease of use, site availability and performance, and email response. To compare customer satisfaction with other sites, benchmarking services can be used.

Channel outcomes
Record of customer
actions taken as a
consequence of a visit to
a site.

Conversion rate
Percentage of site visitors
who perform a particular
action such as making a
purchase.

Channel outcomes

Traditional marketing objectives such as number of sales, number of leads, **conversion rates** and targets for customer acquisition and retention should be set and then compared to other channels. Dell Computer (**www.dell.com**) records on-site sales and also orders generated as a result of site visits, but placed by phone. This is achieved by monitoring calls to a specific phone number unique to the site.

Key marketing outcomes include:

- registration to site or subscriptions to an email newsletter;
- requests for further information such as a brochure or a request for a call-back from a customer service representative;
- responding to a promotion such as an online competition;
- an offline (phone or store) lead or sale influenced by a visit to the site;
- a sale on-site.

Key measure

- Channel contribution (direct and indirect).

A widely used method of assessing channel outcomes is to review the conversion rate, which gives an indication of the percentage of site visitors who take a particular outcome. For example:

- Conversion rate, visitors to purchase = 2 per cent (10,000 visitors, of which 200 make purchases).
- Conversion rate, visitors to registration = 5 per cent (10,000 visitors, of which 500 register).

Attrition rate
Percentage of site visitors
lost at each stage in
making a purchase.

A related concept is the **attrition rate** which describes how many visitors are lost at each step of a conversion funnel from landing page to checkout. Figure 10.4 shows that for a set time period, only a proportion of site visitors will make their way to product information, a small proportion will add an item to a basket and a smaller proportion still will actually make the purchase. A key feature of e-commerce sites is that there is a high attrition rate between a customer adding an item to a basket and subsequently making a purchase. It is surmised that this is due to fears about credit card security, and that customers are merely experimenting.

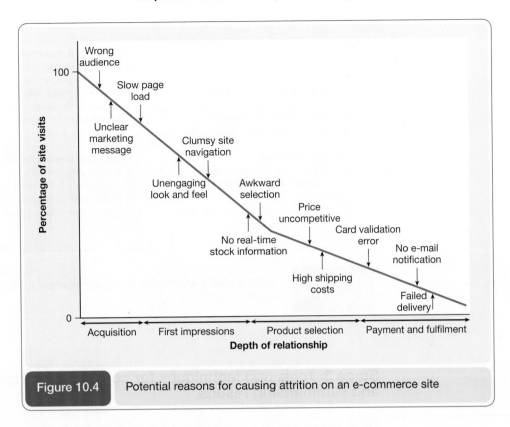

Figure 10.4   Potential reasons for causing attrition on an e-commerce site

Channel profitability
The profitability of the website, taking into account revenue and cost and discounted cash flow

Channel profitability

A contribution to business profitability is always the ultimate aim of e-commerce. To assess this, leading companies set an Internet contribution target of achieving a certain proportion of sales via the channel. Assessing contribution is more difficult for a company that cannot sell products online, but the role of the Internet in influencing leads and purchase should be assessed. Discounted cash flow techniques are used to assess the rate of return over time.

Multichannel evaluation

The frameworks we have presented in this chapter are explained in the context of an individual channel, but with the contribution of the channel highlighted as percentage sales or profitability. But as Wilson (2008) has pointed out, there is a need to evaluate how different channels support each other. Wilson says:

> Traditional metrics have been aligned to channels, measuring resource input or leads in at one end and the value of sales generated by the channel at the other end. For companies that have been operating in a single channel environment, this might have been relatively efficient – but it no longer works when the organisation diversifies to a multichannel approach.

He suggests the most important aspect of multichannel measurement is to measure 'channel cross-over effects'. This involves asking, for example: 'How can the impact of a paid search campaign be measured if it is as likely to generate traffic to a store, salesforce or call centre as to a website?' and 'How can the impact of a direct mail campaign be tracked if it generates website traffic as well as direct responses?'

An example of a balanced scorecard style dashboard developed to assess and compare channel performance for a retailer is presented in Figure 10.5.

Results (6)		Customers & stakeholders (5)	
• Revenue • Multichannel contribution • Degree multichannel sells up • Costs per channel • Degree of sweating assets • Multichannel infrastructure costs		• Overall customer satisfaction • Customer propensity to defect • Customer propensity to purchase • Customer perception of added value • Integration of customer experience	
Core processes (3)		**People and knowledge (4)**	
• Productive multichannel usage • Price (relative to competitors/other channels) • Quality of integrated customer view		• Staff satisfaction • Appropriate behaviours 'Living the brand' • Willingness to diversify/extend the brand • Knowledge of target customer	

Figure 10.5 Multichannel performance scorecard example for a retailer
Source: Wilson (2008)

Stage 3: Tools and techniques for collecting metrics and summarising results

Organisations need to select the most appropriate tools for collecting and reporting metrics which meet requirements such as reporting of marketing performance, accuracy, analysis and visualisation tools, integration with other marketing information systems (import, export and integration using XML standards), ease of use, configuration (e.g. creation of custom dashboards and email alerts), support quality, cost of purchase, configuration and ongoing support.

Techniques to collect metrics include the collection of site-visitor activity data such as that stored in web analytics systems and in site log files; the collection of metrics about outcomes such as online sales or email enquiries and traditional marketing research techniques such as questionnaires and focus groups which collect information on the customer's experience on the website. We start by describing methods for collecting site-visitor activity data and then review more traditional techniques of market research.

Collecting site-visitor activity data

Site-visitor activity data captured in web analytics systems records the number of visitors on the site and the paths or clickstreams they take through the site as they visit different content. The terms used to measure visitor activity are summarised in Table 10.1.

In the early days of Internet marketing, in the mid-1990s, this information was typically collected using log files. The server-based log file is added to every time a user downloads a piece of information (a **hit**) and is analysed using a **log file analyser** (as illustrated by Figure 3.8). Examples of transactions within a log file are:

www.davechaffey.com – [05/Oct/2006:00:00:49 -000] 'GET/index.html HTTP/1.0' 200 33362

www.davechaffey.com – [05/Oct/2006:00:00:49 -000] 'GET/logo.gif HTTP/1.0' 200 54342

Despite their wide use in the media, hits are not a useful measure of website effectiveness since if a page consists of ten graphics, plus text, this is recorded as 11 hits. **Page impressions or page views** and **unique visitors** are better measures of site activity. Auditing companies such as ABC electronic (**www.abce.org.uk**), which audit sites for the purpose

Site-visitor activity data
Information on content and services accessed by e-commerce site visitors.

Hit
Recorded for each graphic or text file requested from a web server. It is not a reliable measure for the number of people viewing a page.

Log file analyser
A separate program such as WebTrends that is used to summarise the information on customer activity in a log file.

Page impression
A more reliable measure than a hit, denoting one person viewing one page. Also known as page view.

Unique visitors
Individual visitors to a site measured through cookies or IP addresses on an individual computer.

Table 10.1	Terminology for key website volume measures	

Measure	Measure	Definition
1 How many? 'audience reach'	Unique users	A unique and valid identifier [for a site visitor]. Sites may use (i) IP + User – Agent, (ii) cookie and/or (iii) registration ID
2 How often? 'frequency metric'	Visit	A series of one or more page impressions, served to one user, which ends when there is a gap of 30 minutes or more between successive page impressions for that user
3 How busy? 'volume metric'	Page impression	A file, or combination of files, sent to a valid user as a result of that user's request being received by the server
4 What see?	Ad impressions	A file or a combination of files sent to a valid user as an individual advertisement as a result of that user's request being received by the server
5 What do?	Ad clicks	An ad impression clicked on by a valid user

Source: ABCe (www.abce.org.uk)

of proving the number of visitors to a site to advertisers, use unique visitors and page impression as the main measures.

An example of visitor volume to a website using different measures based on real, representative data for one month is presented in Figure 10.6. You can see how hits are much higher than page views and unique visitors and are quite misleading in terms of the 'opportunities to see' a message. We can also learn from the ratio between some of these measures – the figure indicates:

- *Pages per visit (PPV)* – the average number of pages viewed per visitor to a site (this is indicative of engagement with a site since the longer a visitor stays on a 'sticky site', the higher this value will be). PPV is a more accurate indication of stickiness than duration on a site in minutes since this figure is skewed upwards by visitors who arrive on a site and are inactive before their session times out at 30 minutes.
- *Visits per (unique) visitor (VPV)* – this suggests the frequency of site visits. Readers will realise that this value is dependent on the period that data are collected over. These data

Figure 10.6	Examples of different measures of visitor volume to a website

are reported for a month during which time one would not expect many returning visitors. So it is often more relevant to present these data across a quarter or a year.

Other information giving detailed knowledge of customer behaviour that can be reported by any web analytics package includes:

- top pages;
- entry and exit pages;
- path or clickstream analysis showing the sequence of pages viewed;
- country of visitor origin (actually dependent on the location of their ISP);
- browser and operating system used;
- referring URL and domain (where the visitor came from).

Digital marketing insight 10.1   Focus on measuring social media marketing

Social media marketing has its own range of specialist measures that can appear confusing, but are best understood in the context of a combination of website and PR measures. These show the volume, quality, sentiment and value of interactions. Analyst Altimeter (2010) has created a useful framework (shown in Figure 10.7) that helps map out different social media measures in the context of level of business management.

    You can see that there are three levels of KPIs:

- *Business-level KPIs to measure contribution from social media*. These KPIs include contribution to revenue through direct sales attributed to social media. Softer measures include reputation and customer satisfaction (CSAT).
- *Reach and influence KPIs to review reach, share-of-voice and sentiment*. These show the relative comparison of a brand's reach.
- *Engagement KPIs to manage social media*. These are the easiest measures to collect, but the least valuable since they don't directly show contribution to business value. Although easy to collect, data on

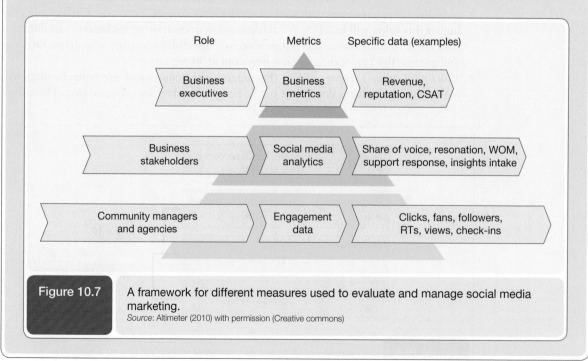

Figure 10.7	A framework for different measures used to evaluate and manage social media marketing.

Source: Altimeter (2010) with permission (Creative commons) interaction with social sites is often supplied separately by the owners of the different social presence and tools for managing social interaction. A new class of social analytics tools have been created to bring this data together. Figure 10.8 shows an example from the social media management tool Hootsuite where sharing of shortened URLs linking to different social media sites have driven traffic back to a main website. Direct traffic is where visitors click direct through from a social media messaging application like Hootsuite or Tweetdeck to the site.

A common question within social media is how to assess the value of a consumer connecting with a brand, by liking on Facebook, following on Twitter or placing in a brand in a circle on Google+. Since the tracking of social media can't show what an individual does on the network, specific value is difficult to establish. Instead what we can assess is the relative purchase rates of visitors from social media sites to websites compared to other channels using measures like conversion rate and revenue per visitor.

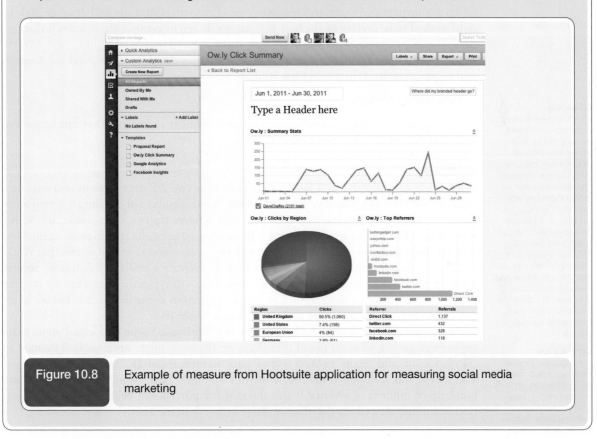

| Figure 10.8 | Example of measure from Hootsuite application for measuring social media marketing |

Design for analysis

Measurement is often highlighted as an issue once the first version of a site has been 'up and running' for a few months, and employees start to ask questions such as 'How many customers are visiting our site, how many sales are we achieving as a result of our site and how can we improve the site to achieve a return on investment?' The consequence of this is that performance measurement is something that is often built into an online presence retrospectively. Preferable is if a technique known as **design for analysis (DFA)** is designed into the site so companies can better understand the types of audience and their decision points. For example, for Dell (**www.dell.com**), the primary navigation on the home page is by customer type. This is a simple example of DFA since it enables Dell to estimate the proportion of different audiences to its site and, at the same time, connect them with relevant content.

Design for analysis (DFA)
The required measures from a site are considered during design to better understand the audience of a site and their decision points.

Other examples of DFA include:

- Breaking up a long page or form into different parts, so you can see which parts people are interested in.
- A URL policy (see Chapter 8) used to recommend entry pages for printed material.
- Group content by audience type or buying decision and setting up content groups of related content within web analytics systems.
- Measure attrition at different points in a customer journey, e.g. exit points on a five-page buying cycle.
- A single exit page to linked sites.

AB and multivariate testing

Often site owners and marketers reviewing the effectiveness of a site will disagree and the only method to be certain of the best-performing design or creative alternatives is through designing and running experiments to evaluate the best to use. Matt Round, then director of personalisation at Amazon, speaking at the e-metrics summit in 2004, said the Amazon philosophy, described further in Case study 10 is:

> Data trumps intuition.

AB testing and multivariate testing are two measurement techniques that can be used to review design effectiveness to improve results.

AB testing

In its simplest form, A/B or **AB testing** refers to testing two different versions of a page or a page element such as a heading, image or button. Some members of the site are served alternately, with the visitors to the page randomly split between the two pages. Hence it is sometimes called 'live split testing'. The goal is to increase page or site effectiveness against key performance indicators including click-through rate, conversion rates and revenue per visit.

When completing AB testing it is important to identify a realistic baseline or **control page** (or audience sample) to compare against. This will typically be an existing landing page. Two new alternatives can be compared to previous control, which is known as an ABC test. Different variables are then applied as in Table 10.2.

An example of the power of AB testing is an experiment Skype performed on its main topbar navigation, where it found that changing the main menu options 'Call Phones' to 'Skype Credit' and 'Shop' to 'Accessories' gave an increase of 18.75 per cent revenue per visit (Skype was speaking at the 2007 e-metrics summit). That's significant when you have hundreds of millions of visitors! It also shows the importance of being direct with navigation and simply describing the offer available rather than the activity.

Multivariate testing

Multivariate testing is a more sophisticated form of AB testing which enables simultaneous testing of pages for different combinations of page elements that are being tested.

AB testing
A/B or AB testing refers to testing two different versions of a page or a page element such as a heading, image or button for effectiveness. The alternatives are served alternately with the visitors to the page randomly split between the two pages. Changes in visitor behaviour can then be compared using different metrics such as click-through rate on page elements like buttons or images, or macro-conversion rates, such as conversion to sale or sign-up.

Control page
The page against which subsequent optimisation will be assessed. Typically a current landing page. When a new page performs better than the existing control page, it becomes the control page in subsequent testing. Also known as 'champion-challenger'

Table 10.2	AB test example	
Test	**A (Control)**	**B (Test page)**
Test 1	Original page	New headline, existing button, existing body copy
Test 2	Original page	Existing headline, new button, existing body copy
Test 3	Original page	Existing headline, existing button, new body copy

This enables selection of the most effective combination of design elements to achieve the desired goal.

An example of a multivariate test is shown in Mini case study 10.1.

Mini case study 10.1	Multivariate testing at National Express Group increases conversion rates

The National Express Group is the leading provider of travel solutions in the UK. Around 1 billion journeys a year are made worldwide on National Express Group's bus, train, light rail and express coach and airport operations. A significant proportion of ticket bookings are made online through the company's website at www.nationalexpress.com/home.aspx.

The company uses multivariate testing provider Maxymiser to run an experiment to improve conversion rate of a fare-selection page which was the penultimate step in booking (Figure 10.9). The analysis team identified a number of subtle alterations to content (labelled A to E) and calls to action on the page with the aim of stimulating visitor engagement and driving a higher percentage of visitors through to successful conversion without changing the structure of the page or National Express brand identity. In order to aid more effective up-sell to insurance add-ons, changes to this call to action were also proposed.

It was decided that a multivariate test would be the most effective approach to determine the best performing combination of content. The variants jointly developed by Maxymiser and the client were tested with all live site visitors and the conversion rate of each combination monitored; 3500 possible page combinations were tried and during the live test the underperforming combinations were taken out to maximise conversion rates at every stage.

At the end of the testing period, after reaching statistical validity, results gave the best combination of elements, showing a 14.11 per cent increase in conversion rates for the page – i.e. 14.11 per cent more visitors

Figure 10.9	National Express page assessed through multivariate testing

were sent through to the fourth and final step in the registration process, immediately hitting bottom line revenue for National Express (Figure 10.10).

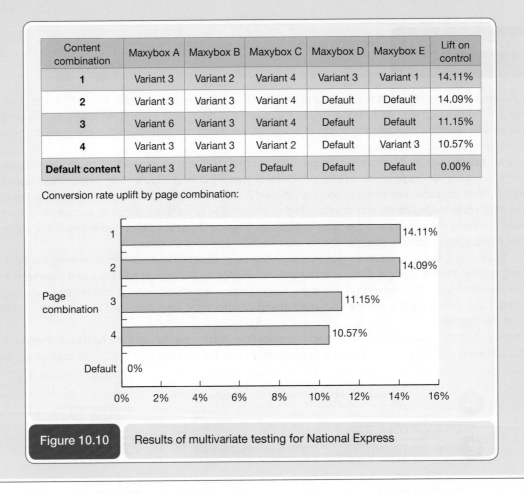

Content combination	Maxybox A	Maxybox B	Maxybox C	Maxybox D	Maxybox E	Lift on control
1	Variant 3	Variant 2	Variant 4	Variant 3	Variant 1	14.11%
2	Variant 3	Variant 3	Variant 4	Default	Default	14.09%
3	Variant 6	Variant 3	Variant 4	Default	Default	11.15%
4	Variant 3	Variant 3	Variant 2	Default	Variant 3	10.57%
Default content	Variant 3	Variant 2	Default	Default	Default	0.00%

Conversion rate uplift by page combination:

Figure 10.10	Results of multivariate testing for National Express

Clickstream analysis and visitor segmentation

Clickstream analysis refers to detailed analysis of visitor behaviour in order to identify improvements to the site. Each web analytics tool differs slightly in its reports and terminology, but all provide similar reports to help companies assess visitor behaviour and diagnose problems and opportunities. Table 10.3 gives an indication of the type of practical questions asked by web analyst and consultant Dave Chaffey (**www.davechaffey.com**) when reviewing clients' sites.

Path analysis

Aggregate clickstreams are usually known within web analytics software as forward or reverse paths. This is a fairly advanced form of analysis, but the principle is straightforward – you seek to learn from the most popular paths.

Viewed at an aggregate level across the site through 'top paths' type reports, this form of clickstream analysis often doesn't appear that useful. It highlights typically paths which are expected and can't really be influenced. The top paths are often:

- Home page: Exit
- Home page: Contact Us: Exit
- News page: Exit

Table 10.3	A summary of how an analyst will interpret web analytics data. GA is terminology for Google Analytics (www.google.com/analytics), one of the most widely used tools	

Analyst question	Typical web analytics report terminology	Diagnosis analyst used to improve performance
How successful is the site at achieving engagement and outcomes?	Conversion goals (GA) Bounce rates (GA) Pages/visit (GA)	• Is engagement and conversion consistent with other sites in sector? • What are maximum engagement and conversion rates from different referrers?
Where are visitors entering the site?	Top entry pages Top landing pages (GA)	• How important is home page compared to other page categories and landing pages? • Does page popularity reflect product popularity? • Review messaging/conversion paths are effective on these pages • Assess source of traffic, in particular keywords from search engines and apply elsewhere
What are the sources of visitors (referrers)?	Referrers Traffic sources Filters set up to segment visitors	• Are the full range of digital media channels relevant for a company represented? • Is the level of search engine traffic consistent with the brand reputation? • What are the main link partners driving free traffic (potential for more?)
What is the most popular content?	Top content (GA)	• Is page popularity as expected? • Are there problems with findability caused by navigation labelling? • Which content is most likely to influence visitors to outcome? • Which content is most popular with returning visitors segment?
Which are the most popular findability methods?	Site search (GA)	• How popular are different forms of navigation, e.g. top menu, sidebar menus, etc? • What are the most popular searches? • Where do searches tend to start? • Are they successfully finding content or converting to sale?
Where do visitors leave the site?	Top exit pages (GA)	• Are these as expected (home page, About Us page, transaction completion)? • Are there error pages (e.g. 404 not found) which cause visitors to leave?
Which clickstreams are taken?	Path analysis Top paths (GA)	• How can attrition in conversion funnels be improved? • What does forward path analysis show are the most effective calls-to-action? • What does reverse path analysis indicate about the pages which influence sales?

Forward path analysis
Reviews the combinations of clicks that occur from a page. This form of analysis is most beneficial from important pages such as the home page, product and directory pages. Use this technique to identify: messaging/navigation combinations which work best to yield the most clicks from a page.

Clickstream analysis becomes more actionable when the analyst reviews clickstreams in the context of a single page – this is **forward path analysis** or **reverse path analysis**.

On-site search effectiveness

On-site search is another crucial part of clickstream analysis on many sites since it is a key way of finding content, so a detailed search analysis will pay dividends. Key search metrics to consider are:

- number of searches;
- average number of searches per visitor or searcher;
- percentage of searches returning zero results;

Reverse path analysis
Reverse path analysis
indicates the most
popular combination of
pages and/or calls-to-
action which lead to a
page. This is particularly
useful for transactional
pages such as the first
checkout page on a
consumer site; a lead
generation or contact us
page on a business-to-
business site; an email
subscription page or a
call-me-back option.

- percentage of site exits from search results;
- percentage of returned searches clicked;
- percentage of returned searches resulting in conversion to sale or other outcome;
- most popular search terms – individual keyword and keyphrases.

Visitor segmentation

Segmentation is a fundamental marketing approach, but is often difficult within web analytics to relate customer segments to web behaviour because the web analytics data isn't integrated with customer or purchase data.

However, all analytics systems have a capability for a different, but valuable form of segmentation where it is possible to create specific filters or profiles to help understand one type of site visitor behaviour. Examples of segments include:

- First- time visitors or returning visitors.
  - Visitors from different referrer types including:
  - Strategic search keyphrases, brand keyphrases, etc.;
  - Display advertising.
- Converters against non-converters.
- Geographic segmentation by country or region (based on IP addresses).
- Type of content accessed, e.g. are some segments more likely to convert? For example, speaking at Ad Tech London '06, MyTravel reported that it segments visitors into:
  - site flirt (two pages or fewer);
  - site browse (two pages or more);
  - saw search results;
  - saw quote;
  - saw payment details;
  - saw booking confirmation details.

Selecting a web analytics tool

There has been consolidation of web analytics tools, such that there is now a basic choice of a free service such as Google Analytics or a paid service from the main providers such as Omniture (owned by Adobe Systems), Coremetrics (owned by IBM) and WebTrends, which may cost hundreds of thousands of dollars a year for a popular site. All will report similar measures for digital marketing activity to those explored earlier in the chapter, so often the selection of the best system will depend on factors such as:

- *Integration with other data sources* (for example, social media marketing, customer data and financial reporting). Figure 10.11 gives an indication of the types of data that need to be integrated; these include operational data, tactical and strategic data.
- *Accuracy*. Potential sources of inaccuracy are reviewed in Table 10.4 comparing traditional *log file analysis* to the more common *browser-based* or *tag-based* measurement system that records access to web pages every time a page is loaded into a user's web browser through running a short script, program or tag inserted into the web page. The key benefit of the browser-based approach is that it is potentially more accurate than server-based approaches. Figure 10.12 indicates how the browser-based approach works. The free version of Google Analytics uses sampling on large sites which can decrease accuracy.
- *Media attribution*. We saw in Chapter 8 that the 'last-click-wins' model of attributing a referral source to sale is inaccurate and weighted models based on the whole customer journey are more accurate. The capability of analytics system to display this is important for companies investing a lot in online media.
- *Visualisation*. How data are displayed through reports and alerts. Vendors continually introduce new features in this area.
- *Customisation facilities*. For creating and distributing new reports and alerts

| Figure 10.11 | Different types of data within a performance management system for Internet marketing |

| Table 10.4 | Inaccuracies caused by server-based log file analysis |

Sources of undercounting	Sources of overcounting
Caching in user's web browsers (when a user accesses a previously accessed file, it is loaded from the user's cache on their PC)	Frames (a user viewing a framed page with three frames will be recorded as three page impressions on a server-based system)
Caching on proxy servers (proxy servers are used within organisations or ISPs to reduce Internet traffic by storing copies of frequently used pages)	Spiders and robots (traversing of a site by spiders from different search engines is recorded as page impressions. These spiders can be excluded, but this is time-consuming)
Firewalls (these do not usually exclude page impressions, but they do assign a single IP address for the user of the page, rather than referring to an individual's PC)	Executable files (these can also be recorded as hits or page impressions unless excluded)
Dynamically generated pages, generated 'on the fly', are difficult to assess with server-based log files	

- *Support services.* For configuration of data feeds and reports and consulting to assist in auctioning the results. In 2011 the free service Google Analytics introduced a premium version for large corporate customers which included account management.
- *Privacy considerations.* Web analytics systems store personal data. As we saw in Chapter 4, it is important that data collection and disclosure about the method of collection by the system follow the latest laws about use of cookies.

Strategic data

Performance management systems for senior managers will give the big picture presented as scorecards or dashboards showing trends in contribution of digital channels to the organisation in terms of sales, revenue and profitability for different products.

An example of the output reporting from a web analytics service is shown in Figure 10.12.

Marketing research using the Internet

Internet-based market research
The use of online questionnaires and focus groups to assess customer perceptions of a website or broader marketing issues.

Internet-based marketing research can help determine the influence of a website and related communications on customer perception of the company and its products and services. But it also has wider applications of gaining feedback from customers about a brand and how it could develop in future. Smart Insights (2010) identifies these five different classes of online feedback tools:

1 *Website feedback tools*. Provide a permanent facility for customers to give feedback by prompts on every page. They are run continuously to enable continuous feedback including ratings on page content, and also products and services.
2 *Site user intent-satisfaction surveys*. These tools measure the gap between what the user had hoped to do on the site and what they actually achieved. We gave the example of 4Q in Chapter 7 that covers four questions to assess site effectiveness.
3 *Crowdsourcing product opinion software*. These are broader than web feedback, enabling customers to comment about potential new services. This is the approach used by Dell in the IdeaStorm (**www.ideastorm.com**).
4 *Simple page or concept feedback tools*. Again a form of crowdsourcing, these tools give feedback from an online panel about page layout, messaging or services.

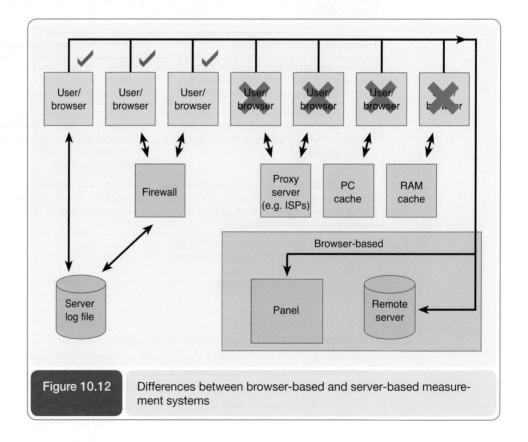

Figure 10.12   Differences between browser-based and server-based measurement systems

5 *General online survey tools.* Tools like Zoomerang (**www.zoomerang.com**) and SurveyMonkey (**www.surveymonkey.com**) enable companies to survey their audience at a low cost.

The full options for conducting survey research include interviews, questionnaires and focus groups are summarised in Table 10.5. Each of these techniques can be conducted offline or online.

We will now briefly review the strengths and weaknesses of the different research techniques and some approaches to best practice.

Table 10.5	A comparison of different online metrics collection and research methods

Technique	Strengths	Weaknesses
Server-based log file analysis of site activity	• Directly records customer behaviour on site plus where they were referred from • Low cost • Gives insight on robot crawling for SEO	• Not based around marketing outcomes such as leads or sales • Size – even summaries may be over 50 pages long • Does not directly record channel satisfaction • Undercounting/overcounting • Misleading unless interpreted carefully • Most site analytics tools are now browser based
Browser-based site activity data	• Greater accuracy than server-based analysis • Counts all users, cf. panel approach	• Relatively expensive method • Similar weaknesses to server-based technique apart from accuracy • Limited demographic information
AB and multivariate testing	• Structured experiments to review influence of on page variables (e.g. messaging and buttons) to improve conversion from a website	• Often requires cost of a separate tool or module from standard web analytics package • Content management systems or page templates may not support AB/multivariate testing
Panel activity and demographic data	• Provides competitor comparisons • Gives demographic profiling representative • Avoids undercounting and overcounting	• Depends on extrapolation from data-limited sample that may not be representative
Outcome data, e.g. enquiries, customer emails	• Records marketing outcomes	• Difficulty of integrating data with other methods of data collection when service collected manually or in other information systems
Online questionnaires Customers are prompted randomly – every *n*th customer or after customer activity or by email	• Can record customer satisfaction and profiles • Relatively cheap to create and analyse	• Difficulty of recruiting respondents who complete accurately • Sample bias – tend to be advocates or disgruntled customers who complete
Online focus groups Synchronous recording	• Relatively cheap to create	• Difficult to moderate and coordinate • No visual cues, as from offline focus groups
Mystery shoppers Example is customers are recruited to evaluate the site, e.g. **www. emysteryshopper.com**	• Structured tests give detailed feedback • Also tests integration with other channels such as email and phone	• Relatively expensive • Sample must be representative

Questionnaires and surveys

Malhotra (1999) suggested that Internet surveys using questionnaires will increase in popularity since the cost is generally lower, they can be less intrusive and they have the ability to target specific populations. Register *et al.* (2014) confirmed that Internet surveys are fast becoming the preferred mode for survey delivery as they afford researchers convenient use of design options such as 'forced answering' (FA) that can virtually eliminate item non-response error.

However, a recent review of the technique by Stern *et al.* (2014) shows that the Internet has failed to deliver in terms of response rates and it can be more challenging to get a representative sample. Questionnaires often take the form of pop-up surveys. The key issues are:

A *Encouraging participation.* Techniques that can be used are:
- interruption on entry – a common approach where every 100th customer is prompted;
- continuous, for example click on a button to complete survey;
- on registration on-site the customer can be profiled;
- after an activity such as sale or customer support, the customer can be prompted for their opinion about the service;
- incentives and promotions (this can also be executed on independent sites);
- by email (an email prompt to visit a website to fill in a survey or a simple email survey).

B *Stages in execution.* It is suggested that there are five stages to a successful questionnaire survey:
1. attract (button, pop-up, email as above);
2. incentivise (prize or offer consistent with required sample and audience);
3. reassure (why the company is doing it – to learn, not too long and that confidentiality is protected);
4. design and execute (brevity, relevance, position);
5. follow-up (feedback).

C *Design.* Grossnickle and Raskin (2001) suggest the following approach to structuring questionnaires:
- easy, interesting questions first;
- cluster questions on same topic;
- flow topic from general to specific;
- flow topic from easier behavioural to more difficult attitudinal questions;
- easy questions last, e.g. demographics or off-putting questions.

Typical questions that can be asked for determining the effectiveness of Internet marketing are:

- *Who is visiting the site?* For example, role in buying decision? Online experience? Access location and speed? Demographics segment?
- *Why are they visiting?* How often do they visit? Which information or service? Did they find it? Actions taken? (Can be determined through web analytics.)
- *What do they think?* Overall opinion? Key areas of satisfaction? Specific likes or dislikes? What was missing that was expected?

Focus groups

Malhotra (1999) noted that the advantage of online focus groups is that they can be used to reach segments that are difficult to access, such as doctors, lawyers and professional people. This author also suggests that costs are lower, they can be arranged more rapidly and can bridge the distance gap when recruiting respondents. Traditional focus groups can be conducted, where customers are brought together in a room and assess a website; this will typically occur pre-launch as part of the prototyping activity. Testing can take the form of random use of the site or, more usefully, the users will be given different scenarios to follow. Focus groups tend to be relatively expensive and time consuming, since rather than simply viewing an advertisement, the customers need to actually interact with the website. Conducting real-world focus groups has the benefit that the reactions of site users can be monitored; the scratch or slap of the head cannot be monitored in the virtual world!

Mystery shoppers

Real-world measurement is also important since the Internet channel does not exist in isolation. It must work in unison with real-world customer service and fulfilment. Chris Russell of eDigitalResearch (**www.edigitalresearch.com**), a company that has completed online customer service surveys for major UK retailers and travel companies, says:

> we also needed to make sure that the bricks-and-mortar customer service support was actually supporting what the clicks-and-mortar side was promising. There is no doubt that an e-commerce site has to be a complete customer service fulfilment picture, it can't just be one bit working online that is not supported offline.

An eMysteryShopper survey involves shoppers not only commenting on site usability, but also on the service quality of email and phone responses together with product fulfilment. Mystery shoppers test these areas:

- site usability;
- e-commerce fulfilment;
- email and phone response (time, accuracy);
- impact on brand.

Customer experience and content management process

As part of the process of continuous improvement in online marketing, it is important to have a clearly defined process for making changes to the online presence of a company. If pages remain static, as is the case with some brochureware sites we still see, then the opportunity to engage customers and prospects with a brand is missed. With search engines and social media sites featuring real-time data posted in blogs, companies that have a static site are missing an opportunity to get better visibility. A static site also has a missed opportunity to make the site more effective at generating value for a business by increasing conversion rates using the AB and multivariate testing approaches we talked about in the last section.

The key to keeping a website dynamic is to have a clear content and e-communications strategy based on a content or social hub, as we have seen in previous chapters. The site and content update process should be understood by all staff contributing content to the site, with their responsibilities clearly identified in their job descriptions. To understand the process, consider the main stages involved in publishing a page. A simple model of the work involved in maintenance is shown in Figure 10.13. It is assumed that the needs of the users and design features of the site have already been defined when the site was originally created (as described in Chapter 7). The model only applies to minor updates to copy, or perhaps updating product or company information. The different tasks involved in the maintenance process are as follows:

1 *Write*. This stage involves writing the marketing copy and, if necessary, designing the layout of copy and associated images.
2 *Review*. An independent review of the copy is necessary to check for errors before a document is published. Depending on the size of organisation, review may be necessary by one person or several people covering different aspects of content quality such as

corporate image, copy-editing text to identify grammatical errors, marketing copy, branding and legality.

3 *Correct*. This stage is straightforward and involves updates necessary as a result of stage 2.

4 *Publish (to test environment)*. The publication stage involves putting the corrected copy on a web page that can be checked further. This will be in a test environment that can only be viewed from inside a company.

5 *Test*. Before the completed web page is made available over the World Wide Web a final test will be required for technical issues such as whether the page loads successfully on different browsers.

6 *Publish (to live environment)*. Once the material has been reviewed and tested and is signed off as satisfactory, it will be published to the main website and will be accessible by customers.

How often should content be updated?

Website content needs to be up-to-date, in line with customer expectations. The web is perceived as a dynamic medium and customers are likely to expect new information to be posted to a site straightaway. If material is inaccurate or 'stale' then the customer may not return to the site.

After a time, the information on a web page naturally becomes outdated and will need to be updated or replaced. It is important to have both a content calendar for publishing future content and a mechanism defining what triggers this update process and leads to the cycle of Figure 10.13. The need for material to be updated has several facets. Trigger procedures should be developed such that when price changes or product specifications are updated in promotional leaflets or catalogues, these changes are also reflected on the website. Without procedures of this type, it is easy for there to be errors on the website. This may sound obvious, but the reality is that the people contributing the updates to the site will have many other tasks to complete, and the website can still be a low priority.

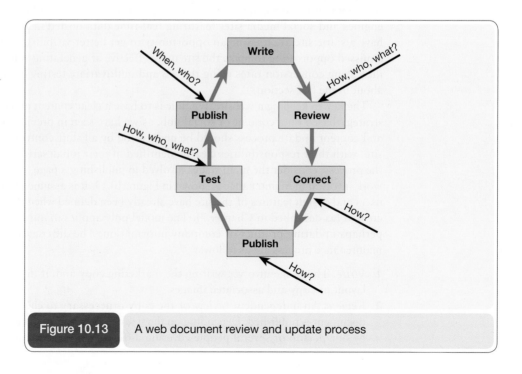

| Figure 10.13 | A web document review and update process |

To ensure site content remains 'fresh', i.e. relevant for the audience and effective for the business, it is useful to consider different types of content and their purpose. Consider different content types for an online retailer. These will include:

- *Product information* – product details on product pages and higher-level groupings of data as category pages. This includes both product descriptions and specifications which are relatively static for a given product and product pricing and availability information which is more dynamic.
- *Brand content (product brands)* – content about an individual brand available as different product may be grouped together.
- *Brand content (retailer brand)* – content about the company, such as its value proposition, trust and history.
- *Promotional content* – 'promotion' in this context referring to information about sales and discounts.
- *Support content* – information about ordering and returns for example.
- *Community content* – user-generated content which may be in a community area or associated with products as reviews and rating.
- *Blog content* – regularly updated content aimed at engaging customers and products, for example showing the latest fashion trends for a clothing retailer. This content may also be useful for search engine optimisation.

Now consider which factors will drive updates of different types of content. For product-related information, it will be new products and changes to pricing or availability. For promotional information, it will be seasonal promotions or other discounts agreed with suppliers. It is a relatively straightforward process to manage these types of content, but less clear for content to engage audiences such as blog-related content. For example, should a company publish one blog post a month, week, day or several per day? There is no 'rule-of-thumb' that helps answer this question for different sizes or types of business. Given the cost of creating content by in-house staff or external writers, a clear cost–benefit must be established to determine which update frequency is right and to determine the quality of content created. Benefits of a blog, for example, may include new or repeat visitors via social media when content is shared or new visits from search engine optimisation. Such content may also increase conversion by increasing desire for products by showing how products are used and the benefits they give.

Editorial calendar
A plan for scheduling the creation of new or updated content for different audiences to support business goals for new visitors or increased conversion as part of content marketing.

As part of content marketing, which requires that existing businesses must act more like publishers, an **editorial calendar** can help agree priorities and schedules for different content types.

Responsibilities for customer experience and site management

Maintenance is easy in a small company with a single person updating the website. Although they may be working on many tasks, one person is able to ensure that the style of the whole site remains consistent. For a large organisation with many different departments and offices in different countries, site maintenance becomes very difficult, and production of a quality site is only possible when there is strong control to establish a team who all follow the same standards. Sterne (2001) suggests that the essence of successful maintenance is to have clearly identified responsibilities for different aspects of updating the website. The questions to ask are:

- Who owns the process?
- Who owns the content?
- Who owns the format?
- Who owns the technology?

We will now consider these in more detail, reviewing the standards required to produce a good-quality website and the different types of responsibilities involved. (**Review of new site functionality is a strategic issue and was covered in Chapter 4.**)

Who owns the process?

One of the first areas to be defined should be the overall process for agreeing new site content and updating the site. But who agrees this process? For the large company it will be necessary to bring together all the interested parties, such as those within the marketing department and the site developers – which may be an external agency or the IT department. Within these groupings there may be many people with an interest such as the marketing manager, the person with responsibility for Internet or new-media marketing, a communications manager who places above-the-line advertising, and product managers who manage the promotion of individual products and services. All of these people should have an input in deciding on the process for updating the website. What, then, is this process? The process will specify responsibilities for different aspects of site management and detail the sequence in which tasks occur for updating the site. A typical update process is outlined in Figure 10.13. If we take a specific example we can illustrate the need for a well-defined process. Imagine that a large organisation is launching a new product – promotional literature is to be distributed to customers, the media are already available, and the company wants to add information about this product to the website. A recently recruited graduate is charged with putting the information on the site. How will this process actually occur? The following process stages need to occur:

1 Graduate reviews promotional literature and rewrites copy on a word processor and modifies graphical elements as appropriate for the website. This is the *write* stage in Figure 10.13.
2 Product and/or marketing manager reviews the revised web-based copy. This is part of the *review* stage in Figure 10.13.
3 Corporate communications manager reviews the copy for suitability. This is also part of the *review* stage in Figure 10.13.
4 Legal adviser reviews copy. This is also part of the *review* stage in Figure 10.13.
5 Copy revised and corrected and then re-reviewed as necessary. This is the *correct* stage in Figure 10.13.
6 Copy converted to web format and then published. This will be performed by a technical person such as a site developer, who will insert a new menu option to help users navigate to the new product. This person will add the HTML formatting and then upload the file using FTP to the test website. This is the first *publish* stage in Figure 10.13.
7 The new copy on the site will be reviewed by the graduate for accuracy, and needs to be tested on different web browsers and screen resolutions if it uses a graphical design different from the standard site template. This type of technical testing will need to be carried out by the webmaster. The new version could also be reviewed on the site by the communications manager or legal adviser at this point. This is part of the *test* stage in Figure 10.13.
8 Once all interested parties agree the new copy is suitable, the pages on the test website can be transferred to the live website and are then available for customers to view. This is the second *publish* stage in Figure 10.13.

Note that in this scenario review of the copy at stages 2 to 4 happens before the copy is actually put onto the test site at stage 6. This is efficient in that it saves the technical person or webmaster having to update the page until the copy is agreed. An alternative would be for the graduate to write the copy at stage 1 and then the webmaster publishes the material before it is reviewed by the various parties. Each approach is equally valid.

Content management systems with workflow capabilities are now commonly used to help achieve review of page updates. Revised copy for a page can be automatically emailed to all reviewers and then the comments received by email can be collated.

To conclude this section, refer to Activity 10.2, which shows a typical website update process and considers possible improvements.

| Activity 10.2 | Optimising a content review process |

Purpose

To assess how quality control and efficiency can be balanced for revisions to web content.

Activity

The extract below and Figure 10.14 illustrate a problem of updating encountered by this company. How can they solve this problem?

Problem description

From the moment the brand manager identifies a need to update copy for their product, the update might happen as follows: brand manager writes the copy (half a day); one day later the web manager reviews the copy. Three days later the marketing manager checks the copy, seven days later the legal department checks the copy, two days later the revised copy is implemented on the test site and two days later the brand manager reviews the test site. The next day the web manager reviews the website, followed by updating and final review, before the copy is added to the live site two days later and over a fortnight from when a relatively minor change to the site was identified!

| Figure 10.14 | An example of a content update review process |

Who owns the content?

For a medium-to-large site where the content is updated regularly, as it should be, it will soon become impossible for one person to update all the content. It is logical and practical to distribute the responsibility for owning and developing different sections of the site to the people in an organisation who have the best skills and knowledge to develop that content. For example, in a large financial services company, the part of the business responsible for a certain product area should update the copy referring to their products. One person will update the copy for each of savings accounts, mortgages, travel insurance, health insurance and investments. For a PC supplier, different **content developers** will be required for the product information, financing, delivery information and customer service facilities. Once the ownership of content is distributed throughout an organisation, it becomes crucial to develop guidelines and standards that help ensure that the site has a coherent 'feel' and appearance. The nature of these guidelines is described in the sections that follow.

As realisation of content as a strategic asset grows, more senior roles are being created to manage content quality as shown by Mini case study 10.2.

Content developer
A person responsible for updating web pages within part of an organisation.

Mini case study 10.2	Logitech appoints a content strategist

Computer peripheral provider Logitech advertised for a content strategist. This job description for a content strategist in a large company helps show us the key aspects of content strategy. These requirements summarise the essence of a sound content strategy:

1 Senior management must understand the importance of content strategy to invest in good-quality resources with high-profile roles.
2 Content must be of exceptional quality to be most effective – the job descriptions says: 'useful, compelling and meaningful'.
3 Involves a strategy for syndication – not limited to company's own site.
4 Blends improving customer experience, customer engagement and SEO.
5 Requires an editorial calendar to manage creation of content.
6 Content quality improved through a continuous process applying analytics and customer satisfaction.
7 Integrates copywriting, web platform design and implementation, marketing communications, PR and SEO resources or teams.
8 Supports goals and essence of company brand.

Content strategist responsibilities

- Drive the development and organisation of content that is useful, compelling and meaningful – directly on **logitech.com** and indirectly through distributed content.
- Create user flows, information hierarchies, wireframes and content strategy for **Logitech.com** in support of campaigns, product launches and ongoing improvement.
- Determine content requirements for **logitech.com**, inventory existing content, identify gaps, evaluate possible sources for additional material, and manage the process of getting that content into production.
- Creatively look for opportunities to improve content, consumer experience and SEO performance.
- Manage the **Logitech.com** editorial calendar to proactively keep content useful and up-to-date.
- Use analytics, consumer and usability testing and business requirements to help improve the experience and the content of **Logitech.com** in the long and short term.
- Work with the web, writing, PR and marcomm teams to determine the most effective ways to support campaigns and product launches on the web.
- Lead projects that make our web and component communication more intuitive and useful to consumers and internal partners.
- Work with brand architecture and terminology to guide the effective organisation of products and activities on **Logitech.com**.
- Drive the architecture of and improvements to the internal product content management system (worldwide product database to fit the needs of the organisation).
- Occasionally write or edit content – particularly meta-data, titles, alt text, and edit general content to optimise or natural search.

Content strategist requirements

- Four-year college degree in a relevant field required, Master's degree preferred.
- Five to seven years of experience in an information architecture role, with two to three years working on complex websites.
- Two to three years of experience being directly responsible for content strategy on a dynamic, complex or ever-evolving website.
- Experience with web content management systems, component content management systems DITA or otherwise and authoring systems XML or other.
- Strong strategic, analytical skills with a solid ability to articulate information requirements clearly.
- A creative and collaborative approach that elevates the creative and communication opportunities – rather than straight analysis.
- Expertise in content strategy – including strong experience in SEO and keyword analysis as well as planning flexible approaches to keep content accurate and fresh.
- Accomplishments in the effective use of syndication (in and out) and user generated content as well as working collaboratively with writers and designers.
- The ability to be measured by hard metrics – views, time on site, consumer feedback – as well as soft metrics – support of the brand vision and architecture, consumer perception.
- Demonstrated ability to visualise and communicate complex information using Microsoft Visio or similar software.
- Deep experience with all levels of UX strategy and testing – but the ability to act quickly on consumer insights and best practices.
- Solid work ethic, ability to perform under pressure, meet deadlines, prioritise and deliver multiple tasks on time.
- Willing to learn and contribute to a strong team environment.
- Enthusiastic about the products and the possibilities of Logitech.

Other information

Logitech knows the value of strategic communication and content and now we're expanding our team to make the most of it. The global marketing team needs an expert who is ready to add his or her brain, talent and creativity to the cause of making our content work smarter, harder and around the globe. This is an opportunity for an IA/content strategy professional to put both strategy and executional excellence into practice every day and make an immediate and visible impact on the efficacy of a global organisation.

This role reports directly to the Global Director of Writing and Brand Architecture, with a direct and ongoing relationship with the Director of Global Web Marketing.

Sources: Job description: Information Architect/Content Strategist for Logitech, posted 29 September 2010 (accessed 2010, no longer available)

Who owns the format?

Site design template(s)
A standard page layout format which is applied to each page of a website for particular page types, e.g. category pages, product or blog pages.

The format refers to different aspects of the design and layout of the site, commonly referred to as its 'look and feel'. The key aim is consistency of format across the whole website. For a large corporate site, with different staff working on different parts of the site, there is a risk that the different areas of the site will not be consistent. Defining a clear format or **site design templates** for the different page or content types means that the quality of the site and customer experience will be better since:

- *The site will be easier to use* – a customer who has become familiar with using one area of the site will be able to confidently use another part of the site.
- *The design elements of the site will be similar* – a user will feel more at home with the site if different parts look similar.
- The corporate image and branding will be consistent with real-world branding (if this is an objective) and similar across the entire site.

Site design templates were reviewed from a site design perspective in Chapter 7.

To achieve a site of this quality it is necessary for written standards to be developed. These may include different standards, such as those shown in Table 10.6. The standards adopted will vary according to the size of the website and company. Typically, larger sites, with more individual content developers, will require more detailed standards.

Who owns the technology?

The technology used to publish a website is important if a company is to utilise fully the power of the Internet. Many standards, such as those in Table 10.6, need to be managed in addition to the technology.

As well as issues of integrating systems, there are detailed technical issues for which the technical staff in the company need to be made responsible. These include:

- availability and performance of the website server;
- checking HTML for validity and correcting broken links;
- managing different versions of web pages in the test and live environments and content management.

Table 10.6	Website standards	
Standard	**Details**	**Applies to**
Site structure	Will specify the main areas of the site, for example products, customer service, press releases, how to place content and who is responsible for each area	Content developers
Navigation	May specify, for instance, that the main menu must always be on the left of the screen. Webmaster usually achieves these with nested (sub-)menus at the foot of the these through site templates screen. The home button should be accessible from every screen at the top-left corner of the screen. See Lynch and Horton (1999) for guidelines on navigation and site design	Website designer/webmaster usually achieves these through site templates
Copy style and page structure	General guidelines, for example reminding those writing copy that web copy needs to be briefer than its paper equivalent and ranking factors for SEO (Chapter 9). Where detail is required, perhaps with product specifications, it should be broken up into chunks that are digestible on-screen. Copy and page structure should also be written for search engine optimisation to keyphrases (Chapter 8).	Individual content developers
Testing standards	Check site functions for: • different browser types and versions • plug-ins • invalid links • speed of download of graphics • spellcheck each page	Website designer/webmaster
Corporate branding	Specifies the appearance of company logos and the colours and typefaces used to convey the brand message design	Website designer/webmaster and graphic design
Process	Web page or updating an existing page. Who is responsible for reviewing and updating?	All
Performance	Availability and download speed figures	Staff managing the server

Content management systems

**Content management
system (CMS)**
A software tool for
creating, editing and
updating documents
accessed by intranet,
extranet or Internet.

Content management systems refers to when software tools (usually browser-based software running on a server) permit business users to contribute web content, while an administrator keeps control of the format and style of the website and the approval process. These tools are used to organise, manage, retrieve and archive information content throughout the life of the site.

Content management systems (CMS) provide these facilities:

- *Structure authoring* – the design and maintenance of content structure (sub-components, templates, etc.), web page structure and website structure.
- *Link management* – the maintenance of internal and external links through content change and the elimination of dead links.
- *Search engine visibility* – the content within the search engine must be stored and linked such that it can be indexed by search engine robots to add it to their index. This was not possible with some first-generation content management systems, but is typical of more recent content management systems.
- *Input and syndication* – the loading (spidering) of externally originating content and the aggregation and dissemination of content from a variety of sources.
- *Versioning* – the crucial task of controlling which edition of a page, page element or the whole site is published. Typically this will be the most recent, but previous editions should be archived and it should be possible to roll back to a previous version at the page, page element or site level.
- *Security and access control* – different permissions can be assigned to different roles of users and some content may only be available through log-in details. In these cases, the CMS maintains a list of users. This facility is useful when a company needs to use the same CMS for an intranet, extranet or public Internet site which may have different levels of permission.
- *Publication workflow* – content destined for a website needs to pass through a publication process to move it from the management environment to the live delivery environment. The process may involve tasks such as format conversion (e.g. to PDF or to WAP), rendering to HTML, editorial authorisation and the construction of composite documents in real time (personalisation and selective dissemination).
- *Tracking and monitoring* – providing logs and statistical analysis of use to provide performance measures, tune the content according to demand and protect against misuse.
- *Navigation and visualisation* – providing an intuitive, clear and attractive representation of the nature and location of content using colour, texture, 3D rendering or even virtual reality.

From this list of features you can see that modern CMSs are complex and many CMSs are expensive investments. Some open-source CMSs are available, without the need to purchase a licence fee, which have many of the features explained in this section. The most popular open-source CMS are Wordpress, Drupal and Django. While these originated mainly for blogging, they can now be used to create more complex sites. For e-commerce sites, Magento is the most widely open-source system.

Initiatives to keep content fresh

It is often said that up-to-date content is crucial to site 'stickiness', but fresh content will not happen by accident, so companies have to consider approaches that can be used to control the quality of information. Generic approaches that we have seen which can work well are:

- Assign responsibility for particular content types of site sections.
- Make the quality of web content produced part of employees' performance appraisal.

- Produce a target schedule for publication of content.
- Identify events which trigger the publication of new content, e.g. a new product launch, price change or a press release.
- Identify stages and responsibilities in updating – who specifies, who creates, who reviews, who checks, who publishes.
- Measure the usage of content through web analytics or get feedback from site users.
- Audit and publish content to show which is up-to-date.

Case Study 10 　 Learning from Amazon's culture of metrics

Context

Why a case study on Amazon? Surely everyone knows about Amazon and what it does? Yes, well, that's maybe true, but this case goes under the surface to review some of the 'insider secrets' of Amazon's early success and a focus on measurement and improvement that remains today.

Like eBay, **Amazon.com** was launched in 1995. The name reflected the vision of founder and CEO Jeff Bezos, to produce a large-scale phenomenon like the Amazon river. This ambition has proved justified since, just eight years later, Amazon passed the $5 billion sales mark – it took WalMart 20 years to achieve this.

Vision and strategy

On its investor relations site Amazon describes its current mission:

> We seek to be Earth's most customer-centric company for four primary customer sets: consumers, sellers, enterprises, and content creators.

This is now a generic statement, but a previous statements from SEC filings in 2008 is more specific:

> Relentlessly focus on customer experience by offering a wide selection of merchandise, low prices and convenience.

This focus on the customer has been there from the start: the 1997 SEC filing said Amazon would 'obsess over the customer'. Success here is shown by consistently high ratings at the American Customer Satisfaction Index (www.theacsi.org/the-american-customer-satisfaction-index#homelogo).

In each SEC filing Amazon explains how it uses an analytical approach to improve satisfaction and business performance by reiterating a comment in a letter to shareholders from Jeff Bezos when Amazon first became a publicly quoted company:

> We will continue to measure our programs and the effectiveness of our investments analytically, to jettison those that do not provide acceptable returns, and to step up our investment in those that work best. We will continue to learn from both our successes and our failures.

More recently, this approach has been applied to a range of business model innovations focussed on hardware and new services: Fire Tablet, Smartphone and TV, Echo (voice-activated speaker), grocery delivery in the West coast of the United States, Prime Instant Video, Prime Music, Amazon Fashion and expansion to Amazon Web Services (AWS). Responding to criticism of the Fire Phone, in an interview with *Business Insider* (2014) Bezos acknowledges that failure will inevitably happen with innovation. He says:

> I've made billions of dollars of failures at Amazon. com. Literally billions of dollars of failures. You might remember Pets.com or Kosmo.com. It was like getting a root canal with no anaesthesia. None of those things are fun. But they also don't matter.

Of course, achieving customer loyalty and repeat purchases has been key to Amazon's success. Many dot-coms failed because they succeeded in achieving awareness, but not loyalty. Amazon achieved both. In its SEC filing the company stresses how it seeks to achieve this:

> We work to earn repeat purchases by providing easy-to-use functionality, fast and reliable fulfilment, timely customer service, feature-rich content, and a trusted transaction environment. Key features of our websites include editorial and customer reviews; manufacturer product information; web pages tailored to individual preferences, such as recommendations and notifications; 1-Click® technology; secure payment systems; image uploads; searching on our websites as well as the Internet; browsing; and the ability to view selected interior pages and citations, and search the entire contents of many of the books we offer with our 'Look Inside the Book' and 'Search Inside the Book' features. Our community of online customers also creates feature-rich content, including product

reviews, online recommendation lists, wish lists, buying guides, and wedding and baby registries.

In fact, as is the practice for many online retailers, the lowest prices are for the most popular products, with less popular products commanding higher prices and a greater margin for Amazon. Free shipping offers are used to encourage increase in basket size since customers have to spend over a certain amount to receive free shipping. The level at which free shipping is set is critical to profitability and Amazon has changed it as competition has changed and for promotional reasons.

Amazon communicates the fulfilment promise in several ways including presentation of latest inventory availability information, delivery date estimates, and options for expedited delivery, as well as delivery shipment notifications and update facilities.

Competition

In its latest SEC filing Amazon describes the environment for its products and services as 'intensely competitive'. It views its main current and potential competitors as: (1) physical-world retailers, catalogue retailers, publishers, vendors, distributors and manufacturers of its products, many of which possess significant brand awareness, sales volume and customer bases, and some of which currently sell, or may sell, products or services through the Internet, mail order or direct marketing; (2) other online e-commerce sites; (3) a number of indirect competitors, including media companies, web portals, comparison shopping websites and web search engines, either directly or in collaboration with other retailers; and (4) companies that provide e-commerce services, including website development, third-party fulfilment and customer service.

Amazon believes the main competitive factors in its market segments include:

selection, price, availability, convenience, information, discovery, brand recognition, personalised services, accessibility, customer service, reliability, speed of fulfilment, ease of use, and ability to adapt to changing conditions, as well as our customers' overall experience and trust in transactions with us and facilitated by us on behalf of third-party sellers.

For services offered to business and individual sellers, additional competitive factors include the quality of services and tools, the ability to generate sales for third parties the company serves and the speed of performance for its services.

From auctions to marketplaces

Amazon auctions (known as 'zShops') were launched in March 1999, in large part as a response to the success of

eBay. They were promoted heavily from the home page, category pages and individual product pages. They give an example of how Amazon will stop initiatives that aren't successful. Today, competitive prices of products are available through third-party sellers in the 'Amazon Marketplace' which are integrated within the standard product listings. The strategy to offer such an auction facility was initially driven by the need to compete with eBay, but now the strategy has been adjusted such that Amazon describes it as part of the approach of low pricing. According to a 2014 interview with Jeff Bezos (Business Insider, 2014) Amazon now sells around 40 per cent of units through sellers, so enabling it to extend its range of products and improve stock availability.

Although it might be thought that Amazon would lose out on enabling its merchants to sell products at lower prices, in fact Amazon makes greater margin on these sales since merchants are charged a commission on each sale and it is the merchant who bears the cost of storing inventory and fulfilling the product to customers. As with eBay, Amazon is just facilitating the exchange of bits and bytes between buyers and sellers without the need to distribute physical products.

Marketing

Amazon does not reveal much about its marketing approach in its annual reports, but there seems to be a focus on online marketing channels. Amazon (2011) states: 'we direct customers to our websites primarily through a number of targeted online marketing channels, such as our Associates program, sponsored search, portal advertising, email marketing campaigns, and other initiatives'. These other initiatives may include outdoor and TV advertising, but they are not mentioned specifically. In this statement they also highlight the importance of customer loyalty tools. They say: 'while costs associated with free shipping are not included in marketing expense, we view free shipping offers and Amazon Prime as effective worldwide marketing tools, and intend to continue offering them indefinitely'.

How Amazon's 'culture of metrics' started

A common theme in Amazon's development is the drive to use a measured approach to all aspects of the business, beyond the finance. Marcus (2004) describes an occasion at a corporate 'boot-camp' in January 1997 when Amazon CEO Jeff Bezos 'saw the light'. 'At Amazon, we will have a Culture of Metrics', he said while addressing his senior staff. He went on to explain how web-based business gave Amazon an 'amazing window into human behaviour'. Marcus says:

Gone were the fuzzy approximations of focus groups, the anecdotal fudging and smoke blowing from the marketing department. A company like Amazon could (and did) record every move a visitor made, every last click and twitch of the mouse. As the data piled up into virtual heaps, hummocks and mountain ranges, you could draw all sorts of conclusions about their chimerical nature, the consumer. In this sense, Amazon was not merely a store, but an immense repository of facts. All we needed were the right equations to plug into them.

Marcus then goes on to give a fascinating insight into a breakout group discussion of how Amazon could better use measures to improve its performance. Marcus was in the Bezos group, brainstorming customer-centric metrics. Marcus (2004) summarises the dialogue, led by Bezos:

'First, we figure out which things we'd like to measure on the site', he said. 'For example, let's say we want a metric for customer enjoyment. How could we calculate that?'

There was silence. Then somebody ventured: 'How much time each customer spends on the site?'

'Not specific enough', Jeff said.

'How about the average number of minutes each customer spends on the site per session', someone else suggested. 'If that goes up, they're having a blast.'

'But how do we factor in purchase?' I [Marcus] said feeling proud of myself. 'Is that a measure of enjoyment?'

'I think we need to consider frequency of visits, too', said a dark-haired woman I didn't recognise. 'Lot of folks are still accessing the web with those creepy-crawly modems. Four short visits from them might be just as good as one visit from a guy with a T-1. Maybe better.'

'Good point', Jeff said. 'And anyway, enjoyment is just the start. In the end, we should be measuring customer ecstasy.'

It is interesting that Amazon was having this debate about the elements of RFM analysis *(described in Chapter 6)* in 1997, after already having achieved $16 million of revenue in the previous year. Of course, this is a minuscule amount compared with today's billions of dollars turnover. The important point was that this was the start of a focus on metrics, which can be seen through the description of Matt Round's work later in this case study.

From human to software-based recommendations

Amazon has developed internal tools to support this 'Culture of Metrics'. Marcus (2004) describes how the 'Creator Metrics' tool shows content creators how well their product listings and product copy are working. For each content editor, such as Marcus, it retrieves all recently posted documents including articles, interviews, booklists and features. For each one it then gives a conversion rate to sale plus the number of page views, adds (added to basket) and repels (content requested, but the back button then used). In time, the work of editorial reviewers, such as Marcus, was marginalised since Amazon found that the majority of visitors used the search tools rather than read editorial and they responded to the personalised recommendations as the matching technology improved (Marcus likens early recommendations techniques to 'going shopping with the village idiot').

Experimentation and testing at Amazon

The 'Culture of Metrics' also led to a test-driven approach to improving results at Amazon. Matt Round, speaking at E-metrics 2004 when he was director of personalisation at Amazon, describes the philosophy as 'data trumps intuitions'. He explained how Amazon used to have a lot of arguments about which content and promotion should go on the all-important home page or category pages. He described how every category VP wanted top-centre and how the Friday meetings about placements for next week were getting 'too long, too loud and lacked performance data'.

But today 'automation replaces intuitions' and real-time experimentation tests are always run to answer these questions since actual consumer behaviour is the best way to decide upon tactics.

Marcus (2004) also notes that Amazon has a culture of experiments of which A/B tests are key components. Examples where A/B tests are used include new home page design, moving features around the page, different algorithms for recommendations, changing search relevance rankings. These involve testing a new treatment against a previous control for a limited time of a few days or a week. The system will randomly show one or more treatments to visitors and measure a range of parameters such as units sold and revenue by category (and total), session time and session length. The new features will usually be launched if the desired metrics are statistically significantly better. Statistical tests are a challenge though, as distributions are not normal (they have a large mass at zero, for example, of no purchase). There are other challenges since multiple A/B tests are running every day and A/B tests may overlap and so conflict. There are also longer-term effects where some features are 'cool' for the first two weeks and the opposite effect where changing navigation may degrade performance temporarily. Amazon also finds that as its users evolve in their online experience, the way they act online has changed. This means that Amazon has to constantly test and evolve its features.

Technology

It follows that the Amazon technology infrastructure must readily support this culture of experimentation and this can be difficult to achieve with standardised content management. Amazon has achieved its competitive advantage through developing its technology internally and with a significant investment in this which may not be available to other organisations without the right focus on the online channels.

As Amazon explains in SEC (2005):

using primarily our own proprietary technologies, as well as technology licensed from third parties, we have implemented numerous features and functionality that simplify and improve the customer shopping experience, enable third parties to sell on our platform, and facilitate our fulfilment and customer service operations. Our current strategy is to focus our development efforts on continuous innovation by creating and enhancing the specialised, proprietary software that is unique to our business, and to license or acquire commercially-developed technology for other applications where available and appropriate. We continually invest in several areas of technology, including our seller platform; **A9.com,** *our wholly-owned subsidiary focussed on search technology on* **www.A9.com** *and other Amazon sites; web services; and digital initiatives.*

Round (2004) describes the technology approach as 'distributed development and deployment'. Pages such as the home page have a number of content 'pods' or 'slots' which call web services for features. This makes it relatively easy to change the content in these pods and even change the location of the pods on-screen. Amazon uses a flowable or fluid page design, unlike many sites, which enables it to make the most of real-estate on-screen.

Technology also supports more standard e-retail facilities. SEC (2005) states:

We use a set of applications for accepting and validating customer orders, placing and tracking orders with suppliers, managing and assigning inventory to customer orders, and ensuring proper shipment of products to customers. Our transaction-processing systems handle millions of items, a number of different status inquiries, multiple shipping addresses, gift wrapping requests and multiple shipment methods. These systems allow the customer to choose whether to receive single or several shipments based on availability and to track the progress of each order. These applications also manage the process of accepting, authorising and charging customer credit cards.

Data-driven automation

Round (2004) said that 'Data is king at Amazon'. He gave many examples of data-driven automation including customer channel preferences, managing the way content is displayed to different user types, such as new releases and top-sellers, merchandising and recommendation (showing related products and promotions) and also advertising through paid search (automatic ad generation and bidding).

The automated search advertising and bidding system for paid search has had a big impact at Amazon. Sponsored links were initially done by humans, but this was unsustainable due to the range of products at Amazon. The automated program generates keywords, writes ad creative, determines best landing page, manages bids, measures conversion rates, profit per converted visitor and updates bids. Again the problem of volume is there: Matt Round described how the book *How to Make Love like a Porn Star* by Jenna Jameson received tens of thousands of clicks from pornography-related searches, but few actually purchased the book. So the update cycle must be quick to avoid large losses.

There is also an automated email measurement and optimisation system. The campaign calendar used to be manually managed with relatively weak measurement and it was costly to schedule and use. A new system:

- automatically optimises content to improve customer experience;
- avoids sending an email campaign that has low click-through or a high unsubscribe rate;
- includes inbox management (avoid sending multiple emails/week);
- has a growing library of automated email programs covering new releases and recommendations.

But there are challenges if promotions are too successful if inventory isn't available.

Your recommendations

'Customers Who Bought X ... also bought Y' is Amazon's signature feature. Round (2004) describes how Amazon relies on acquiring and then crunching a massive amount of data. Every purchase, every page viewed and every search is recorded. So there are now two new versions: 'Customers who shopped for X also shopped for ...', and 'Customers who searched for X also bought ...'. Amazon also has a system codenamed 'Goldbox', which is a cross-sell and awareness-raising tool. Items are discounted to encourage purchases in new categories!

He also describes the challenge of techniques for sifting patterns from noise (sensitivity filtering), and clothing and toy catalogues change frequently so recommendations become out-of-date. The main challenges though are the massive data size arising from millions of customers, millions of items and recommendations made in real time.

Partnership strategy

As Amazon grew, its share price growth enabled partnership or acquisition with a range of companies in different sectors. Marcus (2004) describes how Amazon partnered with **Drugstore.com** (pharmacy), **Living.com** (furniture), **Pets.com** (pet supplies), **Wineshopper.com** (wines), **HomeGrocer.com** (groceries), **Sothebys.com** (auctions) and **Kozmo.com** (urban home delivery). In most cases, Amazon purchased an equity stake in these partners, so that it would share in their prosperity. It also charged them fees for placements on the Amazon site to promote and drive traffic to their sites. Similarly, Amazon charged publishers for prime position to promote books on its site which caused an initial hue-and-cry, but this abated when it was realised that paying for prominent placements was widespread in traditional booksellers and supermarkets. Many of these new online companies failed in 1999 and 2000, but Amazon had covered the potential for growth and was not pulled down by these partners, even though for some, such as **Pets.com**, it had an investment of 50 per cent.

Analysts sometimes refer to 'Amazoning a sector', meaning that one company becomes so dominant in an online sector such as book retail that it becomes very difficult for others to achieve market share. In addition to developing, communicating and delivering a very strong proposition, Amazon has been able to consolidate its strength in different sectors through its partnership arrangements and through using technology to facilitate product promotion and distribution via these partnerships. The Amazon retail platform enables other retailers to sell products online using the Amazon user interface and infrastructure through its 'Syndicated Stores' programme. For example, in the UK, Waterstones (www.waterstones.co.uk) is one of the largest traditional bookstores. It found competition with online so expensive and challenging, that eventually it entered a partnership arrangement where Amazon markets and distributes its books online in return for a commission online. Similarly, in the US the large book retailer Borders used the Amazon merchant platform for distributing its products. Such partnerships help Amazon extend its reach into the customer-base of other suppliers, and of course, customers who buy in one category such as books can be encouraged to purchase into other areas such as clothing or electronics.

Another form of partnership referred to above is the Amazon Marketplace, which enables Amazon customers and other retailers to sell their new and used books and other goods alongside the regular retail listings. A similar partnership approach is the Amazon 'Merchants@' programme which enables third-party merchants (typically larger than those that sell via the Amazon Marketplace) to sell their products via Amazon. Amazon earns money either through fixed fees or sales commissions per unit. This arrangement can help customers, who get a wider choice of products from a range of suppliers with the convenience of purchasing them through a single checkout process.

Finally, Amazon has also facilitated formation of partnerships with smaller companies through its affiliates programme. Internet legend records that Jeff Bezos, the creator of Amazon, was chatting to someone at a cocktail party who wanted to sell books about divorce via her website. Subsequently, **Amazon.com** launched its Associates Program in July 1996 and it is still going strong. Amazon does not use an affiliate network *(explained in Chapter 9)*, which would take commissions from sale, but thanks to the strength of its brand has developed its own affiliate programme. Amazon has created tiered performance-based incentives to encourage affiliates to sell more Amazon products.

Marketing communications

In its SEC filings Amazon states that the aims of its communications strategy are (unsurprisingly) to:

- Increase customer traffic to its websites.
- Create awareness of its products and services.
- Promote repeat purchases.
- Develop incremental product and service revenue opportunities.
- Strengthen and broaden the **Amazon.com** brand name.

Amazon also believes that its most effective marketing communications are a consequence of its focus on continuously improving the customer experience. This then creates word-of-mouth promotion which is effective in acquiring new customers and may also encourage repeat customer visits.

As well as this, Marcus (2004) describes how Amazon used the personalisation enabled through technology to reach out to a difficult-to-reach market which Bezos originally called 'the hard middle'. Bezos's view was that it was easy to reach ten people (you called them on the phone) or the 10 million people who bought the most popular products (you placed a superbowl ad), but more difficult to reach those in between. The search facilities in the search engine and on the Amazon site, together with its product recommendation features, meant that Amazon could connect its products with the interests of these people.

Online advertising techniques include paid search marketing, interactive ads on portals, email campaigns and search engine optimisation. These are automated as far as possible, as described earlier in the case study. As previously mentioned, the affiliate programme is also important in driving visitors to Amazon, and Amazon offers a wide range of methods of linking to its site to help improve conversion. For example, affiliates can use straight text links leading direct to a product page and they also offer a range of dynamic banners which feature different content such as books about Internet marketing or a search box.

Amazon also uses cooperative advertising arrangements, better known as 'contra-deals', with some vendors and other third parties. For example, a print advertisement in 2005 for a particular product such as a wireless router with a free wireless laptop card promotion was to feature a specific Amazon URL in the ad. In product fulfilment packs, Amazon may include a leaflet for a non-competing online company such as **Figleaves.com** (lingerie) or Expedia (travel). In return, Amazon leaflets may be included in customer communications from the partner brands.

The associates programme directs customers to Amazon websites by enabling independent websites to make millions of products available to their audiences with fulfilment performed by Amazon or third parties.

Amazon pays commissions to hundreds of thousands of participants in the associates programme when their customer referrals result in product sales. In addition, Amazon offers everyday free shipping options worldwide and recently announced **Amazon.com** Prime in the US, its first membership programme in which members receive free two-day shipping and discounted overnight shipping. Although marketing expenses do not include the costs of free shipping or promotional offers, Amazon views such offers as effective marketing tools.

Questions

1 By referring to the case study, Amazon's website for your country and your experience of Amazon offline communications evaluate how well Amazon communicates its core proposition and promotional offers.

2 Using the case study, characterise Amazon's approach to marketing communications.

3 Explain what distinguishes Amazon in its uses of technology for competitive advantage.

4 How does the Amazon 'culture of metrics' differ from that in other organisations from your experience.

Summary

1 A structured measurement and improvement programme is necessary to collect measures to assess a website's effectiveness. Action can then be taken to adjust the website strategy or promotional efforts. A measurement programme involves:

- Stage 1: Defining a measurement process.
- Stage 2: Defining a metrics framework.
- Stage 3: Selecting of tools for data collection, reporting, optimisation and analysis.

2 Measures of Internet marketing effectiveness can be categorised as assessing:

- *Level 1: Business effectiveness* – these measure the impact of the website on the whole business, and look at financial measures such as revenue and profit and promotion of corporate awareness.
- *Level 2: Marketing effectiveness* – these measure the number of leads and sales achieved via the Internet and effect of the Internet on retention rates and other aspects of the marketing mix such as branding.
- *Level 3: Internet marketing effectiveness* – these measures assess how well the site is being promoted, and do so by reviewing the popularity of the site and how good it is at delivering customer needs.

3 The measures of effectiveness referred to above are collected in two main ways – online and offline – or in combination.

4 Online measures are obtained from a web-server log file or using browser-based techniques. They indicate the number of visitors to a site, which pages they visit and where they originated from. These also provide a breakdown of visitors through time or by country.

5 Offline measures are marketing outcomes such as enquiries or sales that are directly attributable to the website. Other measures of the effectiveness are available through surveying customers using questionnaires, interviews and focus groups.

6 Managing a website requires clear responsibilities to be identified for different roles. These include the roles of content owners and site developers, and those ensuring that the content conforms with company and legal requirements.

7 To produce a good-quality website, standards are required to enforce uniformity in terms of:

- site look and feel;
- corporate branding;
- quality of content.

Exercises

Self-assessment exercises

1 Why are standards necessary for controlling website management? What aspects of the site do standards seek to control?
2 Explain the difference between hits and page impressions. How are these measured?
3 How should social media marketing effectiveness be assessed?
4 Why should content development be distributed through a large organisation?
5 Describe the different types of measures that should be used to review and improve digital marketing.
6 How can focus groups and interviews be used to assess website effectiveness?
7 Explain how a web log file analyser works. What are its limitations?
8 Why is it useful to integrate the collection of online and offline metrics?

Essay and discussion questions

1 'Corporate standards for a website's format and update process are likely to stifle the creative development of a site and reduce its value to customers.' Discuss.
2 'Most companies collect data about digital marketing activities, but few derive much value from it'. Discuss possible reasons for this assertion.
3 You have been appointed manager of a website for a car manufacturer and have been asked to refine the existing online measurement and improvement programme. Explain, in detail, the steps you would take to develop this programme.
4 The first version of a website for a financial services company has been live for a year. Originally it was developed by a team of two people, and was effectively 'brochureware'. The second version of the site is intended to contain more detailed information, and will involve contributions from ten different product areas. You have been asked to define a procedure for controlling updates to the site. Write a document detailing the update procedure, which also explains the reasons for each control.

Examination questions

1 Why are standards necessary to control the process of updating a website? Give three examples of different aspects of a website that need to be controlled.

2 Explain the following terms concerning measurement of website effectiveness:
   a hits;
   b page impressions;
   c referring pages.
3 Measurement of websites concerns the recording of key events involving customers using a website. Briefly explain five different types of event.
4 Describe and briefly explain the purpose of the different stages involved in updating an existing document on a commercial website.
5 Outline different types of measures for reviewing the effectiveness of social media marketing.
6 Give three reasons explaining why a website may have to integrate with existing marketing information systems and databases within a company.
7 You have been appointed manager of a website and have been asked to develop a metrics programme. Briefly explain the steps you would take to develop this programme.
8 If a customer can be persuaded to register his or her name and email address with a website, how can this information be used for site measurement purposes?

References

Adams, C., Kapashi, N., Neely, A. and Marr, B. (2000) Managing with measures: measuring e-business performance, Accenture white paper. Survey conducted in conjunction with Cranfield School of Management.

Agrawal, V., Arjona, V. and Lemmens, R. (2001) E-performance: the path to rational exuberance, *McKinsey Quarterly*, 1, 31–43.

Altimeter (2010) Framework: the social media ROI pyramid, 13 December 2010, by Jeremiah Owyang; **www.web-strategist.com/blog/2010/12/13/framework-the-social-media-roi-pyramid**.

Amazon (2011) Amazon 2010 full year report/SEC filing, Amazon Investor relations site, published 27 January.

Business Insider (2014) I asked Jeff Bezos the tough questions – no profits, the book controversies, the phone flop – and he showed why Amazon is such a huge success. Interview by Henry Blodget, 13 December 2014, **http://uk.businessinsider.com/amazons-jeff-bezos-on-profits-failure-succession-big-bets-2014–12**.

Chaffey, D. (2000) Achieving Internet marketing success, *The Marketing Review*, 1(1), 35–60.

Friedman, L. and Furey, T. (1999) *The Channel Advantage*, Butterworth-Heinemann, Oxford.

Grossnickle, J. and Raskin, O. (2001) *The Handbook of Online Marketing Research: Knowing your Customer Using the Net*, McGraw-Hill, New York.

Kotler, P. (1997) *Marketing Management – Analysis, Planning, Implementation and Control*, Prentice-Hall, Englewood Cliffs, NJ.

Lynch, P. and Horton, S. (1999) *Web Style Guide: Basic Design Principles for Creating Websites*, Yale University Press, New Haven, CT.

Malhotra, N. (1999) *Marketing Research: An Applied Orientation*, Prentice-Hall, Upper Saddle River, NJ.

Marcus, J. (2004) *Amazonia. Five Years at the Epicentre of the Dot-com Juggernaut*, The New Press, New York.

Neely, A., Adams, C. and Kennerley, M. (2002) *The Performance Prism: The Scorecard for Measuring and Managing Business Success*, Financial Times/Prentice Hall, Harlow.

Register, C.A., Albaum, G. and Smith, S.M. (2014) Topic sensitivity and Internet survey design: a cross-cultural/national study, *Journal of Marketing Theory and Practice*, 22(1), 91–102.

Round, M. (2004) Presentation to E-metrics, London, May 2005, **www.emetrics.org**.

SEC (2005) United States Securities and Exchange Commission Submission Form 10-K from Amazon. For the fiscal year ended 31 December 2004.

SEC (2008) United States Securities and Exchange Commission Submission Form 10-K from Amazon. For the fiscal year ended 31 December 2007.

SmartInsights (2010) Website Feedback Tools Review, Dave Chaffey, **http://bit.ly/ smartfeedback**.

Stern, M.J., Bilgen, I. and Dillman, D.A. (2014) The state of survey methodology challenges, dilemmas, and new frontiers in the era of the tailored design, *Field Methods*, 26(3), 284–301.

Sterne, J. (2001) *World Wide Web Marketing*, 3rd edn, Wiley, New York. Web Analytics Association (2011) Web Analytics Association Outlook: 2011 Survey report, February, **www.webanalyticsassociation.org**.

Wilson, H. (2008) *The Multichannel Challenge*, Butterworth-Heinemann, Oxford. Copyright Elsevier.

Wisner, J. and Fawcett, S. (1991) Link firm strategy to operating decisions through performance measurement, *Production and Inventory Management Journal* (Third Quarter), 5–11.

Weblinks

Web analytics resources

- ABCe (**www.abce.org.uk**). Audited Bureau of Circulation is standard for magazines in the UK. This is the electronic auditing part. Useful for definitions and examples of traffic for UK organisations.
- E-metrics (**www.emetrics.org**). Jim Sterne's site has many resources for online marketing metrics.
- Marketing Experiments (**www.marketingexperiments.com**). Summarises approaches to testing to improve website marketing effectiveness.
- Smart Insights Web Analytics Strategy (**www.smartinsights.com/managing-digital-marketing/web-analytics-strategy**). This Quick Guide from Dave Chaffey's site has all the main resources for students.
- Web Analytics Association (**www.webanalyticsassociation.org**). The site of the trade association for web analytics has useful definitions, articles and forums on this topic.
- Web Analytics Demystified (**www.webanalyticsdemystified.com**). A site to support Eric Petersen's books with a range of content.

Web analytics expertise

- Avinash Kaushik's Occam's Razor blog (**www.kaushik.net**). Avinash is an expert in web analytics and his popular blog shows how web analytics should be used to control and improve return on e-marketing investments.
- Cardinal Path blog (**www.cardinalpath.com/blog**) Practical discussions of web analytics.
- Justin Cutroni (**www.cutroni.com**). A specialist web analytics blog giving guidance on how to tailor Google Analytics.
- Lunametrics (**www.lunametrics.com**) One of the best advanced blogs on Google Analytics giving practical advice.

Social media marketing analytics

These are the blogs of three of the leading commentators on social media marketing who discuss how to measure return from social media marketing.

- Jay Baer (www.convinceandconvert.com)
- Brian Solis (www.briansolis.com)
- Altimeter (www.altimeter.com)

Chapter 11

Business-to-consumer digital marketing practice

Chapter at a glance

Main topics

- The consumer perspective: online consumer behaviour 596
- The retail perspective: online retailing 606
- Implications for e-retail marketing strategy 612

Case studies

Case study 11: ASOS reinvents fashion retail 614

Learning objectives

After reading this chapter, the reader should be able to:

- understand online consumer behaviour, and more specifically how consumer profiles and online experiences shape and influence the extent to which individuals are likely to engage with the digital marketplace
- explain the development of online retailing and describe various types of online retailing activities and strategies
- begin to develop an understanding from a retailer's perspective of the strategic implications of trading online in consumer markets.

Questions for marketers

Key questions for marketing managers related to this chapter are:

- What are the key decisions that a consumer-facing organisation should consider when developing a consumer-facing strategy?
- What are customer expectations of web-based services?
- How can we maximise commercial results for our site?
- How can we integrate social commerce and social media?

Scan code
to find the
latest updates
for topics in
this chapter

Links to other chapters

This chapter builds on concepts and frameworks introduced earlier in the book. The main related chapters are as follows:

- Chapter 2, which provides an introduction to the characteristics of Internet consumer behaviour
- Chapter 4, which introduces strategic approaches to exploiting the Internet
- Chapter 6, which examines customer relationship management issues
- Chapter 7, covering issues relating to successful site development and operations.

Introduction

Business-to-consumer (B2C) markets have made a significant contribution to the commercial development of the Internet, encouraging wide-scale use of transactional e-commerce sites by a diverse and increasingly global range of consumers.

This chapter explores some of the key issues which have an impact on the growth and development of online B2C markets. It focuses on the retail sector and begins with looking at online consumers (who they are, their expectations, how online experiences affect the motivation to shop online) and then retailers (the meaning and scope of the term *online retailing* and the different ways in which digital and Internet technologies are used to create a virtual *retail channel*). The chapter concludes with a discussion of the factors affecting the development of successful e-retail strategies.

We start with a review summary of key digital marketing practice questions which applies to companies discussed in both Chapters 11 and 12. These are key management questions marketers have to review to develop a digital marketing plan (see Digital marketing insight 11.1).

Digital marketing insight 11.1	The Smart Insights planning template for digital strategy development

As an alternative perspective on strategy from that which is covered in Chapters 4 and 5, the RACE Planning framework we introduced in Chapter 1 gives a structure to review the opportunities and challenges for managing digital marketing in the different types of organisations covered in Chapters 11 and 12. These are some of the key strategic questions that need to be addressed by managers and can be viewed as a summary of actions to be taken.

Planning questions

These overview questions review strategies to maximise efficiency and effectiveness of the channel. Key questions to consider are:

Q1. Do we have a clear strategy to support growth of our online channels?

Q2. How do we align our online marketing activities to support our business goals?

Q3. Which audiences are we targeting and how do we attract them to do business with us online?

Q4. Which insights do we have about our customer characteristics (profiles), needs from online services (requirements and intent) and perceptions of our service (quality gap)?

Q5. Have we analysed our marketplace to understand the types of online sites and influencers that affect sales?

Q6. How is our value proposition and brand offer supported by online channels?

Q7. How do we integrate channels to support customer journeys?

Q8. How do we achieve sales growth through customer lifecycle strategies, i.e. reach strategy, interaction and conversion strategy and ongoing engagement strategy.

Reach strategy questions

These questions should be asked to determine approaches to reach prospects, existing customers and raising awareness on a website or other online presences to encourage visits and interaction. Key questions here are:

Q1. Do we have visibility of actual and target performance for volume, quality and value for our online visitors?

Q2. What is the right channel media mix of paid, owned and earned media (inbound/content marketing) to meet our goals?

Q3. Have we maximised the efficiency of each channel? Which are the priorities?

Q4. Which audiences are we targeting or not targeting through online media?

Q5. What are our core messages and offers to encourage use of online channels?

Q6. Are we putting sufficient time into managing relationships with partners and influencers?

Q7. How do we route traffic and manage customer journeys to maximise effectiveness?

Q8. How do we best integrate ALL channels?

Q9. How do we leverage the viral/word-of-mouth effect from viral channels?

Q10. Are our social presences effective and are we measuring reputation?

Act and conversion strategy questions

Act and conversion refers to achieving interaction and participation to deliver sales leads. For a retail site, this is initial engagement with a site to browse products and then add them to product categories. In financial services this is encouraging a quote or application, while in travel it is encouraging interest in destinations. Conversion may happen online or offline, so steps are taken to facilitate these customer journeys. Key questions are:

Q1. How do we appeal to different audiences, needs, behaviour, referrers?

Q2. What are our key value messages?

Q3. How do we improve the customer experience to improve conversion and satisfaction across different hardware and software platforms such as desktop and mobile access?

Q4. How do we reduce friction to make more efficient customer journeys through the right call-to-action?

Q5. Is our content effective in supporting conversion?

Q6. Are social media and user-generated content ineffective in supporting conversion?

Q7. Are we maximising the value generated per visit?

Q8. Are we following up on leads effectively?

Q9. Are we using web analytics effectively to improve results through combining the right metrics, process, people and tools?

Engage and retention strategy questions

The final set of questions refer to approaches to build long-term relationships with customers through online media:

Q1. How well do we know the needs, wants, characteristics and value of existing customers?

Q2. How do we increase customer lifetime value?

Q3. What is the gap between customer satisfaction needs and delivery and do we improve satisfaction?

Q4. What content, offers, experiences will engage different audiences?

Q5. How should we manage customer communities to grow our brand?

Q6. How do we create an integrated lifecycle email + social media customer communications programme?

Q7. How can we use customer advocacy to improve results?

Key themes and concepts

This chapter considers online B2C markets from two distinct perspectives:

- *The consumer perspective* – the first part of the chapter focuses on the online consumer, namely his/her profile, which has been found to strongly influence the extent to which particular consumers shop online and also online shopping experiences, which are likely to shape online shopping intentions.
- *The company perspective* – the second part of the chapter examines the development of online retailing, types of online strategies, factors likely to affect how retailers develop online retailing activities, managerial and strategic challenges.

This chapter provides illustrative case studies, examples of consumer and retailer behaviour and graphics as supporting material. Academic articles are used to support underlying theoretical issues and concepts.

The consumer perspective: online consumer behaviour

Arguably, levels of consumer demand for online shopping and services determine the size of e-retail markets and when or if a market saturation point will be reached for online purchasing. Various influences, such as ease of access to the Internet, levels of competency in use of the technology, perceived benefits of engaging in online shopping and various demographic variables, have been identified as key factors likely to impact on whether an individual shops online or not.

Online retailing, sometimes referred to as e-retailing , offers the consumer an experience which is different from shopping in a physical store. Web-based stores can: be open continuously around the clock; offer instantaneous and individually tailored promotions; use dynamic pricing to enable real-time prices, which reflect current market demand; provide recommendations and reviews from other site users. Indeed, many consumers, even if they do not intend to buy online, turn to the Internet to find information about a product in the early part of the purchase decision-making process. An example of an online brand, which facilitates comparison of products and prices, is **Kelkoo.com**. The origins of the name from the French phrase '*Quel coût?*' can be interpreted as 'At what price?' or even 'What a bargain'. As a result of the innovative characteristics of the online shopping environment, the online consumer experience can become an elective and very goal-orientated activity whereby consumers go to the Internet to seek the particular products and services they wish to buy. Perea *et al.* (2004) suggest there are various factors, including ease of use, enjoyment and individual consumer traits, which will determine whether an individual will become an avid Internet shopper, an occasional shopper, or just a *browser*. The next section explores who are the customers who shop online?

Who are the online customers?

Many researchers have written about online consumer behaviour and a very wide array of factors and variables have been cited as influencing the extent to which individuals are likely to shop online. Hoffman *et al.* (2004), focussed on the impact of demographics, and highlighted inequities of Internet access based on race and gender that still occur. Source *et al.* (2005) looked at age and found that 'while older shoppers search for significantly fewer products than their younger counterparts they actually purchase as much as the younger consumer'. Doherty and Ellis-Chadwick (2006) suggest there is a large body of literature looking at online consumer behaviour and the variables can be grouped into two broad categories: studies of *consumer profiles* and studies of *consumer experiences*.

The consumer profile

A consumer's profile can strongly influence where, when and how an individual shops online and also have important marketing implications. We can break the consumer profile down into two distinct sub-categories: classification variables and character variables.

Classification variables are those personal attributes that tend to remain static throughout an individual's lifetime or evolve slowly over time. These variables are particularly useful for marketers as they can help to *identify* particular consumers and target groups. Moreover, according to Jobber and Ellis-Chadwick (2013), profile segmentation variables can be used to group consumers together in a meaningful way so they can be reached by suitable media communications. See Table 11.1 for a list of classification variables and possible implications for online target marketing. Remember that while many

Table 11.1	Consumer profile: classification variables

Profile variable	Online marketing impact
Age	Age can affect levels of access to technology, computer literacy and, eventually, the extent to which individuals use the Internet as part of their shopping routines
Education	Education can affect how an individual uses the Internet, e.g. university students find it is not only useful for shopping but indispensable to support their studies
Employment status	Employment places time constraints on online shopping behaviour, i.e. when and where individuals can access online shopping channels
Gender	Originally, male consumers made more purchases and bought higher ticket items online than females. But now this has changed; according to research by Comscore (2014) women account for 57 per cent of online sales. This upwards growth trend is likely to continue as typically, (in the UK) women are responsible for 83 per cent of purchases (on- and offline) (Bignell, 2013)
Geography	Location is an important consideration: where people live can affect the potential size of the online market; Asia now has the largest number of Internet users, followed by the European Union. Interestingly the USA no longer has the highest number of Internet users. Also, shoppers living in remote locations are likely to do more online shopping than those who live in or near a large conurbation
Household size	Household size has the potential to affect the number of people involved in purchasing decisions and the direction of influence. For example, research has shown that in Europe children and teenagers can have a strong influence on purchasing based on their levels of computing competency
Household type	Household type has the potential to affect product and service requirements; major shifts towards single-person households have led to a shift in purchasing patterns and times of purchasing. Online, such households can create logistical difficulties when delivering bulky and perishable goods. Interestingly over three-quarters of all households with children have access to the Internet as opposed to just over half of households without children
Income	Income affects purchasing power and also influences whether individuals have access to the Internet. In the UK, AB, C1, C2 socio-economic groups are significantly more likely to have access to the Internet and to subsequently shop online than groupings D, E. Income is positively related to a tendency to shop online
Mobility	Mobility affects channel access; less mobile targets may be encouraged to shop online. This also applies to macro-populations, which are poorly served by public and private transport
Race and ethnicity	Race and ethnicity affects access to technology and economic circumstances. In the US, the number of African Americans with Internet access is increasing to over 50 per cent but this sector of the population still lags behind the Caucasians and Hispanics. See Mini case study 11.1 for further insight into the uptake of online shopping around the globe

consumers have desktop access to the Internet, there will be larger differences in access to smartphone and tablet devices, particularly between different countries, and this will constrain the experiences these enable the merchant to offer.

Mini case study 11.1 — Online retail business is booming in Europe and BRIC nations

Consumers everywhere are 'buying into' the idea of shopping online. Online retailing has been growing at an average of 18 per cent per annum globally since 2010 (Figure 11.1) (Cushman and Wakefield, 2013).

The Internet is a disruptive technological innovation and its impact on retailing has been profound and as a result many businesses are changing the channels they use to sell their goods and services. In some parts of the world, retailers have been quick off the mark in developing their own branded e-commerce stores, whereas in other parts of the globe e-marketplaces dominate. The USA remains ahead of the rest of the globe, with the highest proportion of online shoppers per head of population, but in Western Europe the United Kingdom, Germany and the Netherlands are catching up fast. Retailers in these nations seized the Internet opportunity early and have been engaging in online trade since the mid-1990s and now have well-developed branded retail operations operating across many different retail categories, including food, fashion, health and beauty products. In Russia, China, India and Brazil the Internet has not been seen as a viable channel to market until more recently but these nations are now hot on the heels of the early adopting nations. China is currently the second largest e-retail market on the globe, with India, Russia and Brazil experiencing increasing demand from online shoppers. As online retailing develops it is fascinating to see how communities of businesses and their shoppers are shaping the online shopping experience to suit their own needs. Read online to find out where online shopping is booming.

Branded online shopping in Europe is led by the UK

While there is diversity in the levels of adoption of online retailing, the UK has the most developed online retail industry, which currently accounts for about 13 per cent of retail sales. Individual UK shoppers spend an average of over £1000 a year online. In Germany the average online spend is just under £1000 a year and accounts for around 10 per cent of total retail sales. The French spend just over £700 per annum. In the

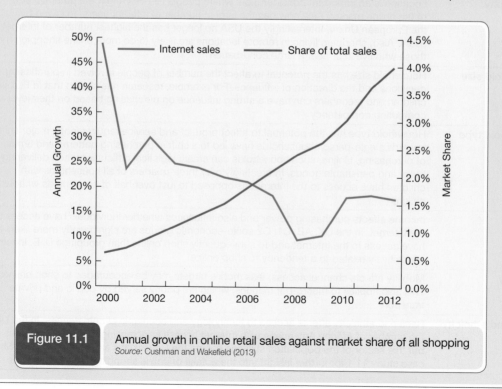

Figure 11.1 — Annual growth in online retail sales against market share of all shopping
Source: Cushman and Wakefield (2013)

Netherlands the figure is just over £600 and in Sweden around £500 average per annum and in all of these nations the prediction is for continuing rapid growth in the number of online shoppers. UK retailers have been meeting the needs of the ever-demanding online consumers and are leading the way in online shopping development. Many leading high-street brands operate highly sophisticated multichannel operations, enabling them to offer shoppers a seamless way to shop at any time of the day; through a computer, a mobile phone or by visiting a store. As there are more shoppers and more retailers offering more products online, consumers are changing their shopping habits and making fewer visits to high street stores. The impact of this shift in preference of where to shop is having far-reaching effects and the Retail Research Centre suggests that by 2018 a fifth of all retail sales in the UK will take place online. This trend is likely to have a significant effect on the shape of the physical High Street and more stores can be expected to disappear.

Russia

Russia is experiencing rapid growth in the number of Internet users, with more unique users online than Germany, France and the UK. While online shopping is in its infancy there is rapidly growing demand for Internet-based services. The economy in Russia has been making the transition from being a centrally planned Soviet system to a more free market-orientated economy. Such major changes to the economy have unique implications and opportunities for adoption and development of online retailing. New technology is adopted and structural challenges from the old regime are being overcome. There is a retail boom taking place and the economic climate is generating opportunities for development both on- and offline. Russian retailers are beginning to develop a vibrant emerging online economy and this has stimulated private consumption online as a result of higher incomes, greater employment and better access to consumer credit. Furthermore, Russians are increasingly becoming homeowners and this is also driving demand for household products and other consumer goods. Indeed, retail industry leaders have reported significant increases in trade – e.g. Magnit (grocery market leader) (Figure 11.2) has seen the company grow by 35 per cent per year – but there are some significant barriers for retailers wishing to expand online, among them access to reliable logistics, reliable financial and payment services. Centres of retailer activity tend to be concentrated in major cities such as Moscow and St Petersburg, leaving large areas of the country without access to any

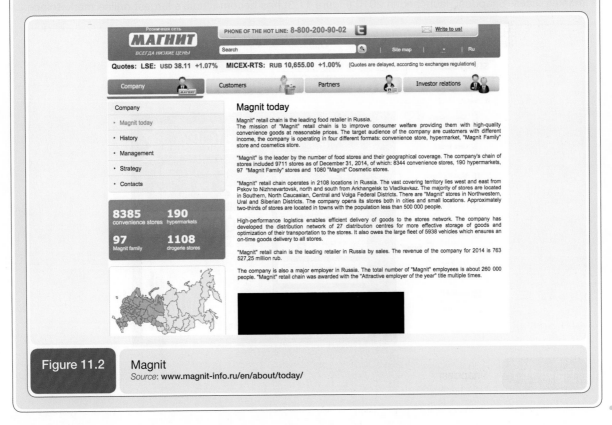

Figure 11.2	Magnit
	Source: www.magnit-info.ru/en/about/today/

substantive retail provision. Given the geographical spread of population in Russia, retail provision is either highly concentrated or highly fragmented. However, this is not deterring online shoppers. The Russians are developing their own unique approach to online retailing to overcome these barriers. Retail showrooms and stores where shoppers can go to collect and pay for pre-ordered goods are becoming increasingly popular.

China

China is rapidly becoming the world's most vibrant market for online shopping, with over $200 billion in sales and an annual growth rate of 120 per cent. The key destination for online shoppers in China is digital marketplaces like Taobao and **360buy.com** rather than individual retail brand websites. Online shopping is changing the economic landscape, with a shift away from an investment-orientated society towards one driven by consumption. Internet retailing is affecting consumption patterns in small and mid-sized cities as well as the largest conurbations and it is suggested that a key driver of the uptake of online shopping in more remote parts of China is access to branded goods, which are otherwise unavailable. Apparel, household and educational products are the most popular online. Arguably, in China, online retailing is set to lead the development of retail markets due to the complexities and geography of setting up a country-wide store-based operation. Online is giving Chinese businesses access to a flexible, responsive and rapidly growing marketplace.

India

The retail sector in India is booming both on- and offline. India is a relative latecomer to the online shopping revolution but it is predicted that online sales will grow by 50 per cent annually in the next few years. The country is already the third largest nation of Internet users, with 120 million Internet users and the rapid uptake of mobile commerce is predicted to increase the number of users to over 330 million by 2015. Social media is helping to drive the development of online retailing. Increasingly wealthy populations of young Internet-savvy customers are spending more time and money online and in doing so are influencing shopping trends. Amongst the popular products online are books, consumer electronics, travel, financial services, apparel and beauty care. Online shopping activity is concentrated in major urban conurbations with Mumbai being the main centre followed by Delhi and Kolkata. A large proportion of the purchases are conducted in online marketplaces. Snapdeal, launched in 2010 (Figure 11.3) has become India's largest online marketplace.

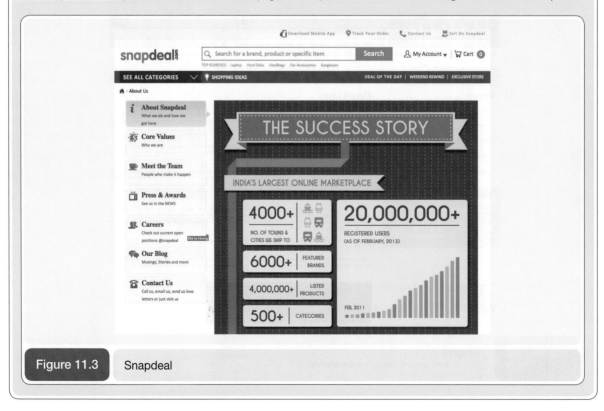

| Figure 11.3 | Snapdeal |

Currently, the Internet accounts for a small proportion of India's GDP but the predictions are that an Internet boom is just around the corner for Internet retailers.

Brazil

Brazil is in the early stages of developing online retailing as more and more consumers gain access to the Internet. However, retailers face difficulties with providing good-quality services, reducing delays in deliveries and returns policies. Online retailing is mainly in the key urban centres. Nevertheless, young Latin Americans are embracing mobile technology, and this is becoming a key driver in the development of online shopping. Brazilian retailers will still have to overcome issues of security, and access to broadband and mobile infrastructure in more remote regions. Also there is still resistance to online shopping from older generations who like to shop in the malls, where they enjoy the personal service offered by retailers (O'Toole, 2013).

Character variables are less straightforward to understand and identify as they comprise any attributes of a consumer's perceptions, beliefs and attitudes, which might influence online behaviour and also shape an individual's intentions to shop online – e.g. innovativeness, enjoyment, skills and experience and emotions. It is important to recognise that character variables are more likely to develop, change and be significantly modified over time by online shopping experiences than classification variables. For example, if a consumer has negative beliefs about, say, privacy and security of online transactions, which are due to *lack of computer skills*, these *beliefs* are likely to shape negative *attitudes* towards the Internet and reduce the *intention* to shop online. Conversely, if a consumer *believes* the Internet is, say, *easy to use*, they are more likely to have a positive *attitude* towards the idea of online shopping and ultimately have an increased *intention* to shop online. Each stance may be continually reinforced by positive or negative feedback from online shopping experiences. See Figure 11.4 for a model of how character variables interact.

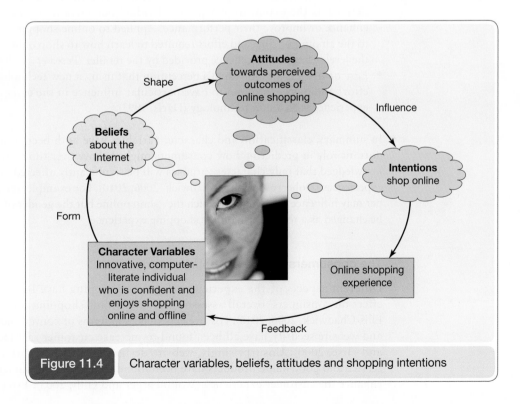

| Figure 11.4 | Character variables, beliefs, attitudes and shopping intentions |

Consumers' beliefs about a range of variables might ultimately shape their attitudes towards the Internet and their purchasing intentions. Examples include:

- *Security and privacy of information* – customers have an expectation that if they are prepared to provide detailed personal and financial information it will be stored securely. If this is not the case, personal belief, attitudes and intentions to shop online are likely to be negatively affected when a case of fraudulent credit card use or stolen identity occurs.
- *Risk* – online consumers are buying into a trading situation laden with uncertainty and a lack of cues to reinforce trading relationships and risk. Bauer (1960) identified six key types of risk likely to affect consumers: financial, product performance, social, psychological, physical and time/convenience loss. Online sales effectiveness can be increased significantly if the perception of risk is reduced. Willingness to purchase is considered to be inversely affected by perceived risk. Stone and Gronhaug (1993) state that 'risk is the subjective expectation of a loss'.
- *Trust* – is a potential outcome of risk reduction. Arguably, it is difficult to completely eliminate risk online therefore a possible strategy is to find ways to increase trust (Chang *et al.*, 2013)(Chang, Cheung and Tang, 2013). If trust is increased and perceived risk decreased consumers can develop positive beliefs in the organisation's online reputation The risk/trust debate should be addressed by online retailers as lack of trust has been found to be a major barrier to online shopping (Chang *et al.*, 2013). Dimensions of trust include service provider expertise, product performance, firm reputations, satisfaction (with past interactions) and similarity. It should be noted that some researchers have suggested that not all online customers respond in the same manner. Newholm *et al.* (2004) conclude that e-retailers should adopt a differential approach to building trust and raise the point that types of customers and products can significantly affect how retailers should develop approaches for handling risk and trust. Indeed 'bargain hunters' are inherently risk takers and in this case it becomes the propensity to engage in risk taking, rather than being risk-averse.
- *Perceived usefulness* – is positively associated with the intention to purchase and is defined as the extent to which an individual perceives that a new technology will enhance or improve their performance. Applied to online shopping, usefulness relates to the amount of time and effort required to learn how to shop online measured against the levels of service excellence provided by the retailer (Perea *et al.*, 2004).
- *Ease of use* – is an individual's perception that using a new technology will be free of effort and has been found to have particular influence in the early stages of a user's experience with a new technology (Davis, 1993).

In summary, classification and character variables have both been found to play an important role in predicting how consumers might behave over time, but it should be acknowledged that only character variables will be significantly affected by online shopping experiences (Doherty and Ellis-Chadwick, 2006, 2010). For example, the gender of a shopper may influence the extent to which they shop online but the gender of a shopper cannot be changed as a result of an online shopping experience.

The consumers' online shopping experiences

Different aspects of the experience of online shopping have been found to have an effect on consumers' overall assessment of the online shopping process (Doherty and Ellis-Chadwick, 2006, 2010). Positive experiences in terms of convenience, service delivery and website security have all been found to increase customer satisfaction (Szymanski and Hise, 2000). Unsurprisingly, website design, ease of navigation, good levels of service and good-value products have been found to increase consumer loyalty and also enhance the customer experience (Wolfinbarger and Gilly, 2003). E-retailers should aim to understand how customer expectations have been raised. Some of the key areas where customers have high expectations are:

- *Delivery* – the critical link between an online order and the delivery of the product is often referred to as the final or last mile. The last mile, including product transportation, is frequently considered the most important element of the order fulfilment process, i.e. 89 per cent of online shoppers rate on-time delivery high in importance and 85 per cent of buyers who receive their order on time would shop at the Internet merchant again. Thus, delivery-related issues have been shown to have a high level of importance to online shoppers (Esper *et al.*, 2003).
- *Timeliness* – the speed of digital communications has raised customer expectations in terms of response times and they expect a speedy shopping experience. It is no longer acceptable to take three or four days to respond to an online customer enquiry; an online customer expects that the response will be instantaneous or at least within a couple of hours. Additionally, they expect to be able to order goods and services at any time.
- *Availability* – the Internet creates a sales environment which is not restricted by space constraints; therefore there is an increased expectation that not only will there be a wider range of goods for sale online but also the goods will be readily available for immediate delivery.
- *Convenience* – it should be easier and quicker to compare prices online; there should be easy access to a wide range of retailers without the inconvenience of having to travel to a number of different locations.
- *Customer service* – customer value is the foremost driver of competitive advantage in the Internet shopping environment and customer service can be measured by the consumer in terms of price savings, service excellence, time savings and experiential values such as entertainment, visual stimulation/reward, levels of interaction. At the start of Chapter 6 we read about the various dimensions of customer loyalty and how they can be translated into website features in Table 11.3. Digital marketing insight 11.2 looks at how Shop Direct is dedicating resource to improving the online consumer experience.

Digital marketing insight 11.2	Shop Direct UX Lab helps understand consumer behaviour

The 20th anniversary of the first online purchase made by a consumer – a music CD by Sting, titled *Ten Summoner's Tales* (Spence, 2014) – was 11 August 2014. Two decades of online retailing have delivered many changes: one in four of us shop online, for a wide range of products (see Figure 11.5).

At an increasing rate, we buy books, clothing, music and travel online, using a computer, laptop or mobile device. Shop Direct is the first UK retailer to make a significant investment (£100,000) into studying online shoppers. Its UX lab is an in-house laboratory dedicated to looking into online users' experiences using a sophisticated research toolkit. The tools and techniques applied allow Shop Direct to see how consumers *shop* websites. The lab provides a facility to observe how customers are moving around websites. It consists of two rooms: one for the shoppers and the viewing room, which allows the retailers researchers to view online shopper behaviour through one-way glass. Shop Direct is keen to know how to get closer to its customers who use its websites: very.co.uk, Littlewoods.com and isme.com. The main aim of the lab is to bring Shop Direct closer to its customers. Of particular importance are the journeys which customers take when they visit the websites and then how they interact with the products on sale (Shop Direct, 2014a). According to Jonathon Wall:

> Having the UX lab on-site has acted as a catalyst for the acceleration of our testing and experimentation programme. Since opening the lab earlier this year, we've doubled the number of monthly lab studies that we undertake. We've also more than doubled the number of split and multivariate tests running across our six transactional websites every month, from 15 to 35 (Shop Direct, 2014b).

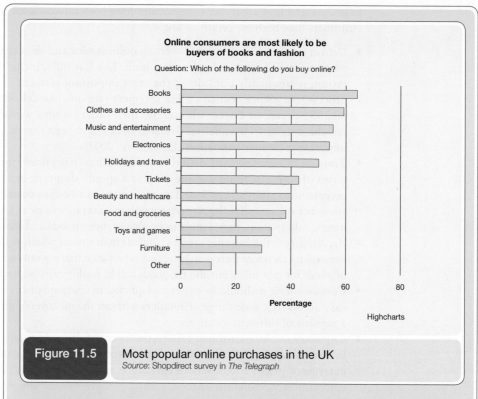

Figure 11.5	Most popular online purchases in the UK
	Source: Shopdirect survey in *The Telegraph*

The UX lab has had a profound impact on Shop Direct. Sam Barton who is Head of the IAB, is quoted as saying 'we're not looking at what our competitors are doing but at what our customers are doing'. The UX lab is enabling Shop Direct to take the guess-work out of online retailing and in doing so building websites which better serve their customers (Figure 11.6).

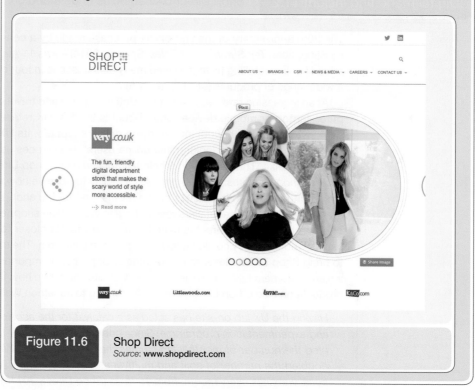

Figure 11.6	Shop Direct
	Source: www.shopdirect.com

It is important to understand that the increase in customer expectations can have quite wide-reaching organisational implications. The gap between customer expectations of the online offer and the actual performance can have a significant impact on online performance. Now read Digital marketing insight 11.3, which explores the relationship between experiences and online success. (Note that the similar E-SERVQUAL and WEBQUAL frameworks are described towards the end of Chapter 7.)

In summary, consumer demand for online shopping continues to grow at a rapid rate. As the Internet infrastructure expands and develops, more parts of the world are able to

---

Digital marketing insight 11.3   eTailQ

There has been a great deal of academic research looking at the relationship between quality and online success in consumer markets. Wolfinbarger and Gilly (2003) used the idea that quality is related to customer satisfaction and retention and ultimately customer loyalty. The study identified four dimensions of e-tailing and in doing so enabled the development of a reliable scale for the measurement of online retail quality called eTailQ. The four key dimensions identified by the study can help managers to understand customer judgements of a company website and how customers shape their attitudes based on their experiences of visiting, say, a retailer's website. The four dimensions in rank order of importance are:

1 *Website design:*
   ● easy navigation;
   ● appropriate levels of information;
   ● effective information search facility;
   ● straightforward ordering;
   ● appropriate personalisation;
   ● appropriate product selection.

2 *Fulfilment/reliability:*
   ● accurate display aimed at ensuring alignment between customer expectations and realisation;
   ● delivery of the right product within promised time frame.

3 *Customer service:*
   ● responsiveness to enquiries;
   ● helpful;
   ● willing service;
   ● immediacy of response.

4 *Privacy/security:*
   ● secure payment facilities;
   ● secure and private personal information.

Customer judgement of the quality of the website visit is an important part of the customer's online experience and the outcome of the evaluation process could determine whether the customer (a) is sufficiently *satisfied* to return and make another purchase, (b) develops *loyalty* intentions and subsequently recommends a site to friends and family and (c) develops a positive relationship with the brand.

You can see that customer concerns from 2003 are similar in many ways to today. Consider which are different. We think that the most significant omissions in this framework are the integration between online and offline presences (click to reserve); integration with social commerce facilities (reviews and ratings); and social networks, although the notion of 'community' is considered.

Table 11.2	Loyalty variables

Loyalty variable	Website feature
Customisation	Personally, tailored product ranges, for example lists of regular grocery purchases, favourite products, brands, etc.
Contact interactivity	Two-way communications that demonstrate the dynamic nature of the online buyer/supplier–customer relationship
Cultivation	Email offers relating to past purchases, informing customers when there is a discount sale on items similar to their previous purchases
Care	Real-time stock-out information/order tracking. Shoppers are looking for evidence that the retailer has paid attention to detail throughout the purchasing process
Community	Product reviews from satisfied customers. Include a facility allowing and encouraging exchange of opinions among shoppers
Choice	Online shoppers expect greater choice online. Therefore, the retailer needs to offer either wide or deep (or both) product and/or service choice
Convenience	Easy access to required information and a simple transaction interface. Over-designed and cognitively complex sites tend to lose visitors before they make a purchase
Character	Symbols, graphics, style, colours, themes can be used to reinforce brand image and convey brand personality

Source: Based on Srinivasan et al. (2002)

have access to the technology, which enables them to shop online. Political and economic development is also playing a part in enabling certain parts of the world to take part in the e-commerce revolution.

At an individual level more is now known about online consumer behaviour and for retail managers and marketers the key to online success is developing better understanding of the *consumer's profile* and the *consumer's behaviour when online shopping*. The web analytics tools we described in Chapter 10 are powerful in reviewing consumer behaviour. Online shoppers tend to have different profiles and characteristics to offline shoppers, which shape their shopping intentions. Online shoppers still tend to be younger, wealthier, better educated, have higher 'computer literacy' and more disposable income than the offline shopper. It is also important when planning e-retail strategies to consider that as the Internet becomes a more mainstream shopping channel there are likely to be a greater range of cultural differences as wider sectors of the global populations have greater access to online shopping channels. The next part of the chapter explores B2C markets from the retailer's perspective and looks at how organisations are developing the online shopping provision.

The retail perspective: online retailing

This section explores online shopping from the retailer's perspective. More specifically, it considers the development of the online trading environment and online retailing activities, trading formats and strategies and the strategic implications of trading online in consumer markets.

Development of online retailing

In the early 1990s, when the development of the Internet as a trading environment began with the first exchanges of commercial email, traditional retailers had little interest in trading online. However, for many retailers it was considered as a remote 'geekish' environment used solely by computer experts and scientists. It was not until the mid-1990s that larger retail companies began to consider how the Internet might impact on trade in the future and the challenges they might face.

In 1995, few retailers considered the Internet to be important as a channel to market, but given the potential of Internet technologies to radically reconfigure the underlying processes of retailing, and because of the highly dynamic and innovative nature of the electronic marketplace, some companies began to test out online trading. Tesco began selling chocolates and flowers, and soon afterwards Sainsbury's and Dixons launched websites. Retailers in well-developed nations, particularly in the US and northern Europe, have spent recent years working out how to best use this new digital phenomenon to support and develop retail trading.

By 2008 most retailers considered it essential to have a website and many offer their customers the option to shop online and where relevant, reserve and collect in-store. In 2015 online retailing has become increasingly popular and important to retailers and consumers around the world. Read Digital marketing insight 11.4 to see how some retailers have made a difference to the development of online retailing.

Digital marketing insight 11.4 | Online retailers that have made their mark on the digital high-street

Amazon, Apple, eBay and **Tesco.com** are high-profile companies that have made their mark on the shape of the digital high street. But these are not the only companies that have changed the way we shop online. Read about some other retailers that have made their mark in online retailing.

Next plc: delivery quality is the key to success

Quality online and quality offline, Next does not deviate from its core values. In the early 1980s George Davis spotted a gap in the fashion market and established the Next brand, providing quality clothing targeting professional working women who were looking for fashion to wear to work. He brought the new concept to market in a few short months and Next plc never looked back. The design and quality ethos driving the growth of the company was used to develop ranges in menswear, children's wear and home products too. By 1988, the company launched the Next Directory. This catalogue was outstanding – clearly differentiated from other catalogue retailers, in terms of both the quality of products and the catalogue itself. The directory was filled with full-colour photographs, which encouraged shopping from home, but this proved (for a while) to be a barrier to the development of the Next website. In the mid-1990s, as competing retailers like Debenhams, Principles and Dorothy Perkins were setting up shop online, Next held back. A key reason for this was the issue of *quality*, so until it was possible to offer the experience of full-colour images of a glossy magazine provided in the Directory, Next stayed offline. However, during this period technology advances were being made every day, if not every hour, and **www.next.co.uk** was launched in 1999. The successful operation of the Next Directory meant that the company was well placed to meet the operational demands of running an e-commerce website. Once established, the website enabled the company to be a pioneer in multichannel retailing. With the launch of the website customers could now shop in-store, by phone and online. But perhaps the biggest contribution to the development of online retailing is the service level agreement Next has with its customers. Since 2001 Next has promised to deliver its customers' orders the following day. Currently, if you place your order by 9pm, you will have the goods the following day and over 3 million loyal customers do just that via the website. Next has brought quality products and customer service agreements and constantly seeks to raise the standards of its online offer.

Sources: Next plc (2013); The Catalogue Shop (2013a)

Great Universal Stores and Experian use their information to change the rules of the game

The power of information; it's not the data you hold but what you do with it that counts. GUS Plc is over a century old and one of the forerunners of large-scale mail order catalogue retailing in the UK. Founded in 1900, for over half a century the business expanded and in doing so acquired other catalogue operations, furniture stores, and well-known fashion brands such as Burberry. By 1983, GUS was operating mail order catalogues, high street stores and manufacturing operations; providing clothing, household goods, finance products, property investment and travel services. GUS was an early adopter of e-commerce and it was well-placed to deal with the operational logistics of distance selling as this was something the company had been excelling at for nearly a century. However, in the early days of online retailing payment methods were a problem for this retailer. Typically, catalogue shoppers would make a number of equal weekly payments in person to a catalogue agent, who would visit the shopper's home, take orders and payments and deliver the goods. This arrangement suited many of GUS's customers as they were typically from low-income families, often with limited finances available for premium goods. But this method of payment was not suited to the world of online shopping where the only method of payment in the early days was by credit card. But GUS was able to use its information resource to assess the credit-worthiness of its customers, a process which would prove to be very valuable in the future.

By 1998, GUS had acquired Argos (which at the time was the UK's second largest online retailer) and also its own online operation was performing successfully. But what set GUS apart from the rest of the online retailers was access to its rich resource of personal data. Analysing the shopping data of millions of shoppers produced vast stores of useful information and in doing so gave unique insight into the behaviour of shoppers and their financial profiles. In 2006, GUS plc was split into two businesses, Home Retail Group and Experian. The Home Retail Group operates well-known high street brands Argos and Homebase. Collectively these brands offer over 65,000 products through over 1000 retail outlets, which makes the business one of the UK's leading home and general merchandise retailers. At the same time, Experian drives the online economy by providing background checks on consumers' financial track records and processing online transactions as well as providing market intelligence for Internet companies, financial information for the mortgage and financial services industry in the UK and around the globe.

From its early beginnings of selling products door-to-door, GUS and then Experian developed the *lubricant* which enabled the smooth operation of the online economy: customer information. Great Universal is now part of the Shop Direct Group.

Sources: Experian (2013); Home Retail group (2013); The Catalogue Shop (2013b)

Iceland Frozen Foods: a fighter brand

Iceland Frozen Foods; a fighter brand and retail pioneer – first to nationwide delivery. Iceland Frozen Foods was founded by Malcolm Walker on a budget of less than you buy a decent meal for two for today. In 1970, in a shop in Oswestry, Shropshire, with his business partner Peter Hinchcliffe, Malcolm put down one month's rent and started selling frozen food by the bag full. The guiding principles of this business were to offer customers value-for-money, good-quality frozen food. And this offer hit the spot with the customers, who typically only had a small freezer compartment in the fridge, as they could buy the *right* quantity of frozen peas, beans and lots of other foodstuffs. The business grew steadily and by the mid-1970s North Wales had over 15 Iceland stores. The business carried on expanding and by 1989 it acquired Bejam and significantly increased the size of the business. It also was a leader in the selling of organic frozen food. However, Iceland did not just revolutionise the selling of frozen foods but was also a pioneer in online grocery retailing. Iceland was the first retailer to offer a nationwide delivery service for its online grocery sales. What Malcolm and his team had realised was that one of the major challenges for high street retailers selling online was the logistical challenges of getting the goods to the consumers, in a decent state. The delivery of frozen foods is particularly challenging as frozen groceries have to be kept at a constant low temperature until they arrive at the customer's doorstep. So Iceland took a phased approach; first customers were invited to shop in-store and then if they spent over £25 they could have their goods delivered to their home. Iceland had a fleet liveried with the Iceland bright red and orange logo, which helped them to establish that it was possible to operate in this manner. In 1999, the next phase was to launch the website and invite customers to shop online. Iceland beat all of the other major supermarkets by offering online delivery for web shoppers. The problem was that many typical Iceland shoppers were not online and so eventually Iceland stopped selling online but continued with the home delivery service.

Currently, Malcolm Walker is back at the helm of Iceland and an online shopping service is on the point of being launched. Iceland is a company which invests in serving its customers and providing its staff with a great place to work and it continues to eschew the values established in the original store in Oswestry: value-for-money, good-quality frozen food.

These four retailers have developed their own unique strategies to develop their online presence. To put it into context and see how the rest of the online retail industry has developed since 1995 in the UK, visit History of online retail (www.open.edu/openlearn/money-management/management/business-studies/history-online-retail).

Source: Iceland (2013)

Online retail formats and strategic approaches

The introduction of online shopping has made classifying retailers by operational formats an increasingly complex task. Traditionally, retailers are classified by: types of retail organisation (e.g. multiples, independent, cooperative) and format (e.g. store-based, home-based), and these features of the operation can also be modified by the breadth and depth of product range offered, target markets served and number of outlets operated. Arguably, online shopping formats have evolved as part of the *natural* progression of the retail life cycle. Davidson *et al.* (1976) introduced the idea of the retail lifecycle to explain the evolution of forms of retailing over time. Based on the premise that styles of retail operation have a lifecycle in much the same way products do and will start from an *introductory* phase where the operational style is innovative, and then move through into a *growth* stage as the business expands, into a *maturity* stage where the company begins to see greater profitability and then finally into a *decline* stage, where the business is overtaken by more innovative competitors offering different retail styles and operational formats.

Operational strategies

E-commerce sparked new thinking about how computer networks might facilitate and increase trade in both business and consumer markets. In the retailer sector new operational strategies were devised which incorporated retail operations and Internet technology. To begin to understand the operational styles and strategies of online retailers it is important to consider three main operational categories:

- *Bricks-and-clicks retailers* are generally long-established retailers operating from bricks-and-mortar stores in, say, the high street and then the Internet is integrated into their businesses either strategically or tactically as a marketing tool or a sales channel. According to Dennis *et al.* (2004), online shoppers prefer shopping at websites operated by established high-street retailers as they understand what a brand means in terms of value and the physical part of the operation gives an increased sense of security.
- *Clicks-and-mortar retailers* tend to be virtual merchants and design their operating format to accommodate consumer demands by trading online supported by a physical distribution infrastructure. Virtual channels have distinct advantages over traditional marketing channels in that they potentially reduce barriers to entry. The location issue, considered to be the key determinant of retail patronage (Finn and Louviere, 1990), is in the physical sense reduced, along with the need for sizeable capital investment in stores. The best-known virtual merchant using this format is **Amazon.com**, the world's largest online bookstore.
- *Pureplay retailers* – 'clicks-only' or virtual retailers operate entirely online. In reality it is almost impossible for a business to operate online without a point of access to the Internet. Therefore, generally speaking, the term 'pureplay' refers to retailers who do not have fixed-location stores and or own physical operational support systems, e.g. distribution warehouses. While this category has produced some very innovative retailers, in reality few retailers actually outsource all warehousing, picking, packing, shipping, returns and replenishment requirement. Perhaps the key difference between these two companies is that one sells products and the other services. In the case of services, the customer takes themselves to the point of consumption rather than having goods delivered to their door.

Retail channel
Retailers' use of the Internet as both a communication and a transactional channel concurrently in business-to-consumer markets.

As retailers develop their usage of the Internet for providing information, customer services and online sales it becomes a **retail channel**. This term was introduced by Doherty *et al.* (1999) to describe companies' multi-purpose adoption of the Internet, using it as both a communication and transactional channel concurrently in business-to-consumer markets. Traditionally the term *channel* describes the flow of a product from source to end user. This definition implies a passive unidirectional system whereby the manufacturer or producer markets through a wholesaler or retailer to the consumer. This move may also suggest a shift towards a bidirectional retailer–consumer relationship, in which more power accrues to the customer (Hagel and Armstrong, 1997). As a result of the technological capacity, e-retailers are becoming increasingly creative with how they are using the Internet and associated digital technologies to serve the needs of their customers. A high proportion of customers are multichannel customers who combine research based on use of a website with physical stores when making a purchase.

Furthermore, the steady growth of online retailing over the last two decades through the applications of these three operational strategies and innovation in mobile technologies and use of social media has influenced the way shoppers wish to connect to their preferred type of shopping. Indeed, according to a report commissioned by eBay, connected consumers are driving the development of retailing as 'consumers want to be able to buy anytime and anywhere' (Guardian, 2015). What this means is that shoppers are interacting with retailers across different channels. As a result it is important not just to operate with one of the three main operation strategies described earlier but to develop a hybrid model which allows shoppers to engage with the brand, products and services at every possible touchpoint in their shopping journeys. This new operational strategy is called omni-channel retailing.

Omni-channel retailing

The way people shop is changing as a result of the interventions of digital technologies and social media. The basic consumer decision-making model discussed in Chapter 3 has become more complex and as a result the shopper's path to purchase can mean that they not only encounter all of the traditional (pre-Internet) purchasing cues but also a range of new digitally enhanced cues. Figure 11.7 shows the potential touchpoints a shopper might encounter prior to purchase (Fulgoni, 2014), where they might encounter cues which can inform their purchase decisions.

To begin with, digital technology has impacted on consumer decision making by providing a vast store of information which shoppers' access to inform their purchase choices. So a path-to-purchase typically begins with an entry in a search engine or a visit to a retailer's website. Digital search tools play a vital role as consumers say they help to save time (Fulgoni, 2014). But digital marketers should not assume that consumers no longer interact with the physical world as they are still likely to watch television and in doing so encounter more traditional advertising. Equally, consumers are also likely to speak to family and friends both on- and offline. Mobile devices facilitate interaction with actual products in physical stores. Indeed, showrooming, where shoppers visit a store to touch and feel actual products but then make their purchases online is becoming increasingly popular. The motivation to buy online is largely driven by seeking lower prices (comScore, 2014). So physical retailers can no longer afford not to operate online as well as offline because if they do they are likely to lose sales. Many physical retailers are beginning to find ways to combat the potentially detrimental effects of showrooming. For example, in November 2014 US department store retailer Macy's, with over 850 physical stores, introduced a smart phone app which enabled shoppers to search to find out whether a particular item was in stock in a local Macy's store. Macy's claims that every dollar it invests in search marketing drives $6 towards a store purchase (Rodriguez, 2014).

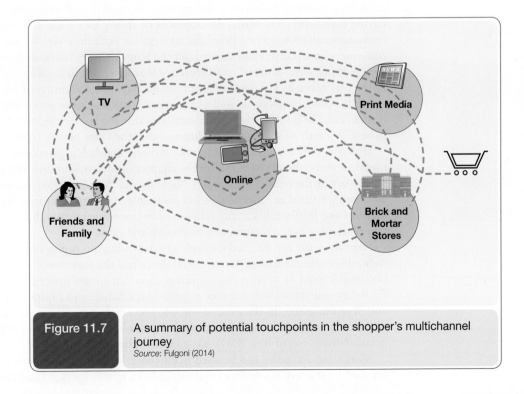

Figure 11.7	A summary of potential touchpoints in the shopper's multichannel journey

Source: Fulgoni (2014)

How do retailers survive in the omni-channel world? According to Fulgoni (2014), there are three priorities retailers should address:

1 *Eliminate silos and create seamless experiences* for consumers all the way along the path-to-purchase. Look for ways to bring together the on- and offline world and avoid isolated marketing campaigns, which do not integrate. If there is any friction along the journey a shopper is likely to defect to another supplier (e.g. if a retailer sells products at different prices online to in-store);

2 *Increase opportunities to digitally interact* – by understanding more about their paths-to purchase (e.g. provide incentives along the way through digital advertising and mobile promotions).

3 *Analyse and measure consumer behaviour* at all touchpoints in order to develop deep and insightful understanding in what is driving shoppers' choices and purchase decisions.

Implications for e-retail marketing strategy

For the retailer, the impact of an increasing number of consumers and businesses accepting the Internet and other forms of digital media as a stable channel to market is an increase in customer expectations, which creates competitive pressures and challenges. In part, this has been caused by new market entrants that have established their market position by, say, offering very wide and deep product choice, dynamic demand-driven pricing or instantaneous real-time purchase and delivery. The result is that retailers are required to adopt a more dynamic and flexible approach to dealing with these raised expectations. Allegra Strategies (2005) identified a number of performance gaps and Table 11.3 presents some of the most significant gaps and the managerial implications.

For the e-retailers it is important to identify any performance gaps and develop strategies which help to close them. For example, in the case of logistics, research has found that utilising carriers (road haulage, air freight) that have higher levels of positive consumer awareness with appropriate online strategies (i.e. offering a choice of carriers) can contribute to the consumer's willingness to buy and overall satisfaction with the online buying experience. Therefore, development of strong awareness and brand image among consumers can prove to be a beneficial strategy for both the e-retailer and the carrier, since consumers have traditionally carried out the home delivery function themselves (i.e. shopping in 'bricks-and-mortar' retail stores). Of course, this in itself raises the expectations of the care taken by the delivery agent, which has the implication of having to introduce better handling of goods as well as the speed with which the goods need to be delivered (Esper *et al.*, 2003). A further consideration is that the retailer and the chosen carrier need to be able jointly to satisfy the consumer so that they may benefit from co-branding.

How the online consumer accesses retailers' goods has given rise to various operational formats (discussed earlier in the chapter) and distribution strategies but this only forms part of the retailer's e-strategy. Nicholls and Watson (2005) discuss the importance of creating e-value in order to develop profitable and long-term strategies and agree that logistics and fulfilment is a core element of online value creation but at two other important platforms: firm structure, and marketing and sales.

Firm structure can be used strategically depending on organisational capabilities and technology infrastructure. Porter (2001) described the emergence of integration and the potential impact on e-value chains. Integration can ensure faster decision making, more flexibility and attract suitable e-management specialists and capital investment (Nicholls and Watson, 2005). In the case of the UK grocery sector, larger retailers have adopted different approaches towards structuring their online operations. (See Case study 11 for a detailed discussion of how ASOS has reinvented fashion retailing online.)

Marketing and sales can be used in customer-centric value creation strategies in the form of interactive marketing communications strategies (see Chapter 9 for a detailed

Table 11.3	Performance gaps and managerial implications	

Performance gap	Commentary	Managerial implications
The disparity between brand strength and website offer	• The gap between Internet use and the lack of website development means there is still the potential to capture browse and buy behaviour	• Companies need to develop websites to meet consumer expectations capture this behaviour • A failure to do so will result in lost sales as consumers browse and/or buy elsewhere, i.e. the effect is both 'on' and 'off' line
The disparity between brand strength offline and online	• Retailer brand strength is frequently not reflected online. This may dilute current brand perception and leaves an opening for competitors to establish a stronger online brand presence even if they are weaker 'offline'	• The first 'dot-com' wave was concerned with establishing first-mover advantage. This second wave is concerned with 'bricks-and-mortar' retailers establishing their brand strengths online, i.e. a 'brand' wave • Any lack of investment will deliver mind share advantages to competitors even if they have a lesser brand. In this second wave it will be difficult to recover a competitive position once any brand advantage has been lost
A lack of alignment between the nature of the online competitive environment and the maturity of consumer demand	• The most advanced entrants are from overseas or national catalogue companies, the larger retailers (to a variable extent) and specialist niche companies	• The market is still at an early stage in many retail categories. There remains a potential competitive advantage for a 'bricks-and-mortar' retailer to 'grab this window of opportunity'
Inertia in decision making	• There is a 'battle for budgets' within retailers, i.e. retrench and invest in core business at the expense of new channels • Some retail cultures run counter to non-traditional means of 'doing business'	• Barriers to customer contact need to be removed. Budgetary constraints are misaligned where the cost of doing nothing means lost opportunity at best, and at worst lost competitive advantage • The maturing outsourcing market may unblock the cost–benefit perception

Source: Allegra Strategies (2005)

discussion) and revenue streams. Indeed, according to Dennis *et al.* (2004), there are four revenue stream business models, which in turn are based on advertising, merchandising and sales, transaction fees and subscriptions.

Strategic implications for retailers wishing to be successful online are far-reaching and require a retailer to develop a carefully informed strategy, which is guided by a business model that can satisfy corporate objectives through deriving value from corporate capabilities while effectively meeting the expectations of the online consumer. The target market and the product category can have a significant influence on success.

In conclusion, it is now widely acknowledged that there is a need for a company to have a coherent e-retail strategy underpinned by a clear vision of how to create sustained competitive advantage if a business is to gain the maximum benefits from operating online. An online retailer's strategy is likely to be affected by the category and operational strategy it adopts, the type of products and services it sells and the market segments it chooses to serve. Traditional offline retailers will need to defend their existing market share as new entrants online are increasingly shaping the future of the Internet as a retail environment. Retailers need to ensure that the value created by online retailing is additional rather than a redistribution of profitability. It has been suggested that by removing the physical aspects of the retail offer the Internet increases competition.

| Case Study 11 | ASOS leads the way with social media and reinvents fashion retailing online |

More than just an online fashion for 20-somethings, ASOS has pioneered social shopping. Currently one of the most successful online fashion retailers founded in the UK, ASOS offers tens of thousands of branded and own-label fashion items to millions of 20-something men and women around the globe. But when the company was first established in the year 2000 the outlook for online businesses selling clothing was bleak. **Boo .com** – the online retailer heralded to change the way we shop – was on the verge of collapse, the dot-com bubble was about to burst and to make matters worse, the word on the digital high street was that no one is going to buy fashion items online anyway.

Nick Robertson and Quinten Griffiths, founders of As Seen On Screen (ASOS), were obviously not deterred by this gloomy outlook. Inspired by watching American TV series *Friends*, Nick and Quinten set about building a website which could sell items that potential customers had seen on television. Initially, ASOS sold copies of clothing worn by celebrities but soon the company began developing its own brand. This focus enabled the company to start to build a reputation that was attractive to young fashion shoppers.

In the past, it has been suggested that it is not possible to develop a successful online fashion business but by 2004 ASOS had introduced its own-label women's wear and in 2006 it was the first company in the UK to launch online catwalk shows. By 2010 ASOS began expanding into European markets and currently the company has offices in Sydney, New York, France, Germany and Russia.

By 2011, ASOS had grown into the UK's largest online fashion retailer and the ASOS Annual Report for 2011 proclaimed that 'Asos was the third most visited fashion website on the planet', averaging 13 million unique visitors a month with 5.3 million registered users and 3.2 million active customers (defined as having shopped in the last 12 months). The main site (www.asos.com) targets the original UK market, but the company has grown: its share in other markets including France (www.asos.fr), Germany (www.asos.de) and the USA (www.us.asos.com). It has increased its country delivery list to 196.

The company's competitive strategy aimed at developing a unique market position by selling a specialist range of products which have 'the designer fashion look'. Nick Robertson, the company's founder, started selling branded clothing as seen in films and on television. Not only did this enable the company the opportunity to create a market but it also benefited from celebrity endorsements in PR and promotional campaigns. ASOS now sells over 50,000 branded and own-label clothing products and offers a much wider product range than its high street competitors. ASOS operates as a fast fashion retailer, which has meant overcoming many challenges to get goods to the customers on time and at the same time manage the high rate of returns. ASOS has set up systems which enable product lines to be replaced quickly. Operating at this level creates many challenges for ASOS, so, in order to deliver the promise of fast designer-look fashion, and to constantly update product ranges, ASOS has established an 'in-house' design team in Europe, which creates catwalk lookalike items that are produced close to the customers, which aids delivery, and helps the higher returns rate of operating online rather than in-store.

ASOS introduced an 'independent designer section', which we established to provide a shop window to new design talent, has been very successful, and we plan to add an additional 30 designers to the 16 designers with whom we currently work.

The most significant development in 2008/9, however, will be the launch of our branded clearance section, ASOSRed. eBay has proved that the Internet can be a very efficient channel for clearing end-of-season and markdown stock. We also know from research that eBay and other sites where this type of stock is available are popular with our customers. We firmly believe that by applying the ASOS presentation techniques to this end of season stock we will be able to enhance the image of the brands and the product and provide an overall better customer experience.

The offer will initially consist of approximately 20 brands, expanding to around 50 brands within six months.

Online value proposition

Product choice is at the core of the ASOS proposition: tens of thousands of branded and own-label products available, with hundreds introduced each week. On pricing, ASOS is price competitive with its Price Promise (a price match offer): if you see a branded (non-ASOS) product cheaper on another website, the company will match that price. ASOS describes its website as 'evolving constantly as we find better ways of presenting our products'. The essence of the brand communicated in its annual report is 'restless innovation for our customers'. The main elements which ASOS aspires to are: 'Inspire and power your fashion discovery'.

| Figure 11.8 | ASOS brand wheel |

Other elements of the 'brand wheel' (see Figure 11.8) are:

- *External*: The world's best fashion, the best fashion experience, the service I want, inspire and engage me.
- *Internal*: Passionate about people, continuous improvement, fashion with integrity.

In 2010 **ASOS.com** launched its marketplace platform, which enables boutiques, vintage collectors, individuals and designers – established or unknown – to trade from their own virtual market stalls to customers across the world. It differs from other online marketplaces like eBay and Amazon in that each vendor can customise their shop front and, for £50 each month, will have access to an account manager at ASOS and some premium promotional spots on Marketplace.

ASOS service

Working with their logistics partner Unipart, Asos says it has been able to improve the speed and accuracy of deliveries to customers. Today, 95 per cent of all orders placed before 2.30 pm leave the warehouse the same day, even if the customer has not opted for next day delivery.

This has had the effect of moving the standard delivery terms from 3–4 days to 1–2 days. In October 2008 new delivery options were introduced including a named day service, including Saturday and both morning and afternoon delivery options. ASOS reported

that it had invested in a customer contact management system which will enable staff to respond to customer care emails more quickly and efficiently. customer care working hours have also been extended to enable the average response time to be reduced from 60 minutes to 30 minutes.

Partnerships

Promotional tie-ups and associations are very important to ASOS. In June 2008 the company launched a limited 100 design collaboration with the London College of Fashion. A capsule collection of 100 one-off pieces each sold on the ASOS website. The promotion received media coverage, including two full-page features in the national press. The collection sold out in minutes.

Marketing communications

In 2011 the ASOS magazine had a circulation of nearly 500,000. ASOS doesn't publish details of online marketing, although it does invest in Google AdWords. The company is now less reliant on affiliate marketing which at one point contributed 30 per cent of revenue. There is much discussion about the value of this. Nick Robertson of ASOS said at the time of stopping the programme (in an incident known in affiliate marketing circles as 'Grubbygate'), 'I'm not saying we couldn't do more in the online marketing space. Next year we'll reintroduce affiliate marketing, but as it should be. No silly commissions being paid to grubby little people in grubby studios growing income at our expense, getting in the way of genuine sales.'

Jess Luthi, who previously worked on the programme, justified investment as follows:

Affiliate refers a new visitor (average order basket at the beginning £35.00) affiliates get £3.50 + network@ £1.05 = total commission payable £4.55. So it's cost ASOS £4.55 for acquiring a new customer? Nope not quite, let's say a customer comes back and orders a further (I will be very generous here) say three times within the cookie of (I can't remember if it was 90 or 120, let's say 120 days) let's keep the basket at £35.00. This new customer has just cost ASOS £18.20 in total, after the cookie expires ASOS own the customer. If we take into account for overheads, let's say the customer cost ASOS, £20.20 (I have added £2.00 for odds and ends). But the customer has bought goods x 4 (goods have markups, they are not selling at cost) ASOS could not as long as I was there tell me what the lifetime value of a customer was, thing is they didn't know then.

Search marketing

The range of terms ASOS targets for search are evident from the <title> and description tags on the home page, which are also used to communicate key brand messages:

<title>ASOS| Shop women's fashion & men's clothing | Free Delivery & Returns</title>

<meta name = "Description" content = "Discover the latest in women's fashion and men's clothing online. Shop from over 40,000 styles, including dresses, jeans, shoes and accessories from ASOS and over 800 brands. ASOS brings you the best fashion clothes online."/>

Social media marketing

The growth of the company in recent years has largely been driven by social media. ASOS has contributed a great deal to the digital high street. Apart from showing that it is possible to sell fashion online profitably, the company has also pioneered *Social shopping*, where customers use online social network sites to share product ideas before they buy. ASOS has successfully used social media to build a community of fashionistas who are prepared to share their views and opinions on Facebook, Twitter and Google plus and to share ideas of what to wear, giving its young shoppers fashion inspiration. With approaching 5 million followers on social media sites, the company has made a significant commitment to community on its own site through the ASOS blogs at **http://community.asos.com/** and the social network sites where it has over 1.3 million Likes on Facebook. It runs regular promotion events integrated across the social networks and email such as #ASOSSavvySunday:

How ASOS has also targeted customers through email marketing

According to the 2008 annual report, email marketing accounted for 9 per cent of sales. Hash Ladha, the ASOS marketing and operations director, told *The Marketer* magazine in April 2009, 'with 20,000 products live on the site at any time and 800 new product lines being added every week, that it's crucial that a customer's marketing message is personalised to include the kind of items they are most likely to buy'.

The company has used the SmartFocus CRM system to define eight different customer types based on purchasing habits including frequent shoppers and those who bought specific brands. There are five female and three male customer profiles that

identify a customer's propensity to spend (a value-based segmentation), their trigger points and whether they tend to shop at the weekend or during the week.

ASOS also ensures that its communications only include items in the appropriate spending bracket since there is a spectrum of goods on sale from bracelets for £5 to £1000 designer handbags. Through data mining, ASOS can even consider the customer's favourite colour.

The communications strategy integrates both online and offline media through:

- a print magazine sent to 500,000 active customers to encourage loyalty, with some content repurposed as a 24-page supplement in magazines such as *Glamour* and *Cosmopolitan*;
- twice-weekly newsletters sent to the site's two million registered users.

Both of these activities are a significant investment, with a team of ten dedicated to the twice-weekly e-newsletters.

The approach to re-activating lapsed customers through email marketing is described by Ladha: 'We have three attempts over several weeks to try to reactivate them. If this fails, we might try a discount to entice them back. After that, they would become a non-target unless we ran a separate reactivation programme.'

Basket analysis

Basket analysis approaches were described in an interview with marketing and operations director Hash Ladha: 'One of the most interesting things we found was that men tend to buy for their partners as well as themselves. We previously thought this might work the other way around.'

Using this data, email content was generated by the company's in-house editorial team. Generic content included a round-up of current fashion trends and 'best buy' recommendations. The personalised content took into account favourite brands and budget, recommending items below a certain price limit. Emails were sent twice a week. Other strategies, such as encouraging customers to refer a friend to the company, and sending viral campaigns, were also used at this time. 'Our best customers visit the site every day. Shopping habits do vary, but most customers like to browse the site between spending', says Ladha. He adds: 'A twice weekly email gives them a direct link straight to the site and keeps it fresh in customers' minds.'

ASOS also wanted to lure lapsed customers back to its website. It targeted these individuals with tailored content that aimed to remind them why they had previously shopped online for designer and high-street clothing.

Ultimately, ASOS has developed a large target audience for its products through the use of digital media and it is able to communicate new product ideas very effectively to keep customers interested. ASOS's innovative use of social media has enabled it to influence the way young shoppers interact with online fashion retailers. Moreover, this is likely to be a massive growth area and social shopping is likely to continue to reshape the way we shop for the foreseeable future. Always keen to be ahead of the competition, ASOS is currently experimenting with Snapchat – the social app for sharing photos – to see how this technology works with its customers. However, it is struggling to find an advertising model which works due to the lack of data provided by Snapchat, which means it is difficult for advertisers to know how well their campaigns are performing (Mortimer, 2015). The main thing for the ASOS team is being where their customers are and being able to engage in the dialogue.

Sources: ASOS (2011, 2013); BBC (2013)

Questions

1 Describe how ASOS applies the marketing mix online?
2 Summarise the integrated communications strategy used by ASOS?
3 What risks do you anticipate as ASOS expands overseas?

Summary

1 This chapter has focussed on online retailing from two perspectives: the consumer and the retailer. In doing so the chapter has raised questions about the different types of customer that shop online and the various types of retail strategies used to create an online presence.

2 Online consumer behaviour is influenced by a number of factors, which shape and influence an individual's intention to shop online and have important managerial implications for retailers when developing target marketing strategies and looking for market development opportunities.

3 The online customer profile is made up of two distinct sub-categories: classification variables and character variables, which are ultimately used to interpret the meaning of any online shopping experiences.

4 Online consumer behaviour is made up of a set of beliefs about the Internet that are shaped from attitudes which influence an individual's intention to shop online. Over time an individual's behaviour can be modified by positive and negative online shopping experiences.

5 Websites that do not deliver a good online experience are unlikely to succeed. Online retailers need to develop a sound understanding of who their customers are and how best to deliver satisfaction via the Internet. In the future, more retailers may begin to develop more strategically focussed websites, integrated into support systems.

6 Trading via the Internet challenges online retailers to pay close attention to the online markets they want to serve and to understand that there are differences between on- and offline customer expectations.

7 Website quality is important as it is a key determinant of customer satisfaction and eventually customer loyalty.

8 Given current levels of growth in adoption from both consumers and retailers, the Internet is developing into a well-established retail channel that provides an innovative and interactive medium for communications and transactions between e-retail businesses and online consumers.

9 The Internet and web present opportunities for companies to adopt different online retail formats to satisfy their customer needs, which may include a mix of Internet and

physical-world offerings – e.g. bricks-and-mortar and pureplay retailers – to form fully integrated channels, which provide opportunities for consumers to interact throughout their paths-to-purchase.

10 Retailers have developed a range of different strategies for using the web to interact with consumers from electronic billboards providing information to highly integrated online shopping and communication channels.

11 The virtual environment created by the Internet and associated technologies is a growing trading platform for retailing. This arena is increasing both in terms of the number of retail businesses that are online and the extent to which the Internet is being integrated into almost every aspect of a retailer's operations. As a result, retailers must choose how they can best employ the Internet in order to serve their customers, rather than whether to adopt the Internet at all.

12 There are strategic advantages to be gained from deploying Internet technologies efficiently and effectively. Leading grocery retailers in the UK have demonstrated some of the opportunities for creating a sustained competitive advantage online based on various applications of IT resources and associated company capabilities.

Exercises

Mapping your path to purchase

Ask a friend or friends to select a product or service that they would like to buy; ideally this will be a completely new purchase, something they have not bought before. Ask them to tell you how they will go about making their purchase decision.

Make notes while they are describing the path-to-purchase as this should help you to identify possible touchpoints, where as a marketer you might interact with the target audience your friend represents.

Once you have gathered your research data from your friend:

a Classify the target audience your friend represents using demographic, psychographic and profile variables.

b Map out the purchase journey your friend intends to take and identify the touchpoints where digital communications, mobile incentives and prompts could be applied.

c Reflect on how different (or similar) your friend's journey is to the classical consumer decision making model.

Self-assessment exercises

1 Make a list of classification variables, which a retailer might use when trying to identify an online target market for (a) high-tech training shoes, (b) organic beauty products.

2 Explain the difference between 'classification' and 'character' variables.

3 Describe three different strategies an e-retailer might develop when creating an online presence.

4 Describe the different types of formats an online retailer might follow.

5 From a resource-based view, explain the difference between 'resources' and 'capabilities'.

Essay and discussion questions

1 Discuss whether you consider that all products on sale in the high street can be sold as easily via the Internet.

2 Select three websites that demonstrate the different ways in which a retailer might use the Internet to interact with its customers. Compare the contents of the websites and explain what the potential benefits are for the customers of each of the sites.

Examination questions

1 It was once predicted that the Internet would replace high street stores and that within ten years the majority of retail purchases would be made online. However, while online shopping is continuing to grow year-on-year it still represents a small part of the total retail spend. Explain why the early predictions have not been met from the perspective of either the consumer or the retailer.

2 **Tesco.com** has established a position of being the world's leading online grocer with an estimated sales turnover of £401 million and profits up 37 per cent to £21 million (as at 21 September 2005). However, Iceland was the first UK retailer to offer nationwide delivery of a range of groceries ordered via the web yet they have ceased to offer this service. Discuss why **Tesco.com** has been able to establish such a dominant market position.

References

Allegra (2005) Allegra Strategies Limited, London WC2N 5BW.

ASOS (2011) Annual Report, 12 months to 31 March 2011, **www.asosplc.com/investors/ financials/annual-interim-results**.

ASOS (2013) Section 1: What we do, **www.asosplc.com/the-basics.aspx#**.

Bauer, R. (1960) Consumer behaviour as risk taking, *Proceedings of the American Marketing Association* (December), 389–98.

BBC (2013) *Robert Peston Goes Shopping*, episode 3, BBC Production, Broadcasting House, London.

Bignell, P. (2013) Shopping? It's all in the gender, *The Independent*, 24 March, **www.inde pendent.co.uk/news/uk/this-britain/shopping-its-all-in-the-gender-8547059.html**.

Chang, M.K., Cheung, W. and Tang, M. (2013) Building trust online: Interactions among trust building mechanisms, *Information and Management*, 50, 439–45.

Comscore (2014) State of the U.S. online retail economy in Q1 2014, 15 May, **www.comscore.com/Insights/Events-and-Webinars/Webinar/2014/State-of-the-US-Online-Retail-Economy-in-Q1–2014**.

Cushman & Wakefield (2013) Global perspective on retail: online retailing, *Cushman & Wakefield Research Publication*, 20 July, **http://media.cushmanwakefield.com/~/media/ global-reports/Global%20Perspective%20on%20Retail%201st%20July%202013.ashx**.

Davidson, W., Bates, A. and Bass, S. (1976) The retail life cycle, *Harvard Business Review*, 54(6), 89–96.

Davis, F.D. (1993) User acceptance of information technology: system characteristics and behavioural aspects, *International Journal of Man–Machine Studies*, 38(3), 475–87.

Dennis, C., Fenech, T. and Merrilees, B. (2004) *Online retailing*, Routledge, Taylor and Francis Group, London.

Doherty, N.F. and Ellis-Chadwick, F.E. (2006) New perspective in Internet retailing: a review and strategic critique of the field, *International Journal of Retail and Distribution Management*, 24(–5), 389–411.

Doherty, N.F. and Ellis-Chadwick, F. (2010) Internet retailing: the past, the present and the future, *International Journal of Retail and Distribution Management*, 38(11–12), 943–65. doi: **http://dx.doi.org/doi:10.1108/09590551011086000**.

Doherty, N.F., Ellis-Chadwick, F.E. and Hart, C.A. (1999) Cyber retailing in the UK: the potential of the Internet as a retail channel, *International Journal of Retail and Distribution Management*, 27(1), 22–36.

Esper, T., Jensen, T., Turnipseed, F. and Burton, S. (2003) The last mile: an examination of effects of online retail delivery strategies on consumers, *Journal of Business Logistics*, 24(2), 177.

Experian (2013) Our history in the UK and Ireland, **www.experian.co.uk/www/pages/about_us/company_history/index.html**.

Finn, A. and Louviere, J. (1990) Shopping centre patronage models; fashioning a consideration set segmentation solution, *Journal of Business Research*, 21, 277–88.

Fulgoni, G. (2014) Omni-channel retail insights and the consumer's path-to-purchase. how digital has transformed the way people make purchasing decisions, *Journal of Advertising Research*, 54(4), 377–80. doi:**10.2501/JAR-54-4-377-380**.

Guardian (2015) The omni-channel opportunity for retailers: what's the story?, *The Guardian*, 14 January, **www.theguardian.com/media-network-partner-zone-ebay/omni-channel-retailers-connected-consumers**.

Hagel, J. III and Armstrong, A.G. (1997) *Net Gain – Expanding Markets through Virtual Communities*, Harvard Business School Press, Boston.

Hoffman, D., Novak, T. and Venkatesh, A. (2004) Has the Internet become indispensable?, *Communications of the ACM*, 47(7), 37–42.

Home Retail Group (2013) About us, **www.homeretailgroup.com/about-us/**.

Iceland (2013) The Iceland story, **www.iceland.co.uk/about-iceland/the-iceland-story/**.

Jobber, D. and Ellis-Chadwick, F. (2013) *Principles and Practice of Marketing*, 7th edn, McGraw-Hill Higher Education, London.

Mortimer, N. (2015) Asos plots further Snapchat activity despite admitting it provides 'virtually no data at all', *The Drum*, 26 January, **www.thedrum.com/news/2015/01/26/asos-plots-further-snapchat-activity-despite-admitting-it-provides-virtually-no-data**.

Newholm, T., McGoldrick, P., Keeling, K., Macaulay, L. and Doherty, J. (2004) Multi-story trust and online retailer strategies, *International Review of Retail, Distribution and Consumer Research*, 14(4), 437–56.

Next PLC (2013) Next Corporate: our history, **www.nextplc.co.uk/about-next/our-history.aspx**.

Nicholls, A. and Watson, A. (2005), *Implementing e-value strategies in UK retailing, International Journal of Retail and Distribution Management*, 33(6) 426–43.

O'Toole, G. (2013). Young Latin Americans embrace the Internet – and start shopping, *The Guardian*, 13 November, **www.theguardian.com/media-network/media-network-blog/2013/nov/13/latin-america-internet-shopping-mobile-online**.

Perea, T., Dellaret, B. and Ruyter, K. (2004) What drives consumers to shop online? A literature review, *International Journal of Service and Industry Management*, 15(1), 102–21.

Porter, M. (2001) Strategy and the Internet, *Harvard Business Review* (March), 62–78.

Rigby, E. (2005) Tesco to open online grocery warehouse, *Financial Times*, 27 October, 22.

Rodriguez, A. (2014) Macy's links with Google to show mobile users what's in stock nearby, *AdAge*, 23 October, **http://adage.com/article/cmo-strategy/macy-s-google-show-mobile-users-stock-nearby/295517/**.

Shop Direct (2014a). Shop Direct celebrates 20 years of online shopping, **www.shopdirect.com/shop-direct-celebrates-20-years-online-shopping/**.

Shop Direct (2014 b). Shop Direct accelerates testing programme with in-house UK lab, 14 May, **www.shopdirect.com/shop-direct-accelerates-testing-programme-in-house-ux-lab/**.

Source, P., Perotti, V. and Widrick, S. (2005) Attitude and age differences in online buying, *International Journal of Retail and Distribution Management*, 33(2), 122–32.

Spence, P. (2014). 20th anniversary of first online sale: how we shop on the web, *Telegraph*, 11 August, **www.telegraph.co.uk/finance/newsbysector/retailandconsumer/11024908/20th-anniversary-of-first-online-sale-how-we-shop-on-the-web.html**.

Srinivasan, S., Anderson, R. and Ponnavolu, K. (2002) Customer loyalty in e-commerce: an exploration of its antecedents and consequences, *Journal of Retailing*, 78, 41–50.

Stone, R. and Gronhaug, K. (1993) Perceived risk: further considerations for the marketing discipline, *European Journal of Marketing*, 27(3), 39–50.

Szymanski, D. and Hise, R. (2000) E-satisfaction: an initial examination, *Journal of Retailing*, 76(3), 309–322.

The Catalogue Shop (2013a) 7 decades of catalogue home shopping, **www.thecatalogshop .co.uk/catalogue-history/next.php.**

The Catalogue shop (2013b) Great Universal Stores now rebranded as K and Co, **www .thecatalogshop.co.uk/catalogue-history/next.php.**

Wolfinbarger, M. and Gilly, M. (2003) eTailQ: dimensionalising, measuring and predicting eTail quality, *Journal of Retailing*, 79, 183–98.

Chapter 12
Business-to-business digital marketing practice

Chapter at a glance

Main topics

- Types of B2B organisational marketing and trading environments 625
- Using digital marketing to support customer acquisition in B2B marketing 627
- Options for online inter-organisational trading 633
- How digital technologies can support B2B marketing 639
- Digital marketing strategies 642

Case studies

Case study 12.1: Covisint – a typical history of a B2B marketplace? 637

Case study 12.2: B2B adoption of the Internet: Inspirational Cosmetics 645

Learning objectives

After reading this chapter, the reader should be able to:

- Explain the differences between online trading between business-to-business and business-to-consumer organisations
- Understand strategic options for organisations seeking to improve their performance in digital markets.

Questions for marketers

Key questions for marketing managers related to this chapter are:

- What are your organisation's sources of competitive advantage and are they applicable in the digital marketplace?
- What is the strategic focus of your organisation's digital marketing strategy?

Scan code
to find the
latest updates
for topics in
this chapter

Links to other chapters

This chapter should be read in conjunction with these chapters:

- Chapter 2 describes the Internet micro-environment
- Chapter 3 looks at the Internet macro-environment
- Chapter 4 explores digital marketing strategy
- Chapter 5 describes the Internet and the marketing mix
- Chapter 11 examines business-to-consumer digital marketing.

Introduction

Although we naturally tend to think of consumer examples when considering the potential for digital marketing, there are many ways digital marketing can support business-to-business organisations. If we return to the typology of website capabilities from Chapter 1, we can see how all of these can be relevant components for a B2B site:

- transactional e-commerce site;
- services-orientated relationship-building website;
- brand-building site;
- portal or media site;
- social network or community site.

To understand how digital marketing concepts frameworks and techniques can be best applied for B2B companies, we need to consider how the buying process operates in different B2B organisations. According to Jobber and Ellis-Chadwick (2013), in organisational markets there are typically fewer customers who are likely to buy goods in bulk quantities and the buyer organisations tend to be larger and subsequently of great value to the supplier. What are the implications of this? Firstly, with fewer buyers, the existence of suppliers and customers tends to be well-known and it can be a very straightforward process to change over to web-based communications and trading. Choice criteria vary: impulse purchases and those based on emotional motives are rare in organisational buying situations as buyers tend to be professionals who use technical and economic choice criteria to inform their decision making. This means that efforts to promote brands are different to those used for consumer brands and price-setting tends to involve more negotiation between the seller and the buyer. Try Activity 12.1 to help understand the differences between B2B and B2C market characteristics.

Activity 12.1	Which market characteristics distinguish B2B from B2C?

Purpose

To introduce the differences between B2B and B2C e-commerce that must be taken into consideration when devising strategy and tactics.

Activity

Consider how you think the characteristics summarised in the first column of Table 12.1 differ for B2C and B2B. Refer to Figure 12.1 when completing your answer.

Table 12.1	Differences in characteristics between B2B and B2C e-commerce

Characteristic	B2C	B2B
Proportion of adopters with access		
Complexity of buying decisions		
Channel		
Purchasing characteristics		
Product characteristic		
Use of content to support customers		
Use of community to support customers		

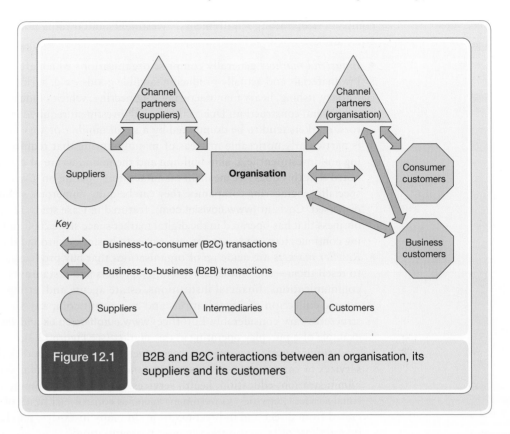

| Figure 12.1 | B2B and B2C interactions between an organisation, its suppliers and its customers |

Kalaignanam *et al.* (2008) highlight that 'a business can leverage the potential of the Internet to enhance the *effectiveness* of its competitive strategy as well as the *efficiency* of its operations and it is therefore important for marketing managers to be fully aware of where sources of competitive advantage can be found'.

Key themes and concepts

This chapter explores business-to business (B2B) use of the Internet by focussing on:

- alternative types of B2B organisational marketing;
- using digital marketing to support customer acquisition;
- using digital marketing to support customer retention;
- e-procurement;
- electronic marketplaces;
- factors that influence B2B adoption of the Internet;
- the development of business strategies.

Types of B2B organisational marketing and trading environments

Traditionally, there are three main types of organisational markets in which businesses primarily trade with other businesses: industrial, reseller and government. These markets cover hundreds of specialist markets which can be reviewed using Standard Industry Codes (SIC). Analysis of the main organisational markets reveals variations in company size, trading requirements, investments and trading potential. The three main types are:

- *Industrial markets* generally comprise organisations which are heavily dependent on raw materials and actually producing tangible goods – e.g. agriculture and hunting and forestry, fishing, heavy manufacturing, engineering, vehicles industry, electricity and gas supply and construction. Due to the capital investment required in many industrial sectors, markets tend to be dominated by a small number of very large companies. This is particularly noticeable in areas of manufacturing that require major capital funding and investment (e.g. ship building and the manufacture of chemicals). It should be noted that this does not mean all manufacturers operate on a vast scale. In the case of specialist engineering companies, they can be quite numerous, small in size and widely dispersed. Covisint (**www.covisint.com**), featured in Case study 12.1, is an example of a business that has operated in the digital market space since 2000 and at the time of writing continues to provide innovative services to businesses around the globe.
- *Reseller markets* are made up of organisations that buy products and services in order to resell them – e.g. wholesalers, retailers, hotels and restaurants, transport, storage, communications, financial institutions, estate agents and letting. This covers a very diverse collection of organisations and as a result company size and market sector structures vary considerably. Euroffice (**www.euroffice.co.uk** and **www.euroffice.it**) is an example of a pureplay operating in this market (see Figure 12.2).
- *Government markets* consist of government agencies and bodies that buy goods and services to carry out specific functions and provide particular services – e.g. public administration, education, health services, armed forces, community, social and personal services activities. Government agencies control vast funds of public money generated from direct and indirect taxation. In many instances, purchasing requirements exceed those of large private commercial organisations.

Mini case study 12.1	Pureplay Euroffice prospers in the office supplies market

The SME office supplies market is estimated to be worth more than £1 billion in the UK. Euroffice was created in 1999 by founders George and Anthony Karibian and Christian Nellemann when the online market was much smaller than today. The company now employs 49 people in both London and Milan. The majority of its suppliers are fulfilled by just three suppliers: Spicers, XMA and Kingfield Heath.

Euroffice uses an Internet-only business model. Its website offers over 27,000 products and services including office supplies, ink and toner cartridges, business machines, computer supplies, furniture and cleaning and maintenance. The core elements of its proposition evident from the site are:

- lowest price guarantee;
- free next-day delivery;
- free returns;
- 30-day free credit accounts.

The company uses state-of-the-art technologies to deliver a high level of service. It has achieved double-digit sales and triple-digit EBITDA growth, even during difficult economic downturns. Euroffice has received many industry awards and has been ranked on *The Sunday Times* Fast Track 100 on three occasions: 2004, 2005 and 2007. By 2010, Euroffice had sold to 250,000 SMEs with 80 per cent of its £30 million revenue from existing customers.

In 2009, Euroffice launched its Italian business in Milan. The following year, Darwin Private Equity acquired a majority stake in the company by backing a management buy-out (MBO) led by CEO Simon Drakeford. In 2013, Euroffice launched in Germany using the same platform as .co.uk and .it.

Google is important to new customer acquisition, with over 300,000 keywords targeted through Adwords and natural search. Euroffice has created its own bidding models and links to Google through APIs to support this. CRM is the main retention channel, using email marketing and personalised web containers to target over 600 customer segments. Euroffice also has a loyalty points system to encourage repeat customer systems and this accounts for around 10 per cent of business.

Sources: Econsultancy (2010) and company Wikipedia page

Figure 12.2   Euroffice (www.euroffice.co.uk)

Using digital marketing to support customer acquisition in B2B marketing

The range of communications tools we introduced in Chapter 1 and detailed in Chapter 9 can also be effective in customer acquisition for B2B markets. Some of the key differences in applying these tools for B2B marketing are:

1 *Search engine marketing*. Within some specialist markets, search volumes can be much lower, meaning that search marketing will deliver few leads although they can potentially be high value. Using the Google Keyword Tool (**see** Chapter 2) can reveal the scale of market demand. This can lead to intense competition, for example within professional services such as solicitors and lawyers leading to high cost-per-click in Google AdWords. In commodity B2B markets like office supplies (Mini case study 12.1) search volumes can be much higher and can be effective in customer acquisition.

2 *Online PR*. Given limited demand through search, online PR can be effective in generating awareness and demand for services. Content marketing based on white papers and videos which inform and educate are key communications tools, particularly in professional services markets (Smart Insights, 2011). According to Rene Power, five options for video marketing in B2B services include corporate videos, staff interviews

or guidance, customer testimonials, video blogging and hosting conferences and presentations. Marketing Automation company Eloqua gives a good example of how content marketing can be used to develop awareness through thought leadership. In early 2013, Eloqua was acquired by Oracle Corporation for $871 million – part of this value was created by the successful use of content marketing to build the company's brand, audience and leads. Before purchase it had a separate resources section with a blog 'All About Revenue' acting as a content hub for different content assets (shown on the Content Marketing Matrix in Chapter 8) shared through social networks such as infographics, charts and Slideshares. Today, the positioning of the blog as part of Oracle has a focus on 'Modern Marketing'.

3 *Online partnerships*. Affiliate marketing tends to be less relevant for B2B marketing since the volumes available for consumer marketing aren't available to appeal to affiliates and often sites aren't e-commerce enabled. There may also be a different purchaser to specifier, meaning that the affiliate can't be credited for the original lead. However, for retail B2B sites like Euroffice (Mini case study 12.1), affiliate marketing is still relevant. Other forms of partnership, particularly with influencers, can be fruitful. For example, Eloqua has an ambassador programme with marketing commentators.

4 *Display advertising*. The use of online ads such as banners and rich media ads to achieve brand awareness and encourage click-through is equally relevant for demand generation in B2B marketers. Well known B2B brands like IBM are active in using this approach on technology trade marketing sites for instance.

5 *Opt-in email marketing*. While using email to build relationships is prevalent within B2B marketing, there are options for using email for acquisition. Renting permission-based email lists or placing ads in third-party e-newsletters can be effective.

6 *Social media marketing*. Specialist communities can be developed within B2B markets. For example, Eloqua has developed an independent 'TopLiners' community and is also active within the main social networks including LinkedIn, the leading B2B social network.

| Figure 12.3 | Eloqua (www.eloqua.com) |

Lead-generation and conversion optimisation for B2B marketing

Many business-to-business websites do not involve e-commerce transactions, unlike the Euroffice example in Figure 12.2. Instead the model used is permission-based and within B2B marketing is often known as an inbound marketing or content marketing approach (explained in Chapters 1 and 6). The marketing model used to acquire customers is:

- *Stage 1*. Inbound marketing focussing on search, online PR and display advertising used to attract website visits.
- *Stage 2*. Engagement devices such as video, white papers or other forms of market education material is used to encourage the visitor to interact with site and share information via social media.
- *Stage 3*. Offering access to permission-based content valuable to the visitor is used to generate leads via encouraging the visitor to register on the site, supplying an email address and profile information or sharing the content via social networks.
- *Stage 4*. Leads are followed up through personalised email sequences or where appropriate outbound phone calls where leads are qualified as valuable.

Cisco is an example of an organisation deploying many of these content marketing approaches across the different social networks and blogs, as shown in Figure 12.4.

Mini case study 12.2	How does Cisco communicate and execute its human network vision in social media?

Cisco started using social media as we know it today back in 2005 when it created the blog. Today it uses a range of tools which support the development of the current brand message 'together, we are the human network'. Writing on this blog, John Earnhardt, director of corporate communications says:

> *We've learnt that we can have richer and more engaging conversations through social media. We are a customer-centric company that doesn't fall in love with any specific technology. We ask customers and deliver what they want. Social media helps us listen and respond.*

Figure 12.4	Social media aggregator (http://socialmedia.cisco.com)

In 2007, Cisco started using video for press releases which are distributed on the Cisco YouTube channel (**www.youtube.com/CSCOPR** and **www.youtube.com/cisco**). One of the most popular videos was used for a campaign about 'the world's most interesting intern'. In 2008, the company started to use 'Twitter channel and currently has various twitter feeds, which target various types of followers (**https://twitter.com/CiscoEnterprise**; **https://twitter.com/CiscoCollab**; **https://twitter.com/CiscoGeeks**). It has over 200,000 followers. Involvement with Twitter was followed by the launch of the official Cisco Facebook fan page.

Today, visitors to the Cisco site can visit the social media aggregator (Figure 12.4; **http://socialmedia.cisco.com/**). This gives access to all of these features:

1 *Corporate blog*. The corporate newsroom is a blog focussing on the company's latest news. It integrates the other blogs to give users easy access into the company.
2 *Twitter*. The@ciscosystems Twitter feed tweets news and information about the company, the Cisco team, and a link to Cisco's support page.
3 *Facebook*. The Cisco Facebook page appears to be more about interaction and entertainment, and ties together video and photographic media. It doesn't just provide information and news. The company also posts contests such as the current 'Super Fan' contest.
4 *YouTube*. The CISCOPR YouTube channel appears to get significant investment with well over 800 videos. There's everything from leadership and learning through to a fun series by the 'World's Most Interesting Intern'.
5 *Flickr*. Cisco's Flickr photostream has more than 50 pages of images and photos related to company events.
6 *Cisco buzz* puts people in touch enabling them to find, follow and friend across the Cisco Social Web.
7 *Community* provides help information, facilitates collaboration and development.
8 *Google+* has news updates and links to various social groups.

In addition to follow-up at Stage 4 where a user completes a form, it is also possible to find information from the IP address of some business users (technically this is known as a reverse domain lookup). Figure 12.5 shows how combining this information with analytics data about the source of the visit and type and amount of content viewed can be used for follow-up.

Customer retention in B2B marketing

Once relationships are formed, email marketing is again important in maintaining a dialogue. Of course, phone and face-to-face interactions are important too. So many companies will use email marketing for lower value customers and traditional channels for higher value customers.

We showed how Euroffice uses segmentation to vary offers through email marketing (Chapter 4) and using the RFM analysis techniques (Chapter 6). The company also uses its 'Office Chatter' blog which is syndicated to Twitter to interact with customers. This contains a blend of content such as 'deal of the day', polls and new product developments in office supplies.

Kalaignanam *et al*. (2008) also suggest three areas of relationship marketing activities where significant efficiency gains can be made:

1 Post-sales customer relationship management

- *Buyer–seller relationships*. Relationships deepen as more and more companies become comfortable with trading in the online environment, and there is more standardisation of communication platforms through the use of Internet technologies. Buyers and

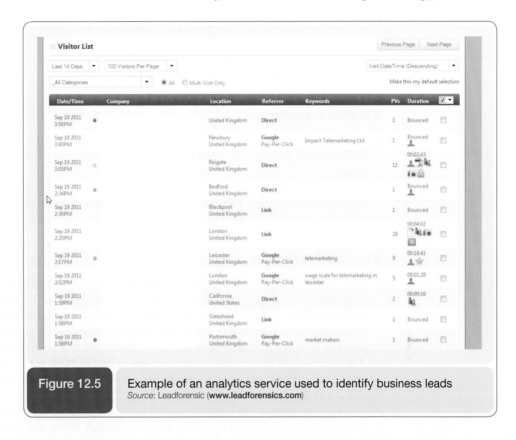

Figure 12.5   Example of an analytics service used to identify business leads
Source: Leadforensic (**www.leadforensics.com**)

sellers develop closer relationships and often work together in a very cooperative manner to achieve benefits for both parties using the Internet. Email and social media marketing can help facilitate these relationships.

- *Electronic billing* – some industries (e.g. telephone, utilities, banking) serve very large customer bases (B2B and B2C) and many of the transactions are typically repeated, for instance quarterly gas bills. For such companies invoicing cost and the production of printed bills is expensive and therefore there is great potential for cost reduction through the application of electronic billing and automated payments. Euroffice featured at the start of this chapter provides tools to make placement of repeat orders more rapid.

- *Self-service technologies* – the airline industry is making significant changes to its cost base and in doing so improving levels of customer service by introducing self-service bag drops, the online check-in and getting flyers to print their own boarding cards. When linked to customer retention strategies (e.g. frequent flyer programmes) the capital cost for the installations of self-service technologies can quickly be redeemed. Self-service is commonly used by business-to-business technology companies, in particular software companies.

- *Online product registrations* – warranties are an important cue for buyers of the value of products and services; moreover, extended warranty schemes can aid customer retention rates and are responsible for a significant percentage of profits in certain industries – but operating such schemes can be very costly. Processing claims against warranties is labour-intensive and time-consuming. Organisations can make significant cost savings through online product registration and warranty claim processing.

- *Online technical support* – in B2B markets customer relationship management is critically important. In high-tech industries much time can be spent dealing with teething problems resulting from the installation of a new software package. If the supplier can set up a system that can diagnose problems electronically then operating cost can be significantly reduced. Hewlett Packard and Dell are examples of companies where significant cost savings have been made as a result of using the website to distribute technical manuals and provide customer support.

2 Market research

- *Online surveys* – the cost of process is also reduced as the need for data input personnel is eliminated, and there is, potentially, improved quality due to reduction of data input errors.
- *Online focus groups* – by conducting electronic focus groups involving geographically dispersed participants, businesses can reduce information processing costs and factor costs but there are potential issues of generalisability and potential bias.

3 Knowledge sharing

- *New product development (NPD) knowledge sharing*. Product development cycles are generally becoming shorter and time to market much faster. The knowledge required for successfully implementing NPD projects often resides in different parts of the business, e.g. accounting, R&D, marketing or production. Consequently, an opportunity exists to leverage the Internet to facilitate sharing of intra-organisational knowledge. The Internet can be integrated into different stages of NPD for information gathering and transfer, both within and outside the organisation – e.g. customers, competitors and channel members.
- *Online advertising knowledge sharing*. The ability to digitise advertising content (e.g. artwork, audio and video files) and share it through online databases among departments within the organisation and with advertising agencies enables streamlining of brand management and considerable savings. In the case of Coca-Cola huge efficiency gains were made by making available via the Internet over 100 years' worth of corporate marketing and advertising icons. This provided easy access for anyone developing new marketing communication projects. Further benefits and efficiencies were gained by centralised storing and updating, and managing and disseminating best advertising practices. The system comprises downloadable video, photographs and marketing and advertising icons. A key benefit of the online knowledge system is that it enhances productivity gains by reusing existing brand knowledge.
- *Online sales knowledge*. Sharing information about sales leads has in the past been an inefficient, inaccurate and time-consuming activity and can result in duplication of effort. However, prospecting and qualifying sales leads and cross-referencing customers through an Internet-based contact management system can help eliminate redundancy and waste and significantly streamline the sales function. An example of other efficiencies related to the sales function occurs at trade shows. The promotional expenditure is the second largest area of spend in a business marketing communications budget and can account for as much as a quarter of the total show budget. Cost efficiencies can be made by using the Internet for pre-announcement of the show promotions, cross-promoting with other advertising and communication campaigns, using email customer invitations.
- *Online service knowledge*. The Internet can be used to act as a platform to enhance the efficiency of intra-organisational learning through establishing problem–solution exchanges, e.g. online customer conflict-resolution centres.
- *Addressability*. The Internet can be used to find users and update customer databases, which can result in great efficiencies in targeting and the profitability of direct mail campaigns. Online communications offer an opportunity to create highly tailored, fast communications that can deliver high information content at comparatively low cost (Gattiker *et al.*, 2000).

Options for online inter-organisational trading

E-commerce trading between organisations usually occurs as part of the procurement process, which is part of the broader business activities of supply chain management. 'Procurement' refers to all activities involved with obtaining items from a supplier; this includes purchasing, but also inbound logistics such as transportation, goods-in and warehousing before the item is used. The key procurement activities and associated information flows within an organisation are shown in Figure 12.6. Online, this process is known as **e-procurement**.

Electronic procurement (e-procurement)
The electronic integration and management of all procurement activities including purchase request, authorisation, ordering, delivery and payment between a purchaser and a supplier.

Knudsen (2003) and Smart (2010) have reviewed a simple classification of different types or applications of e-procurement. These are the main types:

1 *E-sourcing*. Finding potential new suppliers using the Internet during the information gathering step of the procurement process.
2 *E-tendering*. The process of screening suppliers and sending suppliers' requests for information (RFI) or requests for price (RFP).
3 *E-informing*. Qualification of suppliers for suitability. It doesn't involve transactions but instead handles information about the supplier's quality, financial status or delivery capabilities.
4 *E-reverse auctions*. Enable the purchasing company to buy goods and services that have the lowest price or combination of lowest price and other conditions via Internet technology.
5 *E-MRO and web-based ERP*. These involve the purchase and supply of products which are the core of most e-procurement applications. The software used manages the process of creating and approving purchasing requisitions, placing orders and receiving the goods or service ordered.

Digital marketing insight 12.1 shows one example of a company offering an e-procurement solution.

Procuring organisation

Purchase order

Supplier

Invoice and delivery note

Payment

Approver   Requisition   Originator

Buyer

Purchase order copy

Warehouse   Payment to customer   Accountant

| Figure 12.6 | Key procurement activities within an organisation |

| Digital marketing insight 12.1 | Perfect Commerce |

In B2B markets many industrial sectors are made up of businesses which need procurement solutions. Perfect Commerce is a global operation offering sourcing and procurement solutions to business in both the public and private sector (Perfect Commerce, 2015). It has data centres in Australia, the UK, the USA and India and its global footprint enables the company to provide high-quality service to customers on a worldwide basis (Bloomberg Business, 2013). The company is able to turn purchasing into a strategic business function and this is a significant change that has come about as a result of successful application of Internet technologies. Indeed, Perfect Commerce's mission is 'power your profits' by providing bespoke procurement solutions for getting spending under control. Purchasing has become a business driver, due to the growing emphasis on efficient and effective spending. Indeed, according to Fernie *et al*. (2010) the restructuring of supply chains has been aided by the adoption of quick response systems and the rationalisation of primary distribution in conjunction with the steady growth in demand for online purchasing by shoppers. The outcome has been that Internet adoption has spread throughout the supply chain. Retailers are now using logistic solutions – like those offered by Perfect Commerce – to manage purchasing, such solutions are enabling the use of automated warehouses and inventory control (right down to the store level), which greatly reduces costs and stock holding. Internet technologies have facilitated the development of strategic sourcing tools and purchasing processes that deliver significant benefits, e.g. controlling spend, increasing compliance, giving preferred suppliers greater visibility. The advantages for a retailer, for example, are that they can have a fully automated exchange system, which completely revolutionises purchasing, shipping, documentation across the supply chain. Perfect Commerce supplies systems that can handle thousands of suppliers, millions of stock keeping units (products) and billions of pounds worth of transactions.

Source: Fernie *et al*. (2010)

Smart (2010) also reviewed the business benefits of e-procurement through case studies of three companies. He identifies five key drivers or supplier selection criteria for e-procurement adoption related to improving:

1 *Control* – improving compliance, achieving centralisation, raising standards, optimising sourcing strategy and improved auditing of data. Enhanced budgetary control is achieved through rules to limit spending and improved reporting facilities.
2 *Cost* – improved buying leverage through increased supplier competition, monitoring savings targets and transactional cost reduction.
3 *Process* – rationalising and standardisation of e-procurement processes giving reduced cycle time, improved visibility of processes for management and efficient invoice settlement.
4 *Individual performance* – knowledge sharing, value-added productivity and productivity improvements.
5 *Supplier management* – reduced supplier numbers, supplier management and selection and integration.

Process efficiencies result in less staff time spent in searching and ordering products and reconciling deliveries with invoices so potentially leading to reduced costs if employees can be reassigned. Savings also occur due to automated validation of pre-approved spending budgets for individuals or departments, leading to fewer people processing each order, and in less time. It is also possible to reduce the cost of physical materials such as specially printed order forms and invoices.

These potential benefits of e-procurement led to massive interest in the potential of electronic marketplaces to deliver these benefits. In the next section, we will review the evolution of these services.

B2B e-marketplaces

Electronic marketspace
A virtual marketplace such as the Internet in which no direct contact occurs between buyers and sellers.

Rayport and Sviokla (1995) introduced the term **electronic marketspace** and suggested the Internet created a new environment which had significant implications for the way in which businesses trade. The speed of development of computer, network and Internet technologies played a key role in the rapid expansion of the marketspace and subsequently the commercial practice of electronic trading. It should be remembered, however, that electronic trading *per se* is not a new phenomenon; commercial exchanges have taken place using electronic data interchange (EDI) and dedicated data links between organisations for several decades. Nevertheless, what is new is Internet technologies. Communication standards and protocols create a virtual trading environment where any organisation with a computer and access to the Internet has the potential to trade in global markets.

Many innovative marketplace models have developed, although the usage of marketplaces has not been as widespread as was predicted when the idea came to prominence in the late 1990s. For example, in the industrial market *e-auctions* are used by General Electric (GE) to trade with both established and non-established suppliers. The model is a web-based electronic bidding mechanism that operates in a similar way to those held in traditional auction rooms and tendering processes. In the GE case the aim is to drive costs down via a competitive, open-bidding process. The downward movement of prices is sometimes referred to as a 'reverse auction' as opposed to a bidding situation where prices are driven upwards. GE purchasing managers do not always select the lowest bid as they will assess the potential risks associated with the supplier: say, the ability to fulfil the order, quality and requirements for after-sales service issues, rejection rates and quality of goods. An emergent benefit of this model is that e-auctions allow companies to monitor competitive pricing, which helps the organisation reduce total costs.

While e-auctions focus on the sales side of purchasing, e-fulfilment focuses on the delivery of goods in a timely and appropriate fashion and is central to the re-engineering of the supply chain. According to a survey, 'fulfilment' will be an area of significant growth for businesses operating online. However, over 80 per cent of organisations cannot fulfil international orders of tangible goods because of the complexities of shipping, although there are some geographical locations (e.g. parts of Europe and Asia) that are better served by local warehouse support networks than others. Time will inevitably establish the validity of the proposition that online purchasing practices are sustainable business models.

One of the key drivers behind the growth in online marketplaces was the rapid demand for doing business in the digital marketplace (Guo, 2007). Many different types of e-marketplaces emerged as a result of being based on different business models. Perhaps the most straightforward way to classify e-marketplaces is by type of user. For example:

- *B2B independent e-marketplace* – an online platform operated by a third party which is open to buyers or sellers in a particular industry. By registering on an independent e-marketplace, members can access classified advertisements and requests for quotations or bids in a particular industrial sector. In Chapter 2 we looked at how **Alibaba.com**, one of the biggest online marketplaces, had developed. Members will typically be expected to pay a fee or make some form of payment.
- *Buyer-orientated e-marketplace* – an example of a portal which is normally run by a consortium of buyers in order to establish an efficient purchasing environment. Joining as a buyer, this type of marketplace can help lower, say, administrative costs or improve bargaining power with suppliers. As a supplier, an organisation can use a buyer-orientated e-marketplace to advertise and this can prove to be highly effective as the buyers will tend to be from a particular target segment.

- *Supplier-orientated e-marketplace* – sometimes known as a supplier directory, this is established and operated by a group of suppliers who are seeking to establish an efficient sales channel via the Internet to a large number of buyers. They are usually searchable by the product or service being offered. Supplier directories benefit buyers by providing information about suppliers for markets and regions they may not be familiar with. Sellers can use these types of marketplaces to find new leads.

Vertical and horizontal e-marketplaces provide online access to businesses vertically up and down every segment of a particular industry sector such as automotive, chemical, construction or textiles. Buying or selling using a vertical e-marketplace can increase operating efficiency and help to decrease supply chain costs, inventories and cycle time. A horizontal e-marketplace connects buyers and sellers across different industries or regions. You can use a horizontal e-marketplace to purchase indirect products such as office equipment or stationery.

In addition to e-marketplaces there are *online exchanges* or *trading hubs*, which are websites where buyers and sellers trade goods and services online and vary according to the size and number of companies using them and the type of commodity traded. There are already successful exchanges in markets as diverse as energy, textiles and logistics. Like online auctions, online exchanges allow trading between B2B organisations. Key growth factors for this type of trading environment are that large companies can use the exchanges to reduce stock holdings while small companies can bid collectively to earn volume discounts or to jointly deliver a large contract. The operational procedures can vary – for example, in some online exchanges suppliers are invited to provide a quote whereas in others buyers are invited to bid for specific products and services. In addition, there are commodity exchanges, where the price of a standardised commodity such as energy or telecoms bandwidth continuously changes as a result of changes in supply and demand. There are some important considerations for managers thinking about entering into online exchanges:

- Are all the required major suppliers already signed up to the exchange?
- Does the exchange operate a comprehensive list of products and services to facilitate price comparison?
- Could belonging to an exchange destabilise existing customer/supplier relationships?
- Does our organisation have adequate systems in place to support order fulfilment?
- What will be the effect of making information about prices and stock levels available to competitors, as well as potential customers?
- What are the cost comparisons between operating through an online exchange and existing sales and procurement systems?

An example of a trading hub is World Retail Exchange which is part of Global Sources (**www.globalsources.com**). Global Sources is an e-business solution and service within the global retail industry helping facilitate transactions with Asian suppliers through a range of tools varying from identifying and qualifying potential suppliers, to achieving agreement on product specifications, pricing and terms for purchase. This special programme provides an advantage to WWRE members in their Asian sourcing business processes and offers security through the verified buyers' scheme. Currently there are over 1 million international buyers using Global Sources including '95 of the world's top 100 retailers' (Global Sources, 2015).

Drivers of adoption of e-marketplaces

Johnson (2010) investigated the barriers to adoption of online marketplaces. Based on interviews with purchasing managers in a range of sectors, he found the most significant are potentially misguided perceptions of the benefits, risks and trust in partners. He gave one example of a marketplace servicing the aerospace and defence industry where it couldn't recruit sufficient small suppliers because the e-market charged the same fee to all suppliers regardless of their size. The e-market charged suppliers $4000 per year to use its catalogue software tool to create their own electronic catalogues, and a yearly subscription fee of $390. Although most small suppliers could afford the subscription, many could not afford to pay $4000 per year in order to create electronic catalogues on the e-market.

Since this study by Johnson (2010), there have been many changes to the manner in which businesses use digital technology, particularly with larger firms. The emphasis is now much more on how technology can be used to develop strong relationships between buyer and supplier. According to Janita (2013), strong relationships and client loyalty are crucial to a firm's existence, especially in complex digital markets. In this study, several important conclusions were drawn from research which studied B2B use of e-marketplaces in Europe. The findings suggest that *image*, *perceived quality* and *added value* are key to the establishment of an e-marketplace and the development of customer loyalty. But interestingly they found that 'user satisfaction' did not affect client loyalty (Janita, 2013). In this context, *perceived quality* was found to be most influential when seeking to develop loyalty, followed by *image* and then *added value*. *Added value* is a strong trigger to encourage clients to return to a website to conduct their transactions. For e-marketers this research suggests that *image* is a powerful differentiator but this is not sufficient to ensure the establishment of long-term loyal relationships 'as quality is a necessary condition for user satisfaction' (Janita, 2013).

Case study 12.1 shows the history of the automotive marketplace Covisint and how this company has built up its reputation on relationships and loyalty. This pattern of a transition from a marketplace portal to a hosted e-procurement service has been followed by other B2B marketplaces which were prominent around the year 2000, including CommerceOne and Ariba.

Case Study 12.1	Covisint – a typical history of a B2B marketplace?

This case studies a successful marketplace to prompt learning about what makes such a marketplace effective. It also illustrates the importance of online bidding in some industries.

The Covisint marketplace was originally created by Ford, GM and DaimlerChrysler (**www.covisint.com**). Today, Covisint is not a marketplace, but is described by its owners Compuware as a 'connectivity solution' with the strapline of 'trusted information. Anywhere' (Covisint, 2015) (Figure 12.7). Its service is still used by motor manufacturers although they now don't use a single marketplace, rather each manufacturer uses technology to access its suppliers direct. This case study charts the evolution of the service.

2002: Covisint used extensively for bidding

Covisint (2002) described a high level of activity on the exchange. Taking the example of DaimlerChrysler AG, 512 online bidding events processed through Covisint over a 12-month period from 2001 to 2002. In total, this amounted to $10 billion. In May 2001, DaimlerChrysler staged the largest online bidding event ever, with an order volume of $3.5 billion in just four days.

In total, 43 per cent of the total value of the parts for a future Chrysler model series was negotiated online with over 50 online bidding events in the third quarter of 2001 alone. As well as savings in material purchasing prices, DaimlerChrysler succeeded in reducing throughput times in purchasing by approximately 80 per cent, thus saving on process costs. According to Dr Rüdiger Grube, deputy member of the board of management responsible for corporate development:

The economic effects achieved with e-procurement in the first year of implementation have already covered the costs of previous investment in e-business and hold great potential for the future, too. Therefore, we will continue to pursue our e-business activities to the fullest extent in 2002 as well.

With the online catalogue system 'eShop', which was part of the Covisint service at that time, DaimlerChrysler would be able to reduce process costs by 50 per cent after the completion of the blanket rollout, which would give approximately 15,000 users the possibility of ordering several million articles. By the end of 2002 about 1500 business partners would be connected to the

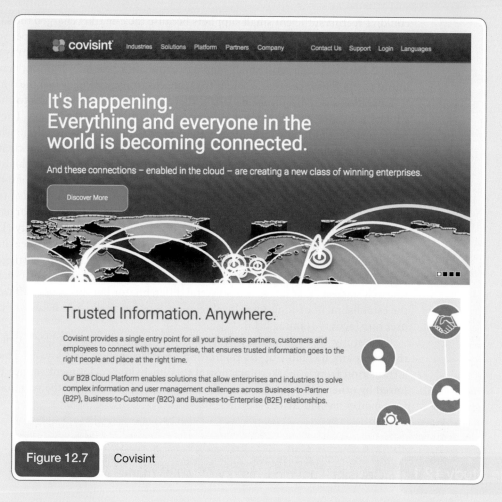

Figure 12.7	Covisint

electronic document exchange system 'eDocs', which would enable them to process approximately 500,000 document transmissions per year. Initial results using the 'FastCar' program for networking change management in automotive development at Chrysler show cuts in communication processes by 60–90 per cent. In 2001, over 600 managers connected to the system developed over 300 product improvement suggestions online with the 'New Product Change Management' used in the development department of Mercedes-Benz.

'e-Business activities are already closely intertwined from development through procurement, logistics, sales and marketing. To a great extent, they are already a part of everyday business', says Olaf Koch, vice president of corporate e-business. Dr Grube adds: 'We're a good deal closer to our goal of making DaimlerChrysler the first automotive company to be networked throughout the entire value chain.'

2004: Covisint purchased by Compuware

Line56 (2004) summarised the acquisition of Covisint by B2B software company Compuware. The article quotes Compuware CEO Pete Karmanos as predicting that the messaging and portal part of Covisint will contribute $20 million in 2005, and will eventually become a $100 million-plus business in the automotive industry alone. The primary e-procurement offering of Covisint is a method of managing purchasing across the many different electronic business document formats including traditional EDI formats like ANSI X12 and EDIFACT along with XML purchasing formats such as OAGIS, STAR, RosettaNet and others. Different suppliers tend to have adopted different exchange formats, so a solution that integrates them is helpful. Covisint continues to offer a portal solution both for manufacturers and their suppliers, who in turn have tier 2 or 3 suppliers. A study for Covisint by AMR Research suggested that the Covisint Communicate service was found to help a company reduce the cost of developing and deploying a portal by up to 80 per cent and reduce the annual cost of maintenance by 50 per cent. You can see the portal solutions at: **https://portal.covisint.com/wps/public/tradingPartners/_l/en/**, one example being the Ford Supplier portal.

2008: Covisint used by more than 45,000 organisations in 96 countries

Covisint describes itself as 'the leading provider of services that enable the integration of vital business information and processes between partners, customers and suppliers'. Many of its customers are still in the automotive industry, but now also in diverse industries including manufacturing, healthcare, aerospace, public-sector and financial services. The scale of operations is evident from these figures:

- translation and secure transportation over 40 million messages annually;
- hosted infrastructure boasts 99.997 per cent uptime;
- provides critical portal, messaging and/or security services for users at over 45,000 organisations worldwide.

2015: Covisint gives access for businesses, their partners, customers and employees to trusted information anywhere around the globe from one single entry point

By using Cloud technology, Covisint has developed solutions which enable its customers to solve complex problems and build stronger relationships.

For each industry it has developed specific services particular to data exchange within these industries. Covisint Connect offers EDI and web EDI facilities for e-procurement. Covisint Communicate has over 300 applications available, some typical modules of which are used by DaimlerChrysler AG including:

- *Accounts payable* – enables suppliers to research past and future payment/information, resolve issues prior to payment due dates and download document information to the desktop for further analysis.
- *Cooperative raw material acquisition* – provides suppliers with access to a cooperative raw material supply programme to leverage customers' purchasing power and maximise operational savings.
- *Product catalogue compilation tool* – collects and distributes information required to produce and update the company's catalogue of products.
- *Request for quote application* – enables customers to issue an online request for quotation process.
- *Supplier profile* – enables customers to maintain an accurate profile consisting of key information about the supplier.

Sources: Covisint website (**www.covisint.com**); Covisint (2002, 2015) and Line56 (2004)

Question

By reviewing the case study and examples of the different supplier portals available on Covisint (**www.covisint.com**), explain why Covisint has prospered as a supplier of e-procurement portals and business document data exchange rather than as a neutral marketplace.

How digital technologies can support B2B marketing

For many years, it has been recognised that the Internet's power, scope and interactivity provide businesses with a unique opportunity to transform their businesses. The Internet has:

- become an important channel for promoting relationships with customers and other partners (Ansari and Mela, 2003; Ding *et al.*, 2011).
- affected all of the elements of the marketing mix – promotion becomes highly interactive, pricing flexible and dynamic, products digital, and place virtual communication strategies of firms (Zettelmeyer, 2000);
- influenced the structure of the competitive market and increased trading opportunities with new partners (Varadarajan and Yadav, 2002);
- increased the capacity to deliver tangible gains through economic efficiencies (Vijayasarathy and Tyler, 1997).

How organisations make efficiency gains

Kalaignanam *et al.* (2008) have suggested there are three distinct areas where efficiency gains in marketing operations:

- *Decision information costs* – efficiencies can result from using information to facilitate decision making and reduce information processing costs.
- *Quality costs* are incurred to ensure that the products or operations conform to specifications. Internet technology can be used to significantly reduce these through gains in efficiency – e.g. if a product does not conform to standards, the customer is likely to return the goods, which has implications for staffing, quality control and can even lead to a breakdown in customer relations.
- *Factor costs* increase in proportion to the level of activity. Traditionally, they are used in the context of production activities encompassing material and labour costs. Factor costs in marketing operations comprise labour costs, material costs and miscellaneous costs (e.g. travel and rentals).

Organisations can use the interactivity of Internet technologies to improve the efficiency of their marketing by focussing on these three types of costs.

The next section considers the factors which determine an organisation's levels of adoption of Internet technologies, which will also tend to determine its capacity to operate efficiently and effectively online.

Analysing the factors which influence the degree of adoption of Internet technologies

Some organisations have wholeheartedly embraced the use of Internet technologies, whereas others 'have been far more timid either developing small scale, experimental applications or completely ignoring the Internet's potential altogether' (Ellis-Chadwick *et al.*, 2002). Table 12.2 summarises the key factors cited as affecting levels of business adoption of the Internet. It is possible to identify four key dimensions within these factors, which are likely to significantly affect online marketing planning and ultimately the effectiveness and efficiency of an organisation's Internet operations. The dimensions (based on Ellis-Chadwick, 2008) are:

- *Financial dimension.* Businesses are beginning to consider carefully the Internet's potential to deliver economic gains. Ashworth *et al.* (2005) have stressed the importance of financial factors and how the extent to which business can benefit from economies of scale is likely to influence rates of Internet adoption. Businesses are also likely to evaluate the cost of operations, the availability of operational and development funding and the timeline of online profitability. The outcome of analysis of financial variables is likely to critically affect the extent to which a business trades online, offers interactive services or invests in using the Internet to support its operations.
- *Operational dimension.* Grewal and Levy (2004) highlighted the importance of the suitability of product range and the impact of logistical complexities of getting goods to buyers at acceptable costs and within an appropriate time frame as key determinants of whether businesses offer the Internet as a channel choice. For successful development of the online channel, businesses also need to have in place a suitable technological infrastructure, and a supportive and technologically integrated supply chain. A business' assessment of operational variables is likely to impact not only on the extent of development of online retail provision but also on the level of the online service provision. Other factors, which can be considered under the operational dimension, are company size and maturity and the choice of online format. Analysis of the operational factors is likely to influence the extent to which a business integrates online and offline channels.

- *Market dimension.* A business' perceptions and understanding of online market potential are cited as important indicators of the level and range of development of online market provision. Businesses tend to develop understanding of the market potential by assessing the suitability of the customer base (Grewal and Levy, 2004). However, researchers suggest it is also important to understand the customer experience in

Table 12.2	Summary of the factors affecting adoption of the Internet

Factors influencing adoption	O'Keefe et al. (1998)	Doherty and Ellis-Chadwick (2003)	Grewal and Levy (2004)	Lunce et al. (2006	Ashworth et al. (2005)	Verdict (2007)	Lee and Kim (2007)	(Princely, 2011)
Capabilities and resources	✓	✓			✓		✓	
Channel – relative advantage		✓						✓
Choice of online format			✓					
Company size	✓			✓				✓
Cost of operating sustainable online retail operations – economies of scale	✓	✓	✓		✓			
Ease of access, use and convenience			✓	✓		✓		
Economies of scale innovativeness					✓		✓	
Internal expertise	✓	✓	✓		✓		✓	✓
Level and type of information provision			✓					
Levels of customer service	✓		✓			✓	✓	
Logistical infrastructure complexities		✓	✓		✓		✓	
Maturity of online market positioning				✓				
Perceived and actual levels of security		✓	✓				✓	
Product category and range	✓		✓	✓		✓		
Size and maturity of target market	✓	✓		✓	✓			✓
Strategic vision and commitment	✓	✓			✓	✓	✓	
Sufficient financial capital				✓	✓			
Suitability of customer base	✓	✓	✓				✓	
Suitable technological infrastructure		✓					✓	
Supply chain management issues					✓	✓		

Source: Gunawan *et al.* (2008)

a multichannel trading environment if the online channel is to be seriously developed. From this viewpoint, businesses should assess customers' perceived ease of use, convenience and levels of security in order to develop a realistic assessment of the market potential. Perceptions of online market potential, knowledge of markets served and market opportunities are likely to influence the extent to which businesses see the Internet as a new virtual world of trading opportunities.

- *Strategic dimension.* According to Doherty and Ellis-Chadwick (2003), strategic vision and leadership are critical to the development of a business' use of Internet and web technologies. However, a clear vision needs to be supported by appropriate competencies and capabilities (Lee and Kim, 2007), say, suitable technological and Internet marketing expertise (Lee and Brandyberry, 2003), appropriate technological, financial and operational resources for a business to use the Internet effectively and efficiently to support its trading activities, develop a competitive positioning and capitalise on the opportunities created by trading in the new virtual world.

The implications are that for organisations wishing to engage successfully in developing transactional operations online there is a need to have certain factors in place. Perhaps most importantly, well-resourced strategic leadership that can navigate a course, which not only creates a clear online positioning but also a sustainable competitive advantage, that is leveraged by maximising operational efficiencies and strategic effectiveness. But in addition, there should be evidence of a rich and fertile target market consisting of buyers who are motivated to buy online.

Digital marketing strategies

The final part of the chapter considers B2B digital marketing strategies. It should be noted that it is not the aim of this section to revisit the process of planning online marketing strategies (which is discussed in Chapter 4), but to consider how digital marketing strategies might be used and integrated into organisational planning activities.

According to Nicholls and Watson (2005), many organisations are developing a better understanding of the importance of strategic thinking and how it can lead to development of successful online trading. In the past, companies have been accused of a lack of strategic planning, which was ultimately said to be the cause of their online failures (Porter, 2001). During the dot-com boom many companies were accused of a lack of strategic planning, which was ultimately said to be the cause of their business failures. E-strategy has been discussed at various levels from business re-engineering, new approaches to marketing planning to analysing and measuring specifics of web-based activities and across an increasingly wide range of industrial sectors around the globe (Razil *et al.*, 2010).

From a strategic planning perspective, Teo and Pian (2003) found that the level of Internet adoption has a significant positive relationship with an organisation's capacity to develop competitive advantage. This is in line with the earlier discussions of the factors, which affect levels of adoption. The implications are that organisations should seriously consider how to develop maximum capacity to benefit from the online trading environment. Organisations that hesitate are likely to be superseded by existing or new competitors. While in the current climate this sounds rather obvious, the business potential that can be derived from adopting Internet technologies is not always immediately clear. This situation helps to reinforce the importance of digital marketing planning as it can help to ensure that organisations reduce the risk of losing their competitive edge by missing out on the benefits of new technology. On the plus side, there are increasing opportunities to benefit from innovation, growth, cost reduction, alliance and differentiation advantages through planned adoption and development of Internet and digital technologies as more trading partners become part of the digital marketspace.

According to Nicholls and Watson (2005), in order to develop an online strategy it is critically important to use Internet technologies effectively and it is also vital to analyse the operational situation. Furthermore, it is important to assess the degree to which the offline and online management infrastructure, marketing and logistics functions are integrated. Figure 12.8 shows a model of e-value creation with key areas, which affect strategy development: the organisation's core strategic objectives, its business characteristics, internal resources and competencies. Different objectives need to be supported by different organisational structures and marketing strategies – e.g. greater cost reduction is likely to be achieved if technologies are integrated throughout the organisation. The characteristics of the organisation are likely to have a significant impact on Internet strategies – e.g. small companies will have to consider carefully how to resource a fully transactional website and handle the logistics. Currently, a good deal of emphasis is placed on the supply side of e-commerce strategies. Streamlining of procurement systems through the use of Internet technologies can make significant cost reductions, which can produce cost saving, managerial efficiencies in the purchasing function and financial benefits.

Mini case study 12.3 gives an example of a B2B services company that has taken a strategic approach to customer-centric strategy.

Figure 12.8	Model of strategic value creation
	Source: Nicholls and Watson (2005)

| Mini case study 12.3 | Customer-centric strategy at Thomson Financial |

The Thomson Corporation is a global provider of integrated information-based solutions to business and professional customers. Thomson serves professionals in the fields of law, tax, accounting, financial services, scientific research and healthcare. Thomson Financial (www.thomson.com/solutions/financial/) provides information and software tools that help its customers make better decisions, faster.

Harrington and Tjan (2008) identified these steps in developing an online customer strategy for Thomson Financial.

Step 1: Map out your real market

Initially, in 2001, Thomson was using third-party reports to estimate market size. The approximately $15 billion financial information market was divided into three categories: firms on the buy side, firms on the sell side and corporate clients.

Using a more sophisticated approach the market was broken down into segments of users. Eight segments were identified and then, using a range of data including competitor reports, interviewing customers, Thomson Financial mapped out its share for each.

Step 2: Understand the customers' objectives and work flow

The next step involved finding out exactly how products were being used by different personas. For example, gathering information not only on the activities of a bank's head of research, who bought the product, but also on the behaviour of analysts doing research for their clients.

Thomson Financial used a combination of traditional survey methods and less traditional methods such as 'day in the life' observations of customers to chart users' activities. Key to this research was an approach called 'three minutes'. What were end users of a product or service doing three minutes before they used it and three minutes after? What were they doing for the next three minutes? Thomson kept asking that until we got a view of the full day. The aim was to make Thomson products part of as much of that day as practical.

Step 3: Develop products that provide what users value most

Once Thomson had a picture of users' needs, candidates for new features that would address unmet needs were identified. Candidate features and information were based on the biggest pain points for end users – which aspects of their jobs were so problematic that customers would pay to make them better? To determine this, Thomson surveyed more than 1200 investment managers, for instance, to find out the features those users valued most in the aggregate. Then they performed a conjoint analysis in which investment managers were asked to make trade-offs among attributes that might enhance the product. This gave a truer picture of their preferences. They saw that within the investment manager group there were three distinct clusters of needs: basic users, advanced users and real-time focussed users. The three clusters valued some but not all of the same things. They then concentrated future development efforts on creating three versions of our solution, each aimed at meeting the needs of one cluster.

Step 4: Keep the focus on users

Thomson highlight the importance of ongoing research and introduction of new functionality when they say:

We are continually evaluating and refining our customer strategy. Implementing it requires a flexible go-to-market plan, which we enable by including sales and product development people right up front in the research; by employing effective customer feedback loops that are built into a periodic review process; and by gradually scaling up the strategy across segments and businesses.

In summary, it is perhaps reasonable to suggest that organisations are beginning to consider use of the Internet from a much more strategic perspective. Organisations operating in B2B sectors are generally well placed to implement online strategies due to having well-established long-standing trading relationships with customers and members of the supply chain.

Case Study 12.2	B2B adoption of the Internet: Inspirational Cosmetics

According to research (Aguila-Obra and Padilla-Meléndez, 2006; Doherty and Ellis-Chadwick, 2010), Internet adoption by organisations is a process which involves different stages, each of which is affected by a number of variables. The stages and the variables are shown in Tables 12.3 and 12.4.

Businesses at the initiation stage are likely to have a very basic level of Internet use but will move towards developing a very basic website and email. By the time the adoption stage is achieved businesses are likely to have their own server in place. Changes to operations and managerial structure will have begun to take place by the time the routinisation stage is reached. Finally, when the infusion stage is reached many changes will have occurred including the development of different organisational units for managing the technology.

In addition to the impact of organisational, external and technology factors, firm size has an impact on the stage and speed of development. In other words, the bigger the firm the more likely it is to have its own website and supporting technology infrastructure. Moreover, the larger the firm the greater the level and intensity of the business activity and the greater the number of employees involved.

Inspirational Cosmetics (IC) is a recently developed subsidiary of the giant pharmaceutical corporation Multichemical. IC is based in Stockholm and produces a range of high-quality cosmetic products and surgical applications. The company specialises in developing products for the 'anti-ageing' market. IC was established when the parent company, Multichemical, acquired a small Swedish company called Abbalaars, which produced highly effective anti-ageing creams from organically grown plants. The organisational structure of IC has been developed using a combination of local and international expertise. Local producers continue to supply high-quality organic materials for the production of facial creams. These producers are

Table 12.3	Factors and variables affecting Internet adoption

Factors affecting adoption	Variables
External factors	• Organisational environment • Industry competition • External support • Internet user expectations • Global electronic markets
Technology factors	• Benefits of technology adoption • Barrier to technology adoption • Comparative advantage • Cost • Technology infrastructure
Organisational factors	• Perceived costs • Internal resources • Skills and expertise • Levels of investment • Business objectives • Organisational structure
Firm size	• Small • Medium • Large

Source: Based on Aguila-Obra and Padilla-Meléndez (2006)

Table 12.4	Stages of internet adoption and influencing factors

Stage	Influencing factors
Initiation	Firms tend to have limited access to technology resources and are unlikely to have internal computer network but firms at this stage are looking at opportunities created by the web. Investment and financial cost are key at this stage
Adoption/adaptation	Firms will already have made an investment in technology but still need external support as they are beginning to use the web Managerial expertise and external networks are key here
Acceptance/routinisation	Firms are likely to have a fairly well-established technology infrastructure and are likely to be using the Internet and the web extensively for internal and external communications
Infusion	By this stage the firms have largely become self-sufficient in terms of operating and developing Internet and web technologies. Managerial skill will also be very well developed

Source: Based on Aguila-Obra and Padilla-Meléndez (2006)

located all around Sweden and vary in size, in terms of number of employees, from 5 to 500. The 'think global, act local' approach to the company development has also been applied to the development of the technology infrastructure. Multichemical provides an Internet infrastructure which is capable of supporting a highly sophisticated range of Internet strategies. However, Abbalaars made limited use of the Internet internally: the company had a computer network linking all parts of the business but externally the website was a static site giving contact details and a short company history. IC has recently appointed an e-commerce director, Henrik Bjornesson, whose responsibility it is to develop online sales revenues and improve communications within the supply chain.

Questions

1 Assess the stage of the Internet adoption for:
   - Multichemical;
   - Inspirational Cosmetics;
   - the organic growers (suppliers).
2 Explain which factor and variables Henrik Bjornesson is most likely to consider when deciding how to achieve the business goals set by Viktor Karlsson, the CEO of Inspirational Cosmetics.
3 Consider the likely stage of adoption of the suppliers of organic produce. Suggest ways in which Inspirational Cosmetics might develop its use of the Internet with these suppliers.

Summary

1 This chapter has examined B2B use of Internet technologies and in doing so it has considered the e-markets, the importance of efficiency and effectiveness to organisations operating online, the factors which affect adoption and has briefly looked at online marketing strategies.

2 We saw how companies can use e-procurement for efficiency.

3 Social media marketing can be applied to B2B markets for lead generation through content and inbound marketing techniques as we saw through the Cisco and Eloqua case studies. The chapter also examined B2B e-markets and considered the importance of e-markets in terms of growth and dispersion of use of Internet technologies across different industrial sectors.

4 We explored different types of e-market places and provided case examples of different types of e-market portals.

5 We summarised the factors that affect Internet adoption and suggested ways in which these factors cluster together into separate dimensions of influencing factors: financial, market, operational and strategic.

6 Digital marketing strategies are not always integrated into a business' wider planning activities. However, this is becoming more important as organisations increasingly integrate Internet technologies into their buying and selling activities.

Exercises

Self-assessment exercises

1 Evaluate and compare the factors likely to affect (a) a construction company, (b) an insurance brokerage contemplating setting up a transactional website aiming to develop online market share.

2 Explain the difference between online market efficiency and online market effectiveness.

Essay and discussion questions

1 Discuss why a business operating in an industrial market might be cautious about putting new product specifications on the company website.
2 Discuss the relevance of social media marketing to B2B organisations.
3 Explain how Internet technologies can contribute to the development of online business strategies.

Examination questions

1 Discuss the extent to which B2B e-marketplaces are fundamentally different from traditional offline markets.
2 Explain the options for applying social media marketing to B2B marketing campaigns.

References

Aguila-Obra, A.R.D. and Padilla-Meléndez, A. (2006) Organisational factors affecting Internet technology adoption, *Internet Research*, 16(1), 91–110.

Ansari, A. and Mela, C.F. (2003) E-customisation, *Journal of Marketing Research*, 40 (May), 131–45.

Ashworth, C. Schmidt, R., Pioche, E. and Hallsworth, A. (2005) An approach to sustainable 'fashion' e-retail: a five stage evolutionary strategy for clicks-and-mortar and pureplay enterprises, *Journal of Retailing and Consumer Service*, 13(4), 289–99.

Bloomberg Business (2013). Perfect commerce expands its global footprint with addition of new operations and data centres, *Bloomberg Business*, 30 July, **www.bloomberg.com /research/stocks/private/snapshot.asp?privcapid=30822995**.

Covisint (2002) Press release, 4 February, **www.covisint.com**.

Covisint (2015) Company home page, **www.covisint.com/en_GB**.

Ding, D., Hu, P. and Sheng, O. (2011) e-SELFQUAL: a scale for measuring online, *Journal of Business Research*, 64(5), 505–15.

Doherty, N.F. and Ellis-Chadwick, F.E. (2003) The relationship between retailers' targeting and e-commerce strategies: an empirical analysis, *Internet Research*, 13(3), 170–82.

Econsultancy (2010) Q&A: Euroffice CEO Simon Drakeford on customer retention, blog post, 10 November, **http://econsultancy.com/uk/blog/6833-q-a-euroffice-ceo-simon-drakeford**.

Ellis-Chadwick, F.E. (2008) Online retailing: open all hours?, *International Journal of Business Environments*, 2(2).

Ellis-Chadwick, F.E., McHardy, P. and Wiesehofer, H. (2002) Online customer relationships in the European financial services sector: a cross-country investigation, *International Journal of Financial Services Marketing*, 6(4).

Fernie, J, Sparks, L. and McKinnon, A. (2010) Retail logistics in the UK: past present and future, *International Journal of Retail Distribution Management*, 38(11–12), 894–914.

Gattiker, U.E., Perlusz, S. and Bohmann, K. (2000) Using the Internet for B2B activities: a review and further direction for research, *Internet Research Electronic Networking Application and Policy*, 10(2), 126–40.

Global Sources (2015). About Global Sources, 28 January 2015, **www.corporate .globalsources.com/profile/bground2.htm**.

Grewal, I. and Levy, M. (2004) Internet retailing: enablers, limiters and market consequences, *Journal of Business Research*, 57(7), 703–13.

Gunawan, G., Ellis-Chadwick, F. and King, M. (2008) An empirical study of the uptake of performance measurement by internet retailers, *Internet Research*, 18(4), 361–81.

Guo, J. (2007). Business-to-business electronic market place selection, *Enterprise Information Systems*, 4(1).

Harrington, R. and Tjan, A. (2008) Transforming strategy one customer at a time, *Harvard Business Review*, 86(3), 62–72.

Janita, A.M. (2013). The antecedents of client loyalty in business-to-business (B2B), *Industrial Marketing Management*, 42, 814–23.

Jobber, D. (2009) *Principles and Practice of Marketing*, 6th edn, McGraw-Hill, London.

Jobber, D. and Ellis-Chadwick, F. (2013) *Principles and Practice of Marketing*, 7th edn, McGraw-Hill Higher Education, London.

Johnson, M. (2010) Barriers to innovation adoption: a study of e-markets, *Industrial Management and Data Systems*, 110(2), 157–74.

Kalaignanam, K., Kushwaha, T. and Varadarajan, P. (2008) Marketing operations efficiency and the Internet: an organizing framework, *Journal of Business Research*, 61(4), 300–308.

Knudsen, D. (2003) Aligning corporate strategy, procurement strategy and e-procurement tools, *International Journal of Physical Distribution and Logistics Management*, 33(8), 720–34.

Lee, S. and Brandyberry, A. (2003) The e-tailer's dilemma, ACM SIGMIS database, 34(2).

Lee, S. and Kim, K.-J. (2007) Factors affecting the implementation success of Internet-based information systems, *Computers in Human Behaviour*, 23(4), 1853–80.

Line56 (2004) Compuware buys last of Covisint, Article by Jim Ericson, *Line56*, 6 February, **www.line56.com**.

Lunce, S., Lunce, L., Kawai, Y. and Balasundrum (2006) Success and failure of pure-play organizations: webvan versus peapod, a comparative analysis, *Industrial Management and Data Systems*, 106(9), 1344–58.

Nicholls, A. and Watson, A. (2005) Implementing e-value strategies in UK retailing, *International Journal of Retail and Distribution Management*, 33(6), 426–43.

O'Keefe, R.M., O'Connor, G. and Kung, H.J. (1998) Early adopters of the web as a retail medium: small company winners and losers, *European Journal of Marketing*, 32(7–8), 629–43.

Perfect Commerce (2015) Who we are, **www.perfect.com/about/who-we-are/**.

Porter, M. (2001) Strategy and the Internet, *Harvard Business Review* (March), 62–78.

Princely, I. (2011). An empirical analysis of factors influencing Internet/e-business technologies adoption by SMES in Canada, *International Journal of Information Technology and Decision Making*, 10(4), doi:**10.1142/S0219622011004543**.

Rayport, J. and Sviokla, J. (1995) Exploiting the virtual value chain, *Harvard Business Review*, November–December, 75–87.

Razil, M., Manaf, Z. and Yassin, A. (2010) Internet business strategies by property companies in Asia. *Property Management*, 28(4), 270–89.

Smart, A. (2010) Exploring the business case for e-procurement, *International Journal of Physical, Distribution and Logistics Management*, 40(3), 181–201.

Smart Insights (2011) Five ways to integrate compelling video into your B2B marketing, blog post by Rene Power, 25 August.

Teo, T. and Pian, Y. (2003) A contingency perspective on Internet adoption and competitive advantage, *European Journal of Information Systems*, 12(2), 78–92.

Varadarajan, R.P. and Yadav, MSC (2002) Marketing strategy and the Internet: an organising framework, *Journal of the Academy of Marketing Science*, 30 (Fall), 296–313.

Verdict Research (2007) *UK e-retail 2007*, Verdict Research limited, Charles House, 108–10 Finchley Road, London, NW3 5JJ.

Vijayasarathy, L. and Tyler, M. (1997) Adoption factors and electronic data interchange use: a survey of retail companies, *International Journal of Retail Distribution and Management*, 25(9), 286–92.

Zettelmeyer, F. (2000) Expanding the internet: pricing and communications strategies when firms compete on multiple channels, *Journal of Marketing Research*, 37 (August), 292–308.

Glossary

3G Third generation of mobile phone technology.

4G Fourth-generation wireless, expected to deliver wireless broadband at 20–40 Mbps (about 10–20 times the current rates of ADSL broadband service).

A

A/B testing A/B or AB testing refers to testing two different versions of a page or a page element such as a heading, image or button. The alternatives are served alternately with the visitors to the page randomly split between the two pages. Hence, it is sometimes called 'live split testing'. Changes in visitor behaviour can then be compared using different metrics such as click-through rate on page elements like buttons or images, or macro-conversion rates, such as conversion to sale or sign-up. AB testing is aimed at increasing page or site effectiveness against key performance indicators including click-through rate, conversion rates and revenue per visit. Since it does not consider combinations of variables tested, for best uplift multivariate testing is increasingly used.

Above the fold A term, derived from printed media, which is used to indicate whether a banner advertisement or other content is displayed on a web page without the need to scroll. This is likely to give higher click-through, but note that the location of the 'fold' within the web browser is dependent on the screen resolution of a user's personal computer.

Access platform A method for customers to access digital media.

Access provider A company providing services to enable a company or individual to access the Internet. Access providers are divided into Internet service providers (ISPs) and online service providers (OSPs).

Accessibility An approach to site design intended to accommodate site usage using different browsers and settings particularly required by the visually impaired and visitors with other disabilities including motor control, learning difficulties and deafness. Users whose first language is not English can also be assisted.

Accessibility legislation Legislation intended to assist users of websites with disabilities including visual disability.

Acquisition *See* **Customer acquisition**.

Activation A prospect or customer takes the first step in actively using an online service after initial registration or purchase.

Active Server Page (ASP) A type of HTML page (denoted by an .asp file name) that includes scripts (small programs) that are processed on a web server before the web page is served to the user's web browser. ASP is a Microsoft technology that usually runs on a Microsoft Internet Information Server (usually on Windows NT). The main use of such programs is to process information supplied by the user in an online form. A query may then be run to provide specific information to the customer such as delivery status on an order, or a personalised web page.

ActiveX A programming language standard developed by Microsoft that permits complex and graphical customer applications to be written and then accessed from a web browser. ActiveX components are standard controls that can be incorporated into websites and are then automatically downloaded for users. Examples are graphics and animation or a calculator form for calculating interest on a loan or a control for graphing stock prices. A competitor to Java.

Adaptive mobile web design Generally a more sophisticated approach than Responsive web design that involves delivering an experience optimised for handsets targeted and splits the code and processing to render on different devices between the client and the server.

Ad creative The design and content of an ad.

Ad impression Similar in concept to a page impression; describes one viewing of an advertisement by a single member of its audience. The same as ad view, a term that is less commonly used.

Ad inventory The total number of ad impressions that a website can sell over time (usually specified per month).

Ad network Ad networks from suppliers such as Blue Lithium or 24-7 Media give advertisers the options of advertising across a network of sites to reach a particular demographic, e.g. female 18–25, but at a lower cost than targeting a single site since the actual site used for the ad placement isn't known (hence these are sometimes known as 'blind network buys').

Ad rotation When advertisements are changed on a website for different user sessions. This may be in response to ad targeting or simply displaying different advertisements from those on a list.

Ad serving The term for displaying an advertisement on a website. Often the advertisement will be served from a web server different from the site on which it is placed. For example, the server URL for displaying the advertisement is http://ad.doubleclick.net.

Ad space The area of a web page that is set aside for banner advertising.

Ad view Similar in concept to a page impression; describes one viewing of an advertisement by a single member of its audience. The same as ad impression, the term that is more commonly used.

Adaptive web design Also known as progressive enhancement, this design technique delivers different layouts and features according to what is supported by browser and screen resolution of the device.

Advertisement Advertisements on websites are usually banner advertisements positioned as a masthead on the page.

Advertising broker *See* **Media broker**.

Advertising networks A collection of independent websites of different companies and media networks, each of which has an arrangement with a single advertising broker (*see* **Media broker**) to place banner advertisements.

Affiliate A company promoting a merchant typically through a commission-based arrangement either direct or through an affiliate network.

Affiliate marketing A commission-based arrangement where referring sites (publishers) receive a commission on sales or leads by merchants (retailers). Commission is usually based on a percentage of product sale price or a fixed amount for each sale (CPA or cost-per-acquisition), but may also sometimes be based on a per-click basis, for example when an aggregator refers visits to merchants.

Affiliate networks Third-party brokers also known as affiliate managers who manage recruitment of affiliates and infrastructure to manage a merchant's affiliate programme in the form of links, tracking and payment of a range of affiliates.

Agents Software programs that can assist people to perform tasks like finding particular information such as the best price for a product.

Aggregated buying A form of customer union where buyers collectively purchase a number of items at the same price and receive a volume discount.

Aggregators An alternative term to *price comparison sites*. Aggregators include product, price and service information comparing competitors within a sector such as financial services, retail or travel. Their revenue models commonly include affiliate revenues (CPA), pay-per-click advertising (CPC) and display advertising (CPM).

Agile software development An iterative approach to developing software and website functionality with the emphasis on face-to-face communications to elicit, define and test requirements. Each iteration or scrum is effectively a mini-software project including stages of planning, requirements analysis, design, coding, testing and documentation.

Allowable cost-per-acquisition A target maximum cost for generating leads or new customers profitably.

Alt tags Alt tags appear after an image tag and contain a phrase associated with that image. For example: <img src="logo.gif" alt="Company name, company products"/>.

Always-on communications Continuous investment in paid, owned and earned digital media to engage prospects and customers and meet purchase intent as they research products through search, social media and publisher sites.

Anchor text (also known as link text) The (usually) clickable text element representing a hyperlink. Or more prosaically, the body copy that is hyperlinked.

Animated banner advertisements (animated GIFs) Early banner advertisements featured only a single advertisement, but today they will typically involve several different images, which are displayed in sequence to help attract attention to the banner and build up a theme, often ending with a call to action and the injunction to click on the banner. These advertisements are achieved through supplying the ad creative as an animated GIF file with different layers or frames, usually a rectangle of 468×60 pixels. Animated banner advertisements are an example of rich-media advertisements.

Announcements *See* **Site announcements**.

Application Programming Interfaces Method of exchanging data between systems such as website services.

Archie A database containing information on what documents and programs are located on FTP servers. It would not be used in a marketing context unless one were looking for a specific piece of software or document name.

Asymmetric encryption Both parties use a related but different key to encode and decode messages.

Atomisation Atomisation in a Web 2.0 context refers to a concept where the content on a site is broken down into smaller fundamental units which can then be distributed via the web through links to other sites. Examples of atomisation include the stories and pages in individual feeds being syndicated to third-party sites and widgets.

Attrition rate Percentage of site visitors who are lost at each stage in making a purchase.

Audit (external) Consideration of the business and economic environment in which the company operates. This includes the economic, political, fiscal, legal, social, cultural and technological factors (usually referred to by the acronym STEP or SLEPT).

Audit (internal) A review of website effectiveness.

Auditors *See* **Site auditors.**

Authentication *See* **Security methods.**

Autoresponders Software tools or agents running on web servers that automatically send a standard reply to the sender of an email message. This may provide information for a standard request sent to, say, price_list@company_name.com, or it could simply state that the message or order has been forwarded to the relevant person and will be answered within two days. (Also known as mailbots.)

Availability *See* **Security methods; Site availability.**

Avatar A term used in computer-mediated environments to mean a 'virtual person'. Derived from the word's original meaning: '*n*. the descendant of a Hindu deity in a visible form; incarnation; supreme glorification of any principle'.

Average order value (AOV) The average amount spent for a single checkout purchase on a retail site for a particular customer group, e.g. first time purchasers.

B

Backbones High-speed communications links used to enable Internet communications across a country and internationally.

Backlinks Hyperlinks which link to a particular web page (or website). Also known as inbound links. Google PageRank and Yahoo! WebRank are methods of enumerating this.

Balanced scorecard A framework for setting and monitoring business performance. Metrics are structured according to customer issues, internal efficiency measures, financial measures and innovation.

Bandwidth Indicates the speed at which data are transferred using a particular network medium. It is measured in bits per second (bps).

- kbps (one kilobit per second or 1000 bps; a modem operates at up to 56.6 kbps).
- Mbps (one megabit per second or 1,000,000 bps; company networks operate at 10 or more Mbps).
- Gbps (one gigabit per second or 1,000,000,000 bps; fibre-optic or satellite links operate at Gbps).

Banner advertisement A typically rectangular graphic displayed on a web page for purposes of brand building or driving traffic to a site. It is normally possible to perform a click-through to access further information from another website. Banners may be static or animated. See **Animated banner advertisements.**

Behavioural ad targeting Enables an advertiser to target ads at a visitor as they move elsewhere on the site or return to the site, thus increasing the frequency or number of impressions served to an individual in the target market.

Behavioural loyalty Loyalty to a brand is demonstrated by repeat sales and response to marketing campaigns.

Behavioural traits of web users Web users can be broadly divided into directed and undirected information seekers.

Bid A commitment by a trader to purchase under certain conditions.

Big Data applications in marketing Big Data refers to applications to gain value from the increasing Volume, Velocity and Variety of data integrated from different sources. These enhance insight to deliver more relevant communications through techniques such as Marketing Automation and Social CRM.

Blog Personal online diary, journal or news source compiled by one person, an internal team or external guest authors. Postings are usually in different categories. Typically comments can be added to each blog posting to help create interactivity and feedback.

Bluecasting Bluecasting involves messages being automatically pushed to a consumer's bluetooth-enabled phone or they can pull or request audio, video or text content to be downloaded from a live advert. In the future ads will be able to respond to those who view them.

Bluejacking Sending a message from a mobile phone or transmitter to another mobile phone which is in close range via Bluetooth technology.

Blueprints Show the relationships between pages and other content components; can be used to portray organisation, navigation and labelling systems.

Bluetooth A standard for wireless transmission of data between devices over short ranges (less than 10m), e.g. a mobile phone or a PDA.

Botnet Independent computers, connected to the Internet, are used together, typically for malicious purposes through controlling software. For example, they may be used to send out spam or for a denial of service attack where they repeatedly access a server to degrade its software. Computers are often initially infected through a virus when effective anti-virus measures are not in place.

Bounce rate Proportion of visitors to a page or site that exit after visiting a single page only, usually expressed as a percentage.

Brand The sum of the characteristics of a product or service perceived by a user.

Brand advocate A customer who has favourable perceptions of a brand who will talk favourably about a brand to their acquaintances to help generate awareness of the brand or influence purchase intent.

Brand equity The brand assets (or liabilities) linked to a brand's name and symbol that add to (or subtract from) a service.

Brand experience The frequency and depth of interactions with a brand can be enhanced through the Internet.

Brand identity The totality of brand associations including name and symbols that must be communicated.

Branding The process of creating and evolving successful brands.

Bricks-and-mortar A traditional organisation with limited online presence.

Broadband technology A term referring to methods of delivering information across the Internet at a higher rate by increasing bandwidth.

Brochureware A website in which a company has simply transferred ('migrated') its existing paper-based promotional literature onto the Internet without recognising the differences required by this medium.

Broker *See* **Media broker**.

Browser *See* **Web browser**.

Bundling Offering complementary services.

Business model A summary of how a company will generate revenue, identifying its product offering, value-added services, revenue sources and target customers.

Business-to-business (B2B) Commercial transactions between an organisation and other organisations (inter-organisational marketing).

Business-to-business exchanges or marketplaces Virtual intermediaries with facilities to enable trading between buyers and sellers.

Business-to-consumer (B2C) Commercial transactions between an organisation and consumers.

Buy-side e-commerce E-commerce transactions between a purchasing organisation and its suppliers.

C

Call centre A location for inbound and outbound telemarketing.

Call-back service A direct response facility available on a website to enable a company to contact a customer by phone at a later time as specified by the customer.

Campaign-based e-communications E-marketing communications that are executed to support a specific marketing campaign such as a product launch, price promotion or a website launch.

Campaign URL (CURL) A web address specific to a particular campaign.

Capabilities Capabilities are intangible and are developed from the combined and coordinated behaviour and activities of an organisation's employees, and it is therefore embedded in the organisation and processes. The definition of a capability is an organisation's ability to 'perform a set of coordinated tasks, utilising organisational resources, for the purposes of achieving a particular end result'.

Card sorting The process of setting up a way of organising objects on the website in a consistent manner.

Cascading style sheets A simple mechanism for adding style (e.g. fonts, colours, spacing) to web documents. CSS enables different style elements to be controlled across an entire site or section of site. Style elements that are commonly controlled include typography, background colour and images, and borders and margins.

Catalogue Catalogues provide a structured listing of registered websites in different categories. They are similar to an electronic version of *Yellow Pages*. Yahoo! and Excite are the best known examples of catalogues. (Also known as directories.) The distinction between search engines and catalogues has become blurred since many sites now include both facilities as part of a portal service.

Certificate A valid copy of a public key of an individual or organisation together with identification information. It is issued by a trusted third party (TTP) or certification authority (CA).

Certification authority (CA) An organisation issuing and managing certificates or public keys and private keys to individuals or organisations together with identification information.

Change management Controls to minimise the risks of project-based and organisational change.

Channel buyer behaviour Describes which content is visited and the time and duration.

Channel conflicts A significant threat arising from the introduction of an Internet channel is that while disintermediation gives the opportunity for a company to sell direct and increase the profitability of products it can also threaten existing distribution arrangements with existing partners.

Channel marketing strategy Defines how a company should set specific objectives for a channel such as the Internet and vary its proposition and communications for this channel.

Channel outcomes Record customer actions taken as a consequence of a visit to a site.

Channel profitability The profitability of a website, taking into account revenue and cost and discounted cash flow.

Channel promotion Measures that assess why customers visit a site – which adverts they have seen, which sites they have been referred from.

Channel satisfaction Evaluation of the customer's opinion of the service quality on the site and supporting services such as email.

Channel structure The configuration of partners in a distribution channel.

Click ecosystem Describes the customer behaviour or flow of online visitors between search engines, media sites, other intermediaries to an organisation and its competitors.

Clicks-and-mortar A business combining online and offline presence.

Clicks-only or Internet pureplay An organisation with principally an online presence.

Clickstream A record of the path a user takes through a website. Clickstreams enable website designers to assess how their site is being used.

Clickstream analysis Reviewing the online behaviour of site visitors based on the sequence of pages that they visit, the navigation and promotion they respond to, the ultimate outcomes and where they leave the site.

Click-through A click-through (ad click) occurs each time a user clicks on a banner advertisement to direct them to a web page that contains further information.

Click-through rate Expressed as a percentage of total ad impressions, and refers to the proportion of users viewing an advertisement who click on it. It is calculated as the number of click-throughs divided by the number of ad impressions.

Click-tracking Java technology can be used to track movements of individual users to a website.

Click ecosystem Describes the customer behaviour or flow of online visitors between search engines, media sites, other intermediaries to an organisation and its competitors.

Client discovery process An initiative to learn what a client or brand needs from a campaign, their strategic initiatives which it must aligned with, their goals and their marketing outcomes.

Client–server The client–server architecture consists of client computers such as PCs sharing resources such as a database stored on a more powerful server computer.

Co-branding An arrangement between two or more companies where they agree to jointly display content and perform joint promotion using brand logos, email marketing or banner advertisements. The aim is that the brands are strengthened if they are seen as complementary. Co-branding is often a reciprocal arrangement which can occur without payment as part of a wider agreement between partners.

Co-marketing A partnership agreement reached between different businesses to promote each other, typically based on sharing content (and potentially promotions) principally to the audience of owned media channels such as social media, blog and email marketing.

Cold list Data about individuals that are rented or sold by a third party.

Collaborative filtering Profiling of customer interest coupled with delivery of specific information and offers, often based on the interests of similar customers.

Commoditisation The process whereby product selection becomes more dependent on price than on differentiating features, benefits and value-added services.

Common Gateway Interface (CGI) A method of processing information on a web server in response to a customer's request. Typically a user will fill in a web-based form and the results will be processed by a CGI script (application). Active Server Pages (ASPs) are an alternative to a CGI script.

Competitive intelligence (CI) A process that transforms disaggregated information into relevant, accurate and usable strategic knowledge about competitors, position, performance, capabilities and intentions.

Competitor analysis Review of Internet marketing services offered by existing and new competitors and adoption by their customers.

Competitor benchmarking A structured analysis of the online services, capabilities and performance of an organisation within the areas of customer acquisition, conversion, retention and growth.

Computer telephony integration The integration of telephony and computing to provide a platform for applications that streamline or enhance business processes.

Confidentiality *See Security methods.*

Consumer-to-business (C2B) Consumers approach the business with an offer.

Consumer-to-consumer (C2C) Informational or financial transactions between consumers, but usually mediated through a business site.

Consumer behaviour Research into the motivations, media consumption preferences and selection processes of consumers as they use digital channels together with traditional channels to purchase online products and use other online services.

Consumer behaviour analysis In digital markets, this type of analysis involves research into the motivations, media consumption preferences and selection processes used by consumers as they use digital channels together with traditional channels to purchase online products and use other online services.

Contact or touch strategy Definition of the sequence and type of outbound communications required at different points in the customer lifecycle.

Content Content is the design, text and graphical information that forms a web page. Good content is the key to attracting customers to a website and retaining their interest or achieving repeat visits.

Content developer A person responsible for updating web pages within part of an organisation.

Content distribution (or delivery) networks (CDNs) A system of servers distributed globally with copies of data stored locally to enable more rapid download of content. Their use has increased with increased use of streaming video and more complex web applications.

Content management Software tools for managing additions and amendments to website content.

Content management system (CMS) A software tool for creating, editing and updating documents accessed by intranet, extranet or Internet.

Content marketing The management of text, rich media, audio and video content aimed at engaging customers and prospects to meet business goals published through print and digital media including web and mobile platforms which is repurposed and syndicated to different forms of web presence such as publisher sites, blogs, social media and comparison sites.

Content marketing hub A central branded location where your audience can access and interact with all your key content marketing assets. In a practical sense, the content hub can be a blog or new section, an online customer magazine or a resource centre.

Content network Sponsored links are displayed by the search engine on third-party sites such as online publishers, aggregators or social networks. Ads can be paid for on a CPC, CPM or CPA basis. There are also options for graphical or video ads in addition to text-based ads.

Content strategy The management of text, rich media, audio and video content aimed at engaging customers and prospects to meet business goals published through print and digital media including web and mobile platforms which is repurposed and syndicated to different forms of web presence such as publisher sites, blogs, social media and comparison sites.

Contextual ads Ads relevant to page content on third-party sites brokered by search ad networks.

Contextual marketing Relevant communications are delivered consistent with the context of the recipient which can depend on their location, time or place.

Continuous e-communications activities Long-term use of e-marketing communications intended to generate site visitors for customer acquisition (such as search engine, and affiliate marketing and online sponsorship) and retention (for example, e-newsletter marketing).

Contra-deals A reciprocal agreement in the form of an exchange where payment doesn't take place. Instead services or ad space promote another company as part of co-branding.

Control page The page against which subsequent optimisation will be assessed. Typically a current landing page. When a new page performs better than the existing control page, it becomes the control page in subsequent testing. Also known as 'champion-challenger'.

Convergence A trend in which different hardware devices such as televisions, computers and telephones merge and have similar functions.

Conversion marketing Using marketing communications to maximise conversion of potential customers to actual customers.

Conversion rate Proportion of visitors to a site, or viewers of an advert, who take an action such as registration or checkout. *See* **Visit conversion rate** and **Visitor conversion rate**.

Conversion rate optimisation (CRO) Improving the commercial returns from a transactional site through increasing conversion to key goals such as sales, quotes or bookings or leads. CRO combines customer and competitor research with evaluation of customer behaviour using web analytics and AB and multivariate testing.

Cookies Cookies are small text files stored on an end user's computer to enable websites to identify the user. They enable a company to identify a previous visitor to a site, and build up a profile of that visitor's behaviour. *See* **Persistent cookies, Session cookies, First-party cookies, Third-party cookies**.

Core product The fundamental features of the product that meet the user's needs.

Core tenants A shopping centre or mall is usually a centrally owned managed facility. In the physical world, the management will aim to include in the mall stores that sell a different but complementary range of merchandise and include a variety of smaller and larger stores. The core tenants, or 'anchor stores' as they are often called, are the dominant large-scale store operators that are expected to draw customers to the centre.

Cost models for Internet advertising These include per-exposure, per-response and per-action costs.

Cost-per-acquisition (CPA) The cost of acquiring a new customer. Typically limited to the communications cost and refers to cost per sale for new customers. May also refer to other outcomes such as cost-per-quote or enquiry.

Cost-per-click (CPC) The cost of each click from a referring site to a destination site, typically from a search engine in pay-per-click search marketing.

Cost-per-targeted mille (CPTM) Cost per targeted thousand for an advertisement. *See* **Targeting**.

Cost per thousand (CPM) Cost per 1000 ad impressions.

Countermediation Creation of a new intermediary by an established company.

Cracker A malicious meddler who tries to discover sensitive information by poking around computer networks.

Cross-media optimisation studies (XMOS) Studies to determine the optimum spend across different media to produce the best results.

Cross-selling Persuading existing customers to purchase products from other categories than their typical purchases.

Customer acquisition Strategies and techniques used to gain new customers.

Customer-centric marketing An approach to marketing based on detailed knowledge of customer behaviour within the target audience which seeks to fulfil the individual needs and wants of customers.

Customer communications channels The range of media used to communicate directly with a customer.

Customer engagement Repeated interactions that strengthen the emotional, psychological or physical investment a customer has in a brand.

Customer engagement strategy A strategy to encourage interaction and participation of consumers with a brand through developing content and experiences with the aim of meeting commercial objectives. It is closely related to the development of content marketing and social media strategy.

Customer experience *See* **Online customer experience**.

Customer Experience Management (CXM) A holistic approach to managing customer experience and customer engagement across digital and non-digital touch-points including web, mobile and social digital platforms, in-store and by call centres.

Customer extension Techniques to encourage customers to increase their involvement with an organisation.

Customer insight Knowledge about customers' needs, characteristics, preferences and behaviours based on analysis of qualitative and quantitative data. Specific insights can be used to inform marketing tactics directed at groups of customers with shared characteristics.

Customer journey A description of modern multichannel buyer behaviour as consumers use different media to select suppliers, make purchases and gain customer support.

Customer lifecycle The stages each customer will pass through in a long-term relationship through acquisition, retention and extension.

Customer loyalty The desire on the part of the customer to continue to do business with a given supplier over time. *See* **Behavioural loyalty** and **Emotional loyalty**.

Customer Preference Centre Profile page(s) which enables customers to tailor the type and frequency of communications they receive.

Customer orientation Providing content and services on a website consistent with the different characteristics of the audience of the site.

Customer profiling Using the website to find out customers' specific interests and characteristics.

Customer relationship management (CRM) A marketing-led approach to building and sustaining long-term business with customers.

Customer retention Techniques to maintain relationships with existing customers.

Customer satisfaction The extent to which a customer's expectations of product quality, service quality and price are met.

Customer scenarios (online customer journeys) Alternative tasks or outcomes required by a visitor to a website. Typically accomplished in a series of stages of different tasks involving different information needs or experiences.

Customer segments Groups of customers sharing similar characteristics, preferences and behaviours who are targeted with different propositions as part of *target marketing strategy*.

Customer selection Identifying key customer segments and targeting them for relationship building.

Customer touch-points Communications channels with which companies interact directly with prospects and customers. Traditional touch-points include face-to-face (in-store or with sales representatives), phone and mail. Digital touch-points include web services, email and, potentially, mobile phone.

Cybermediaries Intermediaries who bring together buyers and sellers or those with particular information or service needs.

Cyberspace and cybermarketing These terms were preferred by science-fiction writers and tabloid writers to indicate the futuristic nature of using the Internet, the prefix 'cyber' indicating a blurring between humans, machines and communications. The terms are not frequently used today since the terms Internet, intranet and World Wide Web are more specific and widely used.

D

Data controller Each company must have a defined person responsible for data protection.

Data fusion The combining of data from different complementary sources (usually geodemographic and lifestyle or market research and lifestyle) to 'build a picture of someone's life' (M. Evans (1998) From 1086 to 1984: direct marketing into the millennium, *Marketing Intelligence and Planning*, 16(1), 56–67).

Data subject The legal term to refer to the individual whose data are held.

Data warehousing and data mining Extracting data from legacy systems and other resources; cleaning, scrubbing and preparing data for decision support; maintaining data in appropriate data stores; accessing and analysing data using a variety of end-user tools; and mining data for significant relationships. The primary purpose of these efforts is to provide easy access to specially prepared data that can be used with decision support applications such as management reports, queries, decision support systems, executive information systems and data mining.

Database marketing The process of systematically collecting, in electronic or optical form, data about past, current and/or potential customers, maintaining the integrity of the data by continually monitoring customer purchases, by enquiring about changing status, and by using the data to formulate marketing strategy and foster personalised relationships with customers.

Decryption The process of decoding (unscrambling) a message that has been encrypted using defined mathematical rules.

Deep linking Jakob Nielsen's term for a user arriving at a site deep within its structure or where search engines index a mirrored copy of content normally inaccessible by search engine spiders.

Deliverability Deliverability refers to ensuring email messages are delivered and aren't blocked by spam filters because the email content or structure falsely identifies a permission-based email as a spammer, or because the sender's IP address has a poor reputation for spam.

Demand analysis Quantitative determination of the potential usage and business value achieved from online customers of an organisation. Qualitative analysis of perceptions of online channels is also assessed.

Demand analysis for e-commerce Assessment of the demand for e-commerce services among existing and potential customer segments using the ratio Access:Choose:Buy online.

Demand Side Platforms (DSPs) A service that enables ads to be managed across multiple ad networks and ad exchanges through a single interface designed for managing reporting and performance.

Demographic characteristics Variations in attributes of the population such as age, sex and social class.

Denial of service attack Also known as a distributed denial of service (DDOS) attack, this involves a hacker group taking control of many 'zombie' computers attached to the Internet whose security has been compromised. This 'botnet' is then used to make many requests to a target server, so overloading it and preventing access to other visitors.

Design for analysis (DFA) The required measures from a site are considered during design to better understand the audience of a site and their decision points.

Design phase (of site construction) The design phase defines how the site will work in the key areas of website structure, navigation and security.

Destination site Frequently used to refer to the site that is visited following a click-through on a banner advertisement. Could also apply to any site visited following a click on a hyperlink.

Destination store A retail store in which the merchandise, selection, presentation, pricing or other unique features act as a magnet for the customer.

Development (of site construction) 'Development' is the term used to describe the creation of a website by programmers. It involves writing the HTML content, creating graphics, and writing any necessary software code such as JavaScript or ActiveX (programming).

DevOps An approach to development of systems which involves a more collaborative and closer relationship between development teams and operations teams with the aim of reducing deployment times and frequency of system updates and improving their stability.

Differential advantage A desirable attribute of a product that is not currently matched by competitor offerings.

Differential pricing Identical products are priced differently for different types of customers, markets or buying situations.

Digital assets The graphical and interactive material that support a campaign displayed on third-party sites and on microsites, they include display ads, email templates, video, audio and other interactive media such as Flash animations.

Digital audio broadcasting (DAB) radio Digital radio with clear sound quality with the facility to transmit text, images and video.

Digital brand A digital brand is a brand identity used for a product or company online that differs from the traditional brand. (Also known as an online brand.)

Digital cash An electronic version of cash in which the buyer of an item is typically anonymous to the seller. (Also referred to as virtual or electronic cash or e-cash.)

Digital certificates (keys) A method of ensuring privacy on the Internet. Certificates consist of keys made up of large numbers that are used to uniquely identify individuals. *See* **Public key**.

Digital customer experience A brand's total digital experience includes a brand's presence on different platforms including desktop website, mobile site and apps, ads on gaming platforms and digital in-store. It is based on the combination of rational and emotional factors of using a company's online services that influences customers' perceptions of a brand online.

Digital marketing This has a similar meaning to 'electronic marketing' – both describe the management and execution of marketing using electronic media such as the web, email, interactive TV, IPTV and wireless media in conjunction with digital data about customers' characteristics and behaviour.

Digital marketing metrics Measures that indicate the effectiveness of digital marketing activities integrated across different channels and platforms in meeting customer, business and marketing objectives.

Digital marketing strategy Definition of the approach by which applying digital technology platforms will support marketing and business objectives.

Digital media Communications are facilitated through content and interactive services delivered by different digital technology platforms including the Internet, web, mobile phone, interactive TV, IPTV and digital signage. *See* **Digital media channels**.

Digital media 'assists' A referrer of a visit to a site before the ultimate sale is credited with the sale, often through a weighting system.

Digital media channels Online communications techniques such as search engine marketing, affiliate marketing and display advertising used to engage web users on third-party sites; encouraging them to visit an organisation's site or purchase through traditional channels such as by phone or in-store.

Digital media de-duplication A single referrer of a visit leading to sale is credited with the sale based on the last-click method of digital media channel attribution.

Digital radio All types of radio broadcast as a digital signal.

Digital rights management (DRM) The use of different technologies to protect the distribution of digital services or content such as software, music, movies or other digital data.

Digital signage The use of interactive digital technologies within billboard and point of sale ads. For example, videos and bluetooth interaction.

Digital signatures The electronic equivalent of written signatures which are used as an online method of identifying individuals or companies using public-key encryption.

Digital television Information is received and displayed on a digital television using binary information (0s and 1s), giving options for better picture and sound quality and providing additional information services based on interactivity. *See* **Interactive digital TV.**

Digital transformation A staged programme of business improvements to People, Process and Tools tools used for integrated digital marketing to maximise the potential contribution of digital technology and media to business growth.

Direct-to-customer model A brand which has previously communicated to its customers via intermediaries such as media sites or wholesalers communicates directly via digital media such as social networks, email and websites.

Direct marketing Marketing to customers using one or more advertising media aimed at achieving measurable response and/or transaction.

Direct response Usually achieved in an Internet marketing context by call-back services.

Directed information seeker Someone who knows what information they are looking for.

Directories Directory websites provide a structured listing of registered websites in different categories. They are similar to an electronic version of *Yellow Pages*. Yahoo! and Excite are the best known examples of directories. (Also known as catalogues.)

Discovery or analysis phase The identification of the requirements of an online service. Techniques to achieve this may include quantitative analysis of digital analytics data and qualitative analysis involving focus groups, questionnaires sent to existing customers or interviews with key accounts.

Disintermediation The removal of intermediaries such as distributors or brokers that formerly linked a company to its customers.

Display advertising Paid ad placements using graphical or *rich media ad units* within a web page to achieve goals of delivering brand awareness, familiarity, favourability and purchase intent. Many ads encourage interaction through prompting the viewer to interact or *rollover* to play videos, complete an online form or to view more details by clicking through to a site.

Display (or content) network Sponsored links are displayed by the search engine on third-party sites such as online publishers, aggregators or social networks. Ads can be paid for on a CPC, CPM or a CPA basis. There are also options for graphical or video ads as well as text-based ads.

Disruptive technologies New technologies that prompt businesses to reappraise their strategic approaches.

Distribution channels The mechanism by which products are directed to customers either through intermediaries or directly.

Domain name The web address that identifies a web server. *See* **Domain name system.**

Domain name registration The process of reserving a unique web address that can be used to refer to the company website.

Domain name system The domain name system (DNS) provides a method of representing Internet Protocol (IP) addresses as text-based names. These are used as web addresses. For example, www.microsoft.com is the representation of site 207.68.156.58. Domain names are divided into the following categories:

- Top-level domain name such as *.com* or *.co.uk*. (Also known as Global (or generic) top-level domain names (gLTD).)
- Second-level domain name. This refers to the company name and is sometimes referred to as the 'enterprise name', e.g. *novell.com*.
- Third-level or sub-enterprise domain name. This may be used to refer to an individual server within an organisation, such as *support.novell.com*.

Doorway pages Specially constructed pages which feature keywords for particular product searches. These often redirect visitors to a home page.

Download The process of retrieving electronic information such as a web page or email from another remote location such as a web server.

Drip irrigation Collecting information about customer needs through their lifetime.

Duplicate content Different pages which are evaluated by the search engine to be similar and so don't rank highly, even though they may be for distinct products or services.

Dynamic pricing Prices can be updated in real time according to the type of customer or current market conditions.

Dynamic web page A page that is created in real time, often with reference to a database query, in response to a user request.

E

Early adopters Companies or departments that invest in new marketing techniques and technologies when they first become available in an attempt to gain a competitive advantage despite the higher risk entailed than that involved in a more cautious approach.

Early (first) mover advantage An early entrant into the marketplace.

Earned media The audience is reached through editorial, comments and sharing online.

Earnings-per-click (EPC) A relative measure of the effectiveness of a site or section of a site in generating revenue for the site owner through affiliate marketing for every 100 outbound clicks generated.

E-business *See* **Electronic business.**

E-cash *See* **Digital cash.**

E-commerce *See* **Electronic commerce.**

Econometric modelling A quantitative technique to evaluate the past influence or predict the future influence on a dependent variable (typically sales in a marketing context) of independent variables which may include product price, promotions and the level and mix of media investments.

Editorial calendar A plan for scheduling the creation of new or updated content for different audiences to support business goals for new visitors or increased conversion as part of content marketing.

Effective cost-per-thousand (eCPM) A measure of the total revenue a site owner can achieve through advertising or other revenue options. eCPM is calculated as advertising revenue achieved for every 1000 pages that are served for the whole site or a section. *See* **EPC.**

Effective frequency The number of exposures or ad impressions (frequency) required for an advertisement to become effective.

Effectiveness Meeting process objectives, delivering the required outputs and outcomes. 'Doing the right thing.'

Efficiency Minimising resources or time needed to complete a process. 'Doing the thing right.'

E-government The use of Internet technologies to provide government services to citizens.

Electronic business (e-business) All electronically mediated information exchanges, both within an organisation and with external stakeholders, supporting the range of business processes.

Electronic cash *See* **Digital cash.**

Electronic commerce (e-commerce) All financial and informational electronically mediated exchanges between an organisation and its external stakeholders. *See* **Buy-side e-commerce** and **Sell-side e-commerce.**

Electronic commerce transactions Transactions in the trading of goods and services conducted using the Internet and other digital media.

Electronic customer relationship management (e-CRM) Using digital communications technologies to maximise sales to existing customers and encourage continued usage of online services.

Electronic data interchange (EDI) The exchange, using digital media, of standardised business documents such as purchase orders and invoices between buyers and sellers.

Electronic mail (email) Sending messages or documents, such as news about a new product or sales promotion between individuals. A primitive form of push channel. Email may be inbound or outbound.

Electronic mail advertising Advertisements contained within email such as newsletters.

Electronic mall *See* **Virtual mall.**

Electronic marketing Achieving marketing objectives through use of electronic communications technology.

Electronic marketspace A virtual marketplace such as the Internet in which no direct contact occurs between buyers and sellers.

Electronic procurement (e-procurement) The electronic integration and management of all procurement activities including purchase request, authorisation, ordering, delivery and payment between a purchaser and a supplier.

Electronic shopping or ES test This test was developed by de Kare-Silver to assess the extent to which consumers are likely to purchase a particular retail product using the Internet.

Electronic tokens Units of digital currency that are in a standard electronic format.

Email marketing Typically applied to outbound communications from a company to prospects or customers to encourage purchase or branding goals. Email marketing is most commonly used for mailing to existing customers on a house-list, but can also be used for mailing prospects on a rented or co-branded list. Emails may be sent as part of a one-off campaign or can be automated event-based triggered emails such as a Welcome strategy which can be broadcast based on rules about intervals and customer characteristics. *See* **Inbound email** and **Outbound email.**

Email service providers (ESPs) Provide a web-based service used by marketers to manage their email activities including hosting email subscription forms, broadcast and tracking.

E-marketing *See* **Electronic marketing**.

Emergent strategy Strategic analysis, strategic development and strategy implementation are interrelated and are developed together.

Emotional loyalty Loyalty to a brand is demonstrated by favourable perceptions, opinions and recommendations.

Encryption The scrambling of information into a form that cannot be interpreted. Decryption is used to make the information readable.

Enterprise application integration The middleware technology that is used to connect together different software applications and their underlying databases is now known as 'enterprise application integration (EAI)'.

Entry page The page at which a visitor enters a website. It is identified by a log file analyser. *See* **Exit page** and **Referring site**.

Environmental scanning and analysis The process of continuously monitoring the environment and analysing events in an organisation's environment(s) which have implications for planning and responding accordingly.

E-retail According to Dennis *et al*. (2004; see Chapter 11), the business of e-retailing is defined as the sale of goods and services via the Internet or other electronic channels for individual consumers. This definition includes all e-commerce and related activities that ultimately result in transactions.

Ethical standards Practices or behaviours which are morally acceptable to society.

Evaluating a website *See* **Website measurement**.

Exchange *See* **Business-to-business exchanges or marketplaces**.

Exit page The page from which a visitor exits a website. It is identified by web analytics services.

Expert reviews An analysis of an existing site or prototype by an experienced usability expert who will identify deficiencies and improvements to a site based on their knowledge of web design principles and best practice.

Exposure-based payment Advertisers pay according to the number of times the ad is viewed.

Extended product Additional features and benefits beyond the core product.

Extension *See* **Customer extension**.

External link building A proactive approach to gain quality links from third-party sites.

Extranet Formed by extending an intranet beyond a company to customers, suppliers, collaborators or even competitors. This is password-protected to prevent access by general Internet users.

F

Facebook commerce (F-commerce) Retailers create an online store within Facebook, often with a limited range of stock.

Faceted navigation Used to enable users to rapidly filter results from a product search based on different ways of classifying the product by their attributes or features. For example by brand, by sub-product category, by price bands.

Feed or RSS feed Blog, news or other content is published by an XML standard and syndicated for other sites or read by users in RSS reader services such as Google Reader, personalised home pages or email systems. RSS stands for *really simple syndication*.

File Transfer Protocol (FTP) A standard method for moving files across the Internet. FTP is available as a feature of web browsers that is sometimes used for marketing applications such as downloading files like product price lists or specifications. Standalone FTP packages such as WSFTP are commonly used to update HTML files on web servers when uploading revisions to the web server.

Findability An assessment of how easy it is for a web user to locate a single content object or to use browse navigation and search system to find content. Like usability it is assessed through efficiency – how long it takes to find the content – and effectiveness – how satisfied the user is with the experience and relevance of the content they find.

Firewall A specialised software application mounted on a server at the point where a company is connected to the Internet. Its purpose is to prevent unauthorised access into the company by outsiders. Firewalls are essential for all companies hosting their own web server.

First-party cookies Served by the site currently in use – typical for e-commerce sites.

Flow Describes a state in which users have a positive experience from readily controlling their navigation and interaction on a website.

Focus groups Online focus groups have been conducted by w3focus.com. These follow a bulletin board or discussion group form where different members of the focus group respond to prompts from the focus group leaders.

Folksonomy A contraction of 'folk taxonomy', a method of classifying content based on tagging that has no hierarchy (i.e. without parent–child relationships).

Form A method on a web page of entering information such as order details.

Forward auctions Item purchased by highest bid made in bidding period.

Forward path analysis Forward path analysis reviews the combinations of clicks that occur from a page. This form of analysis is most beneficial when it is forward from important pages such as the home page, product and directory pages. This technique is used to identify messaging/navigation combinations which work best to yield the most clicks from a page. Similar, effective messaging approaches can then be deployed elsewhere on the site.

Frame A technique used to divide a web page into different parts such as a menu and separate content.

G

Gamification The process of applying game thinking and mechanics to engage an audience by rewarding them for achievements and sharing.

Global (or generic) top-level domain names (gLTD) The part of the domain name that refers to the category of site. The gLTD is usually the rightmost part of the domain name such as .co.uk or .com.

Globalisation The increase of international trading and shared social and cultural values.

Google AdWords Enhanced campaigns An approach introduced by Google in 2013 to simplify the management of ads displayed in different locations, different day parts (times of day) and on different devices.

Google Display Network (GDN) Different types of online publishers agree for Google to display contextual ads on their sites for a fee, for example as part of the AdSense programme.

Google's Product Listing Ads (PLAs) Product information such as pricing and images are uploaded to Google's servers using a product feed in XML or text formats for display in ads within Google AdWords or Google Shopping.

Gopher Gopher is a directory-based structure containing information in certain categories.

GPRS This is approximately five times faster than GSM and is an 'always-on' service which is charged according to usage. Display is still largely text-based and based on the WAP protocol.

Graphic design All factors that govern the physical appearance of a web page.

Graphics Interchange Format (GIF) A graphics format used to display images within web pages. An interlaced GIF is displayed gradually on the screen, building up an image in several passes.

Growth hacking A mindset which focuses marketing activities on increasing the scale and profitability of a business through testing and improving techniques for improving the value of audience touchpoints across the customer lifecycle of Reach, Interactions, Conversion and Engagement.

GSM The digital transmission technique standard used widely for mobile voice data.

H

Hacker Someone who enjoys exploring the details of programmable systems and how to stretch their capabilities.

Halo effect The role of one media channel on influencing sale or uplift in brand metrics. Commonly applied to online display advertising, where exposure to display ads may increase click-through rates when the consumer is later exposed to a brand through other media, for example sponsored links or affiliate ads. It may also improve conversion rates on destination sites through higher confidence in the brand or familiarity with the offer.

Hard launch A site is launched once fully complete with full promotional effort.

Hit A hit is recorded for each graphic or page of text requested from a web server. It is not a reliable measure for the number of people viewing a page. A page impression is a more reliable measure denoting one person viewing one page.

Home page The index page of a website with menu options or links to other resources on the site. Usually denoted by <web address>/index.html.

House list A list of prospect and customer names, email addresses and profile information owned by an organisation.

HTML (Hypertext Markup Language) A standard format used to define the text and layout of web pages. HTML files usually have the extension.HTML or.HTM.

HTTP (Hypertext Transfer Protocol) A standard that defines the way information is transmitted across the Internet.

Hurdle rate The proportion of customers that fall within a particular level of activity. For example, the percentage of members of an email list that click on the email within a 90-day period, or the number of customers that have made a second purchase.

Hype cycle A graphic representation of the maturity, adoption and business application of specific technologies.

Hyperlink A method of moving between one website page and another, indicated to the user by text highlighted by underlining and/or a different colour. Hyperlinks can also be achieved by clicking on a graphic image such as a banner advertisement that is linked to another website.

I

Identity theft The misappropriation of the identity of another person, without their knowledge or consent.

I-Mode A mobile access platform that enables display of colour graphics and content subscription services.

Inbound customer contact strategies Approaches to managing the cost and quality of service related to management of customer enquiries.

Inbound email Email arriving at a company.

Inbound email marketing Management of emails from customers by an organisation.

Inbound Internet-based communications Customers enquire through web-based form and email. *See* **Web self-service**.

Inbound link *See* **Backlink**.

Inbound marketing The consumer is proactive in seeking out information for their needs, and interactions with brands are attracted through content, search and social media marketing.

Incidental offline advertising Driving traffic to the website is not a primary objective of the advert.

Index inclusion Ensuring that as many of the relevant pages from your domain(s) are included within the search engine indexes you are targeting to be listed in.

Infomediary An intermediary business whose main source of revenue derives from capturing consumer information and developing detailed profiles of individual customers for use by third parties.

Information architecture The combination of organisation, labelling and navigation schemes constituting an information system.

Information organisation schemes The structure chosen to group and categorise information.

Initiation of the website project This phase of the project should involve a structured review of the costs and benefits of developing a website (or making a major revision to an existing website). A successful outcome to initiation will be a decision to proceed with the site development phase, with an agreed budget and target completion date.

Insertion order A printed order to run an advertisement campaign. It defines the campaign name, the website

receiving the order and the planner or buyer giving the order, the individual advertisements to be run (or who will provide them), the sizes of the advertisements, the campaign start and end dates, the CPM, the total cost, discounts to be applied, and reporting requirements and possible penalties or stipulations relative to the failure to deliver the impressions.

Integrated marketing communications The coordination of communications channels to deliver a clear, consistent message.

Integrity *See* **Security methods**.

Intellectual property rights (IPRs) Protect the intangible property created by corporations or individuals that is protected under copyright, trade secret and patent laws.

Interactive banner advertisement A banner advertisement that enables the user to enter information.

Interactive digital TV (iDTV) Television displayed using a digital signal delivered by a range of media – cable, satellite, terrestrial (aerial). Interactions can be provided through phone line or cable service.

Interactivity The medium enables a dialogue between company and customer.

Interaction rate (IR) The proportion of ad viewers who interact with an online ad through rolling over it. Some will be involuntary depending on where the ad is placed on screen, so it is highly dependent on placement.

Internal link architecture Structuring and labelling links within a site's navigation to improve the results of SEO.

Intermediaries Online sites that help bring together different parties such as buyers and sellers.

Internet The physical network that links computers across the globe. It consists of the infrastructure of network servers and communication links between them that are used to hold and transport the vast amount of information on the Internet.

Internet-based market research The use of online questionnaires and focus groups to assess customer perceptions of a website or broader marketing issues.

Internet contribution An assessment of the extent to which the Internet contributes to sales is a key measure of the importance of the Internet to a company.

Internet EDI Use of electronic data interchange standards delivered across non-proprietary Internet protocol networks.

Internet governance Control of the operation and use of the Internet.

Internet marketing The application of the Internet and related digital technologies in conjunction with traditional communications to achieve marketing objectives.

Internet marketing metrics *See* **Metrics for Internet marketing.**

Internet marketing strategy Definition of the approach by which Internet marketing will support marketing and business objectives.

Internet Protocol Television (IPTV) Digital television service delivered using Internet protocol, typically by a broadband connection. IPTV can be streamed for real-time viewing or downloaded before playback.

Internet pureplay An organisation with the majority of its customer-facing operations online, e.g. Egg.

Internet Relay Chat (IRC) A communications tool that allows a text-based 'chat' between different users who are logged on at the same time. Of limited use for marketing purposes except for special-interest or youth products.

Internet service provider (ISP) Company that provides home or business users with a connection to access the Internet. It can also host websites or provide a link from web servers to allow other companies and consumers access to a corporate website.

Interruption marketing Marketing communications that disrupt customers' activities.

Interstitial ads Ads that appear between one page and the next.

Intranet A network within a single company that enables access to company information using the familiar tools of the Internet such as web browsers and email. Only staff within a company can access the intranet, which will be password-protected.

J

Java A programming language standard supported by Sun Microsystems, which permits complex and graphical customer applications to be written and then accessed from a web browser. An example might be a form for calculating interest on a loan. A competitor to ActiveX.

Joint Photographics Experts Group (JPEG) A compressed graphics standard specified by the JPEG. Used for graphic images typically requiring use of many colours, such as product photographs where some loss of quality is acceptable. The format allows for some degradation in image quality to enable more rapid download.

K

Key online influencers Celebrities, individuals well known in their niche or publishers that an online target audience listens to and interacts with. Online influencer outreach or 'blogger outreach' can help companies reach and engage a wider audience. Recently video bloggers ('vloggers' or 'YouTubers') have become popular amongst teenage audiences.

Key performance indicators (KPIs) Metrics used to assess the performance of a process and/or whether goals set are achieved.

Keyphrase (keyword phrase) The combination of words users of search engines type into a search box which form a search query.

Knowledge Graph An infrastructure developed by Google to display related information about people, places and objects.

L

Lagging performance indicator A metric which indicates past performance. Corrective action can then be applied to improve performance.

Landing page A destination page when a user clicks on an ad or other form of link from a *referring site*. It can be a home page, but more typically and desirably a landing page is a page with the messaging focussed on the offer in the ad. This will maximise conversion rates and brand favourability.

Last-click method of digital media channel attribution The site which referred a visitor immediately before purchase is credited with the sale. Previous referrals influenced by other customer touch-points on other sites are ignored.

Latency The average length of time that different customer types take between different activities, e.g. log-ins, paying bills, first and second purchase.

Lead Details about a potential customer (prospect). *See* **Qualified lead.**

Leading performance indicator A measure which is suggestive of future performance and so can be used to take proactive action to shape future performance.

Lead generation offers Offered in return for customers providing their contact details and characteristics. Commonly used in B2B marketing where free information such as a report or a seminar will be offered.

Lifetime value (LTV) The total net benefit that a customer or group of customers will provide a company over their total relationship with a company.

Link anchor text The text used to form the blue, underlined hyperlink viewed in a web browser defined in the HTML source. For example: Visit Dave Chaffey's web log is created by the HTML code: <A

HREF="http://www.davechaffey.com">Visit Dave Chaffey's web log</A>.

Link building A proactive approach to gain quality links from third-party sites.

List broker Will source the appropriate email list(s) from the list owner.

List owner Has collected email addresses which are offered for sale.

Live website Current site accessible to customers, as distinct from test website.

Localisation Designing the content of the website in such a way that it is appropriate to different audiences in different countries.

Location-based marketing Location or proximity-based marketing is mobile marketing based on the GPS built into phones or based on interaction with other local digital devices.

Log file A file stored on a web server that records every item downloaded by users.

Log file analysers Web analytics tools that are used to build a picture of the amount of usage of different parts of a website based on the information contained in the log file.

Long tail concept A frequency distribution suggesting the relative variation in popularity of items selected by consumers.

Loyalty techniques Customers sign up to an incentive scheme where they receive points for repeat purchases, which can be converted into offers such as discounts, free products or cash. (Also known as online incentive schemes.)

M

Macro-environment Broader forces affecting all organisations in the marketplace including social, technological, economic, political and legal aspects.

Mailbots *See* **Autoresponders**.

Maintenance process The work involved in running a live website such as updating pages and checking the performance of the site.

Malware Malicious software or toolbars, typically downloaded via the Internet, which act as a 'trojan horse' by executing other unwanted activities such as keylogging of user passwords or viruses which may collect email addresses.

Marketing automation Enables businesses to automate tasks in the marketing and sales process to make the process to deliver more relevant communications typically delivered as personalised emails and website messages.

Marketing intermediaries Firms that can help a company to promote, sell and distribute its products or services.

Marketing-led site design Site design elements are developed to achieve customer acquisition, retention and communication of marketing messages.

Marketing mix The series of seven key variables – Product, Price, Place, Promotion, People, Process and Physical evidence – that are varied by marketers as part of the customer offering.

Marketing planning A logical sequence and a series of activities leading to the setting of marketing objectives and the formulation of plans for achieving them.

Marketplace *See* **Business-to-business exchanges or marketplaces**.

Marketsite eXchange, eHub, metamediaries are terms used to refer to complex websites that facilitate trading exchanges between companies around the globe.

MarketSite™ A trade mark of commerceOne and considered the leading e-marketplace operating environment.

Marketspace A virtual marketplace such as the Internet in which no direct contact occurs between buyers and sellers. (Also known as electronic marketspace.)

Markup language *See* **HTML, XML**.

Mashup Websites, pages or widgets that combine the content or functionality of one website or data source with another to create something offering a different type of value to web users from the separate types of content or functionality.

Mass customisation The ability to create tailored marketing messages or products for individual customers or a group of similar customers (a bespoke service), yet retain the economies of scale and the capacity of mass marketing or production.

Mass marketing One-to-many communication between a company and potential customers, with limited tailoring of the message.

Measurement *See* **Website measurement**.

Media broker A company that places advertisements for companies wishing to advertise by contacting the media owners.

Media buyer The person within a company wishing to advertise who places the advertisement, usually via a media broker.

Media buying The process of purchasing media to meet the media plan requirements at the lowest costs.

Media fragmentation Describes a trend to increasing choice and consumption of a range of media in terms of different channels such as web and mobile and also within channels, for example more TV channels, radio stations, magazines, more websites. Media fragmentation implies increased difficulty in reaching target audiences.

Media multiplier or halo effect The role of one media channel on influencing sale or uplift in brand metrics. Commonly applied to online display advertising, where exposure to display ads may increase click-through rates when the consumer is later exposed to a brand through other media, for example sponsored links or affiliate ads. It may also improve conversion rates on destination sites through higher confidence in the brand or familiarity with the offer.

Media-neutral planning (MNP) An approach to planning ad campaigns to maximise response across different media according to consumer usage of these media.

Media owners The owners of websites (or other media such as newspapers) that accept advertisements.

Media planning The process of selecting the best combination of media to achieve marketing campaign objectives. Answers questions such as 'How many of the audience can I reach through different media?', 'On which media (and ad vehicles) should I place ads?', 'Which frequency should I select?', 'How much money should be spent in each medium?'

Media queries A styling approach within Cascading Style Sheets (CSS3) enabling the layout to change based on type of device at its scale.

Media site Typical location where paid-for ads are placed.

Merchandising *See* **Web merchandising**.

Meta-data Literally, data about data – a format describing the structure and content of data.

Memes An idea, theme or trend that engages an audience and spreads through viral communications.

Meta search engines Meta search engines submit keywords typed by users to a range of search engines in order to increase the number of relevant pages since different search engines may have indexed different sites. An example is the meta-crawler search engine or www.mamma.com.

Meta-tags Text within an HTML file summarising the content of the site (content meta-tag) and relevant keywords (keyword meta-tag), which are matched against the keywords typed into search engines.

Metrics for Internet marketing Measures that indicate the effectiveness of Internet marketing activities in meeting customer, business and marketing objectives.

Micro-environment The *actors* (stakeholders) and their interactions which influence how an organisation responds in its marketplace.

Micropayments (microtransactions) Digital cash systems that allow very small sums of money (fractions of 1p) to be transferred, but with lower security. Such small sums do not warrant a credit card payment, because processing is too costly.

Microformats A semantic definition in XML/HTML of a specific information type within a web page such as a product, event, recipe or review. Schema.org manages some of the most common definitions.

Microsite Specialised content that is part of a website that is not necessarily owned by the organisation. If owned by the company it may be as part of an extranet. *See* **Nested ad content**.

Microsoft Internet Information Server (IIS) Microsoft IIS is a web server developed by Microsoft that runs on Windows NT.

Mixed-mode buying The process by which a customer changes between online and offline channels during the buying process.

Mobile-based apps Designed to run on smartphones and tablet computers, apps provide users with rich mobile content by deploying the handset's multiple native capabilities. Apps are available for download from app stores hosted by the mobile operating systems (e.g. iTunes for iOS, Google Play for Android, Microsoft App Store, BlackBerry App World).

Mobile commerce The use of wireless devices such as mobile phones for informational or monetary transactions.

Mobile marketing Marketing to encourage consumer engagement when using mobile phones (particularly smartphones) or tablet devices.

Multichannel marketing Customer communications and product distribution are supported by a combination of digital and traditional channels at different points in the buying cycle.

Multichannel marketing strategy Defines how different marketing channels should integrate and support each other in terms of their proposition development and communications based on their relative merits for the customer and the company.

Multichannel prioritisation Assesses the strategic significance of the Internet relative to other communications channels and then deploys resources to integrate with marketing channels.

Multiscreening A term used to describe simultaneous use of devices such as digital TV and tablet.

N

Native advertising Online content that it is created to promote or enhance a brand such as a publisher article or social media update. Such content should be disclosed as advertising by law in many countries, but often it isn't.

Natural or organic listings The pages listing results from a search engine query which are displayed in a sequence according to relevance of match between the keyword phrase typed into a search engine and a web page according to a ranking algorithm used by the search engine.

Navigational search Searchers use a search engine such as Google to find information deeper within a company site by appending a qualifier such as a product name to the brand or site name. Organisations need to check that relevant pages are available in the search results pages for these situations.

Near Field Communications (NFC) Enables data exchange through wireless connections between two devices in close proximity to each other. Use of NFC enabled smartphones can facilitate contactless payments.

Nested ad content This refers to the situation when the person undertaking the click-through is not redirected to a corporate or brand site, but is instead taken to a related page on the same site as that on which the advertisement is placed. (Sometimes referred to as microsite.)

Net Promoter Score A measure of the number of advocates a company (or website) has who would recommend it compared to the number of detractors.

Nofollow and Dofollow tags A nofollow tag is a basic piece of HTML. Appended to a hyperlink, it allows webmasters to control whether search engines follow a link or not. For example, the following URL on a page of another site allows search engines to visit Smart Insights' website and credit the website with the link; each link is scored by the search engines, supporting SEO: *<a href="http://www.smartinsights. com/" title="Smart Insights"<Visit Smart Insights</a>* This normal, natural type of link is sometimes known as 'do-followed'! Here's the same hyperlink, now including a nofollow tag (highlighted in red): <a href="http:// www.smartinsights.com/" title="Smart Insights" rel="nofollow" Visit Smart Insights</a>.

Newsjacking A publisher or other brand seeks to take advantage of current topical interest in a story and then add to or subvert it to increase their own publicity.

Non-repudiability *See* **Security methods**.

Notification The process whereby companies register with the data protection register to inform about their data holdings.

O

Offer An incentive in direct marketing or a product offering.

Offline site promotion Traditional techniques such as print and TV advertising used to generate website traffic.

Offline web metric Offline measures are those that are collated by marketing staff recording particular marketing outcomes such as an enquiry or a sale. They are usually collated manually, but could be collated automatically.

One-to-one marketing A unique dialogue that occurs directly between a company and individual customers (or less strictly with groups of customers with similar needs). The dialogue involves a company in listening to customer needs and responding with services to meet these needs.

Online brand *See* **Digital brand**.

Online branding How online channels are used to support brands that, in essence, are the sum of the characteristics of a product or service as perceived by a user.

Online business model A summary of how a company will generate a profit identifying its core product or service value proposition, target customers in different markets, position in the competitive online marketplace or value chain and its projections for revenue and costs.

Online company presence Different forms of online media controlled by a company including their website, blogs, email list and social media presences. Also known as 'owned media'.

Online customer experience The combination of rational and emotional factors in using a company's online services that influences customers' perceptions of a brand online.

Online tactical marketing segmentation Tactical segmentation enables targeting based on customer journey behaviour such as search behaviour, content accessed and contribution to social media.

Online incentive schemes *See* **Loyalty techniques**.

Online influencer outreach Identifying online influencers such as bloggers, media owners or individuals with a large online following in the social networks and then approaching them to partner together to communicate with their audience.

Online influencers and Key Opinion Leaders Online influencers can include any type of online person who has a significant following. They can include journalists, bloggers or celebrities.

Online intermediary sites Websites that facilitate exchanges between consumer and business suppliers.

Online market ecosystem Interactions between different online systems related to a specific hardware or software technology which may be independent or developed by a particular brand.

Online marketplace Exchanges of information and commercial transactions between consumers, businesses and governments completed through different forms of online presence such as search engines, social networks, comparison sites and destination sites.

Online promotion contribution An assessment of the proportion of customers (new or retained) who are reached by online communications and are influenced as a result.

Online PR (e-PR) Maximising favourable mentions of your company, brands, products or websites on third-party websites which are likely to be visited by your target audience. Online PR can extend reach and awareness of a brand within an audience and will also generate backlinks vital to SEO. It can also be used to support viral or word-of-mouth marketing activities in other media.

Online reputation management Controlling the reputation of an organisation through monitoring and controlling messages placed about the organisation.

Online revenue contribution An assessment of the direct contribution of the Internet or other digital media to sales, usually expressed as a percentage of overall sales revenue.

Online service providers (OSPs) An OSP is sometimes used to distinguish large Internet service providers (ISPs) from other access providers. In the UK, AOL, Freeserve, VirginNet and LineOne can be considered OSPs since they have a large amount of specially developed content available to their subscribers. Note that this term is not used as frequently as ISP, and the distinction between ISPs and OSPs is a blurred one since all OSPs are also ISPs and the distinction only occurs according to the amount of premium content (only available to customers) offered as part of the service.

Online service-quality gap The mismatch between what is expected and delivered by an online presence.

Online site promotion Internet-based techniques used to generate website traffic.

Online social network A service facilitating the connection, collaboration and exchange of information between individuals.

Online value proposition (OVP) A statement of the benefits of online services that reinforce the core proposition and differentiate from an organisation's offline offering and that of competitors.

Online voice of customer (VoC) Qualitative assessments of the effectiveness of digital presence based on direct customer feedback. They answer 'who and why' questions about how customers interact with brands online.

Online web metrics Online measures are those that are collected automatically on the web server, often in a server log file.

On-page optimisation Writing copy and applying markup such as the <title> tag and heading tags <h1> to highlight to search engines relevant keyphrases within a document.

Operational effectiveness Performing similar activities better than rivals. This includes efficiency of processes.

Opt-in A customer proactively agrees to receive further information.

Opt-in email The customer is only contacted when he or she has explicitly asked for information to be sent (usually when filling in an on-screen form).

Opt-out A customer declines the offer to receive further information.

Opt-out email The customer is not contacted subsequently if he or she has explicitly stated that he or she does not want to be contacted in future. Opt-out or unsubscribe options are usually available within the email itself.

Outbound email Email sent from a company.

Outbound email marketing Emails are sent to customers and prospects from an organisation.

Outbound Internet-based communications The website and email marketing are used to send personalised communications to customers.

Outsourcing Contracting an outside company to undertake part of the Internet marketing activities.

Overlay Typically an animated ad that moves around the page and is superimposed on the website content.

Overt Typically an animated ad that moves around the page and is superimposed on the website content.

Owned media Different forms of online media controlled by a company including their website, blogs, email list and social media presence.

P

Page impression One page impression occurs when a member of the audience views a web page. *See* **Ad impression** and **Reach**.

PageRank A scale between 0 to 10 used by Google to assess the importance of websites according to the number of inbound links or backlinks.

Page request The process of a user selecting a hyperlink or typing in a uniform resource locator (URL) to retrieve information on a specific web page. Equivalent to page impression.

Page view *See* **Page impression**.

Paid media Also known as bought media, a direct payment occurs to a site owner or an ad network when they serve an ad, a sponsorship or pay for a click, lead or sale generated.

Paid search marketing (pay-per-click PPC) A relevant text ad with a link to a company page is displayed on the SERPs when the user of a search engine types in a specific phrase. A fee is charged for every click of each link, with the amount bid for the click mainly determining its position. Additionally, PPC may involve advertising through a content network of third-party sites (which may be on a CPC, CPM or CPA basis).

Panda and Penguin algorithm updates Changes to Google's algorithm aimed at reducing the impact at webspam. They caused the rankings of many sites to fall. Panda targeted low-quality sites with 'thin' content. Penguin targeted sites using aggressive link building.

Path to purchase The different sites, channels and devices and information sources that consumers use to inform their purchase decision for a product or service. Also known as conversion pathways on a site.

Pay-for-performance communications The wastage from traditional media buys can be reduced online through advertising models where the advertisers only pay for a response (cost-per-click) as in pay-per-click search marketing or for a lead or sale as in affiliate marketing.

Pay-per-click PPC refers to when a company pays for text ads to be displayed on the search engine results pages as a sponsored link (typically above, to the right of or below the natural listings) when a specific keyphrase is entered by the search users. It is so called because the marketer pays each time the hypertext link in the ad is clicked on. If a link is clicked repeatedly, then this will be detected by the search engine as click fraud and the marketer will not be charged.

Payment systems Methods of transferring funds from a customer to a merchant.

People variable The element of the marketing mix that involves the delivery of service to customers during interactions with those customers.

Performance drivers Critical success factors that determine whether business and marketing objectives are achieved.

Performance management system A process used to evaluate and improve the efficiency and effectiveness of an organisation and its processes.

Performance measurement system The process by which metrics are defined, collected, disseminated and actioned.

Performance metrics Measures that are used to evaluate and improve the efficiency and effectiveness of business processes.

Performance of website Performance or quality of service is dependent on its availability and speed of access.

Permission marketing Customers agree (opt in) to be involved in an organisation's marketing activities, usually as a result of an incentive.

Persistent cookies Cookies that remain on a computer after a visitor session has ended. Used to recognise returning visitors.

Personal data Any information about an individual stored by companies concerning their customers or employees.

Personalisation Web-based personalisation involves delivering customised content for the individual through web pages, email or push technology.

Personas A thumbnail summary of the characteristics, needs, motivations and environment of typical website users.

Persuasion marketing Using design elements such as layout, copy and typography together with promotional messages to encourage site users to follow particular paths and specific actions rather than giving them complete choice in their navigation.

Phishing Obtaining personal details online through sites and emails masquerading as legitimate businesses.

Phone-me A call-back facility available on the website for a company to contact a customer by phone at a later time, as specified by the customer.

Physical evidence variable The element of the marketing mix that involves the tangible expression of a product and how it is purchased and used.

Pixel The small dots on a computer screen that are used to represent images and text. Short for 'picture element'. Used to indicate the size of banner advertisements.

Place variable The element of the marketing mix that involves distributing products to customers in line with demand and minimising cost of inventory, transport and storage.

Plug-in A program that must be downloaded to view particular content such as an animation.

Podcasts Individuals and organisations post online media (audio and video) which can be viewed in the appropriate players (including the iPod which first sparked the growth in this technique). The latest podcast updates can be automatically delivered by *Really Simple Syndication*.

Portal A website that acts as a gateway to information and services available on the Internet by providing search engines, directories and other services such as personalised news or free email.

Portfolio analysis Identification, evaluation and selection of desirable marketing applications.

Positioning Customers' perception of the product and brand offering relative to those of competitors.

Predictive Analytics Using data mining and statistical modelling to predict future outcomes, for example by scoring customer propensity to respond to a specific offer.

Prescriptive strategy The three core areas of strategic analysis, strategic development and strategy implementation are linked together sequentially.

Price comparison sites *See* **Aggregators**.

Price dispersion The distribution or range of prices charged for an item across different retailers.

Price elasticity of demand Measure of consumer behaviour that indicates the change in demand for a product or service in response to changes in price.

Price transparency Customer knowledge about pricing increases due to increased availability of pricing information.

Price variable The element of the marketing mix that involves defining product prices and pricing models.

Pricing level The price set for a specific product or range of products.

Pricing model Describes the form of payment such as outright purchase, auction, rental, volume purchases and credit terms.

Primary persona A representation of the typical site user.

Privacy A moral right of individuals to avoid intrusion into their personal affairs. *See* **Security methods**.

Privacy and Electronic Communications Regulations Act A law intended to control the distribution of email and other online communications including cookies.

Privacy statement Information on a website explaining how and why individuals' data are collected, processed and stored.

Process variable The element of the marketing mix that involves the methods and procedures companies use to achieve all marketing functions.

Product variable The element of the marketing mix that involves researching customers' needs and developing appropriate products. *See* **Core product** and **Extended product**.

Profiling *See* **Customer profiling**.

Programmatic Ad Buying Describes the purchase of online display advertising that is aggregated, booked, flighted, analysed and optimised via demand-side software interfaces and algorithms. It includes RTB and also non-RTB methods and buy types such as Facebook Ads API and the Google Display Network.

Promotion (online and offline) Online promotion uses communication via the Internet itself to raise awareness about a site and drive traffic to it. This promotion may take the form of links from other sites, banner advertisements or targeted email messages. Offline promotion uses traditional media such as television or newspaper advertising and word-of-mouth to promote a company's website.

Promotion variable The element of the marketing mix that involves communication with customers and other stakeholders to inform them about the product and the organisation.

Propensity modelling A name given to the approach of evaluating customer characteristics and behaviour and then making recommendations for future products.

Prosumer 'Producer + consumer'. The customer is closely involved in specifying their requirements in a product.

Prototypes and prototyping A prototype is a preliminary version of part (or a framework of all) of a website that can be reviewed by its target audience, or the marketing team. Prototyping is an iterative process where website users suggest modifications before further prototypes are made and the final version of the site is developed.

Proximity marketing Marketing messages are delivered in real time according to customers' presence based on the technology they are carrying, wearing or have embedded. Bluecasting is the best-known example.

Psychographic segmentation A breakdown of customers according to different characteristics.

Public key A unique identifier of a buyer or a seller that is available to other parties to enable secure e-commerce using encryption based on digital certificates.

Public-key encryption An asymmetric form of encryption in which the keys or digital certificates used by the sender and receiver of information are different. The two keys are related, so only the pair of keys can be used together to encrypt and decrypt information.

Public-key infrastructure (PKI) The organisations responsible for issuing and maintaining certificates for public-key security together form the PKI.

Public relations The management of the awareness, understanding and reputation of an organisation or brand, primarily achieved through influencing exposure in the media.

Pull media The consumer is proactive in selection of the message through actively seeking out a website.

Push media Communications are broadcast from an advertiser to consumers of the message, who are passive recipients.

Push technology The delivery of web-based content to the user's desktop without the need for the user to visit a site to download information. Email can also be considered to be a push technology. A particular type of information is a push channel.

Q

Qualified lead Contact and profile information for a customer with an indication of the level of their interest in product categories.

Quality score An assessment in paid search by Google AdWords (and now other search engines) of an individual ad triggered by a keyword which, in combination with the bid amount, determines the ranking of the ad relative to competitors. The primary factor is the click-through rate for each ad, but quality score also considers the match between the keyword and the occurrence of the keyword in the text, historical click-through rates, the engagement of the searcher when they click through to the site and the speed at which the page loads.

Quick Response (QR) code A QR code is a two-dimensional matrix bar code. QR codes were invented in Japan, where they are a popular type of two-dimensional code used for direct response.

R

Reach The number of unique individuals who view an advertisement.

Real-time bidding (RTB) Bids for buying ads against keywords can be managed in real-time in conjunction with a DSP.

Real-time marketing and PR Brands develop an agile, proactive approach to PR, content marketing and advertising to participate in current news and trends to help increase their visibility and influence through positive brand mentions. They also develop a reactive approach to respond to negative brand mentions through social media reputation management.

Really Simple Syndication (RSS) Blog, news or other content is published by an XML standard and syndicated for other sites or read by users in RSS reader software services.

RealNames A service for matching company names and brands with web addresses.

Reciprocal links Links which are agreed between yourself and another organisation.

Referrer The site that a visitor previously visited before following a link.

Referring sites A log file may indicate which site a user visited immediately before visiting the current site. *See* **Click-through, Destination site** and **Exit page.**

Referrer or referring site The source of a visitor to site delivered via a digital media channel. Typically a specific site, e.g. Google AdWords or a media site or an individual ad placement on the site.

Registration (individuals) The process whereby an individual subscribes to a site or requests further information by filling in contact details and his or her needs using an electronic form.

Registration (of domain name) The process of reserving a unique web address that can be used to refer to the company website.

Reintermediation The creation of new intermediaries between customers and suppliers providing services such as supplier search and product evaluation.

Relationship marketing Consistent application of up-to-date knowledge of individual customers to product and service design, which is communicated interactively in order to develop a continuous, mutually beneficial and long-term relationship.

Renderability The capability of an email to display correctly formatted in different email readers.

Repeat visits If an organisation can encourage customers to return to the website then the relationship can be maintained online.

Representation The locations on the Internet where an organisation is located for promoting or selling its services.

Repurposing Developing for a new access platform, such as the web, content which was previously used for a different platform.

Responsive Web Design (RWD) Layout and formatting of website content is modified at the point of rendering to suit different screen resolutions and capabilities to produce a better experience to users of a range of desktop, tablet and smartphone devices using web development methods like CSS and image scaling.

Resource analysis Review of the technological, financial and human resources of an organisation and how they are utilised in business processes.

Resources Resources are defined as physical assets over which an organisation has control. This narrow definition of resources allows them to be clearly distinguished from capabilities.

Results-based payment Advertisers pay according to the number of times the ad is clicked on.

Retail channel Retailers' use of the Internet as both a communication and a transactional channel concurrently in business-to-consumer markets.

Retail format This is the general nature of the retail mix in terms of range of products and services, pricing policy, promotional programmes, operating style or store design and visual merchandising; examples include mail-order retailers (non-store-based) and department-store retailers.

Retention *See* **Customer retention**.

Return on advertising spend (ROAS) This indicates amount of revenue generated from each referrer. ROAS = Total revenue generated from referrer/Amount spent on advertising with referrer.

Return on investment (ROI) This indicates the profitability of any investment, or in an advertising context for each referring site.

  ROI = Profit generated from investment/Cost of investment.

  ROI = Profit generated from referrers/Amount spent on advertising with referrer.

Return path An interaction where the customer sends information to the iDTV provider using a phone line or cable.

Revenue models Describe methods of generating income for an organisation.

Reverse auctions Item purchased from lowest-bidding supplier in bidding period.

Reverse path analysis Indicates the most popular combination of pages and/or calls-to-action which lead to a page. This is particularly useful for transactional pages such as the first checkout page on a consumer site; a lead generation or contact-us page on a business-to-business site; an email subscription page; a call-me-back option.

Rich media Advertisements that are not static, but provide animation, audio, sound or interactivity as a game or form to be completed. An example of this would be a banner display advertisement for a loan in which a customer can type in the amount of loan required, and the cost of the loan is calculated immediately.

Rich Internet Applications (RIA) Interactive applications which provide options such as product selectors or games. They may incorporate video or sound also. Typically built using technologies such as Adobe Flash, Ajax, Flex, Java or Silverlight.

Robot A tool, also known as a spider, that is employed by search engines to index web pages of registered sites on a regular basis. *See* **Spider**.

Run-of-site A situation where a company pays for banner advertisements to promote its services across a website.

S

Sales generation offers Offers that encourage product trial. A coupon redeemed against a purchase is a classic example.

Sales promotions The Internet offers tremendous potential for sales promotions of different types since it is more immediate than any other medium – it is always available for communication, and tactical variations in the details of the promotion can be made at short notice.

Satisficing behaviour Consumers do not behave entirely rationally in product or supplier selection. They will compare alternatives, but then may make their choice given imperfect information.

Scenario-based analysis Models of the future environment are developed from different starting points.

Scenario of use A particular path or flow of events or activities performed by a visitor to a website.

Scripts Scripts can run either on the user's browser (client-side scripts) (*see* **Web browser**) or on the web server (server-side scripts).

Scrum A methodology that supports agile software development based on 15–30-day sprints to implement features from a product backlog. 'Scrum' refers to a daily project status meeting during the sprint.

Search engine Specialised website that uses automatic tools known as spiders or robots to index web pages of registered sites. Users can search the index by typing in keywords to specify their interest. Pages containing these keywords will be listed, and by clicking on a hyperlink the user will be taken to the site.

Search engine listing The list of sites and descriptions returned by a search engine after a user types in keywords.

Search engine marketing (SEM) Promoting an organisation through search engines to meet its objectives by delivering relevant content in the search listings for searchers and encouraging them to click through to a destination site. The two key techniques of SEM are *search engine optimisation (SEO)* to improve results from the natural listings and paid-search marketing to deliver results from the sponsored listings within the search engines through pay-per-click (PPC) paid-search engine marketing and through content-network paid-search marketing (which may be on a PPC basis or on a CPM basis). SEM is about connecting the searchers with information which will help them find what they are looking for and will help site owners generate revenue or disseminate information.

Search engine optimisation (SEO) A structured approach used to increase the position of a company or its products in search engine natural or organic results listings (the main body of the search results page) for selected keywords or phrases.

Search engine ranking The position of a site on a particular search engine.

Search engine results pages (SERPs) The page(s) containing the results after a user types in a keyphrase into a search engine. SERPs contain both natural or organic listings and paid or sponsored listings.

Search engine submission The process of informing search engines that a site should be indexed for listing in the search engine results pages.

Secure Electronic Transaction (SET) A standard for public-key encryption intended to enable secure e-commerce transactions, lead-developed by Mastercard and Visa.

Secure HTTP Encrypted HTTP.

Secure Sockets Layer (SSL) A commonly used encryption technique for scrambling data such as credit card numbers as they are passed across the Internet from a web browser to a web server.

Security methods When systems for electronic commerce are devised, or when existing solutions are selected, the following attributes must be present:

- *Authentication* – are parties to the transaction who they claim to be? This is achieved through the use of digital certificates.
- *Privacy and confidentiality* – are transaction data protected? The consumer may want to make an anonymous purchase. Are all non-essential traces of a transaction removed from the public network and all intermediary records eliminated?

- *Integrity* – checks that the message sent is complete, i.e. that it is not corrupted.
- *Non-repudiability* – ensures sender cannot deny sending message.
- *Availability* – how can threats to the continuity and performance of the system be eliminated?

Seeding The viral campaign is started by sending an email to a targeted group that are likely to propagate the virus.

Segmentation Identification of different groups within a target market in order to develop different offerings for each group.

Sell-side e-commerce E-commerce transactions between a supplier organisation and its customers.

Sense and respond communications Delivering timely, relevant communications to customers as part of a contact strategy based on assessment of their position in the customer lifecycle and monitoring specific interactions with a company's website, emails and staff.

Server log file *See* **Online web metrics**.

Service quality The level of service received on a website. Dependent on reliability, responsiveness and availability of staff and the website service.

Serving Used to describe the process of displaying an advertisement on a website (ad serving) or delivering a web page to a user's web browser. *See* **Web server**.

Session *See* **Visitor session**.

Session cookie A cookie used to manage a single visitor session.

Share of search The audience share of Internet searchers achieved by a particular audience in a particular market.

Share of voice The relative advertising spend of the different competitive brands within the product category. Share of voice (SOV) is calculated by dividing a particular brand's advertising spend by the total category spend.

Short code Five-digit numbers combined with text that can be used by advertisers or broadcasters to encourage consumers to register their interest. They are typically followed up by an automated text message from the advertiser with the option to opt in to further information by email or to link through to a WAP site.

Short Message Service (SMS) The formal name for text messaging.

Single customer view Customer profile information is kept consistent across systems to maintain customer data quality.

Site *See* **Website**.

Site announcements Usually used to describe the dissemination of information about a new or revised website.

Site auditors Auditors accurately measure the usage for different sites as the number of ad impressions and click-through rates. Auditors include ABC (Audit Bureau of Circulation) and BPA (Business Publication Auditor) International.

Site availability An indication of how easy it is to connect to a website as a user. In theory this figure should be 100 per cent, but for technical reasons such as failures in the server hardware or upgrades to software, sometimes users cannot access the site and the figure falls below 90 per cent.

Site design page template(s) A standard page layout format which is applied to each page of a website. Typically defined for different page categories (e.g. category page, product page, search page).

Site map A graphical or text depiction of the relationship between different groups of content on a website.

Site measurement *See* **Website measurement**.

Site navigation scheme Tools provided to the user to move between different information on a website.

Site re-launch Where a website is replaced with a new version with a new 'look and feel'.

Site statistics Collected by log file analysers, these are used to monitor the effectiveness of a website.

Site 'stickiness' An indication of how long a visitor stays on a site. Log file analysers can be used to assess average visit times.

Site visit One site visit records one customer visiting the site. Not equivalent to User session.

Site-visitor activity data Information on content and services accessed by e-commerce site visitors.

Sitemapping tools These tools diagram the layout of the website, which is useful for site management and can be used to assist users.

Situation analysis Collection and review of information about an organisation's external environment and internal processes and resources in order to inform its strategies.

Skunkworks A loosely structured group of people who research and develop innovative opportunities and business benefits.

SMART metrics SMART metrics must be:

- Specific
- Measurable
- Actionable
- Relevant
- Timely.

Smartcards Physical cards containing a memory chip that can be inserted into a smartcard reader before items can be purchased.

Social bookmarking Web users keep a shared version of favourite sites ('Favourites') online. This enables the most popular sites in a category to be identified.

Social commerce Social commerce is a subset of e-commerce which encourages participation and interaction of customers in rating, selecting and buying products through group buying. This participation can occur on an e-commerce site or on third-party sites.

Social CRM The process of managing customer-to-customer conversations to engage existing customers, prospects and other stakeholders with a brand and so enhance customer-relationship management.

Social exclusion Part of society is excluded from the facilities available to the remainder.

Social graph A term popularised by Facebook in 2007 when describing its Facebook platform. The social graph describes the relationship between individuals linked through social networks and other connections such as email or personal contact.

Social location-based marketing Where social media tools give users the option of sharing their location, and hence give businesses the opportunity to use proximity or location-based marketing to deliver targeted offers and messages to consumers and collect data about their preferences and behaviour. Businesses can offer consumers benefits to check-in, for example, to gain points, be the most regular visitor to that location, to gain rewards and prizes from advertisers, to share their location with friends, and, in the case of events, to meet like-minded people. Of course the privacy implications of this relatively new technology must be carefully reviewed.

Social media governance A definition of how companies should respond to social mentions that may give rise to leads or reputational damage.

Social media listening The process of using monitoring tools to review mentions of a brand and related keywords within social networks and other online sites.

Social media marketing Monitoring and facilitating customer–customer interaction and participation throughout the web to encourage positive engagement with a company and its brands. Interactions may occur on a company site, social networks and other third-party sites.

Social media optimisation (SMO) A process to review and improve the effectiveness of social media marketing through reviewing approaches to enhance content and communications quality to generate more business value.

Social media strategy A definition of the marketing communications used to achieve interaction with social network users to meet business goals. The scope of social media optimisation also includes incorporation of social features such as status updates and sharing widgets into company websites.

Social network A site that facilitates peer-to-peer communications within a group or between individuals through providing facilities to develop user-generated content (UGC) and to exchange messages and comments between different users.

Social sign-on A user logs in to a site using a social network service user name and password. This can enable connection between social memberships and company profile information.

Soft launch A trial version of a site launched with limited publicity.

Soft lock-in Electronic linkages between supplier and customer increase switching costs.

Software agents *See* **Agents**.

Software as a Service (SaaS) Business applications and software services are provided through Internet and web protocols with the application managed on a separate server from where it is accessed through a web browser on an end-user's computer with data stored within 'The Cloud'.

Spam Unsolicited email (usually bulk mailed and untargeted).

Spamming Bulk emailing of unsolicited mail.

Specific offline advertising Driving traffic to the website or explaining the online proposition is a primary objective of the advert.

Spider Spiders are software processes, technically known as robots, employed by search engines to index web pages of registered sites on a regular basis. They follow links between pages and record the reference URL of a page for future analysis.

Splash page A preliminary page that precedes the normal home page of a website. Site users can either wait to be redirected to the home page or can follow a link to do this. Splash pages are not now commonly used since they slow down the process of customers finding the information they need.

Sponsorship Sponsorship involves a company paying money to advertise on a website. The arrangement may involve more than advertising. Sponsorship is a similar arrangement to co-branding.

Stage models Models for the development of different levels of Internet marketing services.

Stages in website development The standard stages of creation of a website are initiation, feasibility, analysis, design, development (content creation), testing and maintenance.

Static (fixed) web page A page on the web server that is invariant.

STEP A framework for assessing the macro-environment, standing for Social, Technological, Economic and Political (including legal).

Stickiness An indication of how long a visitor stays on-site.

Storyboarding Using static drawings or screenshots of the different parts of a website to review the design concept with customers or clients.

Strategic agility The capability to innovate and so gain competitive advantage within a marketplace by monitoring changes within an organisation's marketplace to efficiently evaluate alternative strategies and then select, review and implement appropriate candidate strategies.

Strategic analysis Collection and review of information about an organisation's internal processes and resources and external marketplace factors in order to inform strategy definition.

Strategic market segmentation Selection of key audiences to target with value propositions developed for these audiences.

Strategic positioning Performing different activities from rivals or performing similar activities in different ways.

Strategic windows Opportunities arising through a significant change in environment.

Strategy formulation Generation, review and selection of strategies to achieve strategic objectives.

Strategy process model A framework for approaching strategy development.

Streaming media Sound and video that can be experienced within a web browser before the whole clip is downloaded.

Streaming media server A specialist server used to broadcast audio (e.g. podcasts) or video (e.g. IPTV or webcast presentations). Served streams can be unicast (a separate copy of stream is served for each recipient), multicast (recipients share streams) or peer-to-peer where the media is shared between different recipient's computers using a Bitorrent or Kontiki approach.

Style guide A definition of site structure, page design, typography and copy defined within a company. *See* **Graphic design**.

Subject access request A request by a data subject to view personal data from an organisation.

Superstitials Pop-up adverts that require interaction to remove them.

Surfer An undirected information seeker who is often looking for an experience rather than information.

Symmetric encryption Both parties to a transaction use the same key to encode and decode messages.

Syndication Content or product information is distributed to third parties. Online this is commonly achieved through standard XML formats such as RSS.

T

Tagging Tracking of the origin or referring site or of visitors to a site and their spending patterns. Also tagging refers to where users or web page creators categorise content on a site through adding descriptive terms. A common approach in blog posts.

Target marketing strategy Evaluation and selection of appropriate segments and the development of appropriate offers.

Targeting (through banner advertisers) Advertising networks such as DoubleClick offer advertisers the ability to target advertisements dynamically on the World Wide Web through their 'DART' targeting technology. This gives advertisers a means of reaching specific audiences.

Technology convergence A trend in which different hardware devices such as TVs, computers and phone merge and have similar functions.

Telemarketing using the Internet Mainly used for inbound telemarketing, including sales lines, carelines for goods and services and response handling for direct response campaigns.

Telnet A program that allows remote access to data and text-based programs on other computer systems at different locations. For example, a retailer could check to see whether an item was in stock in a warehouse using a telnet application.

Template *See* **Site design page template**.

Test website A parallel version of the site to use before the site is made available to customers as a live website.

Testing Testing involves different aspects of the content such as spelling, validity of links, formatting on different web browsers and dynamic features such as form filling or database queries.

Testing content Testing should be conducted for plug-ins; for interactive facilities and integration with company databases; for spelling and grammar; for adherence to corporate image standards; for implementation of HTML in different web browsers; and to ensure that links to external sites are valid.

Third-party cookies Served by another site to the one being viewed – typical for portals where an ad network will track remotely or where the web analytics software places a cookie.

Tipping point Using the science of social epidemics explains principles that underpin the rapid spread of ideas, products and behaviours through a population.

Trademark A trademark is a unique word or phrase that distinguishes your company. The mark can be registered as plain or designed text, artwork or a combination. In theory, colours, smells and sounds can also be trademarks.

Traffic-building campaign The use of online and offline promotion techniques such as banner advertising, search engine promotion and reciprocal linking to increase the audience of a site (both new and existing customers).

Transactional e-commerce sites Sites that support online sales.

Transaction log file A web server file that records all page requests.

Transfer Control Protocol/Internet Protocol (TCP/IP) The passing of data packets around the Internet occurs via TCP/IP. For a PC to be able to receive web pages or for a server to host web pages it must be configured to support this protocol.

Trialogue The interaction between company, customer and other customers facilitated through online community, social networks, reviews and comments.

Trusted feed A trusted feed is an automated method of putting content into a search engine index or an aggregator database.

Trusted third parties (TTPs) Companies with which an agreement has been reached to share information.

U

Undirected information seeker A person who does not know what information they are looking for – a surfer.

Uniform (universal) resource locator (URL) Text that indicates the web address of a site. A specific domain name is typed into a web browser window and the browser will then locate and load the website. It is in the form of: http://www.domain-name.extension/filename.html.

Unique visitors Individual visitors to a site measured through cookies or IP addresses on an individual computer.

Universal search The *natural listings* incorporate other relevant results from vertical searches related to a query, such as video, books, scholar, news, sitelinks and images.

Unsubscribe An option to opt out from an email newsletter or discussion group.

Upload The transfer of files from a local computer to a server. Usually achieved using FTP. Email or website pages can be uploaded to update a remote server.

Up-selling Persuading existing customers to purchase more expensive products (typically related to existing purchase categories).

URL strategy A defined approach to how content is labelled through placing it in different directories or folders with distinct web addresses.

Usability An approach to website design intended to enable the completion of user tasks.

Usability/user testing Representative users are observed performing representative tasks using a system.

Usenet newsgroup An electronic bulletin board used to discuss a particular topic such as a sport, hobby or business area. Traditionally accessed by special newsreader software, these can now be accessed via a web browser from www.deja.com.

User-centred design Design based on optimising the user experience according to all factors, including the user interface, which affect this.

User journey *See* **Customer scenarios**.

User session Used to specify the frequency of visits to a site. Not equivalent to site visit.

V

Validation Validation services test for errors in HTML code which may cause a web page to be displayed incorrectly or for links to other pages that do not work.

Value chain A model that considers how supply chain activities can add value to products and services delivered to the customer.

Value event scoring Value events are outcomes that occur on the site as indicated by visits to different page or content types which suggest marketing communications are effective. Examples include leads, sales, newsletter registrations and product page views. They can be tagged and scored using many web analytics systems, for example Google refers to them as conversion goals.

Value network The links between an organisation and its strategic and non-strategic partners that form its external value chain.

Value proposition The benefits or value a brand offers to customers in its products and services.

Value proposition of site The benefits or value of a website that are evident to its users.

Vertical portals These are generally business-to-business sites that will host content to help participants in an industry to get their work done by providing industry news, details of business techniques, and product and service reviews.

Video marketing The use of video to gain visibility in search marketing, video hosting sites and to engage site visitors.

View *See* **Page impression**.

View-through A view-through indicates when a user views an ad and subsequently visits a website.

Viral marketing A marketing message is communicated from one person to another, facilitated by different media, such as word of mouth, email or websites. Implies rapid transmission of messages is intended.

Viral referral An 'email a friend or colleague' component to an email campaign or part of website design.

Virtual cash *See* **Digital cash**.

Virtual community An Internet-based forum for special-interest groups to communicate using a bulletin board to post messages.

Virtual mall A website that brings together different electronic retailers at a single virtual (online) location. This contrasts with a fixed-location infrastructure – the traditional arrangement where retail organisations operate from retail stores situated in fixed locations such as real-world shopping malls. (Also known as electronic mall.)

Virtual merchants Retailers such as Amazon that only operate online – they have no fixed-location infrastructure.

Virtual organisation An organisation that uses information and communications technology to allow it to operate without clearly defined physical boundaries between different functions. It provides customised services by outsourcing production and other functions to third parties.

Virtual private network Private network created using the public network infrastructure of the Internet.

Virtualisation The process whereby a company develops more of the characteristics of a virtual organisation.

Visit conversion rate An indication of the capability of a site in converting visitors to defined outcomes such as registration. Calculated by dividing the number of conversion events by the number of visitor sessions within a time period.

Visitor conversion rate An indication of the capability of a site in converting visitors to defined outcomes such as registration. Calculated by dividing the number of conversion events by the number of unique visitors within a defined time period.

Visitor session (visit) A series of one or more page impressions, served to one user, which ends when there is a gap of 30 minutes or more between successive page impressions for that user.

W

Walled garden A limited range of e-commerce services on iDTV (compared to the Internet).

WAP WAP is a technical standard for transferring information to wireless devices, such as mobile phones.

Web 2.0 concept A collection of web services that facilitate interaction of web users with a site to create user-generated content and encouraging certain behaviours online such as community or social network participation and user-generated content, mashups, content rating, use of widgets and tagging.

Web 3.0 concept Next-generation web incorporating high-speed connectivity, complex cross-community interactions and an intelligent or semantic web where automated applications can access data from different online services to assist searchers perform complex tasks of supplier selection.

Web accessibility An approach to site design intended to accommodate site usage using different browsers and settings – particularly required by the visually impaired and visitors with other disabilities including motor control, learning difficulties and deaf users. Users whose first language is not English can also be assisted.

Web addresses Web addresses refer to particular pages on a web server, which is hosted by a company or organisation. The technical name for web addresses is uniform or universal resource locators (URLs).

Web analytics Techniques used to assess and improve the contribution of e-marketing to a business, including reviewing traffic volume, referrals, clickstreams, online reach data, customer satisfaction surveys, leads and sales.

Web application frameworks A standard programming framework based on reusable library functions for creating dynamic websites through a programming language.

Web Application Protocol (WAP) A standard that enables mobile phones to access text from websites.

Web application server Software processes which is accessed by a standard programming interface (API) of a web application framework to serve dynamic website functionality in response to requests received from browsers.

Web browsers Browsers such as Mozilla Firefox and Microsoft Internet Explorer provide an easy method of accessing and viewing information stored as HTML web documents on different web servers.

Webmaster A webmaster is responsible for ensuring the quality of a website. This means achieving suitable availability, speed, working links between pages and connections to company databases. In small companies the webmaster may be responsible for graphic design and content development.

Web merchandising The aims of web merchandising are to maximise sales potential of an online store for each visitor. This means connecting the right products with the right offer to the right visitor, and remembering that the online store is part of a broader experience including online and offline advertising, in-store visits, customer service and delivery.

Web radio Internet radio is when existing broadcasts are streamed via the Internet and listened to using plug-ins such as Real Media or Windows Media Player.

Web response model The website is used as a response mechanism for offline campaign elements such as direct mail or advertising.

Web self-service Content and services provided by an organisation to replace or complement in-store or phone customer enquiries in order to reduce costs and increase customer convenience.

Web servers Web servers are used to store the web pages accessed by web browsers. They may also contain databases of customer or product information, which can be queried and retrieved using a browser.

Website auditors Auditors accurately measure the usage of different sites in terms of the number of ad impressions and click-through rates.

Website content Accessible on the World Wide Web that is created by a particular organisation or individual. The location and identity of a website is indicated by its web address (URL) or domain name. It may be stored on a single server in a single location, or a cluster of servers.

Website measurement The process whereby metrics such as page impressions are collected and evaluated to assess the effectiveness of Internet marketing activities in meeting customers, business and marketing objectives.

Wide Area Information Service (WAIS) An Internet service that has been superseded by the World Wide Web.

Widget A badge or button incorporated into a site or social network space by its owner, with content or services typically served from another site making widgets effectively a mini-software application or web service. Content can be updated in real time since the widget interacts with the server each time it loads.

Wi-Fi ('wireless fidelity') A high-speed wireless local-area network enabling wireless access to the Internet for mobile, office and home users.

Wireframe A simplified outline of a single page template used to define new layout or functionality for part of a website for discussion, iteration and then a brief for implementation.

Word-of-mouth marketing According to the Word-of-Mouth Marketing Association it is giving people a reason to talk about your products and services, and making it easier for that conversation to take place. It is the art and science of building active, mutually beneficial consumer-to-consumer and consumer-to-marketer communications.

World Wide Web A medium for publishing information on the Internet. It is accessed through web browsers, which display web pages and can now be used to run business applications. Company information is stored on web servers, which are usually referred to as websites.

X

XML An advanced markup language giving better control than HTML over format for structured information on web pages.

XMOS (cross-media optimisation studies) XMOS research is designed to help marketers and their agencies answer the question 'What is the optimal mix of advertising vehicles across different media, in terms of frequency, reach and budget allocation, for a given campaign to achieve its marketing goals?' The mix between online and offline spend is varied to maximise campaign metrics such as reach, brand awareness and purchase intent.

Z

Zero Moment of Truth (ZMOT) A summary of today's multichannel consumer decision making for product purchase where they search, review ratings, styles, prices comments on social media before visiting a retailer.

Index

Page numbers in bold refer to glossary entries.

3G **649**
3M 379
4Cs 251, 463, 536
4Ps 250–85
4G **649**
4Q 378
5Is 313
5Ss 18, 198–9, 224
6 Is 37
7Ps 250
7 Ss 26–7, 232–3

A/B testing see AB testing
Aaker, D, 266
AB testing 552, 564, **649**
ABCelectronic (Audit Bureau of Circulation Electronic) 520
above the fold **649**
Abraham, M. 518
acceptance, website information 400
access
    control 401, 581
    to digital platforms 67, 69, 76
    divide 165
    Internet 61, 66, 69, 73
    platforms 44, 45, 386, 398, **649**
    portals 65, 94, 95, 96
    providers **649**
accessibility **649**
    legislation 159, 379, **649**
    websites 378–9, **677**
Account Planning Group 463, 464
accountability 43, 498, 519, 537
accuracy
    personal data 151–2
    web analytics tools 560, 561, 568
acquisition
    customers see customers
    objectives 204, 209
ACT (Access: Choose: Transact) 72
actions 188, 189, 229
Active Server Page (ASP) **648**
ActiveX **649**
activity levels 329
ad creative 521–2, **649**
ad hoc activity 233
ad impression 519, **649**

ad inventory **649**
ad network 515, **650**
ad rotation **650**
ad serving 515, **650**
ad space **650**
ad supported content 258
ad view **650**
Adams, C. 554, 556
adaptability 273
adaptive web design 391, 395, **650**
AdBots-Google 497
addressability 632
addresses, websites see domain names;
        web addresses
adequacy of personal data 151
Adobe Acrobat 128
Adobe Analytics 157
advertisements **650**
advertising 11, 21
    campaigns, dynamic updates 518
    capacity to sell 104
    direct responses 135
    display see display advertising
    fee levels negotiated 104
    integration, advertising-led 465
    law 163–4
    media 16
    networks **650**
    offline see offline advertising
    online 11, 21, 28, 29, 33, 628, 632
    pay-per-click 6, 20, 29, 30
    promotional mix 284
    reputational damage 161
    revenue 21, 24, 47, 103–4
    as revenue model 214
    spend, return on (ROAS) 435, **671**
    standards 154, 163
    text ads 104
    units, number and size 109
    see also entries beginning with ad
Advertising Standards Authority (ASA)
        154, 163
advice-led buying behaviours 86, 87, 88
advocacy
    online 324, 327
    ratings 206, 327
advocates 324, 334
    brands 265, 530, 532, **652**
    customer 534
affiliate commission 100, 103

affiliate marketing 11, 30, 427, 446, 479, 501, 509, 510–13, 536, 541, 542, 628, **650**
affiliate networks 149, 157, 283, 511, 512, **650**
affiliate revenue 103
affiliates 64, 65, **650**
affiliation 278
affluents 334
affordable method of budgeting 451
agents **650**
aggregated buying **650**
aggregators 64–5, 103, 269, 270, 279, 479, 509, 510–11, **650**
Agile Manifesto 367
agile software development 367–8, **650**
agility 93
    strategic 123, **674**
Agrawal, V. 231, 330, 455
Ahmed, N.U. 167
AIDA 448
AJ Bombers 137
Ajax 36
Alba, J. 97
Alexa 66
Alexander, James 168
Alibaba 94–5
Allegra Strategies 612
Allen, E. 252, 277
Alliance & Leicester 420
allowable cost per acquisition 200–1, 435, **650**
alt tags **650**
alternative image text 493
alternative pricing structure or policies 268, 278
Altimeter 562
Amazon 38, 91–2, 102, 103, 108, 141–2, 257, 258, 259, 262, 263, 275, 276, 278, 279, 292, 300, 302, 319, 323, 564, 582–7, 607, 610
Amazon Prime 276
Amazon Web Services 259
ambassadors, brands 530
American Express Open Forum 343
American Customer Satisfaction Index 405
analysis, e-CRM use 311
analysis phase 374, **658**
anchor text **650**

Anderson, C. 261, 262, 277
Android OS 60, 136, 255
animated banner advertisements
    (animated GIFs) **650**
animated graphical information 128
annual marketing communications
    objectives 432
Ansari, A. 639
Ansoff matrix 17, 210
anti-spam legislation 153, 158
AOV (average order value) **651**
API (Application Programming
    Interfaces) 12, 60, 129, 130, 225
appeal 452
Apple 263, 277, 292
Apple iPhone 136, 255
Application Programming Interfaces
    (API) 12, 60, 129, 130, 225
applications service providers (ASP) 276
apps 13, 255, 267, 292, 346, 374, 388, 393,
    394, 395, 396, 480, 509, 617
mobile 60, 65, 135, 136–7, 304, 422, 468,
    469, 611,
Apteco 336
Aguila-Obra, A.R.D. 645
Archie **651**
Arena Flowers 199–200
Argos 212
Armstrong, Arthur 341, 610
Arthur, Charles 506
ASA (Advertising Standards Authority)
    154, 163
ASDA 224, 270
Ashworth, C. 640, 641
ASOS 614–17
ASP (Active Server Page) **649**
ASPs (applications service providers) 276
assets, digital 460–1, **657**
'assists', digital media 458, **657**
association, brand 264, 266
assurance, service quality 405, 406, 407
asymmetric encryption 133, **651**
asynchronous communication 427
atomisation **651**
attention 43, 400, 448
attitudes, shaping 517
attitudinal segmentation 444–5
attractability efficiency 69
attraction 231
    efficiency 455
attributes, e-mail marketing 526
attrition rates 192, 558, **651**
auctions 90, 101
    forward 274, **661**
    prices 251, 267–8293
    reverse see reverse auctions
    sites 94
audiences 63, 64, 70, 76, 78, 79, 99, 101,
    212, 423, 425, 427, 433, 436
    communication with 449
    reach and composition 442, 443

research into 224, 441–2
sales trends compared to market
    audience 206
targeting 215, 421, 443–6
audio standards 128
Audit Bureau of Circulation Electronic
    (ABCelectronic) 520
auditors, websites 520, **673**, **677**
audits 190, 232
    checklist 232
    external **651**
    internal 191, **651**
authentication 132, 134, **672**
authoring 400, 581
autoresponders 287, **651**
availability **672**, **673**
    customer expectations 603
    websites 361, 365, 372, 373–4,
        406, 407
Avast 135
avatars 286, 287, **650**
average order value (AOV) **651**
awareness
    consumers 79, 81–2
    efficiency 69
    generating 84
Azumah, G. 283

B2B see business-to-business
B2C see business-to-consumer
B2G (business-to-government) 21
backbones 126, **651**
backlinks 487, 488, 495, **651**
BagCheck 396
Baker, W. 267, 273
balanced scorecard 205, 206, **651**
Balter, D. 534
bandwidth 372, 386, **651**
Bank of England 144
banking, online 166
banner advertising 479, 514, 515,
    517–22, **651**
    see also display advertising
banner blindness 43, 519, 542
bargaining powers
    buyers 89–90
    suppliers 89, 90
Barlow, John Perry 148
Baron, R. 465
Barrett, T. 399
barriers to entry 90–1
Bart, Y. 86, 87
barter 111
Barton, Sam 199
Bassett, Fred 121–2
Bauer, R. 602
Baye, M. 275, 276
Bazaarvoice 403, 404
Bazett, M. 205
BBH 462
behaviour

channel buyer 557–8, **653**
consumers see consumers
customers see customers
Fogg's Model 375
multichannel 219
satisficing 269, **671**
behavioural ad targeting 520–1, **651**
behavioural email marketing 321
behavioural information 148–9
behavioural loyalty 324, 325, **651**
behavioural targeting 445, 452
behavioural traits of web users **651**
behavioural variables 76
beliefs, consumers 601–2
below-zero customers (BZC) 330–1
benchmarking 91–3, 122, 141, 380, 405,
    558, **654**
benefits
    5Ss 198–9
    intangible 198, 199
    tangible 198, 199
Benjamin, R. 97, 282
Berners-Lee, Sir Tim 29, 37, 123, 127, 143
Berthon, P. 69, 81, 420, 427
Best Buy 305
BEST principles 389, 399
Bevan, Nigel 388–9
Bezos, Jeff 582–6
Bickerton, P. 273
bidding, real-time (RTB) 516, **670**
bids 274, **651**
    management 500–1
billboard strategy 618
Bing 478, 484, 488, 495, 497
Bitner, M. 250
Bjornesson, Henrik 646
Blackcircles.com 57–9
Blanc, Xavier 31
Blanks, Karl 360–1
bleeding edge 141
blind network buys 518
bloggers 12, 65, 111, 126, 252, 503, 504
blogopshere 503, 530
BlogPulse 161
blogs 33, 36, 478, 488, 502–8, 532, **651**
    'blogstorm' 504
    brand blogging 530
    'guest blogging' 495
    monitoring brand conversations in 161
    negative comments 506
    seeding 535
    social commenting in 35
    Über-bloggers 511
Blue Latitude 121
bluecasting **651**
bluejacking **651**
blueprints 383, **652**
    websites 387, 413
Bluetooth 138, **652**
BMW 257, 292
BOGOF (buy-one-get-one-free) 402

boo.com 108–10
bookmarking, social see social
    bookmarking
boomers 143
Booms, B. 250
Borders 273, 586
botnets 132, **652**
Bottomley, Jonathan 462
bounce rates 433, 434, **652**
Bounds, Deirdre 411
Bowen Craggs Index 92
Boyd, D. 34
brand-building sites 24
brand-focused buying behaviours
    64, 73, 87
brand idea-led orchestration 465
brands
    advocates 265, 530, 532, **652**
    alignment 232
    ambassadors 530
    awareness 481
        affiliate marketing 512
        display advertising 515, 516,
            517, 523
        email marketing 522, 523
        enhancing 517
        offline communications 536
        online advertising 517
        online sponsorship 514, 542
    blogging 507
    conversation monitoring in social
        networks and blogs 161
    customer engagement 265
    definitions
        brand advocates **652**
        brand equity 263, **652**
        brand experience 264, **652**
        brand identity 266, **652**
        branding **652**
        brands **652**
    engagement
        customers 265
        longer-term goals 438
        rewarding with offers for 136
    enhancement, online public relations
        505
    equity 263, **652**
        online, indicators of 358–9
    experience 264, 358–9, **652**
    goals 438
    identity 266–7, **652**
    interactions, achieving 518
    loyalists 534
    measures 435
    names 266–7
    objectives 447
    online
        expansion offline 263
        importance 262–3
    online branding 250, **666**
    products 262–3

protection 505
    online public relations 478,
        502, 506
    law 147, 159–61
reach, enhancing 517
reputation 519
    management 161
sites, success factors for 265–6
switching 19
website design 362, 365, 372, 375,
    376–7, 382, 386, 387, 390,
    391–2, 413
Brandyberry, A. 642
Branthwaite, A. 431
Bravo, R. 263
breaking of bulk 225
Brengman, M. 76
bricks and clicks 226, 610
bricks and mortar 610, 612, 613, **652**
Briggs, R. 466
Brin, S. 494
British Phonographic Institute 145
Brittin, Matt 285
broadband technology **652**
brochureware 24, 193, 236, 573,
    588, **652**
Broderick, D. 463, 464
brokered deals 102, 111
bronze customers 332
browse-to-buy ratios 434
browser-based measurement systems 568,
    571, 588
Brynjolfsson, E. 262
BT 145
budgets
    bid management 500–1
    campaigns 432, 451, 454–6, 461,
        465, 518
    gaining 184
    monitoring 500
    online communications mix and
        231–2
    pay-per-click marketing 500
building websites see websites: design
    and build
bulk, breaking of 225
bundling 256–7, 258, 402, **652**
Burt, S. 263
business context 442
business contribution 557
business models 20–2, 99–102, 213–15,
    652, 666
business objectives, support 31–2
business requirements, websites 374–5
business-to-business (B2B) 21, 22, 74, 90,
    91, **652**
    bargaining power of buyers 89–90
    business-to-consumer and, market
        characteristics distinguishing
        624–5
    choice and influence 72–4

conversion optimisation 629–30
customer acquisition 627–32
customer retention 630–2
digital marketing 624–46
digital technologies 639–42
e-marketplaces 635–7
exchanges 90, **652**
independent e-marketplaces 635
intermediaries 94–8, 100
lead-generation 629–30
marketplaces 90, **652**
online intermediaries 89, 94, 95,
    100, 116
online inter-organisational trading
    633–8
organisational marketing and trading
    environments 625–7
strategies 642–4
transactions 74
business-to-consumer (B2C) 21, **652**
    bargaining power of buyers 89–90
    digital marketing practice 594–617
    online intermediaries 89, 94, 95, 100
business-to-government (B2G) 21
Butman, J. 534
buy-in, gaining 184, 232
buy-one-get-one-free (BOGOF) 402
buy-side e-commerce 22–3, **652**
buyers
    bargaining powers 89–90
    channel buyer behaviour 557–8, **653**
    e-marketplaces 635
    seller relationships 630–1
buying
    aggregated **650**
    consumer behaviours see consumers
    hierarchy of response models 80
    mixed-mode see mixed-mode buying
    multichannel 69, 71–2
    online, customer preferences 445
    see also purchases
buzz marketing 529, 530
BuzzParadise 503
BuzzSumo 496
BZC (below-zero customers) 331

C2B (consumer-to-business) 21,
    22, **654**
C2C see consumer-to-consumer
C2G (consumer-to-government) 21
CA (certificate (or certification)
    authorities) 134, **653**
Cahoot 91
call-back service 440, **652**
call-backs 405
call centres **652**
campaign-based e-communications
    231, **652**
campaign-specific communications
    objectives 432
campaign URL (CURL) 439, **652**

campaigns 420–72
  advertising, dynamic updates 518–19
  budgeting 451–62
  competitor activity 442
  customer insight 441, 442–3
  digital media
    characteristics 424–32
    mix selection 464–67
  goal setting and tracking 432–41
  insight 441–3
  integration into overall media
      schedules or plans 428, 463–7
  investment decisions 451–62
  microsites 372
  offers, message development and
      creatives 447–50
  response mechanisms 438–41
  segmentation and targeting 443–7
  terminology for measuring 432–5
capabilities 652
  competitive 92
  digital marketing, stage models of
      193–4
  institutionalising 233
  internal 92
  marketing resources 233
  maturity model 194
  organisational 232–6
  stage models 193–4
capacities, advertising, selling 104
card sorting 382–3, 652
care, loyalty variable 606
Carnegie Mellon Software Engineering
      Institute 194
Cartellieri, C. 516
cascading style sheets (CSS) 127,
      384–6, 652
cash, digital 95, 657
Castells, Manuel 340
catalogues 652
causal marketing 530
ccTLD (country code top-level domains)
      125, 370, 371, 372
CDN (content distribution networks) 372
certificate authorities (CA) 134, 653
certificates 134, 653
CGI (Common Gateway Interface) 130,
      654
Chaffey, D. 17, 18, 22, 24, 32, 33, 69, 80,
      103, 110, 188, 189, 192, 194, 198,
      228, 233, 236, 252, 258, 284, 286,
      314, 317, 319, 387, 391, 404, 407,
      408, 409, 420, 449, 487, 494, 526,
      555, 566
champions 334
change management 233, 653
channels
  business objectives support 31–2
  buyer behaviour 557–8, 653
  chains 81, 98
  communications specific to 178

conflicts 277, 281–2, 653
contribution objectives 200c
coordination 184
customer communications 223, 655
customer preferences 219, 224, 229
definition 30
digital, contribution 232
digital media see digital media
distribution 17, 189, 225, 226, 658
key types 32–4
marketing strategy 178–9, 653
new structures 96–9, 280
objectives specific to 178, 188, 198
outcomes 558, 653
partnerships 180
performance evaluation and
    improvement 550–88
planning 464
preferences 219, 229
profitability 559, 653
promotion 556–7, 653
propositions, differential 178, 208
retail 610, 671
satisfaction 558, 653
social 224
structures 96–9, 653
see also entries beginning with
    multichannel
character variables 601–2
Charles Tyrwhitt 328
Chaston, I. 220, 221
Cheung, C.M.K. 76
Chiquita 310
Chittenden, L. 522
Choi, H. 63
choice, loyalty variable 606
Christodoulides, G. 358
Chromebook 263
churn rates 192, 231
CI (competitive intelligence) 190, 654
CIA 164
Cisco 629–30
Citibank 91
Clarke, Philip 240
classification variables, consumers
    597, 601
click ecosystem 60, 653
click-through 479, 499, 500, 517, 519,
    520, 521, 522, 525, 526, 653
  rates (CTR) 225, 485, 486, 488, 489,
    497, 519–20, 522, 526, 540, 653
click-tracking 653
clicks-and-mortar 227, 610, 653
clicks-only (Internet pureplay) 227,
    610, 653
clickstream analysis 560, 566–8, 653
clickstreams 70, 653
ClickZ.com 137, 514
client–servers 126, 653
Clifton, Anthony 464
Clinton, Bill 146

cloud computing 36
Cluetrain Manifesto 34, 528, 529
clutter 452
CLV (customer lifetime value) 334
CMS (content management systems)
      see content: management
co-alliance model 283
co-branding 514, 515, 523, 653
co-browsing 405
CODAR 448
Cohen, Jack 239
coherence 389, 463, 536
cold campaigns 522–3
cold lists 153, 653
collaboration
  platforms 101
  social CRM 303
collaborative filtering 323, 652
collection tools and techniques 560–73
commerce see electronic commerce;
      social commerce
commercial arrangements 111
commission 512–13
Commission Junction 512
commitment 84–6
commoditisation 90, 269, 653
common customer profiles 319
Common Gateway Interface (CGI)
      130, 654
Common Name, Law of the 266
communications
  change of nature 427
  channel-specific 178
  competitors 356, 380–1, 399
  continuous activities 420, 430, 654
  cross-channel 233
  customers see customers
  data 311
  digital and traditional, relationship
      between 30–1
  digital media channels see digital
      media: channels
  electronic see electronic
      communications
  interactive, goal setting and tracking
      for 432–41
  intermediaries 428
  introduction to 29–49
  key challenges 43
  key concepts 43–5
  marketing mix 251
  mix 29, 30
    and budget 231–2
    planning 442
    tools selection 454–60
  multichannel 228–30
  objectives 228, 239, 432, 436–7,
      447, 451
  online mix and budgets 231–2
  planners 442
  preferences, e-mail marketing 525

sense and respond 38, 302, 309, 319, **672**
social interaction models 86–7
social media marketing strategy 529
style 427
tailored 406
traditional and digital, relationship between 30
viral 138, 155
communities 56, 347
activities 138
loyalty variable 606
marketing 530
own presence, creating 343
sites 25
social networks, creating through 342–3
social niche 35
virtual see virtual communities
compensation 406
competition-based pricing 274
competitive capabilities 93
competitive environments 101
competitive intelligence (CI) 190, **654**
competitive markets 88–91
competitive parity methods of budgeting 451
competitors 88–93
analysis 91–3, 190, 194, **654**
benchmarking 56, 91–3, 111, 194, 224, 232, **654**
campaign activity 442
competitive markets, shape and nature 88–91
marketplace analysis 56, 60, 91
meta-tags and 160
micro-environment 59, 67
performance 443
responding to 43
response capabilities 93
rivalry between 89, 91
websites, reviewing 380–1
complementarities 286, 463, 513, 514, 515, 536
complexity 43, 389
comprehension, website information 400
computer telephony integration **654**
Compuware 637–8
ComScore 66
confidentiality **654**
see also data: protection; privacy
Conlon, Seamus 160
connectivity, Internet, payments for 131
consistency 396, 397, 398, 463, 536, 579
consumer-to-business (C2B) 21, 22, **654**
consumer-to-consumer (C2C) 21, 22, 94, **654**
consumer-to-government (C2G) 21
consumers

awareness 69, 81–2
behaviour **654**
analysis 68
buying 72, 78
digital 68
implications for marketing 76–88
online 64, 72, 78, 596–606
search engines 484
beliefs 601–2
character variables 597, 601, 602
choice and digital influence 72–5
classification variables 597, 601
evaluations by 84
feedback 84
marketing to using independent social networks 308, 317, 342, 343
online behaviour 64, 72, 78, 596–606
online experiences 65, 77–8
online shopping experiences 601–6
post-purchase evaluation 84
profile 597–602
purchases 83
selections by 68, 90, 97
suppliers searches 82, 83, 97
transactions 56, 74
unawareness 81
see also customers
contact 405, 406
centres 407–8, 409
consent 152, 153
control 427
details 155
information 148, 149
interactivity, loyalty variable 606
management 463
strategy 309, 319–22, **654**
content 12, 45, 123, 125, 126, 127, 129, 136, 147, 161, 162, 163, **654**
access platforms 45, 398
consumption, customer preferences 443
control 427
creation profiles, customers 443
delivering 484, 517
design 389, 398–400
developers 365, **654**
development 362, 366, 400–1
distribution networks (CDN) 372, **654**
engagement values 45, 398
freshness 575, 579, 581–2
information 451
management **654**
systems (CMS) 400–1, 581
marketing 44–5, **654**
media 45, 398
mobile-based apps 13
networks 495–6, 500, **654**
ownership 577–8
participation 45, 398
permission-based 629
reviews 573–4

strategists 578–9
strategy 398–9, 413, 573, **654**
syndication 36, 45, 398, 401
testing 362, 400–1, **675**
updating 573, 574–5
context 397
customers 442
power of 261
contextual ads 495, **654**
continuity 463, 536
continuous e-communications 231, 420, **654**
contra-deals 510, 515, **654**
contract law 147, 162–3
control 188
of contact 427
of content 427
costs 43, 435
e-procurement 634
pages 564, **655**
political 145
controllers, data 150, **656**
convenience 259, 602, 603
customer expectations 602–3
loyalty variable 606
convergence **655**
technology 123, 135, **675**
conversation creation 530, 532
conversation monitoring 161
conversion 208, 231, 238, 403–4
customers 180, 181, 356, 375, 411–12
e-mails 523–4
efficiency 69, 207, 380
goals 438
marketing 69, **655**
models 69–72
objectives 204, 209
optimisation, business-to-business 628–30
rates 192, 203, 205, 237, 362, 380, 386–7, 402, 404, 412, 499, 517, **655**
optimisation (CRO) 356, 360–1, 362, 399, **655**
cookies 147, 149, 156–9, 518–19, **655**
Co-operative Bank 212
coordination, channels 184
copy, e-mail marketing 526
copyright 145, 161
copywriting 399
core products 255–7, 262, **655**
core tenants **655**
cost-per-acquisition (CPA) 103, 207, 434–5, **655**
cost-per-click (CPC) 103, 434, 496–7, 498, 499, **655**
cost-per-targeted mille (CPTM) **655**
cost-per-thousand (CPM) 103, 434, 515, 519, **655**
cost-plus pricing 273

costs 43
  allowable costs per acquisition 200–1,
    435, 650
  bases 101
  control 43
  to customers 251
  decision information 640
  delivery 452
  development 452
  e-mail marketing 525
  e-procurement 634
  factor costs 640
  lower, e-CRM use 308–9
  media measures 434, 446
  media selection factor 451
  models for Internet advertising **655**
  objectives 180, 188, 198, 204, 205
  offline communications 536
  online advertising 498, 500, 518, 519,
    523, 524
  online public relations 504
  quality 640
  reduction 180, 199, 225
  stickiness factor 260
Coulter, K. 451–2
countermediation 98, 280, **655**
country code top-level domains (ccTLD)
  124, 125, 370, 371
country of origin principle 162
coverage, media selection factor 452
Covisint 626, 637–9
CPA see cost-per-acquisition
CPC see cost-per-click
CPM see cost-per-thousand
CPT see cost-per-thousand
CPTM (cost-per-targeted mille) **655**
crackers **655**
crawling 400, 485–6
Crawshaw, P. 464
creative 500, 501, 513, 518–22, 525,
  526, 537
creative material 534
creative testing 501
credibility 451–2, 504
CRITICAL 526
critical success factors (CSF) 198, 231
CRM see customer relationship
  management
CRO (conversion rate optimisation) 356,
  360–1, 362, 399, **655**
Cronin, J. 404
cross-channel communications 233
cross-media optimisation studies
  (XMOS) 464–7, 517, **655**, **678**
cross-selling 312, 340, **655**
crowdsourcing 570
cruise.co.uk 160
CRV (customer referral value) 334
cScape 44
CSF (critical success factors) 198, 231
Csikszentmihalyi, Mihaly 395

CSS (cascading style sheets) 127, 365,
  384–6, 393, 398, **652**
CSS ZenGarden 386
CTR (click-through rates) see
  click-through: rates
cultivation, loyalty variable 606
cultural forces 165–7
culturally customised websites 380
CURL (campaign URL) 439, **652**
Currys 82, 83
customer-centric key performance
  indicators 238
customer-centric marketing 300, 304, **655**
customer relationship management
  (CRM) 300, 312, 331, **656**
  electronic see electronic customer
    relationship management
  post-sales, B2B marketing 630–2
  technologies and data 311
customers
  acquisition 312, 314, 332, 340, 341,
    655
    business-to-business 627–30
    growth hacking 369
    marketing-led site design 374–5
    opt-in e-mail marketing options 479,
      522–3
    performance driver 375
    viral effect 346
  advocacy ratings 206
  advocates 534
  analysis, environmental scanning 60
  behaviour
    analysis 60
    metric 557
    online buying 442
    search 442
    web analytics 552, 557, 562, 568
  below-zero (BZC) 330–1
  bronze 332
  channel preferences 219, 229
  characteristics 76–8
  communications
    channels 178–9, 210, 219, 223, 228,
      229, 230, **655**
    management 311
    planners 442
  content consumption preferences 443
  content creation profiles 443
  context 442
  conversion, performance driver 375
  costs to 251
  development 302, 309, 312
  differentiating by value and
    engagement 328–31
  digital profiles 443
  digital usage habits 443
  engagement 44, 223–5, **655**
    brands see brands
    challenge of 308–11
    differentiating by 329, 336

  e-CRM use benefits 308–9
  expectations
    service 603
    understanding 408
  experience 343
    online see online experience below
    implementation 26
    social CRM 303, 324–5
  extension 309, 312–13, 330, 332, **655**
  feedback 255, 259, 286, 361, 378, 382,
    403–4
  general profiles 443
  gold 332
  individual profiles 443
  information
    capture 314, 316, 317, 319
    management and integration 184
  insight 68, 443, **655**
  journeys 11, 16, 39, 61–72, 359, 374,
    376, **655**
  knowledge increases 89
  lifecycles 92, **656**
    management 311–43
  lifecycle groups 218
  lifetime value (CLV) 328, 330, 331–4
  loyalty 311, 312–13, 343, 637, **656**
    behavioural 324, **651**
    digital media use to increase 324
    emotional 324, **660**
    gamification 309
    improvement 211, 220
    programmes 309
    satisfaction and, relationships
      between 325–7, 410
    service quality and, relationships
      between 410
  media consumption 442
  micro-environment 59
  most-growable (MGC) 330
  most-valuable (MVC) 330
  needs 251, 255
  online buying behaviour and
    preferences 442
  online experience **666**
    delivery 356–412
  online journeys 79, 99
  orientation **656**
  perceptions of Internet and different
    media 431
  platinum 332–3
  power, increases 89
  preferences
    channels 219, 229
    content consumption 443
    online buying 442
  profiles 30
    common 319
    demographic characteristics based
      on 218
    information management 302
  profiling 311, 316, 323, **656**

purchase histories 217, 218, 220
ratings 403
referral value (CRV) 334
relationship management see cus-
    tomer relationship management
requirements 17
research 192
response histories 218
retention 312, 330, **656**
    business-to-business 630–2
    loyalty programmes 309
    metric 330
    opt-in e-mail marketing options
        523–4
    performance driver 375
reviews 403, 404, 406
satisfaction **656**
    factors affecting 324–5
    loyalty and, relationship between
        324, 325–7, 410
    metric 326
    ratings 206
    service quality and, relationships
        between 410
    social media marketing KPIs 562
scenarios 79–80, 192, **656**
search behaviour 442
segments 63, 68, 99, **656**
selection 312, 332, **656**
service
    customer expectations 603, 605,
        612
    management 311
    mechanisms 17
    online facilities 302, 309
    quality 375, 404–10
    social 35
silver 332
single customer view 317, **672**
support forums 259
support queries, defining 286–7
touchpoints 179, 308, 316, 317, **656**
understanding 309, 324, 336, 337,
    340
value
    differentiating by 328–31
    digital media use to increase 324
    improvement 211
    proposition 16
voice
    measuring in digital media 327–8,
        378
    online 327
wants 251, 253, 262
see also consumers
customisation
    loyalty variable 606
    mass see mass customisation
    web analytics tools 568
Cutts, Mark 125
cyber crime 132, 133

cybermarketing **656**
cybermediaries 95, **656**
cyberspace **656**

DaimlerChrysler 637–9
Daniel, E. 236
Darwin Private Equity 626
data
    communications 311
    controllers 150, **656**
    customer relationship management
        300, 302, 311
    demographic 571
    direct access 131–2
    fusion **656**
    input, validation 131
    mining 302, 311, 341, **656**
    outcome 571
    output, validation 131
    personal 668
        accuracy 151–2
        adequate, relevant and not excessive
            151
        CRM 311
        fair and lawful processing 150
        integration 37
        processed for limited purposes
            150–1
        processed in accordance with data
            subjects' rights 152
        security 153
        sensitive 150, 159
        retention 159
        transfer of data abroad 153
    planners 442
    poisoning 132
    privacy law 147, 148–9
    problems 554
    profile 311
    protection
        law 147, 148–59
        notification 150, **666**
        principles 150–3
    strategic 568, 569, 570
    subjects 150, 152, **656**
        rights 164
    theft 131
    transaction 311
    warehousing 656
Data Protection Act 150, 153
databases
    building 135
    marketing **656**
    technology 311
Davidow, W.H. 282
Davidson, A. 144
Davis, F.D. 602
Dawson, J. 76
DDOS (distributed denial of service) 132
de Chernatony, L. 357, 358
De Jong, B. 205

decisions
    information costs 640
    strategy 208, 210–36
decoding 427
decryption **656**
de-duplication, digital media 458, **657**
Dee, A. 531
deep linking 397, **656**
deepening relationships 19
Deighton, J. 37, 425
Deise, M. 93, 220–1
Delgado, E. 263
Delicious 35
deliverability **656**
    e-mail marketing 525, 526, 527
delivery
    costs 452
    customer expectations 603
    rates, e-mail marketing 526
Dell 39, 213, 214, 217, 283, 327, 344–6,
    387, 505, 506, 558, 563, 570, 632
Dell, Michael 283, 345
Dell Premier 344–5
demand analysis 68, 69, **656**
demand analysis for e-commerce **656**
demand curves 271–2
Demand Side Platforms (DSP) 516, **657**
dematerialisation 166
democracy 145
demographic characteristics 218, **657**
demographic data 571
demographic segmentation 444
demographic variables 76
demographics 142
denial of service attacks 132, **657**
Dennis, C. 610, 613
Der Zee, J. 205
Derosby, D. 130
design
    for analysis (DFA) 563–4, **657**
    phase 388, 413, **657**
    questionnaires 572
    templates 579–80, **673**
    websites see websites: design and
        build
designers, websites 365, 374, 382, 390,
    391, 397
desktop apps 13
desktop browser-based platform 13
desktop gadgets 509
destination platforms 65
destination sites 65, 94, 103, 446, 515,
    517, 523, **657**
destination stores **657**
detractors, online 327–8
development
    agile software 366–70, **650**
    content 362, 365, 366, 367
    costs 452
    customers 302, 309, 312
    markets 17, 211–12

development (*continued*)
  new products 255, 256, 259–60, 632
  products 17, 211, 212
  of site construction **657**
  of strategy 20–2, 24, 25–9
DFA (design for analysis) 563–4, **657**
Dholakia, U. 229
dialogues 18, 37, 38, 424–5, 427, 430, 465
differential advantage 221–2, **657**
differential pricing 268, 269, 274, 275, **657**
differentiation
  customers by value and engagement 328–31
  strategy 216, 220–3
diffusion–adoption curves 139–40
diffusion
  new products 260–1
  rapid 141
digital assets 460–1, **657**
digital audio broadcasting (DAB) radio **657**
digital brands **657**
digital cash **657**
digital certificates 133, 134, **657**
digital channels see digital media
digital communications
  traditional communications and, relationship between 30
digital divides 165
Digital Economy Act 145
digital marketing 6
  applications 16–17
  benefits 17–19
  communications, introduction to 29–46
  definitions 11–15, **657**
  key challenges 43
  key communications concepts 43–6
  metrics 553
  strategy 16–29, 121–2, 123, 164, 178–239
    URL 125
  transformation of marketing by digital technologies 6–10
digital media 11, **657**
  'assists' 458, **657**
  benefits 37–43
  channels 12, 29, 31–4, 421, 463, 478–538, **657**
  characteristics 424–32
  customer loyalty and value, use to increase 324
  customer voice measurement in 327–8
  de-duplication 458, **657**
  investment in techniques in comparison to offline promotion 451–4
  marketing mix 250–90
  mix selection 454–60
digital natives 131
digital platforms, access to 67
digital profiles, customers 443

digital properties 12
digital radio **657**
digital rights management (DRM) 104, **658**
digital security 130–5
digital signage **658**
digital signatures 133–4, **658**
digital teams, structuring 184
digital technologies
  business-to-business 637–42
  transformation of marketing by 6–10
digital television **658**
digital usage habits, customers 443
digitally augmented word-of-mouth 534
digitisation 166
direct data access 131
direct mail 135, 150, 166, 284
direct marketing 522, 538, **658**
Direct Marketing Association (DMA) 152, 527
direct responses 16, 37, 39, 135, 137, 515, 516, 517, 519, 525, 537, **658**
directed information seekers **658**
directories 95, **658**
disability law 147, 159
disciplines, definition 30
discrimination law 147, 159
disillusionment 140–1
disintermediation 41, 90, 97, 280, 281, **658**
dispersion, prices 273, **669**
displacement 286
display advertising 8, 30, 33, 103, 444, 445, 455, 458, 459, 467, 479, 515–23, 628, **658**
display networks 478, 485, 495, 540, **658**
  Google Display Network (GDN) 498, 516, 517, **661**
disruption, economic 143–4
disruptive technologies **658**
distance selling law 162–3
distributed denial of service (DDOS) 139
distribution
  channels 225–6, **658**
  content distribution networks (CDN) 372, **654**
  multichannel 225–8
diversification 17, 211, 212
Dixons 607
DMA (Direct Marketing Association) 152, 527
DNS see domain names
document meta-data 487
Dodds, S. 87, 534
Doherty, N.F. 68, 76, 97, 143, 192, 240, 241, 278, 596, 602, 610, 641, 642, 645
domain names 108, 124–5, 147, 160, **658**
  registration 159–6, 267, 370–1, **658**
  system (DNS) **658**
  value (monetary) 160

DoNotTrackMe 157
Donthu, N, 76
doorway pages **658**
Dorset Cereals 265
Doubleclick 157
downloads 104, 109, 128, 143, 163, 166, **658**
  apps 136
  illegal 145,
  malware 147, 149
  speeds 138
downstream integration with intermediaries 211, 212
downward pressure on prices 270–4
Drakeford, Simon 626
drip irrigation **658**
DRM (digital rights management) 104, **658**
Drugstore.com 586
DSP (Demand Side Platforms) 516, **657**
duplicate content 489, 493, **658**
duration, of visit 189, 192, 203
Durex 380
Duvall, Richard 168
dynamic pricing 268, 275, **658**
Dynamic Systems Development Methodology 367
dynamic web pages 126, 129, 130, **658**

e-auctions 101, 635
e-business see electronic business
e-commerce see electronic commerce
e-CRM see electronic customer relationship management
e-fulfilment 635
e-government 22, 145, **659**
e-Inclusion 165
e-informing 633
e-mail 645
  advertising 632
  cross-sell support 302
  lists 522–4, 527–8, 535
    'emotionally unsubscribed' members 320–2
    quality 302
  marketing 22, 27, 29, 30–1, 33, 38, 424, 445, 447, 467, 522, 627, 628, 630, 631, **659**
    advantages 524–5
    best practice in planning and managing 525–8
    co-branded e-mails 523
    cold campaigns 522–3
    disadvantages 525
    inbound 522, **662**
    law 147, 148–9, 152, 153, 154–5, 158
    list management 527–8
    management, practical issues 527
    measuring 526
    opt-in see opt-in e-mail marketing

outbound 522, **667**
  success factors 526–7
  third-party e-newsletters 523
pass-along 529
platforms 13
receipt and acknowledgement 287
reliability of response 407
routeing 287
sequences 524, 629
service providers (ESP) 525, **659**
up-sell support 302
e-malls 101
e-marketing mix 37
e-marketplaces 635–7
e-MRO 633
e-newsletters 479, 503, 514, 523, 524
e-permission marketing principles 317
e-PR see online public relations
e-procurement 101, 633–5, **659**
e-retailing 596–601, 603–4, 606–17, **660**
e-reverse auctions 633
E-SERVQUAL 359, 406, 605
e-sourcing 633
e-tendering 633
early adopters 139, 140, 141, **659**
early digital divide 165
early (first) mover advantage 213,
    214, **659**
early majority 139
earned media 11–12
earnings per click (EPC) 106, 513, **659**
easyJet 17, 21, 200, 211, 212, 221
eBay 21, 22, 46–8
ebXML (electronic business XML) 127–8
Ecomom 107
econometric modelling 453–4, **659**
economic disruption 143–4
economic forces 121, 142–4
EConsultancy 26, 27, 65, 106, 184, 200,
    232, 234, 235, 536
eCPM (effective cost-per-thousand)
    106, **659**
Edgar, M. 404, 407, 409
Edgecliff-Johnson, A. 91
EDI see electronic data interchange
eDigitalResearch 573
Edwards, Cory 345–6
effective cost-per-thousand (eCPM)
    106, **659**
effective frequency 520, **659**
effectiveness 191–2, 203, 204, 205–6, 554,
    564, 567–8, **659**
  display advertising measurement
    519–20
  macro-level metrics 555
  marketing 69, 106
  on-site search 567–8
  websites, digital marketing audits
    191–2
efficiency 205–6, 402, 406, 446, 454,
    554, 555, **659**

attraction 557
conversion 69, 207, 238, 380
lead conversion 436, 437
micro-level metrics 555
online advertising 555
sales, online strategy 239
site conversion 436, 437
value chain 180
effort, focusing 233
Egg 91, 110
Eisenberg, Bryan 375
elasticity of demand 269, 271–2, 274, **669**
electronic billing 631
electronic business 22–4, **659**
  strategy formulation 99, 101, 102
electronic business XML (ebXML) 127–8
electronic commerce 22, 24, **659**
  business models 99–106
  greenness 165–7
  revenue models 64, 101, 102, 103–6,
    107
  transactions **659**
electronic communications
  campaign-based 231, **652**
  continuous 231, 239, 420, 428, **654**
  regulations 153–59
electronic customer relationship
    management (e-CRM) 11, 302–3,
    311, **659**
electronic data interchange (EDI) 90,
    635, **659**
electronic mail see e-mail
electronic marketing (definition) **659**
electronic marketspaces 63, 635, 643, **659**
electronic partnerships 283
electronic procurement (e-procurement)
    101, 633–5, 637–9, **659**
electronic shopping or ES test **659**
electronic tokens **659**
Ellis-Chadwick, F.E. 68, 76, 88, 97, 192,
    216, 221, 226, 240, 241, 262, 263,
    278, 284, 596, 597, 602, 640 , 641,
    642, 645
Ellison, N. 34
Eloqua 628
Eltvedt, H. 460
emergent strategy 189, **660**
emerging economies 142, 143
emerging technology 138
emotional appeal 406
emotional connections, offline communi-
    cations 536
emotional loyalty 324–5, **660**
'emotionally unsubscribed' e-mail list
    members 320–2
empathy, service quality 405, 408–9
employment and market growth 142–3
empowered involvement 531
empowerment 532
enabling transactions 517
encoding 427

encryption 133–5, **651, 660, 670 675**
engagement 260
  B2B marketing 629
  brands, longer-term goals 438
  customers see customers
  digital solutions 289
  e-mail marketing 525, 527
  efficiency 69
  rates 434
  social media marketing KPIs 562
  values, content 45, 398
enlightenment, slope of 141
enterprise application integration (EAI)
    660
entry barriers 89, 90–1
entry pages **660**
environment analysis 122
environment mapping 122
environmental changes 123
environmental issues, Internet usage
    165–7
environmental scanning 60, **660**
EPC (earnings per click) 106, 513, **659**
Epson 287
equity, brands see brands
error handling 133
ES test **659**
ESP (e-mail service providers) 525, **659**
Estée Lauder 18
eTailQ 605
ethical standards 147, **660**
Ettorre, B. 97
Euroffice 217, 219, 220, 626–7, 630
Europa 149
European Commission 165
evaluators 95
Evans, P. 277
event-triggered e-mails 524
evidence, physical see physical evidence
excellence 220–1, 260
execution, questionnaires 572
exhibitions, promotional mix 284
exit pages 660
expansion, markets 18
expectations
  customers see customers
  inflated 140–1
experience
  brands 263, 264–5, 358, 359, 391, **652**
  customers see customers
experimentation, rampant 196
Experian Hitwise 63
expert evaluations 92, 93
expert reviews 377, **660**
explanations, offline communications
    536
exposure
  payment based on **660**
  website information 400
extended products 251, 255–6, 258–9, **660**

eXtensible Markup Language (XML) 127–8, **678**

extension, customers 309, 312–13, 330, 332, **655**

external context 442

external link building 488, **660**

external linking 494–5

extranets 129, **660**

Extreme Programming 367

Facebook 8, 10, 11, 20, 25, 34, 37, 161, 199, 213, 304–5, 342, 346, 423, 468–71, 488
  advertising 322, 343, 424, 528
  API (Application Programming Interface) 12, 224, 509, 516
  Cisco 630
  growth 369–70
  hashtags 441
  Insights 225
  'Likes' 314, 317, 342, 421, 563
  'People Like You' 168–9
  Princess Cruises 318
  sharing 421, 509
  status updates 225, 342

Facebook commerce (F-commerce) **660**

faceted navigation 402, **660**

factor costs 632, 640

fair processing of personal data 150

fake clicks 501

fan clubs 95

Faucheux, Scott 310

Fawcett, S. 555

fee levels negotiated 104

feed-based platforms 13

feedback 427
  app refinement 137
  Charles Tyrwhitt 328
  consumers 84
  customers 199, 259, 286, 309, 327, 382, 403
  loops 341, 342, 644
  product development 198, 255, 344
  tools 570

feeds 33, **660**

Fernie, J. 225, 226, 634

few, law of the 260

figleaves.com 403–4

file transfer protocol (FTP) **660**

filename.html 130

Fill, C. 442

filtering, collaborative 323, **653**

financial dimension 640

financial intermediaries 95

financial measures 93

financial performance 380

financial resources 192

Financial Services Authority (FSA) 145

findability 371, 372, 381, 382, 397, 402, **660**

Findlay, Graeme 420

Finn, A. 610

firewalls 135, **660**

firm structure 612

First Direct 259, 445

first mover advantage 213, 226, **659**

first-party cookies 149, 156, 157, **660**

fixation times 447

fixed price sales 102

Fjermestad, J. 252, 277

Flash 123, 128, 137

flexibility 43, 401, 452

Flickr 36

Flores, L. 265, 460

flow 382, 392, 395, 396, 399, 413, **660**

focus groups 259, 283, 558, 570, 571, 572–3, 588, **660**

Fogg, B. 375, 389, 390

Fogg's Behaviour Model 375

folksonomies **660**

Ford 637, 638

formalisation 233, 234

format ownership 579–80

forms **660**

Forrester 86, 88, 308, 324, 529, 531

forums 95

forward auctions 274, **661**

forward path analysis 567, **661**

Fotonatura 438

Foursquare 137

Fox, S. 143

fragmentation, media 308, 319, **664**

frames **661**

Frazier, G. 281

frequency 317, 320, 335, 337, 338, 444, 445, 452, 456, 465, 467
  effective 520, **659**

Friedlein, A. 207

Friedman, L. 556

FSA (Financial Services Authority) 145

FTP (file transfer protocol) **660**

fulfilment 406, 635

functional fit to task 406

Furey, T. 556

Furner, Paul 41–2

G2B (government-to-business) 21

G2C (government-to-consumer 21

G2G (government-to-government) 21

Galbraith, R. 404

gamification 309–10

gaming platforms 13

Garcia, A. 76

Gartner 122, 140

Gatorade 505

Gattiker, U.E. 632

Gemeinschaft 340

general profiles, customers 443

generic strategic approach 187–8

generic top-level domains (gTLD) 124, 658, **661**

George, J. 76

Gesellschaft 340

Geyskens, I. 18

Ghosh, S. 97, 256, 259

GIF (Graphics Interchange Format) 128, 149, **661**

Gilly, M. 77, 602, 605

Gladwell, Malcolm 260–1, 534

global economy growth 131

global positioning system (GPS) 313

Global Sources 636

global top-level domains (gTLD) 124, 658, **661**

globalisation 143, **661**

GM 637

Go Green, Go Online 166

goals
  branding 438
  conversion 436
  display advertising 516
  interaction 436
  longer-term brand engagement 438
  multichannel marketing 438
  setting 196–207, 432–41
    campaigns 441–3
    frameworks for objective setting 205–7
    online revenue contribution 200–2
    SMART objectives 203–5
  strategies to achieve 209, 239
  third-party site reach 438
  tracking, campaigns 432–41, 457
  traffic building 436
  see also objectives

Godin, Seth 44, 313, 314, 317, 425, 534

gold customers 332

Google 6, 30, 43, 44, 60, 61, 63, 71, 103, 213, 260, 263, 264, 290, 362, 372, 421, 470, 484–5, 487, 490, 494, 498, 508, 539–40, 626
  AdBots-Google 497
  ad manager 515
  algorithm 487, 490–1, 494, 495
  apps 13, 136, 395
  ASOS 615–16
  Kaushik, Avinash 551–3
  Knowledge Graph 491, 663
  pay-per-click ads 455
  Product Listing Ads (PLAs) 496, **661**
  quality score 497

Google Adsense 103, 104, 258, 495, 532

Google AdWords 20, 21, 42, 43, 71, 82, 103, 149, 157, 183, 345, 411, 421, 435, 457, 478, 480, 495–7, 517, 521, 615, 626
  Enhanced campaigns 501

Google Alerts 161, 496,

Google Analytics 10, 20, 43, 67, 126, 157, 203, 204, 377, 401, 438, 457, 479, 480, 551–2, 567, 568, 569

Google Base™ 37

Google Checkout 283

Google Chrome 13, 123, 124, 391
Google Display Network (GDN) 498, 517
Google gadgets 509
Google Keyword Tool 491, 492, 627
Google Maps 36
Google Merchant 20, 496
Google My Business 193
Google Music Key 292
Google Orkut 94
Google Product Search 20, 279, 511
Google Reader 33
'Google sandbox effect' 363, 489
Google Shopping 279, 496
Google tools 66
Google Trends data 64, 66
Google Webmaster 20, 401
Google Webmaster Tools 490, 495
Google Website Optimiser 254, 361, 552
Google+ 21, 24, 35, 44, 65, 137, 180, 193, 224, 317, 340, 342, 343, 356, 441, 470, 563, 630
gophers **661**
Gorell, C. 143–4
governance
    Internet 131, 145, **662**
    organisational capabilities 232–6
government markets 626
government-to-business (G2B) 21
government-to-consumer (G2C) 21
government-to-government (G2G) 21
GPRS **661**
GPS (global positioning system) 313
Graham, J. 536
graphic design **661**
graphical images 128
Graphics Interchange Format (GIF) 128, **661**
green issues, Internet usage 165–7
greenhouse gas emissions 165
Grehan, Mike 502
Grewal, D. 640, 641
Gronhaug, K. 602
Grossnickle, J. 572
growth
    hacking 369–70, **661**
    market share 210–1
Grube, Rüdiger 637–8
GSM **661**
gTLD (global (or generic) top-level domains) 124–5, 160, **661**
Guardian 258
Gunawan, G. 205

hackers **661**
Hagel, J. 341, 610
Halligan, B. 37, 424
halo effect see media multiplier: or halo effect
Halvorson, K. 398
Hamilton, Karen 461
hard launch **661**

Harridge-March, S. 252
Harrington, R. 644
Hasan, H. 205
Haven, B. 44
help 449
helper applications 128
herding 87
Hernandez, M. 263
hierarchy of response models 80
high-speed communication links 126, 137
highly localised websites 380
Hise, R. 602
hits, 560–1, 569, 661
Hitwise 508, 535
Hofacker, C, 399, 400
Hoffman, Bob 533
Hoffman, D.L. 22, 76, 395, 426, 427, 456, 520, 596
Hoffman, Reid 68
Holdsworth, Lynn 379
Holzwarth, M. 287
home pages 439, **661**
HomeGrocer.com 586
Honda UK 343
Hootsuite 225
horizontal e-marketplaces 636
horizontal portals 63
Hortal, Roberto 252–5
hosting providers 372–3
hostnames 125
hosts 126
Hotmail 526, 527
house lists 153, 479, 523–5, **661**
HSBC 165–6
Hsieh, Tony 300–2
HTML (Hypertext Markup Language) 127, **661**
HTTP (Hypertext Transfer Protocol) 125, 127, 134, **661**
human resources 192, 193
Humby, C. 240
Hunt, T. 240
hurdle rate 335, 336, **661**
Hussein, I. 443
hygiene factors see entry barriers
hype cycles 140, **661**
hyperlinks 126, 399, 440, 486, 487, 488, 493, 495, **662**
Hypertext Markup Language (HTML) 127, **661**
Hypertext Transfer Protocol (HTTP) 125, 127, 134, **661**

I-mode **662**
I-to-i.com 410–12
IAB (Internet Advertising Bureau) 67, 465, 515, 516
ICANN (Internet Corporation for Assigned Names and Numbers) 124–5, 144

ICO (Information Commissioner's Office) 150
ideas, forming 448
Ideastorm 214, 327, 344, 346, 570
ideavirus 534
identification 313
identity
    brands 266, 652
    online customers 602
    theft 132, 148, **662**
iDTV (interactive digital TV) **662**
IKEA 423–4
IMC (integrated marketing communications) 463–4, **662**
iMediaConnection 518
IMRG (Internet Media in Retail Group) 67
in-sector benchmarking 92
inbound customer contact strategies **662**
inbound e-mail marketing 522, **662**
inbound Internet-based communications 39, **662**
inbound marketing 37, 309, 424, 504, **662**
incentives 314, 316, 319, 521, 522, 526, 538
incidental offline advertising 537, **662**
independence of location 41
independent e-marketplaces 635
independent social networks 343
index inclusion 489–90, **662**
indexing 485–7
indirect responses 517
individual performance, e-procurement 634
individual profiles, customers 443
individualisation 38–9, 313
indoor kiosk-type platforms 13
industrial markets 626
industry restructuring 41
inelastic demand 269, 272
inflated expectations 140–1
influence
    customer engagement 308
    social media marketing KPIs 562
influencer marketing 530
influencer outreach 478, 494, 502–3, 506, 510, 531
influencers 488, 502, 503, 505, 506, 508, 532, 533, 534
influentials hypothesis 534
infomediaries **662**
information
    acquisition 56, 73, 86
    architecture 362, 381–2, **662**
    breadth, increased 309
    brokerage 101
    collected online 149
    customers see customers
    depth, increased 309
    leakage 132
    management, customer profiles 302
    offline communications 537

information (*continued*)
organisation schemes 381, 390– 1, **662**
privacy, consumer beliefs 601, 602
processing, websites 400
quality 406, 490
seekers
directed 88, **658**
undirected **675**
Information Commissioner's Office
(ICO) 150
informing, electronic 633
infrastructure components, Internet
126
ING Direct 91
initiatives, strategy 180–1
innovation 6, 7–8, 537
Google 539–40
marketing value of 139–42
social CRM 303
innovativeness 406
innovators 139, 143
inputs 581
data, validation 132
websites 401
insertion orders **662**
inside-out 366
InsideSales 407
insight
campaigns 441–3
customers 68, 441–3, **655**
Inspirational Cosmetics 645–6
institutionalising capabilities 233
intangible benefits 198, 199
integrated marketing communications
(IMC) 463–4, **662**
integrated strategy 184–6, 221, 232
integration 27, 38–40, 184–6, 211, 307,
313, 560
campaigns into overall media
schedules or plans 428, 440,
463–71
communications 501
customer information 184, 302
digital channels 25
e-mail marketing 525, 526
with intermediaries 212
options for 465
personal data 37
social channels 224,
social sign on 317
with suppliers 212
technology 228
vertical 283
web analytics tools 568
integrity 313, **672**
intellectual property rights (IPR) 147,
161, **662**
intelligence 38
artificial 37
competitive (CI) 190, **654**
inter-organisational trading online 633–9

interaction 37, 324
brand 518
customer engagement 308
customer lifecycle management 313
goals 436
offline communications 537
rates (IR) 519–20, **662**
social communication models 86–7
social networks 65, 304, 528
interactive advertisements 33, 38
Interactive Advertising Bureau (IAB) 67
interactive banner advertisements **662**
interactive communications, goal setting
and tracking for 432–41
interactive digital TV (iDTV) **662**
interactive display advertising 479,
515–22
interactive signage platforms 13
interactivity 37–8, 424–5, 452, **662**
intermediaries 64–5, **662**
analysis 194
downstream integration with
intermediaries 211, 212
financial 95
marketing 94–6, **664**
micro-environment 67
online sites 94–5, 180, 556–7
reintermediation 97–8
revenue models 103–6
search 63–4
internal audits 191–2
internal capabilities 92
internal context 442
internal link architecture 488, **662**
internal structures 233–6
international market growth 142, 143
International Telecoms Union 67
Internet
contribution **662**
definition 123, **662**
disengagement 164, 165
EDI 90, **662**
governance 131, 145, 662
infrastructure components 126
marketing **663**
marketing research based on 570–3
marketing strategy **663**
pureplay see clicks-only (Internet
pureplay)
security 130–3
share of search 64, **672**
technology 121, 123–38
usage, environmental and green issues
165–7
see also websites and entries
beginning with digital; online
Internet Advertising Bureau (IAB) 67, 515
Internet Corporation for Assigned
Names and Numbers (ICANN)
124–5, 144, 160
Internet Media in Retail Group (IMRG) 67

Internet Protocol Television (IPTV) 13,
36, **663**
Internet Relay Chat (IRC) **663**
Internet service providers (ISP) 126,
145, **663**
Internet Shopping Is Safe (ISIS) principles
408
InterNIC 371
interruption marketing 44, 313, **663**
interstitial ads 520, **663**
intimacy, customer engagement 308
intranets 129, **663**
intuitive operations 406
inventories, lower requirements 166
investment 428, 439
digital marketing campaigns 451–62
return on (ROI) 435, **671**
involvement
customer engagement 308
empowered 531
IPA 443, 454, 465
iPhone 8, 136, 255
IPR (intellectual property rights) 147,
161, **662**
IPTV (Internet Protocol Television) 13,
36, **663**
IR (interaction rates) 519–20, **662**
IRC (Internet Relay Chat) **663**
ISIS (Internet Shopping Is Safe)
principles 408
ISP (Internet service providers) 126,
145, **663**
iTunes 13, 277, 292
Iyengar, R. 23

Jackson, Steve 31
Janda, S. 358, 404
Java **663**
JavaScript rollovers 397
Jenkins, F. 537
Jenkinson, A. 30
Jesson, Ben 360–1
Joachimsthaler, E. 266
Jobber, D. 216, 221, 262, 263, 284,
597, 624
Johnson, E. 269
Johnson, M. 636
Joint Photographic Experts Group
(JPEG) 134, **663**
journalists 506, 508
JPEG (Joint Photographic Experts
Group) 134, **663**
jurisdiction, tax 146
JustGiving 532

Kalaignanam, K. 625, 630, 640
Kaplan, R.S. 205
Karibian, Anthony 626
Karibian, George 220, 626
Kaushik, Avinash 551–2
Keen, C. 76

Keiningham, T. 328
key performance indicators (KPI) 192,
        198, 205, 209, 233, 238, 554,
        564, **663**
keyphrase (keyword phrase) 483, 484,
        491–2, 494, 498, 499, 500, **663**
keys see digital certificates
keywords meta-tags 493
Kim, E. 221
Kim, K-J. 641, 642
Kindle 91
kiosk-type platforms 13
Kirby, Justin 534
Kirby, K. 328
Klein, L. 193, 260, 269
knowledge
    customers, increases 89
    online sales 632
    online service 632
    sharing, B2B marketing 632
    social 35
Koch, Olaf 638
Kolesar, M. 404
Kotler, P. 79, 451, 463, 554, 555
Kozmo.com 586
KPI see key performance indicators
Kumar, N. 227, 281, 282
Kumar, V. 328, 331, 334, 532

labelling 371, 381, 382, 383, 400
Ladha, Hash 616
laggards 139
lagging performance indicators 206–7,
        663
Lancaster, Alison 356
landing pages 30, 31, 360, 386–8, 404,
        411, 497, 499, 501, 526, **663**
last-click method of digital media
        channel attribution 456, 458, **663**
Lastminute.com 256, 280
late majority 139
latency 335, 660
Lautenborn, R. 251
law 147–64
Law of the Common Name 266
law of the few 260
Law of the Proper Name 266
lawful processing of personal data 150
leads **663**
    conversion efficiency 436, 437
    generation 68, 81
        business-to-business 629–30
        method 17
        offers 314, **663**
    qualified **670**
Leadforensic 631
leading performance indicators 206,
        663
Leahy, Terry 240
lean-forward media 427
Lee, G. 456, 458

Lee, S. 641, 642
legal forces 121, 147–64
legibility 389
lending 167–9
levels of pricing 271, 272, **669**
Levine, R. 34, 528
Lewis, M. 276
Lewis, Martin 65
Lexus 85
lifecycles
    customers see customers
    groups 218
    management grid 238–9
    stages, targeting 444, 445
lifetime value (LTV) 331–4, 435, **663**
limited purposes, personal data
        processing 150–1
link anchor text 486, 494, **663**
link building 488, 491, 495, **664**
link management 401, 581
Link Share 512
LinkedIn 11, 13, 24, 25, 35, 44, 65, 68,
        303, 317, 340, 342, 369
links 487–9, 494–7, 513
list brokers **664**
list owners **664**
lists, e-mail see e-mail
live chat 405, 412
live split testing see AB testing
live websites **664**
Living.com 586
localisation 280, 379–80, **664**
location
    independence of 41
    of trading 103–4
location-based marketing 13, 137
location-based services 135, 136, 138
Location Optimised Commerce
        on the Internet (LOCI) 146
lock-in, soft 89, 90, **674**
log files 560, **664**
    analysers 560, **664**
    analysis 568, 569, 571
Logitech 578–9
Logophilia WordSpy 257
Loiacono, E. 359, 405
Lonely Planet 258
long tail concept 261–2, **664**
look to book 434
Loomis, C.P. 340
Louviere, J. 610
loyalists, brand 534
loyalty
    customers see customers
    programmes 309
    techniques **664**
    variables 606
LTV (lifetime value) 330, 331–6,
        435–6, **663**
Lunce, S. 641
Lynx 461–2

Ma, Jack 94–5
Macafee 142
macro-environment 59–60, 120–68, **664**
    cultural forces 165–7
    economic forces 121, 142–4
    environmental changes 123
    legal forces 121, 147–64
    political forces 121, 144–6
    social forces 121, 164–5
    technological forces 121, 123–42
macro-level effectiveness metrics 555
Macromedia Flash and Shockwave
        products 128
MAD 517
magazine publishers 94
Magretta, J. 283
mailbot see autoresponders
mainstream new media sites or portals
        63, 65
maintenance
    process **664**
    websites 573–87
majority clicks 226
Makienko, I. 403
Malhotra, N. 572
malicious file execution 132
malls
    e-malls 101
    virtual **676**
Malmsten, Ernst 108–10
Malone, M.S. 282
Malone, T.W. 97
malware 130, 147, 149, **664**
management
    affiliate marketing best practice 512–13
    customer communications 311
    customer information 184, 199
    customer lifecycles 311–46
    customer service 302, 304–9, 311
    of digital marketing xiii–xv
    digital rights 104
    display advertising best practice 519–22
    e-mail marketing best practice 525–8
    information refinement 233
    online public relations best practice
        506–9
    paid search marketing (pay-per-click)
        best practice 499–501
    performance see performance
    search engine optimisation (SEO) best
        practice 489–95
    of strategy 25–7
    systems, content 400–1
    viral marketing best practice 534–5
    websites see websites
manufacturers 262, 281–2
many-to-many communications 426–7
mapping
    environment 122
    market 98
    sitemapping tools **673**

maps, site 381, 383, **673**
Marcus, J. 583–6
market alliance model 283
market and product development
    strategies 210–11
market audience, sales trends compared
    to 206
market development 17, 211–12
market dimension 641
market expansion 18
market growth 57, 142–3
market mapping 98
market-oriented pricing 274
market penetration 17, 210–11
market place structure changes 228
market research, B2B marketing 632
market share growth 210–11
marketing, definition 17
marketing intermediaries 94–6, **664**
marketing-led site design 383–4, 661
marketing mix 37, 250–292, **664**
marketing outcomes 557–8, 588
marketing planning 187, 216, **664**
marketing research, Internet-based
    570–3, **662**
marketing resources, capabilities 233
marketing value of innovations 139–42
marketplaces
    analysis 56–110, 121–2, 232
    performance 380
    portals 96
    positioning 101, 102, 380
    third-party 101
    virtual representation 278
markets, online competitive 88–91
    see also entries beginning with market
MarketSite™ **664**
marketsites **664**
marketspaces 63, 111, **664**
    electronic 635, 643, **659**
Marks and Spencer 159
Marsden, P. 260, 530
Marshak, R. 79
Marshall, P. 283
mashups 506, 508, **664**
mass customisation 256, 313, 322–3,
    425, **664**
mass marketing **664**
Maxymiser 565
McAfee 408
McCarthy, Jerome 250
McDonald, M. 37, 98, 187, 237, 272, 276
McDonald's 137
McKinsey 26
McLuhan, Marshall 340
measurement
    e-mail marketing 479, 522–8, 530, 542
    performance see performance
    social media marketing 562–3
media
    advertising 16

attribution, web analytics tools 568
brokers **664**
buyers **664**
buying **664**
consumption, customers 442
content 45, 398
cost measures 434
definition 27
digital see digital media
digital channels see digital media:
    channels
direct-response 16
earned 11–12, 342, 356
fragmentation 308, **664**
mix 451–62, 465–6
multiplier or halo effect 517, **661**, **665**
owned 11–12, 342, 356
owners **665**
paid 11–12, 356
planning 420–71, **665**
portals 24, 65, 96
range of 463, 464
relationship building 17
rich see rich media
selection, key activities 464–7
sites 12, 16, 22, 24, 29, 56, 60, 63,
    64, 65, **665**
website content 398
media-neutral planning (MNP) 464, **665**
Mela, C.F. 639
menu options, websites 396–7
merchandising
    online retail 402–4
    promotional mix 284
    web 359, **677**
merchants, virtual see virtual merchants
meta search engines **665**
meta-tags 160, 489, 493, **665**
meta-data 127–8, 487, 493, **665**
metrics
    for Internet marketing **665**
    performance see performance
Meyer, D. 263
MGC (most-growable customers)
    313, 330
micro-environment 59, 67, 68, **665**
    see also marketplaces: analysis
micro-level efficiency metrics 555
micro-targeting 43
micropayments **665**
microsites 438, 439, 461–2, 515, 526, **665**
Microsoft 127–8, 495, 497, 532
Microsoft Internet Information Server
    (IIS) **665**
Microstrategy 444
misers 334
mixed-mode buying 40, 438, **665**
MNP (media-neutral planning) 464, **665**
mobile apps 136–7, 395, **665**
mobile-based apps 13, **665**
mobile commerce **665**

mobile marketing 13, **665**
mobile phones 135–7,
    mobile apps 144–5
    platforms 13
    QR codes 137
    texting (SMS messaging) 135–6, 528
    web addresses 124
Mobile shopping (M-shopping) 73
mobile text messaging 135–6, 528
monetary value 335
monetise 104
monitoring 29, 401, 581
monologue 424–5
Morrisons 208, 240
Morville, P. 381, 383, 388
most-growable customers (MGC) 313,
    330
most-valuable customers (MVC) 330
Mougayer, W. 146
M-shopping 73
multichannel behaviour 219
multichannel buying models 84
multichannel communications 228–32
    service quality preferences 407–8
multichannel conversion models 71–2
multichannel customer experience 303,
    307, 324–5, 343–6
multichannel distribution 225–8
multichannel evaluation 559–60
multichannel marketing 11–12, 16, **665**
    goals 438
    Internet role 38–40
    strategy 179, **665**
multichannel prioritisation 223, **665**
Multilingual 380
multivariate testing 552, 564–6, 571
MVC (most-valuable customers) 330
MySpace 7
mystery shoppers 571, 573
mySupermarket 270, 278
MyTravel 568

names
    brands 264, 266–7
    domain see domain names
Napster 290, 292
National Express Group 565–6
natural or organic listings 484, 502, **666**
navigation 395–9, 401, 402, 580, 581, **673**
navigational search 484, **666**
needs, customers 251, 253, 255
Neely, Andy 553, 554
Nees Reisen 160
negotiated deals 102, 111
Negroponte, Nicholas 340
Neighbourhoods 47
Nellemann, Christian 626
nested ad content 515, **666**
net generations 131
net promoter score (NPS) 206, 327–8,
    346, 530, 531, **666**

New Media Age 420
new pricing approaches 268, 274–6
new products see products
Newholm, T. 602
news 24, 33, 35, 65
newspaper publishers 94
niche affiliates 65
niche communities 35
niche media sites 63
Nicholls, A. 612, 642, 643
Nicholson, David 168
Niederberger, Matthew 378
Nielsen 63, 66, 136
Nielsen BuzzMetrics 161
Nielsen, J. 375, 377, 389, 397, 400, 483
Nitish, S. 380
NMA 461
noise 427
Nominet 371
non-financial measures 93
non-repudiability **672**
Norton, D.P. 205
notification, data protection 150, **666**
Novak, T.P. 22, 395, 426, 427, 456, 520
Novo, J. 335, 336
NPD (new product development)
    see products: new
NPS see net promoter score

objective and task method of
    budgeting 451
objectives 18, 28, 180, 188, 198
    5Ss 189
    acquisition 205, 209, 219
    annual marketing communications
        432
    business, support 31–2
    campaign-specific communications
        432
    channel-specific 178
    communications 239, 432, 436
    conversion 204, 209
    costs 205
    digital marketing 196–207
    growth 205, 209
    penetration 205
    retention 204, 205, 209
    setting, frameworks for 205–7
    SMART 198, 203–5
    see also goals
O'Brien, Mike 422–4
Ocado 270
Ofcom 145
offers 274, **666**
    campaigns, message development and
        creatives 447–50
    lead generation 314, **663**
    sales generation 314, **671**
offline advertising
    incidental 537, **662**
    specific 537, **674**

offline promotion 535–40, **669**
offline responses 440
offline sales impact strategy 238, 239
offline site promotion 436, **666**
offline web metrics **666**
O'Keefe, R.M. 641
O'Malley, L. 314
Omar, A. 146
Omidyar, Pierre 46
omni-channel retailing 611–12
on-pack 135
on-page optimisation 478, , 487, 489,
    492–4, **667**
on-site search effectiveness 567–8
One in a Million Limited 159–60
one-to-many communications 425–7
one-to-one communications 425–7
one-to-one marketing 300, **666**
online advocacy 324, 327
online branding 250, **666**
online company presence 11, **666**
online completeness 406
online customer journeys 61–6, 79
online detractors 327
online exchanges 636
online focus groups 558, 560, 570, 571,
    572–3, 632
online influencer outreach 478, 494,
    502–3, 506, 531, **666**
Online Influencer Relations Program 346
online intermediary sites 94, **667**
online inter-organisational trading
    633–6
online lifecycle management grid 238–9
online market ecosystem 60
online marketplaces 46, 121–2
online ordering systems 157
online partnerships 33, 479, 510–15, 628
online presence 24–5, 537, 541
online product registrations 631
online promotion **669**
    contribution 201, **667**
online public relations (e-PR) 478,
    502–9, **667**
online questionnaires 558, 570, 571
online reputation management 503, **667**
online response mechanisms 439–40
online retail merchandising 402–4
online revenue contribution **667**
online sales
    efficiency strategy 239
    knowledge 632
online service
    knowledge 632
    providers (OSP) **667**
    quality gap 406, **667**
online shopping experiences 602–6
online site promotion 436, **667**
online social networks 65, 94, **667**
online sponsorship 479, 513–14
online surveys 632

online tactical marketing segmentation
    210, **666**
online targeted reach strategy 239
online technical support 631–2
online value propositions (OVP) 16, 222,
    239, **667**
online voice of customer 327, **667**
online web metrics **667**
OPA Europe 517
open-bid arrangements 274
open rates, e-mail marketing 526
operating environment see
    micro-environment
operating system gadgets 509
operational categories, e-retailing 610
operational dimension 640
operational effectiveness 640, 642
operational strategies, e-retailing
    610–11
Opinion Labs 327
opportunities 16–17, 28
    assessments 195–6
    see also SWOT analysis
opt-in 153, 154–5, 159, 314, **667**
    cookies 158
    e-mail 667
        marketing see opt-in e-mail
            marketing
    house list 523, **661**
    incentives 319
    selective 317
    social networks 314, 317
opt-in e-mail marketing 33, 479, 522–4,
    542
    B2B marketing 628
    customers 522–4
    prospect conversion options 523–4
opt-out 153, 155–6, 158, 159, 314, 319,
    409, **667**
opt-out e-mail **667**
optimisation
    campaigns, pay-per-click marketing
        501
    cross-media studies (XMOS) 517,
        655, 678
    on-page 487, 489, 492–4, **667**
    pay-per-click 500–1
    search engines see search engines
orchestration 465
ORCI 538
orders
    average order value (AOV) **651**
    conversion rates 434
O'Reilly, Tim 36
organisational capabilities 232–6
organisational governance 232–6
organisational marketing environments,
    business-to-business 625–6
organisational structures 101, 232, 233–4
organisational trading environments,
    business-to-business 625–7

organisations
  channel preferences 229
  virtual 282–3
OSP (online service providers) **667**
Out-Law 162
out-of-sector benchmarking 92
outbound contact strategy 319,
outbound e-mail **667**
outbound e-mail marketing 30, 522, **667**
outbound Internet-based
    communications 38, **667**
outcome data 571
outcomes, channels 558, **653**
outdoor kiosk-type platforms 13
output data, validation 131–2
outside-in 377
outsourcing 282–3, 286, 294, 365–6, **667**
overlays 520, **667**
overts **667**
OVP *see* online value propositions
owned media 11–12, 342, 356
ownership
  conflicts 184
  content 585
  technology 580
  websites 365, 379

packaging 166, 253, 284
Padilla-Meléndez, A. 645
page impressions 560–1, 569, **668**
Page, L. 494
page requests 126, **668**
page templates 363, 367, 384–7, 398, 401
page views see page impressions
PageRank 486–7, 494, **668**
pages per visit (PPV) 561
paid media 11–12, **668**
paid search marketing (pay-per-click
    (PPC)) see search engines
paid search networks 283
panel activity 571
Parasuraman, A. 404
Parry, K. 538
Parsons A. 233
participant print 443
participation
  community 30, 33, 36, 430
  content 45, 398
  customers 22, 33, 44
  orchestration led by 465
  questionnaires 572
  website content 398
partner networks 12
partnerships
  channels 180
  electronic 283
  online *see* online partnerships
  strategic 228, 252
pass-along 452
path analysis 566–8, **661, 671**
paths 125, 132

pay-for-performance communications
    427, **668**
pay-per-click (PPC) 29–30, 427, 434, 445,
    452, **668**
  ad networks 149, 157
  marketing 161, **668**
  paid search marketing *see* search
    engines
pay-per-performance 104
pay-per-view 258
payments
  mechanisms 279–80
  results-based 515, **671**
  secure electronic transaction (SET)
    134–5, **672**
  systems **668**
PayPal 8, 46, 103, 279, 283
PDSA 336
peak of inflated expectations 140–1
penetration
  markets 17, 210–11
  objectives 205
people
  customers defining support queries
    286–7
  e-mails
    receipt and acknowledgement 287
    routeing 287
  follow-up 288
  responses 287–8
  social media marketing 536
  variable in marketing mix 250,
    286–8, **664**
Peppard, J. 259
Peppers, D. 313, 330
perceived usefulness, consumer beliefs
    602
percentage of sales methods of
    budgeting 451
perceptions
  customers, of Internet and different
    media 431–2
  service delivery 404
  website information 408
Perea, T. 596, 602
Pereira, A. 379
Perfect Commerce 634
perfectly elastic demand 272
perfectly inelastic demand 272
performance
  channels, evaluation and
    improvement 550–87
  competitors 443
  customer acquisition driver 375
  customer conversion driver 375
  customer retention driver 375
  digital marketing 28
  digital strategy development 9–10
  drivers 198, 206, 231, 238, **668**
  e-procurement 634
  gaps 558, 570, 605, 612–13

  Google Analytics 20
  improvement process 25
  lagging indicators 206–7, **663**
  leading indicators 206–7, **663**
  management
    digital channels 553–73
    grid 238
    systems 553–5, 569, 570, **668**
  marketplace 380
  measurement
    definition 554
    systems 554, 570, **668**
  metrics 205, **668**
    collection tools and techniques
      560–73
    framework definition 555–60
  prices, excellence 220
  products, excellence 220
  relationships, excellence 231
  site management 575–82
  transactions, excellence 221
  websites 580, **668**
    optimisation 372–3
  see also key performance indicators
Performics 484
permanent beta see agile software
    development
permission-based content 629
permission marketing 30, 44, 155, 265,
    309, 313–19, 343, **668**
Permissive Marketing 153
persistent cookies 156, 157, **668**
personal data see data
personal response 440
personalisation 38, 139, 141, 209, 220,
    236–7, 302, 313, 317, 322–3,
    425, **668**
  customer lifecycles 322
  e-mail marketing 425, 525, 537
  media selection 430, 452
  offline communications 537
  one-to-many communications 425
  products 256
  technology 309
personality, websites 390
personas 79–80, 122, 192, 368, 481, **668**
persuasion marketing 375, **668**
PEST 120
PESTLE 120
Peters, L. 425, 427
Petersen, Eric 433
Pets.com 582, 586
phishing 132, **668**
phone
  personalisation 395
  response (home page design) 377
  service delivery 405, 407
  website design 377
  see also mobile phones
phone-me **668**
photo sharing sites 508

physical evidence variable in marketing mix 250, 252, 288, **668**
physical reminders 538
Pian, Y. 642
Pickton, A. 463, 464
Pieterse, Jurie 518
Pincott, G. 466
Pinsent Mason 162
Pirie, Kane 41
pixels **668**
Pixmania 275
PKI (public key infrastructure) 134
place
    channel conflicts 281–2
    new channel structures 280
    of purchase 277–80
    variable in marketing mix 277–83, **669**
    virtual organisations 282–3
planning
    affiliate marketing best practice 512–13
    channel 464
    communications-mix 464
    demand analysis 69
    display advertising best practice 519–22
    e-mail marketing best practice 525–8
    e-marketing 232, 285
    environmental scanning 60
    implementation 29
    integrated marketing communications 464, 463–4
    key media activities 464–7
    marketing 187, **664**
    media 463–7, **665**
    media-neutral (MNP) 464, **665**
    online public relations 506–9
    organisational capabilities 232
    paid search marketing (pay-per-click) best practice 499–501
    search engine optimisation best practice 489–99
    target marketing 215–19
    viral marketing best practice 534–5
    website design and build 362–70
plans see planning
plateau of productivity 140, 141
platforms 11–15
    collaboration 101
    content access 45
    destination sites and 65
platinum customers 332–3
Plaxo 21
plug-ins 128, 401, **669**
PNG (Portable Network Graphics) 128
podcasts 33, 44, 508, **669**
poisoning, data 132
political control 145
political forces 121, 144–6
Portable Network Graphics (PNG) 128
portals 24, 65, 94, 96, **669**

Porter, Michael xiii, 56, 89, 92, 178, 186, 196, 208, 221, 612, 642
portfolio analysis 236–7, **669**
ports 125
positioning 16, **669**
    marketplace 101, 380
    strategy 216, 220–3
    target marketing 215
    value chain 101
POST 529
post-purchase evaluation, consumers 84
power
    customers, increases 89
    of context 261
Power, Rene 627
PPC see pay-per-click
PPV (pages per visit) 561
PR see public relations
pre-development tasks, websites 362
precision 273
predictive modelling 122
preferences
    channels 219, 229
    communications, e-mail marketing 525
    customers see customers
    multichannel communications, service quality 407–8
    tone and style 219
premium pricing 274
prescriptive strategy 189, **669**
Pricerunner 270
prices
    alternative pricing structure or policies 276
    auctions 274
    comparison sites 56, 64, 65, 69, 89, 94, 101, 103
    competition-based pricing 274
    cost-plus pricing 273
    definitions
        differential pricing **657**
        price dispersion **669**
        price elasticity of demand **669**
        price transparency **669**
        price variable **669**
        pricing levels 271, **669**
        pricing models **669**
    differential pricing 269, **657**
    dispersion 273, **669**
    downward pressure on 270–4
    dynamic pricing 268, 275, **658**
    elasticity of demand 269, 271–2, 274, **669**
    levels of pricing 271, **669**
    market-oriented pricing 274
    new pricing approaches 274–6
    performance, excellence 220
    premium pricing 274
    pricing models 251, 267, **669**
    skimming the market 274

target-profit pricing 274
testing 275
transparency 269–70, **669**
variable in marketing mix 267–76, **669**
primary digital divide 165
primary messages 447–9
primary personas 80, 665
Princess Cruises 318
printed materials 166
printing 398
privacy 406, 408, **669**
    commercial organisations providing protection services 135
    cookies 156–8
    data 149–53, 155
    electronic communications 153–4, 158–9, **669**
    Electronic Frontier Foundation 148
    Facebook 471
    independent third parties 135
    laws controlling 147, 148–59
    Secure Electronic Transaction (SET) 134–5
    Secure Sockets Layer protocol (SSL) 134
    service quality 409
    social location-based marketing 137
    statements 149, 158, 159, 408, **669**
    viral marketing 155, **676**
    web analytics tools 569
Privacy and Electronic Communications (EC Directive) Regulations 153–4
process, e-procurement 633–5, 637–9, **659**
process models, strategy 187–9, **674**
process variable in marketing mix 288, **669**
processing, straight-through 405
productivity, plateau of 140–1
products
    bestselling 402
    branding 250, 262–7
    core 255–7, 262, **655**
    development 17, 210–1, 212
    digital, options for offering 257–8
    experience 448, 449
    extended 251, 258–9, **660**
    long tail concept 261–2, **664**
    new
        development 259, 260, 632
        diffusion 260–1
    online registrations 631
    performance, excellence 220
    personalisation 256
    recommendations 302, 323, 330, 340, 370, 388
    registrations 631
    related 388, 340
    research online 256, 259–60
    substitute 88, 89, 90
    support 84
    variable in marketing mix 255–67, **669**
    visualisation systems 401, 403

profiles
  capturing 314, 316
  consumers 597–602
  customers see customers
  data 311
  demographic characteristics 218
  information 148, 149
profitability
  channels 206, 559, **653**
  sales 207
projects
  different, assessing 236–7
  initiation 370–4, **662**
  managers, websites 365, 367
  website 362–74
promotion
  channels 556–7, **653**
  mix 451, 463
  offline 535–8, **669**
  offline site 436, **666**
  online see online promotion
  online site 436, **667**
  tools 463
  variable in marketing mix 284–5, **669**
  websites 363, 370, 404
propensity modelling 336, 340, **669**
Proper Name, Law of the 266
propositions, differential channel 178
prospect conversion, opt-in e-mail
    marketing options 523–4
prosumers **669**
protection
  brands see brands
  data see data
protocols 125, 127, 134
prototypes 366–7, 369, **669**
Prouse, Robin 336
proximity marketing 137, 138, **669**
Prussakov, E. 513, 514
psychographic segmentation 444–5, **669**
psychographic variables 76
public key **669–70**
  encryption 133–4, **670**
  infrastructure (PKI) 134, **670**
public relations (PR) 29, 30, 33, 101, 109,
    529, 531, 537–8, **670**
  online see online public relations
  promotional mix 284
publication workflow 401, 581
publisher sites 64
publishers 65, 94, 101, 102
  online 96, 103
publishing, social 35
Pulizzi, J. 399
pull media 37, 38, 424, **670**
purchases
  consumers 83
  decisions, suppliers assisting 83
  facilitation of 83
  histories, customers 217, 218, 220
  place of 277–80

see also buyers; buying
pureplay retailers see clicks-only (Internet
    pureplay)
Purinton, E. 389
push media 37, 38, 424, 425, 430, **670**
push technology **670**

QR (Quick Response) codes 137, **670**
qualified lead **670**
qualitative assessments 92
quality
  costs 640
  e-mails lists 302
  information 406
  measures 203, 433
  media selection factor 451–2
  scores 497–8, **670**
  service see service
  of use, divide stemming from 165
quantitative analysis 92
Quelch, J. 193, 260, 269
query requests 486
questionnaires 309, 374, 413, 558, 560,
    570, 571, 572
Quick Response (QR) codes 137, **670**
quick wins 233

RACE 31–2
radio 138
rampant experimentation 196
ranking 484–9, 491–8
rapid diffusion 141
Raskin, O. 572
ratings, customers 403
Rayport, J. 285, 286, 635
reach 93, 277, 452, 504, **670**
  brands, enhancing 517
  offline communications 536
  online public relations 504
  social media marketing KPIs 562
  targeted strategy 238, 239
reactivation 312
real-time bidding (RTB) 516, **670**
really simple syndication (RSS) feeds 33,
    508, **660**, **670**
RealNames **670**
REAN 31
recency 335
recency frequency monetary value (RFM)
    analysis 335, 337, 338
reciprocal links **670**
referral programmes 530
referral value, customers (CRV) 334
referrals 312
referrer or referring sites 421, **670**
referrers 421, 557, **670**
registration
  domain names see domain names
  individuals **670**
  products 631
Reichheld, F. 300, 327

reintermediation 41, 97–8, 280, **670**
related businesses, diversification into
    211, 212
related products 340
relationship marketing 300–43, **670**
  customer engagement challenge
    308–11
  customer lifecycle management
    311–43
relationships
  building 448
    media 17
  buyer–seller 630–2
  with companies, targeting 444
  customers, management see customer
    relationship management
  deepening 19
  excellence 221
  marketing see relationship marketing
relative advantage 406
re-launch, websites **673**
relevance
  e-mail marketing 526
  personal data 151
reliability
  e-mail response 407
  service quality 405, 406, 409
  website 406, 407
remote environment see
    macro-environment
Renault 503, 506
renderability **670**
  e-mail marketing 525, 527
repeat-customer base 330
repeat sales metrics 206
repeat visits 192, **670**
reporting consistency 184
reporting refinement 233
representation 101, **670**
repurposing **670**
reputation
  brands see brands
  damage 148, 153, 161
  management 161
    brands 161
    online 503, **667**
  social media marketing KPIs 562
requests for information (RFI) 633
requests for price (RFP) 633
research, customers 192
resellers 281–2, 626
re-selling 312
residence countries 146
resizing 398
resources **671**
  analysis 192–3, **671**
  e-mail marketing 525
  financial 192
  human 193
  issues, performance management 554
  technology infrastructure 192–3

responses
  capabilities, competitors 93
  decay, e-mail marketing 525
  direct 525
  e-mail marketing 526–7, 528
  going viral 531
  histories, customers 218
  indirect 517
  mechanisms 438–41, 537
  offline 440, 467, 537
  soliciting 517
  times 406, 409
responsiveness 405
restructuring, industry 41
results-based payment 515, **671**
results delivery 29
results serving 486
retail channels 610, **671**
retail format **671**
retail merchandising 402–4
retention 231
  customers see customers
  efficiency 70
  encouraging 517
  objectives 204, 205, 209
  of personal data 159
  rate metrics 330
Rettie, R. 395, 396, 522, 528
return on advertising spend (ROAS)
    435, **671**
return on investment (ROI) 435, **671**
return paths **671**
revenue
  advertising 64, 103, 104
  affiliate 103
  per click (RPC) 103, 106
  contribution 200–2
  generation 180
  models 64, 101, 102, 103–7, 213,
    380, **671**
    electronic commerce 99–102
    strategy 213–5
  sales 200
  stream 100
  transaction fees 103
  per transaction of repeat customers
    330
reverse auctions 274, 278, 633, 635, **671**
reverse path analysis 566, 567, 568, **671**
review sites 511
reviews
  content 573–4, 576, 577, 580
  customers 390, 398, 403, 404, 406
  expert 377, **660**
rewards 136, 137, 511
RFI (requests for information) 633
RFM (recency frequency monetary value
    analysis) 335, 337, 338
RFP (requests for price) 633
rich internet applications (RIA) 45,
    398, **671**

rich media 30, 31, 33, 44, 45, 123, 128,
    265, 274, **671**
richness 278
Ries, A. 265, 266
Ries, L. 265, 266
Rigby, D. 410
'right touching' through developing
    online contact strategies 319–20
rights
  data subjects 150–3
  management, digital 104
risk, consumer beliefs 602
risk–reward analysis 237
rivalry between competitors 89, 91
ROAS (return on advertising spend)
    435, **671**
Robertson, J. 383
Robertson, Nick 614–15
Robinson, H. 516, 521
robots 372, 400, 485, 488–90, **671**
Rogers, E. 139
Rogers, M. 313, 330
Rohm, A. 180
ROI (return on investment) 435,
    671
ROPO 72
Rosen, D. 389
Rosenfeld, L. 381, 383, 388
Rossiter, J.R. 241
Round, M. 564, 584–5
Roxio 290
RPC (revenue per click) 103, 106
RS Components 211, 221, 316
RSS (really simple syndication) feeds 33,
    508, **660**, **670**
RTB (real-time bidding) 516, **670**
Rued-Sabater, E. 130
run-of-site 515, **671**
Ryan, J. 514
Rylander, A. 259

Safe Harbor Scheme 153
Sain, B. 30
Sainsbury's 208, 226, 240, 607
sales
  activation 448
  e-retailing strategies 606, 612–13
  efficiency, online strategy 239
  force automation (SFA) 311
  generation offers 314, **671**
  impact, offline strategy 239
  influence, attributing to digital media
    channels 456
  offline impact strategy 239
  online see online sales
  process management 311
  profitability 207
  promotions 135, **671**
    promotional mix 284
  repeat, metrics 206
  representatives 311, 344

revenue 200
social CRM 303
transactions, platforms 17
trends compared to market audience
    trends 206
volumes 206, 207, 210, 238
samplings 135
Samson, A. 328
Santander 420
Sarah Matthews 168
Sarkar, M. 95, 96, 101
satisfaction
  channels 558, **653**
  customers see customers
  surveys 550, 570
satisficing behaviour 269, **671**
save (5 Ss) 198, 205
Scan Alert 408
scanning, environmental 60, **660**
scenario-based analysis **671**
scenario of use **671**
scenarios, customers 79–80, 192, **656**
Schefter, P. 300
schematics see wireframes
Schramm, W. 427–8
SciVisum 373–4
scoring 486
  value event see value event scoring
scripts **671**
scrum 367, **671**
sealed-bid arrangements 274
search engines 63, 64, 82, 84, 95,
    103, **671**
  listing 478, 484–5, 493, 495–9,
    502, **672**
  marketing (SEM) 32–3, 64, 82, 478,
    484–5, 491, 495, 499, 627, **672**
  meta **665**
  optimisation (SEO) 20, 30, 377, 380,
    382, 401, 478, 484, 504, **672**
    advantages 488
    best practice in planning and
      managing 489–95
    disadvantages 488–9
    online public relations 504
  paid search marketing (pay-per-click
    (PPC)) 485, 495–8, **668**
    advantages 498
    best practice in planning and
      managing 499–501
    disadvantages 498–9
  pay-per-click marketing 484–5, 506,
    542
    optimisation 500
  ranking **672**
  ranking factors 487–8
  results pages (SERPs) 484–5, 511,
    672
  robot crawling 400
  submission 489, **672**
  visibility 581

searches
customer behaviour 309, 517–18, 520
engines see search engines
on-site effectiveness 567–8
phrases 64
portals 96
share of 64, **672**
social media 33–4
terms in body copy 492–3
Sears Social 317
SEAT 523
second level domains (SLD) 125
secondary digital divide 165
secret key encryption see symmetric encryption
Secure Electronic Transactions (SET) 134–5, **672**
Secure Sockets Layer (SSL) 134, **672**
security
access control 581
consumer beliefs 601–2
Internet 130–5
methods 667
personal data 149–53
verified buyers' scheme 636
websites 131–3, 408
Sedley, Richard 308
seeding 533–4, 535, **672**
segmentation **672**
attitudinal 444–5
campaigns 443–4
customers 63, 79, 312, **656**
demographic 444
psychographic 444–5, **669**
target marketing 215–18, 229
visitors 557
selection
customers 312, 332, **656**
media 451–2, 464–7
selective opt-in 317
self-identification 217
self-service technologies 631
sell (5 Ss) 189, 198, 205
sell-side e-commerce 22, **672**
selling
promotional mix 284
re-selling 312
see also cross-selling; up-selling
SEM (search engine marketing) see search engines
semantic web 36, 37
semi-localised websites 379
senior management
commitment 232
myopia 554
sense and respond communications 38, 302, 309, 311, 319, **672**
sensitive personal data 150, 159
SEO (search engine optimisation) see search engines

sequences, e-mail 629
SERPs (search engine results pages) 484–5, 511, **672**
serve (5 Ss) 198, 205
server-based log file analysis 560, 569
service
customers see customers
online see online service
online quality 302, 312
gap 406, **667**
promise 406, 408–9
quality 58, 404–10, **672**
services-oriented relationship-building websites 24
serving **672**
see also ad serving; web servers
SERVQUAL 404, 406, 408, 409
session conversion rates 404, 433
session cookies 156, 158, **672**
session management, websites 132
SET (Secure Electronic Transactions) 134–5, **672**
Seybold, P. 79
SFA (sales force automation) 311
SGML (Standard Generalised Markup Language) 127
Shah, D, 37, 424
share buttons 509
share of search 64, **672**
share of voice **672**
shareable social objects 535
shipping fees 276
Shiu, E. 76
Shop Direct 603–4
shopping, mobile 73
short codes 136, **672**
Short Message Service (SMS) 135–6, **672**
SIC (Standard Industry Codes) 625
Sidh, Inder 144
Siikavirta, H. 165
silver customers 332
Simon, Herbert 269
simple page feedback tools 570
simplicity 389, 396–7
Singh, N. 379
single customer view 317, **672**
site auditors see websites: auditors
sitemapping tools **673**
site navigation schemes 395–9
sites see websites
situation analysis 56–7, 121–2, 188, 190–1, 194, **673**
Sivakumar, K. 395
sizzle (5 Ss) 189, 199, 205
skills xv
skimming the market 274
Sky 535
SLD (second level domains) 125
SLEPT 120
slide sharing sites 508
slope of enlightenment 140–1

Slyke, C.V. 76
Smart, A. 633, 634
Smart Insights 20, 23, 24, 25, 31, 32, 45, 129, 158, 314, 315, 317, 321, 342, 534, 627
SMART objectives 198, 203–4, 436, **673**
smartcards **673**
smartphones 8, 12, 15, 61, 73, 124, 136, 182, 304, 362, 372, 386, 390, 392–3, 395, 396, 468, 598
Smile 91, 212–13
Smith, D. 395
Smith, P.R. 17–18, 32, 33, 80, 188, 189, 192, 198, 252, 258, 284, 286, 387, 408, 420, 494
SMO (social media optimisation) 225, **673**
SMS marketing 528
SMS (Short Message Service) 135–6, **672**
sneezers 534
SNS (social networking sites) 34
social blogging 36
social bookmarking 35, 508, **673**
social channels 224
social commerce 22, 23, 35, 47, **673**
social CRM 302–3, 305–6, 324, **673**
social customer service 35
social exclusion 164–5, **673**
social forces 121, 164–5
social graphs 488, **673**
social interaction communication models 86–8
social isolation 164
social knowledge 35, 33
social location-based marketing 137, **673**
social media
governance 504, **673**
listening 504, **673**
marketing 9, 11–12, 29, 31, 33–7, 41, 479, 482, 528–9, **673**
B2B marketing 628
communications strategy 529
measuring 562–3
tools 34–7
optimisation (SMO) 225, **673**
strategy 233–5
social network-related viral marketing 531–2
social networking sites (SNS) 21, 25, 33
social networks 25, 33, 56, 64, 65, 68, 86, 87, 508–9, **674**
communities creating through 342–3
for CRM 340–4
cross-sell support 302
independent 343
monitoring brand conversations in 161
online 94, **667**
opt-in 314, 317
up-sell support 302
virtual communities 101, 340–2, **676**
social news 33, 35

social niche communities 35
social objects, shareable 535
social presence 302, 427
social publishing 35
social sharing widgets 509
social streaming 35
soft closes 274
soft launch 362, **674**
soft lock-in 89, 90, **674**
software, agile *see* agile software
    development
Sorge, Joe 137
SOSTAC® 188, 189, 529
Sothebys.com 586
source countries 146
Source, P. 596
sourcing, electronic 633
spam 153, 154, 158, 489, 490–1, 523, 524,
    527, **674**
Sparrow, A. 162
speak (5 Ss) 189, 198, 205
specific offline advertising 537, **674**
spiders 485–6, **674**
splash pages **674**
sponsors, websites 364–5
sponsorship **674**
    fixed run-of-site 105
    promotional mix 284
    site section or content types 103
Spotify 290–2
sprints 367
Srinivasan, S. 606
SSL (Secure Sockets Layer) 134, **672**
stage models 24, **674**
stakeholders, websites 365
Standard Generalised Markup Language
    (SGML) 127
Standard Industry Codes (SIC) 625
standardised websites 379
standards, websites 580
star alliance model 283
Starbucks 137
Starkis, J. 451
start-ups 90, 99, 100, 106, 107
static (fixed) web pages 126, **674**
statistics, websites **673**
STEP **674**
Stephens, Guy 304–7
Sterne, J. 575
stickiness 260, 558, 561, 581, **674**
stimulation 451
Stone, R. 602
storyboarding 387, **674**
straight-through processing 405
strategic agility 123, **674**
strategic analysis **674**
strategic data 568, 570
strategic dimension 642
strategic market segmentation 216, **674**
strategic positioning **674**
strategic windows 189, **674**

strategists, content 578–9
strategy 178–90, 197
    approach selection 29
    business models 213–15
    business-to-business 642–3
    challenges in developing and
        managing 25–7
    channel marketing 178–9
    customer engagement 223–5
    decisions 210–36
    differentiation 220–3
    e-retailing 612–13
    emergent 189, **660**
    formulation 208–39, **674**
    framework for developing 27–9
    generic approach 187–8
    goal setting 196–207
    implementation 236–9
    initiatives 181
    integrated 184–6
    market development 211–12
    multichannel communications
        228–30
    multichannel distribution 225–8
    online communications mix and
        budgets 231–2
    organisational capabilities and
        governance 232–6
    positioning 216, 220–2
    prescriptive 189, **669**
    process models 187–8, **674**
    product development 210–12
    revenue models 213–5
    scope 179–80
    situation analysis 188, 190–6
    social media 223–5
    social media marketing 528–9
    target marketing 16, 215–18, **675**
    uniform (universal) resource locators
        123, 124, **675**
    see also marketing mix, relationship
        marketing
streamed video 35
streaming media **674**
streaming media servers 124, **674**
streaming, social 32, 33
strengths 193
    see also SWOT analysis
structures 193
    authoring 581
    internal 233–6
    organisational 101, 233–4
    websites 389–90
style guides **674**
style preferences 219
subdomains 125
subjects, data *see* data
submission, search engines 489, **672**
subscriptions 212, 257, 258
    access to content or services 90, 104,
        290–2

substitute products and services 89, 90
substitution 285–6
success
    barriers to 91
    factors 198, 207, 209, 231
        brand sites 265–6
        critical (CSF) 198, 209, 231
        e-mail marketing 526–7
        online customer experience 357–9
Sullivan, U. 98
Sultan, F. 180
Sun Microsystems 128
super-affiliates 65
superstitials 520, **674**
suppliers 96
    bargaining powers 89–90
    intermediaries 59, 67, 89
    marketing intermediaries 94–6
    micro-environment 59
    oriented e-marketplaces 635
    upstream integration with 211, 212
support
    forums 259
    products 84
    services, web analytics tools 554, 569
    social CRM 302–3
surfers 71, **675**
surveys 86, 92, 259
    UX Lab 603–4
    online 632
Sviokla, J. 635
Swaminathan, V. 76
switching brands 19, 62
switching supplier 90, 91
SWOT analysis 188, 193, 195–6, 197
symmetric encryption 133–4, **675**
synchronous communications 427
synchronous recording 571
syndication 36, 279, 401, 579, 581, **675**
    content 45, 398
    RSS (Really Simple Syndication) 33
    technology 317
system architecture and configuration
    132
system information leakage 132
Szymanski, D. 602

tablet platforms 13
tag-based measurement systems 568
tagging 424, 456, 458, 460, **675**
tailored communications 406
TalkTalk 145
tangible benefits 198, 199
tangibles, service quality 405, 407
Taobao 94–5
Tapp, A. 464
target audiences 224
target marketing strategy 16, 215–20,
    675
target-profit pricing 284
targeted reach strategy 274

targeting
advertisements **675**
behavioural 445, 452
behavioural ad 520–1, **651**
campaigns 443–4
cost-effective 308
display advertising 519–20
e-mail marketing 525, 526
interactive ad 520–1
lifecycle stages 444, 445
micro 43
offline communications 537
online advertising 517, 518
pay-per-click marketing 498–9, 500
relationships with companies 444
value 444, 445
taxation 145–6
Taylor, Geoff 145
Taylor, S. 404
TCP/IP (Transfer Control Protocol/
Internet Protocol) **675**
technical support 631
technological forces 121, 123–42
technology
Bluetooth wireless applications 138
changes, responding to 43
convergence 135, **675**
customer relationship management
311
databases 311
emerging 138
infrastructure 187, 192, 218, 227,
232, 236
integration 228
Internet 123–38
marketing value of innovations
139–42
mobile apps 136–7
ownership 580
QR (Quick Response) codes 137
self-service 631
social media marketing 479
syndication 317
triggers 140
WiFi (wireless fidelity) 137
telemarketing using the Internet **675**
television 138
telnet **675**
temporary cookies *see* session cookies
tendering, electronic 633
tensions between teams 184
Teo, T. 642
Tesco 15, 65, 157, 208, 213, 215, 222,
225, 226, 239–41, 263, 270, 309,
513, 607
test website **675**
testing 43, **675**
AB *see* AB testing
content 362, 400–1, **675**
creative 501
e-mail marketing 525

multivariate *see* multivariate testing
prices 275
website content 388, 401
websites 388–9
text ads 103
text information and data 127–8
texting 135–6
theft
data 131–2
identity 148
third-parties
cookies 149, **675**
e-newsletters 523
sites, reach goals 438
see also trusted third parties
Thomas Cook Netherlands 378
Thomas, J. 98
Thomson 382
Thomson Financial 644
Threadless 425
threats
assessments 195–6
see also SWOT analysis
Tibbits, H. 205
time, media selection factor 452
timeliness, customer expectations 603
timing, e-mail marketing 526
Timmers, P. 100, 101, 102
tipping points 260–1, **675**
Tjan, A. 237, 644
TLD (top-level domains) 124–5, 658,
661
Toffler, Alvin 265
tone preferences 229
Tonnies, Ferdinand 352
top-level domains (TLD) 124–5, 658, **661**
touch marketing funnel 220
touch strategy 319
touchpoints, customers 179, 230, 308,
316, 317, 324, 611
tracking 59, 479–81, 508, 511
ClickTracks 553
cookies 168–9, 510, 513, 518
cross-channel 98
e-commerce 204
eye 361, 377
Facebook 471
metrics 238
online activity 66, 218, 225, 289, 357,
457–60, 516, 520
orders 585
real-time experience (RET) 85–6
tags 456,–60, 508
viral marketing 535
website 401,
content 399, 581
Trade Doubler 512
trademarks **675**
meta-tags 160
pay-per-click advertising 161
protection law 125, 147, 159, 161

traditional communications
digital and, relationship between 30–1
traffic building 420, 436, **675**
traffic volumes 104, 433
transactional e-commerce sites 24,
65, **675**
transactions
Alibaba.com 94–5
business-to-business 74
commercial arrangements for 111
consumers 74
data 311, 341
excellence 221
fee revenue 103
log files 126, **675**
per repeat customer 330
purchase 279
regular/emergency 255
security risks 130
Transfer Control Protocol/Internet
Protocol (TCP/IP) **675**
transfer of personal data abroad 153
transparency, prices 269, **669**
Transversal 407
Travel Republic 41–2
trialogue 424–5, **675**
triggers, technology 218, 240–1
TripAdvisor 96
Trocchia, P. 358, 404
trough of disillusionment 141
trust 77, 78, 87, 406
consumer beliefs 602
models 84–6
segmentation based on 88
TRUSTe 101, 135, 144, 408
trusted feeds 496, **675**
trusted third parties (TTP) 134, **675**
certificates 133, 134
Trustpilot 58
Tweetburner 225
Twitter 11, 13, 14, 15, 33, 34, 304, 305,
307, 317, 342, 346, 356, 481, 482,
488, 528, 563
Tyler, M. 639
Tynan, C. 314

über-bloggers 511
UGC (user-generated content) 33, 84
Ultralase 376–7
unawareness, consumers 81–2
unclear responsibilities 554
undirected information-seekers **675**
uniform (universal) resource locators
(URL) 123, 124, 370, 371
components 125, 371
parameters 125, 371
strategy 125, 446, **676**
see also domain names
unique selling points (USP) 57, 199
unique visitors 66, 110, 192, 203, 238,
421, 433–4, 560–1, 566, **675**

uniqueness 260
unit elastic demand 272
unitary elastic demand 272
United Nations 164
units, number and size 104
universal resource locators *see* uniform
    (universal) resource locators
universal search 484, **675**
unrelated businesses, diversification into
    211, 212
unsubscribing 153, 155, 159, **676**
up-selling 302, 312, 336, 340, **676**
uploads **676**
upstream integration with suppliers 212
Upton, N. 407–8
URL *see* uniform (universal) resource
    locators
usability **676**
    requirements 375–7
    testing 356, 360, 361, 377, 382, **676**
    websites 377, 416–17
usenet newsgroups **676**
user-centred design 374, 388, **676**
user-generated content (UGC) 33, 84
USP (unique selling points) 57, 199

validation **676**
    of input and output data 131–3
value
    customers *see* customers
    lifetime *see* lifetime value
    targeting 444, 445
value alliance model 283
value chains 97, 100, 101, 180, **676**
value event scoring 437, **676**
value measures 435
value networks **676**
value propositions 99, 101, **676**
    customers 16
    online *see* online value propositions
    websites **676**
values, domain names 160
van Duyne, D. 340
Varadarajan, R.P. 639
Varian, H. 63
Varianini, V. 192, 454
Varley, R. 142
Vaturi, D. 192, 454
vehicles
    definition 31
    miles 166
Venkatraman, N. 100
VeriSign 134, 135
versioning 401, 581
vertical e-marketplaces 636
vertical media sites 65
vertical portals **676**
video marketing 13, 36
video sharing sites 508
video standards 128
video, streamed 35

view-through 520, **676**
Vijayasarathy, L. 639
viral agents 479, 532, 534, 542
viral amplification 509
viral communications 138
viral marketing 33, 82, 84, 155, 260,
    528–35, **676**
viral referrals **676**
Virgin Wines 222
virtual communities 95, 101, 340–3, **676**
virtual malls **676**
virtual marketplace representation 278
virtual merchants 97, 610, **676**
virtual organisations 282–3, **676**
virtual private networks **676**
virtual resellers 95
The Virtual Revolution 148
virtual worlds 37
virtualisation 282, 283, **676**
virtuous circles 341
vision 197, 232
Vision Express 480–2
visit conversion rates 433–4, **676**
VisitBritain 96
visitors
    conversion rates 433–4, **676**
    engagement 104
    segmentation 566, 568
    sessions 433–4, **677**
    unique *see* unique visitors
visits per (unique) visitor (VPV) 561
visual appeal 406, 407, 409
visual design 390–1
visualisation 401, 568, 581
    systems, products 403
    web analytics tools 553, 560
Vodafone 72, 161
volume measures 433
volumes, sales 206, 207, 210
voucher code sites 511
VPV (visits per (unique) visitor) 561–2

W3C *see* World Wide Web Consortium
WAIS (Wide Area Information Service) **677**
Waite, Chris 41
walled gardens 423, **677**
wants, customers 251, 253, 262
WAP *see* Web Application Protocol
wastage
    affiliate marketing 510
    offline communications 536
    paid search marketing 498
waste, less 166
Waterman, R.H. 26
Waterstones 586
Watson, A. 612, 642, 643
Watts, D. 91, 534
weaknesses 179, 193, 195
    see also SWOT analysis
Weathers, D. 403
Web 2.0 concept 36, 502, 506–7, **677**

Web 3.0 concept 36, **677**
web addresses 123–4, 371, 439, **677**
    see also domain names
web analytics 31, 43, 126, 148, 157, 260,
    566–8, **677**
    tool selection 568–9
Web Analytics Association 554
Web Application Protocol (WAP) **677**
web applications 36
    frameworks 129–30, **677**
    servers 130, **677**
web-based ERP 633
web browsers 123, 124, 126, 129, **677**
Web Certain 380
web classification *see* card sorting
web-facilitated viral marketing 529–35
web functionality 367
web merchandising 402–4, **677**
web page standards 126
web radio **677**
web response model 440, **677**
web servers 123–6, 132, **677**
web widgets 509
Webb, Kate 480–3
WebInsights™ 557
webmasters 365, **677**
WEBQUAL 405–6, 605
Website Accessibility Initiative 379
websites
    accessibility 379, 386, **677**
    addresses *see* domain names; web
        addresses
    announcements **673**
    auditors 520, **673**, **677**
    authentication 132
    availability 373–4, **673**
    blueprints 383, 384, 387
    business requirements 374–5
    card sorting 382–3
    of competitors, reviewing 380–1
    content *see* content
    conversion efficiency 436, 437
    customer development use for 302
    design and build
        adaptive web design 391
        content 381–2, 386–8, 398–401
        defining site or app requirements
            374–88
        elements of design 389–91
        evaluating designs 389
        page design 397–8
        planning 362–6
        project initiation 370–4, **662**
        user experience 388–93
        visual design 390–1
    design page templates 398, **673**
    design templates 579–80, **675**
    development 400–2, **657**
        stages **674**
    digital marketing effectiveness audits
        191–2

websites (*continued*)
feedback tools 570–1
format ownership 579–80
information architecture design 381–2
landing pages 386–8
localisation 379–80
maintenance 573–5
management
  process 581–2
  responsibilities 575–81
maps 383, 413, **673**
measurement **677**
menu options 396–7
navigation 381, 383, 387, 390
  schemes 395–7, **673**
online retail merchandising 409–13
paths *see* clickstreams
performance optimisation 372–3
personality 390
pre-development tasks 362
promotion 363, 366, 402, 404
re-launch **673**
security risks 131–3
service quality 404–6
sessions 192
standards 575
statistics **673**
structure 389–90
styles 390
technology ownership 580
testing 401
usability 375, 377
user intent-satisfaction surveys 570
value propositions **676**
visitor activity data 560–2, **673**

visits 192, **673**
wireframes 383–7, **678**
see also Internet and entries
    beginning with digital; online
WebTrends 514
WeBuyAnyCar 222
Weinberg, T. 35
Welch, Michael 57–9
Wertime, K. 443
WHSmith 321
Whatis.com 397
Whiteman, N. 514
wholesalers 281
Wi-Fi (wireless fidelity) 137–8, **678**
Wide Area Information Service
    (WAIS) **677**
widgets 401, 509, **677**
WIFM factor 526
Wigand, R. 97, 282
Wilson, H. 37, 98, 237, 559, 560
Wineshopper.com 586
wireframes 367, 375, 383–7, **678**
wireless fidelity (Wi-Fi) 137–8, **678**
Wisner, J. 555
Wodtke, C. 80, 383
Wolfinbarger, M. 77, 602, 605
Wolin, L.D. 76
WOM see word-of-mouth
WOMMA (Word-of-Mouth Marketing
    Association) 530–1
Wood, S. 387
Wood, Z. 240
word-of-mouth (WOM)
  digitally augmented 534
  marketing 530–1, **678**

promotional mix 284
Word-of-Mouth Marketing Association
    (WOMMA) 530–1
working patterns 143
World Wide Web 123, **678**
World Wide Web Consortium (W3C)
    127, 128, 379
WorldWide Retail Exchange (WWRE) 636
Wroblewski, Luke 391, 396
Wurster, T.S. 277
WWRE (WorldWide Retail Exchange)
    636
Wynne, Will 200

Xing, X. 267, 272
XML (eXtensible Markup Language)
    127–8, **678**
XMOS *see* cross-media optimisation
    studies

Yadav, M.S. 639
Yahoo! 63, 82, 94, 95, 101, 102, 110, 487,
    495, 497, 508, 527
yielding, website information 400
YouTube 8, 15, 21, 36, 44, 304–7, 342,
    343, 356, 365, 478, 484, 498, 508,
    531, 533, 540

Zappos 300–2
Zed Media 455–6
Zeithaml, V. 404, 406
Zettelmeyer, F. 639
Zipf, George Kingsley 261
Zopa 167–9
Zuckerberg, Mark 468–71